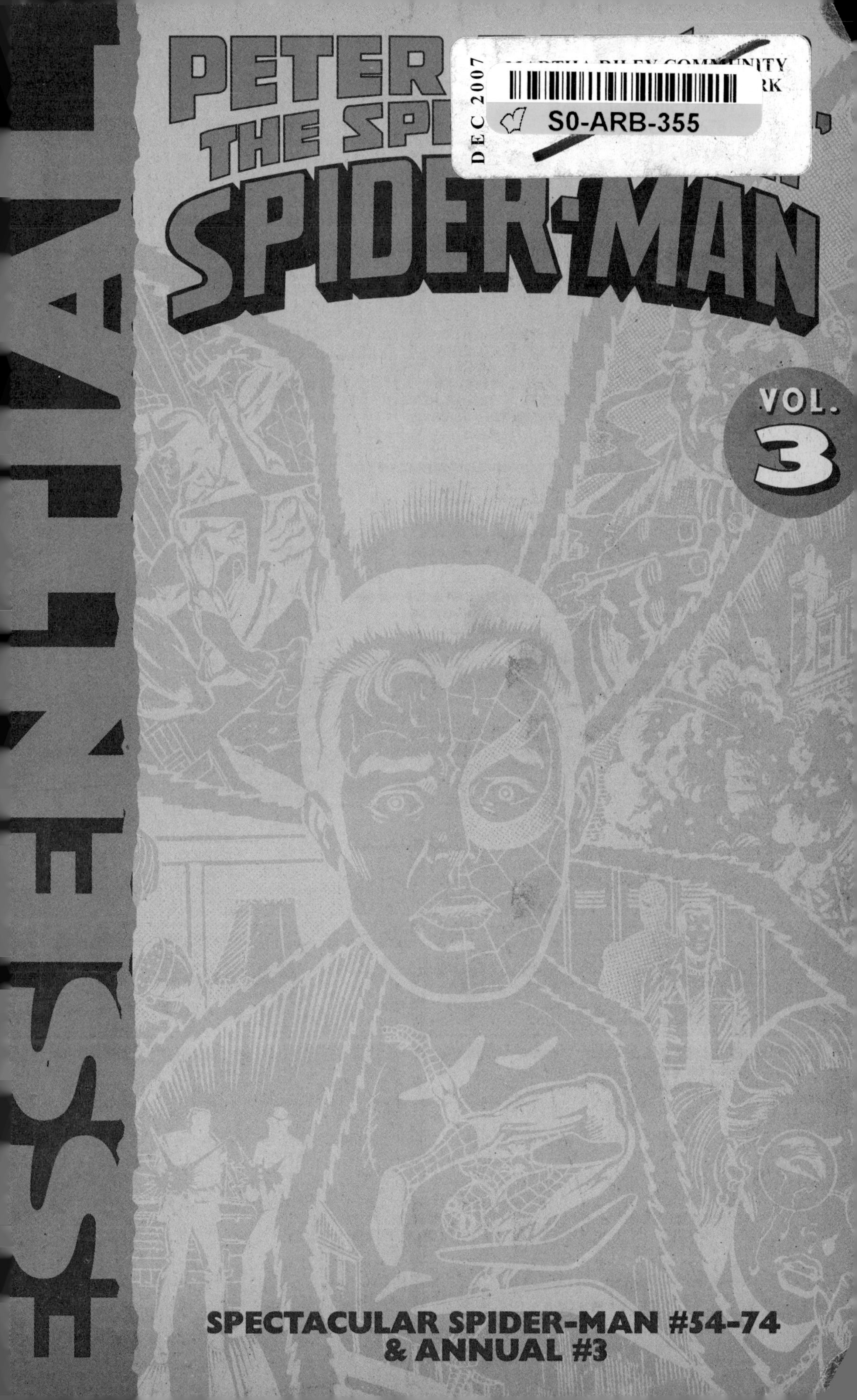
ESSENTIAL
PETER
THE SP
SPIDER-MAN
VOL. 3
SPECTACULAR SPIDER-MAN #54-74
& ANNUAL #3

SPECTACULAR SPIDER-MAN #54
SCRIPT: ROGER STERN
PLOT & PENCILER: MARIE SEVERIN
INKER: JIM MOONEY
LETTERER: JIM NOVAK
EDITOR: DENNY O'NEIL

SPECTACULAR SPIDER-MAN #61
PLOT: ROGER STERN
SCRIPT: BILL MANTLO
PENCILER: ED HANNIGAN
INKER: JIM MOONEY
LETTERER: JEAN SIMEK
EDITOR: TOM DEFALCO

SPECTACULAR SPIDER-MAN #69
WRITER: BILL MANTLO
PENCILER: ED HANNIGAN
INKER: AL MILGROM
LETTERER: JOE ROSEN
EDITOR: TOM DEFALCO

SPECTACULAR SPIDER-MAN #55
WRITER: ROGER STERN
PENCILER: LUKE MCDONNELL
INKER: JIM MOONEY
LETTERER: JOHN MORELLI
EDITOR: DENNY O'NEIL

SPECTACULAR SPIDER-MAN #62
WRITER: BILL MANTLO
PENCILER: ED HANNIGAN
INKER: JIM MOONEY
LETTERER: DIANA ALBERS
EDITOR: TOM DEFALCO

SPECTACULAR SPIDER-MAN #70
WRITER: BILL MANTLO
PENCILER: ED HANNIGAN
INKER: AL MILGROM
LETTERER: JOE ROSEN
EDITOR: TOM DEFALCO

SPECTACULAR SPIDER-MAN #56
WRITER: ROGER STERN
LAYOUTS: JIM SHOOTER
FINISHES: JIM MOONEY
LETTERER: JANICE CHIANG
EDITOR: DENNY O'NEIL

SPECTACULAR SPIDER-MAN #63
WRITER: BILL MANTLO
PENCILER: GREG LAROCQUE
INKER: JIM MOONEY
LETTERER: DIANA ALBERS
EDITOR: TOM DEFALCO

SPECTACULAR SPIDER-MAN #71
WRITER: BILL MANTLO
PENCILER: RICK LEONARDI
INKER: JIM MOONEY
LETTERER: JOE ROSEN
EDITOR: TOM DEFALCO

SPECTACULAR SPIDER-MAN #57
WRITER: ROGER STERN
LAYOUTS: JIM SHOOTER
FINISHES: JIM MOONEY
LETTERER: JIM NOVAK
EDITOR: DENNY O'NEIL

SPECTACULAR SPIDER-MAN #64
WRITER: BILL MANTLO
PENCILER: ED HANNIGAN
INKER: JIM MOONEY
LETTERER: JOE ROSEN
EDITOR: TOM DEFALCO

SPECTACULAR SPIDER-MAN #72
WRITER: BILL MANTLO
PENCILER: ED HANNIGAN
INKERS: AL MILGROM &
  RICK MAGYAR
LETTERER: JIM NOVAK
EDITOR: TOM DEFALCO

SPECTACULAR SPIDER-MAN #58
WRITER: ROGER STERN
PENCILER: JOHN BYRNE
INKER: VINCE COLLETTA
LETTERER: JEAN SIMEK
EDITOR: TOM DEFALCO

SPECTACULAR SPIDER-MAN #65
WRITER: BILL MANTLO
PENCILER: BOB HALL
INKER: JIM MOONEY
LETTERER: JIM NOVAK
EDITOR: TOM DEFALCO

SPECTACULAR SPIDER-MAN #73
WRITER: BILL MANTLO
PENCILER: AL MILGROM
INKER: JIM MOONEY
LETTERER: DIANA ALBERS
EDITOR: TOM DEFALCO

SPECTACULAR SPIDER-MAN #59
WRITER: ROGER STERN
LAYOUTS: JIM SHOOTER
FINISHES: JIM MOONEY
LETTERER JEAN SIMEK
EDITOR: TOM DEFALCO

SPECTACULAR SPIDER-MAN #66
WRITER: BILL MANTLO
PENCILER: ED HANNIGAN
INKER: JIM MOONEY
LETTERER: DIANA ALBERS
EDITOR: TOM DEFALCO

SPECTACULAR SPIDER-MAN #74
WRITER: BILL MANTLO
PENCILER: BOB HALL
INKER: JIM MOONEY
LETTERER: DIANA ALBERS
EDITOR: TOM DEFALCO

SPECTACULAR SPIDER-MAN #60
WRITER: ROGER STERN
PENCILER: ED HANNIGAN
INKER: JIM MOONEY
LETTERER: DIANA ALBERS
EDITOR: TOM DEFALCO

SPECTACULAR SPIDER-MAN #67
WRITER: BILL MANTLO
PENCILER: ED HANNIGAN
INKER: AL MILGROM
LETTERER: JIM NOVAK
EDITOR: TOM DEFALCO

SPECTACULAR SPIDER-MAN
ANNUAL #3
WRITER: DAVID KRAFT
PENCILERS: JIM SHERMAN &
AL WEISS
INKER: STEVE MITCHELL
LETTERER: DIANA ALBERS
EDITOR: TOM DEFALCO

SPECTACULAR SPIDER-MAN #68
WRITER: BILL MANTLO
LAYOUTS: LUKE MCDONNELL
FINISHES: JIM MOONEY
LETTERER DIANA ALBERS
EDITOR: TOM DEFALCO

REPRINT CREDITS

MARVEL ESSENTIAL DESIGN: JOHN
"JG" ROSHELL OF COMICRAFT
FRONT COVER ART:
FRANK MILLER
BACK COVER ART:
ED HANNIGAN
COVER COLORS:
CHRIS SOTOMAYOR
COLLECTION EDITOR:
MARK D. BEAZLEY
ASSISTANT EDITOR:
MICHAEL SHORT
ASSOCIATE EDITOR:
JENNIFER GRÜNWALD

SENIOR EDITOR, SPECIAL PROJECTS:
JEFF YOUNGQUIST
PRODUCTION:
JERRON QUALITY COLOR
SENIOR VICE PRESIDENT OF SALES:
DAVID GABRIEL
CREATIVE DIRECTOR:
TOM MARVELLI
EDITOR IN CHIEF:
JOE QUESADA
PUBLISHER:
DAN BUCKLEY

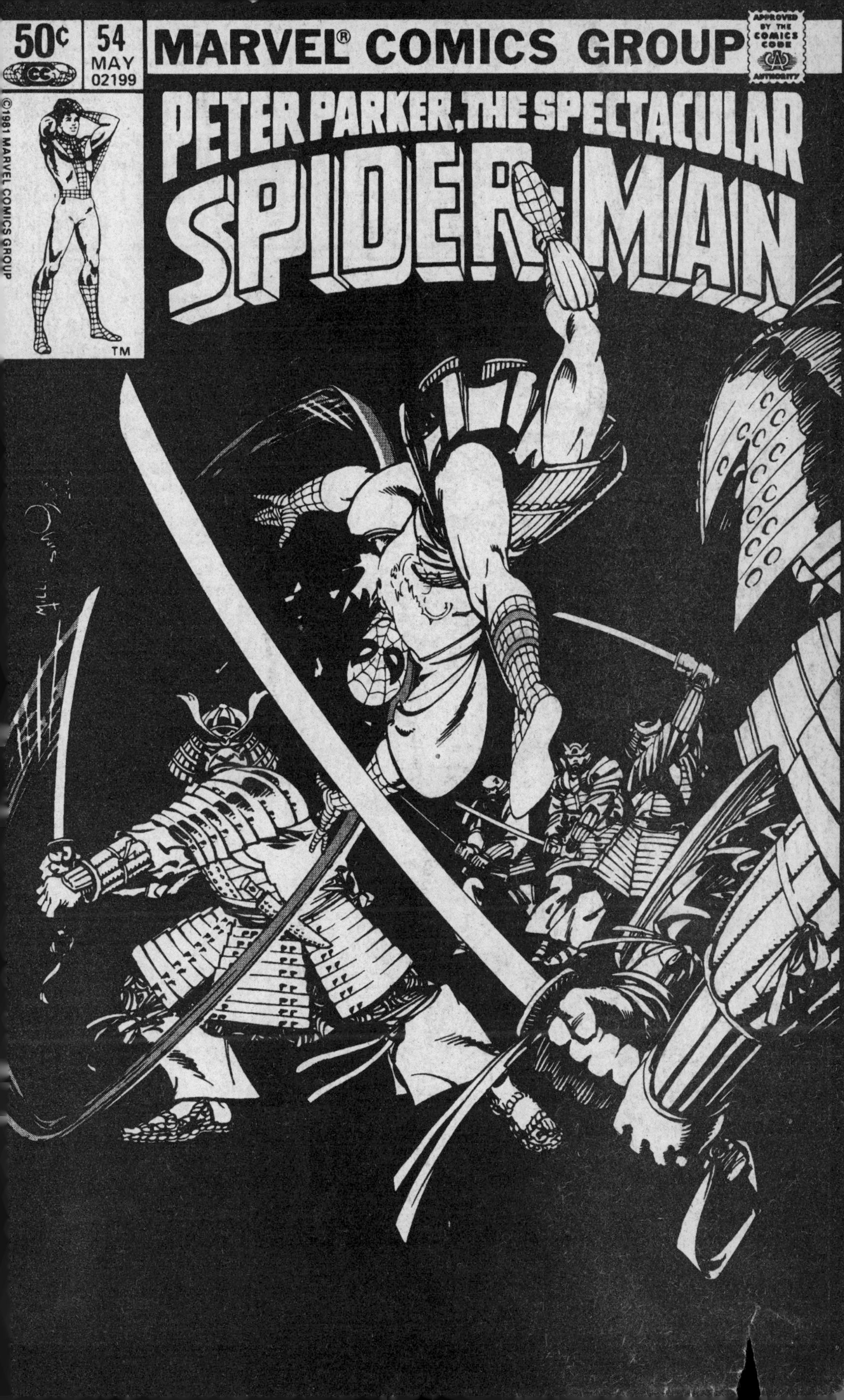
50¢
54
MAY
02199
MARVEL® COMICS GROUP
APPROVED BY THE COMICS CODE AUTHORITY
PETER PARKER, THE SPECTACULAR
SPIDER-MAN
©1981 MARVEL COMICS GROUP
TM

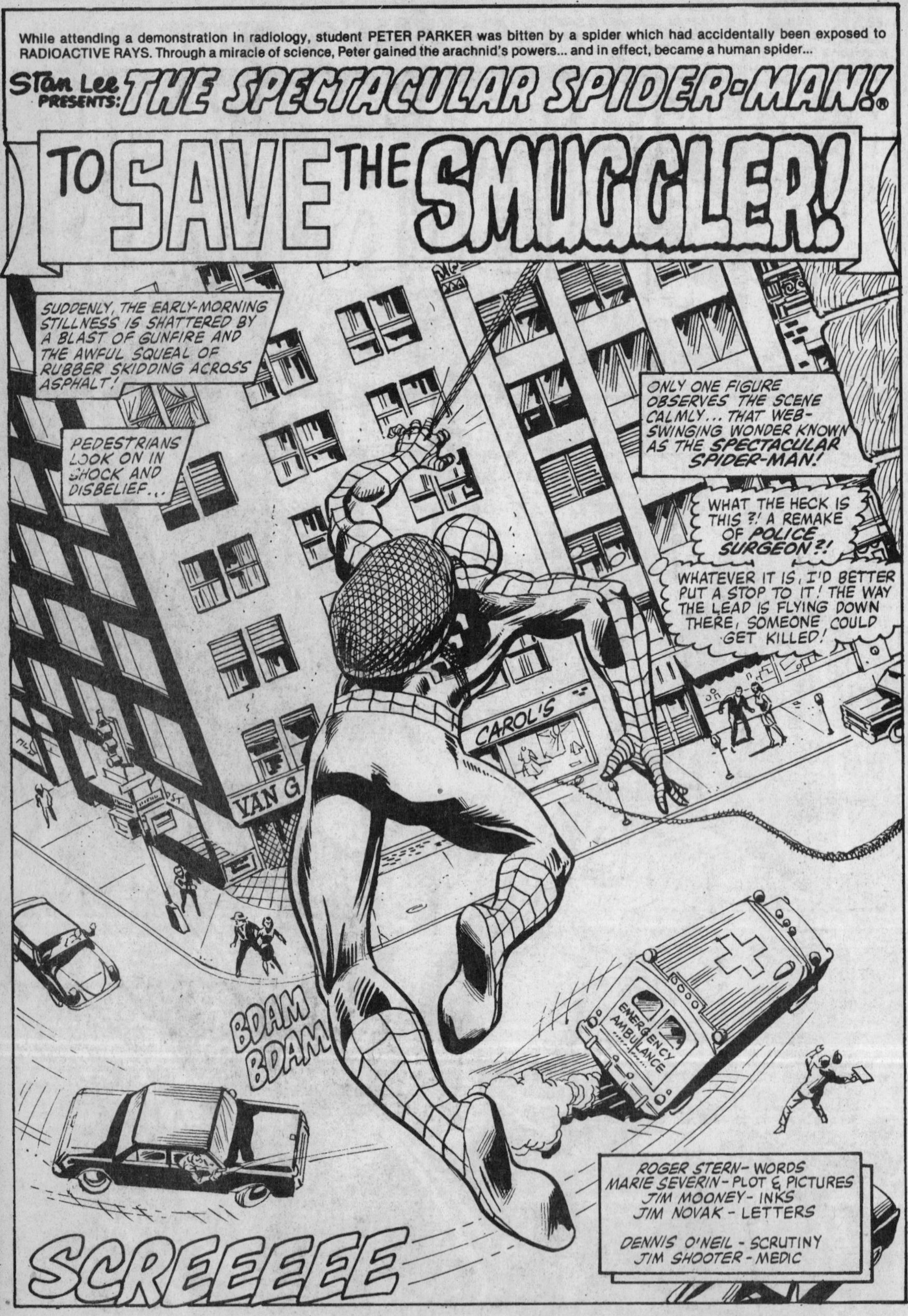
While attending a demonstration in radiology, student PETER PARKER was bitten by a spider which had accidentally been exposed to RADIOACTIVE RAYS. Through a miracle of science, Peter gained the arachnid's powers... and in effect, became a human spider...
Stan Lee PRESENTS: THE SPECTACULAR SPIDER-MAN!®
TO SAVE THE SMUGGLER!
SUDDENLY, THE EARLY-MORNING STILLNESS IS SHATTERED BY A BLAST OF GUNFIRE AND THE AWFUL SQUEAL OF RUBBER SKIDDING ACROSS ASPHALT!
PEDESTRIANS LOOK ON IN SHOCK AND DISBELIEF...
ONLY ONE FIGURE OBSERVES THE SCENE CALMLY... THAT WEB-SWINGING WONDER KNOWN AS THE SPECTACULAR SPIDER-MAN!
WHAT THE HECK IS THIS ?! A REMAKE OF POLICE SURGEON ?!
WHATEVER IT IS, I'D BETTER PUT A STOP TO IT! THE WAY THE LEAD IS FLYING DOWN THERE, SOMEONE COULD GET KILLED!
CAROL'S
VAN G
BDAM BDAM
EMERGENCY AMBULANCE
SCREEEEEE
ROGER STERN- WORDS
MARIE SEVERIN- PLOT & PICTURES
JIM MOONEY- INKS
JIM NOVAK - LETTERS
DENNIS O'NEIL - SCRUTINY
JIM SHOOTER - MEDIC

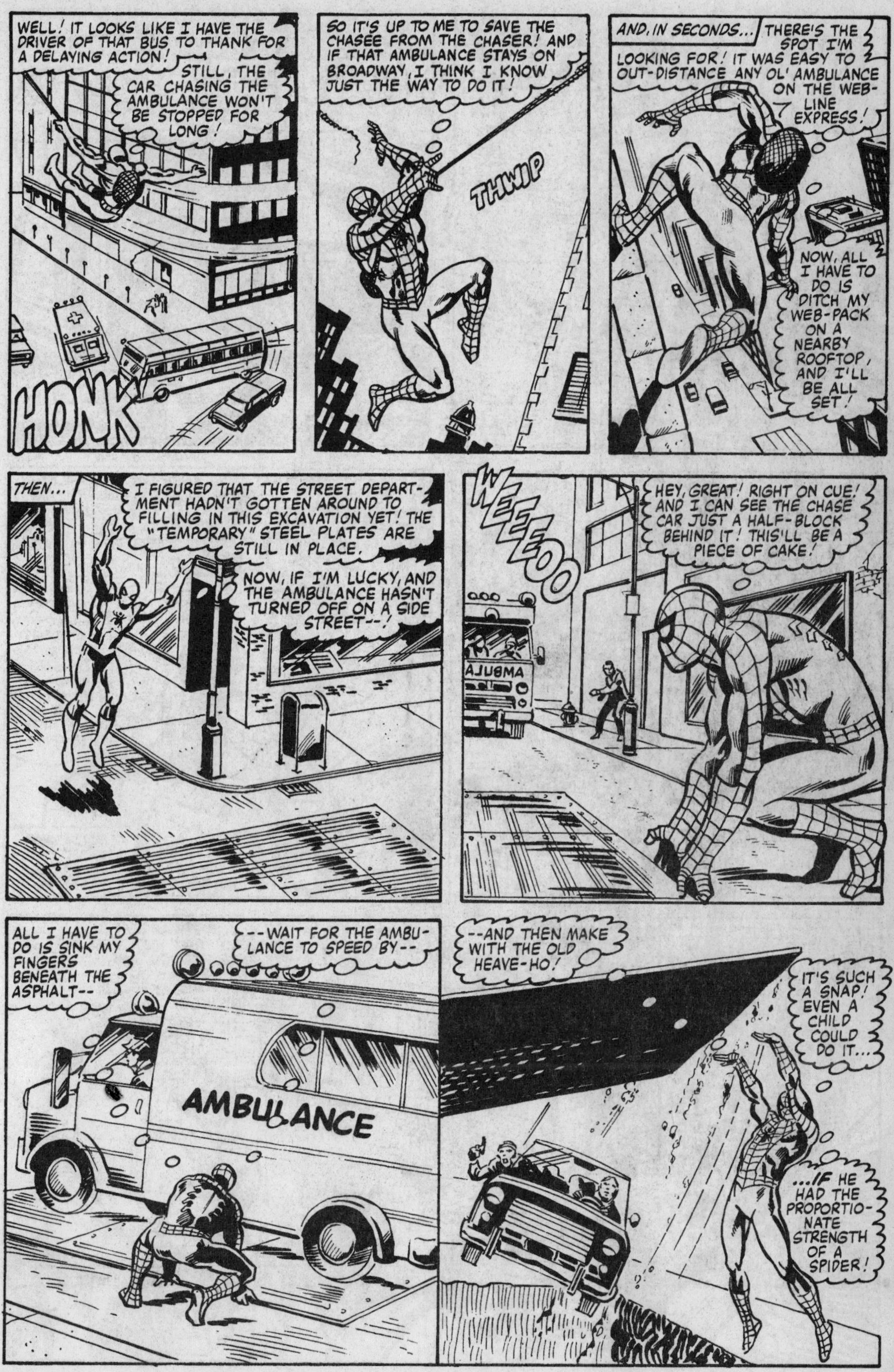
WELL! IT LOOKS LIKE I HAVE THE DRIVER OF THAT BUS TO THANK FOR A DELAYING ACTION!
STILL, THE CAR CHASING THE AMBULANCE WON'T BE STOPPED FOR LONG!
HONK
SO IT'S UP TO ME TO SAVE THE CHASEE FROM THE CHASER! AND IF THAT AMBULANCE STAYS ON BROADWAY, I THINK I KNOW JUST THE WAY TO DO IT!
THWIP
AND, IN SECONDS...
THERE'S THE SPOT I'M LOOKING FOR! IT WAS EASY TO OUT-DISTANCE ANY OL' AMBULANCE ON THE WEB-LINE EXPRESS!
NOW, ALL I HAVE TO DO IS DITCH MY WEB-PACK ON A NEARBY ROOFTOP, AND I'LL BE ALL SET!
THEN...
I FIGURED THAT THE STREET DEPARTMENT HADN'T GOTTEN AROUND TO FILLING IN THIS EXCAVATION YET! THE "TEMPORARY" STEEL PLATES ARE STILL IN PLACE.
NOW, IF I'M LUCKY, AND THE AMBULANCE HASN'T TURNED OFF ON A SIDE STREET--!
WEEEOO
HEY, GREAT! RIGHT ON CUE! AND I CAN SEE THE CHASE CAR JUST A HALF-BLOCK BEHIND IT! THIS'LL BE A PIECE OF CAKE!
AJUBMA
ALL I HAVE TO DO IS SINK MY FINGERS BENEATH THE ASPHALT--
--WAIT FOR THE AMBULANCE TO SPEED BY--
AMBULANCE
--AND THEN MAKE WITH THE OLD HEAVE-HO!
IT'S SUCH A SNAP! EVEN A CHILD COULD DO IT...
...IF HE HAD THE PROPORTIONATE STRENGTH OF A SPIDER!

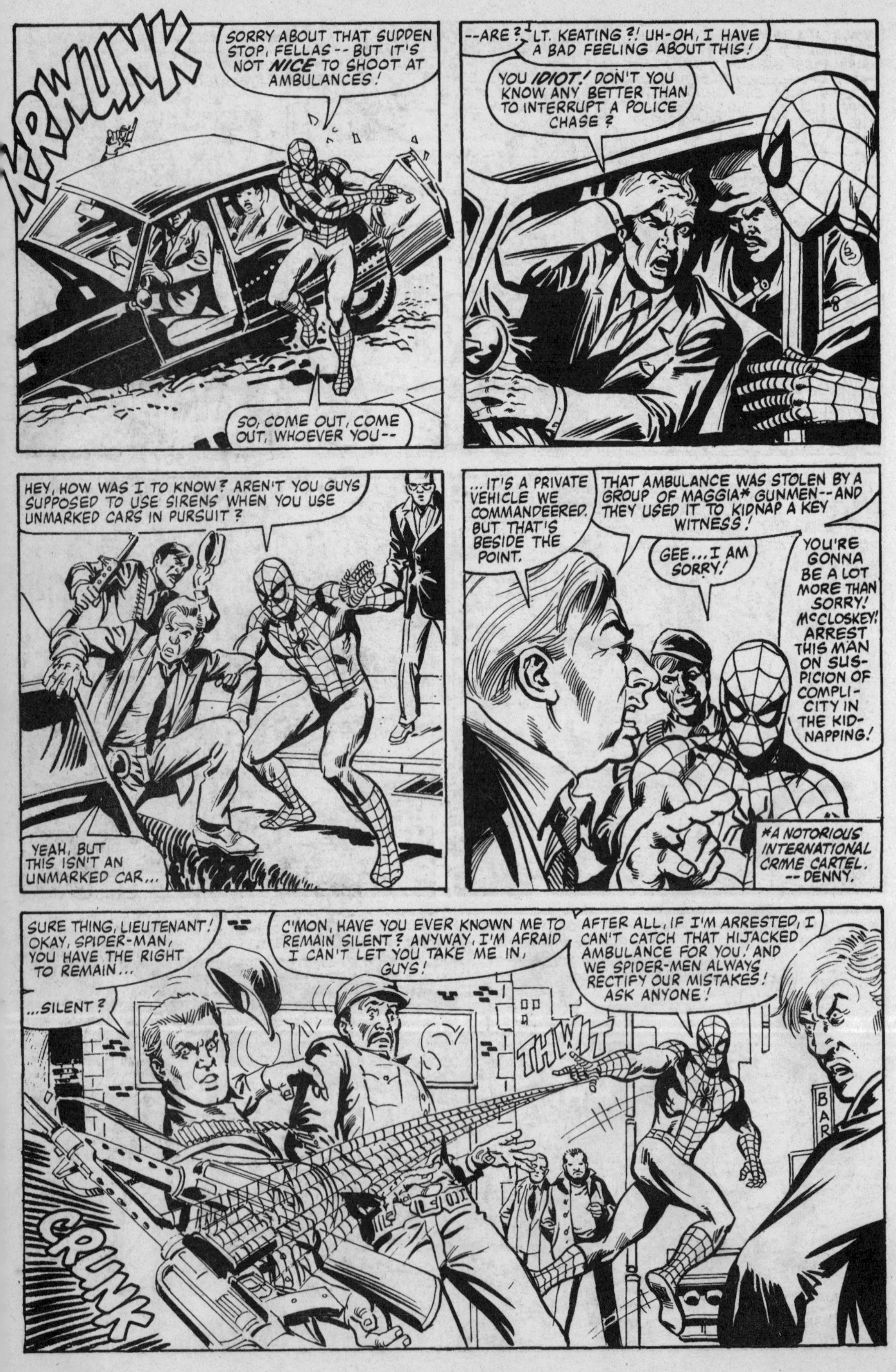
KRWHUNK
SORRY ABOUT THAT SUDDEN STOP, FELLAS -- BUT IT'S NOT NICE TO SHOOT AT AMBULANCES!
SO, COME OUT, COME OUT, WHOEVER YOU--
--ARE?
YOU IDIOT! DON'T YOU KNOW ANY BETTER THAN TO INTERRUPT A POLICE CHASE?
LT. KEATING?! UH-OH, I HAVE A BAD FEELING ABOUT THIS!
HEY, HOW WAS I TO KNOW? AREN'T YOU GUYS SUPPOSED TO USE SIRENS WHEN YOU USE UNMARKED CARS IN PURSUIT?
YEAH, BUT THIS ISN'T AN UNMARKED CAR...
...IT'S A PRIVATE VEHICLE WE COMMANDEERED. BUT THAT'S BESIDE THE POINT.
THAT AMBULANCE WAS STOLEN BY A GROUP OF MAGGIA* GUNMEN--AND THEY USED IT TO KIDNAP A KEY WITNESS!
GEE... I AM SORRY!
YOU'RE GONNA BE A LOT MORE THAN SORRY! McCLOSKEY! ARREST THIS MAN ON SUSPICION OF COMPLICITY IN THE KIDNAPPING!
*A NOTORIOUS INTERNATIONAL CRIME CARTEL. -- DENNY.
SURE THING, LIEUTENANT! OKAY, SPIDER-MAN, YOU HAVE THE RIGHT TO REMAIN...
...SILENT?
C'MON, HAVE YOU EVER KNOWN ME TO REMAIN SILENT? ANYWAY, I'M AFRAID I CAN'T LET YOU TAKE ME IN, GUYS!
AFTER ALL, IF I'M ARRESTED, I CAN'T CATCH THAT HIJACKED AMBULANCE FOR YOU! AND WE SPIDER-MEN ALWAYS RECTIFY OUR MISTAKES! ASK ANYONE!
THWIT
BAR
CRUNK

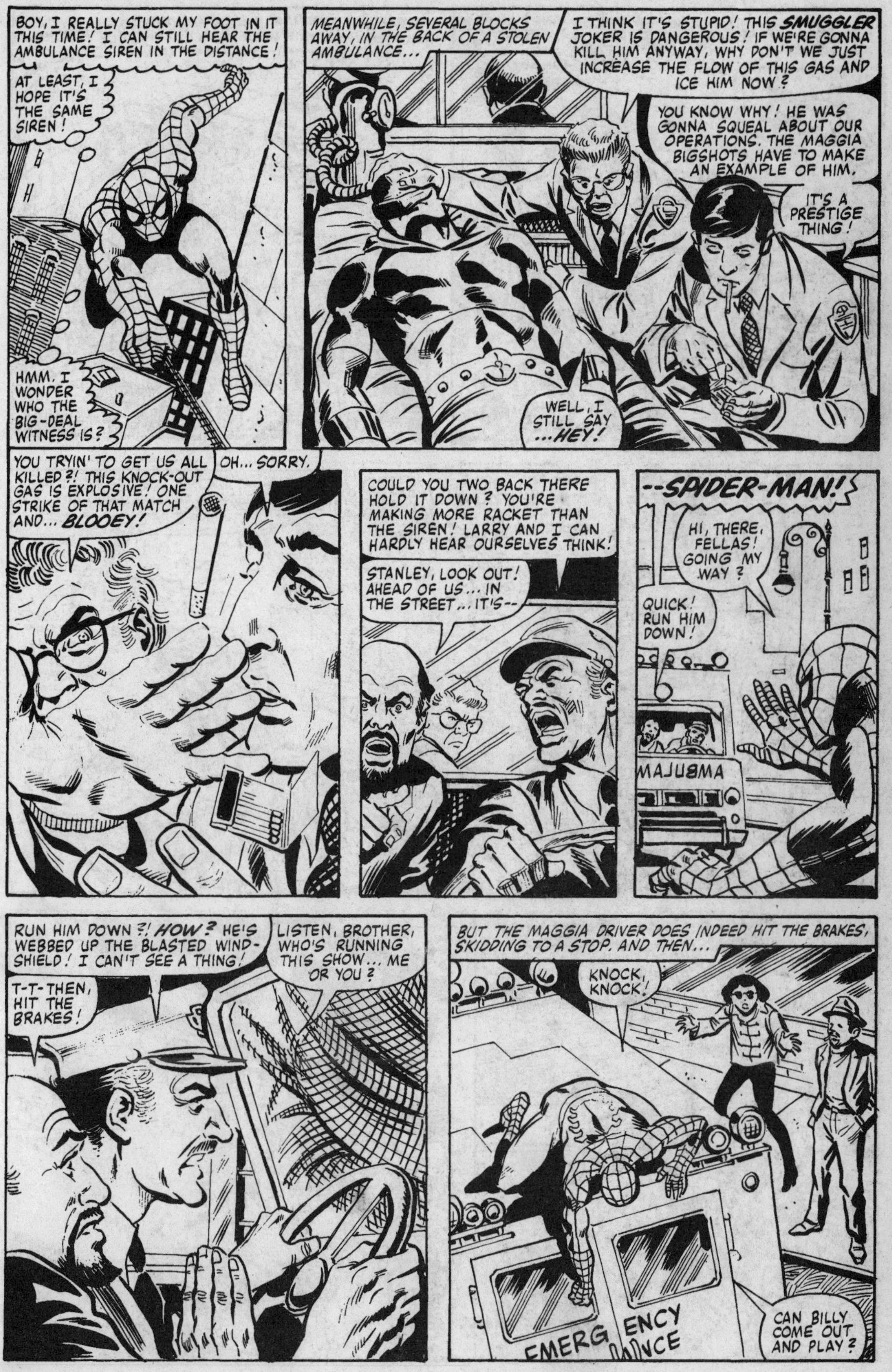
BOY, I REALLY STUCK MY FOOT IN IT THIS TIME! I CAN STILL HEAR THE AMBULANCE SIREN IN THE DISTANCE!
AT LEAST, I HOPE IT'S THE SAME SIREN!
HMM. I WONDER WHO THE BIG-DEAL WITNESS IS?
MEANWHILE, SEVERAL BLOCKS AWAY, IN THE BACK OF A STOLEN AMBULANCE...
I THINK IT'S STUPID! THIS SMUGGLER JOKER IS DANGEROUS! IF WE'RE GONNA KILL HIM ANYWAY, WHY DON'T WE JUST INCREASE THE FLOW OF THIS GAS AND ICE HIM NOW?
YOU KNOW WHY! HE WAS GONNA SQUEAL ABOUT OUR OPERATIONS. THE MAGGIA BIGSHOTS HAVE TO MAKE AN EXAMPLE OF HIM.
IT'S A PRESTIGE THING!
WELL, I STILL SAY ...HEY!
YOU TRYIN' TO GET US ALL KILLED?! THIS KNOCK-OUT GAS IS EXPLOSIVE! ONE STRIKE OF THAT MATCH AND... BLOOEY!
OH... SORRY.
COULD YOU TWO BACK THERE HOLD IT DOWN? YOU'RE MAKING MORE RACKET THAN THE SIREN! LARRY AND I CAN HARDLY HEAR OURSELVES THINK!
STANLEY, LOOK OUT! AHEAD OF US... IN THE STREET... IT'S--
--SPIDER-MAN!
HI, THERE, FELLAS! GOING MY WAY?
QUICK! RUN HIM DOWN!
AMBULANCE
RUN HIM DOWN?! HOW? HE'S WEBBED UP THE BLASTED WIND-SHIELD! I CAN'T SEE A THING!
T-T-THEN, HIT THE BRAKES!
LISTEN, BROTHER, WHO'S RUNNING THIS SHOW... ME OR YOU?
BUT THE MAGGIA DRIVER DOES INDEED HIT THE BRAKES, SKIDDING TO A STOP. AND THEN...
KNOCK, KNOCK!
CAN BILLY COME OUT AND PLAY?
EMERG ENCY
...NCE

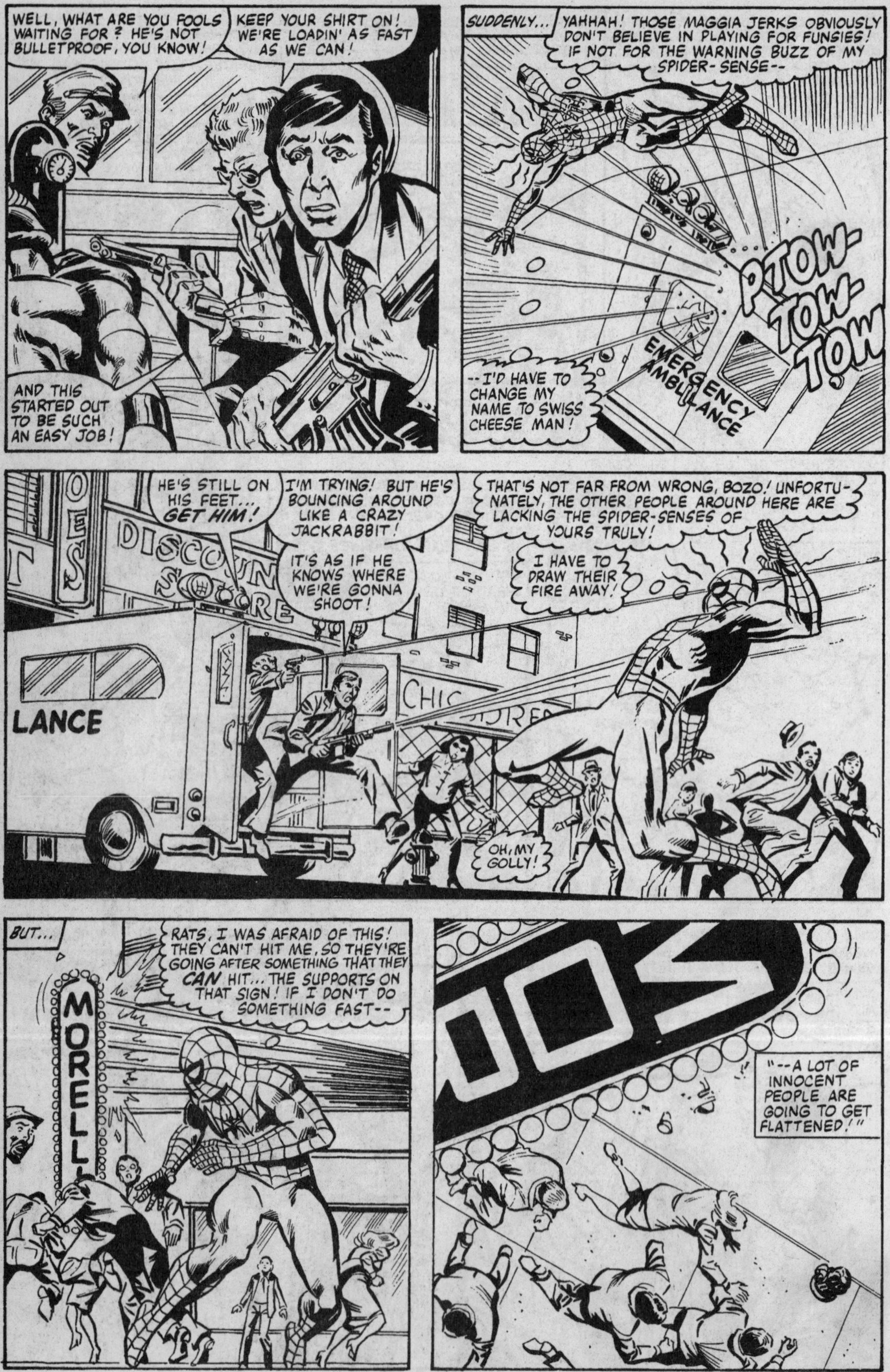
WELL, WHAT ARE YOU FOOLS WAITING FOR? HE'S NOT BULLETPROOF, YOU KNOW!
KEEP YOUR SHIRT ON! WE'RE LOADIN' AS FAST AS WE CAN!
AND THIS STARTED OUT TO BE SUCH AN EASY JOB!
SUDDENLY...
YAHHAH! THOSE MAGGIA JERKS OBVIOUSLY DON'T BELIEVE IN PLAYING FOR FUNSIES! IF NOT FOR THE WARNING BUZZ OF MY SPIDER-SENSE--
P'TOW-TOW-TOW
EMERGENCY AMBULANCE
--I'D HAVE TO CHANGE MY NAME TO SWISS CHEESE MAN!
HE'S STILL ON HIS FEET... GET HIM!
I'M TRYING! BUT HE'S BOUNCING AROUND LIKE A CRAZY JACKRABBIT!
IT'S AS IF HE KNOWS WHERE WE'RE GONNA SHOOT!
THAT'S NOT FAR FROM WRONG, BOZO! UNFORTUNATELY, THE OTHER PEOPLE AROUND HERE ARE LACKING THE SPIDER-SENSES OF YOURS TRULY!
I HAVE TO DRAW THEIR FIRE AWAY!
LANCE
OH, MY GOLLY!
BUT...
RATS, I WAS AFRAID OF THIS! THEY CAN'T HIT ME, SO THEY'RE GOING AFTER SOMETHING THAT THEY CAN HIT... THE SUPPORTS ON THAT SIGN! IF I DON'T DO SOMETHING FAST--
MORELLI
"--A LOT OF INNOCENT PEOPLE ARE GOING TO GET FLATTENED!"

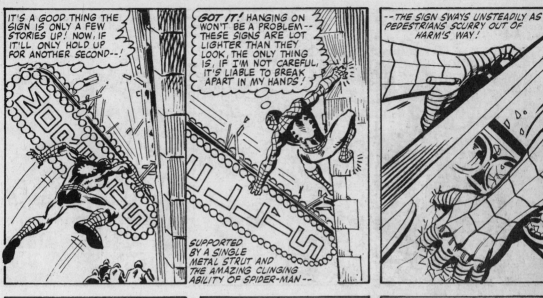

IT'S A GOOD THING THE SIGN IS ONLY A FEW STORIES UP! NOW, IF IT'LL ONLY HOLD UP FOR ANOTHER SECOND--!

GOT IT! HANGING ON WON'T BE A PROBLEM-- THESE SIGNS ARE A LOT LIGHTER THAN THEY LOOK, THE ONLY THING IS, IF I'M NOT CAREFUL, IT'S LIABLE TO BREAK APART IN MY HANDS!

SUPPORTED BY A SINGLE METAL STRUT AND THE AMAZING CLINGING ABILITY OF SPIDER-MAN--

--THE SIGN SWAYS UNSTEADILY AS PEDESTRIANS SCURRY OUT OF HARM'S WAY!

MINUTES LATER... MAN! I THOUGHT THAT CROWD WOULD NEVER CLEAR!

NOW, I CAN FINALLY SET THIS THING DOWN AND GET AFTER THOSE MAGGIA CLOWNS AGAIN!

MEANWHILE... C'MON, YOU TWO! DON'T BOTHER PICKING HIM OFF... THE SMUGGLER'S MORE IMPORTANT!

Y-YEAH! THERE'S A CAR AT THE END OF THIS ALLEY! IF WE CAN JUMP-START IT--!

THUS, AT THIS MOMENT, SPIDER-MAN'S PREY IS ALREADY BLOCKS AWAY...

AND... I DON'T BELIEVE IT! DIDN'T ANY OF YOU SEE WHICH WAY THE GUNMEN WENT?

NAW! WE WAS TOO BUSY WATCHIN' YOU, MAN!

GREAT! JUST GREAT!

GROCERY

IT'S PROBABLY A WASTE OF TIME, BUT I MIGHT AS WELL CHECK OUT THE AMBULANCE. I DON'T KNOW WHAT I EXPECT TO FIND... I DOUBT THAT THEY LEFT A MAP TO THEIR HIDEOUT!

EH? WHAT'S THIS?

HMPH! JUST A MATCHBOOK FROM SOME ORIENTAL PLACE. THAT DOESN'T TELL ME MUCH.

STILL, I SUPPOSE I'D BETTER HOLD ONTO IT. IT COULD BE A CLUE, I GUESS.

CHRYSANTHEMUM AND THE SWORD

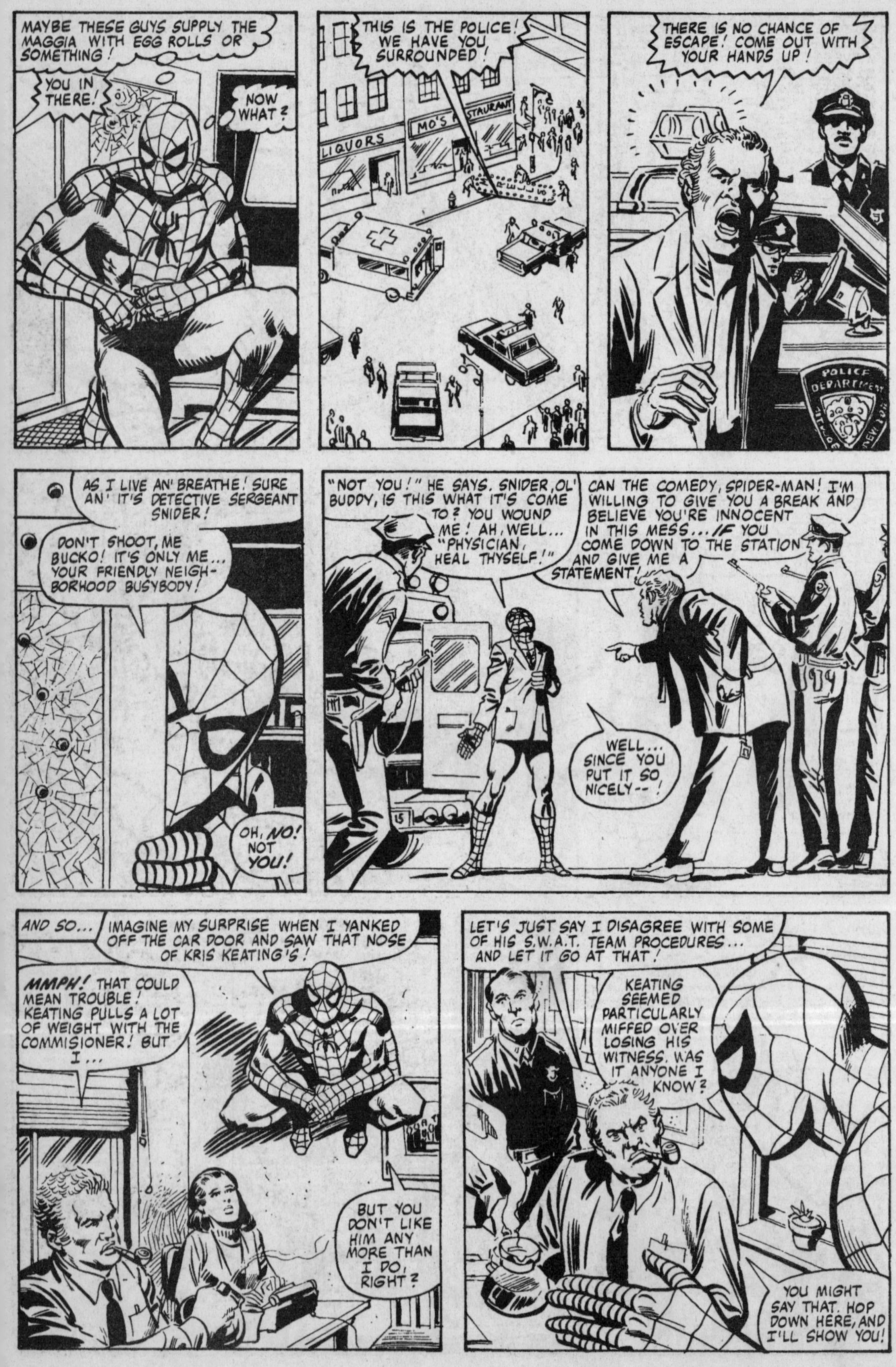
MAYBE THESE GUYS SUPPLY THE MAGGIA WITH EGG ROLLS OR SOMETHING!
YOU IN THERE!
NOW WHAT?
THIS IS THE POLICE! WE HAVE YOU SURROUNDED!
LIQUORS
THERE IS NO CHANCE OF ESCAPE! COME OUT WITH YOUR HANDS UP!
POLICE DEPARTMENT
AS I LIVE AN' BREATHE! SURE AN' IT'S DETECTIVE SERGEANT SNIDER!
DON'T SHOOT, ME BUCKO! IT'S ONLY ME... YOUR FRIENDLY NEIGHBORHOOD BUSYBODY!
OH, NO! NOT YOU!
"NOT YOU!" HE SAYS. SNIDER, OL' BUDDY, IS THIS WHAT IT'S COME TO? YOU WOUND ME! AH, WELL... "PHYSICIAN, HEAL THYSELF!"
CAN THE COMEDY, SPIDER-MAN! I'M WILLING TO GIVE YOU A BREAK AND BELIEVE YOU'RE INNOCENT IN THIS MESS... IF YOU COME DOWN TO THE STATION AND GIVE ME A STATEMENT!
WELL... SINCE YOU PUT IT SO NICELY--!
AND SO...
IMAGINE MY SURPRISE WHEN I YANKED OFF THE CAR DOOR AND SAW THAT NOSE OF KRIS KEATING'S!
MMPH! THAT COULD MEAN TROUBLE! KEATING PULLS A LOT OF WEIGHT WITH THE COMMISIONER! BUT I...
BUT YOU DON'T LIKE HIM ANY MORE THAN I DO, RIGHT?
LET'S JUST SAY I DISAGREE WITH SOME OF HIS S.W.A.T. TEAM PROCEDURES... AND LET IT GO AT THAT!
KEATING SEEMED PARTICULARLY MIFFED OVER LOSING HIS WITNESS. WAS IT ANYONE I KNOW?
YOU MIGHT SAY THAT. HOP DOWN HERE, AND I'LL SHOW YOU!

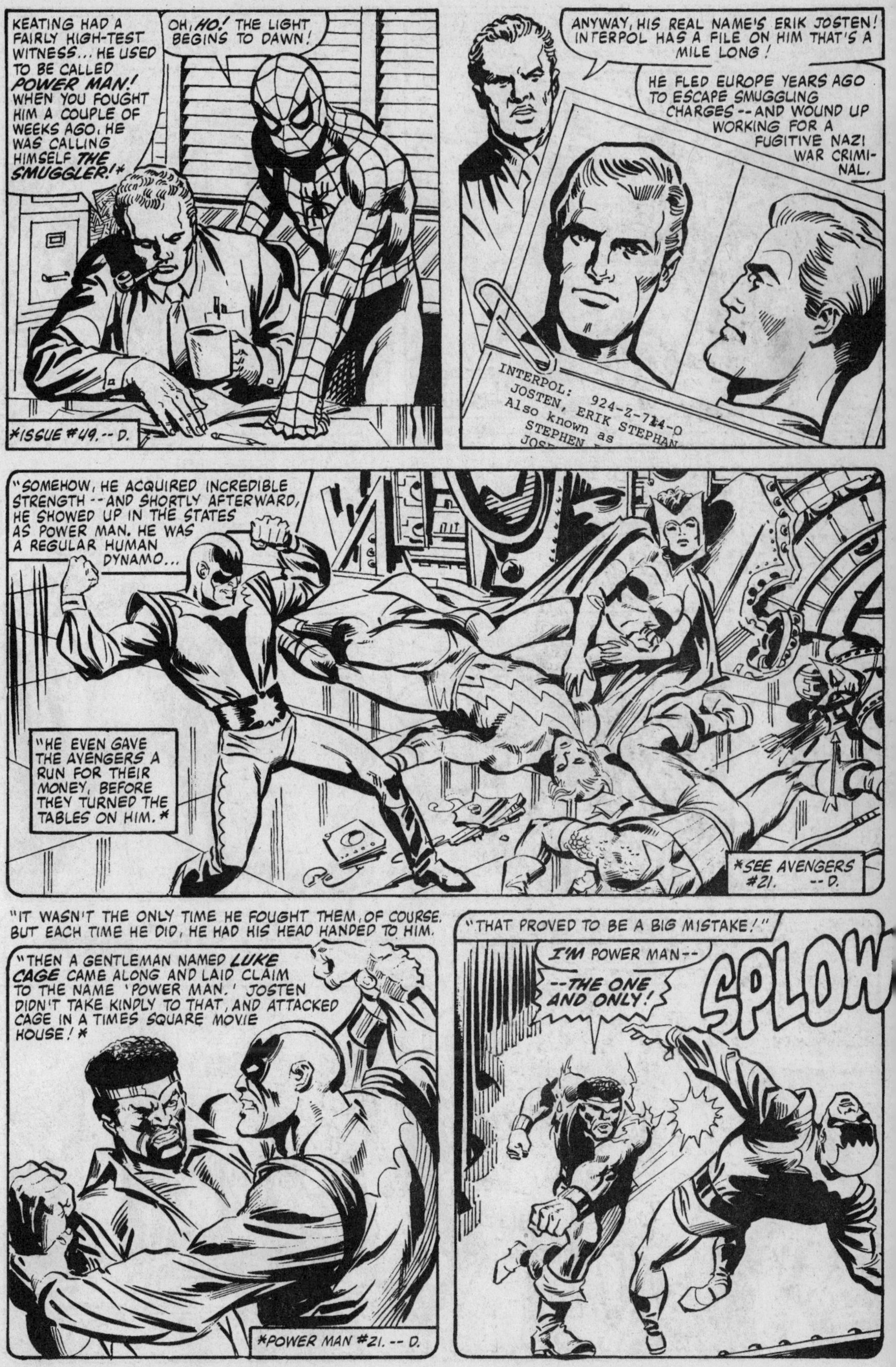
KEATING HAD A FAIRLY HIGH-TEST WITNESS... HE USED TO BE CALLED POWER MAN! WHEN YOU FOUGHT HIM A COUPLE OF WEEKS AGO, HE WAS CALLING HIMSELF THE SMUGGLER!*
OH, HO! THE LIGHT BEGINS TO DAWN!
*ISSUE #49. -- D.
ANYWAY, HIS REAL NAME'S ERIK JOSTEN! INTERPOL HAS A FILE ON HIM THAT'S A MILE LONG!
HE FLED EUROPE YEARS AGO TO ESCAPE SMUGGLING CHARGES -- AND WOUND UP WORKING FOR A FUGITIVE NAZI WAR CRIMINAL.
INTERPOL: 924-Z-714-0
JOSTEN, ERIK STEPHAN
Also known as
STEPHEN
"SOMEHOW, HE ACQUIRED INCREDIBLE STRENGTH -- AND SHORTLY AFTERWARD, HE SHOWED UP IN THE STATES AS POWER MAN. HE WAS A REGULAR HUMAN DYNAMO...
"HE EVEN GAVE THE AVENGERS A RUN FOR THEIR MONEY, BEFORE THEY TURNED THE TABLES ON HIM.*
*SEE AVENGERS #21. -- D.
"IT WASN'T THE ONLY TIME HE FOUGHT THEM, OF COURSE. BUT EACH TIME HE DID, HE HAD HIS HEAD HANDED TO HIM.
"THEN A GENTLEMAN NAMED LUKE CAGE CAME ALONG AND LAID CLAIM TO THE NAME 'POWER MAN.' JOSTEN DIDN'T TAKE KINDLY TO THAT, AND ATTACKED CAGE IN A TIMES SQUARE MOVIE HOUSE!*
*POWER MAN #21. -- D.
"THAT PROVED TO BE A BIG MISTAKE!"
I'M POWER MAN--
--THE ONE AND ONLY!
SPLOW

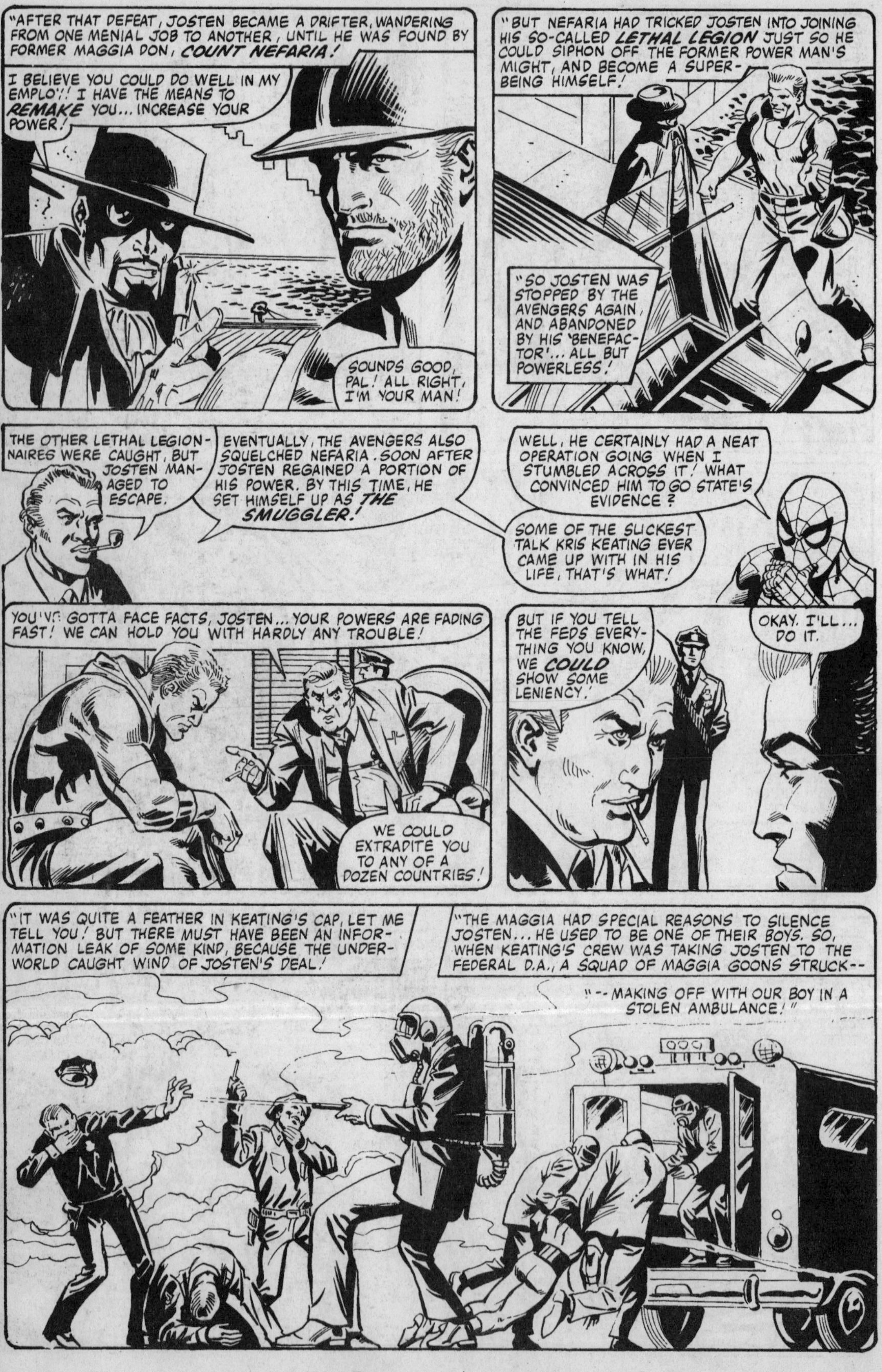
"AFTER THAT DEFEAT, JOSTEN BECAME A DRIFTER, WANDERING FROM ONE MENIAL JOB TO ANOTHER, UNTIL HE WAS FOUND BY FORMER MAGGIA DON, COUNT NEFARIA!
I BELIEVE YOU COULD DO WELL IN MY EMPLOY! I HAVE THE MEANS TO REMAKE YOU... INCREASE YOUR POWER!
SOUNDS GOOD, PAL! ALL RIGHT, I'M YOUR MAN!
"BUT NEFARIA HAD TRICKED JOSTEN INTO JOINING HIS SO-CALLED LETHAL LEGION JUST SO HE COULD SIPHON OFF THE FORMER POWER MAN'S MIGHT, AND BECOME A SUPER-BEING HIMSELF!
"SO JOSTEN WAS STOPPED BY THE AVENGERS AGAIN, AND ABANDONED BY HIS 'BENEFACTOR'... ALL BUT POWERLESS!
THE OTHER LETHAL LEGIONNAIRES WERE CAUGHT, BUT JOSTEN MANAGED TO ESCAPE.
EVENTUALLY, THE AVENGERS ALSO SQUELCHED NEFARIA. SOON AFTER JOSTEN REGAINED A PORTION OF HIS POWER. BY THIS TIME, HE SET HIMSELF UP AS THE SMUGGLER!
WELL, HE CERTAINLY HAD A NEAT OPERATION GOING WHEN I STUMBLED ACROSS IT! WHAT CONVINCED HIM TO GO STATE'S EVIDENCE?
SOME OF THE SLICKEST TALK KRIS KEATING EVER CAME UP WITH IN HIS LIFE, THAT'S WHAT!
YOU'VE GOTTA FACE FACTS, JOSTEN... YOUR POWERS ARE FADING FAST! WE CAN HOLD YOU WITH HARDLY ANY TROUBLE!
WE COULD EXTRADITE YOU TO ANY OF A DOZEN COUNTRIES!
BUT IF YOU TELL THE FEDS EVERYTHING YOU KNOW, WE COULD SHOW SOME LENIENCY!
OKAY. I'LL... DO IT.
"IT WAS QUITE A FEATHER IN KEATING'S CAP, LET ME TELL YOU! BUT THERE MUST HAVE BEEN AN INFORMATION LEAK OF SOME KIND, BECAUSE THE UNDERWORLD CAUGHT WIND OF JOSTEN'S DEAL!
"THE MAGGIA HAD SPECIAL REASONS TO SILENCE JOSTEN... HE USED TO BE ONE OF THEIR BOYS. SO, WHEN KEATING'S CREW WAS TAKING JOSTEN TO THE FEDERAL D.A., A SQUAD OF MAGGIA GOONS STRUCK--
"--MAKING OFF WITH OUR BOY IN A STOLEN AMBULANCE!"

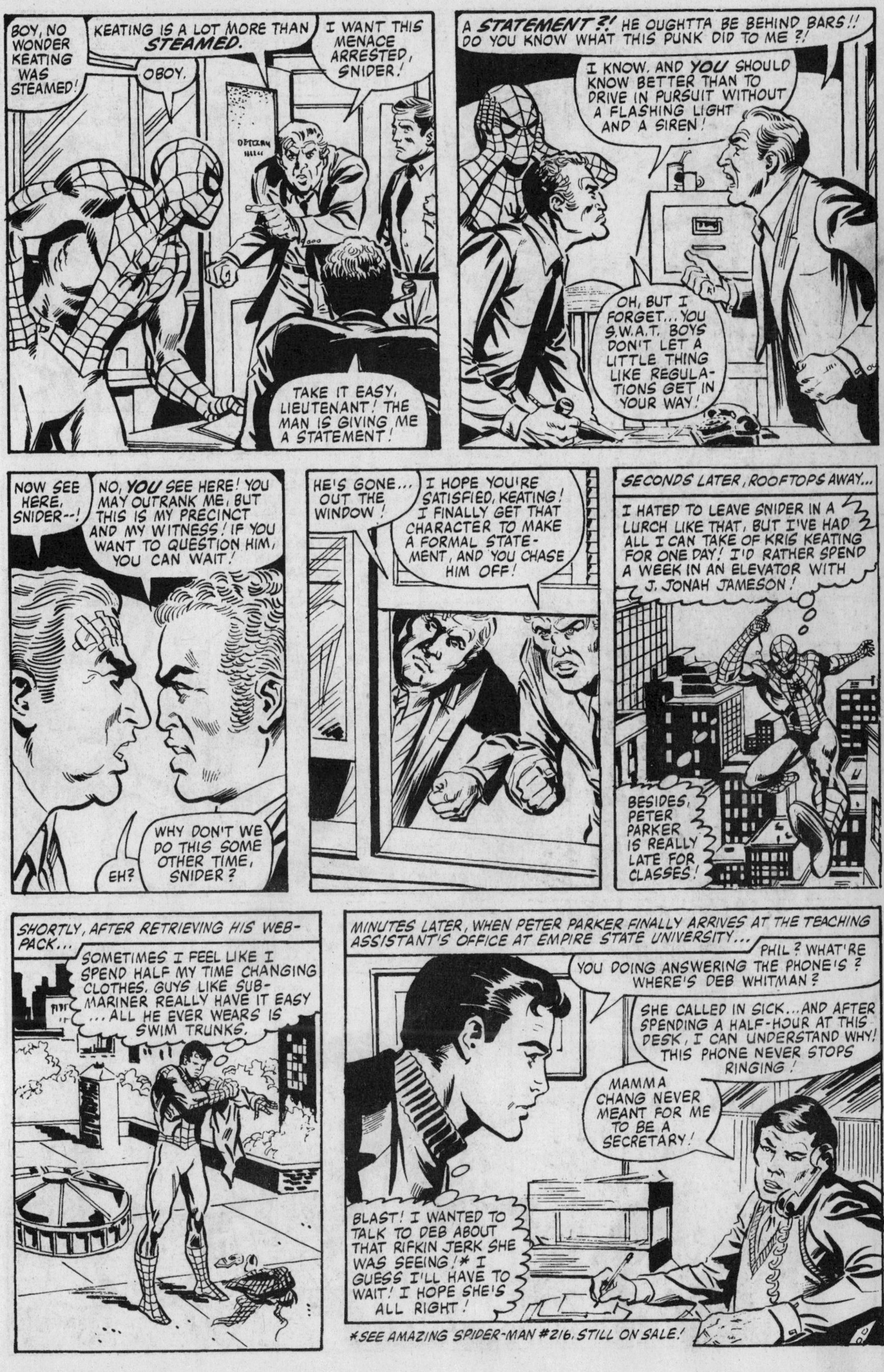
BOY, NO WONDER KEATING WAS STEAMED!
KEATING IS A LOT MORE THAN STEAMED.
OBOY.
I WANT THIS MENACE ARRESTED, SNIDER!
TAKE IT EASY, LIEUTENANT! THE MAN IS GIVING ME A STATEMENT!
A STATEMENT?! HE OUGHTTA BE BEHIND BARS!! DO YOU KNOW WHAT THIS PUNK DID TO ME?!
I KNOW. AND YOU SHOULD KNOW BETTER THAN TO DRIVE IN PURSUIT WITHOUT A FLASHING LIGHT AND A SIREN!
OH, BUT I FORGET... YOU S.W.A.T. BOYS DON'T LET A LITTLE THING LIKE REGULATIONS GET IN YOUR WAY!
NOW SEE HERE, SNIDER--!
NO, YOU SEE HERE! YOU MAY OUTRANK ME, BUT THIS IS MY PRECINCT AND MY WITNESS! IF YOU WANT TO QUESTION HIM, YOU CAN WAIT!
WHY DON'T WE DO THIS SOME OTHER TIME, SNIDER?
EH?
HE'S GONE... OUT THE WINDOW!
I HOPE YOU'RE SATISFIED, KEATING! I FINALLY GET THAT CHARACTER TO MAKE A FORMAL STATEMENT, AND YOU CHASE HIM OFF!
SECONDS LATER, ROOFTOPS AWAY...
I HATED TO LEAVE SNIDER IN A LURCH LIKE THAT, BUT I'VE HAD ALL I CAN TAKE OF KRIS KEATING FOR ONE DAY! I'D RATHER SPEND A WEEK IN AN ELEVATOR WITH J. JONAH JAMESON!
BESIDES, PETER PARKER IS REALLY LATE FOR CLASSES!
SHORTLY, AFTER RETRIEVING HIS WEB-PACK...
SOMETIMES I FEEL LIKE I SPEND HALF MY TIME CHANGING CLOTHES. GUYS LIKE SUB-MARINER REALLY HAVE IT EASY ... ALL HE EVER WEARS IS SWIM TRUNKS.
MINUTES LATER, WHEN PETER PARKER FINALLY ARRIVES AT THE TEACHING ASSISTANT'S OFFICE AT EMPIRE STATE UNIVERSITY...
PHIL? WHAT'RE YOU DOING ANSWERING THE PHONE'S? WHERE'S DEB WHITMAN?
SHE CALLED IN SICK... AND AFTER SPENDING A HALF-HOUR AT THIS DESK, I CAN UNDERSTAND WHY! THIS PHONE NEVER STOPS RINGING!
MAMMA CHANG NEVER MEANT FOR ME TO BE A SECRETARY!
BLAST! I WANTED TO TALK TO DEB ABOUT THAT RIFKIN JERK SHE WAS SEEING!* I GUESS I'LL HAVE TO WAIT! I HOPE SHE'S ALL RIGHT!
*SEE AMAZING SPIDER-MAN #216, STILL ON SALE!

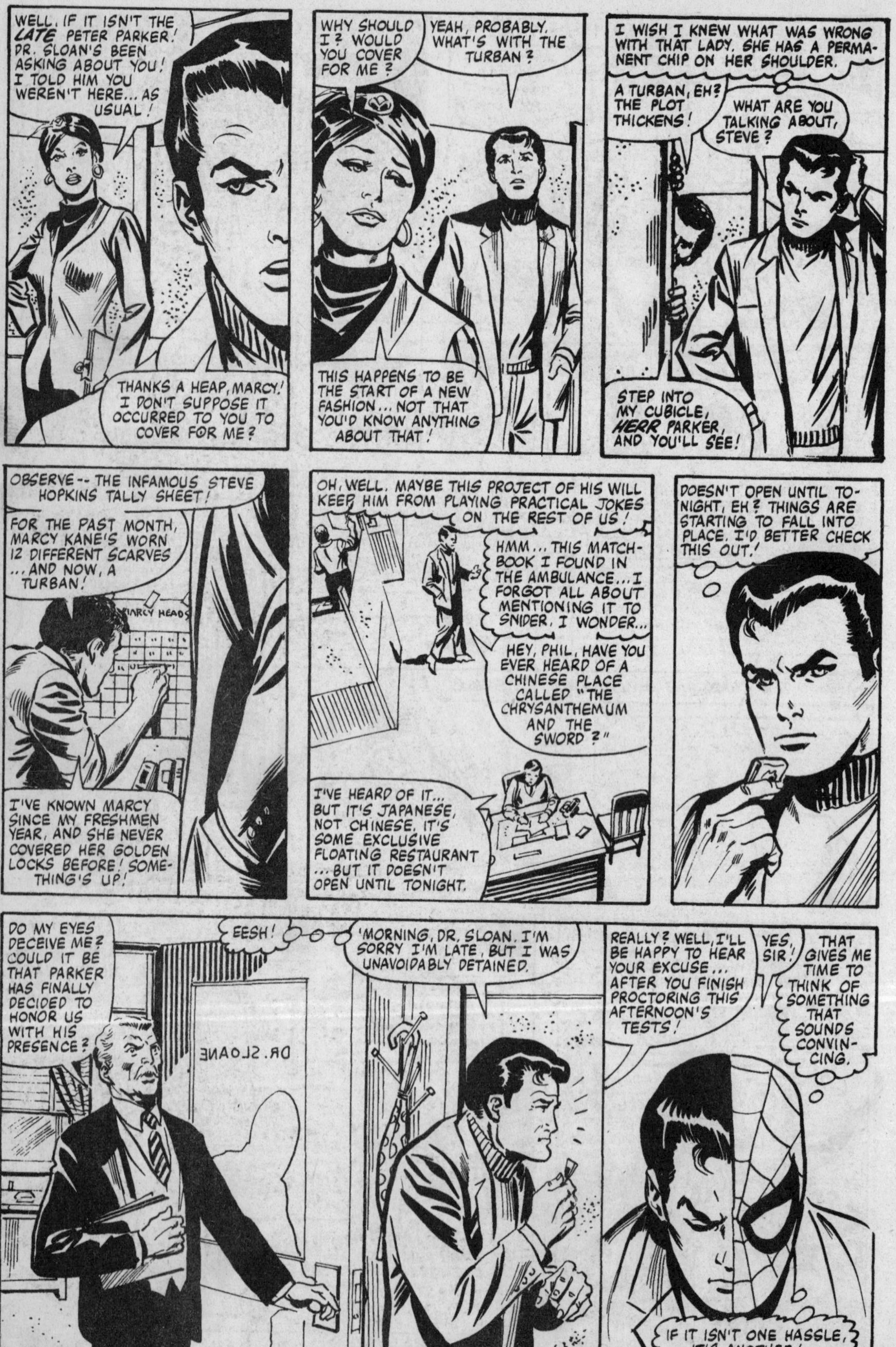
WELL, IF IT ISN'T THE LATE PETER PARKER! DR. SLOAN'S BEEN ASKING ABOUT YOU! I TOLD HIM YOU WEREN'T HERE... AS USUAL!
THANKS A HEAP, MARCY! I DON'T SUPPOSE IT OCCURRED TO YOU TO COVER FOR ME?
WHY SHOULD I? WOULD YOU COVER FOR ME?
YEAH, PROBABLY. WHAT'S WITH THE TURBAN?
THIS HAPPENS TO BE THE START OF A NEW FASHION... NOT THAT YOU'D KNOW ANYTHING ABOUT THAT!
I WISH I KNEW WHAT WAS WRONG WITH THAT LADY. SHE HAS A PERMANENT CHIP ON HER SHOULDER.
A TURBAN, EH? THE PLOT THICKENS!
WHAT ARE YOU TALKING ABOUT, STEVE?
STEP INTO MY CUBICLE, HERR PARKER, AND YOU'LL SEE!
OBSERVE -- THE INFAMOUS STEVE HOPKINS TALLY SHEET!
FOR THE PAST MONTH, MARCY KANE'S WORN 12 DIFFERENT SCARVES ... AND NOW, A TURBAN!
MARCY HEADS
I'VE KNOWN MARCY SINCE MY FRESHMEN YEAR, AND SHE NEVER COVERED HER GOLDEN LOCKS BEFORE! SOMETHING'S UP!
OH, WELL. MAYBE THIS PROJECT OF HIS WILL KEEP HIM FROM PLAYING PRACTICAL JOKES ON THE REST OF US!
HMM... THIS MATCHBOOK I FOUND IN THE AMBULANCE... I FORGOT ALL ABOUT MENTIONING IT TO SNIDER. I WONDER...
HEY, PHIL, HAVE YOU EVER HEARD OF A CHINESE PLACE CALLED "THE CHRYSANTHEMUM AND THE SWORD?"
I'VE HEARD OF IT... BUT IT'S JAPANESE, NOT CHINESE. IT'S SOME EXCLUSIVE FLOATING RESTAURANT ... BUT IT DOESN'T OPEN UNTIL TONIGHT.
DOESN'T OPEN UNTIL TONIGHT, EH? THINGS ARE STARTING TO FALL INTO PLACE. I'D BETTER CHECK THIS OUT!
DO MY EYES DECEIVE ME? COULD IT BE THAT PARKER HAS FINALLY DECIDED TO HONOR US WITH HIS PRESENCE?
DR. SLOANE
EESH!
'MORNING, DR. SLOAN. I'M SORRY I'M LATE, BUT I WAS UNAVOIDABLY DETAINED.
REALLY? WELL, I'LL BE HAPPY TO HEAR YOUR EXCUSE... AFTER YOU FINISH PROCTORING THIS AFTERNOON'S TESTS!
YES, SIR!
THAT GIVES ME TIME TO THINK OF SOMETHING THAT SOUNDS CONVINCING.
IF IT ISN'T ONE HASSLE, IT'S ANOTHER!

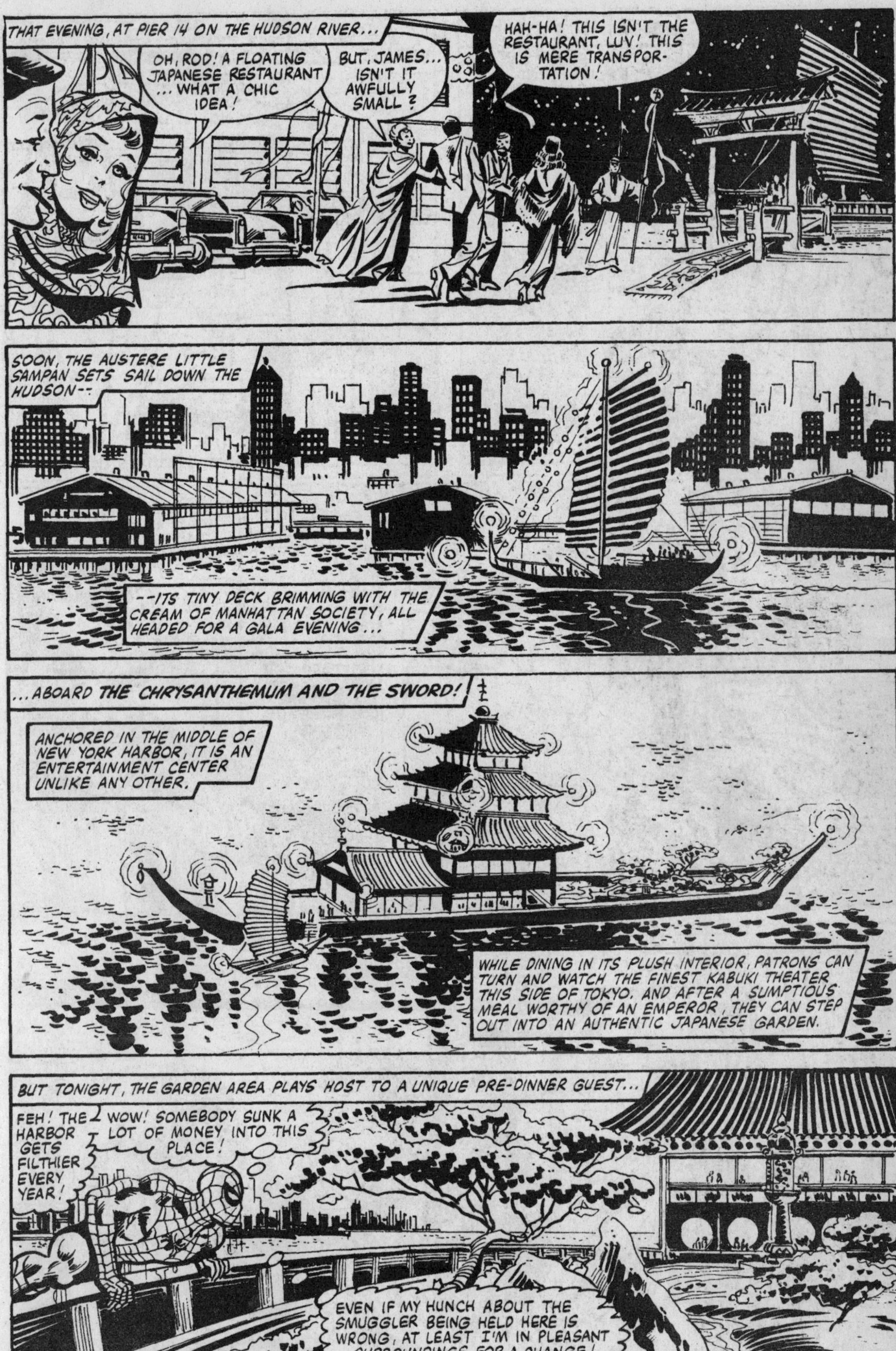

THAT EVENING, AT PIER 14 ON THE HUDSON RIVER...
OH, ROD! A FLOATING JAPANESE RESTAURANT ... WHAT A CHIC IDEA!
BUT, JAMES... ISN'T IT AWFULLY SMALL?
HAH-HA! THIS ISN'T THE RESTAURANT, LUV! THIS IS MERE TRANSPORTATION!
SOON, THE AUSTERE LITTLE SAMPAN SETS SAIL DOWN THE HUDSON--
--ITS TINY DECK BRIMMING WITH THE CREAM OF MANHATTAN SOCIETY, ALL HEADED FOR A GALA EVENING...
...ABOARD THE CHRYSANTHEMUM AND THE SWORD!
ANCHORED IN THE MIDDLE OF NEW YORK HARBOR, IT IS AN ENTERTAINMENT CENTER UNLIKE ANY OTHER.
WHILE DINING IN ITS PLUSH INTERIOR, PATRONS CAN TURN AND WATCH THE FINEST KABUKI THEATER THIS SIDE OF TOKYO. AND AFTER A SUMPTIOUS MEAL WORTHY OF AN EMPEROR, THEY CAN STEP OUT INTO AN AUTHENTIC JAPANESE GARDEN.
BUT TONIGHT, THE GARDEN AREA PLAYS HOST TO A UNIQUE PRE-DINNER GUEST...
FEH! THE HARBOR GETS FILTHIER EVERY YEAR!
WOW! SOMEBODY SUNK A LOT OF MONEY INTO THIS PLACE!
EVEN IF MY HUNCH ABOUT THE SMUGGLER BEING HELD HERE IS WRONG, AT LEAST I'M IN PLEASANT SURROUNDINGS FOR A CHANGE!

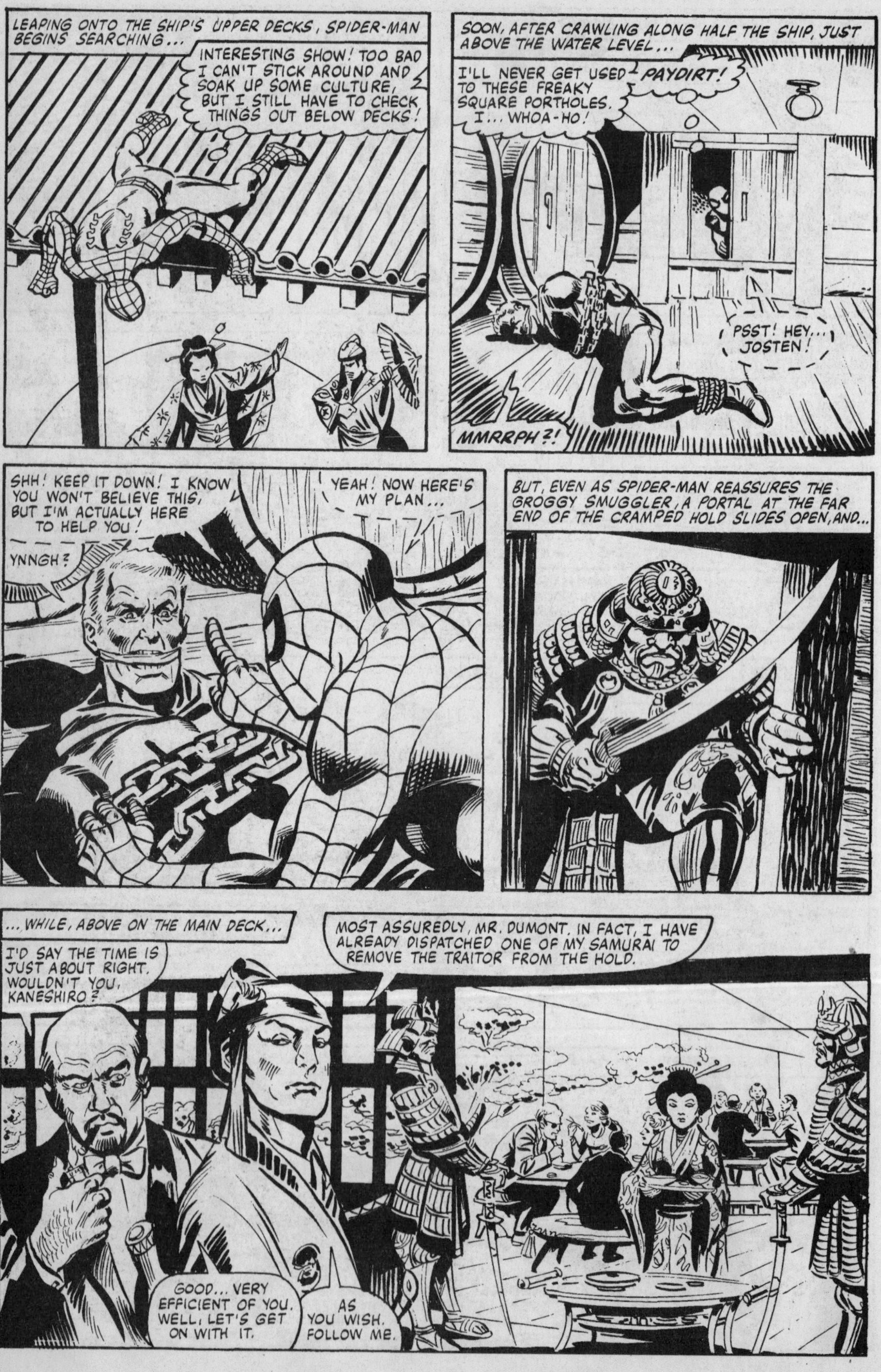

LEAPING ONTO THE SHIP'S UPPER DECKS, SPIDER-MAN BEGINS SEARCHING...
INTERESTING SHOW! TOO BAD I CAN'T STICK AROUND AND SOAK UP SOME CULTURE, BUT I STILL HAVE TO CHECK THINGS OUT BELOW DECKS!
SOON, AFTER CRAWLING ALONG HALF THE SHIP, JUST ABOVE THE WATER LEVEL...
I'LL NEVER GET USED TO THESE FREAKY SQUARE PORTHOLES. I... WHOA-HO!
PAYDIRT!
PSST! HEY... JOSTEN!
MMRRPH?!
SHH! KEEP IT DOWN! I KNOW YOU WON'T BELIEVE THIS, BUT I'M ACTUALLY HERE TO HELP YOU!
YNNGH?
YEAH! NOW HERE'S MY PLAN...
BUT, EVEN AS SPIDER-MAN REASSURES THE GROGGY SMUGGLER, A PORTAL AT THE FAR END OF THE CRAMPED HOLD SLIDES OPEN, AND...
...WHILE, ABOVE ON THE MAIN DECK...
I'D SAY THE TIME IS JUST ABOUT RIGHT. WOULDN'T YOU, KANESHIRO?
MOST ASSUREDLY, MR. DUMONT. IN FACT, I HAVE ALREADY DISPATCHED ONE OF MY SAMURAI TO REMOVE THE TRAITOR FROM THE HOLD.
GOOD... VERY EFFICIENT OF YOU. WELL, LET'S GET ON WITH IT.
AS YOU WISH. FOLLOW ME.

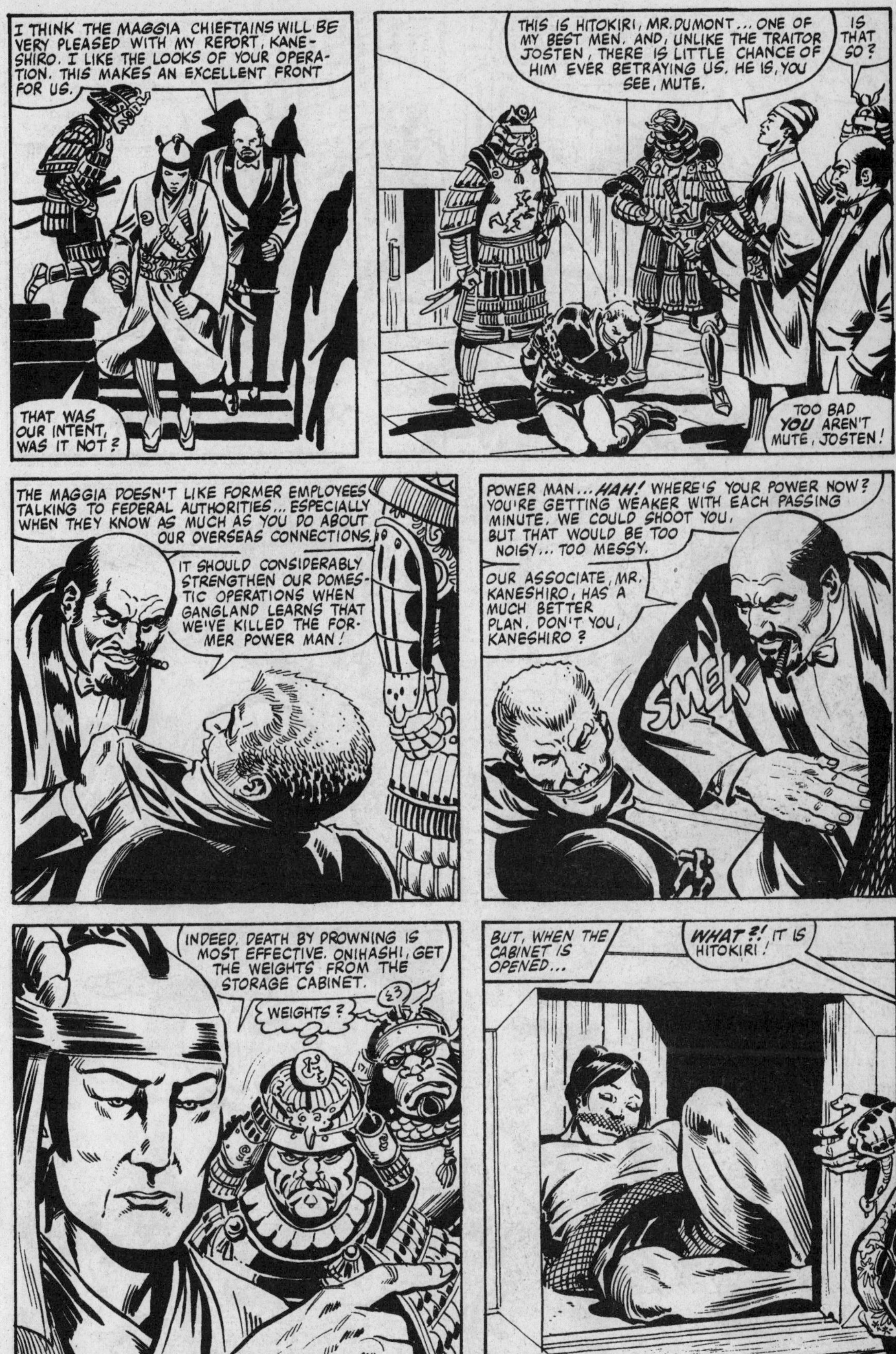

I THINK THE MAGGIA CHIEFTAINS WILL BE VERY PLEASED WITH MY REPORT, KANESHIRO. I LIKE THE LOOKS OF YOUR OPERATION. THIS MAKES AN EXCELLENT FRONT FOR US.
THAT WAS OUR INTENT, WAS IT NOT?
THIS IS HITOKIRI, MR. DUMONT... ONE OF MY BEST MEN. AND, UNLIKE THE TRAITOR JOSTEN, THERE IS LITTLE CHANCE OF HIM EVER BETRAYING US. HE IS, YOU SEE, MUTE.
IS THAT SO?
TOO BAD YOU AREN'T MUTE, JOSTEN!
THE MAGGIA DOESN'T LIKE FORMER EMPLOYEES TALKING TO FEDERAL AUTHORITIES... ESPECIALLY WHEN THEY KNOW AS MUCH AS YOU DO ABOUT OUR OVERSEAS CONNECTIONS.
IT SHOULD CONSIDERABLY STRENGTHEN OUR DOMESTIC OPERATIONS WHEN GANGLAND LEARNS THAT WE'VE KILLED THE FORMER POWER MAN!
POWER MAN... HAH! WHERE'S YOUR POWER NOW? YOU'RE GETTING WEAKER WITH EACH PASSING MINUTE. WE COULD SHOOT YOU, BUT THAT WOULD BE TOO NOISY... TOO MESSY.
OUR ASSOCIATE, MR. KANESHIRO, HAS A MUCH BETTER PLAN, DON'T YOU, KANESHIRO?
SMEK
INDEED. DEATH BY DROWNING IS MOST EFFECTIVE. ONIHASHI, GET THE WEIGHTS FROM THE STORAGE CABINET.
WEIGHTS?
BUT, WHEN THE CABINET IS OPENED...
WHAT?! IT IS HITOKIRI!

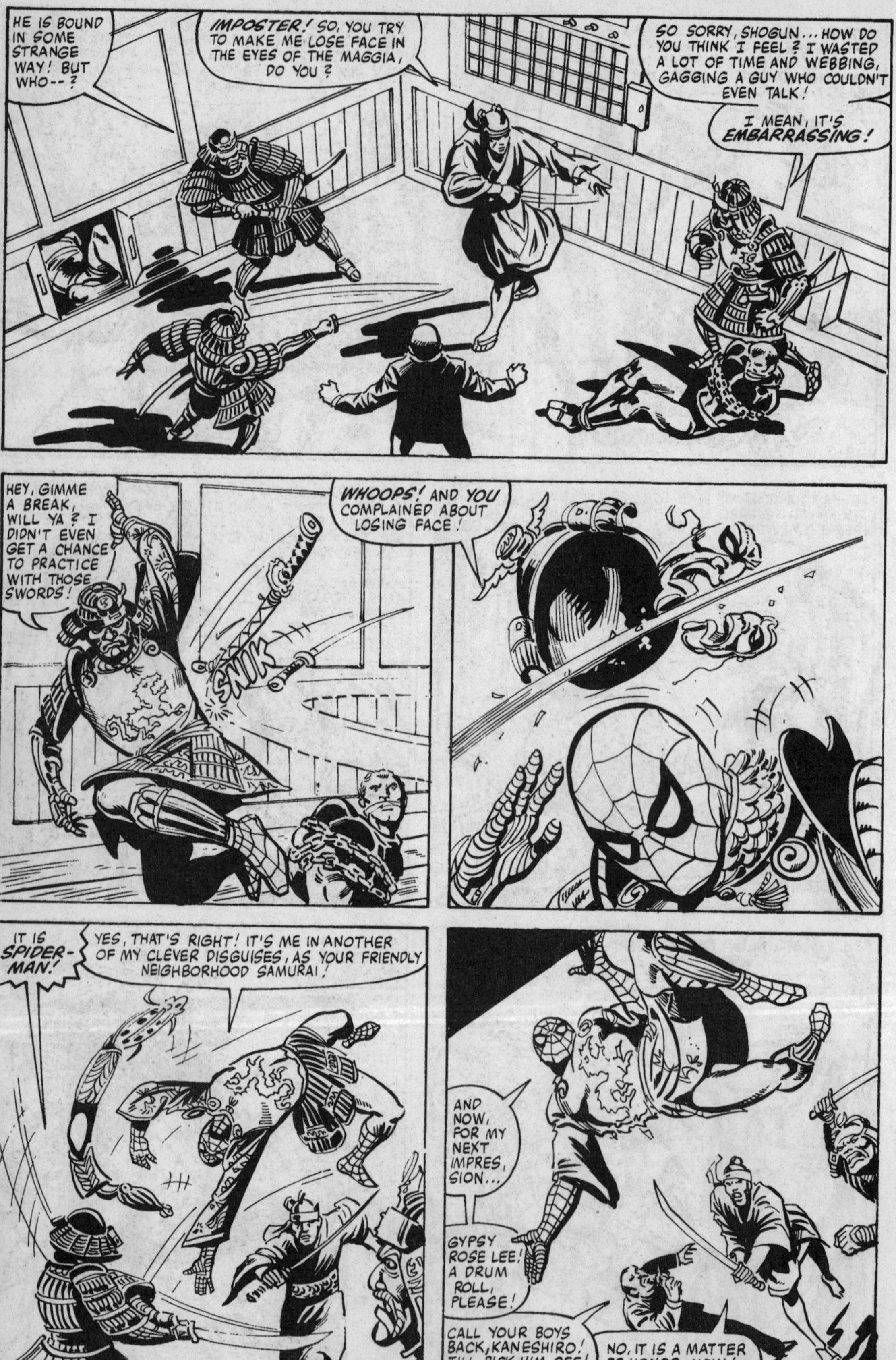
HE IS BOUND IN SOME STRANGE WAY! BUT WHO--?
IMPOSTER! SO, YOU TRY TO MAKE ME LOSE FACE IN THE EYES OF THE MAGGIA, DO YOU?
SO SORRY, SHOGUN... HOW DO YOU THINK I FEEL? I WASTED A LOT OF TIME AND WEBBING, GAGGING A GUY WHO COULDN'T EVEN TALK!
I MEAN, IT'S EMBARRASSING!
HEY, GIMME A BREAK, WILL YA? I DIDN'T EVEN GET A CHANCE TO PRACTICE WITH THOSE SWORDS!
SNIK
WHOOPS! AND YOU COMPLAINED ABOUT LOSING FACE!
IT IS SPIDER-MAN!
YES, THAT'S RIGHT! IT'S ME IN ANOTHER OF MY CLEVER DISGUISES, AS YOUR FRIENDLY NEIGHBORHOOD SAMURAI!
AND NOW, FOR MY NEXT IMPRES-SION...
GYPSY ROSE LEE! A DRUM ROLL, PLEASE!
CALL YOUR BOYS BACK, KANESHIRO! I'LL PICK HIM OFF!
NO, IT IS A MATTER OF HONOR, NOW!

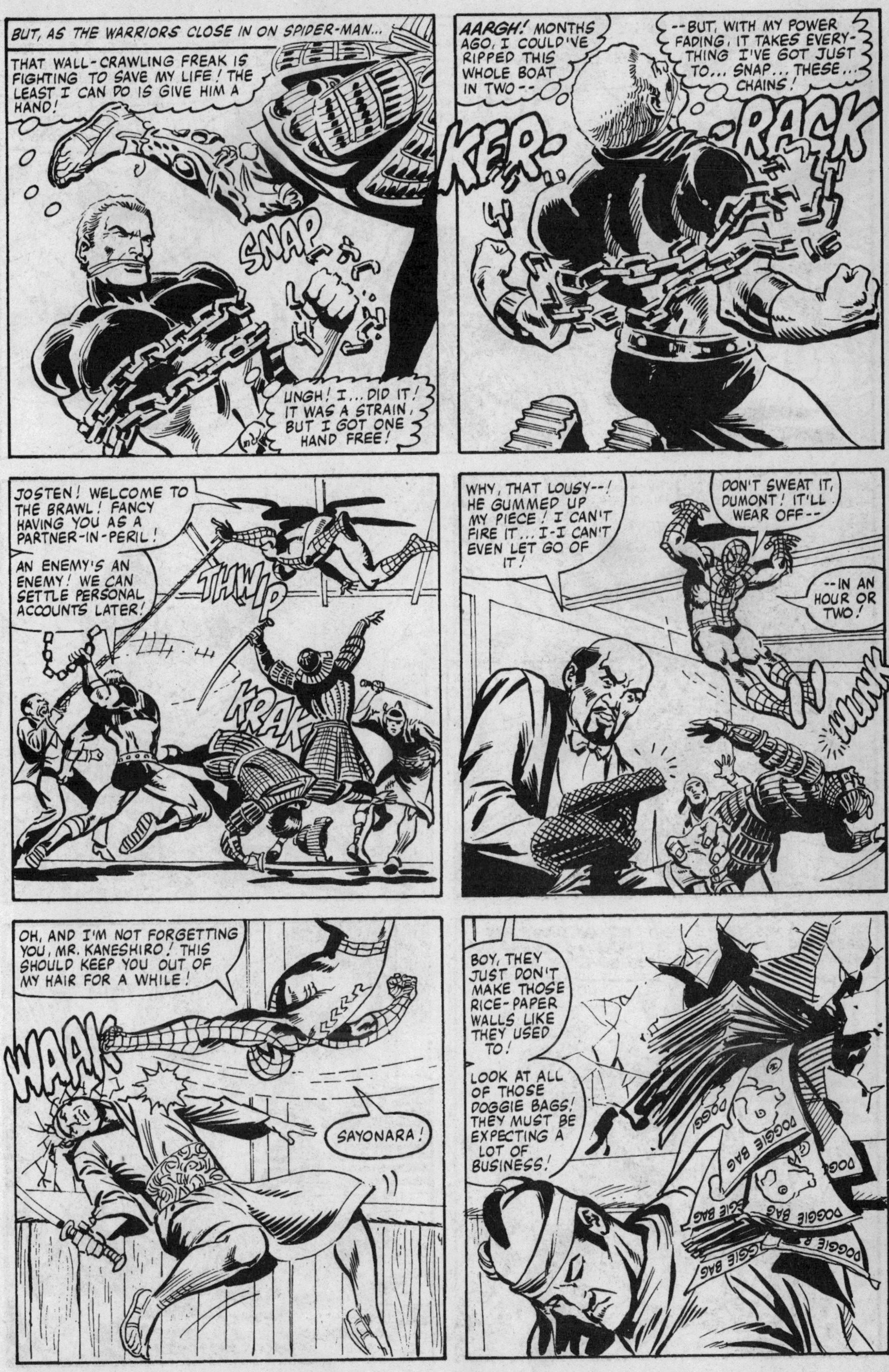

BUT, AS THE WARRIORS CLOSE IN ON SPIDER-MAN...
THAT WALL-CRAWLING FREAK IS FIGHTING TO SAVE MY LIFE! THE LEAST I CAN DO IS GIVE HIM A HAND!
SNAP
UNGH! I... DID IT! IT WAS A STRAIN, BUT I GOT ONE HAND FREE!
AARGH! MONTHS AGO, I COULD'VE RIPPED THIS WHOLE BOAT IN TWO--
--BUT, WITH MY POWER FADING, IT TAKES EVERYTHING I'VE GOT JUST TO... SNAP... THESE... CHAINS!
KER-RACK
JOSTEN! WELCOME TO THE BRAWL! FANCY HAVING YOU AS A PARTNER-IN-PERIL!
AN ENEMY'S AN ENEMY! WE CAN SETTLE PERSONAL ACCOUNTS LATER!
THWIP
KRAK
WHY, THAT LOUSY--! HE GUMMED UP MY PIECE! I CAN'T FIRE IT... I-I CAN'T EVEN LET GO OF IT!
DON'T SWEAT IT, DUMONT! IT'LL WEAR OFF--
--IN AN HOUR OR TWO!
WUNK
OH, AND I'M NOT FORGETTING YOU, MR. KANESHIRO! THIS SHOULD KEEP YOU OUT OF MY HAIR FOR A WHILE!
WAAK
SAYONARA!
BOY, THEY JUST DON'T MAKE THOSE RICE-PAPER WALLS LIKE THEY USED TO!
LOOK AT ALL OF THOSE DOGGIE BAGS! THEY MUST BE EXPECTING A LOT OF BUSINESS!
DOGGIE BAG

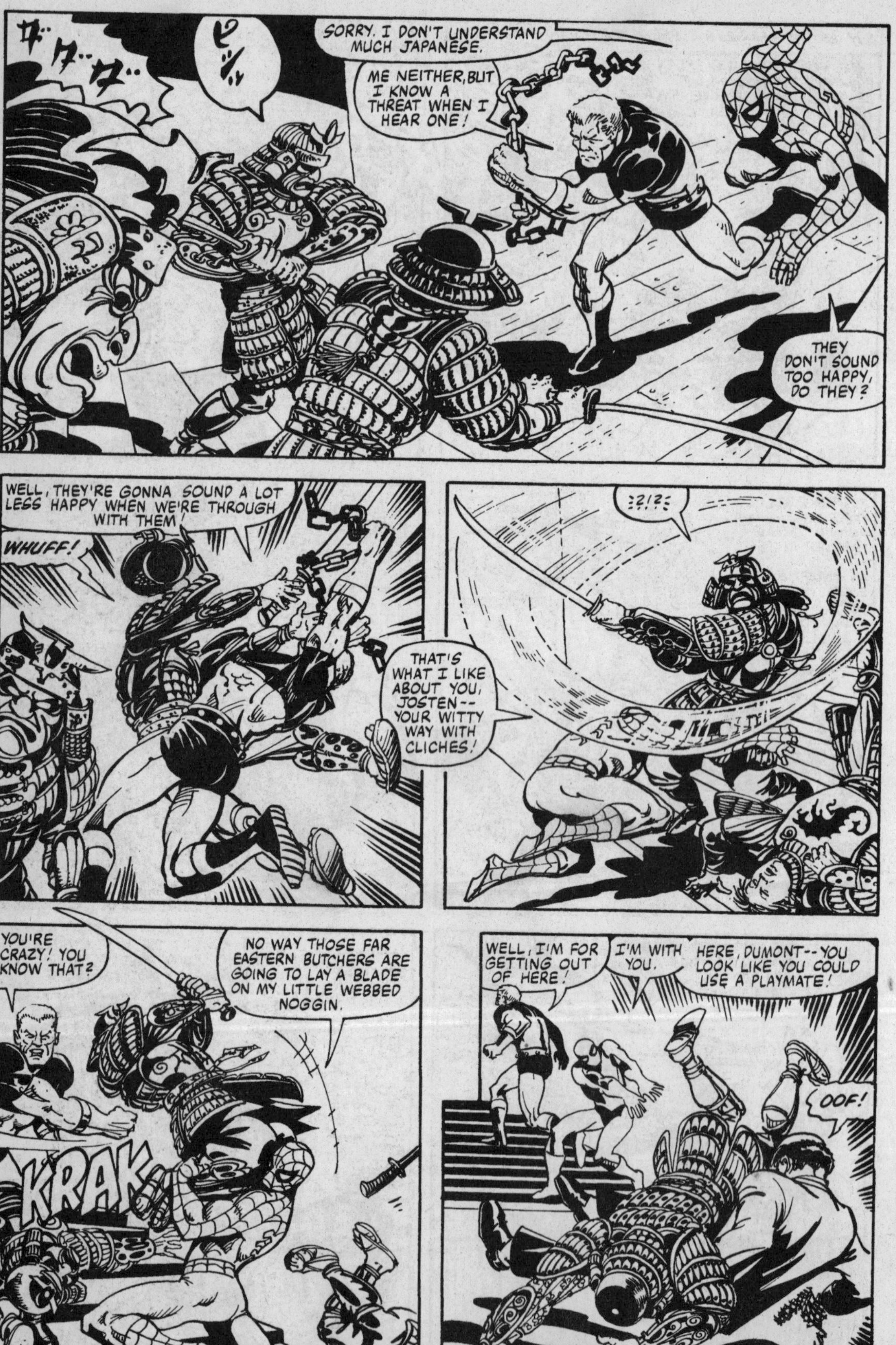
SORRY. I DON'T UNDERSTAND MUCH JAPANESE.
ME NEITHER, BUT I KNOW A THREAT WHEN I HEAR ONE!
THEY DON'T SOUND TOO HAPPY, DO THEY?
WELL, THEY'RE GONNA SOUND A LOT LESS HAPPY WHEN WE'RE THROUGH WITH THEM!
WHUFF!
THAT'S WHAT I LIKE ABOUT YOU, JOSTEN-- YOUR WITTY WAY WITH CLICHES!
?!?
YOU'RE CRAZY! YOU KNOW THAT?
NO WAY THOSE FAR EASTERN BUTCHERS ARE GOING TO LAY A BLADE ON MY LITTLE WEBBED NOGGIN.
KRAK
WELL, I'M FOR GETTING OUT OF HERE!
I'M WITH YOU.
HERE, DUMONT--YOU LOOK LIKE YOU COULD USE A PLAYMATE!
OOF!

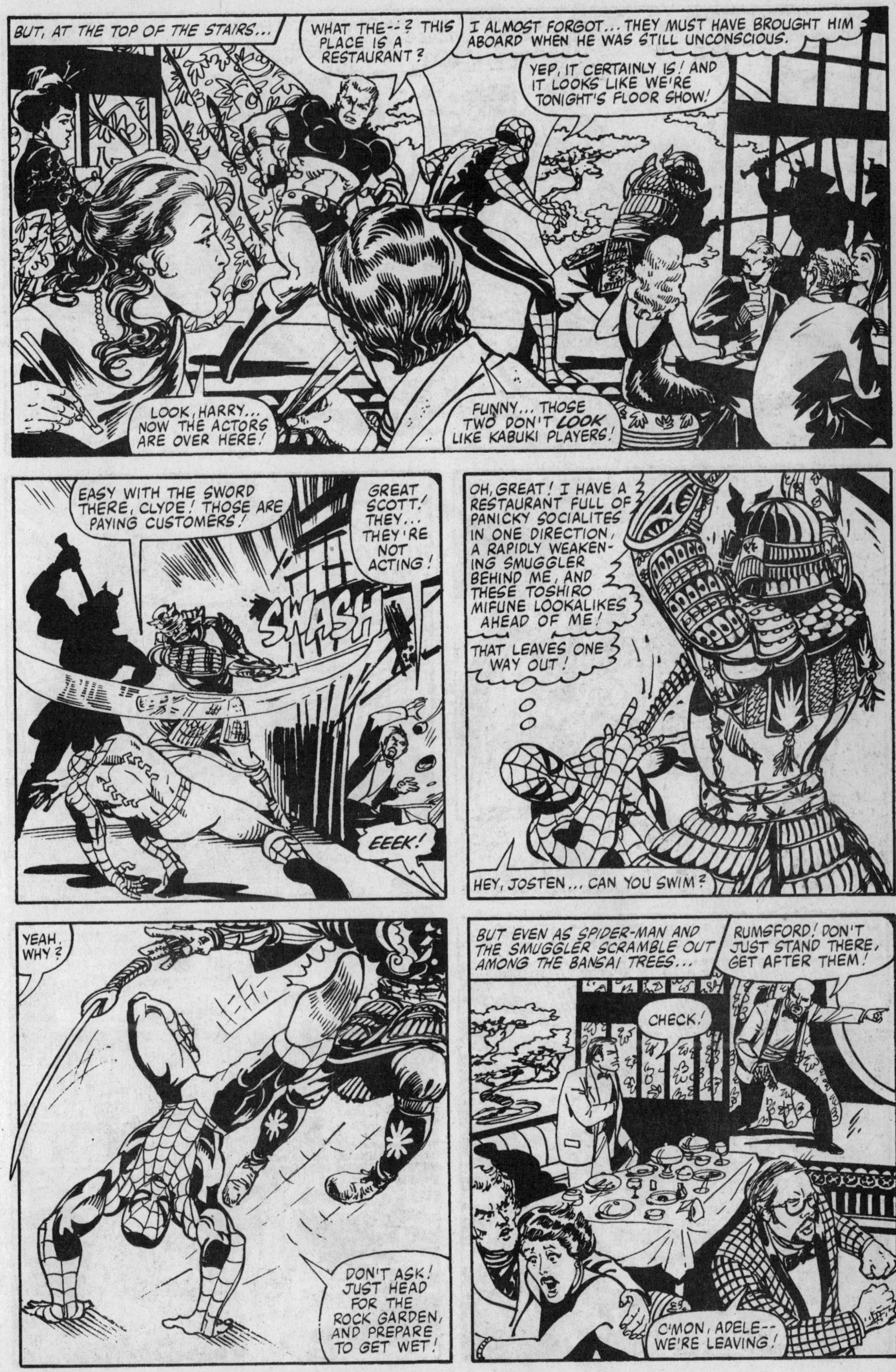
BUT, AT THE TOP OF THE STAIRS...
WHAT THE--? THIS PLACE IS A RESTAURANT?
I ALMOST FORGOT... THEY MUST HAVE BROUGHT HIM ABOARD WHEN HE WAS STILL UNCONSCIOUS.
YEP, IT CERTAINLY IS! AND IT LOOKS LIKE WE'RE TONIGHT'S FLOOR SHOW!
LOOK, HARRY... NOW THE ACTORS ARE OVER HERE!
FUNNY... THOSE TWO DON'T LOOK LIKE KABUKI PLAYERS!
EASY WITH THE SWORD THERE, CLYDE! THOSE ARE PAYING CUSTOMERS!
GREAT SCOTT! THEY... THEY'RE NOT ACTING!
SWASH
EEEK!
OH, GREAT! I HAVE A RESTAURANT FULL OF PANICKY SOCIALITES IN ONE DIRECTION, A RAPIDLY WEAKENING SMUGGLER BEHIND ME, AND THESE TOSHIRO MIFUNE LOOKALIKES AHEAD OF ME!
THAT LEAVES ONE WAY OUT!
HEY, JOSTEN... CAN YOU SWIM?
YEAH. WHY?
DON'T ASK! JUST HEAD FOR THE ROCK GARDEN, AND PREPARE TO GET WET!
BUT EVEN AS SPIDER-MAN AND THE SMUGGLER SCRAMBLE OUT AMONG THE BANSAI TREES...
RUMSFORD! DON'T JUST STAND THERE, GET AFTER THEM!
CHECK!
C'MON, ADELE-- WE'RE LEAVING!

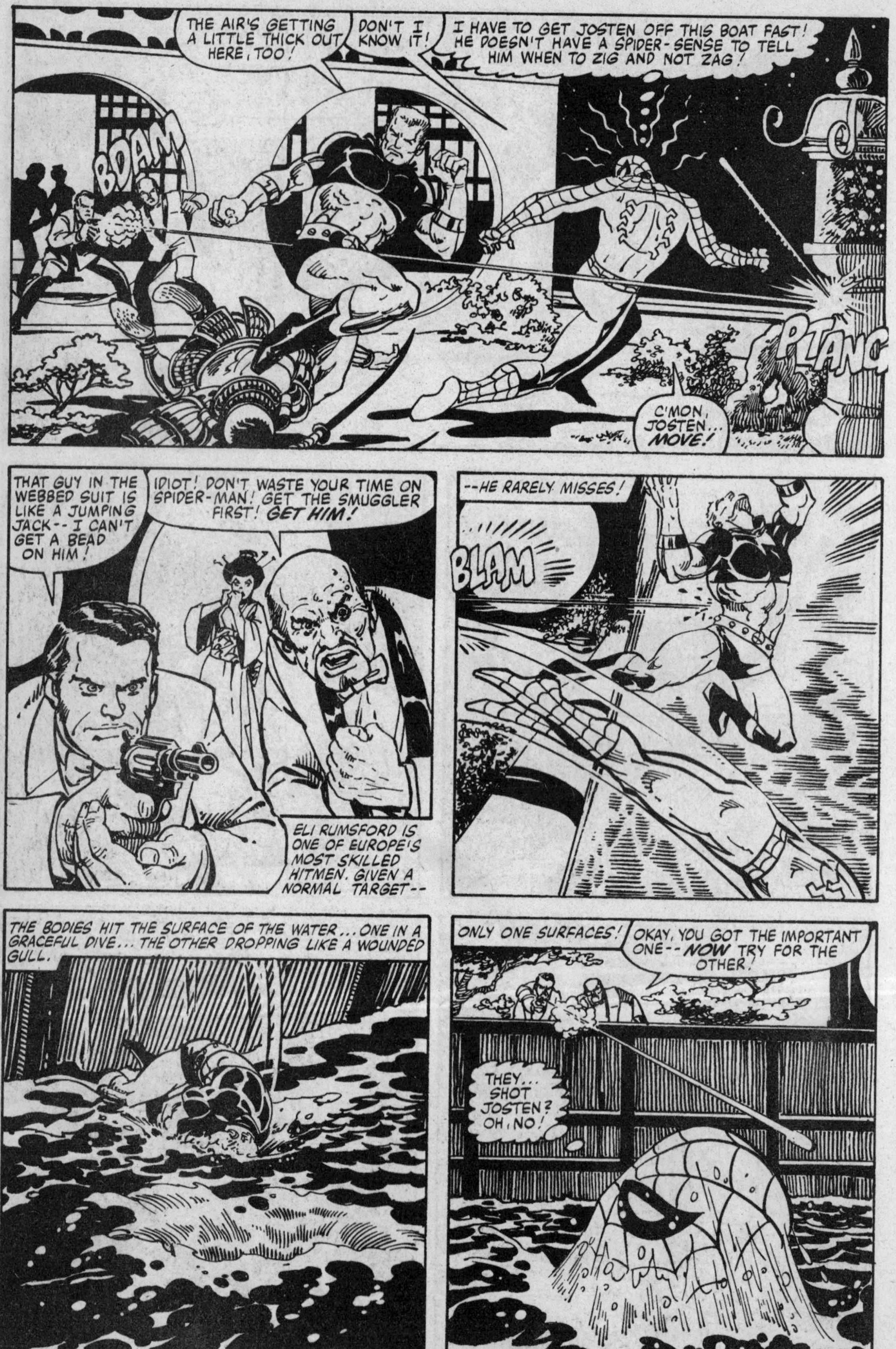
THE AIR'S GETTING A LITTLE THICK OUT HERE, TOO!
DON'T I KNOW IT!
I HAVE TO GET JOSTEN OFF THIS BOAT FAST! HE DOESN'T HAVE A SPIDER-SENSE TO TELL HIM WHEN TO ZIG AND NOT ZAG!
BOAM
PTANG
C'MON, JOSTEN... MOVE!
THAT GUY IN THE WEBBED SUIT IS LIKE A JUMPING JACK-- I CAN'T GET A BEAD ON HIM!
IDIOT! DON'T WASTE YOUR TIME ON SPIDER-MAN! GET THE SMUGGLER FIRST! GET HIM!
ELI RUMSFORD IS ONE OF EUROPE'S MOST SKILLED HITMEN. GIVEN A NORMAL TARGET--
--HE RARELY MISSES!
BLAM
THE BODIES HIT THE SURFACE OF THE WATER... ONE IN A GRACEFUL DIVE... THE OTHER DROPPING LIKE A WOUNDED GULL.
ONLY ONE SURFACES!
OKAY, YOU GOT THE IMPORTANT ONE-- NOW TRY FOR THE OTHER!
THEY... SHOT JOSTEN? OH, NO!

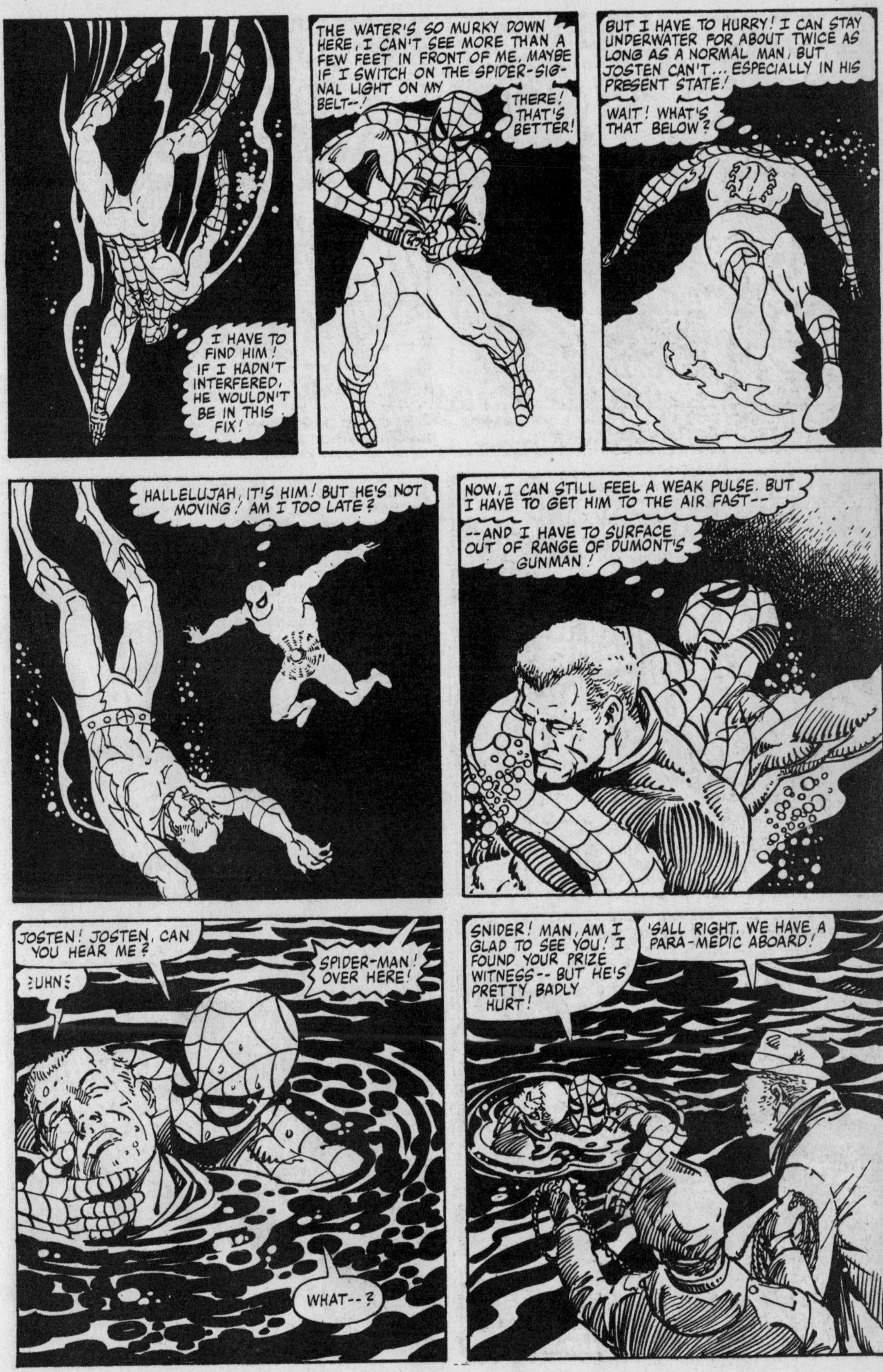
I HAVE TO FIND HIM! IF I HADN'T INTERFERED, HE WOULDN'T BE IN THIS FIX!
THE WATER'S SO MURKY DOWN HERE, I CAN'T SEE MORE THAN A FEW FEET IN FRONT OF ME. MAYBE IF I SWITCH ON THE SPIDER-SIGNAL LIGHT ON MY BELT--!
THERE! THAT'S BETTER!
BUT I HAVE TO HURRY! I CAN STAY UNDERWATER FOR ABOUT TWICE AS LONG AS A NORMAL MAN, BUT JOSTEN CAN'T... ESPECIALLY IN HIS PRESENT STATE!
WAIT! WHAT'S THAT BELOW?
HALLELUJAH, IT'S HIM! BUT HE'S NOT MOVING! AM I TOO LATE?
NOW, I CAN STILL FEEL A WEAK PULSE. BUT I HAVE TO GET HIM TO THE AIR FAST--
--AND I HAVE TO SURFACE OUT OF RANGE OF DUMONT'S GUNMAN!
JOSTEN! JOSTEN, CAN YOU HEAR ME?
UHN
SPIDER-MAN! OVER HERE!
WHAT--?
SNIDER! MAN, AM I GLAD TO SEE YOU! I FOUND YOUR PRIZE WITNESS-- BUT HE'S PRETTY BADLY HURT!
'SALL RIGHT. WE HAVE A PARA-MEDIC ABOARD!

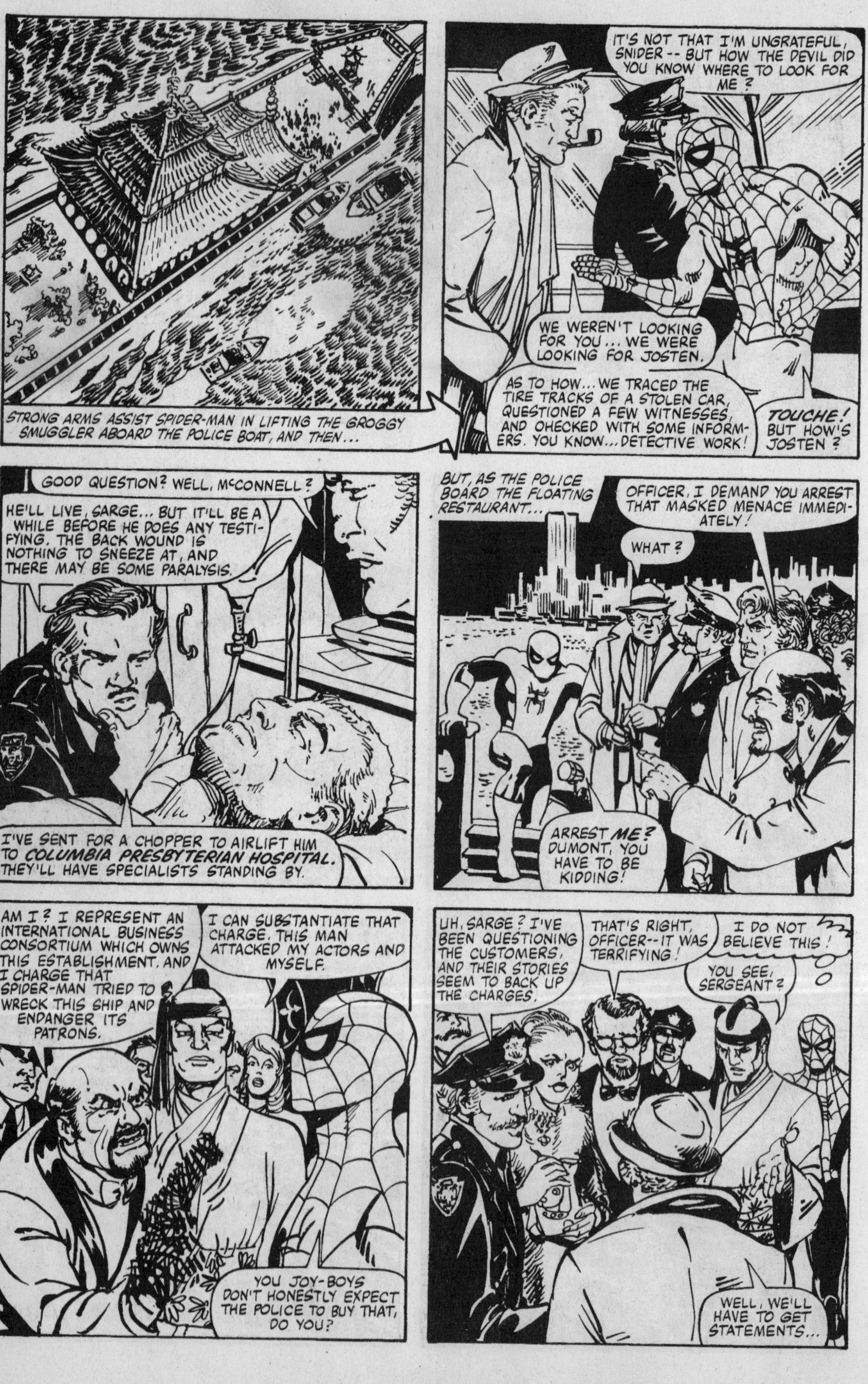
STRONG ARMS ASSIST SPIDER-MAN IN LIFTING THE GROGGY SMUGGLER ABOARD THE POLICE BOAT, AND THEN...
IT'S NOT THAT I'M UNGRATEFUL, SNIDER -- BUT HOW THE DEVIL DID YOU KNOW WHERE TO LOOK FOR ME ?
WE WEREN'T LOOKING FOR YOU... WE WERE LOOKING FOR JOSTEN.
AS TO HOW... WE TRACED THE TIRE TRACKS OF A STOLEN CAR, QUESTIONED A FEW WITNESSES, AND OHECKED WITH SOME INFORMERS. YOU KNOW... DETECTIVE WORK!
TOUCHE! BUT HOW'S JOSTEN ?
GOOD QUESTION? WELL, McCONNELL?
HE'LL LIVE, SARGE... BUT IT'LL BE A WHILE BEFORE HE DOES ANY TESTIFYING. THE BACK WOUND IS NOTHING TO SNEEZE AT, AND THERE MAY BE SOME PARALYSIS.
I'VE SENT FOR A CHOPPER TO AIRLIFT HIM TO COLUMBIA PRESBYTERIAN HOSPITAL. THEY'LL HAVE SPECIALISTS STANDING BY.
BUT, AS THE POLICE BOARD THE FLOATING RESTAURANT...
OFFICER, I DEMAND YOU ARREST THAT MASKED MENACE IMMEDIATELY!
WHAT?
ARREST ME? DUMONT, YOU HAVE TO BE KIDDING!
AM I? I REPRESENT AN INTERNATIONAL BUSINESS CONSORTIUM WHICH OWNS THIS ESTABLISHMENT, AND I CHARGE THAT SPIDER-MAN TRIED TO WRECK THIS SHIP AND ENDANGER ITS PATRONS.
I CAN SUBSTANTIATE THAT CHARGE. THIS MAN ATTACKED MY ACTORS AND MYSELF.
YOU JOY-BOYS DON'T HONESTLY EXPECT THE POLICE TO BUY THAT, DO YOU?
UH, SARGE? I'VE BEEN QUESTIONING THE CUSTOMERS, AND THEIR STORIES SEEM TO BACK UP THE CHARGES.
THAT'S RIGHT, OFFICER--IT WAS TERRIFYING!
I DO NOT BELIEVE THIS!
YOU SEE, SERGEANT?
WELL, WE'LL HAVE TO GET STATEMENTS...

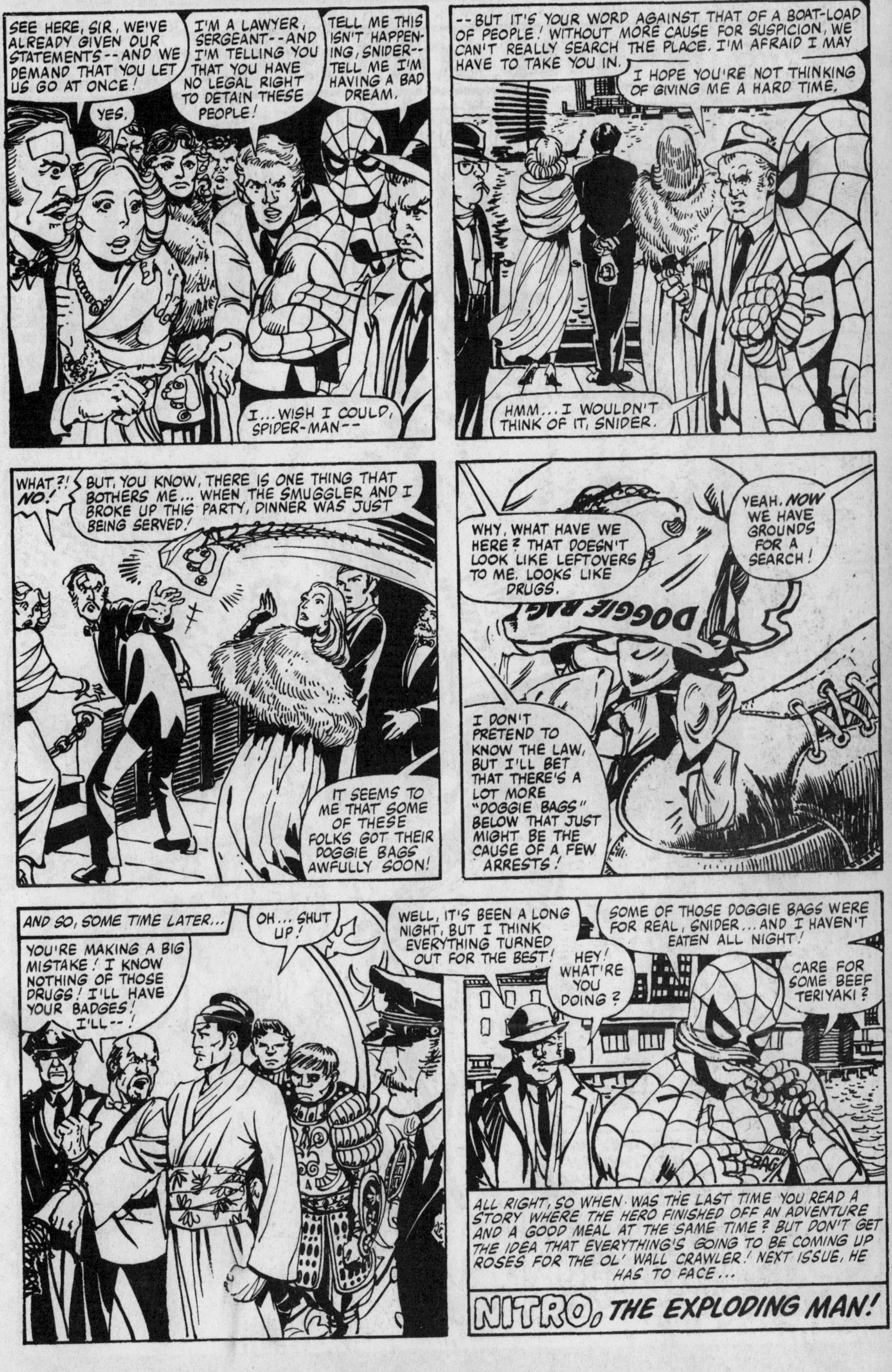

SEE HERE, SIR, WE'VE ALREADY GIVEN OUR STATEMENTS--AND WE DEMAND THAT YOU LET US GO AT ONCE!
YES.
I'M A LAWYER, SERGEANT--AND I'M TELLING YOU THAT YOU HAVE NO LEGAL RIGHT TO DETAIN THESE PEOPLE!
TELL ME THIS ISN'T HAPPENING, SNIDER--TELL ME I'M HAVING A BAD DREAM.
I...WISH I COULD, SPIDER-MAN--
--BUT IT'S YOUR WORD AGAINST THAT OF A BOAT-LOAD OF PEOPLE! WITHOUT MORE CAUSE FOR SUSPICION, WE CAN'T REALLY SEARCH THE PLACE. I'M AFRAID I MAY HAVE TO TAKE YOU IN.
I HOPE YOU'RE NOT THINKING OF GIVING ME A HARD TIME.
HMM...I WOULDN'T THINK OF IT, SNIDER.
WHAT?! NO!
BUT, YOU KNOW, THERE IS ONE THING THAT BOTHERS ME... WHEN THE SMUGGLER AND I BROKE UP THIS PARTY, DINNER WAS JUST BEING SERVED!
IT SEEMS TO ME THAT SOME OF THESE FOLKS GOT THEIR DOGGIE BAGS AWFULLY SOON!
WHY, WHAT HAVE WE HERE? THAT DOESN'T LOOK LIKE LEFTOVERS TO ME. LOOKS LIKE DRUGS.
YEAH. NOW WE HAVE GROUNDS FOR A SEARCH!
DOGGIE BAG
I DON'T PRETEND TO KNOW THE LAW, BUT I'LL BET THAT THERE'S A LOT MORE "DOGGIE BAGS" BELOW THAT JUST MIGHT BE THE CAUSE OF A FEW ARRESTS!
AND SO, SOME TIME LATER...
YOU'RE MAKING A BIG MISTAKE! I KNOW NOTHING OF THOSE DRUGS! I'LL HAVE YOUR BADGES! I'LL--!
OH... SHUT UP!
WELL, IT'S BEEN A LONG NIGHT, BUT I THINK EVERYTHING TURNED OUT FOR THE BEST!
SOME OF THOSE DOGGIE BAGS WERE FOR REAL, SNIDER...AND I HAVEN'T EATEN ALL NIGHT!
HEY! WHAT'RE YOU DOING?
CARE FOR SOME BEEF TERIYAKI?
BAG
ALL RIGHT, SO WHEN WAS THE LAST TIME YOU READ A STORY WHERE THE HERO FINISHED OFF AN ADVENTURE AND A GOOD MEAL AT THE SAME TIME? BUT DON'T GET THE IDEA THAT EVERYTHING'S GOING TO BE COMING UP ROSES FOR THE OL' WALL CRAWLER! NEXT ISSUE, HE HAS TO FACE...
NITRO, THE EXPLODING MAN!

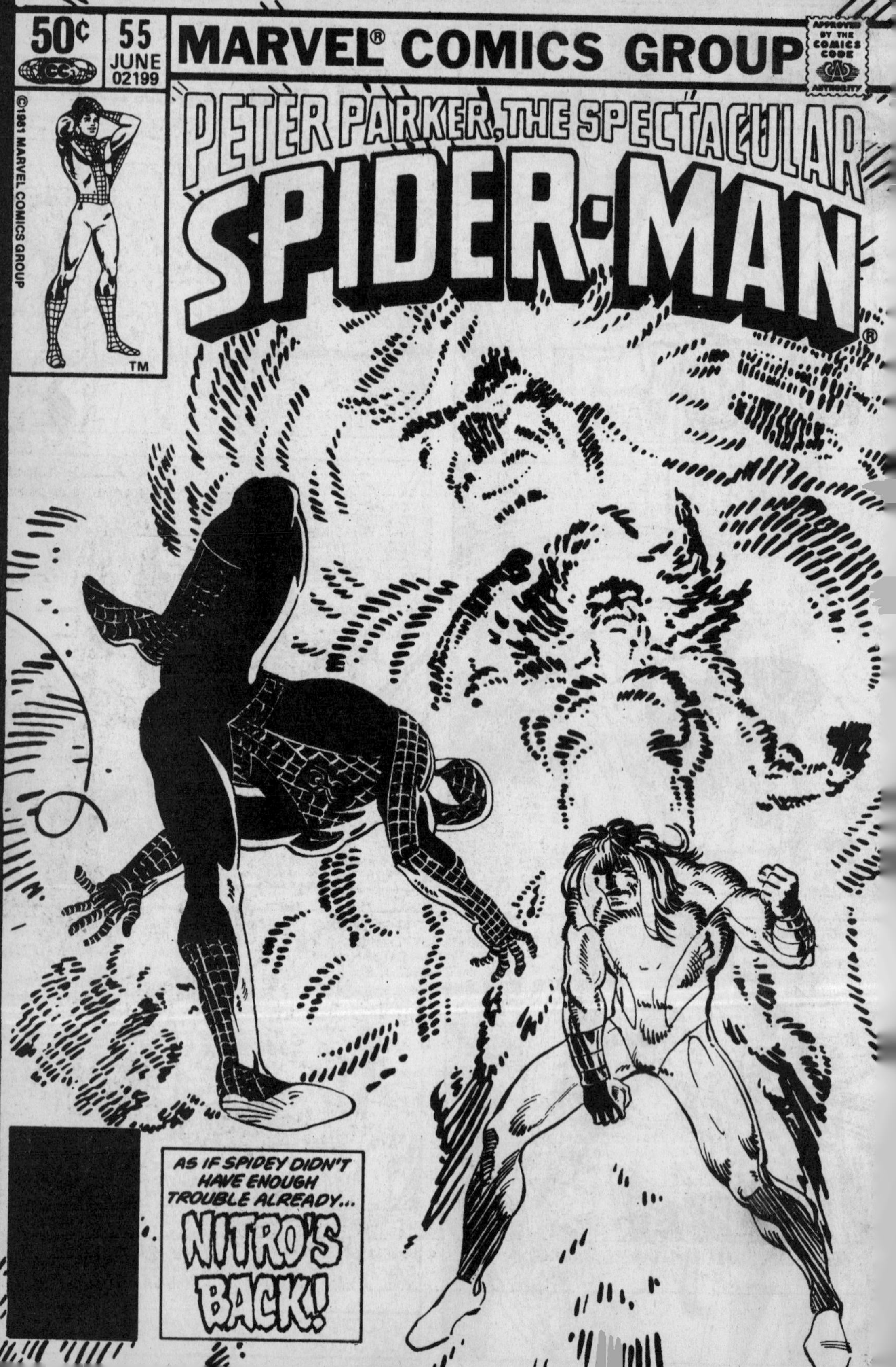
50¢
55
JUNE
02199
MARVEL COMICS GROUP
APPROVED BY THE COMICS CODE AUTHORITY
©1981 MARVEL COMICS GROUP
TM
PETER PARKER, THE SPECTACULAR
SPIDER-MAN
AS IF SPIDEY DIDN'T HAVE ENOUGH TROUBLE ALREADY...
NITRO'S BACK!

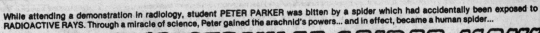

While attending a demonstration in radiology, student PETER PARKER was bitten by a spider which had accidentally been exposed to RADIOACTIVE RAYS. Through a miracle of science, Peter gained the arachnid's powers... and in effect, became a human spider...

Stan Lee PRESENTS: **THE SPECTACULAR SPIDER-MAN!**®

The BIG BLOW OUT

DESPITE WHAT EARLY RISERS TELL YOU, SEVEN O'CLOCK IN THE MORNING IS *NOT* A PLEASANT TIME TO WAKE UP... ESPECIALLY FOR A FELLOW LIKE PETER PARKER!

MAYBE IT WOULDN'T BE SO BAD IF PETE WERE JUST A GRADUATE STUDENT. BUT IT SO HAPPENS THAT HE'S ALSO A TEACHING ASSISTANT, A PART-TIME PHOTOGRAPHER FOR THE *DAILY BUGLE*, AND-- OH, YES--SPIDER-MAN!

AND LEADING FOUR LIVES CAN BE TIRING, EVEN FOR A MAN WITH THE PROPORTIONATE POWERS OF A SPIDER!

GNRRR

HUH?! WHAT?!

ROGER STERN	LUKE McDONNELL	JIM MOONEY	JOHN MORELLI	ROG SLIFER	DENNY O'NEIL	JIM SHOOTER
WRITER	PENCILER	INKER	LETTERER	COLORIST	EDITOR	WAKE-UP CALLS

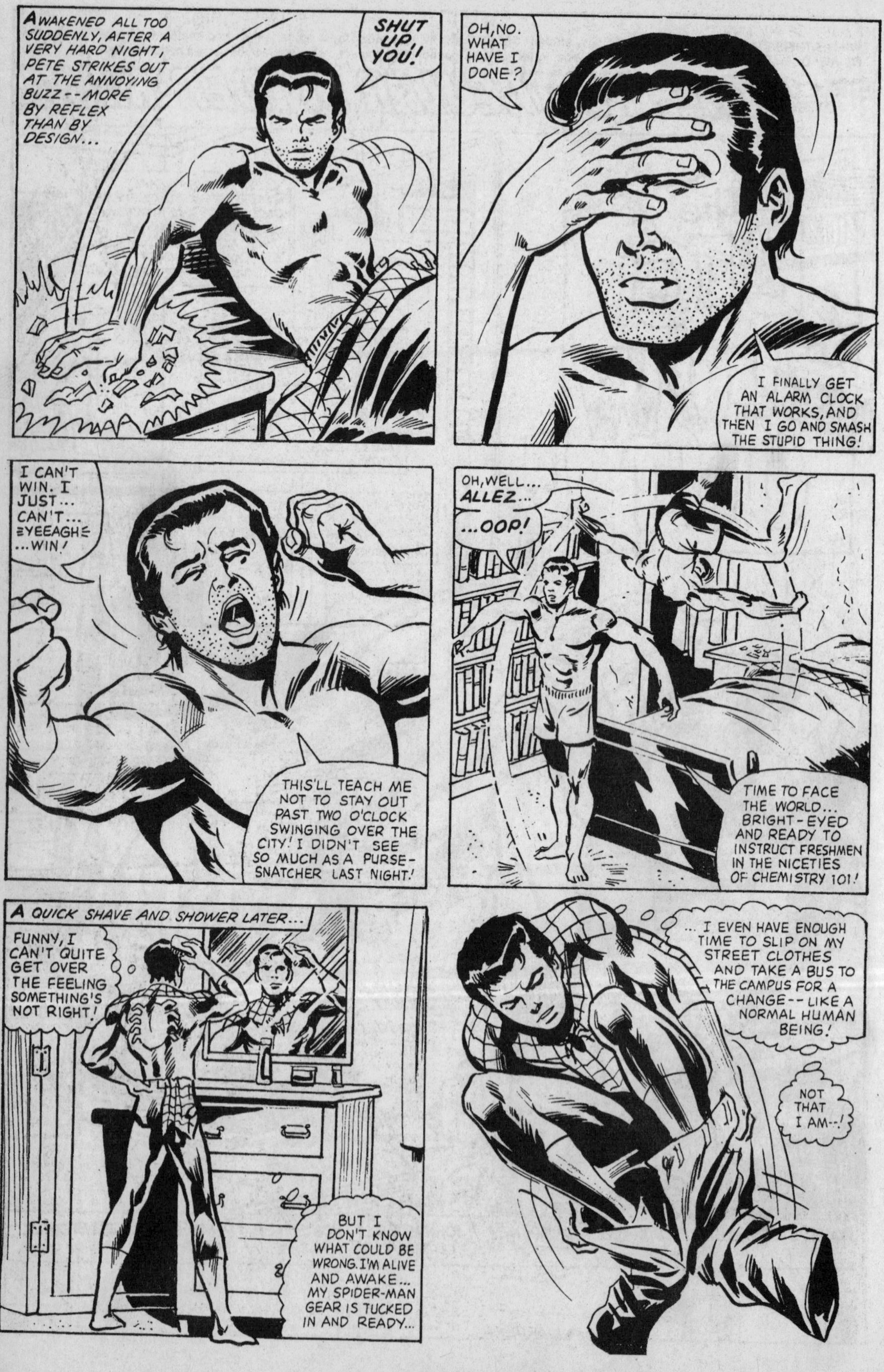

AWAKENED ALL TOO SUDDENLY, AFTER A VERY HARD NIGHT, PETE STRIKES OUT AT THE ANNOYING BUZZ--MORE BY REFLEX THAN BY DESIGN...
SHUT UP, YOU!
OH, NO. WHAT HAVE I DONE?
I FINALLY GET AN ALARM CLOCK THAT WORKS, AND THEN I GO AND SMASH THE STUPID THING!
I CAN'T WIN. I JUST... CAN'T... =YEEAGH= ...WIN!
THIS'LL TEACH ME NOT TO STAY OUT PAST TWO O'CLOCK SWINGING OVER THE CITY! I DIDN'T SEE SO MUCH AS A PURSE-SNATCHER LAST NIGHT!
OH, WELL... ALLEZ...
...OOP!
TIME TO FACE THE WORLD... BRIGHT-EYED AND READY TO INSTRUCT FRESHMEN IN THE NICETIES OF CHEMISTRY 101!
A QUICK SHAVE AND SHOWER LATER...
FUNNY, I CAN'T QUITE GET OVER THE FEELING SOMETHING'S NOT RIGHT!
BUT I DON'T KNOW WHAT COULD BE WRONG. I'M ALIVE AND AWAKE... MY SPIDER-MAN GEAR IS TUCKED IN AND READY...
...I EVEN HAVE ENOUGH TIME TO SLIP ON MY STREET CLOTHES AND TAKE A BUS TO THE CAMPUS FOR A CHANGE--LIKE A NORMAL HUMAN BEING!
NOT THAT I AM--!

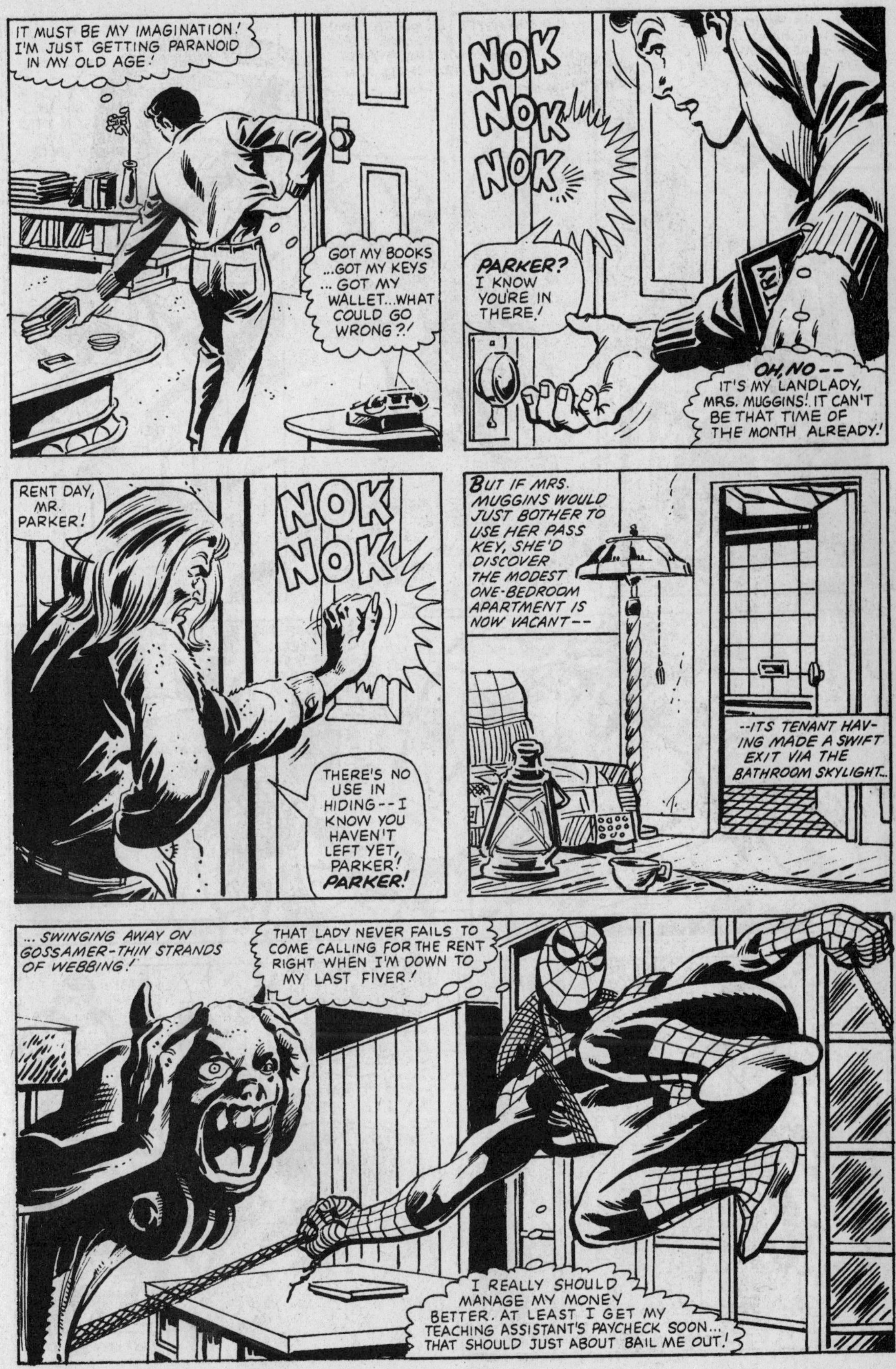
IT MUST BE MY IMAGINATION! I'M JUST GETTING PARANOID IN MY OLD AGE!
GOT MY BOOKS ...GOT MY KEYS ... GOT MY WALLET...WHAT COULD GO WRONG?!
NOK NOK NOK
PARKER? I KNOW YOU'RE IN THERE!
OH, NO -- IT'S MY LANDLADY, MRS. MUGGINS! IT CAN'T BE THAT TIME OF THE MONTH ALREADY!
RENT DAY, MR. PARKER!
NOK NOK
THERE'S NO USE IN HIDING--I KNOW YOU HAVEN'T LEFT YET, PARKER! PARKER!
BUT IF MRS. MUGGINS WOULD JUST BOTHER TO USE HER PASS KEY, SHE'D DISCOVER THE MODEST ONE-BEDROOM APARTMENT IS NOW VACANT--
--ITS TENANT HAVING MADE A SWIFT EXIT VIA THE BATHROOM SKYLIGHT...
... SWINGING AWAY ON GOSSAMER-THIN STRANDS OF WEBBING!
THAT LADY NEVER FAILS TO COME CALLING FOR THE RENT RIGHT WHEN I'M DOWN TO MY LAST FIVER!
I REALLY SHOULD MANAGE MY MONEY BETTER. AT LEAST I GET MY TEACHING ASSISTANT'S PAYCHECK SOON... THAT SHOULD JUST ABOUT BAIL ME OUT!

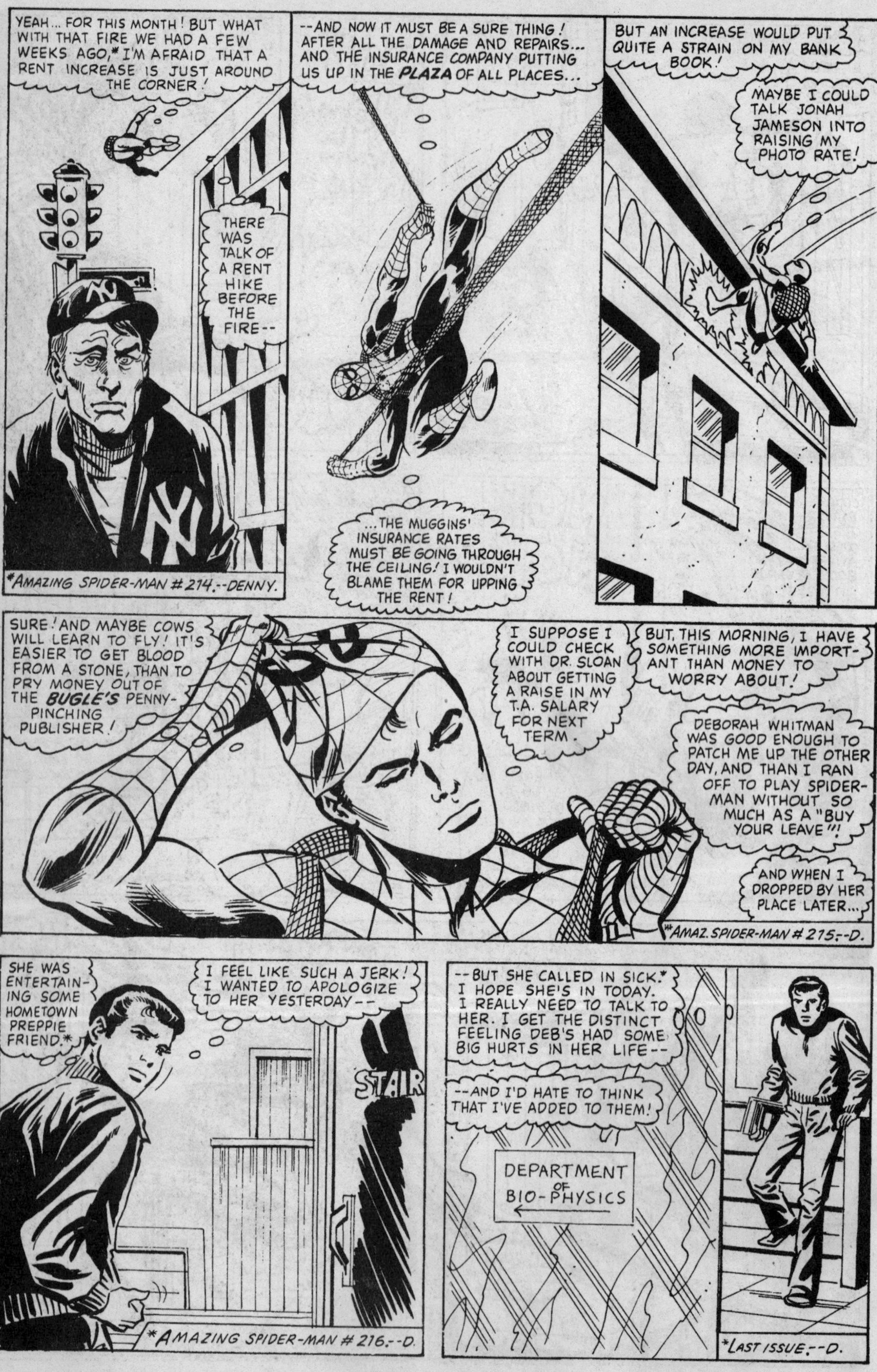
YEAH... FOR THIS MONTH! BUT WHAT WITH THAT FIRE WE HAD A FEW WEEKS AGO,* I'M AFRAID THAT A RENT INCREASE IS JUST AROUND THE CORNER!
THERE WAS TALK OF A RENT HIKE BEFORE THE FIRE--
*AMAZING SPIDER-MAN #214.--DENNY.
--AND NOW IT MUST BE A SURE THING! AFTER ALL THE DAMAGE AND REPAIRS... AND THE INSURANCE COMPANY PUTTING US UP IN THE PLAZA OF ALL PLACES...
...THE MUGGINS' INSURANCE RATES MUST BE GOING THROUGH THE CEILING! I WOULDN'T BLAME THEM FOR UPPING THE RENT!
BUT AN INCREASE WOULD PUT QUITE A STRAIN ON MY BANK BOOK!
MAYBE I COULD TALK JONAH JAMESON INTO RAISING MY PHOTO RATE!
SURE! AND MAYBE COWS WILL LEARN TO FLY! IT'S EASIER TO GET BLOOD FROM A STONE, THAN TO PRY MONEY OUT OF THE BUGLE'S PENNY-PINCHING PUBLISHER!
I SUPPOSE I COULD CHECK WITH DR. SLOAN ABOUT GETTING A RAISE IN MY T.A. SALARY FOR NEXT TERM.
BUT, THIS MORNING, I HAVE SOMETHING MORE IMPORT-ANT THAN MONEY TO WORRY ABOUT!
DEBORAH WHITMAN WAS GOOD ENOUGH TO PATCH ME UP THE OTHER DAY, AND THAN I RAN OFF TO PLAY SPIDER-MAN WITHOUT SO MUCH AS A "BUY YOUR LEAVE"*!
AND WHEN I DROPPED BY HER PLACE LATER...
*AMAZ. SPIDER-MAN #215.--D.
SHE WAS ENTERTAIN-ING SOME HOMETOWN PREPPIE FRIEND.*
I FEEL LIKE SUCH A JERK! I WANTED TO APOLOGIZE TO HER YESTERDAY--
STAIR
*AMAZING SPIDER-MAN #216.--D.
--BUT SHE CALLED IN SICK.* I HOPE SHE'S IN TODAY. I REALLY NEED TO TALK TO HER. I GET THE DISTINCT FEELING DEB'S HAD SOME BIG HURTS IN HER LIFE--
--AND I'D HATE TO THINK THAT I'VE ADDED TO THEM!
DEPARTMENT OF BIO-PHYSICS
*LAST ISSUE.--D.

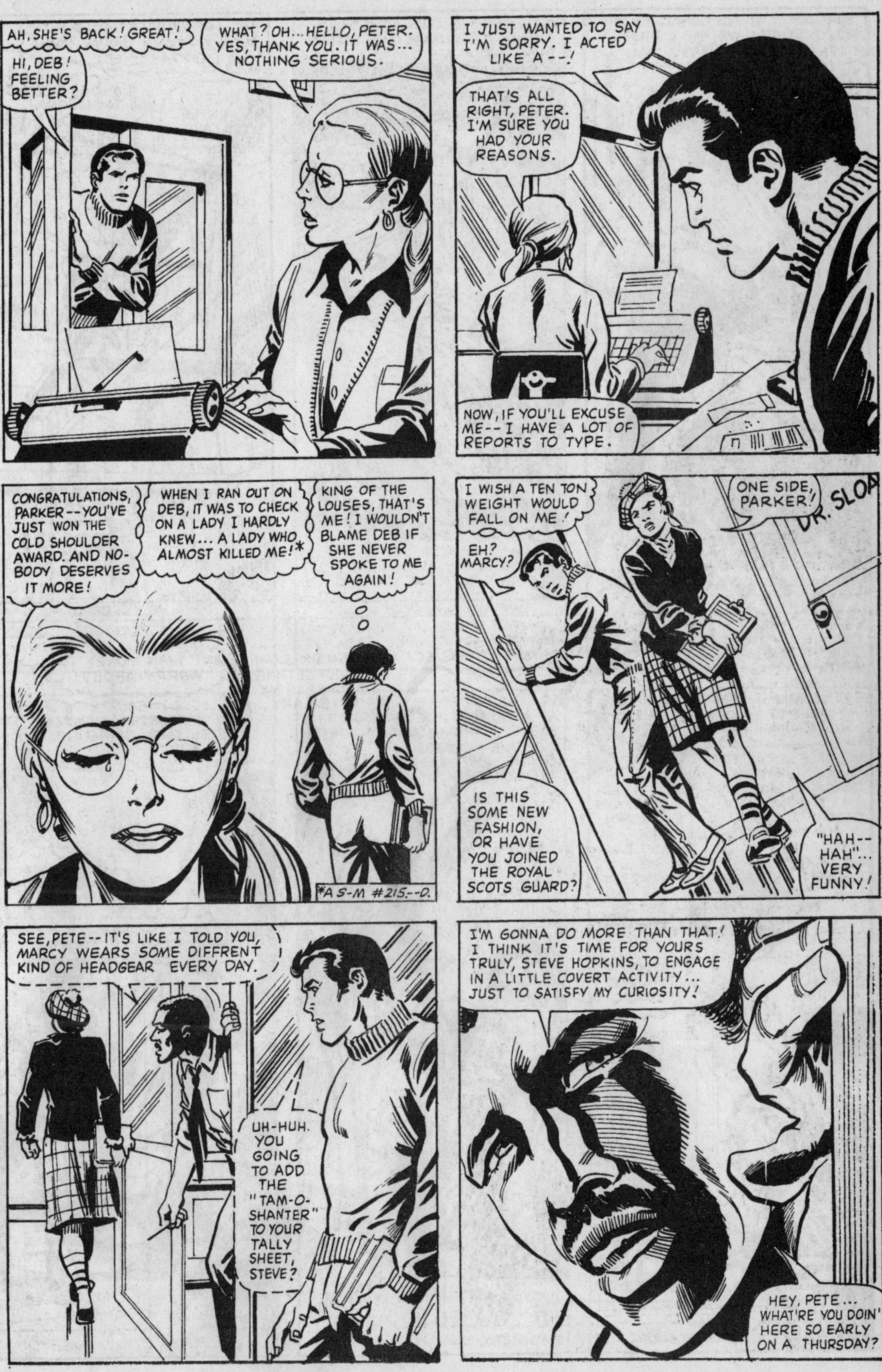
AH, SHE'S BACK! GREAT!
HI, DEB! FEELING BETTER?
WHAT? OH... HELLO, PETER. YES, THANK YOU. IT WAS... NOTHING SERIOUS.
I JUST WANTED TO SAY I'M SORRY. I ACTED LIKE A --!
THAT'S ALL RIGHT, PETER. I'M SURE YOU HAD YOUR REASONS.
NOW, IF YOU'LL EXCUSE ME-- I HAVE A LOT OF REPORTS TO TYPE.
CONGRATULATIONS, PARKER--YOU'VE JUST WON THE COLD SHOULDER AWARD. AND NOBODY DESERVES IT MORE!
WHEN I RAN OUT ON DEB, IT WAS TO CHECK ON A LADY I HARDLY KNEW... A LADY WHO ALMOST KILLED ME!*
KING OF THE LOUSES, THAT'S ME! I WOULDN'T BLAME DEB IF SHE NEVER SPOKE TO ME AGAIN!
*A S-M #215.--D.
I WISH A TEN TON WEIGHT WOULD FALL ON ME!
ONE SIDE, PARKER!
DR. SLOA
EH? MARCY?
IS THIS SOME NEW FASHION, OR HAVE YOU JOINED THE ROYAL SCOTS GUARD?
"HAH--HAH"... VERY FUNNY!
SEE, PETE--IT'S LIKE I TOLD YOU, MARCY WEARS SOME DIFFRENT KIND OF HEADGEAR EVERY DAY.
UH-HUH. YOU GOING TO ADD THE "TAM-O-SHANTER" TO YOUR TALLY SHEET, STEVE?
I'M GONNA DO MORE THAN THAT! I THINK IT'S TIME FOR YOURS TRULY, STEVE HOPKINS, TO ENGAGE IN A LITTLE COVERT ACTIVITY... JUST TO SATISFY MY CURIOSITY!
HEY, PETE... WHAT'RE YOU DOIN' HERE SO EARLY ON A THURSDAY?

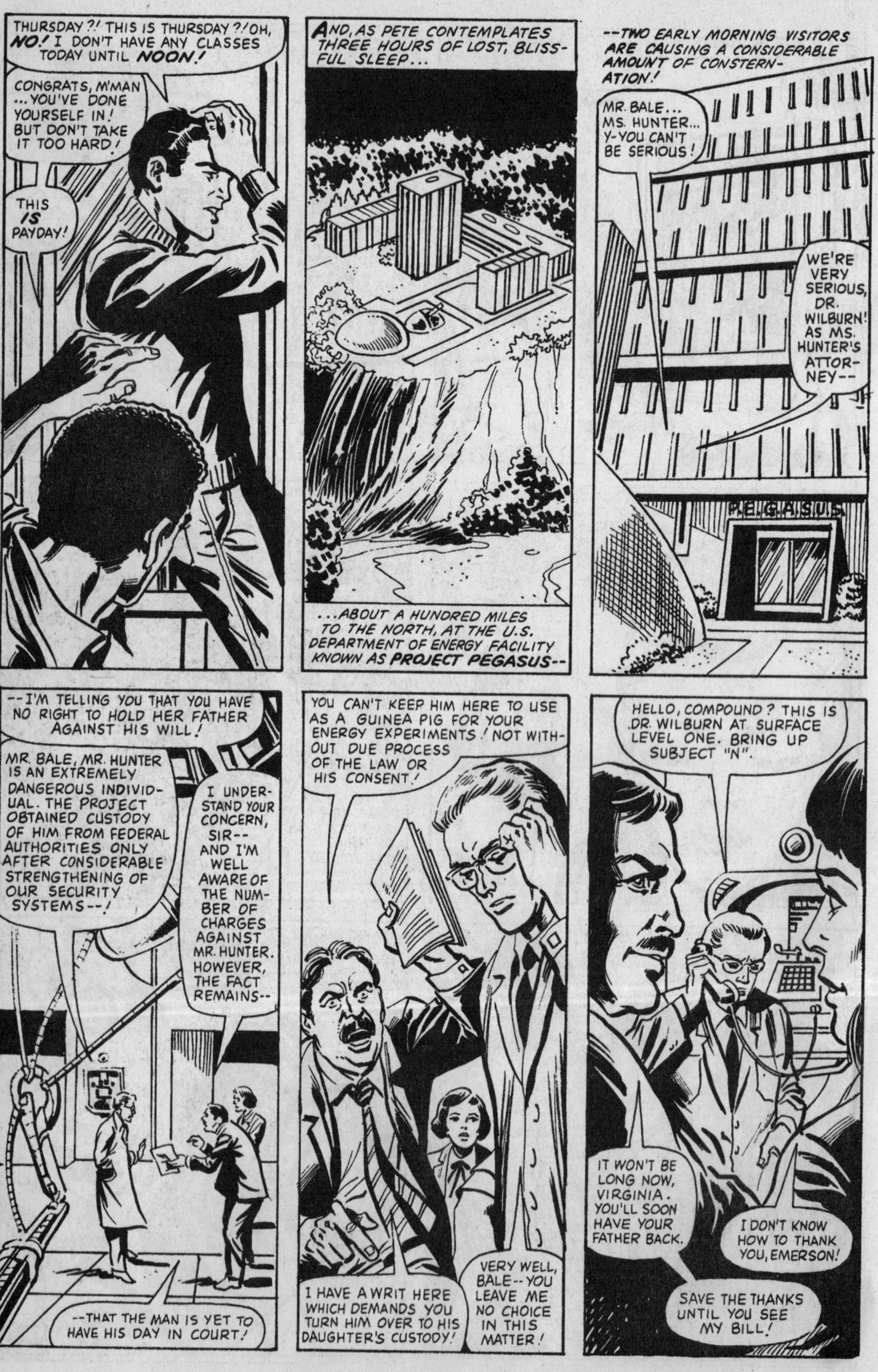
THURSDAY?! THIS IS THURSDAY?! OH, NO! I DON'T HAVE ANY CLASSES TODAY UNTIL NOON!
CONGRATS, M'MAN ...YOU'VE DONE YOURSELF IN! BUT DON'T TAKE IT TOO HARD!
THIS IS PAYDAY!
AND, AS PETE CONTEMPLATES THREE HOURS OF LOST, BLISSFUL SLEEP...
...ABOUT A HUNDRED MILES TO THE NORTH, AT THE U.S. DEPARTMENT OF ENERGY FACILITY KNOWN AS PROJECT PEGASUS--
--TWO EARLY MORNING VISITORS ARE CAUSING A CONSIDERABLE AMOUNT OF CONSTERNATION!
MR. BALE... MS. HUNTER... Y-YOU CAN'T BE SERIOUS!
WE'RE VERY SERIOUS, DR. WILBURN! AS MS. HUNTER'S ATTORNEY--
P.E.G.A.S.U.S.
--I'M TELLING YOU THAT YOU HAVE NO RIGHT TO HOLD HER FATHER AGAINST HIS WILL!
MR. BALE, MR. HUNTER IS AN EXTREMELY DANGEROUS INDIVIDUAL. THE PROJECT OBTAINED CUSTODY OF HIM FROM FEDERAL AUTHORITIES ONLY AFTER CONSIDERABLE STRENGTHENING OF OUR SECURITY SYSTEMS--!
I UNDERSTAND YOUR CONCERN, SIR--AND I'M WELL AWARE OF THE NUMBER OF CHARGES AGAINST MR. HUNTER. HOWEVER, THE FACT REMAINS--
--THAT THE MAN IS YET TO HAVE HIS DAY IN COURT!
YOU CAN'T KEEP HIM HERE TO USE AS A GUINEA PIG FOR YOUR ENERGY EXPERIMENTS! NOT WITHOUT DUE PROCESS OF THE LAW OR HIS CONSENT!
I HAVE A WRIT HERE WHICH DEMANDS YOU TURN HIM OVER TO HIS DAUGHTER'S CUSTODY!
VERY WELL, BALE--YOU LEAVE ME NO CHOICE IN THIS MATTER!
HELLO, COMPOUND? THIS IS DR. WILBURN AT SURFACE LEVEL ONE. BRING UP SUBJECT "N".
IT WON'T BE LONG NOW, VIRGINIA. YOU'LL SOON HAVE YOUR FATHER BACK.
I DON'T KNOW HOW TO THANK YOU, EMERSON!
SAVE THE THANKS UNTIL YOU SEE MY BILL!

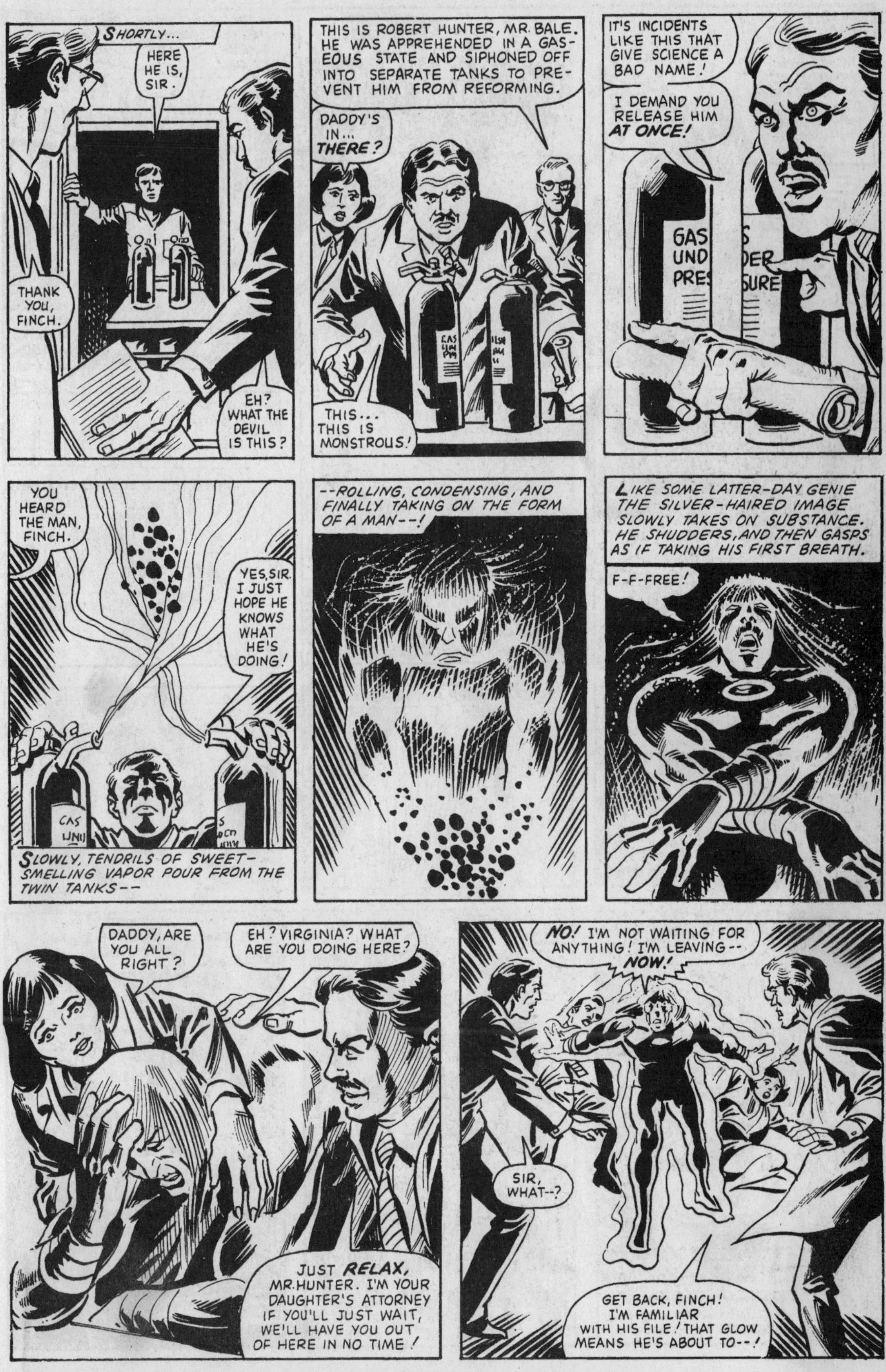
SHORTLY...
HERE HE IS, SIR.
THANK YOU, FINCH.
EH? WHAT THE DEVIL IS THIS?
THIS IS ROBERT HUNTER, MR. BALE. HE WAS APPREHENDED IN A GASEOUS STATE AND SIPHONED OFF INTO SEPARATE TANKS TO PREVENT HIM FROM REFORMING.
DADDY'S IN... THERE?
THIS... THIS IS MONSTROUS!
IT'S INCIDENTS LIKE THIS THAT GIVE SCIENCE A BAD NAME!
I DEMAND YOU RELEASE HIM AT ONCE!
YOU HEARD THE MAN, FINCH.
YES, SIR. I JUST HOPE HE KNOWS WHAT HE'S DOING!
SLOWLY, TENDRILS OF SWEET-SMELLING VAPOR POUR FROM THE TWIN TANKS--
--ROLLING, CONDENSING, AND FINALLY TAKING ON THE FORM OF A MAN--!
LIKE SOME LATTER-DAY GENIE THE SILVER-HAIRED IMAGE SLOWLY TAKES ON SUBSTANCE. HE SHUDDERS, AND THEN GASPS AS IF TAKING HIS FIRST BREATH.
F-F-FREE!
DADDY, ARE YOU ALL RIGHT?
EH? VIRGINIA? WHAT ARE YOU DOING HERE?
JUST RELAX, MR. HUNTER. I'M YOUR DAUGHTER'S ATTORNEY IF YOU'LL JUST WAIT, WE'LL HAVE YOU OUT OF HERE IN NO TIME!
NO! I'M NOT WAITING FOR ANYTHING! I'M LEAVING-- NOW!
SIR, WHAT--?
GET BACK, FINCH! I'M FAMILIAR WITH HIS FILE! THAT GLOW MEANS HE'S ABOUT TO--!

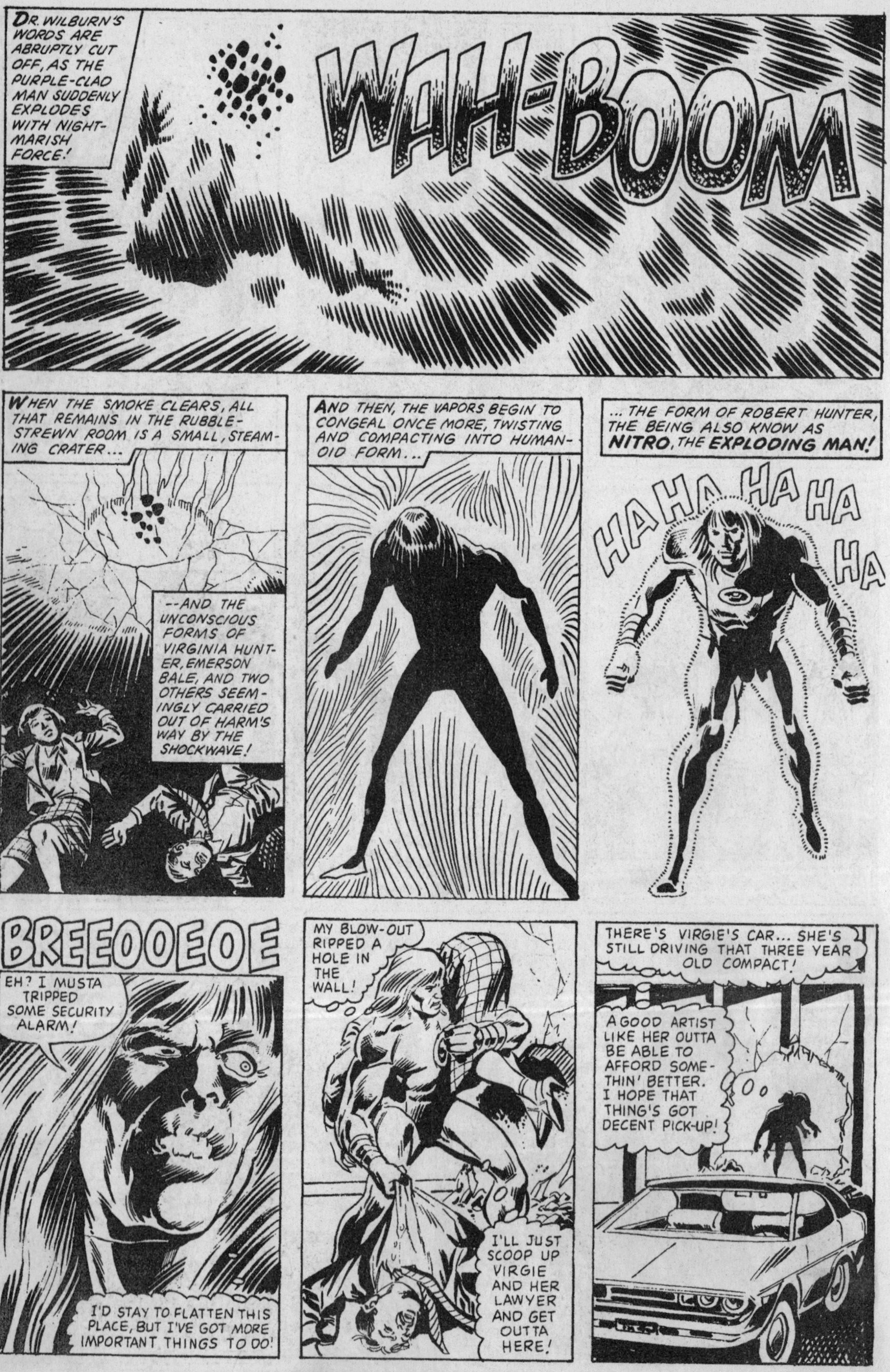
DR. WILBURN'S WORDS ARE ABRUPTLY CUT OFF, AS THE PURPLE-CLAD MAN SUDDENLY EXPLODES WITH NIGHTMARISH FORCE!
WAH-BOOM
WHEN THE SMOKE CLEARS, ALL THAT REMAINS IN THE RUBBLE-STREWN ROOM IS A SMALL, STEAMING CRATER...
--AND THE UNCONSCIOUS FORMS OF VIRGINIA HUNTER, EMERSON BALE, AND TWO OTHERS SEEMINGLY CARRIED OUT OF HARM'S WAY BY THE SHOCKWAVE!
AND THEN, THE VAPORS BEGIN TO CONGEAL ONCE MORE, TWISTING AND COMPACTING INTO HUMANOID FORM...
...THE FORM OF ROBERT HUNTER, THE BEING ALSO KNOW AS NITRO, THE EXPLODING MAN!
HA HA HA HA HA HA
BREEOOEOE
EH? I MUSTA TRIPPED SOME SECURITY ALARM!
I'D STAY TO FLATTEN THIS PLACE, BUT I'VE GOT MORE IMPORTANT THINGS TO DO!
MY BLOW-OUT RIPPED A HOLE IN THE WALL!
I'LL JUST SCOOP UP VIRGIE AND HER LAWYER AND GET OUTTA HERE!
THERE'S VIRGIE'S CAR... SHE'S STILL DRIVING THAT THREE YEAR OLD COMPACT!
A GOOD ARTIST LIKE HER OUTTA BE ABLE TO AFFORD SOMETHIN' BETTER. I HOPE THAT THING'S GOT DECENT PICK-UP!

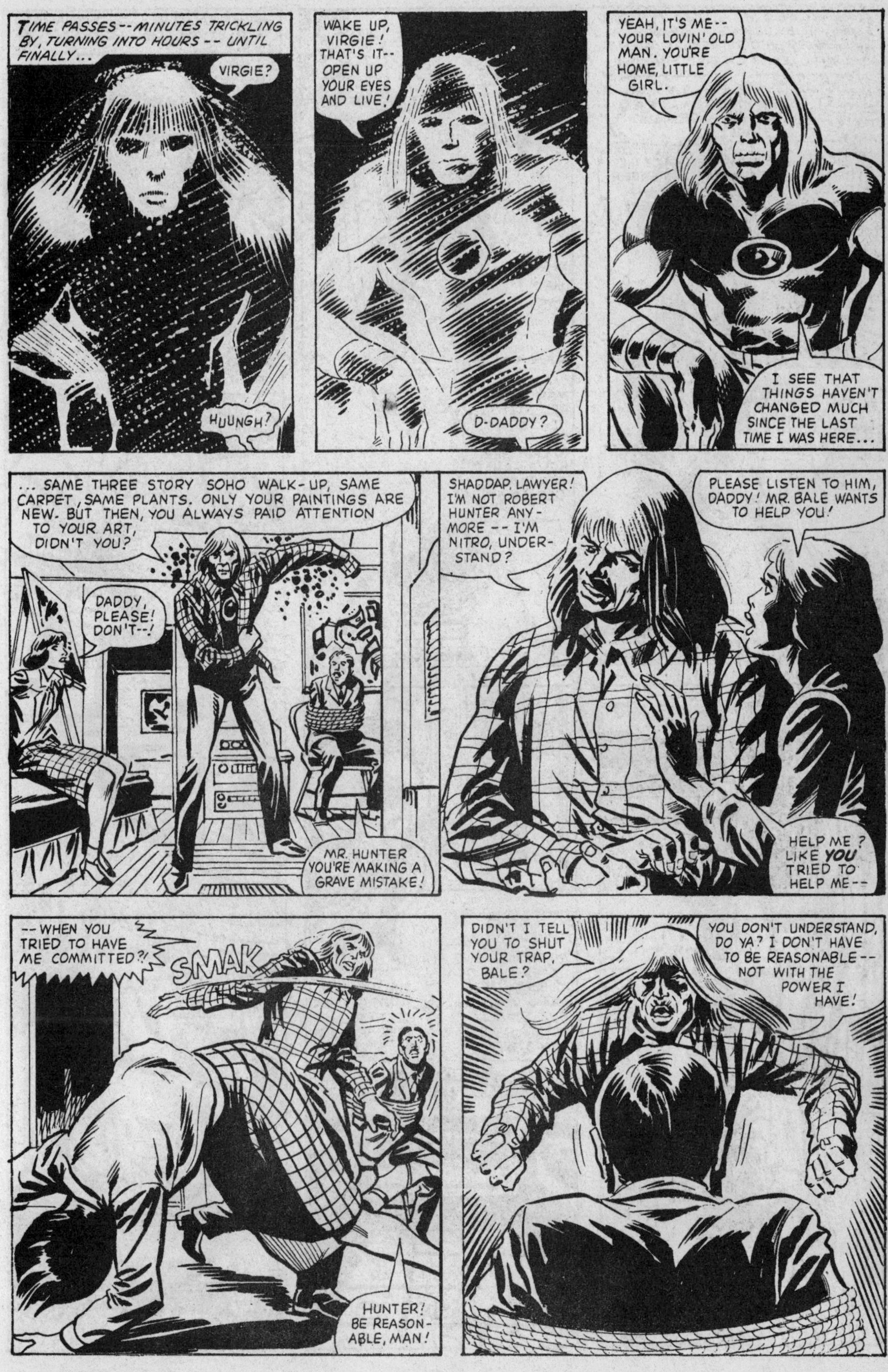
TIME PASSES--MINUTES TRICKLING BY, TURNING INTO HOURS -- UNTIL FINALLY...
VIRGIE?
HUUNGH?
WAKE UP, VIRGIE! THAT'S IT--OPEN UP YOUR EYES AND LIVE!
D-DADDY?
YEAH, IT'S ME--YOUR LOVIN' OLD MAN. YOU'RE HOME, LITTLE GIRL.
I SEE THAT THINGS HAVEN'T CHANGED MUCH SINCE THE LAST TIME I WAS HERE...
... SAME THREE STORY SOHO WALK-UP, SAME CARPET, SAME PLANTS. ONLY YOUR PAINTINGS ARE NEW. BUT THEN, YOU ALWAYS PAID ATTENTION TO YOUR ART, DIDN'T YOU?
DADDY, PLEASE! DON'T--!
MR. HUNTER YOU'RE MAKING A GRAVE MISTAKE!
SHADDAP, LAWYER! I'M NOT ROBERT HUNTER ANY-MORE -- I'M NITRO, UNDER-STAND?
PLEASE LISTEN TO HIM, DADDY! MR. BALE WANTS TO HELP YOU!
HELP ME? LIKE YOU TRIED TO HELP ME--
--WHEN YOU TRIED TO HAVE ME COMMITTED?!
SMAK
HUNTER! BE REASON-ABLE, MAN!
DIDN'T I TELL YOU TO SHUT YOUR TRAP, BALE?
YOU DON'T UNDERSTAND, DO YA? I DON'T HAVE TO BE REASONABLE -- NOT WITH THE POWER I HAVE!

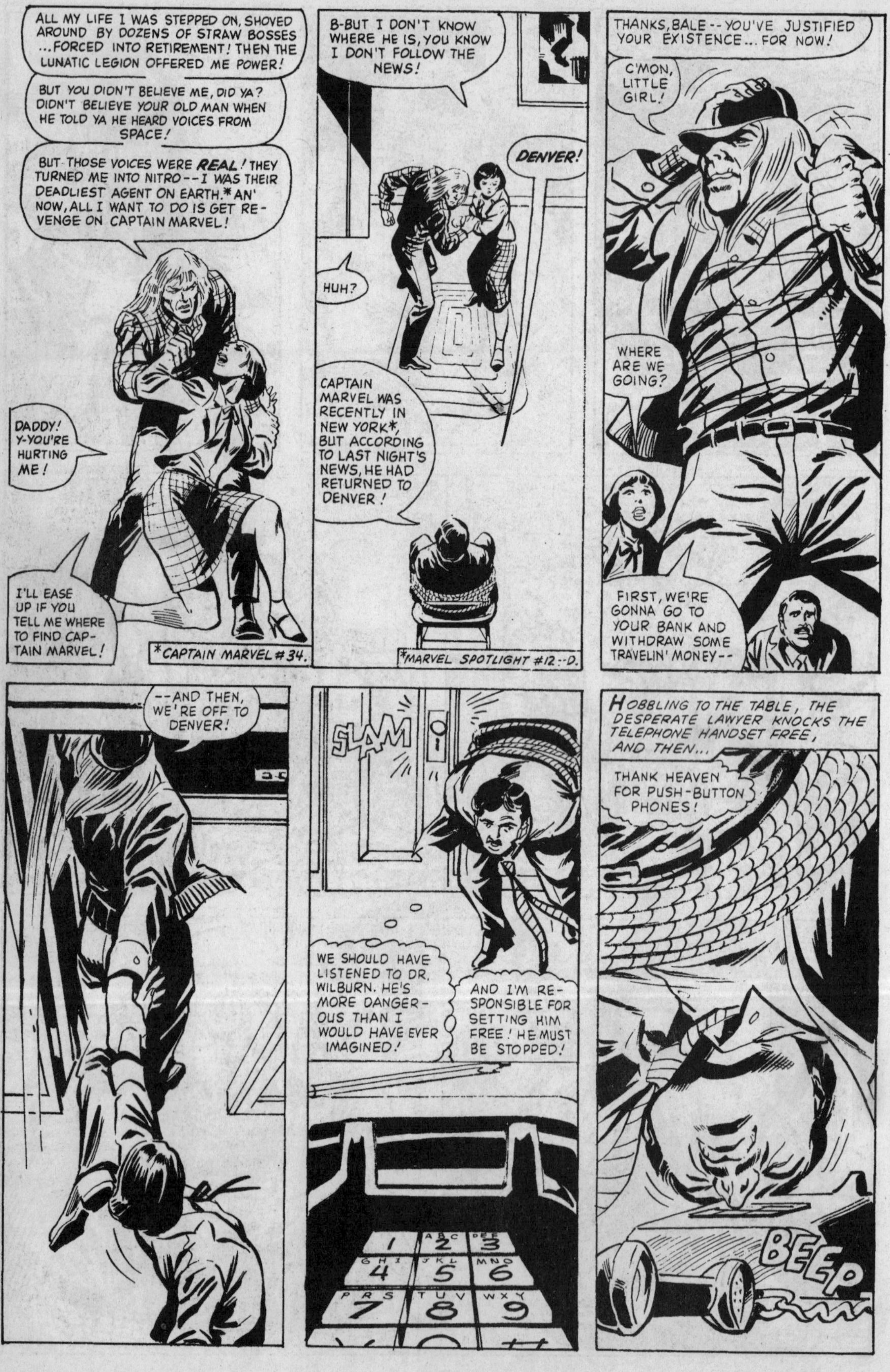
ALL MY LIFE I WAS STEPPED ON, SHOVED AROUND BY DOZENS OF STRAW BOSSES ...FORCED INTO RETIREMENT! THEN THE LUNATIC LEGION OFFERED ME POWER!
BUT YOU DIDN'T BELIEVE ME, DID YA? DIDN'T BELIEVE YOUR OLD MAN WHEN HE TOLD YA HE HEARD VOICES FROM SPACE!
BUT THOSE VOICES WERE REAL! THEY TURNED ME INTO NITRO--I WAS THEIR DEADLIEST AGENT ON EARTH.* AN' NOW, ALL I WANT TO DO IS GET REVENGE ON CAPTAIN MARVEL!
DADDY! Y-YOU'RE HURTING ME!
I'LL EASE UP IF YOU TELL ME WHERE TO FIND CAPTAIN MARVEL!
*CAPTAIN MARVEL #34.
B-BUT I DON'T KNOW WHERE HE IS, YOU KNOW I DON'T FOLLOW THE NEWS!
DENVER!
HUH?
CAPTAIN MARVEL WAS RECENTLY IN NEW YORK*, BUT ACCORDING TO LAST NIGHT'S NEWS, HE HAD RETURNED TO DENVER!
*MARVEL SPOTLIGHT #12.--D.
THANKS, BALE--YOU'VE JUSTIFIED YOUR EXISTENCE... FOR NOW!
C'MON, LITTLE GIRL!
WHERE ARE WE GOING?
FIRST, WE'RE GONNA GO TO YOUR BANK AND WITHDRAW SOME TRAVELIN' MONEY--
--AND THEN, WE'RE OFF TO DENVER!
SLAM
WE SHOULD HAVE LISTENED TO DR. WILBURN. HE'S MORE DANGEROUS THAN I WOULD HAVE EVER IMAGINED!
AND I'M RESPONSIBLE FOR SETTING HIM FREE! HE MUST BE STOPPED!
HOBBLING TO THE TABLE, THE DESPERATE LAWYER KNOCKS THE TELEPHONE HANDSET FREE, AND THEN...
THANK HEAVEN FOR PUSH-BUTTON PHONES!
BEEP

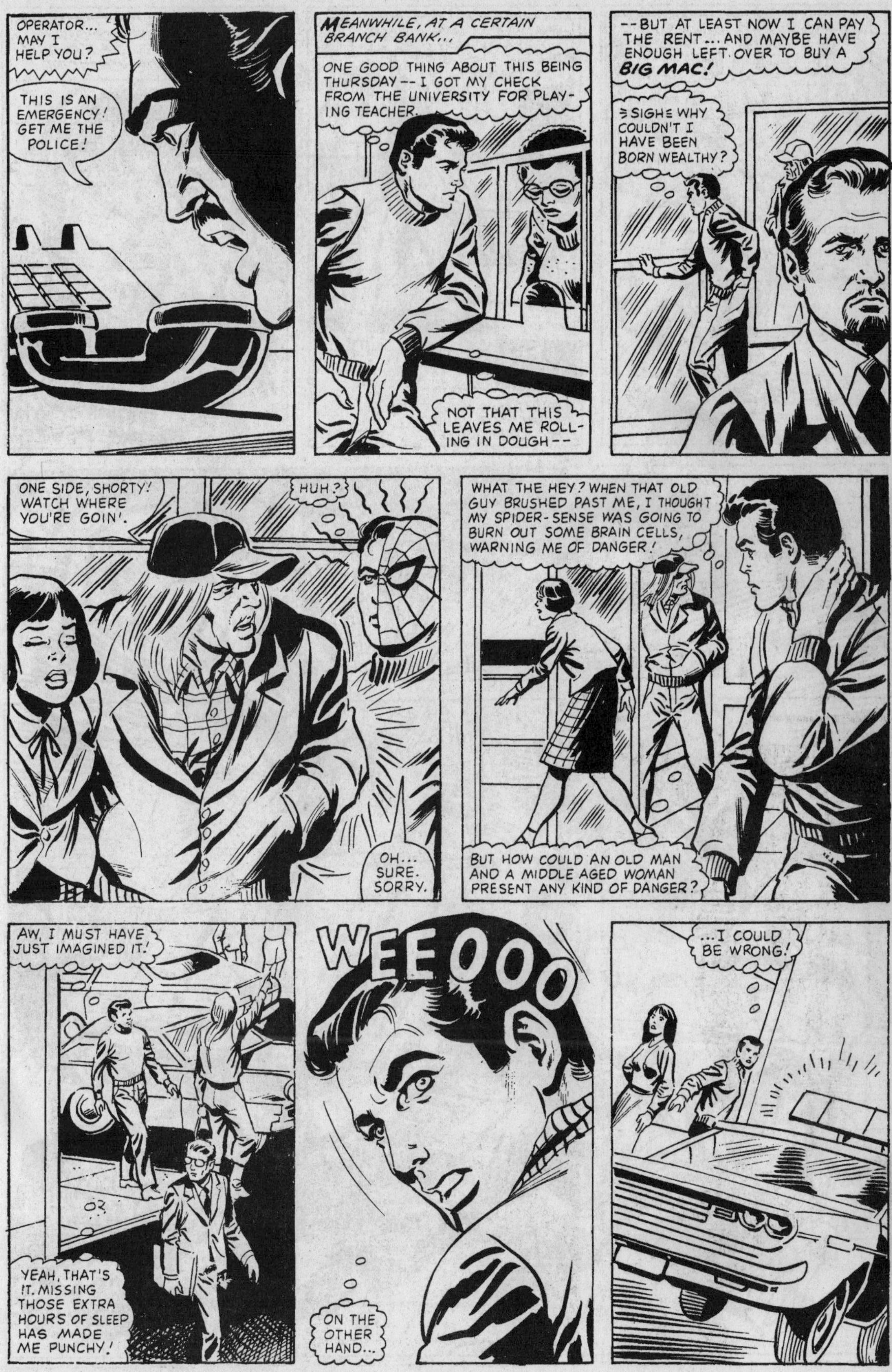
OPERATOR... MAY I HELP YOU?
THIS IS AN EMERGENCY! GET ME THE POLICE!
MEANWHILE, AT A CERTAIN BRANCH BANK...
ONE GOOD THING ABOUT THIS BEING THURSDAY -- I GOT MY CHECK FROM THE UNIVERSITY FOR PLAYING TEACHER.
NOT THAT THIS LEAVES ME ROLLING IN DOUGH --
-- BUT AT LEAST NOW I CAN PAY THE RENT... AND MAYBE HAVE ENOUGH LEFT OVER TO BUY A BIG MAC!
≡SIGH≡ WHY COULDN'T I HAVE BEEN BORN WEALTHY?
ONE SIDE, SHORTY! WATCH WHERE YOU'RE GOIN'.
HUH?
OH... SURE. SORRY.
WHAT THE HEY? WHEN THAT OLD GUY BRUSHED PAST ME, I THOUGHT MY SPIDER-SENSE WAS GOING TO BURN OUT SOME BRAIN CELLS, WARNING ME OF DANGER!
BUT HOW COULD AN OLD MAN AND A MIDDLE AGED WOMAN PRESENT ANY KIND OF DANGER?
AW, I MUST HAVE JUST IMAGINED IT!
YEAH, THAT'S IT. MISSING THOSE EXTRA HOURS OF SLEEP HAS MADE ME PUNCHY!
WEEOOO
ON THE OTHER HAND...
...I COULD BE WRONG!

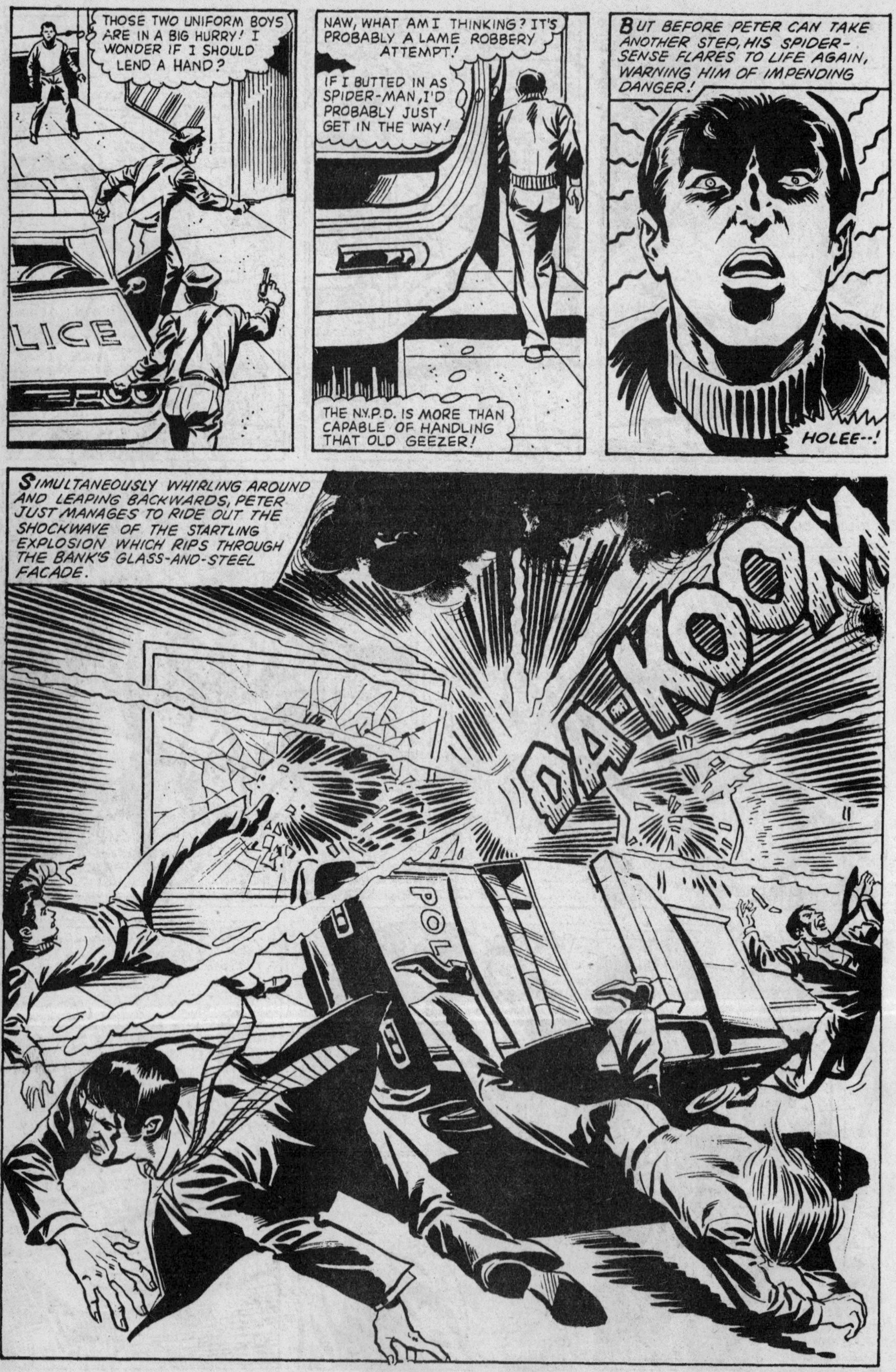
THOSE TWO UNIFORM BOYS ARE IN A BIG HURRY! I WONDER IF I SHOULD LEND A HAND?
LICE
NAW, WHAT AM I THINKING? IT'S PROBABLY A LAME ROBBERY ATTEMPT!
IF I BUTTED IN AS SPIDER-MAN, I'D PROBABLY JUST GET IN THE WAY!
THE N.Y.P.D. IS MORE THAN CAPABLE OF HANDLING THAT OLD GEEZER!
BUT BEFORE PETER CAN TAKE ANOTHER STEP, HIS SPIDER-SENSE FLARES TO LIFE AGAIN, WARNING HIM OF IMPENDING DANGER!
HOLEE--!
SIMULTANEOUSLY WHIRLING AROUND AND LEAPING BACKWARDS, PETER JUST MANAGES TO RIDE OUT THE SHOCKWAVE OF THE STARTLING EXPLOSION WHICH RIPS THROUGH THE BANK'S GLASS-AND-STEEL FACADE.
DA-KOOOM
POL

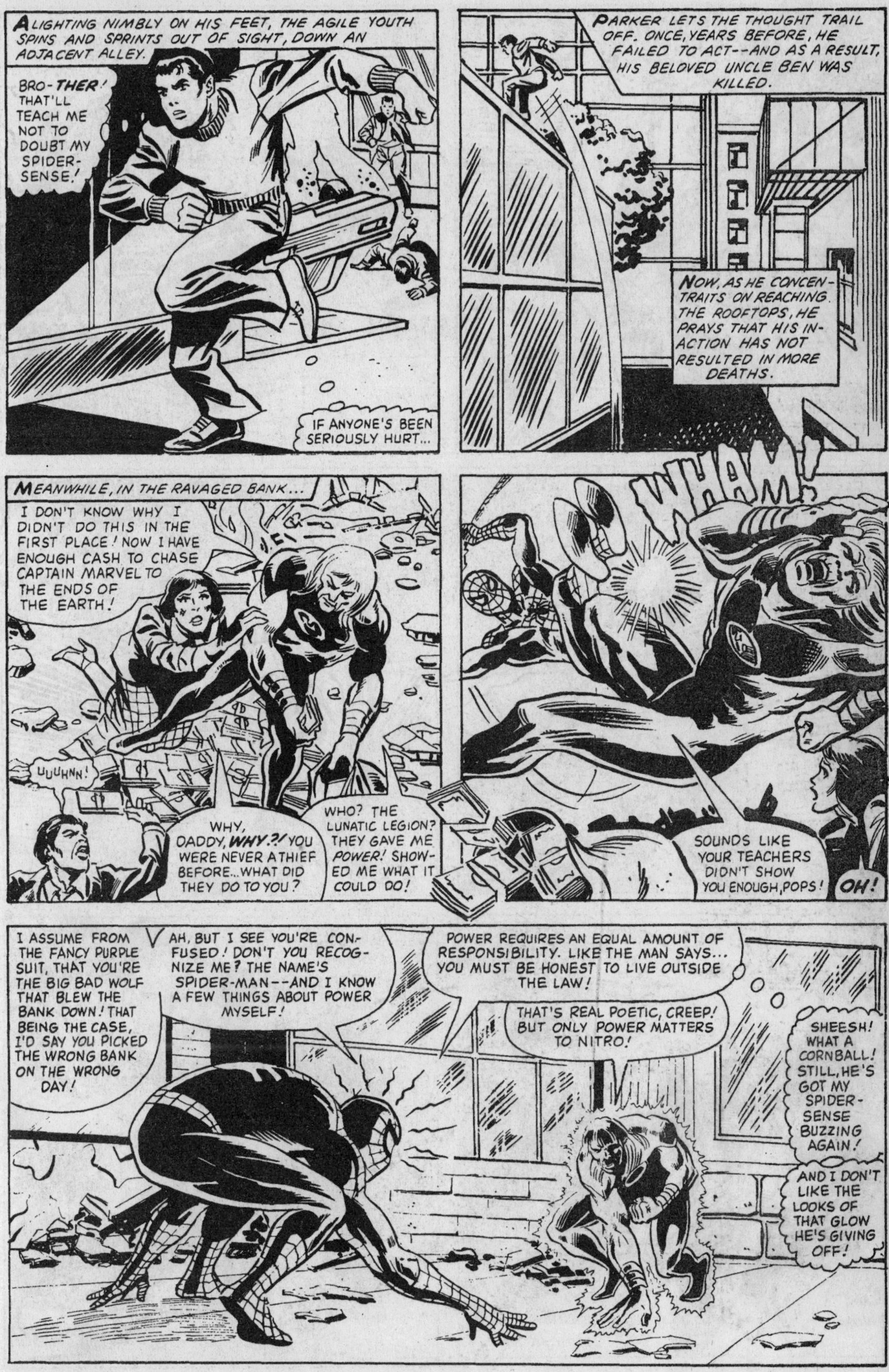

ALIGHTING NIMBLY ON HIS FEET, THE AGILE YOUTH SPINS AND SPRINTS OUT OF SIGHT, DOWN AN ADJACENT ALLEY.
BRO-THER! THAT'LL TEACH ME NOT TO DOUBT MY SPIDER-SENSE!
IF ANYONE'S BEEN SERIOUSLY HURT...
PARKER LETS THE THOUGHT TRAIL OFF. ONCE, YEARS BEFORE, HE FAILED TO ACT--AND AS A RESULT, HIS BELOVED UNCLE BEN WAS KILLED.
NOW, AS HE CONCENTRAITS ON REACHING THE ROOFTOPS, HE PRAYS THAT HIS INACTION HAS NOT RESULTED IN MORE DEATHS.
MEANWHILE, IN THE RAVAGED BANK...
I DON'T KNOW WHY I DIDN'T DO THIS IN THE FIRST PLACE! NOW I HAVE ENOUGH CASH TO CHASE CAPTAIN MARVEL TO THE ENDS OF THE EARTH!
UUUHNN!
WHY, DADDY, WHY?! YOU WERE NEVER A THIEF BEFORE...WHAT DID THEY DO TO YOU?
WHO? THE LUNATIC LEGION? THEY GAVE ME POWER! SHOWED ME WHAT IT COULD DO!
WHAM!
SOUNDS LIKE YOUR TEACHERS DIDN'T SHOW YOU ENOUGH, POPS!
OH!
I ASSUME FROM THE FANCY PURPLE SUIT, THAT YOU'RE THE BIG BAD WOLF THAT BLEW THE BANK DOWN! THAT BEING THE CASE, I'D SAY YOU PICKED THE WRONG BANK ON THE WRONG DAY!
AH, BUT I SEE YOU'RE CONFUSED! DON'T YOU RECOGNIZE ME? THE NAME'S SPIDER-MAN--AND I KNOW A FEW THINGS ABOUT POWER MYSELF!
POWER REQUIRES AN EQUAL AMOUNT OF RESPONSIBILITY. LIKE THE MAN SAYS... YOU MUST BE HONEST TO LIVE OUTSIDE THE LAW!
THAT'S REAL POETIC, CREEP! BUT ONLY POWER MATTERS TO NITRO!
SHEESH! WHAT A CORNBALL! STILL, HE'S GOT MY SPIDER-SENSE BUZZING AGAIN!
AND I DON'T LIKE THE LOOKS OF THAT GLOW HE'S GIVING OFF!

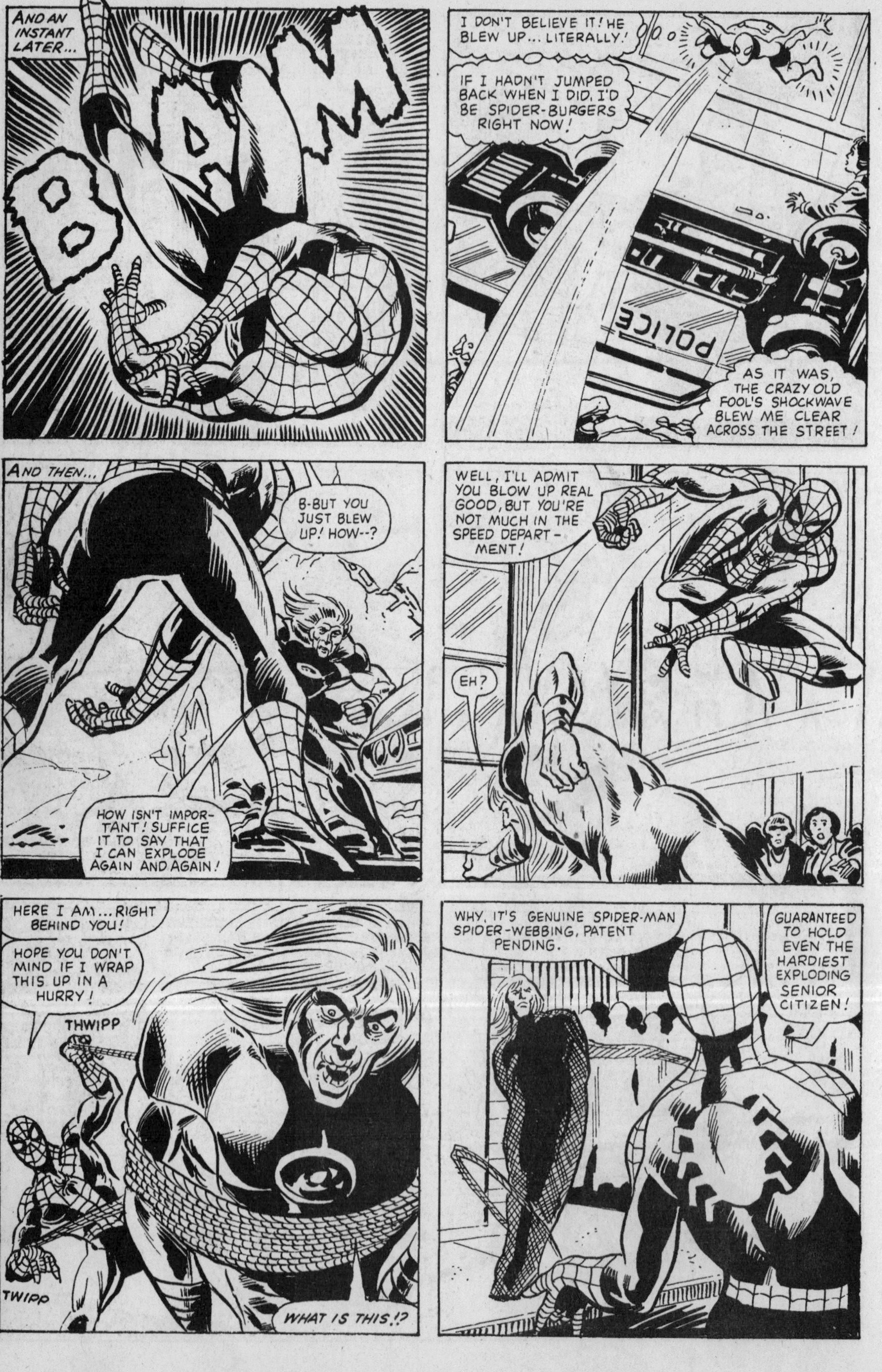
AND AN INSTANT LATER...
BAM
I DON'T BELIEVE IT! HE BLEW UP... LITERALLY!
IF I HADN'T JUMPED BACK WHEN I DID, I'D BE SPIDER-BURGERS RIGHT NOW!
POLICE
AS IT WAS, THE CRAZY OLD FOOL'S SHOCKWAVE BLEW ME CLEAR ACROSS THE STREET!
AND THEN...
B-BUT YOU JUST BLEW UP! HOW--?
HOW ISN'T IMPORTANT! SUFFICE IT TO SAY THAT I CAN EXPLODE AGAIN AND AGAIN!
WELL, I'LL ADMIT YOU BLOW UP REAL GOOD, BUT YOU'RE NOT MUCH IN THE SPEED DEPARTMENT!
EH?
HERE I AM... RIGHT BEHIND YOU!
HOPE YOU DON'T MIND IF I WRAP THIS UP IN A HURRY!
THWIPP
TWIPP
WHAT IS THIS!?
WHY, IT'S GENUINE SPIDER-MAN SPIDER-WEBBING, PATENT PENDING.
GUARANTEED TO HOLD EVEN THE HARDIEST EXPLODING SENIOR CITIZEN!

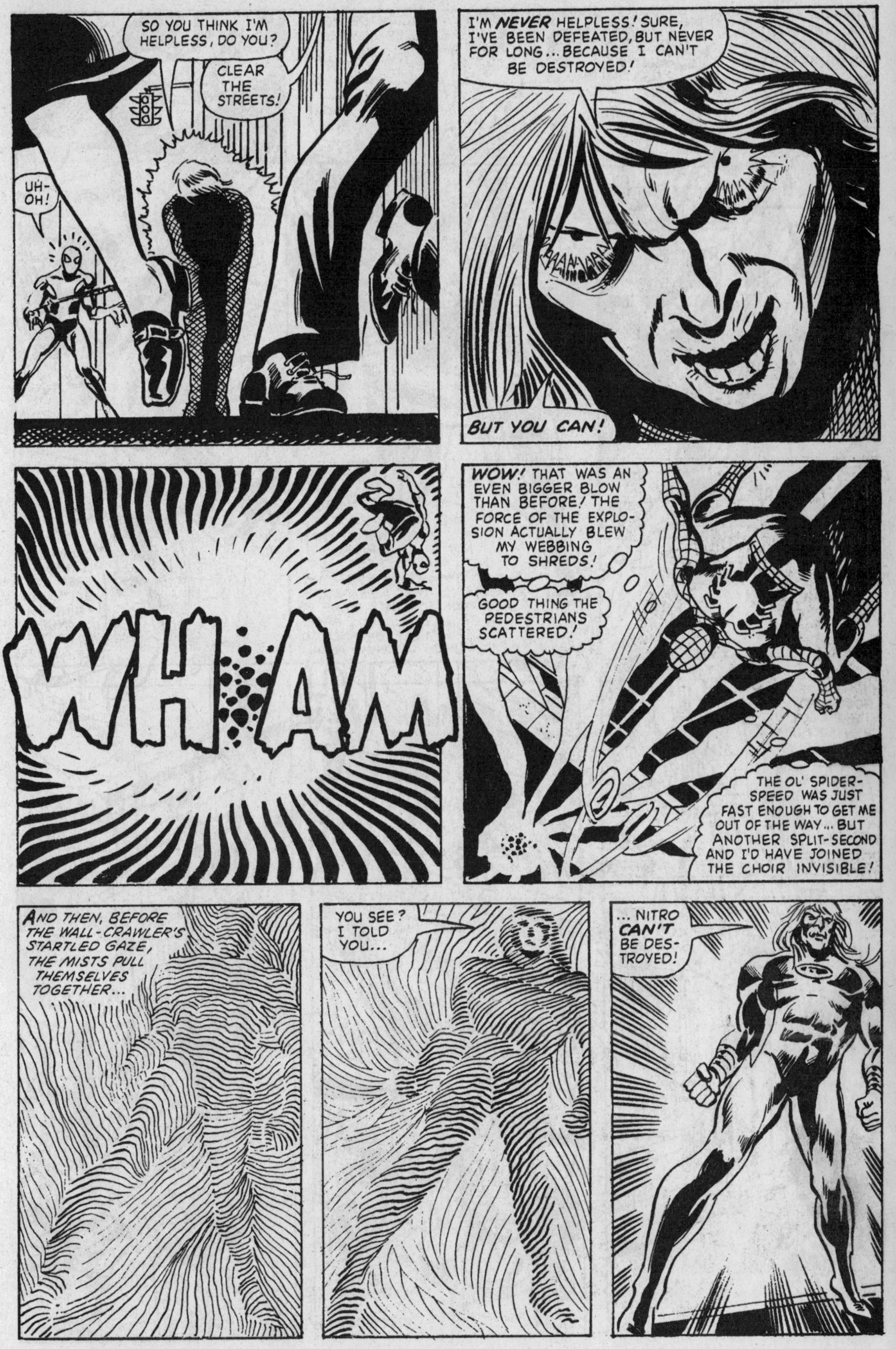
SO YOU THINK I'M HELPLESS, DO YOU?
CLEAR THE STREETS!
UH-OH!
I'M NEVER HELPLESS! SURE, I'VE BEEN DEFEATED, BUT NEVER FOR LONG... BECAUSE I CAN'T BE DESTROYED!
BUT YOU CAN!
WHAM
WOW! THAT WAS AN EVEN BIGGER BLOW THAN BEFORE! THE FORCE OF THE EXPLOSION ACTUALLY BLEW MY WEBBING TO SHREDS!
GOOD THING THE PEDESTRIANS SCATTERED!
THE OL' SPIDER-SPEED WAS JUST FAST ENOUGH TO GET ME OUT OF THE WAY... BUT ANOTHER SPLIT-SECOND AND I'D HAVE JOINED THE CHOIR INVISIBLE!
AND THEN, BEFORE THE WALL-CRAWLER'S STARTLED GAZE, THE MISTS PULL THEMSELVES TOGETHER...
YOU SEE? I TOLD YOU...
...NITRO CAN'T BE DESTROYED!

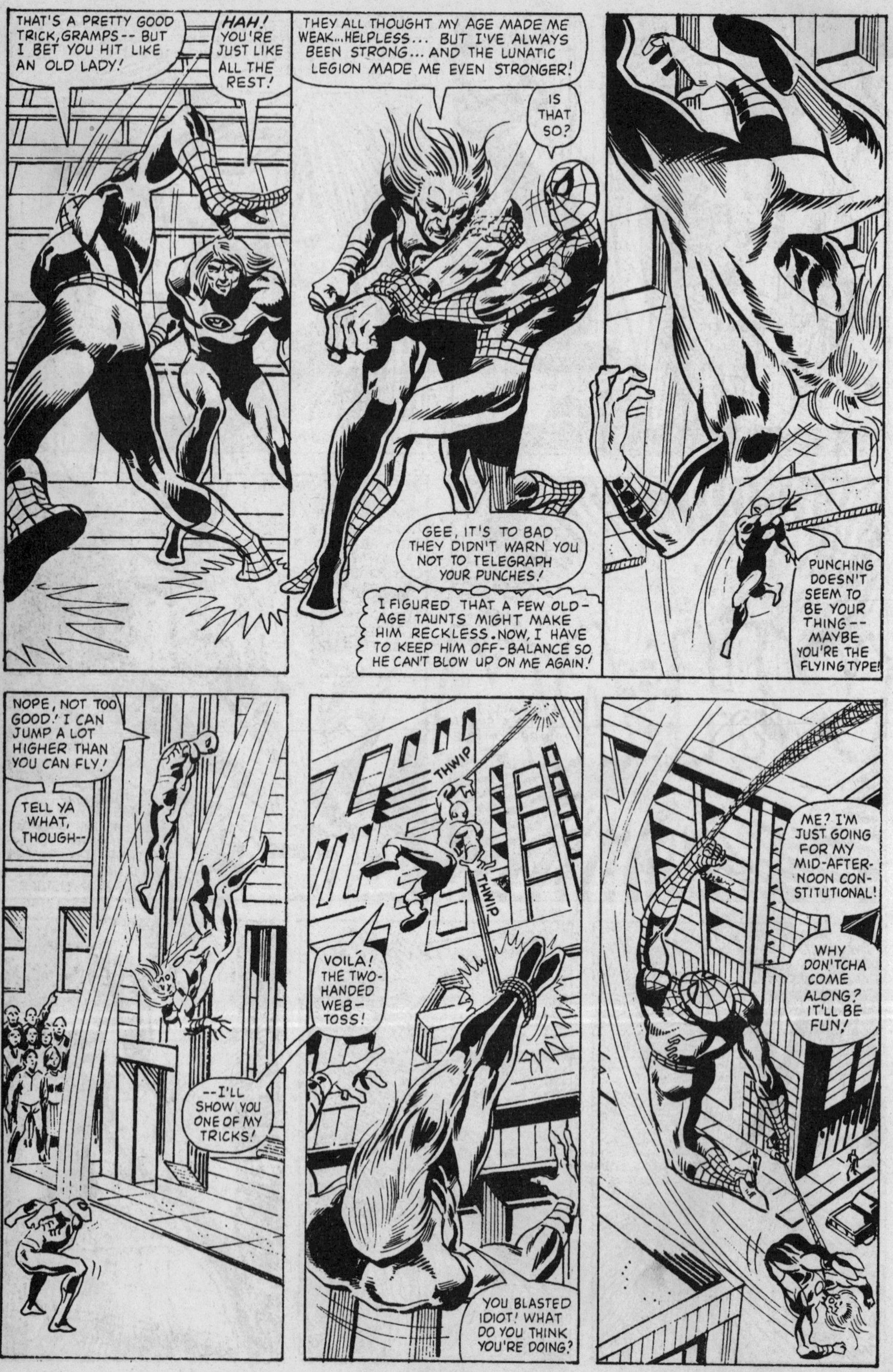
THAT'S A PRETTY GOOD TRICK, GRAMPS -- BUT I BET YOU HIT LIKE AN OLD LADY!
HAH! YOU'RE JUST LIKE ALL THE REST!
THEY ALL THOUGHT MY AGE MADE ME WEAK...HELPLESS... BUT I'VE ALWAYS BEEN STRONG... AND THE LUNATIC LEGION MADE ME EVEN STRONGER!
IS THAT SO?
GEE, IT'S TO BAD THEY DIDN'T WARN YOU NOT TO TELEGRAPH YOUR PUNCHES!
I FIGURED THAT A FEW OLD-AGE TAUNTS MIGHT MAKE HIM RECKLESS. NOW, I HAVE TO KEEP HIM OFF-BALANCE SO HE CAN'T BLOW UP ON ME AGAIN!
PUNCHING DOESN'T SEEM TO BE YOUR THING -- MAYBE YOU'RE THE FLYING TYPE!
NOPE, NOT TOO GOOD! I CAN JUMP A LOT HIGHER THAN YOU CAN FLY!
TELL YA WHAT, THOUGH--
--I'LL SHOW YOU ONE OF MY TRICKS!
THWIP
THWIP
VOILÁ! THE TWO-HANDED WEB-TOSS!
YOU BLASTED IDIOT! WHAT DO YOU THINK YOU'RE DOING?
ME? I'M JUST GOING FOR MY MID-AFTER-NOON CON-STITUTIONAL!
WHY DON'TCHA COME ALONG? IT'LL BE FUN!

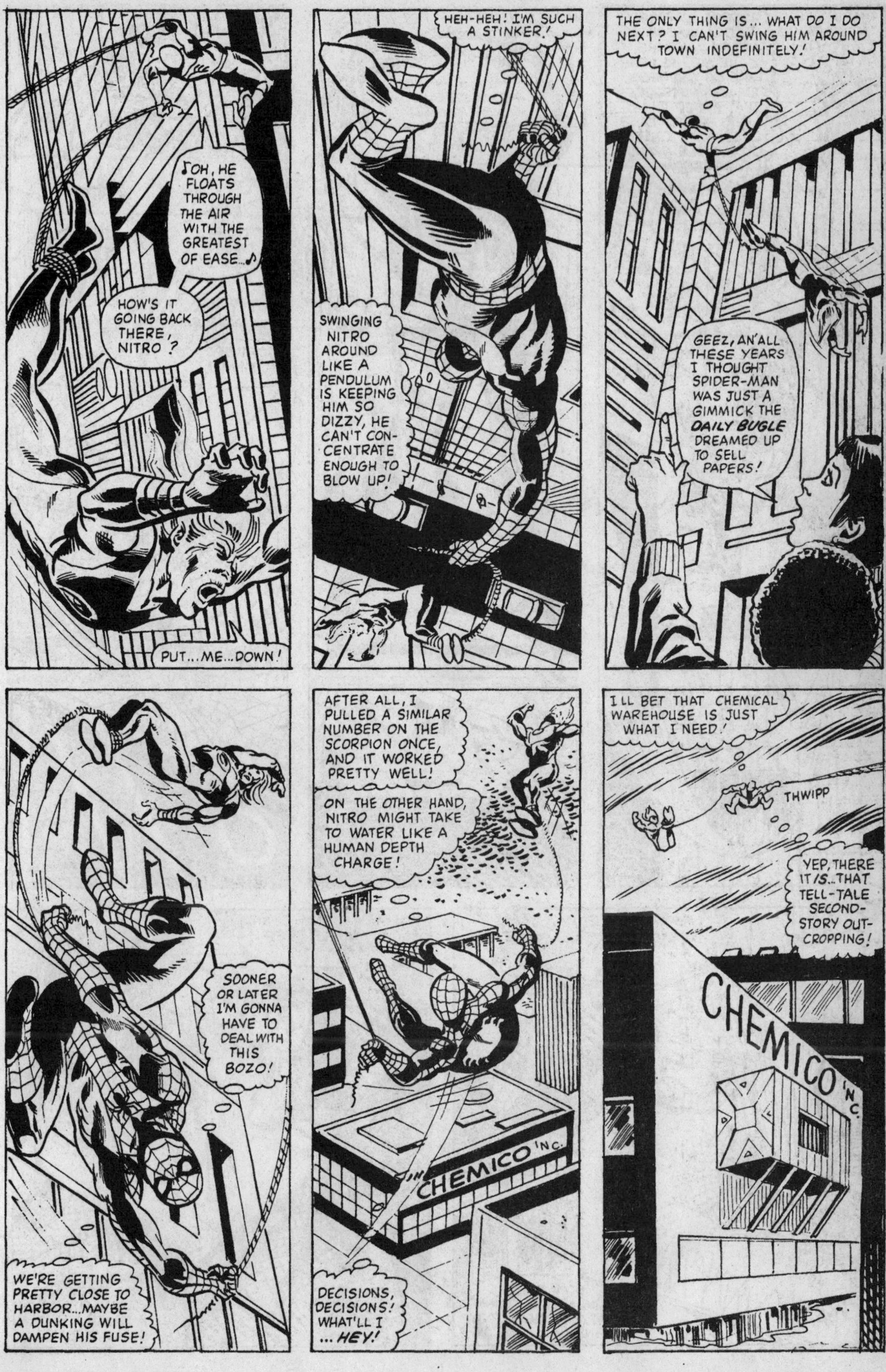
♪OH, HE FLOATS THROUGH THE AIR WITH THE GREATEST OF EASE...♪
HOW'S IT GOING BACK THERE, NITRO?
PUT...ME...DOWN!
HEH-HEH! I'M SUCH A STINKER!
SWINGING NITRO AROUND LIKE A PENDULUM IS KEEPING HIM SO DIZZY, HE CAN'T CONCENTRATE ENOUGH TO BLOW UP!
THE ONLY THING IS... WHAT DO I DO NEXT? I CAN'T SWING HIM AROUND TOWN INDEFINITELY!
GEEZ, AN'ALL THESE YEARS I THOUGHT SPIDER-MAN WAS JUST A GIMMICK THE DAILY BUGLE DREAMED UP TO SELL PAPERS!
SOONER OR LATER I'M GONNA HAVE TO DEAL WITH THIS BOZO!
WE'RE GETTING PRETTY CLOSE TO HARBOR...MAYBE A DUNKING WILL DAMPEN HIS FUSE!
AFTER ALL, I PULLED A SIMILAR NUMBER ON THE SCORPION ONCE, AND IT WORKED PRETTY WELL!
ON THE OTHER HAND, NITRO MIGHT TAKE TO WATER LIKE A HUMAN DEPTH CHARGE!
CHEMICO INC.
DECISIONS, DECISIONS! WHAT'LL I ...HEY!
I'LL BET THAT CHEMICAL WAREHOUSE IS JUST WHAT I NEED!
THWIPP
YEP, THERE IT IS...THAT TELL-TALE SECOND-STORY OUT-CROPPING!
CHEMICO INC.

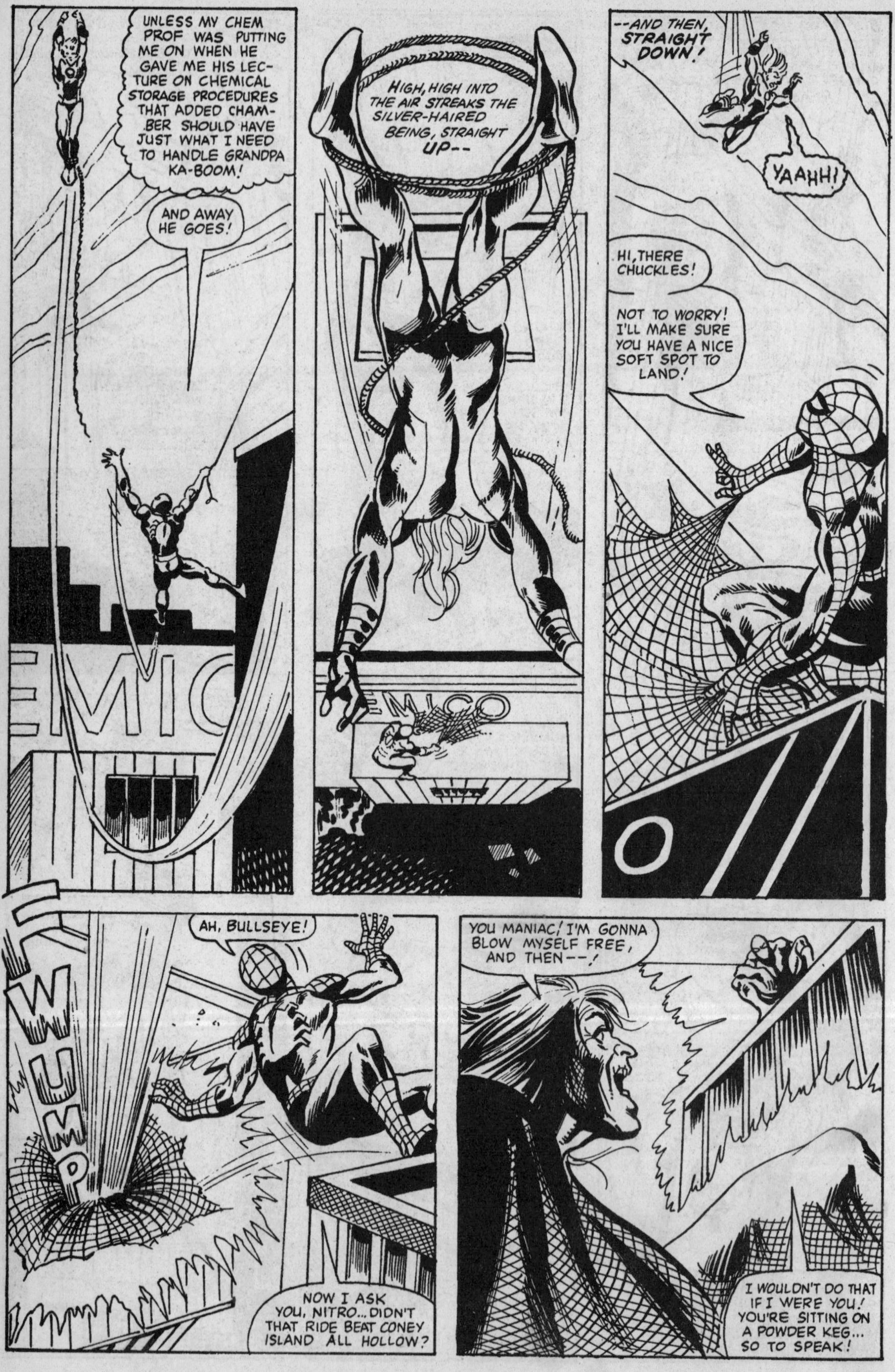
UNLESS MY CHEM PROF WAS PUTTING ME ON WHEN HE GAVE ME HIS LECTURE ON CHEMICAL STORAGE PROCEDURES THAT ADDED CHAMBER SHOULD HAVE JUST WHAT I NEED TO HANDLE GRANDPA KA-BOOM!
AND AWAY HE GOES!
EMIC
HIGH, HIGH INTO THE AIR STREAKS THE SILVER-HAIRED BEING, STRAIGHT UP--
EMICO
--AND THEN, STRAIGHT DOWN!
YAAHH!
HI, THERE CHUCKLES!
NOT TO WORRY! I'LL MAKE SURE YOU HAVE A NICE SOFT SPOT TO LAND!
WWUMP
AH, BULLSEYE!
NOW I ASK YOU, NITRO... DIDN'T THAT RIDE BEAT CONEY ISLAND ALL HOLLOW?
YOU MANIAC! I'M GONNA BLOW MYSELF FREE, AND THEN--!
I WOULDN'T DO THAT IF I WERE YOU! YOU'RE SITTING ON A POWDER KEG... SO TO SPEAK!

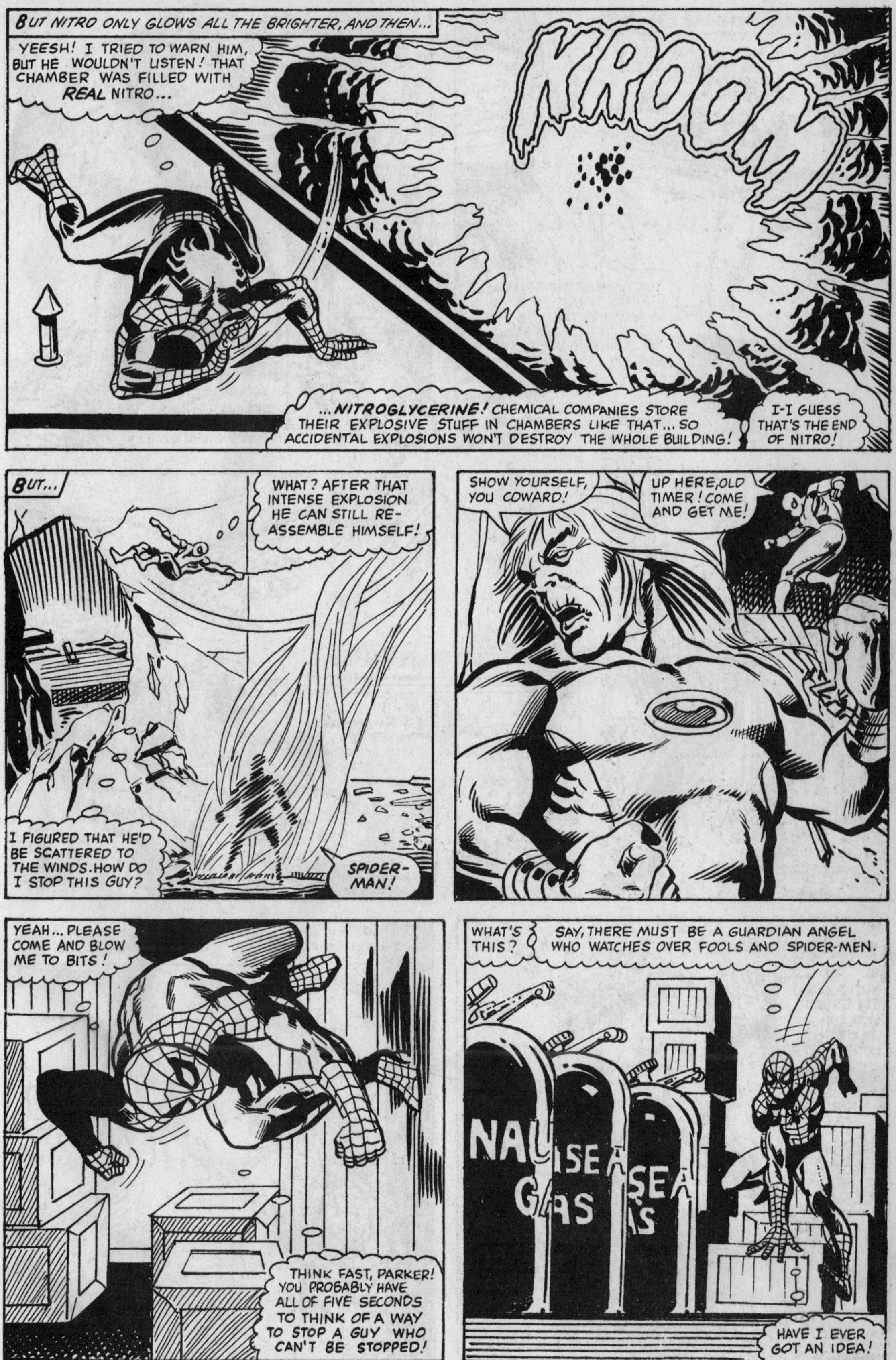
BUT NITRO ONLY GLOWS ALL THE BRIGHTER, AND THEN...
YEESH! I TRIED TO WARN HIM, BUT HE WOULDN'T LISTEN! THAT CHAMBER WAS FILLED WITH REAL NITRO...
KROOM
...NITROGLYCERINE! CHEMICAL COMPANIES STORE THEIR EXPLOSIVE STUFF IN CHAMBERS LIKE THAT... SO ACCIDENTAL EXPLOSIONS WON'T DESTROY THE WHOLE BUILDING!
I-I GUESS THAT'S THE END OF NITRO!
BUT...
WHAT? AFTER THAT INTENSE EXPLOSION HE CAN STILL RE-ASSEMBLE HIMSELF!
I FIGURED THAT HE'D BE SCATTERED TO THE WINDS. HOW DO I STOP THIS GUY?
SPIDER-MAN!
SHOW YOURSELF, YOU COWARD!
UP HERE, OLD TIMER! COME AND GET ME!
YEAH... PLEASE COME AND BLOW ME TO BITS!
THINK FAST, PARKER! YOU PROBABLY HAVE ALL OF FIVE SECONDS TO THINK OF A WAY TO STOP A GUY WHO CAN'T BE STOPPED!
WHAT'S THIS?
SAY, THERE MUST BE A GUARDIAN ANGEL WHO WATCHES OVER FOOLS AND SPIDER-MEN.
NAUSEA GAS
HAVE I EVER GOT AN IDEA!

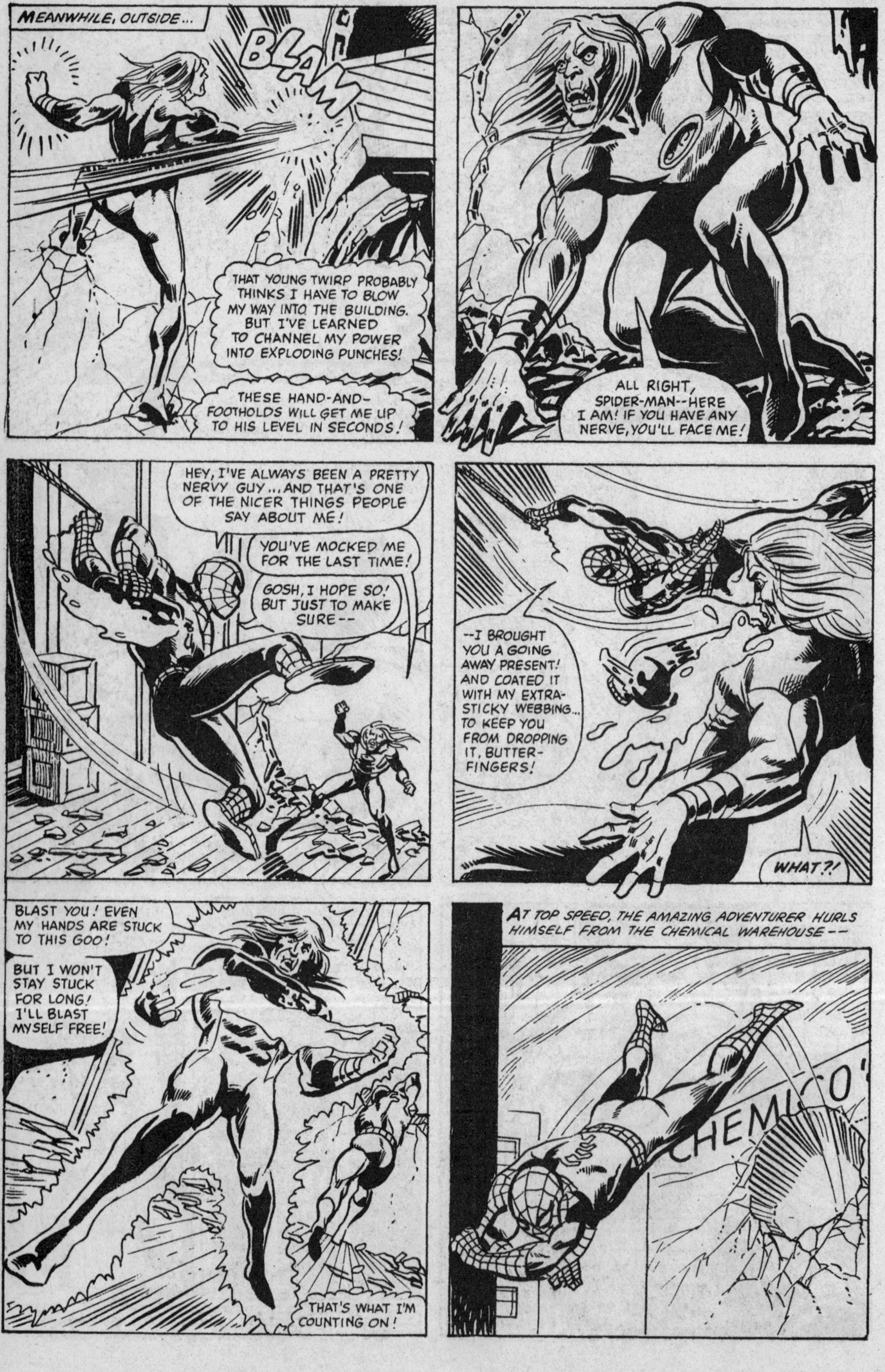
MEANWHILE, OUTSIDE...
BLAM
THAT YOUNG TWIRP PROBABLY THINKS I HAVE TO BLOW MY WAY INTO THE BUILDING. BUT I'VE LEARNED TO CHANNEL MY POWER INTO EXPLODING PUNCHES!
THESE HAND-AND-FOOTHOLDS WILL GET ME UP TO HIS LEVEL IN SECONDS!
ALL RIGHT, SPIDER-MAN--HERE I AM! IF YOU HAVE ANY NERVE, YOU'LL FACE ME!
HEY, I'VE ALWAYS BEEN A PRETTY NERVY GUY... AND THAT'S ONE OF THE NICER THINGS PEOPLE SAY ABOUT ME!
YOU'VE MOCKED ME FOR THE LAST TIME!
GOSH, I HOPE SO! BUT JUST TO MAKE SURE--
--I BROUGHT YOU A GOING AWAY PRESENT! AND COATED IT WITH MY EXTRA-STICKY WEBBING... TO KEEP YOU FROM DROPPING IT, BUTTER-FINGERS!
WHAT?!
BLAST YOU! EVEN MY HANDS ARE STUCK TO THIS GOO!
BUT I WON'T STAY STUCK FOR LONG! I'LL BLAST MYSELF FREE!
THAT'S WHAT I'M COUNTING ON!
AT TOP SPEED, THE AMAZING ADVENTURER HURLS HIMSELF FROM THE CHEMICAL WAREHOUSE--
CHEMCO

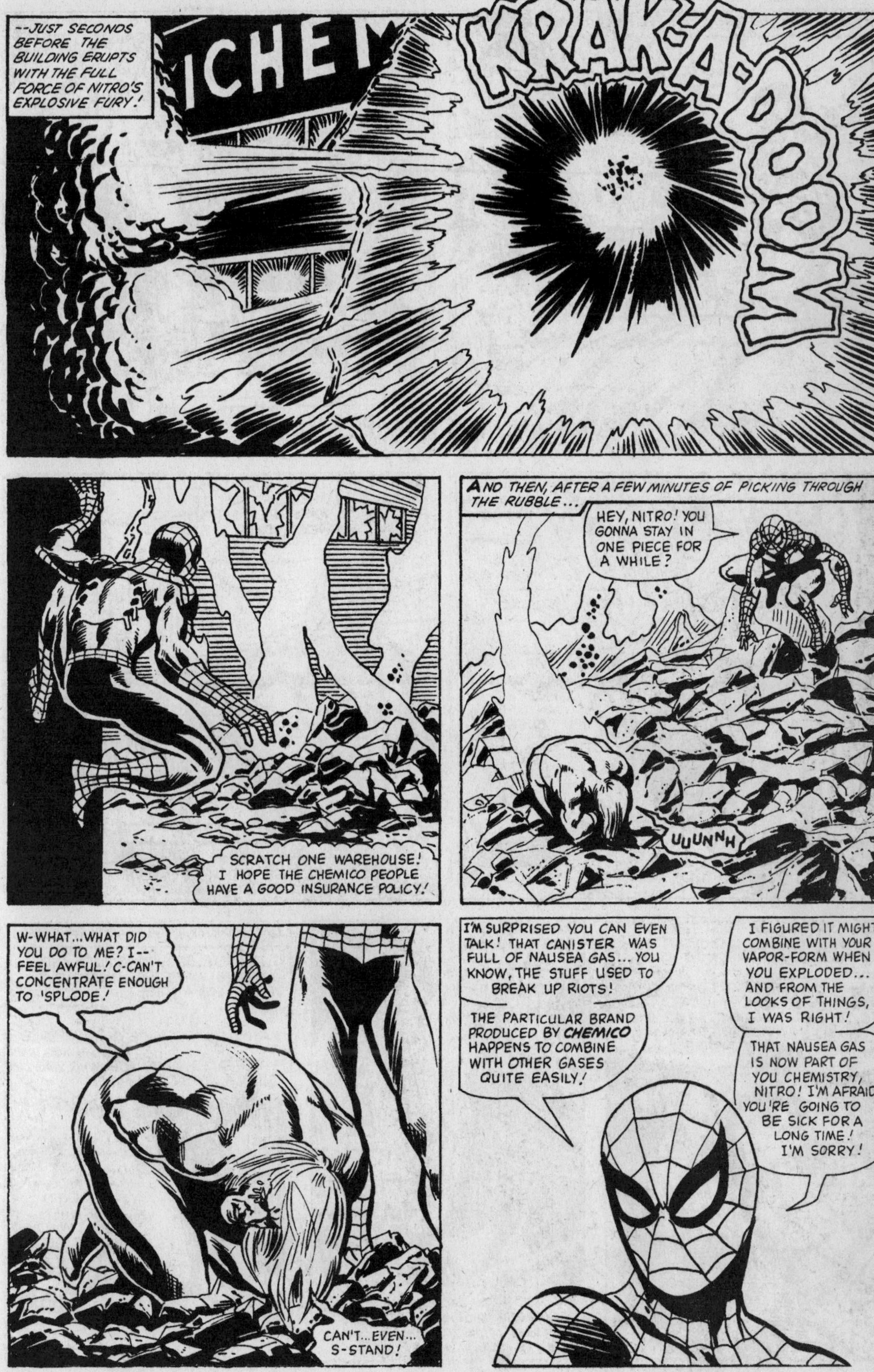
--JUST SECONDS BEFORE THE BUILDING ERUPTS WITH THE FULL FORCE OF NITRO'S EXPLOSIVE FURY!
CHEM
KRAK-A-DOOM
SCRATCH ONE WAREHOUSE! I HOPE THE CHEMICO PEOPLE HAVE A GOOD INSURANCE POLICY!
AND THEN, AFTER A FEW MINUTES OF PICKING THROUGH THE RUBBLE...
HEY, NITRO! YOU GONNA STAY IN ONE PIECE FOR A WHILE?
UUUNNH
W-WHAT...WHAT DID YOU DO TO ME? I-- FEEL AWFUL! C-CAN'T CONCENTRATE ENOUGH TO 'SPLODE!
CAN'T...EVEN... S-STAND!
I'M SURPRISED YOU CAN EVEN TALK! THAT CANISTER WAS FULL OF NAUSEA GAS... YOU KNOW, THE STUFF USED TO BREAK UP RIOTS!
THE PARTICULAR BRAND PRODUCED BY CHEMICO HAPPENS TO COMBINE WITH OTHER GASES QUITE EASILY!
I FIGURED IT MIGHT COMBINE WITH YOUR VAPOR-FORM WHEN YOU EXPLODED... AND FROM THE LOOKS OF THINGS, I WAS RIGHT!
THAT NAUSEA GAS IS NOW PART OF YOU CHEMISTRY, NITRO! I'M AFRAID YOU'RE GOING TO BE SICK FOR A LONG TIME! I'M SORRY!

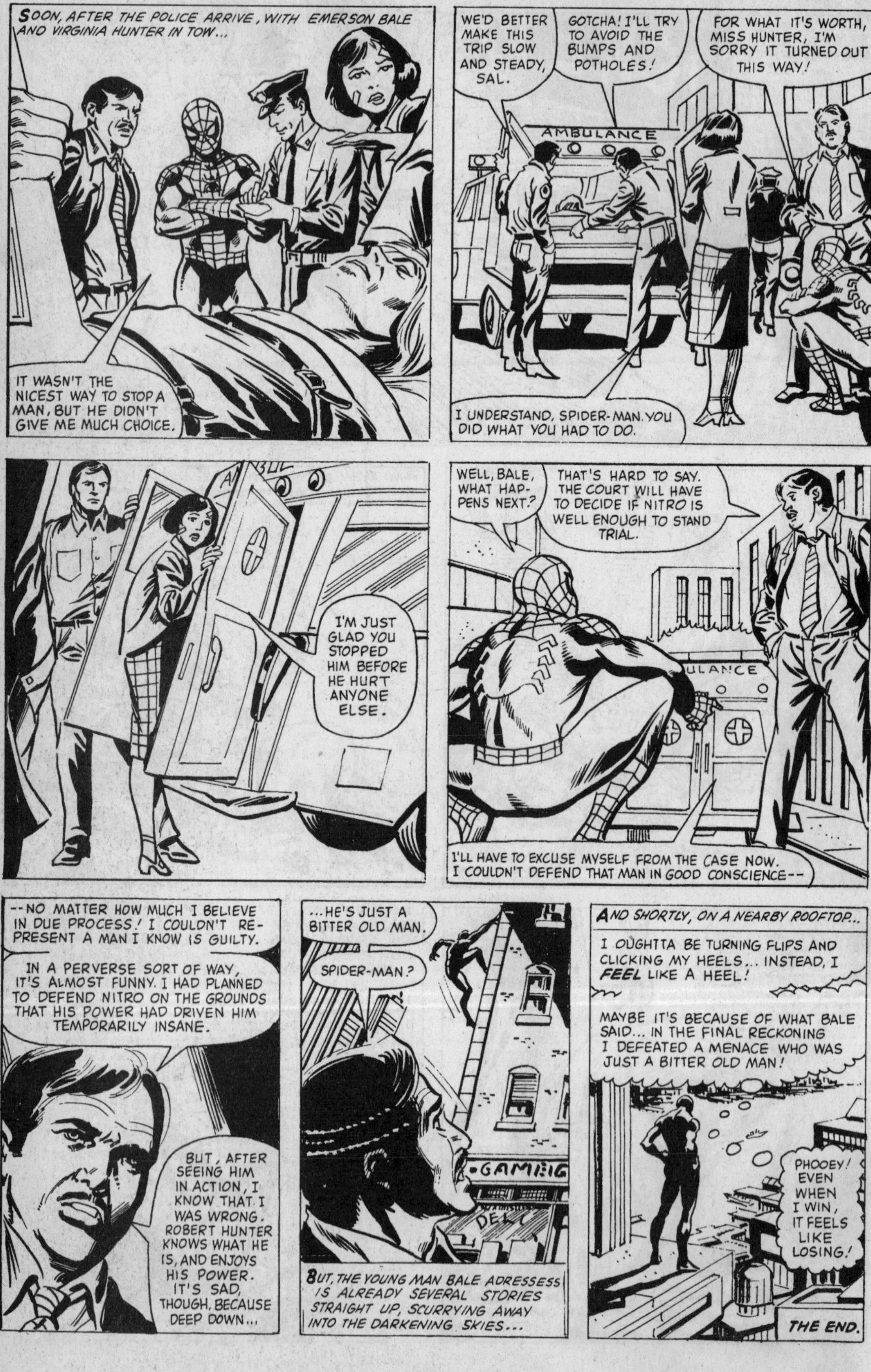
SOON, AFTER THE POLICE ARRIVE, WITH EMERSON BALE AND VIRGINIA HUNTER IN TOW...
IT WASN'T THE NICEST WAY TO STOP A MAN, BUT HE DIDN'T GIVE ME MUCH CHOICE.
WE'D BETTER MAKE THIS TRIP SLOW AND STEADY, SAL.
GOTCHA! I'LL TRY TO AVOID THE BUMPS AND POTHOLES!
FOR WHAT IT'S WORTH, MISS HUNTER, I'M SORRY IT TURNED OUT THIS WAY!
AMBULANCE
I UNDERSTAND, SPIDER-MAN. YOU DID WHAT YOU HAD TO DO.
I'M JUST GLAD YOU STOPPED HIM BEFORE HE HURT ANYONE ELSE.
WELL, BALE, WHAT HAPPENS NEXT?
THAT'S HARD TO SAY. THE COURT WILL HAVE TO DECIDE IF NITRO IS WELL ENOUGH TO STAND TRIAL.
I'LL HAVE TO EXCUSE MYSELF FROM THE CASE NOW. I COULDN'T DEFEND THAT MAN IN GOOD CONSCIENCE--
--NO MATTER HOW MUCH I BELIEVE IN DUE PROCESS! I COULDN'T REPRESENT A MAN I KNOW IS GUILTY.
IN A PERVERSE SORT OF WAY, IT'S ALMOST FUNNY. I HAD PLANNED TO DEFEND NITRO ON THE GROUNDS THAT HIS POWER HAD DRIVEN HIM TEMPORARILY INSANE.
BUT, AFTER SEEING HIM IN ACTION, I KNOW THAT I WAS WRONG. ROBERT HUNTER KNOWS WHAT HE IS, AND ENJOYS HIS POWER. IT'S SAD, THOUGH, BECAUSE DEEP DOWN...
...HE'S JUST A BITTER OLD MAN.
SPIDER-MAN?
BUT, THE YOUNG MAN BALE ADRESSESS IS ALREADY SEVERAL STORIES STRAIGHT UP, SCURRYING AWAY INTO THE DARKENING SKIES...
AND SHORTLY, ON A NEARBY ROOFTOP...
I OUGHTTA BE TURNING FLIPS AND CLICKING MY HEELS... INSTEAD, I FEEL LIKE A HEEL!
MAYBE IT'S BECAUSE OF WHAT BALE SAID... IN THE FINAL RECKONING I DEFEATED A MENACE WHO WAS JUST A BITTER OLD MAN!
PHOOEY! EVEN WHEN I WIN, IT FEELS LIKE LOSING!
THE END.

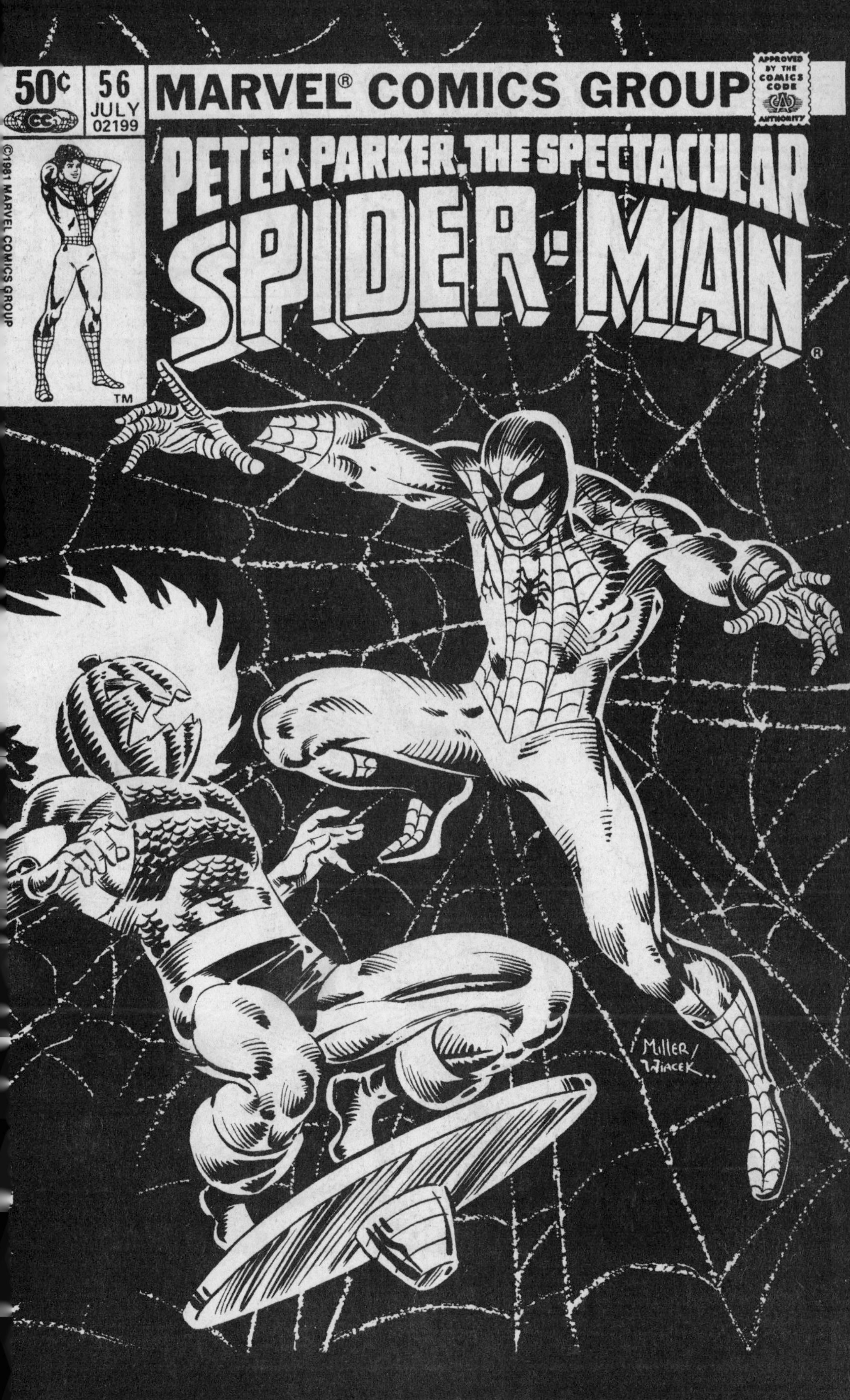
50¢
56
JULY
02199
MARVEL® COMICS GROUP
APPROVED BY THE COMICS CODE AUTHORITY
©1981 MARVEL COMICS GROUP
PETER PARKER, THE SPECTACULAR
SPIDER-MAN®
TM
MILLER/
WIACEK

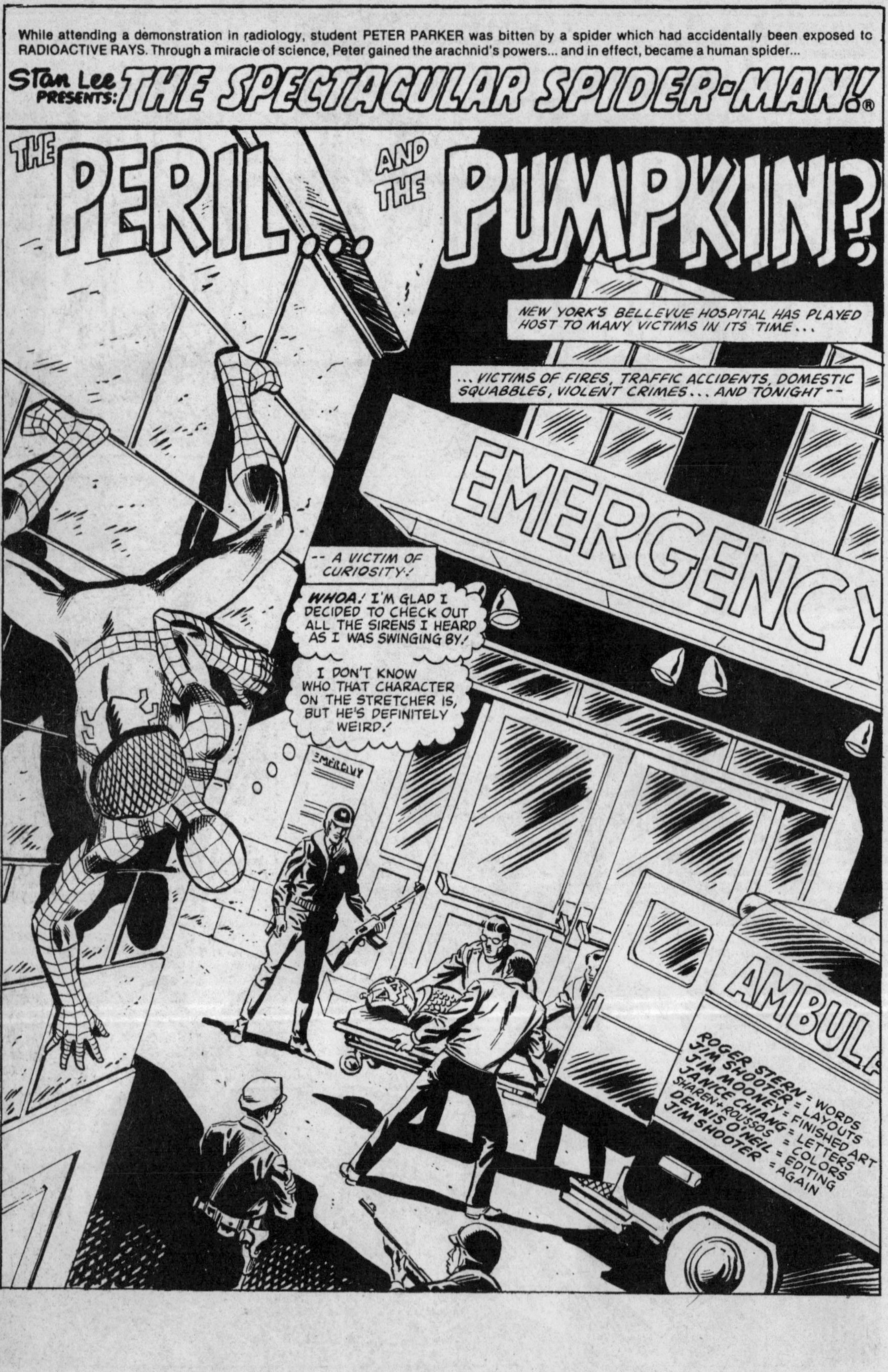

While attending a demonstration in radiology, student PETER PARKER was bitten by a spider which had accidentally been exposed to RADIOACTIVE RAYS. Through a miracle of science, Peter gained the arachnid's powers... and in effect, became a human spider...
Stan Lee PRESENTS: THE SPECTACULAR SPIDER-MAN!®
THE PERIL... AND THE PUMPKIN?
NEW YORK'S BELLEVUE HOSPITAL HAS PLAYED HOST TO MANY VICTIMS IN ITS TIME...
...VICTIMS OF FIRES, TRAFFIC ACCIDENTS, DOMESTIC SQUABBLES, VIOLENT CRIMES... AND TONIGHT --
EMERGENCY
-- A VICTIM OF CURIOSITY!
WHOA! I'M GLAD I DECIDED TO CHECK OUT ALL THE SIRENS I HEARD AS I WAS SWINGING BY!
I DON'T KNOW WHO THAT CHARACTER ON THE STRETCHER IS, BUT HE'S DEFINITELY WEIRD!
AMBUL
ROGER STERN = WORDS
JIM SHOOTER = LAYOUTS
JIM MOONEY = FINISHED ART
JANICE CHIANG = LETTERS
SHAREN+ROUSSOS = COLORS
DENNIS O'NEIL = EDITING
JIM SHOOTER = AGAIN

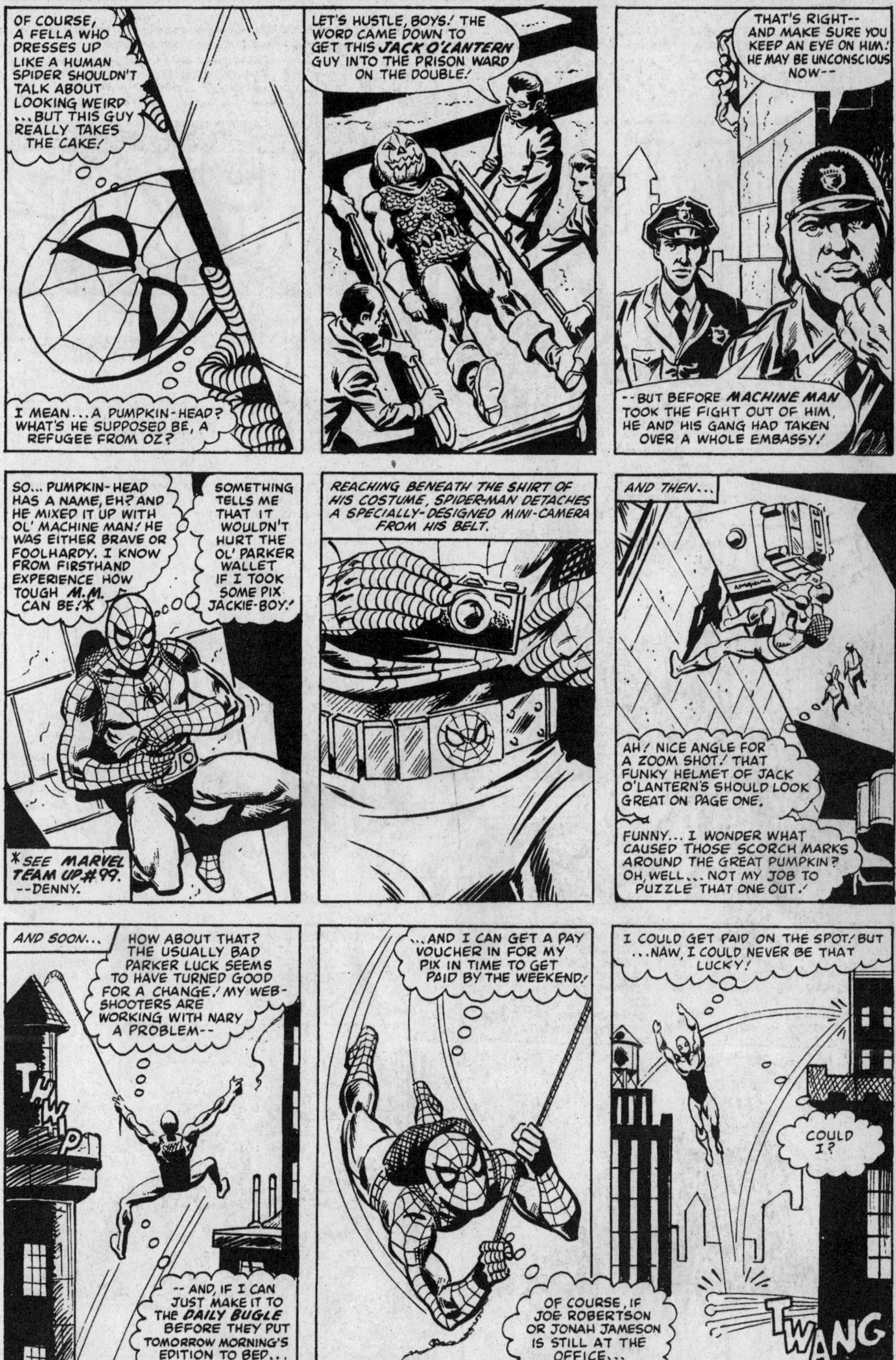
OF COURSE, A FELLA WHO DRESSES UP LIKE A HUMAN SPIDER SHOULDN'T TALK ABOUT LOOKING WEIRD ...BUT THIS GUY REALLY TAKES THE CAKE!
I MEAN... A PUMPKIN-HEAD? WHAT'S HE SUPPOSED BE, A REFUGEE FROM OZ?
LET'S HUSTLE, BOYS! THE WORD CAME DOWN TO GET THIS JACK O'LANTERN GUY INTO THE PRISON WARD ON THE DOUBLE!
THAT'S RIGHT-- AND MAKE SURE YOU KEEP AN EYE ON HIM! HE MAY BE UNCONSCIOUS NOW--
--BUT BEFORE MACHINE MAN TOOK THE FIGHT OUT OF HIM, HE AND HIS GANG HAD TAKEN OVER A WHOLE EMBASSY!
SO... PUMPKIN-HEAD HAS A NAME, EH? AND HE MIXED IT UP WITH OL' MACHINE MAN! HE WAS EITHER BRAVE OR FOOLHARDY. I KNOW FROM FIRSTHAND EXPERIENCE HOW TOUGH M.M. CAN BE!*
SOMETHING TELLS ME THAT IT WOULDN'T HURT THE OL' PARKER WALLET IF I TOOK SOME PIX JACKIE-BOY!
*SEE MARVEL TEAM UP #99. --DENNY.
REACHING BENEATH THE SHIRT OF HIS COSTUME, SPIDER-MAN DETACHES A SPECIALLY-DESIGNED MINI-CAMERA FROM HIS BELT.
AND THEN...
AH! NICE ANGLE FOR A ZOOM SHOT! THAT FUNKY HELMET OF JACK O'LANTERN'S SHOULD LOOK GREAT ON PAGE ONE.
FUNNY... I WONDER WHAT CAUSED THOSE SCORCH MARKS AROUND THE GREAT PUMPKIN? OH, WELL... NOT MY JOB TO PUZZLE THAT ONE OUT!
AND SOON...
HOW ABOUT THAT? THE USUALLY BAD PARKER LUCK SEEMS TO HAVE TURNED GOOD FOR A CHANGE! MY WEB-SHOOTERS ARE WORKING WITH NARY A PROBLEM--
THWIP
--AND, IF I CAN JUST MAKE IT TO THE DAILY BUGLE BEFORE THEY PUT TOMORROW MORNING'S EDITION TO BED...
...AND I CAN GET A PAY VOUCHER IN FOR MY PIX IN TIME TO GET PAID BY THE WEEKEND!
OF COURSE, IF JOE ROBERTSON OR JONAH JAMESON IS STILL AT THE OFFICE...
I COULD GET PAID ON THE SPOT! BUT ...NAW, I COULD NEVER BE THAT LUCKY!
COULD I?
TWANG

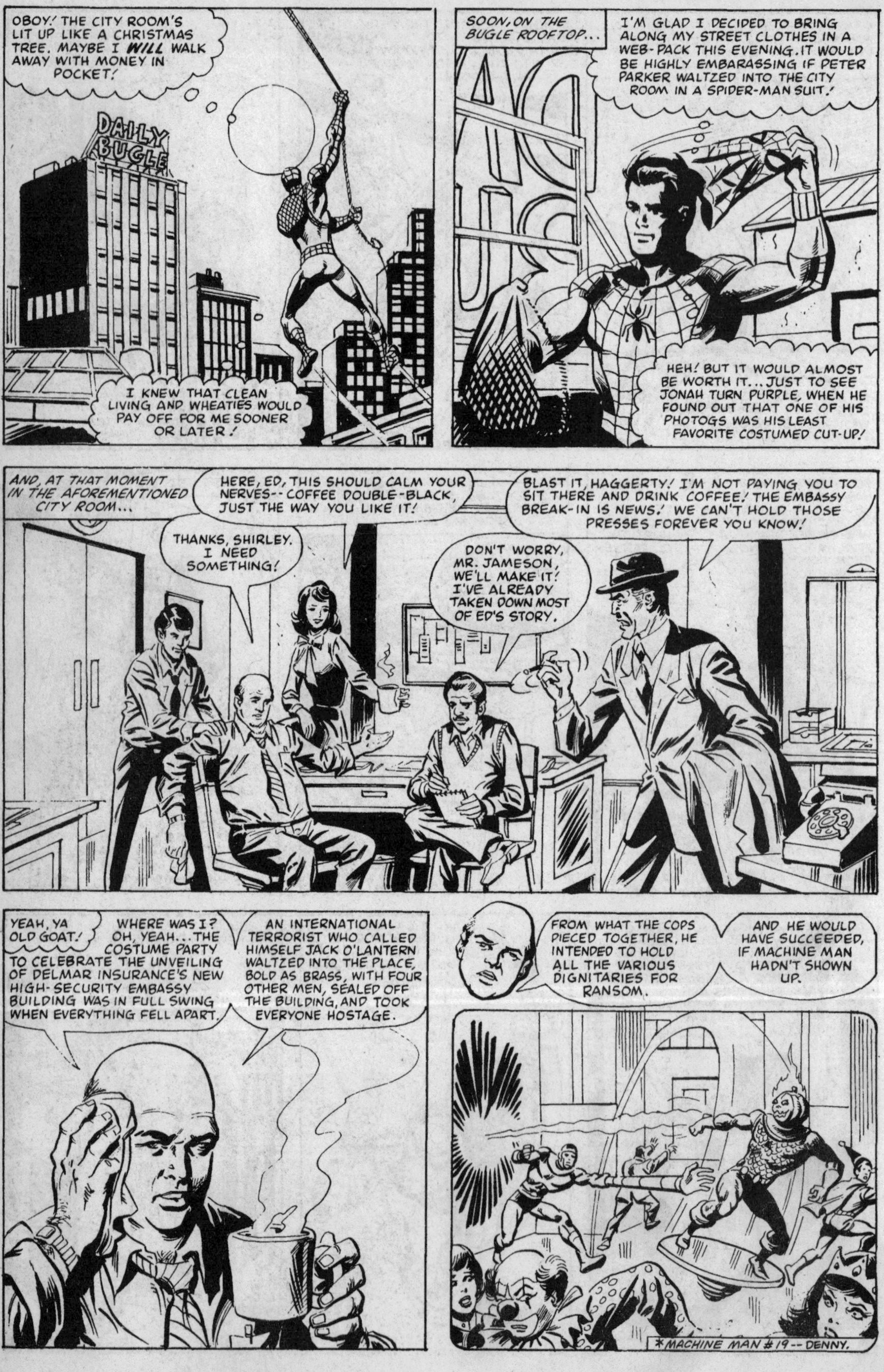
OBOY! THE CITY ROOM'S LIT UP LIKE A CHRISTMAS TREE. MAYBE I WILL WALK AWAY WITH MONEY IN POCKET!
DAILY BUGLE
I KNEW THAT CLEAN LIVING AND WHEATIES WOULD PAY OFF FOR ME SOONER OR LATER!
SOON, ON THE BUGLE ROOFTOP...
I'M GLAD I DECIDED TO BRING ALONG MY STREET CLOTHES IN A WEB-PACK THIS EVENING. IT WOULD BE HIGHLY EMBARASSING IF PETER PARKER WALTZED INTO THE CITY ROOM IN A SPIDER-MAN SUIT!
HEH! BUT IT WOULD ALMOST BE WORTH IT... JUST TO SEE JONAH TURN PURPLE, WHEN HE FOUND OUT THAT ONE OF HIS PHOTOGS WAS HIS LEAST FAVORITE COSTUMED CUT-UP!
AND, AT THAT MOMENT IN THE AFOREMENTIONED CITY ROOM...
HERE, ED, THIS SHOULD CALM YOUR NERVES-- COFFEE DOUBLE-BLACK, JUST THE WAY YOU LIKE IT!
THANKS, SHIRLEY. I NEED SOMETHING!
BLAST IT, HAGGERTY! I'M NOT PAYING YOU TO SIT THERE AND DRINK COFFEE! THE EMBASSY BREAK-IN IS NEWS! WE CAN'T HOLD THOSE PRESSES FOREVER YOU KNOW!
DON'T WORRY, MR. JAMESON, WE'LL MAKE IT! I'VE ALREADY TAKEN DOWN MOST OF ED'S STORY.
YEAH, YA OLD GOAT!
WHERE WAS I? OH, YEAH... THE COSTUME PARTY TO CELEBRATE THE UNVEILING OF DELMAR INSURANCE'S NEW HIGH-SECURITY EMBASSY BUILDING WAS IN FULL SWING WHEN EVERYTHING FELL APART.
AN INTERNATIONAL TERRORIST WHO CALLED HIMSELF JACK O'LANTERN WALTZED INTO THE PLACE, BOLD AS BRASS, WITH FOUR OTHER MEN, SEALED OFF THE BUILDING, AND TOOK EVERYONE HOSTAGE.
FROM WHAT THE COPS PIECED TOGETHER, HE INTENDED TO HOLD ALL THE VARIOUS DIGNITARIES FOR RANSOM.
AND HE WOULD HAVE SUCCEEDED, IF MACHINE MAN HADN'T SHOWN UP.
*MACHINE MAN #19 -- DENNY.

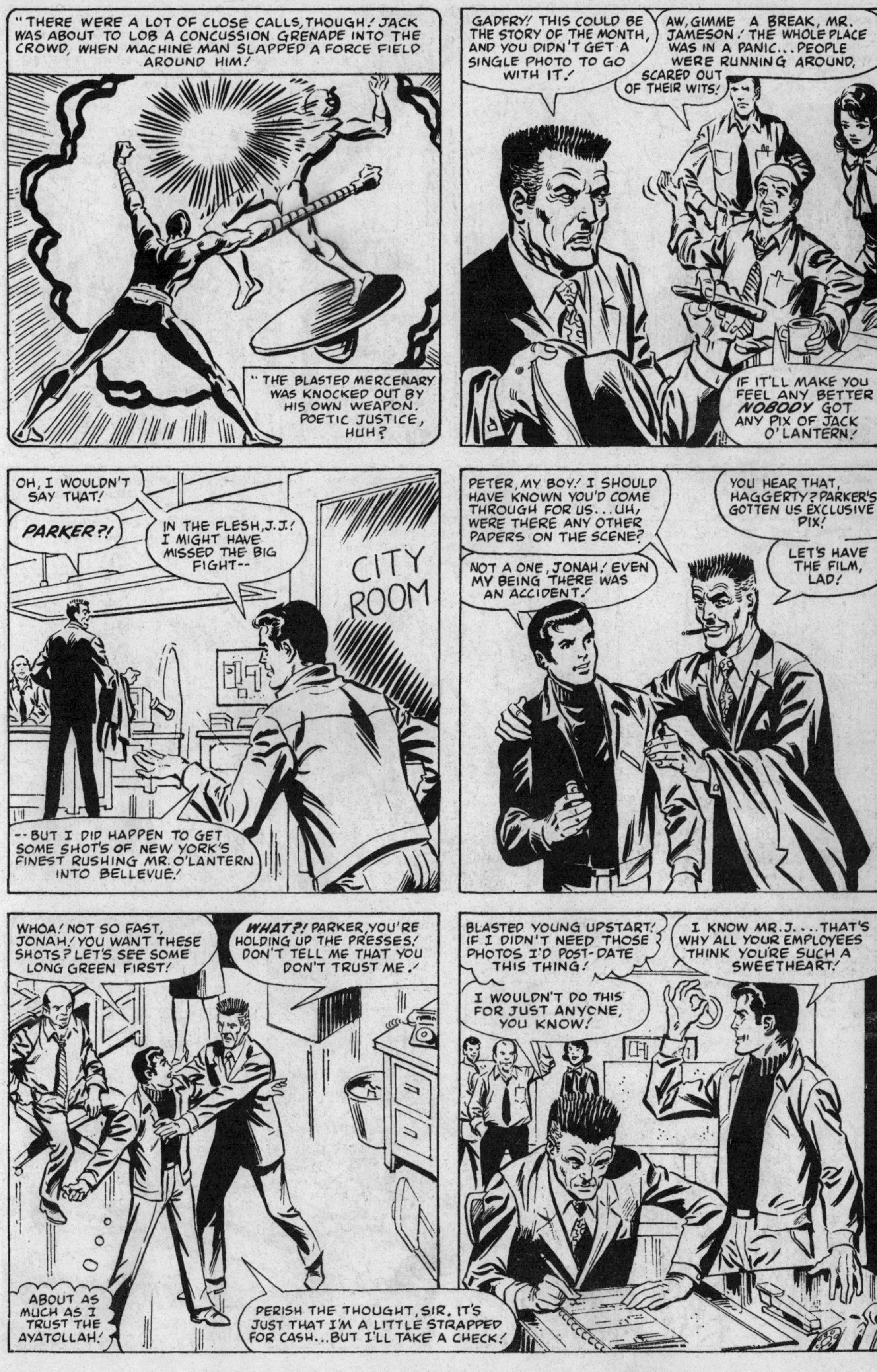
"THERE WERE A LOT OF CLOSE CALLS, THOUGH! JACK WAS ABOUT TO LOB A CONCUSSION GRENADE INTO THE CROWD, WHEN MACHINE MAN SLAPPED A FORCE FIELD AROUND HIM!
"THE BLASTED MERCENARY WAS KNOCKED OUT BY HIS OWN WEAPON. POETIC JUSTICE, HUH?
GADFRY! THIS COULD BE THE STORY OF THE MONTH, AND YOU DIDN'T GET A SINGLE PHOTO TO GO WITH IT!
AW, GIMME A BREAK, MR. JAMESON! THE WHOLE PLACE WAS IN A PANIC... PEOPLE WERE RUNNING AROUND, SCARED OUT OF THEIR WITS!
IF IT'LL MAKE YOU FEEL ANY BETTER NOBODY GOT ANY PIX OF JACK O'LANTERN!
OH, I WOULDN'T SAY THAT!
PARKER?!
IN THE FLESH, J.J.! I MIGHT HAVE MISSED THE BIG FIGHT--
CITY ROOM
--BUT I DID HAPPEN TO GET SOME SHOT'S OF NEW YORK'S FINEST RUSHING MR. O'LANTERN INTO BELLEVUE!
PETER, MY BOY! I SHOULD HAVE KNOWN YOU'D COME THROUGH FOR US... UH, WERE THERE ANY OTHER PAPERS ON THE SCENE?
NOT A ONE, JONAH! EVEN MY BEING THERE WAS AN ACCIDENT!
YOU HEAR THAT, HAGGERTY? PARKER'S GOTTEN US EXCLUSIVE PIX!
LET'S HAVE THE FILM, LAD!
WHOA! NOT SO FAST, JONAH! YOU WANT THESE SHOTS? LET'S SEE SOME LONG GREEN FIRST!
WHAT?! PARKER, YOU'RE HOLDING UP THE PRESSES! DON'T TELL ME THAT YOU DON'T TRUST ME.
ABOUT AS MUCH AS I TRUST THE AYATOLLAH!
PERISH THE THOUGHT, SIR. IT'S JUST THAT I'M A LITTLE STRAPPED FOR CASH... BUT I'LL TAKE A CHECK!
BLASTED YOUNG UPSTART! IF I DIDN'T NEED THOSE PHOTOS I'D POST-DATE THIS THING!
I WOULDN'T DO THIS FOR JUST ANYONE, YOU KNOW!
I KNOW MR. J... THAT'S WHY ALL YOUR EMPLOYEES THINK YOU'RE SUCH A SWEETHEART!

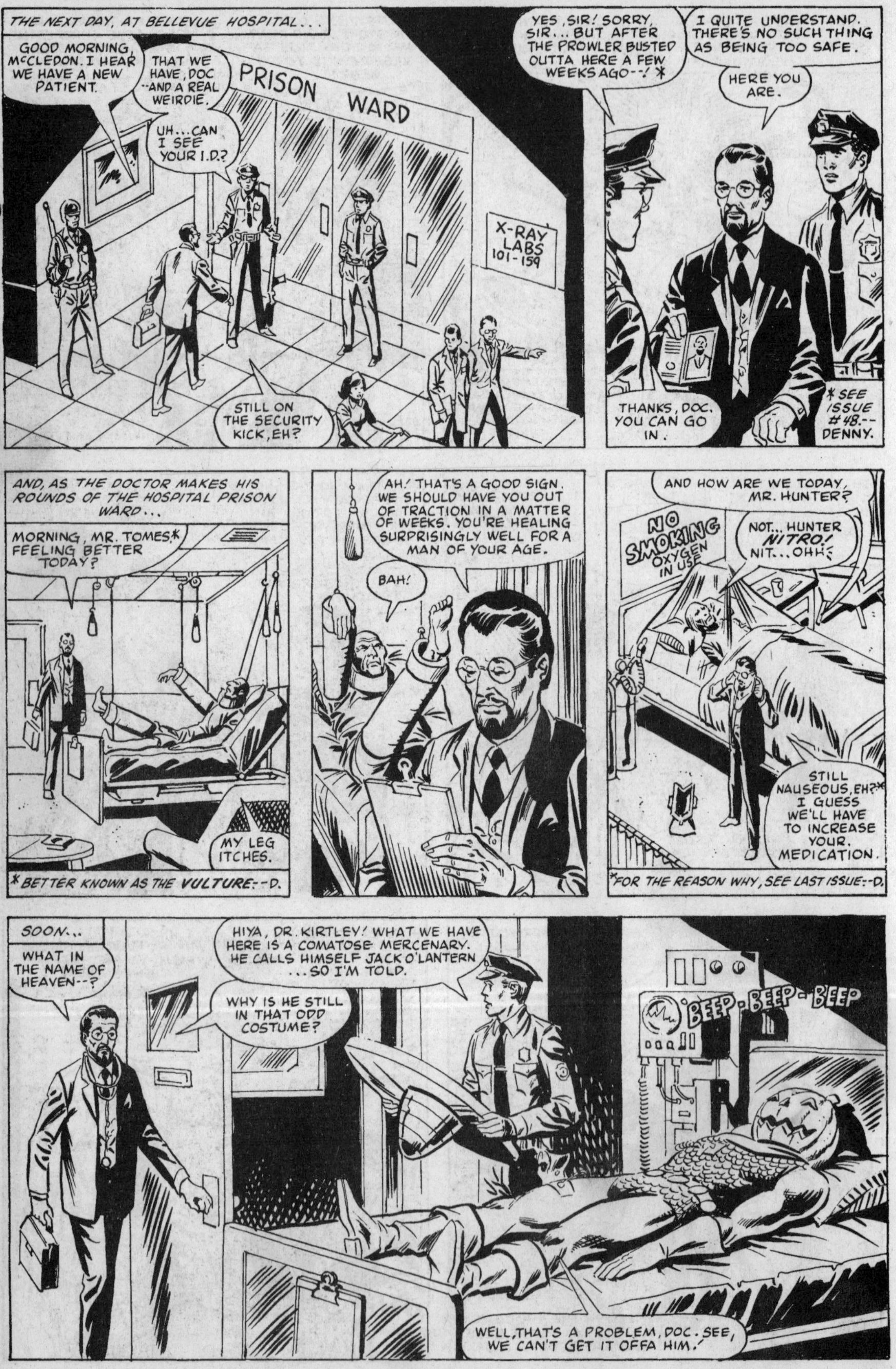
THE NEXT DAY, AT BELLEVUE HOSPITAL...
GOOD MORNING, McCLEDON. I HEAR WE HAVE A NEW PATIENT.
THAT WE HAVE, DOC --AND A REAL WEIRDIE.
PRISON WARD
UH...CAN I SEE YOUR I.D.?
STILL ON THE SECURITY KICK, EH?
X-RAY LABS 101-159
YES, SIR! SORRY, SIR... BUT AFTER THE PROWLER BUSTED OUTTA HERE A FEW WEEKS AGO--! *
I QUITE UNDERSTAND. THERE'S NO SUCH THING AS BEING TOO SAFE.
HERE YOU ARE.
THANKS, DOC. YOU CAN GO IN.
* SEE ISSUE #48.-- DENNY.
AND, AS THE DOCTOR MAKES HIS ROUNDS OF THE HOSPITAL PRISON WARD...
MORNING, MR. TOMES.* FEELING BETTER TODAY?
MY LEG ITCHES.
* BETTER KNOWN AS THE VULTURE.--D.
AH! THAT'S A GOOD SIGN. WE SHOULD HAVE YOU OUT OF TRACTION IN A MATTER OF WEEKS. YOU'RE HEALING SURPRISINGLY WELL FOR A MAN OF YOUR AGE.
BAH!
AND HOW ARE WE TODAY, MR. HUNTER?
NO SMOKING OXYGEN IN USE
NOT... HUNTER NITRO! NIT...OHH
STILL NAUSEOUS, EH?* I GUESS WE'LL HAVE TO INCREASE YOUR MEDICATION.
* FOR THE REASON WHY, SEE LAST ISSUE.--D.
SOON...
WHAT IN THE NAME OF HEAVEN--?
HIYA, DR. KIRTLEY! WHAT WE HAVE HERE IS A COMATOSE MERCENARY. HE CALLS HIMSELF JACK O'LANTERN ...SO I'M TOLD.
WHY IS HE STILL IN THAT ODD COSTUME?
BEEP - BEEP - BEEP
WELL, THAT'S A PROBLEM, DOC. SEE, WE CAN'T GET IT OFFA HIM!

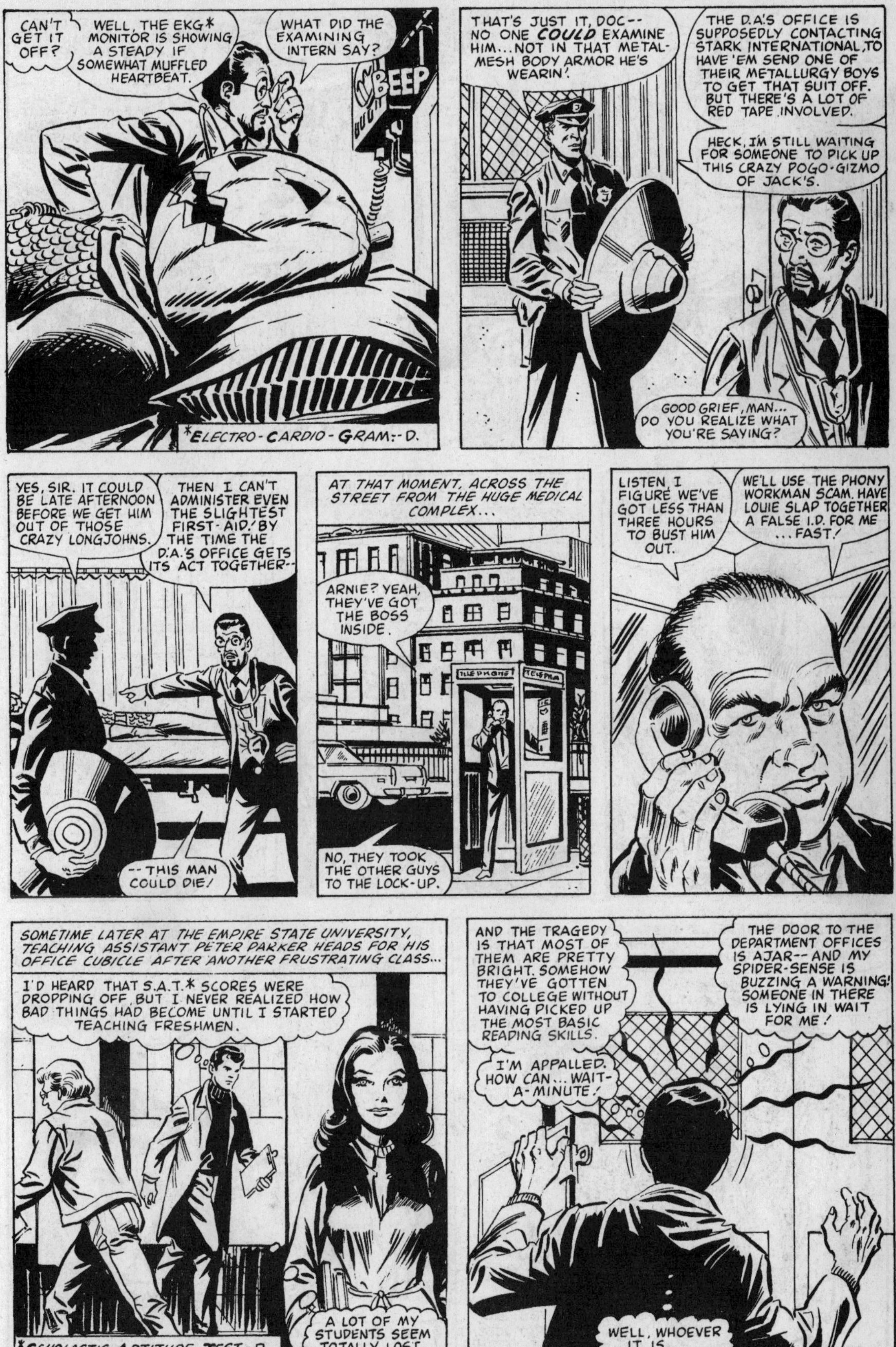
CAN'T GET IT OFF?
WELL, THE EKG* MONITOR IS SHOWING A STEADY IF SOMEWHAT MUFFLED HEARTBEAT.
WHAT DID THE EXAMINING INTERN SAY?
BEEP
*ELECTRO-CARDIO-GRAM:-D.
THAT'S JUST IT, DOC-- NO ONE COULD EXAMINE HIM... NOT IN THAT METAL-MESH BODY ARMOR HE'S WEARIN'.
THE D.A.'S OFFICE IS SUPPOSEDLY CONTACTING STARK INTERNATIONAL, TO HAVE 'EM SEND ONE OF THEIR METALLURGY BOYS TO GET THAT SUIT OFF. BUT THERE'S A LOT OF RED TAPE INVOLVED.
HECK, I'M STILL WAITING FOR SOMEONE TO PICK UP THIS CRAZY POGO-GIZMO OF JACK'S.
GOOD GRIEF, MAN... DO YOU REALIZE WHAT YOU'RE SAYING?
YES, SIR. IT COULD BE LATE AFTERNOON BEFORE WE GET HIM OUT OF THOSE CRAZY LONGJOHNS.
THEN I CAN'T ADMINISTER EVEN THE SLIGHTEST FIRST-AID! BY THE TIME THE D.A.'S OFFICE GETS ITS ACT TOGETHER--
--THIS MAN COULD DIE!
AT THAT MOMENT, ACROSS THE STREET FROM THE HUGE MEDICAL COMPLEX...
ARNIE? YEAH, THEY'VE GOT THE BOSS INSIDE.
NO, THEY TOOK THE OTHER GUYS TO THE LOCK-UP.
LISTEN. I FIGURE WE'VE GOT LESS THAN THREE HOURS TO BUST HIM OUT.
WE'LL USE THE PHONY WORKMAN SCAM. HAVE LOUIE SLAP TOGETHER A FALSE I.D. FOR ME ...FAST!
SOMETIME LATER AT THE EMPIRE STATE UNIVERSITY, TEACHING ASSISTANT PETER PARKER HEADS FOR HIS OFFICE CUBICLE AFTER ANOTHER FRUSTRATING CLASS...
I'D HEARD THAT S.A.T.* SCORES WERE DROPPING OFF, BUT I NEVER REALIZED HOW BAD THINGS HAD BECOME UNTIL I STARTED TEACHING FRESHMEN.
A LOT OF MY STUDENTS SEEM TOTALLY LOST.
*SCHOLASTIC APTITUDE TEST.-D.
AND THE TRAGEDY IS THAT MOST OF THEM ARE PRETTY BRIGHT. SOMEHOW THEY'VE GOTTEN TO COLLEGE WITHOUT HAVING PICKED UP THE MOST BASIC READING SKILLS.
THE DOOR TO THE DEPARTMENT OFFICES IS AJAR-- AND MY SPIDER-SENSE IS BUZZING A WARNING! SOMEONE IN THERE IS LYING IN WAIT FOR ME!
I'M APPALLED. HOW CAN... WAIT-A-MINUTE!
WELL, WHOEVER IT IS...

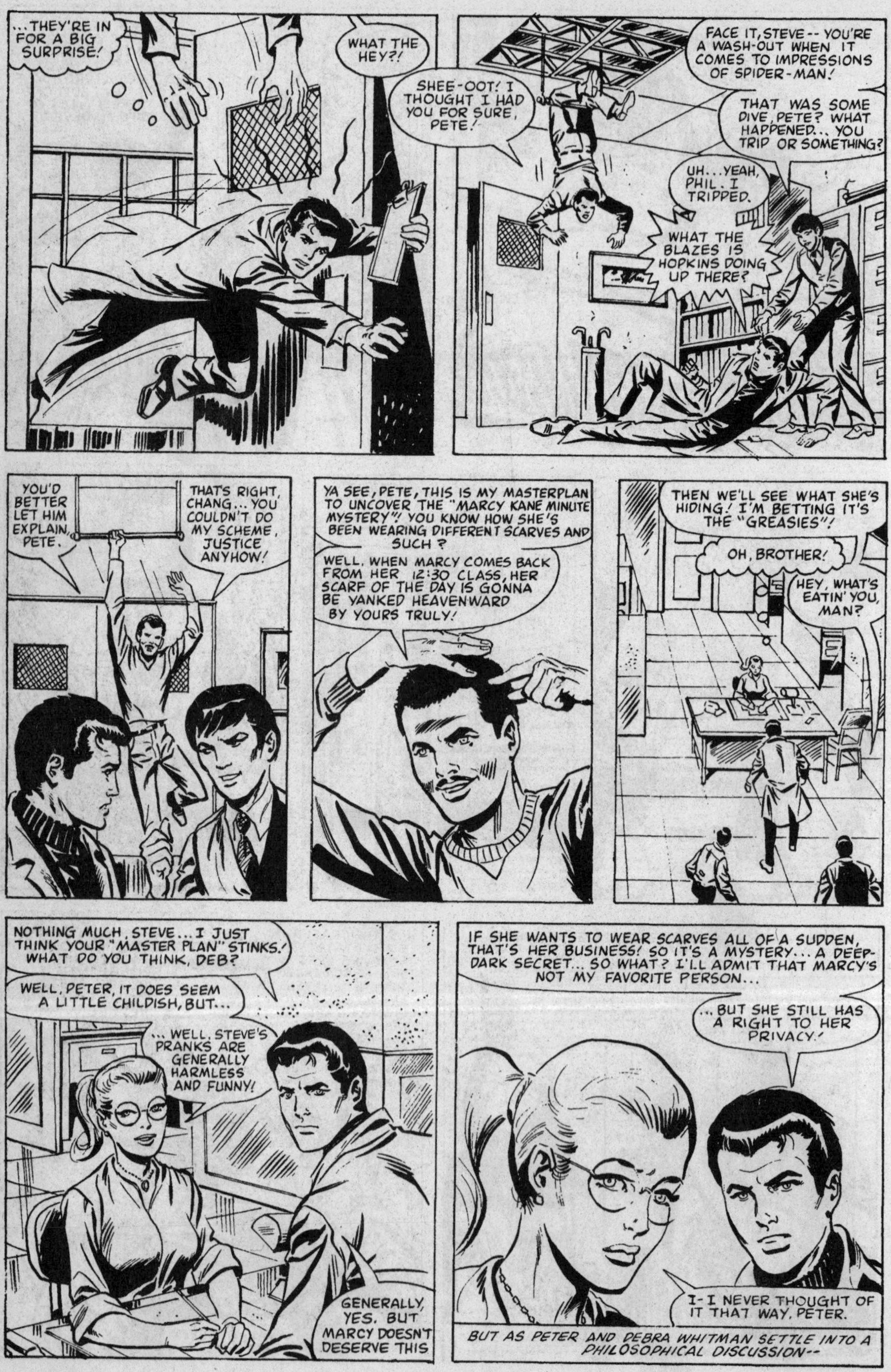
...THEY'RE IN FOR A BIG SURPRISE!
WHAT THE HEY?!
SHEE-OOT! I THOUGHT I HAD YOU FOR SURE, PETE!
FACE IT, STEVE-- YOU'RE A WASH-OUT WHEN IT COMES TO IMPRESSIONS OF SPIDER-MAN!
THAT WAS SOME DIVE, PETE? WHAT HAPPENED... YOU TRIP OR SOMETHING?
UH...YEAH, PHIL. I TRIPPED.
WHAT THE BLAZES IS HOPKINS DOING UP THERE?
YOU'D BETTER LET HIM EXPLAIN, PETE.
THAT'S RIGHT, CHANG... YOU COULDN'T DO MY SCHEME JUSTICE ANYHOW!
YA SEE, PETE, THIS IS MY MASTERPLAN TO UNCOVER THE "MARCY KANE MINUTE MYSTERY"! YOU KNOW HOW SHE'S BEEN WEARING DIFFERENT SCARVES AND SUCH?
WELL, WHEN MARCY COMES BACK FROM HER 12:30 CLASS, HER SCARF OF THE DAY IS GONNA BE YANKED HEAVENWARD BY YOURS TRULY!
THEN WE'LL SEE WHAT SHE'S HIDING! I'M BETTING IT'S THE "GREASIES"!
OH, BROTHER!
HEY, WHAT'S EATIN' YOU, MAN?
NOTHING MUCH, STEVE... I JUST THINK YOUR "MASTER PLAN" STINKS! WHAT DO YOU THINK, DEB?
WELL, PETER, IT DOES SEEM A LITTLE CHILDISH, BUT...
...WELL, STEVE'S PRANKS ARE GENERALLY HARMLESS AND FUNNY!
GENERALLY, YES. BUT MARCY DOESN'T DESERVE THIS
IF SHE WANTS TO WEAR SCARVES ALL OF A SUDDEN, THAT'S HER BUSINESS! SO IT'S A MYSTERY... A DEEP-DARK SECRET... SO WHAT? I'LL ADMIT THAT MARCY'S NOT MY FAVORITE PERSON...
...BUT SHE STILL HAS A RIGHT TO HER PRIVACY!
I- I NEVER THOUGHT OF IT THAT WAY, PETER.
BUT AS PETER AND DEBRA WHITMAN SETTLE INTO A PHILOSOPHICAL DISCUSSION--

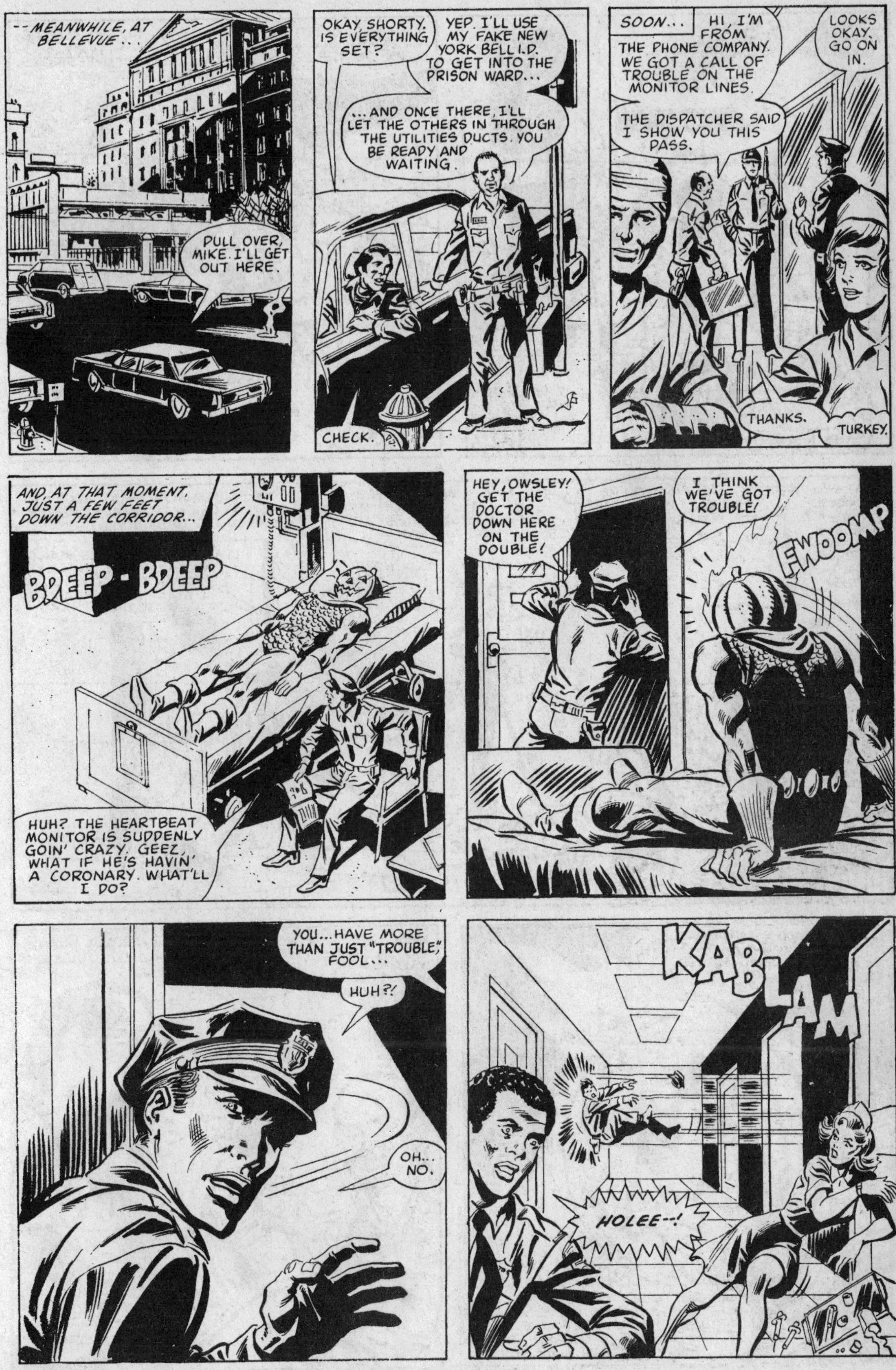
--MEANWHILE, AT BELLEVUE...
PULL OVER, MIKE. I'LL GET OUT HERE.
OKAY, SHORTY. IS EVERYTHING SET?
YEP. I'LL USE MY FAKE NEW YORK BELL I.D. TO GET INTO THE PRISON WARD...
...AND ONCE THERE, I'LL LET THE OTHERS IN THROUGH THE UTILITIES DUCTS. YOU BE READY AND WAITING.
CHECK.
SOON...
HI, I'M FROM THE PHONE COMPANY. WE GOT A CALL OF TROUBLE ON THE MONITOR LINES.
THE DISPATCHER SAID I SHOW YOU THIS PASS.
LOOKS OKAY. GO ON IN.
THANKS.
TURKEY.
AND, AT THAT MOMENT, JUST A FEW FEET DOWN THE CORRIDOR...
BDEEP-BDEEP
HUH? THE HEARTBEAT MONITOR IS SUDDENLY GOIN' CRAZY. GEEZ, WHAT IF HE'S HAVIN' A CORONARY. WHAT'LL I DO?
HEY, OWSLEY! GET THE DOCTOR DOWN HERE ON THE DOUBLE!
I THINK WE'VE GOT TROUBLE!
FWOOMP
YOU...HAVE MORE THAN JUST "TROUBLE," FOOL...
HUH?!
OH... NO.
KABLAM
HOLEE--!

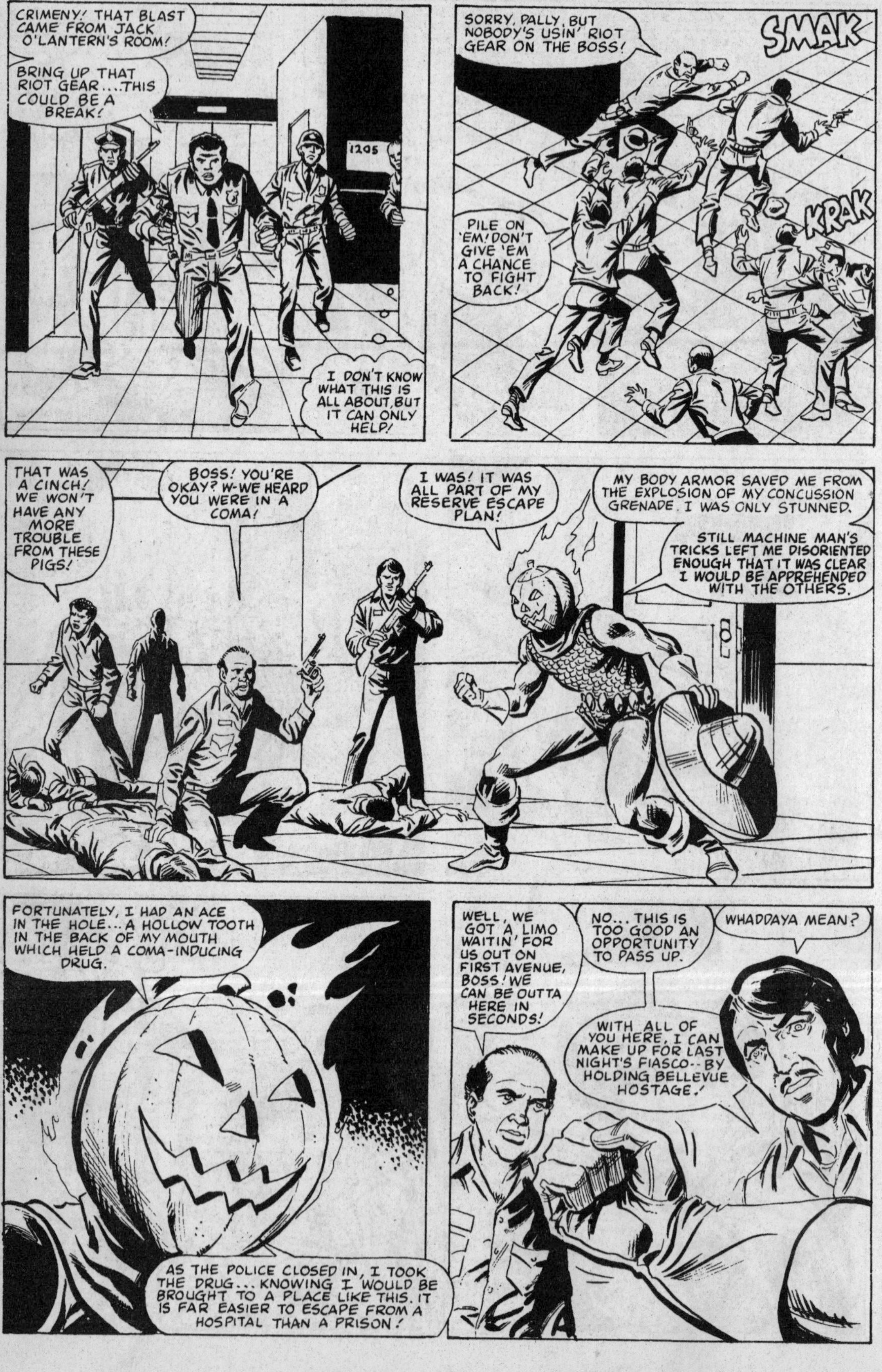
CRIMENY! THAT BLAST CAME FROM JACK O'LANTERN'S ROOM!
BRING UP THAT RIOT GEAR....THIS COULD BE A BREAK!
1205
I DON'T KNOW WHAT THIS IS ALL ABOUT, BUT IT CAN ONLY HELP!
SORRY, PALLY, BUT NOBODY'S USIN' RIOT GEAR ON THE BOSS!
SMAK
PILE ON 'EM! DON'T GIVE 'EM A CHANCE TO FIGHT BACK!
KRAK
THAT WAS A CINCH! WE WON'T HAVE ANY MORE TROUBLE FROM THESE PIGS!
BOSS! YOU'RE OKAY? W-WE HEARD YOU WERE IN A COMA!
I WAS! IT WAS ALL PART OF MY RESERVE ESCAPE PLAN!
MY BODY ARMOR SAVED ME FROM THE EXPLOSION OF MY CONCUSSION GRENADE. I WAS ONLY STUNNED.
STILL MACHINE MAN'S TRICKS LEFT ME DISORIENTED ENOUGH THAT IT WAS CLEAR I WOULD BE APPREHENDED WITH THE OTHERS.
FORTUNATELY, I HAD AN ACE IN THE HOLE... A HOLLOW TOOTH IN THE BACK OF MY MOUTH WHICH HELD A COMA-INDUCING DRUG.
AS THE POLICE CLOSED IN, I TOOK THE DRUG... KNOWING I WOULD BE BROUGHT TO A PLACE LIKE THIS. IT IS FAR EASIER TO ESCAPE FROM A HOSPITAL THAN A PRISON!
WELL, WE GOT A LIMO WAITIN' FOR US OUT ON FIRST AVENUE, BOSS! WE CAN BE OUTTA HERE IN SECONDS!
NO... THIS IS TOO GOOD AN OPPORTUNITY TO PASS UP.
WHADDAYA MEAN?
WITH ALL OF YOU HERE, I CAN MAKE UP FOR LAST NIGHT'S FIASCO-- BY HOLDING BELLEVUE HOSTAGE!

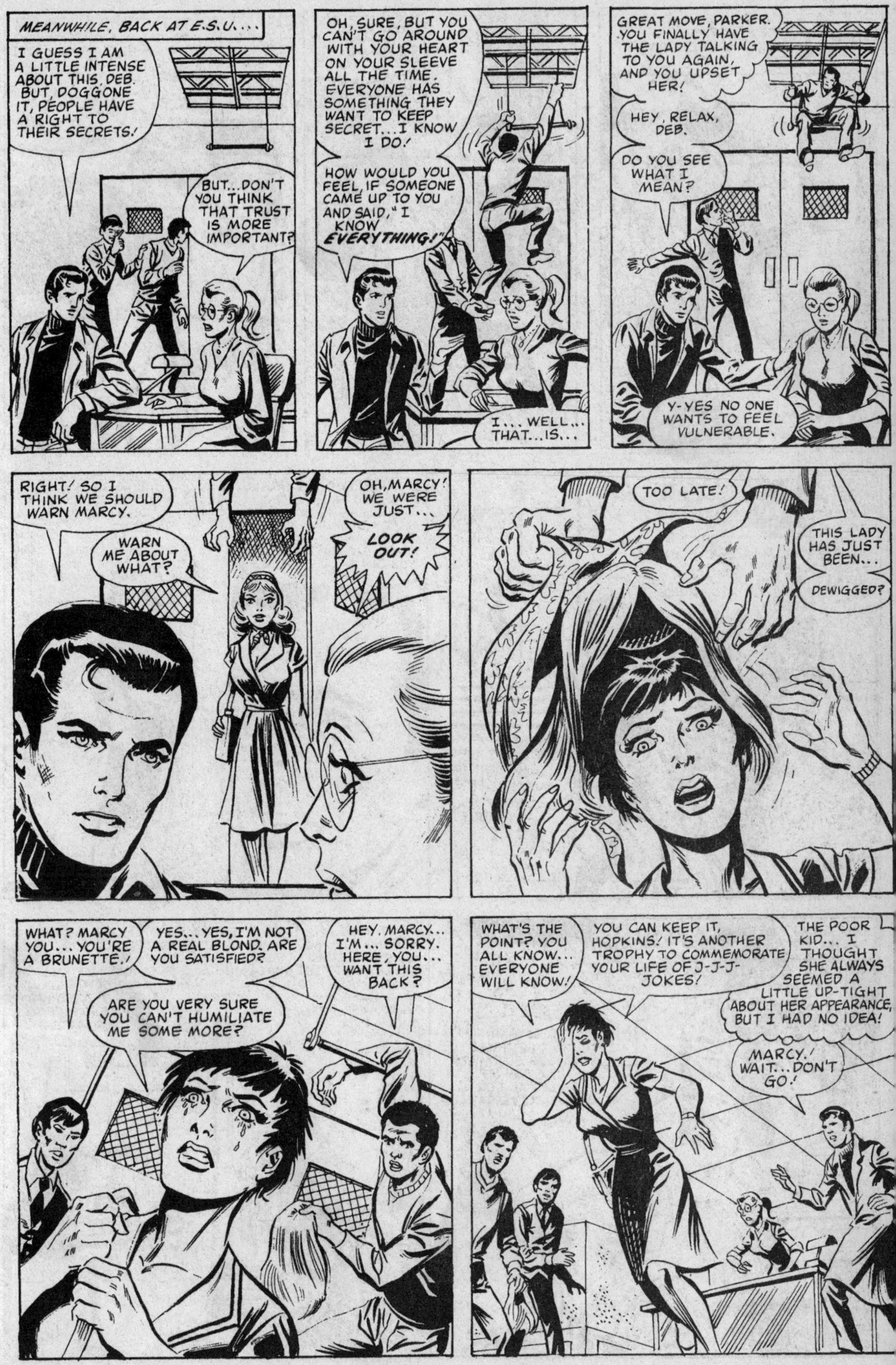
MEANWHILE, BACK AT E.S.U. . . .
I GUESS I AM A LITTLE INTENSE ABOUT THIS, DEB. BUT, DOGGONE IT, PEOPLE HAVE A RIGHT TO THEIR SECRETS!
BUT... DON'T YOU THINK THAT TRUST IS MORE IMPORTANT?
OH, SURE, BUT YOU CAN'T GO AROUND WITH YOUR HEART ON YOUR SLEEVE ALL THE TIME. EVERYONE HAS SOMETHING THEY WANT TO KEEP SECRET... I KNOW I DO!
HOW WOULD YOU FEEL, IF SOMEONE CAME UP TO YOU AND SAID, "I KNOW EVERYTHING!"
I... WELL... THAT... IS...
GREAT MOVE, PARKER. YOU FINALLY HAVE THE LADY TALKING TO YOU AGAIN, AND YOU UPSET HER!
HEY, RELAX, DEB.
DO YOU SEE WHAT I MEAN?
Y-YES NO ONE WANTS TO FEEL VULNERABLE.
RIGHT! SO I THINK WE SHOULD WARN MARCY.
WARN ME ABOUT WHAT?
OH, MARCY! WE WERE JUST...
LOOK OUT!
TOO LATE!
THIS LADY HAS JUST BEEN...
DEWIGGED?
WHAT? MARCY YOU... YOU'RE A BRUNETTE!
YES... YES, I'M NOT A REAL BLOND. ARE YOU SATISFIED?
ARE YOU VERY SURE YOU CAN'T HUMILIATE ME SOME MORE?
HEY, MARCY... I'M... SORRY. HERE, YOU... WANT THIS BACK?
WHAT'S THE POINT? YOU ALL KNOW... EVERYONE WILL KNOW!
YOU CAN KEEP IT, HOPKINS! IT'S ANOTHER TROPHY TO COMMEMORATE YOUR LIFE OF J-J-J-JOKES!
THE POOR KID... I THOUGHT SHE ALWAYS SEEMED A LITTLE UP-TIGHT ABOUT HER APPEARANCE, BUT I HAD NO IDEA!
MARCY! WAIT... DON'T GO!

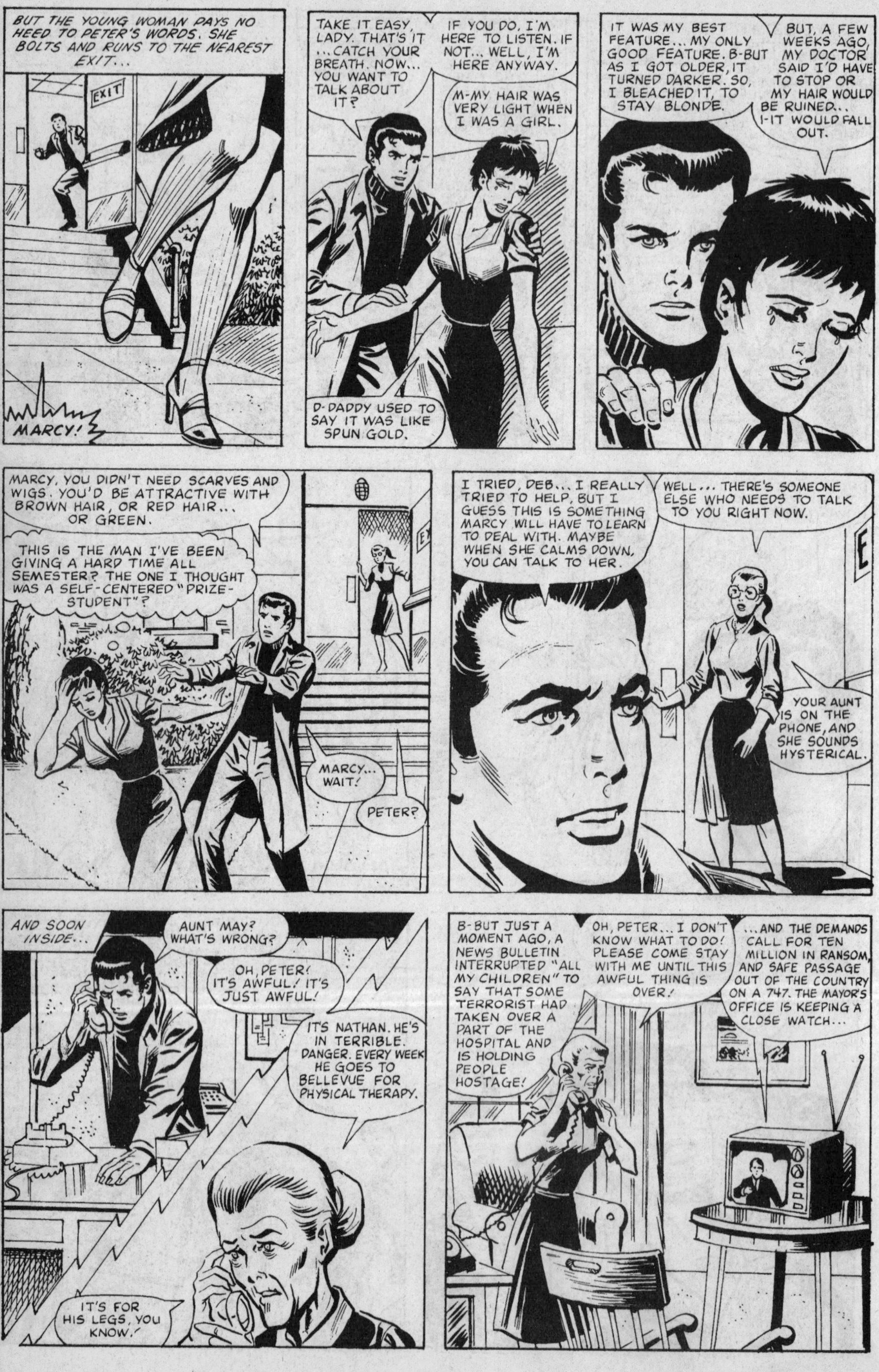
BUT THE YOUNG WOMAN PAYS NO HEED TO PETER'S WORDS. SHE BOLTS AND RUNS TO THE NEAREST EXIT...
EXIT
MARCY!
TAKE IT EASY, LADY. THAT'S IT ...CATCH YOUR BREATH. NOW... YOU WANT TO TALK ABOUT IT?
IF YOU DO, I'M HERE TO LISTEN. IF NOT... WELL, I'M HERE ANYWAY.
M-MY HAIR WAS VERY LIGHT WHEN I WAS A GIRL.
D-DADDY USED TO SAY IT WAS LIKE SPUN GOLD.
IT WAS MY BEST FEATURE... MY ONLY GOOD FEATURE. B-BUT AS I GOT OLDER, IT TURNED DARKER. SO, I BLEACHED IT, TO STAY BLONDE.
BUT, A FEW WEEKS AGO, MY DOCTOR SAID I'D HAVE TO STOP OR MY HAIR WOULD BE RUINED... I-IT WOULD FALL OUT.
MARCY, YOU DIDN'T NEED SCARVES AND WIGS. YOU'D BE ATTRACTIVE WITH BROWN HAIR, OR RED HAIR... OR GREEN.
THIS IS THE MAN I'VE BEEN GIVING A HARD TIME ALL SEMESTER? THE ONE I THOUGHT WAS A SELF-CENTERED "PRIZE-STUDENT"?
MARCY... WAIT!
PETER?
I TRIED, DEB... I REALLY TRIED TO HELP, BUT I GUESS THIS IS SOMETHING MARCY WILL HAVE TO LEARN TO DEAL WITH. MAYBE WHEN SHE CALMS DOWN, YOU CAN TALK TO HER.
WELL... THERE'S SOMEONE ELSE WHO NEEDS TO TALK TO YOU RIGHT NOW.
YOUR AUNT IS ON THE PHONE, AND SHE SOUNDS HYSTERICAL.
AND SOON INSIDE...
AUNT MAY? WHAT'S WRONG?
OH, PETER! IT'S AWFUL! IT'S JUST AWFUL!
IT'S NATHAN. HE'S IN TERRIBLE DANGER. EVERY WEEK HE GOES TO BELLEVUE FOR PHYSICAL THERAPY.
IT'S FOR HIS LEGS, YOU KNOW.
B-BUT JUST A MOMENT AGO, A NEWS BULLETIN INTERRUPTED "ALL MY CHILDREN" TO SAY THAT SOME TERRORIST HAD TAKEN OVER A PART OF THE HOSPITAL AND IS HOLDING PEOPLE HOSTAGE!
OH, PETER... I DON'T KNOW WHAT TO DO! PLEASE COME STAY WITH ME UNTIL THIS AWFUL THING IS OVER!
...AND THE DEMANDS CALL FOR TEN MILLION IN RANSOM, AND SAFE PASSAGE OUT OF THE COUNTRY ON A 747. THE MAYOR'S OFFICE IS KEEPING A CLOSE WATCH...

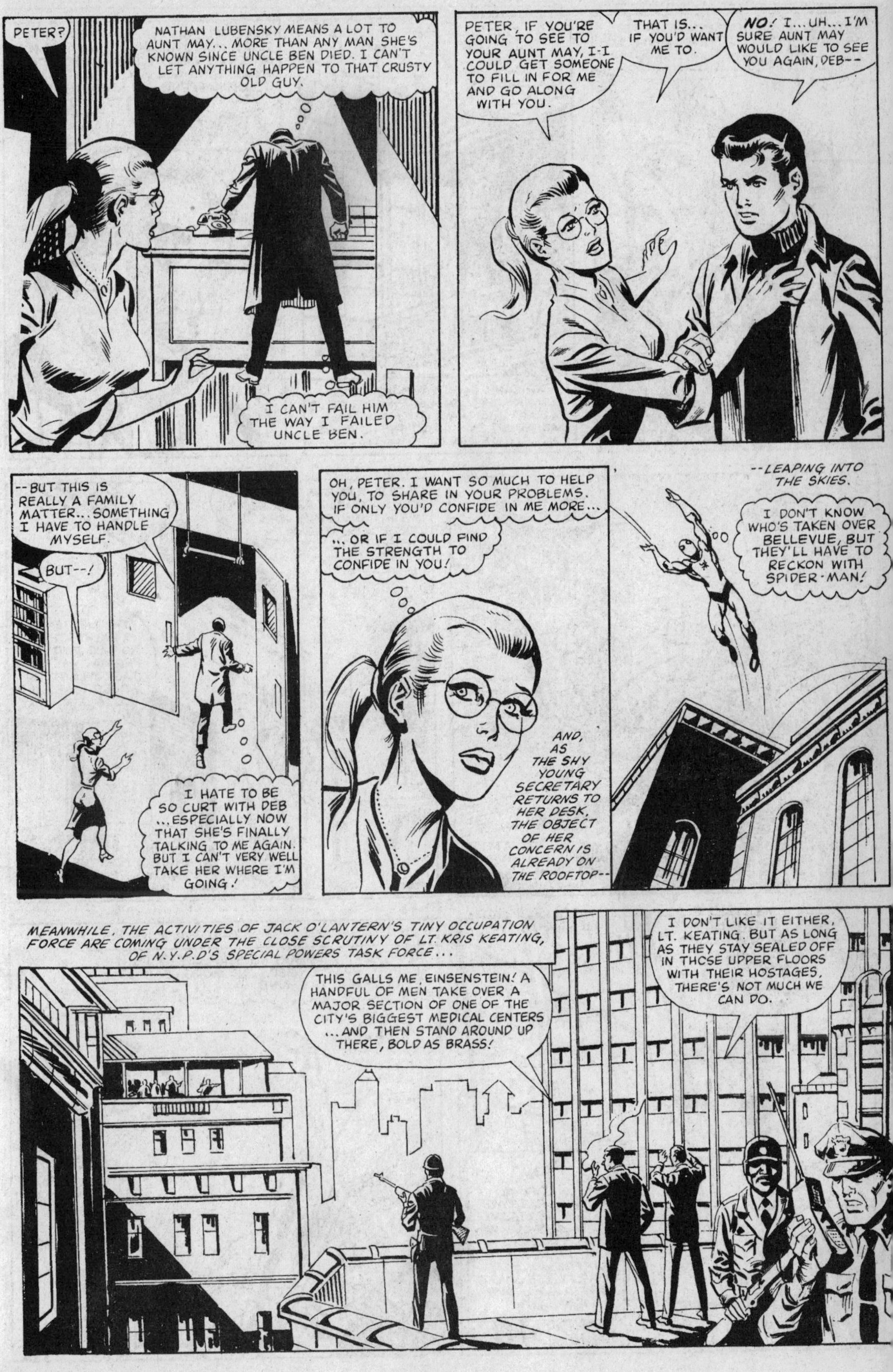
PETER?
NATHAN LUBENSKY MEANS A LOT TO AUNT MAY... MORE THAN ANY MAN SHE'S KNOWN SINCE UNCLE BEN DIED. I CAN'T LET ANYTHING HAPPEN TO THAT CRUSTY OLD GUY.
I CAN'T FAIL HIM THE WAY I FAILED UNCLE BEN.
PETER, IF YOU'RE GOING TO SEE TO YOUR AUNT MAY, I-I COULD GET SOMEONE TO FILL IN FOR ME AND GO ALONG WITH YOU.
THAT IS... IF YOU'D WANT ME TO.
NO! I... UH... I'M SURE AUNT MAY WOULD LIKE TO SEE YOU AGAIN, DEB--
--BUT THIS IS REALLY A FAMILY MATTER... SOMETHING I HAVE TO HANDLE MYSELF.
BUT--!
I HATE TO BE SO CURT WITH DEB ...ESPECIALLY NOW THAT SHE'S FINALLY TALKING TO ME AGAIN. BUT I CAN'T VERY WELL TAKE HER WHERE I'M GOING!
OH, PETER. I WANT SO MUCH TO HELP YOU, TO SHARE IN YOUR PROBLEMS. IF ONLY YOU'D CONFIDE IN ME MORE...
...OR IF I COULD FIND THE STRENGTH TO CONFIDE IN YOU!
AND, AS THE SHY YOUNG SECRETARY RETURNS TO HER DESK, THE OBJECT OF HER CONCERN IS ALREADY ON THE ROOFTOP--
--LEAPING INTO THE SKIES.
I DON'T KNOW WHO'S TAKEN OVER BELLEVUE, BUT THEY'LL HAVE TO RECKON WITH SPIDER-MAN!
MEANWHILE, THE ACTIVITIES OF JACK O'LANTERN'S TINY OCCUPATION FORCE ARE COMING UNDER THE CLOSE SCRUTINY OF LT. KRIS KEATING, OF N.Y.P.D'S SPECIAL POWERS TASK FORCE...
THIS GALLS ME, EINSENSTEIN! A HANDFUL OF MEN TAKE OVER A MAJOR SECTION OF ONE OF THE CITY'S BIGGEST MEDICAL CENTERS ...AND THEN STAND AROUND UP THERE, BOLD AS BRASS!
I DON'T LIKE IT EITHER, LT. KEATING. BUT AS LONG AS THEY STAY SEALED OFF IN THOSE UPPER FLOORS WITH THEIR HOSTAGES, THERE'S NOT MUCH WE CAN DO.

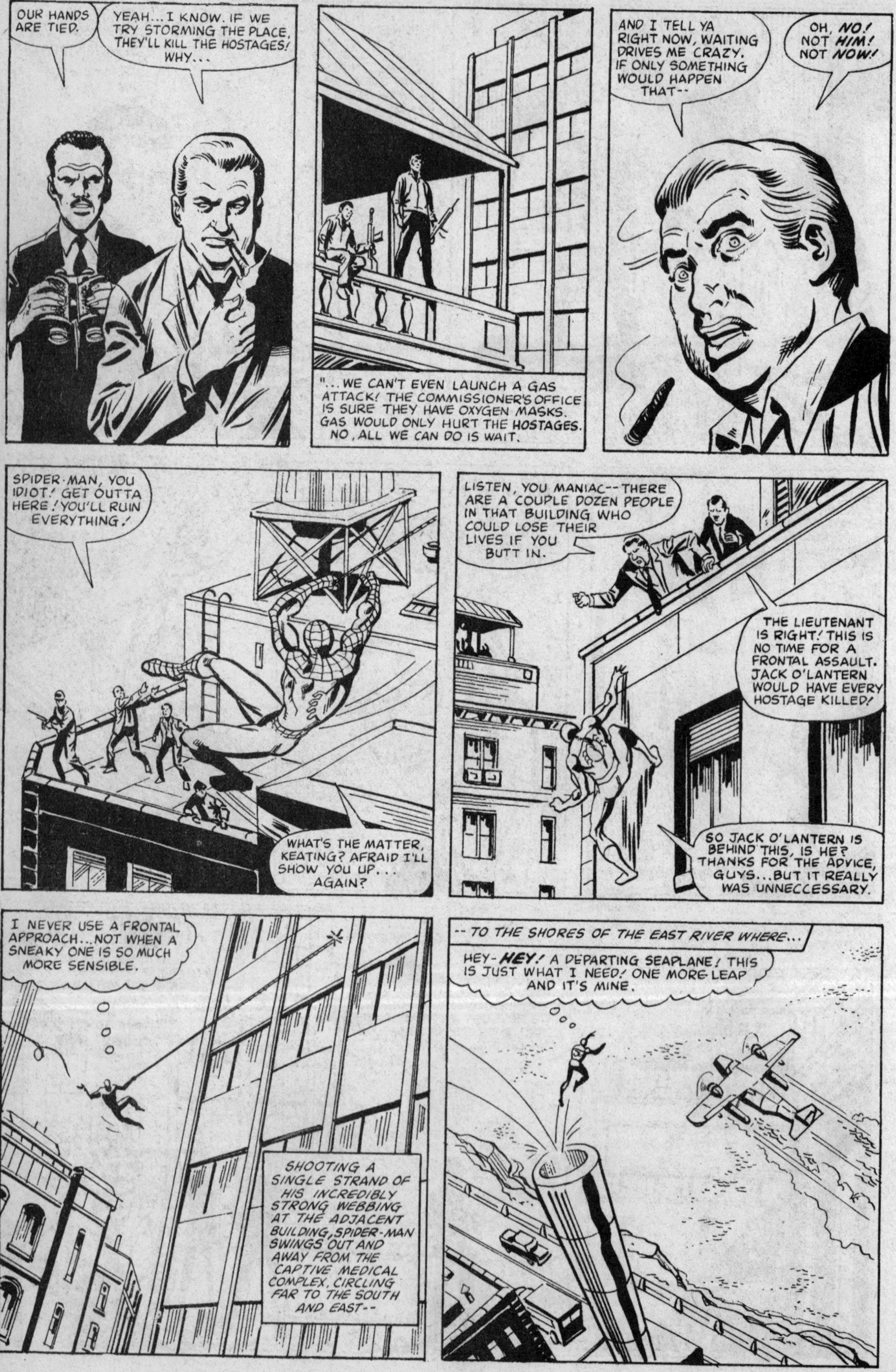
OUR HANDS ARE TIED.
YEAH... I KNOW. IF WE TRY STORMING THE PLACE, THEY'LL KILL THE HOSTAGES! WHY...
"...WE CAN'T EVEN LAUNCH A GAS ATTACK! THE COMMISSIONER'S OFFICE IS SURE THEY HAVE OXYGEN MASKS. GAS WOULD ONLY HURT THE HOSTAGES. NO, ALL WE CAN DO IS WAIT.
AND I TELL YA RIGHT NOW, WAITING DRIVES ME CRAZY. IF ONLY SOMETHING WOULD HAPPEN THAT--
OH, NO! NOT HIM! NOT NOW!
SPIDER-MAN, YOU IDIOT! GET OUTTA HERE! YOU'LL RUIN EVERYTHING!
WHAT'S THE MATTER, KEATING? AFRAID I'LL SHOW YOU UP... AGAIN?
LISTEN, YOU MANIAC--THERE ARE A COUPLE DOZEN PEOPLE IN THAT BUILDING WHO COULD LOSE THEIR LIVES IF YOU BUTT IN.
THE LIEUTENANT IS RIGHT! THIS IS NO TIME FOR A FRONTAL ASSAULT. JACK O'LANTERN WOULD HAVE EVERY HOSTAGE KILLED!
SO JACK O'LANTERN IS BEHIND THIS, IS HE? THANKS FOR THE ADVICE, GUYS... BUT IT REALLY WAS UNNECCESSARY.
I NEVER USE A FRONTAL APPROACH... NOT WHEN A SNEAKY ONE IS SO MUCH MORE SENSIBLE.
SHOOTING A SINGLE STRAND OF HIS INCREDIBLY STRONG WEBBING AT THE ADJACENT BUILDING, SPIDER-MAN SWINGS OUT AND AWAY FROM THE CAPTIVE MEDICAL COMPLEX, CIRCLING FAR TO THE SOUTH AND EAST--
--TO THE SHORES OF THE EAST RIVER WHERE...
HEY-HEY! A DEPARTING SEAPLANE! THIS IS JUST WHAT I NEED! ONE MORE LEAP AND IT'S MINE.

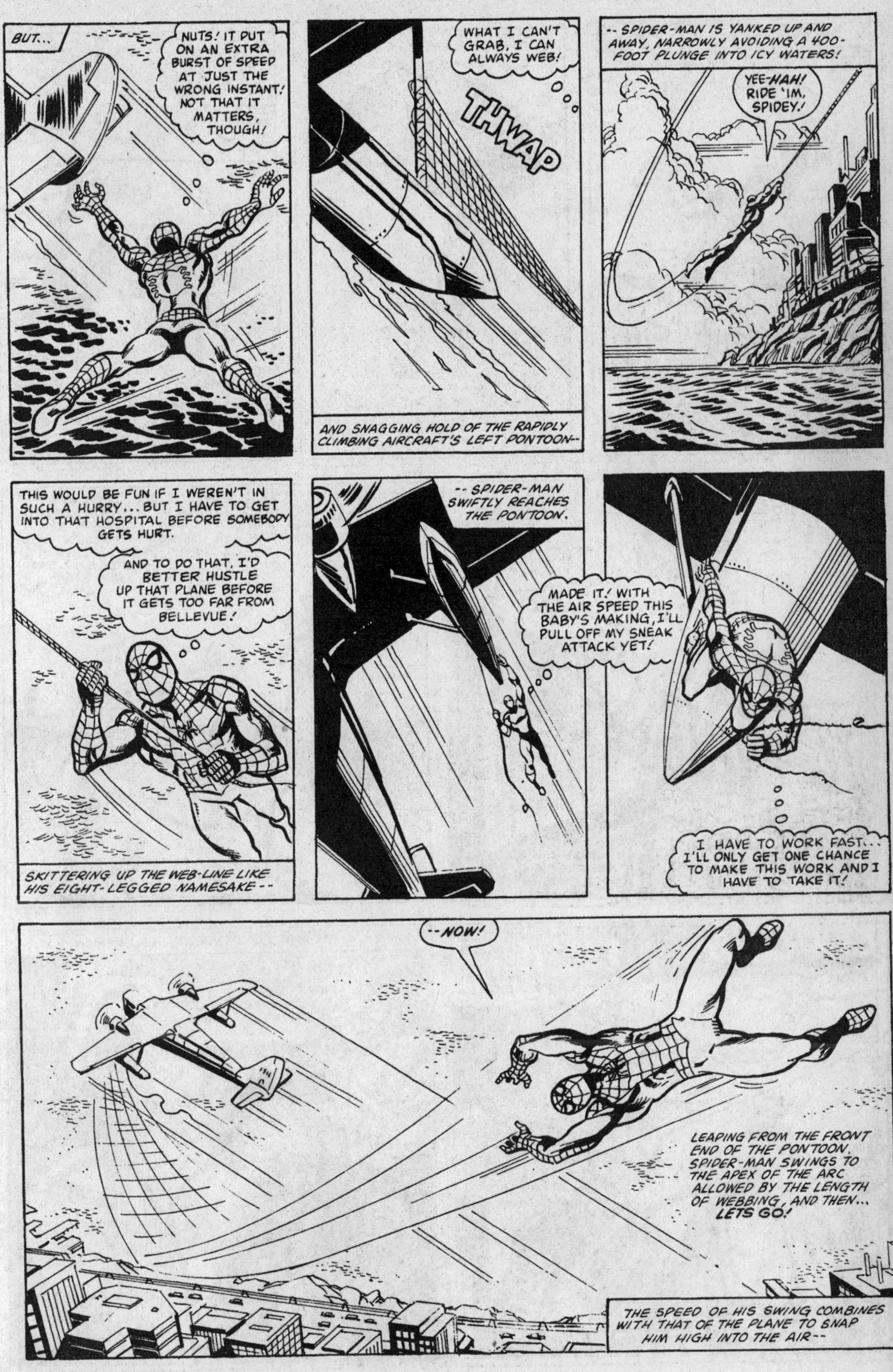

BUT...
NUTS! IT PUT ON AN EXTRA BURST OF SPEED AT JUST THE WRONG INSTANT! NOT THAT IT MATTERS, THOUGH!
WHAT I CAN'T GRAB, I CAN ALWAYS WEB!
THWAP
AND SNAGGING HOLD OF THE RAPIDLY CLIMBING AIRCRAFT'S LEFT PONTOON--
-- SPIDER-MAN IS YANKED UP AND AWAY, NARROWLY AVOIDING A 400-FOOT PLUNGE INTO ICY WATERS!
YEE-HAH! RIDE 'IM, SPIDEY!
THIS WOULD BE FUN IF I WEREN'T IN SUCH A HURRY... BUT I HAVE TO GET INTO THAT HOSPITAL BEFORE SOMEBODY GETS HURT.
AND TO DO THAT, I'D BETTER HUSTLE UP THAT PLANE BEFORE IT GETS TOO FAR FROM BELLEVUE!
SKITTERING UP THE WEB-LINE LIKE HIS EIGHT-LEGGED NAMESAKE--
-- SPIDER-MAN SWIFTLY REACHES THE PONTOON.
MADE IT! WITH THE AIR SPEED THIS BABY'S MAKING, I'LL PULL OFF MY SNEAK ATTACK YET!
I HAVE TO WORK FAST... I'LL ONLY GET ONE CHANCE TO MAKE THIS WORK AND I HAVE TO TAKE IT!
--NOW!
LEAPING FROM THE FRONT END OF THE PONTOON, SPIDER-MAN SWINGS TO THE APEX OF THE ARC ALLOWED BY THE LENGTH OF WEBBING, AND THEN... LETS GO!
THE SPEED OF HIS SWING COMBINES WITH THAT OF THE PLANE TO SNAP HIM HIGH INTO THE AIR--

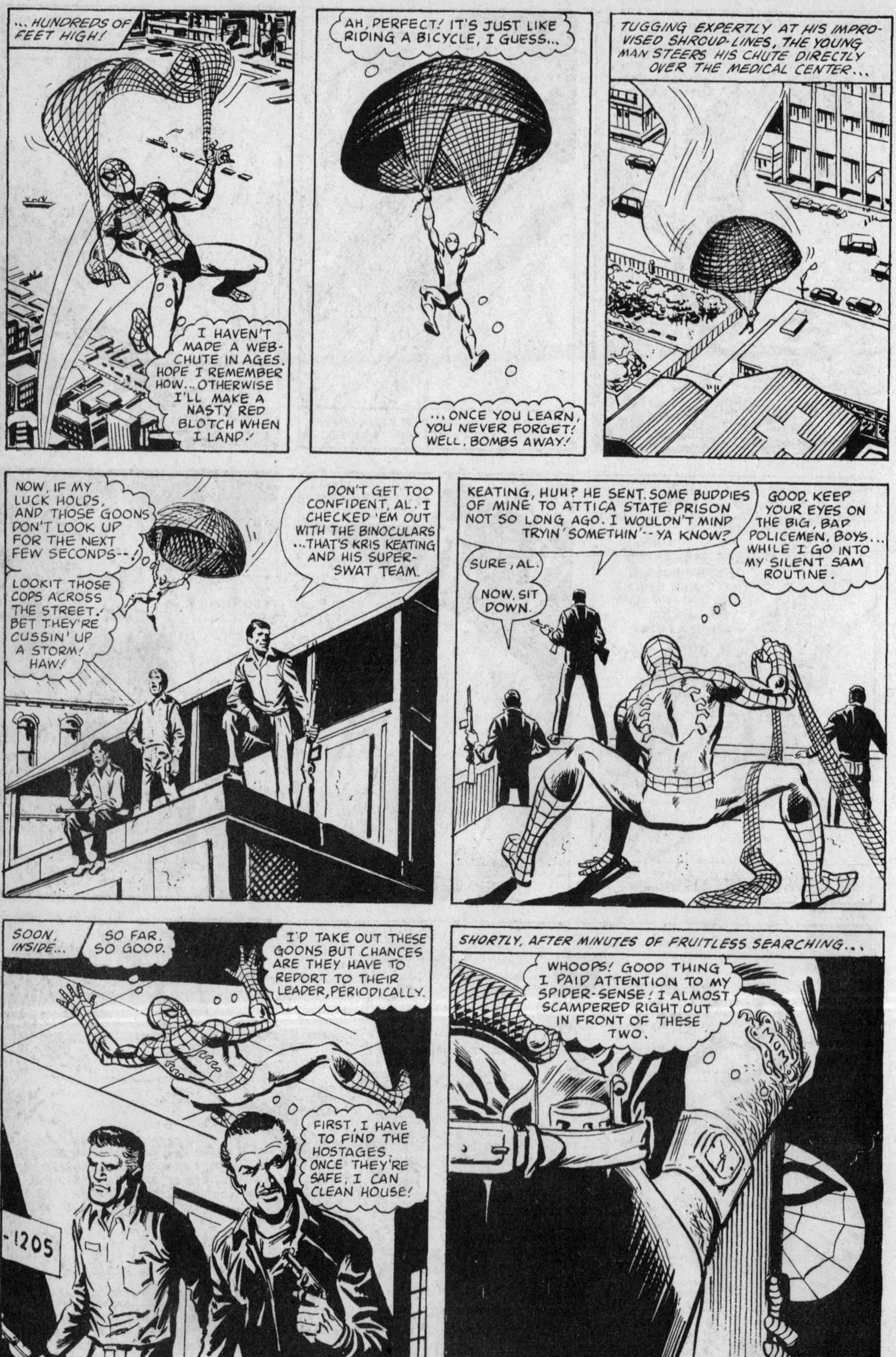
...HUNDREDS OF FEET HIGH!
I HAVEN'T MADE A WEB-CHUTE IN AGES. HOPE I REMEMBER HOW...OTHERWISE I'LL MAKE A NASTY RED BLOTCH WHEN I LAND!
AH, PERFECT! IT'S JUST LIKE RIDING A BICYCLE, I GUESS...
...ONCE YOU LEARN, YOU NEVER FORGET! WELL, BOMBS AWAY!
TUGGING EXPERTLY AT HIS IMPROVISED SHROUD-LINES, THE YOUNG MAN STEERS HIS CHUTE DIRECTLY OVER THE MEDICAL CENTER...
NOW, IF MY LUCK HOLDS, AND THOSE GOONS DON'T LOOK UP FOR THE NEXT FEW SECONDS--!
LOOKIT THOSE COPS ACROSS THE STREET! BET THEY'RE CUSSIN' UP A STORM! HAW!
DON'T GET TOO CONFIDENT, AL. I CHECKED 'EM OUT WITH THE BINOCULARS ...THAT'S KRIS KEATING AND HIS SUPER-SWAT TEAM.
KEATING, HUH? HE SENT SOME BUDDIES OF MINE TO ATTICA STATE PRISON NOT SO LONG AGO. I WOULDN'T MIND TRYIN' SOMETHIN'--YA KNOW?
SURE, AL.
NOW, SIT DOWN.
GOOD. KEEP YOUR EYES ON THE BIG, BAD POLICEMEN, BOYS... WHILE I GO INTO MY SILENT SAM ROUTINE.
SOON, INSIDE...
SO FAR, SO GOOD.
I'D TAKE OUT THESE GOONS BUT CHANCES ARE THEY HAVE TO REPORT TO THEIR LEADER, PERIODICALLY.
FIRST, I HAVE TO FIND THE HOSTAGES. ONCE THEY'RE SAFE, I CAN CLEAN HOUSE!
-1205
SHORTLY, AFTER MINUTES OF FRUITLESS SEARCHING...
WHOOPS! GOOD THING I PAID ATTENTION TO MY SPIDER-SENSE! I ALMOST SCAMPERED RIGHT OUT IN FRONT OF THESE TWO.
MOM

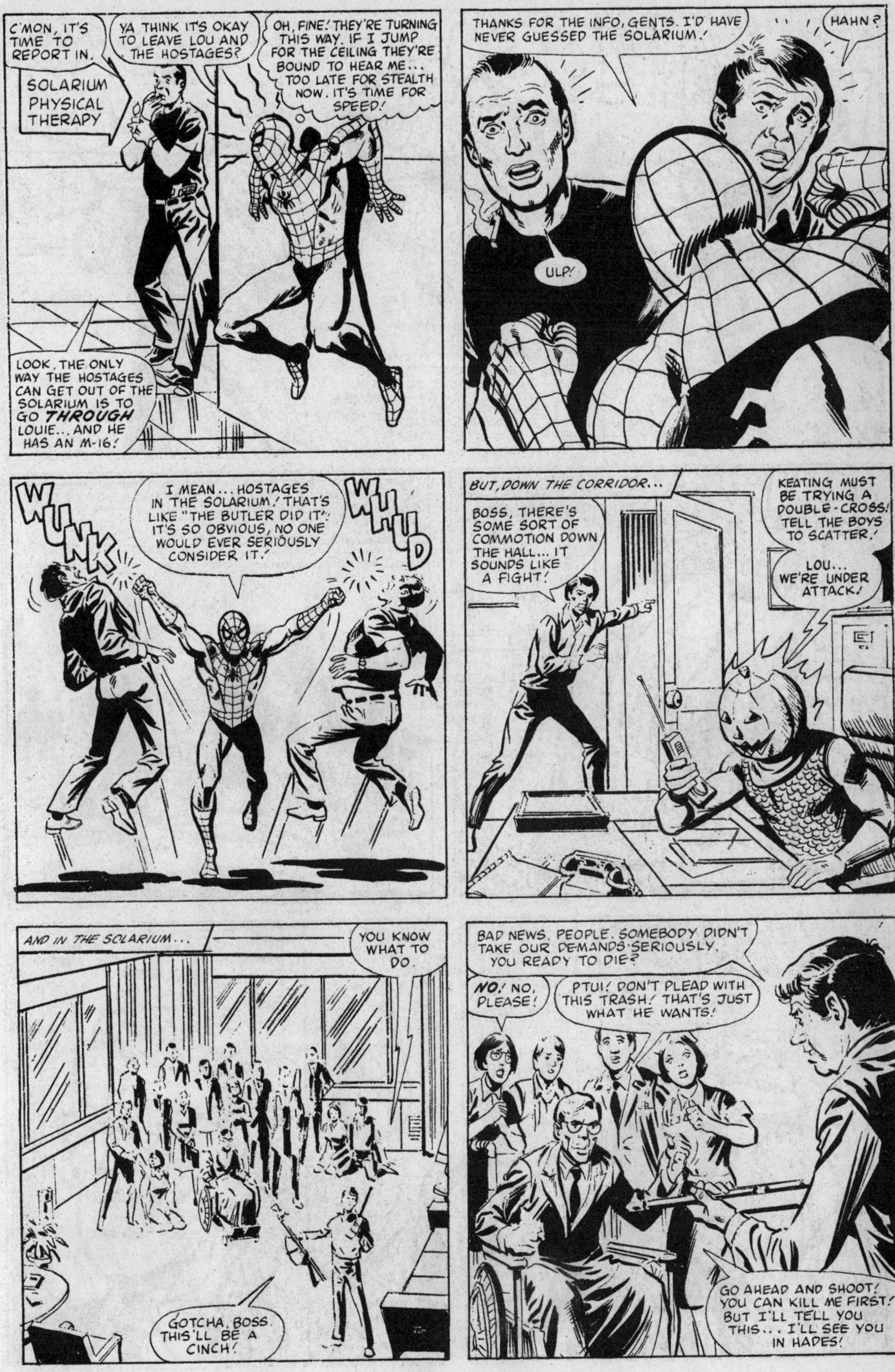

C'MON, IT'S TIME TO REPORT IN.
YA THINK IT'S OKAY TO LEAVE LOU AND THE HOSTAGES?
OH, FINE! THEY'RE TURNING THIS WAY. IF I JUMP FOR THE CEILING THEY'RE BOUND TO HEAR ME... TOO LATE FOR STEALTH NOW. IT'S TIME FOR SPEED!
SOLARIUM PHYSICAL THERAPY
LOOK, THE ONLY WAY THE HOSTAGES CAN GET OUT OF THE SOLARIUM IS TO GO THROUGH LOUIE... AND HE HAS AN M-16!
THANKS FOR THE INFO, GENTS. I'D HAVE NEVER GUESSED THE SOLARIUM!
HAHN?
ULP!
WUNK
I MEAN... HOSTAGES IN THE SOLARIUM! THAT'S LIKE "THE BUTLER DID IT"! IT'S SO OBVIOUS, NO ONE WOULD EVER SERIOUSLY CONSIDER IT!
WHUD
BUT, DOWN THE CORRIDOR...
BOSS, THERE'S SOME SORT OF COMMOTION DOWN THE HALL... IT SOUNDS LIKE A FIGHT!
KEATING MUST BE TRYING A DOUBLE-CROSS! TELL THE BOYS TO SCATTER!
LOU... WE'RE UNDER ATTACK!
AND IN THE SOLARIUM...
YOU KNOW WHAT TO DO.
GOTCHA, BOSS. THIS'LL BE A CINCH!
BAD NEWS, PEOPLE. SOMEBODY DIDN'T TAKE OUR DEMANDS SERIOUSLY. YOU READY TO DIE?
NO! NO, PLEASE!
PTUI! DON'T PLEAD WITH THIS TRASH! THAT'S JUST WHAT HE WANTS!
GO AHEAD AND SHOOT! YOU CAN KILL ME FIRST! BUT I'LL TELL YOU THIS... I'LL SEE YOU IN HADES!

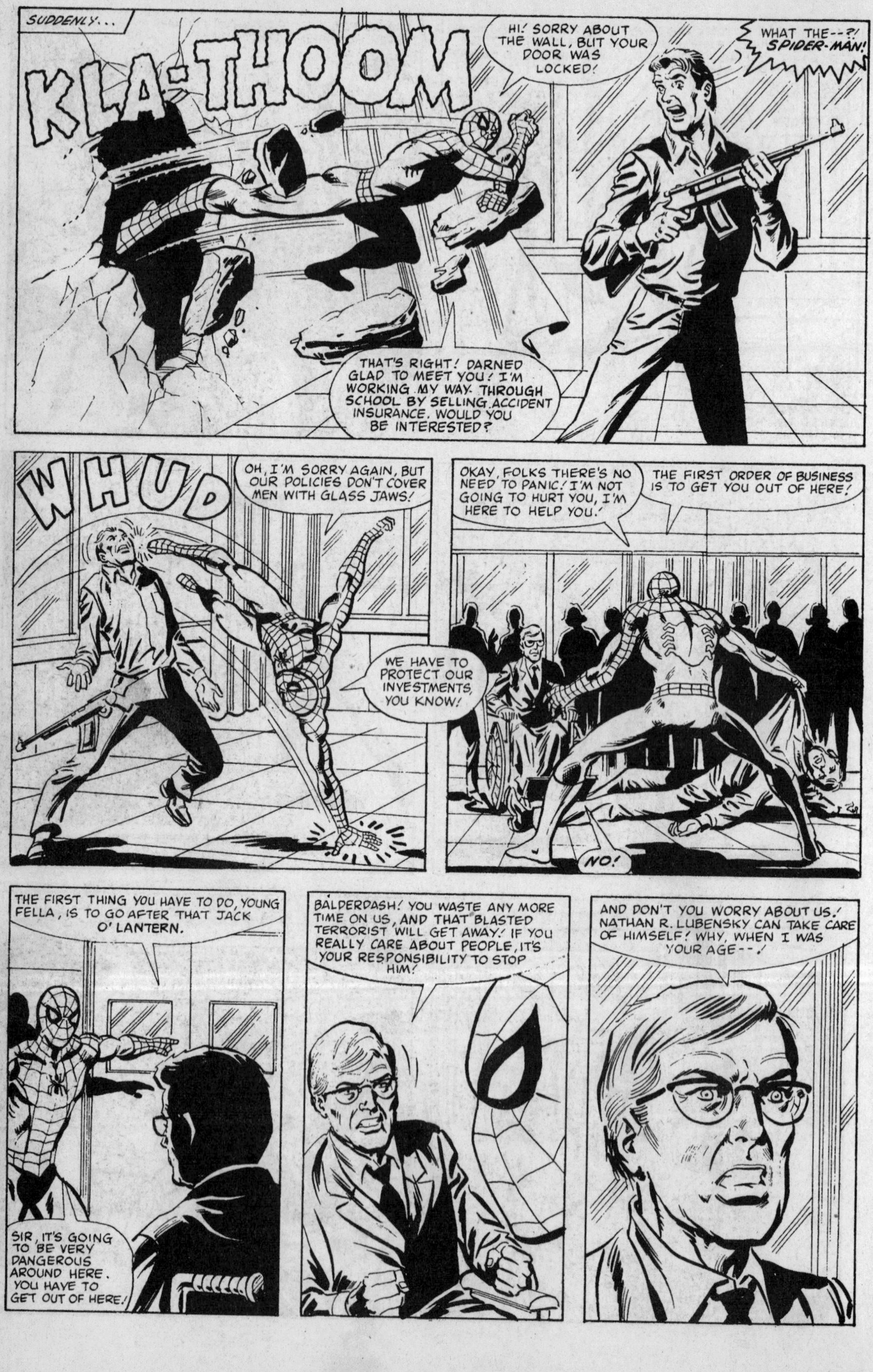
SUDDENLY...
KLA-THOOM
HI! SORRY ABOUT THE WALL, BUT YOUR DOOR WAS LOCKED!
WHAT THE--?! SPIDER-MAN!
THAT'S RIGHT! DARNED GLAD TO MEET YOU! I'M WORKING MY WAY THROUGH SCHOOL BY SELLING ACCIDENT INSURANCE. WOULD YOU BE INTERESTED?
WHUD
OH, I'M SORRY AGAIN, BUT OUR POLICIES DON'T COVER MEN WITH GLASS JAWS!
WE HAVE TO PROTECT OUR INVESTMENTS, YOU KNOW!
OKAY, FOLKS THERE'S NO NEED TO PANIC! I'M NOT GOING TO HURT YOU, I'M HERE TO HELP YOU.
THE FIRST ORDER OF BUSINESS IS TO GET YOU OUT OF HERE!
NO!
THE FIRST THING YOU HAVE TO DO, YOUNG FELLA, IS TO GO AFTER THAT JACK O' LANTERN.
SIR, IT'S GOING TO BE VERY DANGEROUS AROUND HERE. YOU HAVE TO GET OUT OF HERE!
BALDERDASH! YOU WASTE ANY MORE TIME ON US, AND THAT BLASTED TERRORIST WILL GET AWAY! IF YOU REALLY CARE ABOUT PEOPLE, IT'S YOUR RESPONSIBILITY TO STOP HIM!
AND DON'T YOU WORRY ABOUT US! NATHAN R. LUBENSKY CAN TAKE CARE OF HIMSELF! WHY, WHEN I WAS YOUR AGE--!

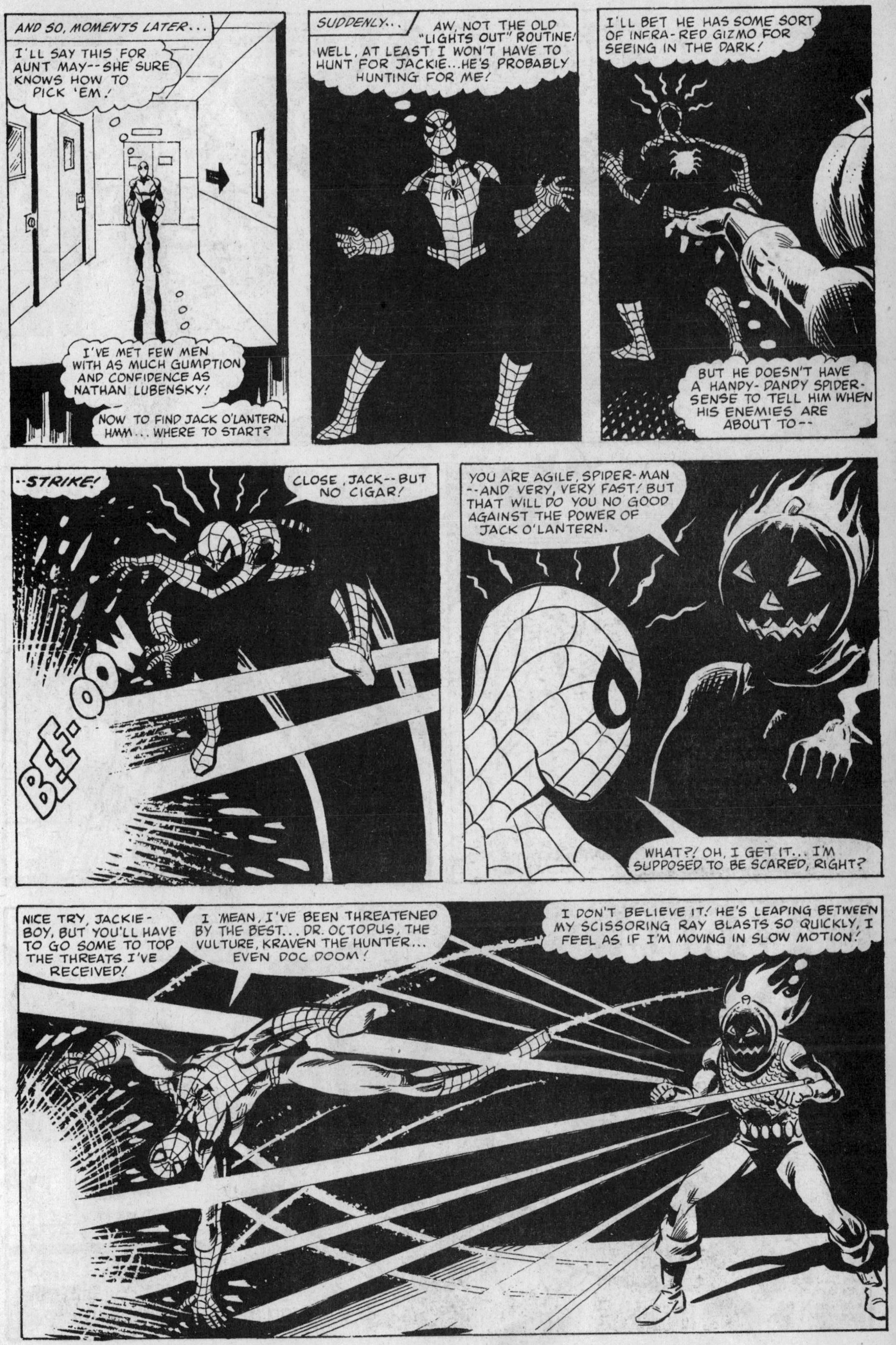
AND SO, MOMENTS LATER...
I'LL SAY THIS FOR AUNT MAY--SHE SURE KNOWS HOW TO PICK 'EM!
I'VE MET FEW MEN WITH AS MUCH GUMPTION AND CONFIDENCE AS NATHAN LUBENSKY!
NOW TO FIND JACK O'LANTERN. HMM... WHERE TO START?
SUDDENLY...
AW, NOT THE OLD "LIGHTS OUT" ROUTINE! WELL, AT LEAST I WON'T HAVE TO HUNT FOR JACKIE...HE'S PROBABLY HUNTING FOR ME!
I'LL BET HE HAS SOME SORT OF INFRA-RED GIZMO FOR SEEING IN THE DARK!
BUT HE DOESN'T HAVE A HANDY-DANDY SPIDER-SENSE TO TELL HIM WHEN HIS ENEMIES ARE ABOUT TO--
--STRIKE!
CLOSE, JACK--BUT NO CIGAR!
BEE-OOW
YOU ARE AGILE, SPIDER-MAN--AND VERY, VERY FAST! BUT THAT WILL DO YOU NO GOOD AGAINST THE POWER OF JACK O'LANTERN.
WHAT?! OH, I GET IT... I'M SUPPOSED TO BE SCARED, RIGHT?
NICE TRY, JACKIE-BOY, BUT YOU'LL HAVE TO GO SOME TO TOP THE THREATS I'VE RECEIVED!
I MEAN, I'VE BEEN THREATENED BY THE BEST... DR. OCTOPUS, THE VULTURE, KRAVEN THE HUNTER... EVEN DOC DOOM!
I DON'T BELIEVE IT! HE'S LEAPING BETWEEN MY SCISSORING RAY BLASTS SO QUICKLY, I FEEL AS IF I'M MOVING IN SLOW MOTION!

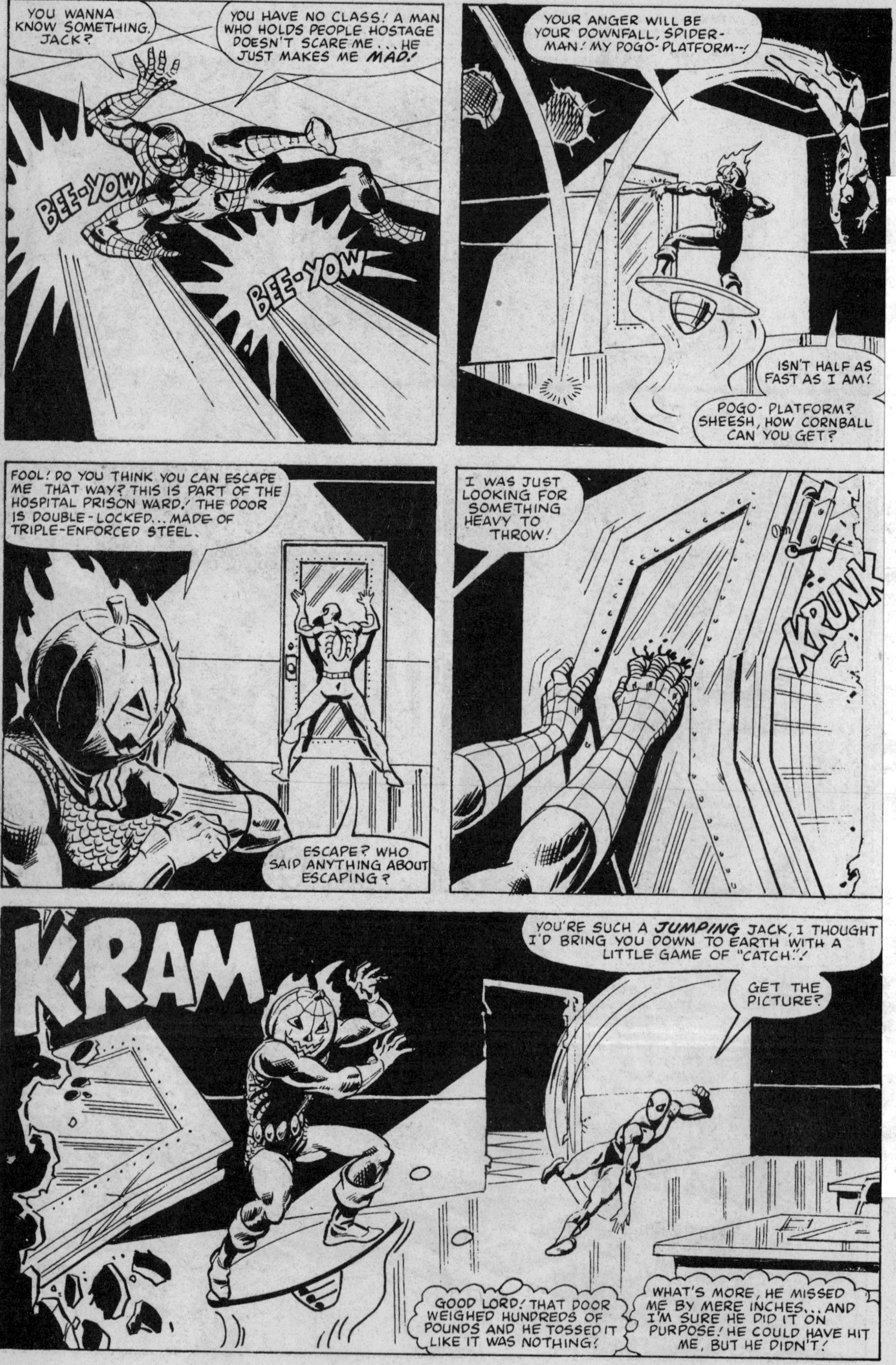
YOU WANNA KNOW SOMETHING, JACK?
YOU HAVE NO CLASS! A MAN WHO HOLDS PEOPLE HOSTAGE DOESN'T SCARE ME... HE JUST MAKES ME MAD!
BEE-YOW
BEE-YOW
YOUR ANGER WILL BE YOUR DOWNFALL, SPIDER-MAN! MY POGO-PLATFORM--!
ISN'T HALF AS FAST AS I AM!
POGO-PLATFORM? SHEESH, HOW CORNBALL CAN YOU GET?
FOOL! DO YOU THINK YOU CAN ESCAPE ME THAT WAY? THIS IS PART OF THE HOSPITAL PRISON WARD! THE DOOR IS DOUBLE-LOCKED... MADE OF TRIPLE-ENFORCED STEEL.
ESCAPE? WHO SAID ANYTHING ABOUT ESCAPING?
I WAS JUST LOOKING FOR SOMETHING HEAVY TO THROW!
KRUNK
KRAM
YOU'RE SUCH A JUMPING JACK, I THOUGHT I'D BRING YOU DOWN TO EARTH WITH A LITTLE GAME OF "CATCH"!
GET THE PICTURE?
GOOD LORD! THAT DOOR WEIGHED HUNDREDS OF POUNDS AND HE TOSSED IT LIKE IT WAS NOTHING!
WHAT'S MORE, HE MISSED ME BY MERE INCHES... AND I'M SURE HE DID IT ON PURPOSE! HE COULD HAVE HIT ME, BUT HE DIDN'T!

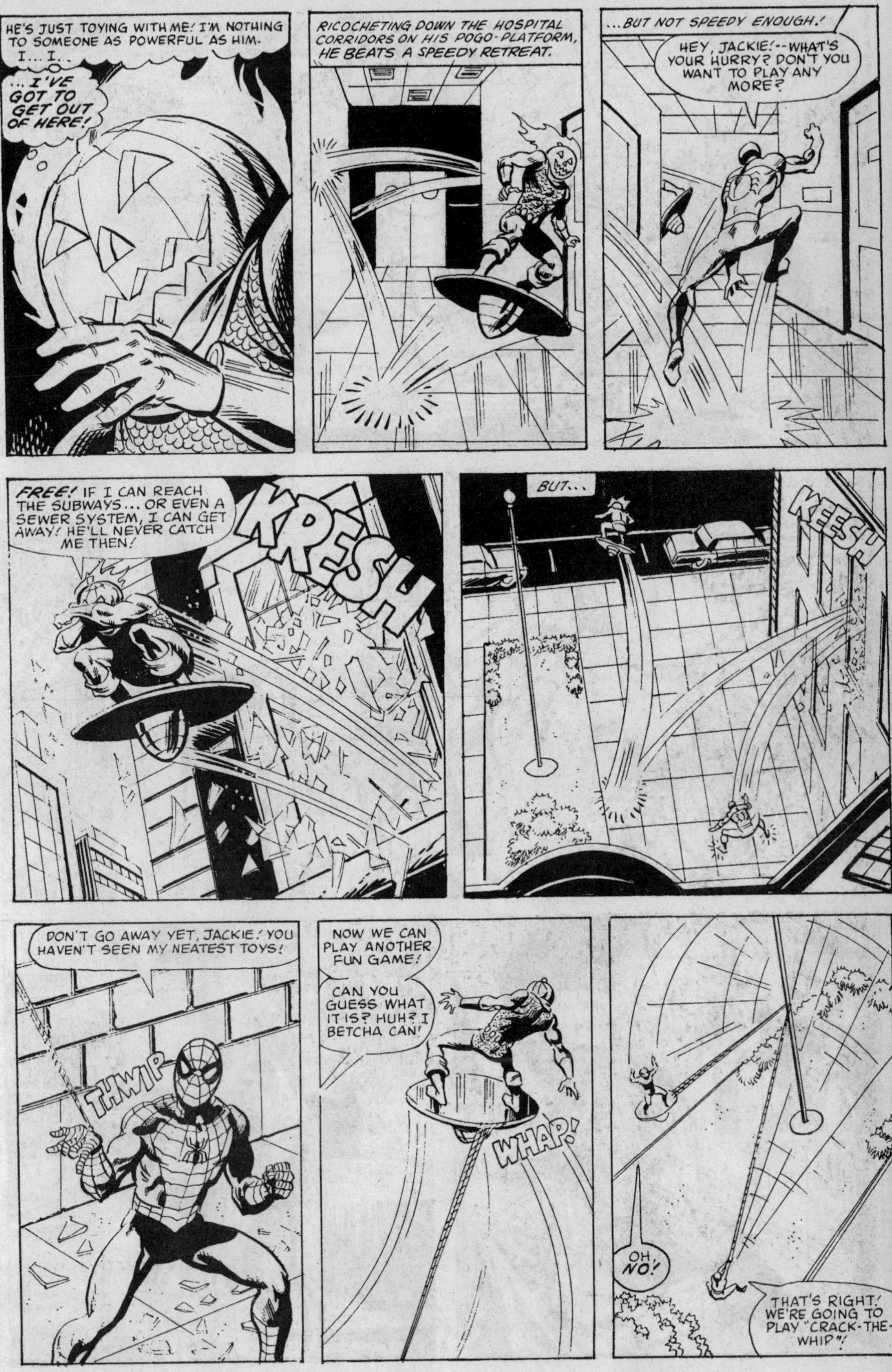
HE'S JUST TOYING WITH ME! I'M NOTHING TO SOMEONE AS POWERFUL AS HIM. I... I...
... I'VE GOT TO GET OUT OF HERE!
RICOCHETING DOWN THE HOSPITAL CORRIDORS ON HIS POGO-PLATFORM, HE BEATS A SPEEDY RETREAT.
...BUT NOT SPEEDY ENOUGH!
HEY, JACKIE!--WHAT'S YOUR HURRY? DON'T YOU WANT TO PLAY ANY MORE?
FREE! IF I CAN REACH THE SUBWAYS... OR EVEN A SEWER SYSTEM, I CAN GET AWAY! HE'LL NEVER CATCH ME THEN!
KRESH
BUT...
KEESH
DON'T GO AWAY YET, JACKIE! YOU HAVEN'T SEEN MY NEATEST TOYS!
THWIP
NOW WE CAN PLAY ANOTHER FUN GAME!
CAN YOU GUESS WHAT IT IS? HUH? I BETCHA CAN!
WHAP!
OH NO!
THAT'S RIGHT! WE'RE GOING TO PLAY "CRACK-THE-WHIP"!

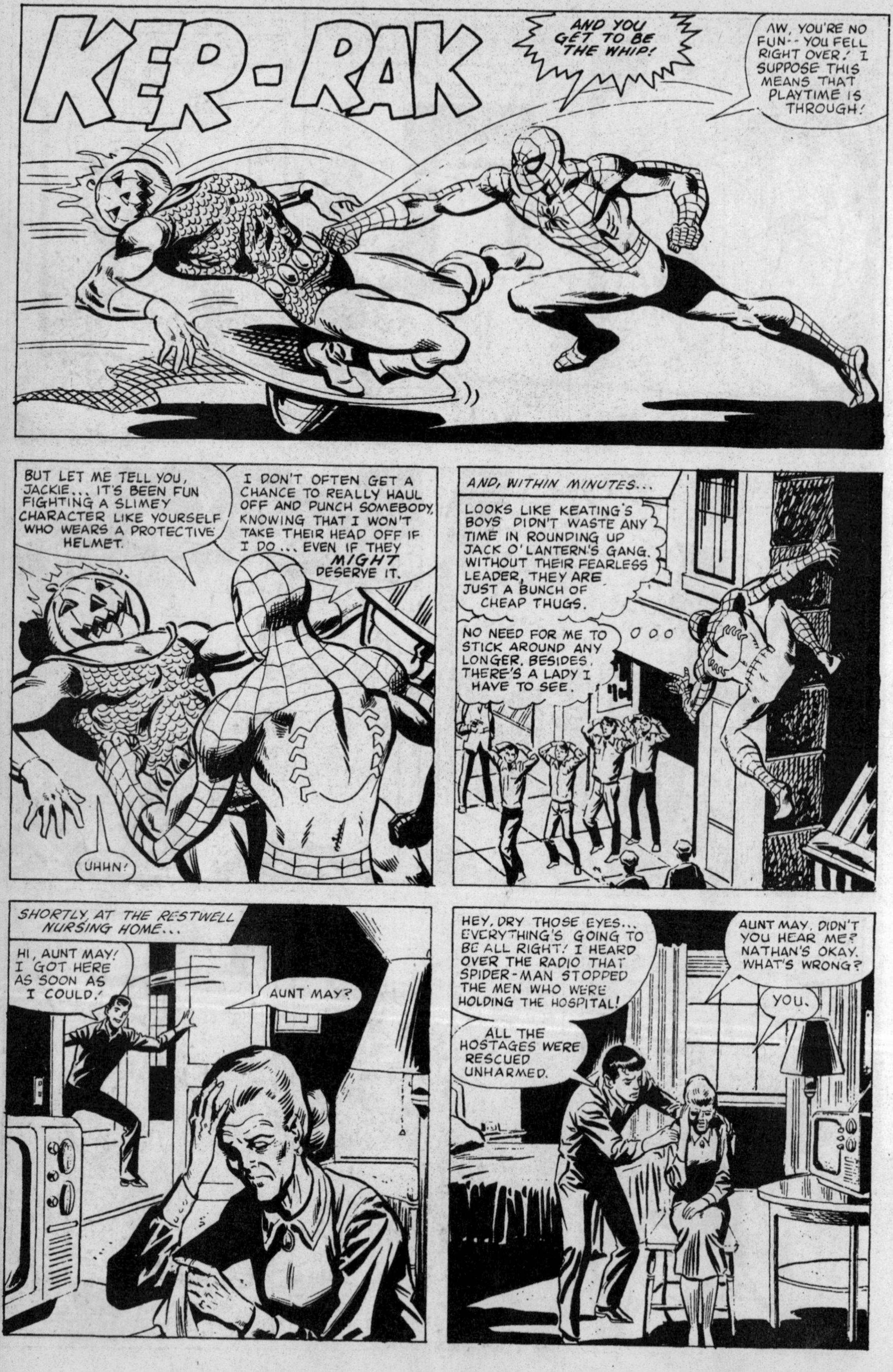
KER-RAK
AND YOU GET TO BE THE WHIP!
AW, YOU'RE NO FUN--YOU FELL RIGHT OVER! I SUPPOSE THIS MEANS THAT PLAYTIME IS THROUGH!
BUT LET ME TELL YOU, JACKIE... IT'S BEEN FUN FIGHTING A SLIMEY CHARACTER LIKE YOURSELF WHO WEARS A PROTECTIVE HELMET.
I DON'T OFTEN GET A CHANCE TO REALLY HAUL OFF AND PUNCH SOMEBODY, KNOWING THAT I WON'T TAKE THEIR HEAD OFF IF I DO... EVEN IF THEY MIGHT DESERVE IT.
UHHN!
AND, WITHIN MINUTES...
LOOKS LIKE KEATING'S BOYS DIDN'T WASTE ANY TIME IN ROUNDING UP JACK O'LANTERN'S GANG. WITHOUT THEIR FEARLESS LEADER, THEY ARE JUST A BUNCH OF CHEAP THUGS.
NO NEED FOR ME TO STICK AROUND ANY LONGER. BESIDES, THERE'S A LADY I HAVE TO SEE.
SHORTLY, AT THE RESTWELL NURSING HOME...
HI, AUNT MAY! I GOT HERE AS SOON AS I COULD!
AUNT MAY?
HEY, DRY THOSE EYES... EVERYTHING'S GOING TO BE ALL RIGHT! I HEARD OVER THE RADIO THAT SPIDER-MAN STOPPED THE MEN WHO WERE HOLDING THE HOSPITAL!
ALL THE HOSTAGES WERE RESCUED UNHARMED.
AUNT MAY, DIDN'T YOU HEAR ME? NATHAN'S OKAY. WHAT'S WRONG?
YOU.

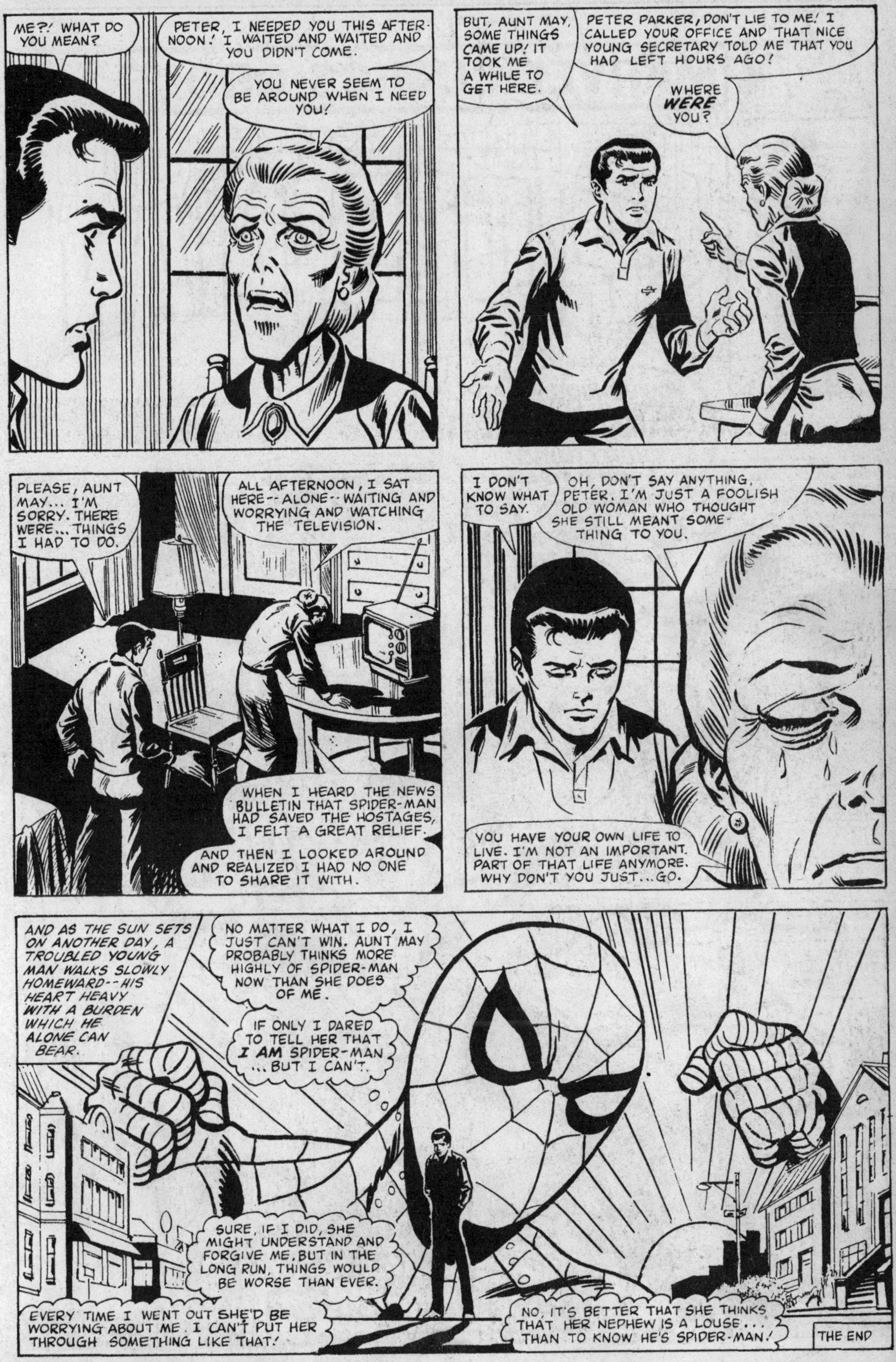

ME?!' WHAT DO YOU MEAN?
PETER, I NEEDED YOU THIS AFTERNOON! I WAITED AND WAITED AND YOU DIDN'T COME.
YOU NEVER SEEM TO BE AROUND WHEN I NEED YOU!
BUT, AUNT MAY, SOME THINGS CAME UP! IT TOOK ME A WHILE TO GET HERE.
PETER PARKER, DON'T LIE TO ME! I CALLED YOUR OFFICE AND THAT NICE YOUNG SECRETARY TOLD ME THAT YOU HAD LEFT HOURS AGO!
WHERE ***WERE*** YOU?
PLEASE, AUNT MAY... I'M SORRY. THERE WERE... THINGS I HAD TO DO.
ALL AFTERNOON, I SAT HERE--ALONE--WAITING AND WORRYING AND WATCHING THE TELEVISION.
WHEN I HEARD THE NEWS BULLETIN THAT SPIDER-MAN HAD SAVED THE HOSTAGES, I FELT A GREAT RELIEF.
AND THEN I LOOKED AROUND AND REALIZED I HAD NO ONE TO SHARE IT WITH.
I DON'T KNOW WHAT TO SAY.
OH, DON'T SAY ANYTHING, PETER. I'M JUST A FOOLISH OLD WOMAN WHO THOUGHT SHE STILL MEANT SOMETHING TO YOU.
YOU HAVE YOUR OWN LIFE TO LIVE. I'M NOT AN IMPORTANT PART OF THAT LIFE ANYMORE. WHY DON'T YOU JUST... GO.
AND AS THE SUN SETS ON ANOTHER DAY, A TROUBLED YOUNG MAN WALKS SLOWLY HOMEWARD--HIS HEART HEAVY WITH A BURDEN WHICH HE ALONE CAN BEAR.
NO MATTER WHAT I DO, I JUST CAN'T WIN. AUNT MAY PROBABLY THINKS MORE HIGHLY OF SPIDER-MAN NOW THAN SHE DOES OF ME.
IF ONLY I DARED TO TELL HER THAT ***I AM*** SPIDER-MAN ...BUT I CAN'T.
SURE, IF I DID, SHE MIGHT UNDERSTAND AND FORGIVE ME, BUT IN THE LONG RUN, THINGS WOULD BE WORSE THAN EVER.
EVERY TIME I WENT OUT SHE'D BE WORRYING ABOUT ME. I CAN'T PUT HER THROUGH SOMETHING LIKE THAT!
NO, IT'S BETTER THAT SHE THINKS THAT HER NEPHEW IS A LOUSE... THAN TO KNOW HE'S SPIDER-MAN!
THE END

50¢
57
AUG
02199
MARVEL® COMICS GROUP
APPROVED BY THE COMICS CODE AUTHORITY
©1981 MARVEL COMICS GROUP
PETER PARKER, THE SPECTACULAR
SPIDER-MAN®
TM
YOU'VE KIDNAPPED THE WOMAN I LOVE ...YOU'VE DESTROYED EVERYTHING I HOLD DEAR--
--AND I'LL MAKE YOU PAY!
FEATURING: A DECIDEDLY DIFFERENT SIDE OF J. JONAH JAMESON!

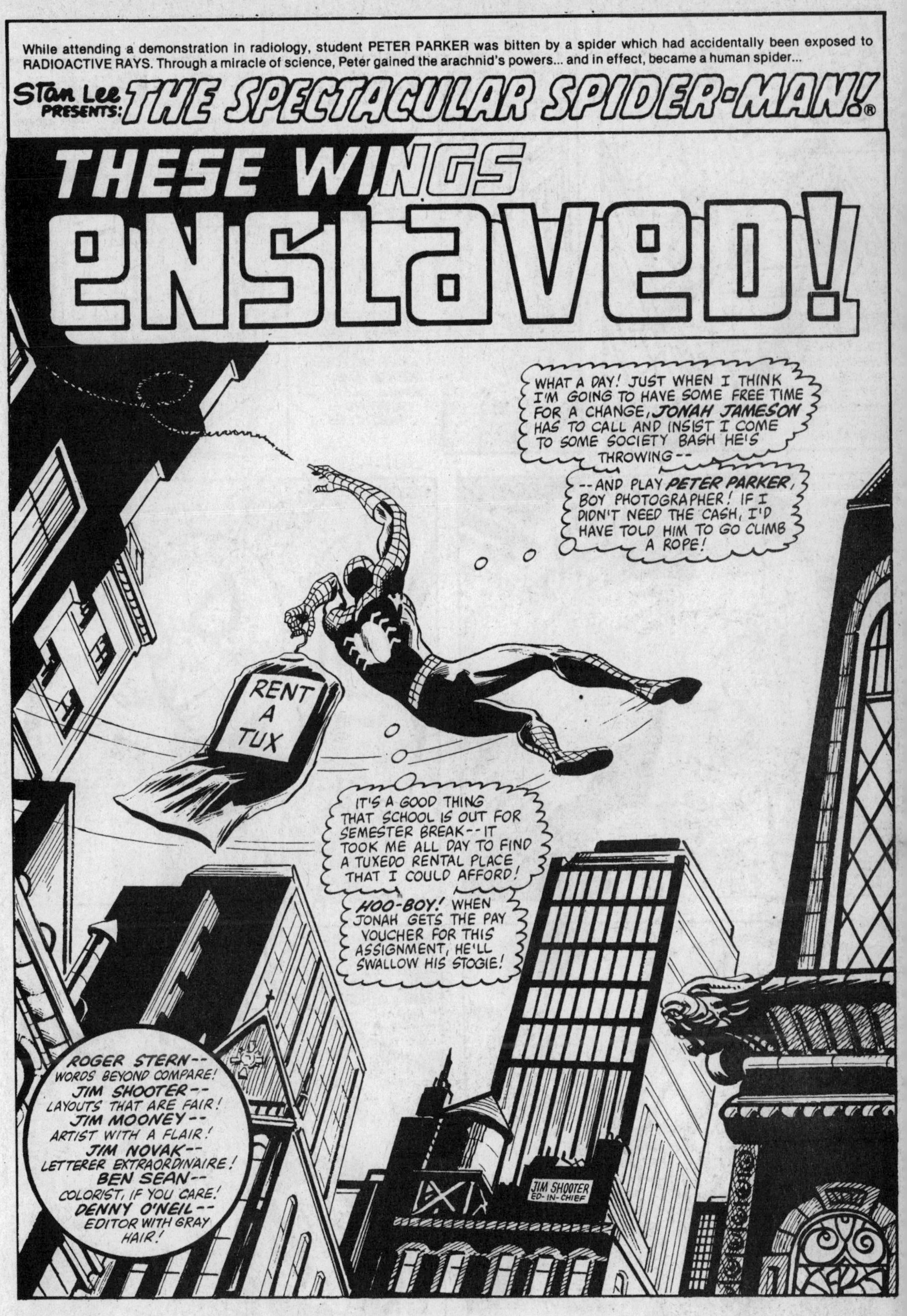
While attending a demonstration in radiology, student PETER PARKER was bitten by a spider which had accidentally been exposed to RADIOACTIVE RAYS. Through a miracle of science, Peter gained the arachnid's powers... and in effect, became a human spider...
STAN LEE PRESENTS: THE SPECTACULAR SPIDER-MAN!®
THESE WINGS ENSLAVED!
WHAT A DAY! JUST WHEN I THINK I'M GOING TO HAVE SOME FREE TIME FOR A CHANGE, JONAH JAMESON HAS TO CALL AND INSIST I COME TO SOME SOCIETY BASH HE'S THROWING--
--AND PLAY PETER PARKER, BOY PHOTOGRAPHER! IF I DIDN'T NEED THE CASH, I'D HAVE TOLD HIM TO GO CLIMB A ROPE!
RENT A TUX
IT'S A GOOD THING THAT SCHOOL IS OUT FOR SEMESTER BREAK--IT TOOK ME ALL DAY TO FIND A TUXEDO RENTAL PLACE THAT I COULD AFFORD!
HOO-BOY! WHEN JONAH GETS THE PAY VOUCHER FOR THIS ASSIGNMENT, HE'LL SWALLOW HIS STOGIE!
ROGER STERN-- WORDS BEYOND COMPARE! JIM SHOOTER-- LAYOUTS THAT ARE FAIR! JIM MOONEY-- ARTIST WITH A FLAIR! JIM NOVAK-- LETTERER EXTRAORDINAIRE! BEN SEAN-- COLORIST, IF YOU CARE! DENNY O'NEIL-- EDITOR WITH GRAY HAIR!
JIM SHOOTER ED-IN-CHIEF

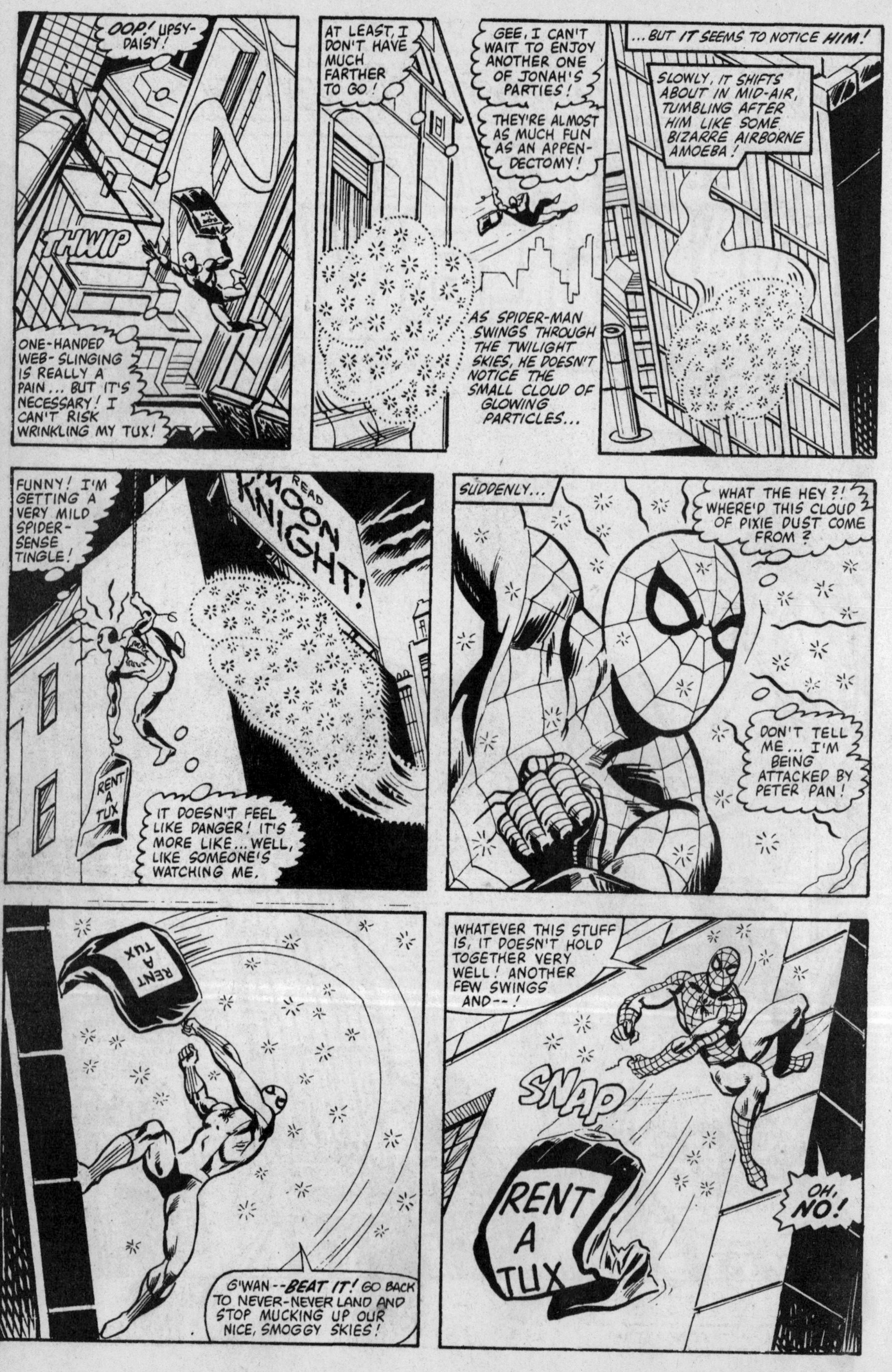
OOP! UPSY-DAISY!
THWIP
ONE-HANDED WEB-SLINGING IS REALLY A PAIN... BUT IT'S NECESSARY! I CAN'T RISK WRINKLING MY TUX!
AT LEAST, I DON'T HAVE MUCH FARTHER TO GO!
GEE, I CAN'T WAIT TO ENJOY ANOTHER ONE OF JONAH'S PARTIES!
THEY'RE ALMOST AS MUCH FUN AS AN APPENDECTOMY!
AS SPIDER-MAN SWINGS THROUGH THE TWILIGHT SKIES, HE DOESN'T NOTICE THE SMALL CLOUD OF GLOWING PARTICLES...
...BUT IT SEEMS TO NOTICE HIM!
SLOWLY, IT SHIFTS ABOUT IN MID-AIR, TUMBLING AFTER HIM LIKE SOME BIZARRE AIRBORNE AMOEBA!
FUNNY! I'M GETTING A VERY MILD SPIDER-SENSE TINGLE!
READ MOON KNIGHT!
RENT A TUX
IT DOESN'T FEEL LIKE DANGER! IT'S MORE LIKE... WELL, LIKE SOMEONE'S WATCHING ME.
SUDDENLY...
WHAT THE HEY?! WHERE'D THIS CLOUD OF PIXIE DUST COME FROM?
DON'T TELL ME... I'M BEING ATTACKED BY PETER PAN!
RENT A TUX
G'WAN--BEAT IT! GO BACK TO NEVER-NEVER LAND AND STOP MUCKING UP OUR NICE, SMOGGY SKIES!
WHATEVER THIS STUFF IS, IT DOESN'T HOLD TOGETHER VERY WELL! ANOTHER FEW SWINGS AND--!
SNAP
RENT A TUX
OH, NO!

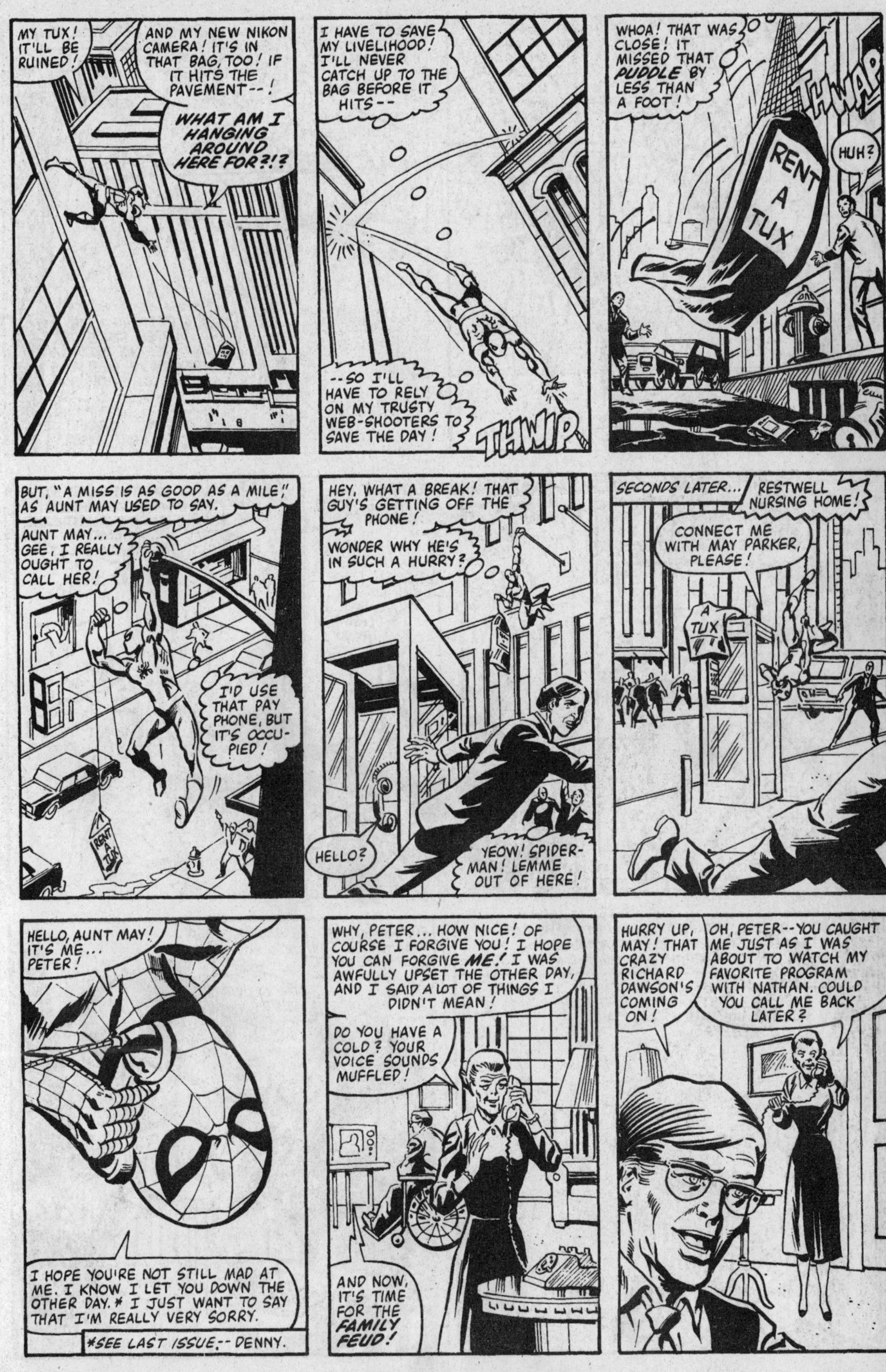
MY TUX! IT'LL BE RUINED!
AND MY NEW NIKON CAMERA! IT'S IN THAT BAG, TOO! IF IT HITS THE PAVEMENT--!
WHAT AM I HANGING AROUND HERE FOR?!?
I HAVE TO SAVE MY LIVELIHOOD! I'LL NEVER CATCH UP TO THE BAG BEFORE IT HITS--
--SO I'LL HAVE TO RELY ON MY TRUSTY WEB-SHOOTERS TO SAVE THE DAY!
THWIP
WHOA! THAT WAS CLOSE! IT MISSED THAT PUDDLE BY LESS THAN A FOOT!
THWAP
RENT A TUX
HUH?
BUT, "A MISS IS AS GOOD AS A MILE," AS AUNT MAY USED TO SAY.
AUNT MAY... GEE, I REALLY OUGHT TO CALL HER!
I'D USE THAT PAY PHONE, BUT IT'S OCCUPIED!
RENT A TUX
HEY, WHAT A BREAK! THAT GUY'S GETTING OFF THE PHONE!
WONDER WHY HE'S IN SUCH A HURRY?
HELLO?
YEOW! SPIDER-MAN! LEMME OUT OF HERE!
SECONDS LATER...
RESTWELL NURSING HOME!
CONNECT ME WITH MAY PARKER, PLEASE!
A TUX
HELLO, AUNT MAY! IT'S ME... PETER!
I HOPE YOU'RE NOT STILL MAD AT ME. I KNOW I LET YOU DOWN THE OTHER DAY.* I JUST WANT TO SAY THAT I'M REALLY VERY SORRY.
*SEE LAST ISSUE.--DENNY.
WHY, PETER... HOW NICE! OF COURSE I FORGIVE YOU! I HOPE YOU CAN FORGIVE ME! I WAS AWFULLY UPSET THE OTHER DAY, AND I SAID A LOT OF THINGS I DIDN'T MEAN!
DO YOU HAVE A COLD? YOUR VOICE SOUNDS MUFFLED!
AND NOW, IT'S TIME FOR THE FAMILY FEUD!
HURRY UP, MAY! THAT CRAZY RICHARD DAWSON'S COMING ON!
OH, PETER--YOU CAUGHT ME JUST AS I WAS ABOUT TO WATCH MY FAVORITE PROGRAM WITH NATHAN. COULD YOU CALL ME BACK LATER?

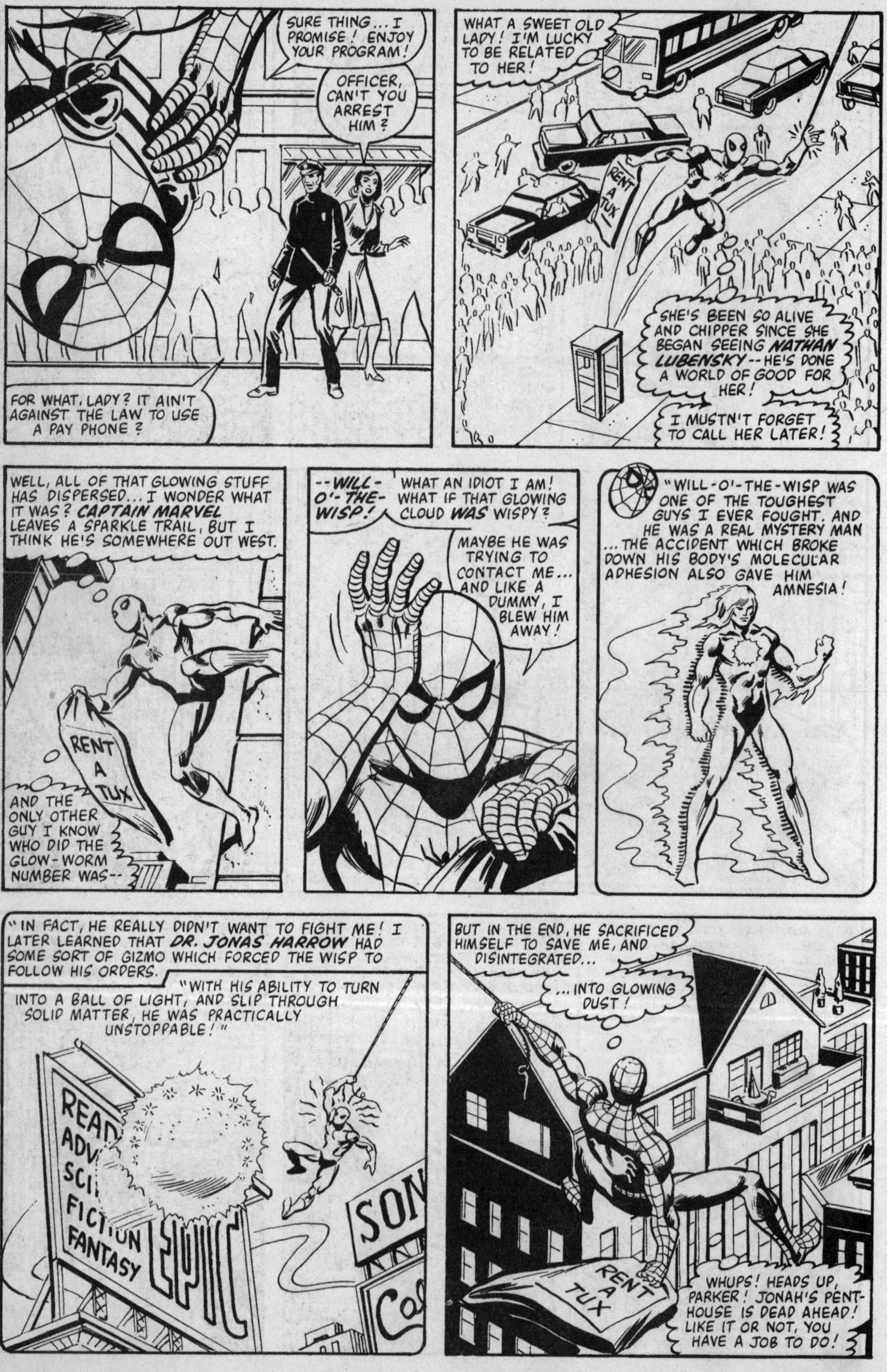

SURE THING... I PROMISE! ENJOY YOUR PROGRAM!
OFFICER, CAN'T YOU ARREST HIM?
FOR WHAT, LADY? IT AIN'T AGAINST THE LAW TO USE A PAY PHONE?
WHAT A SWEET OLD LADY! I'M LUCKY TO BE RELATED TO HER!
RENT A TUX
SHE'S BEEN SO ALIVE AND CHIPPER SINCE SHE BEGAN SEEING NATHAN LUBENSKY--HE'S DONE A WORLD OF GOOD FOR HER!
I MUSTN'T FORGET TO CALL HER LATER!
WELL, ALL OF THAT GLOWING STUFF HAS DISPERSED... I WONDER WHAT IT WAS? CAPTAIN MARVEL LEAVES A SPARKLE TRAIL, BUT I THINK HE'S SOMEWHERE OUT WEST.
RENT A TUX
AND THE ONLY OTHER GUY I KNOW WHO DID THE GLOW-WORM NUMBER WAS--
--WILL-O'-THE-WISP!
WHAT AN IDIOT I AM! WHAT IF THAT GLOWING CLOUD WAS WISPY?
MAYBE HE WAS TRYING TO CONTACT ME... AND LIKE A DUMMY, I BLEW HIM AWAY!
"WILL-O'-THE-WISP WAS ONE OF THE TOUGHEST GUYS I EVER FOUGHT, AND HE WAS A REAL MYSTERY MAN ...THE ACCIDENT WHICH BROKE DOWN HIS BODY'S MOLECULAR ADHESION ALSO GAVE HIM AMNESIA!
"IN FACT, HE REALLY DIDN'T WANT TO FIGHT ME! I LATER LEARNED THAT DR. JONAS HARROW HAD SOME SORT OF GIZMO WHICH FORCED THE WISP TO FOLLOW HIS ORDERS.
"WITH HIS ABILITY TO TURN INTO A BALL OF LIGHT, AND SLIP THROUGH SOLID MATTER, HE WAS PRACTICALLY UNSTOPPABLE!"
FANTASY
EPIC
BUT IN THE END, HE SACRIFICED HIMSELF TO SAVE ME, AND DISINTEGRATED...
...INTO GLOWING DUST!
RENT A TUX
WHUPS! HEADS UP, PARKER! JONAH'S PENTHOUSE IS DEAD AHEAD! LIKE IT OR NOT, YOU HAVE A JOB TO DO!

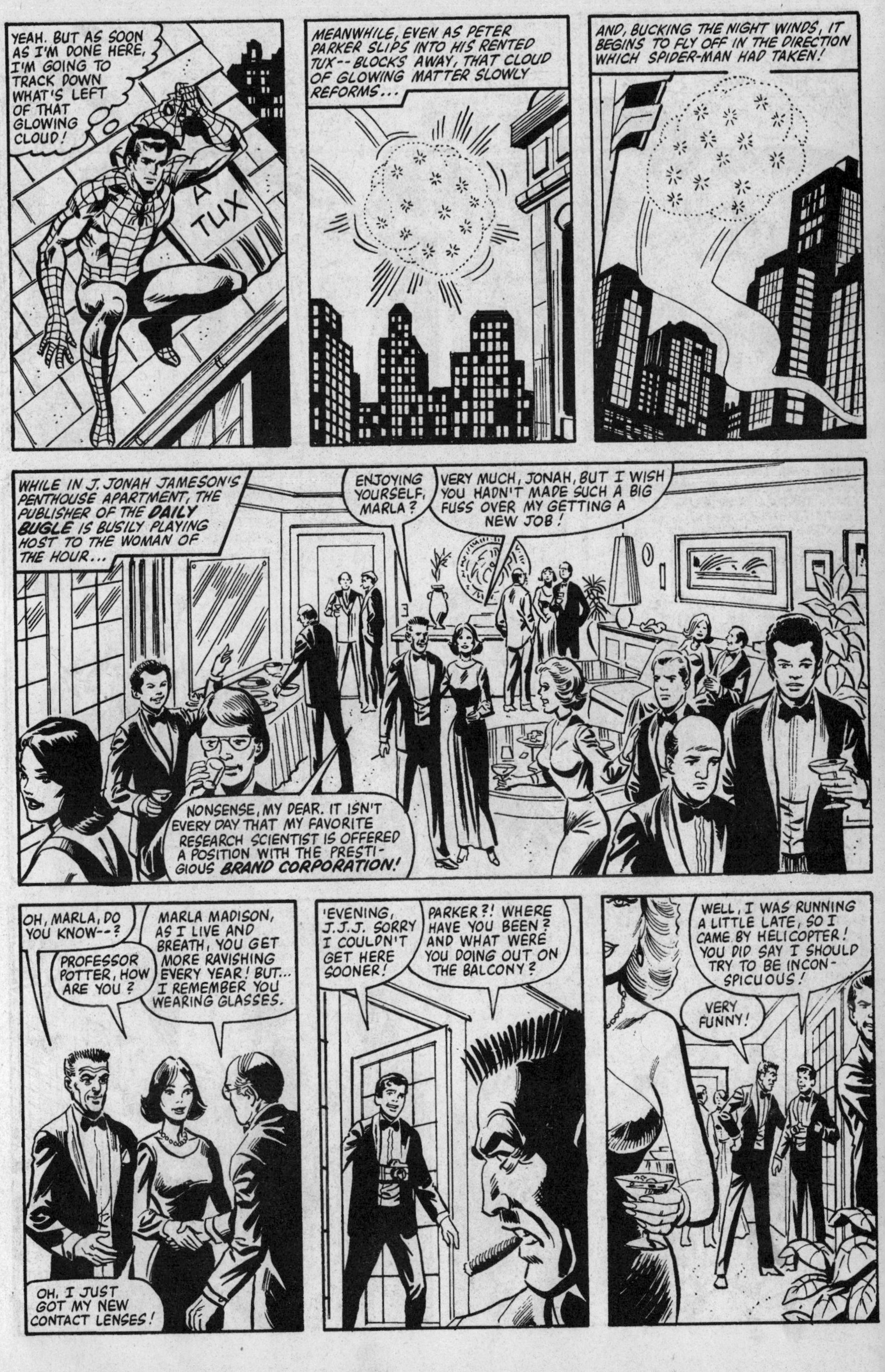
YEAH. BUT AS SOON AS I'M DONE HERE, I'M GOING TO TRACK DOWN WHAT'S LEFT OF THAT GLOWING CLOUD!
A TUX
MEANWHILE, EVEN AS PETER PARKER SLIPS INTO HIS RENTED TUX-- BLOCKS AWAY, THAT CLOUD OF GLOWING MATTER SLOWLY REFORMS...
AND, BUCKING THE NIGHT WINDS, IT BEGINS TO FLY OFF IN THE DIRECTION WHICH SPIDER-MAN HAD TAKEN!
WHILE IN J. JONAH JAMESON'S PENTHOUSE APARTMENT, THE PUBLISHER OF THE DAILY BUGLE IS BUSILY PLAYING HOST TO THE WOMAN OF THE HOUR...
ENJOYING YOURSELF, MARLA?
VERY MUCH, JONAH, BUT I WISH YOU HADN'T MADE SUCH A BIG FUSS OVER MY GETTING A NEW JOB!
NONSENSE, MY DEAR. IT ISN'T EVERY DAY THAT MY FAVORITE RESEARCH SCIENTIST IS OFFERED A POSITION WITH THE PRESTIGIOUS BRAND CORPORATION!
OH, MARLA, DO YOU KNOW--?
PROFESSOR POTTER, HOW ARE YOU?
MARLA MADISON, AS I LIVE AND BREATH, YOU GET MORE RAVISHING EVERY YEAR! BUT... I REMEMBER YOU WEARING GLASSES.
OH, I JUST GOT MY NEW CONTACT LENSES!
'EVENING, J.J.J. SORRY I COULDN'T GET HERE SOONER!
PARKER?! WHERE HAVE YOU BEEN? AND WHAT WERE YOU DOING OUT ON THE BALCONY?
WELL, I WAS RUNNING A LITTLE LATE, SO I CAME BY HELICOPTER! YOU DID SAY I SHOULD TRY TO BE INCONSPICUOUS!
VERY FUNNY!

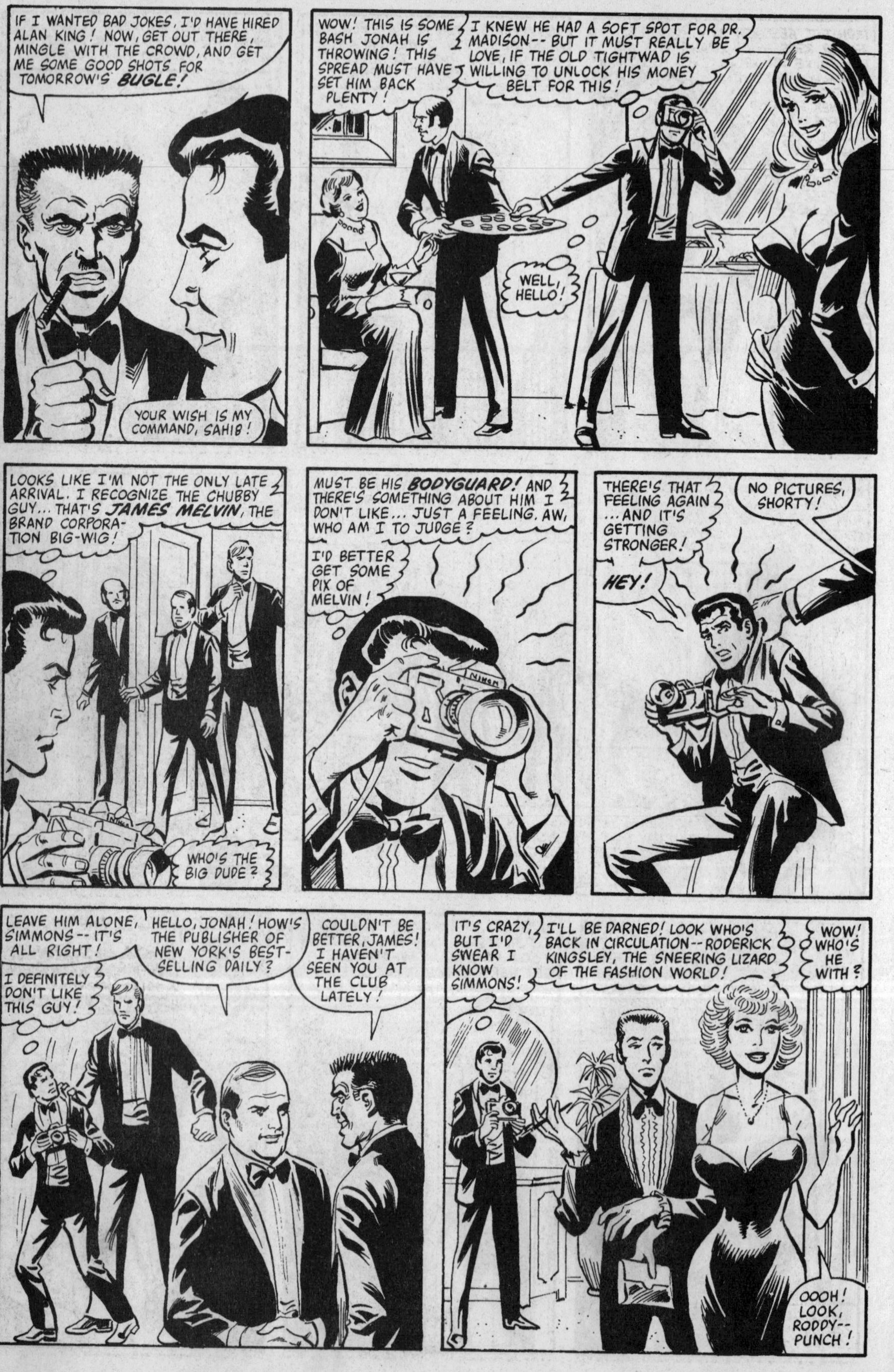

IF I WANTED BAD JOKES, I'D HAVE HIRED ALAN KING! NOW, GET OUT THERE, MINGLE WITH THE CROWD, AND GET ME SOME GOOD SHOTS FOR TOMORROW'S BUGLE!
YOUR WISH IS MY COMMAND, SAHIB!
WOW! THIS IS SOME BASH JONAH IS THROWING! THIS SPREAD MUST HAVE SET HIM BACK PLENTY!
I KNEW HE HAD A SOFT SPOT FOR DR. MADISON-- BUT IT MUST REALLY BE LOVE, IF THE OLD TIGHTWAD IS WILLING TO UNLOCK HIS MONEY BELT FOR THIS!
WELL, HELLO!
LOOKS LIKE I'M NOT THE ONLY LATE ARRIVAL. I RECOGNIZE THE CHUBBY GUY... THAT'S JAMES MELVIN, THE BRAND CORPORATION BIG-WIG!
WHO'S THE BIG DUDE?
MUST BE HIS BODYGUARD! AND THERE'S SOMETHING ABOUT HIM I DON'T LIKE... JUST A FEELING. AW, WHO AM I TO JUDGE?
I'D BETTER GET SOME PIX OF MELVIN!
THERE'S THAT FEELING AGAIN ...AND IT'S GETTING STRONGER!
HEY!
NO PICTURES, SHORTY!
LEAVE HIM ALONE, SIMMONS-- IT'S ALL RIGHT!
I DEFINITELY DON'T LIKE THIS GUY!
HELLO, JONAH! HOW'S THE PUBLISHER OF NEW YORK'S BEST-SELLING DAILY?
COULDN'T BE BETTER, JAMES! I HAVEN'T SEEN YOU AT THE CLUB LATELY!
IT'S CRAZY, BUT I'D SWEAR I KNOW SIMMONS!
I'LL BE DARNED! LOOK WHO'S BACK IN CIRCULATION-- RODERICK KINGSLEY, THE SNEERING LIZARD OF THE FASHION WORLD!
WOW! WHO'S HE WITH?
OOOH! LOOK, RODDY-- PUNCH!

Panel 1 (top left):
DIDN'T I SEE HER IN A *CENTERFOLD* RECENTLY? HOW'D A SCRAWNY WIMP LIKE KINGSLEY EVER LATCH ONTO HER?

I NEVER FIGURED HIM FOR A LADIES' MAN. I GUESS THIS PROVES THAT YOU CAN'T GO BY APPEARANCES!

HELLO, ROD! IS THIS YOUR NEW LADY? SHE'S...CUTE.

Panel 2 (top middle):
WELCOME TO THE CLUB, DEAR. I'M MARJORIE DuPREY.

CLUB? WHAT ARE YOU TALKING ABOUT?

SHUT UP, MARGE!

Panel 3 (top right):

WHY, HAVEN'T YOU HEARD OF "KINGSLEY'S KOZY KOMPANIONS"? WE'RE A SELECT GROUP... THERE ARE ONLY 19 OF US... 20, COUNTING YOU!

I DON'T UNDERSTAND.

YOU WILL... WHEN HE DROPS YOU FOR THE *NEXT* SKIRT THAT CATCHES HIS EYE!

Panel 4 (middle left):

RODDY?

BUT--!

IGNORE HER, DAPHNE. SHE'S DRUNK!

HAH-HA! SO RODDY-BOY'S A SOCIAL LOUSE, AS WELL AS A PROFESSIONAL ONE! I BET HE WON'T BE SEEING THAT LADY MUCH LONGER!

Panel 5 (middle right):

YES, JONAH, I HAD GREAT HOPES FOR THE NEW ADMINISTRATION. BUT THEY'RE JUST NOT DOING ENOUGH FOR BUSINESS.

I SEE YOUR POINT, BUT SURELY YOU MUST AGREE THAT--!

I CAN'T TAKE MUCH MORE OF THIS! I NEED SOME AIR... AND A SMOKE!

Panel 6 (bottom left):

THAT'S BETTER! I DON'T KNOW WHO'S THE BIGGER WINDBAG... JAMESON OR THE BOSS!

HAROLD SIMMONS RELAXES, NOT SEEING THE GLOWING CLOUD WHICH DRAWS NEAR.

Panel 7 (bottom middle):

BOBBING AND WEAVING, IT SEARCHES FOR SPIDER-MAN, FOLLOWING THE RAPIDLY FADING TRAIL OF HIS PARTICULAR ELECTRICAL AURA. JUST THEN, SOMETHING ELSE ATTRACTS IT...

Panel 8 (bottom right):

FOR A MOMENT, IT PAUSES. AND THEN, IT TURNS...

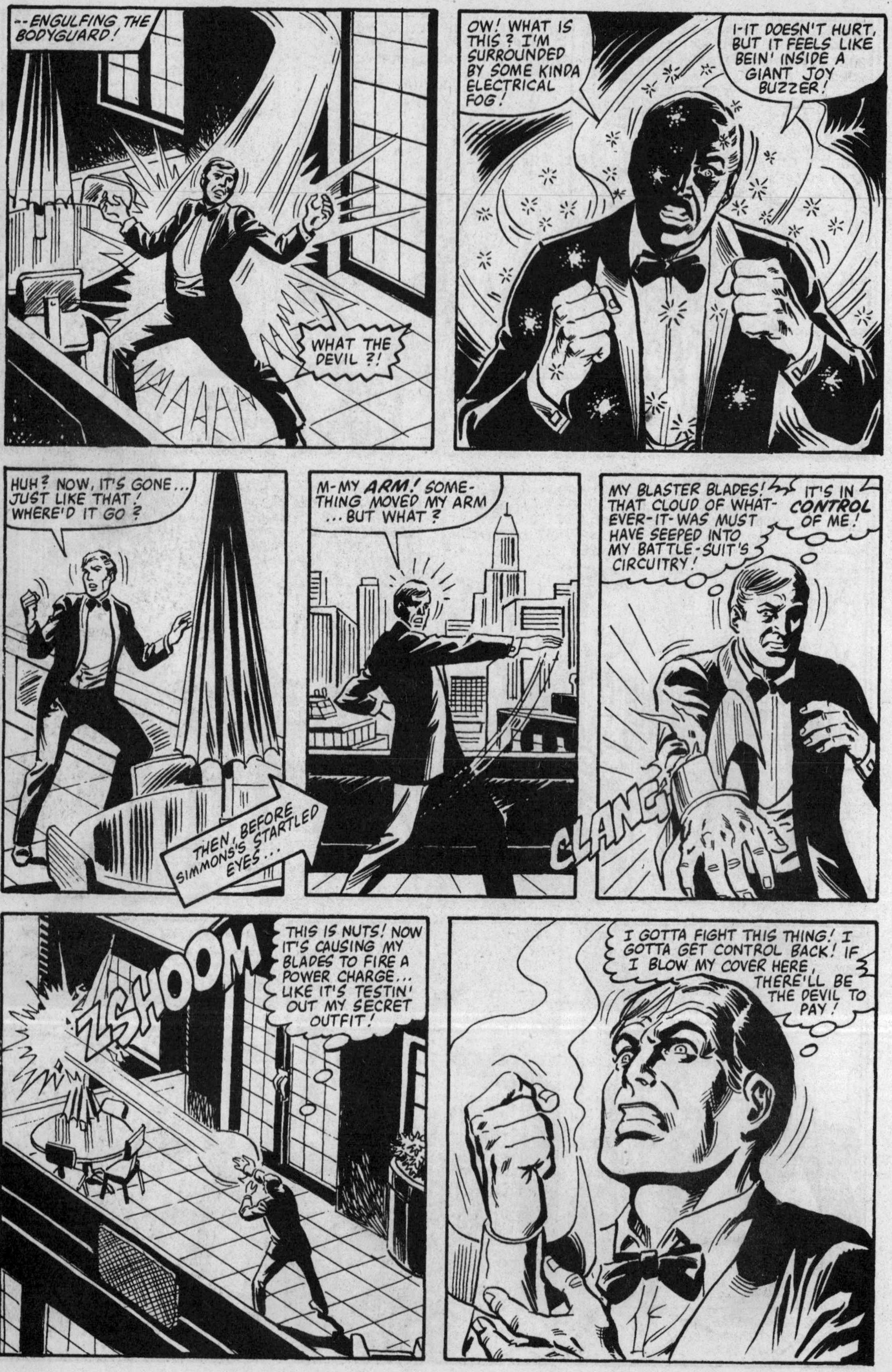
--ENGULFING THE BODYGUARD!
WHAT THE DEVIL ?!
OW! WHAT IS THIS ? I'M SURROUNDED BY SOME KINDA ELECTRICAL FOG!
I-IT DOESN'T HURT, BUT IT FEELS LIKE BEIN' INSIDE A GIANT JOY BUZZER!
HUH? NOW, IT'S GONE... JUST LIKE THAT! WHERE'D IT GO ?
THEN, BEFORE SIMMONS'S STARTLED EYES...
M-MY ARM! SOMETHING MOVED MY ARM ... BUT WHAT ?
MY BLASTER BLADES! THAT CLOUD OF WHATEVER-IT-WAS MUST HAVE SEEPED INTO MY BATTLE-SUIT'S CIRCUITRY!
IT'S IN CONTROL OF ME!
CLANG!
ZSHOOM
THIS IS NUTS! NOW IT'S CAUSING MY BLADES TO FIRE A POWER CHARGE... LIKE IT'S TESTIN' OUT MY SECRET OUTFIT!
I GOTTA FIGHT THIS THING! I GOTTA GET CONTROL BACK! IF I BLOW MY COVER HERE, THERE'LL BE THE DEVIL TO PAY!

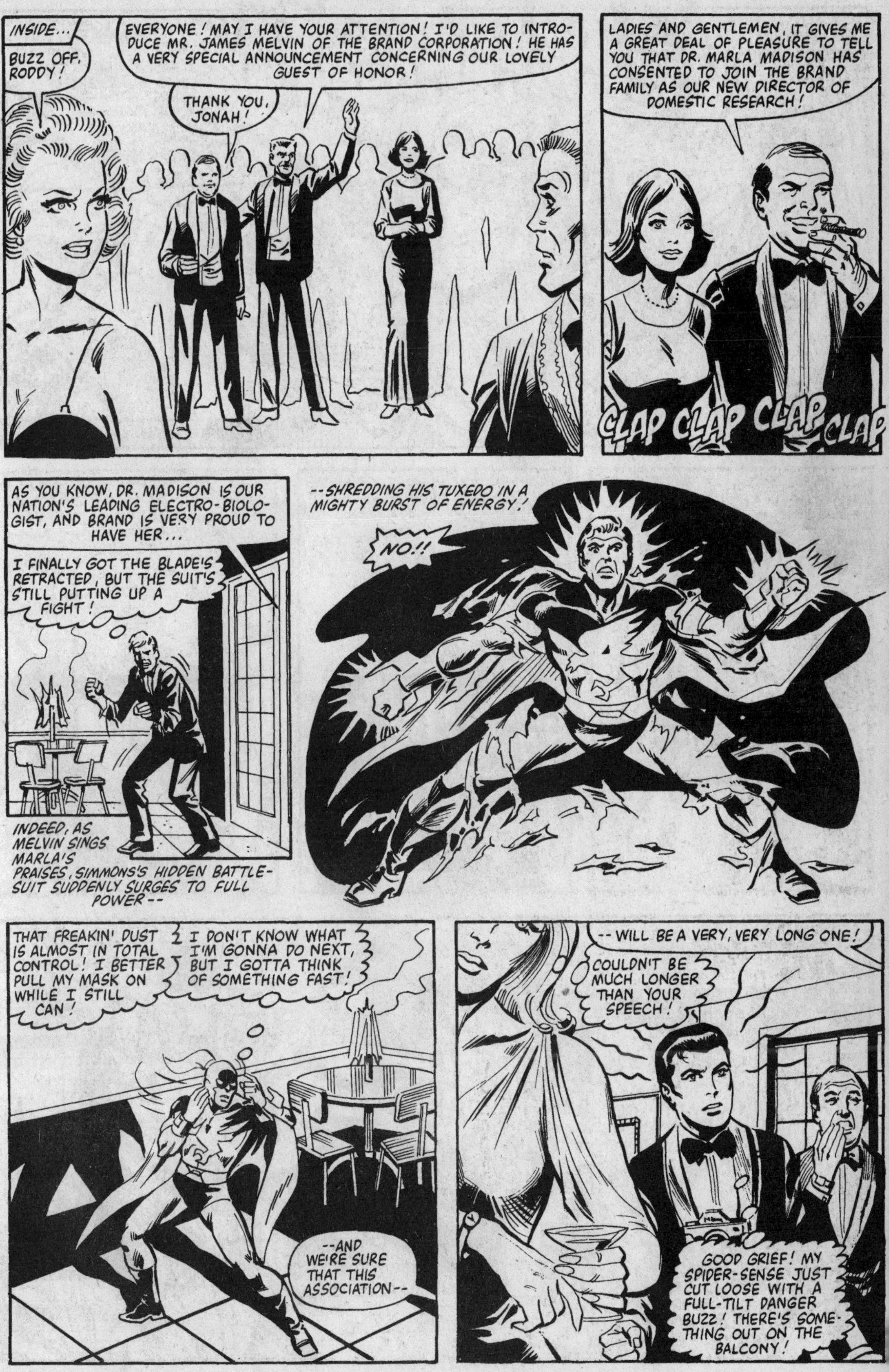
INSIDE...
BUZZ OFF, RODDY!
EVERYONE! MAY I HAVE YOUR ATTENTION! I'D LIKE TO INTRODUCE MR. JAMES MELVIN OF THE BRAND CORPORATION! HE HAS A VERY SPECIAL ANNOUNCEMENT CONCERNING OUR LOVELY GUEST OF HONOR!
THANK YOU, JONAH!
LADIES AND GENTLEMEN, IT GIVES ME A GREAT DEAL OF PLEASURE TO TELL YOU THAT DR. MARLA MADISON HAS CONSENTED TO JOIN THE BRAND FAMILY AS OUR NEW DIRECTOR OF DOMESTIC RESEARCH!
CLAP CLAP CLAP CLAP
AS YOU KNOW, DR. MADISON IS OUR NATION'S LEADING ELECTRO-BIOLOGIST, AND BRAND IS VERY PROUD TO HAVE HER...
I FINALLY GOT THE BLADE'S RETRACTED, BUT THE SUIT'S STILL PUTTING UP A FIGHT!
INDEED, AS MELVIN SINGS MARLA'S PRAISES, SIMMONS'S HIDDEN BATTLE-SUIT SUDDENLY SURGES TO FULL POWER--
--SHREDDING HIS TUXEDO IN A MIGHTY BURST OF ENERGY!
NO!!
THAT FREAKIN' DUST IS ALMOST IN TOTAL CONTROL! I BETTER PULL MY MASK ON WHILE I STILL CAN!
I DON'T KNOW WHAT I'M GONNA DO NEXT, BUT I GOTTA THINK OF SOMETHING FAST!
--AND WE'RE SURE THAT THIS ASSOCIATION--
--WILL BE A VERY, VERY LONG ONE!
COULDN'T BE MUCH LONGER THAN YOUR SPEECH!
GOOD GRIEF! MY SPIDER-SENSE JUST CUT LOOSE WITH A FULL-TILT DANGER BUZZ! THERE'S SOMETHING OUT ON THE BALCONY!

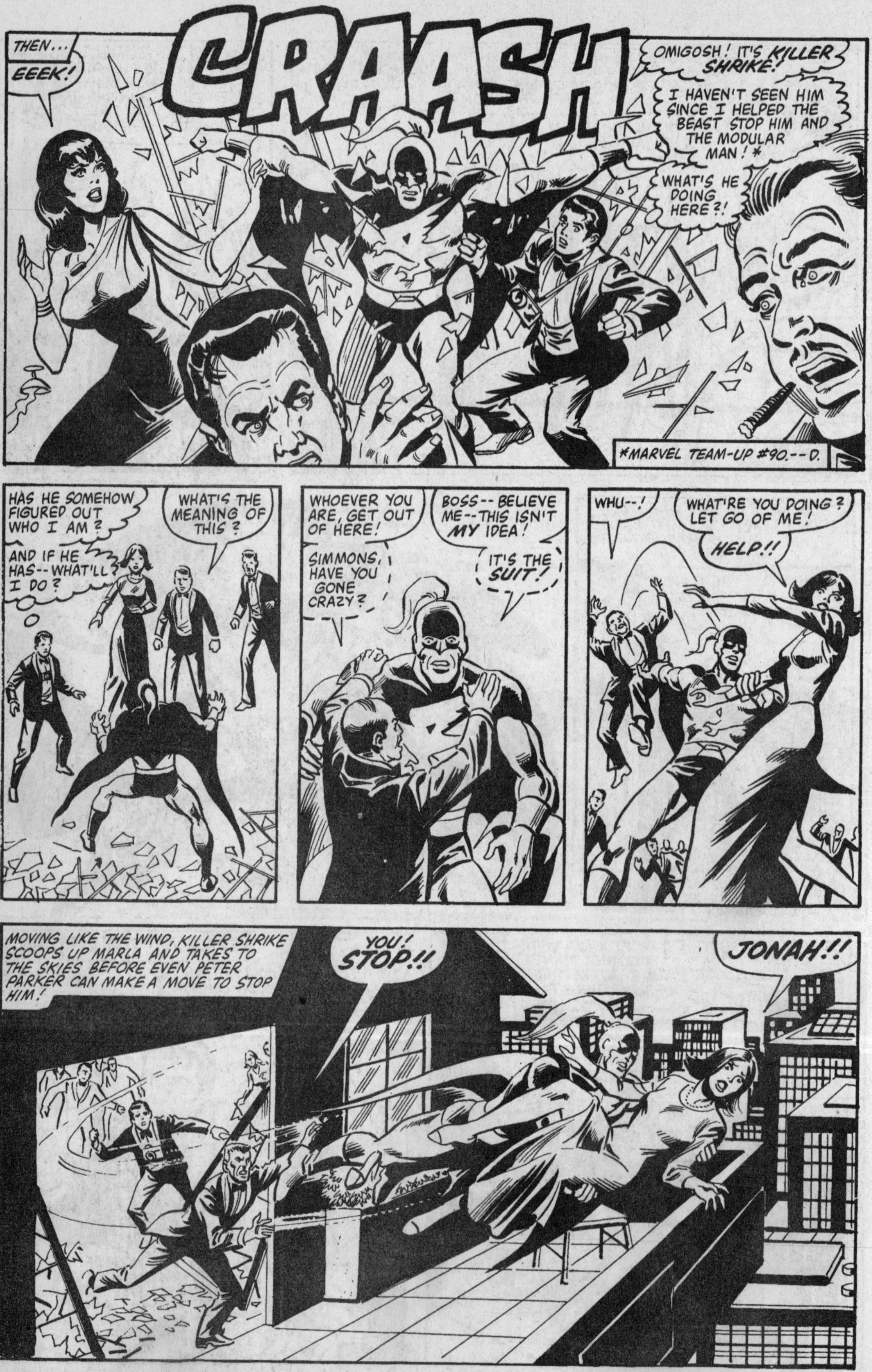
THEN...
EEEK!
CRAASH
OMIGOSH! IT'S KILLER SHRIKE!
I HAVEN'T SEEN HIM SINCE I HELPED THE BEAST STOP HIM AND THE MODULAR MAN! *
WHAT'S HE DOING HERE?!
*MARVEL TEAM-UP #90.--D.
HAS HE SOMEHOW FIGURED OUT WHO I AM?
AND IF HE HAS--WHAT'LL I DO?
WHAT'S THE MEANING OF THIS?
WHOEVER YOU ARE, GET OUT OF HERE!
SIMMONS, HAVE YOU GONE CRAZY?
BOSS--BELIEVE ME--THIS ISN'T MY IDEA!
IT'S THE SUIT!
WHU--!
WHAT'RE YOU DOING? LET GO OF ME!
HELP!!
MOVING LIKE THE WIND, KILLER SHRIKE SCOOPS UP MARLA AND TAKES TO THE SKIES BEFORE EVEN PETER PARKER CAN MAKE A MOVE TO STOP HIM!
YOU! STOP!!
JONAH!!

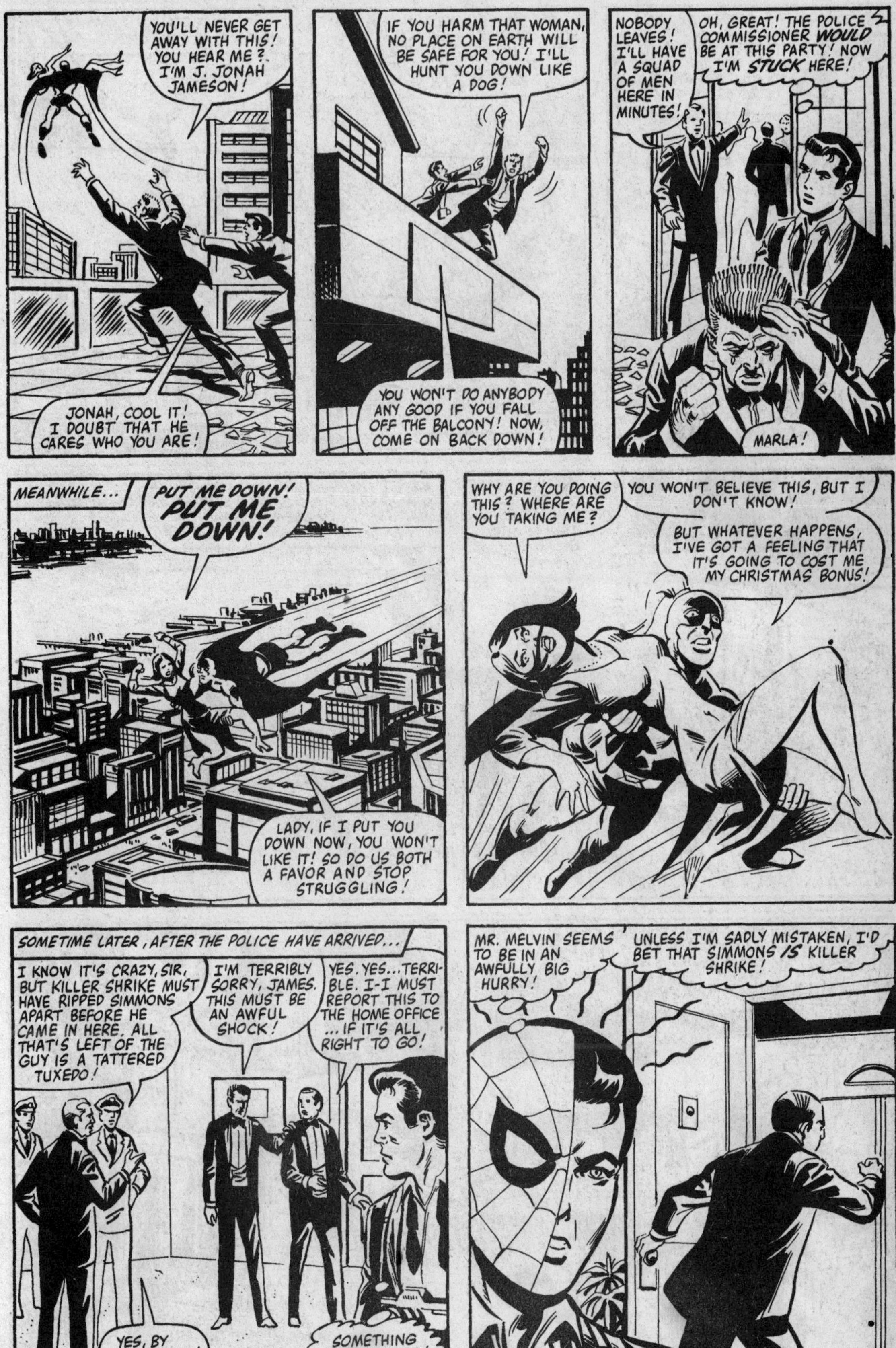
YOU'LL NEVER GET AWAY WITH THIS! YOU HEAR ME?. I'M J. JONAH JAMESON!
JONAH, COOL IT! I DOUBT THAT HE CARES WHO YOU ARE!
IF YOU HARM THAT WOMAN, NO PLACE ON EARTH WILL BE SAFE FOR YOU! I'LL HUNT YOU DOWN LIKE A DOG!
YOU WON'T DO ANYBODY ANY GOOD IF YOU FALL OFF THE BALCONY! NOW, COME ON BACK DOWN!
NOBODY LEAVES! I'LL HAVE A SQUAD OF MEN HERE IN MINUTES!
OH, GREAT! THE POLICE COMMISSIONER WOULD BE AT THIS PARTY! NOW I'M STUCK HERE!
MARLA!
MEANWHILE...
PUT ME DOWN! PUT ME DOWN!
LADY, IF I PUT YOU DOWN NOW, YOU WON'T LIKE IT! SO DO US BOTH A FAVOR AND STOP STRUGGLING!
WHY ARE YOU DOING THIS? WHERE ARE YOU TAKING ME?
YOU WON'T BELIEVE THIS, BUT I DON'T KNOW!
BUT WHATEVER HAPPENS, I'VE GOT A FEELING THAT IT'S GOING TO COST ME MY CHRISTMAS BONUS!
SOMETIME LATER, AFTER THE POLICE HAVE ARRIVED...
I KNOW IT'S CRAZY, SIR, BUT KILLER SHRIKE MUST HAVE RIPPED SIMMONS APART BEFORE HE CAME IN HERE. ALL THAT'S LEFT OF THE GUY IS A TATTERED TUXEDO!
YES, BY ALL MEANS!
I'M TERRIBLY SORRY, JAMES. THIS MUST BE AN AWFUL SHOCK!
YES. YES... TERRIBLE. I-I MUST REPORT THIS TO THE HOME OFFICE ... IF IT'S ALL RIGHT TO GO!
SOMETHING STINKS HERE!
MR. MELVIN SEEMS TO BE IN AN AWFULLY BIG HURRY!
UNLESS I'M SADLY MISTAKEN, I'D BET THAT SIMMONS IS KILLER SHRIKE!

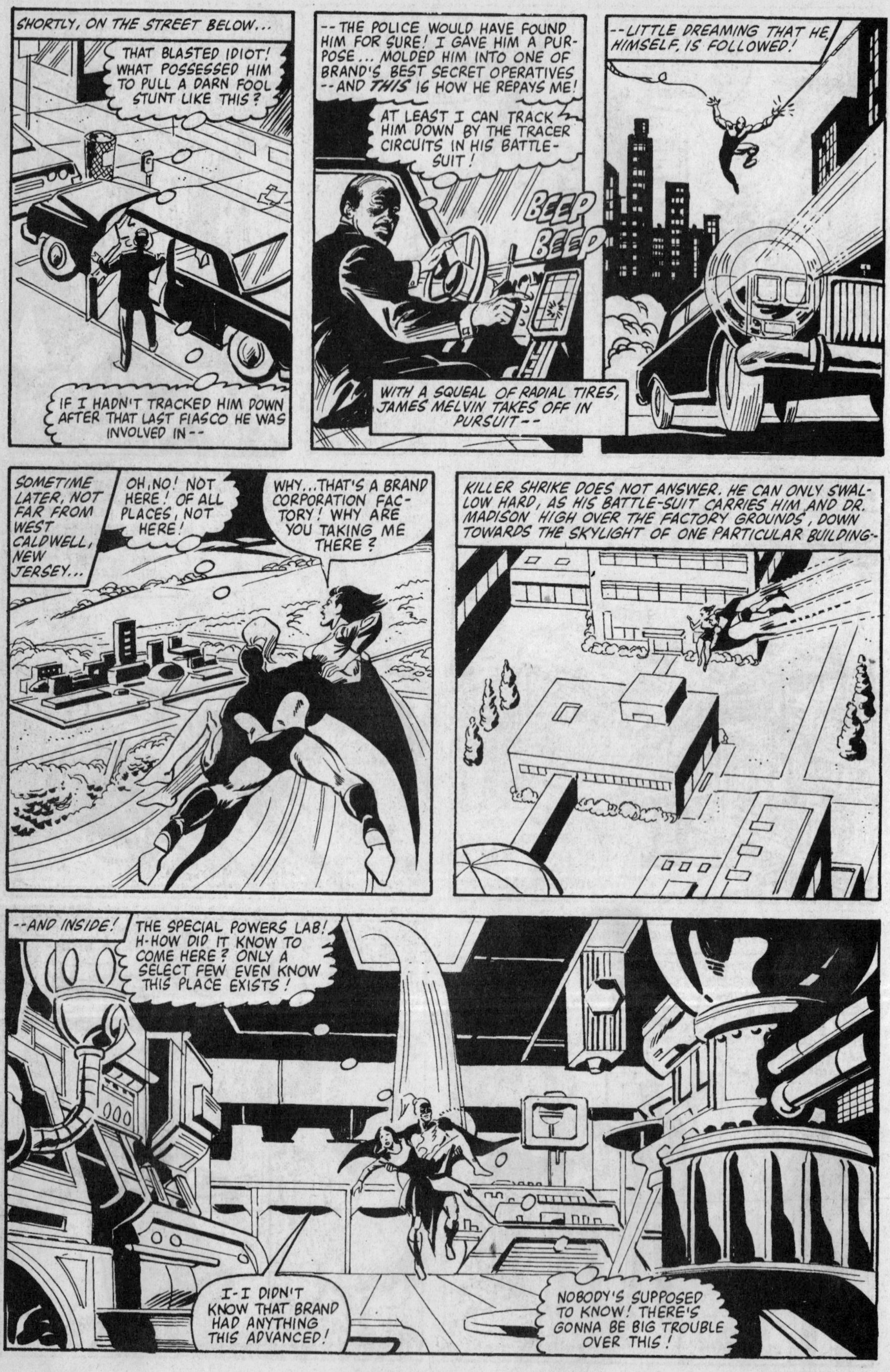
SHORTLY, ON THE STREET BELOW...
THAT BLASTED IDIOT! WHAT POSSESSED HIM TO PULL A DARN FOOL STUNT LIKE THIS?
IF I HADN'T TRACKED HIM DOWN AFTER THAT LAST FIASCO HE WAS INVOLVED IN--
--THE POLICE WOULD HAVE FOUND HIM FOR SURE! I GAVE HIM A PURPOSE... MOLDED HIM INTO ONE OF BRAND'S BEST SECRET OPERATIVES --AND THIS IS HOW HE REPAYS ME!
AT LEAST I CAN TRACK HIM DOWN BY THE TRACER CIRCUITS IN HIS BATTLE-SUIT!
BEEP BEEP
WITH A SQUEAL OF RADIAL TIRES, JAMES MELVIN TAKES OFF IN PURSUIT--
--LITTLE DREAMING THAT HE, HIMSELF, IS FOLLOWED!
SOMETIME LATER, NOT FAR FROM WEST CALDWELL, NEW JERSEY...
OH, NO! NOT HERE! OF ALL PLACES, NOT HERE!
WHY...THAT'S A BRAND CORPORATION FACTORY! WHY ARE YOU TAKING ME THERE?
KILLER SHRIKE DOES NOT ANSWER. HE CAN ONLY SWALLOW HARD, AS HIS BATTLE-SUIT CARRIES HIM AND DR. MADISON HIGH OVER THE FACTORY GROUNDS, DOWN TOWARDS THE SKYLIGHT OF ONE PARTICULAR BUILDING--
--AND INSIDE!
THE SPECIAL POWERS LAB! H-HOW DID IT KNOW TO COME HERE? ONLY A SELECT FEW EVEN KNOW THIS PLACE EXISTS!
I-I DIDN'T KNOW THAT BRAND HAD ANYTHING THIS ADVANCED!
NOBODY'S SUPPOSED TO KNOW! THERE'S GONNA BE BIG TROUBLE OVER THIS!

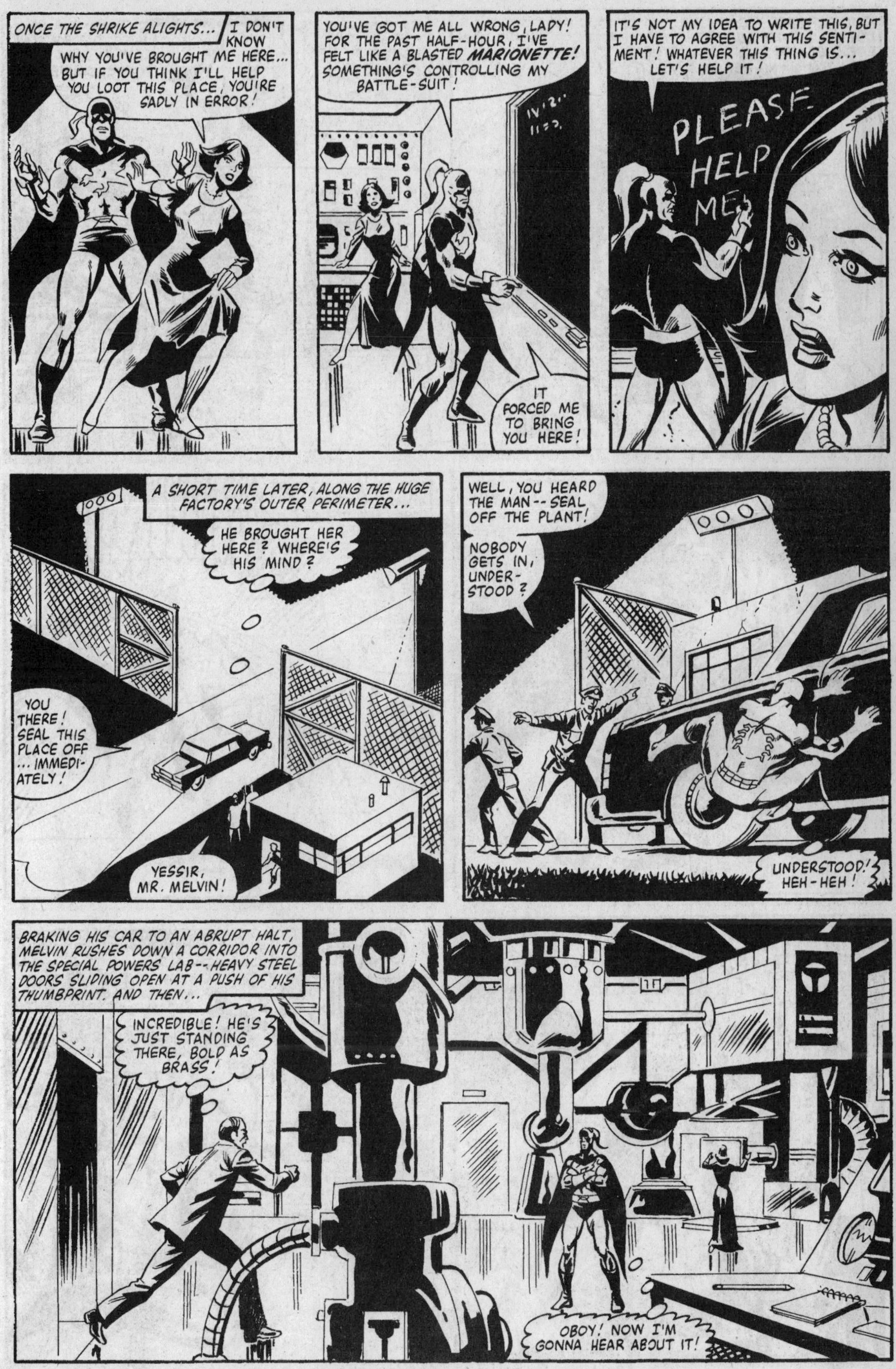
ONCE THE SHRIKE ALIGHTS...
I DON'T KNOW WHY YOU'VE BROUGHT ME HERE... BUT IF YOU THINK I'LL HELP YOU LOOT THIS PLACE, YOU'RE SADLY IN ERROR!
YOU'VE GOT ME ALL WRONG, LADY! FOR THE PAST HALF-HOUR, I'VE FELT LIKE A BLASTED MARIONETTE! SOMETHING'S CONTROLLING MY BATTLE-SUIT!
IT FORCED ME TO BRING YOU HERE!
IT'S NOT MY IDEA TO WRITE THIS, BUT I HAVE TO AGREE WITH THIS SENTIMENT! WHATEVER THIS THING IS... LET'S HELP IT!
PLEASE HELP ME!
A SHORT TIME LATER, ALONG THE HUGE FACTORY'S OUTER PERIMETER...
HE BROUGHT HER HERE? WHERE'S HIS MIND?
YOU THERE! SEAL THIS PLACE OFF... IMMEDIATELY!
YESSIR, MR. MELVIN!
WELL, YOU HEARD THE MAN--SEAL OFF THE PLANT!
NOBODY GETS IN, UNDERSTOOD?
UNDERSTOOD! HEH-HEH!
BRAKING HIS CAR TO AN ABRUPT HALT, MELVIN RUSHES DOWN A CORRIDOR INTO THE SPECIAL POWERS LAB--HEAVY STEEL DOORS SLIDING OPEN AT A PUSH OF HIS THUMBPRINT. AND THEN...
INCREDIBLE! HE'S JUST STANDING THERE, BOLD AS BRASS!
OBOY! NOW I'M GONNA HEAR ABOUT IT!

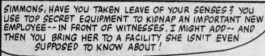

SIMMONS, HAVE YOU TAKEN LEAVE OF YOUR SENSES? YOU USE TOP SECRET EQUIPMENT TO KIDNAP AN IMPORTANT NEW EMPLOYEE -- IN FRONT OF WITNESSES, I MIGHT ADD -- AND THEN YOU BRING HER TO A FACILITY SHE ISN'T EVEN SUPPOSED TO KNOW ABOUT!

BOSS, IT WASN'T MY IDEA, HONEST! SOMETHING IS CONTROLLING MY SUIT...AND I'D BACK OFF IF I WERE YOU!

I DON'T THINK IT WANTS YOU TO BOTHER DR. MADISON!

DID I HEAR SOMEONE SAY THEY WANTED TO BE BOTHERED?

WHO--?

I THINK OUR PAL WITH THE PONYTAIL CAN ANSWER THAT ONE, CHUBBINS!

SPIDER-MAN!

SEE? I THOUGHT HE'D REMEMBER ME!

UNFORTUNATELY, THAT'S NOT ALL HE CAN DO!

BETTER GET DOWN, IF YOU DON'T WANT TO BE FRICASSEED!

ZZAK ZZOW

YEP, OL' K.S. IS PRETTY TOUGH WITH THAT SUIT AND THOSE BLASTERS!

BUT IF YOU HIT HIM IN THE CHIN, HE STILL FALLS DOWN WITH THE BEST OF THEM!

WHUMP

AWK!

KILLER SHRIKE WON'T BOTHER YOU ANY MORE DR. MADISON! LET'S GET OUT OF HERE!

I'M NOT LEAVING WITH ANYONE, SPIDER-MAN -- LEAST OF ALL YOU! I HAVE IMPORTANT WORK TO DO HERE!

WHAT? BUT DIDN'T THE SHRIKE KIDNAP YOU?

NO, HE DID NOT!

AM I GOING CRAZY? I SAW HIM FLY OFF WITH HER MYSELF!

YEAH, I MUST BE CRAZY! MY SPIDER-SENSE IS BUZZING AGAIN ... BUT THE ONLY THING THAT'S BEHIND ME IS SHRIKE, AND HE'S OUT COLD!

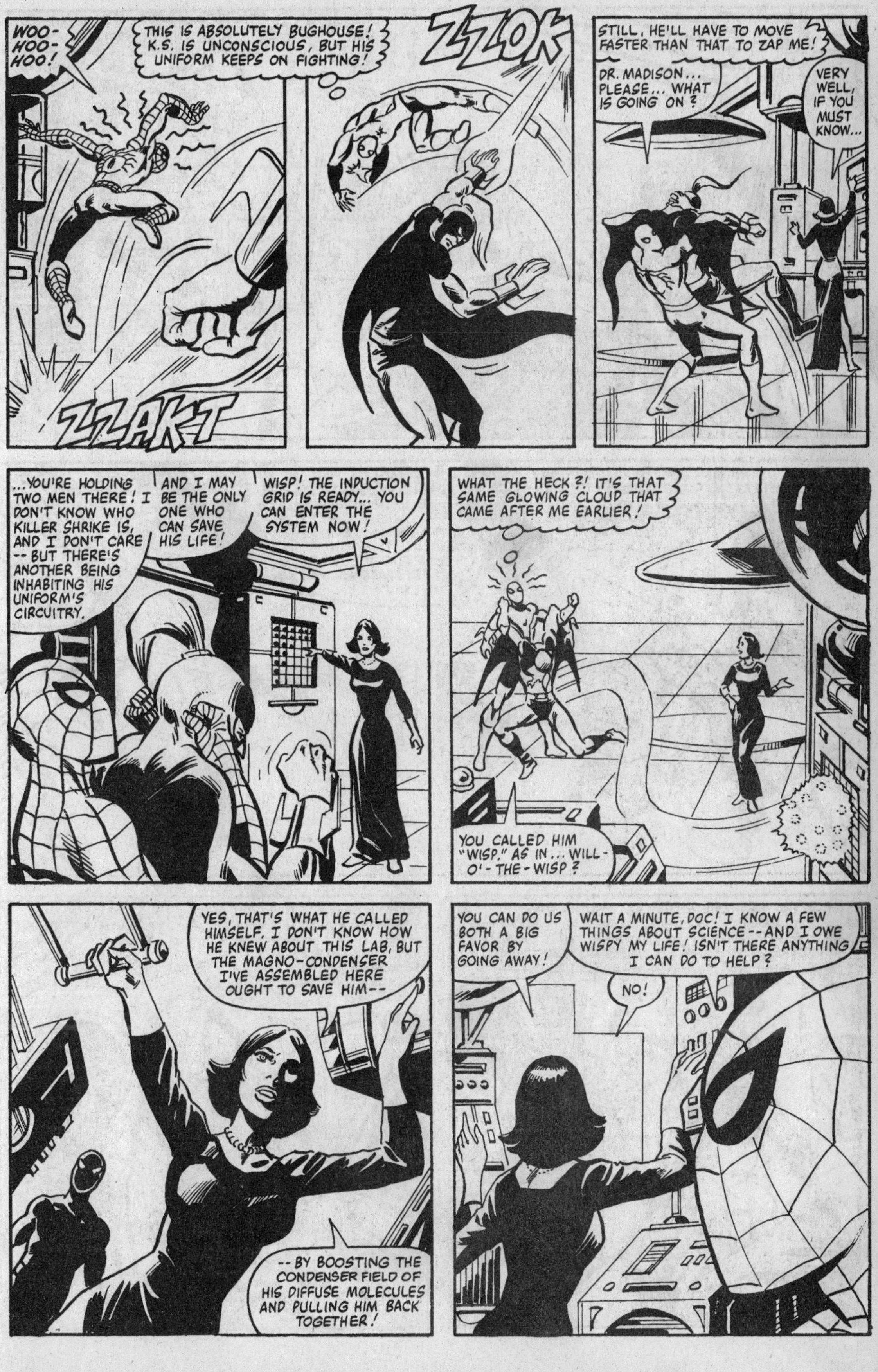
WOO-HOO-HOO-HOO!
THIS IS ABSOLUTELY BUGHOUSE! K.S. IS UNCONSCIOUS, BUT HIS UNIFORM KEEPS ON FIGHTING!
ZZLAKT
ZZLOK
STILL, HE'LL HAVE TO MOVE FASTER THAN THAT TO ZAP ME!
DR. MADISON... PLEASE... WHAT IS GOING ON?
VERY WELL, IF YOU MUST KNOW...
...YOU'RE HOLDING TWO MEN THERE! I DON'T KNOW WHO KILLER SHRIKE IS, AND I DON'T CARE -- BUT THERE'S ANOTHER BEING INHABITING HIS UNIFORM'S CIRCUITRY.
AND I MAY BE THE ONLY ONE WHO CAN SAVE HIS LIFE!
WISP! THE INDUCTION GRID IS READY... YOU CAN ENTER THE SYSTEM NOW!
WHAT THE HECK?! IT'S THAT SAME GLOWING CLOUD THAT CAME AFTER ME EARLIER!
YOU CALLED HIM "WISP." AS IN... WILL-O'-THE-WISP?
YES, THAT'S WHAT HE CALLED HIMSELF. I DON'T KNOW HOW HE KNEW ABOUT THIS LAB, BUT THE MAGNO-CONDENSER I'VE ASSEMBLED HERE OUGHT TO SAVE HIM--
--BY BOOSTING THE CONDENSER FIELD OF HIS DIFFUSE MOLECULES AND PULLING HIM BACK TOGETHER!
YOU CAN DO US BOTH A BIG FAVOR BY GOING AWAY!
WAIT A MINUTE, DOC! I KNOW A FEW THINGS ABOUT SCIENCE--AND I OWE WISPY MY LIFE! ISN'T THERE ANYTHING I CAN DO TO HELP?
NO!

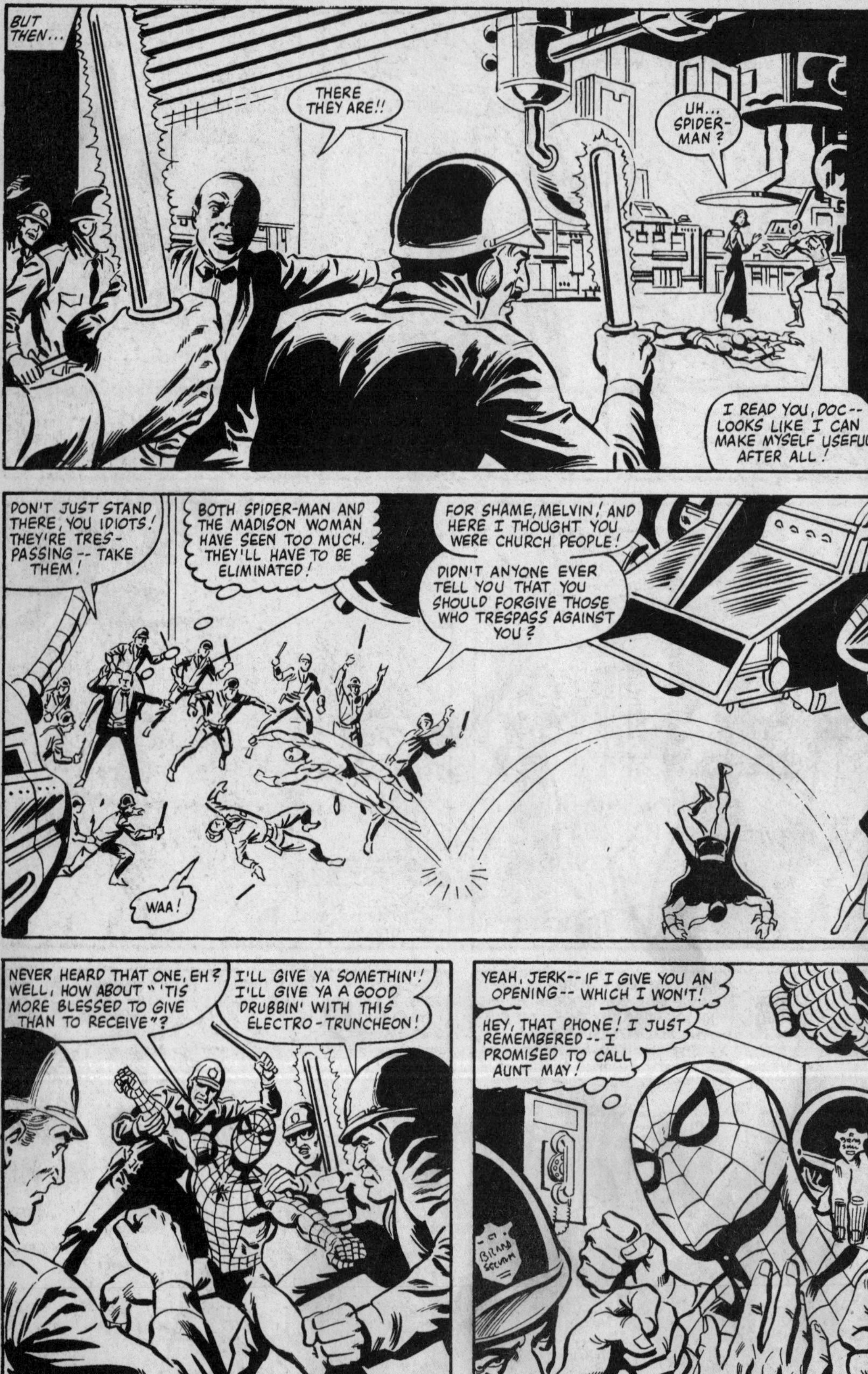
BUT THEN...
THERE THEY ARE!!
UH... SPIDER-MAN?
I READ YOU, DOC-- LOOKS LIKE I CAN MAKE MYSELF USEFUL AFTER ALL!
DON'T JUST STAND THERE, YOU IDIOTS! THEY'RE TRES-PASSING -- TAKE THEM!
BOTH SPIDER-MAN AND THE MADISON WOMAN HAVE SEEN TOO MUCH. THEY'LL HAVE TO BE ELIMINATED!
FOR SHAME, MELVIN! AND HERE I THOUGHT YOU WERE CHURCH PEOPLE!
DIDN'T ANYONE EVER TELL YOU THAT YOU SHOULD FORGIVE THOSE WHO TRESPASS AGAINST YOU?
WAA!
NEVER HEARD THAT ONE, EH? WELL, HOW ABOUT "'TIS MORE BLESSED TO GIVE THAN TO RECEIVE"?
I'LL GIVE YA SOMETHIN'! I'LL GIVE YA A GOOD DRUBBIN' WITH THIS ELECTRO-TRUNCHEON!
YEAH, JERK-- IF I GIVE YOU AN OPENING-- WHICH I WON'T!
HEY, THAT PHONE! I JUST REMEMBERED-- I PROMISED TO CALL AUNT MAY!

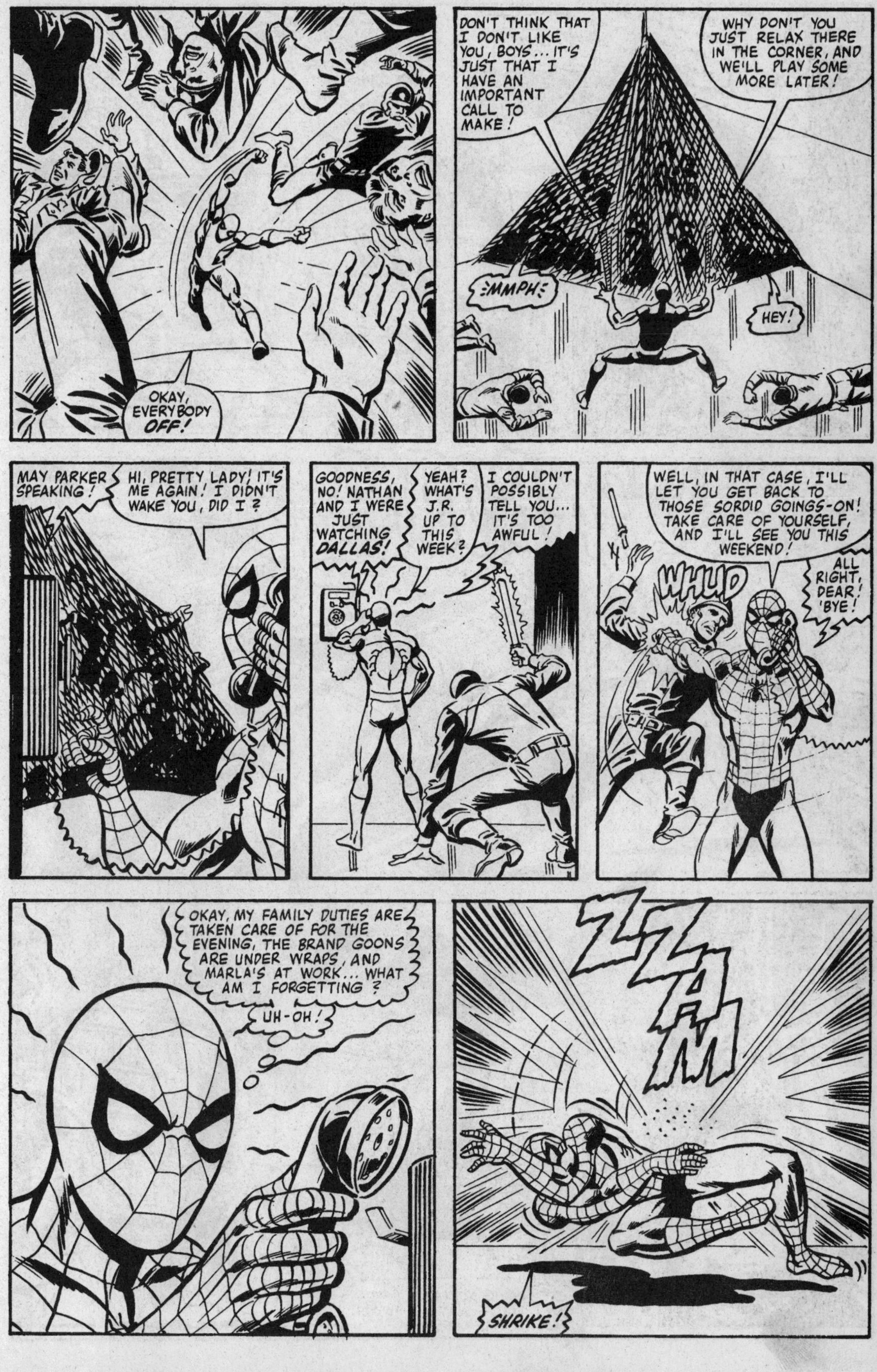
OKAY, EVERYBODY OFF!
DON'T THINK THAT I DON'T LIKE YOU, BOYS... IT'S JUST THAT I HAVE AN IMPORTANT CALL TO MAKE!
WHY DON'T YOU JUST RELAX THERE IN THE CORNER, AND WE'LL PLAY SOME MORE LATER!
MMPH!
HEY!
MAY PARKER SPEAKING!
HI, PRETTY LADY! IT'S ME AGAIN! I DIDN'T WAKE YOU, DID I?
GOODNESS, NO! NATHAN AND I WERE JUST WATCHING DALLAS!
YEAH? WHAT'S J.R. UP TO THIS WEEK?
I COULDN'T POSSIBLY TELL YOU... IT'S TOO AWFUL!
WELL, IN THAT CASE, I'LL LET YOU GET BACK TO THOSE SORDID GOINGS-ON! TAKE CARE OF YOURSELF, AND I'LL SEE YOU THIS WEEKEND!
WHUD
ALL RIGHT, DEAR! 'BYE!
OKAY, MY FAMILY DUTIES ARE TAKEN CARE OF FOR THE EVENING, THE BRAND GOONS ARE UNDER WRAPS, AND MARLA'S AT WORK... WHAT AM I FORGETTING?
UH-OH!
ZZZAM
SHRIKE!

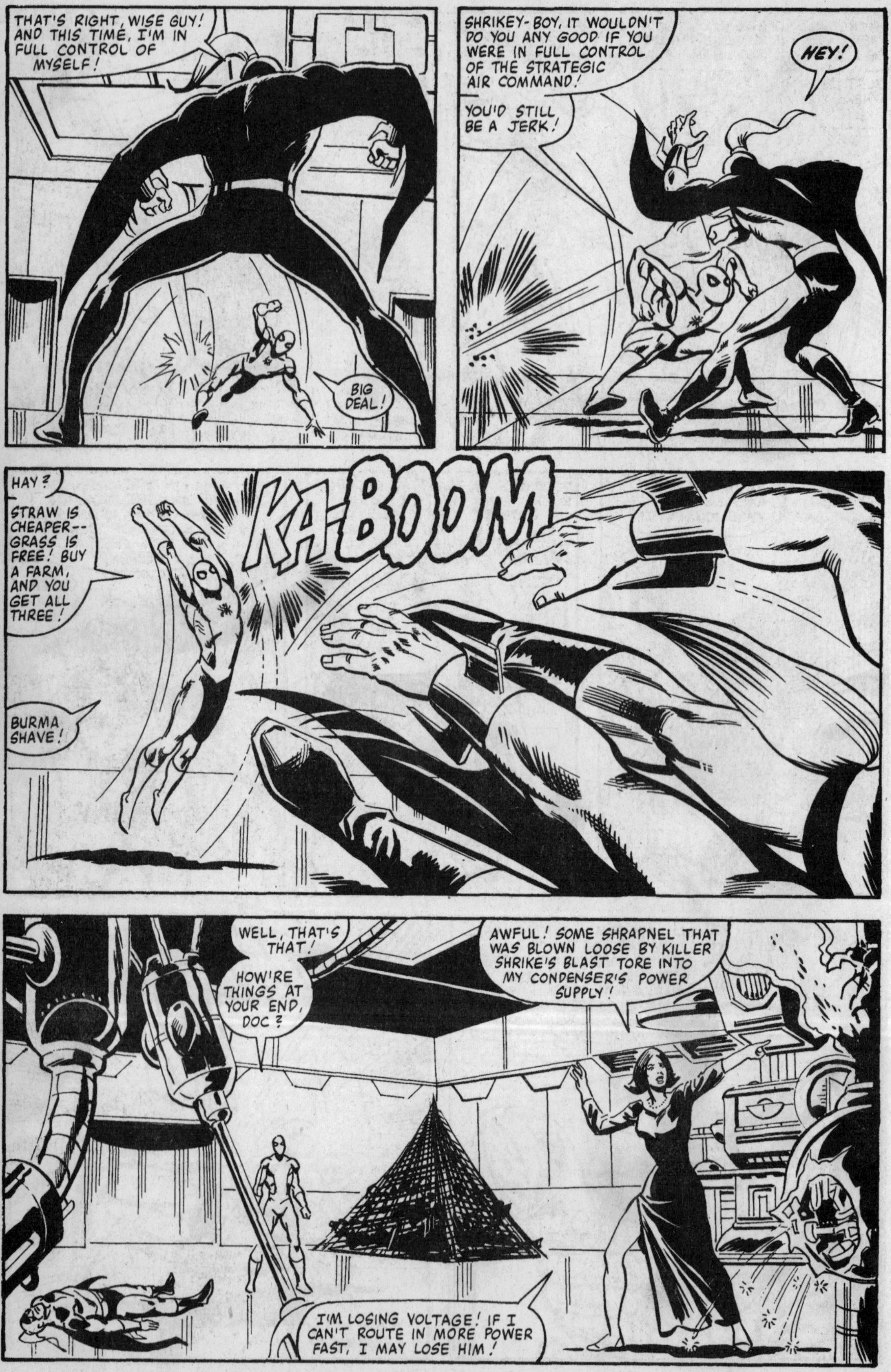
THAT'S RIGHT, WISE GUY! AND THIS TIME, I'M IN FULL CONTROL OF MYSELF!
BIG DEAL!
SHRIKEY-BOY, IT WOULDN'T DO YOU ANY GOOD IF YOU WERE IN FULL CONTROL OF THE STRATEGIC AIR COMMAND!
YOU'D STILL BE A JERK!
HEY!
HAY?
STRAW IS CHEAPER--GRASS IS FREE! BUY A FARM, AND YOU GET ALL THREE!
BURMA SHAVE!
KA-BOOM
WELL, THAT'S THAT!
HOW'RE THINGS AT YOUR END, DOC?
AWFUL! SOME SHRAPNEL THAT WAS BLOWN LOOSE BY KILLER SHRIKE'S BLAST TORE INTO MY CONDENSER'S POWER SUPPLY!
I'M LOSING VOLTAGE! IF I CAN'T ROUTE IN MORE POWER FAST, I MAY LOSE HIM!

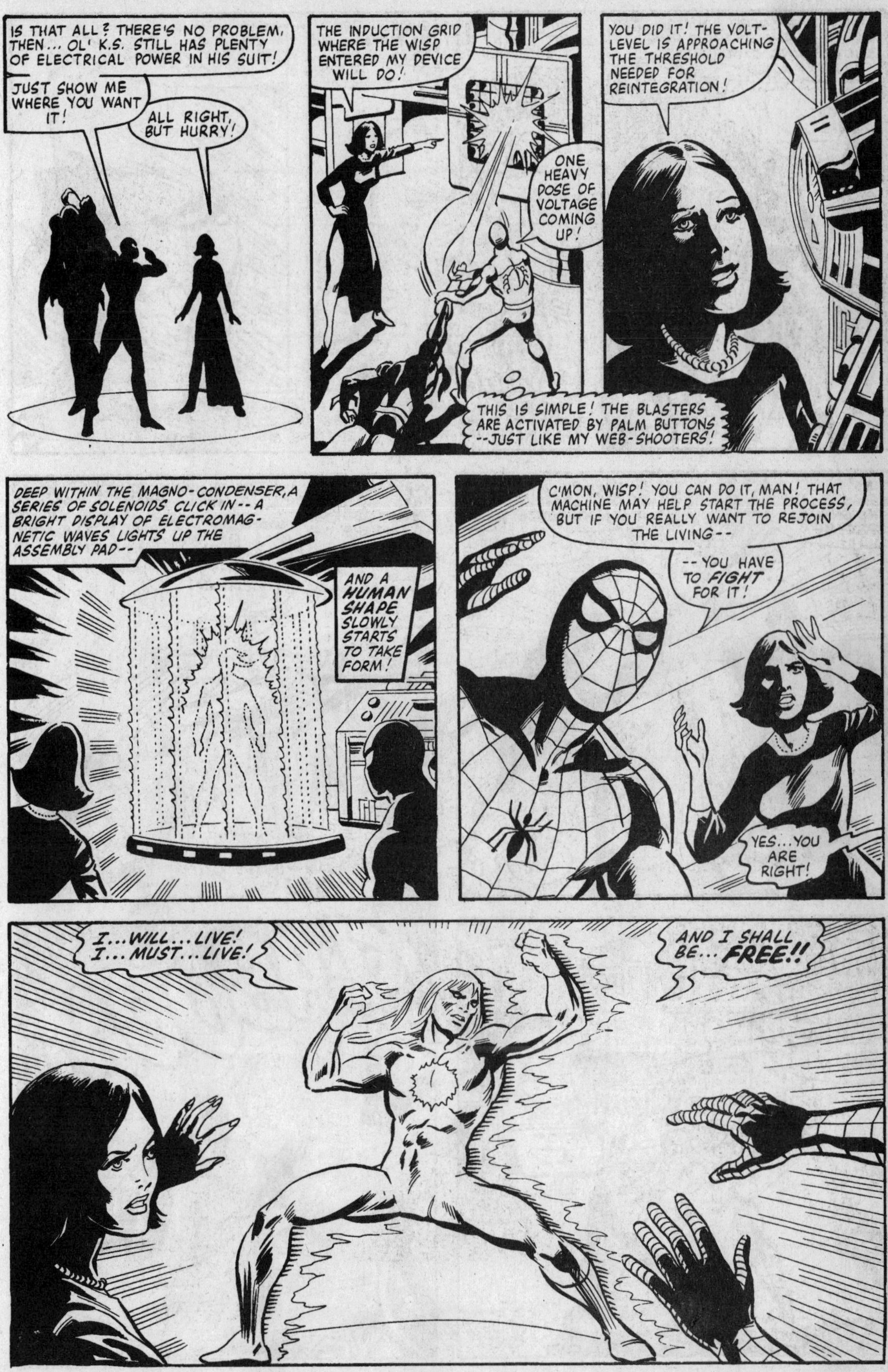
IS THAT ALL? THERE'S NO PROBLEM, THEN... OL' K.S. STILL HAS PLENTY OF ELECTRICAL POWER IN HIS SUIT!
JUST SHOW ME WHERE YOU WANT IT!
ALL RIGHT, BUT HURRY!
THE INDUCTION GRID WHERE THE WISP ENTERED MY DEVICE WILL DO!
ONE HEAVY DOSE OF VOLTAGE COMING UP!
THIS IS SIMPLE! THE BLASTERS ARE ACTIVATED BY PALM BUTTONS --JUST LIKE MY WEB-SHOOTERS!
YOU DID IT! THE VOLT-LEVEL IS APPROACHING THE THRESHOLD NEEDED FOR REINTEGRATION!
DEEP WITHIN THE MAGNO-CONDENSER, A SERIES OF SOLENOIDS CLICK IN-- A BRIGHT DISPLAY OF ELECTROMAGNETIC WAVES LIGHTS UP THE ASSEMBLY PAD--
AND A HUMAN SHAPE SLOWLY STARTS TO TAKE FORM!
C'MON, WISP! YOU CAN DO IT, MAN! THAT MACHINE MAY HELP START THE PROCESS, BUT IF YOU REALLY WANT TO REJOIN THE LIVING--
--YOU HAVE TO FIGHT FOR IT!
YES... YOU ARE RIGHT!
I... WILL... LIVE! I... MUST... LIVE!
AND I SHALL BE... FREE!!

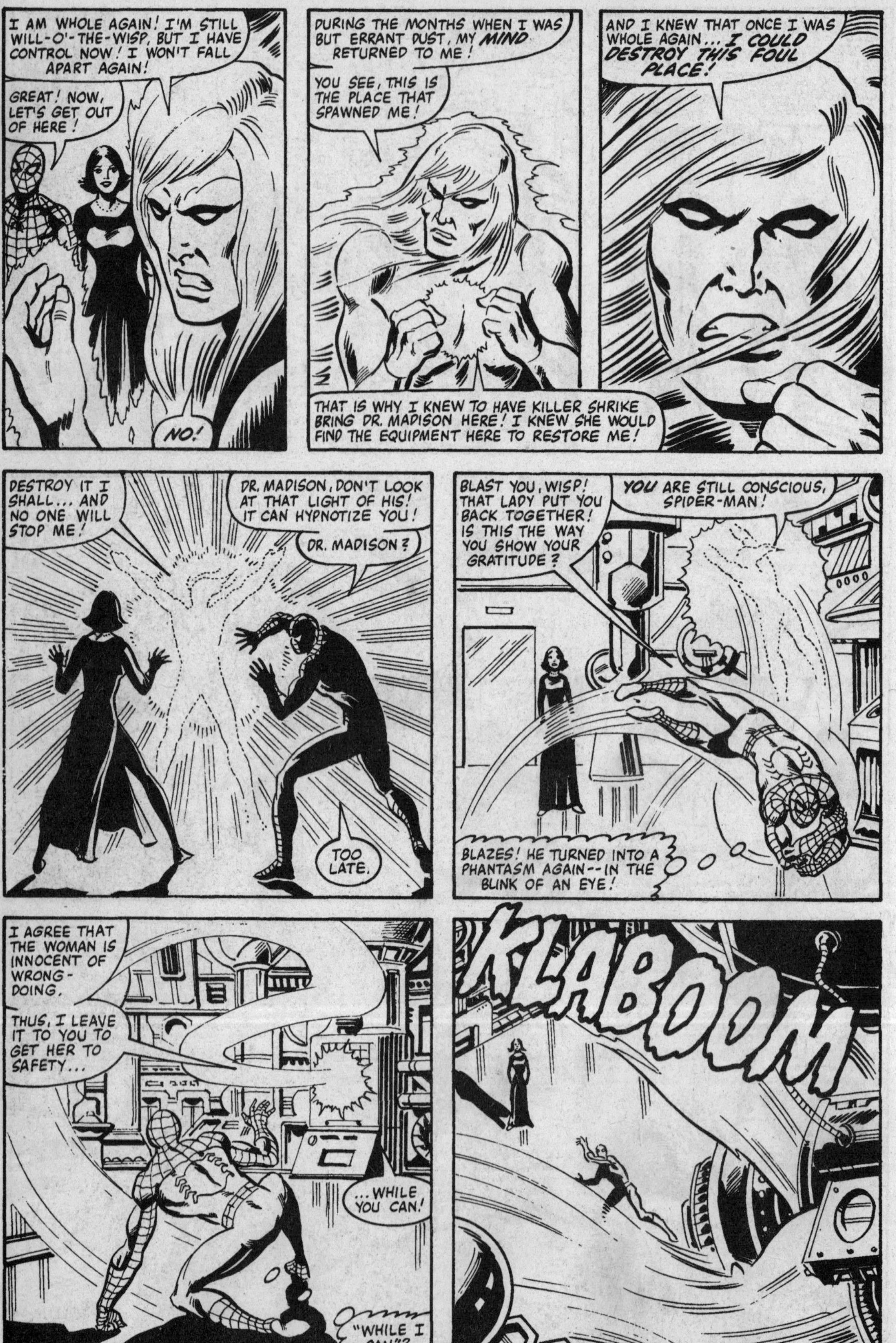

I AM WHOLE AGAIN! I'M STILL WILL-O'-THE-WISP, BUT I HAVE CONTROL NOW! I WON'T FALL APART AGAIN!
GREAT! NOW, LET'S GET OUT OF HERE!
NO!
DURING THE MONTHS WHEN I WAS BUT ERRANT DUST, MY MIND RETURNED TO ME!
YOU SEE, THIS IS THE PLACE THAT SPAWNED ME!
AND I KNEW THAT ONCE I WAS WHOLE AGAIN... I COULD DESTROY THIS FOUL PLACE!
THAT IS WHY I KNEW TO HAVE KILLER SHRIKE BRING DR. MADISON HERE! I KNEW SHE WOULD FIND THE EQUIPMENT HERE TO RESTORE ME!
DESTROY IT I SHALL... AND NO ONE WILL STOP ME!
DR. MADISON, DON'T LOOK AT THAT LIGHT OF HIS! IT CAN HYPNOTIZE YOU!
DR. MADISON?
TOO LATE.
BLAST YOU, WISP! THAT LADY PUT YOU BACK TOGETHER! IS THIS THE WAY YOU SHOW YOUR GRATITUDE?
YOU ARE STILL CONSCIOUS, SPIDER-MAN!
BLAZES! HE TURNED INTO A PHANTASM AGAIN--IN THE BLINK OF AN EYE!
I AGREE THAT THE WOMAN IS INNOCENT OF WRONG-DOING.
THUS, I LEAVE IT TO YOU TO GET HER TO SAFETY...
...WHILE YOU CAN!
"WHILE I CAN"?
KLABOOM

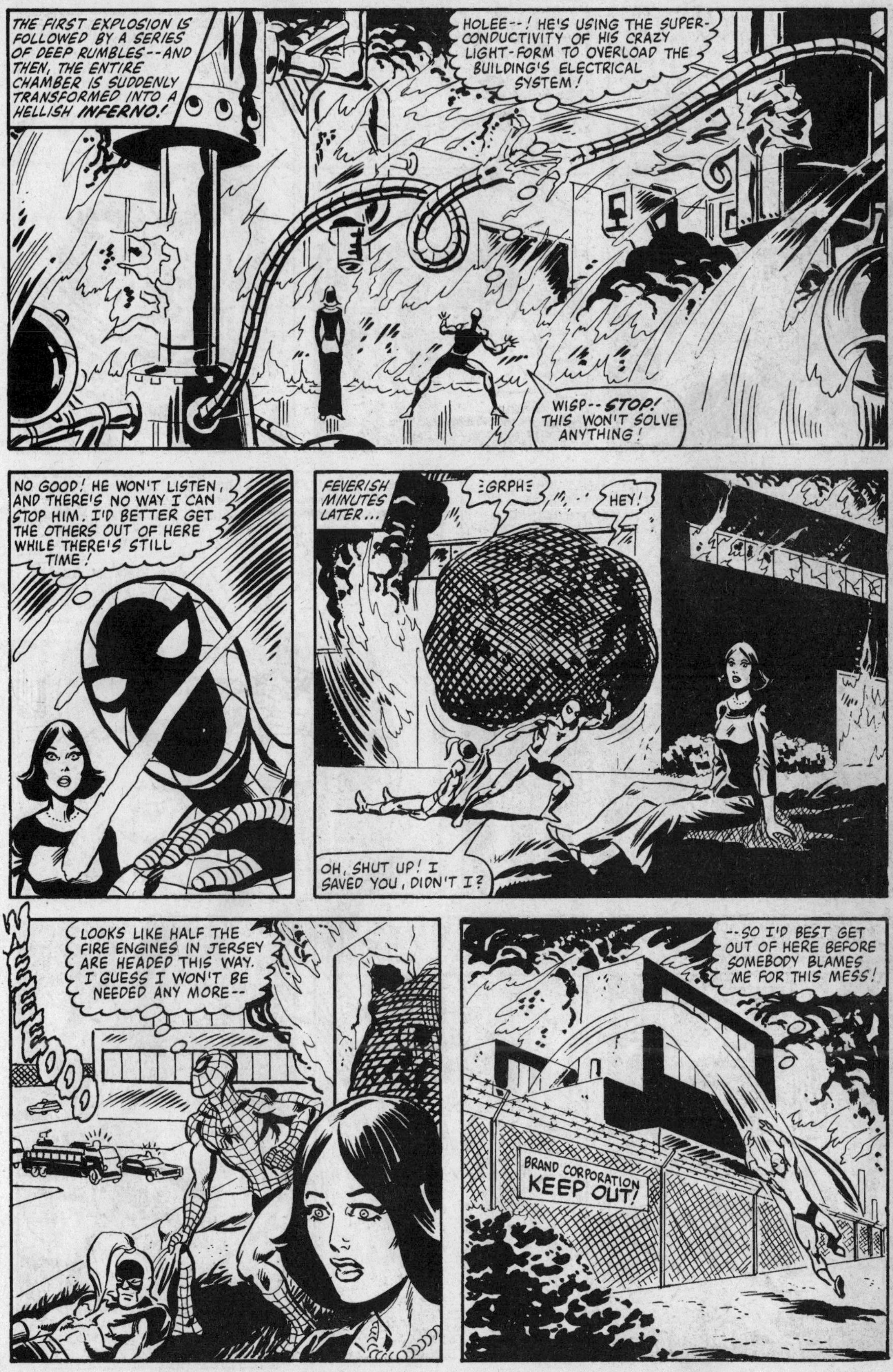
THE FIRST EXPLOSION IS FOLLOWED BY A SERIES OF DEEP RUMBLES--AND THEN, THE ENTIRE CHAMBER IS SUDDENLY TRANSFORMED INTO A HELLISH INFERNO!
HOLEE--! HE'S USING THE SUPER-CONDUCTIVITY OF HIS CRAZY LIGHT-FORM TO OVERLOAD THE BUILDING'S ELECTRICAL SYSTEM!
WISP--STOP! THIS WON'T SOLVE ANYTHING!
NO GOOD! HE WON'T LISTEN, AND THERE'S NO WAY I CAN STOP HIM. I'D BETTER GET THE OTHERS OUT OF HERE WHILE THERE'S STILL TIME!
FEVERISH MINUTES LATER...
GRPH
HEY!
OH, SHUT UP! I SAVED YOU, DIDN'T I?
LOOKS LIKE HALF THE FIRE ENGINES IN JERSEY ARE HEADED THIS WAY. I GUESS I WON'T BE NEEDED ANY MORE--
--SO I'D BEST GET OUT OF HERE BEFORE SOMEBODY BLAMES ME FOR THIS MESS!
BRAND CORPORATION
KEEP OUT!

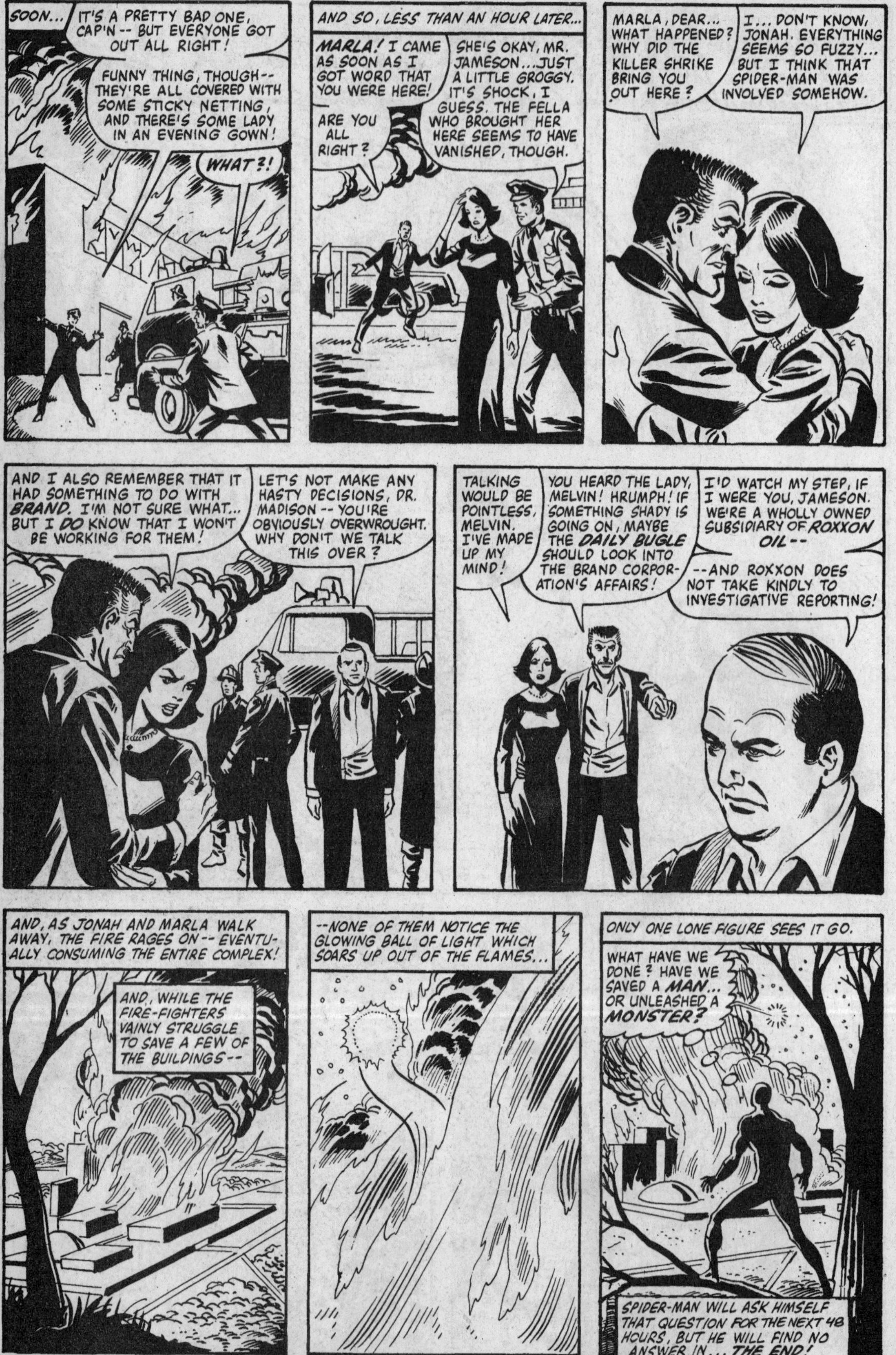
SOON...
IT'S A PRETTY BAD ONE, CAP'N -- BUT EVERYONE GOT OUT ALL RIGHT!
FUNNY THING, THOUGH-- THEY'RE ALL COVERED WITH SOME STICKY NETTING, AND THERE'S SOME LADY IN AN EVENING GOWN!
WHAT?!
AND SO, LESS THAN AN HOUR LATER...
MARLA! I CAME AS SOON AS I GOT WORD THAT YOU WERE HERE!
ARE YOU ALL RIGHT?
SHE'S OKAY, MR. JAMESON... JUST A LITTLE GROGGY. IT'S SHOCK, I GUESS. THE FELLA WHO BROUGHT HER HERE SEEMS TO HAVE VANISHED, THOUGH.
MARLA, DEAR... WHAT HAPPENED? WHY DID THE KILLER SHRIKE BRING YOU OUT HERE?
I... DON'T KNOW, JONAH. EVERYTHING SEEMS SO FUZZY... BUT I THINK THAT SPIDER-MAN WAS INVOLVED SOMEHOW.
AND I ALSO REMEMBER THAT IT HAD SOMETHING TO DO WITH BRAND. I'M NOT SURE WHAT... BUT I DO KNOW THAT I WON'T BE WORKING FOR THEM!
LET'S NOT MAKE ANY HASTY DECISIONS, DR. MADISON -- YOU'RE OBVIOUSLY OVERWROUGHT. WHY DON'T WE TALK THIS OVER?
TALKING WOULD BE POINTLESS, MELVIN. I'VE MADE UP MY MIND!
YOU HEARD THE LADY, MELVIN! HRUMPH! IF SOMETHING SHADY IS GOING ON, MAYBE THE DAILY BUGLE SHOULD LOOK INTO THE BRAND CORPORATION'S AFFAIRS!
I'D WATCH MY STEP, IF I WERE YOU, JAMESON. WE'RE A WHOLLY OWNED SUBSIDIARY OF ROXXON OIL--
--AND ROXXON DOES NOT TAKE KINDLY TO INVESTIGATIVE REPORTING!
AND, AS JONAH AND MARLA WALK AWAY, THE FIRE RAGES ON-- EVENTUALLY CONSUMING THE ENTIRE COMPLEX!
AND, WHILE THE FIRE-FIGHTERS VAINLY STRUGGLE TO SAVE A FEW OF THE BUILDINGS--
--NONE OF THEM NOTICE THE GLOWING BALL OF LIGHT WHICH SOARS UP OUT OF THE FLAMES...
ONLY ONE LONE FIGURE SEES IT GO.
WHAT HAVE WE DONE? HAVE WE SAVED A MAN... OR UNLEASHED A MONSTER?
SPIDER-MAN WILL ASK HIMSELF THAT QUESTION FOR THE NEXT 48 HOURS, BUT HE WILL FIND NO ANSWER IN... THE END!

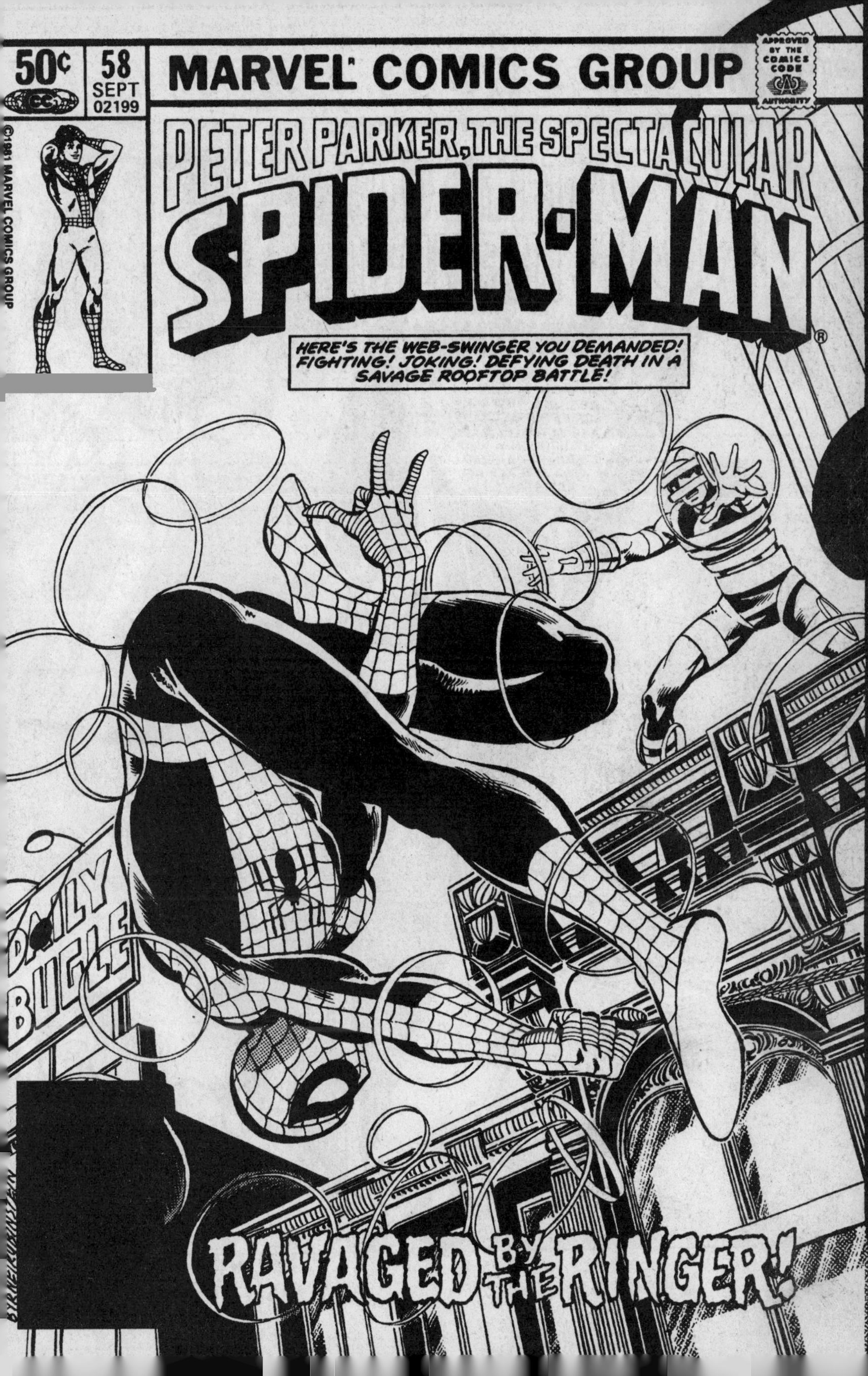

50¢
58
SEPT
02199
MARVEL COMICS GROUP
APPROVED BY THE COMICS CODE AUTHORITY
©1981 MARVEL COMICS GROUP
PETER PARKER, THE SPECTACULAR
SPIDER-MAN
HERE'S THE WEB-SWINGER YOU DEMANDED! FIGHTING! JOKING! DEFYING DEATH IN A SAVAGE ROOFTOP BATTLE!
DAILY BUGLE
RAVAGED BY THE RINGER!

While attending a demonstration in radiology, student PETER PARKER was bitten by a spider which had accidentally been exposed to RADIOACTIVE RAYS. Through a miracle of science, Peter gained the arachnid's powers... and in effect, became a human spider...

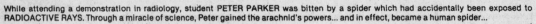

STAN LEE PRESENTS: THE SPECTACULAR SPIDER-MAN!®

RING OUT THE OLD, IN THE NEW!

I CAN'T BELIEVE THAT IT'S THE BEGINNING OF A NEW SEMESTER ALREADY! I'VE ACTUALLY MADE IT THROUGH A WHOLE TERM, AS A GRAD AND A TEACHING ASSISTANT!

SOMEHOW, I'VE SURVIVED THAT WHILE STILL PULLING IN A REASONABLE LIVING AS A FREE-LANCE PHOTOGRAPHER AND PLAYING SPIDER-MAN ON THE SIDE!

I MUST BE OUT OF MY MIND TO TRY LIVING FOUR LIVES AT ONCE! IT'S REALLY BEEN A HECKUVA STRAIN, BUT SOMEHOW I SEEM TO BE MAKING IT!

WRITER: ROGER STERN
PENCILER: JOHN BYRNE
INKER: VINCE COLLETTA
LETTERER: JEAN SIMEK
COLORIST: BEN SEAN
EDITOR: TOM DE FALCO
EDITOR-IN-CHIEF: JIM SHOOTER

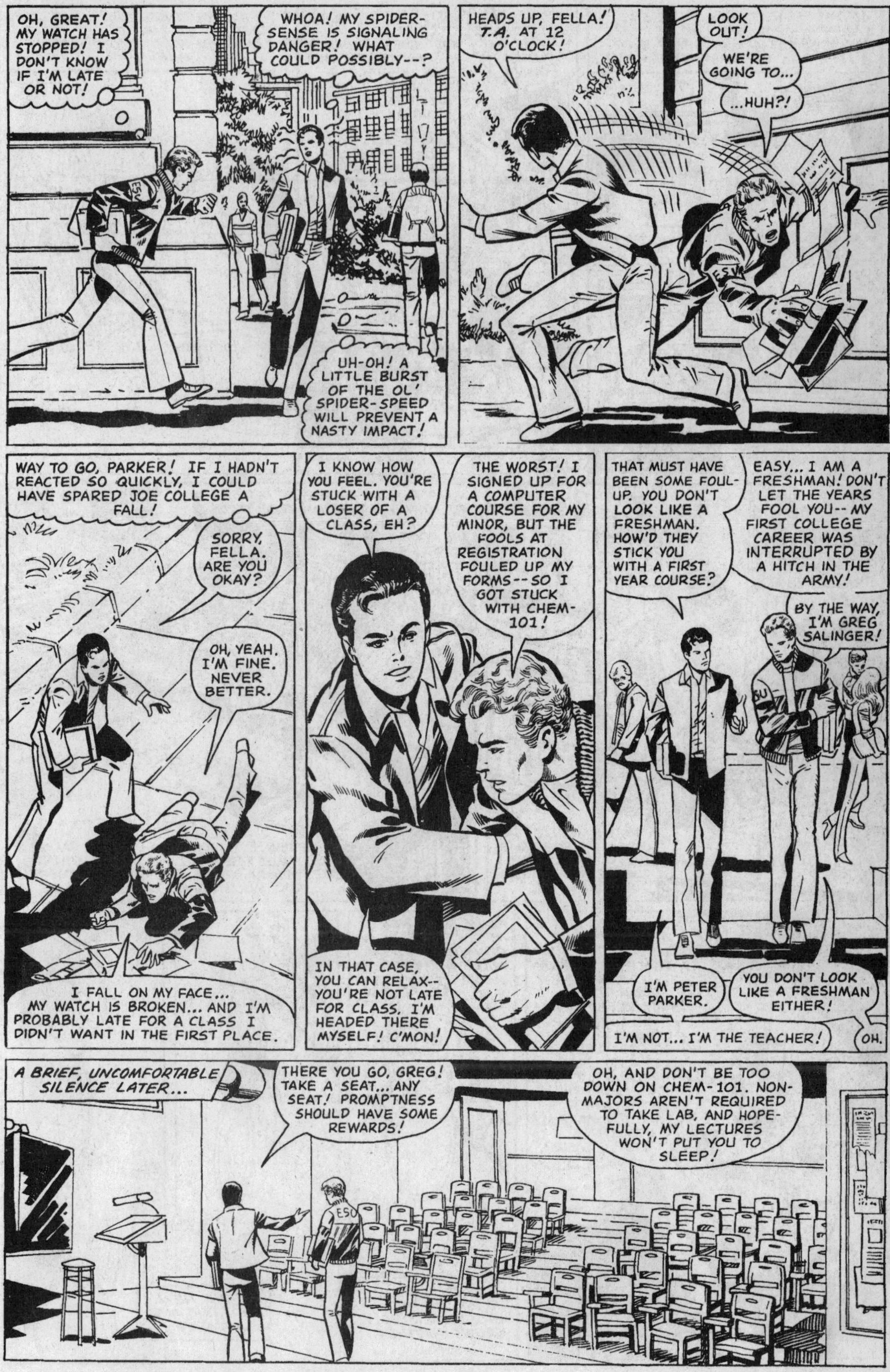

OH, GREAT! MY WATCH HAS STOPPED! I DON'T KNOW IF I'M LATE OR NOT!
WHOA! MY SPIDER-SENSE IS SIGNALING DANGER! WHAT COULD POSSIBLY--?
UH-OH! A LITTLE BURST OF THE OL' SPIDER-SPEED WILL PREVENT A NASTY IMPACT!
HEADS UP, FELLA! T.A. AT 12 O'CLOCK!
LOOK OUT!
WE'RE GOING TO...
...HUH?!
WAY TO GO, PARKER! IF I HADN'T REACTED SO QUICKLY, I COULD HAVE SPARED JOE COLLEGE A FALL!
SORRY, FELLA. ARE YOU OKAY?
OH, YEAH. I'M FINE. NEVER BETTER.
I FALL ON MY FACE... MY WATCH IS BROKEN... AND I'M PROBABLY LATE FOR A CLASS I DIDN'T WANT IN THE FIRST PLACE.
I KNOW HOW YOU FEEL. YOU'RE STUCK WITH A LOSER OF A CLASS, EH?
THE WORST! I SIGNED UP FOR A COMPUTER COURSE FOR MY MINOR, BUT THE FOOLS AT REGISTRATION FOULED UP MY FORMS--SO I GOT STUCK WITH CHEM-101!
IN THAT CASE, YOU CAN RELAX--YOU'RE NOT LATE FOR CLASS. I'M HEADED THERE MYSELF! C'MON!
THAT MUST HAVE BEEN SOME FOUL-UP. YOU DON'T LOOK LIKE A FRESHMAN. HOW'D THEY STICK YOU WITH A FIRST YEAR COURSE?
EASY... I AM A FRESHMAN! DON'T LET THE YEARS FOOL YOU--MY FIRST COLLEGE CAREER WAS INTERRUPTED BY A HITCH IN THE ARMY!
BY THE WAY, I'M GREG SALINGER!
I'M PETER PARKER.
YOU DON'T LOOK LIKE A FRESHMAN EITHER!
I'M NOT... I'M THE TEACHER!
OH.
A BRIEF, UNCOMFORTABLE SILENCE LATER...
THERE YOU GO, GREG! TAKE A SEAT... ANY SEAT! PROMPTNESS SHOULD HAVE SOME REWARDS!
OH, AND DON'T BE TOO DOWN ON CHEM-101. NON-MAJORS AREN'T REQUIRED TO TAKE LAB, AND HOPE-FULLY, MY LECTURES WON'T PUT YOU TO SLEEP!

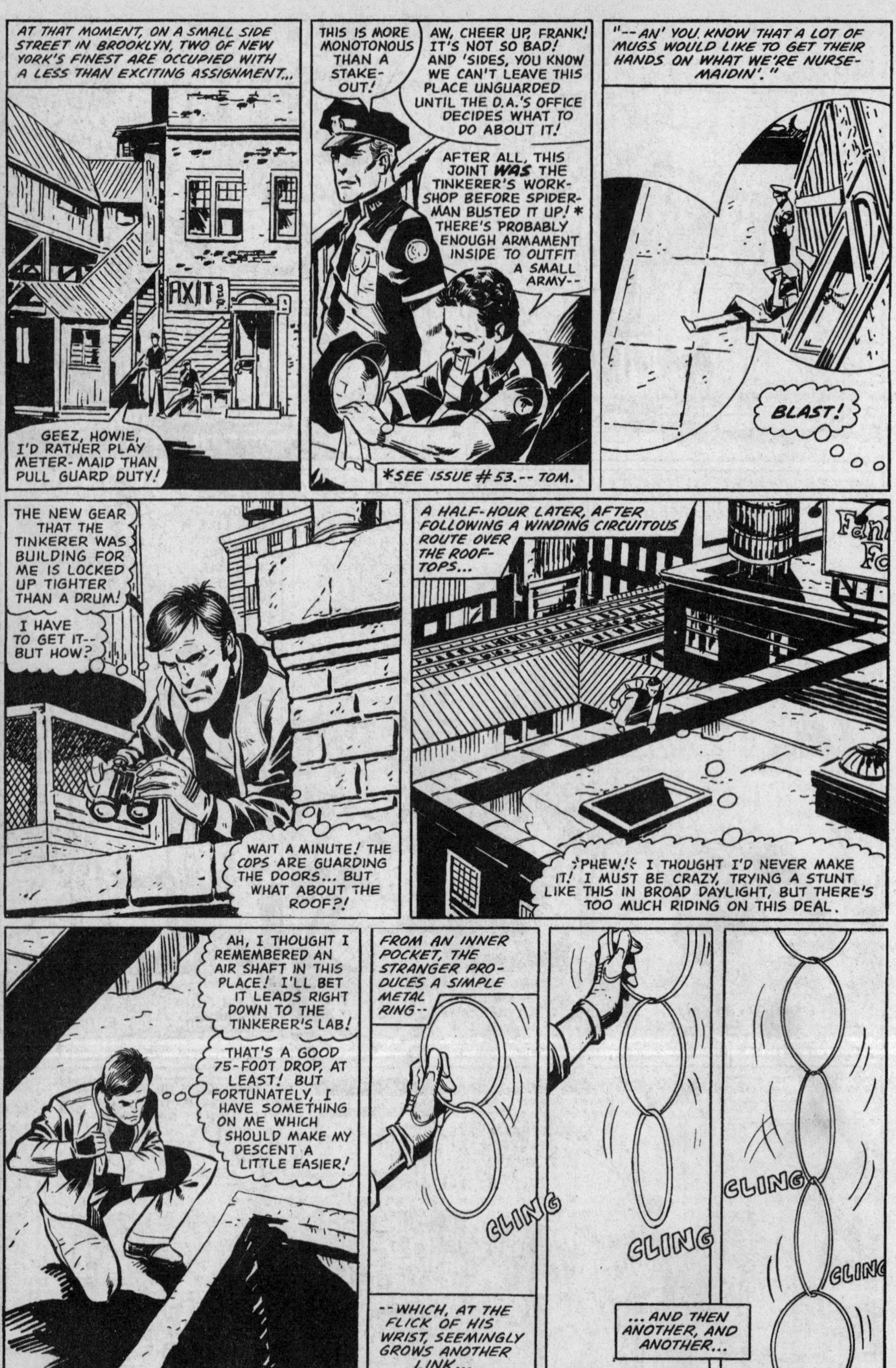

AT THAT MOMENT, ON A SMALL SIDE STREET IN BROOKLYN, TWO OF NEW YORK'S FINEST ARE OCCUPIED WITH A LESS THAN EXCITING ASSIGNMENT...
AXIT
GEEZ, HOWIE, I'D RATHER PLAY METER-MAID THAN PULL GUARD DUTY!
THIS IS MORE MONOTONOUS THAN A STAKE-OUT!
AW, CHEER UP, FRANK! IT'S NOT SO BAD! AND 'SIDES, YOU KNOW WE CAN'T LEAVE THIS PLACE UNGUARDED UNTIL THE D.A.'S OFFICE DECIDES WHAT TO DO ABOUT IT!
AFTER ALL, THIS JOINT WAS THE TINKERER'S WORK-SHOP BEFORE SPIDER-MAN BUSTED IT UP!* THERE'S PROBABLY ENOUGH ARMAMENT INSIDE TO OUTFIT A SMALL ARMY--
*SEE ISSUE #53.-- TOM.
"--AN' YOU KNOW THAT A LOT OF MUGS WOULD LIKE TO GET THEIR HANDS ON WHAT WE'RE NURSE-MAIDIN'."
BLAST!
THE NEW GEAR THAT THE TINKERER WAS BUILDING FOR ME IS LOCKED UP TIGHTER THAN A DRUM!
I HAVE TO GET IT-- BUT HOW?
WAIT A MINUTE! THE COPS ARE GUARDING THE DOORS... BUT WHAT ABOUT THE ROOF?!
A HALF-HOUR LATER, AFTER FOLLOWING A WINDING CIRCUITOUS ROUTE OVER THE ROOF-TOPS...
PHEW! I THOUGHT I'D NEVER MAKE IT! I MUST BE CRAZY, TRYING A STUNT LIKE THIS IN BROAD DAYLIGHT, BUT THERE'S TOO MUCH RIDING ON THIS DEAL.
AH, I THOUGHT I REMEMBERED AN AIR SHAFT IN THIS PLACE! I'LL BET IT LEADS RIGHT DOWN TO THE TINKERER'S LAB!
THAT'S A GOOD 75-FOOT DROP, AT LEAST! BUT FORTUNATELY, I HAVE SOMETHING ON ME WHICH SHOULD MAKE MY DESCENT A LITTLE EASIER!
FROM AN INNER POCKET, THE STRANGER PRODUCES A SIMPLE METAL RING--
CLING
--WHICH, AT THE FLICK OF HIS WRIST, SEEMINGLY GROWS ANOTHER LINK...
CLING
CLING
CLING
...AND THEN ANOTHER, AND ANOTHER...

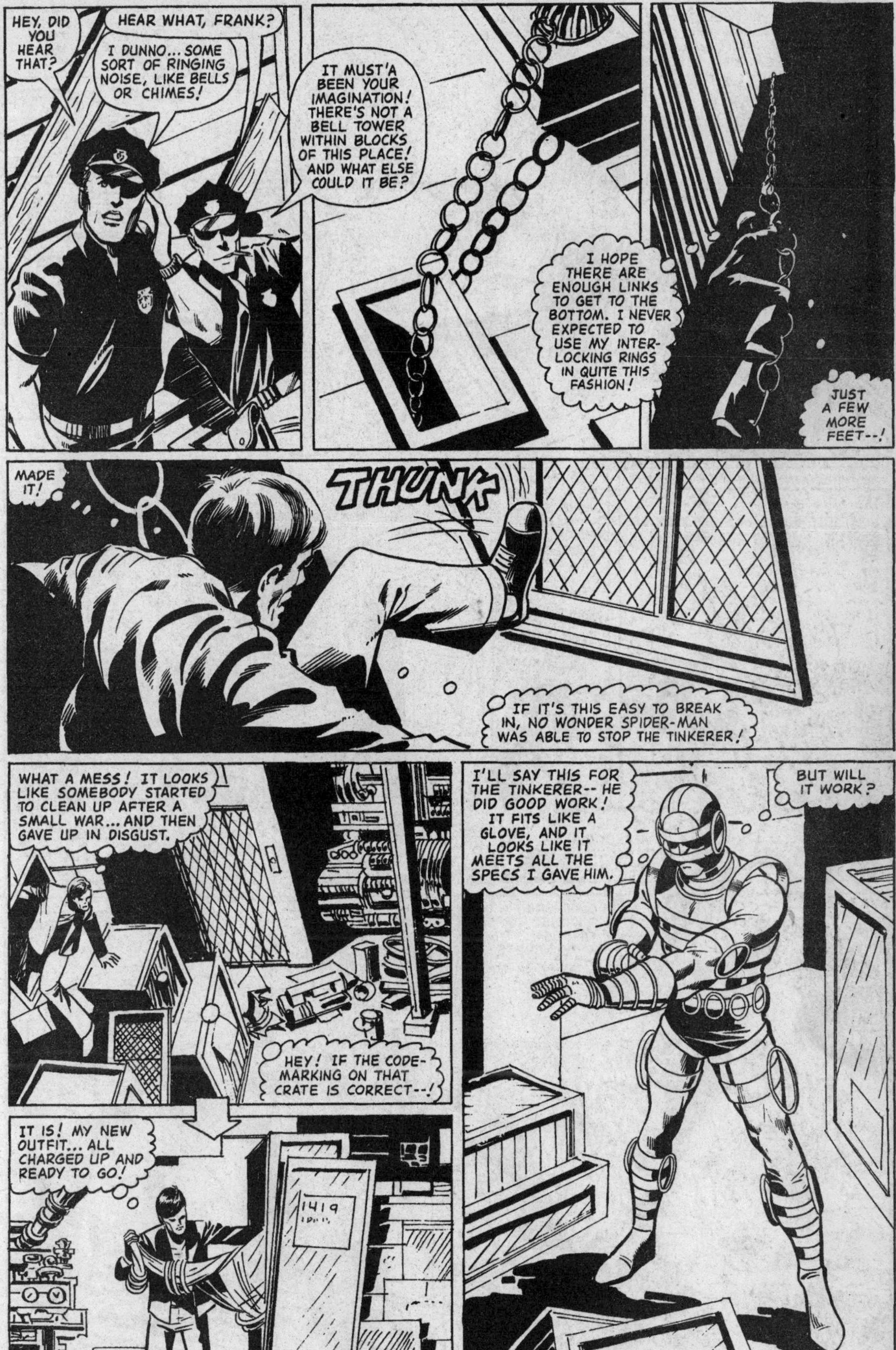
HEY, DID YOU HEAR THAT?
HEAR WHAT, FRANK?
I DUNNO... SOME SORT OF RINGING NOISE, LIKE BELLS OR CHIMES!
IT MUST'A BEEN YOUR IMAGINATION! THERE'S NOT A BELL TOWER WITHIN BLOCKS OF THIS PLACE! AND WHAT ELSE COULD IT BE?
I HOPE THERE ARE ENOUGH LINKS TO GET TO THE BOTTOM. I NEVER EXPECTED TO USE MY INTER-LOCKING RINGS IN QUITE THIS FASHION!
JUST A FEW MORE FEET--!
MADE IT!
THUNK
IF IT'S THIS EASY TO BREAK IN, NO WONDER SPIDER-MAN WAS ABLE TO STOP THE TINKERER!
WHAT A MESS! IT LOOKS LIKE SOMEBODY STARTED TO CLEAN UP AFTER A SMALL WAR... AND THEN GAVE UP IN DISGUST.
HEY! IF THE CODE-MARKING ON THAT CRATE IS CORRECT--!
IT IS! MY NEW OUTFIT... ALL CHARGED UP AND READY TO GO!
1419
I'LL SAY THIS FOR THE TINKERER-- HE DID GOOD WORK! IT FITS LIKE A GLOVE, AND IT LOOKS LIKE IT MEETS ALL THE SPECS I GAVE HIM.
BUT WILL IT WORK?

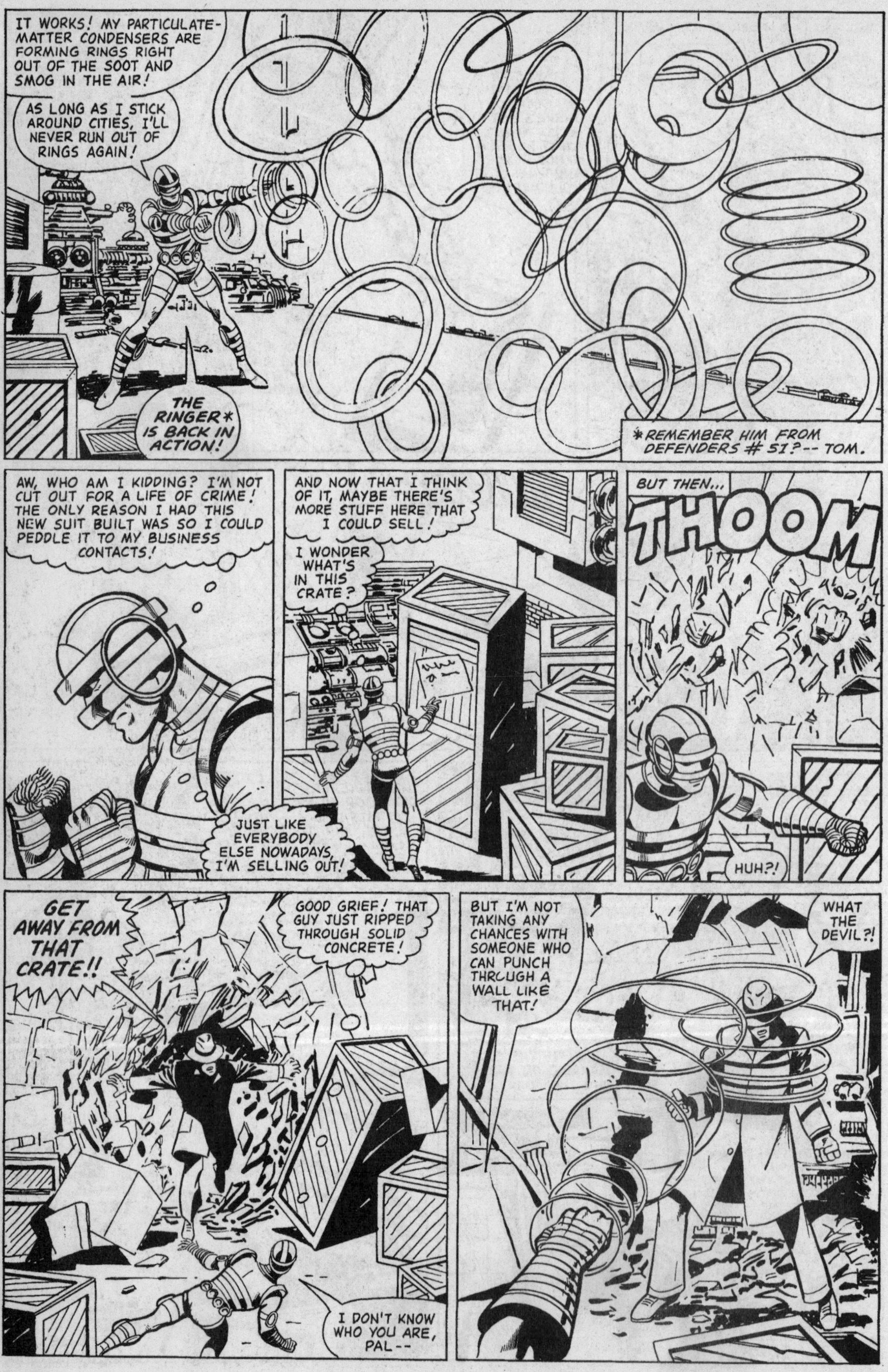
IT WORKS! MY PARTICULATE-MATTER CONDENSERS ARE FORMING RINGS RIGHT OUT OF THE SOOT AND SMOG IN THE AIR!
AS LONG AS I STICK AROUND CITIES, I'LL NEVER RUN OUT OF RINGS AGAIN!
THE RINGER* IS BACK IN ACTION!
*REMEMBER HIM FROM DEFENDERS # 51?-- TOM.
AW, WHO AM I KIDDING? I'M NOT CUT OUT FOR A LIFE OF CRIME! THE ONLY REASON I HAD THIS NEW SUIT BUILT WAS SO I COULD PEDDLE IT TO MY BUSINESS CONTACTS!
AND NOW THAT I THINK OF IT, MAYBE THERE'S MORE STUFF HERE THAT I COULD SELL!
I WONDER WHAT'S IN THIS CRATE?
JUST LIKE EVERYBODY ELSE NOWADAYS, I'M SELLING OUT!
BUT THEN...
THOOM
HUH?!
GET AWAY FROM THAT CRATE!!
GOOD GRIEF! THAT GUY JUST RIPPED THROUGH SOLID CONCRETE!
I DON'T KNOW WHO YOU ARE, PAL--
BUT I'M NOT TAKING ANY CHANCES WITH SOMEONE WHO CAN PUNCH THROUGH A WALL LIKE THAT!
WHAT THE DEVIL?!

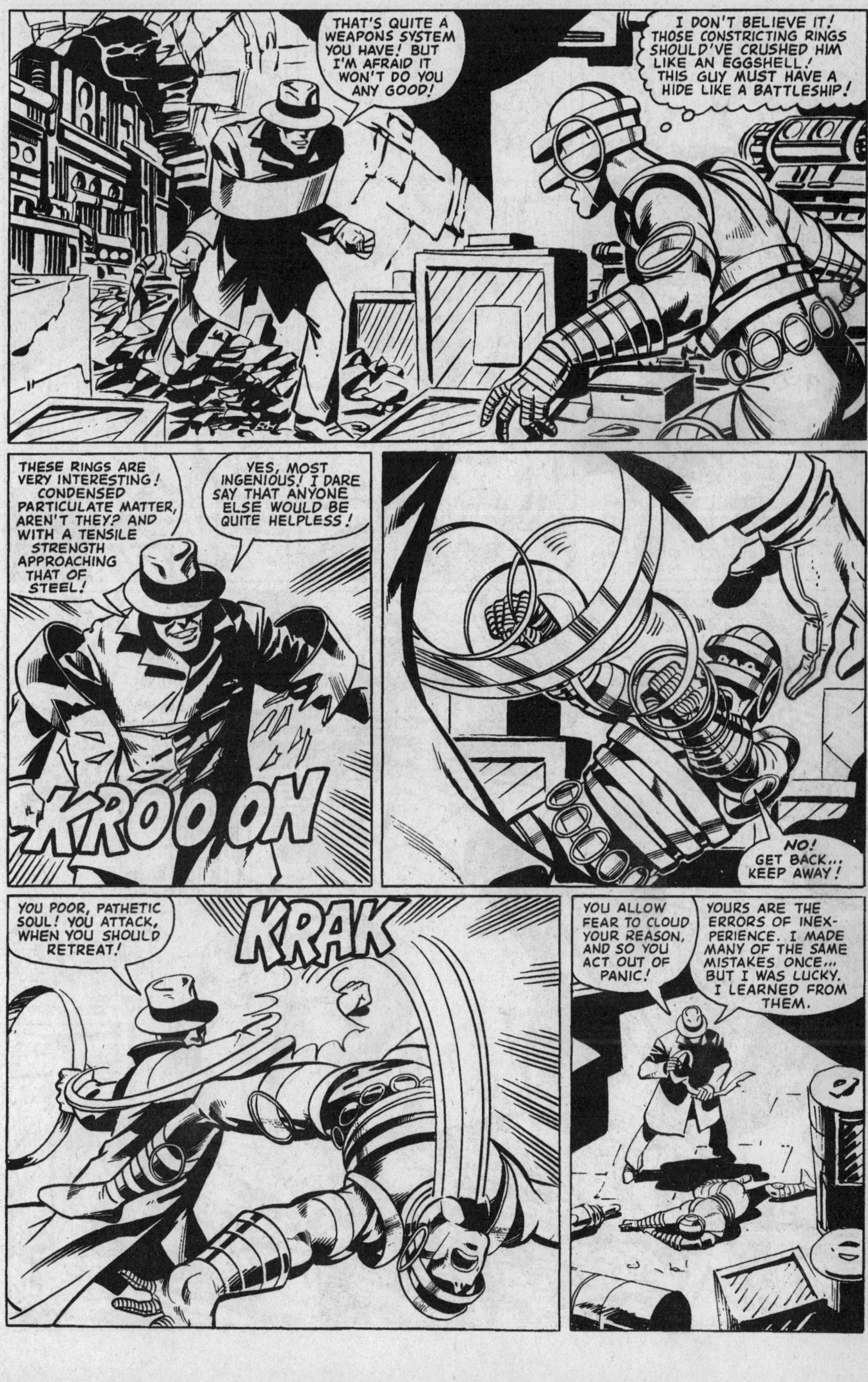
THAT'S QUITE A WEAPONS SYSTEM YOU HAVE! BUT I'M AFRAID IT WON'T DO YOU ANY GOOD!
I DON'T BELIEVE IT! THOSE CONSTRICTING RINGS SHOULD'VE CRUSHED HIM LIKE AN EGGSHELL! THIS GUY MUST HAVE A HIDE LIKE A BATTLESHIP!
THESE RINGS ARE VERY INTERESTING! CONDENSED PARTICULATE MATTER, AREN'T THEY? AND WITH A TENSILE STRENGTH APPROACHING THAT OF STEEL!
YES, MOST INGENIOUS! I DARE SAY THAT ANYONE ELSE WOULD BE QUITE HELPLESS!
KROO OM
NO! GET BACK... KEEP AWAY!
YOU POOR, PATHETIC SOUL! YOU ATTACK, WHEN YOU SHOULD RETREAT!
KRAK
YOU ALLOW FEAR TO CLOUD YOUR REASON, AND SO YOU ACT OUT OF PANIC!
YOURS ARE THE ERRORS OF INEX-PERIENCE. I MADE MANY OF THE SAME MISTAKES ONCE... BUT I WAS LUCKY. I LEARNED FROM THEM.

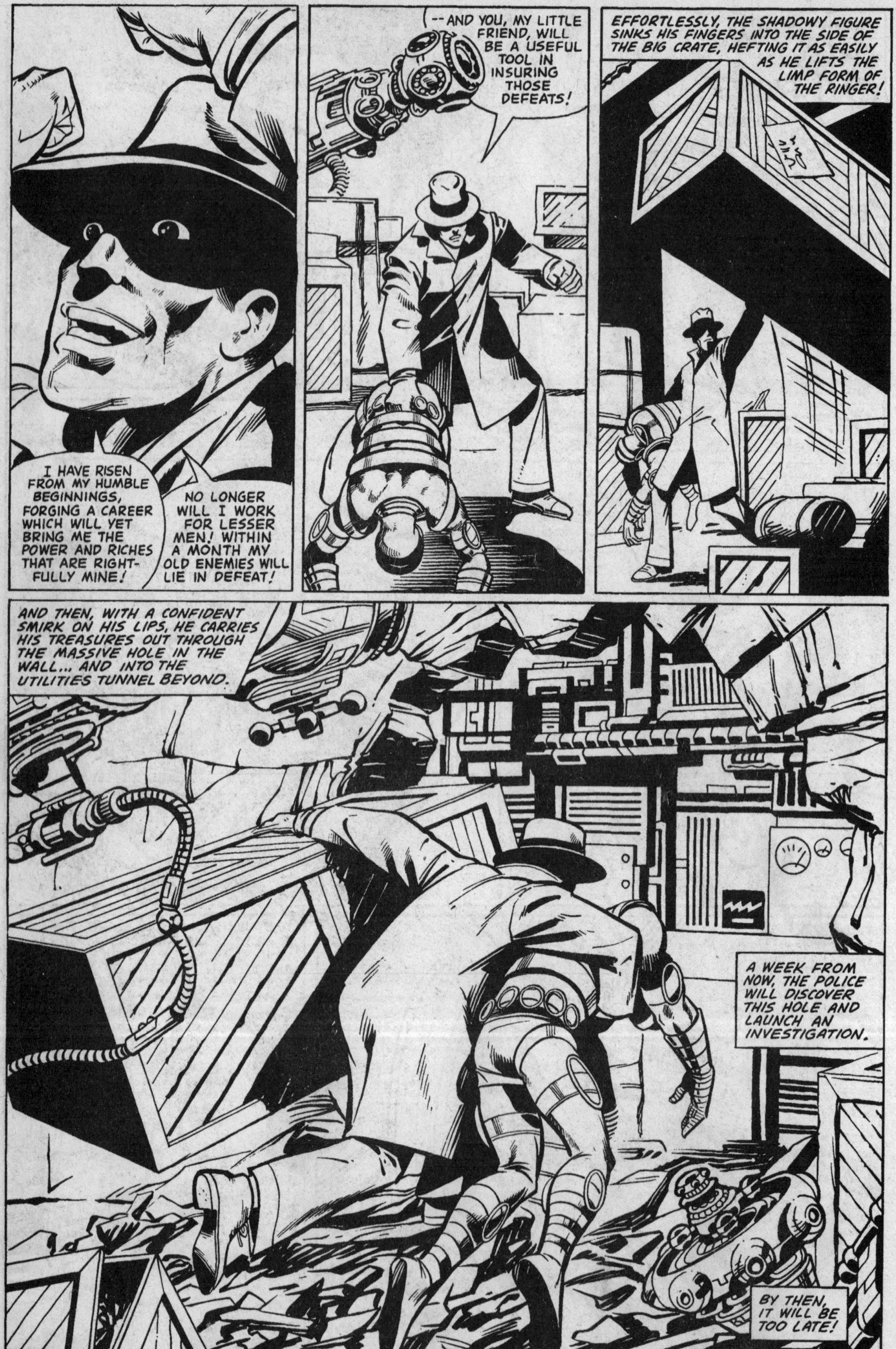
I HAVE RISEN FROM MY HUMBLE BEGINNINGS, FORGING A CAREER WHICH WILL YET BRING ME THE POWER AND RICHES THAT ARE RIGHTFULLY MINE!
NO LONGER WILL I WORK FOR LESSER MEN! WITHIN A MONTH MY OLD ENEMIES WILL LIE IN DEFEAT!
--AND YOU, MY LITTLE FRIEND, WILL BE A USEFUL TOOL IN INSURING THOSE DEFEATS!
EFFORTLESSLY, THE SHADOWY FIGURE SINKS HIS FINGERS INTO THE SIDE OF THE BIG CRATE, HEFTING IT AS EASILY AS HE LIFTS THE LIMP FORM OF THE RINGER!
AND THEN, WITH A CONFIDENT SMIRK ON HIS LIPS, HE CARRIES HIS TREASURES OUT THROUGH THE MASSIVE HOLE IN THE WALL... AND INTO THE UTILITIES TUNNEL BEYOND.
A WEEK FROM NOW, THE POLICE WILL DISCOVER THIS HOLE AND LAUNCH AN INVESTIGATION.
BY THEN, IT WILL BE TOO LATE!

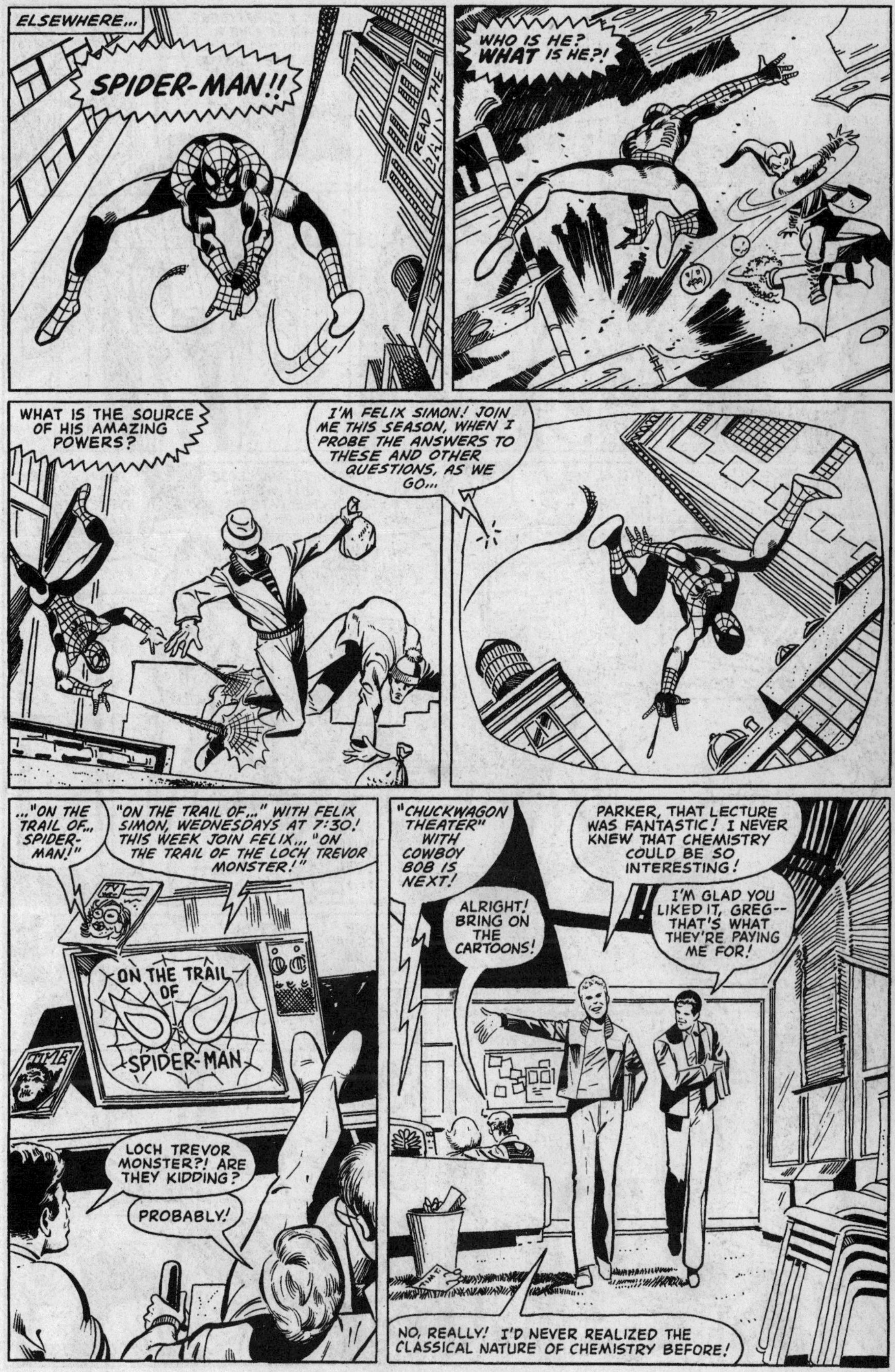
ELSEWHERE...
SPIDER-MAN!!
READ THE DAILY
WHO IS HE? WHAT IS HE?!
WHAT IS THE SOURCE OF HIS AMAZING POWERS?
I'M FELIX SIMON! JOIN ME THIS SEASON, WHEN I PROBE THE ANSWERS TO THESE AND OTHER QUESTIONS, AS WE GO...
..."ON THE TRAIL OF... SPIDER-MAN!"
"ON THE TRAIL OF..." WITH FELIX SIMON, WEDNESDAYS AT 7:30! THIS WEEK JOIN FELIX... "ON THE TRAIL OF THE LOCH TREVOR MONSTER!"
ON THE TRAIL OF SPIDER-MAN
TIME
LOCH TREVOR MONSTER?! ARE THEY KIDDING?
PROBABLY!
"CHUCKWAGON THEATER" WITH COWBOY BOB IS NEXT!
ALRIGHT! BRING ON THE CARTOONS!
PARKER, THAT LECTURE WAS FANTASTIC! I NEVER KNEW THAT CHEMISTRY COULD BE SO INTERESTING!
I'M GLAD YOU LIKED IT, GREG-- THAT'S WHAT THEY'RE PAYING ME FOR!
NO, REALLY! I'D NEVER REALIZED THE CLASSICAL NATURE OF CHEMISTRY BEFORE!

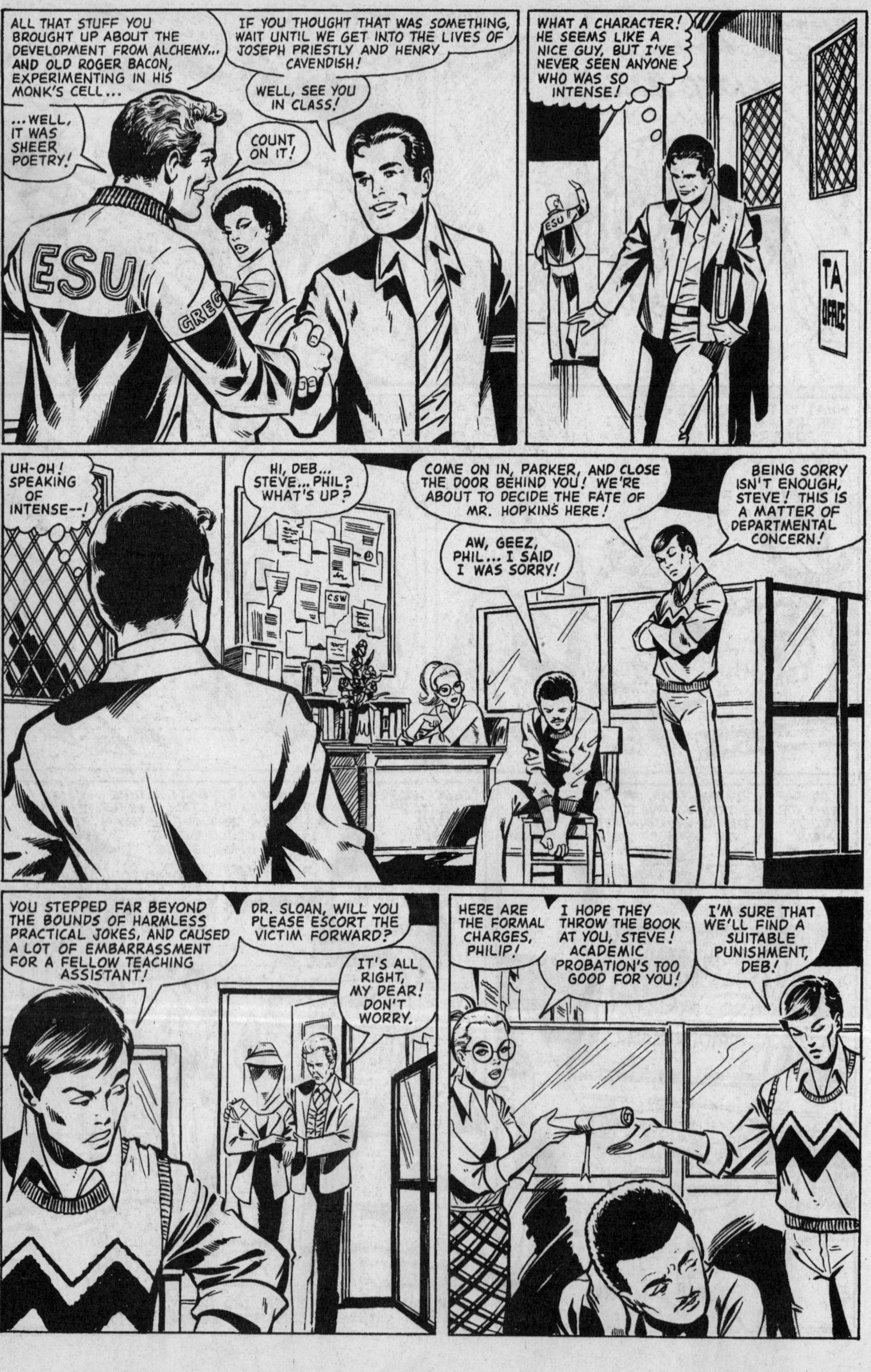

ALL THAT STUFF YOU BROUGHT UP ABOUT THE DEVELOPMENT FROM ALCHEMY... AND OLD ROGER BACON, EXPERIMENTING IN HIS MONK'S CELL...
...WELL, IT WAS SHEER POETRY!
IF YOU THOUGHT THAT WAS SOMETHING, WAIT UNTIL WE GET INTO THE LIVES OF JOSEPH PRIESTLY AND HENRY CAVENDISH!
WELL, SEE YOU IN CLASS!
COUNT ON IT!
ESU
GREG
WHAT A CHARACTER! HE SEEMS LIKE A NICE GUY, BUT I'VE NEVER SEEN ANYONE WHO WAS SO INTENSE!
ESU
TA OFFICE
UH-OH! SPEAKING OF INTENSE--!
HI, DEB... STEVE... PHIL? WHAT'S UP?
COME ON IN, PARKER, AND CLOSE THE DOOR BEHIND YOU! WE'RE ABOUT TO DECIDE THE FATE OF MR. HOPKINS HERE!
AW, GEEZ, PHIL... I SAID I WAS SORRY!
BEING SORRY ISN'T ENOUGH, STEVE! THIS IS A MATTER OF DEPARTMENTAL CONCERN!
CSW
YOU STEPPED FAR BEYOND THE BOUNDS OF HARMLESS PRACTICAL JOKES, AND CAUSED A LOT OF EMBARRASSMENT FOR A FELLOW TEACHING ASSISTANT!
DR. SLOAN, WILL YOU PLEASE ESCORT THE VICTIM FORWARD?
IT'S ALL RIGHT, MY DEAR! DON'T WORRY.
HERE ARE THE FORMAL CHARGES, PHILIP!
I HOPE THEY THROW THE BOOK AT YOU, STEVE! ACADEMIC PROBATION'S TOO GOOD FOR YOU!
I'M SURE THAT WE'LL FIND A SUITABLE PUNISHMENT, DEB!

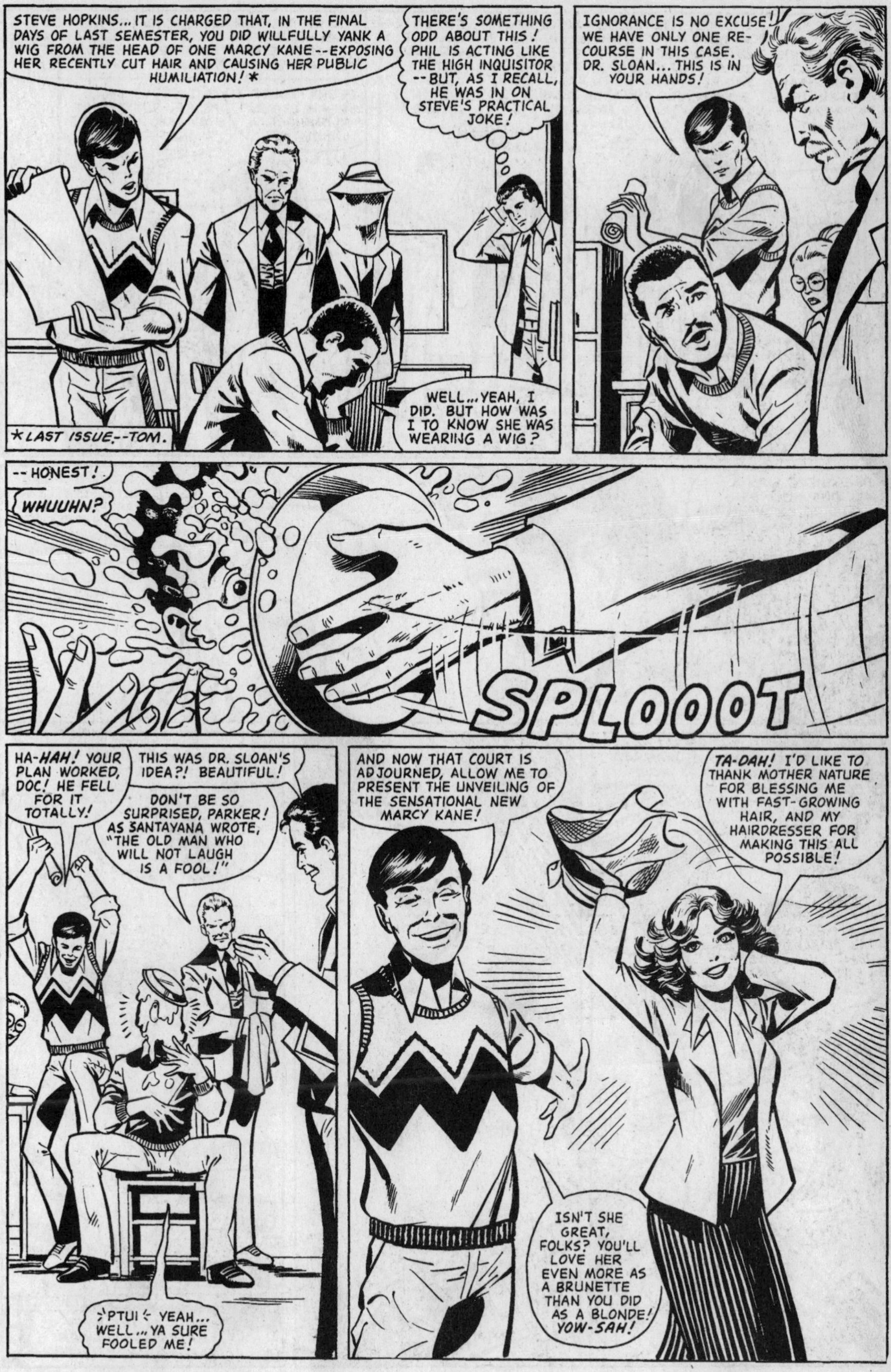
STEVE HOPKINS... IT IS CHARGED THAT, IN THE FINAL DAYS OF LAST SEMESTER, YOU DID WILLFULLY YANK A WIG FROM THE HEAD OF ONE MARCY KANE--EXPOSING HER RECENTLY CUT HAIR AND CAUSING HER PUBLIC HUMILIATION! *
THERE'S SOMETHING ODD ABOUT THIS! PHIL IS ACTING LIKE THE HIGH INQUISITOR --BUT, AS I RECALL, HE WAS IN ON STEVE'S PRACTICAL JOKE!
WELL... YEAH, I DID. BUT HOW WAS I TO KNOW SHE WAS WEARING A WIG?
*LAST ISSUE.--TOM.
IGNORANCE IS NO EXCUSE! WE HAVE ONLY ONE RECOURSE IN THIS CASE. DR. SLOAN... THIS IS IN YOUR HANDS!
--HONEST!
WHUUHN?
SPLOOOT
HA-HAH! YOUR PLAN WORKED, DOC! HE FELL FOR IT TOTALLY!
THIS WAS DR. SLOAN'S IDEA?! BEAUTIFUL!
DON'T BE SO SURPRISED, PARKER! AS SANTAYANA WROTE, "THE OLD MAN WHO WILL NOT LAUGH IS A FOOL!"
PTUI YEAH... WELL... YA SURE FOOLED ME!
AND NOW THAT COURT IS ADJOURNED, ALLOW ME TO PRESENT THE UNVEILING OF THE SENSATIONAL NEW MARCY KANE!
TA-DAH! I'D LIKE TO THANK MOTHER NATURE FOR BLESSING ME WITH FAST-GROWING HAIR, AND MY HAIRDRESSER FOR MAKING THIS ALL POSSIBLE!
ISN'T SHE GREAT, FOLKS? YOU'LL LOVE HER EVEN MORE AS A BRUNETTE THAN YOU DID AS A BLONDE! YOW-SAH!

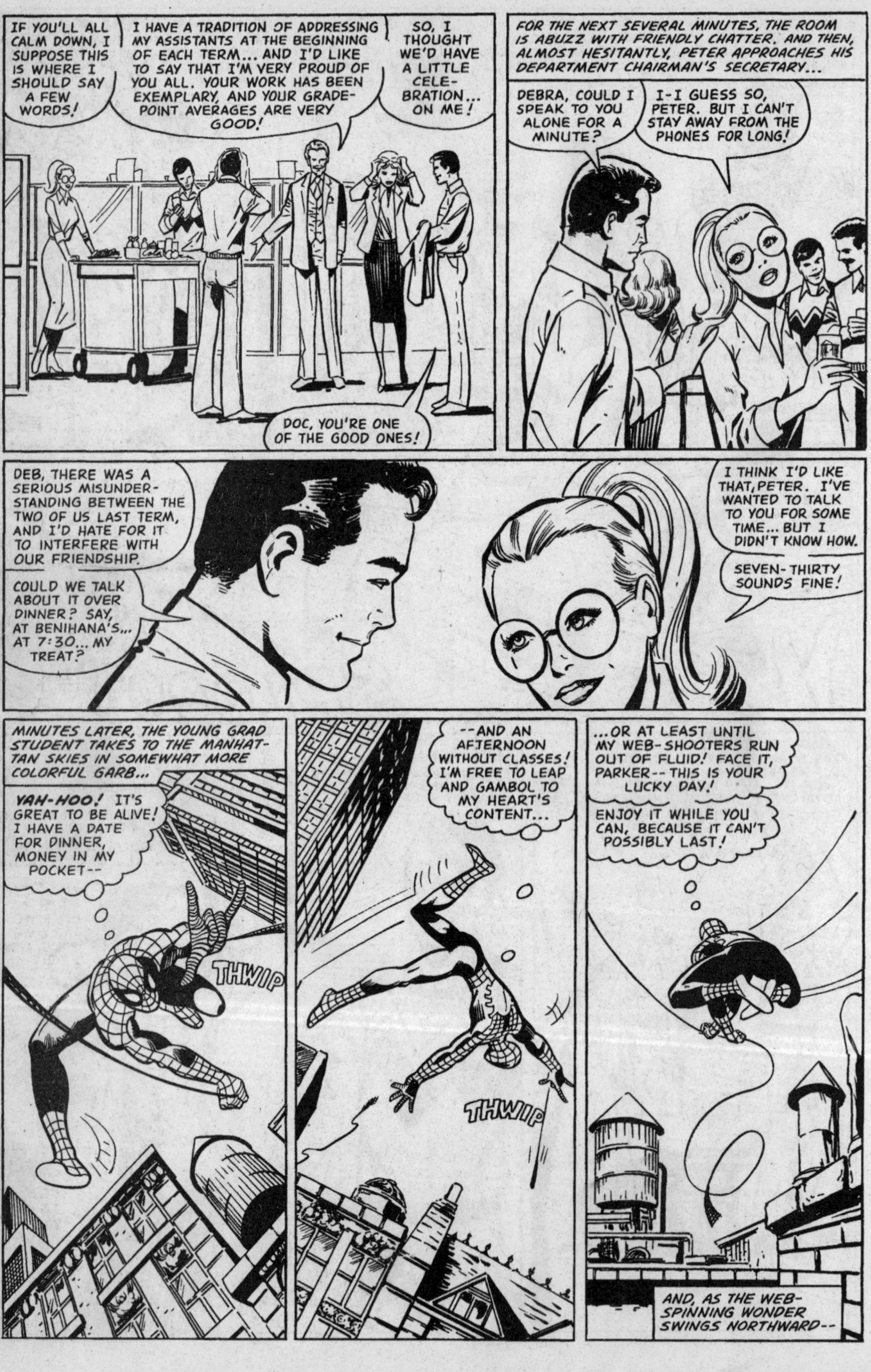
IF YOU'LL ALL CALM DOWN, I SUPPOSE THIS IS WHERE I SHOULD SAY A FEW WORDS!
I HAVE A TRADITION OF ADDRESSING MY ASSISTANTS AT THE BEGINNING OF EACH TERM... AND I'D LIKE TO SAY THAT I'M VERY PROUD OF YOU ALL. YOUR WORK HAS BEEN EXEMPLARY, AND YOUR GRADE-POINT AVERAGES ARE VERY GOOD!
SO, I THOUGHT WE'D HAVE A LITTLE CELE-BRATION... ON ME!
DOC, YOU'RE ONE OF THE GOOD ONES!
FOR THE NEXT SEVERAL MINUTES, THE ROOM IS ABUZZ WITH FRIENDLY CHATTER. AND THEN, ALMOST HESITANTLY, PETER APPROACHES HIS DEPARTMENT CHAIRMAN'S SECRETARY...
DEBRA, COULD I SPEAK TO YOU ALONE FOR A MINUTE?
I-I GUESS SO, PETER. BUT I CAN'T STAY AWAY FROM THE PHONES FOR LONG!
DEB, THERE WAS A SERIOUS MISUNDER-STANDING BETWEEN THE TWO OF US LAST TERM, AND I'D HATE FOR IT TO INTERFERE WITH OUR FRIENDSHIP.
COULD WE TALK ABOUT IT OVER DINNER? SAY, AT BENIHANA'S... AT 7:30... MY TREAT?
I THINK I'D LIKE THAT, PETER. I'VE WANTED TO TALK TO YOU FOR SOME TIME... BUT I DIDN'T KNOW HOW.
SEVEN-THIRTY SOUNDS FINE!
MINUTES LATER, THE YOUNG GRAD STUDENT TAKES TO THE MANHAT-TAN SKIES IN SOMEWHAT MORE COLORFUL GARB...
YAH-HOO! IT'S GREAT TO BE ALIVE! I HAVE A DATE FOR DINNER, MONEY IN MY POCKET--
THWIP
--AND AN AFTERNOON WITHOUT CLASSES! I'M FREE TO LEAP AND GAMBOL TO MY HEART'S CONTENT...
THWIP
...OR AT LEAST UNTIL MY WEB-SHOOTERS RUN OUT OF FLUID! FACE IT, PARKER-- THIS IS YOUR LUCKY DAY!
ENJOY IT WHILE YOU CAN, BECAUSE IT CAN'T POSSIBLY LAST!
AND, AS THE WEB-SPINNING WONDER SWINGS NORTHWARD--

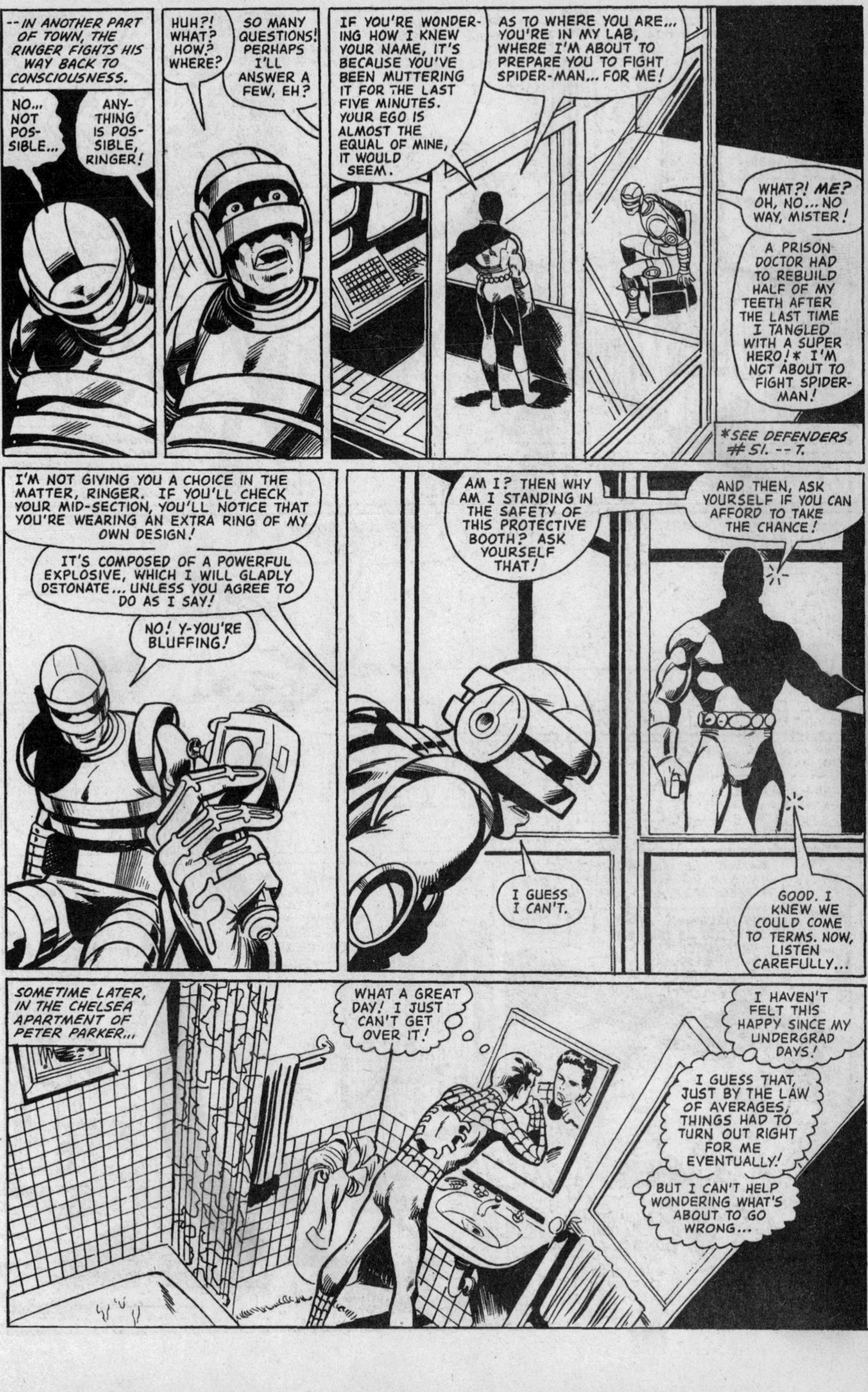

--IN ANOTHER PART OF TOWN, THE RINGER FIGHTS HIS WAY BACK TO CONSCIOUSNESS.
NO... NOT POSSIBLE...
ANYTHING IS POSSIBLE, RINGER!
HUH?! WHAT? HOW? WHERE?
SO MANY QUESTIONS! PERHAPS I'LL ANSWER A FEW, EH?
IF YOU'RE WONDERING HOW I KNEW YOUR NAME, IT'S BECAUSE YOU'VE BEEN MUTTERING IT FOR THE LAST FIVE MINUTES. YOUR EGO IS ALMOST THE EQUAL OF MINE, IT WOULD SEEM.
AS TO WHERE YOU ARE... YOU'RE IN MY LAB, WHERE I'M ABOUT TO PREPARE YOU TO FIGHT SPIDER-MAN... FOR ME!
WHAT?! ME? OH, NO... NO WAY, MISTER!
A PRISON DOCTOR HAD TO REBUILD HALF OF MY TEETH AFTER THE LAST TIME I TANGLED WITH A SUPER HERO!* I'M NOT ABOUT TO FIGHT SPIDER-MAN!
*SEE DEFENDERS #51. --T.
I'M NOT GIVING YOU A CHOICE IN THE MATTER, RINGER. IF YOU'LL CHECK YOUR MID-SECTION, YOU'LL NOTICE THAT YOU'RE WEARING AN EXTRA RING OF MY OWN DESIGN!
IT'S COMPOSED OF A POWERFUL EXPLOSIVE, WHICH I WILL GLADLY DETONATE... UNLESS YOU AGREE TO DO AS I SAY!
NO! Y-YOU'RE BLUFFING!
AM I? THEN WHY AM I STANDING IN THE SAFETY OF THIS PROTECTIVE BOOTH? ASK YOURSELF THAT!
AND THEN, ASK YOURSELF IF YOU CAN AFFORD TO TAKE THE CHANCE!
I GUESS I CAN'T.
GOOD. I KNEW WE COULD COME TO TERMS. NOW, LISTEN CAREFULLY...
SOMETIME LATER, IN THE CHELSEA APARTMENT OF PETER PARKER...
WHAT A GREAT DAY! I JUST CAN'T GET OVER IT!
I HAVEN'T FELT THIS HAPPY SINCE MY UNDERGRAD DAYS!
I GUESS THAT, JUST BY THE LAW OF AVERAGES, THINGS HAD TO TURN OUT RIGHT FOR ME EVENTUALLY!
BUT I CAN'T HELP WONDERING WHAT'S ABOUT TO GO WRONG...

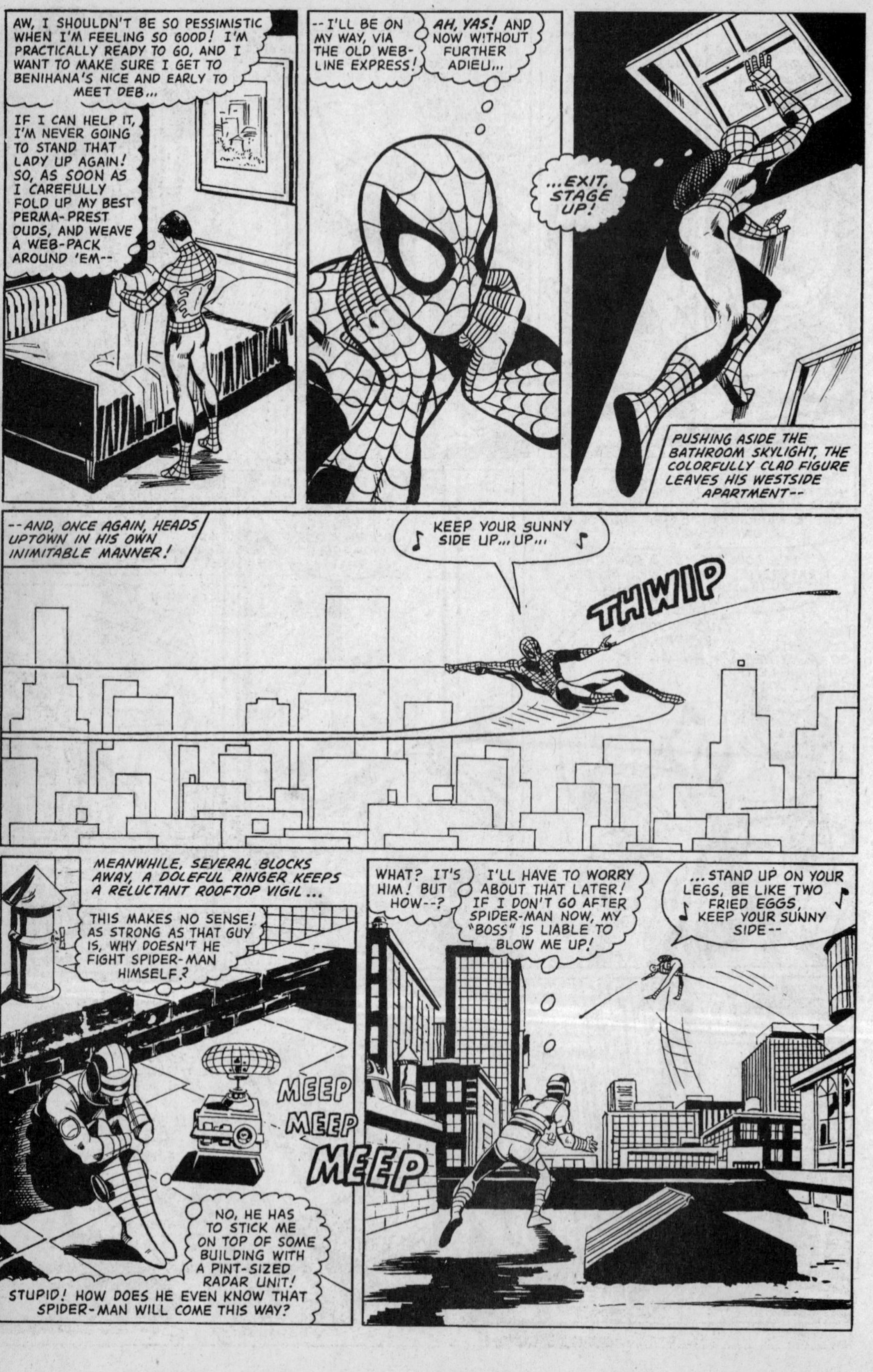
AW, I SHOULDN'T BE SO PESSIMISTIC WHEN I'M FEELING SO GOOD! I'M PRACTICALLY READY TO GO, AND I WANT TO MAKE SURE I GET TO BENIHANA'S NICE AND EARLY TO MEET DEB...
IF I CAN HELP IT, I'M NEVER GOING TO STAND THAT LADY UP AGAIN! SO, AS SOON AS I CAREFULLY FOLD UP MY BEST PERMA-PREST DUDS, AND WEAVE A WEB-PACK AROUND 'EM--
--I'LL BE ON MY WAY, VIA THE OLD WEB-LINE EXPRESS!
AH, YAS! AND NOW WITHOUT FURTHER ADIEU...
...EXIT, STAGE UP!
PUSHING ASIDE THE BATHROOM SKYLIGHT, THE COLORFULLY CLAD FIGURE LEAVES HIS WESTSIDE APARTMENT--
--AND, ONCE AGAIN, HEADS UPTOWN IN HIS OWN INIMITABLE MANNER!
♪ KEEP YOUR SUNNY SIDE UP... UP... ♪
THWIP
MEANWHILE, SEVERAL BLOCKS AWAY, A DOLEFUL RINGER KEEPS A RELUCTANT ROOFTOP VIGIL...
THIS MAKES NO SENSE! AS STRONG AS THAT GUY IS, WHY DOESN'T HE FIGHT SPIDER-MAN HIMSELF?
MEEP
MEEP
MEEP
NO, HE HAS TO STICK ME ON TOP OF SOME BUILDING WITH A PINT-SIZED RADAR UNIT!
STUPID! HOW DOES HE EVEN KNOW THAT SPIDER-MAN WILL COME THIS WAY?
WHAT? IT'S HIM! BUT HOW--?
I'LL HAVE TO WORRY ABOUT THAT LATER! IF I DON'T GO AFTER SPIDER-MAN NOW, MY "BOSS" IS LIABLE TO BLOW ME UP!
...STAND UP ON YOUR LEGS, BE LIKE TWO FRIED EGGS, ♪ KEEP YOUR SUNNY SIDE-- ♪

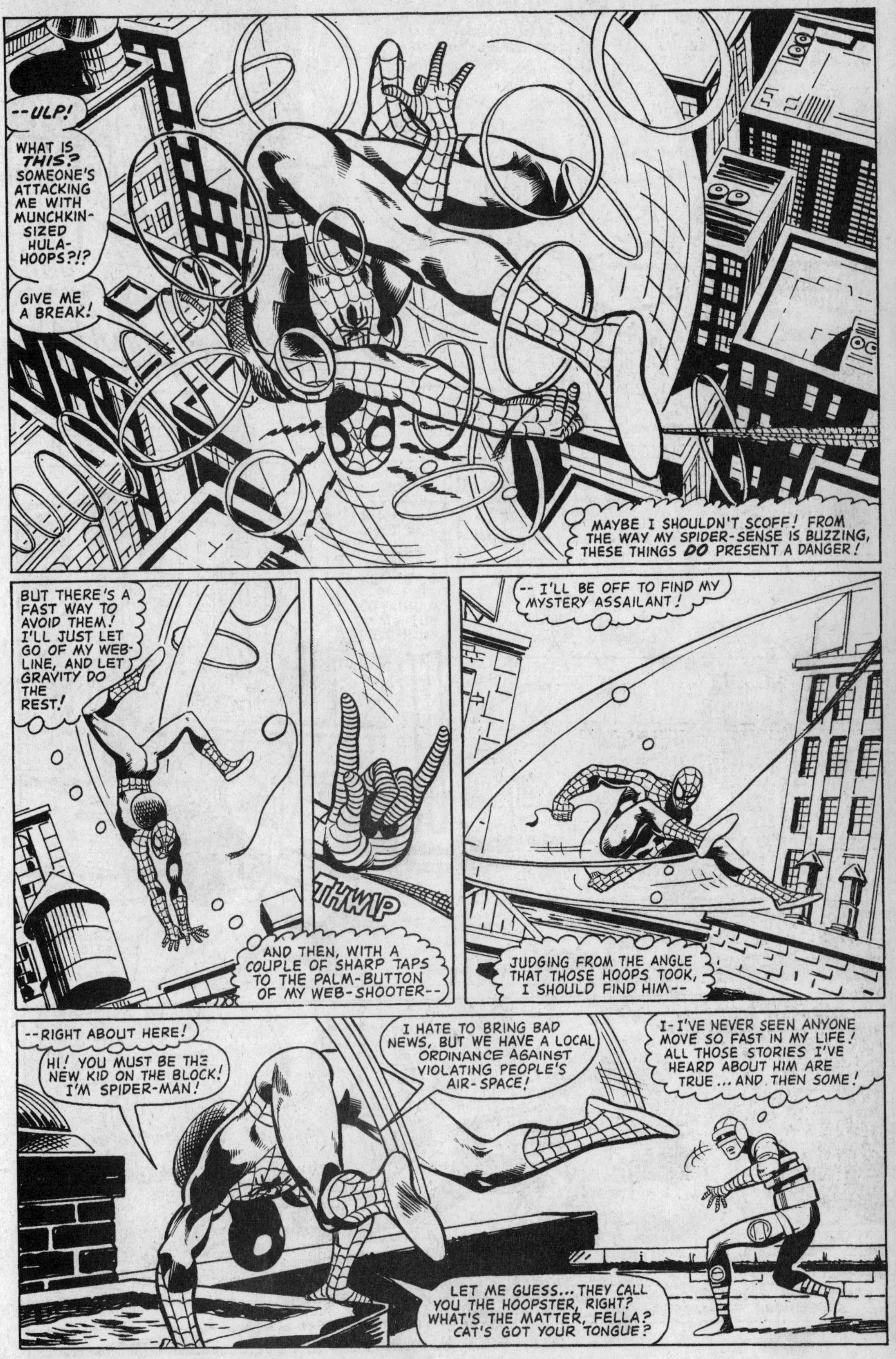
--ULP!
WHAT IS THIS? SOMEONE'S ATTACKING ME WITH MUNCHKIN-SIZED HULA-HOOPS?!?
GIVE ME A BREAK!
MAYBE I SHOULDN'T SCOFF! FROM THE WAY MY SPIDER-SENSE IS BUZZING, THESE THINGS DO PRESENT A DANGER!
BUT THERE'S A FAST WAY TO AVOID THEM! I'LL JUST LET GO OF MY WEB-LINE, AND LET GRAVITY DO THE REST!
THWIP
AND THEN, WITH A COUPLE OF SHARP TAPS TO THE PALM-BUTTON OF MY WEB-SHOOTER--
-- I'LL BE OFF TO FIND MY MYSTERY ASSAILANT!
JUDGING FROM THE ANGLE THAT THOSE HOOPS TOOK, I SHOULD FIND HIM--
--RIGHT ABOUT HERE!
HI! YOU MUST BE THE NEW KID ON THE BLOCK! I'M SPIDER-MAN!
I HATE TO BRING BAD NEWS, BUT WE HAVE A LOCAL ORDINANCE AGAINST VIOLATING PEOPLE'S AIR-SPACE!
I-I'VE NEVER SEEN ANYONE MOVE SO FAST IN MY LIFE! ALL THOSE STORIES I'VE HEARD ABOUT HIM ARE TRUE... AND THEN SOME!
LET ME GUESS... THEY CALL YOU THE HOOPSTER, RIGHT? WHAT'S THE MATTER, FELLA? CAT'S GOT YOUR TONGUE?

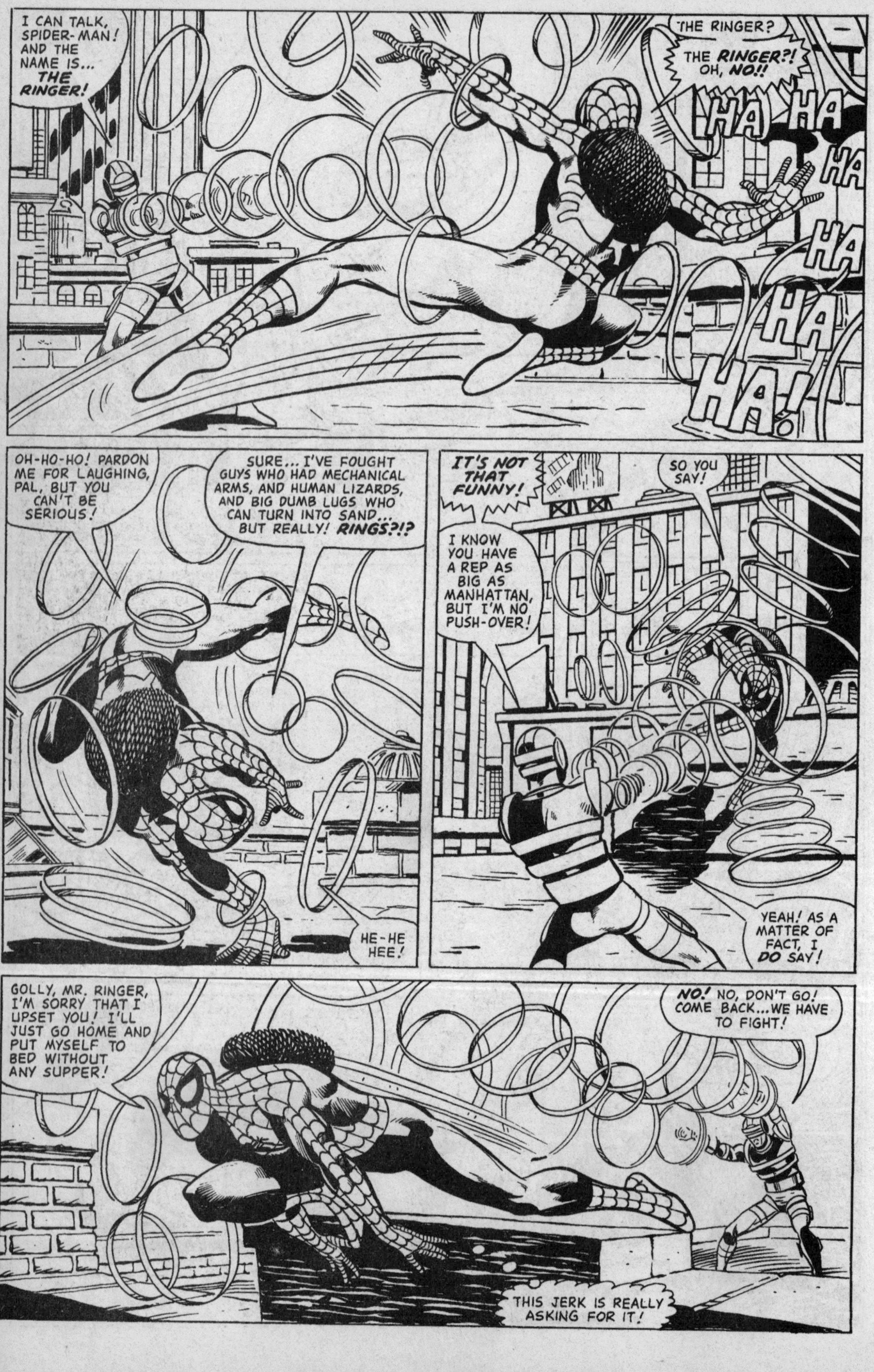

I CAN TALK, SPIDER-MAN! AND THE NAME IS... THE RINGER!
THE RINGER?
THE RINGER?! OH, NO!!
HA HA HA HA HA HA!
OH-HO-HO! PARDON ME FOR LAUGHING, PAL, BUT YOU CAN'T BE SERIOUS!
SURE... I'VE FOUGHT GUYS WHO HAD MECHANICAL ARMS, AND HUMAN LIZARDS, AND BIG DUMB LUGS WHO CAN TURN INTO SAND... BUT REALLY! RINGS?!?
HE-HE HEE!
IT'S NOT THAT FUNNY!
I KNOW YOU HAVE A REP AS BIG AS MANHATTAN, BUT I'M NO PUSH-OVER!
SO YOU SAY!
YEAH! AS A MATTER OF FACT, I DO SAY!
GOLLY, MR. RINGER, I'M SORRY THAT I UPSET YOU! I'LL JUST GO HOME AND PUT MYSELF TO BED WITHOUT ANY SUPPER!
NO! NO, DON'T GO! COME BACK... WE HAVE TO FIGHT!
THIS JERK IS REALLY ASKING FOR IT!

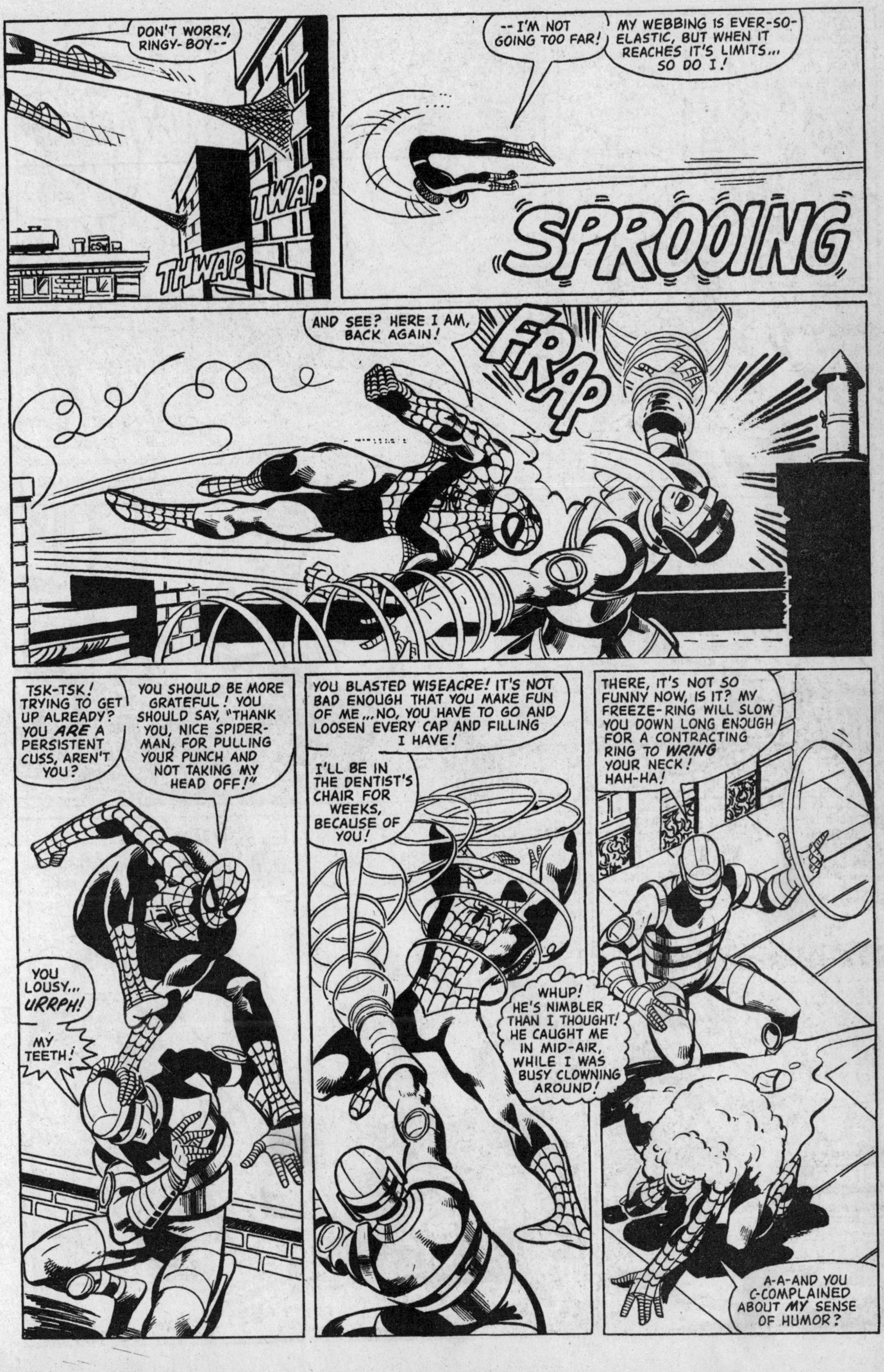
DON'T WORRY, RINGY-BOY--
TWAP
THWAP
-- I'M NOT GOING TOO FAR!
MY WEBBING IS EVER-SO-ELASTIC, BUT WHEN IT REACHES IT'S LIMITS... SO DO I!
SPROOING
AND SEE? HERE I AM, BACK AGAIN!
FRAP
TSK-TSK! TRYING TO GET UP ALREADY? YOU ARE A PERSISTENT CUSS, AREN'T YOU?
YOU SHOULD BE MORE GRATEFUL! YOU SHOULD SAY, "THANK YOU, NICE SPIDER-MAN, FOR PULLING YOUR PUNCH AND NOT TAKING MY HEAD OFF!"
YOU LOUSY... URRPH!
MY TEETH!
YOU BLASTED WISEACRE! IT'S NOT BAD ENOUGH THAT YOU MAKE FUN OF ME... NO, YOU HAVE TO GO AND LOOSEN EVERY CAP AND FILLING I HAVE!
I'LL BE IN THE DENTIST'S CHAIR FOR WEEKS, BECAUSE OF YOU!
WHUP! HE'S NIMBLER THAN I THOUGHT! HE CAUGHT ME IN MID-AIR, WHILE I WAS BUSY CLOWNING AROUND!
THERE, IT'S NOT SO FUNNY NOW, IS IT? MY FREEZE-RING WILL SLOW YOU DOWN LONG ENOUGH FOR A CONTRACTING RING TO WRING YOUR NECK! HAH-HA!
A-A-AND YOU C-COMPLAINED ABOUT MY SENSE OF HUMOR?

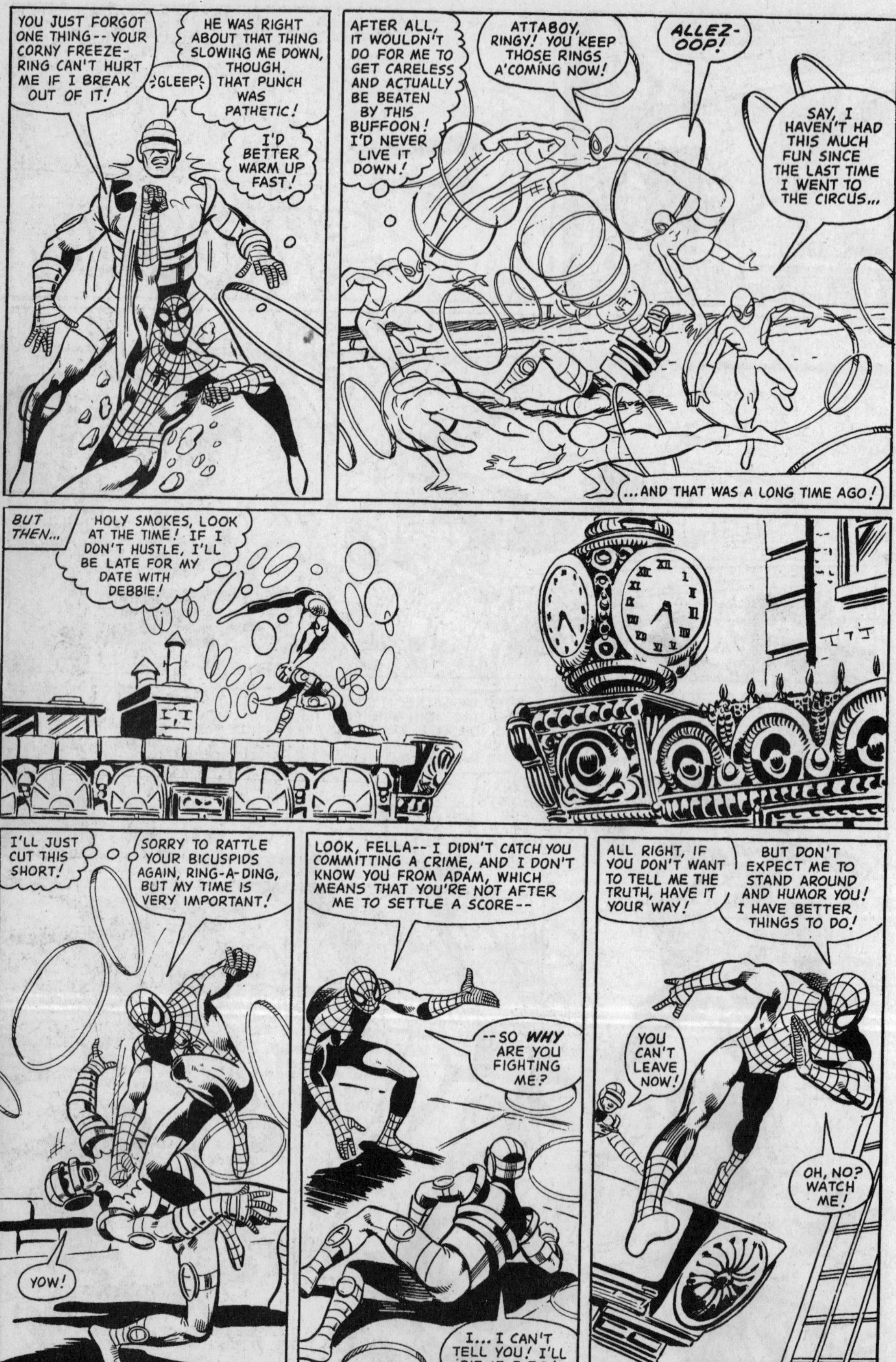
YOU JUST FORGOT ONE THING-- YOUR CORNY FREEZE-RING CAN'T HURT ME IF I BREAK OUT OF IT!
HE WAS RIGHT ABOUT THAT THING SLOWING ME DOWN, THOUGH. THAT PUNCH WAS PATHETIC!
GLEEP
I'D BETTER WARM UP FAST!
AFTER ALL, IT WOULDN'T DO FOR ME TO GET CARELESS AND ACTUALLY BE BEATEN BY THIS BUFFOON! I'D NEVER LIVE IT DOWN!
ATTABOY, RINGY! YOU KEEP THOSE RINGS A'COMING NOW!
ALLEZ-OOP!
SAY, I HAVEN'T HAD THIS MUCH FUN SINCE THE LAST TIME I WENT TO THE CIRCUS...
...AND THAT WAS A LONG TIME AGO!
BUT THEN...
HOLY SMOKES, LOOK AT THE TIME! IF I DON'T HUSTLE, I'LL BE LATE FOR MY DATE WITH DEBBIE!
I'LL JUST CUT THIS SHORT!
SORRY TO RATTLE YOUR BICUSPIDS AGAIN, RING-A-DING, BUT MY TIME IS VERY IMPORTANT!
YOW!
LOOK, FELLA-- I DIDN'T CATCH YOU COMMITTING A CRIME, AND I DON'T KNOW YOU FROM ADAM, WHICH MEANS THAT YOU'RE NOT AFTER ME TO SETTLE A SCORE--
--SO WHY ARE YOU FIGHTING ME?
I... I CAN'T TELL YOU! I'LL DIE IF I DO!
ALL RIGHT, IF YOU DON'T WANT TO TELL ME THE TRUTH, HAVE IT YOUR WAY!
BUT DON'T EXPECT ME TO STAND AROUND AND HUMOR YOU! I HAVE BETTER THINGS TO DO!
YOU CAN'T LEAVE NOW!
OH, NO? WATCH ME!

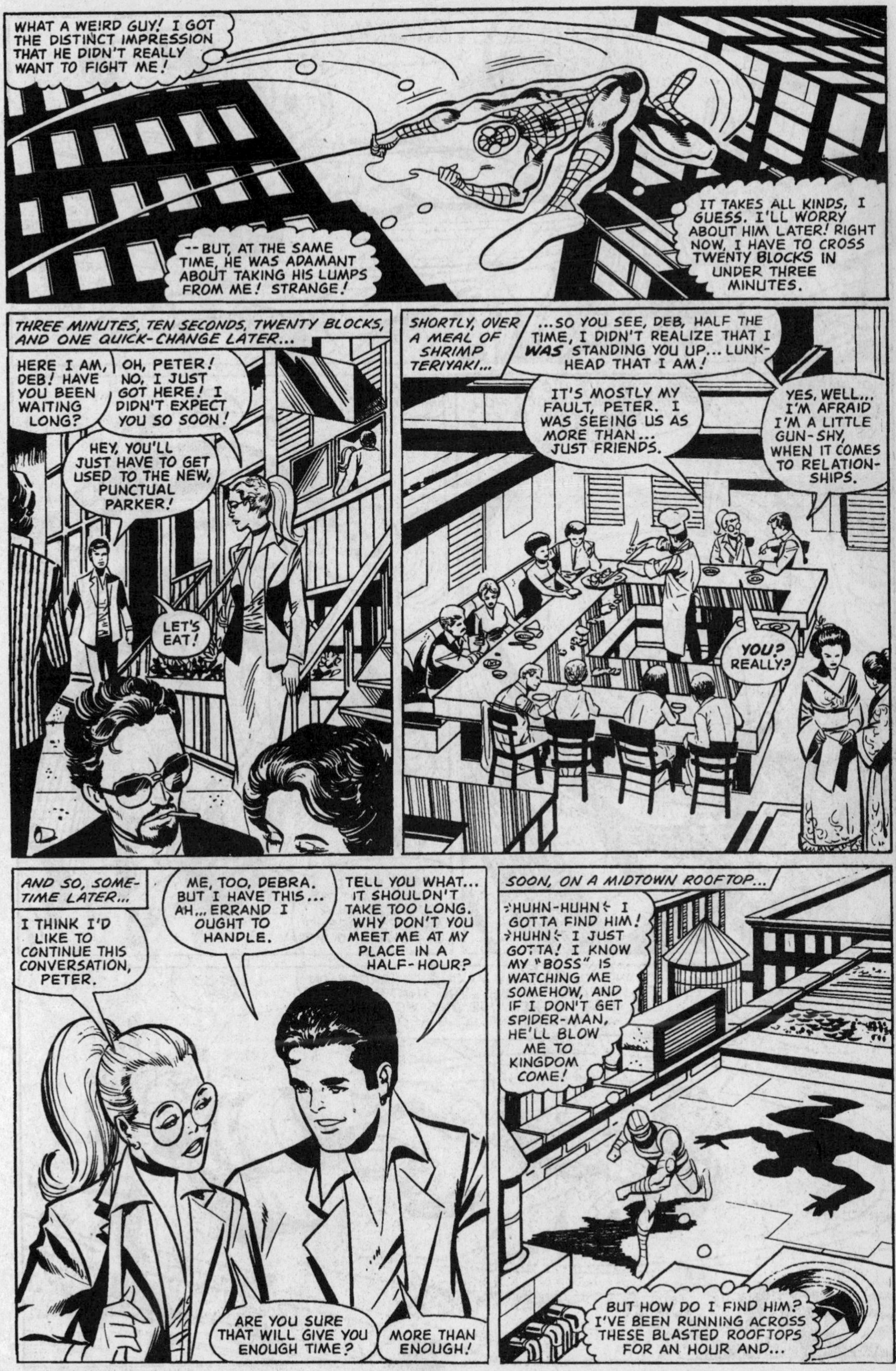
WHAT A WEIRD GUY! I GOT THE DISTINCT IMPRESSION THAT HE DIDN'T REALLY WANT TO FIGHT ME!
--BUT, AT THE SAME TIME, HE WAS ADAMANT ABOUT TAKING HIS LUMPS FROM ME! STRANGE!
IT TAKES ALL KINDS, I GUESS. I'LL WORRY ABOUT HIM LATER! RIGHT NOW, I HAVE TO CROSS TWENTY BLOCKS IN UNDER THREE MINUTES.
THREE MINUTES, TEN SECONDS, TWENTY BLOCKS, AND ONE QUICK-CHANGE LATER...
HERE I AM, DEB! HAVE YOU BEEN WAITING LONG?
OH, PETER! NO, I JUST GOT HERE! I DIDN'T EXPECT YOU SO SOON!
HEY, YOU'LL JUST HAVE TO GET USED TO THE NEW, PUNCTUAL PARKER!
LET'S EAT!
SHORTLY, OVER A MEAL OF SHRIMP TERIYAKI...
...SO YOU SEE, DEB, HALF THE TIME, I DIDN'T REALIZE THAT I WAS STANDING YOU UP... LUNK-HEAD THAT I AM!
IT'S MOSTLY MY FAULT, PETER. I WAS SEEING US AS MORE THAN... JUST FRIENDS.
YES, WELL... I'M AFRAID I'M A LITTLE GUN-SHY, WHEN IT COMES TO RELATION-SHIPS.
YOU? REALLY?
AND SO, SOME-TIME LATER...
I THINK I'D LIKE TO CONTINUE THIS CONVERSATION, PETER.
ME, TOO, DEBRA. BUT I HAVE THIS... AH... ERRAND I OUGHT TO HANDLE.
TELL YOU WHAT... IT SHOULDN'T TAKE TOO LONG. WHY DON'T YOU MEET ME AT MY PLACE IN A HALF-HOUR?
ARE YOU SURE THAT WILL GIVE YOU ENOUGH TIME?
MORE THAN ENOUGH!
SOON, ON A MIDTOWN ROOFTOP...
HUHN-HUHN I GOTTA FIND HIM! HUHN I JUST GOTTA! I KNOW MY "BOSS" IS WATCHING ME SOMEHOW, AND IF I DON'T GET SPIDER-MAN, HE'LL BLOW ME TO KINGDOM COME!
BUT HOW DO I FIND HIM? I'VE BEEN RUNNING ACROSS THESE BLASTED ROOFTOPS FOR AN HOUR AND...

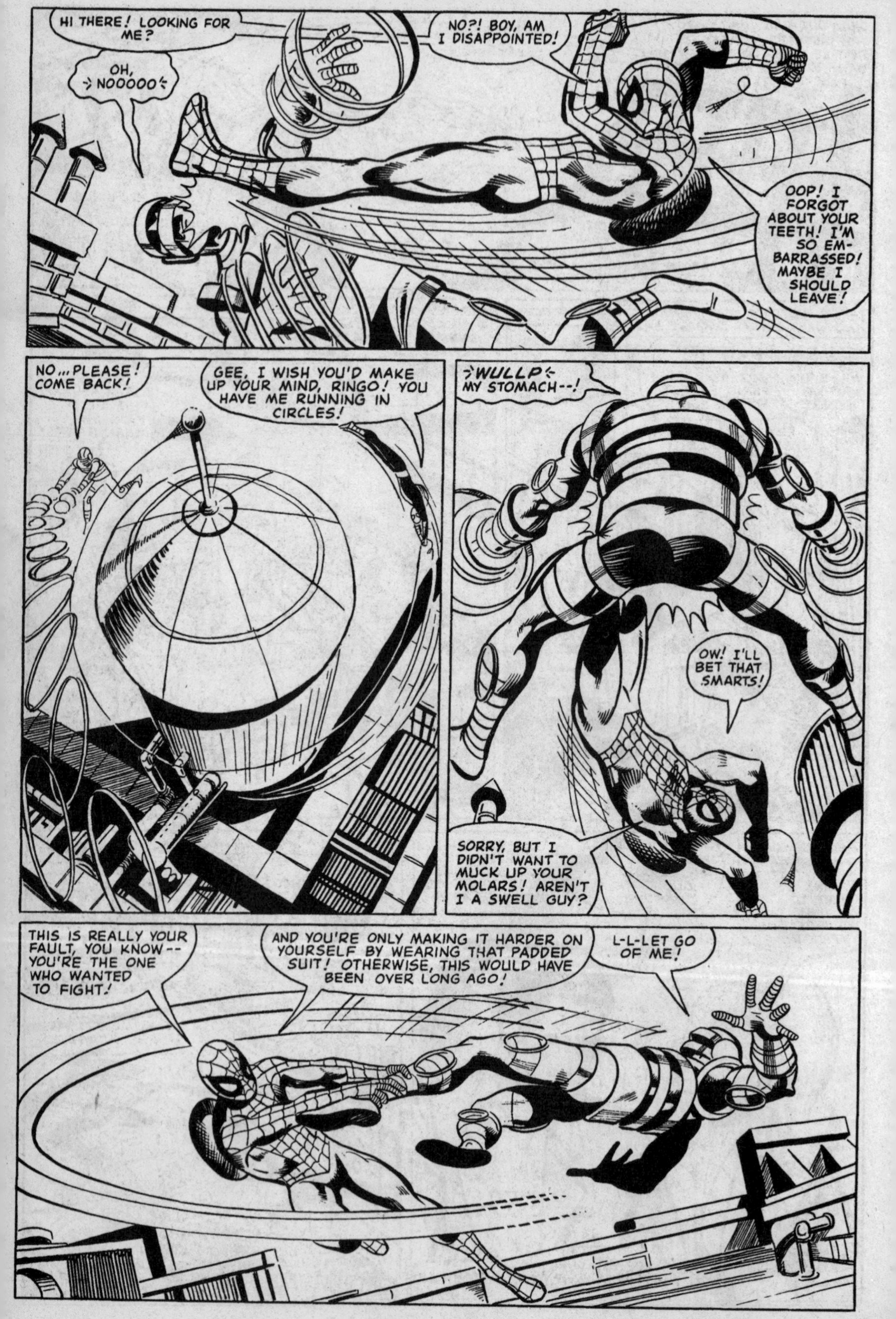
HI THERE! LOOKING FOR ME?
OH, NOOOOO!
NO?! BOY, AM I DISAPPOINTED!
OOP! I FORGOT ABOUT YOUR TEETH! I'M SO EMBARRASSED! MAYBE I SHOULD LEAVE!
NO... PLEASE! COME BACK!
GEE, I WISH YOU'D MAKE UP YOUR MIND, RINGO! YOU HAVE ME RUNNING IN CIRCLES!
WULLP
MY STOMACH--!
OW! I'LL BET THAT SMARTS!
SORRY, BUT I DIDN'T WANT TO MUCK UP YOUR MOLARS! AREN'T I A SWELL GUY?
THIS IS REALLY YOUR FAULT, YOU KNOW-- YOU'RE THE ONE WHO WANTED TO FIGHT!
AND YOU'RE ONLY MAKING IT HARDER ON YOURSELF BY WEARING THAT PADDED SUIT! OTHERWISE, THIS WOULD HAVE BEEN OVER LONG AGO!
L-L-LET GO OF ME!

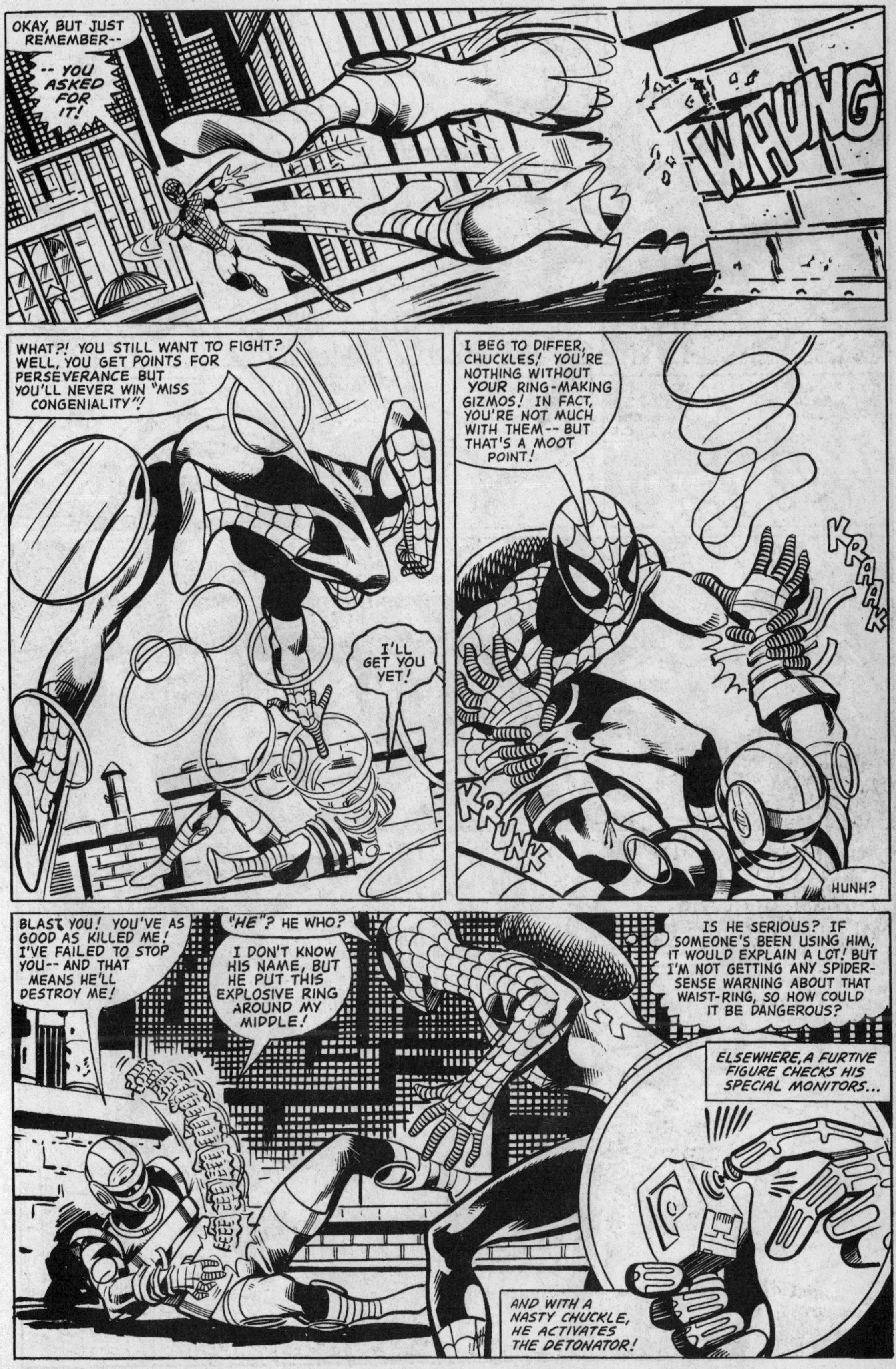
OKAY, BUT JUST REMEMBER--
-- YOU ASKED FOR IT!
WHUNG
WHAT?! YOU STILL WANT TO FIGHT? WELL, YOU GET POINTS FOR PERSEVERANCE BUT YOU'LL NEVER WIN "MISS CONGENIALITY"!
I'LL GET YOU YET!
I BEG TO DIFFER, CHUCKLES! YOU'RE NOTHING WITHOUT YOUR RING-MAKING GIZMOS! IN FACT, YOU'RE NOT MUCH WITH THEM -- BUT THAT'S A MOOT POINT!
KRAAK
KRUNK
HUNH?
BLAST YOU! YOU'VE AS GOOD AS KILLED ME! I'VE FAILED TO STOP YOU-- AND THAT MEANS HE'LL DESTROY ME!
"HE"? HE WHO?
I DON'T KNOW HIS NAME, BUT HE PUT THIS EXPLOSIVE RING AROUND MY MIDDLE!
IS HE SERIOUS? IF SOMEONE'S BEEN USING HIM, IT WOULD EXPLAIN A LOT! BUT I'M NOT GETTING ANY SPIDER-SENSE WARNING ABOUT THAT WAIST-RING, SO HOW COULD IT BE DANGEROUS?
ELSEWHERE, A FURTIVE FIGURE CHECKS HIS SPECIAL MONITORS...
AND WITH A NASTY CHUCKLE, HE ACTIVATES THE DETONATOR!

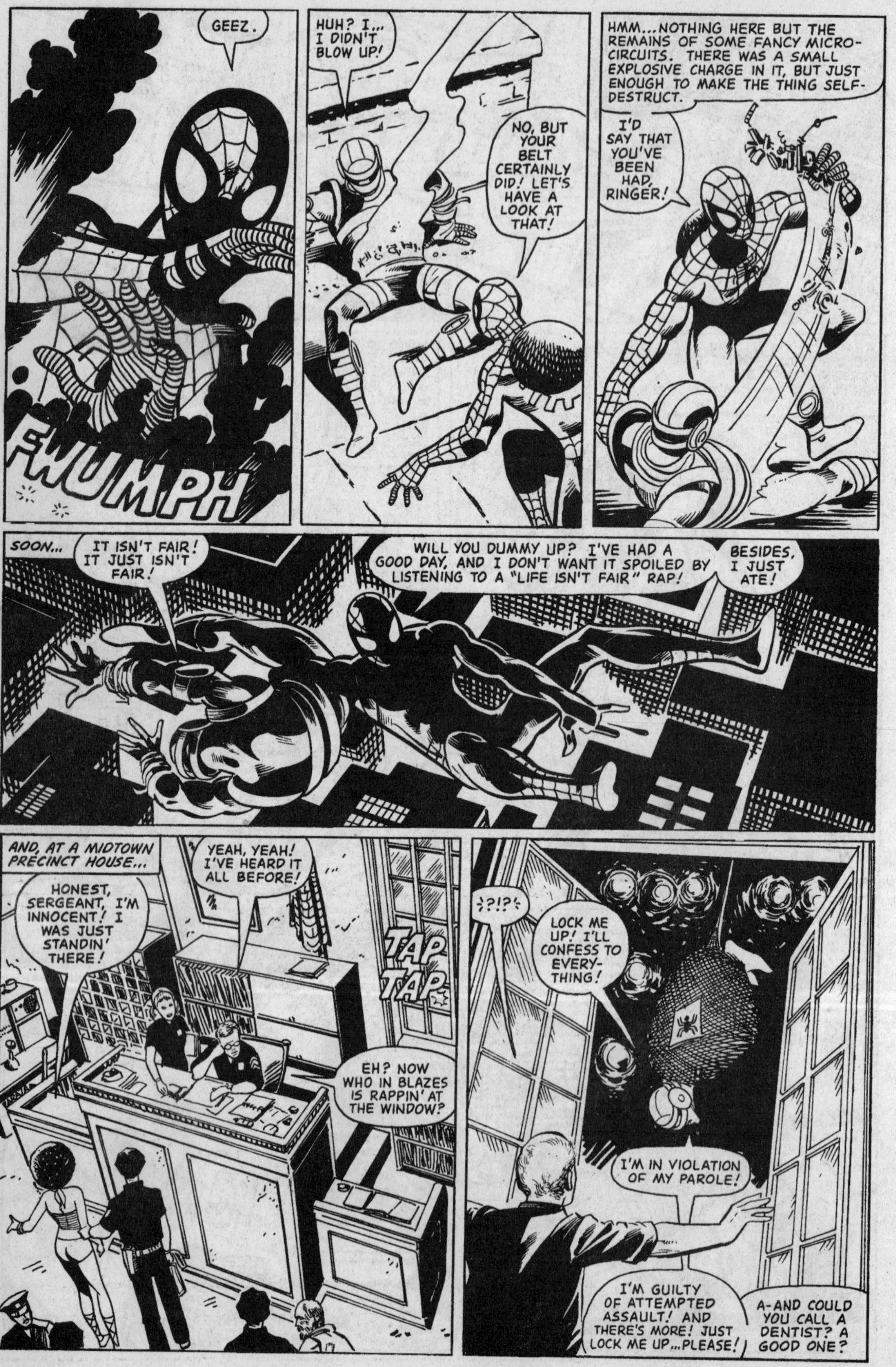
GEEZ.
FWUMPH
HUH? I... I DIDN'T BLOW UP!
NO, BUT YOUR BELT CERTAINLY DID! LET'S HAVE A LOOK AT THAT!
HMM... NOTHING HERE BUT THE REMAINS OF SOME FANCY MICRO-CIRCUITS. THERE WAS A SMALL EXPLOSIVE CHARGE IN IT, BUT JUST ENOUGH TO MAKE THE THING SELF-DESTRUCT.
I'D SAY THAT YOU'VE BEEN HAD, RINGER!
SOON...
IT ISN'T FAIR! IT JUST ISN'T FAIR!
WILL YOU DUMMY UP? I'VE HAD A GOOD DAY, AND I DON'T WANT IT SPOILED BY LISTENING TO A "LIFE ISN'T FAIR" RAP!
BESIDES, I JUST ATE!
AND, AT A MIDTOWN PRECINCT HOUSE...
HONEST, SERGEANT, I'M INNOCENT! I WAS JUST STANDIN' THERE!
YEAH, YEAH! I'VE HEARD IT ALL BEFORE!
TAP TAP
EH? NOW WHO IN BLAZES IS RAPPIN' AT THE WINDOW?
?!?!
LOCK ME UP! I'LL CONFESS TO EVERY-THING!
I'M IN VIOLATION OF MY PAROLE!
I'M GUILTY OF ATTEMPTED ASSAULT! AND THERE'S MORE! JUST LOCK ME UP... PLEASE!
A-AND COULD YOU CALL A DENTIST? A GOOD ONE?

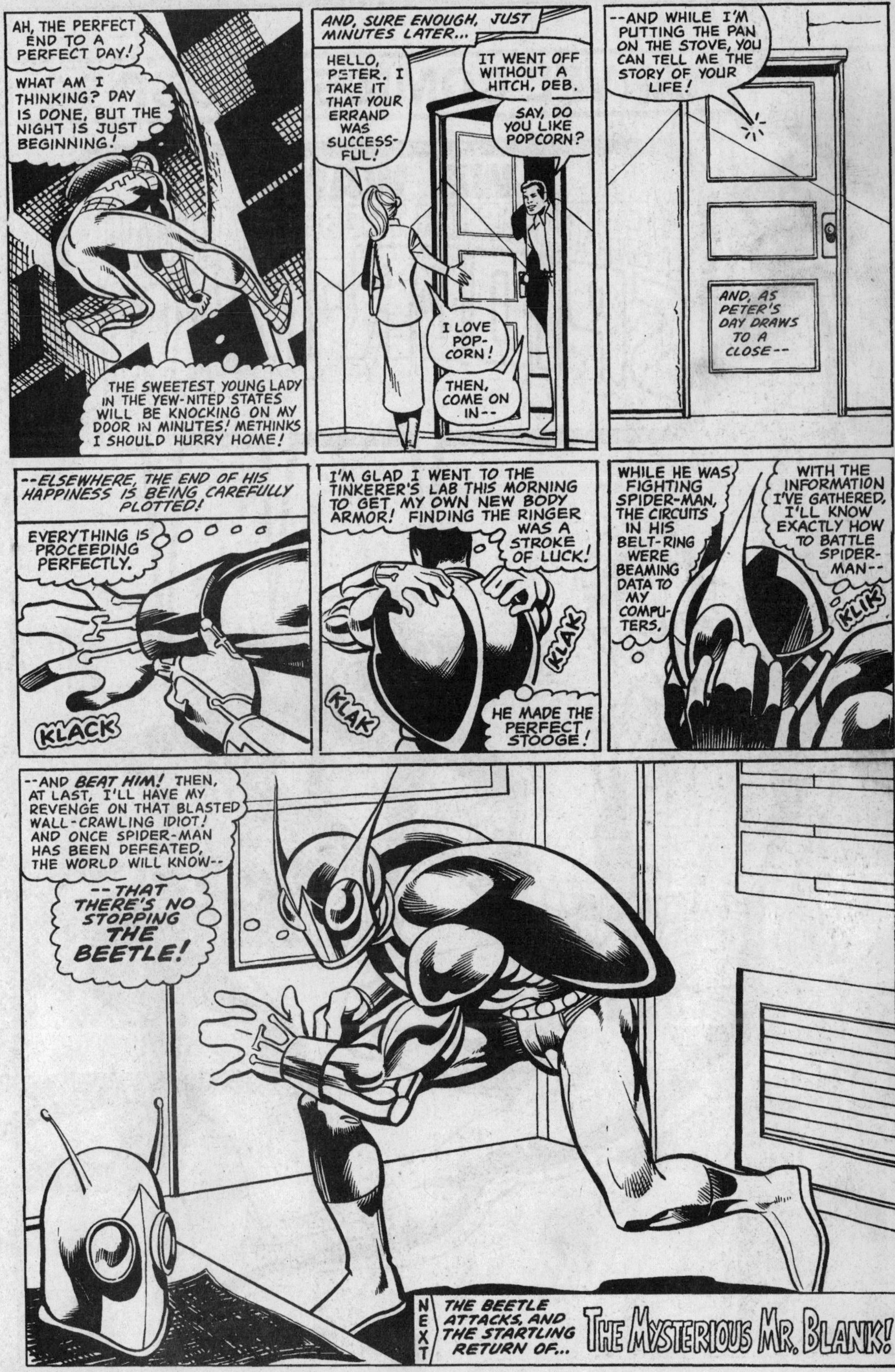
AH, THE PERFECT END TO A PERFECT DAY!
WHAT AM I THINKING? DAY IS DONE, BUT THE NIGHT IS JUST BEGINNING!
THE SWEETEST YOUNG LADY IN THE YEW-NITED STATES WILL BE KNOCKING ON MY DOOR IN MINUTES! METHINKS I SHOULD HURRY HOME!
AND, SURE ENOUGH, JUST MINUTES LATER...
HELLO, PETER. I TAKE IT THAT YOUR ERRAND WAS SUCCESSFUL!
IT WENT OFF WITHOUT A HITCH, DEB.
SAY, DO YOU LIKE POPCORN?
I LOVE POPCORN!
THEN, COME ON IN--
--AND WHILE I'M PUTTING THE PAN ON THE STOVE, YOU CAN TELL ME THE STORY OF YOUR LIFE!
AND, AS PETER'S DAY DRAWS TO A CLOSE--
--ELSEWHERE, THE END OF HIS HAPPINESS IS BEING CAREFULLY PLOTTED!
EVERYTHING IS PROCEEDING PERFECTLY.
KLACK
I'M GLAD I WENT TO THE TINKERER'S LAB THIS MORNING TO GET MY OWN NEW BODY ARMOR! FINDING THE RINGER WAS A STROKE OF LUCK!
KLAK
KLAK
HE MADE THE PERFECT STOOGE!
WHILE HE WAS FIGHTING SPIDER-MAN, THE CIRCUITS IN HIS BELT-RING WERE BEAMING DATA TO MY COMPUTERS.
WITH THE INFORMATION I'VE GATHERED, I'LL KNOW EXACTLY HOW TO BATTLE SPIDER-MAN--
KLIK
--AND BEAT HIM! THEN, AT LAST, I'LL HAVE MY REVENGE ON THAT BLASTED WALL-CRAWLING IDIOT! AND ONCE SPIDER-MAN HAS BEEN DEFEATED, THE WORLD WILL KNOW--
--THAT THERE'S NO STOPPING THE BEETLE!
NEXT
THE BEETLE ATTACKS, AND THE STARTLING RETURN OF...
THE MYSTERIOUS MR. BLANK!

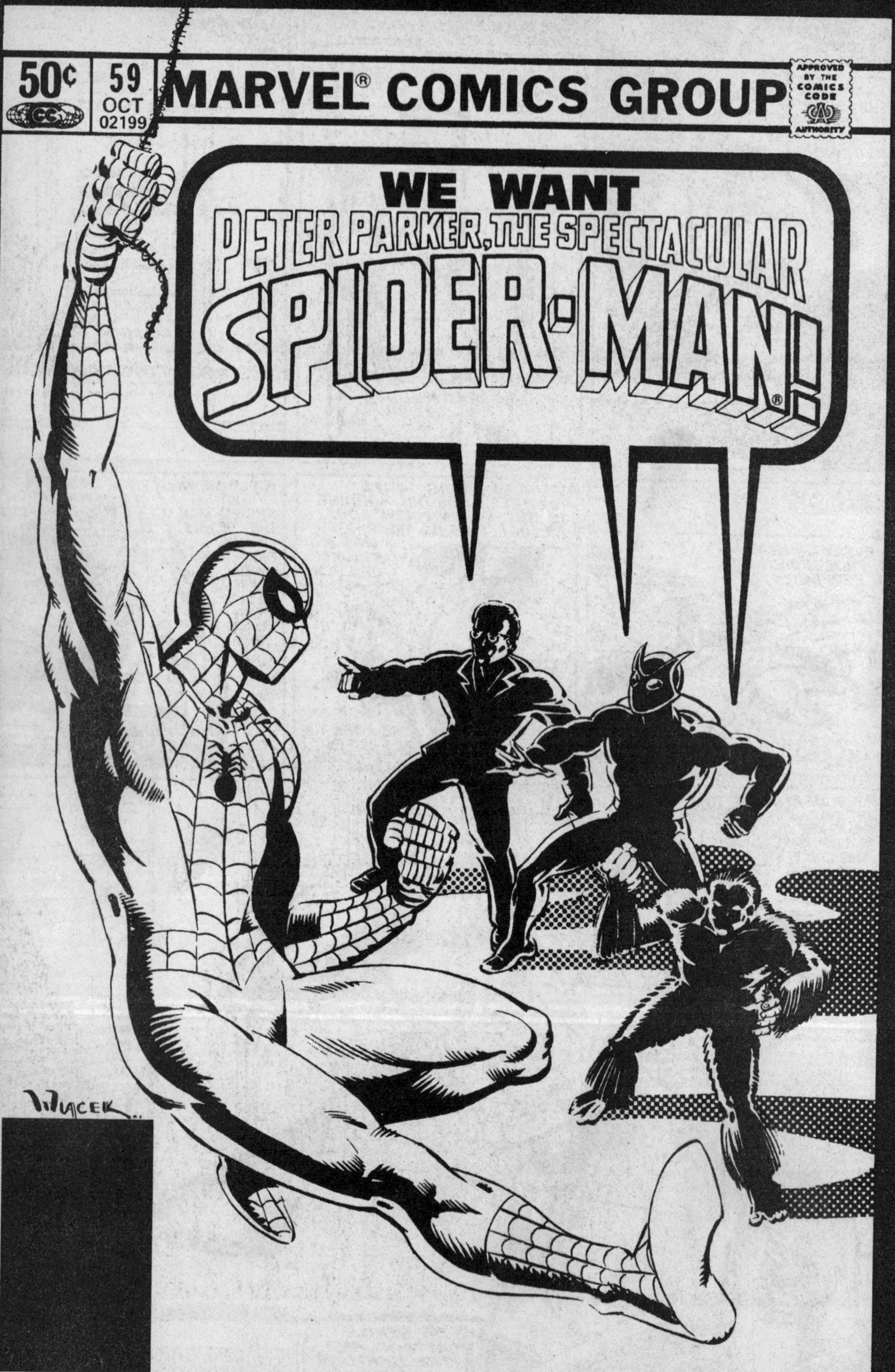
50¢
59
OCT
02199
MARVEL® COMICS GROUP
APPROVED BY THE COMICS CODE AUTHORITY
WE WANT
PETER PARKER, THE SPECTACULAR
SPIDER-MAN!

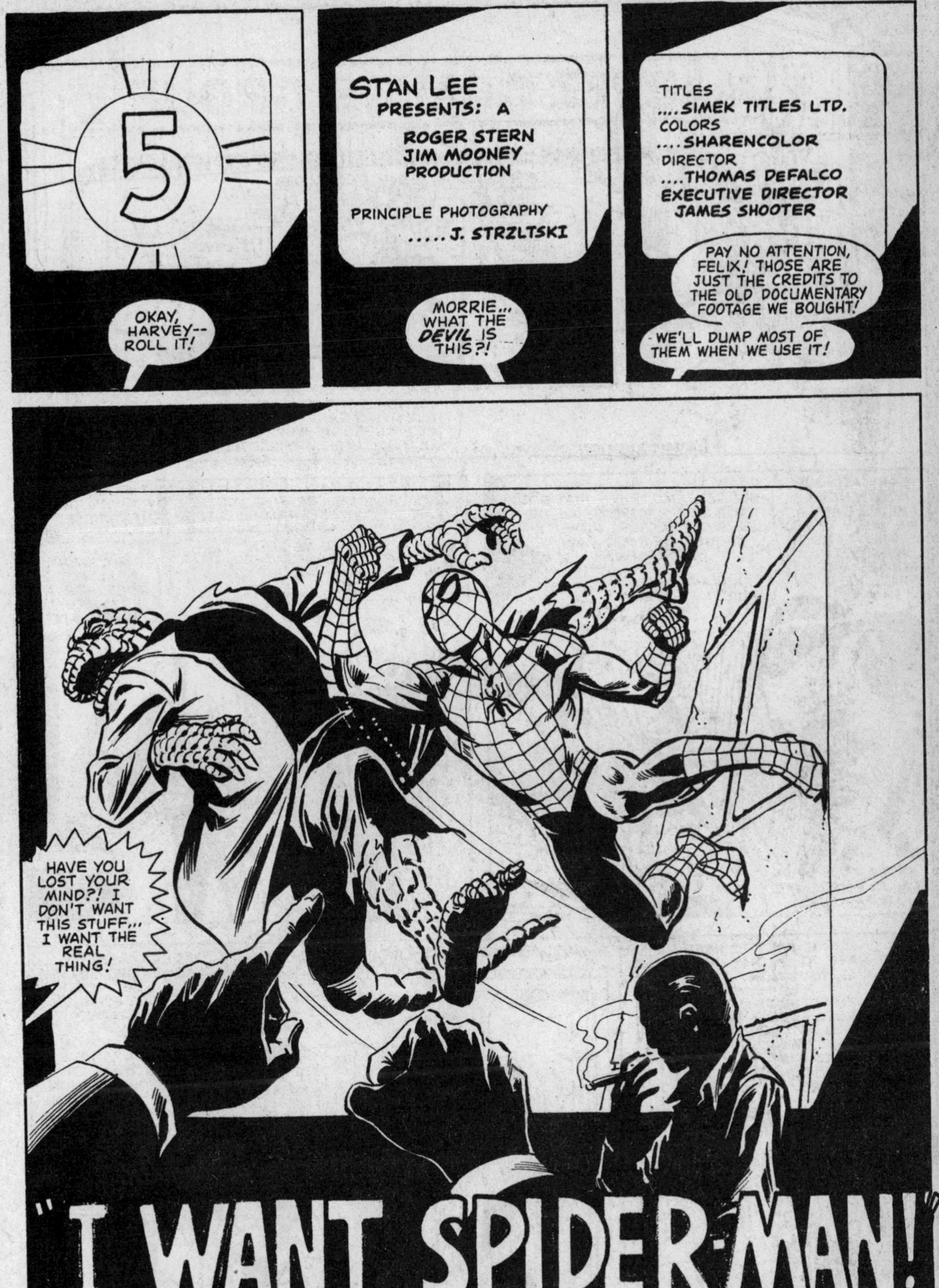
5
OKAY, HARVEY-- ROLL IT!
STAN LEE PRESENTS: A
ROGER STERN
JIM MOONEY
PRODUCTION
PRINCIPLE PHOTOGRAPHY
..... J. STRZLTSKI
MORRIE... WHAT THE DEVIL IS THIS?!
TITLES
....SIMEK TITLES LTD.
COLORS
....SHARENCOLOR
DIRECTOR
....THOMAS DEFALCO
EXECUTIVE DIRECTOR
JAMES SHOOTER
PAY NO ATTENTION, FELIX! THOSE ARE JUST THE CREDITS TO THE OLD DOCUMENTARY FOOTAGE WE BOUGHT!
WE'LL DUMP MOST OF THEM WHEN WE USE IT!
HAVE YOU LOST YOUR MIND?! I DON'T WANT THIS STUFF... I WANT THE REAL THING!
"I WANT SPIDER-MAN!"

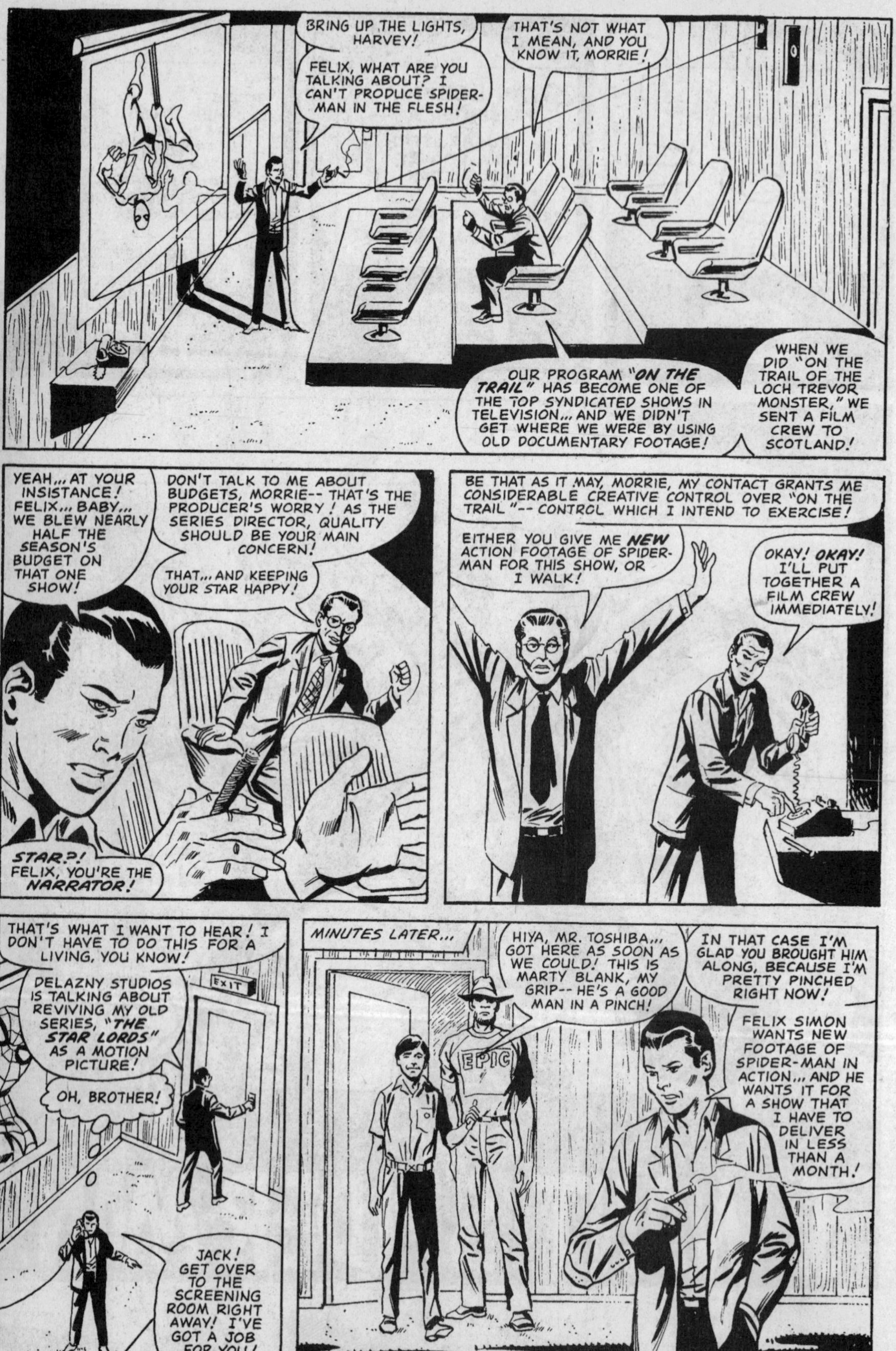
BRING UP THE LIGHTS, HARVEY!
FELIX, WHAT ARE YOU TALKING ABOUT? I CAN'T PRODUCE SPIDER-MAN IN THE FLESH!
THAT'S NOT WHAT I MEAN, AND YOU KNOW IT, MORRIE!
OUR PROGRAM "ON THE TRAIL" HAS BECOME ONE OF THE TOP SYNDICATED SHOWS IN TELEVISION... AND WE DIDN'T GET WHERE WE WERE BY USING OLD DOCUMENTARY FOOTAGE!
WHEN WE DID "ON THE TRAIL OF THE LOCH TREVOR MONSTER," WE SENT A FILM CREW TO SCOTLAND!
YEAH... AT YOUR INSISTANCE! FELIX... BABY... WE BLEW NEARLY HALF THE SEASON'S BUDGET ON THAT ONE SHOW!
DON'T TALK TO ME ABOUT BUDGETS, MORRIE-- THAT'S THE PRODUCER'S WORRY! AS THE SERIES DIRECTOR, QUALITY SHOULD BE YOUR MAIN CONCERN!
THAT... AND KEEPING YOUR STAR HAPPY!
STAR?! FELIX, YOU'RE THE NARRATOR!
BE THAT AS IT MAY, MORRIE, MY CONTACT GRANTS ME CONSIDERABLE CREATIVE CONTROL OVER "ON THE TRAIL"-- CONTROL WHICH I INTEND TO EXERCISE!
EITHER YOU GIVE ME NEW ACTION FOOTAGE OF SPIDER-MAN FOR THIS SHOW, OR I WALK!
OKAY! OKAY! I'LL PUT TOGETHER A FILM CREW IMMEDIATELY!
THAT'S WHAT I WANT TO HEAR! I DON'T HAVE TO DO THIS FOR A LIVING, YOU KNOW!
DELAZNY STUDIOS IS TALKING ABOUT REVIVING MY OLD SERIES, "THE STAR LORDS" AS A MOTION PICTURE!
EXIT
OH, BROTHER!
JACK! GET OVER TO THE SCREENING ROOM RIGHT AWAY! I'VE GOT A JOB FOR YOU!
MINUTES LATER...
HIYA, MR. TOSHIBA... GOT HERE AS SOON AS WE COULD! THIS IS MARTY BLANK, MY GRIP-- HE'S A GOOD MAN IN A PINCH!
EPIC
IN THAT CASE I'M GLAD YOU BROUGHT HIM ALONG, BECAUSE I'M PRETTY PINCHED RIGHT NOW!
FELIX SIMON WANTS NEW FOOTAGE OF SPIDER-MAN IN ACTION... AND HE WANTS IT FOR A SHOW THAT I HAVE TO DELIVER IN LESS THAN A MONTH!

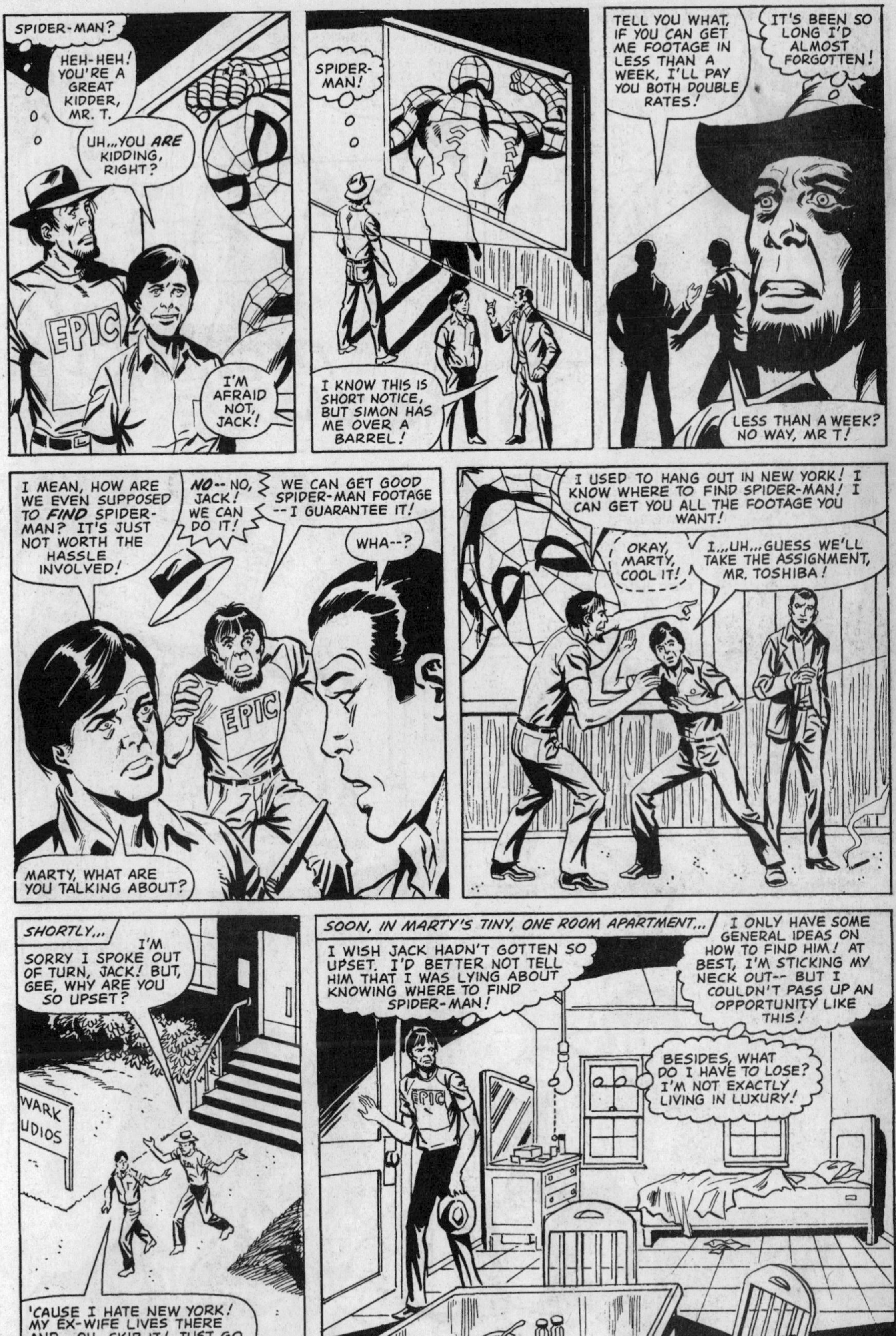
SPIDER-MAN?
HEH-HEH! YOU'RE A GREAT KIDDER, MR. T.
UH...YOU ARE KIDDING, RIGHT?
I'M AFRAID NOT, JACK!
SPIDER-MAN!
I KNOW THIS IS SHORT NOTICE, BUT SIMON HAS ME OVER A BARREL!
TELL YOU WHAT, IF YOU CAN GET ME FOOTAGE IN LESS THAN A WEEK, I'LL PAY YOU BOTH DOUBLE RATES!
IT'S BEEN SO LONG I'D ALMOST FORGOTTEN!
LESS THAN A WEEK? NO WAY, MR T!
I MEAN, HOW ARE WE EVEN SUPPOSED TO FIND SPIDER-MAN? IT'S JUST NOT WORTH THE HASSLE INVOLVED!
NO-- NO, JACK! WE CAN DO IT!
WE CAN GET GOOD SPIDER-MAN FOOTAGE -- I GUARANTEE IT!
WHA--?
MARTY, WHAT ARE YOU TALKING ABOUT?
I USED TO HANG OUT IN NEW YORK! I KNOW WHERE TO FIND SPIDER-MAN! I CAN GET YOU ALL THE FOOTAGE YOU WANT!
OKAY, MARTY, COOL IT!
I...UH...GUESS WE'LL TAKE THE ASSIGNMENT, MR. TOSHIBA!
SHORTLY...
I'M SORRY I SPOKE OUT OF TURN, JACK! BUT, GEE, WHY ARE YOU SO UPSET?
WARK UDIOS
'CAUSE I HATE NEW YORK! MY EX-WIFE LIVES THERE AND... OH, SKIP IT! JUST GO HOME AND PACK! OKAY?
SOON, IN MARTY'S TINY, ONE ROOM APARTMENT...
I WISH JACK HADN'T GOTTEN SO UPSET. I'D BETTER NOT TELL HIM THAT I WAS LYING ABOUT KNOWING WHERE TO FIND SPIDER-MAN!
I ONLY HAVE SOME GENERAL IDEAS ON HOW TO FIND HIM! AT BEST, I'M STICKING MY NECK OUT-- BUT I COULDN'T PASS UP AN OPPORTUNITY LIKE THIS!
BESIDES, WHAT DO I HAVE TO LOSE? I'M NOT EXACTLY LIVING IN LUXURY!

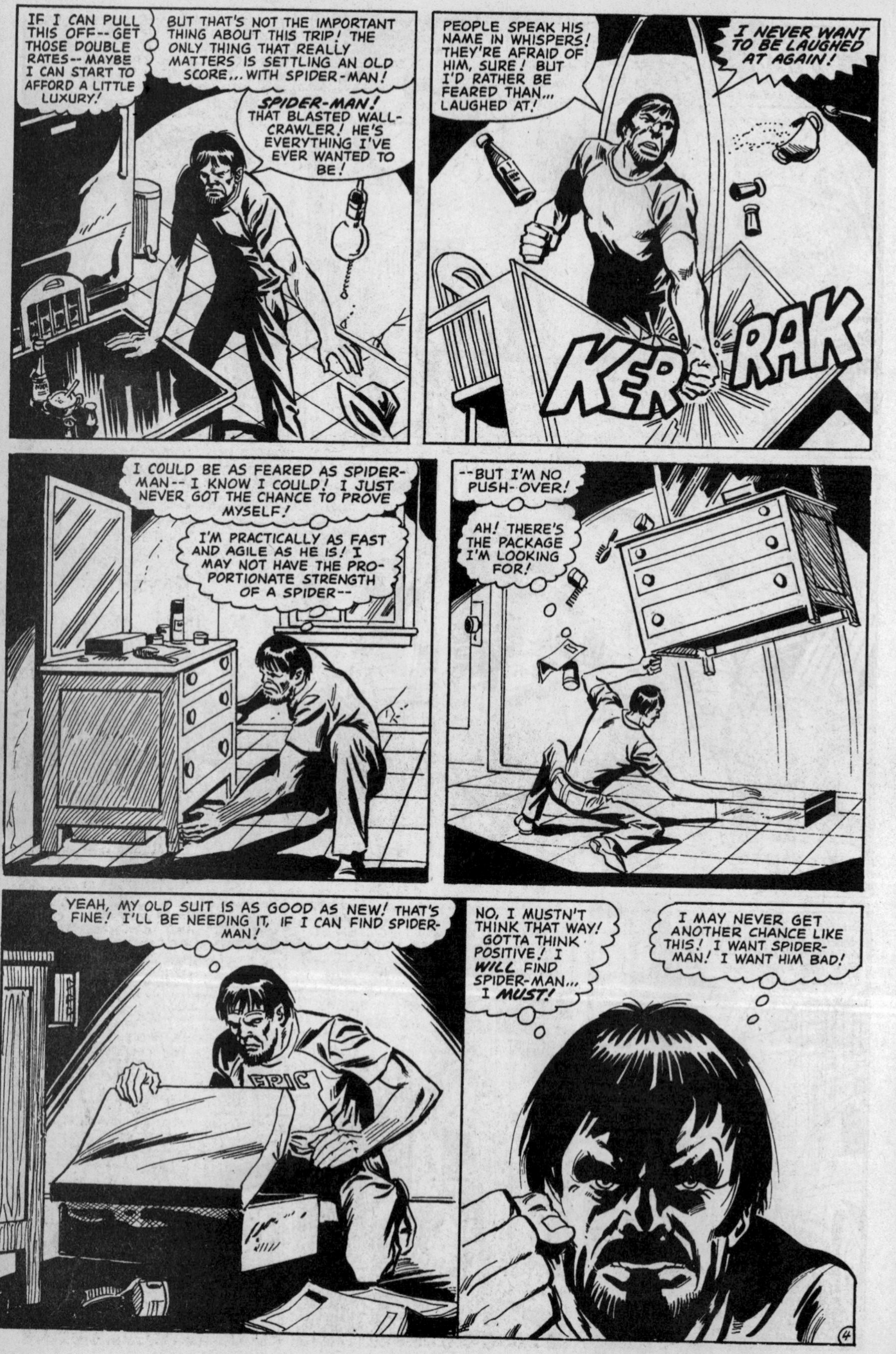

IF I CAN PULL THIS OFF--GET THOSE DOUBLE RATES--MAYBE I CAN START TO AFFORD A LITTLE LUXURY!
BUT THAT'S NOT THE IMPORTANT THING ABOUT THIS TRIP! THE ONLY THING THAT REALLY MATTERS IS SETTLING AN OLD SCORE... WITH SPIDER-MAN!
SPIDER-MAN! THAT BLASTED WALL-CRAWLER! HE'S EVERYTHING I'VE EVER WANTED TO BE!
PEOPLE SPEAK HIS NAME IN WHISPERS! THEY'RE AFRAID OF HIM, SURE! BUT I'D RATHER BE FEARED THAN... LAUGHED AT!
I NEVER WANT TO BE LAUGHED AT AGAIN!
KER RAK
I COULD BE AS FEARED AS SPIDER-MAN-- I KNOW I COULD! I JUST NEVER GOT THE CHANCE TO PROVE MYSELF!
I'M PRACTICALLY AS FAST AND AGILE AS HE IS! I MAY NOT HAVE THE PROPORTIONATE STRENGTH OF A SPIDER--
--BUT I'M NO PUSH-OVER!
AH! THERE'S THE PACKAGE I'M LOOKING FOR!
YEAH, MY OLD SUIT IS AS GOOD AS NEW! THAT'S FINE! I'LL BE NEEDING IT, IF I CAN FIND SPIDER-MAN!
EPIC
NO, I MUSTN'T THINK THAT WAY! GOTTA THINK POSITIVE! I WILL FIND SPIDER-MAN... I MUST!
I MAY NEVER GET ANOTHER CHANCE LIKE THIS! I WANT SPIDER-MAN! I WANT HIM BAD!

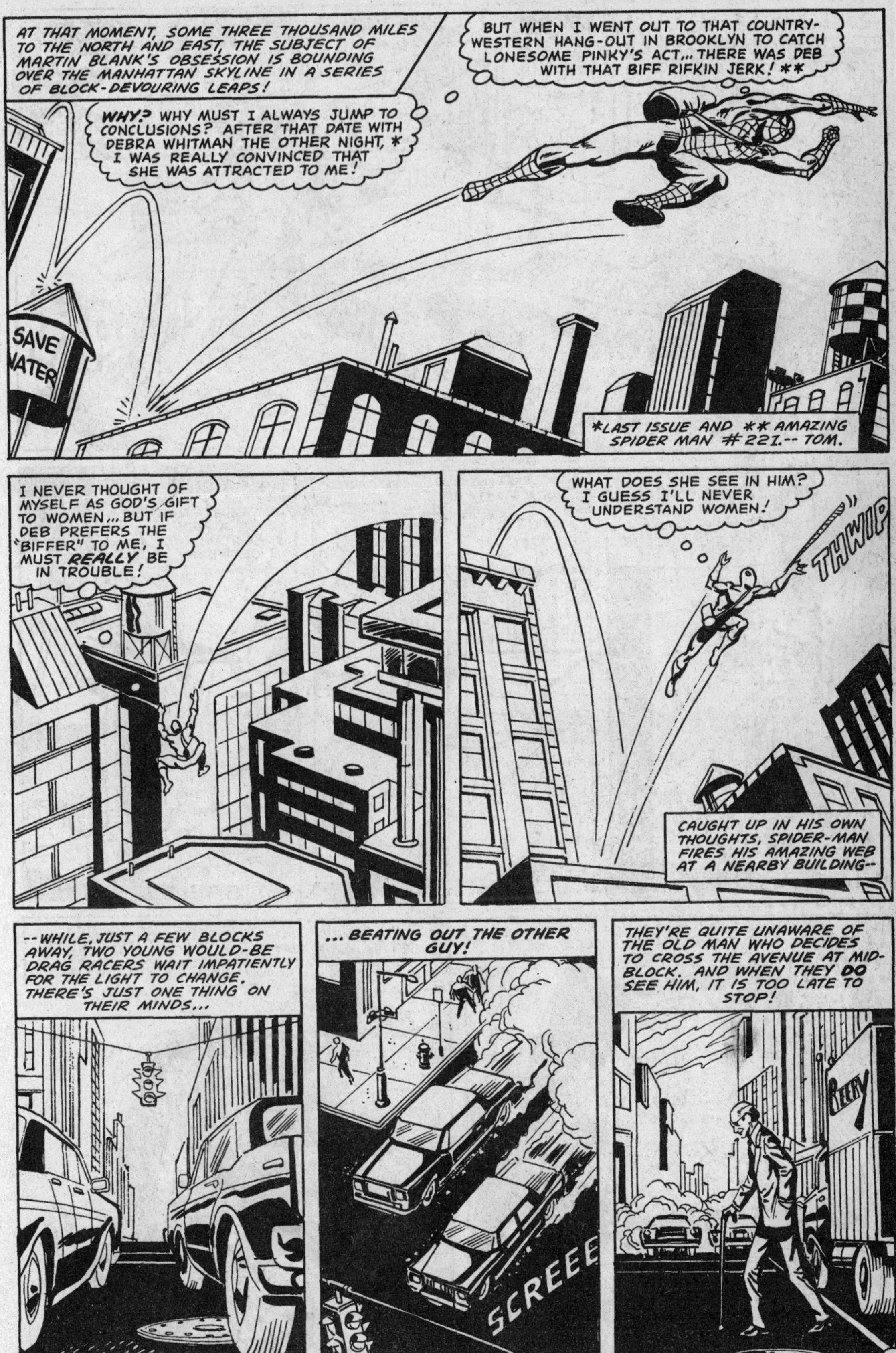
AT THAT MOMENT, SOME THREE THOUSAND MILES TO THE NORTH AND EAST, THE SUBJECT OF MARTIN BLANK'S OBSESSION IS BOUNDING OVER THE MANHATTAN SKYLINE IN A SERIES OF BLOCK-DEVOURING LEAPS!
WHY? WHY MUST I ALWAYS JUMP TO CONCLUSIONS? AFTER THAT DATE WITH DEBRA WHITMAN THE OTHER NIGHT,* I WAS REALLY CONVINCED THAT SHE WAS ATTRACTED TO ME!
BUT WHEN I WENT OUT TO THAT COUNTRY-WESTERN HANG-OUT IN BROOKLYN TO CATCH LONESOME PINKY'S ACT... THERE WAS DEB WITH THAT BIFF RIFKIN JERK! **
SAVE WATER
*LAST ISSUE AND ** AMAZING SPIDER MAN #221.-- TOM.
I NEVER THOUGHT OF MYSELF AS GOD'S GIFT TO WOMEN... BUT IF DEB PREFERS THE "BIFFER" TO ME, I MUST REALLY BE IN TROUBLE!
WHAT DOES SHE SEE IN HIM? I GUESS I'LL NEVER UNDERSTAND WOMEN!
THWIP
CAUGHT UP IN HIS OWN THOUGHTS, SPIDER-MAN FIRES HIS AMAZING WEB AT A NEARBY BUILDING--
--WHILE, JUST A FEW BLOCKS AWAY, TWO YOUNG WOULD-BE DRAG RACERS WAIT IMPATIENTLY FOR THE LIGHT TO CHANGE. THERE'S JUST ONE THING ON THEIR MINDS...
...BEATING OUT THE OTHER GUY!
SCREEE
THEY'RE QUITE UNAWARE OF THE OLD MAN WHO DECIDES TO CROSS THE AVENUE AT MID-BLOCK. AND WHEN THEY DO SEE HIM, IT IS TOO LATE TO STOP!
BEERY

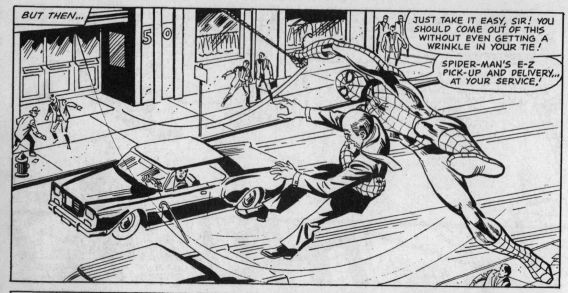

BUT THEN...

JUST TAKE IT EASY, SIR! YOU SHOULD COME OUT OF THIS WITHOUT EVEN GETTING A WRINKLE IN YOUR TIE!

SPIDER-MAN'S E-Z PICK-UP AND DELIVERY... AT YOUR SERVICE!

I... I COULD HAVE BEEN KILLED!

YES, THAT *WAS* A DISTINCT POSSIBILITY! I THINK THERE ARE A COUPLE OF HOT RODDERS WHO ARE DUE FOR A LESSON IN TRAFFIC SAFETY!

BUT... FIRST THINGS FIRST!

YOUR CANE, SIR!

THWIP

⸮ULP⸮ T-THANK YOU!

DON'T MENTION IT!

BUT REMEMBER-- CROSS AT THE GREEN AND NOT IN BETWEEN!

THWIP

TA-TAH!

SECONDS LATER, THE TWO SPEEDING DRIVERS SUDDENLY FIND THEIR WAY BLOCKED BY A COLORFUL FIGURE...

HEY! GET OUTTA THE STREET!

HONK HONK

OH, I'M SORRY! DID I GET IN YOUR WAY? HERE, LET ME MAKE IT UP TO YOU ...

... LET ME WASH YOUR WINDSHIELDS!

WHA--?

OOPS! SILLY ME! THAT'S NOT WATER, IS IT?!

I CAN'T SEE!

6

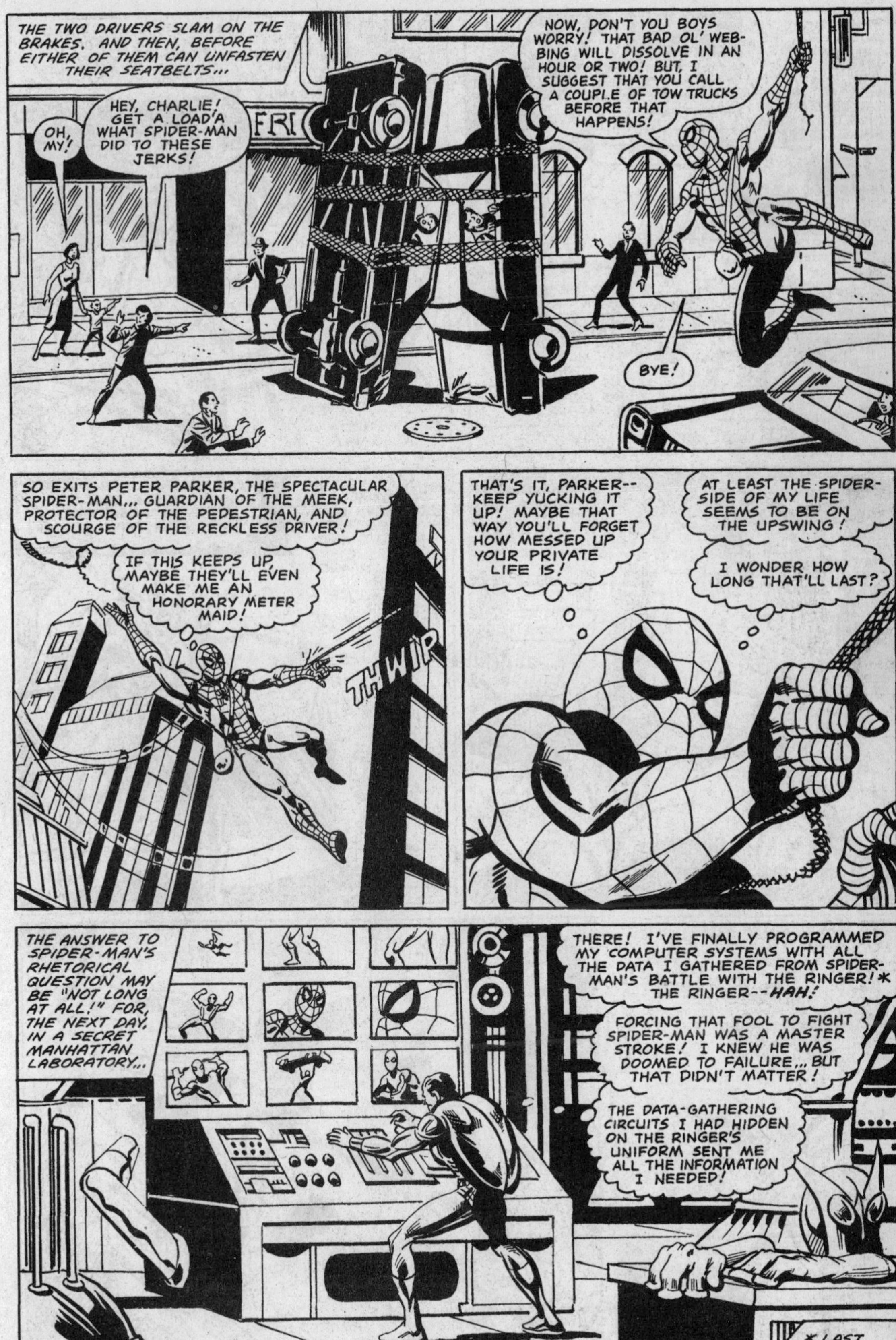
THE TWO DRIVERS SLAM ON THE BRAKES. AND THEN, BEFORE EITHER OF THEM CAN UNFASTEN THEIR SEATBELTS...
OH, MY!
HEY, CHARLIE! GET A LOAD'A WHAT SPIDER-MAN DID TO THESE JERKS!
NOW, DON'T YOU BOYS WORRY! THAT BAD OL' WEBBING WILL DISSOLVE IN AN HOUR OR TWO! BUT, I SUGGEST THAT YOU CALL A COUPLE OF TOW TRUCKS BEFORE THAT HAPPENS!
BYE!
SO EXITS PETER PARKER, THE SPECTACULAR SPIDER-MAN... GUARDIAN OF THE MEEK, PROTECTOR OF THE PEDESTRIAN, AND SCOURGE OF THE RECKLESS DRIVER!
IF THIS KEEPS UP, MAYBE THEY'LL EVEN MAKE ME AN HONORARY METER MAID!
THWIP
THAT'S IT, PARKER-- KEEP YUCKING IT UP! MAYBE THAT WAY YOU'LL FORGET HOW MESSED UP YOUR PRIVATE LIFE IS!
AT LEAST THE SPIDER-SIDE OF MY LIFE SEEMS TO BE ON THE UPSWING!
I WONDER HOW LONG THAT'LL LAST?
THE ANSWER TO SPIDER-MAN'S RHETORICAL QUESTION MAY BE "NOT LONG AT ALL!" FOR, THE NEXT DAY, IN A SECRET MANHATTAN LABORATORY...
THERE! I'VE FINALLY PROGRAMMED MY COMPUTER SYSTEMS WITH ALL THE DATA I GATHERED FROM SPIDER-MAN'S BATTLE WITH THE RINGER!* THE RINGER--HAH!
FORCING THAT FOOL TO FIGHT SPIDER-MAN WAS A MASTER STROKE! I KNEW HE WAS DOOMED TO FAILURE... BUT THAT DIDN'T MATTER!
THE DATA-GATHERING CIRCUITS I HAD HIDDEN ON THE RINGER'S UNIFORM SENT ME ALL THE INFORMATION I NEEDED!
*LAST ISSUE.--T.
7

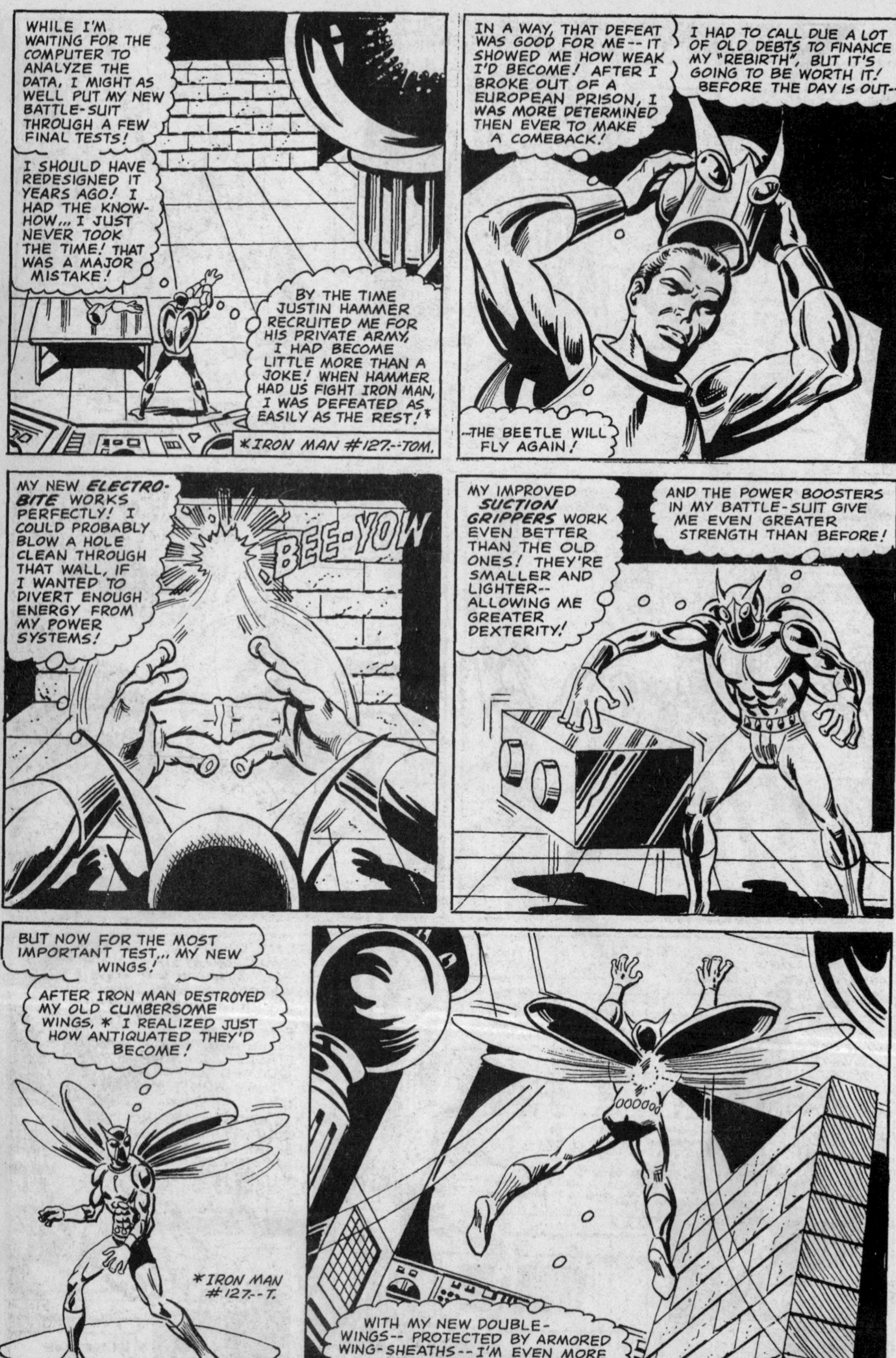

WHILE I'M WAITING FOR THE COMPUTER TO ANALYZE THE DATA, I MIGHT AS WELL PUT MY NEW BATTLE-SUIT THROUGH A FEW FINAL TESTS!
I SHOULD HAVE REDESIGNED IT YEARS AGO! I HAD THE KNOW-HOW... I JUST NEVER TOOK THE TIME! THAT WAS A MAJOR MISTAKE!
BY THE TIME JUSTIN HAMMER RECRUITED ME FOR HIS PRIVATE ARMY, I HAD BECOME LITTLE MORE THAN A JOKE! WHEN HAMMER HAD US FIGHT IRON MAN, I WAS DEFEATED AS EASILY AS THE REST!*
*IRON MAN #127.--TOM.
IN A WAY, THAT DEFEAT WAS GOOD FOR ME-- IT SHOWED ME HOW WEAK I'D BECOME! AFTER I BROKE OUT OF A EUROPEAN PRISON, I WAS MORE DETERMINED THEN EVER TO MAKE A COMEBACK!
I HAD TO CALL DUE A LOT OF OLD DEBTS TO FINANCE MY "REBIRTH", BUT IT'S GOING TO BE WORTH IT! BEFORE THE DAY IS OUT--
--THE BEETLE WILL FLY AGAIN!
MY NEW ELECTRO-BITE WORKS PERFECTLY! I COULD PROBABLY BLOW A HOLE CLEAN THROUGH THAT WALL, IF I WANTED TO DIVERT ENOUGH ENERGY FROM MY POWER SYSTEMS!
BEE-YOW
MY IMPROVED SUCTION GRIPPERS WORK EVEN BETTER THAN THE OLD ONES! THEY'RE SMALLER AND LIGHTER-- ALLOWING ME GREATER DEXTERITY!
AND THE POWER BOOSTERS IN MY BATTLE-SUIT GIVE ME EVEN GREATER STRENGTH THAN BEFORE!
BUT NOW FOR THE MOST IMPORTANT TEST... MY NEW WINGS!
AFTER IRON MAN DESTROYED MY OLD CUMBERSOME WINGS,* I REALIZED JUST HOW ANTIQUATED THEY'D BECOME!
*IRON MAN #127.--T.
WITH MY NEW DOUBLE-WINGS-- PROTECTED BY ARMORED WING-SHEATHS--I'M EVEN MORE LIKE A HUMAN BEETLE!

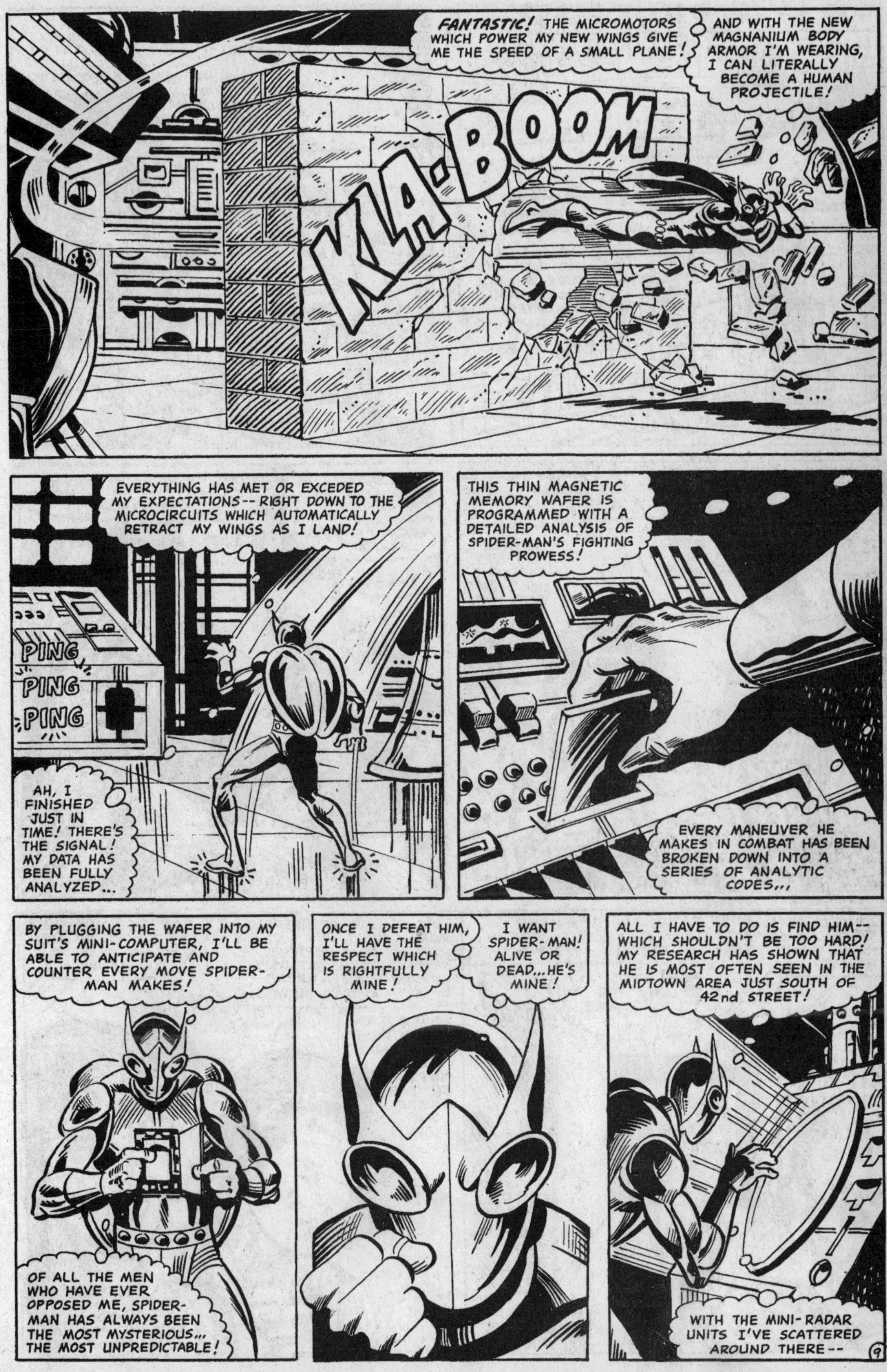
FANTASTIC! THE MICROMOTORS WHICH POWER MY NEW WINGS GIVE ME THE SPEED OF A SMALL PLANE!
AND WITH THE NEW MAGNANIUM BODY ARMOR I'M WEARING, I CAN LITERALLY BECOME A HUMAN PROJECTILE!
KLA-BOOM
EVERYTHING HAS MET OR EXCEDED MY EXPECTATIONS-- RIGHT DOWN TO THE MICROCIRCUITS WHICH AUTOMATICALLY RETRACT MY WINGS AS I LAND!
PING
PING
PING
AH, I FINISHED JUST IN TIME! THERE'S THE SIGNAL! MY DATA HAS BEEN FULLY ANALYZED...
THIS THIN MAGNETIC MEMORY WAFER IS PROGRAMMED WITH A DETAILED ANALYSIS OF SPIDER-MAN'S FIGHTING PROWESS!
EVERY MANEUVER HE MAKES IN COMBAT HAS BEEN BROKEN DOWN INTO A SERIES OF ANALYTIC CODES,,,
BY PLUGGING THE WAFER INTO MY SUIT'S MINI-COMPUTER, I'LL BE ABLE TO ANTICIPATE AND COUNTER EVERY MOVE SPIDER-MAN MAKES!
OF ALL THE MEN WHO HAVE EVER OPPOSED ME, SPIDER-MAN HAS ALWAYS BEEN THE MOST MYSTERIOUS... THE MOST UNPREDICTABLE!
ONCE I DEFEAT HIM, I'LL HAVE THE RESPECT WHICH IS RIGHTFULLY MINE!
I WANT SPIDER-MAN! ALIVE OR DEAD... HE'S MINE!
ALL I HAVE TO DO IS FIND HIM-- WHICH SHOULDN'T BE TOO HARD! MY RESEARCH HAS SHOWN THAT HE IS MOST OFTEN SEEN IN THE MIDTOWN AREA JUST SOUTH OF 42nd STREET!
WITH THE MINI-RADAR UNITS I'VE SCATTERED AROUND THERE--
9

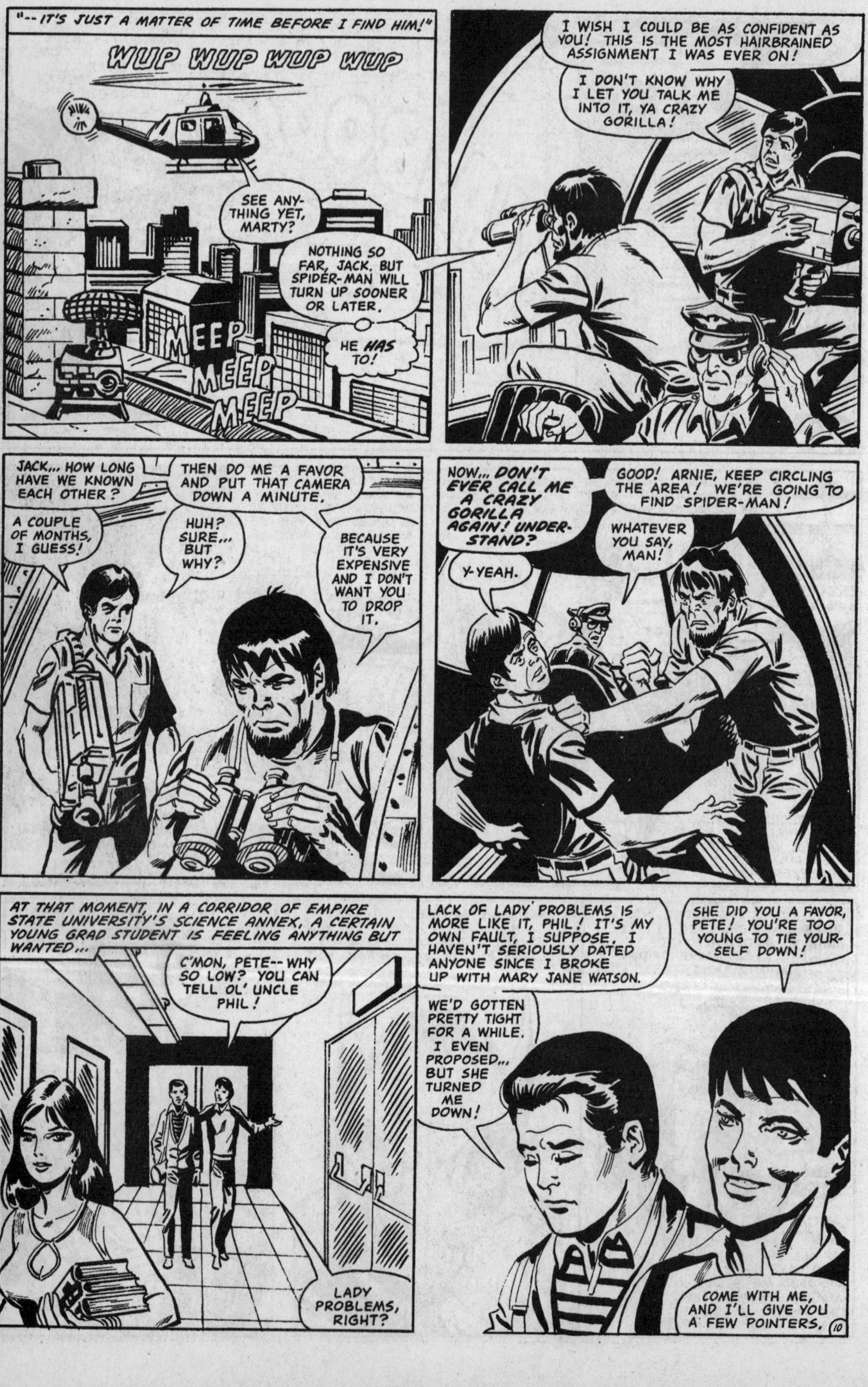
"-- IT'S JUST A MATTER OF TIME BEFORE I FIND HIM!"
WUP WUP WUP WUP
SEE ANYTHING YET, MARTY?
NOTHING SO FAR, JACK. BUT SPIDER-MAN WILL TURN UP SOONER OR LATER.
HE HAS TO!
MEEP MEEP MEEP
I WISH I COULD BE AS CONFIDENT AS YOU! THIS IS THE MOST HAIRBRAINED ASSIGNMENT I WAS EVER ON!
I DON'T KNOW WHY I LET YOU TALK ME INTO IT, YA CRAZY GORILLA!
JACK... HOW LONG HAVE WE KNOWN EACH OTHER?
A COUPLE OF MONTHS, I GUESS!
THEN DO ME A FAVOR AND PUT THAT CAMERA DOWN A MINUTE.
HUH? SURE... BUT WHY?
BECAUSE IT'S VERY EXPENSIVE AND I DON'T WANT YOU TO DROP IT.
NOW... DON'T EVER CALL ME A CRAZY GORILLA AGAIN! UNDERSTAND?
Y-YEAH.
GOOD! ARNIE, KEEP CIRCLING THE AREA! WE'RE GOING TO FIND SPIDER-MAN!
WHATEVER YOU SAY, MAN!
AT THAT MOMENT, IN A CORRIDOR OF EMPIRE STATE UNIVERSITY'S SCIENCE ANNEX, A CERTAIN YOUNG GRAD STUDENT IS FEELING ANYTHING BUT WANTED...
C'MON, PETE-- WHY SO LOW? YOU CAN TELL OL' UNCLE PHIL!
LADY PROBLEMS, RIGHT?
LACK OF LADY PROBLEMS IS MORE LIKE IT, PHIL! IT'S MY OWN FAULT, I SUPPOSE. I HAVEN'T SERIOUSLY DATED ANYONE SINCE I BROKE UP WITH MARY JANE WATSON.
WE'D GOTTEN PRETTY TIGHT FOR A WHILE. I EVEN PROPOSED... BUT SHE TURNED ME DOWN!
SHE DID YOU A FAVOR, PETE! YOU'RE TOO YOUNG TO TIE YOURSELF DOWN!
COME WITH ME, AND I'LL GIVE YOU A FEW POINTERS.
10

BUT, AS PETER FOLLOWS PHIL CHANG OUT THROUGH A SIDE EXIT...

WHOA! I DON'T KNOW WHO THOSE BIG GUYS ARE, BUT THE FELLOW THEY'VE CORNERED IS GREG SALINGER-- A FRESHMAN IN MY CHEMISTRY CLASS!

FEEL THAT SUNSHINE, PARKER! DOESN'T IT JUST MAKE YOU WANT TO HIT THE STREET AND CRUISE FOR CUTIES?

UH... YEAH!

SURE.

MAYBE SOME OTHER TIME!

I JUST REMEMBERED SOMETHING! SEE YA!

WHAT? BUT, PETE--!

WHAT'S HIS PROBLEM? IS HE AFRAID OF WOMEN?

DASHING BACK INTO THE BUILDING, PETER TAKES A QUICK TURN INTO A LITTLE USED STAIRWELL...

I HATED TO RUN OUT ON PHIL LIKE THAT, BUT IT COULDN'T BE HELPED!

SOMETIMES IT SEEMS LIKE I'M ALWAYS RUNNING OUT ON FRIENDS TO BECOME SPIDER-MAN! MAYBE I'M SUBCONSCIOUSLY AFRAID OF FRIENDSHIP, AND I USE OL' SPIDEY AS AN ESCAPE!

WOW, I MISSED MY CALLING-- I SHOULD'VE BEEN A PSYCHOLO-GIST!

AH, WELL-- I'LL WORRY ABOUT THE STATE OF MY MIND LATER!

LET'S SEE... MY WEB-SHOOTERS ARE ALL LOADED AND READY...

...AND THE MASK IS IN PLACE! NOW I CAN FIND OUT WHY THOSE BIG DUDES ARE HASSLING SALINGER!

GREG'S A NICE GUY... I'D HATE TO THINK THAT HE'S GOTTEN MIXED UP IN SOMETHING SHADY!

BOUNDING UP THE STAIRCASE, SPIDER-MAN EXITS INTO AN UPPER-FLOOR HALLWAY, WHERE...

EEEKK! IT'S SPIDER-MAN!

HEH-HEH! HI, FOLKS! DON'T MIND ME-- I'M JUST PASSING THROUGH!

WELL, THAT WAS A BONEHEADED MOVE! I'D BETTER GET OUT OF HERE BEFORE SOMEONE GETS A GOOD LOOK AT MY SHOULDER BAG AND NOTICES ITS SIMILARITY TO PETER PARKER'S!

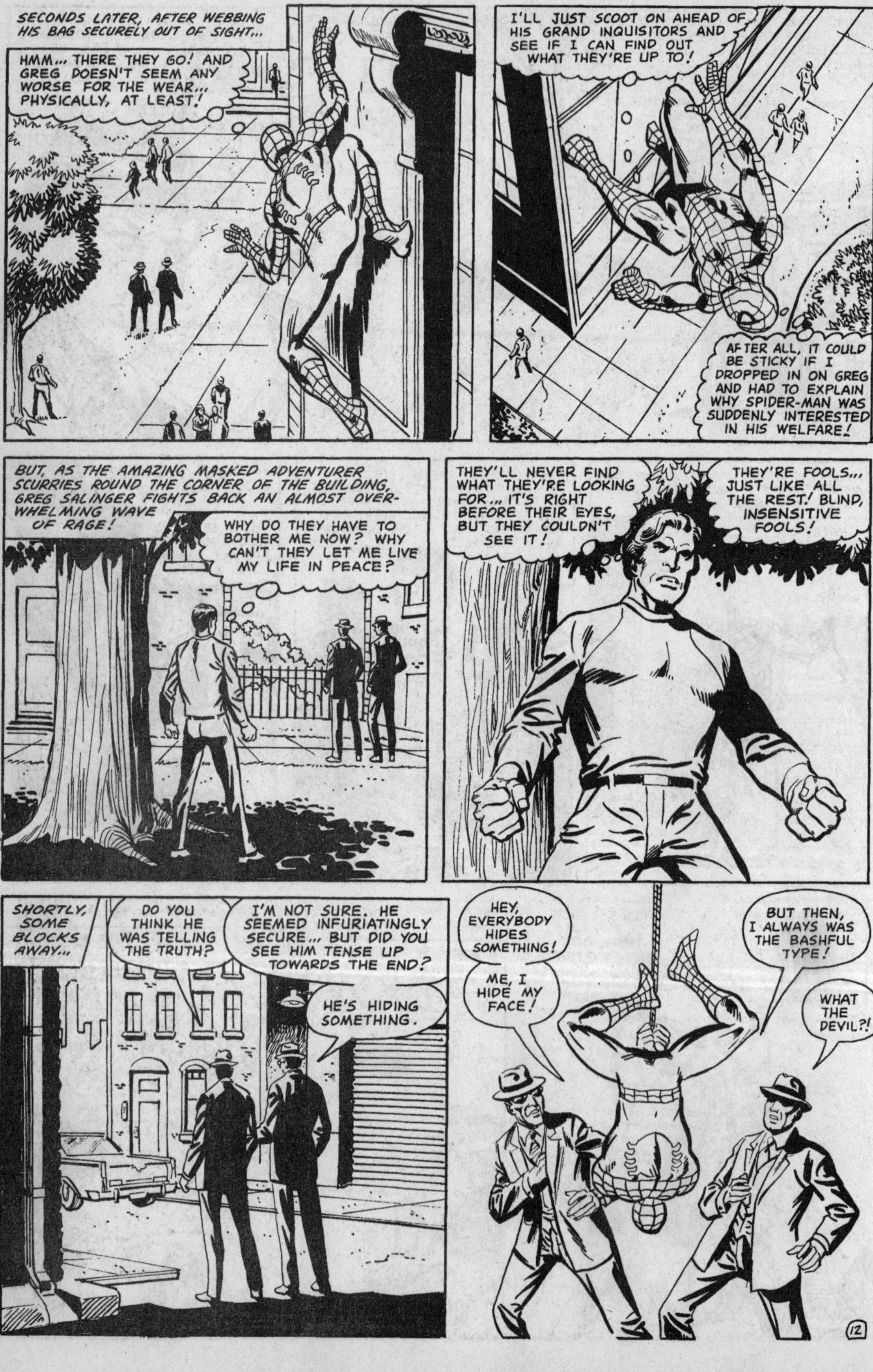

SECONDS LATER, AFTER WEBBING HIS BAG SECURELY OUT OF SIGHT...
HMM... THERE THEY GO! AND GREG DOESN'T SEEM ANY WORSE FOR THE WEAR... PHYSICALLY, AT LEAST!
I'LL JUST SCOOT ON AHEAD OF HIS GRAND INQUISITORS AND SEE IF I CAN FIND OUT WHAT THEY'RE UP TO!
AFTER ALL, IT COULD BE STICKY IF I DROPPED IN ON GREG AND HAD TO EXPLAIN WHY SPIDER-MAN WAS SUDDENLY INTERESTED IN HIS WELFARE!
BUT, AS THE AMAZING MASKED ADVENTURER SCURRIES ROUND THE CORNER OF THE BUILDING, GREG SALINGER FIGHTS BACK AN ALMOST OVER-WHELMING WAVE OF RAGE!
WHY DO THEY HAVE TO BOTHER ME NOW? WHY CAN'T THEY LET ME LIVE MY LIFE IN PEACE?
THEY'LL NEVER FIND WHAT THEY'RE LOOKING FOR... IT'S RIGHT BEFORE THEIR EYES, BUT THEY COULDN'T SEE IT!
THEY'RE FOOLS... JUST LIKE ALL THE REST! BLIND, INSENSITIVE FOOLS!
SHORTLY, SOME BLOCKS AWAY...
DO YOU THINK HE WAS TELLING THE TRUTH?
I'M NOT SURE. HE SEEMED INFURIATINGLY SECURE... BUT DID YOU SEE HIM TENSE UP TOWARDS THE END?
HE'S HIDING SOMETHING.
HEY, EVERYBODY HIDES SOMETHING!
ME, I HIDE MY FACE!
BUT THEN, I ALWAYS WAS THE BASHFUL TYPE!
WHAT THE DEVIL?!

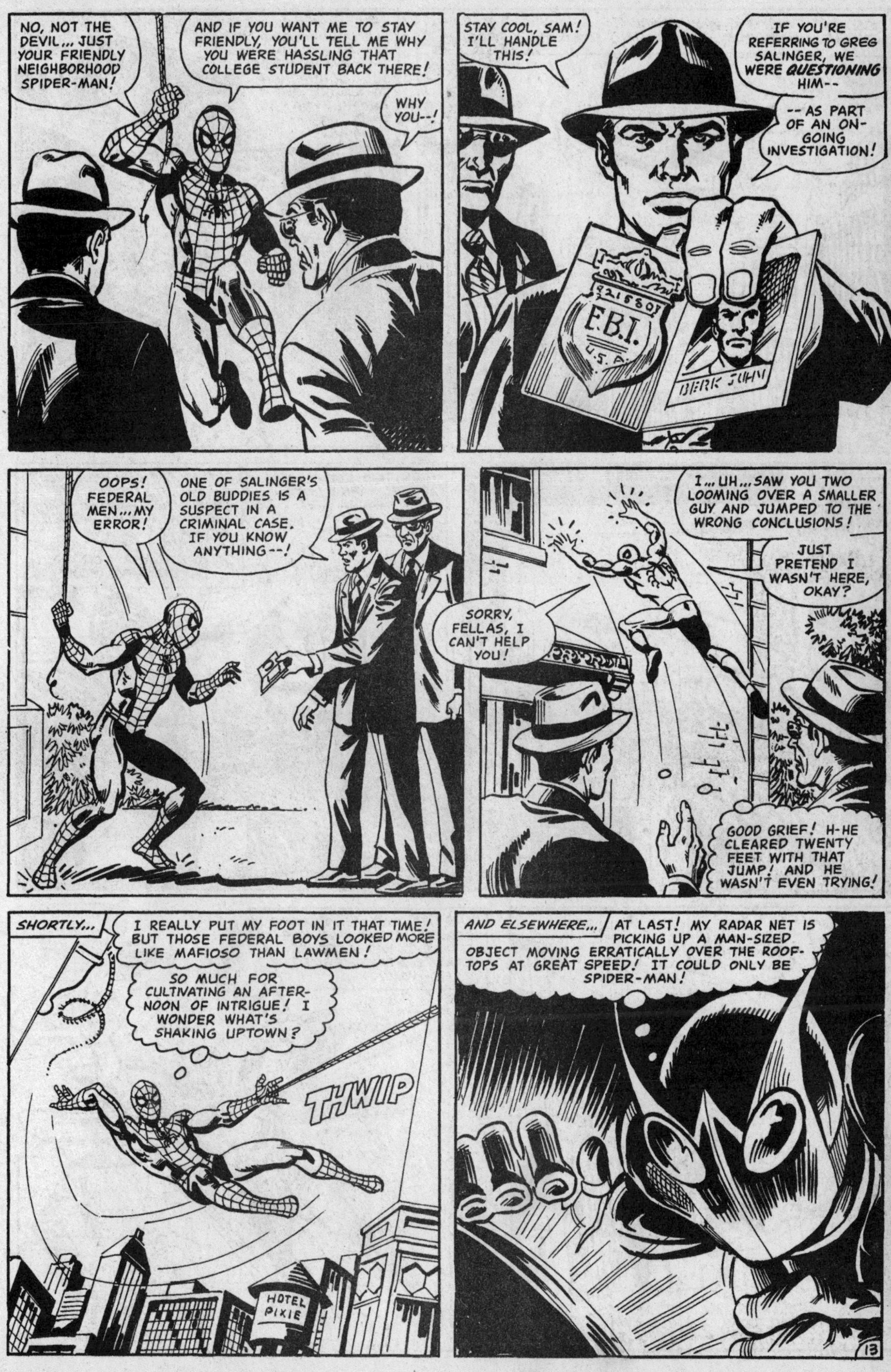
NO, NOT THE DEVIL... JUST YOUR FRIENDLY NEIGHBORHOOD SPIDER-MAN!
AND IF YOU WANT ME TO STAY FRIENDLY, YOU'LL TELL ME WHY YOU WERE HASSLING THAT COLLEGE STUDENT BACK THERE!
WHY YOU--!
STAY COOL, SAM! I'LL HANDLE THIS!
IF YOU'RE REFERRING TO GREG SALINGER, WE WERE QUESTIONING HIM--
--AS PART OF AN ON-GOING INVESTIGATION!
F.B.I.
U.S.A.
BERK JUHN
OOPS! FEDERAL MEN... MY ERROR!
ONE OF SALINGER'S OLD BUDDIES IS A SUSPECT IN A CRIMINAL CASE. IF YOU KNOW ANYTHING--!
SORRY, FELLAS, I CAN'T HELP YOU!
I... UH... SAW YOU TWO LOOMING OVER A SMALLER GUY AND JUMPED TO THE WRONG CONCLUSIONS!
JUST PRETEND I WASN'T HERE, OKAY?
GOOD GRIEF! H-HE CLEARED TWENTY FEET WITH THAT JUMP! AND HE WASN'T EVEN TRYING!
SHORTLY...
I REALLY PUT MY FOOT IN IT THAT TIME! BUT THOSE FEDERAL BOYS LOOKED MORE LIKE MAFIOSO THAN LAWMEN!
SO MUCH FOR CULTIVATING AN AFTER-NOON OF INTRIGUE! I WONDER WHAT'S SHAKING UPTOWN?
THWIP
HOTEL PIXIE
AND ELSEWHERE...
AT LAST! MY RADAR NET IS PICKING UP A MAN-SIZED OBJECT MOVING ERRATICALLY OVER THE ROOF-TOPS AT GREAT SPEED! IT COULD ONLY BE SPIDER-MAN!

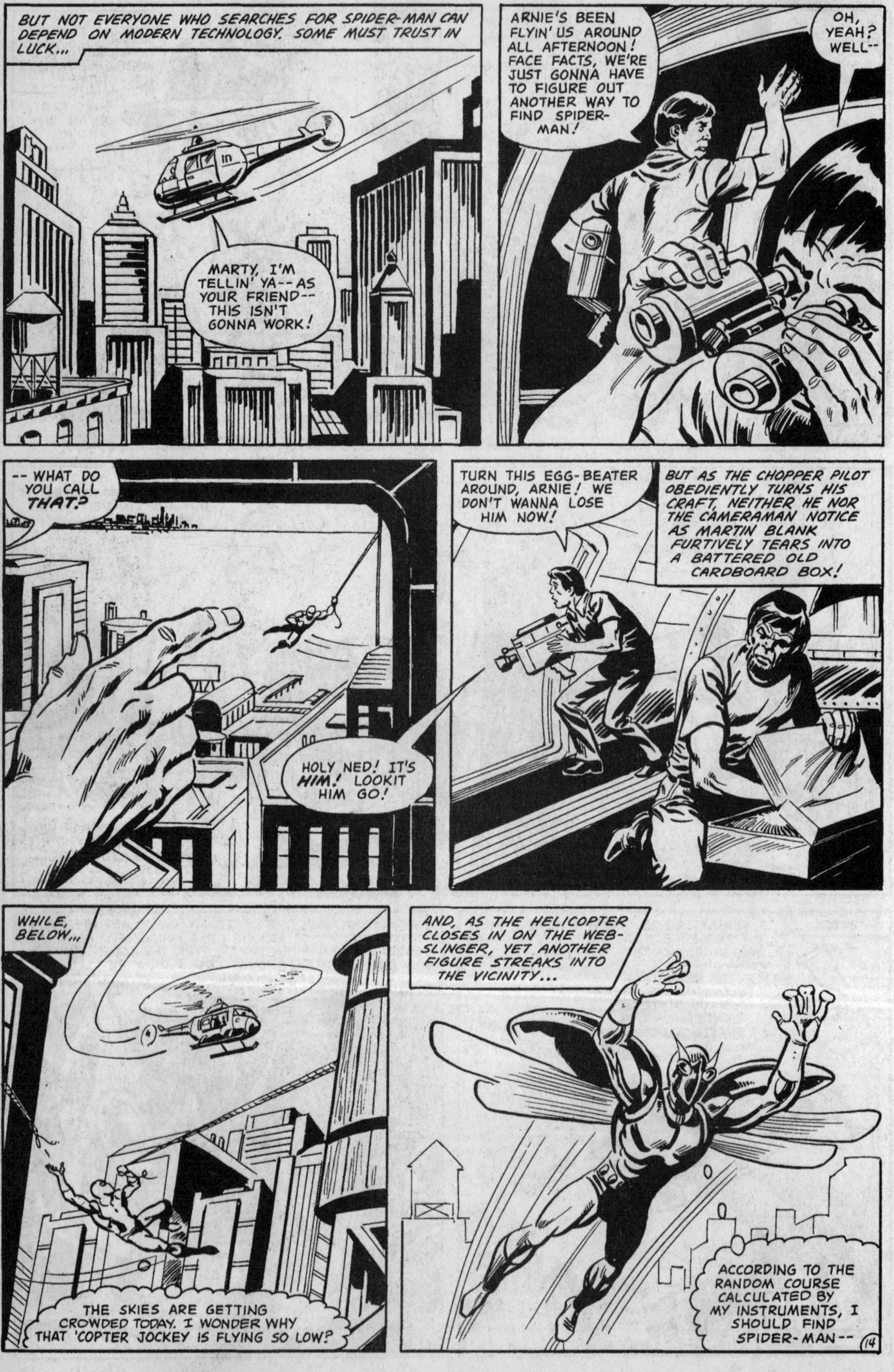
BUT NOT EVERYONE WHO SEARCHES FOR SPIDER-MAN CAN DEPEND ON MODERN TECHNOLOGY. SOME MUST TRUST IN LUCK...
MARTY, I'M TELLIN' YA--AS YOUR FRIEND--THIS ISN'T GONNA WORK!
ARNIE'S BEEN FLYIN' US AROUND ALL AFTERNOON! FACE FACTS, WE'RE JUST GONNA HAVE TO FIGURE OUT ANOTHER WAY TO FIND SPIDER-MAN!
OH, YEAH? WELL--
--WHAT DO YOU CALL THAT?
HOLY NED! IT'S HIM! LOOKIT HIM GO!
TURN THIS EGG-BEATER AROUND, ARNIE! WE DON'T WANNA LOSE HIM NOW!
BUT AS THE CHOPPER PILOT OBEDIENTLY TURNS HIS CRAFT, NEITHER HE NOR THE CAMERAMAN NOTICE AS MARTIN BLANK FURTIVELY TEARS INTO A BATTERED OLD CARDBOARD BOX!
WHILE, BELOW...
THE SKIES ARE GETTING CROWDED TODAY. I WONDER WHY THAT 'COPTER JOCKEY IS FLYING SO LOW?
AND, AS THE HELICOPTER CLOSES IN ON THE WEB-SLINGER, YET ANOTHER FIGURE STREAKS INTO THE VICINITY...
ACCORDING TO THE RANDOM COURSE CALCULATED BY MY INSTRUMENTS, I SHOULD FIND SPIDER-MAN--
14

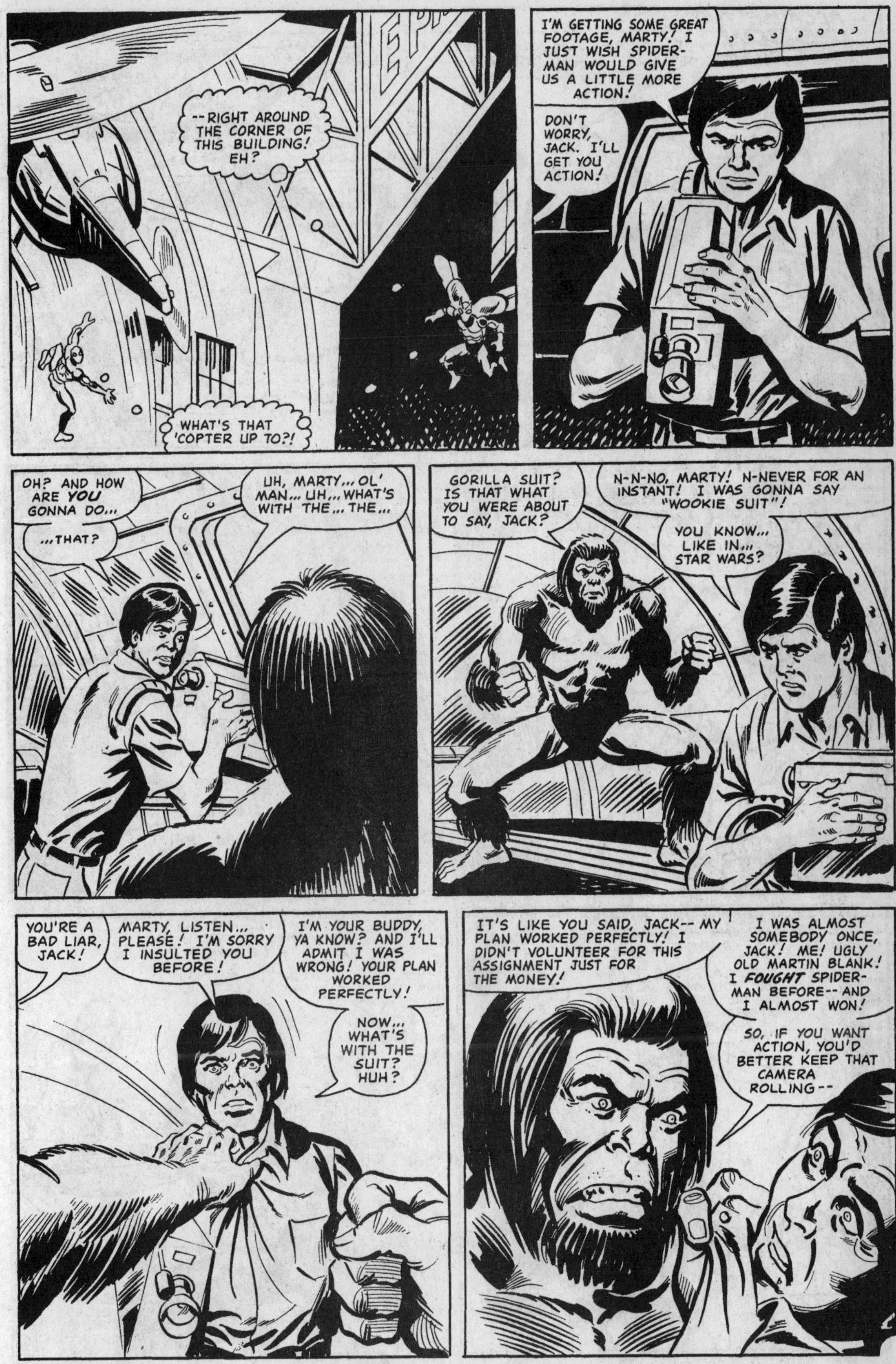
--RIGHT AROUND THE CORNER OF THIS BUILDING! EH?
WHAT'S THAT 'COPTER UP TO?!
I'M GETTING SOME GREAT FOOTAGE, MARTY! I JUST WISH SPIDER-MAN WOULD GIVE US A LITTLE MORE ACTION!
DON'T WORRY, JACK. I'LL GET YOU ACTION!
OH? AND HOW ARE YOU GONNA DO...
...THAT?
UH, MARTY... OL' MAN... UH... WHAT'S WITH THE... THE...
GORILLA SUIT? IS THAT WHAT YOU WERE ABOUT TO SAY, JACK?
N-N-NO, MARTY! N-NEVER FOR AN INSTANT! I WAS GONNA SAY "WOOKIE SUIT"!
YOU KNOW... LIKE IN... STAR WARS?
YOU'RE A BAD LIAR, JACK!
MARTY, LISTEN... PLEASE! I'M SORRY I INSULTED YOU BEFORE!
I'M YOUR BUDDY, YA KNOW? AND I'LL ADMIT I WAS WRONG! YOUR PLAN WORKED PERFECTLY!
NOW... WHAT'S WITH THE SUIT? HUH?
IT'S LIKE YOU SAID, JACK-- MY PLAN WORKED PERFECTLY! I DIDN'T VOLUNTEER FOR THIS ASSIGNMENT JUST FOR THE MONEY!
I WAS ALMOST SOMEBODY ONCE, JACK! ME! UGLY OLD MARTIN BLANK! I FOUGHT SPIDER-MAN BEFORE-- AND I ALMOST WON!
SO, IF YOU WANT ACTION, YOU'D BETTER KEEP THAT CAMERA ROLLING--

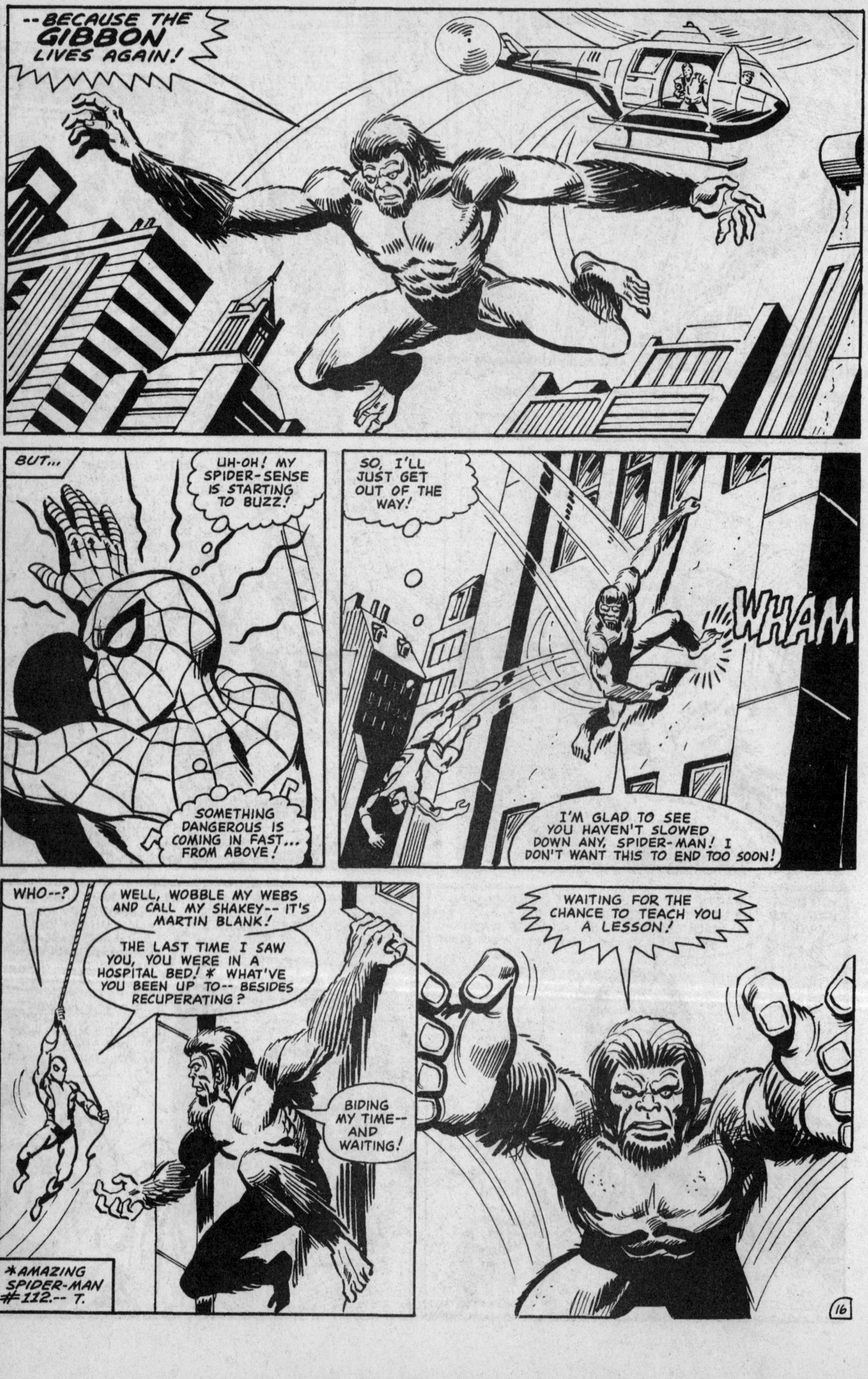
--BECAUSE THE GIBBON LIVES AGAIN!
BUT...
UH-OH! MY SPIDER-SENSE IS STARTING TO BUZZ!
SOMETHING DANGEROUS IS COMING IN FAST... FROM ABOVE!
SO, I'LL JUST GET OUT OF THE WAY!
WHAM
I'M GLAD TO SEE YOU HAVEN'T SLOWED DOWN ANY, SPIDER-MAN! I DON'T WANT THIS TO END TOO SOON!
WHO--?
WELL, WOBBLE MY WEBS AND CALL MY SHAKEY-- IT'S MARTIN BLANK!
THE LAST TIME I SAW YOU, YOU WERE IN A HOSPITAL BED! * WHAT'VE YOU BEEN UP TO-- BESIDES RECUPERATING?
BIDING MY TIME-- AND WAITING!
WAITING FOR THE CHANCE TO TEACH YOU A LESSON!
*AMAZING SPIDER-MAN #112.-- T.

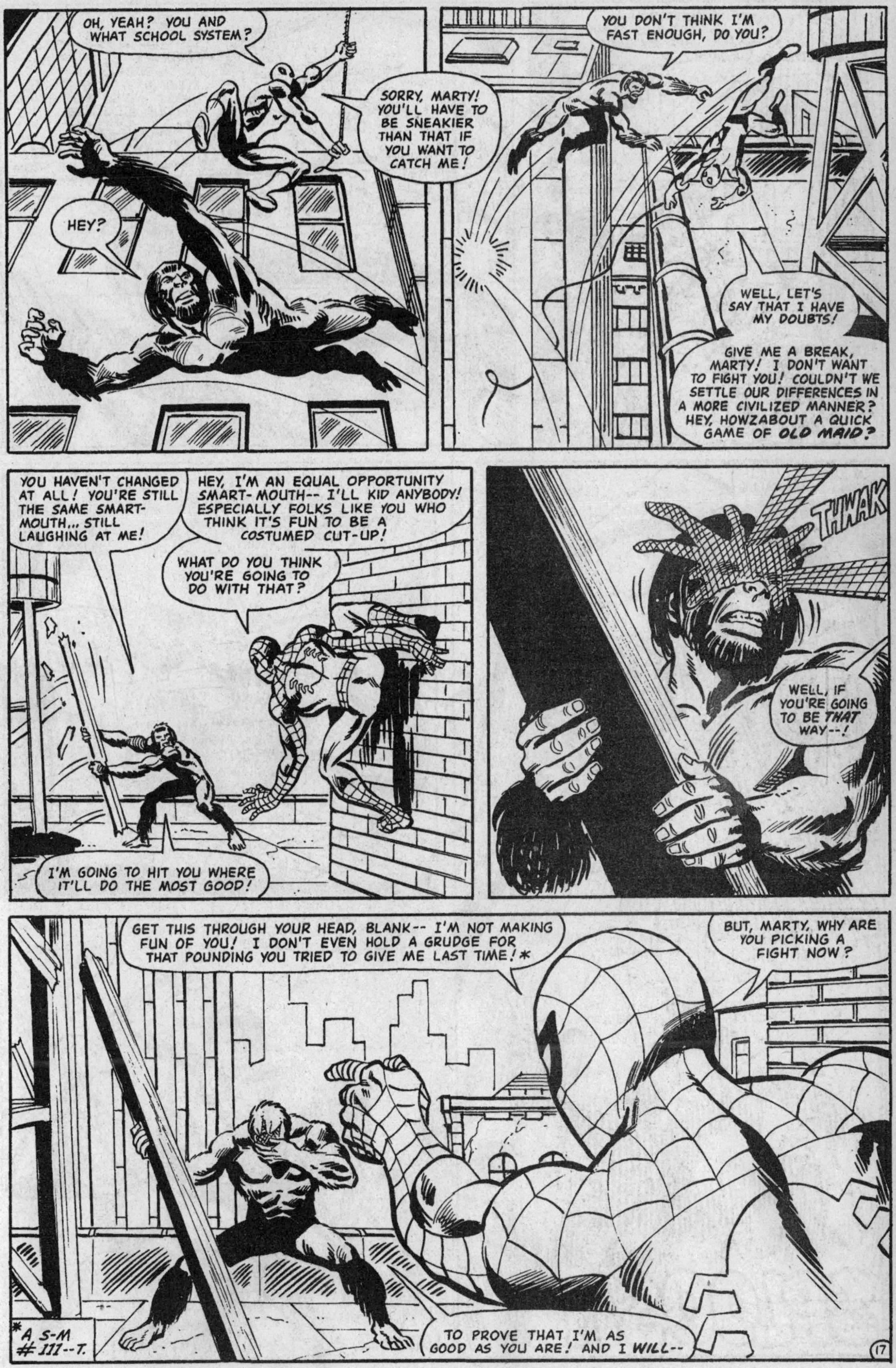
OH, YEAH? YOU AND WHAT SCHOOL SYSTEM?
SORRY, MARTY! YOU'LL HAVE TO BE SNEAKIER THAN THAT IF YOU WANT TO CATCH ME!
HEY?
YOU DON'T THINK I'M FAST ENOUGH, DO YOU?
WELL, LET'S SAY THAT I HAVE MY DOUBTS!
GIVE ME A BREAK, MARTY! I DON'T WANT TO FIGHT YOU! COULDN'T WE SETTLE OUR DIFFERENCES IN A MORE CIVILIZED MANNER? HEY, HOWZABOUT A QUICK GAME OF OLD MAID?
YOU HAVEN'T CHANGED AT ALL! YOU'RE STILL THE SAME SMART-MOUTH... STILL LAUGHING AT ME!
HEY, I'M AN EQUAL OPPORTUNITY SMART-MOUTH-- I'LL KID ANYBODY! ESPECIALLY FOLKS LIKE YOU WHO THINK IT'S FUN TO BE A COSTUMED CUT-UP!
WHAT DO YOU THINK YOU'RE GOING TO DO WITH THAT?
I'M GOING TO HIT YOU WHERE IT'LL DO THE MOST GOOD!
THWAK
WELL, IF YOU'RE GOING TO BE THAT WAY--!
GET THIS THROUGH YOUR HEAD, BLANK-- I'M NOT MAKING FUN OF YOU! I DON'T EVEN HOLD A GRUDGE FOR THAT POUNDING YOU TRIED TO GIVE ME LAST TIME! *
BUT, MARTY, WHY ARE YOU PICKING A FIGHT NOW?
TO PROVE THAT I'M AS GOOD AS YOU ARE! AND I WILL--
*A S-M #111--T.

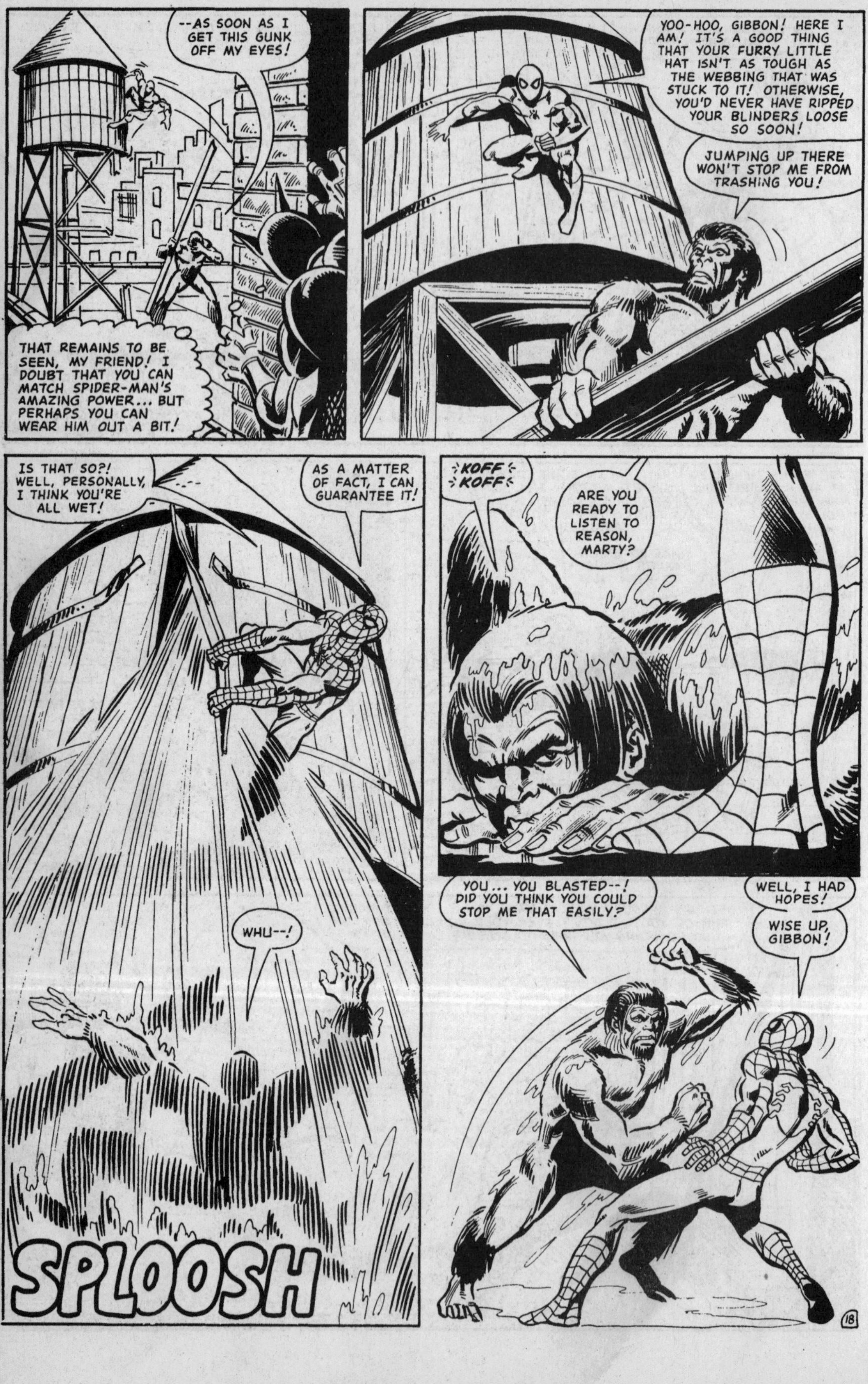
--AS SOON AS I GET THIS GUNK OFF MY EYES!
THAT REMAINS TO BE SEEN, MY FRIEND! I DOUBT THAT YOU CAN MATCH SPIDER-MAN'S AMAZING POWER... BUT PERHAPS YOU CAN WEAR HIM OUT A BIT!
YOO-HOO, GIBBON! HERE I AM! IT'S A GOOD THING THAT YOUR FURRY LITTLE HAT ISN'T AS TOUGH AS THE WEBBING THAT WAS STUCK TO IT! OTHERWISE, YOU'D NEVER HAVE RIPPED YOUR BLINDERS LOOSE SO SOON!
JUMPING UP THERE WON'T STOP ME FROM TRASHING YOU!
IS THAT SO?! WELL, PERSONALLY, I THINK YOU'RE ALL WET!
AS A MATTER OF FACT, I CAN GUARANTEE IT!
WHU--!
SPLOOSH
KOFF KOFF
ARE YOU READY TO LISTEN TO REASON, MARTY?
YOU... YOU BLASTED--! DID YOU THINK YOU COULD STOP ME THAT EASILY?
WELL, I HAD HOPES!
WISE UP, GIBBON!
18

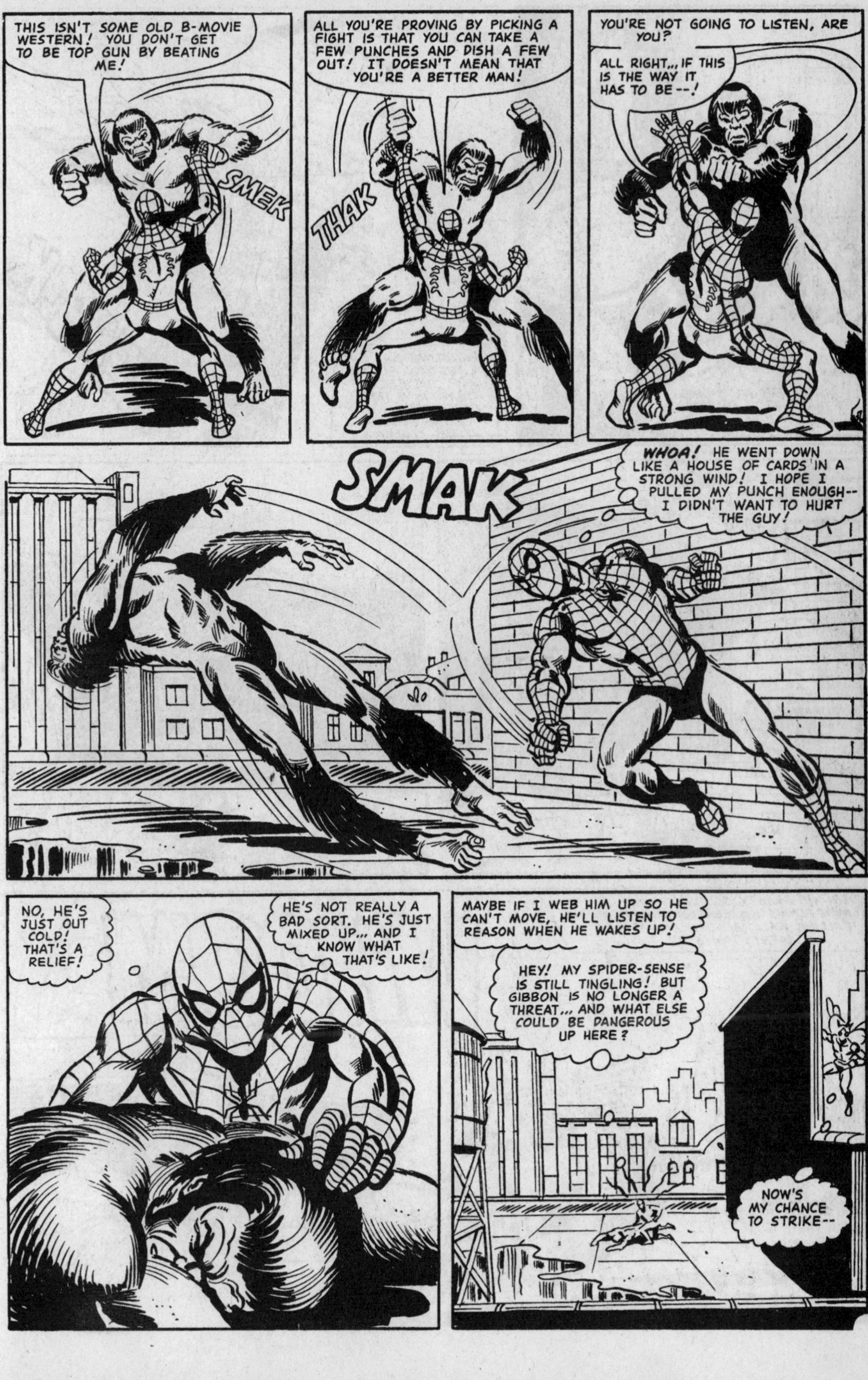
THIS ISN'T SOME OLD B-MOVIE WESTERN! YOU DON'T GET TO BE TOP GUN BY BEATING ME!
SMEK
ALL YOU'RE PROVING BY PICKING A FIGHT IS THAT YOU CAN TAKE A FEW PUNCHES AND DISH A FEW OUT! IT DOESN'T MEAN THAT YOU'RE A BETTER MAN!
THAK
YOU'RE NOT GOING TO LISTEN, ARE YOU?
ALL RIGHT... IF THIS IS THE WAY IT HAS TO BE--!
SMAK
WHOA! HE WENT DOWN LIKE A HOUSE OF CARDS IN A STRONG WIND! I HOPE I PULLED MY PUNCH ENOUGH-- I DIDN'T WANT TO HURT THE GUY!
NO, HE'S JUST OUT COLD! THAT'S A RELIEF!
HE'S NOT REALLY A BAD SORT. HE'S JUST MIXED UP... AND I KNOW WHAT THAT'S LIKE!
MAYBE IF I WEB HIM UP SO HE CAN'T MOVE, HE'LL LISTEN TO REASON WHEN HE WAKES UP!
HEY! MY SPIDER-SENSE IS STILL TINGLING! BUT GIBBON IS NO LONGER A THREAT... AND WHAT ELSE COULD BE DANGEROUS UP HERE?
NOW'S MY CHANCE TO STRIKE--

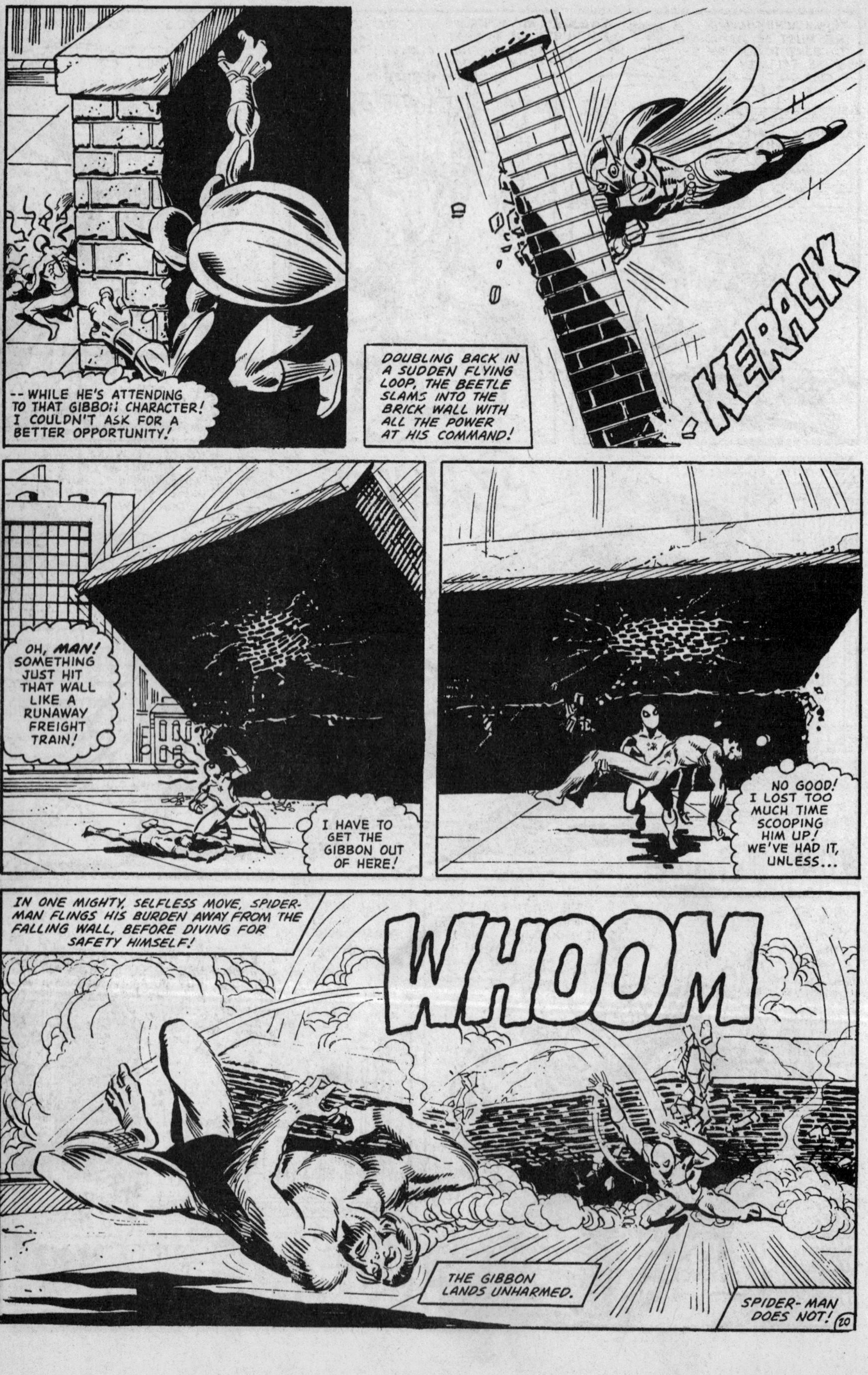
-- WHILE HE'S ATTENDING TO THAT GIBBON CHARACTER! I COULDN'T ASK FOR A BETTER OPPORTUNITY!
DOUBLING BACK IN A SUDDEN FLYING LOOP, THE BEETLE SLAMS INTO THE BRICK WALL WITH ALL THE POWER AT HIS COMMAND!
KERACK
OH, MAN! SOMETHING JUST HIT THAT WALL LIKE A RUNAWAY FREIGHT TRAIN!
I HAVE TO GET THE GIBBON OUT OF HERE!
NO GOOD! I LOST TOO MUCH TIME SCOOPING HIM UP! WE'VE HAD IT, UNLESS...
IN ONE MIGHTY, SELFLESS MOVE, SPIDER-MAN FLINGS HIS BURDEN AWAY FROM THE FALLING WALL, BEFORE DIVING FOR SAFETY HIMSELF!
WHOOM
THE GIBBON LANDS UNHARMED.
SPIDER-MAN DOES NOT!

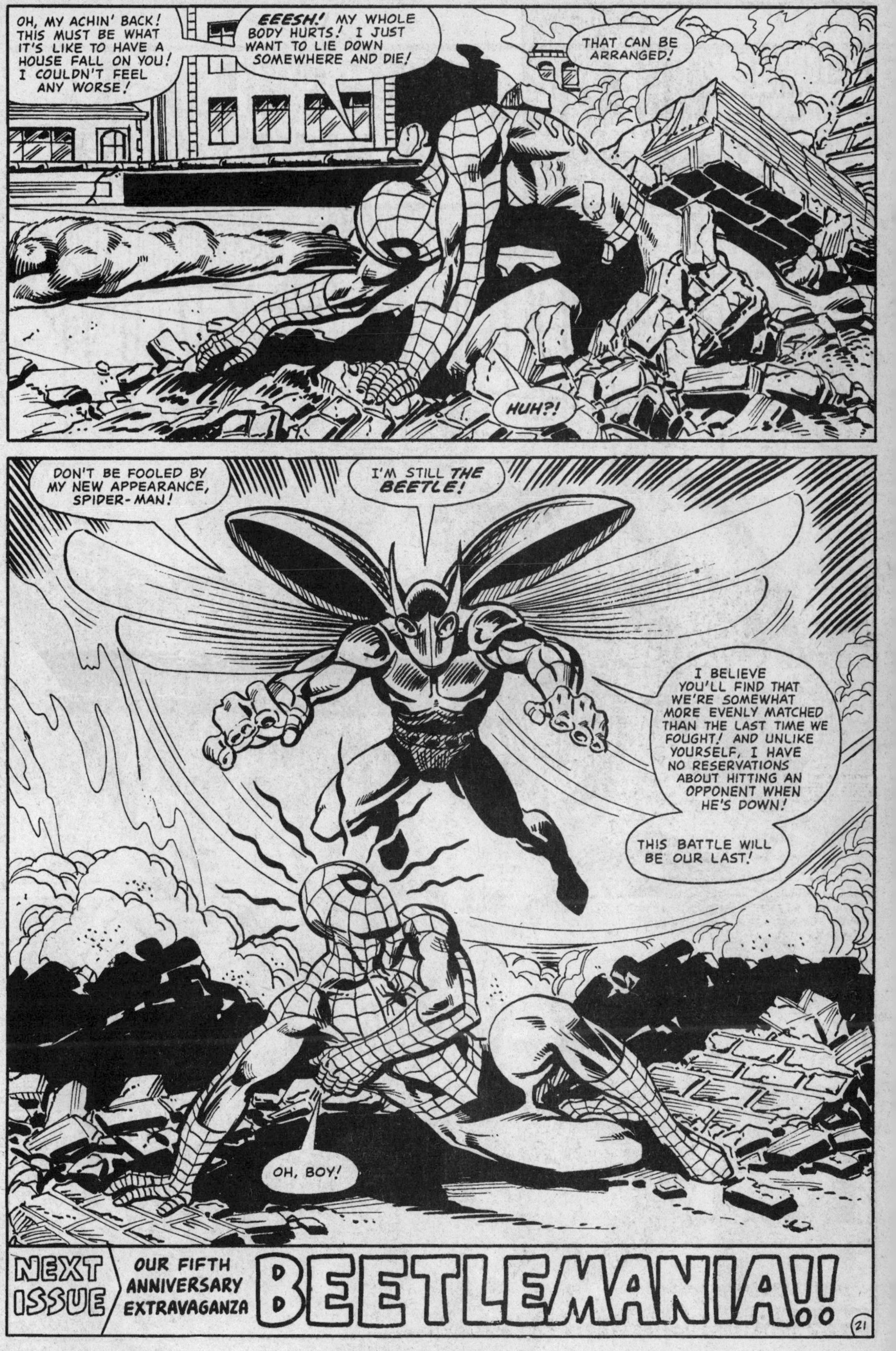
OH, MY ACHIN' BACK! THIS MUST BE WHAT IT'S LIKE TO HAVE A HOUSE FALL ON YOU! I COULDN'T FEEL ANY WORSE!
EEESH! MY WHOLE BODY HURTS! I JUST WANT TO LIE DOWN SOMEWHERE AND DIE!
THAT CAN BE ARRANGED!
HUH?!
DON'T BE FOOLED BY MY NEW APPEARANCE, SPIDER-MAN!
I'M STILL THE BEETLE!
I BELIEVE YOU'LL FIND THAT WE'RE SOMEWHAT MORE EVENLY MATCHED THAN THE LAST TIME WE FOUGHT! AND UNLIKE YOURSELF, I HAVE NO RESERVATIONS ABOUT HITTING AN OPPONENT WHEN HE'S DOWN!
THIS BATTLE WILL BE OUR LAST!
OH, BOY!

NEXT ISSUE OUR FIFTH ANNIVERSARY EXTRAVAGANZA BEETLEMANIA!!

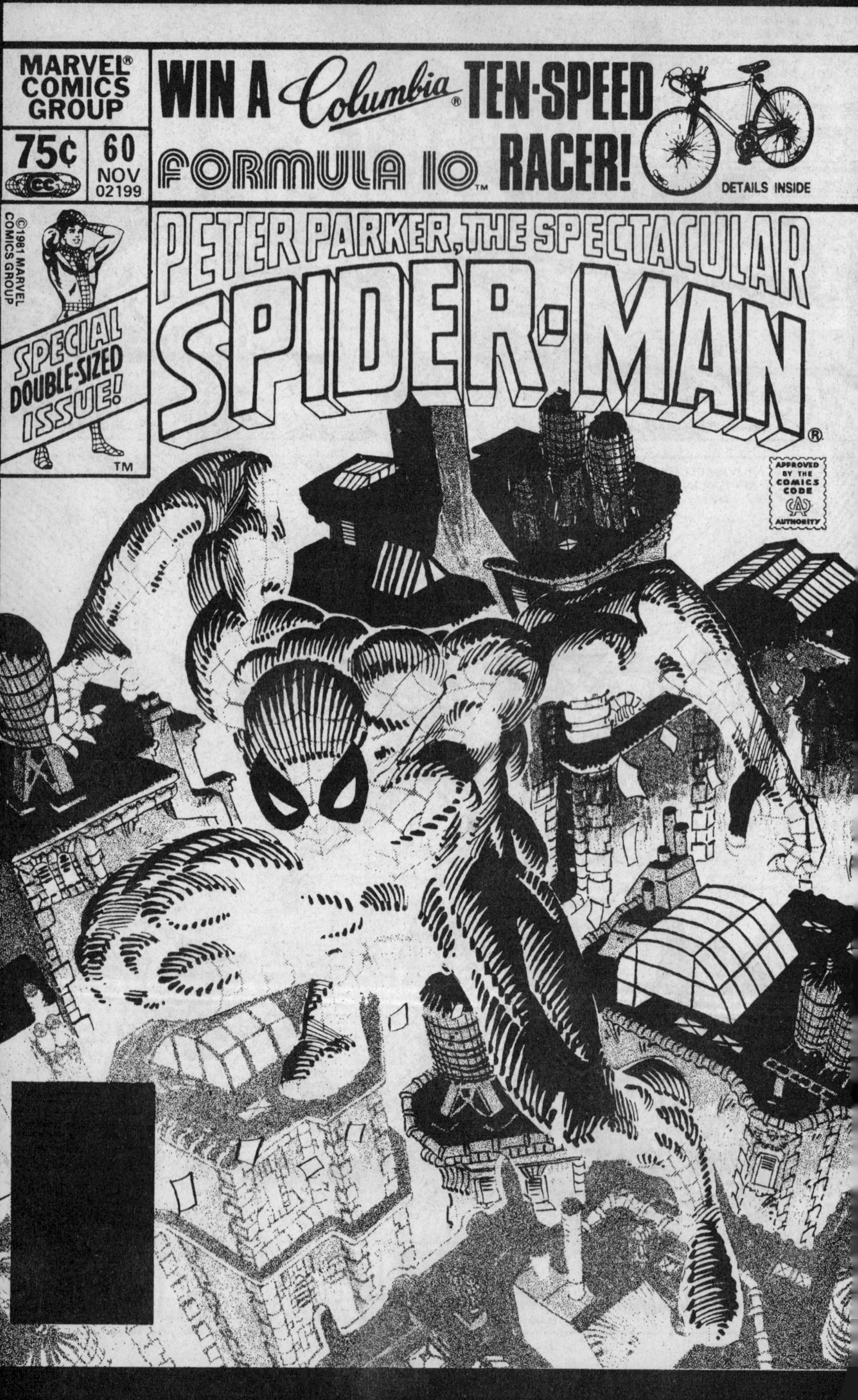
MARVEL® COMICS GROUP
75¢
60
NOV
02199
WIN A Columbia® TEN-SPEED RACER!
FORMULA 10™
DETAILS INSIDE
©1981 MARVEL COMICS GROUP
SPECIAL DOUBLE-SIZED ISSUE!
TM
PETER PARKER, THE SPECTACULAR
SPIDER-MAN®
APPROVED BY THE COMICS CODE AUTHORITY

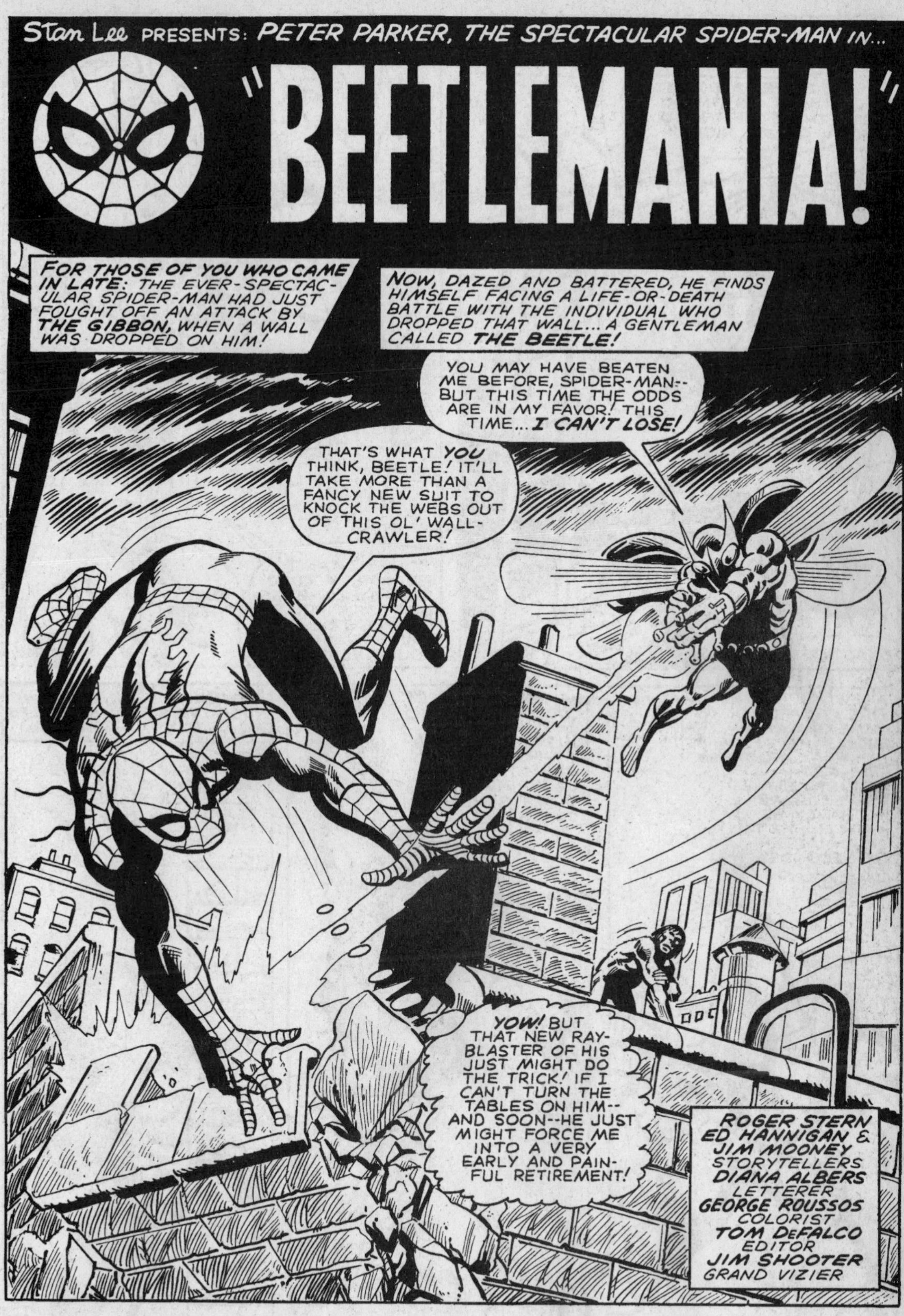
Stan Lee PRESENTS: PETER PARKER, THE SPECTACULAR SPIDER-MAN IN...
"BEETLEMANIA!"
FOR THOSE OF YOU WHO CAME IN LATE: THE EVER-SPECTACULAR SPIDER-MAN HAD JUST FOUGHT OFF AN ATTACK BY THE GIBBON, WHEN A WALL WAS DROPPED ON HIM!
NOW, DAZED AND BATTERED, HE FINDS HIMSELF FACING A LIFE-OR-DEATH BATTLE WITH THE INDIVIDUAL WHO DROPPED THAT WALL... A GENTLEMAN CALLED THE BEETLE!
YOU MAY HAVE BEATEN ME BEFORE, SPIDER-MAN--BUT THIS TIME THE ODDS ARE IN MY FAVOR! THIS TIME... I CAN'T LOSE!
THAT'S WHAT YOU THINK, BEETLE! IT'LL TAKE MORE THAN A FANCY NEW SUIT TO KNOCK THE WEBS OUT OF THIS OL' WALL-CRAWLER!
YOW! BUT THAT NEW RAY-BLASTER OF HIS JUST MIGHT DO THE TRICK! IF I CAN'T TURN THE TABLES ON HIM--AND SOON--HE JUST MIGHT FORCE ME INTO A VERY EARLY AND PAINFUL RETIREMENT!
ROGER STERN ED HANNIGAN & JIM MOONEY STORYTELLERS
DIANA ALBERS LETTERER
GEORGE ROUSSOS COLORIST
TOM DeFALCO EDITOR
JIM SHOOTER GRAND VIZIER

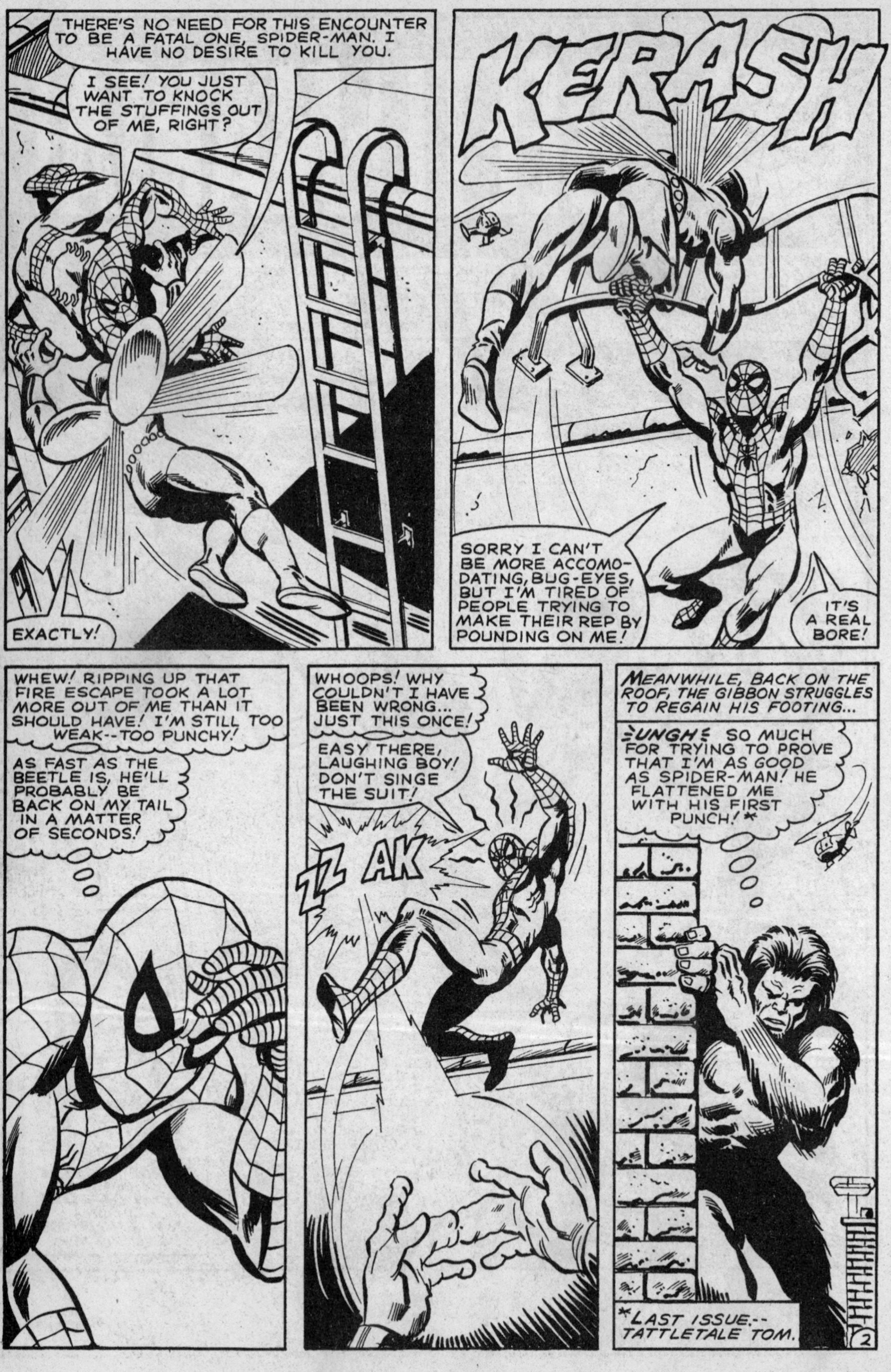
THERE'S NO NEED FOR THIS ENCOUNTER TO BE A FATAL ONE, SPIDER-MAN. I HAVE NO DESIRE TO KILL YOU.
I SEE! YOU JUST WANT TO KNOCK THE STUFFINGS OUT OF ME, RIGHT?
EXACTLY!
KERASH
SORRY I CAN'T BE MORE ACCOMODATING, BUG-EYES, BUT I'M TIRED OF PEOPLE TRYING TO MAKE THEIR REP BY POUNDING ON ME!
IT'S A REAL BORE!
WHEW! RIPPING UP THAT FIRE ESCAPE TOOK A LOT MORE OUT OF ME THAN IT SHOULD HAVE! I'M STILL TOO WEAK--TOO PUNCHY!
AS FAST AS THE BEETLE IS, HE'LL PROBABLY BE BACK ON MY TAIL IN A MATTER OF SECONDS!
WHOOPS! WHY COULDN'T I HAVE BEEN WRONG... JUST THIS ONCE!
EASY THERE, LAUGHING BOY! DON'T SINGE THE SUIT!
ZZ AK
MEANWHILE, BACK ON THE ROOF, THE GIBBON STRUGGLES TO REGAIN HIS FOOTING...
UNGH SO MUCH FOR TRYING TO PROVE THAT I'M AS GOOD AS SPIDER-MAN! HE FLATTENED ME WITH HIS FIRST PUNCH!*
*LAST ISSUE.-- TATTLETALE TOM.
2

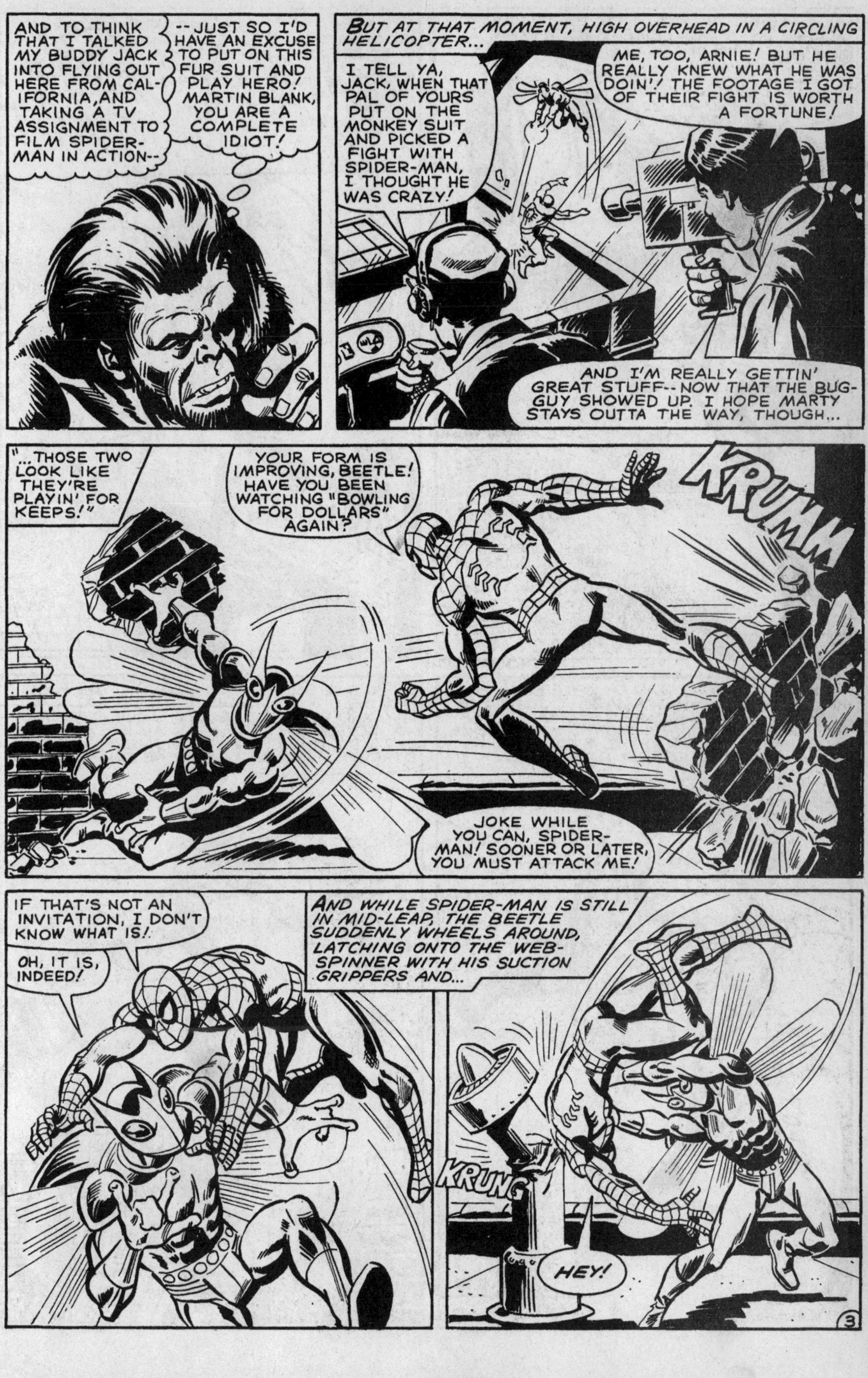
AND TO THINK THAT I TALKED MY BUDDY JACK INTO FLYING OUT HERE FROM CALIFORNIA, AND TAKING A TV ASSIGNMENT TO FILM SPIDER-MAN IN ACTION--
--JUST SO I'D HAVE AN EXCUSE TO PUT ON THIS FUR SUIT AND PLAY HERO! MARTIN BLANK, YOU ARE A COMPLETE IDIOT!
BUT AT THAT MOMENT, HIGH OVERHEAD IN A CIRCLING HELICOPTER...
I TELL YA, JACK, WHEN THAT PAL OF YOURS PUT ON THE MONKEY SUIT AND PICKED A FIGHT WITH SPIDER-MAN, I THOUGHT HE WAS CRAZY!
ME, TOO, ARNIE! BUT HE REALLY KNEW WHAT HE WAS DOIN'! THE FOOTAGE I GOT OF THEIR FIGHT IS WORTH A FORTUNE!
AND I'M REALLY GETTIN' GREAT STUFF--NOW THAT THE BUG-GUY SHOWED UP. I HOPE MARTY STAYS OUTTA THE WAY, THOUGH...
"...THOSE TWO LOOK LIKE THEY'RE PLAYIN' FOR KEEPS!"
YOUR FORM IS IMPROVING, BEETLE! HAVE YOU BEEN WATCHING "BOWLING FOR DOLLARS" AGAIN?
KRUMM
JOKE WHILE YOU CAN, SPIDER-MAN! SOONER OR LATER, YOU MUST ATTACK ME!
IF THAT'S NOT AN INVITATION, I DON'T KNOW WHAT IS!
OH, IT IS, INDEED!
AND WHILE SPIDER-MAN IS STILL IN MID-LEAP, THE BEETLE SUDDENLY WHEELS AROUND, LATCHING ONTO THE WEB-SPINNER WITH HIS SUCTION GRIPPERS AND...
KRUNG
HEY!

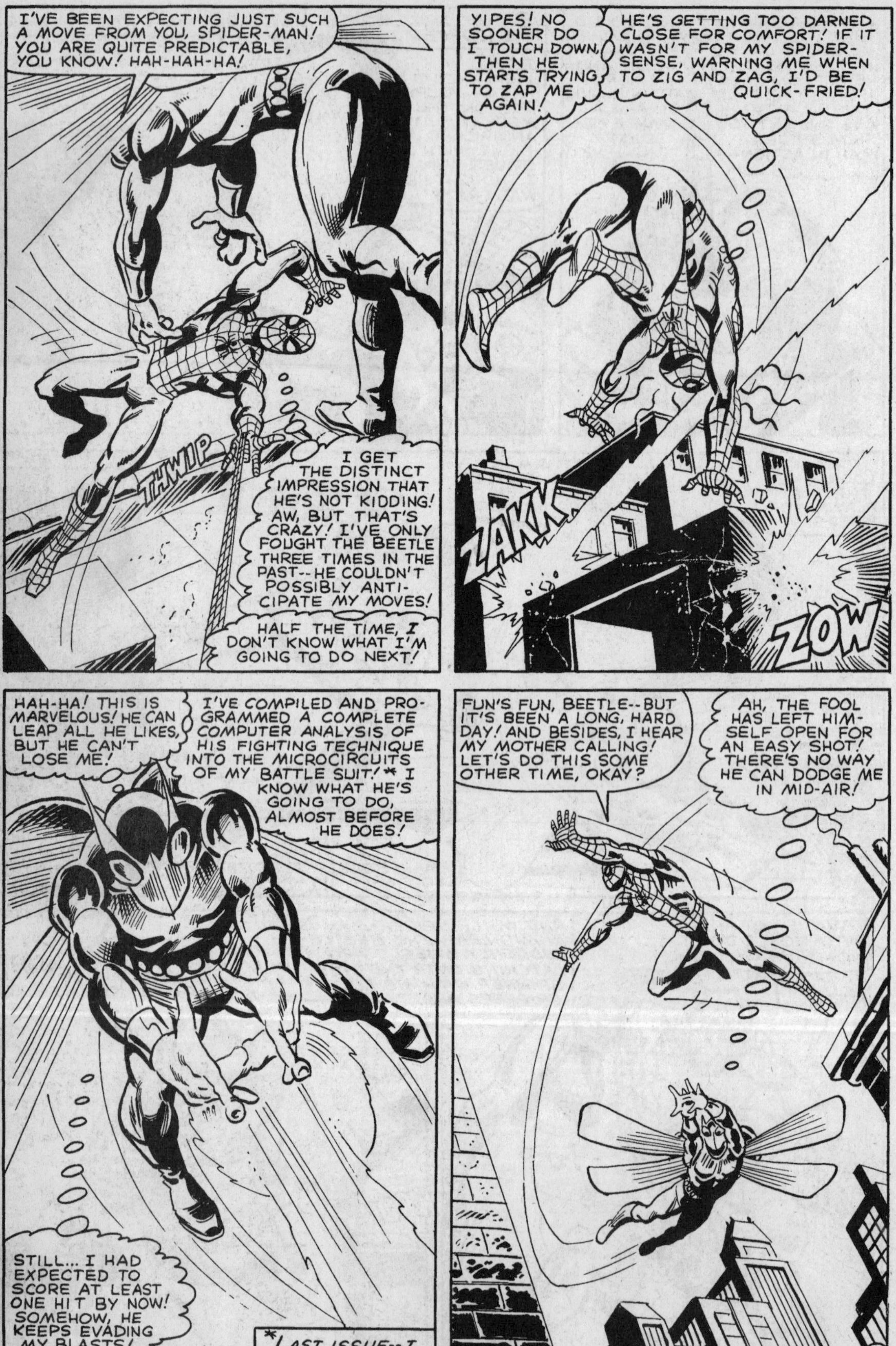

I'VE BEEN EXPECTING JUST SUCH A MOVE FROM YOU, SPIDER-MAN! YOU ARE QUITE PREDICTABLE, YOU KNOW! HAH-HAH-HA!
THWIP
I GET THE DISTINCT IMPRESSION THAT HE'S NOT KIDDING! AW, BUT THAT'S CRAZY! I'VE ONLY FOUGHT THE BEETLE THREE TIMES IN THE PAST--HE COULDN'T POSSIBLY ANTI-CIPATE MY MOVES!
HALF THE TIME, I DON'T KNOW WHAT I'M GOING TO DO NEXT!
YIPES! NO SOONER DO I TOUCH DOWN, THEN HE STARTS TRYING TO ZAP ME AGAIN!
HE'S GETTING TOO DARNED CLOSE FOR COMFORT! IF IT WASN'T FOR MY SPIDER-SENSE, WARNING ME WHEN TO ZIG AND ZAG, I'D BE QUICK-FRIED!
ZAKK
ZOW
HAH-HA! THIS IS MARVELOUS! HE CAN LEAP ALL HE LIKES, BUT HE CAN'T LOSE ME!
I'VE COMPILED AND PRO-GRAMMED A COMPLETE COMPUTER ANALYSIS OF HIS FIGHTING TECHNIQUE INTO THE MICROCIRCUITS OF MY BATTLE SUIT!* I KNOW WHAT HE'S GOING TO DO, ALMOST BEFORE HE DOES!
STILL... I HAD EXPECTED TO SCORE AT LEAST ONE HIT BY NOW! SOMEHOW, HE KEEPS EVADING MY BLASTS!
*LAST ISSUE:-T.
FUN'S FUN, BEETLE--BUT IT'S BEEN A LONG, HARD DAY! AND BESIDES, I HEAR MY MOTHER CALLING! LET'S DO THIS SOME OTHER TIME, OKAY?
AH, THE FOOL HAS LEFT HIM-SELF OPEN FOR AN EASY SHOT! THERE'S NO WAY HE CAN DODGE ME IN MID-AIR!
4

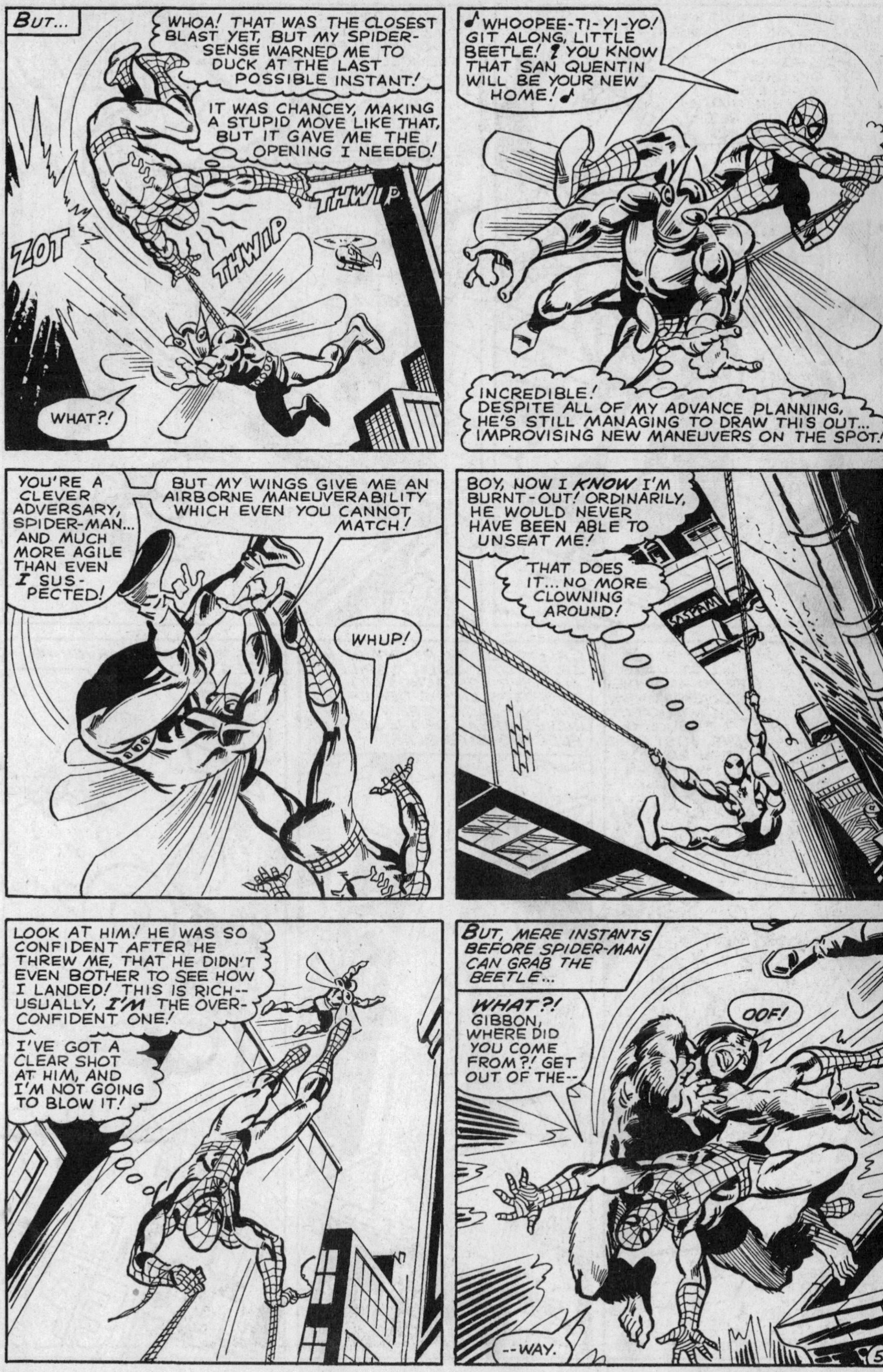
BUT...
WHOA! THAT WAS THE CLOSEST BLAST YET, BUT MY SPIDER-SENSE WARNED ME TO DUCK AT THE LAST POSSIBLE INSTANT!
IT WAS CHANCEY, MAKING A STUPID MOVE LIKE THAT, BUT IT GAVE ME THE OPENING I NEEDED!
THWIP
ZOT
THWIP
WHAT?!
♪WHOOPEE-TI-YI-YO! GIT ALONG, LITTLE BEETLE! ♪ YOU KNOW THAT SAN QUENTIN WILL BE YOUR NEW HOME!♪
INCREDIBLE! DESPITE ALL OF MY ADVANCE PLANNING, HE'S STILL MANAGING TO DRAW THIS OUT... IMPROVISING NEW MANEUVERS ON THE SPOT!
YOU'RE A CLEVER ADVERSARY, SPIDER-MAN... AND MUCH MORE AGILE THAN EVEN I SUSPECTED!
BUT MY WINGS GIVE ME AN AIRBORNE MANEUVERABILITY WHICH EVEN YOU CANNOT MATCH!
WHUP!
BOY, NOW I KNOW I'M BURNT-OUT! ORDINARILY, HE WOULD NEVER HAVE BEEN ABLE TO UNSEAT ME!
THAT DOES IT... NO MORE CLOWNING AROUND!
LOOK AT HIM! HE WAS SO CONFIDENT AFTER HE THREW ME, THAT HE DIDN'T EVEN BOTHER TO SEE HOW I LANDED! THIS IS RICH-- USUALLY, I'M THE OVER-CONFIDENT ONE!
I'VE GOT A CLEAR SHOT AT HIM, AND I'M NOT GOING TO BLOW IT!
BUT, MERE INSTANTS BEFORE SPIDER-MAN CAN GRAB THE BEETLE...
WHAT?! GIBBON, WHERE DID YOU COME FROM?! GET OUT OF THE--
OOF!
--WAY.
5

HE...WASN'T PAYING ATTENTION... TO ME. I... THOUGHT I... COULD HELP!

OH, GREAT! MARTY'S PUNCHIER THAN I AM, AND HE'S *STILL* TRYING TO PROVE HIMSELF!

UH-OH! HERE COMES THE BEETLE... SWOOPING IN FOR THE KILL!

I HAVE TO GET THE GIBBON OUT OF THE WAY, SO I CAN JUMP OUT OF RANGE! OTHERWISE, I'LL GET--!

YEEEOW!

THAT BLAST MUST HAVE FRIED HALF THE NERVE ENDINGS IN MY BODY! I FEEL LIKE I'VE JUST GONE TEN ROUNDS WITH THE HULK!

THWIP

I HAVE TO KEEP MOVING! IF HE ZAPS ME AGAIN, IT'LL BE ALL OVER!

CALLING ON EVERY IOTA OF HIS SPIDERLIKE AGILITY, SPIDER-MAN SPRINGS ACROSS THE ROOFTOPS LIKE A DEMENTED JUMPING-JACK, KEEPING JUST INCHES AHEAD OF THE BEETLE'S ELECTRO-BITE BLAST!

BUT, INEVITABLY, EVEN HE TIRES. AND THEN...

Z

EPIC

6

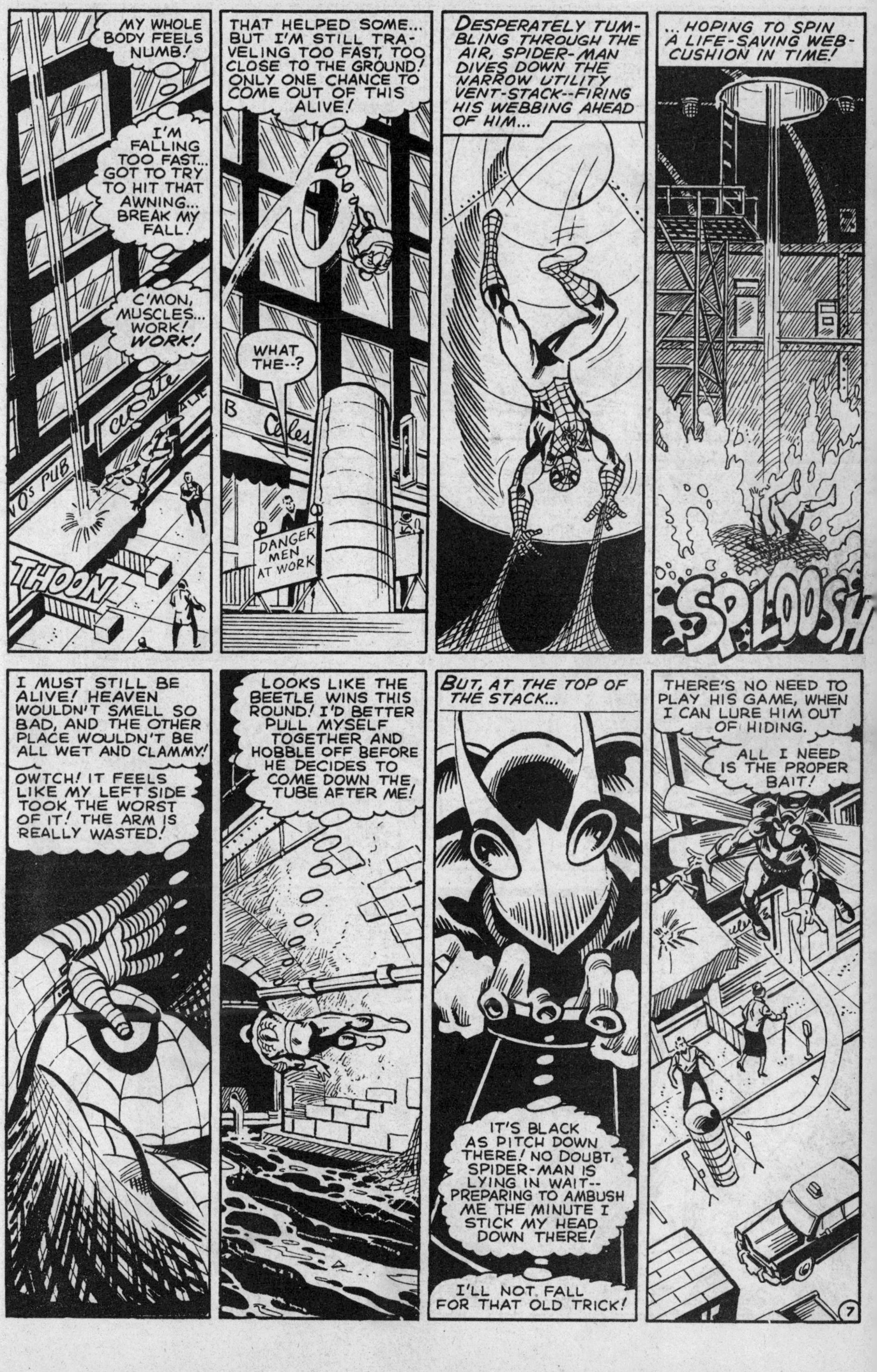
MY WHOLE BODY FEELS NUMB!
I'M FALLING TOO FAST... GOT TO TRY TO HIT THAT AWNING... BREAK MY FALL!
C'MON, MUSCLES... WORK! WORK!
THOON
THAT HELPED SOME... BUT I'M STILL TRAVELING TOO FAST, TOO CLOSE TO THE GROUND! ONLY ONE CHANCE TO COME OUT OF THIS ALIVE!
WHAT THE--?
DANGER MEN AT WORK
DESPERATELY TUMBLING THROUGH THE AIR, SPIDER-MAN DIVES DOWN THE NARROW UTILITY VENT-STACK--FIRING HIS WEBBING AHEAD OF HIM...
... HOPING TO SPIN A LIFE-SAVING WEB-CUSHION IN TIME!
SPLOOSH
I MUST STILL BE ALIVE! HEAVEN WOULDN'T SMELL SO BAD, AND THE OTHER PLACE WOULDN'T BE ALL WET AND CLAMMY!
OWTCH! IT FEELS LIKE MY LEFT SIDE TOOK THE WORST OF IT! THE ARM IS REALLY WASTED!
LOOKS LIKE THE BEETLE WINS THIS ROUND! I'D BETTER PULL MYSELF TOGETHER AND HOBBLE OFF BEFORE HE DECIDES TO COME DOWN THE TUBE AFTER ME!
BUT, AT THE TOP OF THE STACK...
IT'S BLACK AS PITCH DOWN THERE! NO DOUBT, SPIDER-MAN IS LYING IN WAIT--PREPARING TO AMBUSH ME THE MINUTE I STICK MY HEAD DOWN THERE!
I'LL NOT FALL FOR THAT OLD TRICK!
THERE'S NO NEED TO PLAY HIS GAME, WHEN I CAN LURE HIM OUT OF HIDING.
ALL I NEED IS THE PROPER BAIT!
7

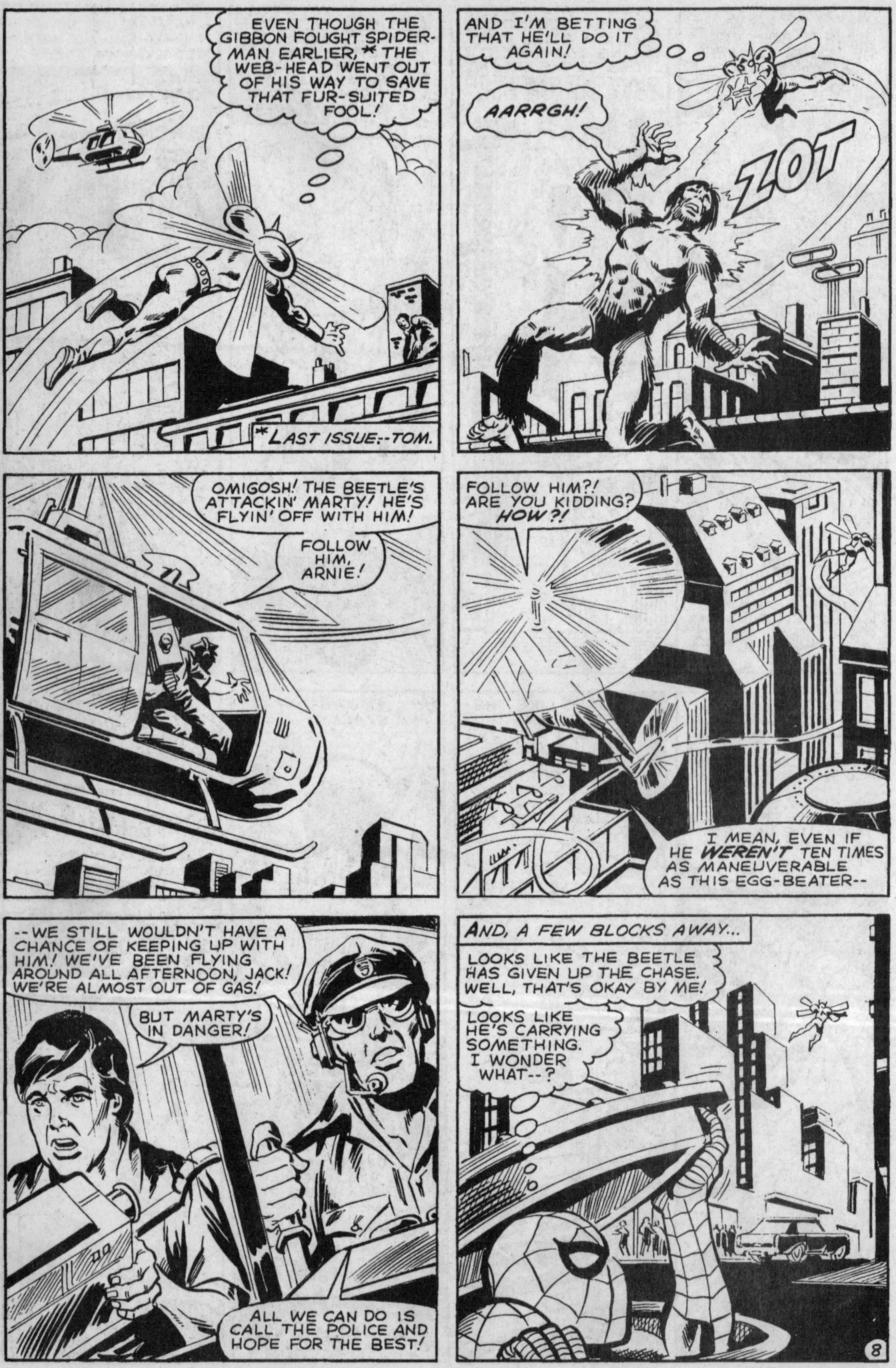
EVEN THOUGH THE GIBBON FOUGHT SPIDER-MAN EARLIER,* THE WEB-HEAD WENT OUT OF HIS WAY TO SAVE THAT FUR-SUITED FOOL!
*LAST ISSUE:--TOM.
AND I'M BETTING THAT HE'LL DO IT AGAIN!
AARRGH!
ZOT
OMIGOSH! THE BEETLE'S ATTACKIN' MARTY! HE'S FLYIN' OFF WITH HIM!
FOLLOW HIM, ARNIE!
FOLLOW HIM?! ARE YOU KIDDING? HOW?!
I MEAN, EVEN IF HE WEREN'T TEN TIMES AS MANEUVERABLE AS THIS EGG-BEATER--
--WE STILL WOULDN'T HAVE A CHANCE OF KEEPING UP WITH HIM! WE'VE BEEN FLYING AROUND ALL AFTERNOON, JACK! WE'RE ALMOST OUT OF GAS!
BUT MARTY'S IN DANGER!
ALL WE CAN DO IS CALL THE POLICE AND HOPE FOR THE BEST!
AND, A FEW BLOCKS AWAY...
LOOKS LIKE THE BEETLE HAS GIVEN UP THE CHASE. WELL, THAT'S OKAY BY ME!
LOOKS LIKE HE'S CARRYING SOMETHING. I WONDER WHAT--?
8

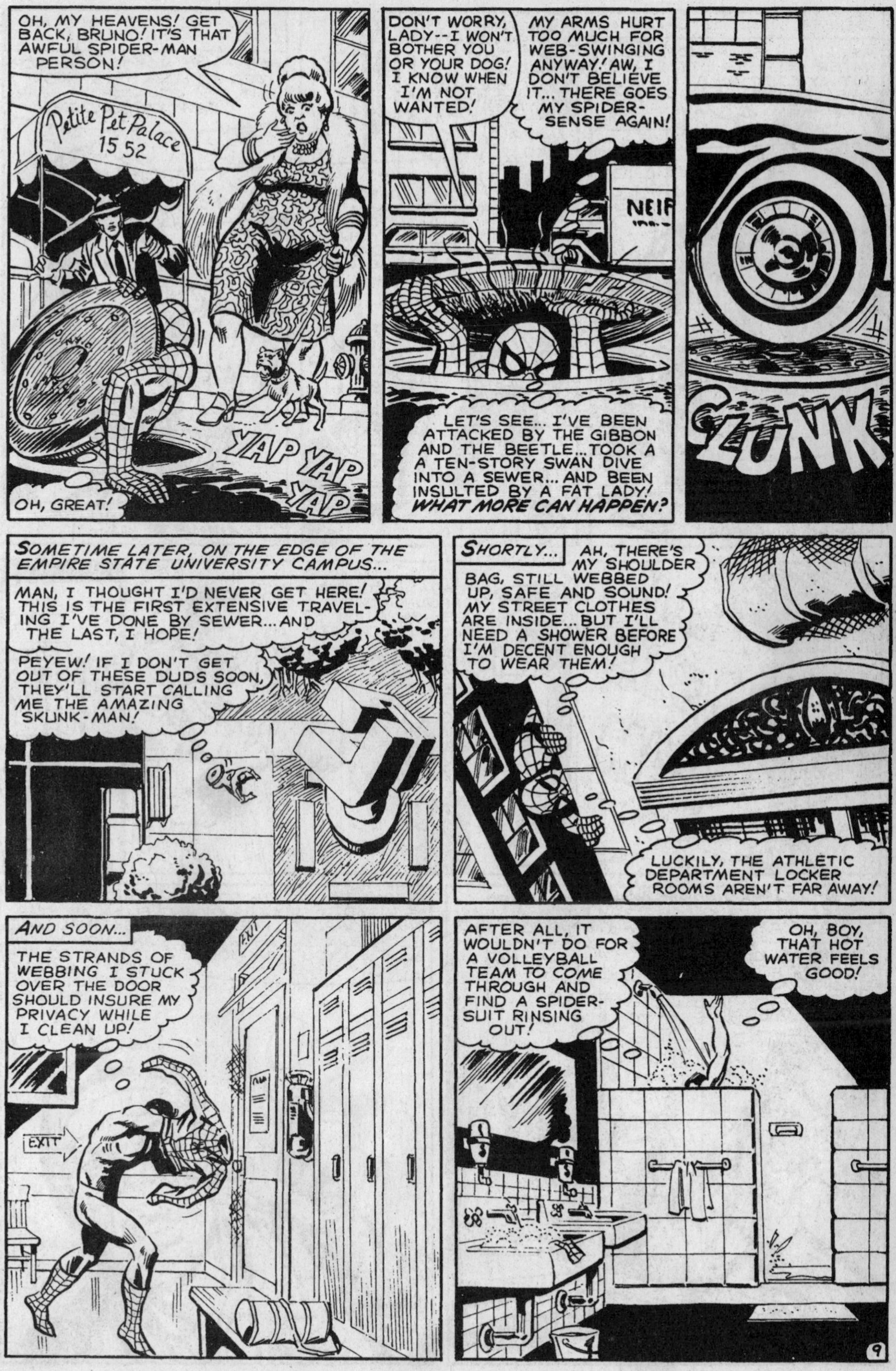

OH, MY HEAVENS! GET BACK, BRUNO! IT'S THAT AWFUL SPIDER-MAN PERSON!
Petite Pet Palace 15 52
YAP YAP YAP
OH, GREAT!
DON'T WORRY, LADY--I WON'T BOTHER YOU OR YOUR DOG! I KNOW WHEN I'M NOT WANTED!
MY ARMS HURT TOO MUCH FOR WEB-SWINGING ANYWAY! AW, I DON'T BELIEVE IT... THERE GOES MY SPIDER-SENSE AGAIN!
NEIF
LET'S SEE... I'VE BEEN ATTACKED BY THE GIBBON AND THE BEETLE... TOOK A A TEN-STORY SWAN DIVE INTO A SEWER... AND BEEN INSULTED BY A FAT LADY! WHAT MORE CAN HAPPEN?
CLUNK
SOMETIME LATER, ON THE EDGE OF THE EMPIRE STATE UNIVERSITY CAMPUS...
MAN, I THOUGHT I'D NEVER GET HERE! THIS IS THE FIRST EXTENSIVE TRAVELING I'VE DONE BY SEWER... AND THE LAST, I HOPE!
PEYEW! IF I DON'T GET OUT OF THESE DUDS SOON, THEY'LL START CALLING ME THE AMAZING SKUNK-MAN!
SHORTLY...
AH, THERE'S MY SHOULDER BAG, STILL WEBBED UP, SAFE AND SOUND! MY STREET CLOTHES ARE INSIDE... BUT I'LL NEED A SHOWER BEFORE I'M DECENT ENOUGH TO WEAR THEM!
LUCKILY, THE ATHLETIC DEPARTMENT LOCKER ROOMS AREN'T FAR AWAY!
AND SOON...
THE STRANDS OF WEBBING I STUCK OVER THE DOOR SHOULD INSURE MY PRIVACY WHILE I CLEAN UP!
EXIT
AFTER ALL, IT WOULDN'T DO FOR A VOLLEYBALL TEAM TO COME THROUGH AND FIND A SPIDER-SUIT RINSING OUT!
OH, BOY, THAT HOT WATER FEELS GOOD!

SEVERAL MINUTES LATER...

WELL, THE SOAP AND WATER HELPED A LITTLE, BUT MY COSTUME STILL SMELLS LIKE A BAD MISTAKE!

I SHOULD GIVE SOME THOUGHT TO MAKING A NEW ONE.

HEY?! WHO LOCKED THE DOOR?

BAM BAM BAM

WHOOPS! A BELLOW THAT LOUD COULD ONLY BELONG--

"-- TO THE EVER-POPULAR COACH BARNSTORM!"*

#%+=@!! NOBODY'S AUTHOR-IZED TO LOCK THIS DOOR BUT ME! OPEN UP, YA HEAR? OPEN THIS DOOR!!

*LAST SEEN IN MARVEL TEAM-UP #108.-- T.

BAM BAM BAM

THAT'S IT, LEAD-HEAD! JUST KEEP ON POUNDING AND SEE HOW MUCH GOOD IT... DOES?

HOO-BOY! I MUST HAVE BEEN UNDER THE SHOWER LONGER THAN I THOUGHT! MY WEBBING IS STARTING TO BREAK DOWN!

AJAX FIRE CLASS A

OFFICE

WITH AN ASTOUNDING BURST OF SPEED, PETER PARKER CROSSES THE ROOM, PLUNKS THE EVAPORATING WEBBING FROM THE DOOR, AND...

THERE YOU GO, COACH! THE DOOR WASN'T LOCKED, JUST... AH... JAMMED!

WHU--?

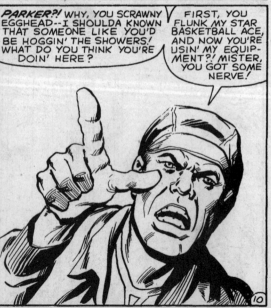

PARKER?! WHY, YOU SCRAWNY EGGHEAD--I SHOULDA KNOWN THAT SOMEONE LIKE YOU'D BE HOGGIN' THE SHOWERS! WHAT DO YOU THINK YOU'RE DOIN' HERE?

FIRST, YOU FLUNK MY STAR BASKETBALL ACE, AND NOW YOU'RE USIN' MY EQUIP-MENT?! MISTER, YOU GOT SOME NERVE!

10

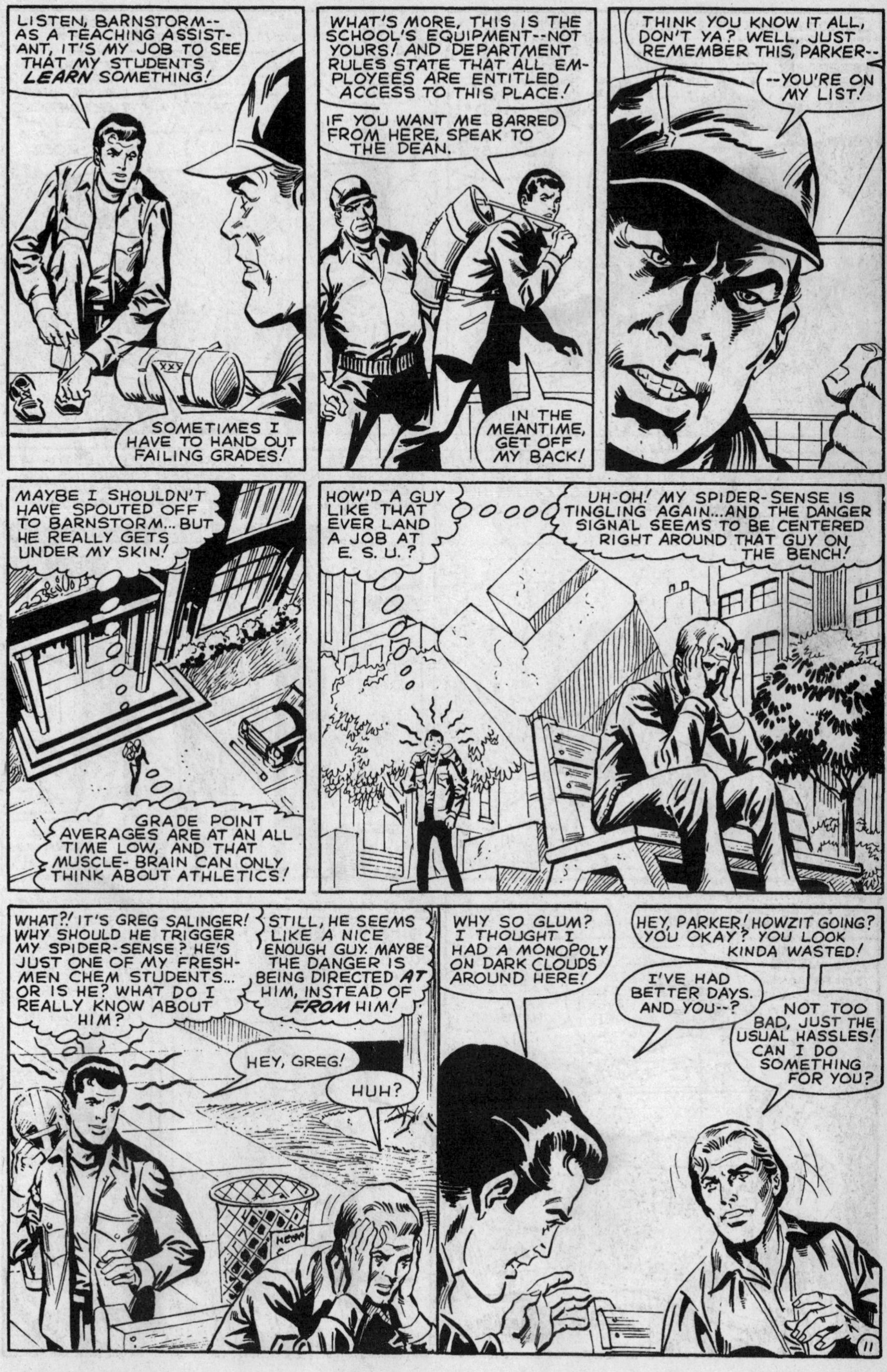
LISTEN, BARNSTORM-- AS A TEACHING ASSISTANT, IT'S MY JOB TO SEE THAT MY STUDENTS LEARN SOMETHING!
SOMETIMES I HAVE TO HAND OUT FAILING GRADES!
WHAT'S MORE, THIS IS THE SCHOOL'S EQUIPMENT--NOT YOURS! AND DEPARTMENT RULES STATE THAT ALL EMPLOYEES ARE ENTITLED ACCESS TO THIS PLACE!
IF YOU WANT ME BARRED FROM HERE, SPEAK TO THE DEAN.
IN THE MEANTIME, GET OFF MY BACK!
THINK YOU KNOW IT ALL, DON'T YA? WELL, JUST REMEMBER THIS, PARKER--
--YOU'RE ON MY LIST!
MAYBE I SHOULDN'T HAVE SPOUTED OFF TO BARNSTORM... BUT HE REALLY GETS UNDER MY SKIN!
GRADE POINT AVERAGES ARE AT AN ALL TIME LOW, AND THAT MUSCLE-BRAIN CAN ONLY THINK ABOUT ATHLETICS!
HOW'D A GUY LIKE THAT EVER LAND A JOB AT E. S. U.?
UH-OH! MY SPIDER-SENSE IS TINGLING AGAIN... AND THE DANGER SIGNAL SEEMS TO BE CENTERED RIGHT AROUND THAT GUY ON THE BENCH!
WHAT?! IT'S GREG SALINGER! WHY SHOULD HE TRIGGER MY SPIDER-SENSE? HE'S JUST ONE OF MY FRESHMEN CHEM STUDENTS... OR IS HE? WHAT DO I REALLY KNOW ABOUT HIM?
STILL, HE SEEMS LIKE A NICE ENOUGH GUY. MAYBE THE DANGER IS BEING DIRECTED AT HIM, INSTEAD OF FROM HIM!
HEY, GREG!
HUH?
WHY SO GLUM? I THOUGHT I HAD A MONOPOLY ON DARK CLOUDS AROUND HERE!
HEY, PARKER! HOWZIT GOING? YOU OKAY? YOU LOOK KINDA WASTED!
I'VE HAD BETTER DAYS. AND YOU--?
NOT TOO BAD, JUST THE USUAL HASSLES! CAN I DO SOMETHING FOR YOU?
11

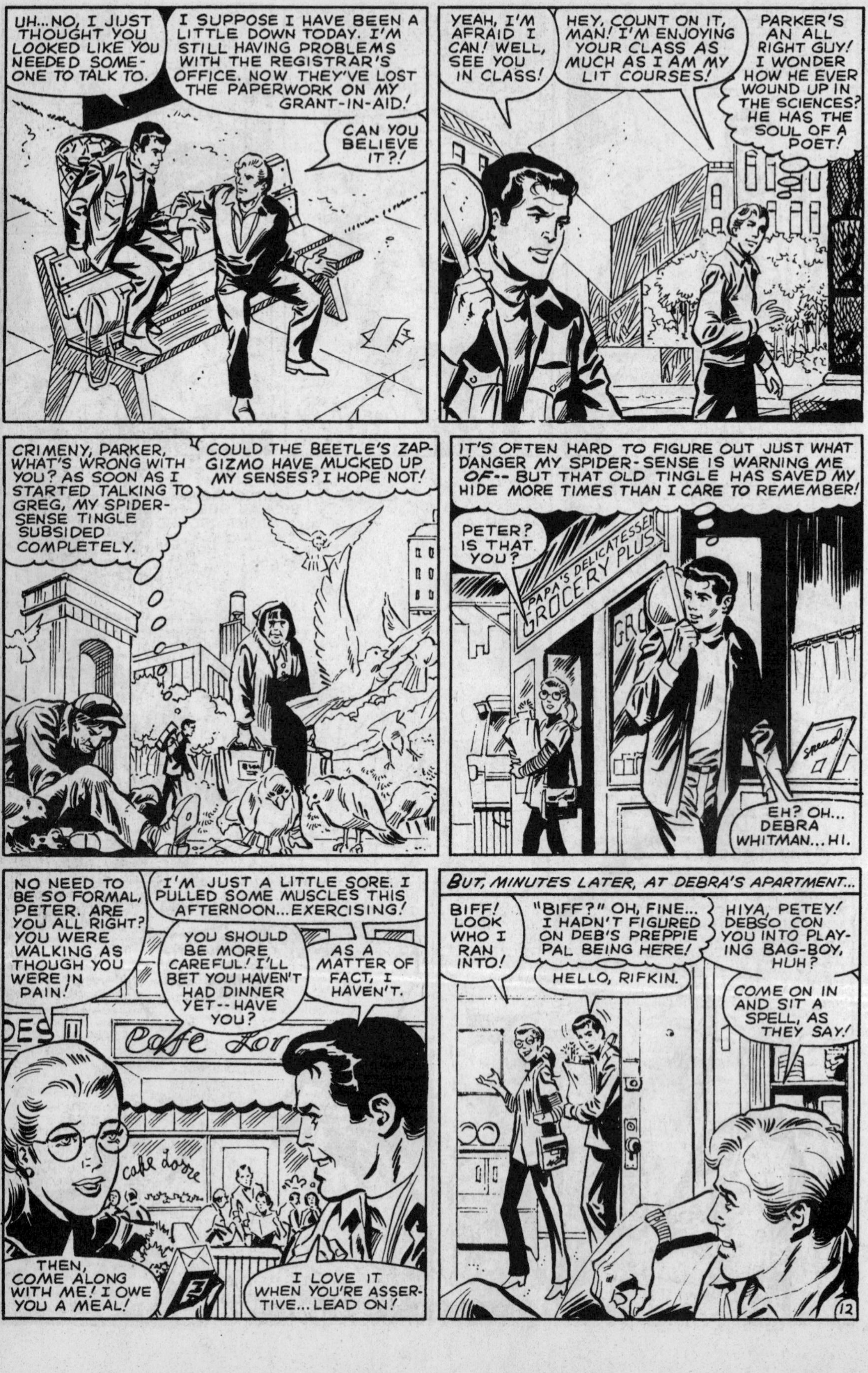
UH... NO, I JUST THOUGHT YOU LOOKED LIKE YOU NEEDED SOME-ONE TO TALK TO.
I SUPPOSE I HAVE BEEN A LITTLE DOWN TODAY. I'M STILL HAVING PROBLEMS WITH THE REGISTRAR'S OFFICE. NOW THEY'VE LOST THE PAPERWORK ON MY GRANT-IN-AID!
CAN YOU BELIEVE IT?!
YEAH, I'M AFRAID I CAN! WELL, SEE YOU IN CLASS!
HEY, COUNT ON IT, MAN! I'M ENJOYING YOUR CLASS AS MUCH AS I AM MY LIT COURSES!
PARKER'S AN ALL RIGHT GUY! I WONDER HOW HE EVER WOUND UP IN THE SCIENCES? HE HAS THE SOUL OF A POET!
CRIMENY, PARKER, WHAT'S WRONG WITH YOU? AS SOON AS I STARTED TALKING TO GREG, MY SPIDER-SENSE TINGLE SUBSIDED COMPLETELY.
COULD THE BEETLE'S ZAP-GIZMO HAVE MUCKED UP MY SENSES? I HOPE NOT!
IT'S OFTEN HARD TO FIGURE OUT JUST WHAT DANGER MY SPIDER-SENSE IS WARNING ME OF-- BUT THAT OLD TINGLE HAS SAVED MY HIDE MORE TIMES THAN I CARE TO REMEMBER!
PETER? IS THAT YOU?
PAPA'S DELICATESSEN
GROCERY PLUS
EH? OH... DEBRA WHITMAN... HI.
NO NEED TO BE SO FORMAL, PETER. ARE YOU ALL RIGHT? YOU WERE WALKING AS THOUGH YOU WERE IN PAIN!
I'M JUST A LITTLE SORE. I PULLED SOME MUSCLES THIS AFTERNOON... EXERCISING!
YOU SHOULD BE MORE CAREFUL! I'LL BET YOU HAVEN'T HAD DINNER YET-- HAVE YOU?
AS A MATTER OF FACT, I HAVEN'T.
Cafe Lorre
THEN, COME ALONG WITH ME! I OWE YOU A MEAL!
I LOVE IT WHEN YOU'RE ASSERTIVE... LEAD ON!
BUT, MINUTES LATER, AT DEBRA'S APARTMENT...
BIFF! LOOK WHO I RAN INTO!
"BIFF?" OH, FINE... I HADN'T FIGURED ON DEB'S PREPPIE PAL BEING HERE!
HELLO, RIFKIN.
HIYA, PETEY! DEBSO CON YOU INTO PLAY-ING BAG-BOY, HUH?
COME ON IN AND SIT A SPELL, AS THEY SAY!
12

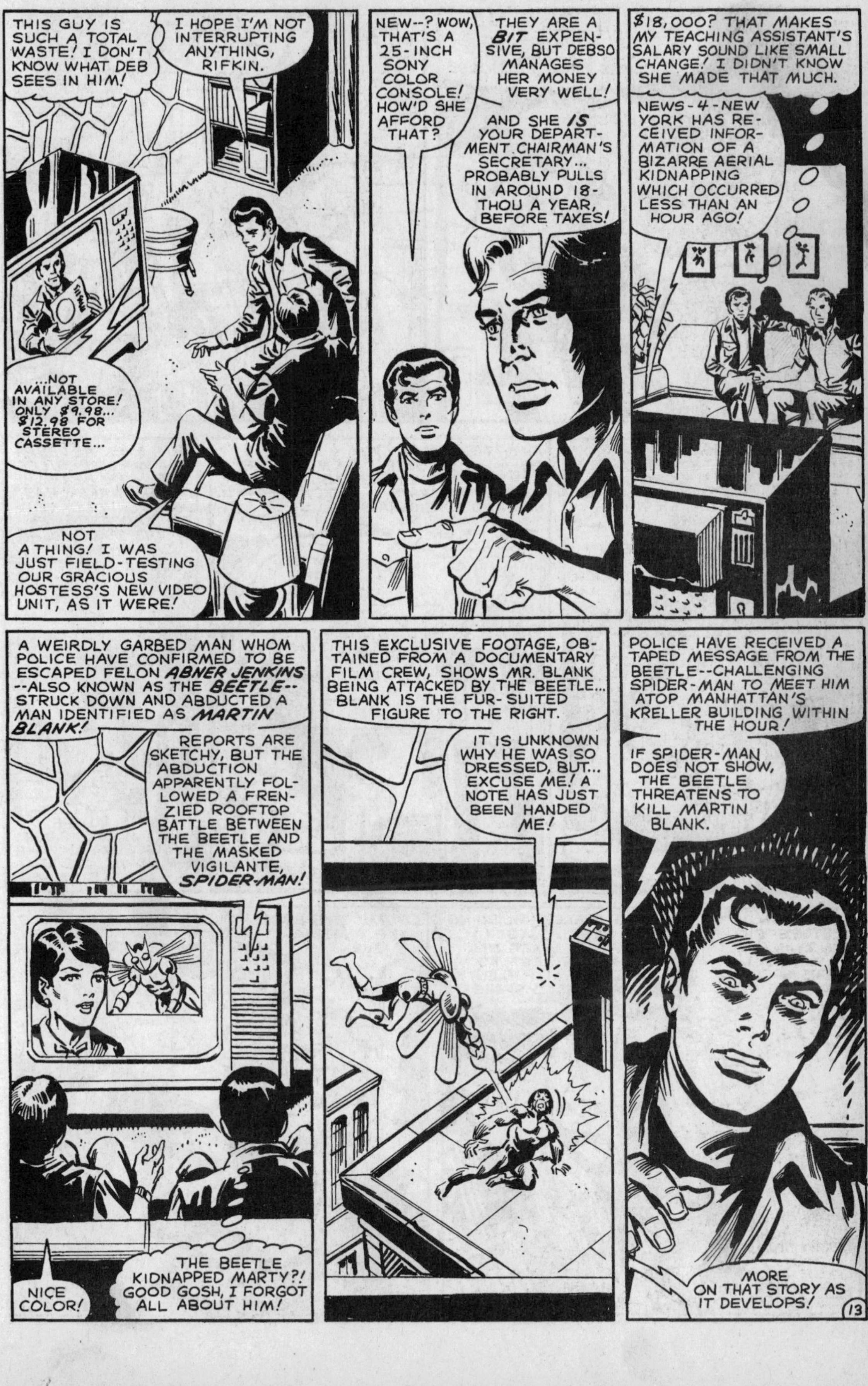
THIS GUY IS SUCH A TOTAL WASTE! I DON'T KNOW WHAT DEB SEES IN HIM!
I HOPE I'M NOT INTERRUPTING ANYTHING, RIFKIN.
...NOT AVAILABLE IN ANY STORE! ONLY $9.98... $12.98 FOR STEREO CASSETTE...
NOT A THING! I WAS JUST FIELD-TESTING OUR GRACIOUS HOSTESS'S NEW VIDEO UNIT, AS IT WERE!
NEW--? WOW, THAT'S A 25-INCH SONY COLOR CONSOLE! HOW'D SHE AFFORD THAT?
THEY ARE A BIT EXPENSIVE, BUT DEBSO MANAGES HER MONEY VERY WELL!
AND SHE IS YOUR DEPARTMENT CHAIRMAN'S SECRETARY... PROBABLY PULLS IN AROUND 18-THOU A YEAR, BEFORE TAXES!
$18,000? THAT MAKES MY TEACHING ASSISTANT'S SALARY SOUND LIKE SMALL CHANGE! I DIDN'T KNOW SHE MADE THAT MUCH.
NEWS-4-NEW YORK HAS RECEIVED INFORMATION OF A BIZARRE AERIAL KIDNAPPING WHICH OCCURRED LESS THAN AN HOUR AGO!
A WEIRDLY GARBED MAN WHOM POLICE HAVE CONFIRMED TO BE ESCAPED FELON ABNER JENKINS --ALSO KNOWN AS THE BEETLE-- STRUCK DOWN AND ABDUCTED A MAN IDENTIFIED AS MARTIN BLANK!
REPORTS ARE SKETCHY, BUT THE ABDUCTION APPARENTLY FOLLOWED A FRENZIED ROOFTOP BATTLE BETWEEN THE BEETLE AND THE MASKED VIGILANTE, SPIDER-MAN!
NICE COLOR!
THE BEETLE KIDNAPPED MARTY?! GOOD GOSH, I FORGOT ALL ABOUT HIM!
THIS EXCLUSIVE FOOTAGE, OBTAINED FROM A DOCUMENTARY FILM CREW, SHOWS MR. BLANK BEING ATTACKED BY THE BEETLE... BLANK IS THE FUR-SUITED FIGURE TO THE RIGHT.
IT IS UNKNOWN WHY HE WAS SO DRESSED, BUT... EXCUSE ME! A NOTE HAS JUST BEEN HANDED ME!
POLICE HAVE RECEIVED A TAPED MESSAGE FROM THE BEETLE--CHALLENGING SPIDER-MAN TO MEET HIM ATOP MANHATTAN'S KRELLER BUILDING WITHIN THE HOUR!
IF SPIDER-MAN DOES NOT SHOW, THE BEETLE THREATENS TO KILL MARTIN BLANK.
MORE ON THAT STORY AS IT DEVELOPS!
13

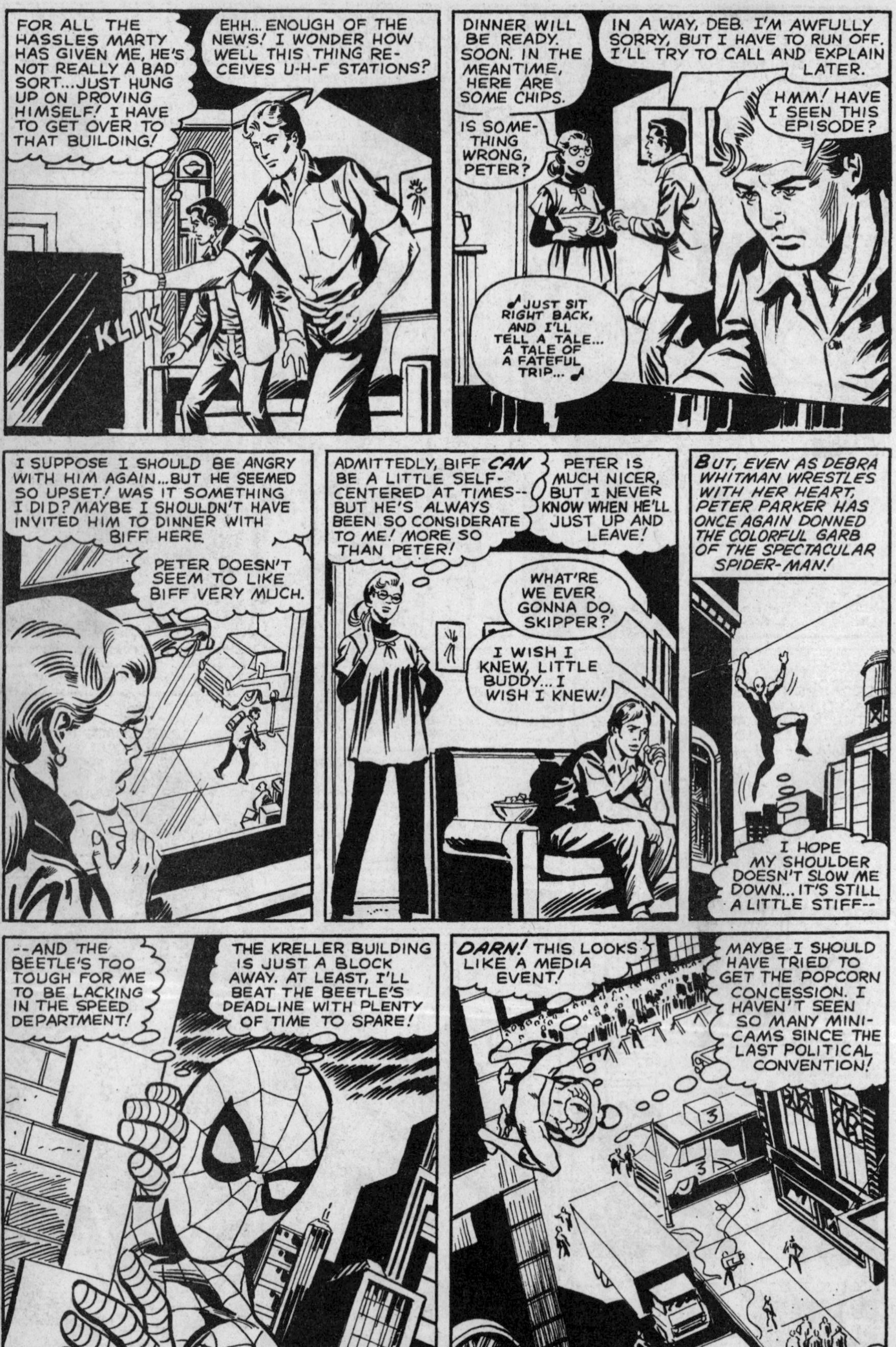

FOR ALL THE HASSLES MARTY HAS GIVEN ME, HE'S NOT REALLY A BAD SORT... JUST HUNG UP ON PROVING HIMSELF! I HAVE TO GET OVER TO THAT BUILDING!
EHH... ENOUGH OF THE NEWS! I WONDER HOW WELL THIS THING RECEIVES U-H-F STATIONS?
KLIK
DINNER WILL BE READY. SOON. IN THE MEANTIME, HERE ARE SOME CHIPS.
IN A WAY, DEB. I'M AWFULLY SORRY, BUT I HAVE TO RUN OFF. I'LL TRY TO CALL AND EXPLAIN LATER.
IS SOMETHING WRONG, PETER?
HMM! HAVE I SEEN THIS EPISODE?
JUST SIT RIGHT BACK, AND I'LL TELL A TALE... A TALE OF A FATEFUL TRIP...
I SUPPOSE I SHOULD BE ANGRY WITH HIM AGAIN... BUT HE SEEMED SO UPSET! WAS IT SOMETHING I DID? MAYBE I SHOULDN'T HAVE INVITED HIM TO DINNER WITH BIFF HERE.
PETER DOESN'T SEEM TO LIKE BIFF VERY MUCH.
ADMITTEDLY, BIFF CAN BE A LITTLE SELF-CENTERED AT TIMES-- BUT HE'S ALWAYS BEEN SO CONSIDERATE TO ME! MORE SO THAN PETER!
PETER IS MUCH NICER, BUT I NEVER KNOW WHEN HE'LL JUST UP AND LEAVE!
WHAT'RE WE EVER GONNA DO, SKIPPER?
I WISH I KNEW, LITTLE BUDDY... I WISH I KNEW!
BUT, EVEN AS DEBRA WHITMAN WRESTLES WITH HER HEART, PETER PARKER HAS ONCE AGAIN DONNED THE COLORFUL GARB OF THE SPECTACULAR SPIDER-MAN!
I HOPE MY SHOULDER DOESN'T SLOW ME DOWN... IT'S STILL A LITTLE STIFF--
--AND THE BEETLE'S TOO TOUGH FOR ME TO BE LACKING IN THE SPEED DEPARTMENT!
THE KRELLER BUILDING IS JUST A BLOCK AWAY. AT LEAST, I'LL BEAT THE BEETLE'S DEADLINE WITH PLENTY OF TIME TO SPARE!
DARN! THIS LOOKS LIKE A MEDIA EVENT!
MAYBE I SHOULD HAVE TRIED TO GET THE POPCORN CONCESSION. I HAVEN'T SEEN SO MANY MINI-CAMS SINCE THE LAST POLITICAL CONVENTION!
3
14

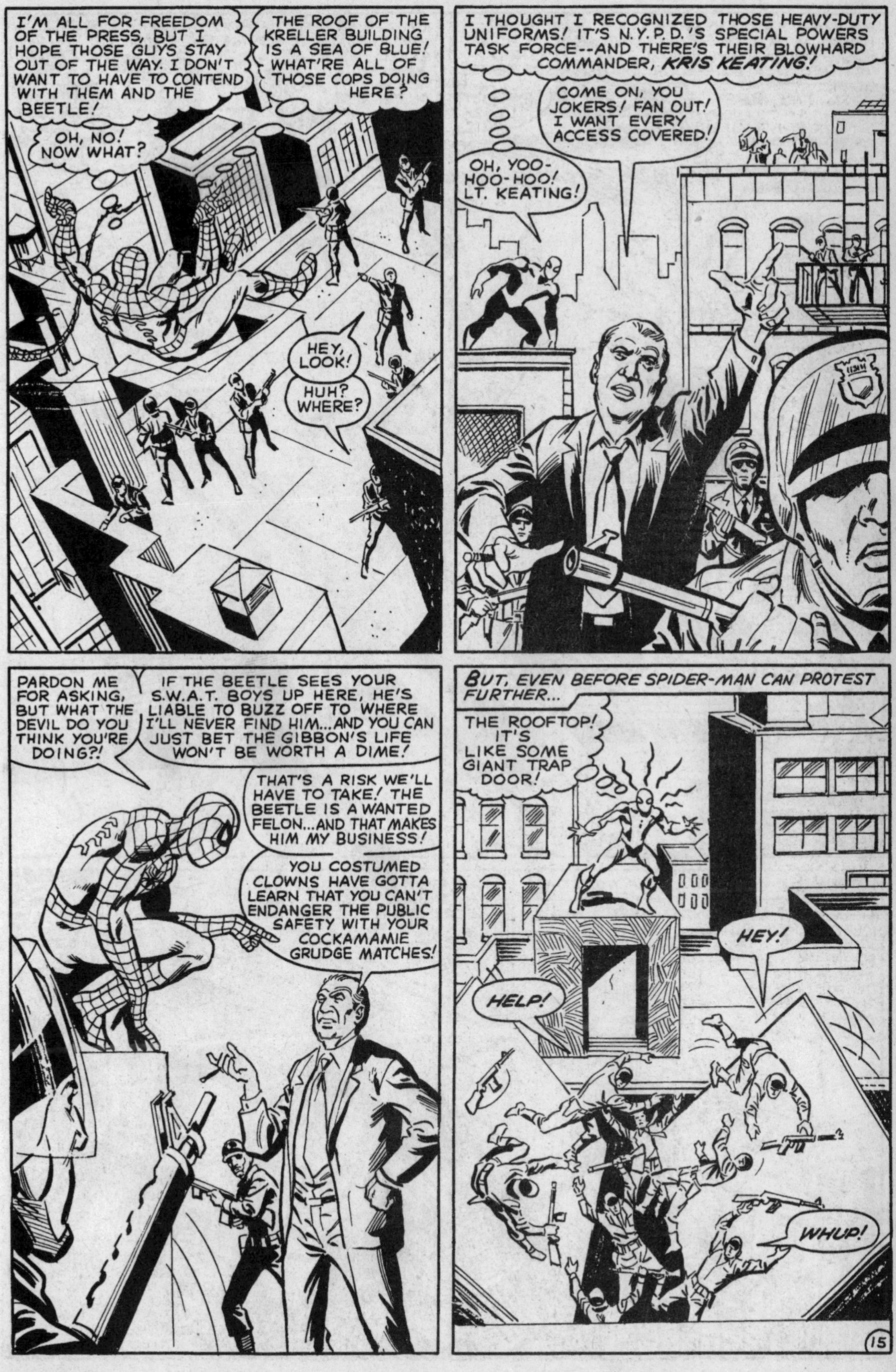
I'M ALL FOR FREEDOM OF THE PRESS, BUT I HOPE THOSE GUYS STAY OUT OF THE WAY. I DON'T WANT TO HAVE TO CONTEND WITH THEM AND THE BEETLE!
THE ROOF OF THE KRELLER BUILDING IS A SEA OF BLUE! WHAT'RE ALL OF THOSE COPS DOING HERE?
OH, NO! NOW WHAT?
HEY, LOOK!
HUH? WHERE?
I THOUGHT I RECOGNIZED THOSE HEAVY-DUTY UNIFORMS! IT'S N.Y.P.D.'S SPECIAL POWERS TASK FORCE--AND THERE'S THEIR BLOWHARD COMMANDER, KRIS KEATING!
COME ON, YOU JOKERS! FAN OUT! I WANT EVERY ACCESS COVERED!
OH, YOO-HOO-HOO! LT. KEATING!
PARDON ME FOR ASKING, BUT WHAT THE DEVIL DO YOU THINK YOU'RE DOING?!
IF THE BEETLE SEES YOUR S.W.A.T. BOYS UP HERE, HE'S LIABLE TO BUZZ OFF TO WHERE I'LL NEVER FIND HIM...AND YOU CAN JUST BET THE GIBBON'S LIFE WON'T BE WORTH A DIME!
THAT'S A RISK WE'LL HAVE TO TAKE! THE BEETLE IS A WANTED FELON...AND THAT MAKES HIM MY BUSINESS!
YOU COSTUMED CLOWNS HAVE GOTTA LEARN THAT YOU CAN'T ENDANGER THE PUBLIC SAFETY WITH YOUR COCKAMAMIE GRUDGE MATCHES!
BUT, EVEN BEFORE SPIDER-MAN CAN PROTEST FURTHER...
THE ROOFTOP! IT'S LIKE SOME GIANT TRAP DOOR!
HEY!
HELP!
WHUP!
15

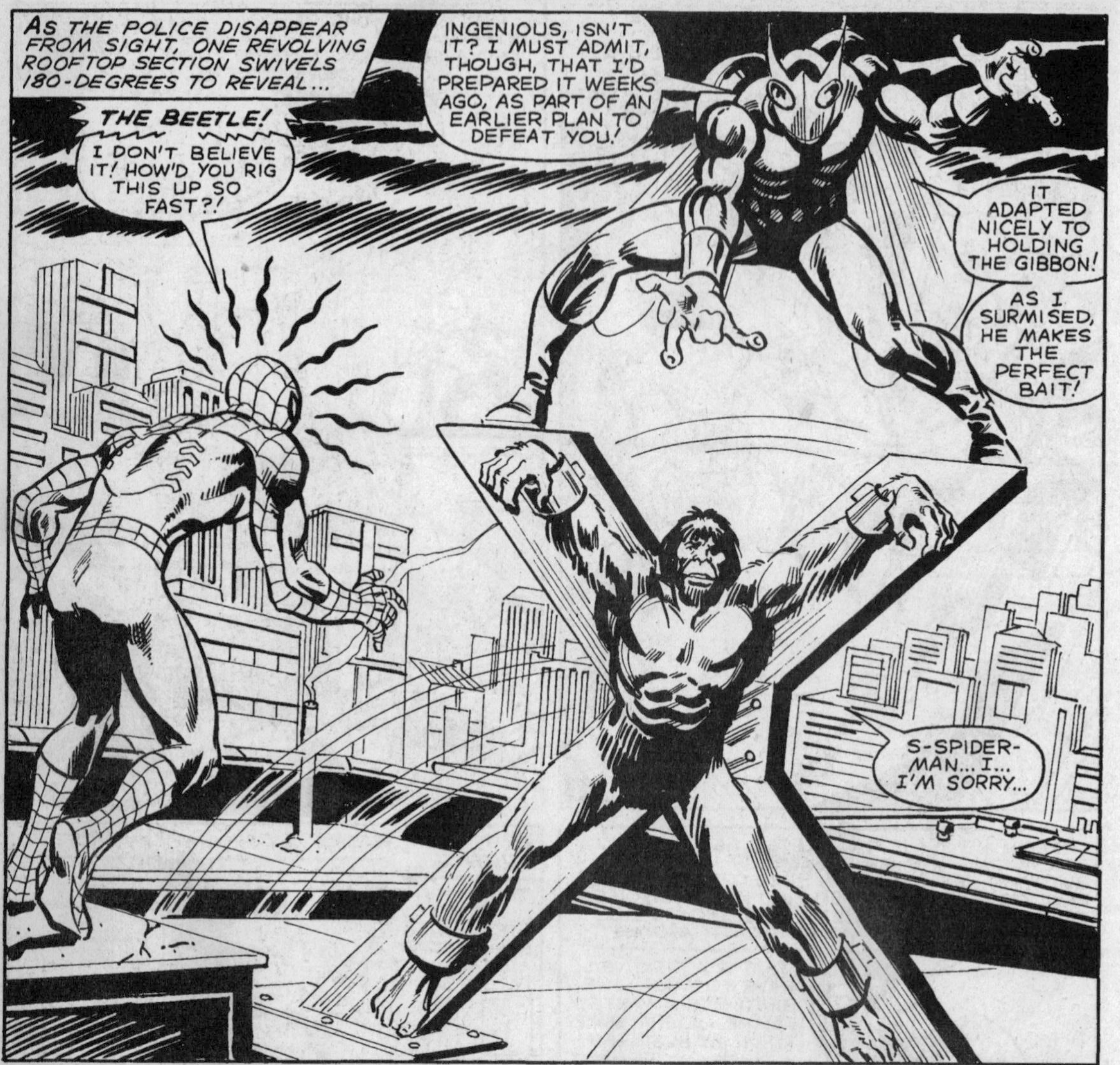
AS THE POLICE DISAPPEAR FROM SIGHT, ONE REVOLVING ROOFTOP SECTION SWIVELS 180-DEGREES TO REVEAL...
THE BEETLE!
I DON'T BELIEVE IT! HOW'D YOU RIG THIS UP SO FAST?!
INGENIOUS, ISN'T IT? I MUST ADMIT, THOUGH, THAT I'D PREPARED IT WEEKS AGO, AS PART OF AN EARLIER PLAN TO DEFEAT YOU!
IT ADAPTED NICELY TO HOLDING THE GIBBON!
AS I SURMISED, HE MAKES THE PERFECT BAIT!
S-SPIDER-MAN... I... I'M SORRY...

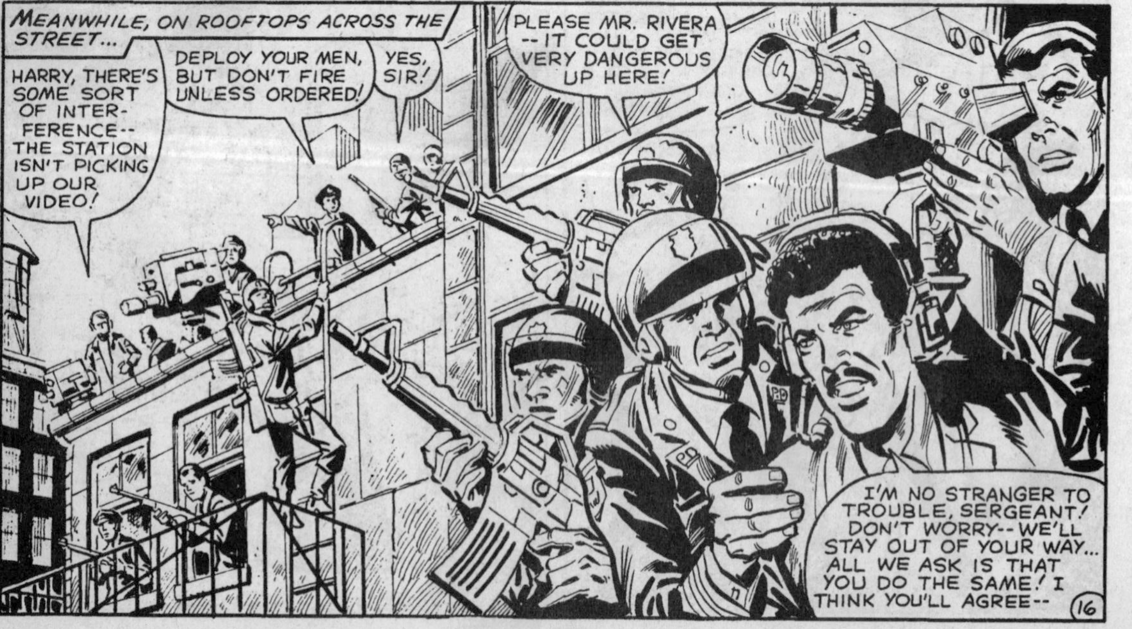
MEANWHILE, ON ROOFTOPS ACROSS THE STREET...
HARRY, THERE'S SOME SORT OF INTERFERENCE-- THE STATION ISN'T PICKING UP OUR VIDEO!
DEPLOY YOUR MEN, BUT DON'T FIRE UNLESS ORDERED!
YES, SIR!
PLEASE MR. RIVERA --IT COULD GET VERY DANGEROUS UP HERE!
I'M NO STRANGER TO TROUBLE, SERGEANT! DON'T WORRY--WE'LL STAY OUT OF YOUR WAY... ALL WE ASK IS THAT YOU DO THE SAME! I THINK YOU'LL AGREE--
16

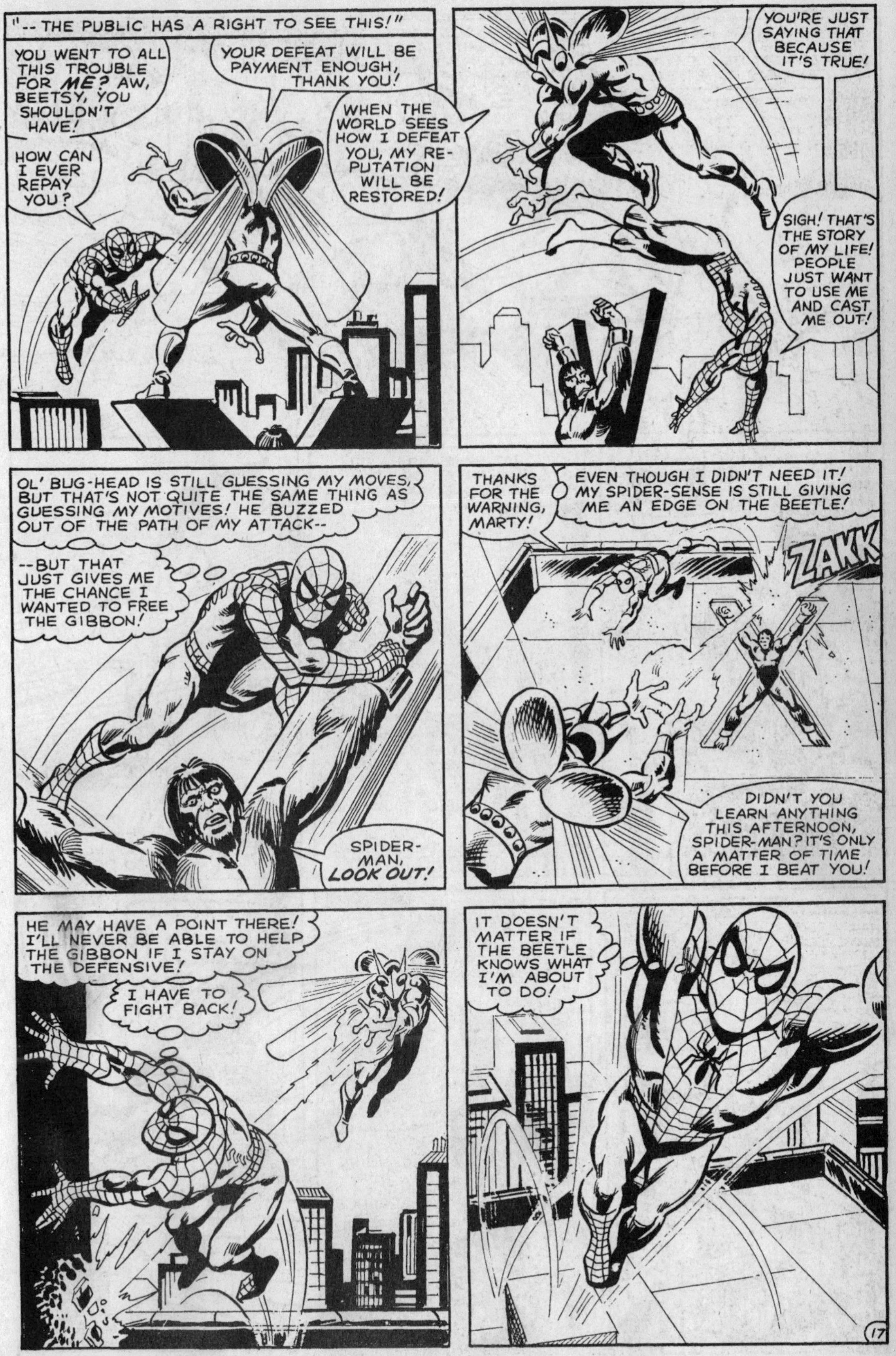
"-- THE PUBLIC HAS A RIGHT TO SEE THIS!"
YOU WENT TO ALL THIS TROUBLE FOR ME? AW, BEETSY, YOU SHOULDN'T HAVE!
HOW CAN I EVER REPAY YOU?
YOUR DEFEAT WILL BE PAYMENT ENOUGH, THANK YOU!
WHEN THE WORLD SEES HOW I DEFEAT YOU, MY REPUTATION WILL BE RESTORED!
YOU'RE JUST SAYING THAT BECAUSE IT'S TRUE!
SIGH! THAT'S THE STORY OF MY LIFE! PEOPLE JUST WANT TO USE ME AND CAST ME OUT!
OL' BUG-HEAD IS STILL GUESSING MY MOVES, BUT THAT'S NOT QUITE THE SAME THING AS GUESSING MY MOTIVES! HE BUZZED OUT OF THE PATH OF MY ATTACK--
--BUT THAT JUST GIVES ME THE CHANCE I WANTED TO FREE THE GIBBON!
SPIDER-MAN, LOOK OUT!
THANKS FOR THE WARNING, MARTY!
EVEN THOUGH I DIDN'T NEED IT! MY SPIDER-SENSE IS STILL GIVING ME AN EDGE ON THE BEETLE!
ZAKK
DIDN'T YOU LEARN ANYTHING THIS AFTERNOON, SPIDER-MAN? IT'S ONLY A MATTER OF TIME BEFORE I BEAT YOU!
HE MAY HAVE A POINT THERE! I'LL NEVER BE ABLE TO HELP THE GIBBON IF I STAY ON THE DEFENSIVE!
I HAVE TO FIGHT BACK!
IT DOESN'T MATTER IF THE BEETLE KNOWS WHAT I'M ABOUT TO DO!
17

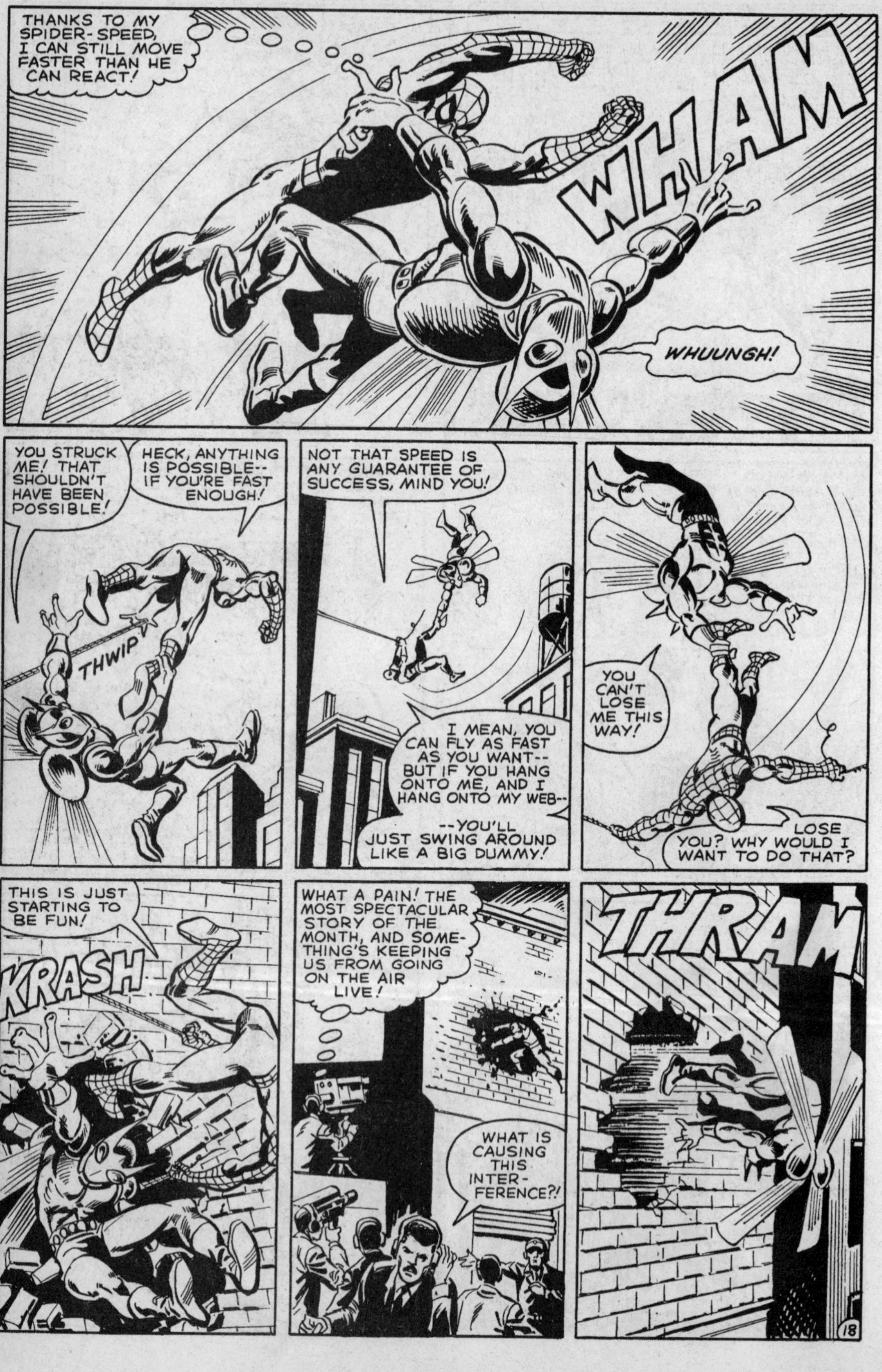
THANKS TO MY SPIDER-SPEED, I CAN STILL MOVE FASTER THAN HE CAN REACT!
WHAM
WHUUNGH!
YOU STRUCK ME! THAT SHOULDN'T HAVE BEEN POSSIBLE!
HECK, ANYTHING IS POSSIBLE-- IF YOU'RE FAST ENOUGH!
THWIP
NOT THAT SPEED IS ANY GUARANTEE OF SUCCESS, MIND YOU!
I MEAN, YOU CAN FLY AS FAST AS YOU WANT-- BUT IF YOU HANG ONTO ME, AND I HANG ONTO MY WEB--
--YOU'LL JUST SWING AROUND LIKE A BIG DUMMY!
YOU CAN'T LOSE ME THIS WAY!
LOSE YOU? WHY WOULD I WANT TO DO THAT?
THIS IS JUST STARTING TO BE FUN!
KRASH
WHAT A PAIN! THE MOST SPECTACULAR STORY OF THE MONTH, AND SOMETHING'S KEEPING US FROM GOING ON THE AIR LIVE!
WHAT IS CAUSING THIS INTERFERENCE?!
THRAM
18

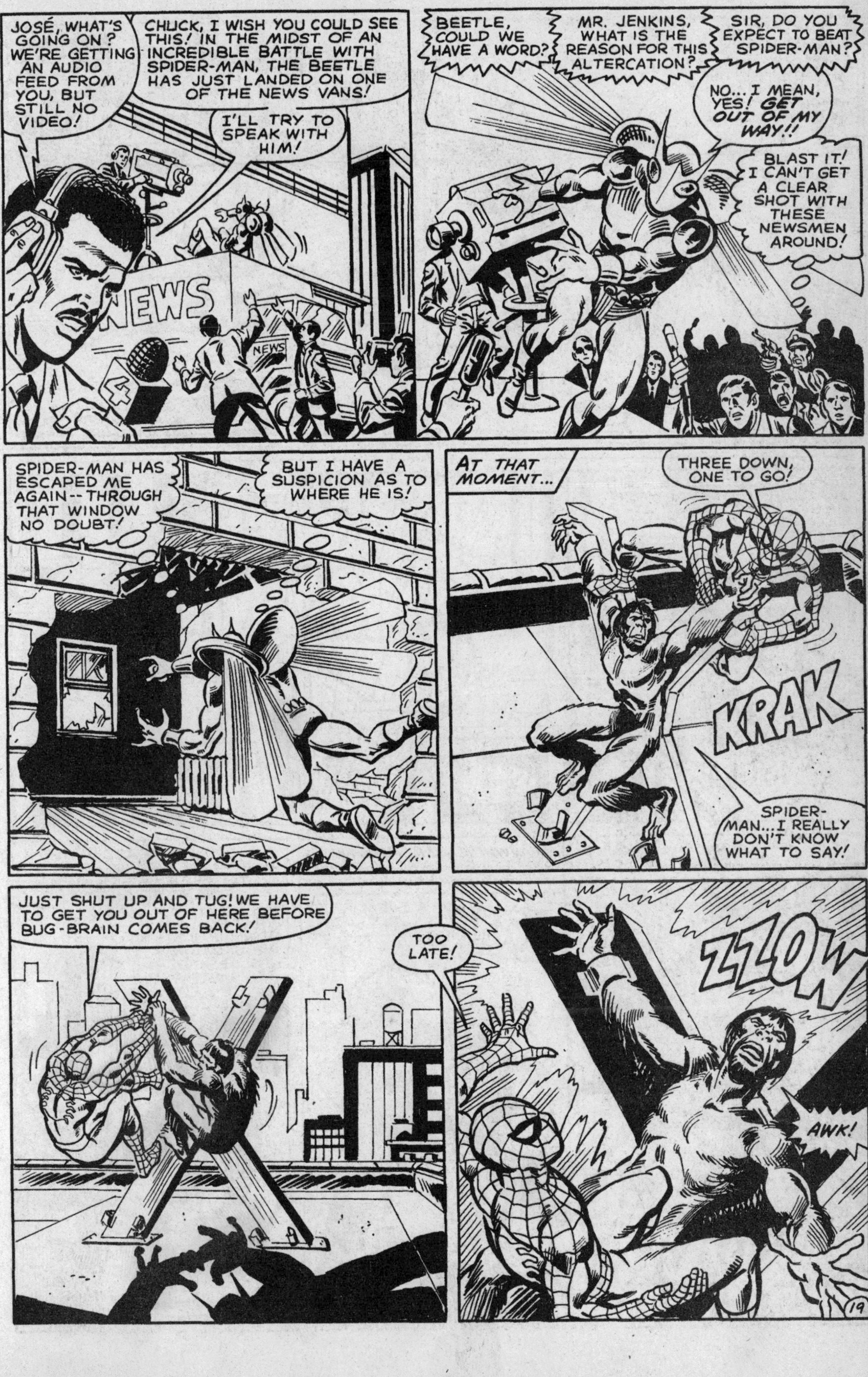

JOSÉ, WHAT'S GOING ON? WE'RE GETTING AN AUDIO FEED FROM YOU, BUT STILL NO VIDEO!
CHUCK, I WISH YOU COULD SEE THIS! IN THE MIDST OF AN INCREDIBLE BATTLE WITH SPIDER-MAN, THE BEETLE HAS JUST LANDED ON ONE OF THE NEWS VANS!
I'LL TRY TO SPEAK WITH HIM!
NEWS
NEWS
4
BEETLE, COULD WE HAVE A WORD?
MR. JENKINS, WHAT IS THE REASON FOR THIS ALTERCATION?
SIR, DO YOU EXPECT TO BEAT SPIDER-MAN?
NO... I MEAN, YES! GET OUT OF MY WAY!!
BLAST IT! I CAN'T GET A CLEAR SHOT WITH THESE NEWSMEN AROUND!
SPIDER-MAN HAS ESCAPED ME AGAIN--THROUGH THAT WINDOW NO DOUBT!
BUT I HAVE A SUSPICION AS TO WHERE HE IS!
AT THAT MOMENT...
THREE DOWN, ONE TO GO!
KRAK
SPIDER-MAN... I REALLY DON'T KNOW WHAT TO SAY!
JUST SHUT UP AND TUG! WE HAVE TO GET YOU OUT OF HERE BEFORE BUG-BRAIN COMES BACK!
TOO LATE!
ZZOW
AWK!

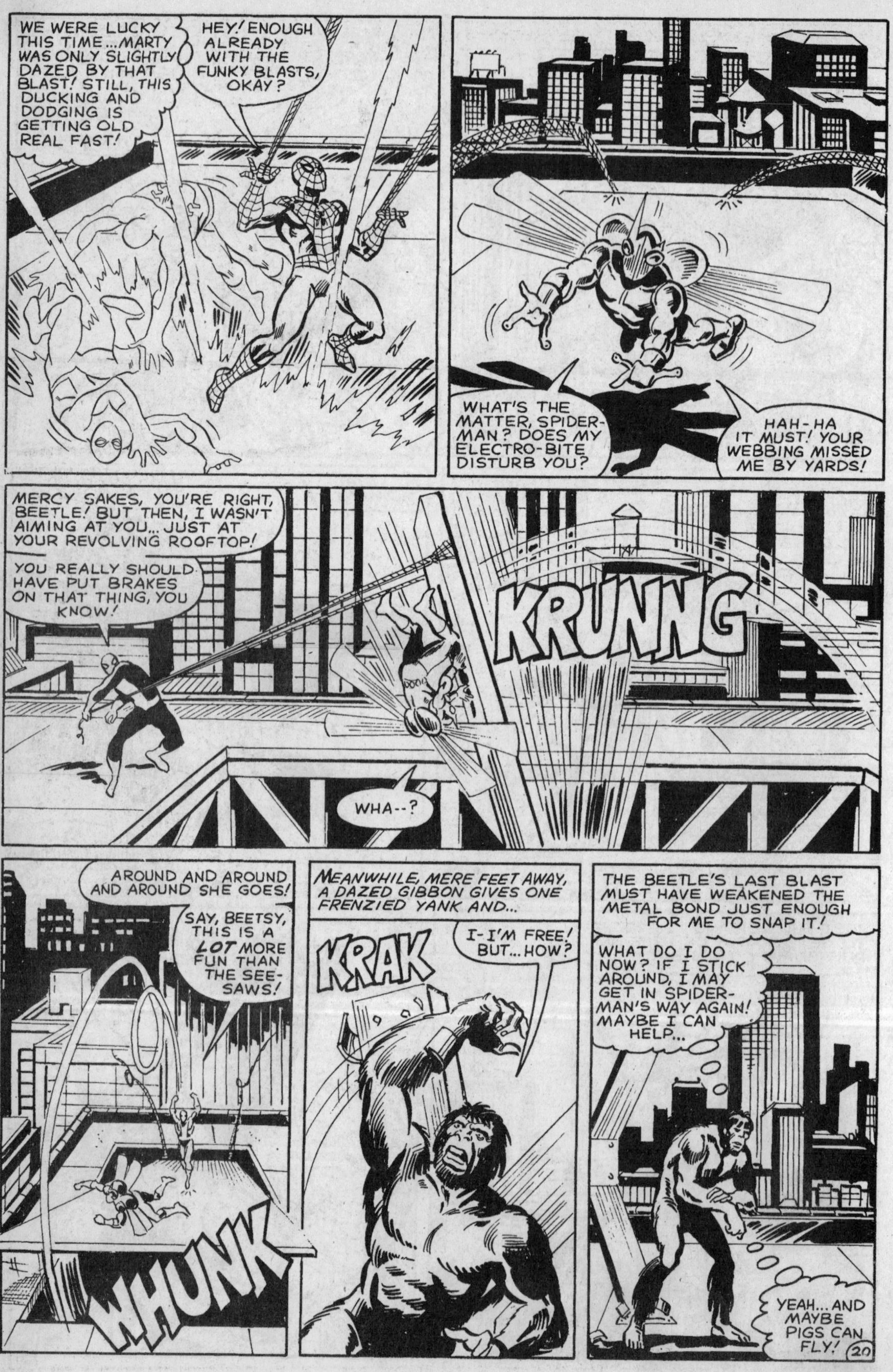

WE WERE LUCKY THIS TIME... MARTY WAS ONLY SLIGHTLY DAZED BY THAT BLAST! STILL, THIS DUCKING AND DODGING IS GETTING OLD REAL FAST!
HEY! ENOUGH ALREADY WITH THE FUNKY BLASTS, OKAY?
WHAT'S THE MATTER, SPIDER-MAN? DOES MY ELECTRO-BITE DISTURB YOU?
HAH-HA IT MUST! YOUR WEBBING MISSED ME BY YARDS!
MERCY SAKES, YOU'RE RIGHT, BEETLE! BUT THEN, I WASN'T AIMING AT YOU... JUST AT YOUR REVOLVING ROOFTOP!
YOU REALLY SHOULD HAVE PUT BRAKES ON THAT THING, YOU KNOW!
KRUNNG
WHA--?
AROUND AND AROUND AND AROUND SHE GOES!
SAY, BEETSY, THIS IS A LOT MORE FUN THAN THE SEE-SAWS!
WHUNK
MEANWHILE, MERE FEET AWAY, A DAZED GIBBON GIVES ONE FRENZIED YANK AND...
KRAK
I-I'M FREE! BUT... HOW?
THE BEETLE'S LAST BLAST MUST HAVE WEAKENED THE METAL BOND JUST ENOUGH FOR ME TO SNAP IT!
WHAT DO I DO NOW? IF I STICK AROUND, I MAY GET IN SPIDER-MAN'S WAY AGAIN! MAYBE I CAN HELP...
YEAH... AND MAYBE PIGS CAN FLY!
20

AT THAT MOMENT, UNAWARE OF THE GIBBON'S ESCAPE...

I'M A LITTLE TIRED OF WALTZING AROUND WITH YOU, BEETLE! IF YOU REALLY WANT TO FIGHT, THEN LET'S DO IT!

VERY WELL!

I AM MORE THAN WILLING TO TEST THE MIGHT OF MY BATTLE SUIT AGAINST YOUR MUCH-VAUNTED SPIDER-STRENGTH!

GOOD AS YOU ARE, YOU ARE NOTHING BEFORE MY POWER! AND ONCE I GET HOLD OF YOU WITH MY SUCTION-GRIPPERS--

--I SHALL RIP YOU IN TWO!

YOU PUT A LOT OF STOCK IN THIS SUIT OF YOURS, BEETLE-BRAIN--BUT IT DOESN'T LOOK SO HOT TO ME!

SEE? LOOK HOW CHEAP IT IS!

SNAP

NO, NOT THE ANTENNA! THAT'S THE FOCUSING POINT FOR MY POWER SOURCE!

YAARRGH!

AND AS THE BEETLE'S BATTLE SUIT DISCHARGES, THE NEARBY NEWSMEN DISCOVER...

HEY, THE STATION IS FINALLY PICKING UP OUR VIDEO SIGNAL!

I'LL BET IT WAS THE BEETLE! HIS SUIT MUST HAVE BEEN PUTTING OUT MICROWAVE INTERFERENCE!

NEVER MIND THAT! NOW SWING YOUR CAMERAS OVER THERE...

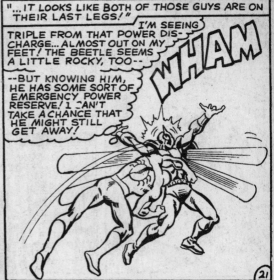

"...IT LOOKS LIKE BOTH OF THOSE GUYS ARE ON THEIR LAST LEGS!"

I'M SEEING TRIPLE FROM THAT POWER DISCHARGE... ALMOST OUT ON MY FEET! THE BEETLE SEEMS A LITTLE ROCKY, TOO--

--BUT KNOWING HIM, HE HAS SOME SORT OF EMERGENCY POWER RESERVE! I CAN'T TAKE A CHANCE THAT HE MIGHT STILL GET AWAY!

WHAM

21

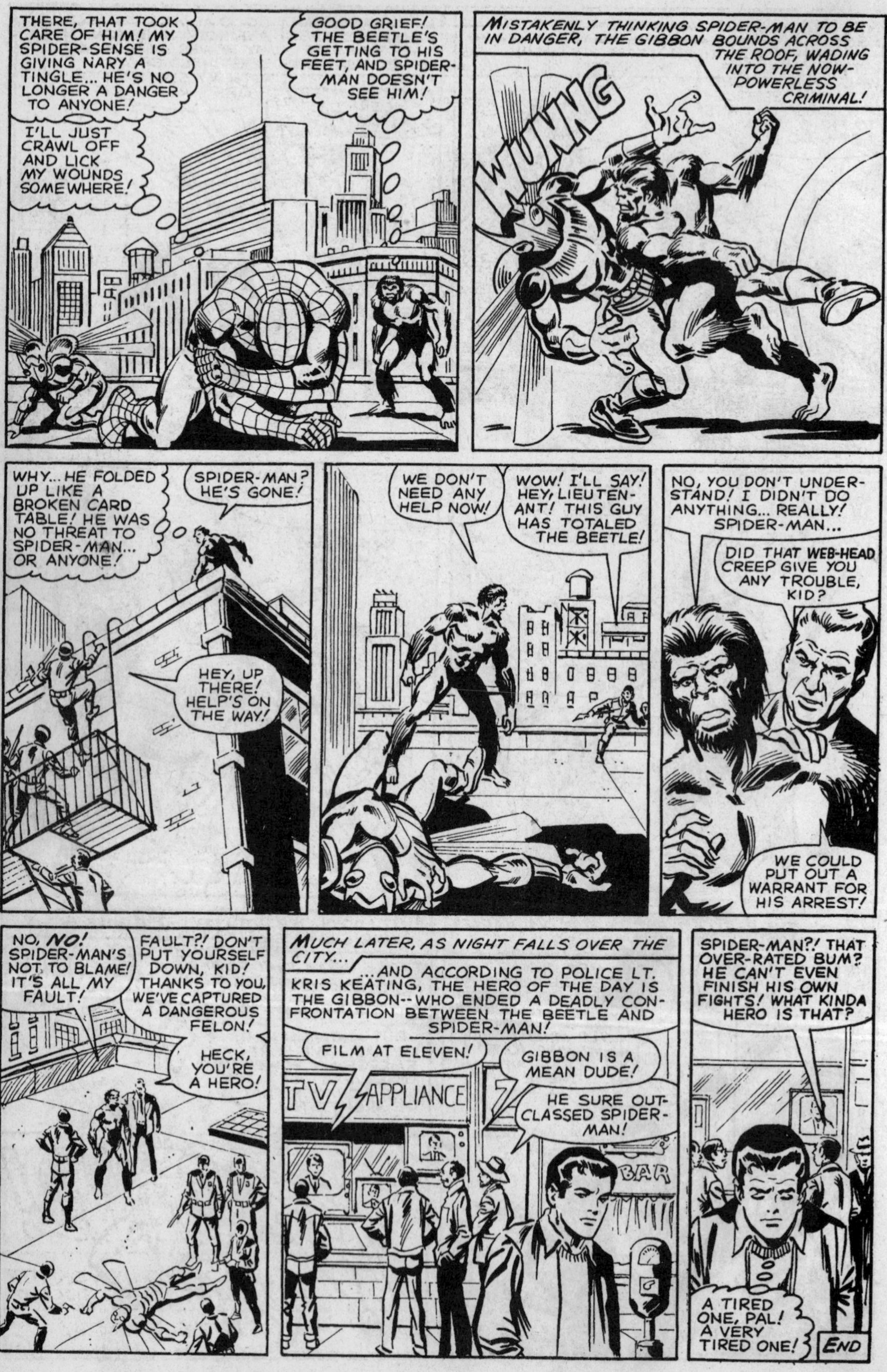
THERE, THAT TOOK CARE OF HIM! MY SPIDER-SENSE IS GIVING NARY A TINGLE... HE'S NO LONGER A DANGER TO ANYONE!
I'LL JUST CRAWL OFF AND LICK MY WOUNDS SOMEWHERE!
GOOD GRIEF! THE BEETLE'S GETTING TO HIS FEET, AND SPIDER-MAN DOESN'T SEE HIM!
MISTAKENLY THINKING SPIDER-MAN TO BE IN DANGER, THE GIBBON BOUNDS ACROSS THE ROOF, WADING INTO THE NOW-POWERLESS CRIMINAL!
WUNNG
WHY... HE FOLDED UP LIKE A BROKEN CARD TABLE! HE WAS NO THREAT TO SPIDER-MAN... OR ANYONE!
SPIDER-MAN? HE'S GONE!
HEY, UP THERE! HELP'S ON THE WAY!
WE DON'T NEED ANY HELP NOW!
WOW! I'LL SAY! HEY, LIEUTENANT! THIS GUY HAS TOTALED THE BEETLE!
NO, YOU DON'T UNDERSTAND! I DIDN'T DO ANYTHING... REALLY! SPIDER-MAN...
DID THAT WEB-HEAD CREEP GIVE YOU ANY TROUBLE, KID?
WE COULD PUT OUT A WARRANT FOR HIS ARREST!
NO, NO! SPIDER-MAN'S NOT TO BLAME! IT'S ALL MY FAULT!
FAULT?! DON'T PUT YOURSELF DOWN, KID! THANKS TO YOU, WE'VE CAPTURED A DANGEROUS FELON!
HECK, YOU'RE A HERO!
MUCH LATER, AS NIGHT FALLS OVER THE CITY...
...AND ACCORDING TO POLICE LT. KRIS KEATING, THE HERO OF THE DAY IS THE GIBBON--WHO ENDED A DEADLY CONFRONTATION BETWEEN THE BEETLE AND SPIDER-MAN!
FILM AT ELEVEN!
GIBBON IS A MEAN DUDE!
HE SURE OUTCLASSED SPIDER-MAN!
TV APPLIANCE
BAR
SPIDER-MAN?! THAT OVER-RATED BUM? HE CAN'T EVEN FINISH HIS OWN FIGHTS! WHAT KINDA HERO IS THAT?
A TIRED ONE, PAL! A VERY TIRED ONE!
END

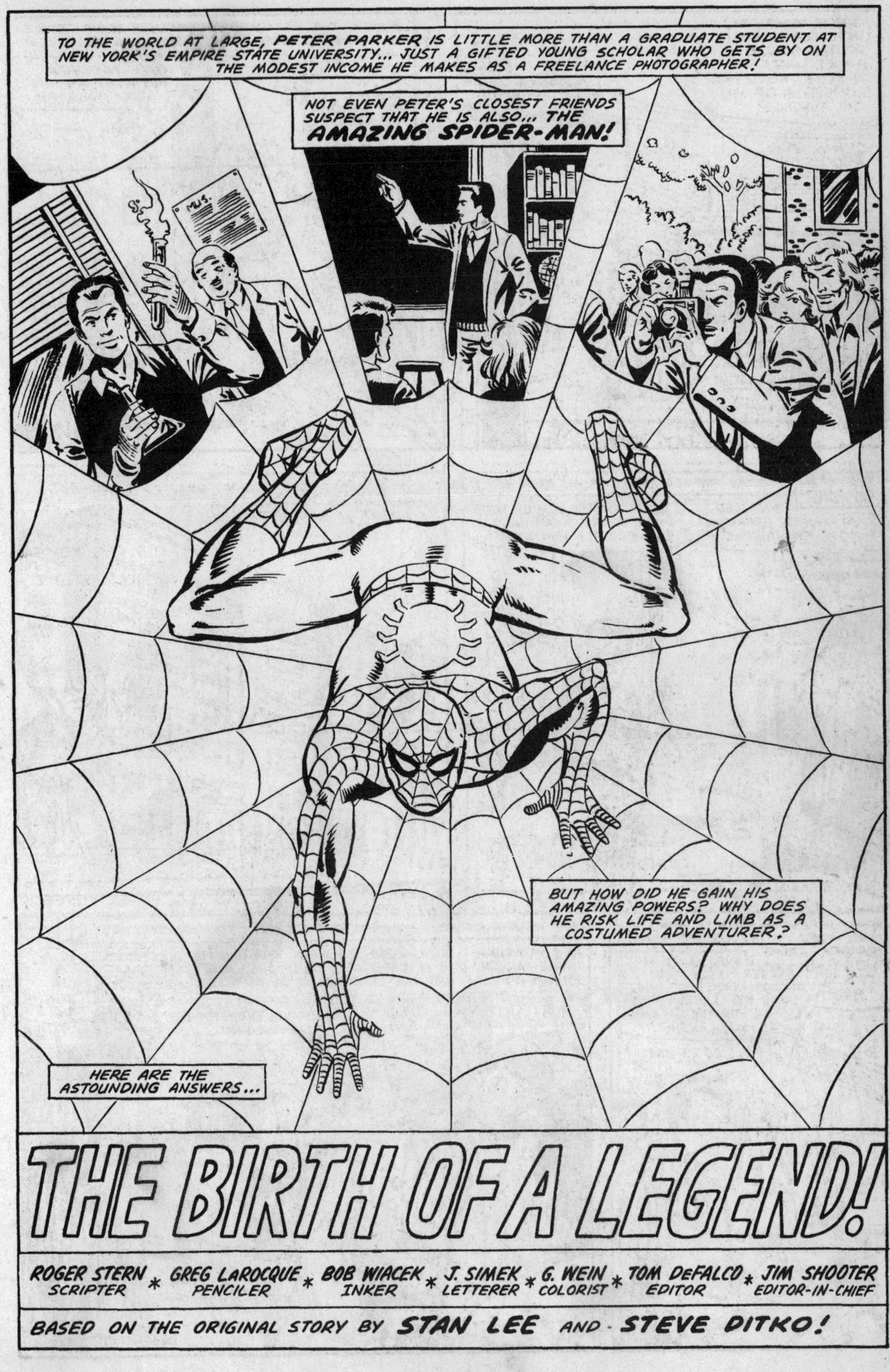
TO THE WORLD AT LARGE, PETER PARKER IS LITTLE MORE THAN A GRADUATE STUDENT AT NEW YORK'S EMPIRE STATE UNIVERSITY... JUST A GIFTED YOUNG SCHOLAR WHO GETS BY ON THE MODEST INCOME HE MAKES AS A FREELANCE PHOTOGRAPHER!
NOT EVEN PETER'S CLOSEST FRIENDS SUSPECT THAT HE IS ALSO... THE AMAZING SPIDER-MAN!
BUT HOW DID HE GAIN HIS AMAZING POWERS? WHY DOES HE RISK LIFE AND LIMB AS A COSTUMED ADVENTURER?
HERE ARE THE ASTOUNDING ANSWERS...
THE BIRTH OF A LEGEND!
ROGER STERN SCRIPTER * GREG LAROCQUE PENCILER * BOB WIACEK INKER * J. SIMEK LETTERER * G. WEIN COLORIST * TOM DEFALCO EDITOR * JIM SHOOTER EDITOR-IN-CHIEF
BASED ON THE ORIGINAL STORY BY STAN LEE AND STEVE DITKO!

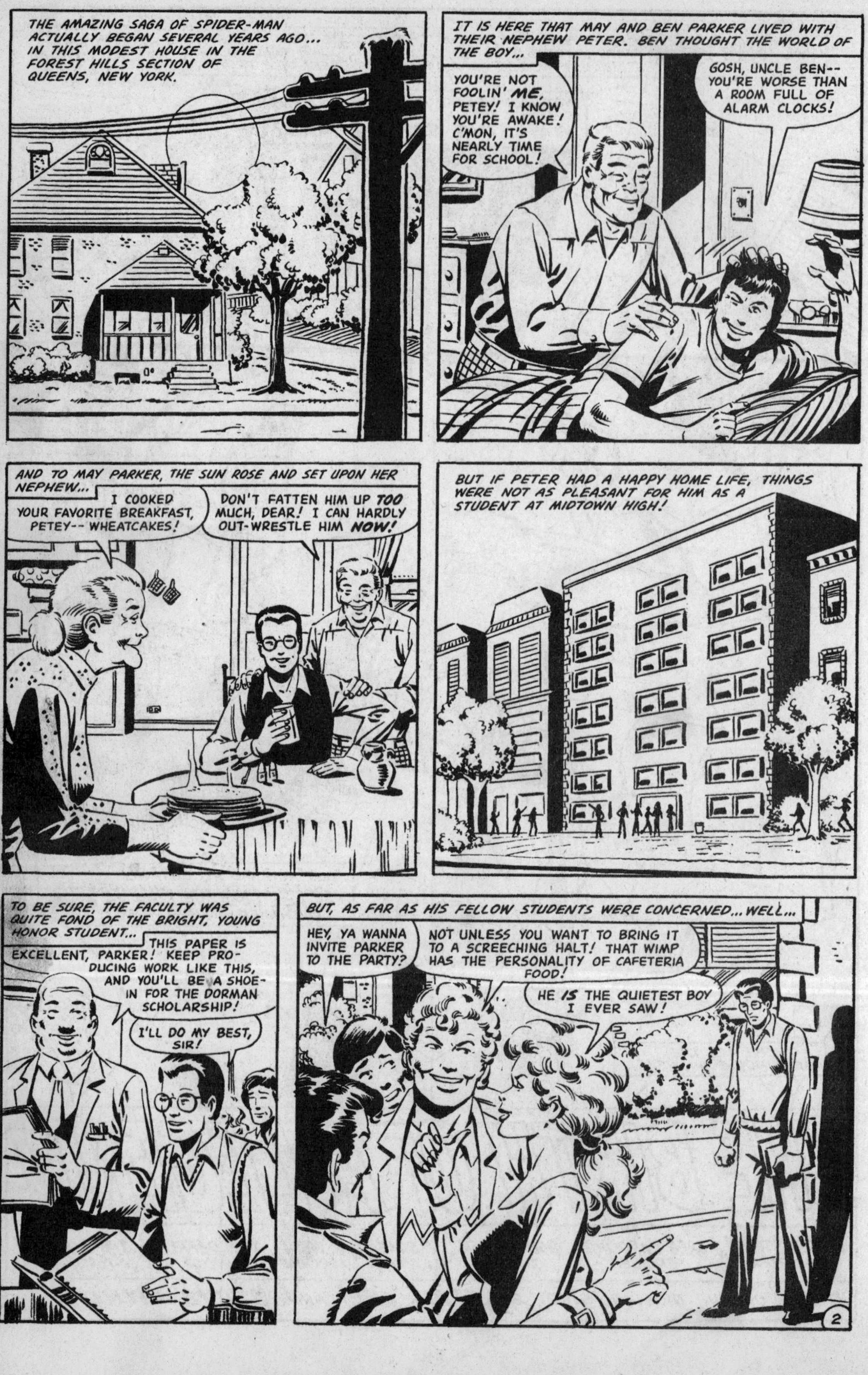
THE AMAZING SAGA OF SPIDER-MAN ACTUALLY BEGAN SEVERAL YEARS AGO... IN THIS MODEST HOUSE IN THE FOREST HILLS SECTION OF QUEENS, NEW YORK.
IT IS HERE THAT MAY AND BEN PARKER LIVED WITH THEIR NEPHEW PETER. BEN THOUGHT THE WORLD OF THE BOY...
YOU'RE NOT FOOLIN' ME, PETEY! I KNOW YOU'RE AWAKE! C'MON, IT'S NEARLY TIME FOR SCHOOL!
GOSH, UNCLE BEN-- YOU'RE WORSE THAN A ROOM FULL OF ALARM CLOCKS!
AND TO MAY PARKER, THE SUN ROSE AND SET UPON HER NEPHEW...
I COOKED YOUR FAVORITE BREAKFAST, PETEY-- WHEATCAKES!
DON'T FATTEN HIM UP TOO MUCH, DEAR! I CAN HARDLY OUT-WRESTLE HIM NOW!
BUT IF PETER HAD A HAPPY HOME LIFE, THINGS WERE NOT AS PLEASANT FOR HIM AS A STUDENT AT MIDTOWN HIGH!
TO BE SURE, THE FACULTY WAS QUITE FOND OF THE BRIGHT, YOUNG HONOR STUDENT...
THIS PAPER IS EXCELLENT, PARKER! KEEP PRODUCING WORK LIKE THIS, AND YOU'LL BE A SHOE-IN FOR THE DORMAN SCHOLARSHIP!
I'LL DO MY BEST, SIR!
BUT, AS FAR AS HIS FELLOW STUDENTS WERE CONCERNED... WELL...
HEY, YA WANNA INVITE PARKER TO THE PARTY?
NOT UNLESS YOU WANT TO BRING IT TO A SCREECHING HALT! THAT WIMP HAS THE PERSONALITY OF CAFETERIA FOOD!
HE IS THE QUIETEST BOY I EVER SAW!
2

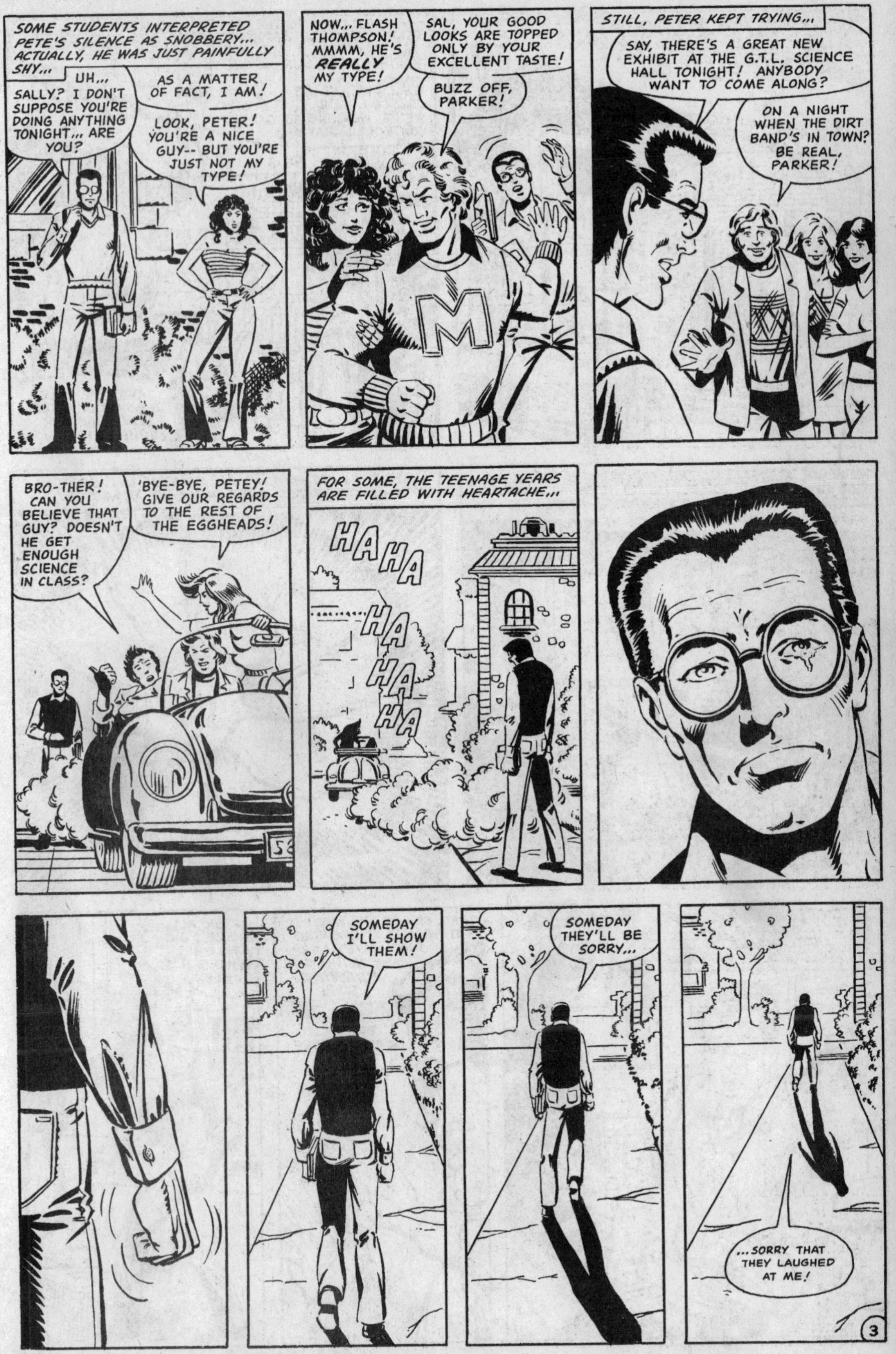

SOME STUDENTS INTERPRETED PETE'S SILENCE AS SNOBBERY... ACTUALLY, HE WAS JUST PAINFULLY SHY...
UH... SALLY? I DON'T SUPPOSE YOU'RE DOING ANYTHING TONIGHT... ARE YOU?
AS A MATTER OF FACT, I AM!
LOOK, PETER! YOU'RE A NICE GUY-- BUT YOU'RE JUST NOT MY TYPE!
NOW... FLASH THOMPSON! MMMM, HE'S REALLY MY TYPE!
SAL, YOUR GOOD LOOKS ARE TOPPED ONLY BY YOUR EXCELLENT TASTE!
BUZZ OFF, PARKER!
STILL, PETER KEPT TRYING...
SAY, THERE'S A GREAT NEW EXHIBIT AT THE G.T.L. SCIENCE HALL TONIGHT! ANYBODY WANT TO COME ALONG?
ON A NIGHT WHEN THE DIRT BAND'S IN TOWN? BE REAL, PARKER!
BRO-THER! CAN YOU BELIEVE THAT GUY? DOESN'T HE GET ENOUGH SCIENCE IN CLASS?
'BYE-BYE, PETEY! GIVE OUR REGARDS TO THE REST OF THE EGGHEADS!
FOR SOME, THE TEENAGE YEARS ARE FILLED WITH HEARTACHE...
HAHA HA HA HA
SOMEDAY I'LL SHOW THEM!
SOMEDAY THEY'LL BE SORRY...
...SORRY THAT THEY LAUGHED AT ME!

WHENEVER THE TAUNTS OF HIS CLASSMATES BECAME TOO MUCH TO BEAR, PETER WOULD ESCAPE INTO A WORLD HE COULD BETTER UNDERSTAND-- THE FASCINATING WORLD OF SCIENCE!

GOOD AFTER-NOON--

-- AND WELCOME TO THE GENERAL TECHTRONICS "EXPERIMENT IN RADIOACTIVITY!" I'M SURE YOU'RE ALL CONCERNED ABOUT THE GROWING LEVELS OF RADIATION IN OUR SOCIETY!

WELL, WE AT G.T.L. SHARE YOUR CONCERN. AND THAT'S WHY WE'RE WORKING TO SAFELY CONTROL RADIATION.

AND NOW, I'LL DEMONSTRATE JUST HOW SAFE OUR EQUIPMENT IS!

HOWEVER, DESPITE ALL THE PRECAUTIONS TAKEN BY THE SCIENCE HALL STAFF, THERE WERE NO SAFE-GUARDS TO PREVENT A TINY SPIDER FROM DESCENDING FROM THE CEILING...

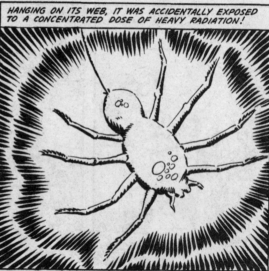

HANGING ON ITS WEB, IT WAS ACCIDENTALLY EXPOSED TO A CONCENTRATED DOSE OF HEAVY RADIATION!

IN AGONY, THE DYING SPIDER SPUN ABOUT-- WAFTING THROUGH THE AIR, AND LANDING ON THE UNSUSPECTING HIGHSCHOOLER...

OW!

THAT SPIDER BIT ME! BUT WHY IS IT GLOWING THAT WAY? AND WHY IS THE BITE BURNING SO?!

BETTER BRUSH IT OFF BEFORE IT BITES AGAIN!

AFTER ALL, THERE'S NO TELLING WHERE IT'S BEEN!

THUUP

4

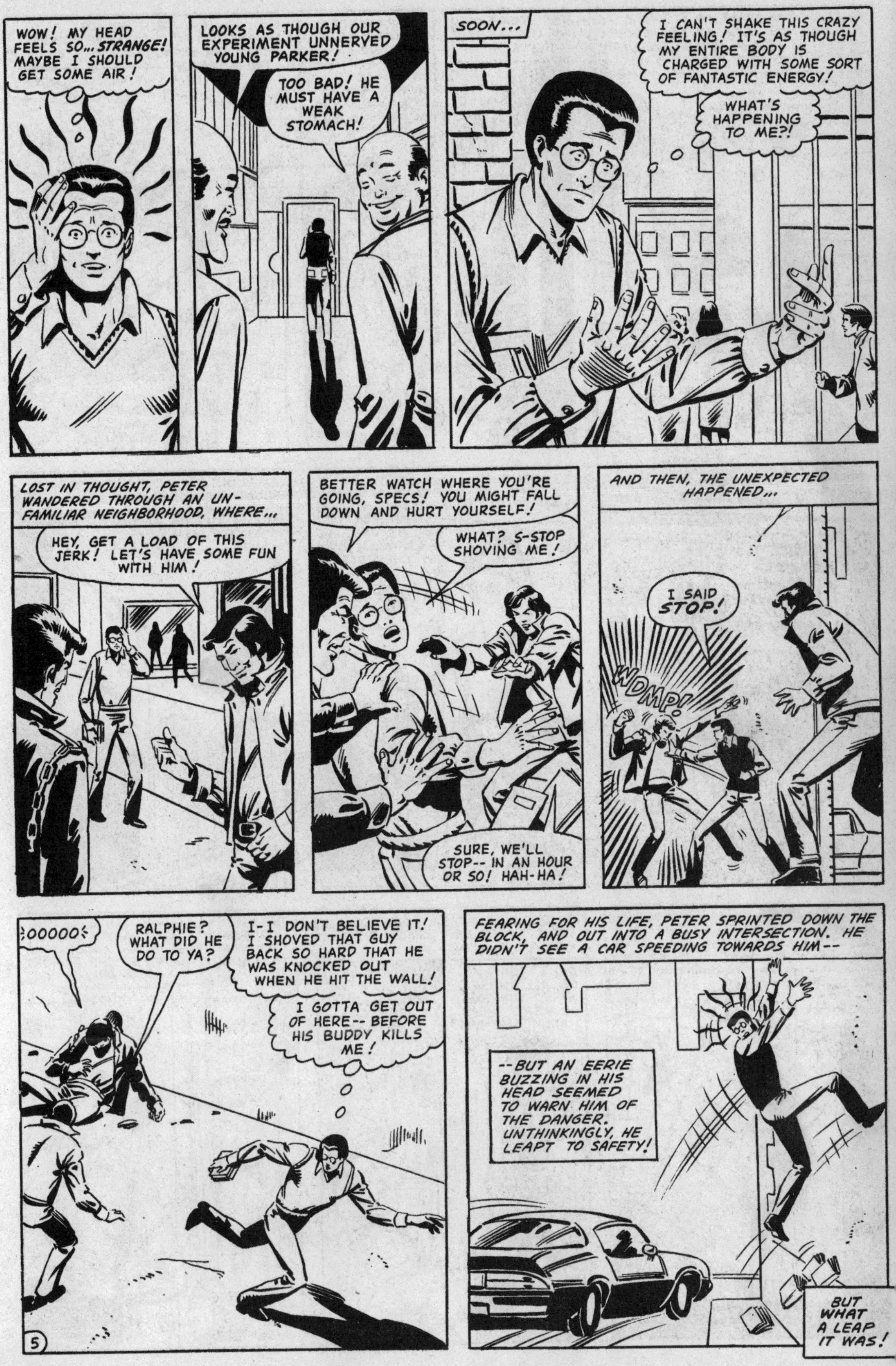
WOW! MY HEAD FEELS SO... STRANGE! MAYBE I SHOULD GET SOME AIR!
LOOKS AS THOUGH OUR EXPERIMENT UNNERVED YOUNG PARKER!
TOO BAD! HE MUST HAVE A WEAK STOMACH!
SOON...
I CAN'T SHAKE THIS CRAZY FEELING! IT'S AS THOUGH MY ENTIRE BODY IS CHARGED WITH SOME SORT OF FANTASTIC ENERGY!
WHAT'S HAPPENING TO ME?!
LOST IN THOUGHT, PETER WANDERED THROUGH AN UN-FAMILIAR NEIGHBORHOOD, WHERE...
HEY, GET A LOAD OF THIS JERK! LET'S HAVE SOME FUN WITH HIM!
BETTER WATCH WHERE YOU'RE GOING, SPECS! YOU MIGHT FALL DOWN AND HURT YOURSELF!
WHAT? S-STOP SHOVING ME!
SURE, WE'LL STOP-- IN AN HOUR OR SO! HAH-HA!
AND THEN, THE UNEXPECTED HAPPENED...
I SAID STOP!
WDMP!
OOOOO
RALPHIE? WHAT DID HE DO TO YA?
I-I DON'T BELIEVE IT! I SHOVED THAT GUY BACK SO HARD THAT HE WAS KNOCKED OUT WHEN HE HIT THE WALL!
I GOTTA GET OUT OF HERE-- BEFORE HIS BUDDY KILLS ME!
FEARING FOR HIS LIFE, PETER SPRINTED DOWN THE BLOCK, AND OUT INTO A BUSY INTERSECTION. HE DIDN'T SEE A CAR SPEEDING TOWARDS HIM--
--BUT AN EERIE BUZZING IN HIS HEAD SEEMED TO WARN HIM OF THE DANGER. UNTHINKINGLY, HE LEAPT TO SAFETY!
BUT WHAT A LEAP IT WAS!
5

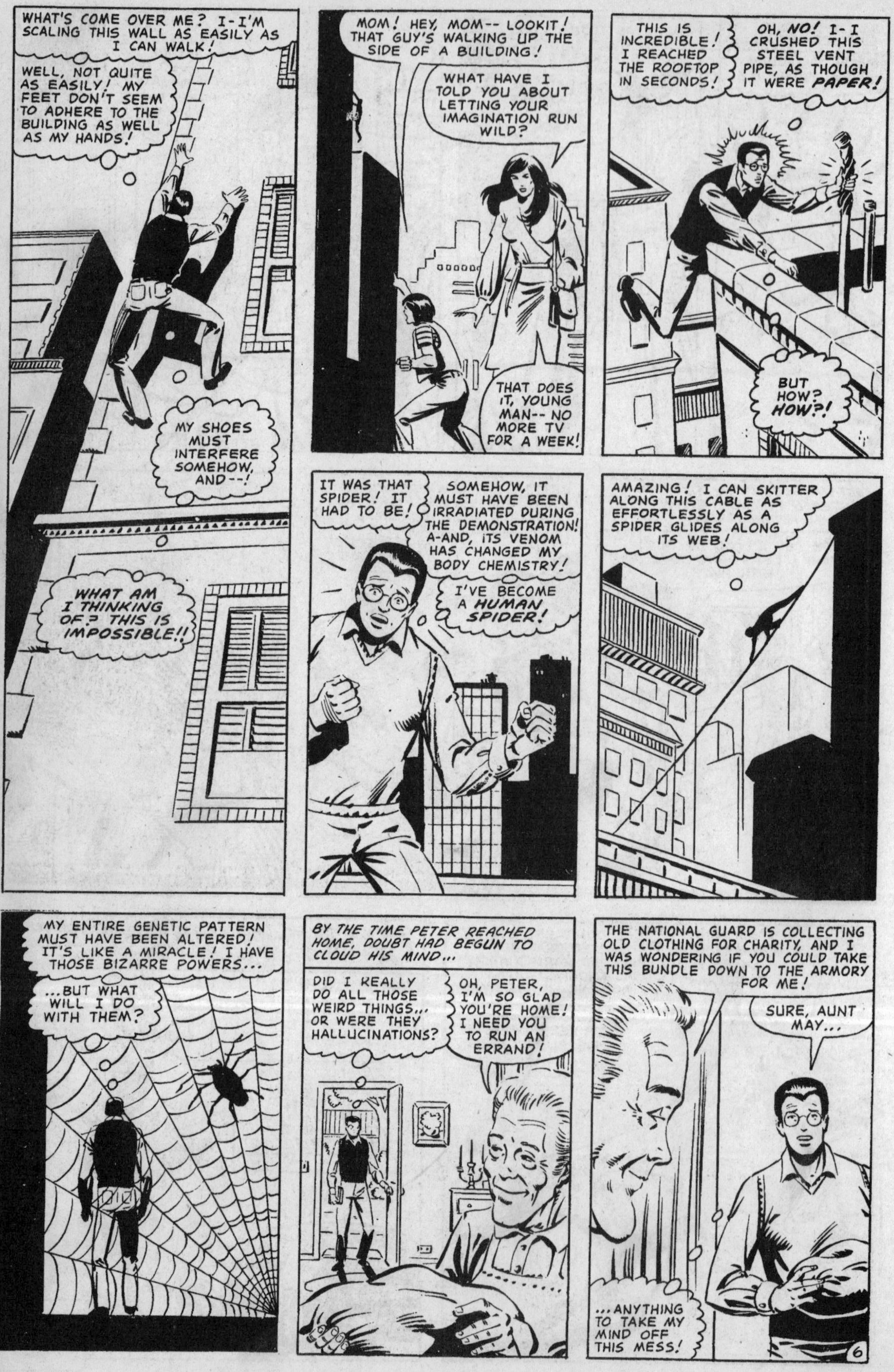

WHAT'S COME OVER ME? I-I'M SCALING THIS WALL AS EASILY AS I CAN WALK!
WELL, NOT QUITE AS EASILY! MY FEET DON'T SEEM TO ADHERE TO THE BUILDING AS WELL AS MY HANDS!
MY SHOES MUST INTERFERE SOMEHOW, AND--!
WHAT AM I THINKING OF? THIS IS IMPOSSIBLE!!
MOM! HEY, MOM-- LOOKIT! THAT GUY'S WALKING UP THE SIDE OF A BUILDING!
WHAT HAVE I TOLD YOU ABOUT LETTING YOUR IMAGINATION RUN WILD?
THAT DOES IT, YOUNG MAN-- NO MORE TV FOR A WEEK!
THIS IS INCREDIBLE! I REACHED THE ROOFTOP IN SECONDS!
OH, NO! I-I CRUSHED THIS STEEL VENT PIPE, AS THOUGH IT WERE PAPER!
BUT HOW? HOW?!
IT WAS THAT SPIDER! IT HAD TO BE!
SOMEHOW, IT MUST HAVE BEEN IRRADIATED DURING THE DEMONSTRATION! A-AND, ITS VENOM HAS CHANGED MY BODY CHEMISTRY!
I'VE BECOME A HUMAN SPIDER!
AMAZING! I CAN SKITTER ALONG THIS CABLE AS EFFORTLESSLY AS A SPIDER GLIDES ALONG ITS WEB!
MY ENTIRE GENETIC PATTERN MUST HAVE BEEN ALTERED! IT'S LIKE A MIRACLE! I HAVE THOSE BIZARRE POWERS...
...BUT WHAT WILL I DO WITH THEM?
BY THE TIME PETER REACHED HOME, DOUBT HAD BEGUN TO CLOUD HIS MIND...
DID I REALLY DO ALL THOSE WEIRD THINGS... OR WERE THEY HALLUCINATIONS?
OH, PETER, I'M SO GLAD YOU'RE HOME! I NEED YOU TO RUN AN ERRAND!
THE NATIONAL GUARD IS COLLECTING OLD CLOTHING FOR CHARITY, AND I WAS WONDERING IF YOU COULD TAKE THIS BUNDLE DOWN TO THE ARMORY FOR ME!
SURE, AUNT MAY...
...ANYTHING TO TAKE MY MIND OFF THIS MESS!
6

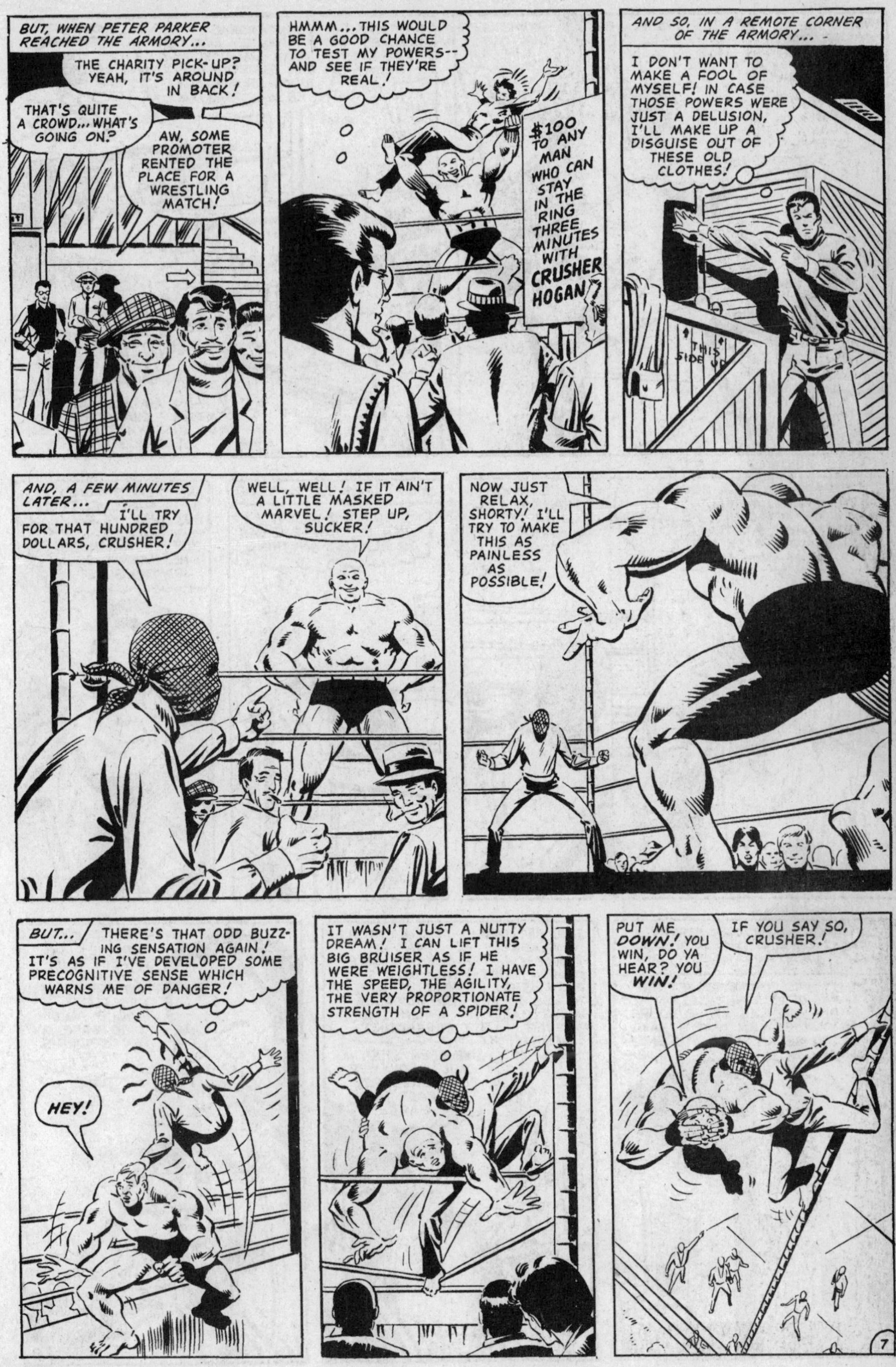

BUT, WHEN PETER PARKER REACHED THE ARMORY...
THE CHARITY PICK-UP? YEAH, IT'S AROUND IN BACK!
THAT'S QUITE A CROWD... WHAT'S GOING ON?
AW, SOME PROMOTER RENTED THE PLACE FOR A WRESTLING MATCH!
HMMM... THIS WOULD BE A GOOD CHANCE TO TEST MY POWERS-- AND SEE IF THEY'RE REAL!
$100 TO ANY MAN WHO CAN STAY IN THE RING THREE MINUTES WITH CRUSHER HOGAN
AND SO, IN A REMOTE CORNER OF THE ARMORY...
I DON'T WANT TO MAKE A FOOL OF MYSELF! IN CASE THOSE POWERS WERE JUST A DELUSION, I'LL MAKE UP A DISGUISE OUT OF THESE OLD CLOTHES!
THIS SIDE UP
AND, A FEW MINUTES LATER...
I'LL TRY FOR THAT HUNDRED DOLLARS, CRUSHER!
WELL, WELL! IF IT AIN'T A LITTLE MASKED MARVEL! STEP UP, SUCKER!
NOW JUST RELAX, SHORTY! I'LL TRY TO MAKE THIS AS PAINLESS AS POSSIBLE!
BUT...
THERE'S THAT ODD BUZZING SENSATION AGAIN! IT'S AS IF I'VE DEVELOPED SOME PRECOGNITIVE SENSE WHICH WARNS ME OF DANGER!
HEY!
IT WASN'T JUST A NUTTY DREAM! I CAN LIFT THIS BIG BRUISER AS IF HE WERE WEIGHTLESS! I HAVE THE SPEED, THE AGILITY, THE VERY PROPORTIONATE STRENGTH OF A SPIDER!
PUT ME DOWN! YOU WIN, DO YA HEAR? YOU WIN!
IF YOU SAY SO, CRUSHER!

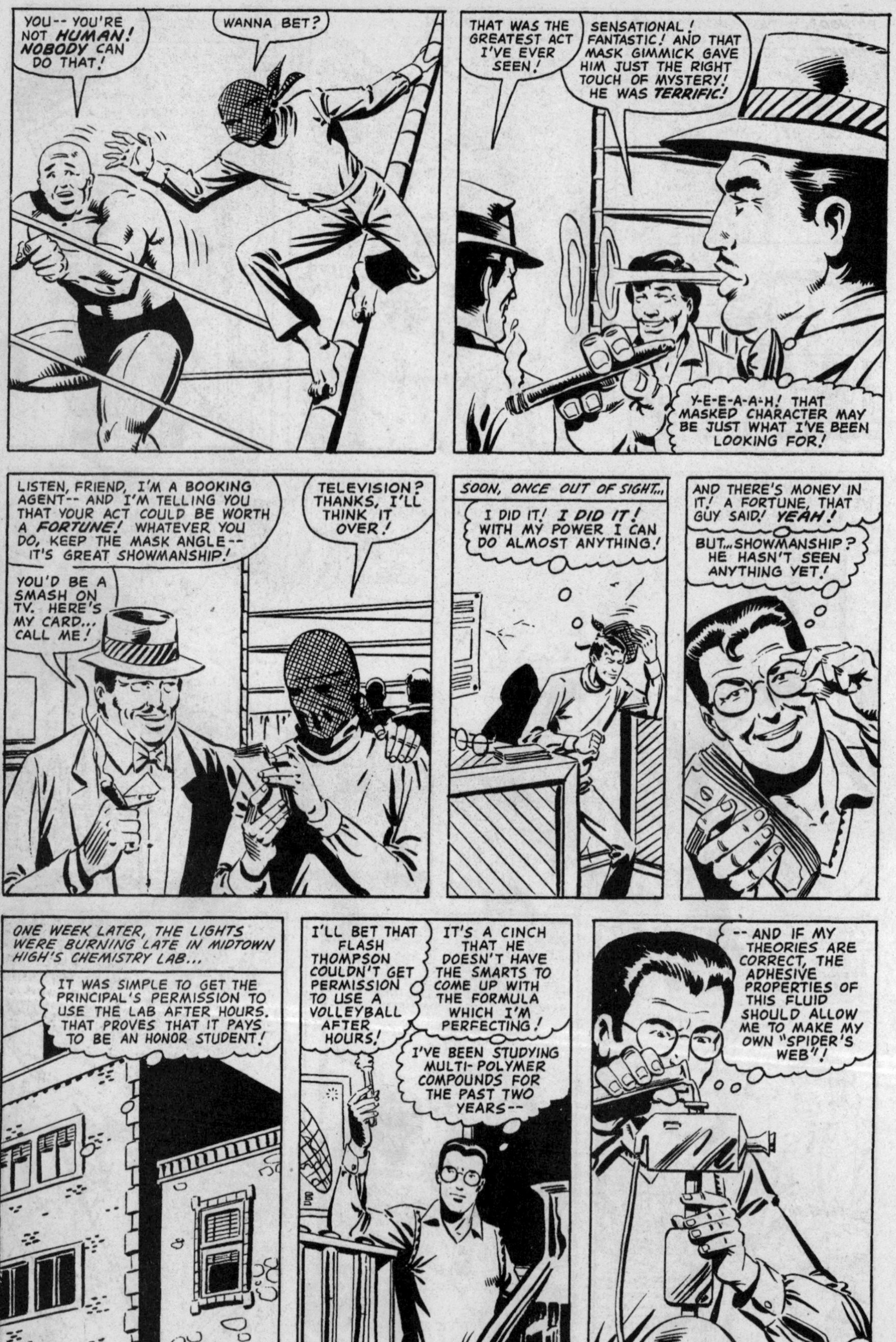
YOU-- YOU'RE NOT **HUMAN!** **NOBODY** CAN DO THAT!
WANNA BET?
THAT WAS THE GREATEST ACT I'VE EVER SEEN!
SENSATIONAL! FANTASTIC! AND THAT MASK GIMMICK GAVE HIM JUST THE RIGHT TOUCH OF MYSTERY! HE WAS **TERRIFIC!**
Y-E-E-A-A-H! THAT MASKED CHARACTER MAY BE JUST WHAT I'VE BEEN LOOKING FOR!
LISTEN, FRIEND, I'M A BOOKING AGENT-- AND I'M TELLING YOU THAT YOUR ACT COULD BE WORTH A **FORTUNE!** WHATEVER YOU DO, KEEP THE MASK ANGLE-- IT'S GREAT SHOWMANSHIP!
YOU'D BE A SMASH ON TV. HERE'S MY CARD... CALL ME!
TELEVISION? THANKS, I'LL THINK IT OVER!
SOON, ONCE OUT OF SIGHT...
I DID IT! **I DID IT!** WITH MY POWER I CAN DO ALMOST ANYTHING!
AND THERE'S MONEY IN IT! A FORTUNE, THAT GUY SAID! **YEAH!**
BUT...SHOWMANSHIP? HE HASN'T SEEN ANYTHING YET!
ONE WEEK LATER, THE LIGHTS WERE BURNING LATE IN MIDTOWN HIGH'S CHEMISTRY LAB...
IT WAS SIMPLE TO GET THE PRINCIPAL'S PERMISSION TO USE THE LAB AFTER HOURS. THAT PROVES THAT IT PAYS TO BE AN HONOR STUDENT!
I'LL BET THAT FLASH THOMPSON COULDN'T GET PERMISSION TO USE A VOLLEYBALL AFTER HOURS!
IT'S A CINCH THAT HE DOESN'T HAVE THE SMARTS TO COME UP WITH THE FORMULA WHICH I'M PERFECTING!
I'VE BEEN STUDYING MULTI-POLYMER COMPOUNDS FOR THE PAST TWO YEARS--
--AND IF MY THEORIES ARE CORRECT, THE ADHESIVE PROPERTIES OF THIS FLUID SHOULD ALLOW ME TO MAKE MY OWN "SPIDER'S WEB"!
8

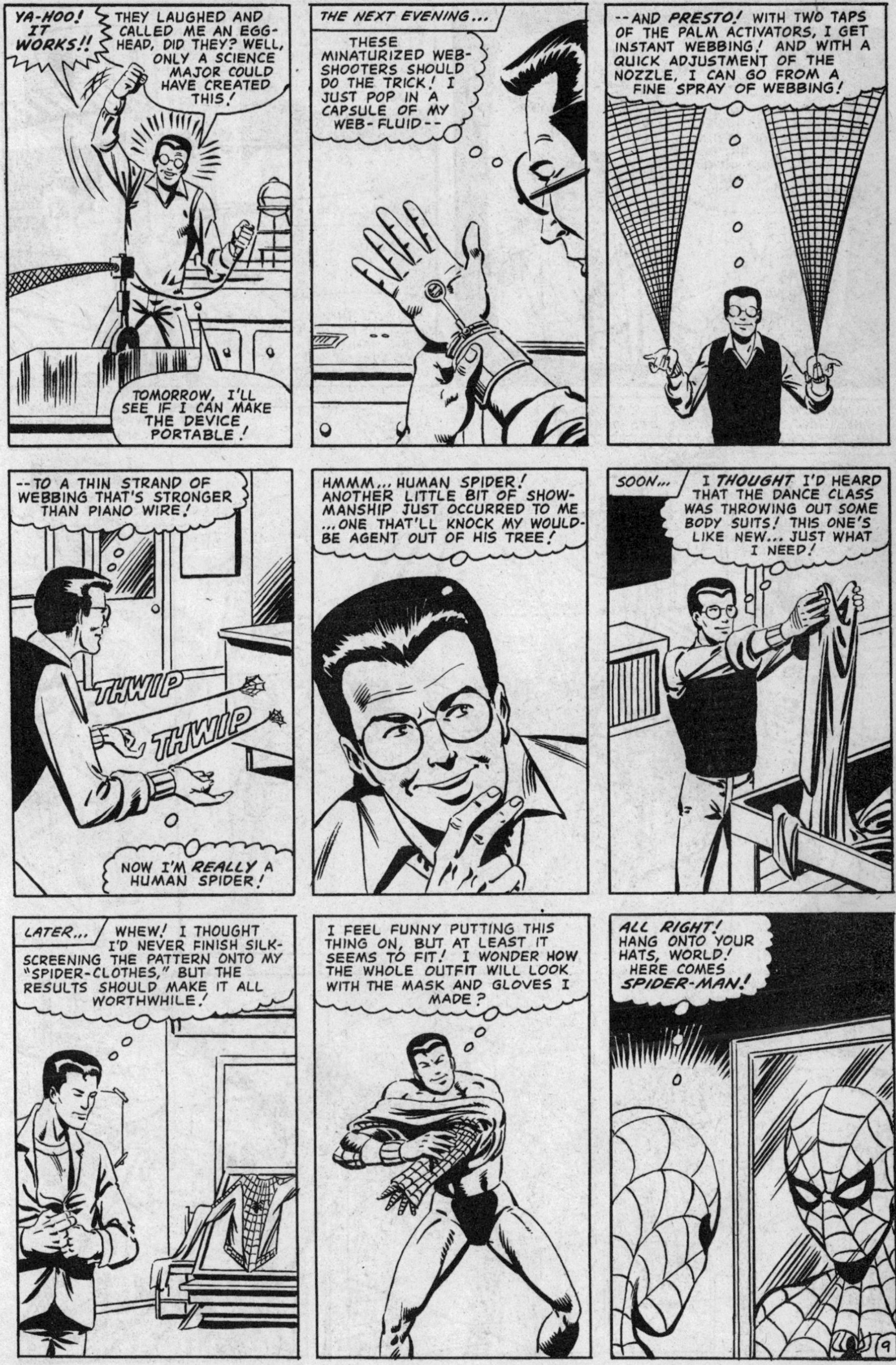

YA-HOO! IT WORKS!!
THEY LAUGHED AND CALLED ME AN EGG-HEAD, DID THEY? WELL, ONLY A SCIENCE MAJOR COULD HAVE CREATED THIS!
TOMORROW, I'LL SEE IF I CAN MAKE THE DEVICE PORTABLE!
THE NEXT EVENING...
THESE MINATURIZED WEB-SHOOTERS SHOULD DO THE TRICK! I JUST POP IN A CAPSULE OF MY WEB-FLUID--
--AND PRESTO! WITH TWO TAPS OF THE PALM ACTIVATORS, I GET INSTANT WEBBING! AND WITH A QUICK ADJUSTMENT OF THE NOZZLE, I CAN GO FROM A FINE SPRAY OF WEBBING!
--TO A THIN STRAND OF WEBBING THAT'S STRONGER THAN PIANO WIRE!
THWIP
THWIP
NOW I'M REALLY A HUMAN SPIDER!
HMMM... HUMAN SPIDER! ANOTHER LITTLE BIT OF SHOW-MANSHIP JUST OCCURRED TO ME ...ONE THAT'LL KNOCK MY WOULD-BE AGENT OUT OF HIS TREE!
SOON...
I THOUGHT I'D HEARD THAT THE DANCE CLASS WAS THROWING OUT SOME BODY SUITS! THIS ONE'S LIKE NEW... JUST WHAT I NEED!
LATER...
WHEW! I THOUGHT I'D NEVER FINISH SILK-SCREENING THE PATTERN ONTO MY "SPIDER-CLOTHES," BUT THE RESULTS SHOULD MAKE IT ALL WORTHWHILE!
I FEEL FUNNY PUTTING THIS THING ON, BUT AT LEAST IT SEEMS TO FIT! I WONDER HOW THE WHOLE OUTFIT WILL LOOK WITH THE MASK AND GLOVES I MADE?
ALL RIGHT! HANG ONTO YOUR HATS, WORLD! HERE COMES SPIDER-MAN!
9

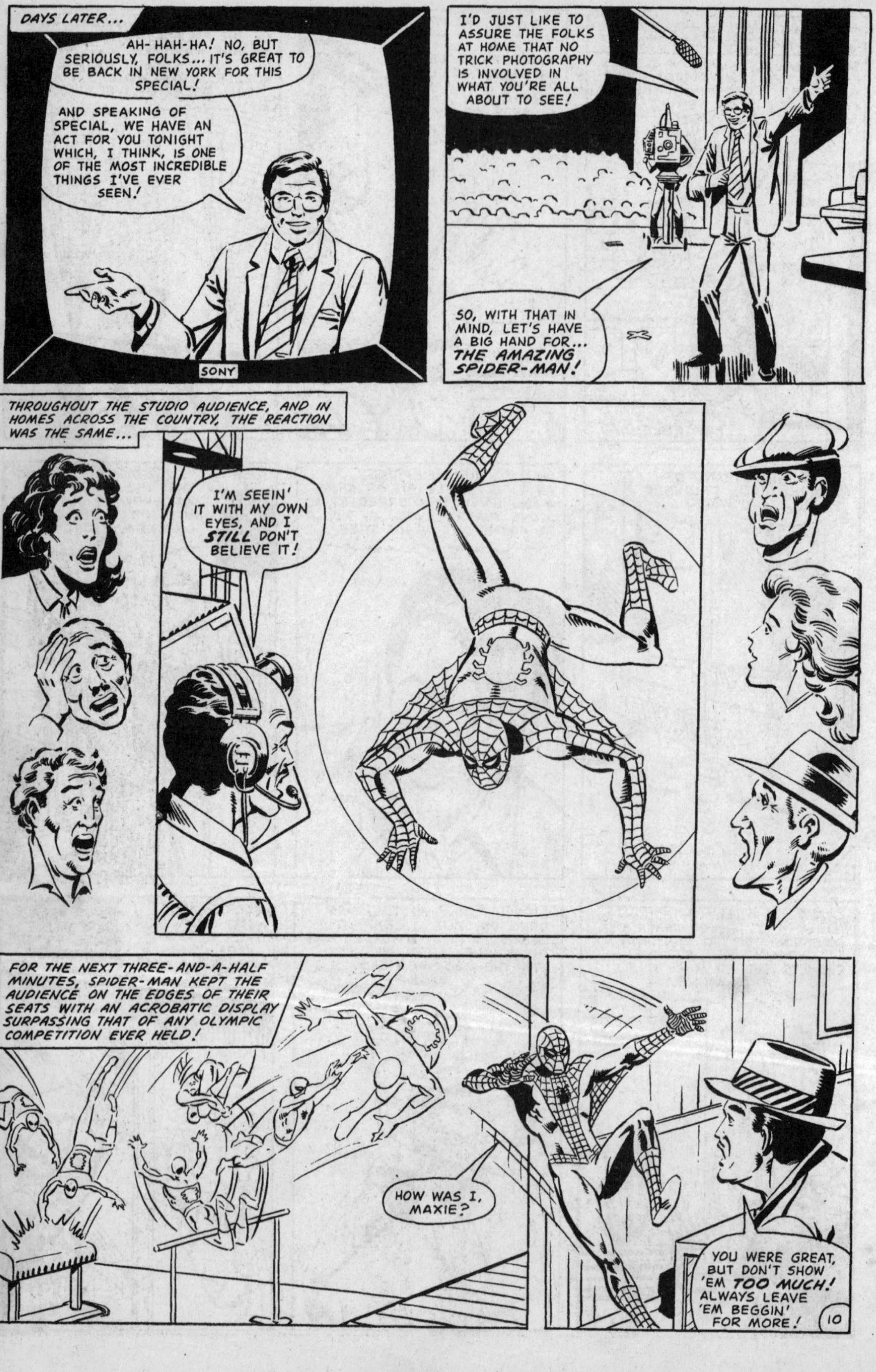
DAYS LATER...
AH-HAH-HA! NO, BUT SERIOUSLY, FOLKS... IT'S GREAT TO BE BACK IN NEW YORK FOR THIS SPECIAL!
AND SPEAKING OF SPECIAL, WE HAVE AN ACT FOR YOU TONIGHT WHICH, I THINK, IS ONE OF THE MOST INCREDIBLE THINGS I'VE EVER SEEN!
SONY
I'D JUST LIKE TO ASSURE THE FOLKS AT HOME THAT NO TRICK PHOTOGRAPHY IS INVOLVED IN WHAT YOU'RE ALL ABOUT TO SEE!
SO, WITH THAT IN MIND, LET'S HAVE A BIG HAND FOR... THE AMAZING SPIDER-MAN!
THROUGHOUT THE STUDIO AUDIENCE, AND IN HOMES ACROSS THE COUNTRY, THE REACTION WAS THE SAME...
I'M SEEIN' IT WITH MY OWN EYES, AND I STILL DON'T BELIEVE IT!
FOR THE NEXT THREE-AND-A-HALF MINUTES, SPIDER-MAN KEPT THE AUDIENCE ON THE EDGES OF THEIR SEATS WITH AN ACROBATIC DISPLAY SURPASSING THAT OF ANY OLYMPIC COMPETITION EVER HELD!
HOW WAS I, MAXIE?
YOU WERE GREAT, BUT DON'T SHOW 'EM TOO MUCH! ALWAYS LEAVE 'EM BEGGIN' FOR MORE!

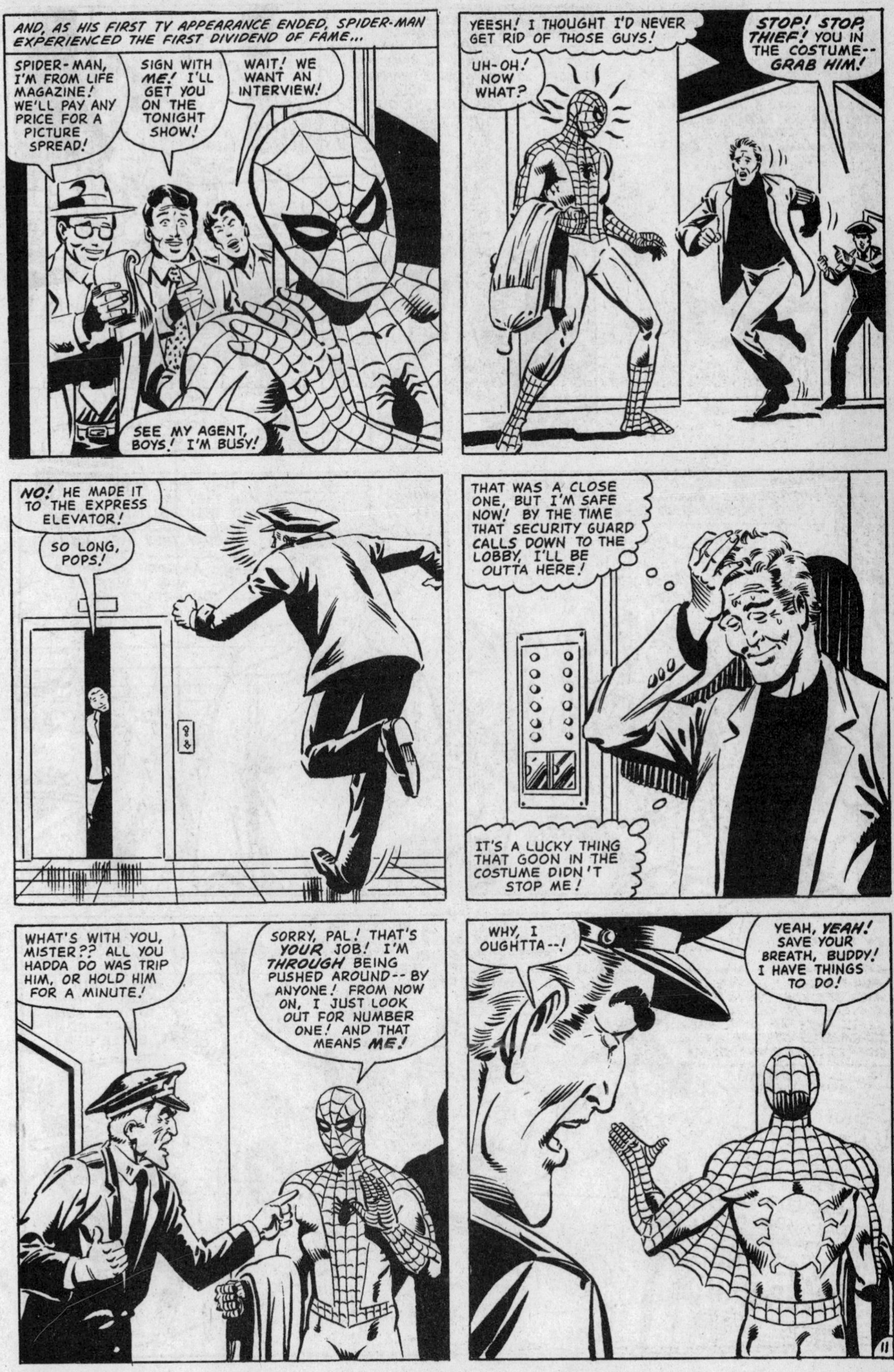
AND, AS HIS FIRST TV APPEARANCE ENDED, SPIDER-MAN EXPERIENCED THE FIRST DIVIDEND OF FAME...
SPIDER-MAN, I'M FROM LIFE MAGAZINE! WE'LL PAY ANY PRICE FOR A PICTURE SPREAD!
SIGN WITH ME! I'LL GET YOU ON THE TONIGHT SHOW!
WAIT! WE WANT AN INTERVIEW!
SEE MY AGENT, BOYS! I'M BUSY!
YEESH! I THOUGHT I'D NEVER GET RID OF THOSE GUYS!
UH-OH! NOW WHAT?
STOP! STOP, THIEF! YOU IN THE COSTUME-- GRAB HIM!
NO! HE MADE IT TO THE EXPRESS ELEVATOR!
SO LONG, POPS!
THAT WAS A CLOSE ONE, BUT I'M SAFE NOW! BY THE TIME THAT SECURITY GUARD CALLS DOWN TO THE LOBBY, I'LL BE OUTTA HERE!
IT'S A LUCKY THING THAT GOON IN THE COSTUME DIDN'T STOP ME!
WHAT'S WITH YOU, MISTER?? ALL YOU HADDA DO WAS TRIP HIM, OR HOLD HIM FOR A MINUTE!
SORRY, PAL! THAT'S YOUR JOB! I'M THROUGH BEING PUSHED AROUND-- BY ANYONE! FROM NOW ON, I JUST LOOK OUT FOR NUMBER ONE! AND THAT MEANS ME!
WHY, I OUGHTTA--!
YEAH, YEAH! SAVE YOUR BREATH, BUDDY! I HAVE THINGS TO DO!
11

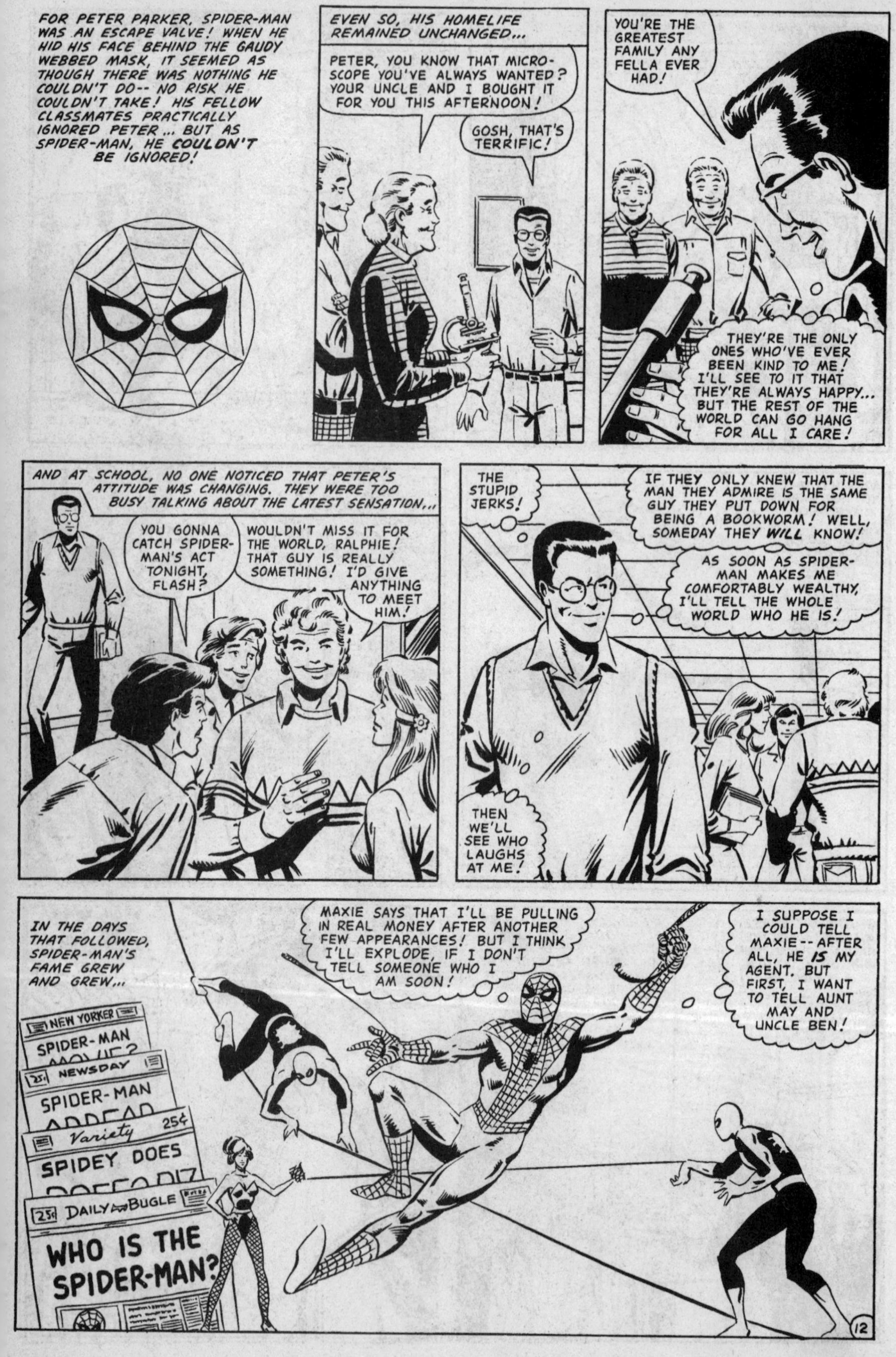
FOR PETER PARKER, SPIDER-MAN WAS AN ESCAPE VALVE! WHEN HE HID HIS FACE BEHIND THE GAUDY WEBBED MASK, IT SEEMED AS THOUGH THERE WAS NOTHING HE COULDN'T DO-- NO RISK HE COULDN'T TAKE! HIS FELLOW CLASSMATES PRACTICALLY IGNORED PETER ... BUT AS SPIDER-MAN, HE COULDN'T BE IGNORED!
EVEN SO, HIS HOMELIFE REMAINED UNCHANGED...
PETER, YOU KNOW THAT MICRO-SCOPE YOU'VE ALWAYS WANTED? YOUR UNCLE AND I BOUGHT IT FOR YOU THIS AFTERNOON!
GOSH, THAT'S TERRIFIC!
YOU'RE THE GREATEST FAMILY ANY FELLA EVER HAD!
THEY'RE THE ONLY ONES WHO'VE EVER BEEN KIND TO ME! I'LL SEE TO IT THAT THEY'RE ALWAYS HAPPY... BUT THE REST OF THE WORLD CAN GO HANG FOR ALL I CARE!
AND AT SCHOOL, NO ONE NOTICED THAT PETER'S ATTITUDE WAS CHANGING. THEY WERE TOO BUSY TALKING ABOUT THE LATEST SENSATION...
YOU GONNA CATCH SPIDER-MAN'S ACT TONIGHT, FLASH?
WOULDN'T MISS IT FOR THE WORLD, RALPHIE! THAT GUY IS REALLY SOMETHING! I'D GIVE ANYTHING TO MEET HIM!
THE STUPID JERKS!
IF THEY ONLY KNEW THAT THE MAN THEY ADMIRE IS THE SAME GUY THEY PUT DOWN FOR BEING A BOOKWORM! WELL, SOMEDAY THEY WILL KNOW!
AS SOON AS SPIDER-MAN MAKES ME COMFORTABLY WEALTHY, I'LL TELL THE WHOLE WORLD WHO HE IS!
THEN WE'LL SEE WHO LAUGHS AT ME!
IN THE DAYS THAT FOLLOWED, SPIDER-MAN'S FAME GREW AND GREW...
MAXIE SAYS THAT I'LL BE PULLING IN REAL MONEY AFTER ANOTHER FEW APPEARANCES! BUT I THINK I'LL EXPLODE, IF I DON'T TELL SOMEONE WHO I AM SOON!
I SUPPOSE I COULD TELL MAXIE-- AFTER ALL, HE IS MY AGENT. BUT FIRST, I WANT TO TELL AUNT MAY AND UNCLE BEN!
NEW YORKER
SPIDER-MAN
25¢ NEWSDAY
SPIDER-MAN
Variety 25¢
SPIDEY DOES
25¢ DAILY BUGLE
WHO IS THE SPIDER-MAN?

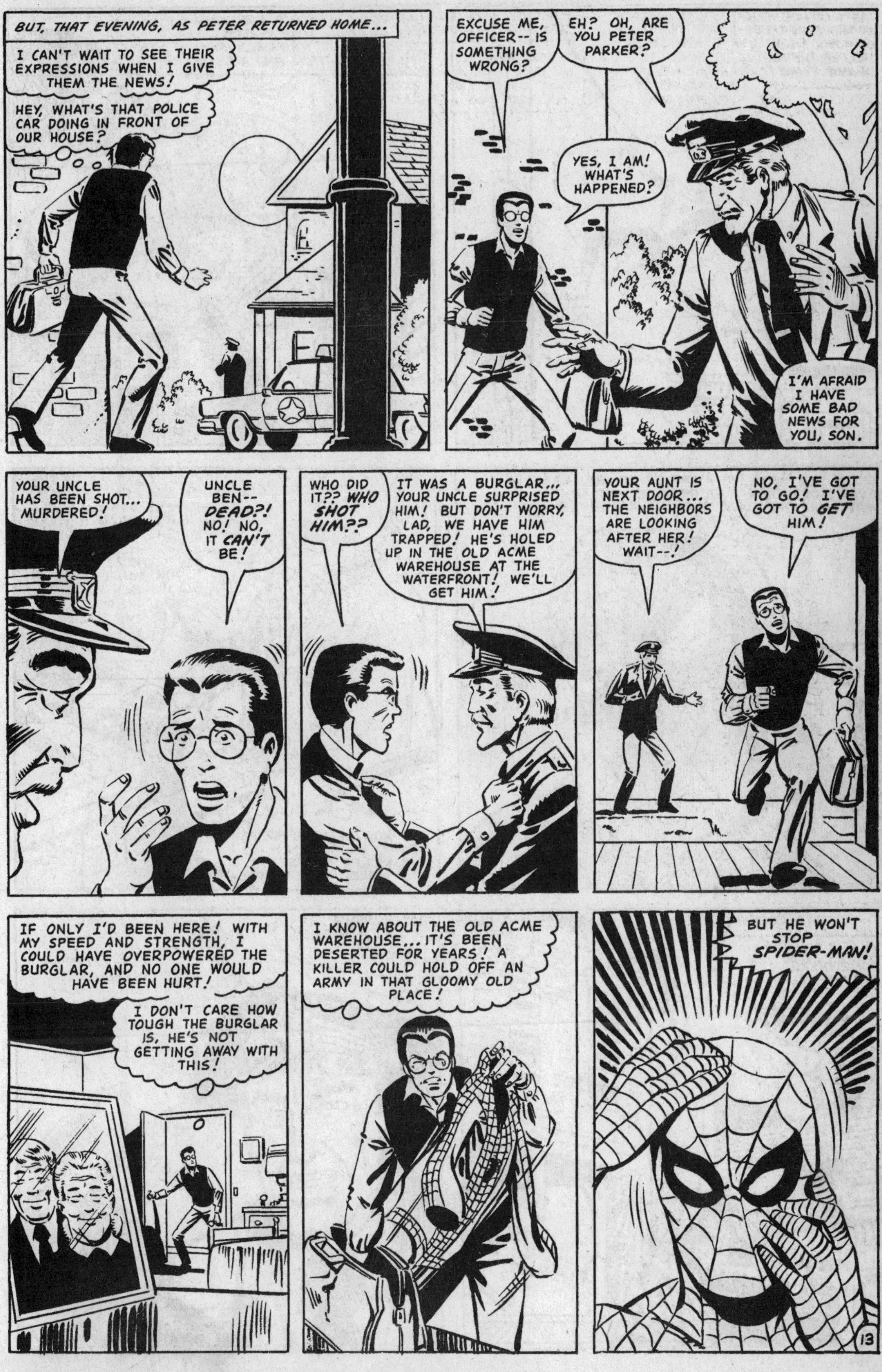
BUT, THAT EVENING, AS PETER RETURNED HOME...
I CAN'T WAIT TO SEE THEIR EXPRESSIONS WHEN I GIVE THEM THE NEWS!
HEY, WHAT'S THAT POLICE CAR DOING IN FRONT OF OUR HOUSE?
EXCUSE ME, OFFICER-- IS SOMETHING WRONG?
EH? OH, ARE YOU PETER PARKER?
YES, I AM! WHAT'S HAPPENED?
I'M AFRAID I HAVE SOME BAD NEWS FOR YOU, SON.
YOUR UNCLE HAS BEEN SHOT... MURDERED!
UNCLE BEN-- DEAD?! NO! NO, IT CAN'T BE!
WHO DID IT?? WHO SHOT HIM??
IT WAS A BURGLAR... YOUR UNCLE SURPRISED HIM! BUT DON'T WORRY, LAD, WE HAVE HIM TRAPPED! HE'S HOLED UP IN THE OLD ACME WAREHOUSE AT THE WATERFRONT! WE'LL GET HIM!
YOUR AUNT IS NEXT DOOR... THE NEIGHBORS ARE LOOKING AFTER HER! WAIT--!
NO, I'VE GOT TO GO! I'VE GOT TO GET HIM!
IF ONLY I'D BEEN HERE! WITH MY SPEED AND STRENGTH, I COULD HAVE OVERPOWERED THE BURGLAR, AND NO ONE WOULD HAVE BEEN HURT!
I DON'T CARE HOW TOUGH THE BURGLAR IS, HE'S NOT GETTING AWAY WITH THIS!
I KNOW ABOUT THE OLD ACME WAREHOUSE... IT'S BEEN DESERTED FOR YEARS! A KILLER COULD HOLD OFF AN ARMY IN THAT GLOOMY OLD PLACE!
BUT HE WON'T STOP SPIDER-MAN!

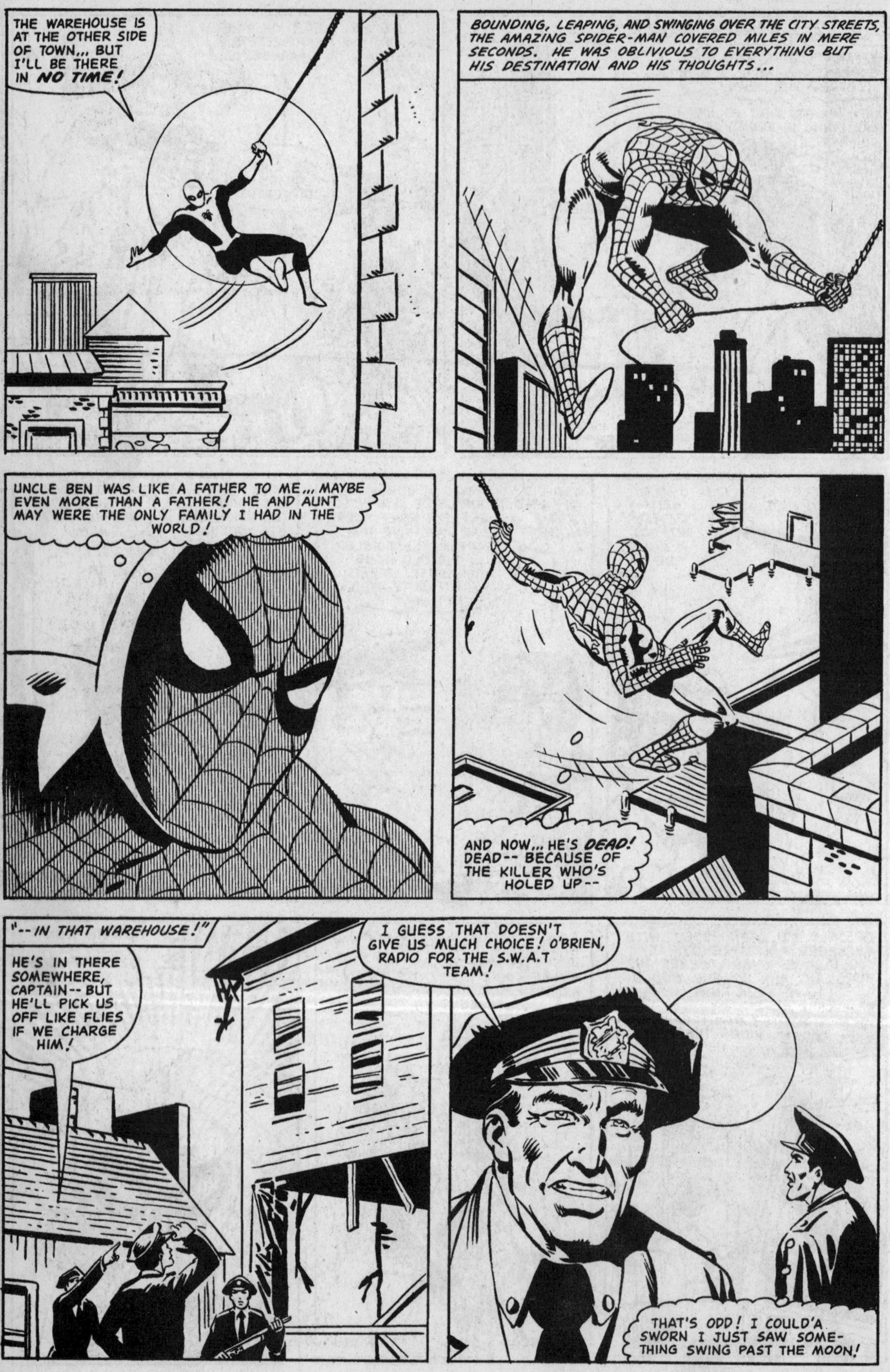
THE WAREHOUSE IS AT THE OTHER SIDE OF TOWN... BUT I'LL BE THERE IN NO TIME!
BOUNDING, LEAPING, AND SWINGING OVER THE CITY STREETS, THE AMAZING SPIDER-MAN COVERED MILES IN MERE SECONDS. HE WAS OBLIVIOUS TO EVERYTHING BUT HIS DESTINATION AND HIS THOUGHTS...
UNCLE BEN WAS LIKE A FATHER TO ME... MAYBE EVEN MORE THAN A FATHER! HE AND AUNT MAY WERE THE ONLY FAMILY I HAD IN THE WORLD!
AND NOW... HE'S DEAD! DEAD-- BECAUSE OF THE KILLER WHO'S HOLED UP--
"--IN THAT WAREHOUSE!"
HE'S IN THERE SOMEWHERE, CAPTAIN-- BUT HE'LL PICK US OFF LIKE FLIES IF WE CHARGE HIM!
I GUESS THAT DOESN'T GIVE US MUCH CHOICE! O'BRIEN, RADIO FOR THE S.W.A.T TEAM!
THAT'S ODD! I COULD'A SWORN I JUST SAW SOME-THING SWING PAST THE MOON!

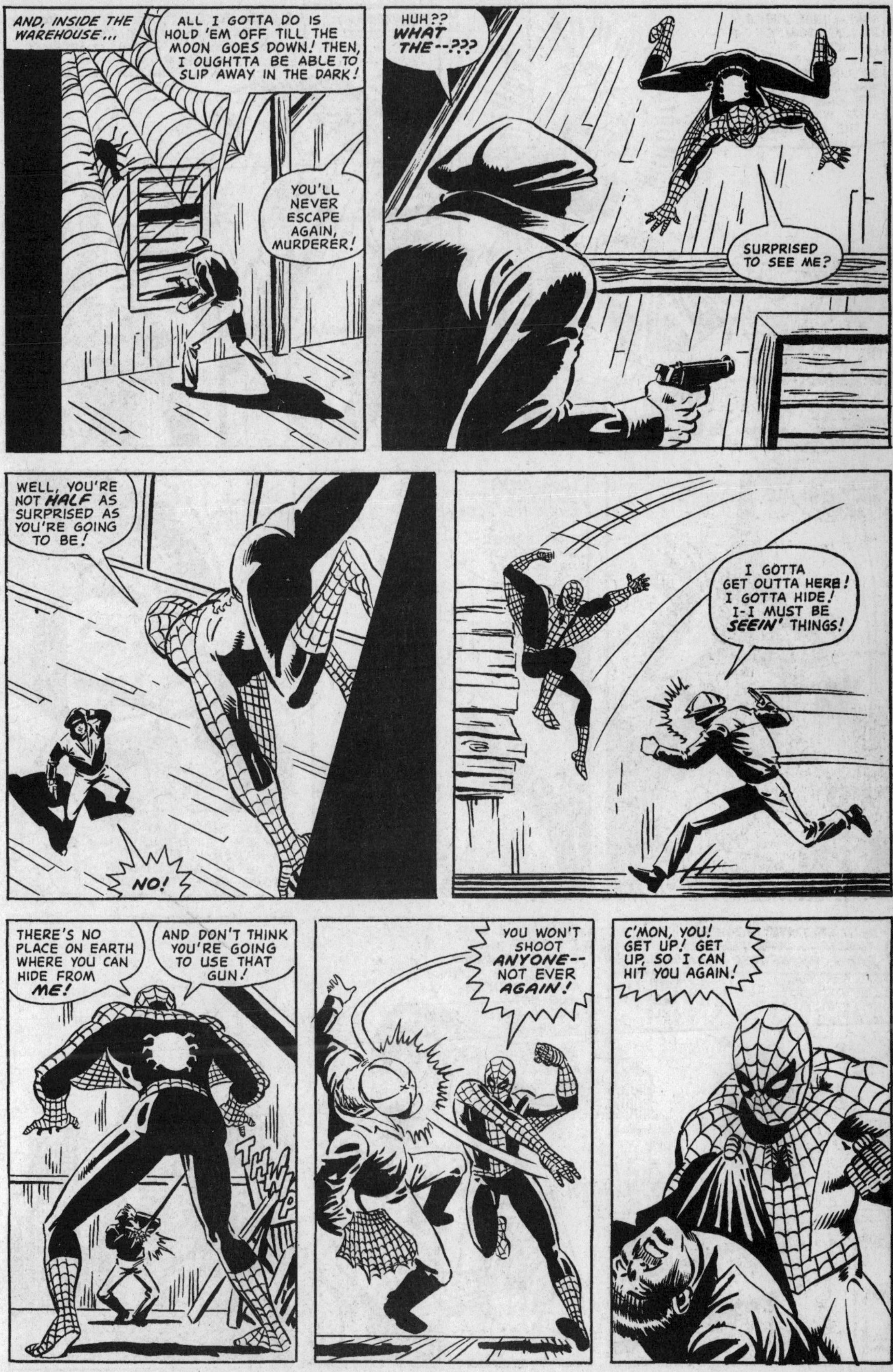
AND, INSIDE THE WAREHOUSE...
ALL I GOTTA DO IS HOLD 'EM OFF TILL THE MOON GOES DOWN! THEN, I OUGHTTA BE ABLE TO SLIP AWAY IN THE DARK!
YOU'LL NEVER ESCAPE AGAIN, MURDERER!
HUH?? WHAT THE--???
SURPRISED TO SEE ME?
WELL, YOU'RE NOT HALF AS SURPRISED AS YOU'RE GOING TO BE!
NO!
I GOTTA GET OUTTA HERE! I GOTTA HIDE! I-I MUST BE SEEIN' THINGS!
THERE'S NO PLACE ON EARTH WHERE YOU CAN HIDE FROM ME!
AND DON'T THINK YOU'RE GOING TO USE THAT GUN!
THWIP
YOU WON'T SHOOT ANYONE-- NOT EVER AGAIN!
C'MON, YOU! GET UP! GET UP, SO I CAN HIT YOU AGAIN!

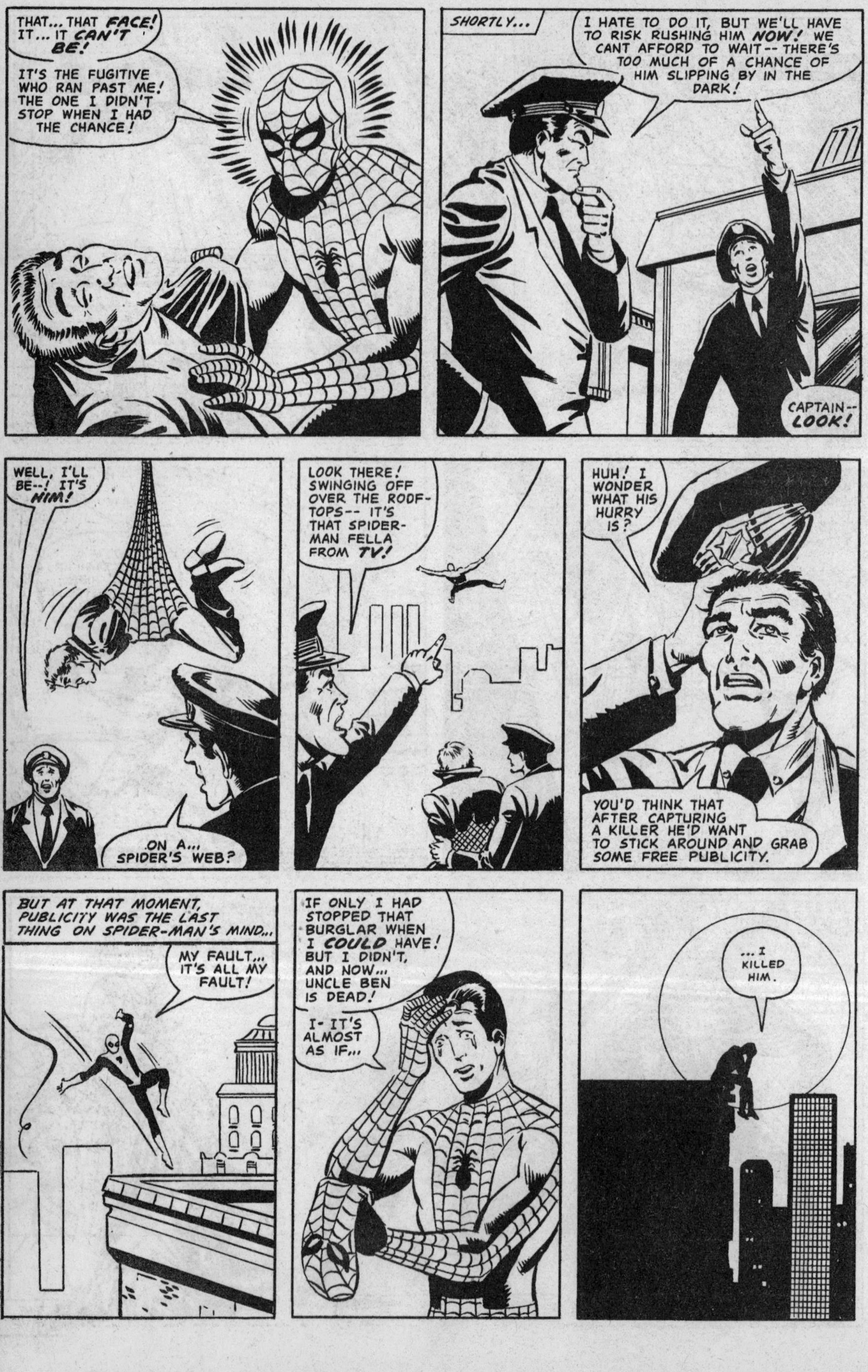
THAT... THAT FACE! IT... IT CAN'T BE!
IT'S THE FUGITIVE WHO RAN PAST ME! THE ONE I DIDN'T STOP WHEN I HAD THE CHANCE!
SHORTLY...
I HATE TO DO IT, BUT WE'LL HAVE TO RISK RUSHING HIM NOW! WE CANT AFFORD TO WAIT -- THERE'S TOO MUCH OF A CHANCE OF HIM SLIPPING BY IN THE DARK!
CAPTAIN -- LOOK!
WELL, I'LL BE--! IT'S HIM!
...ON A... SPIDER'S WEB?
LOOK THERE! SWINGING OFF OVER THE ROOF-TOPS-- IT'S THAT SPIDER-MAN FELLA FROM TV!
HUH! I WONDER WHAT HIS HURRY IS?
YOU'D THINK THAT AFTER CAPTURING A KILLER HE'D WANT TO STICK AROUND AND GRAB SOME FREE PUBLICITY.
BUT AT THAT MOMENT, PUBLICITY WAS THE LAST THING ON SPIDER-MAN'S MIND...
MY FAULT... IT'S ALL MY FAULT!
IF ONLY I HAD STOPPED THAT BURGLAR WHEN I COULD HAVE! BUT I DIDN'T, AND NOW... UNCLE BEN IS DEAD!
I- IT'S ALMOST AS IF...
...I KILLED HIM.

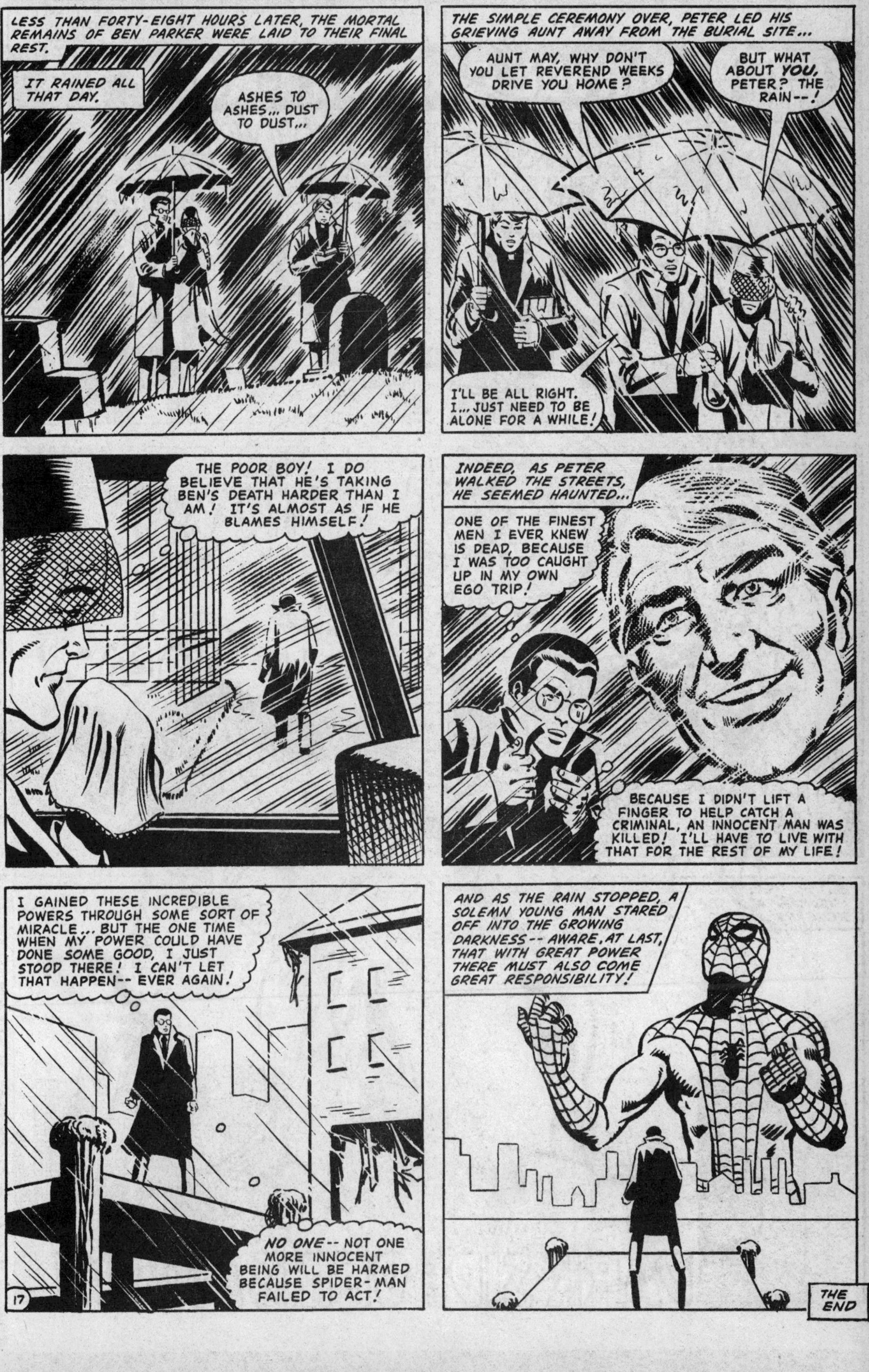
LESS THAN FORTY-EIGHT HOURS LATER, THE MORTAL REMAINS OF BEN PARKER WERE LAID TO THEIR FINAL REST.
IT RAINED ALL THAT DAY.
ASHES TO ASHES... DUST TO DUST...
THE SIMPLE CEREMONY OVER, PETER LED HIS GRIEVING AUNT AWAY FROM THE BURIAL SITE...
AUNT MAY, WHY DON'T YOU LET REVEREND WEEKS DRIVE YOU HOME?
BUT WHAT ABOUT YOU, PETER? THE RAIN--!
I'LL BE ALL RIGHT. I... JUST NEED TO BE ALONE FOR A WHILE!
THE POOR BOY! I DO BELIEVE THAT HE'S TAKING BEN'S DEATH HARDER THAN I AM! IT'S ALMOST AS IF HE BLAMES HIMSELF!
INDEED, AS PETER WALKED THE STREETS, HE SEEMED HAUNTED...
ONE OF THE FINEST MEN I EVER KNEW IS DEAD, BECAUSE I WAS TOO CAUGHT UP IN MY OWN EGO TRIP!
BECAUSE I DIDN'T LIFT A FINGER TO HELP CATCH A CRIMINAL, AN INNOCENT MAN WAS KILLED! I'LL HAVE TO LIVE WITH THAT FOR THE REST OF MY LIFE!
I GAINED THESE INCREDIBLE POWERS THROUGH SOME SORT OF MIRACLE... BUT THE ONE TIME WHEN MY POWER COULD HAVE DONE SOME GOOD, I JUST STOOD THERE! I CAN'T LET THAT HAPPEN-- EVER AGAIN!
NO ONE -- NOT ONE MORE INNOCENT BEING WILL BE HARMED BECAUSE SPIDER-MAN FAILED TO ACT!
17
AND AS THE RAIN STOPPED, A SOLEMN YOUNG MAN STARED OFF INTO THE GROWING DARKNESS -- AWARE, AT LAST, THAT WITH GREAT POWER THERE MUST ALSO COME GREAT RESPONSIBILITY!
THE END

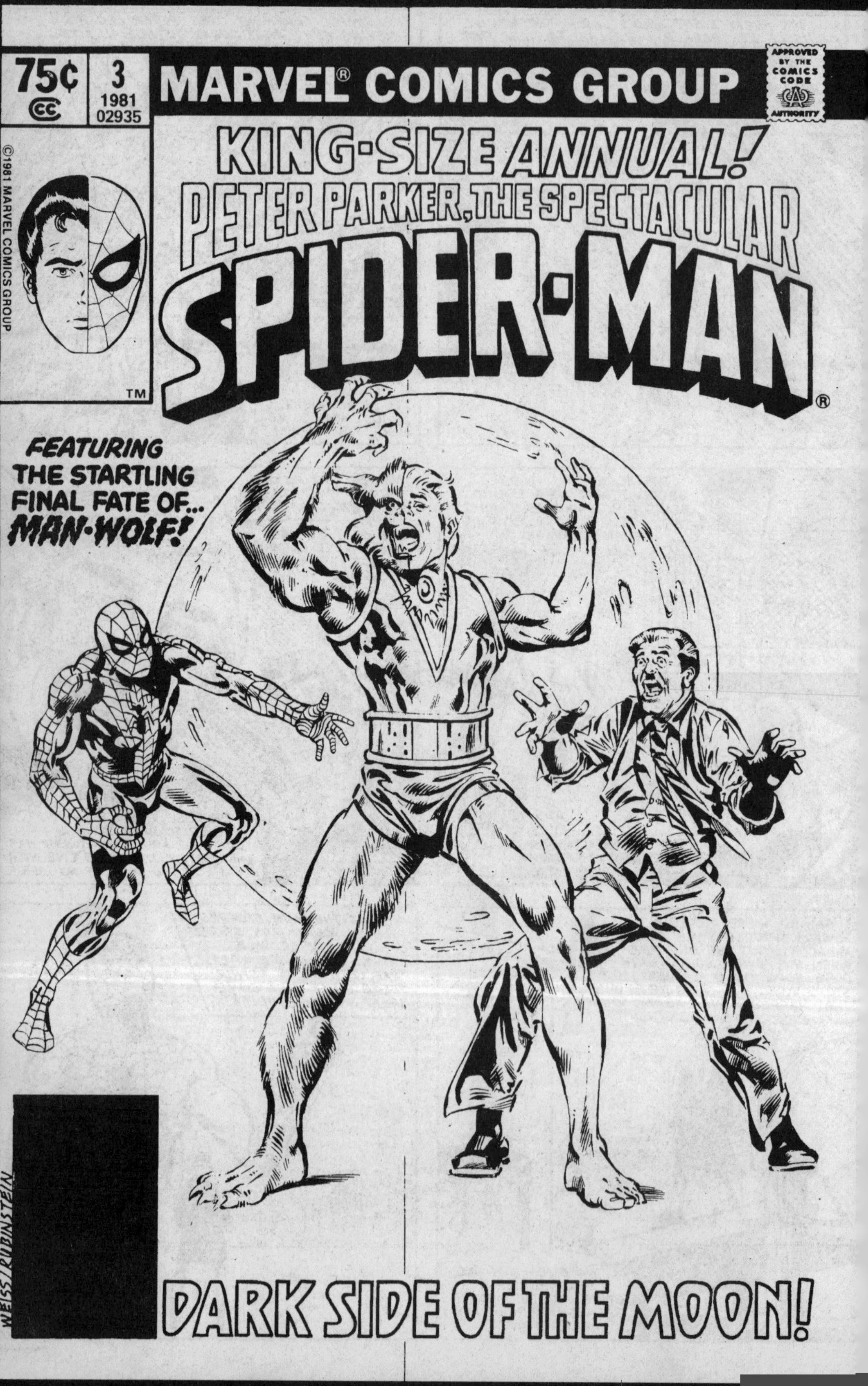

75¢
3
1981
02935
MARVEL® COMICS GROUP
APPROVED BY THE COMICS CODE AUTHORITY
©1981 MARVEL COMICS GROUP
KING-SIZE ANNUAL!
PETER PARKER, THE SPECTACULAR
SPIDER-MAN®
FEATURING THE STARTLING FINAL FATE OF... MAN-WOLF!
WEISS/RUBINSTEIN
DARK SIDE OF THE MOON!

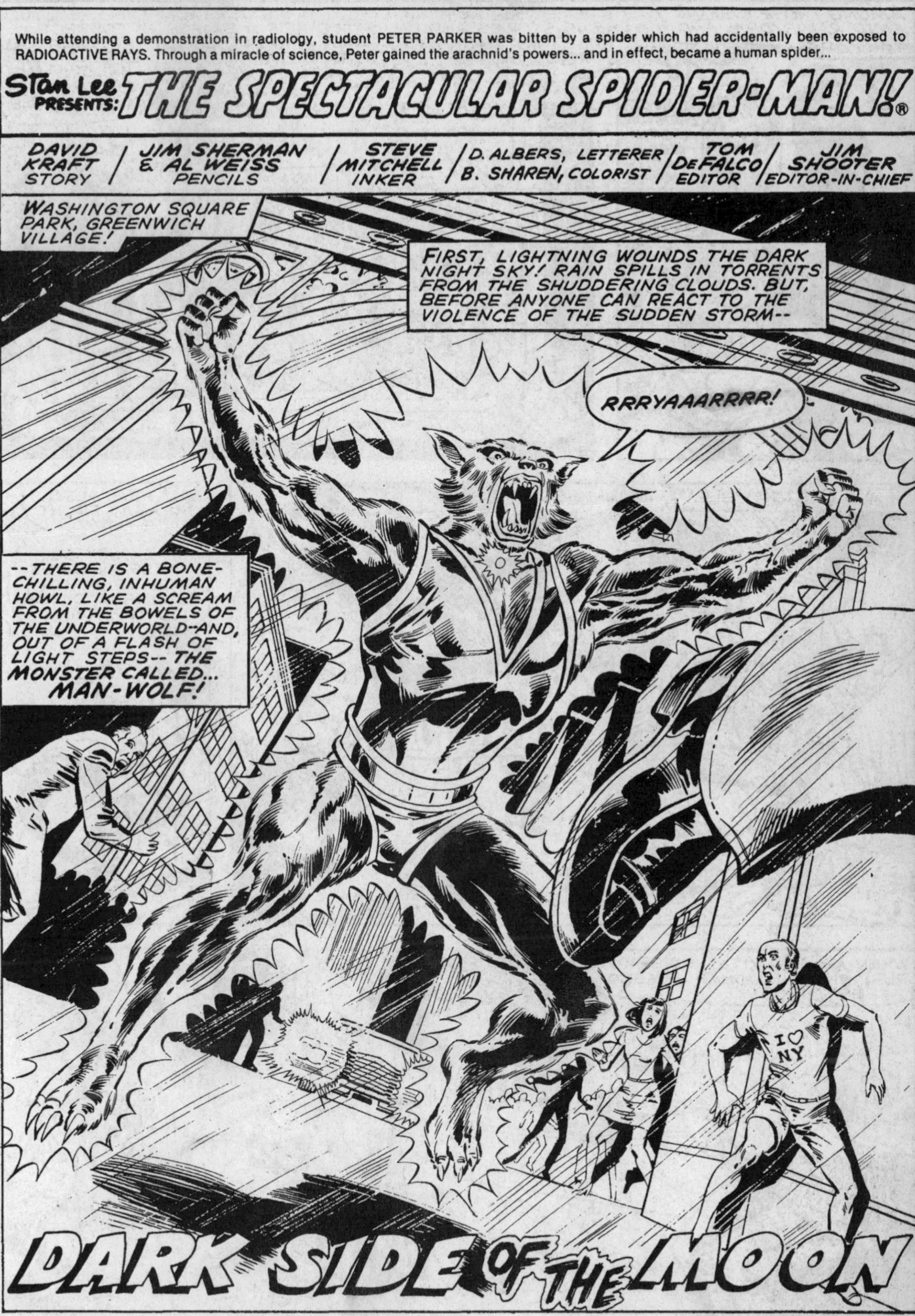

While attending a demonstration in radiology, student PETER PARKER was bitten by a spider which had accidentally been exposed to RADIOACTIVE RAYS. Through a miracle of science, Peter gained the arachnid's powers... and in effect, became a human spider...
Stan Lee PRESENTS: THE SPECTACULAR SPIDER-MAN!®
DAVID KRAFT STORY
JIM SHERMAN & AL WEISS PENCILS
STEVE MITCHELL INKER
D. ALBERS, LETTERER
B. SHAREN, COLORIST
TOM DeFALCO EDITOR
JIM SHOOTER EDITOR-IN-CHIEF
WASHINGTON SQUARE PARK, GREENWICH VILLAGE!
FIRST, LIGHTNING WOUNDS THE DARK NIGHT SKY! RAIN SPILLS IN TORRENTS FROM THE SHUDDERING CLOUDS. BUT, BEFORE ANYONE CAN REACT TO THE VIOLENCE OF THE SUDDEN STORM--
RRRYAAARRRR!
--THERE IS A BONE-CHILLING, INHUMAN HOWL, LIKE A SCREAM FROM THE BOWELS OF THE UNDERWORLD--AND, OUT OF A FLASH OF LIGHT STEPS-- THE MONSTER CALLED... MAN-WOLF!
I ♥ NY
DARK SIDE OF THE MOON

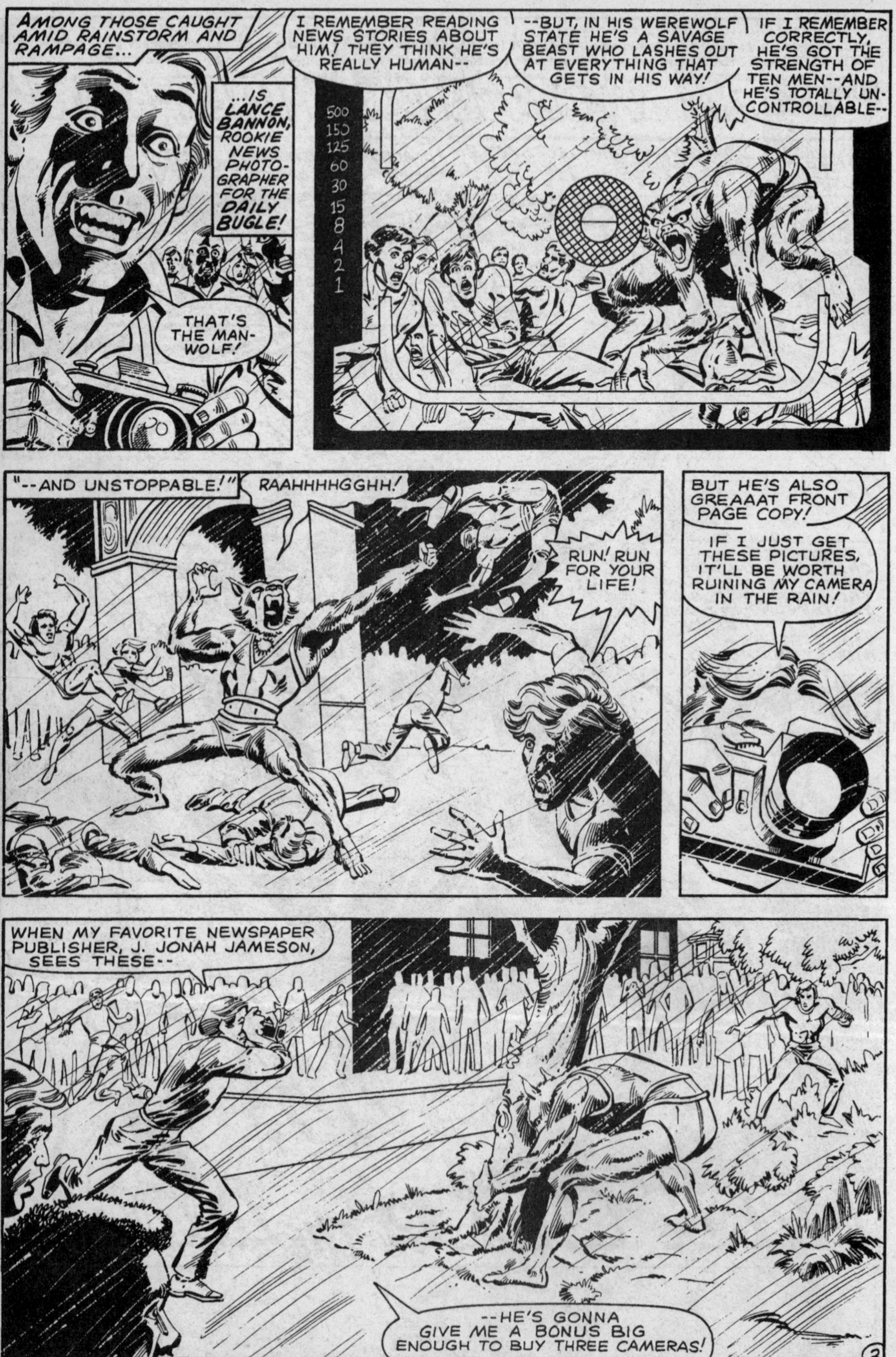
AMONG THOSE CAUGHT AMID RAINSTORM AND RAMPAGE...
...IS LANCE BANNON, ROOKIE NEWS PHOTOGRAPHER FOR THE DAILY BUGLE!
THAT'S THE MAN-WOLF!
I REMEMBER READING NEWS STORIES ABOUT HIM! THEY THINK HE'S REALLY HUMAN--
--BUT, IN HIS WEREWOLF STATE HE'S A SAVAGE BEAST WHO LASHES OUT AT EVERYTHING THAT GETS IN HIS WAY!
IF I REMEMBER CORRECTLY, HE'S GOT THE STRENGTH OF TEN MEN--AND HE'S TOTALLY UNCONTROLLABLE--
500
150
125
60
30
15
8
4
2
1
"--AND UNSTOPPABLE!"
RAAHHHHGGHH!
RUN! RUN FOR YOUR LIFE!
BUT HE'S ALSO GREAAAT FRONT PAGE COPY!
IF I JUST GET THESE PICTURES, IT'LL BE WORTH RUINING MY CAMERA IN THE RAIN!
WHEN MY FAVORITE NEWSPAPER PUBLISHER, J. JONAH JAMESON, SEES THESE--
--HE'S GONNA GIVE ME A BONUS BIG ENOUGH TO BUY THREE CAMERAS!

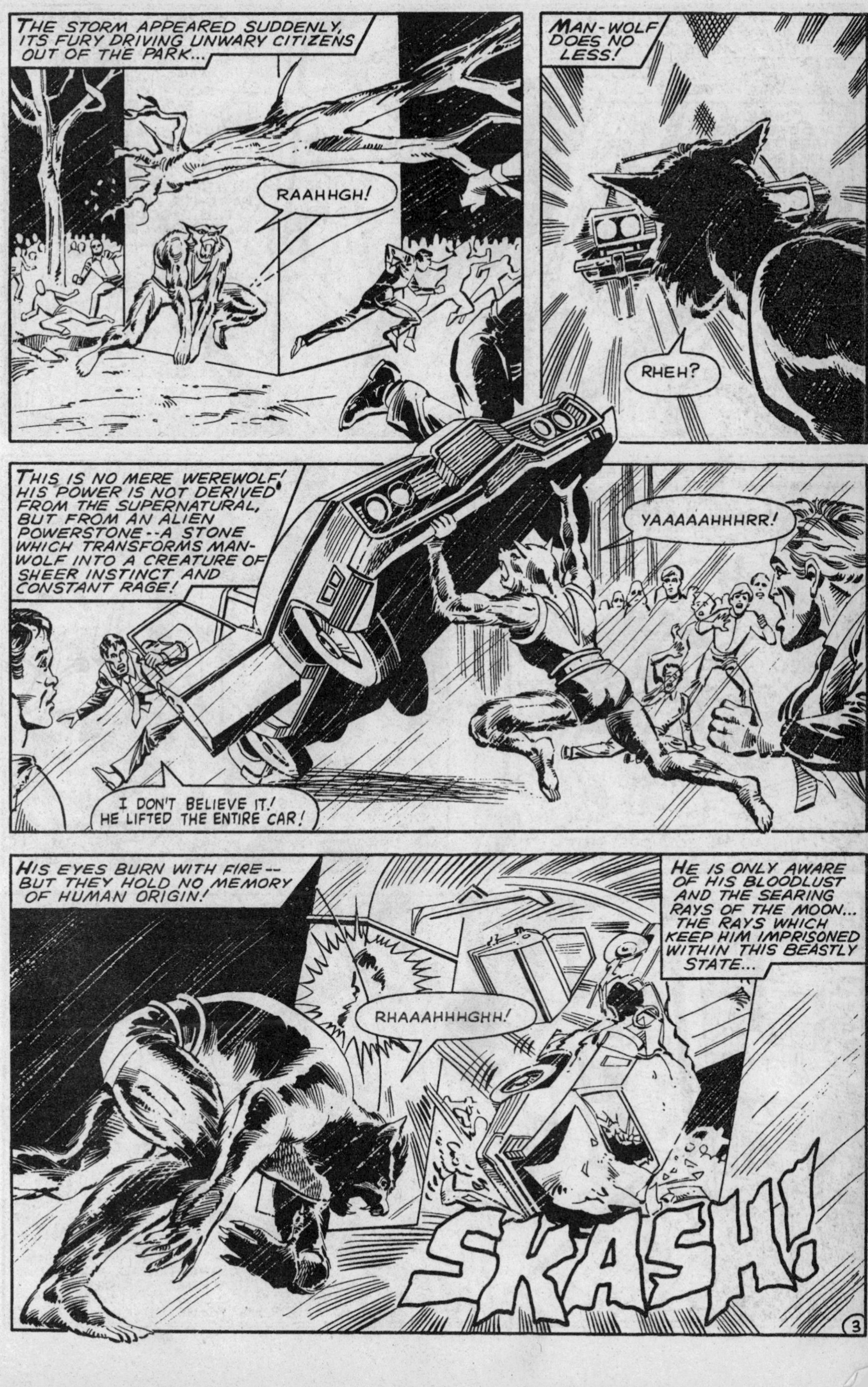
THE STORM APPEARED SUDDENLY, ITS FURY DRIVING UNWARY CITIZENS OUT OF THE PARK...
RAAHHGH!
MAN-WOLF DOES NO LESS!
RHEH?
THIS IS NO MERE WEREWOLF! HIS POWER IS NOT DERIVED FROM THE SUPERNATURAL, BUT FROM AN ALIEN POWERSTONE--A STONE WHICH TRANSFORMS MAN-WOLF INTO A CREATURE OF SHEER INSTINCT AND CONSTANT RAGE!
YAAAAAHHHRR!
I DON'T BELIEVE IT! HE LIFTED THE ENTIRE CAR!
HIS EYES BURN WITH FIRE--BUT THEY HOLD NO MEMORY OF HUMAN ORIGIN!
HE IS ONLY AWARE OF HIS BLOODLUST AND THE SEARING RAYS OF THE MOON... THE RAYS WHICH KEEP HIM IMPRISONED WITHIN THIS BEASTLY STATE...
RHAAAHHHGHH!
SKASH!

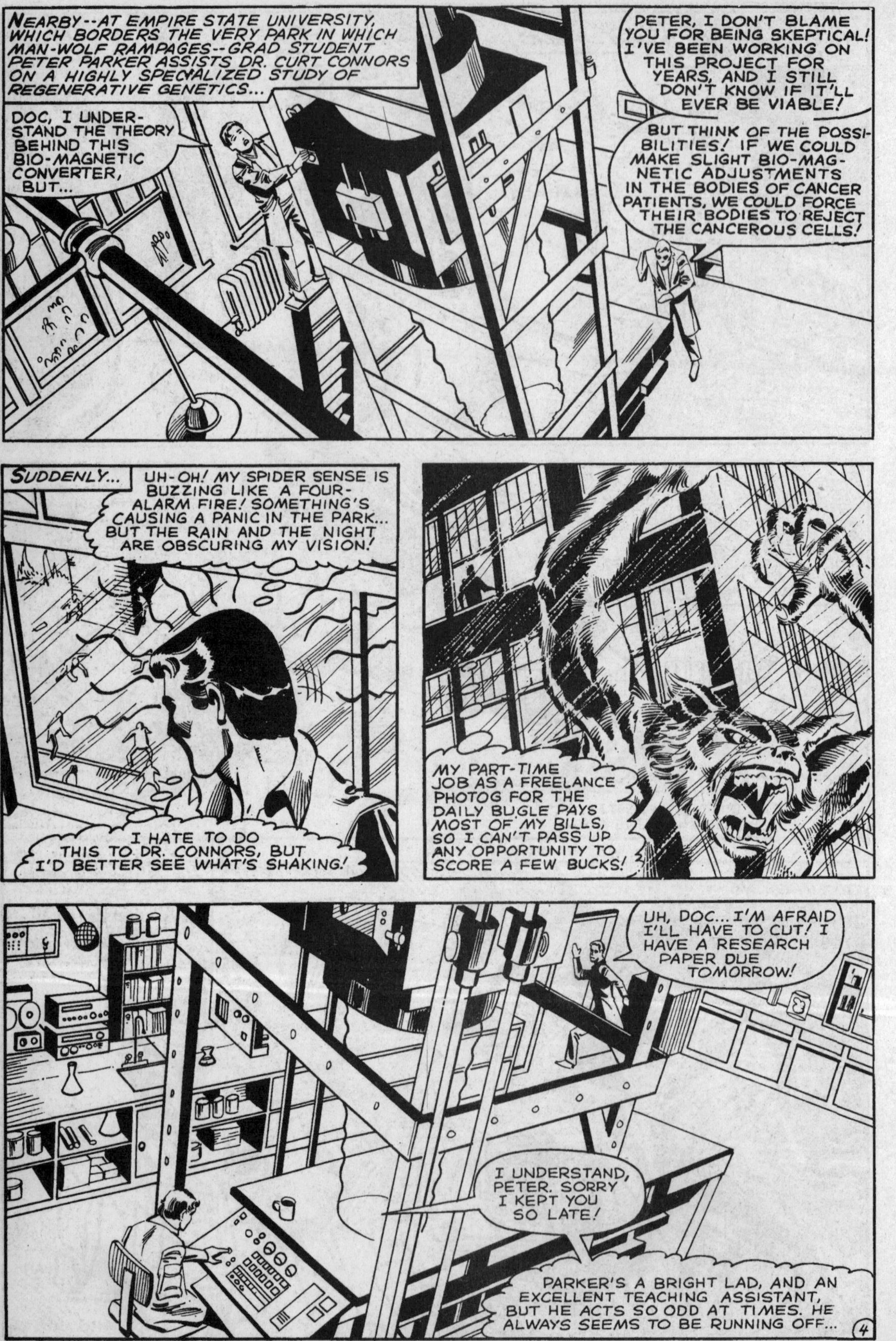
NEARBY--AT EMPIRE STATE UNIVERSITY, WHICH BORDERS THE VERY PARK IN WHICH MAN-WOLF RAMPAGES--GRAD STUDENT PETER PARKER ASSISTS DR. CURT CONNORS ON A HIGHLY SPECIALIZED STUDY OF REGENERATIVE GENETICS...
DOC, I UNDERSTAND THE THEORY BEHIND THIS BIO-MAGNETIC CONVERTER, BUT...
PETER, I DON'T BLAME YOU FOR BEING SKEPTICAL! I'VE BEEN WORKING ON THIS PROJECT FOR YEARS, AND I STILL DON'T KNOW IF IT'LL EVER BE VIABLE!
BUT THINK OF THE POSSIBILITIES! IF WE COULD MAKE SLIGHT BIO-MAGNETIC ADJUSTMENTS IN THE BODIES OF CANCER PATIENTS, WE COULD FORCE THEIR BODIES TO REJECT THE CANCEROUS CELLS!
SUDDENLY...
UH-OH! MY SPIDER SENSE IS BUZZING LIKE A FOUR-ALARM FIRE! SOMETHING'S CAUSING A PANIC IN THE PARK... BUT THE RAIN AND THE NIGHT ARE OBSCURING MY VISION!
I HATE TO DO THIS TO DR. CONNORS, BUT I'D BETTER SEE WHAT'S SHAKING!
MY PART-TIME JOB AS A FREELANCE PHOTOG FOR THE DAILY BUGLE PAYS MOST OF MY BILLS, SO I CAN'T PASS UP ANY OPPORTUNITY TO SCORE A FEW BUCKS!
UH, DOC... I'M AFRAID I'LL HAVE TO CUT! I HAVE A RESEARCH PAPER DUE TOMORROW!
I UNDERSTAND, PETER. SORRY I KEPT YOU SO LATE!
PARKER'S A BRIGHT LAD, AND AN EXCELLENT TEACHING ASSISTANT, BUT HE ACTS SO ODD AT TIMES. HE ALWAYS SEEMS TO BE RUNNING OFF...

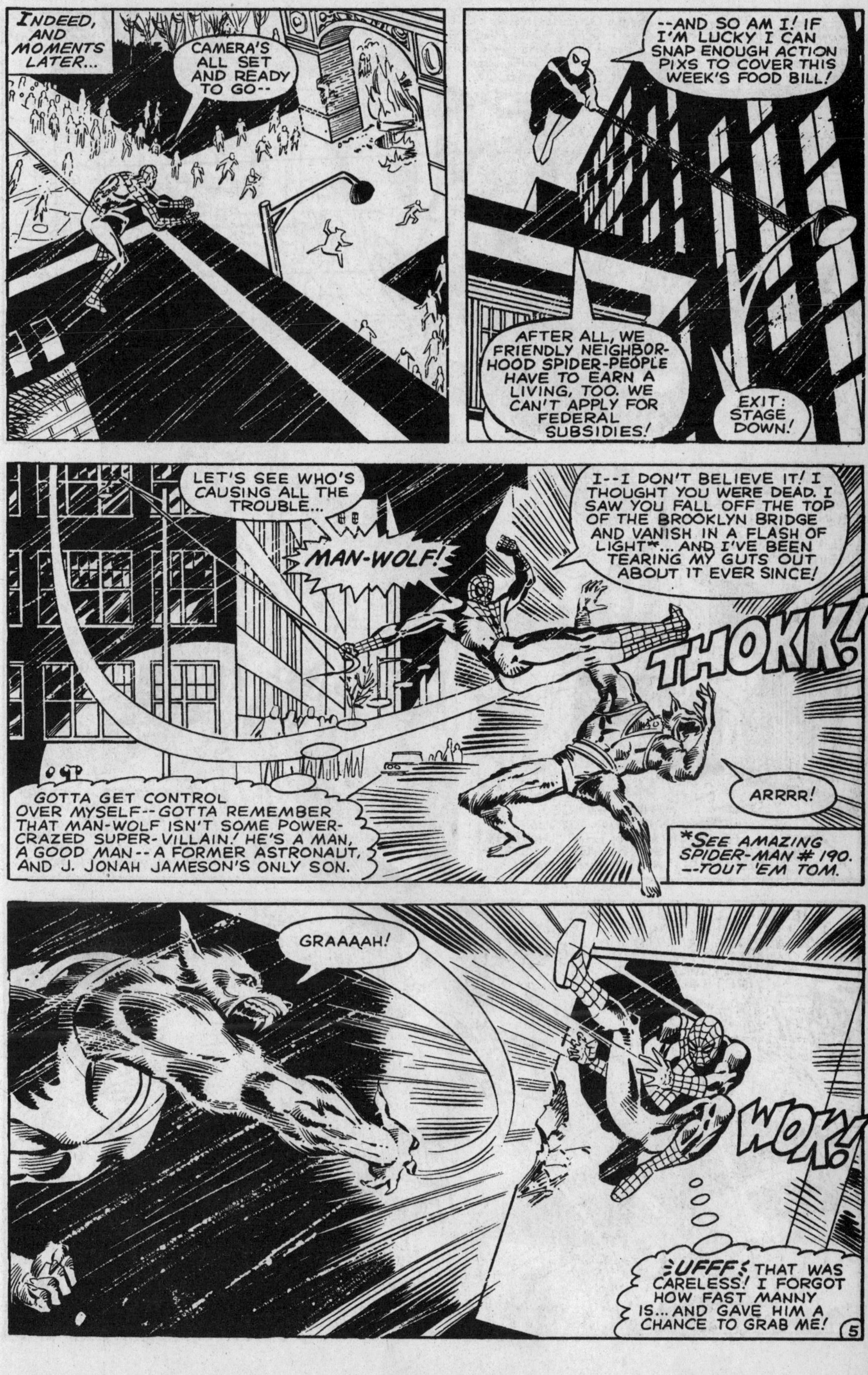

INDEED, AND MOMENTS LATER...
CAMERA'S ALL SET AND READY TO GO--
--AND SO AM I! IF I'M LUCKY I CAN SNAP ENOUGH ACTION PIXS TO COVER THIS WEEK'S FOOD BILL!
AFTER ALL, WE FRIENDLY NEIGHBOR-HOOD SPIDER-PEOPLE HAVE TO EARN A LIVING, TOO. WE CAN'T APPLY FOR FEDERAL SUBSIDIES!
EXIT: STAGE DOWN!
LET'S SEE WHO'S CAUSING ALL THE TROUBLE...
MAN-WOLF!
I--I DON'T BELIEVE IT! I THOUGHT YOU WERE DEAD. I SAW YOU FALL OFF THE TOP OF THE BROOKLYN BRIDGE AND VANISH IN A FLASH OF LIGHT*... AND I'VE BEEN TEARING MY GUTS OUT ABOUT IT EVER SINCE!
THOKK!
GOTTA GET CONTROL OVER MYSELF--GOTTA REMEMBER THAT MAN-WOLF ISN'T SOME POWER-CRAZED SUPER-VILLAIN! HE'S A MAN, A GOOD MAN--A FORMER ASTRONAUT, AND J. JONAH JAMESON'S ONLY SON.
ARRRR!
*SEE AMAZING SPIDER-MAN # 190. --TOUT 'EM TOM.
GRAAAAH!
WOK!
UFFF! THAT WAS CARELESS! I FORGOT HOW FAST MANNY IS... AND GAVE HIM A CHANCE TO GRAB ME!

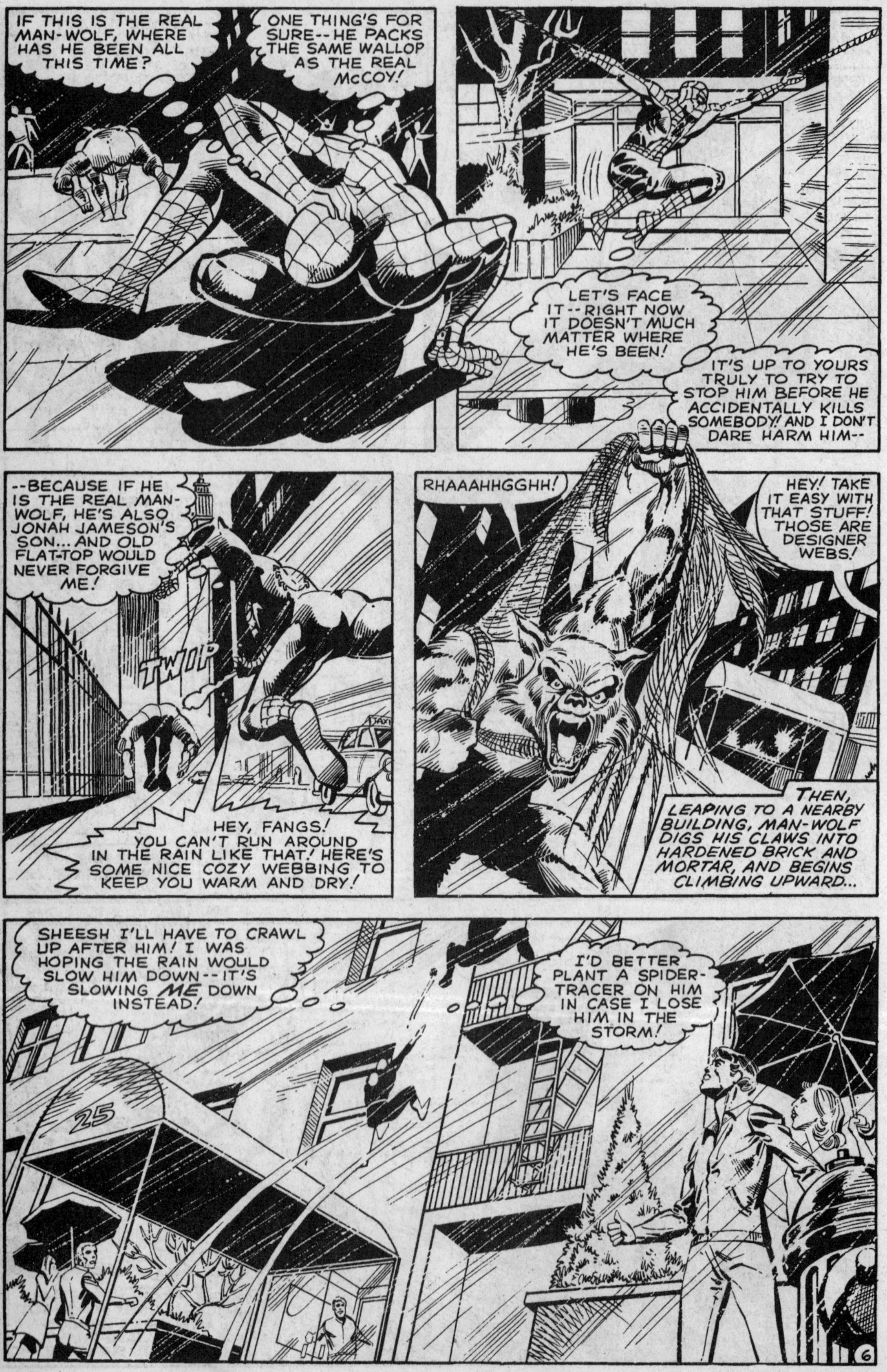
IF THIS IS THE REAL MAN-WOLF, WHERE HAS HE BEEN ALL THIS TIME?
ONE THING'S FOR SURE--HE PACKS THE SAME WALLOP AS THE REAL McCOY!
LET'S FACE IT--RIGHT NOW IT DOESN'T MUCH MATTER WHERE HE'S BEEN!
IT'S UP TO YOURS TRULY TO TRY TO STOP HIM BEFORE HE ACCIDENTALLY KILLS SOMEBODY! AND I DON'T DARE HARM HIM--
--BECAUSE IF HE IS THE REAL MAN-WOLF, HE'S ALSO JONAH JAMESON'S SON... AND OLD FLAT-TOP WOULD NEVER FORGIVE ME!
TWIP
TAXI
HEY, FANGS! YOU CAN'T RUN AROUND IN THE RAIN LIKE THAT! HERE'S SOME NICE COZY WEBBING TO KEEP YOU WARM AND DRY!
RHAAAHHGGHH!
HEY! TAKE IT EASY WITH THAT STUFF! THOSE ARE DESIGNER WEBS!
THEN, LEAPING TO A NEARBY BUILDING, MAN-WOLF DIGS HIS CLAWS INTO HARDENED BRICK AND MORTAR, AND BEGINS CLIMBING UPWARD...
SHEESH I'LL HAVE TO CRAWL UP AFTER HIM! I WAS HOPING THE RAIN WOULD SLOW HIM DOWN--IT'S SLOWING ME DOWN INSTEAD!
I'D BETTER PLANT A SPIDER-TRACER ON HIM IN CASE I LOSE HIM IN THE STORM!
25
6

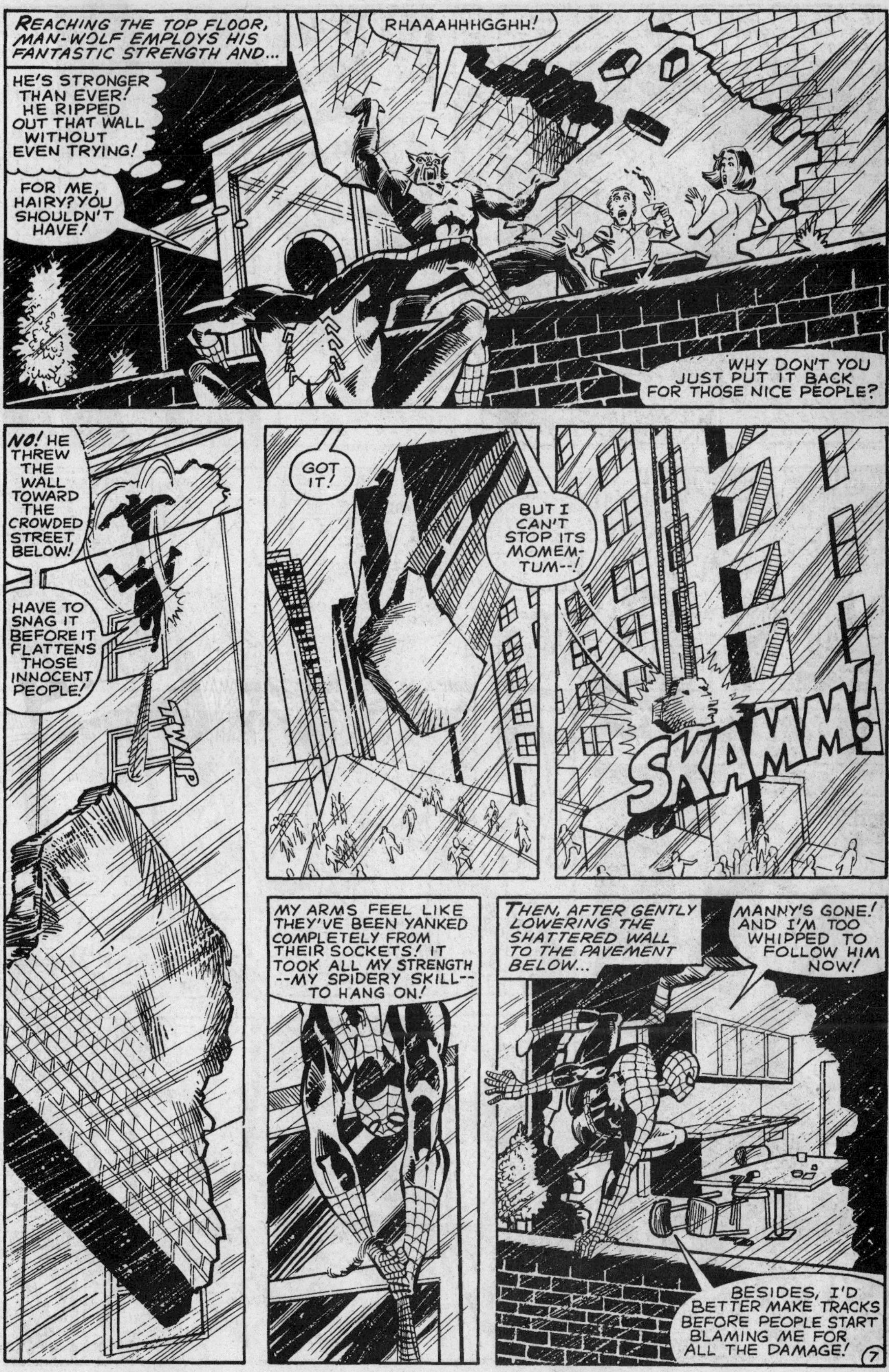

REACHING THE TOP FLOOR, MAN-WOLF EMPLOYS HIS FANTASTIC STRENGTH AND...
RHAAAHHHGGHH!
HE'S STRONGER THAN EVER! HE RIPPED OUT THAT WALL WITHOUT EVEN TRYING!
FOR ME, HAIRY? YOU SHOULDN'T HAVE!
WHY DON'T YOU JUST PUT IT BACK FOR THOSE NICE PEOPLE?
NO! HE THREW THE WALL TOWARD THE CROWDED STREET BELOW!
HAVE TO SNAG IT BEFORE IT FLATTENS THOSE INNOCENT PEOPLE!
TWIP
GOT IT!
BUT I CAN'T STOP ITS MOMEMTUM--!
SKAMM!
MY ARMS FEEL LIKE THEY'VE BEEN YANKED COMPLETELY FROM THEIR SOCKETS! IT TOOK ALL MY STRENGTH --MY SPIDERY SKILL-- TO HANG ON!
THEN, AFTER GENTLY LOWERING THE SHATTERED WALL TO THE PAVEMENT BELOW...
MANNY'S GONE! AND I'M TOO WHIPPED TO FOLLOW HIM NOW!
BESIDES, I'D BETTER MAKE TRACKS BEFORE PEOPLE START BLAMING ME FOR ALL THE DAMAGE!

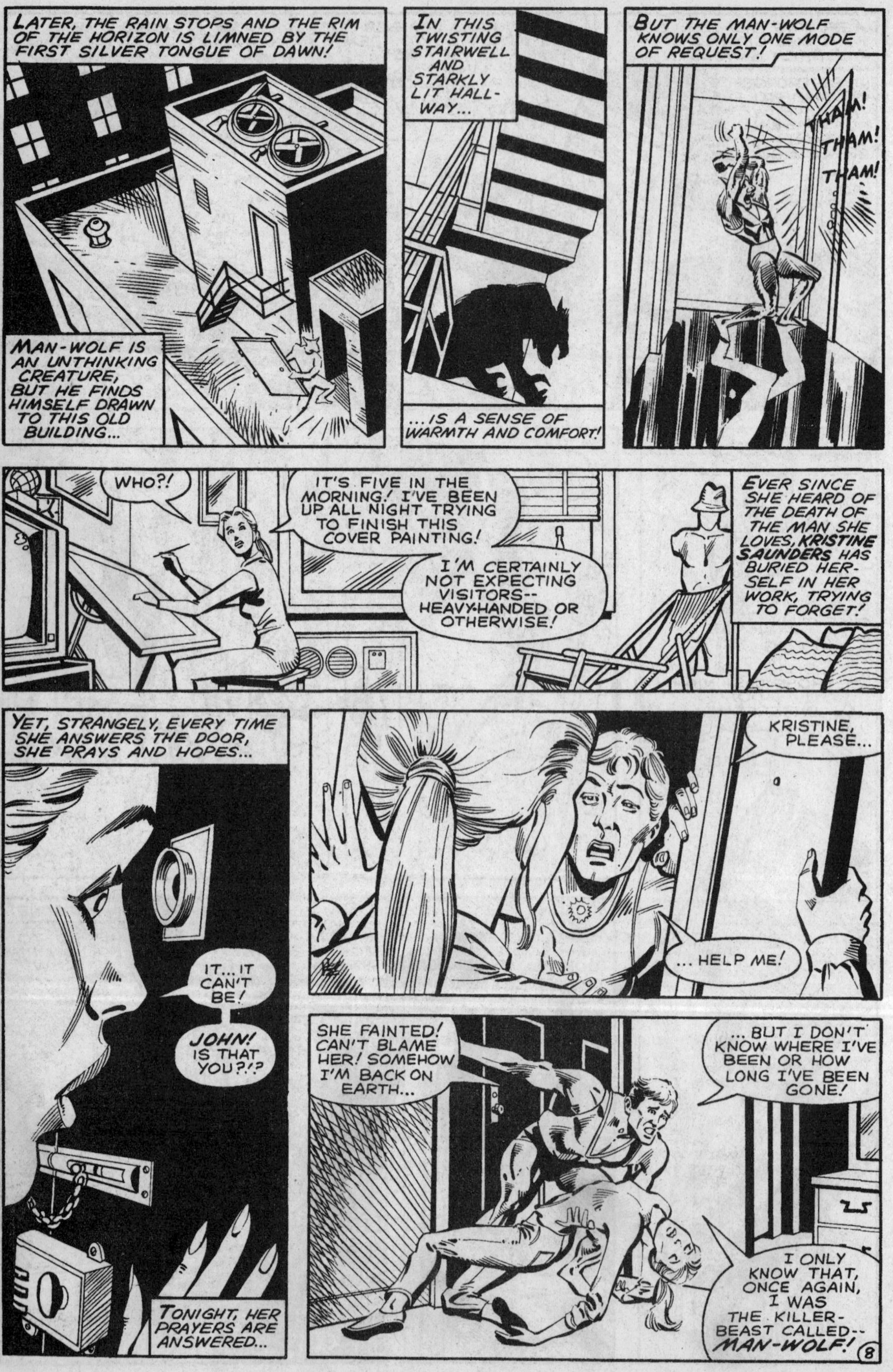

LATER, THE RAIN STOPS AND THE RIM OF THE HORIZON IS LIMNED BY THE FIRST SILVER TONGUE OF DAWN!
MAN-WOLF IS AN UNTHINKING CREATURE, BUT HE FINDS HIMSELF DRAWN TO THIS OLD BUILDING...
IN THIS TWISTING STAIRWELL AND STARKLY LIT HALL-WAY...
...IS A SENSE OF WARMTH AND COMFORT!
BUT THE MAN-WOLF KNOWS ONLY ONE MODE OF REQUEST!
THAM! THAM! THAM!
WHO?!
IT'S FIVE IN THE MORNING! I'VE BEEN UP ALL NIGHT TRYING TO FINISH THIS COVER PAINTING!
I'M CERTAINLY NOT EXPECTING VISITORS-- HEAVY-HANDED OR OTHERWISE!
EVER SINCE SHE HEARD OF THE DEATH OF THE MAN SHE LOVES, KRISTINE SAUNDERS HAS BURIED HER-SELF IN HER WORK, TRYING TO FORGET!
YET, STRANGELY, EVERY TIME SHE ANSWERS THE DOOR, SHE PRAYS AND HOPES...
IT... IT CAN'T BE!
JOHN! IS THAT YOU?!?
TONIGHT, HER PRAYERS ARE ANSWERED...
KRISTINE, PLEASE...
... HELP ME!
SHE FAINTED! CAN'T BLAME HER! SOMEHOW I'M BACK ON EARTH...
... BUT I DON'T KNOW WHERE I'VE BEEN OR HOW LONG I'VE BEEN GONE!
I ONLY KNOW THAT, ONCE AGAIN, I WAS THE KILLER-BEAST CALLED-- MAN-WOLF!
8

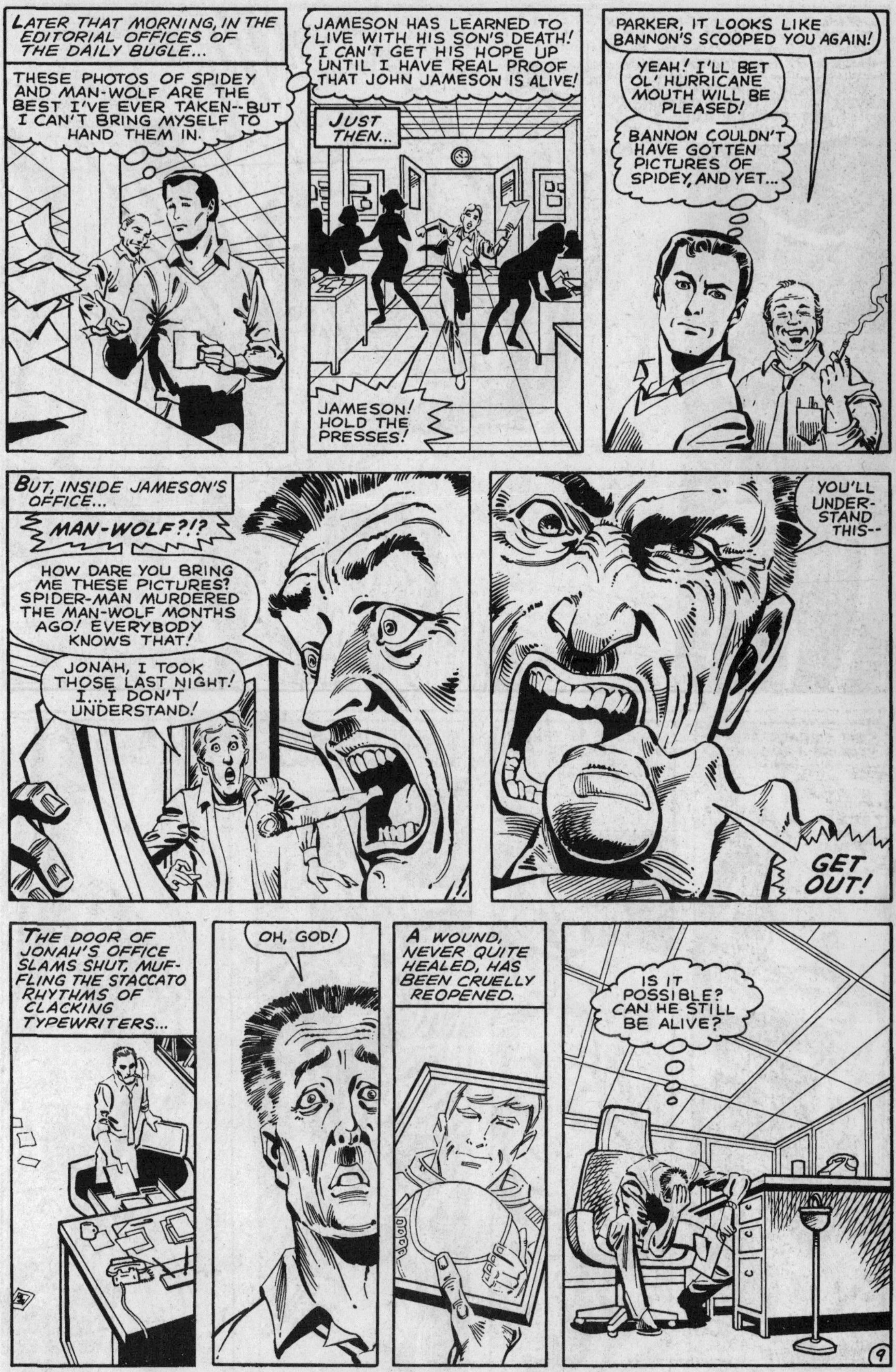
LATER THAT MORNING, IN THE EDITORIAL OFFICES OF THE DAILY BUGLE...
THESE PHOTOS OF SPIDEY AND MAN-WOLF ARE THE BEST I'VE EVER TAKEN--BUT I CAN'T BRING MYSELF TO HAND THEM IN.
JAMESON HAS LEARNED TO LIVE WITH HIS SON'S DEATH! I CAN'T GET HIS HOPE UP UNTIL I HAVE REAL PROOF THAT JOHN JAMESON IS ALIVE!
JUST THEN...
JAMESON! HOLD THE PRESSES!
PARKER, IT LOOKS LIKE BANNON'S SCOOPED YOU AGAIN!
YEAH! I'LL BET OL' HURRICANE MOUTH WILL BE PLEASED!
BANNON COULDN'T HAVE GOTTEN PICTURES OF SPIDEY, AND YET...
BUT, INSIDE JAMESON'S OFFICE...
MAN-WOLF?!?
HOW DARE YOU BRING ME THESE PICTURES? SPIDER-MAN MURDERED THE MAN-WOLF MONTHS AGO! EVERYBODY KNOWS THAT!
JONAH, I TOOK THOSE LAST NIGHT! I... I DON'T UNDERSTAND!
YOU'LL UNDERSTAND THIS--
GET OUT!
THE DOOR OF JONAH'S OFFICE SLAMS SHUT, MUFFLING THE STACCATO RHYTHMS OF CLACKING TYPEWRITERS...
OH, GOD!
A WOUND, NEVER QUITE HEALED, HAS BEEN CRUELLY REOPENED.
IS IT POSSIBLE? CAN HE STILL BE ALIVE?
9

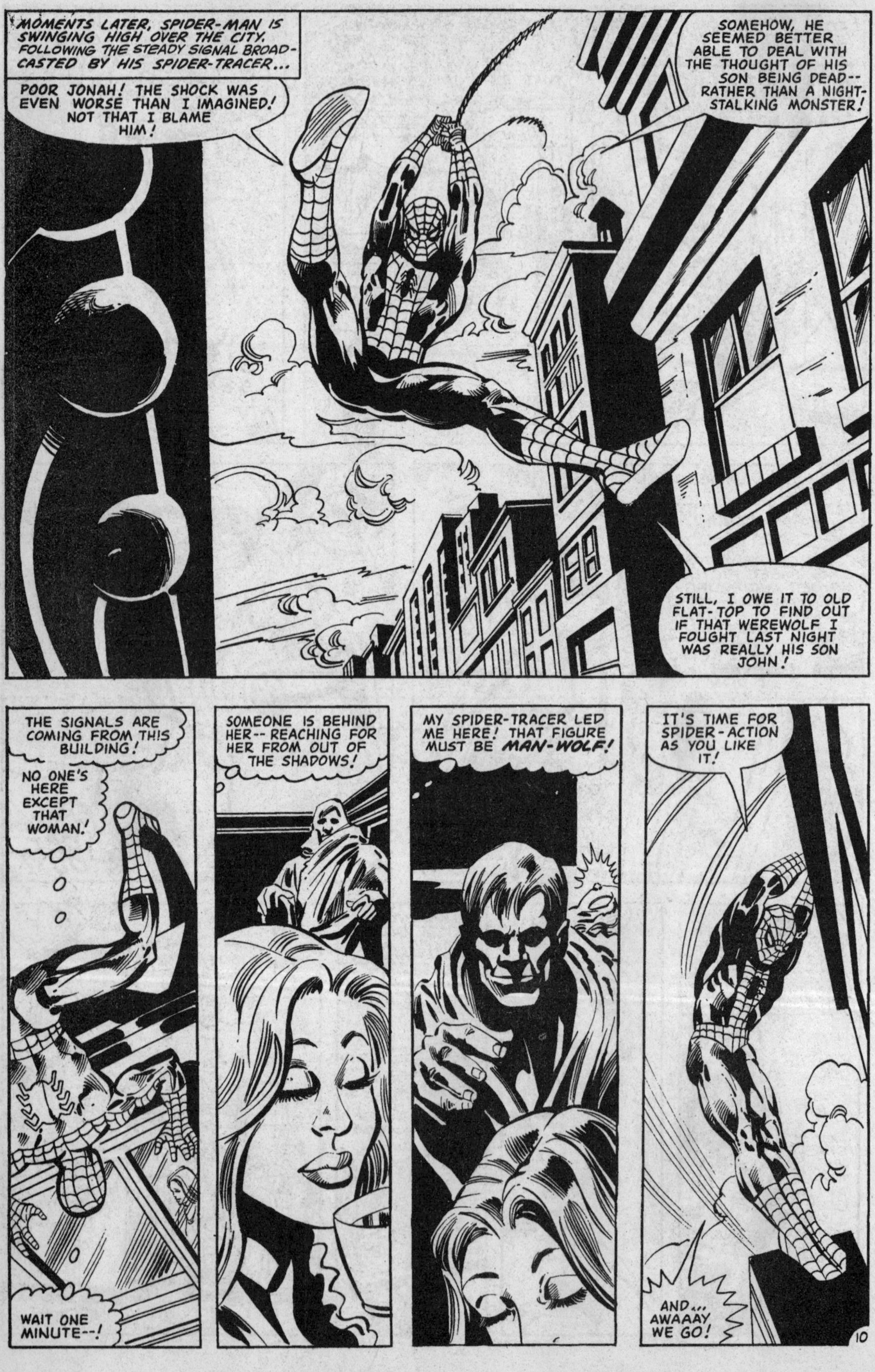

MOMENTS LATER, SPIDER-MAN IS SWINGING HIGH OVER THE CITY, FOLLOWING THE STEADY SIGNAL BROADCASTED BY HIS SPIDER-TRACER...
POOR JONAH! THE SHOCK WAS EVEN WORSE THAN I IMAGINED! NOT THAT I BLAME HIM!
SOMEHOW, HE SEEMED BETTER ABLE TO DEAL WITH THE THOUGHT OF HIS SON BEING DEAD-- RATHER THAN A NIGHT-STALKING MONSTER!
STILL, I OWE IT TO OLD FLAT-TOP TO FIND OUT IF THAT WEREWOLF I FOUGHT LAST NIGHT WAS REALLY HIS SON JOHN!
THE SIGNALS ARE COMING FROM THIS BUILDING!
NO ONE'S HERE EXCEPT THAT WOMAN!
WAIT ONE MINUTE--!
SOMEONE IS BEHIND HER-- REACHING FOR HER FROM OUT OF THE SHADOWS!
MY SPIDER-TRACER LED ME HERE! THAT FIGURE MUST BE MAN-WOLF!
IT'S TIME FOR SPIDER-ACTION AS YOU LIKE IT!
AND... AWAAAY WE GO!
10

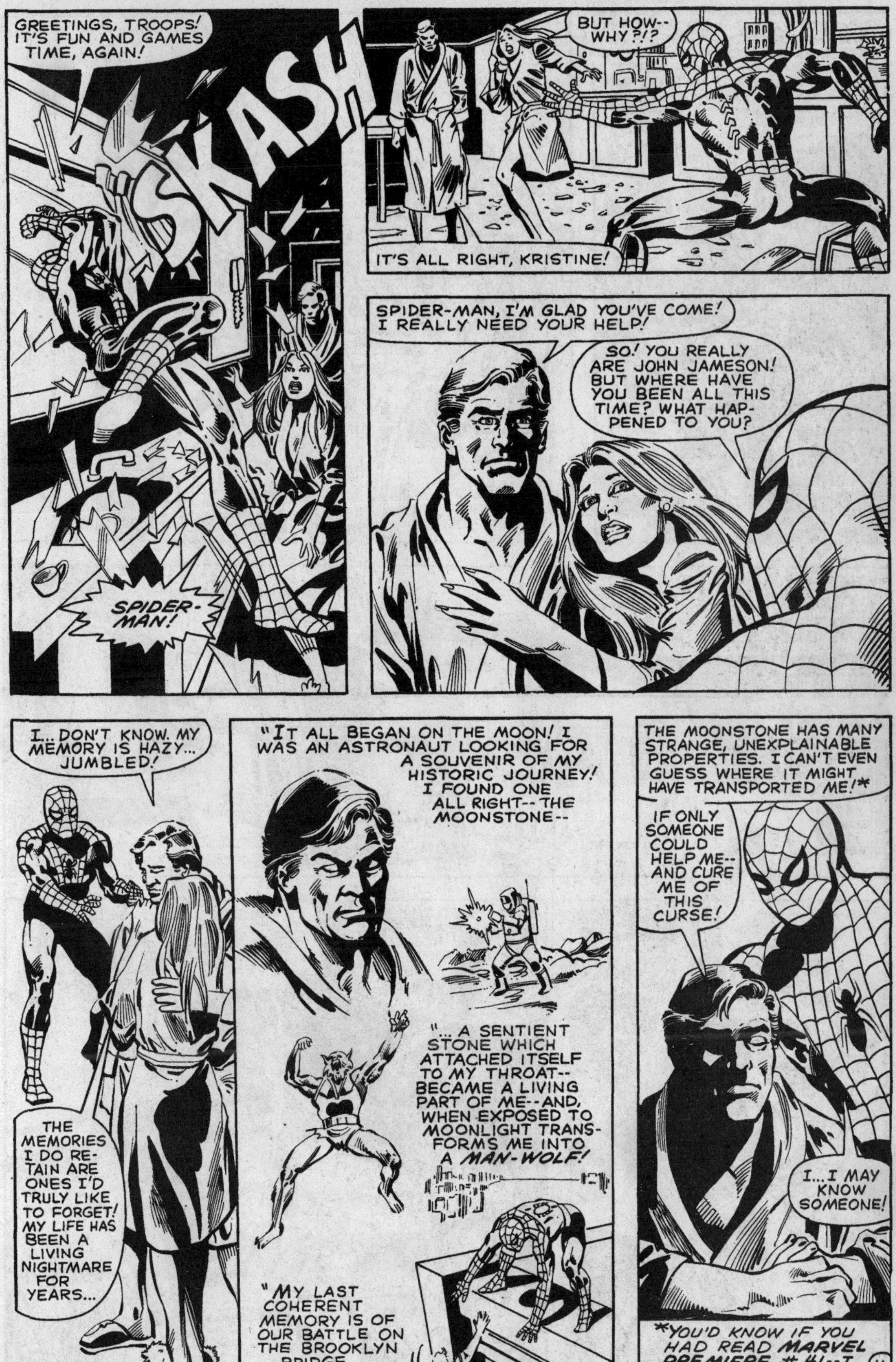
GREETINGS, TROOPS! IT'S FUN AND GAMES TIME, AGAIN!
SKASH
SPIDER-MAN!
BUT HOW-- WHY?!?
IT'S ALL RIGHT, KRISTINE!
SPIDER-MAN, I'M GLAD YOU'VE COME! I REALLY NEED YOUR HELP!
SO! YOU REALLY ARE JOHN JAMESON! BUT WHERE HAVE YOU BEEN ALL THIS TIME? WHAT HAPPENED TO YOU?
I... DON'T KNOW. MY MEMORY IS HAZY... JUMBLED!
THE MEMORIES I DO RETAIN ARE ONES I'D TRULY LIKE TO FORGET! MY LIFE HAS BEEN A LIVING NIGHTMARE FOR YEARS...
"IT ALL BEGAN ON THE MOON! I WAS AN ASTRONAUT LOOKING FOR A SOUVENIR OF MY HISTORIC JOURNEY! I FOUND ONE ALL RIGHT-- THE MOONSTONE--
"... A SENTIENT STONE WHICH ATTACHED ITSELF TO MY THROAT-- BECAME A LIVING PART OF ME--AND, WHEN EXPOSED TO MOONLIGHT TRANSFORMS ME INTO A MAN-WOLF!
"MY LAST COHERENT MEMORY IS OF OUR BATTLE ON THE BROOKLYN BRIDGE...
THE MOONSTONE HAS MANY STRANGE, UNEXPLAINABLE PROPERTIES. I CAN'T EVEN GUESS WHERE IT MIGHT HAVE TRANSPORTED ME!*
IF ONLY SOMEONE COULD HELP ME-- AND CURE ME OF THIS CURSE!
I... I MAY KNOW SOMEONE!
*YOU'D KNOW IF YOU HAD READ MARVEL PREMIERE # 41.--T.
11

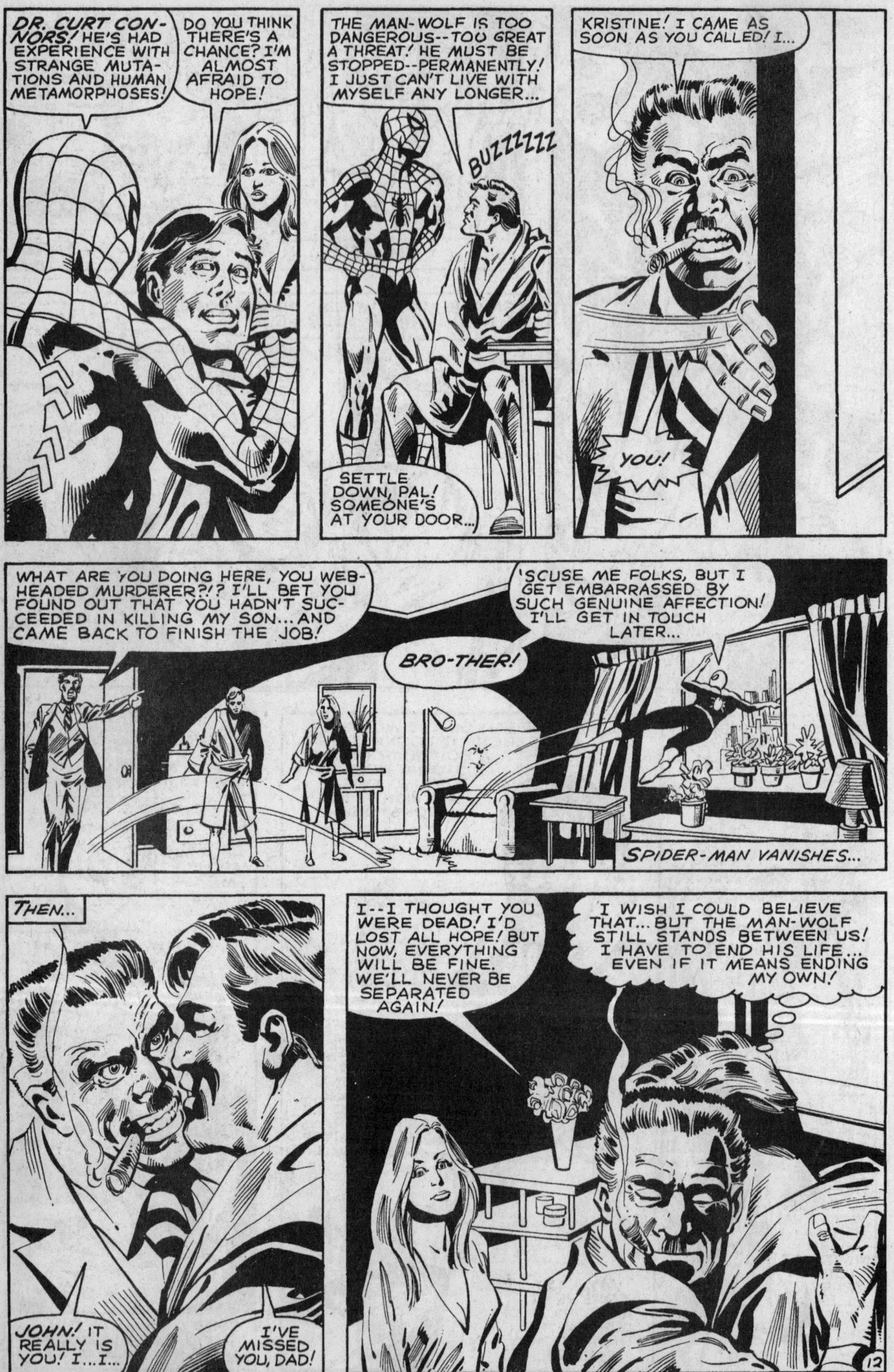
DR. CURT CONNORS! HE'S HAD EXPERIENCE WITH STRANGE MUTATIONS AND HUMAN METAMORPHOSES!
DO YOU THINK THERE'S A CHANCE? I'M ALMOST AFRAID TO HOPE!
THE MAN-WOLF IS TOO DANGEROUS--TOO GREAT A THREAT! HE MUST BE STOPPED--PERMANENTLY! I JUST CAN'T LIVE WITH MYSELF ANY LONGER...
BUZZZZZZ
SETTLE DOWN, PAL! SOMEONE'S AT YOUR DOOR...
KRISTINE! I CAME AS SOON AS YOU CALLED! I...
YOU!
WHAT ARE YOU DOING HERE, YOU WEB-HEADED MURDERER?!? I'LL BET YOU FOUND OUT THAT YOU HADN'T SUCCEEDED IN KILLING MY SON... AND CAME BACK TO FINISH THE JOB!
'SCUSE ME FOLKS, BUT I GET EMBARRASSED BY SUCH GENUINE AFFECTION! I'LL GET IN TOUCH LATER...
BRO-THER!
SPIDER-MAN VANISHES...
THEN...
JOHN! IT REALLY IS YOU! I...I...
I'VE MISSED YOU, DAD!
I--I THOUGHT YOU WERE DEAD! I'D LOST ALL HOPE! BUT NOW, EVERYTHING WILL BE FINE. WE'LL NEVER BE SEPARATED AGAIN!
I WISH I COULD BELIEVE THAT... BUT THE MAN-WOLF STILL STANDS BETWEEN US! I HAVE TO END HIS LIFE... EVEN IF IT MEANS ENDING MY OWN!
12

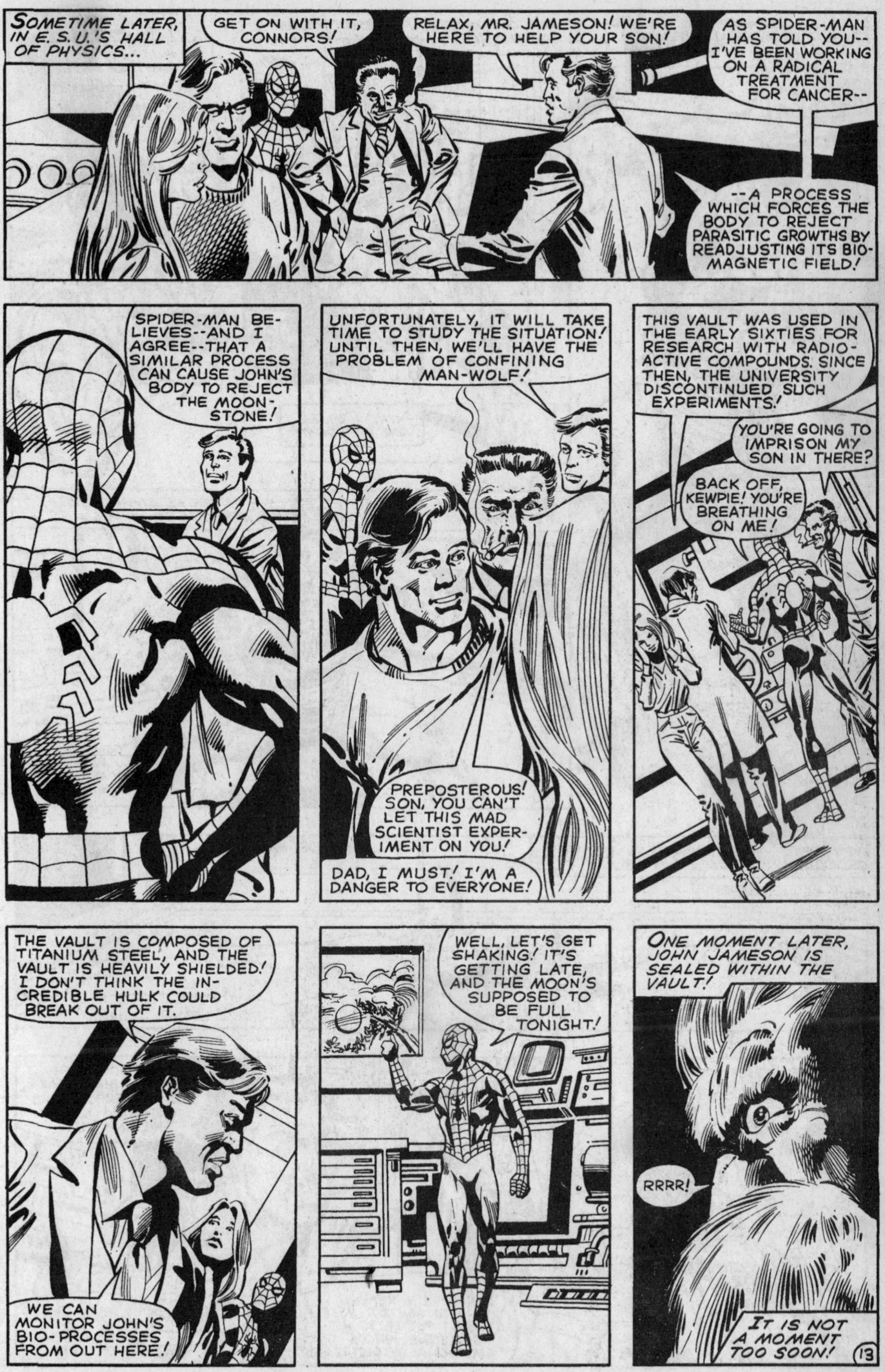
SOMETIME LATER, IN E.S.U.'S HALL OF PHYSICS...
GET ON WITH IT, CONNORS!
RELAX, MR. JAMESON! WE'RE HERE TO HELP YOUR SON!
AS SPIDER-MAN HAS TOLD YOU-- I'VE BEEN WORKING ON A RADICAL TREATMENT FOR CANCER--
--A PROCESS WHICH FORCES THE BODY TO REJECT PARASITIC GROWTHS BY READJUSTING ITS BIO-MAGNETIC FIELD!
SPIDER-MAN BELIEVES--AND I AGREE--THAT A SIMILAR PROCESS CAN CAUSE JOHN'S BODY TO REJECT THE MOON-STONE!
UNFORTUNATELY, IT WILL TAKE TIME TO STUDY THE SITUATION! UNTIL THEN, WE'LL HAVE THE PROBLEM OF CONFINING MAN-WOLF!
PREPOSTEROUS! SON, YOU CAN'T LET THIS MAD SCIENTIST EXPERIMENT ON YOU!
DAD, I MUST! I'M A DANGER TO EVERYONE!
THIS VAULT WAS USED IN THE EARLY SIXTIES FOR RESEARCH WITH RADIO-ACTIVE COMPOUNDS. SINCE THEN, THE UNIVERSITY DISCONTINUED SUCH EXPERIMENTS!
YOU'RE GOING TO IMPRISON MY SON IN THERE?
BACK OFF, KEWPIE! YOU'RE BREATHING ON ME!
THE VAULT IS COMPOSED OF TITANIUM STEEL, AND THE VAULT IS HEAVILY SHIELDED! I DON'T THINK THE INCREDIBLE HULK COULD BREAK OUT OF IT.
WE CAN MONITOR JOHN'S BIO-PROCESSES FROM OUT HERE!
WELL, LET'S GET SHAKING! IT'S GETTING LATE, AND THE MOON'S SUPPOSED TO BE FULL TONIGHT!
ONE MOMENT LATER, JOHN JAMESON IS SEALED WITHIN THE VAULT!
RRRR!
IT IS NOT A MOMENT TOO SOON!
13

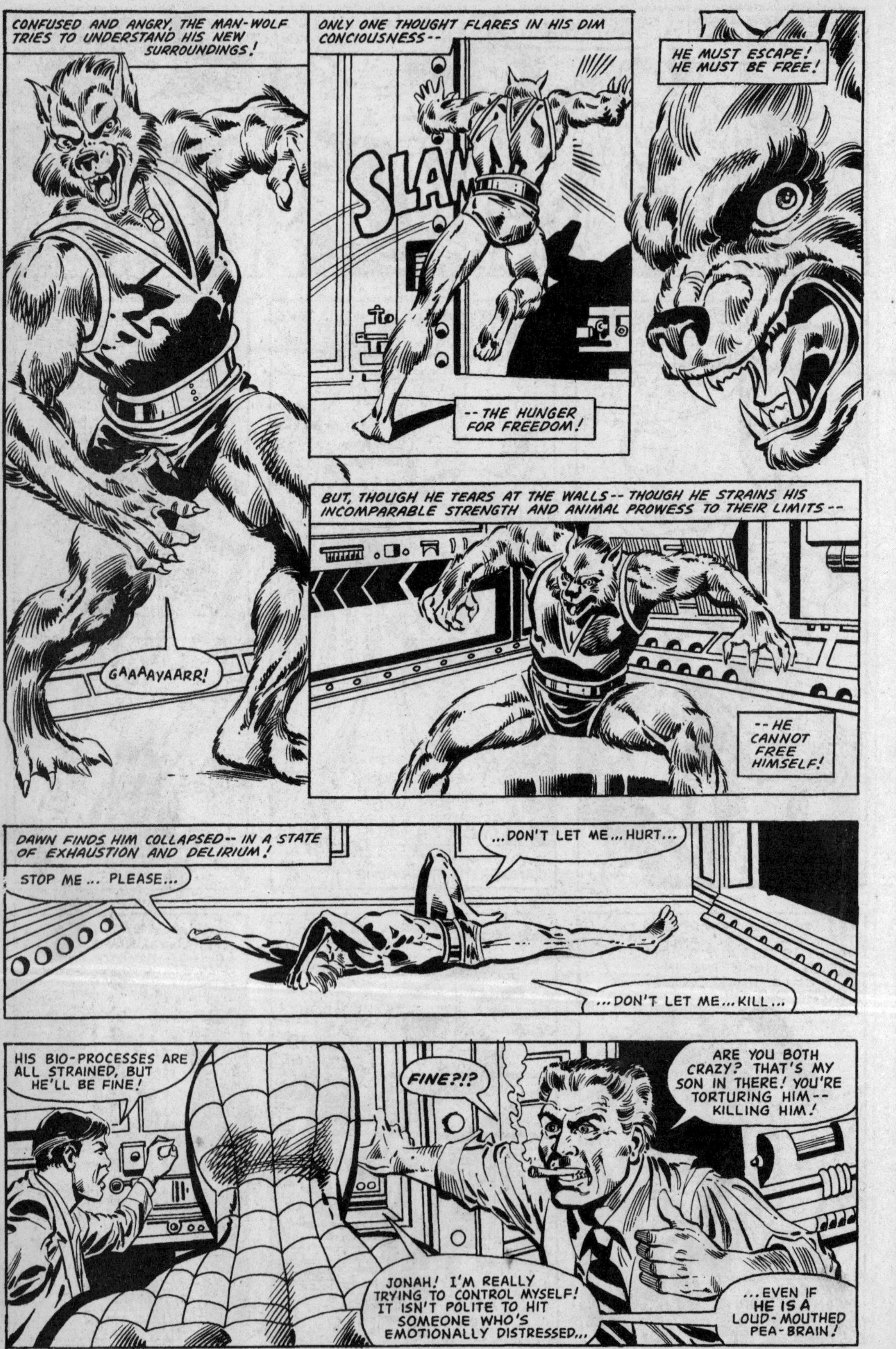

CONFUSED AND ANGRY, THE MAN-WOLF TRIES TO UNDERSTAND HIS NEW SURROUNDINGS!
GAAAAYAARR!
ONLY ONE THOUGHT FLARES IN HIS DIM CONCIOUSNESS--
SLAM
--THE HUNGER FOR FREEDOM!
HE MUST ESCAPE! HE MUST BE FREE!
BUT, THOUGH HE TEARS AT THE WALLS--THOUGH HE STRAINS HIS INCOMPARABLE STRENGTH AND ANIMAL PROWESS TO THEIR LIMITS--
--HE CANNOT FREE HIMSELF!
DAWN FINDS HIM COLLAPSED--IN A STATE OF EXHAUSTION AND DELIRIUM!
STOP ME ... PLEASE...
...DON'T LET ME...HURT...
...DON'T LET ME...KILL...
HIS BIO-PROCESSES ARE ALL STRAINED, BUT HE'LL BE FINE!
FINE?!?
ARE YOU BOTH CRAZY? THAT'S MY SON IN THERE! YOU'RE TORTURING HIM--KILLING HIM!
JONAH! I'M REALLY TRYING TO CONTROL MYSELF! IT ISN'T POLITE TO HIT SOMEONE WHO'S EMOTIONALLY DISTRESSED...
...EVEN IF HE IS A LOUD-MOUTHED PEA-BRAIN!

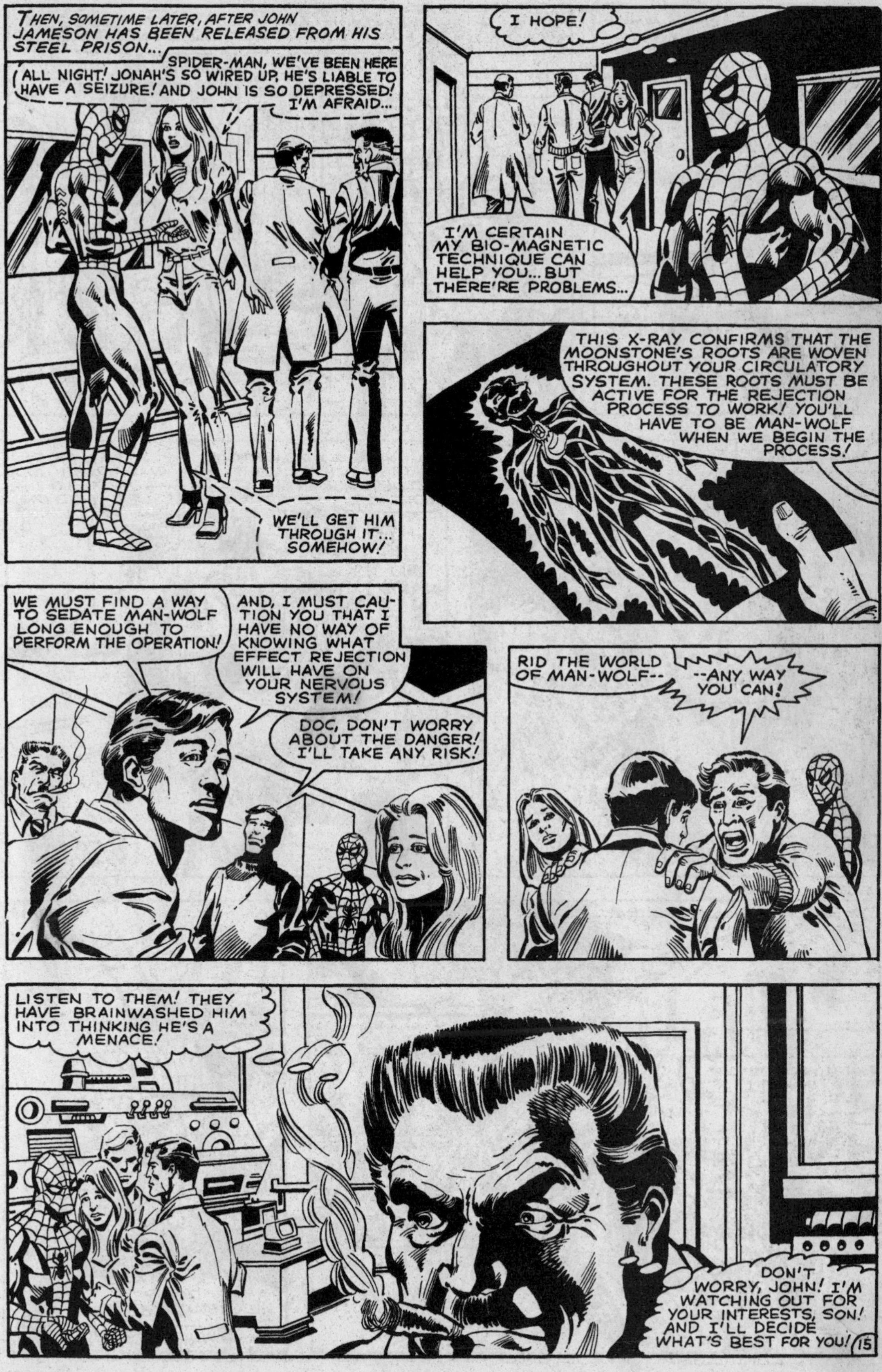
THEN, SOMETIME LATER, AFTER JOHN JAMESON HAS BEEN RELEASED FROM HIS STEEL PRISON...
SPIDER-MAN, WE'VE BEEN HERE ALL NIGHT! JONAH'S SO WIRED UP, HE'S LIABLE TO HAVE A SEIZURE! AND JOHN IS SO DEPRESSED! I'M AFRAID...
WE'LL GET HIM THROUGH IT... SOMEHOW!
I HOPE!
I'M CERTAIN MY BIO-MAGNETIC TECHNIQUE CAN HELP YOU... BUT THERE'RE PROBLEMS...
THIS X-RAY CONFIRMS THAT THE MOONSTONE'S ROOTS ARE WOVEN THROUGHOUT YOUR CIRCULATORY SYSTEM. THESE ROOTS MUST BE ACTIVE FOR THE REJECTION PROCESS TO WORK! YOU'LL HAVE TO BE MAN-WOLF WHEN WE BEGIN THE PROCESS!
WE MUST FIND A WAY TO SEDATE MAN-WOLF LONG ENOUGH TO PERFORM THE OPERATION!
AND, I MUST CAUTION YOU THAT I HAVE NO WAY OF KNOWING WHAT EFFECT REJECTION WILL HAVE ON YOUR NERVOUS SYSTEM!
DOC, DON'T WORRY ABOUT THE DANGER! I'LL TAKE ANY RISK!
RID THE WORLD OF MAN-WOLF--
--ANY WAY YOU CAN!
LISTEN TO THEM! THEY HAVE BRAINWASHED HIM INTO THINKING HE'S A MENACE!
DON'T WORRY, JOHN! I'M WATCHING OUT FOR YOUR INTERESTS, SON! AND I'LL DECIDE WHAT'S BEST FOR YOU!

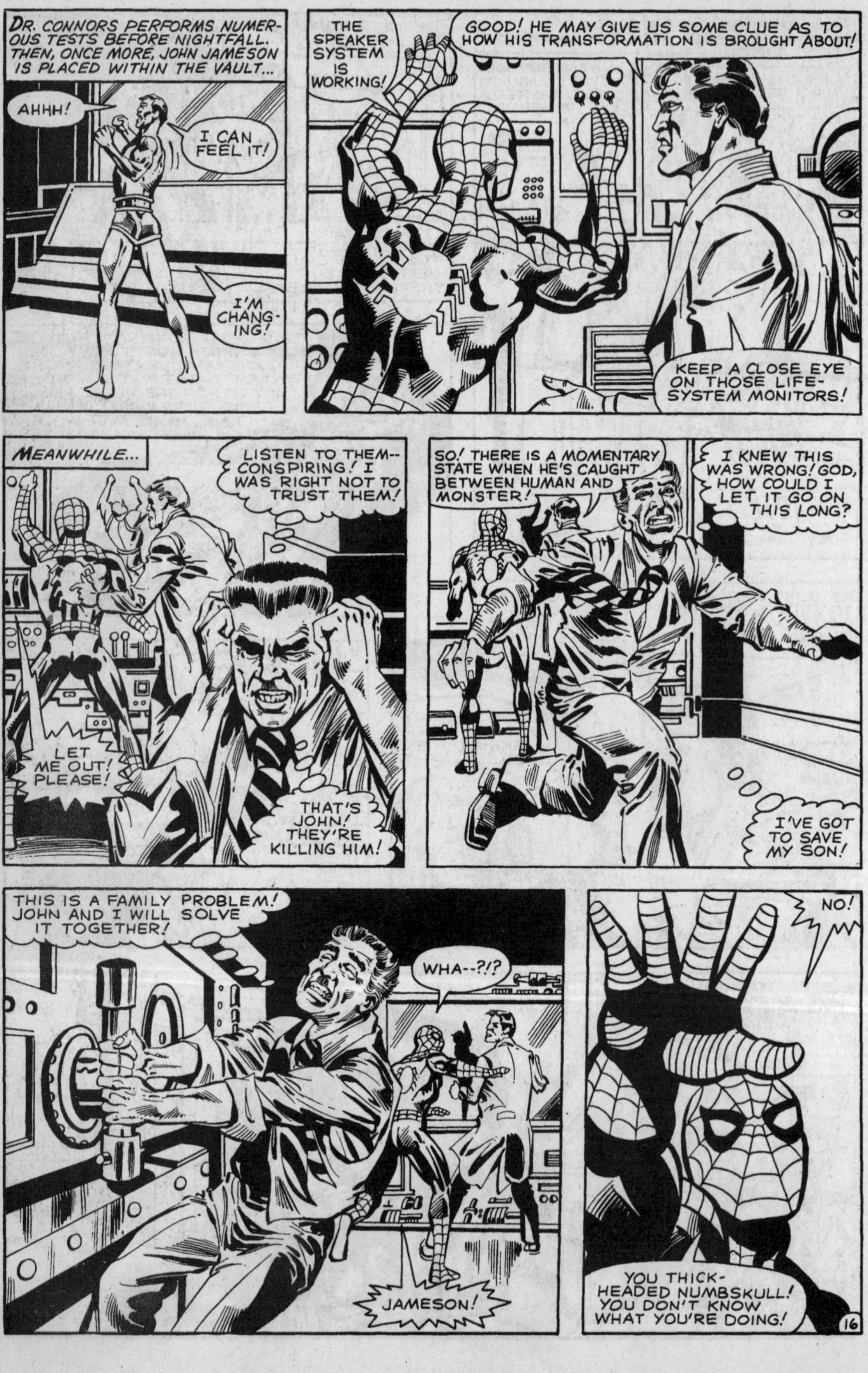

DR. CONNORS PERFORMS NUMEROUS TESTS BEFORE NIGHTFALL. THEN, ONCE MORE, JOHN JAMESON IS PLACED WITHIN THE VAULT...
AHHH!
I CAN FEEL IT!
I'M CHANGING!
THE SPEAKER SYSTEM IS WORKING!
GOOD! HE MAY GIVE US SOME CLUE AS TO HOW HIS TRANSFORMATION IS BROUGHT ABOUT!
KEEP A CLOSE EYE ON THOSE LIFE-SYSTEM MONITORS!
MEANWHILE...
LISTEN TO THEM-- CONSPIRING! I WAS RIGHT NOT TO TRUST THEM!
LET ME OUT! PLEASE!
THAT'S JOHN! THEY'RE KILLING HIM!
SO! THERE IS A MOMENTARY STATE WHEN HE'S CAUGHT BETWEEN HUMAN AND MONSTER!
I KNEW THIS WAS WRONG! GOD, HOW COULD I LET IT GO ON THIS LONG?
I'VE GOT TO SAVE MY SON!
THIS IS A FAMILY PROBLEM! JOHN AND I WILL SOLVE IT TOGETHER!
WHA--?!?
JAMESON!
NO!
YOU THICK-HEADED NUMBSKULL! YOU DON'T KNOW WHAT YOU'RE DOING!
16

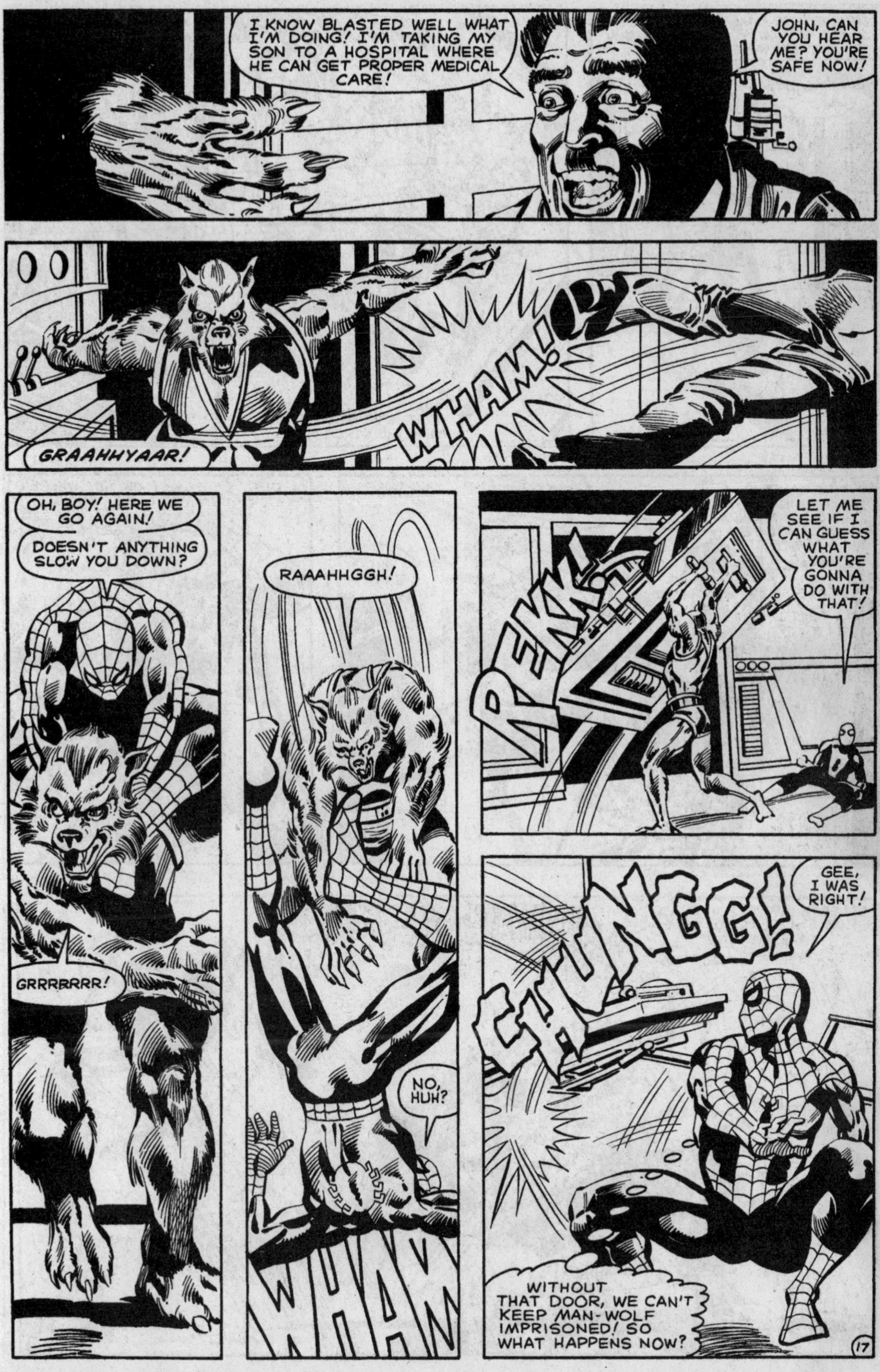
I KNOW BLASTED WELL WHAT I'M DOING! I'M TAKING MY SON TO A HOSPITAL WHERE HE CAN GET PROPER MEDICAL CARE!
JOHN, CAN YOU HEAR ME? YOU'RE SAFE NOW!
WHAM!
GRAAHHYAAR!
OH, BOY! HERE WE GO AGAIN!
DOESN'T ANYTHING SLOW YOU DOWN?
GRRRRRRR!
RAAAHHGGH!
NO, HUH?
WHAM
REKK!
LET ME SEE IF I CAN GUESS WHAT YOU'RE GONNA DO WITH THAT!
CHUNGG!
GEE, I WAS RIGHT!
WITHOUT THAT DOOR, WE CAN'T KEEP MAN-WOLF IMPRISONED! SO WHAT HAPPENS NOW?

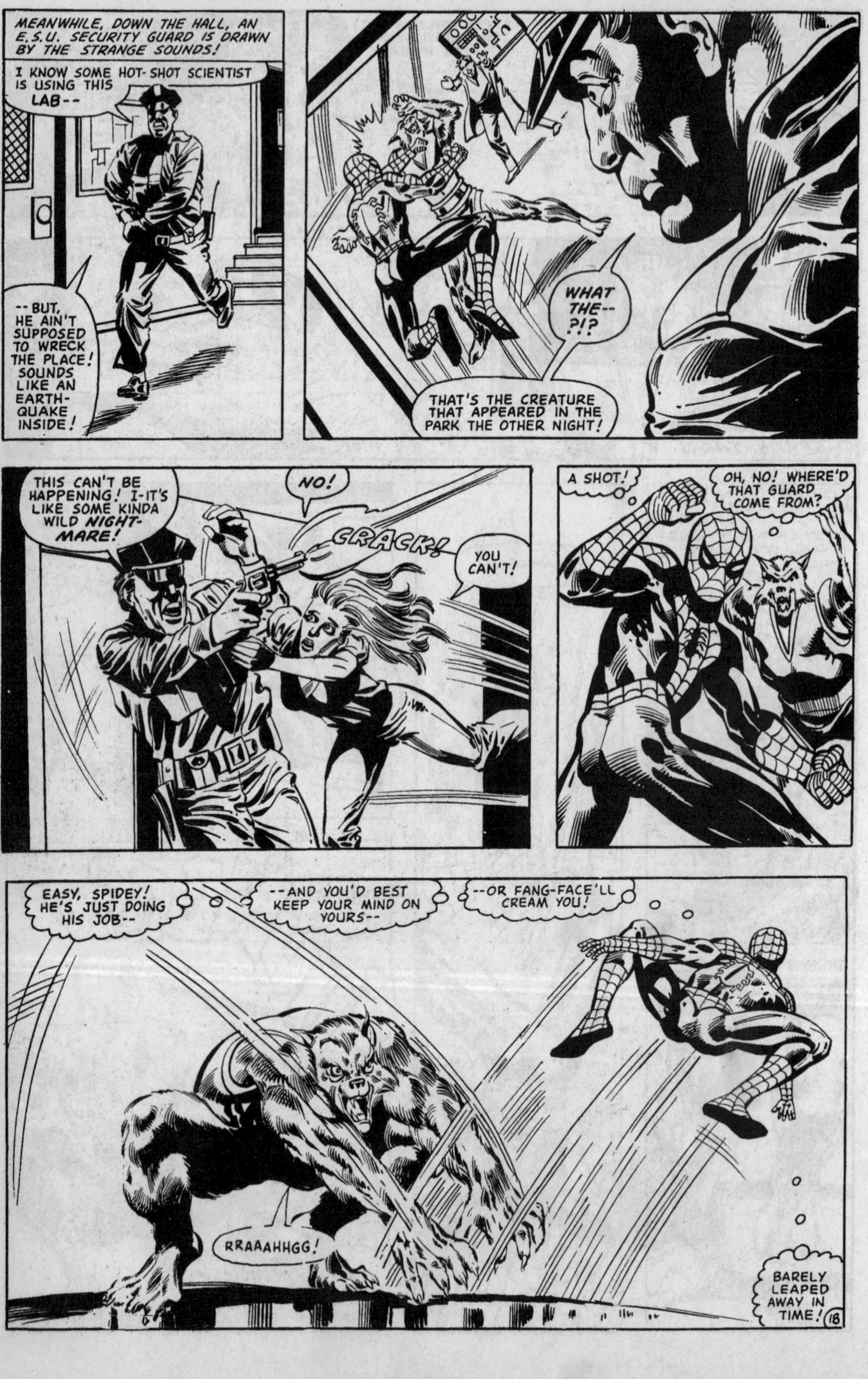
MEANWHILE, DOWN THE HALL, AN E.S.U. SECURITY GUARD IS DRAWN BY THE STRANGE SOUNDS!
I KNOW SOME HOT-SHOT SCIENTIST IS USING THIS LAB--
--BUT, HE AIN'T SUPPOSED TO WRECK THE PLACE! SOUNDS LIKE AN EARTH-QUAKE INSIDE!
WHAT THE--?!?
THAT'S THE CREATURE THAT APPEARED IN THE PARK THE OTHER NIGHT!
THIS CAN'T BE HAPPENING! I-IT'S LIKE SOME KINDA WILD NIGHT-MARE!
NO!
CRACK!
YOU CAN'T!
A SHOT!
OH, NO! WHERE'D THAT GUARD COME FROM?
EASY, SPIDEY! HE'S JUST DOING HIS JOB--
--AND YOU'D BEST KEEP YOUR MIND ON YOURS--
--OR FANG-FACE'LL CREAM YOU!
RRAAAHHGG!
BARELY LEAPED AWAY IN TIME!
18

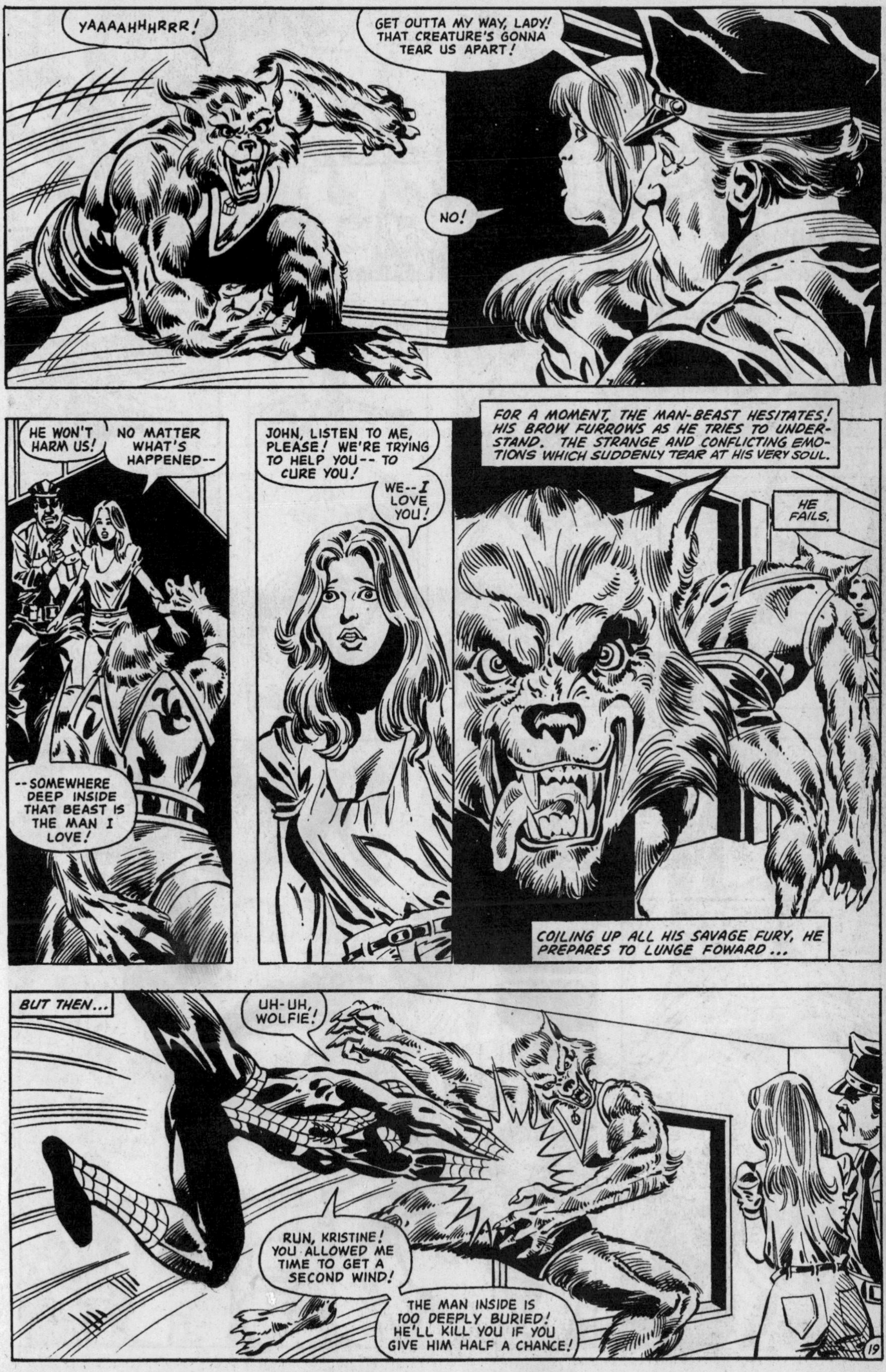

YAAAAHHHRRR!
GET OUTTA MY WAY, LADY! THAT CREATURE'S GONNA TEAR US APART!
NO!
HE WON'T HARM US!
NO MATTER WHAT'S HAPPENED--
--SOMEWHERE DEEP INSIDE THAT BEAST IS THE MAN I LOVE!
JOHN, LISTEN TO ME, PLEASE! WE'RE TRYING TO HELP YOU-- TO CURE YOU!
WE--I LOVE YOU!
FOR A MOMENT, THE MAN-BEAST HESITATES! HIS BROW FURROWS AS HE TRIES TO UNDERSTAND. THE STRANGE AND CONFLICTING EMOTIONS WHICH SUDDENLY TEAR AT HIS VERY SOUL.
HE FAILS.
COILING UP ALL HIS SAVAGE FURY, HE PREPARES TO LUNGE FOWARD...
BUT THEN...
UH-UH, WOLFIE!
RUN, KRISTINE! YOU ALLOWED ME TIME TO GET A SECOND WIND!
THE MAN INSIDE IS TOO DEEPLY BURIED! HE'LL KILL YOU IF YOU GIVE HIM HALF A CHANCE!
19

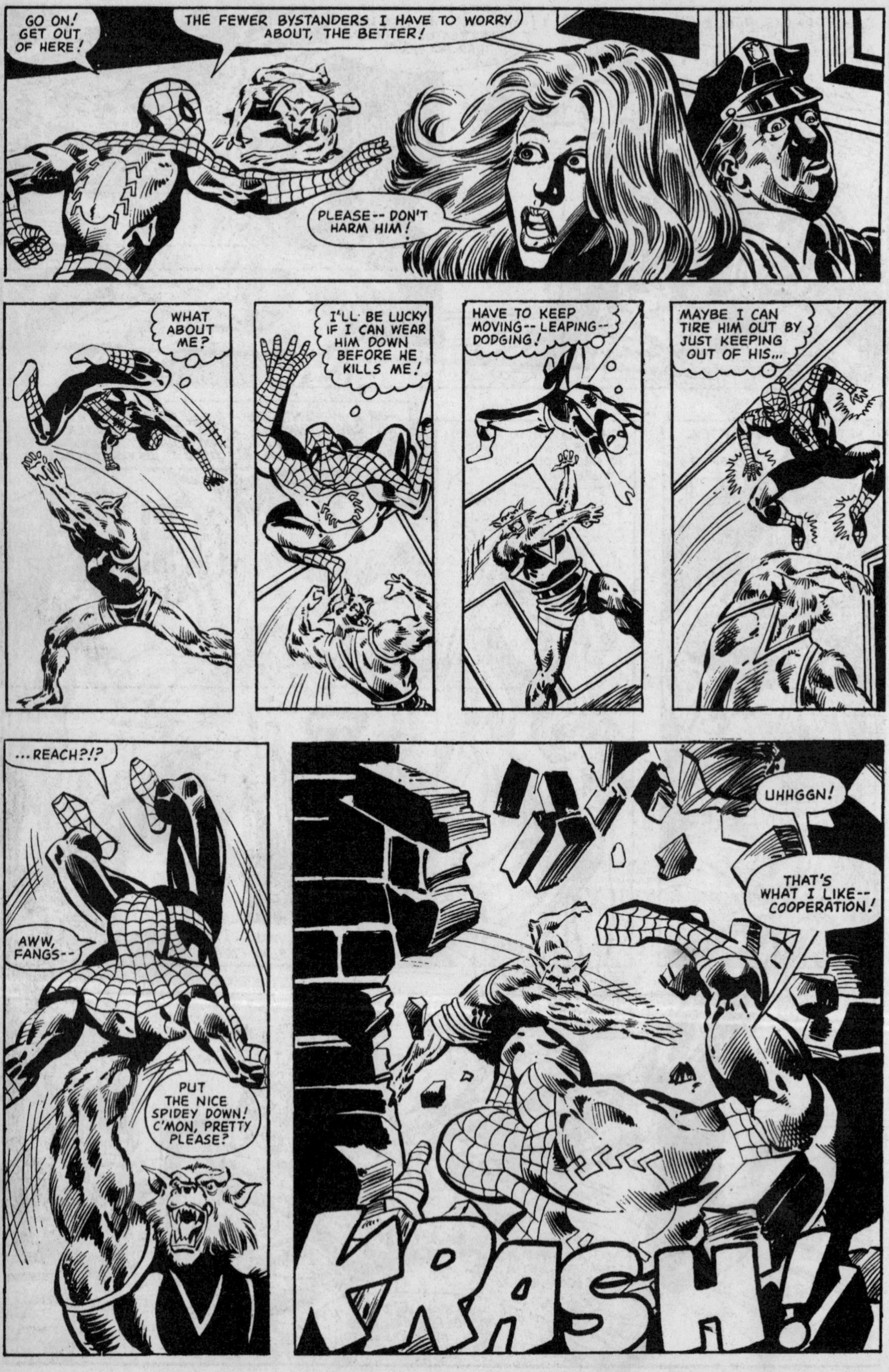
GO ON! GET OUT OF HERE!
THE FEWER BYSTANDERS I HAVE TO WORRY ABOUT, THE BETTER!
PLEASE-- DON'T HARM HIM!
WHAT ABOUT ME?
I'LL BE LUCKY IF I CAN WEAR HIM DOWN BEFORE HE KILLS ME!
HAVE TO KEEP MOVING-- LEAPING-- DODGING!
MAYBE I CAN TIRE HIM OUT BY JUST KEEPING OUT OF HIS...
...REACH?!?
AWW, FANGS--
PUT THE NICE SPIDEY DOWN! C'MON, PRETTY PLEASE?
UHHGGN!
THAT'S WHAT I LIKE-- COOPERATION!
KRASH!

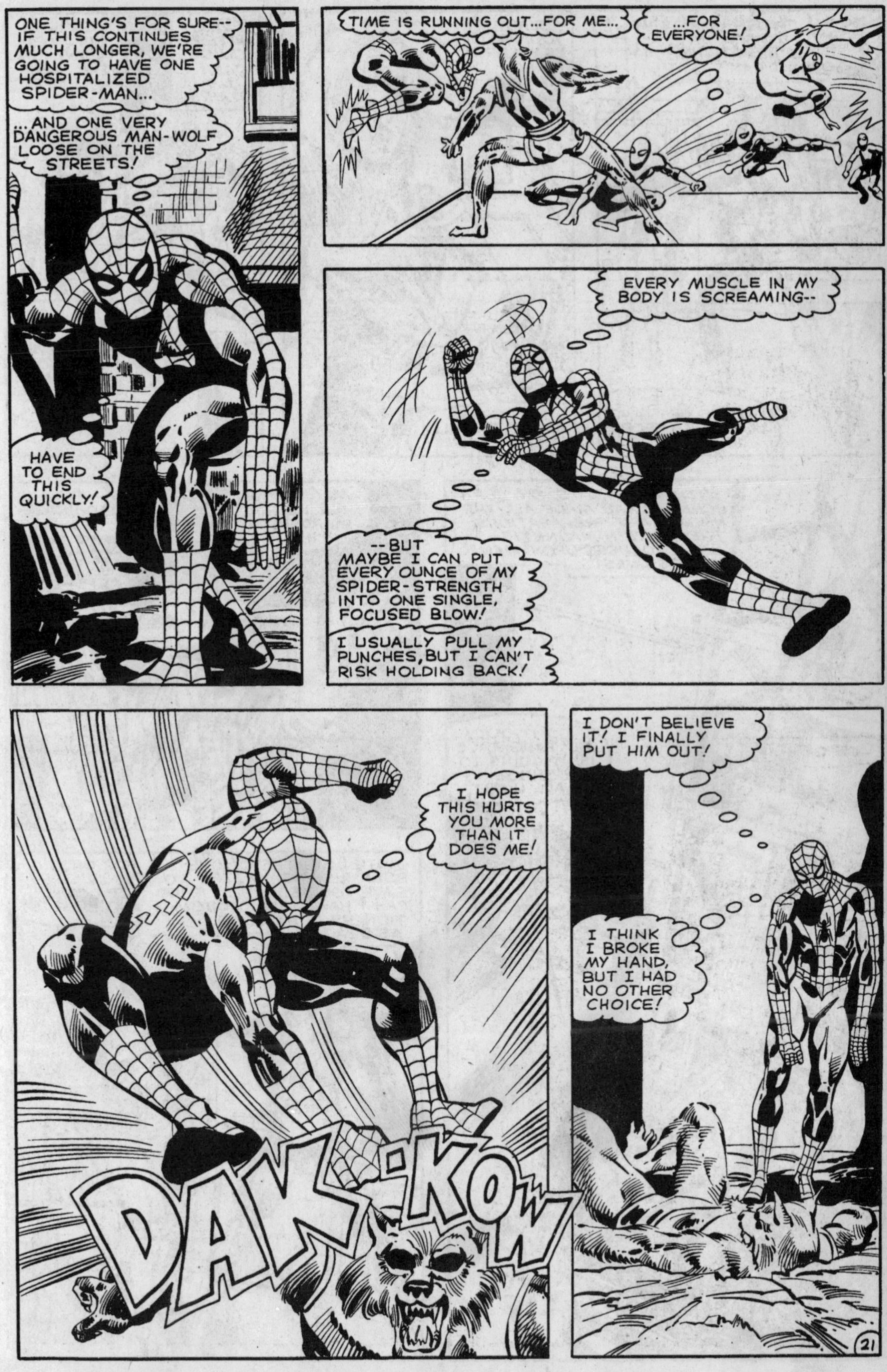
ONE THING'S FOR SURE-- IF THIS CONTINUES MUCH LONGER, WE'RE GOING TO HAVE ONE HOSPITALIZED SPIDER-MAN...
...AND ONE VERY DANGEROUS MAN-WOLF LOOSE ON THE STREETS!
HAVE TO END THIS QUICKLY!
TIME IS RUNNING OUT...FOR ME...
...FOR EVERYONE!
EVERY MUSCLE IN MY BODY IS SCREAMING--
--BUT MAYBE I CAN PUT EVERY OUNCE OF MY SPIDER-STRENGTH INTO ONE SINGLE, FOCUSED BLOW!
I USUALLY PULL MY PUNCHES, BUT I CAN'T RISK HOLDING BACK!
I HOPE THIS HURTS YOU MORE THAN IT DOES ME!
DAK-KOW
I DON'T BELIEVE IT! I FINALLY PUT HIM OUT!
I THINK I BROKE MY HAND, BUT I HAD NO OTHER CHOICE!
21

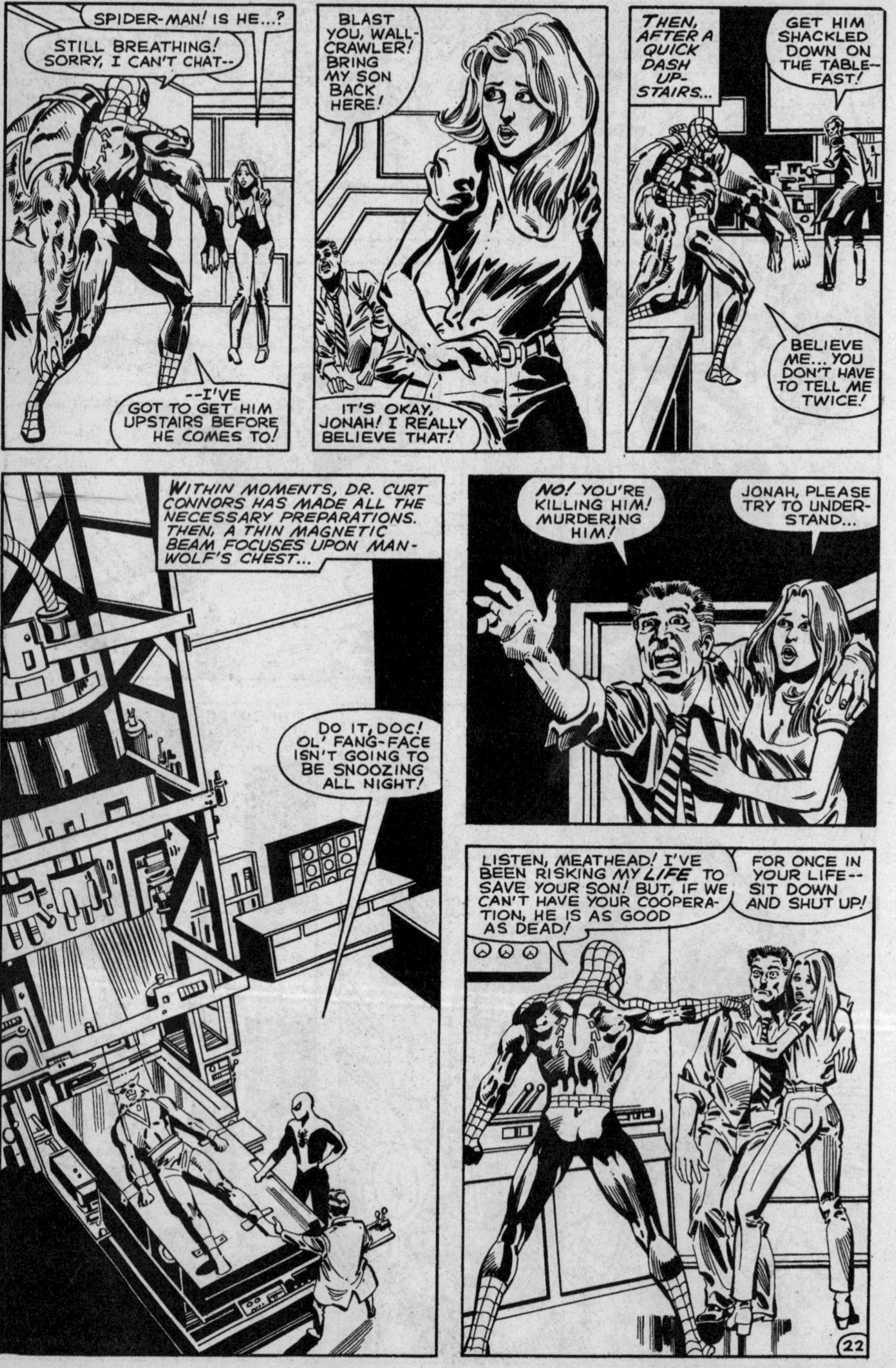
SPIDER-MAN! IS HE...?
STILL BREATHING! SORRY, I CAN'T CHAT--
--I'VE GOT TO GET HIM UPSTAIRS BEFORE HE COMES TO!
BLAST YOU, WALL-CRAWLER! BRING MY SON BACK HERE!
IT'S OKAY, JONAH! I REALLY BELIEVE THAT!
THEN, AFTER A QUICK DASH UP-STAIRS...
GET HIM SHACKLED DOWN ON THE TABLE--FAST!
BELIEVE ME... YOU DON'T HAVE TO TELL ME TWICE!
WITHIN MOMENTS, DR. CURT CONNORS HAS MADE ALL THE NECESSARY PREPARATIONS. THEN, A THIN MAGNETIC BEAM FOCUSES UPON MAN-WOLF'S CHEST...
DO IT, DOC! OL' FANG-FACE ISN'T GOING TO BE SNOOZING ALL NIGHT!
NO! YOU'RE KILLING HIM! MURDERING HIM!
JONAH, PLEASE TRY TO UNDER-STAND...
LISTEN, MEATHEAD! I'VE BEEN RISKING MY LIFE TO SAVE YOUR SON! BUT, IF WE CAN'T HAVE YOUR COOPERA-TION, HE IS AS GOOD AS DEAD!
FOR ONCE IN YOUR LIFE--SIT DOWN AND SHUT UP!
22

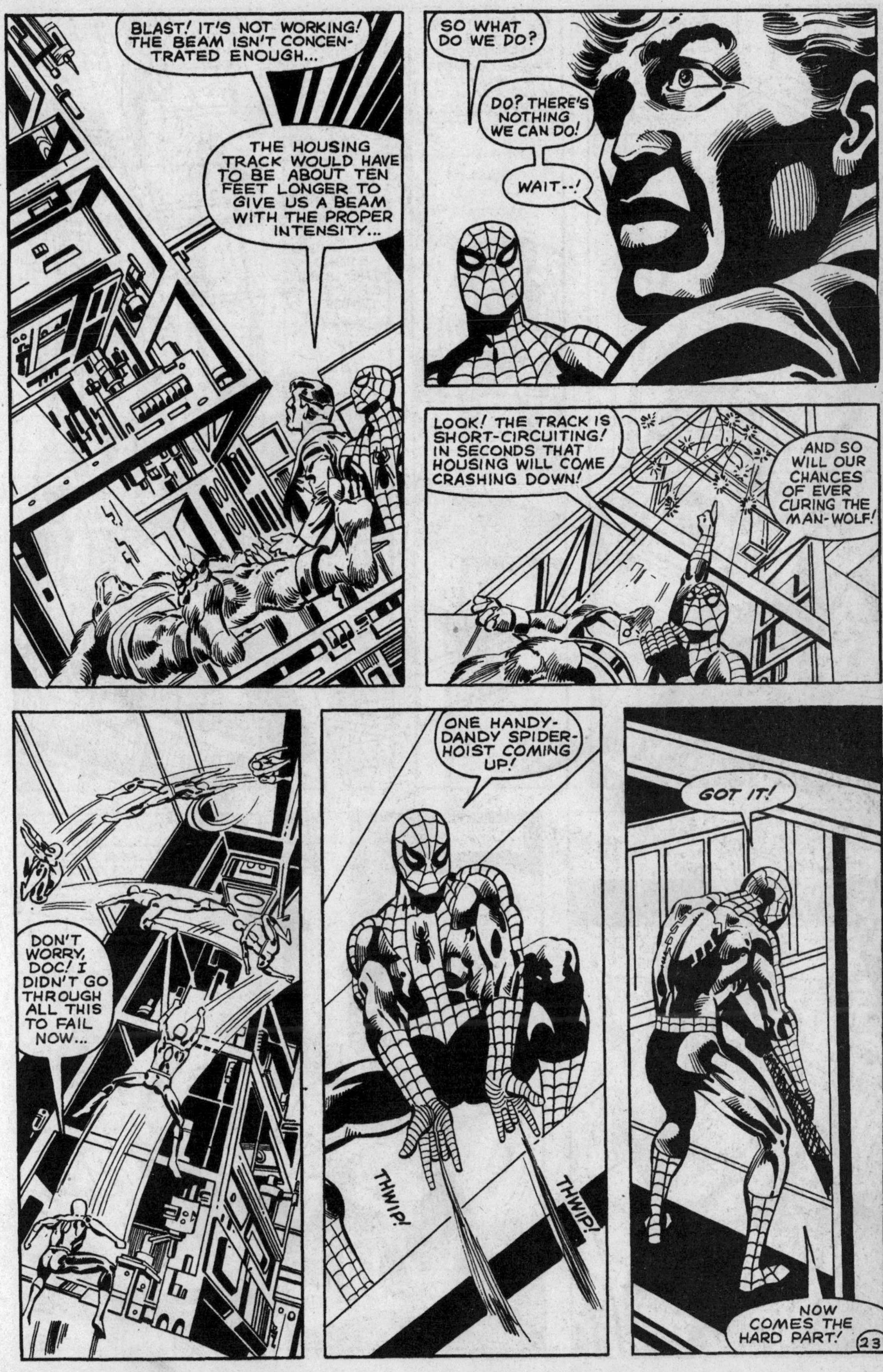
BLAST! IT'S NOT WORKING! THE BEAM ISN'T CONCENTRATED ENOUGH...
THE HOUSING TRACK WOULD HAVE TO BE ABOUT TEN FEET LONGER TO GIVE US A BEAM WITH THE PROPER INTENSITY...
SO WHAT DO WE DO?
DO? THERE'S NOTHING WE CAN DO!
WAIT--!
LOOK! THE TRACK IS SHORT-CIRCUITING! IN SECONDS THAT HOUSING WILL COME CRASHING DOWN!
AND SO WILL OUR CHANCES OF EVER CURING THE MAN-WOLF!
DON'T WORRY, DOC! I DIDN'T GO THROUGH ALL THIS TO FAIL NOW...
ONE HANDY-DANDY SPIDER-HOIST COMING UP!
THWIP!
THWIP!
GOT IT!
NOW COMES THE HARD PART!

STRAINING EVERY FIBER OF HIS BEING, SPIDER-MAN BEGINS PULLING THE HOUSING BACK INTO POSITION...

DESPITE THE PAIN IN HIS LIMBS, DESPITE THE EXHAUSTION WHICH NUMBS HIM, HE KEEPS GOING...

I'M SWAYING ALREADY--CAN HARDLY KEEP MY BALANCE! BUT THERE'S ONLY ONE WAY TO SAVE JOHN JAMESON!

HAVE TO PULL THIS HOUSING UP BEYOND THE LIMIT OF ITS TRACK--

--AND GIVE DR. CONNORS THE ADDITIONAL TEN FEET HE NEEDS!

AT THAT MOMENT, BELOW, THE MAN-WOLF WAKENS. THERE IS A DULL THROBBING IN HIS HEAD. IT MAKES HIM ANGRY!

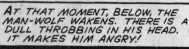

THEN...

SWAKK!

GRAHHHH!

BUT, SUDDENLY, THE CONCENTRATED BIO-MAGNETIC BEAM FOCUSES ON THE MOONSTONE...

SZAAAKK!

24

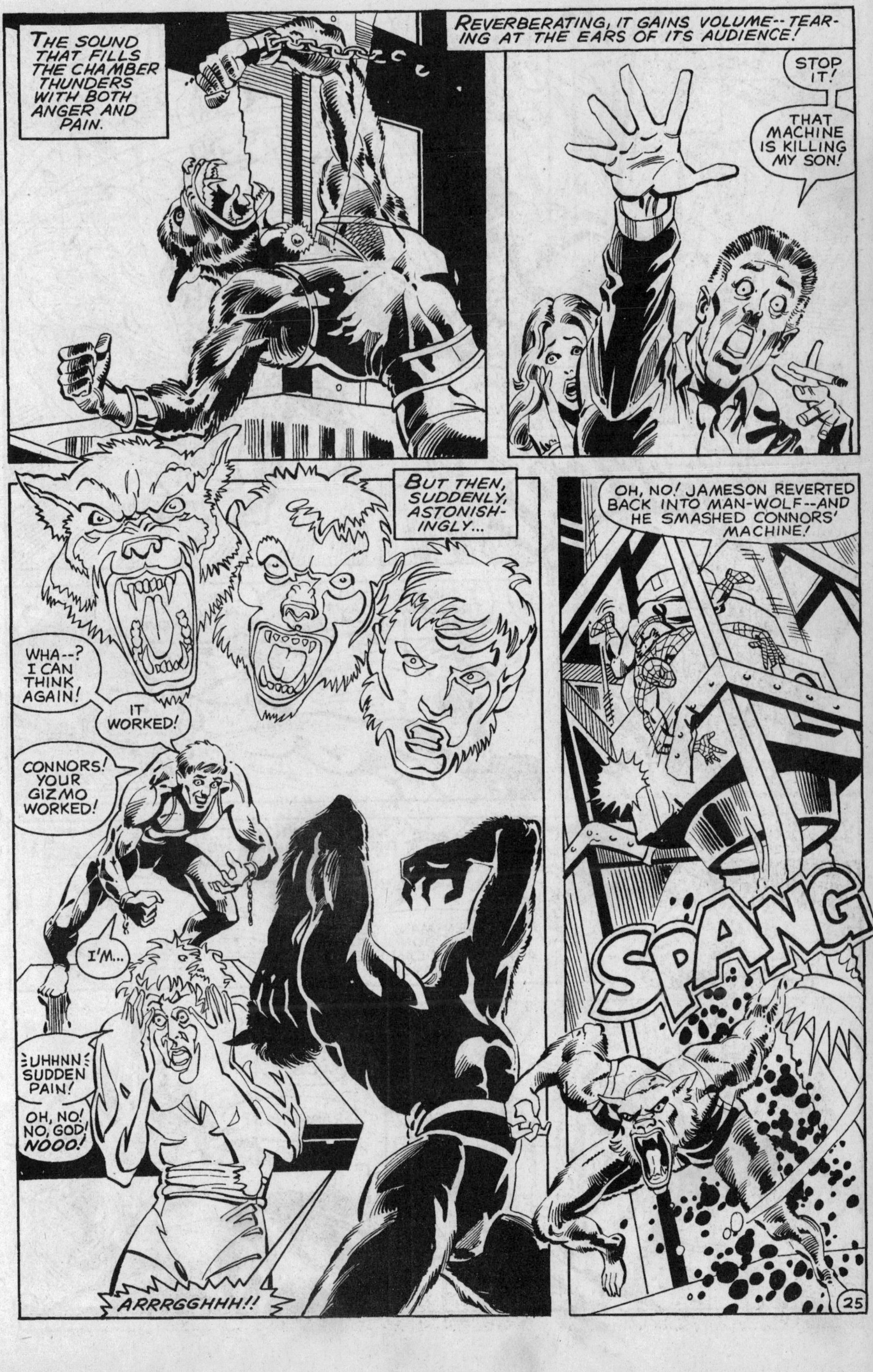

THE SOUND THAT FILLS THE CHAMBER THUNDERS WITH BOTH ANGER AND PAIN.
REVERBERATING, IT GAINS VOLUME--TEARING AT THE EARS OF ITS AUDIENCE!
STOP IT!
THAT MACHINE IS KILLING MY SON!
BUT THEN, SUDDENLY, ASTONISHINGLY...
WHA--? I CAN THINK AGAIN!
IT WORKED!
CONNORS! YOUR GIZMO WORKED!
I'M...
UHHNN SUDDEN PAIN!
OH, NO! NO, GOD! NOOO!
ARRRGGHHH!!
OH, NO! JAMESON REVERTED BACK INTO MAN-WOLF--AND HE SMASHED CONNORS' MACHINE!
SPANG

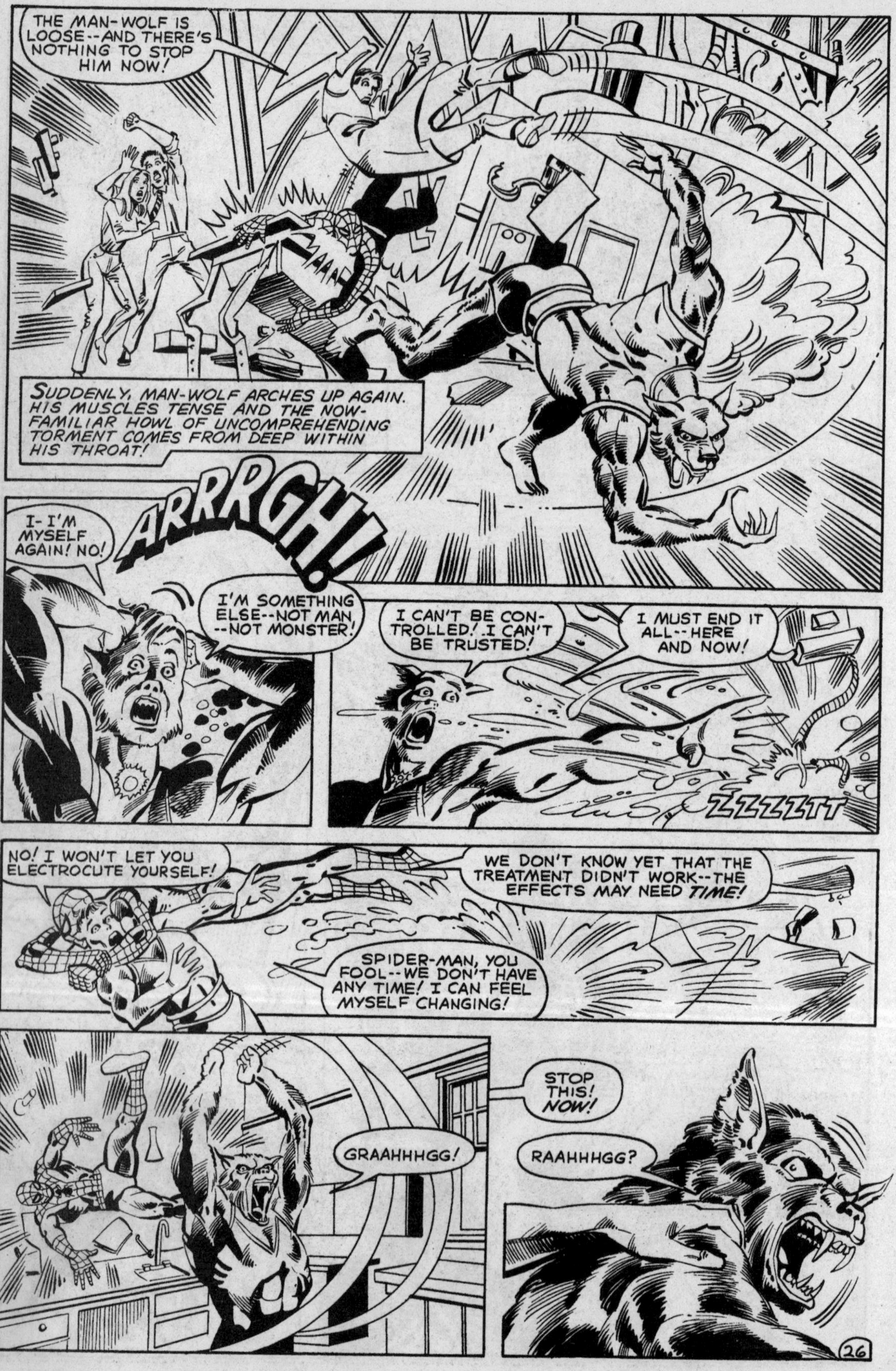
THE MAN-WOLF IS LOOSE--AND THERE'S NOTHING TO STOP HIM NOW!
SUDDENLY, MAN-WOLF ARCHES UP AGAIN. HIS MUSCLES TENSE AND THE NOW-FAMILIAR HOWL OF UNCOMPREHENDING TORMENT COMES FROM DEEP WITHIN HIS THROAT!
ARRRGH!
I- I'M MYSELF AGAIN! NO!
I'M SOMETHING ELSE--NOT MAN --NOT MONSTER!
I CAN'T BE CONTROLLED! I CAN'T BE TRUSTED!
I MUST END IT ALL--HERE AND NOW!
ZZZZZTT
NO! I WON'T LET YOU ELECTROCUTE YOURSELF!
WE DON'T KNOW YET THAT THE TREATMENT DIDN'T WORK--THE EFFECTS MAY NEED TIME!
SPIDER-MAN, YOU FOOL--WE DON'T HAVE ANY TIME! I CAN FEEL MYSELF CHANGING!
GRAAHHHGG!
STOP THIS! NOW!
RAAHHHGG?
26

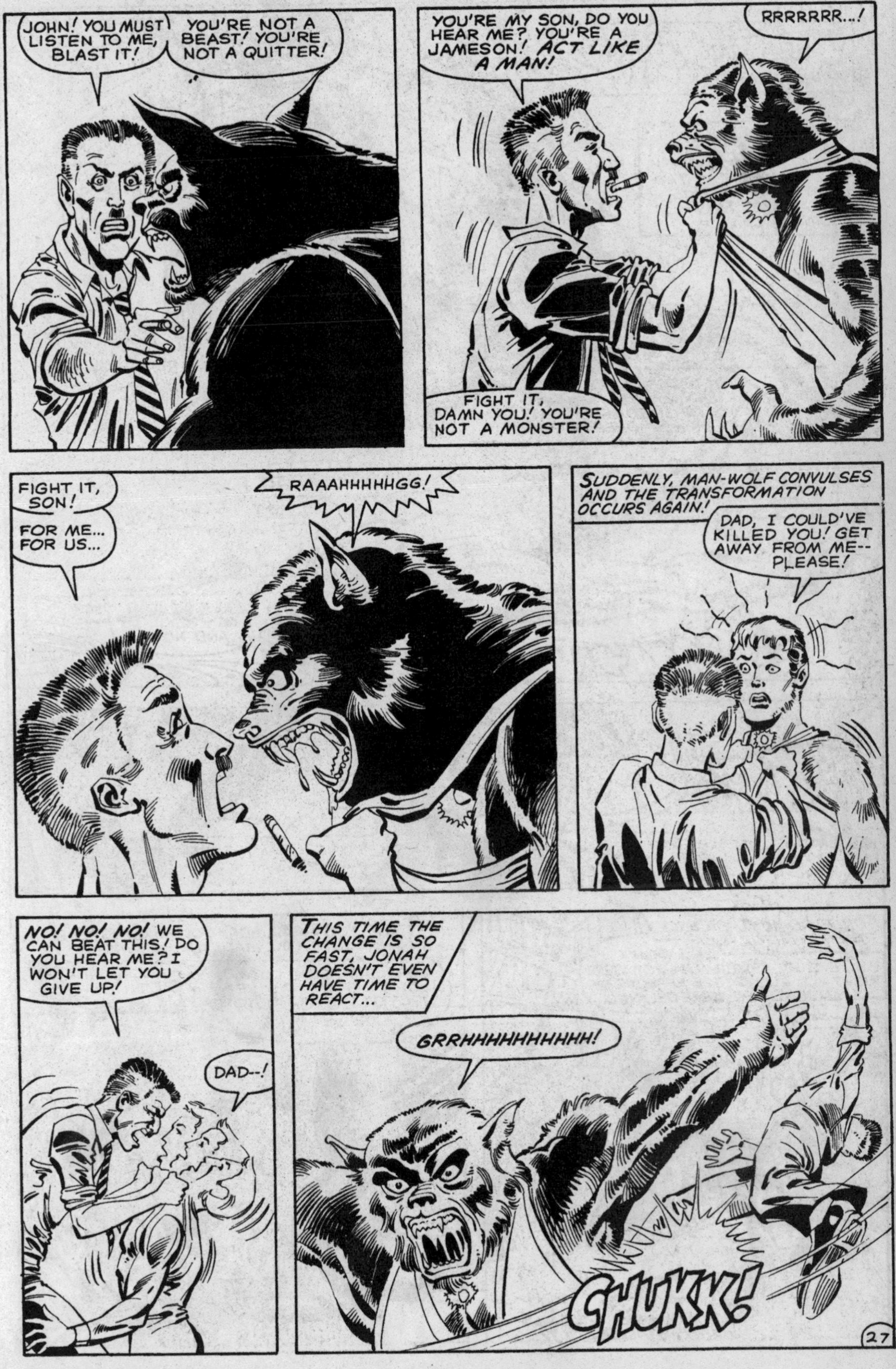
JOHN! YOU MUST LISTEN TO ME, BLAST IT!
YOU'RE NOT A BEAST! YOU'RE NOT A QUITTER!
YOU'RE MY SON, DO YOU HEAR ME? YOU'RE A JAMESON! ACT LIKE A MAN!
RRRRRRR...!
FIGHT IT, DAMN YOU! YOU'RE NOT A MONSTER!
FIGHT IT, SON!
FOR ME... FOR US...
RAAAHHHHHGG!
SUDDENLY, MAN-WOLF CONVULSES AND THE TRANSFORMATION OCCURS AGAIN!
DAD, I COULD'VE KILLED YOU! GET AWAY FROM ME-- PLEASE!
NO! NO! NO! WE CAN BEAT THIS! DO YOU HEAR ME? I WON'T LET YOU GIVE UP!
DAD--!
THIS TIME THE CHANGE IS SO FAST, JONAH DOESN'T EVEN HAVE TIME TO REACT...
GRRHHHHHHHHHH!
CHUKK!

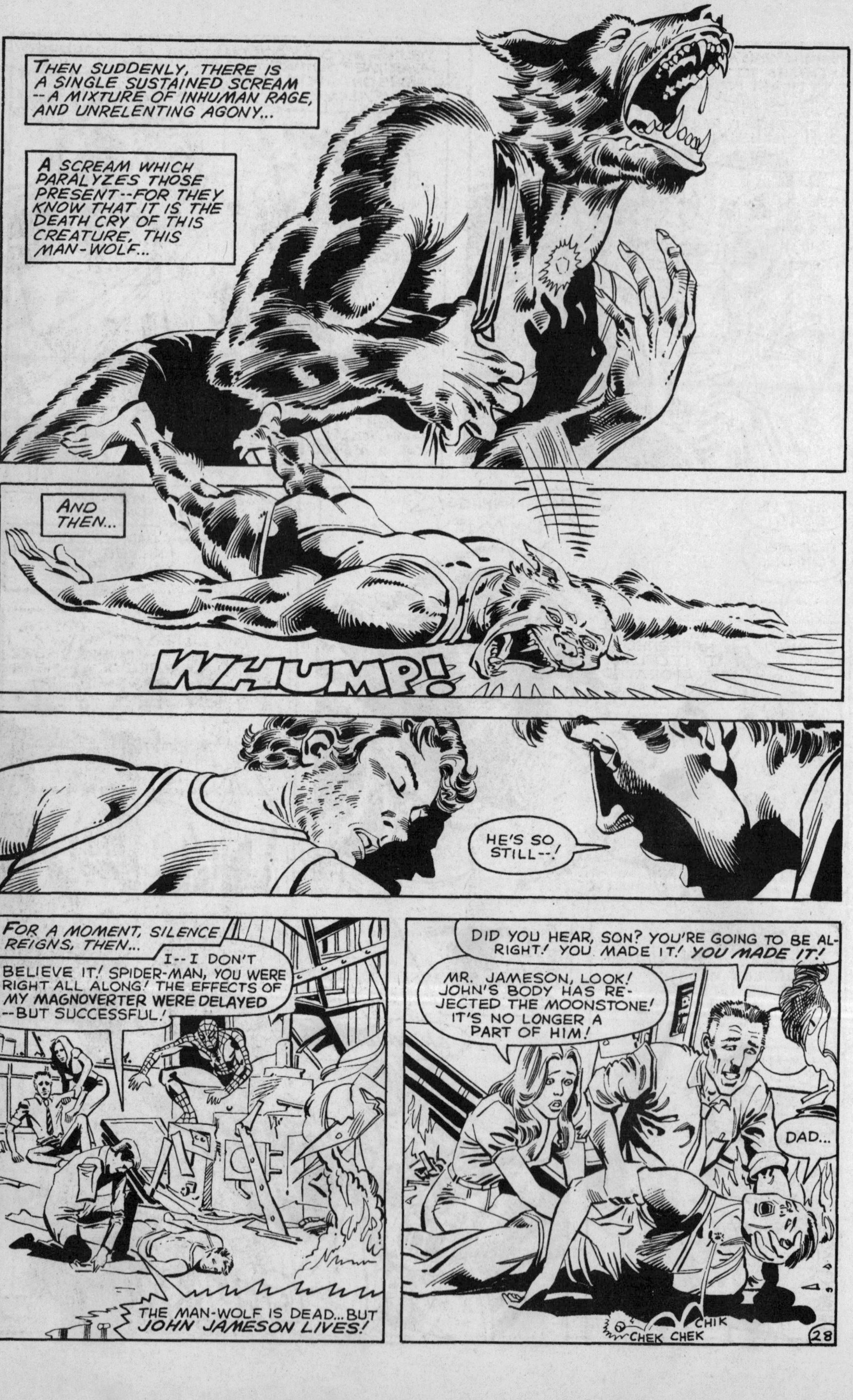
THEN SUDDENLY, THERE IS A SINGLE SUSTAINED SCREAM --A MIXTURE OF INHUMAN RAGE, AND UNRELENTING AGONY...
A SCREAM WHICH PARALYZES THOSE PRESENT--FOR THEY KNOW THAT IT IS THE DEATH CRY OF THIS CREATURE, THIS MAN-WOLF...
AND THEN...
WHUMP!
HE'S SO STILL--!
FOR A MOMENT, SILENCE REIGNS, THEN...
I--I DON'T BELIEVE IT! SPIDER-MAN, YOU WERE RIGHT ALL ALONG! THE EFFECTS OF MY MAGNOVERTER WERE DELAYED --BUT SUCCESSFUL!
THE MAN-WOLF IS DEAD...BUT JOHN JAMESON LIVES!
DID YOU HEAR, SON? YOU'RE GOING TO BE AL-RIGHT! YOU MADE IT! YOU MADE IT!
MR. JAMESON, LOOK! JOHN'S BODY HAS RE-JECTED THE MOONSTONE! IT'S NO LONGER A PART OF HIM!
DAD...
CHIK
CHEK CHEK

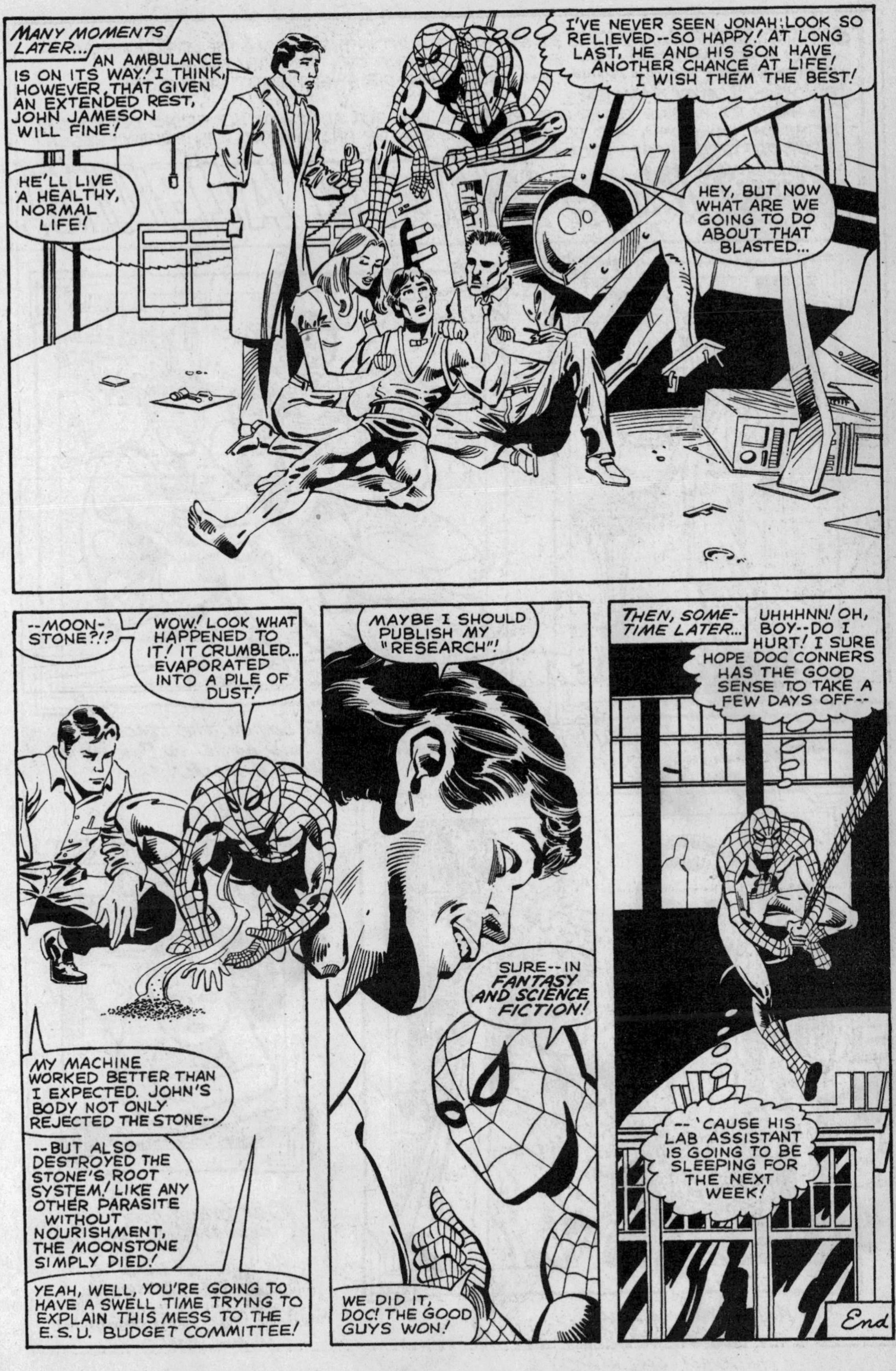
MANY MOMENTS LATER...
AN AMBULANCE IS ON ITS WAY! I THINK, HOWEVER, THAT GIVEN AN EXTENDED REST, JOHN JAMESON WILL FINE!
HE'LL LIVE A HEALTHY, NORMAL LIFE!
I'VE NEVER SEEN JONAH LOOK SO RELIEVED--SO HAPPY! AT LONG LAST, HE AND HIS SON HAVE ANOTHER CHANCE AT LIFE! I WISH THEM THE BEST!
HEY, BUT NOW WHAT ARE WE GOING TO DO ABOUT THAT BLASTED...
--MOON-STONE?!?
WOW! LOOK WHAT HAPPENED TO IT! IT CRUMBLED... EVAPORATED INTO A PILE OF DUST!
MY MACHINE WORKED BETTER THAN I EXPECTED. JOHN'S BODY NOT ONLY REJECTED THE STONE--
--BUT ALSO DESTROYED THE STONE'S ROOT SYSTEM! LIKE ANY OTHER PARASITE WITHOUT NOURISHMENT, THE MOONSTONE SIMPLY DIED!
YEAH, WELL, YOU'RE GOING TO HAVE A SWELL TIME TRYING TO EXPLAIN THIS MESS TO THE E.S.U. BUDGET COMMITTEE!
MAYBE I SHOULD PUBLISH MY "RESEARCH"!
SURE--IN FANTASY AND SCIENCE FICTION!
WE DID IT, DOC! THE GOOD GUYS WON!
THEN, SOME-TIME LATER...
UHHHHN! OH, BOY--DO I HURT! I SURE HOPE DOC CONNERS HAS THE GOOD SENSE TO TAKE A FEW DAYS OFF--
--'CAUSE HIS LAB ASSISTANT IS GOING TO BE SLEEPING FOR THE NEXT WEEK!
End

CERTAINLY, THE AWARD FOR THE MOST DOTING AUNT IN THE ANNALS OF COMICDOM HAS TO GO TO THAT PIN-UP GIRL OF THE SENIOR CITIZENS CENTER...THAT PEERLESS PURVEYOR OF CHICKEN SOUP...THAT NEVER-SAY-DIE SWEETHEART OF THE GREY PANTHERS... **MAY PARKER!**
IT'S HARD TO IMAGINE PETER PARKER'S LIFE WITHOUT AUNT MAY HOVERING SOMEWHERE IN THE BACKGROUND. AND SO, FOR YOUR GREATER ENJOYMENT, WE HEREBY PRESENT A FEW TATTERED PAGES FROM...

Aunt May's PHOTO ALBUM!

My coming-out party! I was the hit of the dance hall!

I met the nicest boy on the beach at Atlantic City...his name is Ben Parker! Quite a sheik!

My Wedding Day... Ben has made me the happiest girl alive!

Our brand-new nephew...Peter!

He weighed in at 8 pounds, 3 ounces!

He's the very image of his father!

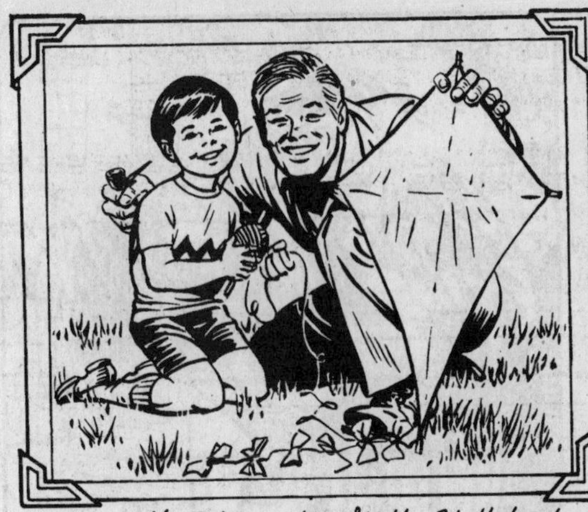

Ben with Peter on his Sixth Birthday! My, how that boy is growing! I'm so glad he came to live with us!

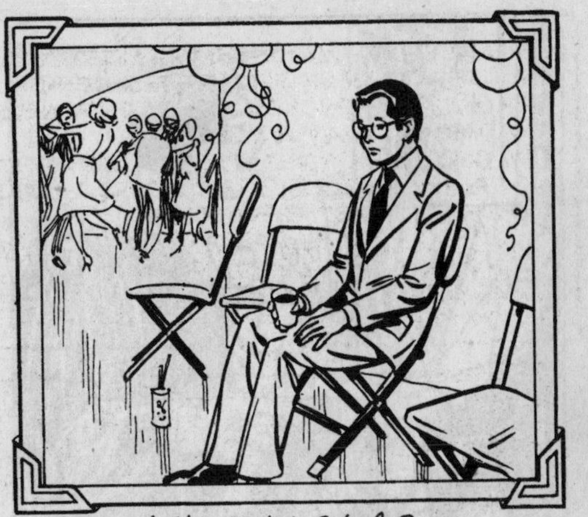

Peter at the Jr. High School Dance. I'm afraid our nephew isn't much of a mixer.

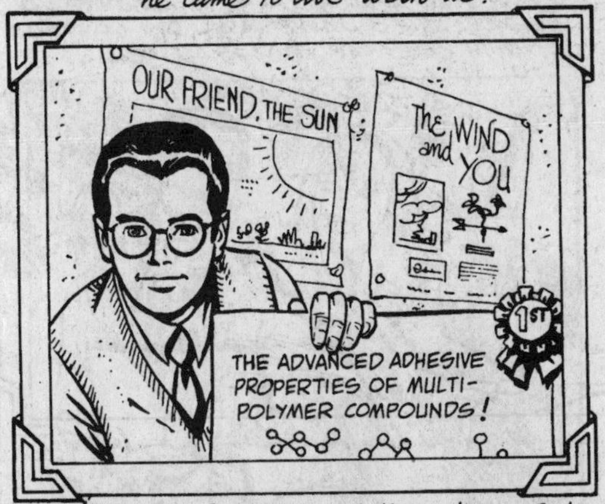
OUR FRIEND, THE SUN
The WIND and YOU
1ST
THE ADVANCED ADHESIVE PROPERTIES OF MULTI-POLYMER COMPOUNDS!

Peter took first prize at the Science Fair again this year... he's such a bright boy.

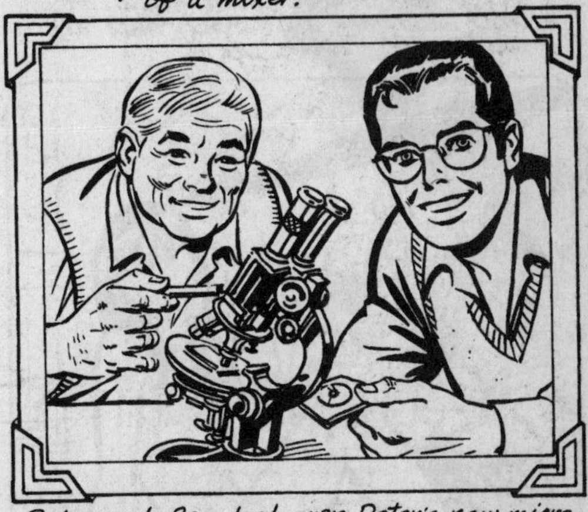

Peter and Ben look over Peter's new microscope. It was a little expensive, but the smile on his face made it all worthwhile!

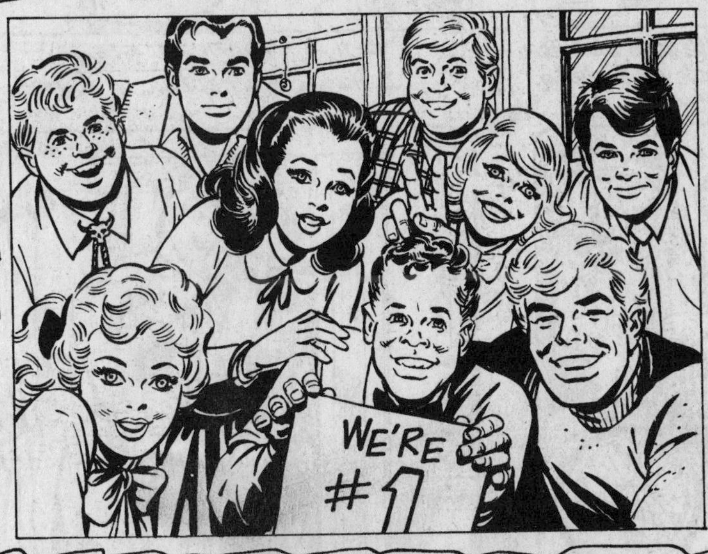
WE'RE
#1

MIDTOWN HIGH STUDENTS CAPTURE TOP HONORS

Nine local students are among the fifty winners of the Empire State Awards for meritorious academic and athletic performance. They are (shown here from left to right) Elizabeth Allen, Peter Doman, Eugene "Flash" Thompson (first row), William Oakes, Alice Tucker, Nyra Siler, Robert Hinds (second row), Peter Parker, and Richard Thacher (third row).

Peter and his classmates! He looks so handsome without his glasses... I'm glad he outgrew them!

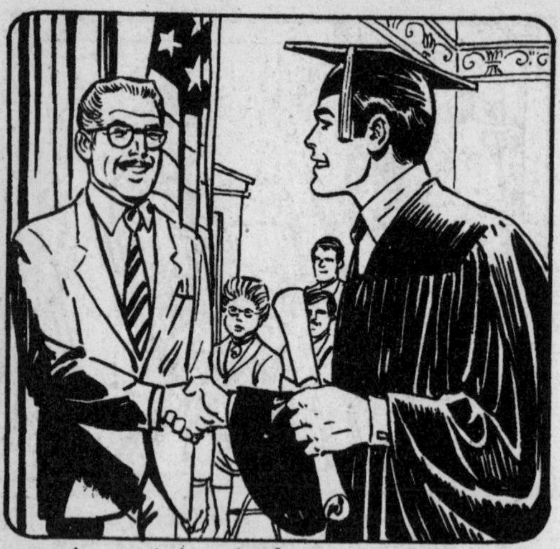

Peter's High School Graduation. It seems like only yesterday that he came to live with us.

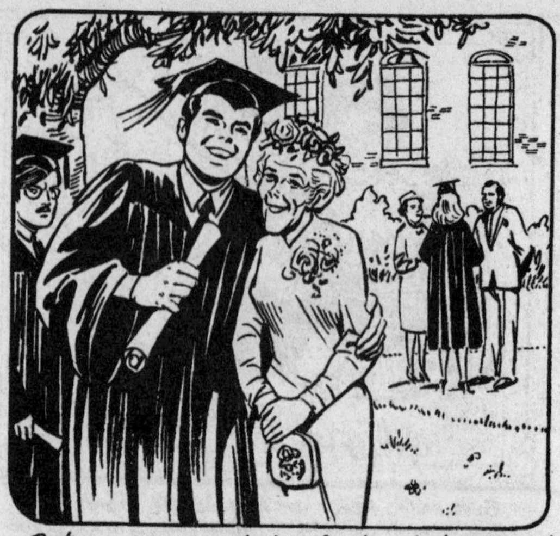

Peter was awarded a full scholarship to Empire State University! I'm so proud! If only Ben were here to see this...

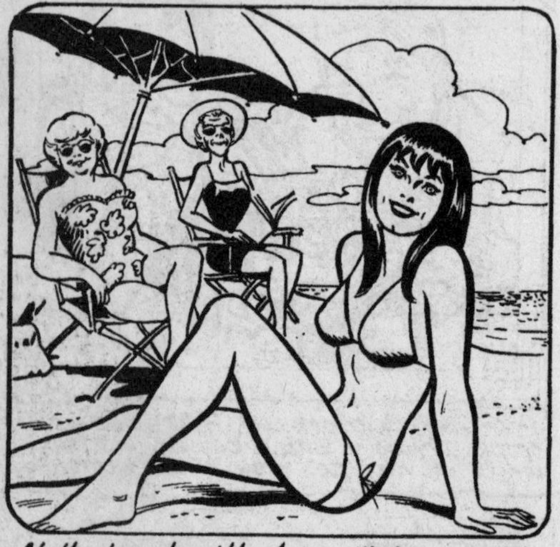

At the beach with Anna Watson and her niece, Mary Jane. Peter took an awfully long time taking this picture!

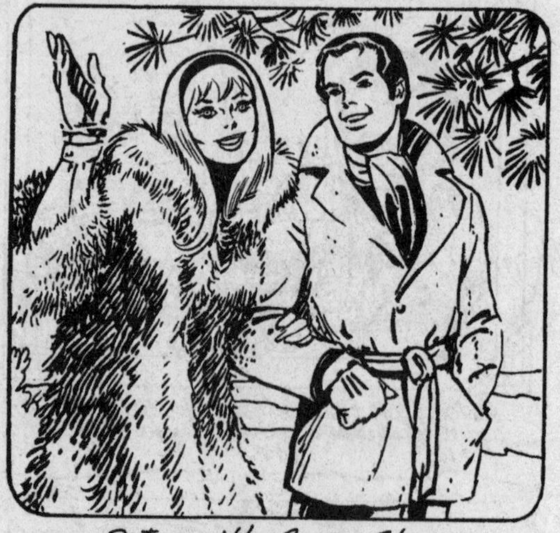

Peter with Gwen Stacy... I think my nephew is in love!

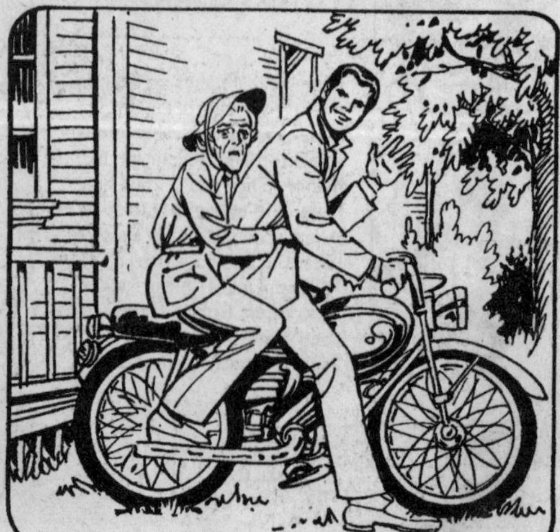

Peter takes me for a ride on his motorcycle... NEVER AGAIN!

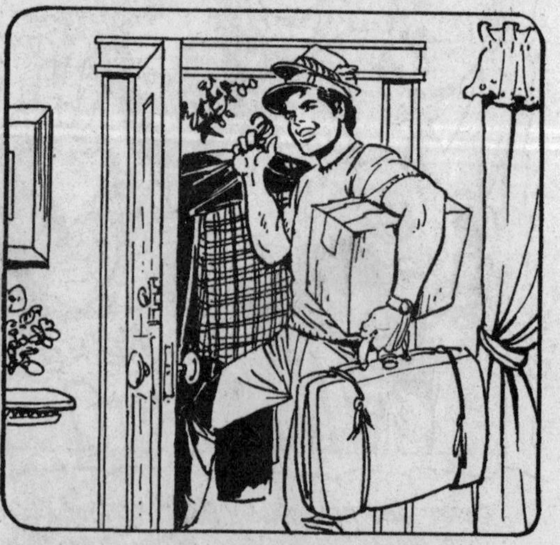

Peter moves out to his own apartment. My boy has become a man...

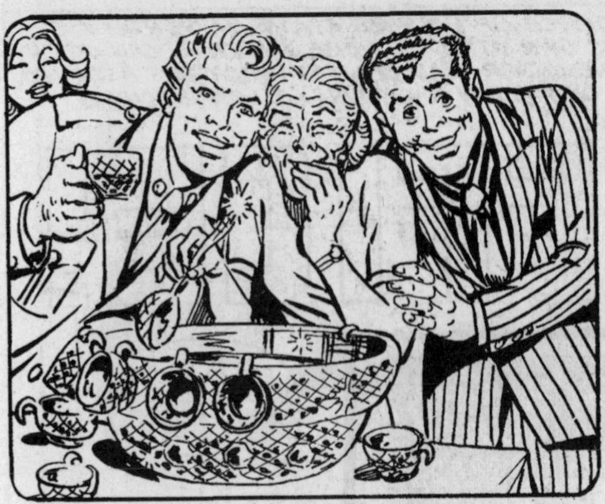

Peter threw this surprise party for his friend, Harry Osborn -- but the way I was treated, you'd have thought it was for **ME**!

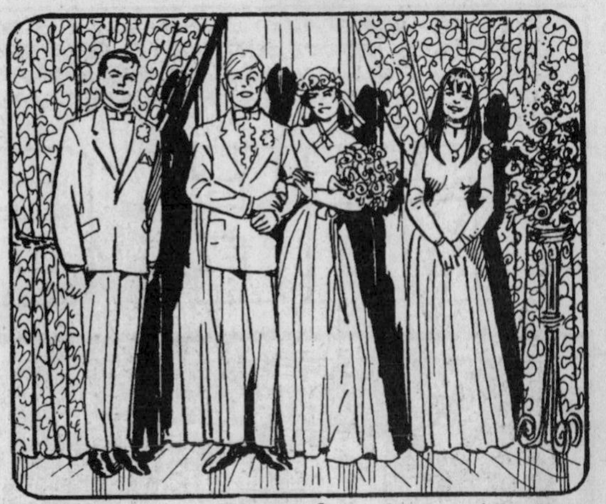

That nice Betty Brant finally tied the knot with Ned Leeds! Peter was the best man --

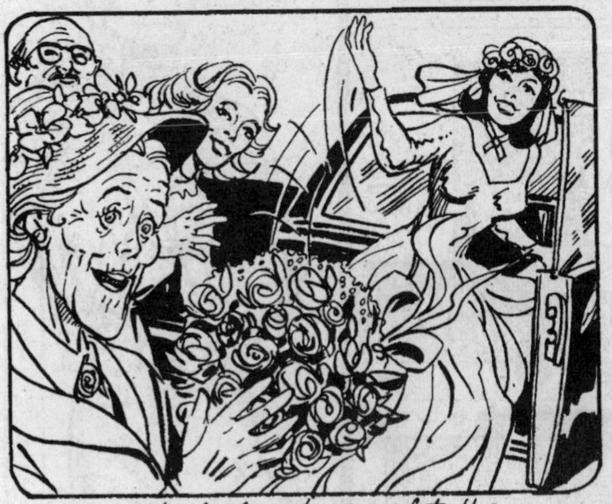

-- and look who caught the bridal bouquet!

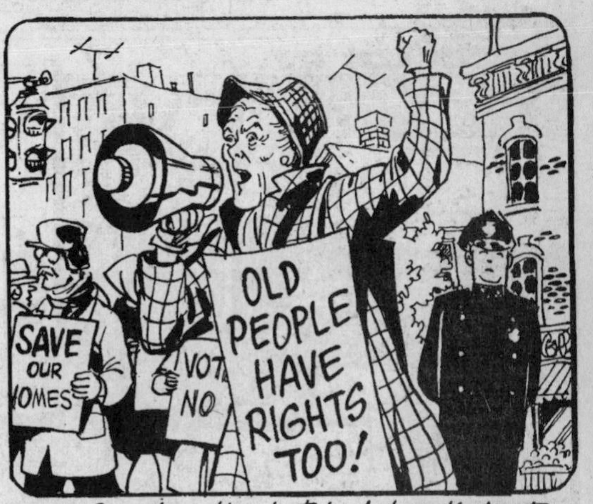
SAVE OUR HOMES
VOT NO
OLD PEOPLE HAVE RIGHTS TOO!

Our landlord tried to eliminate rent control in our building... but we stopped him!

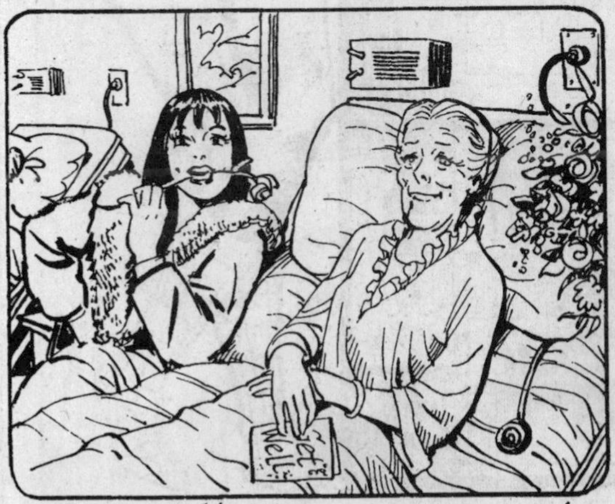

Recuperating from my coronary by-pass operation... Mary Jane's visits were such a comfort!

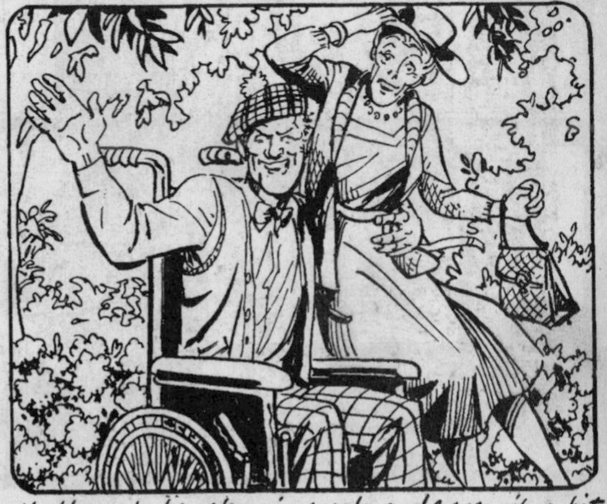

Nathan Lubensky is such a dear--if a bit of a rounder! He reminds me so much of my beloved Ben! I wonder... can a woman find such love **TWICE** in her life?

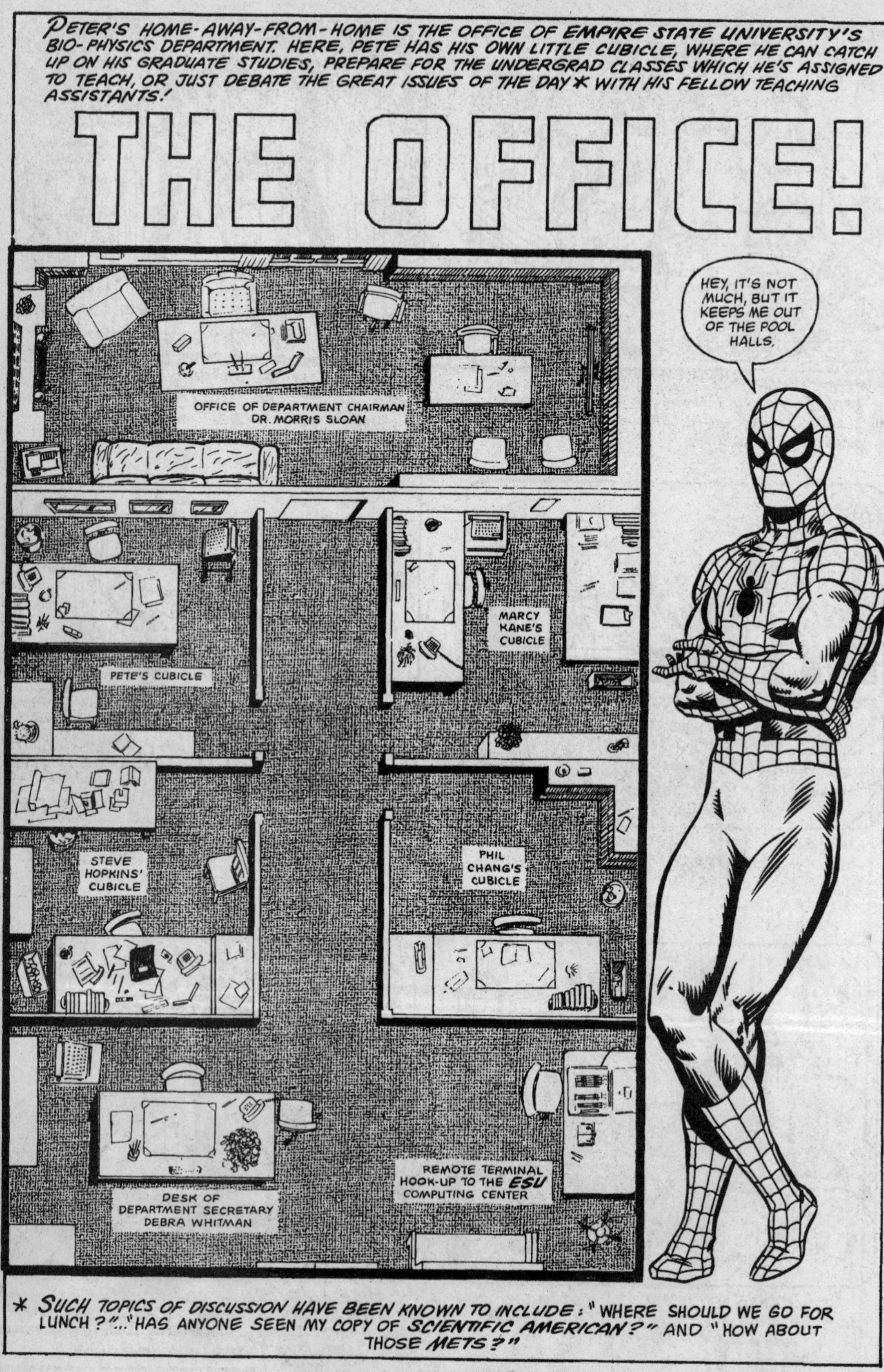
PETER'S HOME-AWAY-FROM-HOME IS THE OFFICE OF EMPIRE STATE UNIVERSITY'S BIO-PHYSICS DEPARTMENT. HERE, PETE HAS HIS OWN LITTLE CUBICLE, WHERE HE CAN CATCH UP ON HIS GRADUATE STUDIES, PREPARE FOR THE UNDERGRAD CLASSES WHICH HE'S ASSIGNED TO TEACH, OR JUST DEBATE THE GREAT ISSUES OF THE DAY* WITH HIS FELLOW TEACHING ASSISTANTS!
THE OFFICE!
HEY, IT'S NOT MUCH, BUT IT KEEPS ME OUT OF THE POOL HALLS.
OFFICE OF DEPARTMENT CHAIRMAN DR. MORRIS SLOAN
MARCY KANE'S CUBICLE
PETE'S CUBICLE
STEVE HOPKINS' CUBICLE
PHIL CHANG'S CUBICLE
REMOTE TERMINAL HOOK-UP TO THE ESU COMPUTING CENTER
DESK OF DEPARTMENT SECRETARY DEBRA WHITMAN
* SUCH TOPICS OF DISCUSSION HAVE BEEN KNOWN TO INCLUDE: "WHERE SHOULD WE GO FOR LUNCH?"..."HAS ANYONE SEEN MY COPY OF SCIENTIFIC AMERICAN?" AND "HOW ABOUT THOSE METS?"

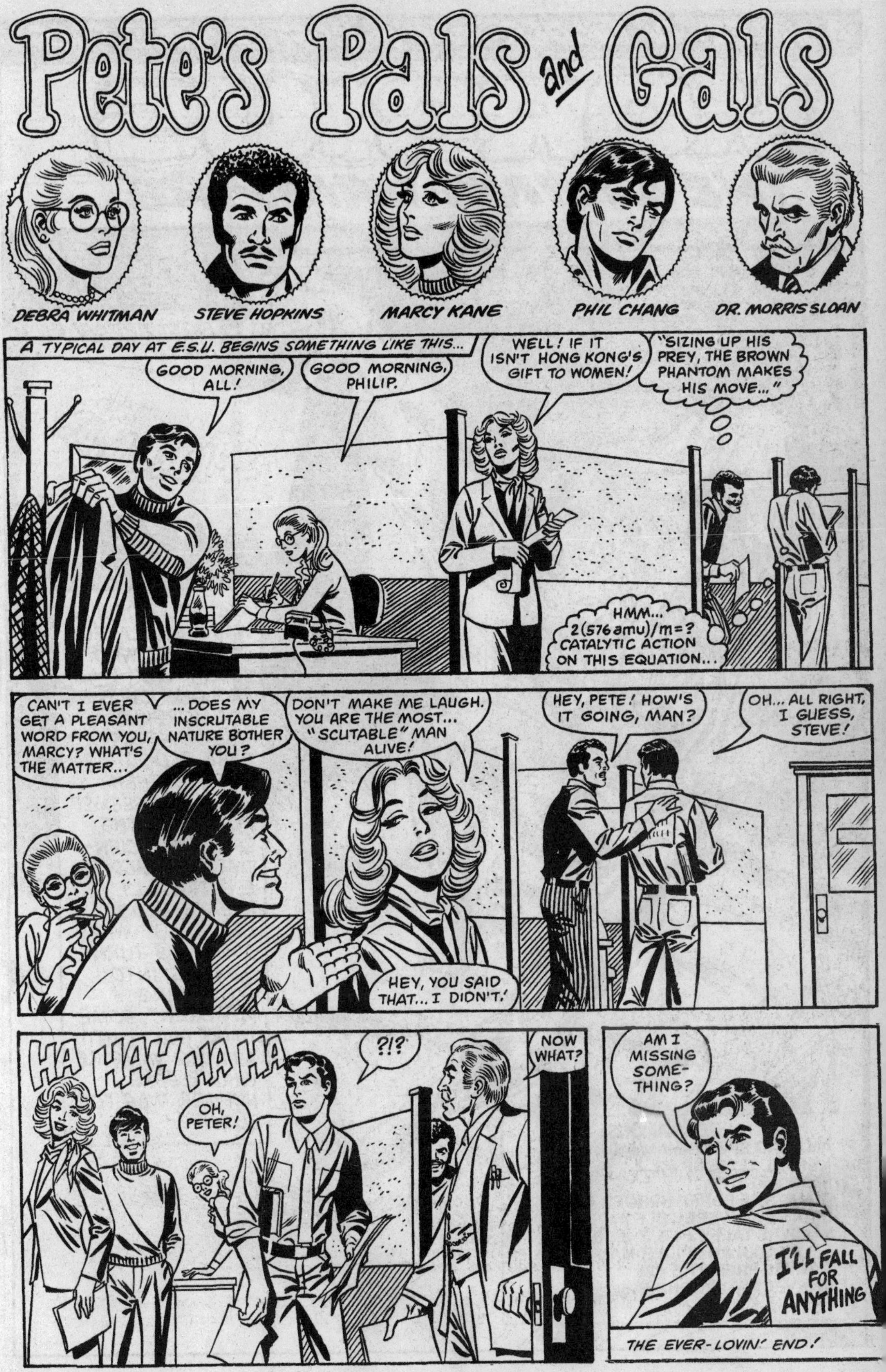
Pete's Pals and Gals
DEBRA WHITMAN
STEVE HOPKINS
MARCY KANE
PHIL CHANG
DR. MORRIS SLOAN
A TYPICAL DAY AT E.S.U. BEGINS SOMETHING LIKE THIS...
GOOD MORNING, ALL!
GOOD MORNING, PHILIP.
WELL! IF IT ISN'T HONG KONG'S GIFT TO WOMEN!
"SIZING UP HIS PREY, THE BROWN PHANTOM MAKES HIS MOVE..."
HMM... 2(576 amu)/m=? CATALYTIC ACTION ON THIS EQUATION...
CAN'T I EVER GET A PLEASANT WORD FROM YOU, MARCY? WHAT'S THE MATTER...
...DOES MY INSCRUTABLE NATURE BOTHER YOU?
DON'T MAKE ME LAUGH. YOU ARE THE MOST... "SCUTABLE" MAN ALIVE!
HEY, YOU SAID THAT... I DIDN'T.!
HEY, PETE! HOW'S IT GOING, MAN?
OH... ALL RIGHT, I GUESS, STEVE!
HA HAH HA HA
OH, PETER!
?!?
NOW WHAT?
AM I MISSING SOME-THING?
I'LL FALL FOR ANYTHING
THE EVER-LOVIN' END!

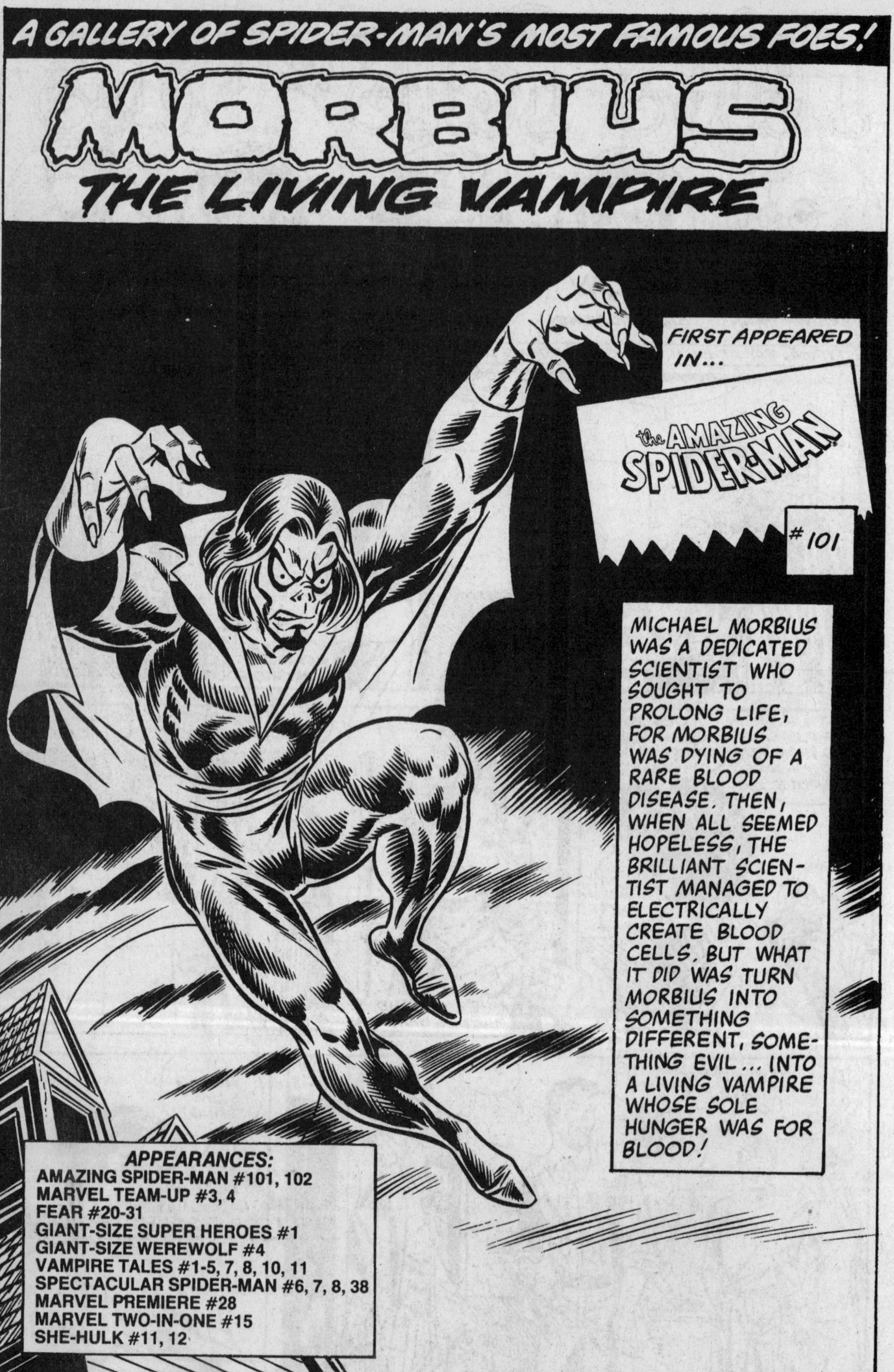
A GALLERY OF SPIDER-MAN'S MOST FAMOUS FOES!
MORBIUS
THE LIVING VAMPIRE
FIRST APPEARED IN...
the AMAZING SPIDER-MAN
#101
MICHAEL MORBIUS WAS A DEDICATED SCIENTIST WHO SOUGHT TO PROLONG LIFE, FOR MORBIUS WAS DYING OF A RARE BLOOD DISEASE. THEN, WHEN ALL SEEMED HOPELESS, THE BRILLIANT SCIENTIST MANAGED TO ELECTRICALLY CREATE BLOOD CELLS. BUT WHAT IT DID WAS TURN MORBIUS INTO SOMETHING DIFFERENT, SOMETHING EVIL... INTO A LIVING VAMPIRE WHOSE SOLE HUNGER WAS FOR BLOOD!
APPEARANCES:
AMAZING SPIDER-MAN #101, 102
MARVEL TEAM-UP #3, 4
FEAR #20-31
GIANT-SIZE SUPER HEROES #1
GIANT-SIZE WEREWOLF #4
VAMPIRE TALES #1-5, 7, 8, 10, 11
SPECTACULAR SPIDER-MAN #6, 7, 8, 38
MARVEL PREMIERE #28
MARVEL TWO-IN-ONE #15
SHE-HULK #11, 12

A GALLERY OF SPIDER-MAN'S MOST FAMOUS FOES!

GIBBON

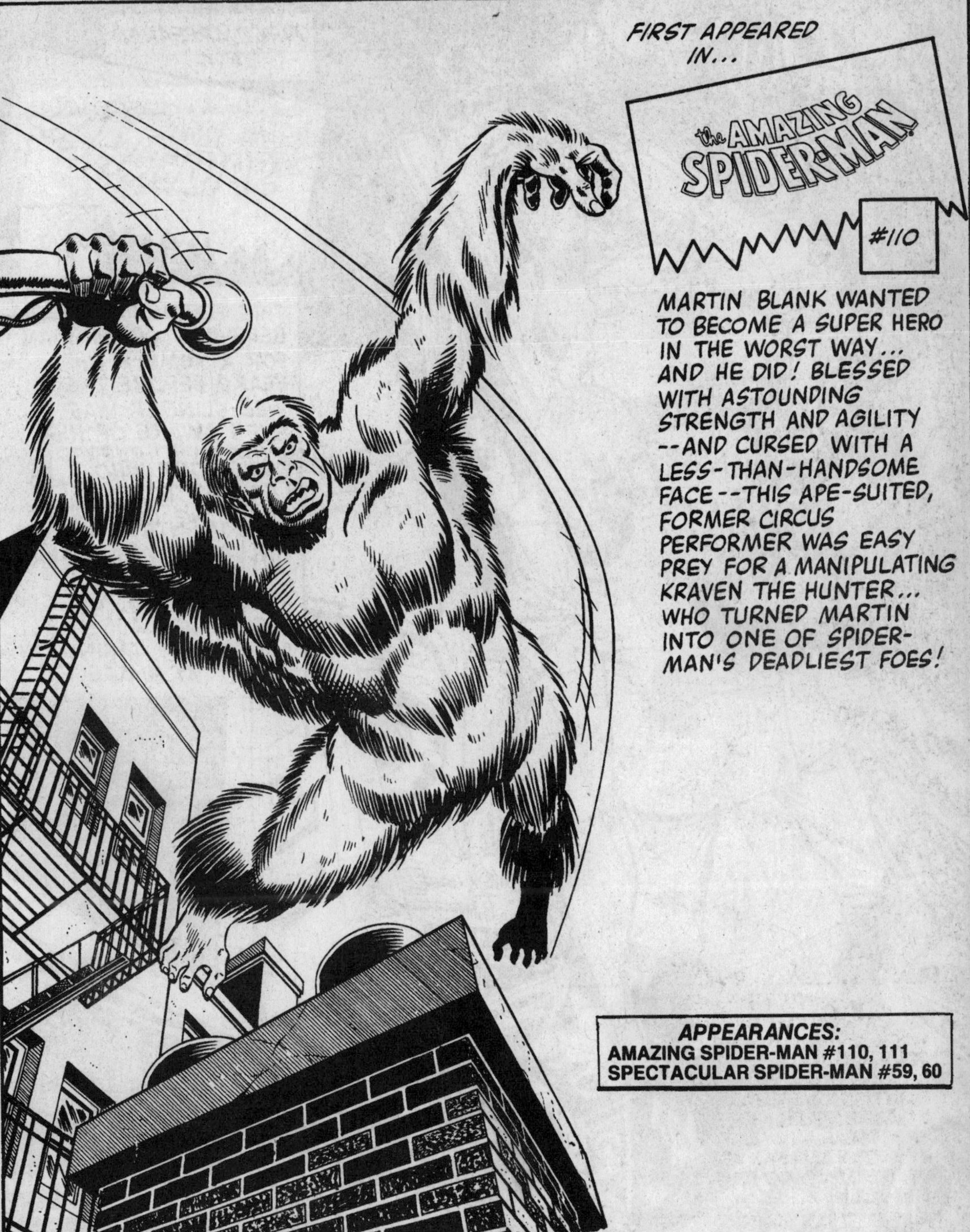
FIRST APPEARED IN...
the AMAZING SPIDER-MAN
#110
MARTIN BLANK WANTED TO BECOME A SUPER HERO IN THE WORST WAY... AND HE DID! BLESSED WITH ASTOUNDING STRENGTH AND AGILITY --AND CURSED WITH A LESS-THAN-HANDSOME FACE--THIS APE-SUITED, FORMER CIRCUS PERFORMER WAS EASY PREY FOR A MANIPULATING KRAVEN THE HUNTER... WHO TURNED MARTIN INTO ONE OF SPIDER-MAN'S DEADLIEST FOES!
APPEARANCES:
AMAZING SPIDER-MAN #110, 111
SPECTACULAR SPIDER-MAN #59, 60

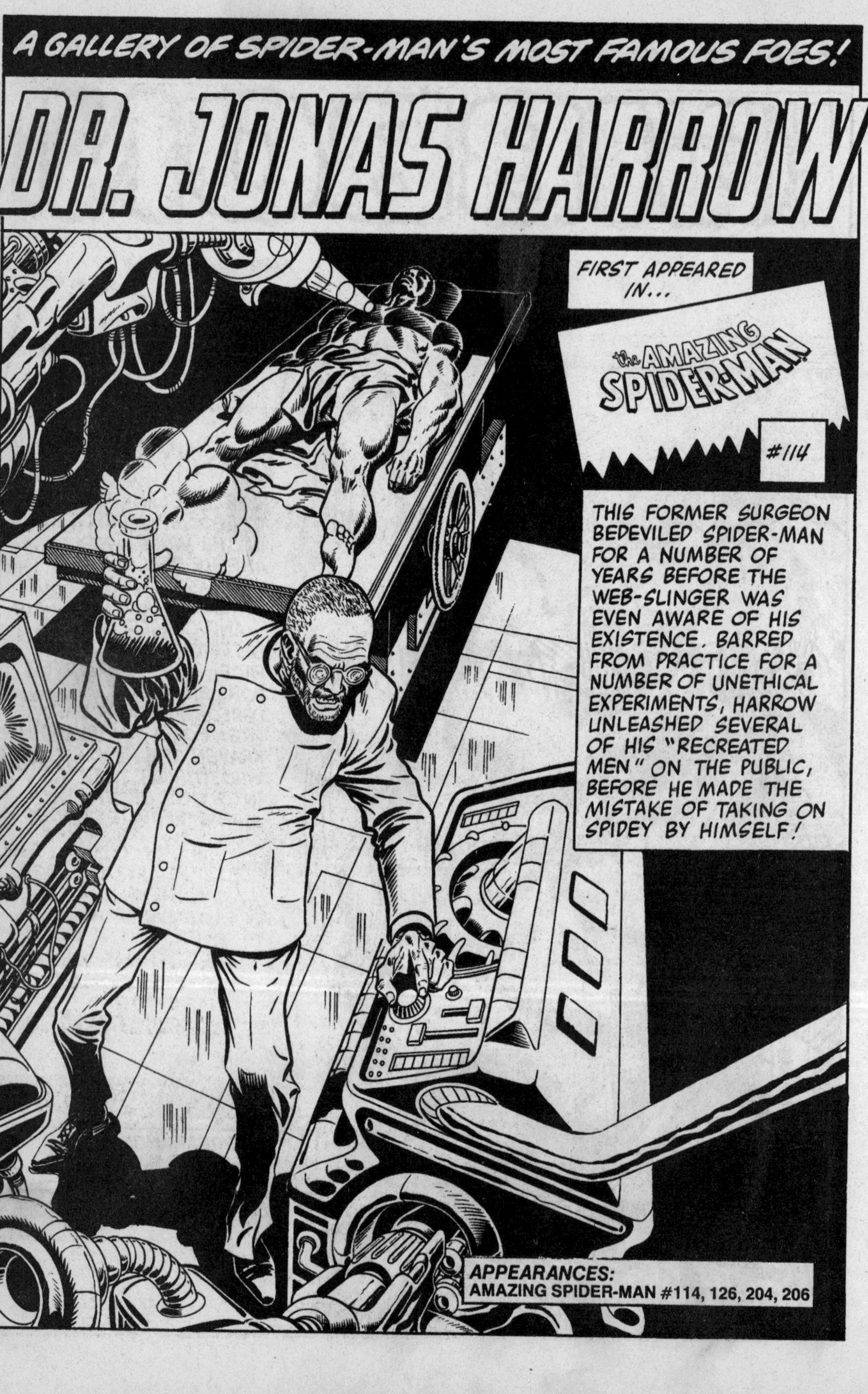
A GALLERY OF SPIDER-MAN'S MOST FAMOUS FOES!
DR. JONAS HARROW
FIRST APPEARED IN...
the AMAZING SPIDER-MAN
#114
THIS FORMER SURGEON BEDEVILED SPIDER-MAN FOR A NUMBER OF YEARS BEFORE THE WEB-SLINGER WAS EVEN AWARE OF HIS EXISTENCE. BARRED FROM PRACTICE FOR A NUMBER OF UNETHICAL EXPERIMENTS, HARROW UNLEASHED SEVERAL OF HIS "RECREATED MEN" ON THE PUBLIC, BEFORE HE MADE THE MISTAKE OF TAKING ON SPIDEY BY HIMSELF!
APPEARANCES:
AMAZING SPIDER-MAN #114, 126, 204, 206

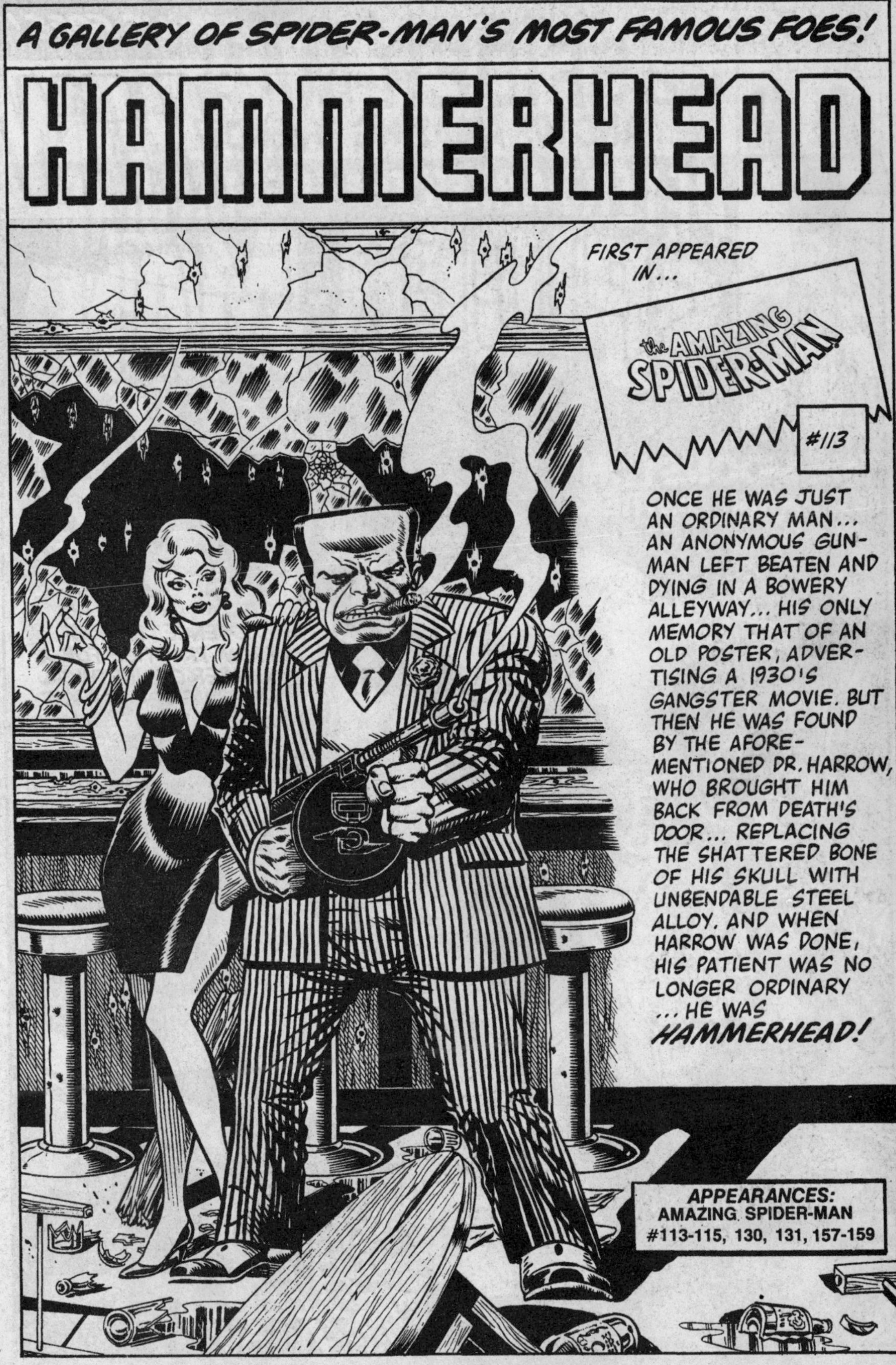

A GALLERY OF SPIDER-MAN'S MOST FAMOUS FOES!
HAMMERHEAD
FIRST APPEARED IN...
the AMAZING SPIDER-MAN
#113
ONCE HE WAS JUST AN ORDINARY MAN... AN ANONYMOUS GUNMAN LEFT BEATEN AND DYING IN A BOWERY ALLEYWAY... HIS ONLY MEMORY THAT OF AN OLD POSTER, ADVERTISING A 1930'S GANGSTER MOVIE. BUT THEN HE WAS FOUND BY THE AFOREMENTIONED DR. HARROW, WHO BROUGHT HIM BACK FROM DEATH'S DOOR... REPLACING THE SHATTERED BONE OF HIS SKULL WITH UNBENDABLE STEEL ALLOY. AND WHEN HARROW WAS DONE, HIS PATIENT WAS NO LONGER ORDINARY ...HE WAS HAMMERHEAD!
APPEARANCES: AMAZING SPIDER-MAN #113-115, 130, 131, 157-159

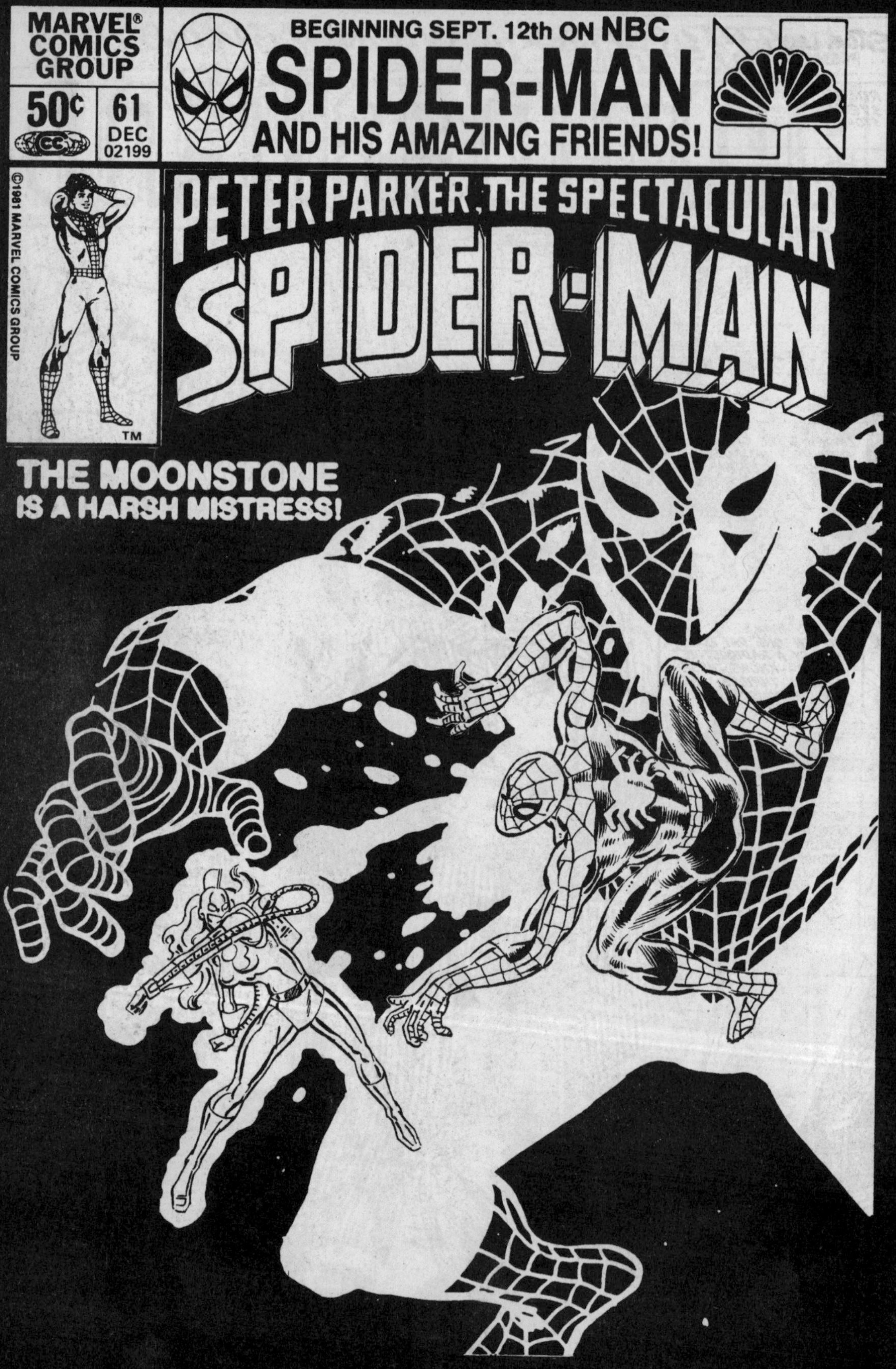

MARVEL® COMICS GROUP
50¢
61
DEC
02199
BEGINNING SEPT. 12th ON NBC
SPIDER-MAN
AND HIS AMAZING FRIENDS!
©1981 MARVEL COMICS GROUP
PETER PARKER, THE SPECTACULAR
SPIDER-MAN
TM
THE MOONSTONE
IS A HARSH MISTRESS!

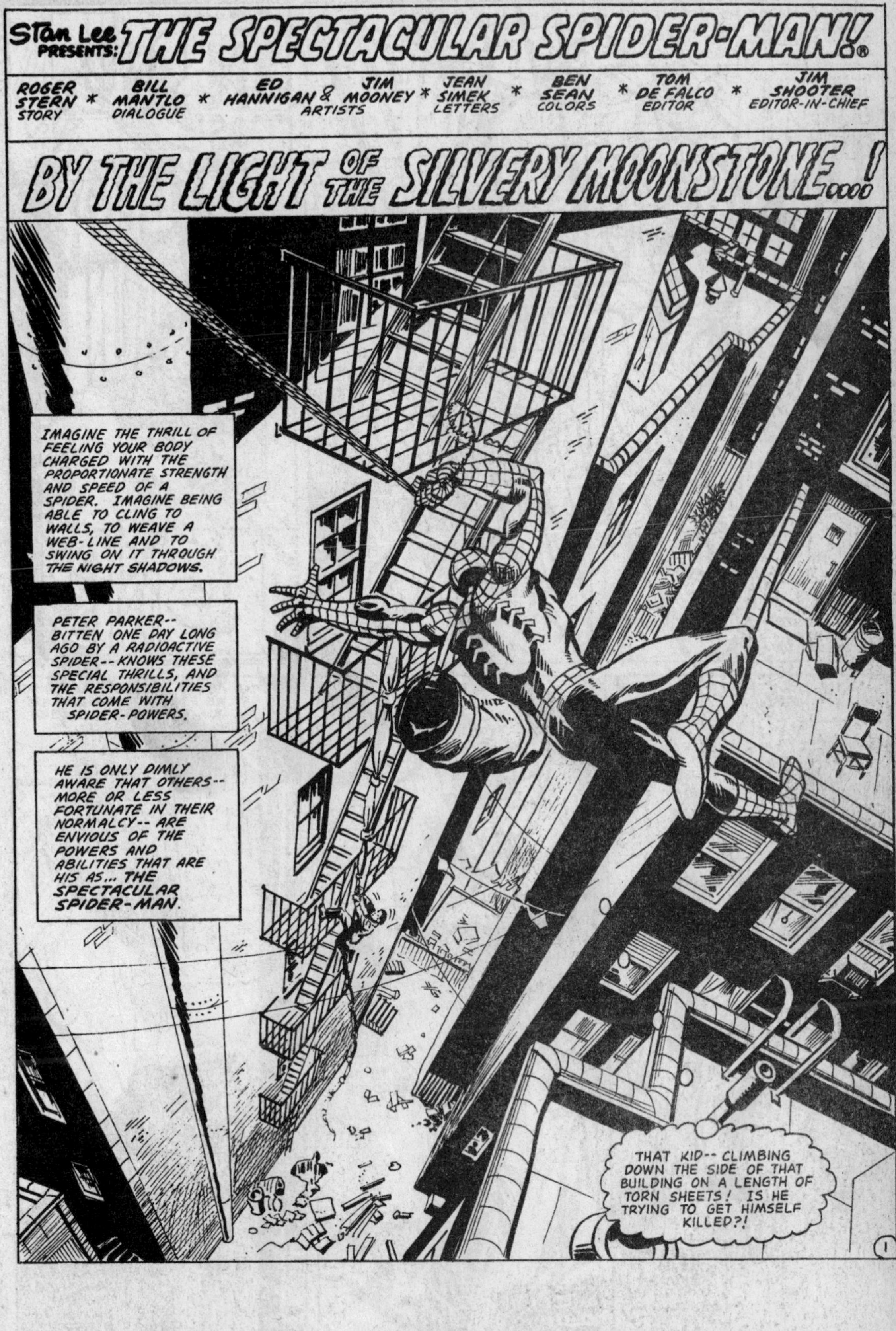
STAN LEE PRESENTS: THE SPECTACULAR SPIDER-MAN!®
ROGER STERN STORY * BILL MANTLO DIALOGUE * ED HANNIGAN & JIM MOONEY ARTISTS * JEAN SIMEK LETTERS * BEN SEAN COLORS * TOM DE FALCO EDITOR * JIM SHOOTER EDITOR-IN-CHIEF
BY THE LIGHT OF THE SILVERY MOONSTONE...!
IMAGINE THE THRILL OF FEELING YOUR BODY CHARGED WITH THE PROPORTIONATE STRENGTH AND SPEED OF A SPIDER. IMAGINE BEING ABLE TO CLING TO WALLS, TO WEAVE A WEB-LINE AND TO SWING ON IT THROUGH THE NIGHT SHADOWS.
PETER PARKER-- BITTEN ONE DAY LONG AGO BY A RADIOACTIVE SPIDER--KNOWS THESE SPECIAL THRILLS, AND THE RESPONSIBILITIES THAT COME WITH SPIDER-POWERS.
HE IS ONLY DIMLY AWARE THAT OTHERS-- MORE OR LESS FORTUNATE IN THEIR NORMALCY-- ARE ENVIOUS OF THE POWERS AND ABILITIES THAT ARE HIS AS... THE SPECTACULAR SPIDER-MAN.
THAT KID-- CLIMBING DOWN THE SIDE OF THAT BUILDING ON A LENGTH OF TORN SHEETS! IS HE TRYING TO GET HIMSELF KILLED?!
1

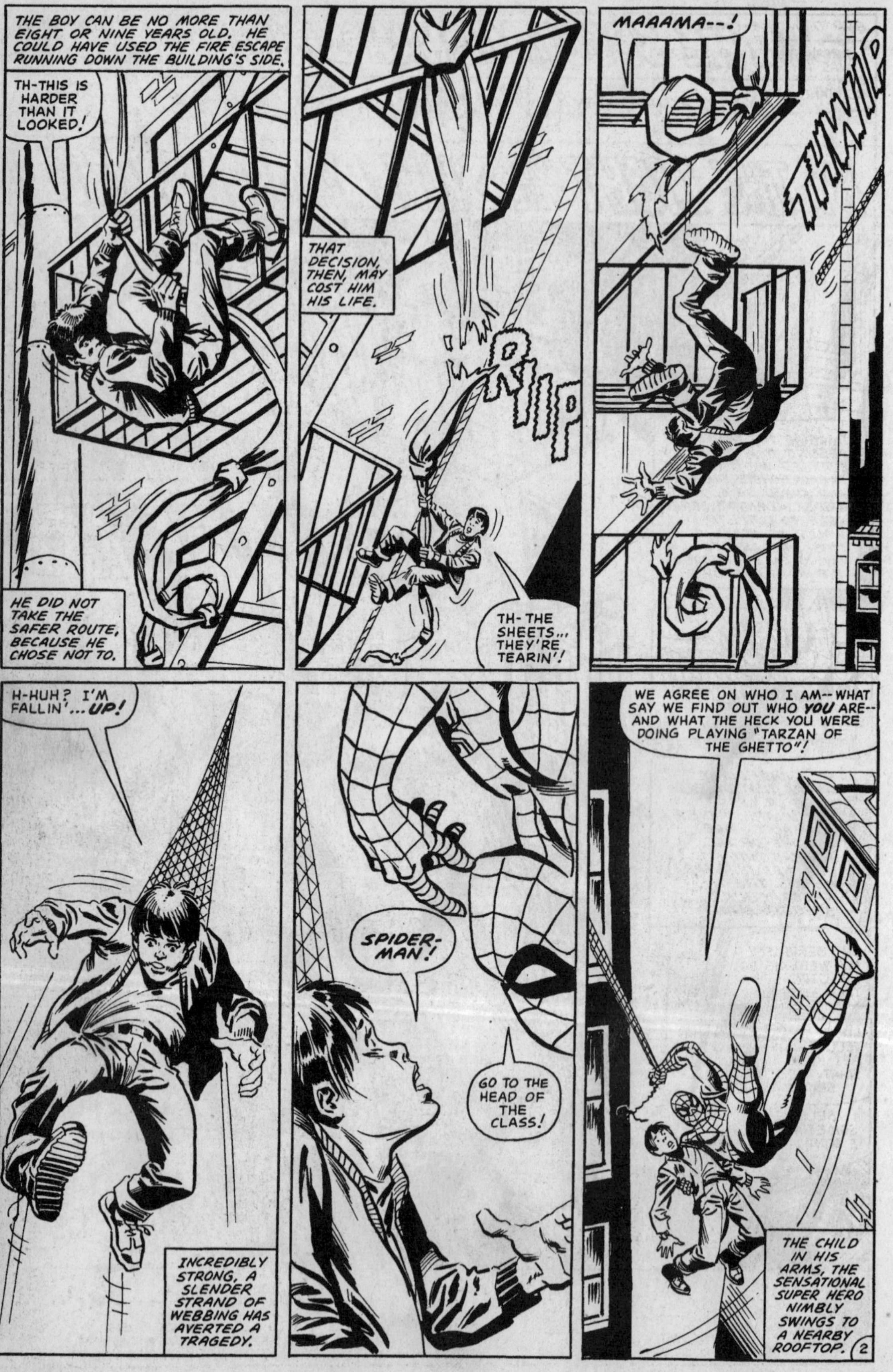
THE BOY CAN BE NO MORE THAN EIGHT OR NINE YEARS OLD. HE COULD HAVE USED THE FIRE ESCAPE RUNNING DOWN THE BUILDING'S SIDE.
TH-THIS IS HARDER THAN IT LOOKED!
HE DID NOT TAKE THE SAFER ROUTE, BECAUSE HE CHOSE NOT TO.
THAT DECISION, THEN, MAY COST HIM HIS LIFE.
RIP
TH- THE SHEETS... THEY'RE TEARIN'!
MAAAMA--!
THWIP
H-HUH? I'M FALLIN'... UP!
INCREDIBLY STRONG, A SLENDER STRAND OF WEBBING HAS AVERTED A TRAGEDY.
SPIDER-MAN!
GO TO THE HEAD OF THE CLASS!
WE AGREE ON WHO I AM--WHAT SAY WE FIND OUT WHO YOU ARE-- AND WHAT THE HECK YOU WERE DOING PLAYING "TARZAN OF THE GHETTO"!
THE CHILD IN HIS ARMS, THE SENSATIONAL SUPER HERO NIMBLY SWINGS TO A NEARBY ROOFTOP.
2

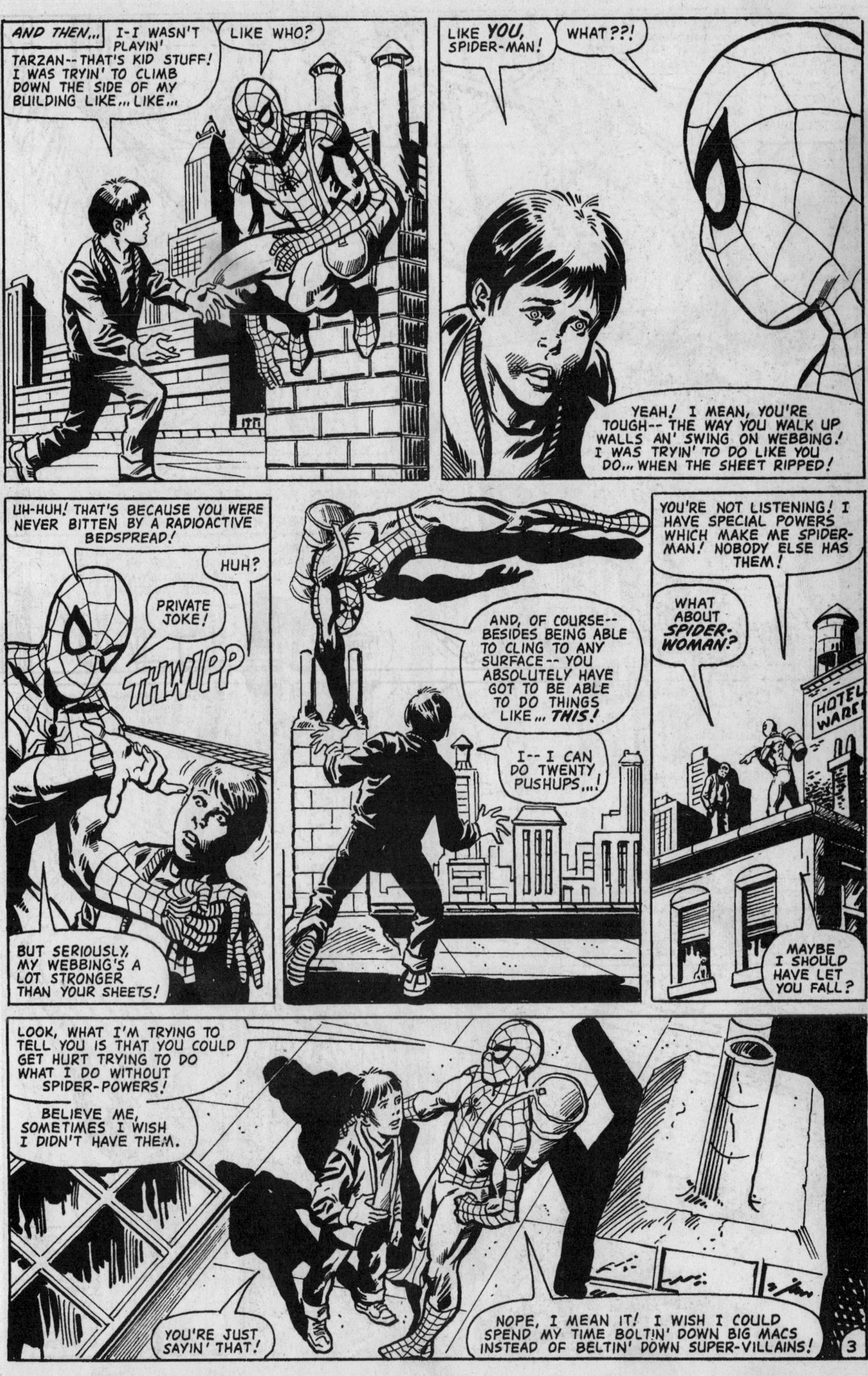
AND THEN...
I-I WASN'T PLAYIN' TARZAN--THAT'S KID STUFF! I WAS TRYIN' TO CLIMB DOWN THE SIDE OF MY BUILDING LIKE... LIKE...
LIKE WHO?
LIKE YOU, SPIDER-MAN!
WHAT??!
YEAH! I MEAN, YOU'RE TOUGH-- THE WAY YOU WALK UP WALLS AN' SWING ON WEBBING! I WAS TRYIN' TO DO LIKE YOU DO... WHEN THE SHEET RIPPED!
UH-HUH! THAT'S BECAUSE YOU WERE NEVER BITTEN BY A RADIOACTIVE BEDSPREAD!
HUH?
PRIVATE JOKE!
THWIPP
BUT SERIOUSLY, MY WEBBING'S A LOT STRONGER THAN YOUR SHEETS!
AND, OF COURSE-- BESIDES BEING ABLE TO CLING TO ANY SURFACE-- YOU ABSOLUTELY HAVE GOT TO BE ABLE TO DO THINGS LIKE... THIS!
I-- I CAN DO TWENTY PUSHUPS...!
YOU'RE NOT LISTENING! I HAVE SPECIAL POWERS WHICH MAKE ME SPIDER-MAN! NOBODY ELSE HAS THEM!
WHAT ABOUT SPIDER-WOMAN?
HOTEL WARE
MAYBE I SHOULD HAVE LET YOU FALL?
LOOK, WHAT I'M TRYING TO TELL YOU IS THAT YOU COULD GET HURT TRYING TO DO WHAT I DO WITHOUT SPIDER-POWERS!
BELIEVE ME, SOMETIMES I WISH I DIDN'T HAVE THEM.
YOU'RE JUST SAYIN' THAT!
NOPE, I MEAN IT! I WISH I COULD SPEND MY TIME BOLTIN' DOWN BIG MACS INSTEAD OF BELTIN' DOWN SUPER-VILLAINS!

CHECK IT OUT! SUPER HEROES DON'T GET OFF WHEN THE THREE O'CLOCK BELL RINGS! IT'S A FULL TIME JOB... WITHOUT PAY!

GEE, EVEN I GET AN ALLOWANCE!

LUCKY YOU!

SCOOT ALONG HOME -- USE THE STAIRS, NOT THE SHEETS -- AND KEEP OFF THE CEILING, OKAY?

OKAY, SPIDER-MAN... AND THANKS!

NICE KID! HOPE I PAINTED A GRIM ENOUGH PICTURE OF SUPER-HEROING TO SEND HIM BACK TO HIS HOMEWORK!

SPEAKING OF WHICH, I DIDN'T HAVE TIME TO DO MINE TONIGHT!

I DON'T THINK THAT DR. SLOAN, MY DEPARTMENT CHAIRMAN, IS GOING TO ACCEPT PETER PARKER'S STORY --

-- THAT HE COULDN'T FINISH HIS CHEM ASSIGNMENT BECAUSE HE WAS OUT SAVING A KID'S LIFE AS SPIDER-MAN!

EMPIRE STATE UNIVERSITY...

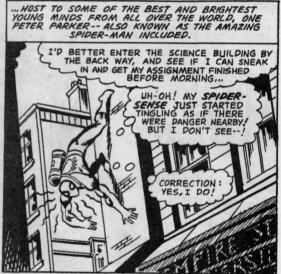

...HOST TO SOME OF THE BEST AND BRIGHTEST YOUNG MINDS FROM ALL OVER THE WORLD, ONE PETER PARKER -- ALSO KNOWN AS THE AMAZING SPIDER-MAN INCLUDED.

I'D BETTER ENTER THE SCIENCE BUILDING BY THE BACK WAY, AND SEE IF I CAN SNEAK IN AND GET MY ASSIGNMENT FINISHED BEFORE MORNING...

UH-OH! MY SPIDER-SENSE JUST STARTED TINGLING AS IF THERE WERE DANGER NEARBY! BUT I DON'T SEE --!

CORRECTION: YES, I DO!

THROUGH ONE-WAY EYE LENSES, SPIDER-MAN SPIES A FURTIVE FIGURE APPROACHING THE REAR EXIT OF THE ESU SCIENCE BUILDING.

SCIENCE BUILDING REAR LANDING

NO ADMITTANCE

NO PAR

THAT DOOR IS ALWAYS LOCKED! WHOEVER HE IS, HE'LL NEVER GET IN --

NO ADM

SCIENCE BUILDIN

-- THAT WAY???

HOLY COW! HE'S WALKING RIGHT THROUGH THE WALL!

NO ADM

4

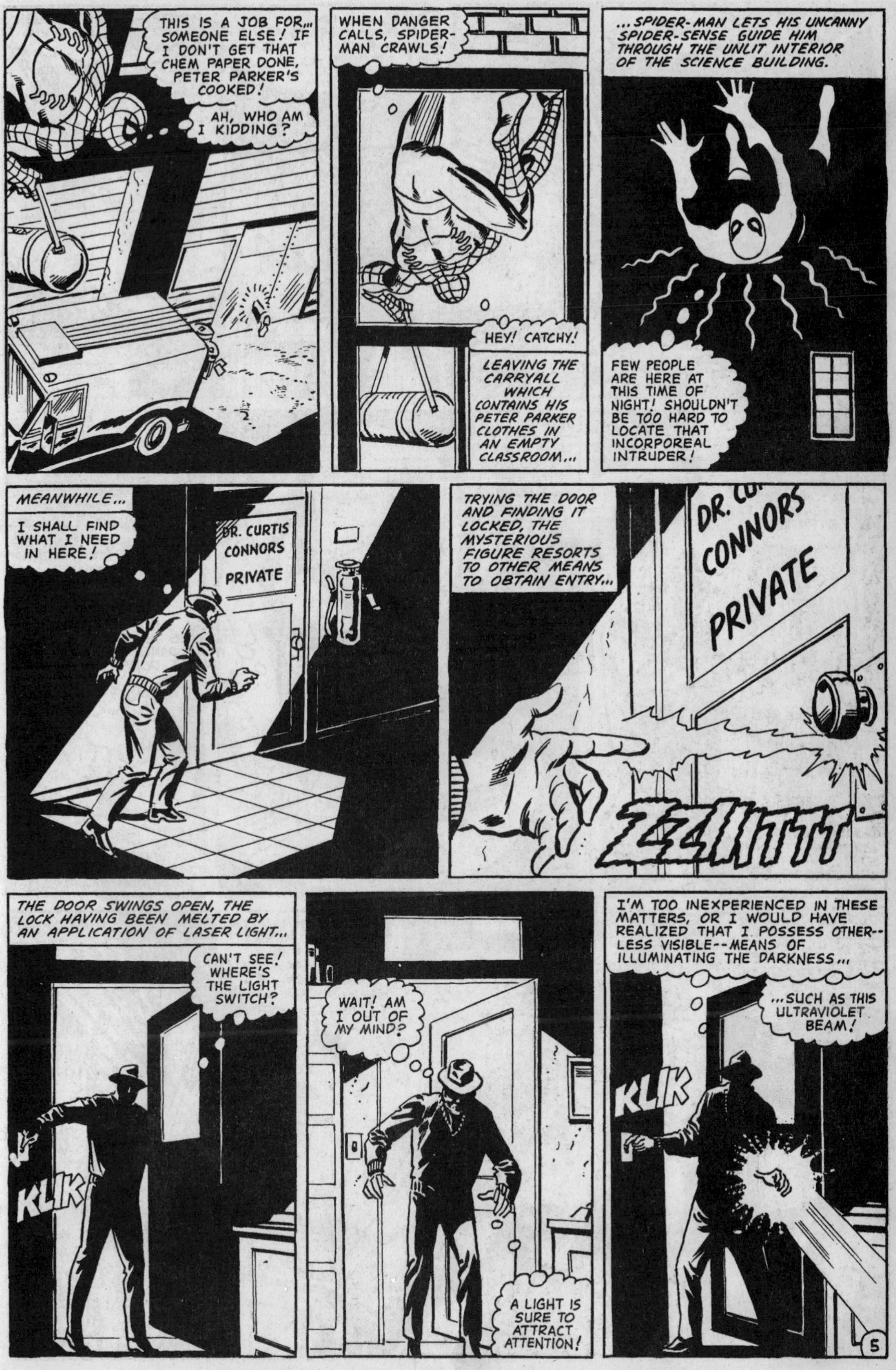
THIS IS A JOB FOR... SOMEONE ELSE! IF I DON'T GET THAT CHEM PAPER DONE, PETER PARKER'S COOKED!
AH, WHO AM I KIDDING?
WHEN DANGER CALLS, SPIDER-MAN CRAWLS!
HEY! CATCHY!
LEAVING THE CARRYALL WHICH CONTAINS HIS PETER PARKER CLOTHES IN AN EMPTY CLASSROOM...
...SPIDER-MAN LETS HIS UNCANNY SPIDER-SENSE GUIDE HIM THROUGH THE UNLIT INTERIOR OF THE SCIENCE BUILDING.
FEW PEOPLE ARE HERE AT THIS TIME OF NIGHT! SHOULDN'T BE TOO HARD TO LOCATE THAT INCORPOREAL INTRUDER!
MEANWHILE...
I SHALL FIND WHAT I NEED IN HERE!
DR. CURTIS CONNORS PRIVATE
TRYING THE DOOR AND FINDING IT LOCKED, THE MYSTERIOUS FIGURE RESORTS TO OTHER MEANS TO OBTAIN ENTRY...
CONNORS PRIVATE
ZZAHTTT
THE DOOR SWINGS OPEN, THE LOCK HAVING BEEN MELTED BY AN APPLICATION OF LASER LIGHT...
CAN'T SEE! WHERE'S THE LIGHT SWITCH?
KLIK
WAIT! AM I OUT OF MY MIND?
A LIGHT IS SURE TO ATTRACT ATTENTION!
I'M TOO INEXPERIENCED IN THESE MATTERS, OR I WOULD HAVE REALIZED THAT I POSSESS OTHER--LESS VISIBLE--MEANS OF ILLUMINATING THE DARKNESS...
...SUCH AS THIS ULTRAVIOLET BEAM!
KLIK
5

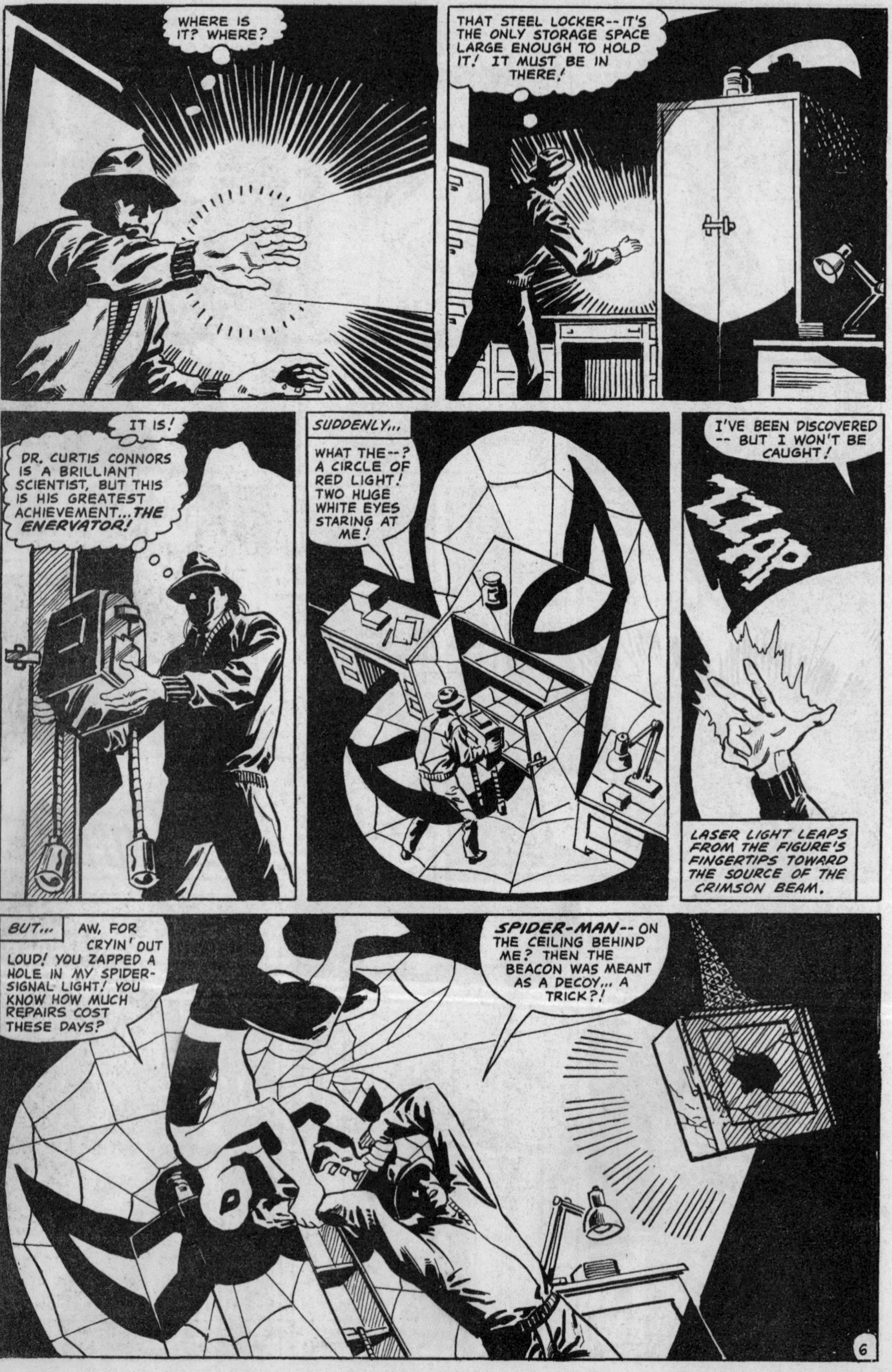
WHERE IS IT? WHERE?
THAT STEEL LOCKER-- IT'S THE ONLY STORAGE SPACE LARGE ENOUGH TO HOLD IT! IT MUST BE IN THERE!
IT IS!
DR. CURTIS CONNORS IS A BRILLIANT SCIENTIST, BUT THIS IS HIS GREATEST ACHIEVEMENT... THE ENERVATOR!
SUDDENLY...
WHAT THE--? A CIRCLE OF RED LIGHT! TWO HUGE WHITE EYES STARING AT ME!
I'VE BEEN DISCOVERED -- BUT I WON'T BE CAUGHT!
ZZAP
LASER LIGHT LEAPS FROM THE FIGURE'S FINGERTIPS TOWARD THE SOURCE OF THE CRIMSON BEAM.
BUT...
AW, FOR CRYIN' OUT LOUD! YOU ZAPPED A HOLE IN MY SPIDER-SIGNAL LIGHT! YOU KNOW HOW MUCH REPAIRS COST THESE DAYS?
SPIDER-MAN-- ON THE CEILING BEHIND ME? THEN THE BEACON WAS MEANT AS A DECOY... A TRICK?!
6

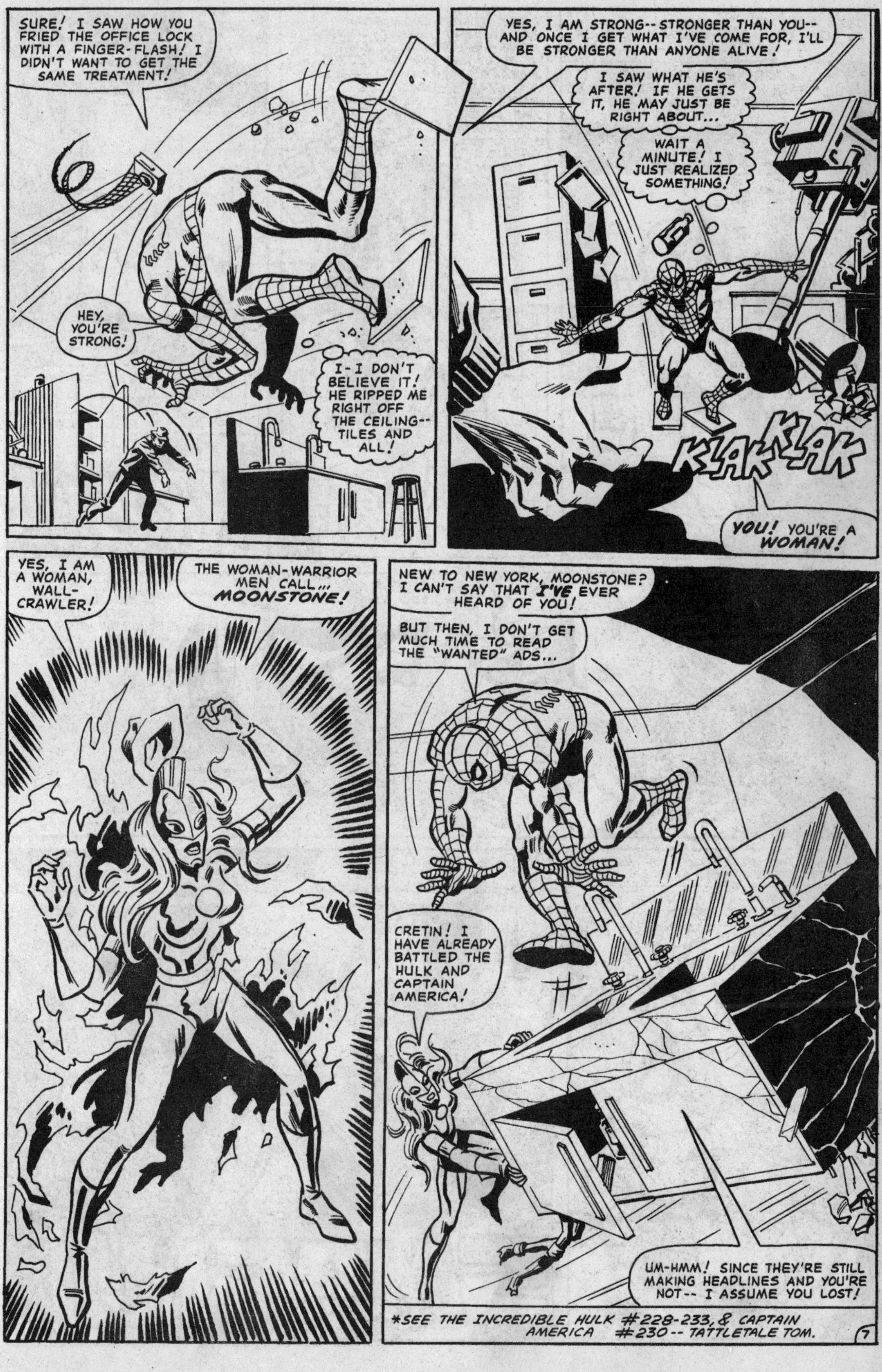
SURE! I SAW HOW YOU FRIED THE OFFICE LOCK WITH A FINGER-FLASH! I DIDN'T WANT TO GET THE SAME TREATMENT!
HEY, YOU'RE STRONG!
I-I DON'T BELIEVE IT! HE RIPPED ME RIGHT OFF THE CEILING--TILES AND ALL!
YES, I AM STRONG--STRONGER THAN YOU--AND ONCE I GET WHAT I'VE COME FOR, I'LL BE STRONGER THAN ANYONE ALIVE!
I SAW WHAT HE'S AFTER! IF HE GETS IT, HE MAY JUST BE RIGHT ABOUT...
WAIT A MINUTE! I JUST REALIZED SOMETHING!
KLAK KLAK
YOU! YOU'RE A WOMAN!
YES, I AM A WOMAN, WALL-CRAWLER!
THE WOMAN-WARRIOR MEN CALL... MOONSTONE!
NEW TO NEW YORK, MOONSTONE? I CAN'T SAY THAT I'VE EVER HEARD OF YOU!
BUT THEN, I DON'T GET MUCH TIME TO READ THE "WANTED" ADS...
CRETIN! I HAVE ALREADY BATTLED THE HULK AND CAPTAIN AMERICA!
UM-HMM! SINCE THEY'RE STILL MAKING HEADLINES AND YOU'RE NOT-- I ASSUME YOU LOST!
*SEE THE INCREDIBLE HULK #228-233, & CAPTAIN AMERICA #230 -- TATTLETALE TOM.
7

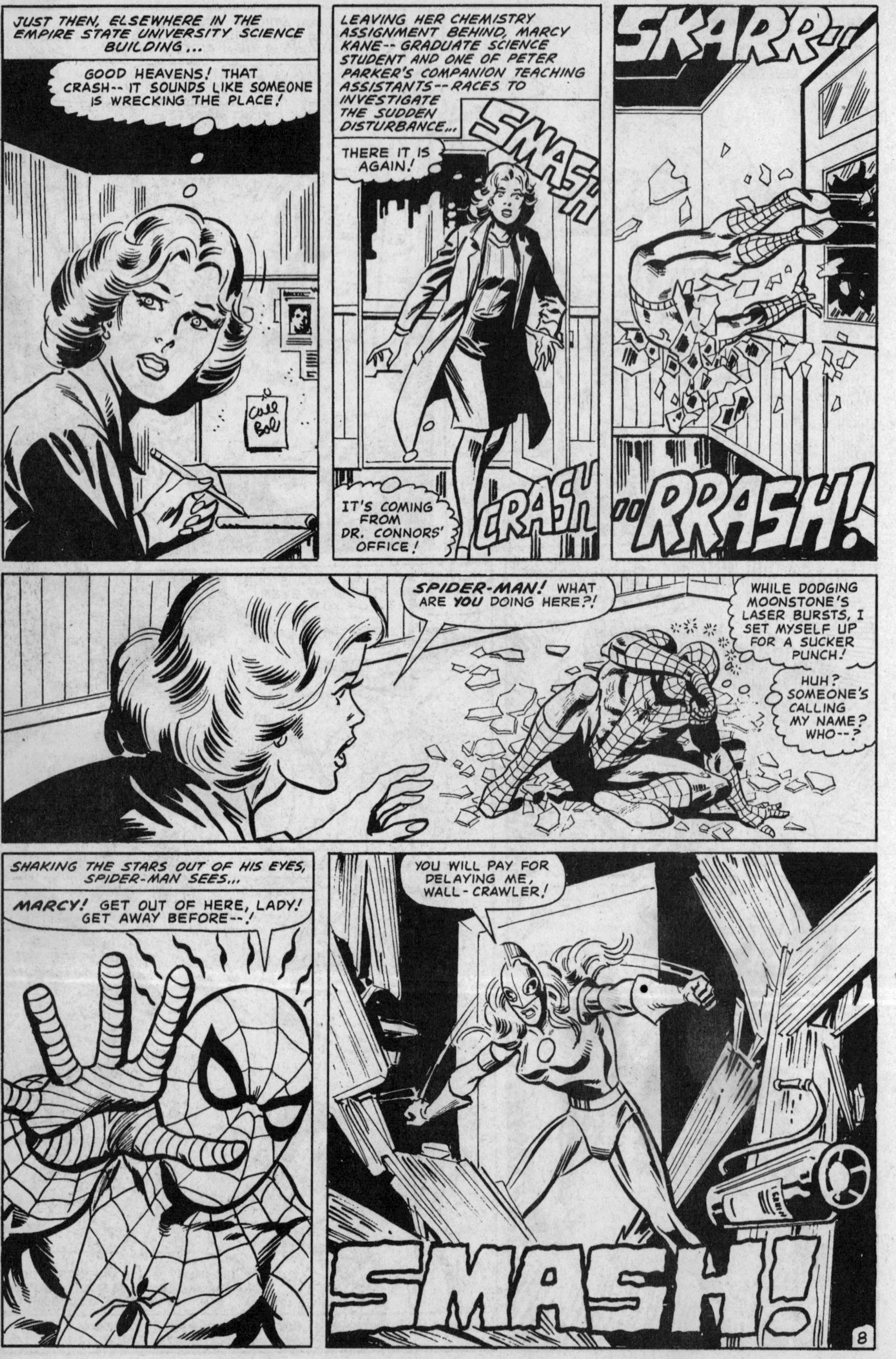

JUST THEN, ELSEWHERE IN THE EMPIRE STATE UNIVERSITY SCIENCE BUILDING...
GOOD HEAVENS! THAT CRASH-- IT SOUNDS LIKE SOMEONE IS WRECKING THE PLACE!
LEAVING HER CHEMISTRY ASSIGNMENT BEHIND, MARCY KANE-- GRADUATE SCIENCE STUDENT AND ONE OF PETER PARKER'S COMPANION TEACHING ASSISTANTS--RACES TO INVESTIGATE THE SUDDEN DISTURBANCE...
SMASH
THERE IT IS AGAIN!
IT'S COMING FROM DR. CONNORS' OFFICE!
CRASH
SKARR-..
..RRASH!
SPIDER-MAN! WHAT ARE YOU DOING HERE?!
WHILE DODGING MOONSTONE'S LASER BURSTS, I SET MYSELF UP FOR A SUCKER PUNCH!
HUH? SOMEONE'S CALLING MY NAME? WHO--?
SHAKING THE STARS OUT OF HIS EYES, SPIDER-MAN SEES...
MARCY! GET OUT OF HERE, LADY! GET AWAY BEFORE--!
YOU WILL PAY FOR DELAYING ME, WALL-CRAWLER!
SMASH!

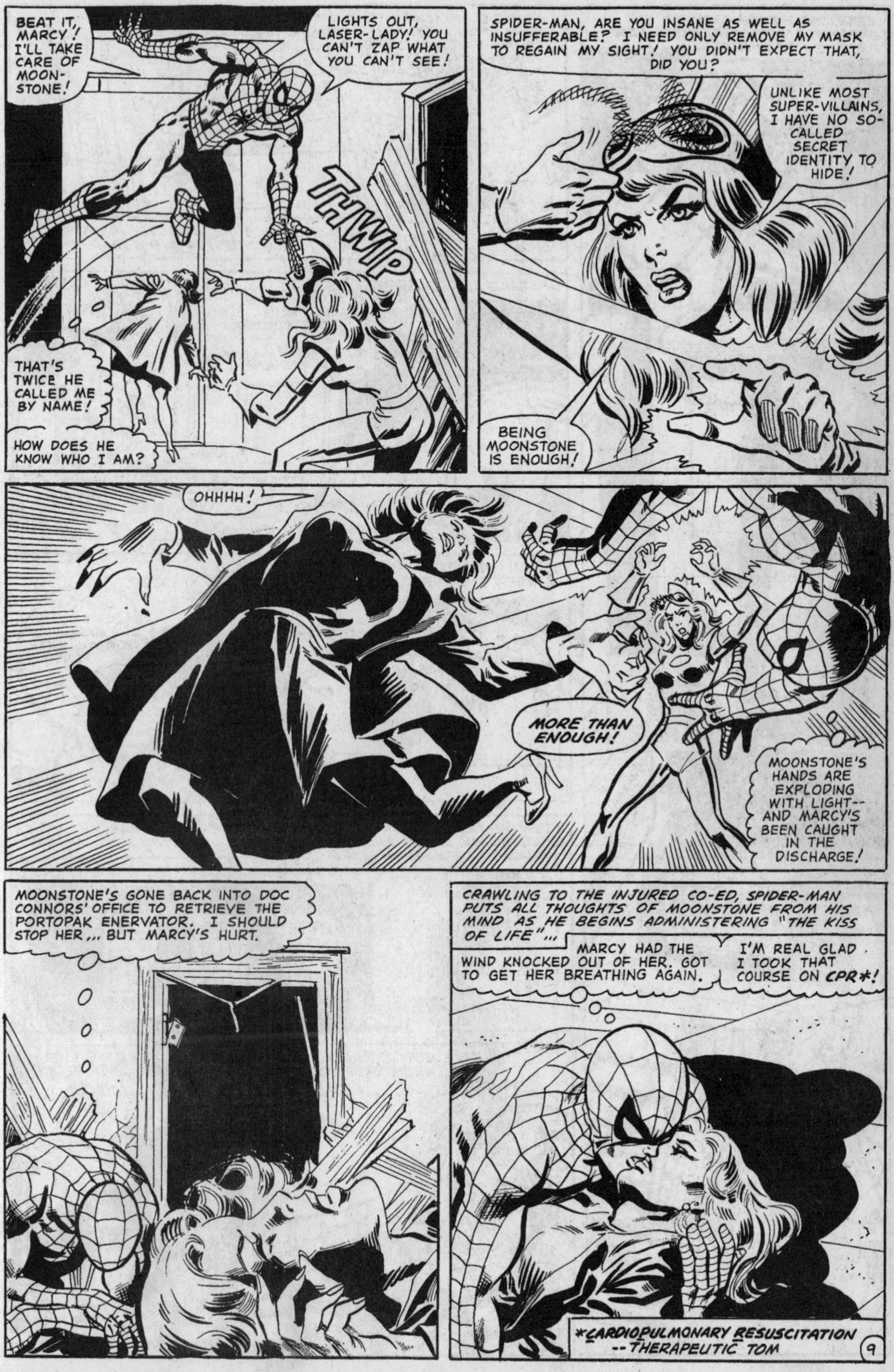

BEAT IT, MARCY! I'LL TAKE CARE OF MOON-STONE!
LIGHTS OUT, LASER-LADY! YOU CAN'T ZAP WHAT YOU CAN'T SEE!
THWIP
THAT'S TWICE HE CALLED ME BY NAME!
HOW DOES HE KNOW WHO I AM?
SPIDER-MAN, ARE YOU INSANE AS WELL AS INSUFFERABLE? I NEED ONLY REMOVE MY MASK TO REGAIN MY SIGHT! YOU DIDN'T EXPECT THAT, DID YOU?
UNLIKE MOST SUPER-VILLAINS, I HAVE NO SO-CALLED SECRET IDENTITY TO HIDE!
BEING MOONSTONE IS ENOUGH!
OHHHH!
MORE THAN ENOUGH!
MOONSTONE'S HANDS ARE EXPLODING WITH LIGHT-- AND MARCY'S BEEN CAUGHT IN THE DISCHARGE!
MOONSTONE'S GONE BACK INTO DOC CONNORS' OFFICE TO RETRIEVE THE PORTOPAK ENERVATOR. I SHOULD STOP HER... BUT MARCY'S HURT.
CRAWLING TO THE INJURED CO-ED, SPIDER-MAN PUTS ALL THOUGHTS OF MOONSTONE FROM HIS MIND AS HE BEGINS ADMINISTERING "THE KISS OF LIFE"...
MARCY HAD THE WIND KNOCKED OUT OF HER. GOT TO GET HER BREATHING AGAIN.
I'M REAL GLAD I TOOK THAT COURSE ON CPR*!
*CARDIOPULMONARY RESUSCITATION --THERAPEUTIC TOM

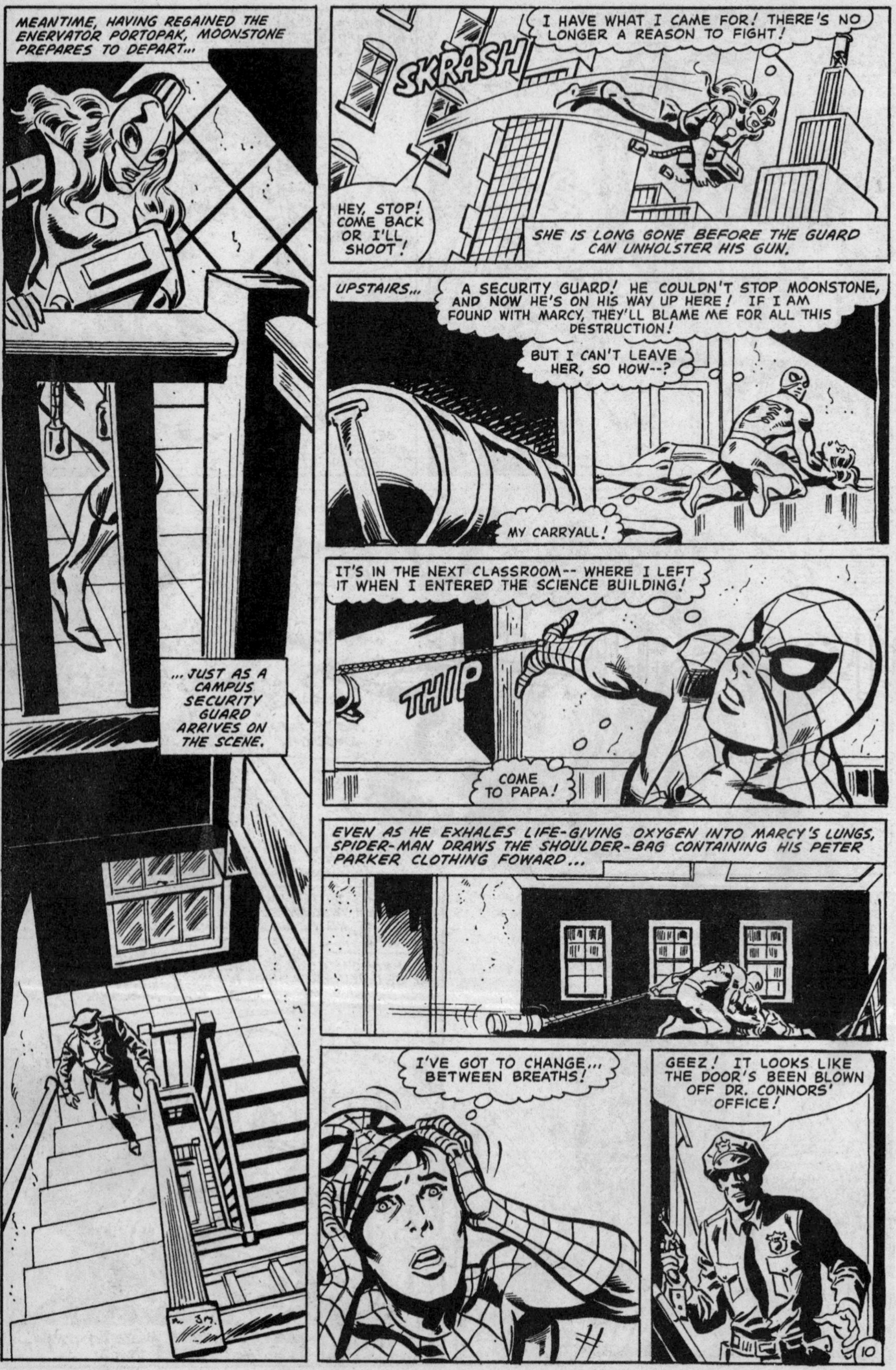

MEANTIME, HAVING REGAINED THE ENERVATOR PORTOPAK, MOONSTONE PREPARES TO DEPART...
...JUST AS A CAMPUS SECURITY GUARD ARRIVES ON THE SCENE.
I HAVE WHAT I CAME FOR! THERE'S NO LONGER A REASON TO FIGHT!
SKRASH
HEY, STOP! COME BACK OR I'LL SHOOT!
SHE IS LONG GONE BEFORE THE GUARD CAN UNHOLSTER HIS GUN.
UPSTAIRS...
A SECURITY GUARD! HE COULDN'T STOP MOONSTONE, AND NOW HE'S ON HIS WAY UP HERE! IF I AM FOUND WITH MARCY, THEY'LL BLAME ME FOR ALL THIS DESTRUCTION!
BUT I CAN'T LEAVE HER, SO HOW--?
MY CARRYALL!
IT'S IN THE NEXT CLASSROOM-- WHERE I LEFT IT WHEN I ENTERED THE SCIENCE BUILDING!
THIP
COME TO PAPA!
EVEN AS HE EXHALES LIFE-GIVING OXYGEN INTO MARCY'S LUNGS, SPIDER-MAN DRAWS THE SHOULDER-BAG CONTAINING HIS PETER PARKER CLOTHING FOWARD...
I'VE GOT TO CHANGE... BETWEEN BREATHS!
GEEZ! IT LOOKS LIKE THE DOOR'S BEEN BLOWN OFF DR. CONNORS' OFFICE!

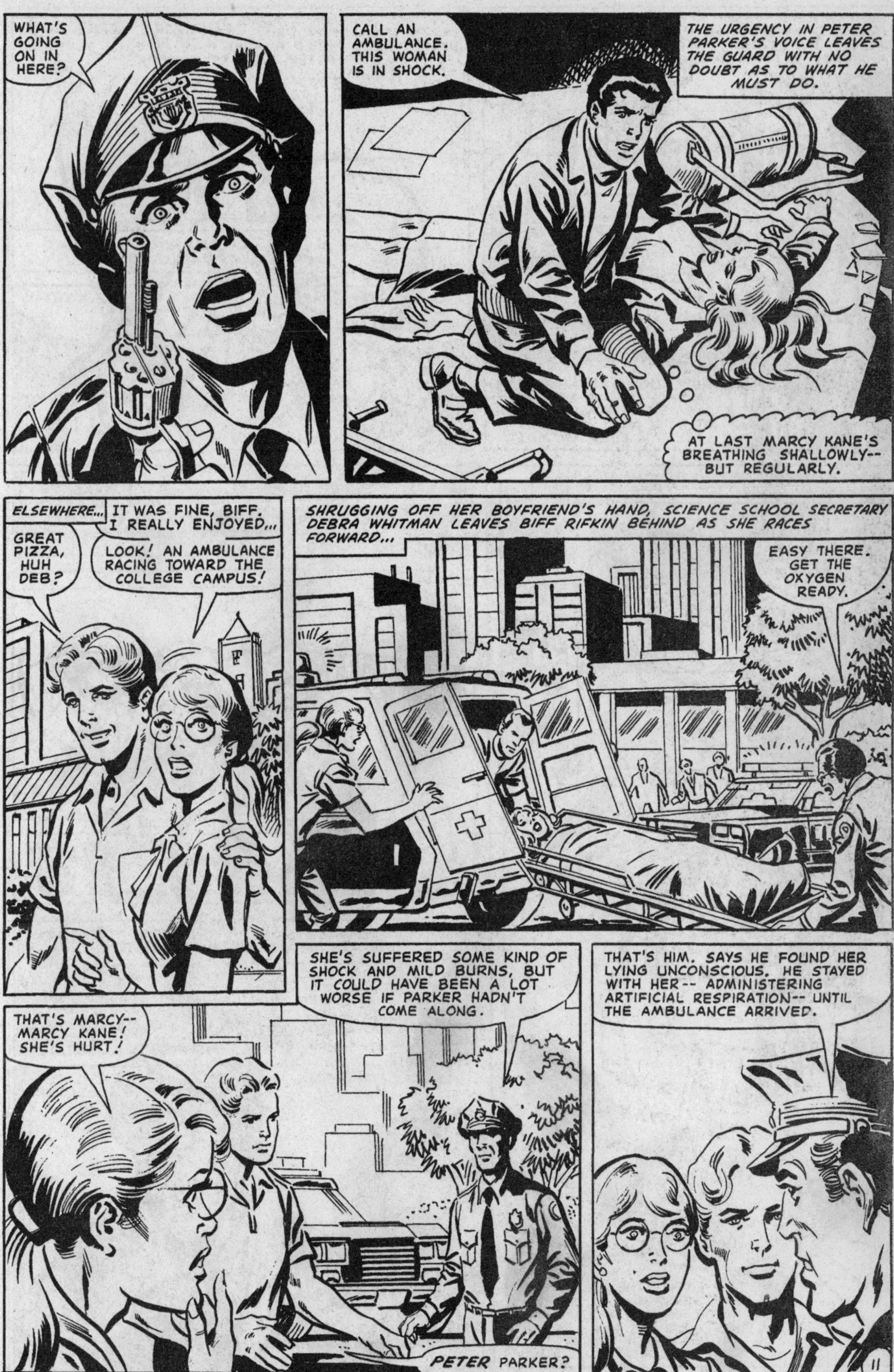
WHAT'S GOING ON IN HERE?
CALL AN AMBULANCE. THIS WOMAN IS IN SHOCK.
THE URGENCY IN PETER PARKER'S VOICE LEAVES THE GUARD WITH NO DOUBT AS TO WHAT HE MUST DO.
AT LAST MARCY KANE'S BREATHING SHALLOWLY-- BUT REGULARLY.
ELSEWHERE...
GREAT PIZZA, HUH DEB?
IT WAS FINE, BIFF. I REALLY ENJOYED...
LOOK! AN AMBULANCE RACING TOWARD THE COLLEGE CAMPUS!
SHRUGGING OFF HER BOYFRIEND'S HAND, SCIENCE SCHOOL SECRETARY DEBRA WHITMAN LEAVES BIFF RIFKIN BEHIND AS SHE RACES FORWARD...
EASY THERE. GET THE OXYGEN READY.
THAT'S MARCY-- MARCY KANE! SHE'S HURT!
SHE'S SUFFERED SOME KIND OF SHOCK AND MILD BURNS, BUT IT COULD HAVE BEEN A LOT WORSE IF PARKER HADN'T COME ALONG.
PETER PARKER?
THAT'S HIM. SAYS HE FOUND HER LYING UNCONSCIOUS. HE STAYED WITH HER-- ADMINISTERING ARTIFICIAL RESPIRATION-- UNTIL THE AMBULANCE ARRIVED.
11

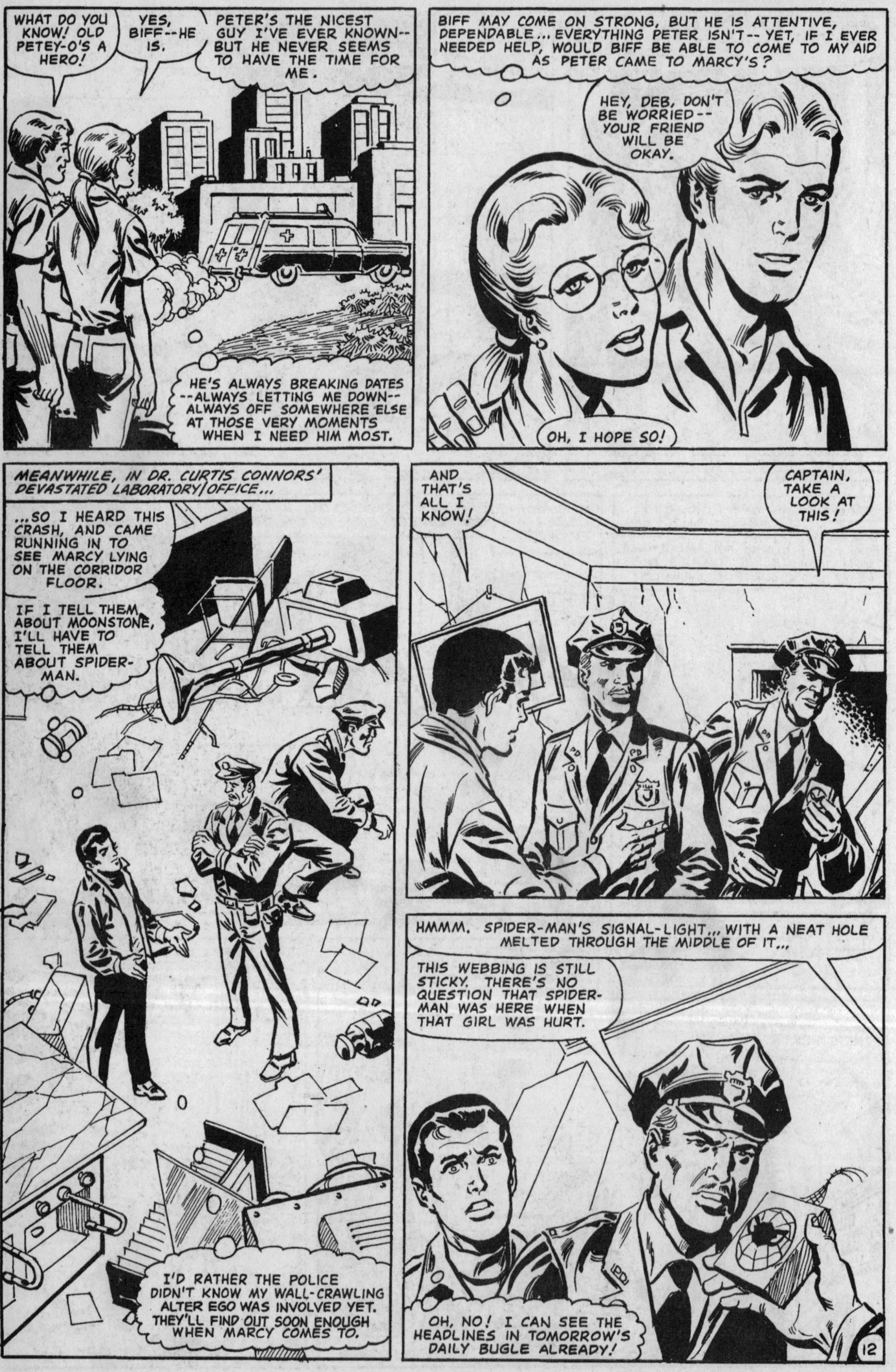
WHAT DO YOU KNOW! OLD PETEY-O'S A HERO!
YES, BIFF--HE IS.
PETER'S THE NICEST GUY I'VE EVER KNOWN--BUT HE NEVER SEEMS TO HAVE THE TIME FOR ME.
HE'S ALWAYS BREAKING DATES --ALWAYS LETTING ME DOWN--ALWAYS OFF SOMEWHERE ELSE AT THOSE VERY MOMENTS WHEN I NEED HIM MOST.
BIFF MAY COME ON STRONG, BUT HE IS ATTENTIVE, DEPENDABLE... EVERYTHING PETER ISN'T-- YET, IF I EVER NEEDED HELP, WOULD BIFF BE ABLE TO COME TO MY AID AS PETER CAME TO MARCY'S?
HEY, DEB, DON'T BE WORRIED-- YOUR FRIEND WILL BE OKAY.
OH, I HOPE SO!
MEANWHILE, IN DR. CURTIS CONNORS' DEVASTATED LABORATORY/OFFICE...
...SO I HEARD THIS CRASH, AND CAME RUNNING IN TO SEE MARCY LYING ON THE CORRIDOR FLOOR.
IF I TELL THEM ABOUT MOONSTONE, I'LL HAVE TO TELL THEM ABOUT SPIDER-MAN.
I'D RATHER THE POLICE DIDN'T KNOW MY WALL-CRAWLING ALTER EGO WAS INVOLVED YET. THEY'LL FIND OUT SOON ENOUGH WHEN MARCY COMES TO.
AND THAT'S ALL I KNOW!
CAPTAIN, TAKE A LOOK AT THIS!
HMMM. SPIDER-MAN'S SIGNAL-LIGHT... WITH A NEAT HOLE MELTED THROUGH THE MIDDLE OF IT...
THIS WEBBING IS STILL STICKY. THERE'S NO QUESTION THAT SPIDER-MAN WAS HERE WHEN THAT GIRL WAS HURT.
OH, NO! I CAN SEE THE HEADLINES IN TOMORROW'S DAILY BUGLE ALREADY!
12

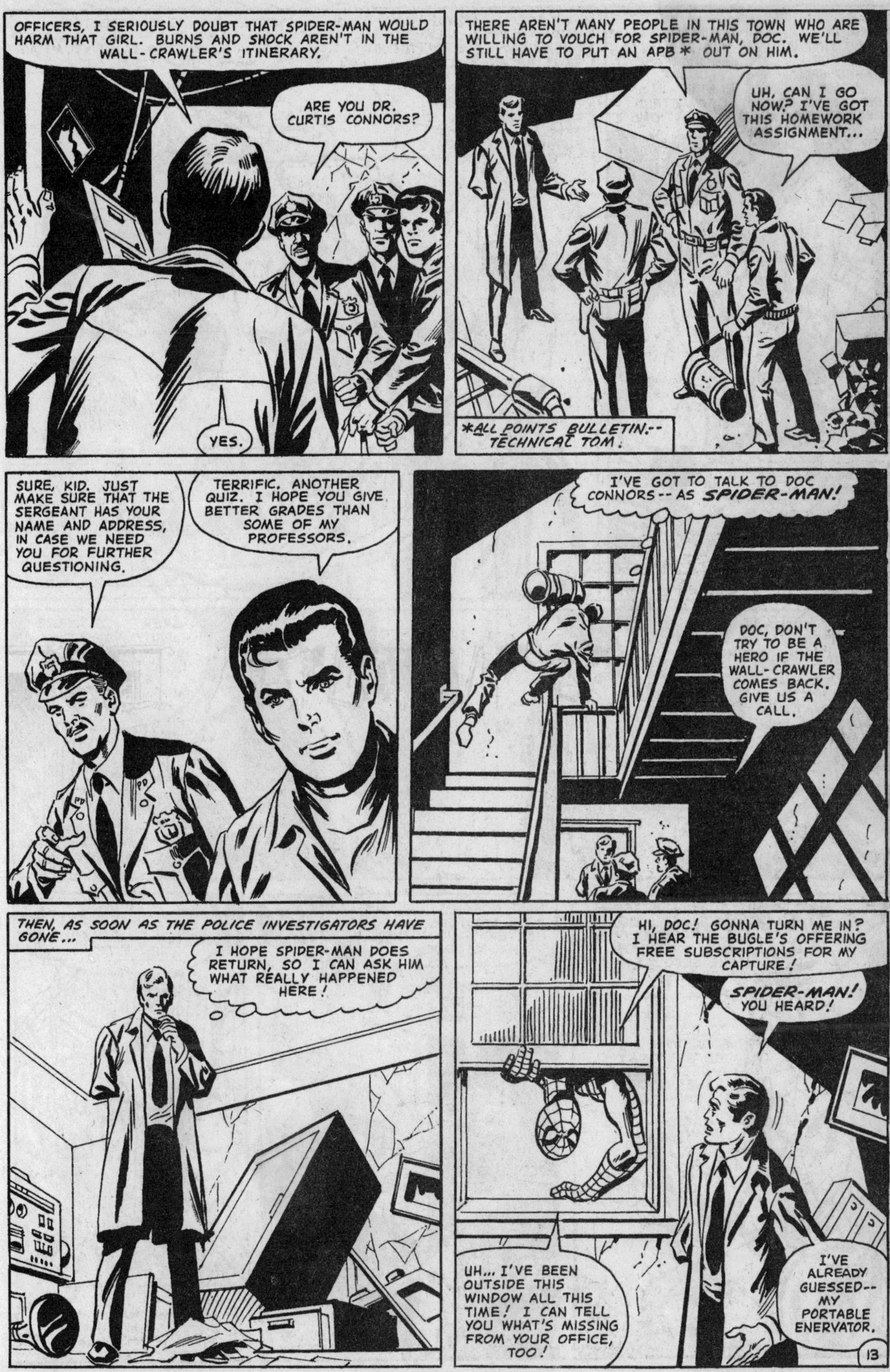
OFFICERS, I SERIOUSLY DOUBT THAT SPIDER-MAN WOULD HARM THAT GIRL. BURNS AND SHOCK AREN'T IN THE WALL-CRAWLER'S ITINERARY.
ARE YOU DR. CURTIS CONNORS?
YES.
THERE AREN'T MANY PEOPLE IN THIS TOWN WHO ARE WILLING TO VOUCH FOR SPIDER-MAN, DOC. WE'LL STILL HAVE TO PUT AN APB* OUT ON HIM.
UH, CAN I GO NOW? I'VE GOT THIS HOMEWORK ASSIGNMENT...
*ALL POINTS BULLETIN.-- TECHNICAL TOM.
SURE, KID. JUST MAKE SURE THAT THE SERGEANT HAS YOUR NAME AND ADDRESS, IN CASE WE NEED YOU FOR FURTHER QUESTIONING.
TERRIFIC. ANOTHER QUIZ. I HOPE YOU GIVE BETTER GRADES THAN SOME OF MY PROFESSORS.
I'VE GOT TO TALK TO DOC CONNORS -- AS SPIDER-MAN!
DOC, DON'T TRY TO BE A HERO IF THE WALL-CRAWLER COMES BACK. GIVE US A CALL.
THEN, AS SOON AS THE POLICE INVESTIGATORS HAVE GONE...
I HOPE SPIDER-MAN DOES RETURN, SO I CAN ASK HIM WHAT REALLY HAPPENED HERE!
HI, DOC! GONNA TURN ME IN? I HEAR THE BUGLE'S OFFERING FREE SUBSCRIPTIONS FOR MY CAPTURE!
SPIDER-MAN! YOU HEARD!
UH... I'VE BEEN OUTSIDE THIS WINDOW ALL THIS TIME! I CAN TELL YOU WHAT'S MISSING FROM YOUR OFFICE, TOO!
I'VE ALREADY GUESSED-- MY PORTABLE ENERVATOR.
13

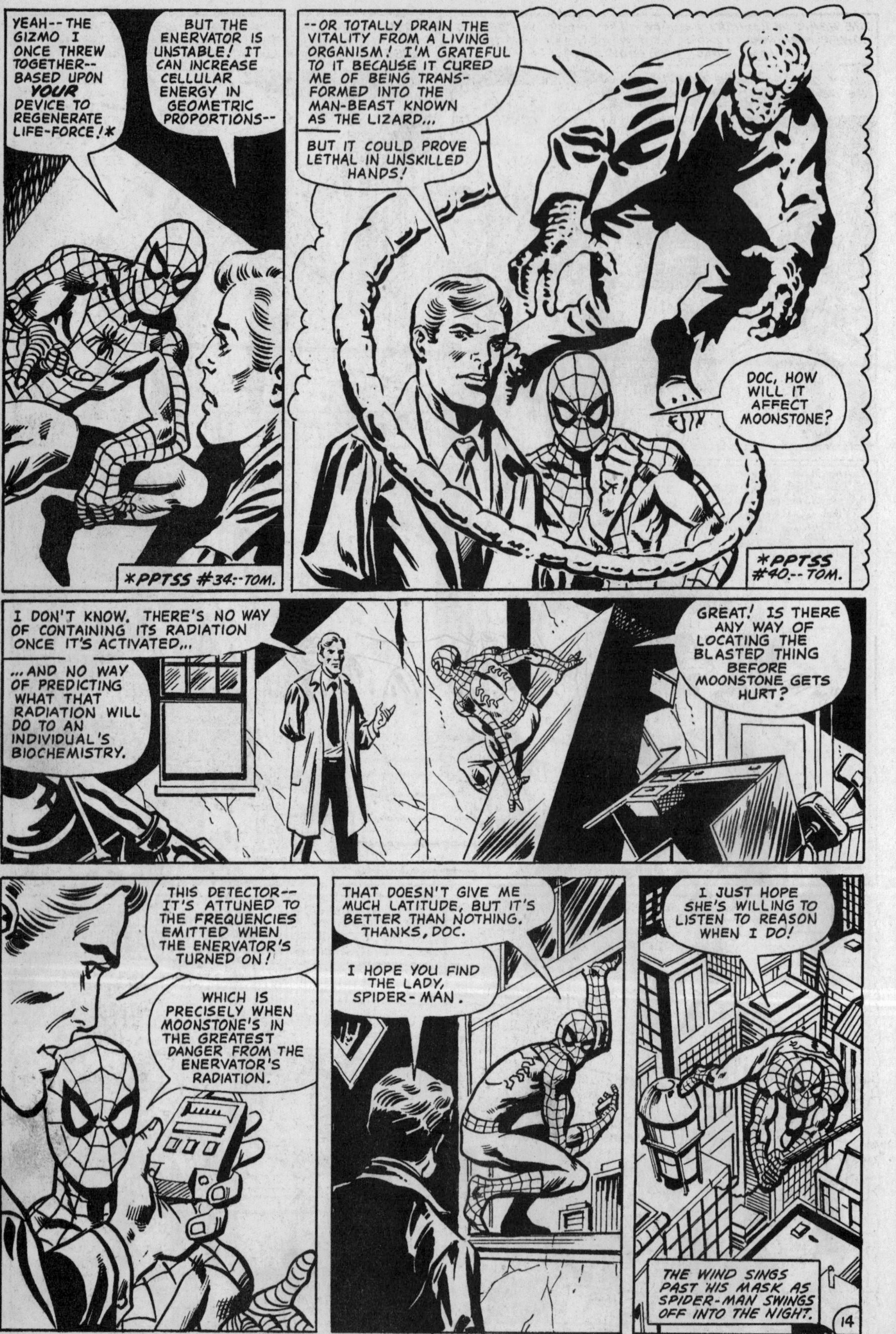
YEAH--THE GIZMO I ONCE THREW TOGETHER--BASED UPON YOUR DEVICE TO REGENERATE LIFE-FORCE!*
BUT THE ENERVATOR IS UNSTABLE! IT CAN INCREASE CELLULAR ENERGY IN GEOMETRIC PROPORTIONS--
*PPTSS #34.--TOM.
--OR TOTALLY DRAIN THE VITALITY FROM A LIVING ORGANISM! I'M GRATEFUL TO IT BECAUSE IT CURED ME OF BEING TRANSFORMED INTO THE MAN-BEAST KNOWN AS THE LIZARD...
BUT IT COULD PROVE LETHAL IN UNSKILLED HANDS!
DOC, HOW WILL IT AFFECT MOONSTONE?
*PPTSS #40.--TOM.
I DON'T KNOW. THERE'S NO WAY OF CONTAINING ITS RADIATION ONCE IT'S ACTIVATED...
...AND NO WAY OF PREDICTING WHAT THAT RADIATION WILL DO TO AN INDIVIDUAL'S BIOCHEMISTRY.
GREAT! IS THERE ANY WAY OF LOCATING THE BLASTED THING BEFORE MOONSTONE GETS HURT?
THIS DETECTOR--IT'S ATTUNED TO THE FREQUENCIES EMITTED WHEN THE ENERVATOR'S TURNED ON!
WHICH IS PRECISELY WHEN MOONSTONE'S IN THE GREATEST DANGER FROM THE ENERVATOR'S RADIATION.
THAT DOESN'T GIVE ME MUCH LATITUDE, BUT IT'S BETTER THAN NOTHING. THANKS, DOC.
I HOPE YOU FIND THE LADY, SPIDER-MAN.
I JUST HOPE SHE'S WILLING TO LISTEN TO REASON WHEN I DO!
THE WIND SINGS PAST HIS MASK AS SPIDER-MAN SWINGS OFF INTO THE NIGHT.
14

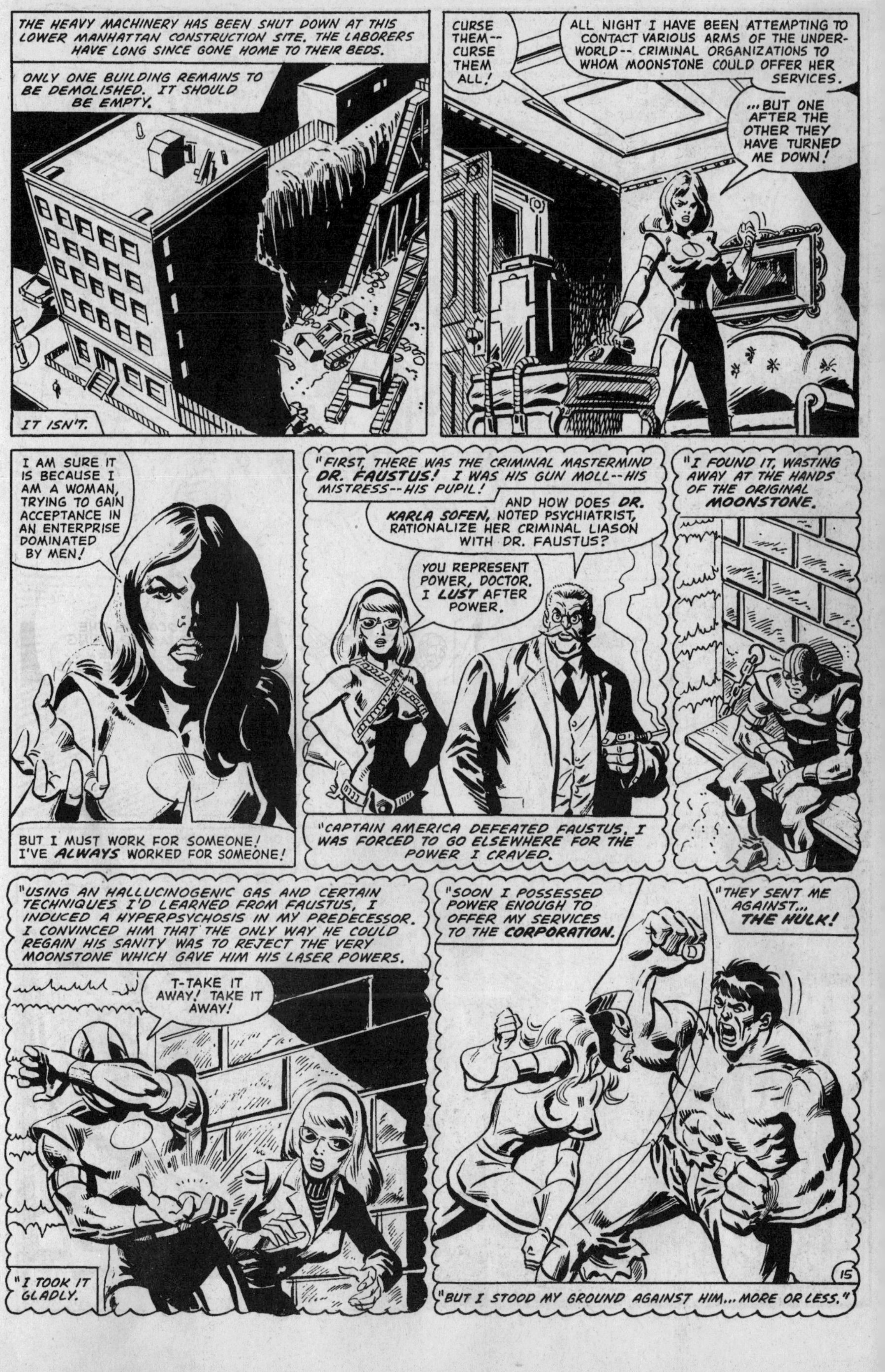
THE HEAVY MACHINERY HAS BEEN SHUT DOWN AT THIS LOWER MANHATTAN CONSTRUCTION SITE. THE LABORERS HAVE LONG SINCE GONE HOME TO THEIR BEDS.
ONLY ONE BUILDING REMAINS TO BE DEMOLISHED. IT SHOULD BE EMPTY.
IT ISN'T.
CURSE THEM-- CURSE THEM ALL!
ALL NIGHT I HAVE BEEN ATTEMPTING TO CONTACT VARIOUS ARMS OF THE UNDERWORLD-- CRIMINAL ORGANIZATIONS TO WHOM MOONSTONE COULD OFFER HER SERVICES.
...BUT ONE AFTER THE OTHER THEY HAVE TURNED ME DOWN!
I AM SURE IT IS BECAUSE I AM A WOMAN, TRYING TO GAIN ACCEPTANCE IN AN ENTERPRISE DOMINATED BY MEN!
BUT I MUST WORK FOR SOMEONE! I'VE ALWAYS WORKED FOR SOMEONE!
"FIRST, THERE WAS THE CRIMINAL MASTERMIND DR. FAUSTUS! I WAS HIS GUN MOLL--HIS MISTRESS--HIS PUPIL!
AND HOW DOES DR. KARLA SOFEN, NOTED PSYCHIATRIST, RATIONALIZE HER CRIMINAL LIASON WITH DR. FAUSTUS?
YOU REPRESENT POWER, DOCTOR. I LUST AFTER POWER.
"CAPTAIN AMERICA DEFEATED FAUSTUS. I WAS FORCED TO GO ELSEWHERE FOR THE POWER I CRAVED.
"I FOUND IT, WASTING AWAY AT THE HANDS OF THE ORIGINAL MOONSTONE.
"USING AN HALLUCINOGENIC GAS AND CERTAIN TECHNIQUES I'D LEARNED FROM FAUSTUS, I INDUCED A HYPERPSYCHOSIS IN MY PREDECESSOR. I CONVINCED HIM THAT THE ONLY WAY HE COULD REGAIN HIS SANITY WAS TO REJECT THE VERY MOONSTONE WHICH GAVE HIM HIS LASER POWERS.
T-TAKE IT AWAY! TAKE IT AWAY!
"I TOOK IT GLADLY.
"SOON I POSSESSED POWER ENOUGH TO OFFER MY SERVICES TO THE CORPORATION.
"THEY SENT ME AGAINST... THE HULK!
15
"BUT I STOOD MY GROUND AGAINST HIM... MORE OR LESS."

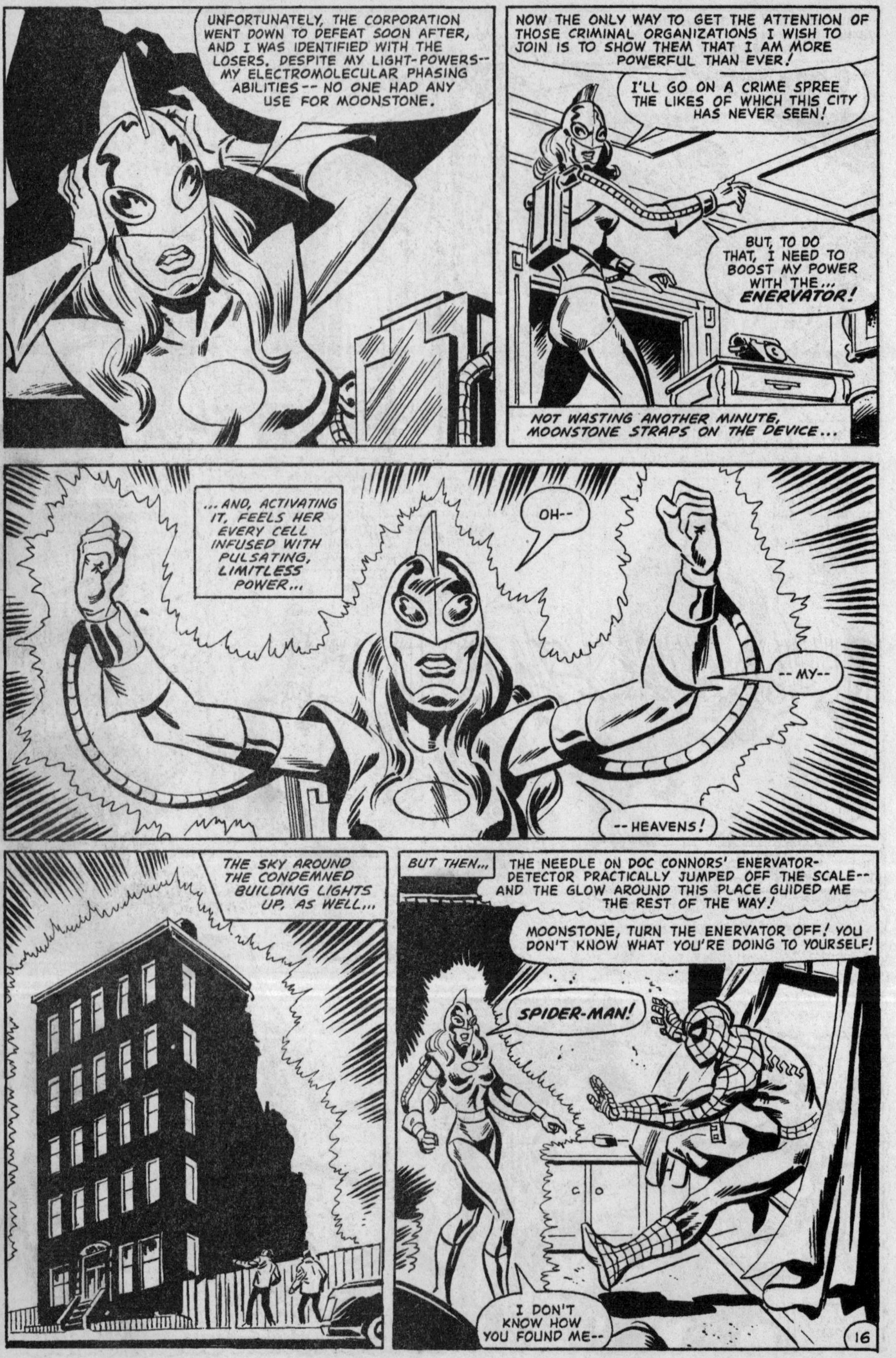

UNFORTUNATELY, THE CORPORATION WENT DOWN TO DEFEAT SOON AFTER, AND I WAS IDENTIFIED WITH THE LOSERS. DESPITE MY LIGHT-POWERS-- MY ELECTROMOLECULAR PHASING ABILITIES-- NO ONE HAD ANY USE FOR MOONSTONE.
NOW THE ONLY WAY TO GET THE ATTENTION OF THOSE CRIMINAL ORGANIZATIONS I WISH TO JOIN IS TO SHOW THEM THAT I AM MORE POWERFUL THAN EVER!
I'LL GO ON A CRIME SPREE THE LIKES OF WHICH THIS CITY HAS NEVER SEEN!
BUT, TO DO THAT, I NEED TO BOOST MY POWER WITH THE... ENERVATOR!
NOT WASTING ANOTHER MINUTE, MOONSTONE STRAPS ON THE DEVICE...
...AND, ACTIVATING IT, FEELS HER EVERY CELL INFUSED WITH PULSATING, LIMITLESS POWER...
OH--
--MY--
--HEAVENS!
THE SKY AROUND THE CONDEMNED BUILDING LIGHTS UP, AS WELL...
BUT THEN...
THE NEEDLE ON DOC CONNORS' ENERVATOR-DETECTOR PRACTICALLY JUMPED OFF THE SCALE-- AND THE GLOW AROUND THIS PLACE GUIDED ME THE REST OF THE WAY!
MOONSTONE, TURN THE ENERVATOR OFF! YOU DON'T KNOW WHAT YOU'RE DOING TO YOURSELF!
SPIDER-MAN!
I DON'T KNOW HOW YOU FOUND ME--

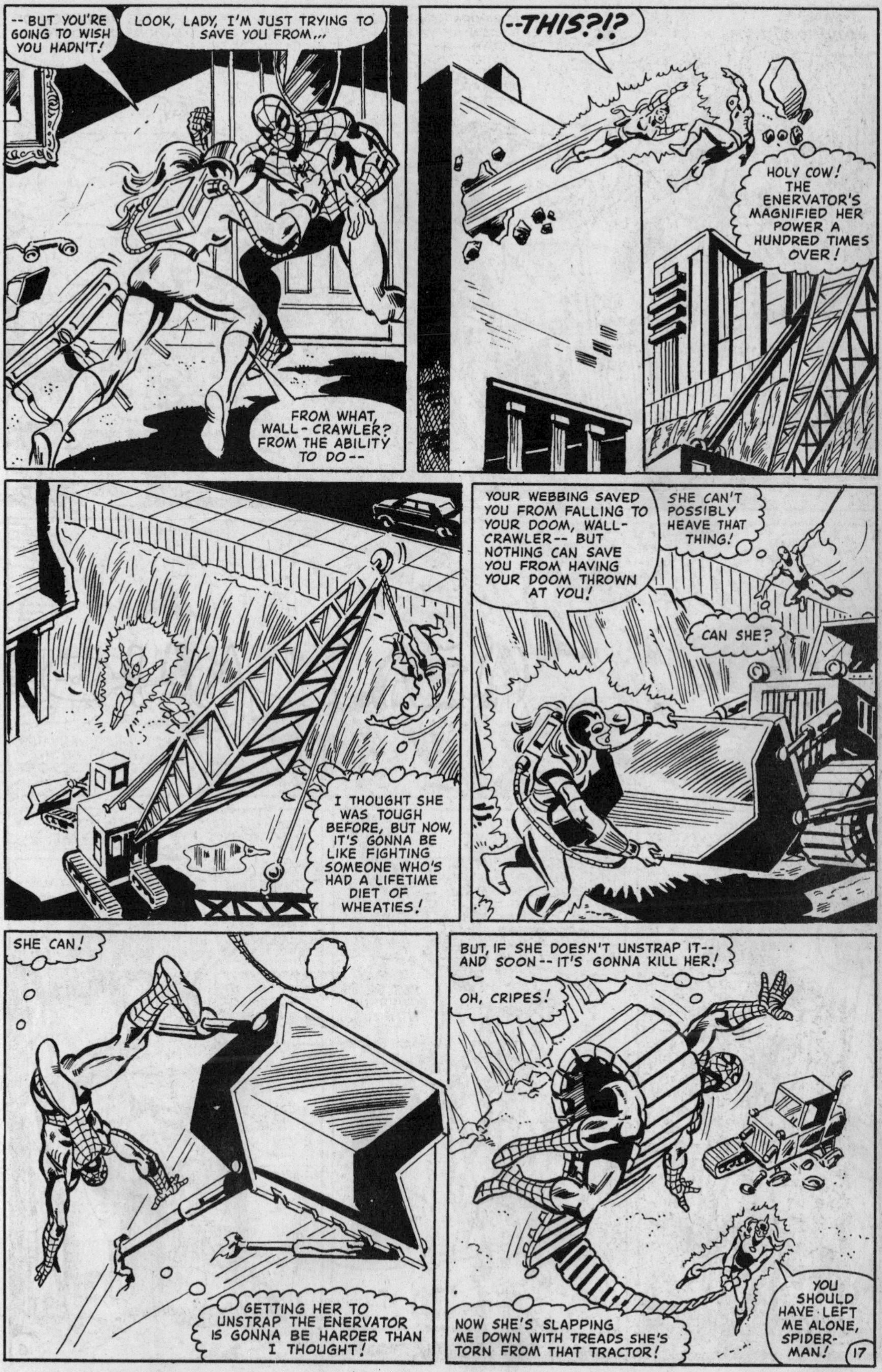
-- BUT YOU'RE GOING TO WISH YOU HADN'T!
LOOK, LADY, I'M JUST TRYING TO SAVE YOU FROM...
FROM WHAT, WALL-CRAWLER? FROM THE ABILITY TO DO--
--THIS?!?
HOLY COW! THE ENERVATOR'S MAGNIFIED HER POWER A HUNDRED TIMES OVER!
I THOUGHT SHE WAS TOUGH BEFORE, BUT NOW, IT'S GONNA BE LIKE FIGHTING SOMEONE WHO'S HAD A LIFETIME DIET OF WHEATIES!
YOUR WEBBING SAVED YOU FROM FALLING TO YOUR DOOM, WALL-CRAWLER-- BUT NOTHING CAN SAVE YOU FROM HAVING YOUR DOOM THROWN AT YOU!
SHE CAN'T POSSIBLY HEAVE THAT THING!
CAN SHE?
SHE CAN!
GETTING HER TO UNSTRAP THE ENERVATOR IS GONNA BE HARDER THAN I THOUGHT!
BUT, IF SHE DOESN'T UNSTRAP IT-- AND SOON-- IT'S GONNA KILL HER!
OH, CRIPES!
NOW SHE'S SLAPPING ME DOWN WITH TREADS SHE'S TORN FROM THAT TRACTOR!
YOU SHOULD HAVE LEFT ME ALONE, SPIDER-MAN!

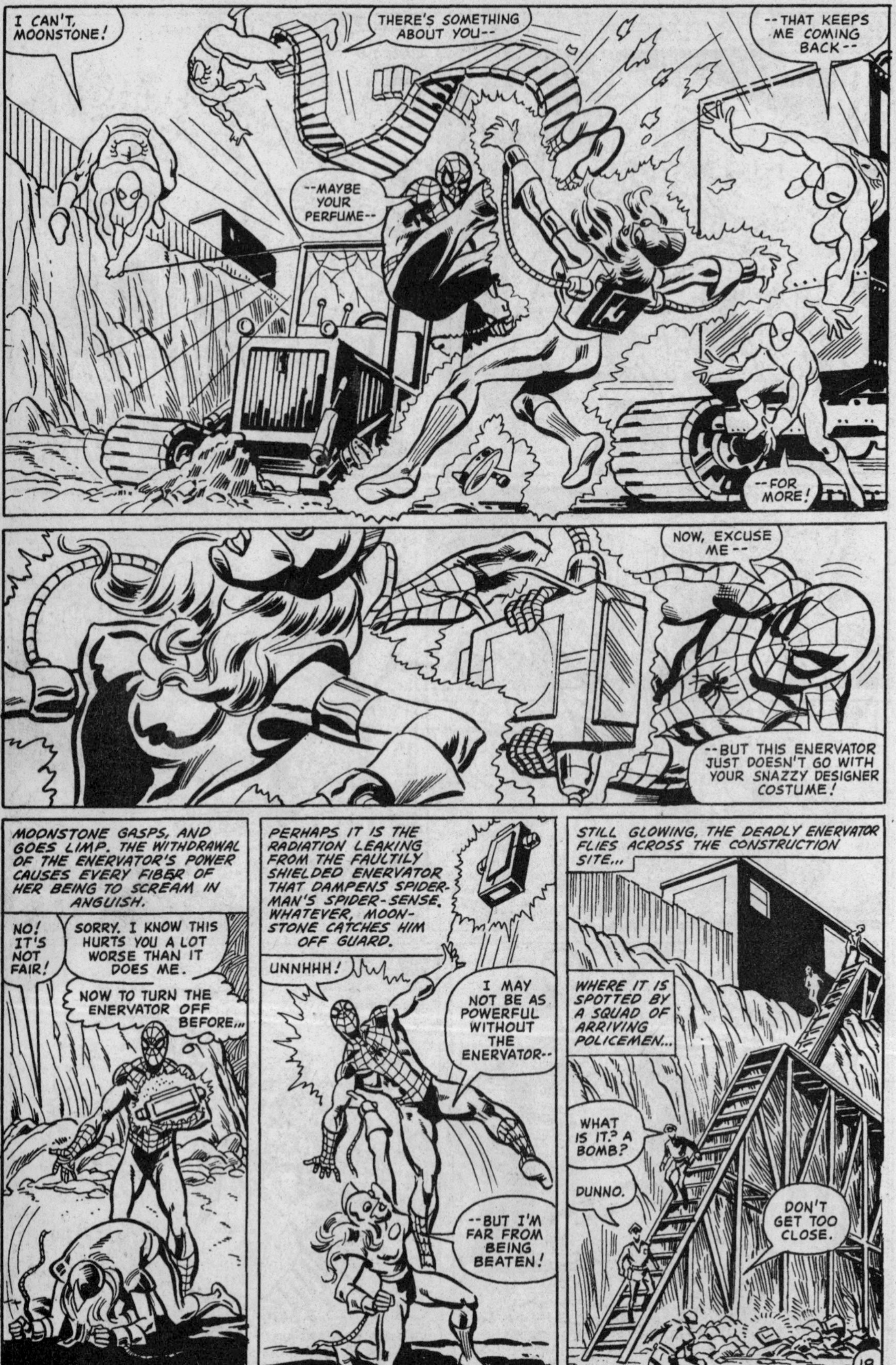

I CAN'T, MOONSTONE!
THERE'S SOMETHING ABOUT YOU--
--THAT KEEPS ME COMING BACK--
--MAYBE YOUR PERFUME--
--FOR MORE!
NOW, EXCUSE ME--
--BUT THIS ENERVATOR JUST DOESN'T GO WITH YOUR SNAZZY DESIGNER COSTUME!
MOONSTONE GASPS, AND GOES LIMP. THE WITHDRAWAL OF THE ENERVATOR'S POWER CAUSES EVERY FIBER OF HER BEING TO SCREAM IN ANGUISH.
NO! IT'S NOT FAIR!
SORRY. I KNOW THIS HURTS YOU A LOT WORSE THAN IT DOES ME.
NOW TO TURN THE ENERVATOR OFF BEFORE...
PERHAPS IT IS THE RADIATION LEAKING FROM THE FAULTILY SHIELDED ENERVATOR THAT DAMPENS SPIDER-MAN'S SPIDER-SENSE. WHATEVER, MOONSTONE CATCHES HIM OFF GUARD.
UNNHHH!
I MAY NOT BE AS POWERFUL WITHOUT THE ENERVATOR--
--BUT I'M FAR FROM BEING BEATEN!
STILL GLOWING, THE DEADLY ENERVATOR FLIES ACROSS THE CONSTRUCTION SITE...
WHERE IT IS SPOTTED BY A SQUAD OF ARRIVING POLICEMEN...
WHAT IS IT? A BOMB?
DUNNO.
DON'T GET TOO CLOSE.
18

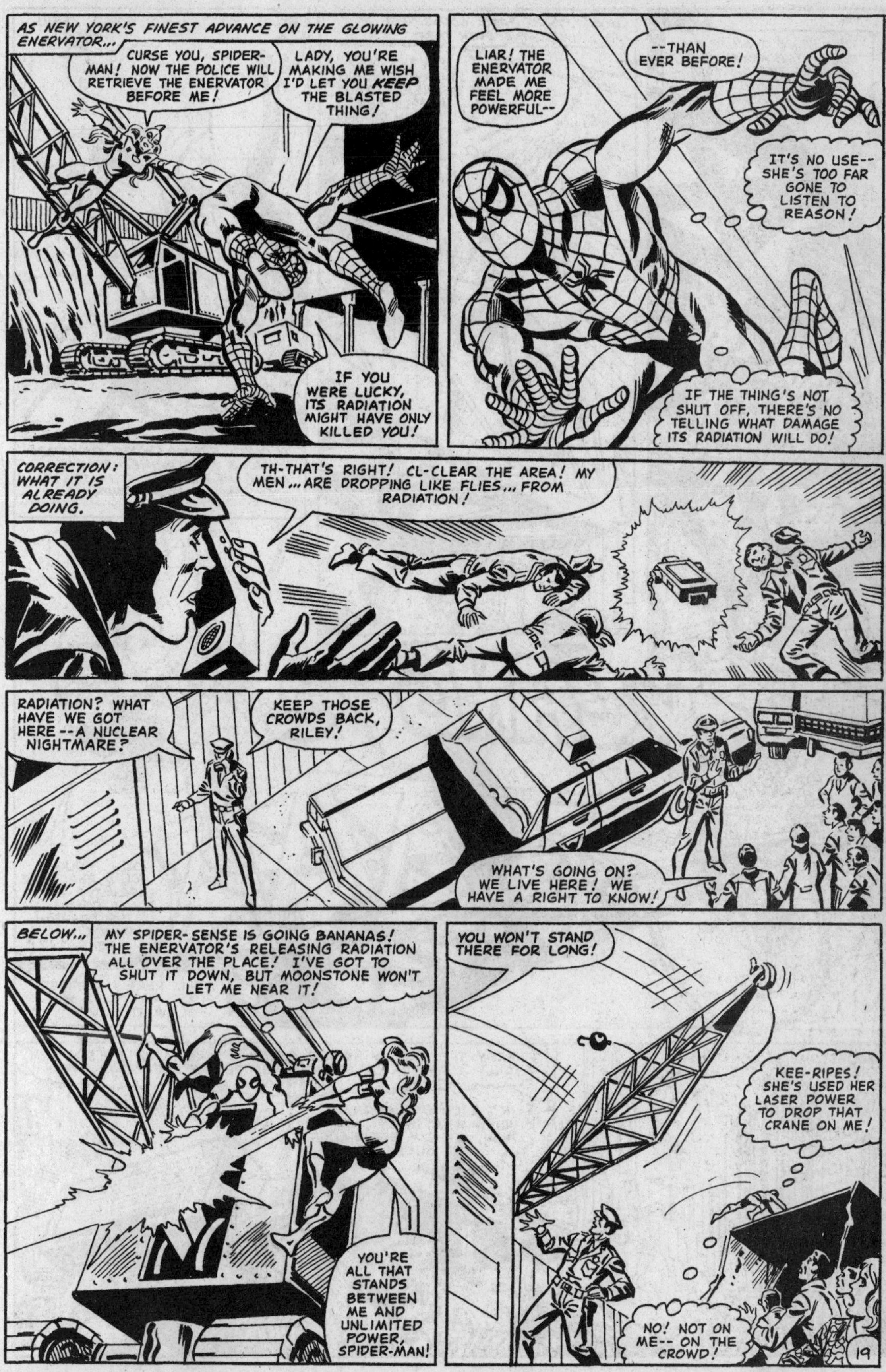
AS NEW YORK'S FINEST ADVANCE ON THE GLOWING ENERVATOR...
CURSE YOU, SPIDER-MAN! NOW THE POLICE WILL RETRIEVE THE ENERVATOR BEFORE ME!
LADY, YOU'RE MAKING ME WISH I'D LET YOU KEEP THE BLASTED THING!
IF YOU WERE LUCKY, ITS RADIATION MIGHT HAVE ONLY KILLED YOU!
LIAR! THE ENERVATOR MADE ME FEEL MORE POWERFUL--
--THAN EVER BEFORE!
IT'S NO USE-- SHE'S TOO FAR GONE TO LISTEN TO REASON!
IF THE THING'S NOT SHUT OFF, THERE'S NO TELLING WHAT DAMAGE ITS RADIATION WILL DO!
CORRECTION: WHAT IT IS ALREADY DOING.
TH-THAT'S RIGHT! CL-CLEAR THE AREA! MY MEN... ARE DROPPING LIKE FLIES... FROM RADIATION!
RADIATION? WHAT HAVE WE GOT HERE--A NUCLEAR NIGHTMARE?
KEEP THOSE CROWDS BACK, RILEY!
WHAT'S GOING ON? WE LIVE HERE! WE HAVE A RIGHT TO KNOW!
BELOW...
MY SPIDER-SENSE IS GOING BANANAS! THE ENERVATOR'S RELEASING RADIATION ALL OVER THE PLACE! I'VE GOT TO SHUT IT DOWN, BUT MOONSTONE WON'T LET ME NEAR IT!
YOU'RE ALL THAT STANDS BETWEEN ME AND UNLIMITED POWER, SPIDER-MAN!
YOU WON'T STAND THERE FOR LONG!
KEE-RIPES! SHE'S USED HER LASER POWER TO DROP THAT CRANE ON ME!
NO! NOT ON ME-- ON THE CROWD!

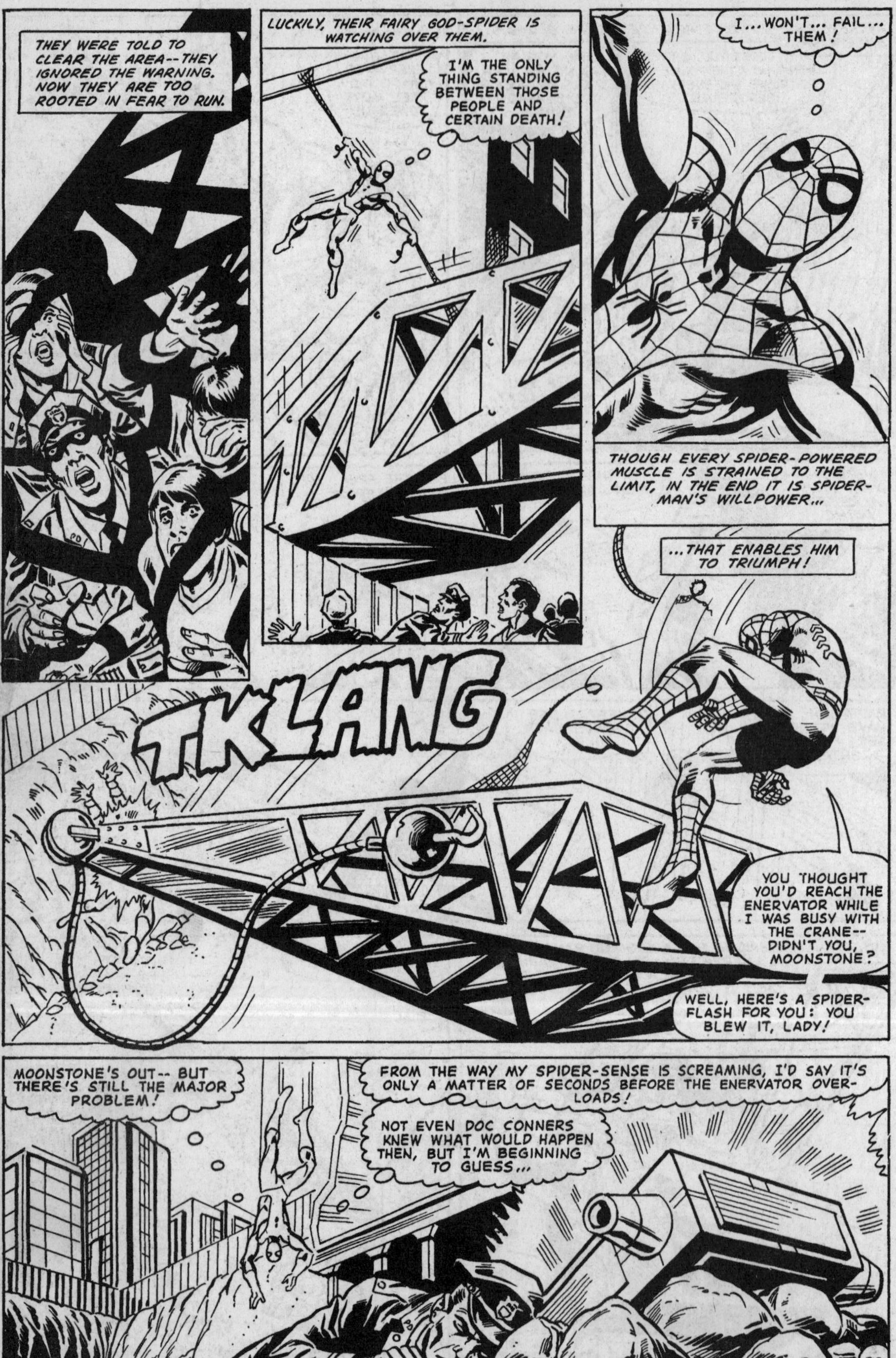
THEY WERE TOLD TO CLEAR THE AREA--THEY IGNORED THE WARNING. NOW THEY ARE TOO ROOTED IN FEAR TO RUN.
LUCKILY, THEIR FAIRY GOD-SPIDER IS WATCHING OVER THEM.
I'M THE ONLY THING STANDING BETWEEN THOSE PEOPLE AND CERTAIN DEATH!
I... WON'T... FAIL... THEM!
THOUGH EVERY SPIDER-POWERED MUSCLE IS STRAINED TO THE LIMIT, IN THE END IT IS SPIDER-MAN'S WILLPOWER...
...THAT ENABLES HIM TO TRIUMPH!
TKLANG
YOU THOUGHT YOU'D REACH THE ENERVATOR WHILE I WAS BUSY WITH THE CRANE-- DIDN'T YOU, MOONSTONE?
WELL, HERE'S A SPIDER-FLASH FOR YOU: YOU BLEW IT, LADY!
MOONSTONE'S OUT-- BUT THERE'S STILL THE MAJOR PROBLEM!
FROM THE WAY MY SPIDER-SENSE IS SCREAMING, I'D SAY IT'S ONLY A MATTER OF SECONDS BEFORE THE ENERVATOR OVER-LOADS!
NOT EVEN DOC CONNERS KNEW WHAT WOULD HAPPEN THEN, BUT I'M BEGINNING TO GUESS...

...AND I'VE GOT A HUNCH IT WON'T BE NICE! THE ENERVATOR SHOULD BE FAR AWAY FROM ANYTHING LIVING WHEN IT EXPLODES!

A SLENDER WEBLINE SNATCHES THE GLOWING DEVICE... AND WHIPS IT UNDER THE CONDEMNED BUILDING.

RRRRRMMMMMMBLLLLLE SHROOM!

SUNNUVAGUN! THE ENERVATOR CAUSED THE BUILDING TO COLLAPSE! 'MOONSTONE DOESN'T KNOW HOW LUCKY SHE IS -- BUT I EXPECT THE WARDEN WILL TELL HER!

THE NEXT MORNING, AT ST. LUKE'S HOSPITAL...

...AND ALL I REMEMBER IS SPIDER-MAN TRYING TO SAVE ME FROM SOME CRAZY WOMAN IN A WILD COSTUME.

YEP, THAT FITS THE STORY AS WE'VE BEEN ABLE TO PIECE IT TOGETHER, MS. KANE. WE'VE GOT MOONSTONE, SO I GUESS SPIDER-MAN'S IN THE CLEAR.

UH, HI! AM I INTERRUPTING ANYTHING?

THE POLICE INVESTIGATOR LEAVES...

...AND MARCY KANE TRIES TO FIND THE WORDS TO THANK PETER PARKER FOR SAVING HER LIFE.

PETER, I-I'VE GIVEN YOU A HARD TIME SINCE THE DAY YOU GOT INTO GRAD SCHOOL. I'M SORRY.

NO APOLOGIES NECESSARY. WE'RE BOTH UNDER A LOT OF PRESSURE.

PETER, YOU KNOW WHAT I WISH?

WHAT, MARCY?

I WISH THAT IT HAD BEEN YOU WHO'D BEEN ZAPPED BY MOONSTONE INSTEAD OF ME!

HUH?!

I SHOULD HAVE KNOWN! FOR A MINUTE I THOUGHT I ALMOST DETECTED WARMTH EMANATING FROM MS. MARCY "ICE QUEEN" KANE!

HEY, PETER-- THAT WAS A JOKE!

A JOKE?

FROM YOU?!

NOT BAD FOR A FIRST TRY. GIVE ME A CHANCE, MAYBE I'LL GET BETTER AT IT.

A CHANCE?

LADY, YOU'VE GOT IT!

AND SO IT BEGINS... AGAIN.

21

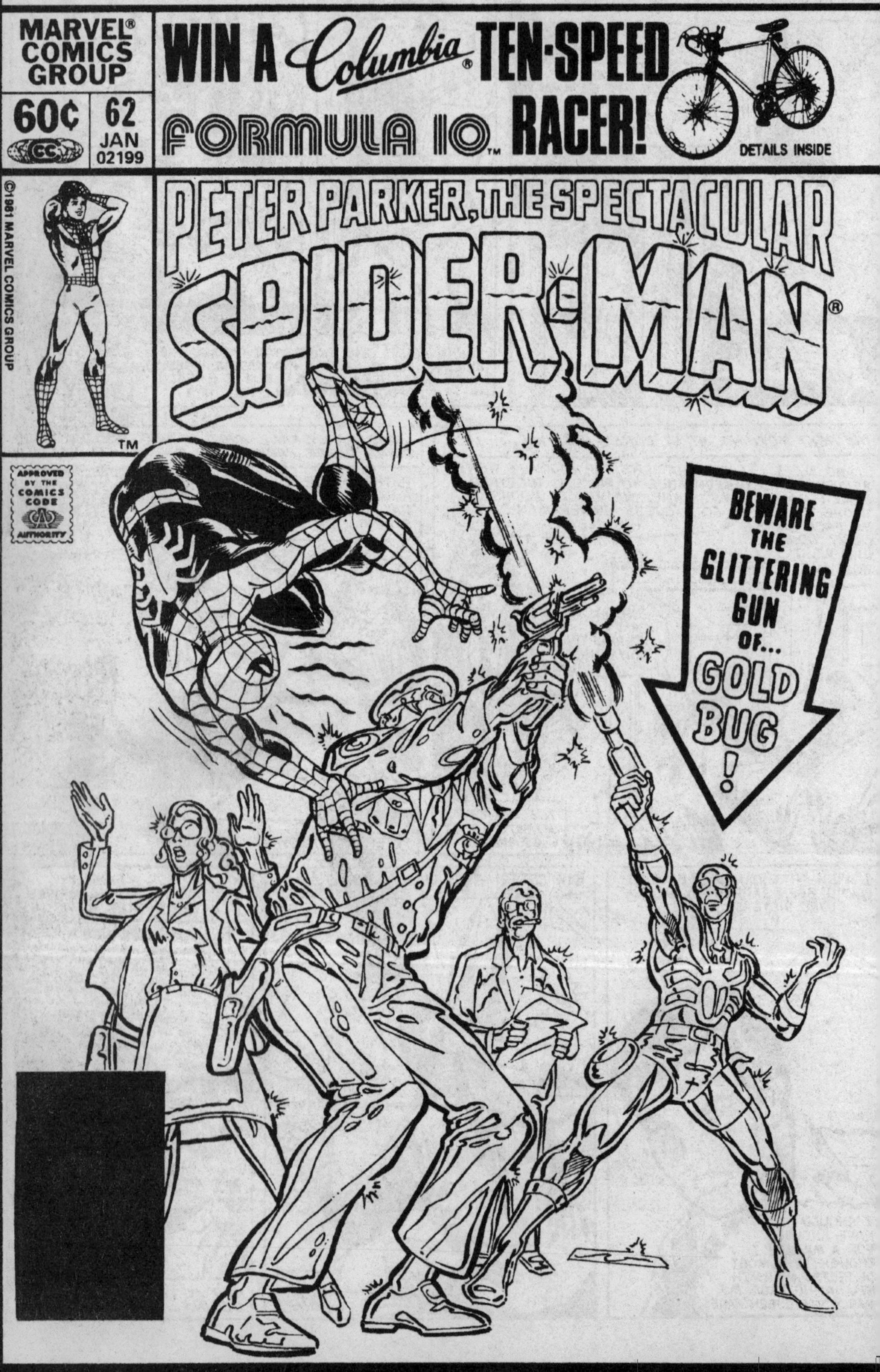
MARVEL® COMICS GROUP
60¢
62 JAN 02199
WIN A Columbia® TEN-SPEED FORMULA 10™ RACER!
DETAILS INSIDE
PETER PARKER, THE SPECTACULAR SPIDER-MAN®
©1981 MARVEL COMICS GROUP
TM
APPROVED BY THE COMICS CODE AUTHORITY
BEWARE THE GLITTERING GUN OF... GOLD BUG!

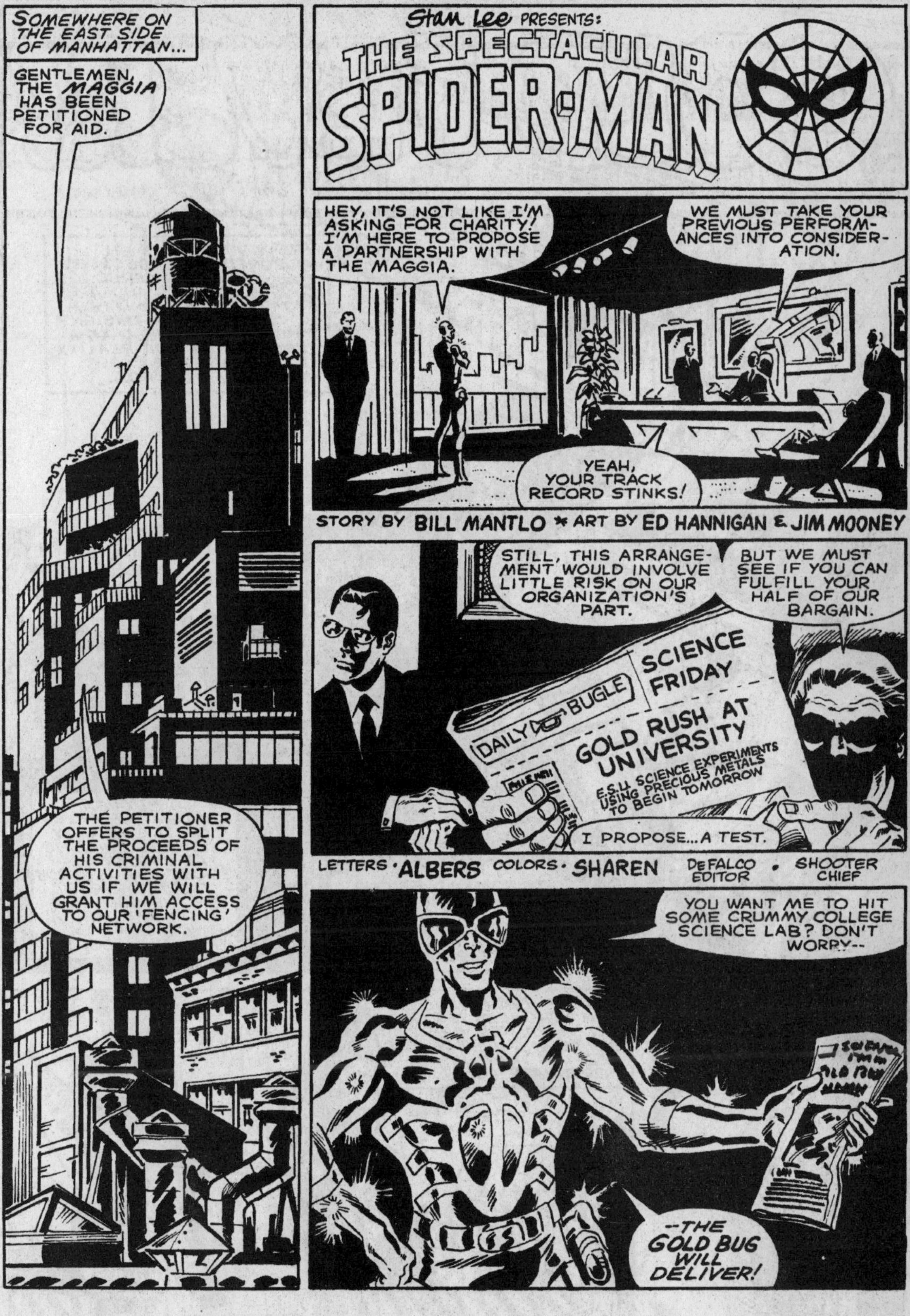
SOMEWHERE ON THE EAST SIDE OF MANHATTAN...
GENTLEMEN, THE MAGGIA HAS BEEN PETITIONED FOR AID.
THE PETITIONER OFFERS TO SPLIT THE PROCEEDS OF HIS CRIMINAL ACTIVITIES WITH US IF WE WILL GRANT HIM ACCESS TO OUR 'FENCING' NETWORK.
Stan Lee PRESENTS:
THE SPECTACULAR SPIDER-MAN
HEY, IT'S NOT LIKE I'M ASKING FOR CHARITY! I'M HERE TO PROPOSE A PARTNERSHIP WITH THE MAGGIA.
WE MUST TAKE YOUR PREVIOUS PERFORMANCES INTO CONSIDERATION.
YEAH, YOUR TRACK RECORD STINKS!
STORY BY BILL MANTLO * ART BY ED HANNIGAN & JIM MOONEY
STILL, THIS ARRANGEMENT WOULD INVOLVE LITTLE RISK ON OUR ORGANIZATION'S PART.
BUT WE MUST SEE IF YOU CAN FULFILL YOUR HALF OF OUR BARGAIN.
DAILY BUGLE
SCIENCE FRIDAY
GOLD RUSH AT UNIVERSITY
E.S.U. SCIENCE EXPERIMENTS USING PRECIOUS METALS TO BEGIN TOMORROW
I PROPOSE...A TEST.
LETTERS · ALBERS COLORS · SHAREN DEFALCO EDITOR · SHOOTER CHIEF
YOU WANT ME TO HIT SOME CRUMMY COLLEGE SCIENCE LAB? DON'T WORRY--
--THE GOLD BUG WILL DELIVER!

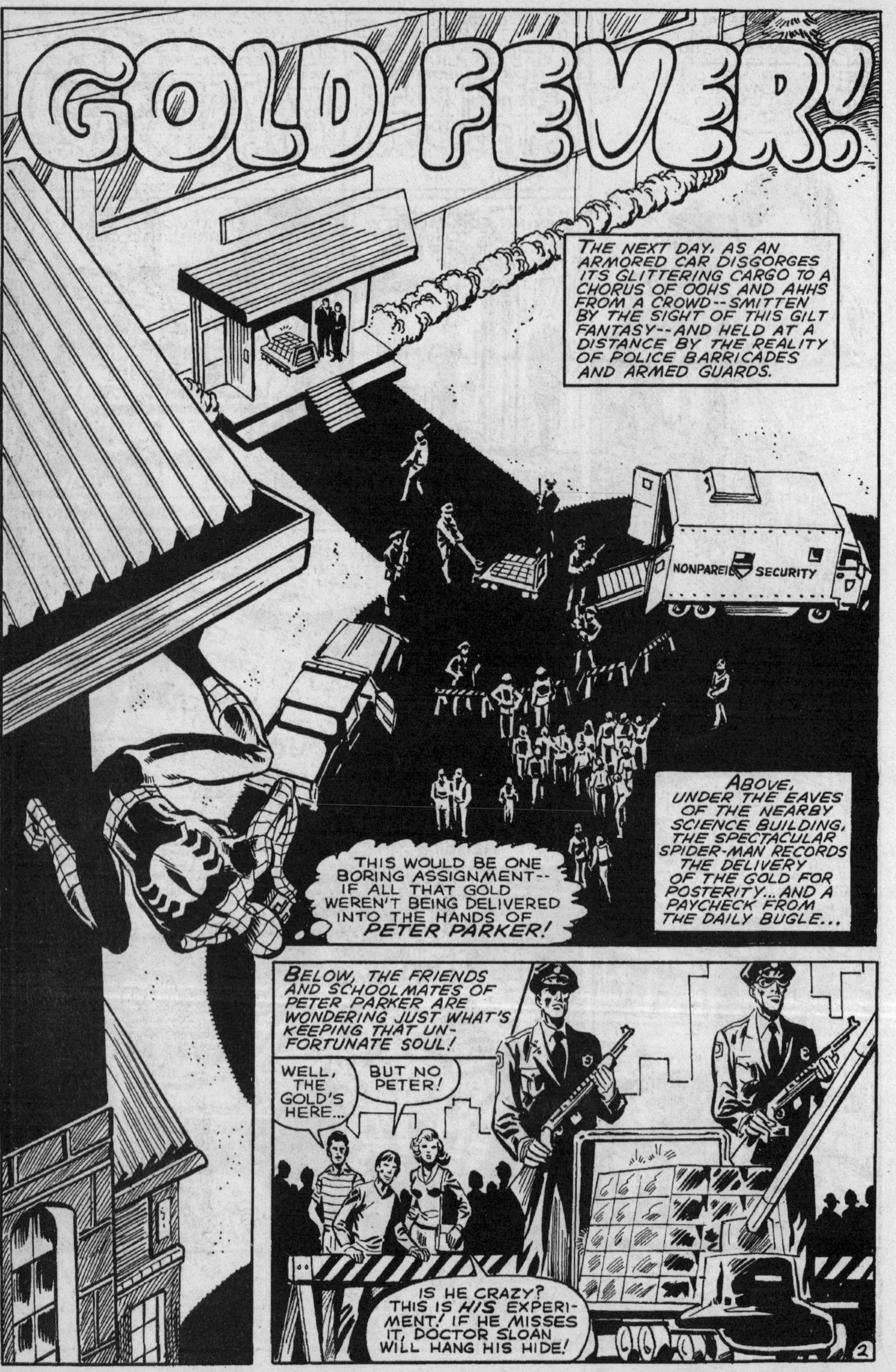
GOLD FEVER!
THE NEXT DAY, AS AN ARMORED CAR DISGORGES ITS GLITTERING CARGO TO A CHORUS OF OOHS AND AHHS FROM A CROWD--SMITTEN BY THE SIGHT OF THIS GILT FANTASY--AND HELD AT A DISTANCE BY THE REALITY OF POLICE BARRICADES AND ARMED GUARDS.
NONPAREIL SECURITY
ABOVE, UNDER THE EAVES OF THE NEARBY SCIENCE BUILDING, THE SPECTACULAR SPIDER-MAN RECORDS THE DELIVERY OF THE GOLD FOR POSTERITY... AND A PAYCHECK FROM THE DAILY BUGLE...
THIS WOULD BE ONE BORING ASSIGNMENT-- IF ALL THAT GOLD WEREN'T BEING DELIVERED INTO THE HANDS OF PETER PARKER!
BELOW, THE FRIENDS AND SCHOOLMATES OF PETER PARKER ARE WONDERING JUST WHAT'S KEEPING THAT UNFORTUNATE SOUL!
WELL, THE GOLD'S HERE...
BUT NO PETER!
IS HE CRAZY? THIS IS HIS EXPERIMENT! IF HE MISSES IT, DOCTOR SLOAN WILL HANG HIS HIDE!
2

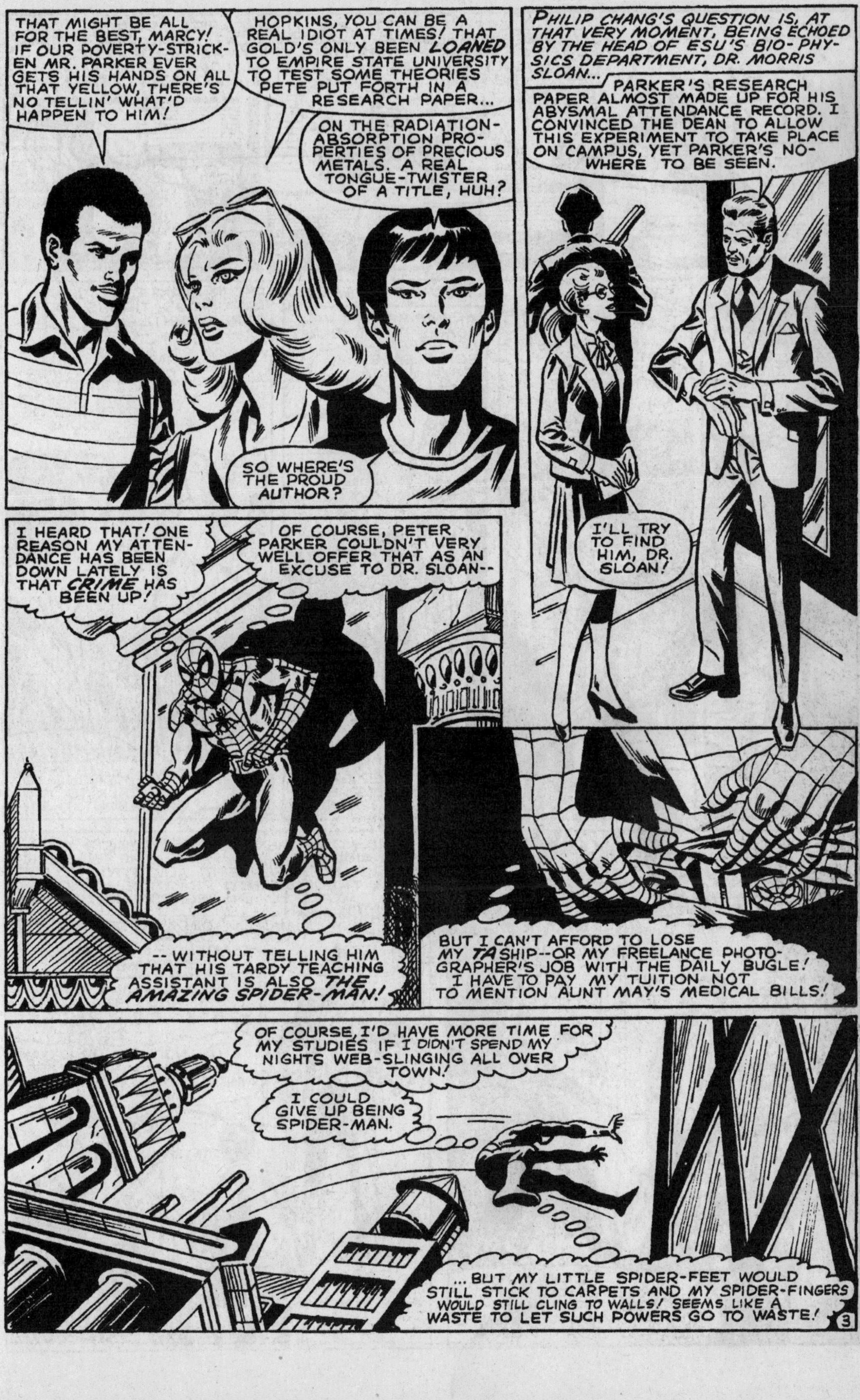
THAT MIGHT BE ALL FOR THE BEST, MARCY! IF OUR POVERTY-STRICKEN MR. PARKER EVER GETS HIS HANDS ON ALL THAT YELLOW, THERE'S NO TELLIN' WHAT'D HAPPEN TO HIM!
HOPKINS, YOU CAN BE A REAL IDIOT AT TIMES! THAT GOLD'S ONLY BEEN LOANED TO EMPIRE STATE UNIVERSITY TO TEST SOME THEORIES PETE PUT FORTH IN A RESEARCH PAPER...
ON THE RADIATION-ABSORPTION PROPERTIES OF PRECIOUS METALS. A REAL TONGUE-TWISTER OF A TITLE, HUH?
SO WHERE'S THE PROUD AUTHOR?
PHILIP CHANG'S QUESTION IS, AT THAT VERY MOMENT, BEING ECHOED BY THE HEAD OF ESU'S BIO-PHYSICS DEPARTMENT, DR. MORRIS SLOAN...
PARKER'S RESEARCH PAPER ALMOST MADE UP FOR HIS ABYSMAL ATTENDANCE RECORD. I CONVINCED THE DEAN TO ALLOW THIS EXPERIMENT TO TAKE PLACE ON CAMPUS, YET PARKER'S NOWHERE TO BE SEEN.
I'LL TRY TO FIND HIM, DR. SLOAN!
I HEARD THAT! ONE REASON MY ATTENDANCE HAS BEEN DOWN LATELY IS THAT CRIME HAS BEEN UP!
OF COURSE, PETER PARKER COULDN'T VERY WELL OFFER THAT AS AN EXCUSE TO DR. SLOAN--
--WITHOUT TELLING HIM THAT HIS TARDY TEACHING ASSISTANT IS ALSO THE AMAZING SPIDER-MAN!
BUT I CAN'T AFFORD TO LOSE MY TA SHIP--OR MY FREELANCE PHOTOGRAPHER'S JOB WITH THE DAILY BUGLE! I HAVE TO PAY MY TUITION NOT TO MENTION AUNT MAY'S MEDICAL BILLS!
OF COURSE, I'D HAVE MORE TIME FOR MY STUDIES IF I DIDN'T SPEND MY NIGHTS WEB-SLINGING ALL OVER TOWN!
I COULD GIVE UP BEING SPIDER-MAN.
...BUT MY LITTLE SPIDER-FEET WOULD STILL STICK TO CARPETS AND MY SPIDER-FINGERS WOULD STILL CLING TO WALLS! SEEMS LIKE A WASTE TO LET SUCH POWERS GO TO WASTE!
3

SO I GUESS I'LL JUST HAVE TO KEEP JUGGLING THE MANY LIVES OF PETER PARKER LIKE A TRAINED SEAL ON A BEACHBALL!

WEBBED BENEATH A VENTILATION DUCT ON THE ROOF OF THE ESU PHYSICS BUILDING, SPIDER-MAN'S SHOULDER BAG AWAITS HIM...

...CONTAINING THE LESS-THAN-STYLISH PARAPHERNALIA OF HIS PETER PARKER IDENTITY.

I'VE GOT TO REPORT TO DR. SLOAN--

--BEFORE HE BEGINS *MY* EXPERIMENT WITHOUT ME!

SECONDS LATER...

AND IF HE COMES IN, MR. ROBERTSON, PLEASE HAVE HIM CALL...

HI, THERE!

PETER! YES, HE'S HERE, MR. ROBERTSON!

PETER PARKER, DR. SLOAN IS FURIOUS! THIS IS YOUR EXPERIMENT, AND...

I GOT HERE AS FAST AS I COULD, DEB! SAY, HOW'RE THINGS WITH YOU AND THAT PREPPIE BOYFRIEND OF YOURS?

BIFF? PETER, I'VE BEEN MEANING TO TALK TO YOU ABOUT THAT--

MR. PARKER, HOW NICE OF YOU TO GRACE THESE HALLOWED WALLS WITH YOUR PRESENCE.

DR. SLOAN!

I DO NOT UNDERSTAND YOU, PETER. YOU ARE A BRILLIANT STUDENT, WHEN YOU DEIGN TO SHOW UP FOR CLASS--

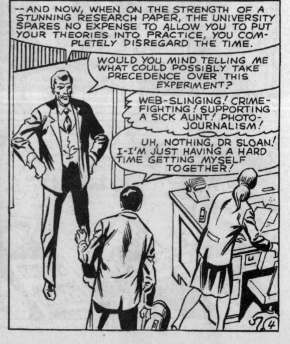

--AND NOW, WHEN ON THE STRENGTH OF A STUNNING RESEARCH PAPER, THE UNIVERSITY SPARES NO EXPENSE TO ALLOW YOU TO PUT YOUR THEORIES INTO PRACTICE, YOU COMPLETELY DISREGARD THE TIME.

WOULD YOU MIND TELLING ME WHAT COULD POSSIBLY TAKE PRECEDENCE OVER THIS EXPERIMENT?

WEB-SLINGING! CRIME-FIGHTING! SUPPORTING A SICK AUNT! PHOTOJOURNALISM!

UH, NOTHING, DR SLOAN! I-I'M JUST HAVING A HARD TIME GETTING MYSELF TOGETHER!

5 4

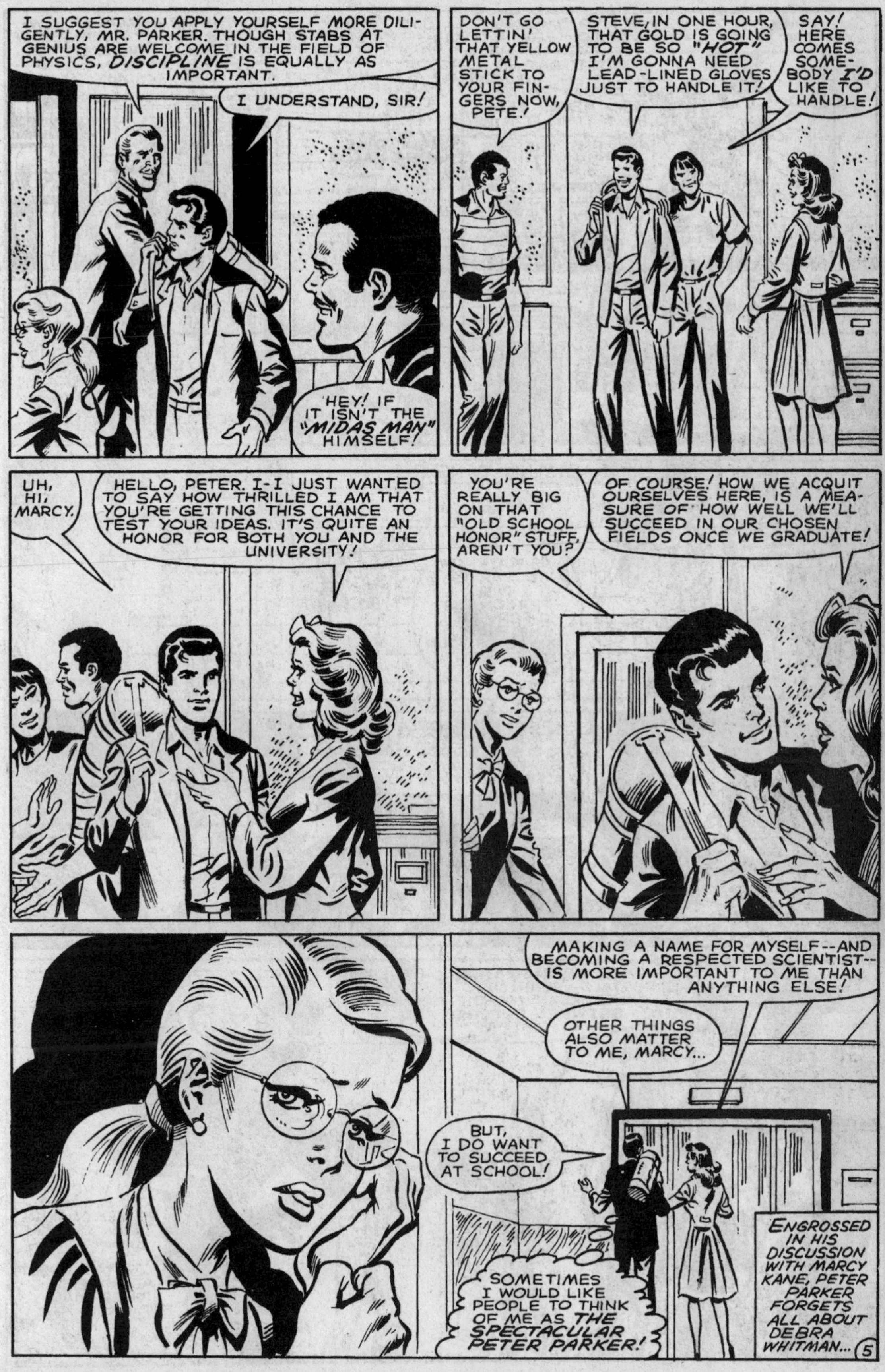

I SUGGEST YOU APPLY YOURSELF MORE DILIGENTLY, MR. PARKER. THOUGH STABS AT GENIUS ARE WELCOME IN THE FIELD OF PHYSICS, DISCIPLINE IS EQUALLY AS IMPORTANT.
I UNDERSTAND, SIR!
'HEY! IF IT ISN'T THE "MIDAS MAN" HIMSELF!
DON'T GO LETTIN' THAT YELLOW METAL STICK TO YOUR FINGERS NOW, PETE!
STEVE, IN ONE HOUR, THAT GOLD IS GOING TO BE SO "HOT" I'M GONNA NEED LEAD-LINED GLOVES JUST TO HANDLE IT!
SAY! HERE COMES SOMEBODY I'D LIKE TO HANDLE!
UH, HI, MARCY.
HELLO, PETER. I-I JUST WANTED TO SAY HOW THRILLED I AM THAT YOU'RE GETTING THIS CHANCE TO TEST YOUR IDEAS. IT'S QUITE AN HONOR FOR BOTH YOU AND THE UNIVERSITY!
YOU'RE REALLY BIG ON THAT "OLD SCHOOL HONOR" STUFF, AREN'T YOU?
OF COURSE! HOW WE ACQUIT OURSELVES HERE, IS A MEASURE OF HOW WELL WE'LL SUCCEED IN OUR CHOSEN FIELDS ONCE WE GRADUATE!
MAKING A NAME FOR MYSELF--AND BECOMING A RESPECTED SCIENTIST--IS MORE IMPORTANT TO ME THAN ANYTHING ELSE!
OTHER THINGS ALSO MATTER TO ME, MARCY...
BUT, I DO WANT TO SUCCEED AT SCHOOL!
SOMETIMES I WOULD LIKE PEOPLE TO THINK OF ME AS THE SPECTACULAR PETER PARKER!
ENGROSSED IN HIS DISCUSSION WITH MARCY KANE, PETER PARKER FORGETS ALL ABOUT DEBRA WHITMAN...
5

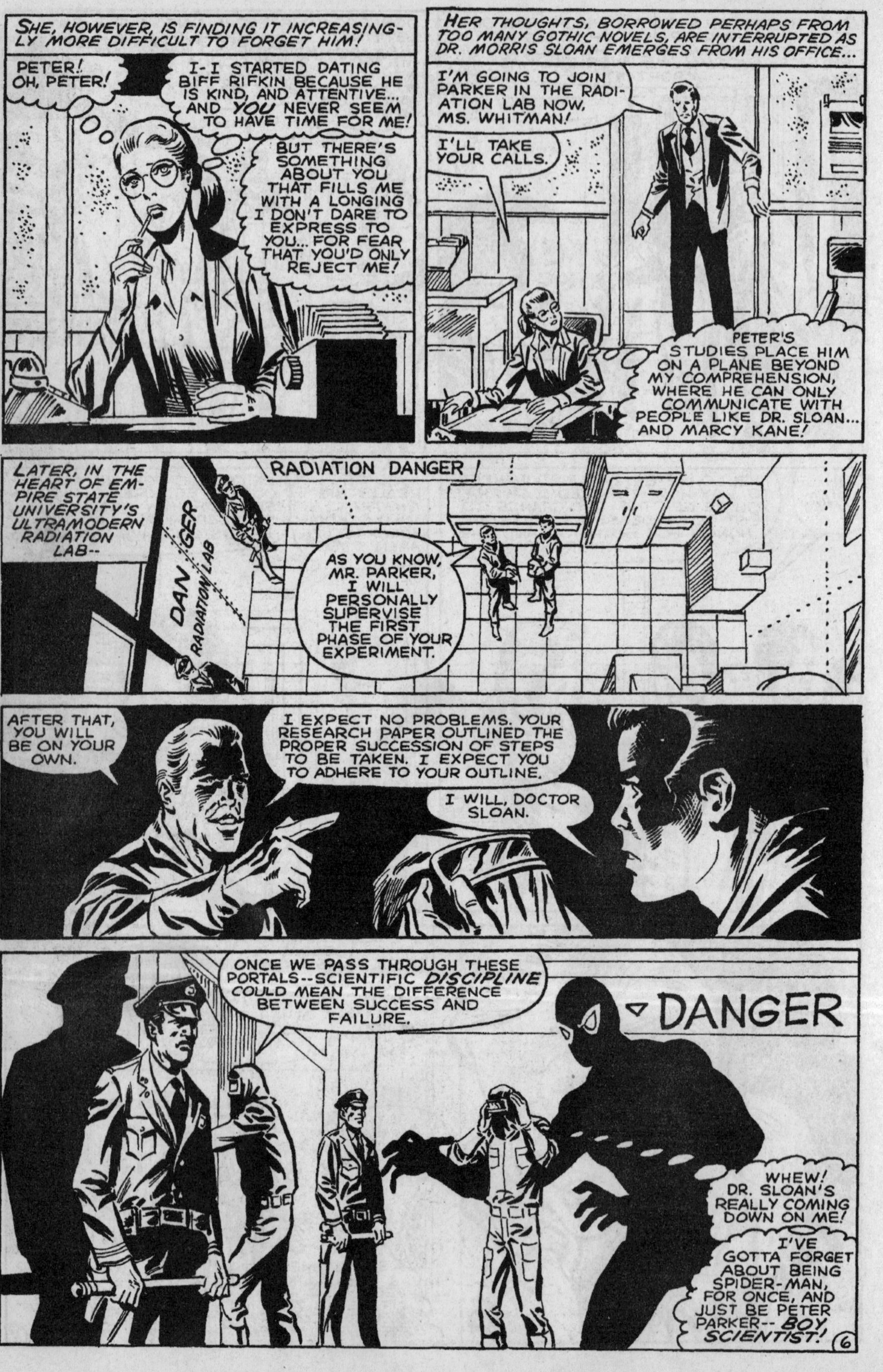
SHE, HOWEVER, IS FINDING IT INCREASINGLY MORE DIFFICULT TO FORGET HIM!
PETER! OH, PETER!
I-I STARTED DATING BIFF RIFKIN BECAUSE HE IS KIND, AND ATTENTIVE... AND YOU NEVER SEEM TO HAVE TIME FOR ME!
BUT THERE'S SOMETHING ABOUT YOU THAT FILLS ME WITH A LONGING I DON'T DARE TO EXPRESS TO YOU... FOR FEAR THAT YOU'D ONLY REJECT ME!
HER THOUGHTS, BORROWED PERHAPS FROM TOO MANY GOTHIC NOVELS, ARE INTERRUPTED AS DR. MORRIS SLOAN EMERGES FROM HIS OFFICE...
I'M GOING TO JOIN PARKER IN THE RADIATION LAB NOW, MS. WHITMAN!
I'LL TAKE YOUR CALLS.
PETER'S STUDIES PLACE HIM ON A PLANE BEYOND MY COMPREHENSION, WHERE HE CAN ONLY COMMUNICATE WITH PEOPLE LIKE DR. SLOAN... AND MARCY KANE!
LATER, IN THE HEART OF EMPIRE STATE UNIVERSITY'S ULTRAMODERN RADIATION LAB--
RADIATION DANGER
DANGER
RADIATION LAB
AS YOU KNOW, MR. PARKER, I WILL PERSONALLY SUPERVISE THE FIRST PHASE OF YOUR EXPERIMENT.
AFTER THAT, YOU WILL BE ON YOUR OWN.
I EXPECT NO PROBLEMS. YOUR RESEARCH PAPER OUTLINED THE PROPER SUCCESSION OF STEPS TO BE TAKEN. I EXPECT YOU TO ADHERE TO YOUR OUTLINE.
I WILL, DOCTOR SLOAN.
ONCE WE PASS THROUGH THESE PORTALS--SCIENTIFIC DISCIPLINE COULD MEAN THE DIFFERENCE BETWEEN SUCCESS AND FAILURE.
DANGER
WHEW! DR. SLOAN'S REALLY COMING DOWN ON ME!
I'VE GOTTA FORGET ABOUT BEING SPIDER-MAN, FOR ONCE, AND JUST BE PETER PARKER-- BOY SCIENTIST!
6

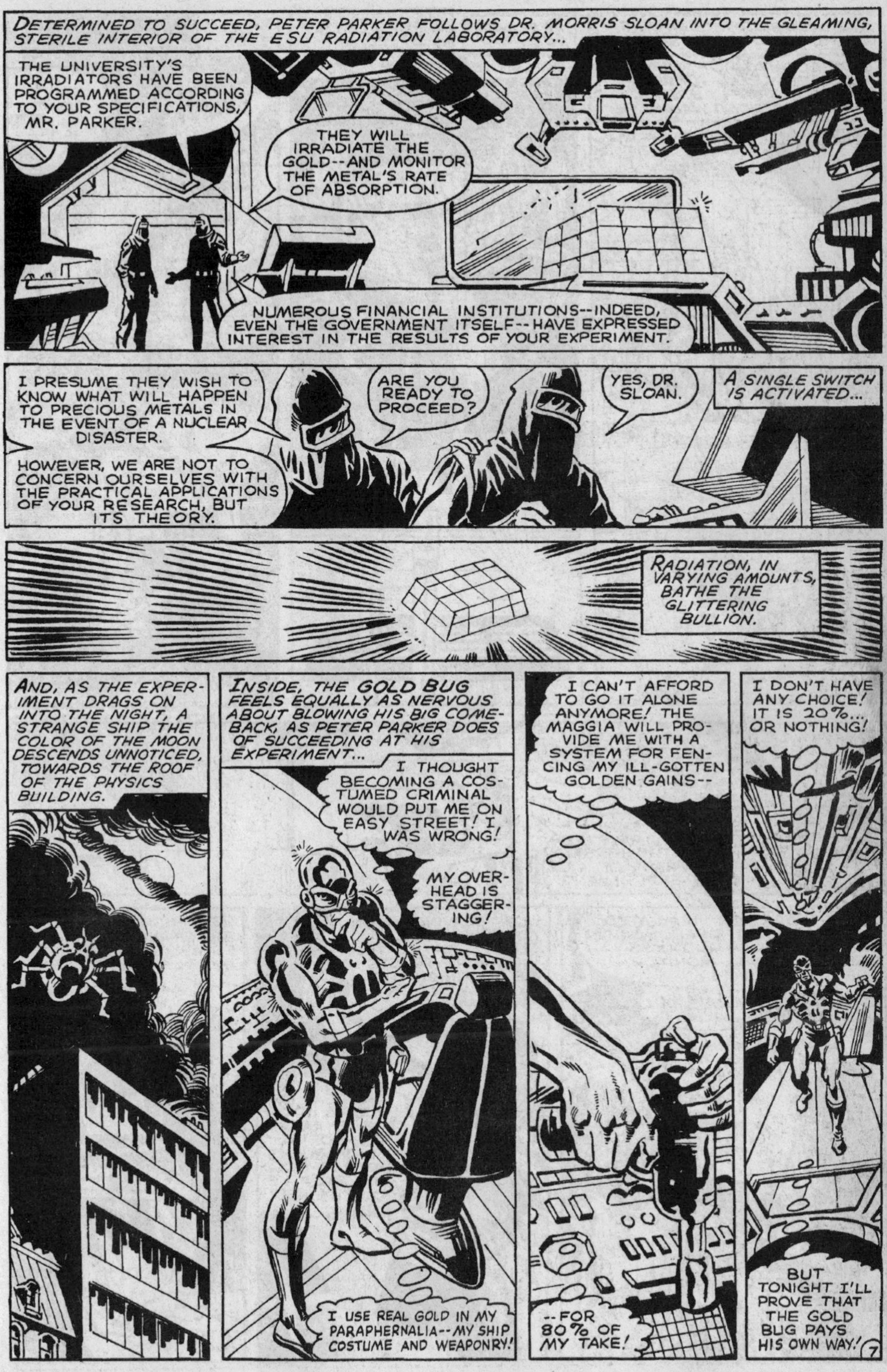
DETERMINED TO SUCCEED, PETER PARKER FOLLOWS DR. MORRIS SLOAN INTO THE GLEAMING, STERILE INTERIOR OF THE ESU RADIATION LABORATORY...
THE UNIVERSITY'S IRRADIATORS HAVE BEEN PROGRAMMED ACCORDING TO YOUR SPECIFICATIONS, MR. PARKER.
THEY WILL IRRADIATE THE GOLD--AND MONITOR THE METAL'S RATE OF ABSORPTION.
NUMEROUS FINANCIAL INSTITUTIONS--INDEED, EVEN THE GOVERNMENT ITSELF--HAVE EXPRESSED INTEREST IN THE RESULTS OF YOUR EXPERIMENT.
I PRESUME THEY WISH TO KNOW WHAT WILL HAPPEN TO PRECIOUS METALS IN THE EVENT OF A NUCLEAR DISASTER.
HOWEVER, WE ARE NOT TO CONCERN OURSELVES WITH THE PRACTICAL APPLICATIONS OF YOUR RESEARCH, BUT ITS THEORY.
ARE YOU READY TO PROCEED?
YES, DR. SLOAN.
A SINGLE SWITCH IS ACTIVATED...
RADIATION, IN VARYING AMOUNTS, BATHE THE GLITTERING BULLION.
AND, AS THE EXPERIMENT DRAGS ON INTO THE NIGHT, A STRANGE SHIP THE COLOR OF THE MOON DESCENDS UNNOTICED, TOWARDS THE ROOF OF THE PHYSICS BUILDING.
INSIDE, THE GOLD BUG FEELS EQUALLY AS NERVOUS ABOUT BLOWING HIS BIG COMEBACK, AS PETER PARKER DOES OF SUCCEEDING AT HIS EXPERIMENT...
I THOUGHT BECOMING A COSTUMED CRIMINAL WOULD PUT ME ON EASY STREET! I WAS WRONG!
MY OVERHEAD IS STAGGERING!
I USE REAL GOLD IN MY PARAPHERNALIA--MY SHIP COSTUME AND WEAPONRY!
I CAN'T AFFORD TO GO IT ALONE ANYMORE! THE MAGGIA WILL PROVIDE ME WITH A SYSTEM FOR FENCING MY ILL-GOTTEN GOLDEN GAINS--
--FOR 80% OF MY TAKE!
I DON'T HAVE ANY CHOICE! IT IS 20%... OR NOTHING!
BUT TONIGHT I'LL PROVE THAT THE GOLD BUG PAYS HIS OWN WAY!
7

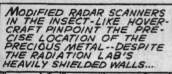

MODIFIED RADAR SCANNERS IN THE INSECT-LIKE HOVERCRAFT PINPOINT THE PRECISE LOCATION OF THE PRECIOUS METAL--DESPITE THE RADIATION LAB'S HEAVILY SHIELDED WALLS....

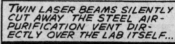

TWIN LASER BEAMS SILENTLY CUT AWAY THE STEEL AIR-PURIFICATION VENT DIRECTLY OVER THE LAB ITSELF...

AND THEN...

SHIP'S DONE ALL IT CAN!

IT'S TIME FOR A MORE *PERSONAL* TOUCH!

MEANWHILE, UNAWARE OF ANY IMPENDING DANGER..

GOOD, MR. PARKER! VERY GOOD!

THAT COMPLETES THE FIRST PHASE OF YOUR EXPERIMENT.

THE GOLD IS NOW IRRADIATED. THE INSTRUMENTS WILL MONITOR THE ABSORPTION AND LOSS RATES. *YOU* WILL MONITOR THE INSTRUMENTS.

ALONE, DR. SLOAN?

I WOULD LIKE TO HAVE MY SUPPER, MR. PARKER.

YES, SIR!

WOW! LEAVING ME ON MY OWN IS DOC SLOAN'S WAY OF TELLING ME HE TRUSTS ME TO FINISH THE EXPERIMENT ON MY OWN!

AND I GUESS THAT HE FIGURES THAT THE FEAR OF LOUSING UP ON THE DE-RADIATING OF A MILLION BUCKS WORTH OF GOLD WILL KEEP ME 'DISCIPLINED'!

HE'S RIGHT! THIS IS MY BIG CHANCE TO RE-ESTABLISH CREDIBILITY IN DOC SLOAN'S EYES!

I WON'T BLOW IT!

8

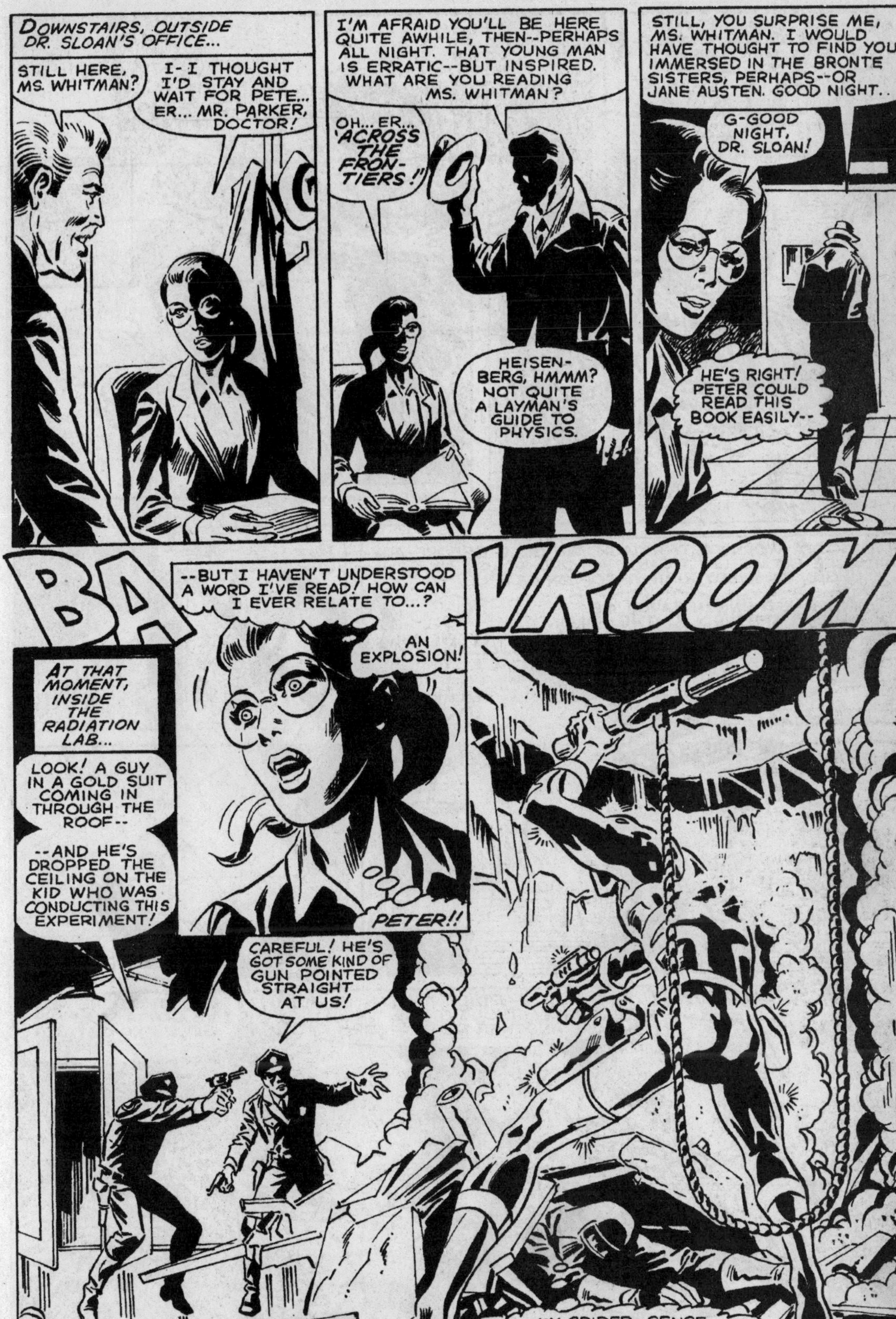

DOWNSTAIRS, OUTSIDE DR. SLOAN'S OFFICE...
STILL HERE, MS. WHITMAN?
I- I THOUGHT I'D STAY AND WAIT FOR PETE... ER... MR. PARKER, DOCTOR!
I'M AFRAID YOU'LL BE HERE QUITE AWHILE, THEN--PERHAPS ALL NIGHT. THAT YOUNG MAN IS ERRATIC--BUT INSPIRED. WHAT ARE YOU READING MS. WHITMAN?
OH... ER... 'ACROSS THE FRONTIERS!'
HEISENBERG, HMMM? NOT QUITE A LAYMAN'S GUIDE TO PHYSICS.
STILL, YOU SURPRISE ME, MS. WHITMAN. I WOULD HAVE THOUGHT TO FIND YOU IMMERSED IN THE BRONTE SISTERS, PERHAPS--OR JANE AUSTEN. GOOD NIGHT..
G-GOOD NIGHT, DR. SLOAN!
HE'S RIGHT! PETER COULD READ THIS BOOK EASILY--
BA VROOM
--BUT I HAVEN'T UNDERSTOOD A WORD I'VE READ! HOW CAN I EVER RELATE TO...?
AN EXPLOSION!
PETER!!
AT THAT MOMENT, INSIDE THE RADIATION LAB...
LOOK! A GUY IN A GOLD SUIT COMING IN THROUGH THE ROOF--
--AND HE'S DROPPED THE CEILING ON THE KID WHO WAS CONDUCTING THIS EXPERIMENT!
CAREFUL! HE'S GOT SOME KIND OF GUN POINTED STRAIGHT AT US!
MY SPIDER-SENSE WARNED ME OF DANGER! BUT THIS RADIATION SUIT HINDERED MY REFLEXES! COULDN'T REACT IN TIME!
9

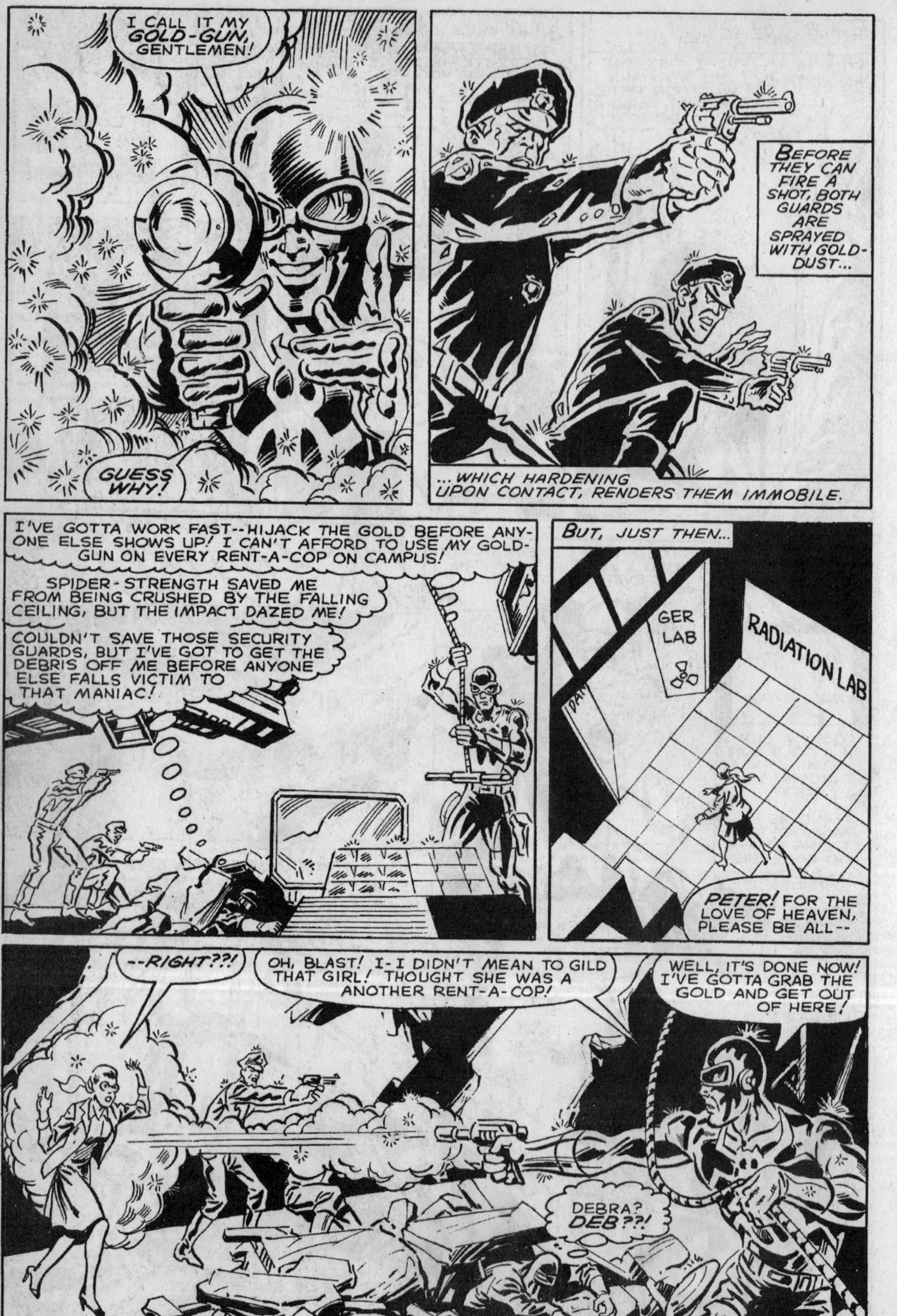
I CALL IT MY GOLD-GUN, GENTLEMEN!
GUESS WHY!
BEFORE THEY CAN FIRE A SHOT, BOTH GUARDS ARE SPRAYED WITH GOLD-DUST...
...WHICH HARDENING UPON CONTACT, RENDERS THEM IMMOBILE.
I'VE GOTTA WORK FAST--HIJACK THE GOLD BEFORE ANYONE ELSE SHOWS UP! I CAN'T AFFORD TO USE MY GOLD-GUN ON EVERY RENT-A-COP ON CAMPUS!
SPIDER-STRENGTH SAVED ME FROM BEING CRUSHED BY THE FALLING CEILING, BUT THE IMPACT DAZED ME!
COULDN'T SAVE THOSE SECURITY GUARDS, BUT I'VE GOT TO GET THE DEBRIS OFF ME BEFORE ANYONE ELSE FALLS VICTIM TO THAT MANIAC!
BUT, JUST THEN...
GER LAB
RADIATION LAB
PETER! FOR THE LOVE OF HEAVEN, PLEASE BE ALL--
--RIGHT??!
OH, BLAST! I-I DIDN'T MEAN TO GILD THAT GIRL! THOUGHT SHE WAS A ANOTHER RENT-A-COP!
WELL, IT'S DONE NOW! I'VE GOTTA GRAB THE GOLD AND GET OUT OF HERE!
DEBRA? DEB??!
10

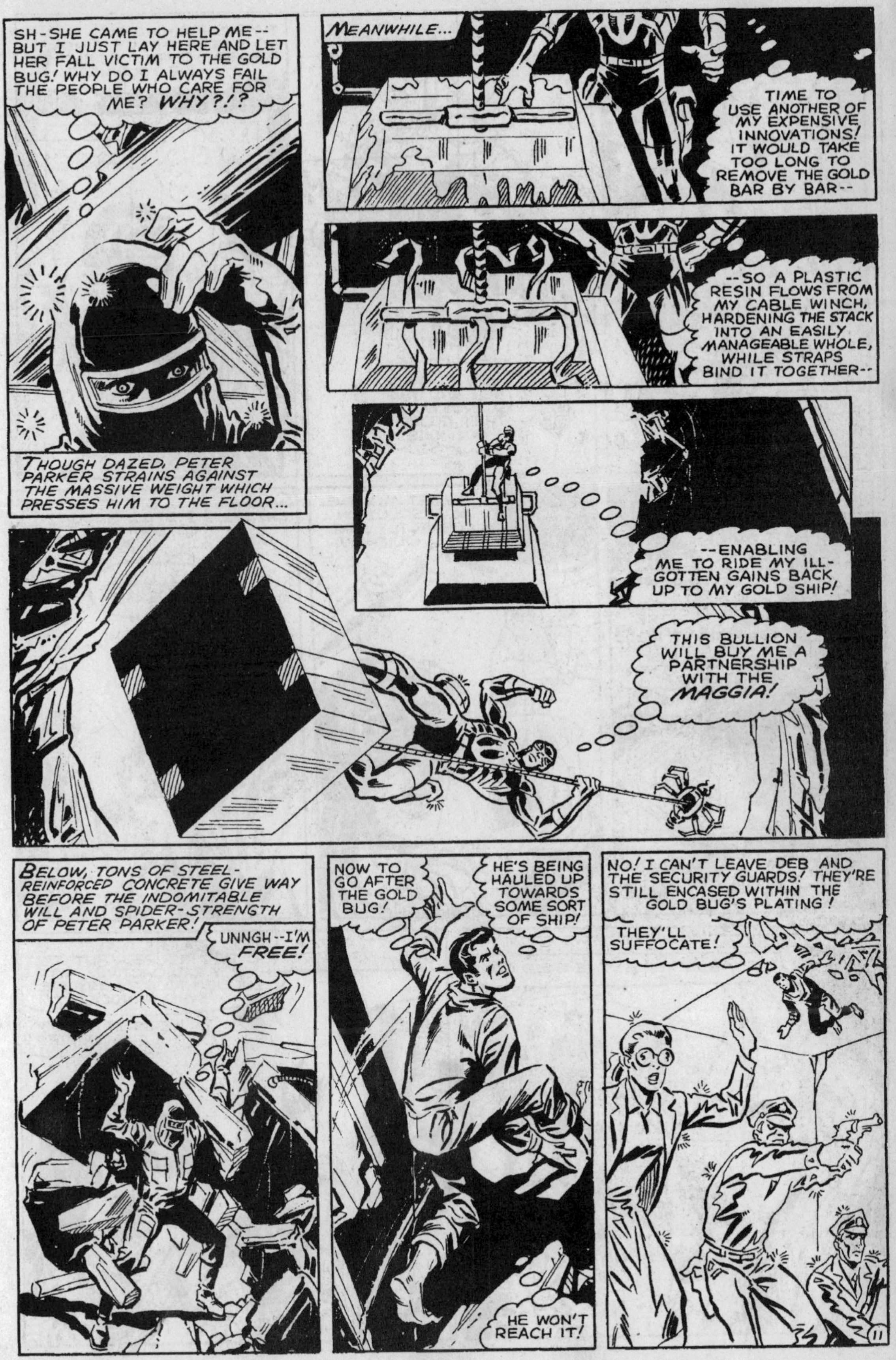
SH-SHE CAME TO HELP ME-- BUT I JUST LAY HERE AND LET HER FALL VICTIM TO THE GOLD BUG! WHY DO I ALWAYS FAIL THE PEOPLE WHO CARE FOR ME? WHY?!?
THOUGH DAZED, PETER PARKER STRAINS AGAINST THE MASSIVE WEIGHT WHICH PRESSES HIM TO THE FLOOR...
MEANWHILE...
TIME TO USE ANOTHER OF MY EXPENSIVE INNOVATIONS! IT WOULD TAKE TOO LONG TO REMOVE THE GOLD BAR BY BAR--
--SO A PLASTIC RESIN FLOWS FROM MY CABLE WINCH, HARDENING THE STACK INTO AN EASILY MANAGEABLE WHOLE, WHILE STRAPS BIND IT TOGETHER--
--ENABLING ME TO RIDE MY ILL-GOTTEN GAINS BACK UP TO MY GOLD SHIP!
THIS BULLION WILL BUY ME A PARTNERSHIP WITH THE MAGGIA!
BELOW, TONS OF STEEL-REINFORCED CONCRETE GIVE WAY BEFORE THE INDOMITABLE WILL AND SPIDER-STRENGTH OF PETER PARKER!
UNNGH--I'M FREE!
NOW TO GO AFTER THE GOLD BUG!
HE'S BEING HAULED UP TOWARDS SOME SORT OF SHIP!
HE WON'T REACH IT!
NO! I CAN'T LEAVE DEB AND THE SECURITY GUARDS! THEY'RE STILL ENCASED WITHIN THE GOLD BUG'S PLATING!
THEY'LL SUFFOCATE!
11

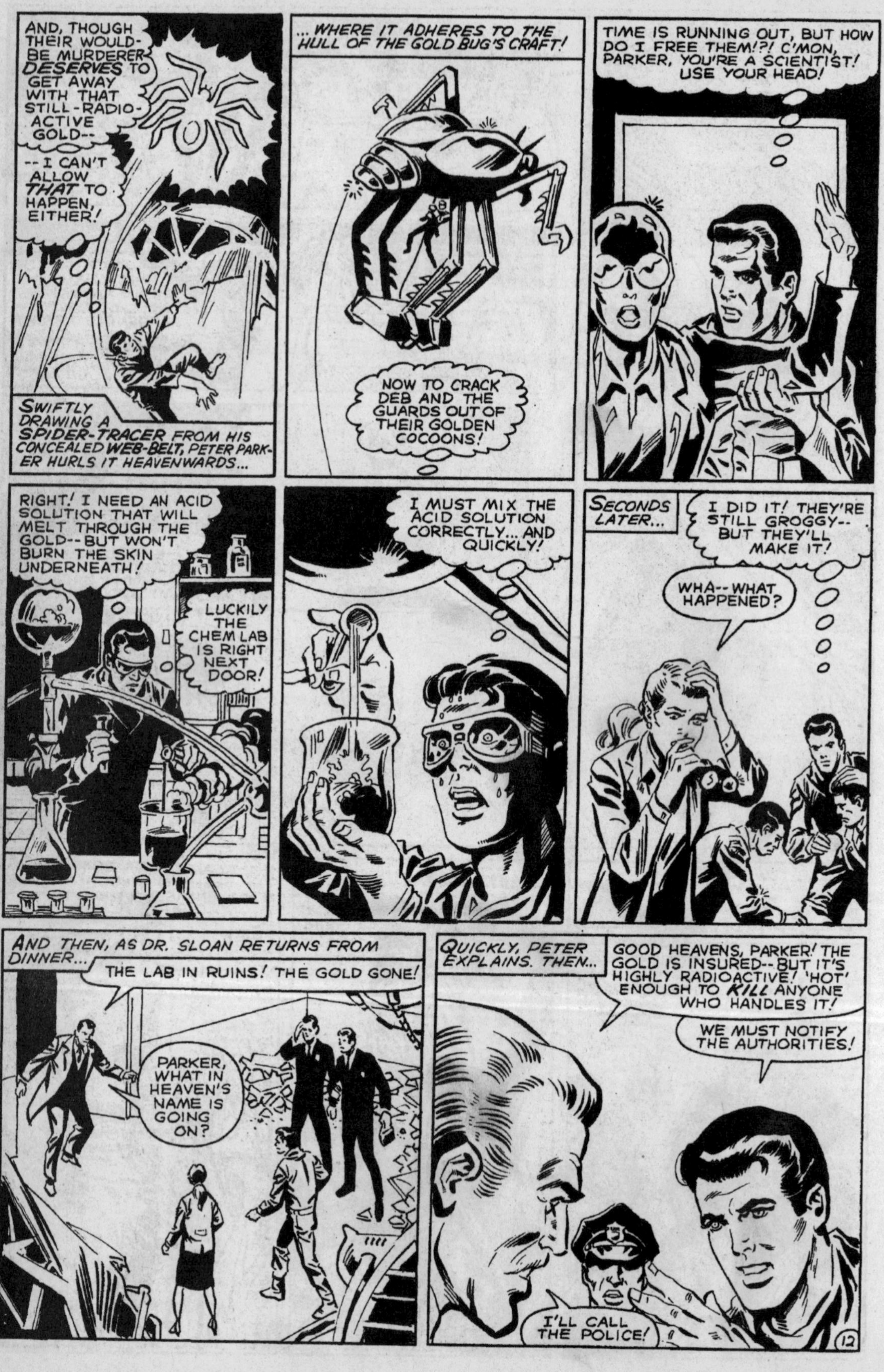
AND, THOUGH THEIR WOULD-BE MURDERER DESERVES TO GET AWAY WITH THAT STILL-RADIO-ACTIVE GOLD--
-- I CAN'T ALLOW THAT TO HAPPEN, EITHER!
SWIFTLY DRAWING A SPIDER-TRACER FROM HIS CONCEALED WEB-BELT, PETER PARKER HURLS IT HEAVENWARDS...
...WHERE IT ADHERES TO THE HULL OF THE GOLD BUG'S CRAFT!
NOW TO CRACK DEB AND THE GUARDS OUT OF THEIR GOLDEN COCOONS!
TIME IS RUNNING OUT, BUT HOW DO I FREE THEM!?! C'MON, PARKER, YOU'RE A SCIENTIST! USE YOUR HEAD!
RIGHT! I NEED AN ACID SOLUTION THAT WILL MELT THROUGH THE GOLD-- BUT WON'T BURN THE SKIN UNDERNEATH!
LUCKILY THE CHEM LAB IS RIGHT NEXT DOOR!
I MUST MIX THE ACID SOLUTION CORRECTLY... AND QUICKLY!
SECONDS LATER...
I DID IT! THEY'RE STILL GROGGY-- BUT THEY'LL MAKE IT!
WHA-- WHAT HAPPENED?
AND THEN, AS DR. SLOAN RETURNS FROM DINNER...
THE LAB IN RUINS! THE GOLD GONE!
PARKER, WHAT IN HEAVEN'S NAME IS GOING ON?
QUICKLY, PETER EXPLAINS. THEN...
GOOD HEAVENS, PARKER! THE GOLD IS INSURED-- BUT IT'S HIGHLY RADIOACTIVE! 'HOT' ENOUGH TO KILL ANYONE WHO HANDLES IT!
WE MUST NOTIFY THE AUTHORITIES!
I'LL CALL THE POLICE!
12

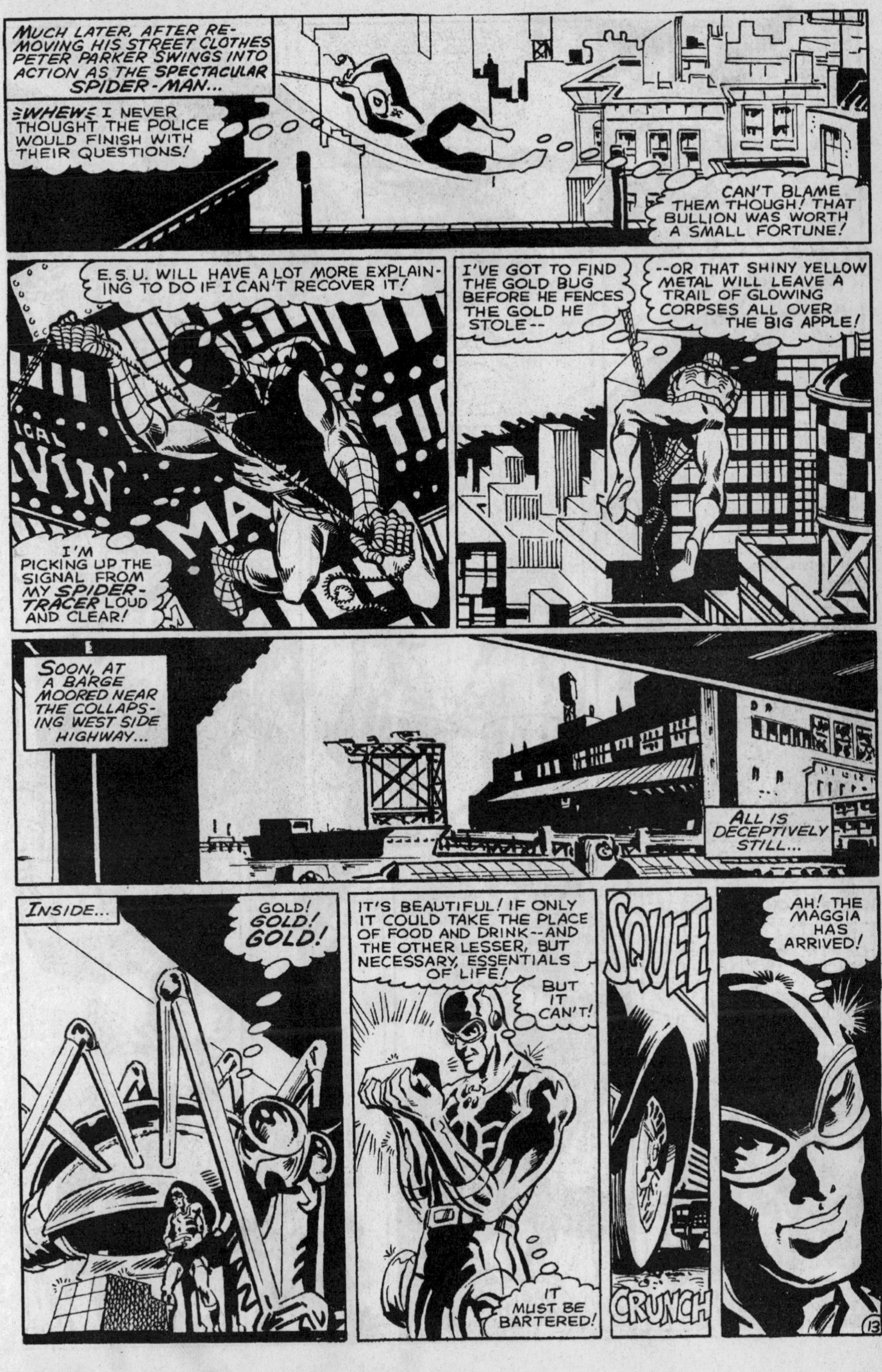

MUCH LATER, AFTER RE-MOVING HIS STREET CLOTHES PETER PARKER SWINGS INTO ACTION AS THE SPECTACULAR SPIDER-MAN...
WHEW I NEVER THOUGHT THE POLICE WOULD FINISH WITH THEIR QUESTIONS!
CAN'T BLAME THEM THOUGH! THAT BULLION WAS WORTH A SMALL FORTUNE!
E.S.U. WILL HAVE A LOT MORE EXPLAIN-ING TO DO IF I CAN'T RECOVER IT!
I'M PICKING UP THE SIGNAL FROM MY SPIDER-TRACER LOUD AND CLEAR!
I'VE GOT TO FIND THE GOLD BUG BEFORE HE FENCES THE GOLD HE STOLE--
--OR THAT SHINY YELLOW METAL WILL LEAVE A TRAIL OF GLOWING CORPSES ALL OVER THE BIG APPLE!
SOON, AT A BARGE MOORED NEAR THE COLLAPS-ING WEST SIDE HIGHWAY...
ALL IS DECEPTIVELY STILL...
INSIDE...
GOLD! GOLD! GOLD!
IT'S BEAUTIFUL! IF ONLY IT COULD TAKE THE PLACE OF FOOD AND DRINK--AND THE OTHER LESSER, BUT NECESSARY, ESSENTIALS OF LIFE!
BUT IT CAN'T!
IT MUST BE BARTERED!
SQUEE
CRUNCH
AH! THE MAGGIA HAS ARRIVED!
13

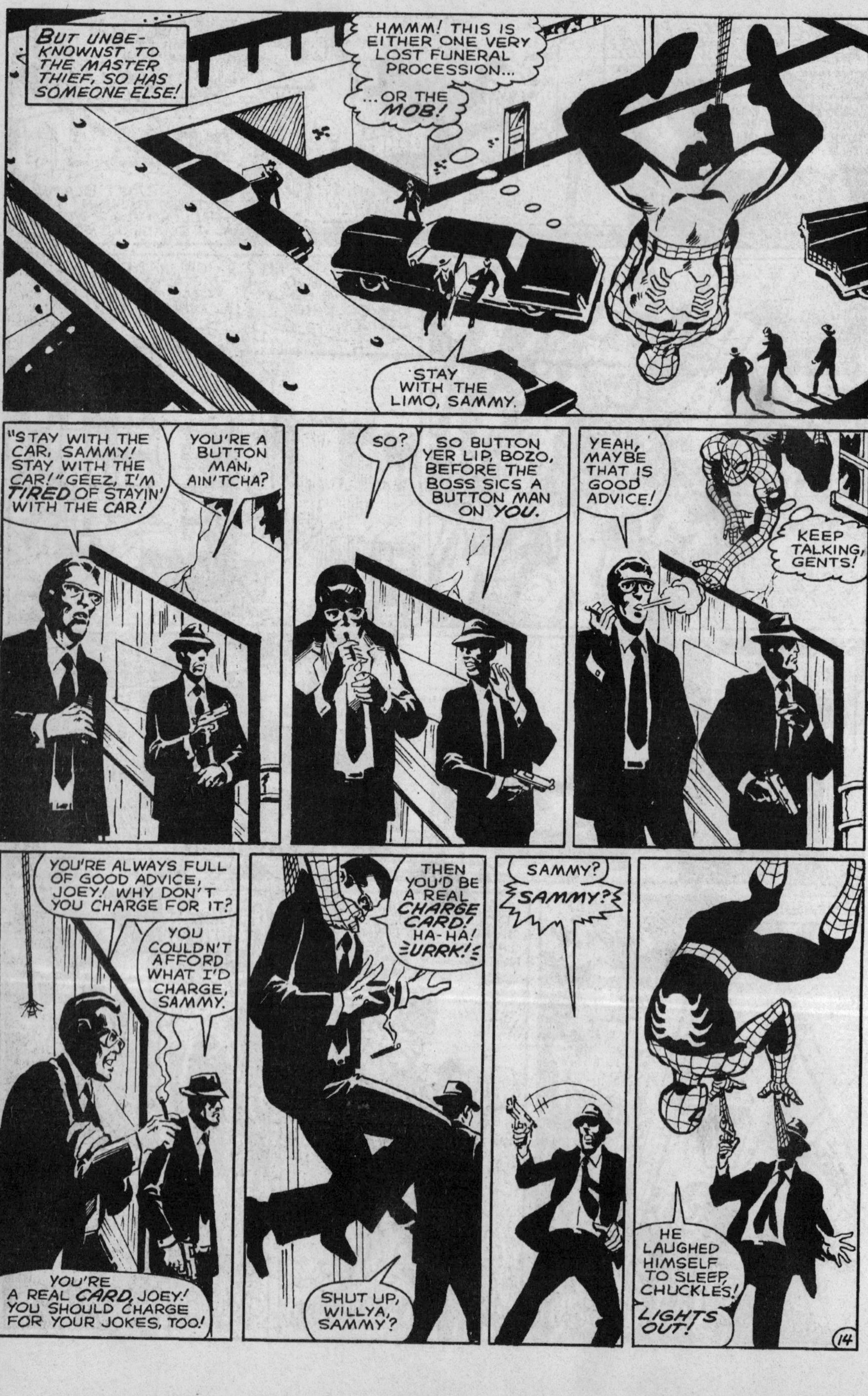
BUT UNBE-KNOWNST TO THE MASTER THIEF, SO HAS SOMEONE ELSE!
HMMM! THIS IS EITHER ONE VERY LOST FUNERAL PROCESSION...
...OR THE MOB!
STAY WITH THE LIMO, SAMMY.
"STAY WITH THE CAR, SAMMY! STAY WITH THE CAR!" GEEZ, I'M TIRED OF STAYIN' WITH THE CAR!
YOU'RE A BUTTON MAN, AIN'TCHA?
SO?
SO BUTTON YER LIP, BOZO, BEFORE THE BOSS SICS A BUTTON MAN ON YOU.
YEAH, MAYBE THAT IS GOOD ADVICE!
KEEP TALKING, GENTS!
YOU'RE ALWAYS FULL OF GOOD ADVICE, JOEY! WHY DON'T YOU CHARGE FOR IT?
YOU COULDN'T AFFORD WHAT I'D CHARGE, SAMMY.
YOU'RE A REAL CARD, JOEY! YOU SHOULD CHARGE FOR YOUR JOKES, TOO!
THEN YOU'D BE A REAL CHARGE CARD! HA-HA! URRK!
SHUT UP, WILLYA, SAMMY?
SAMMY?
SAMMY?
HE LAUGHED HIMSELF TO SLEEP, CHUCKLES!
LIGHTS OUT!
14

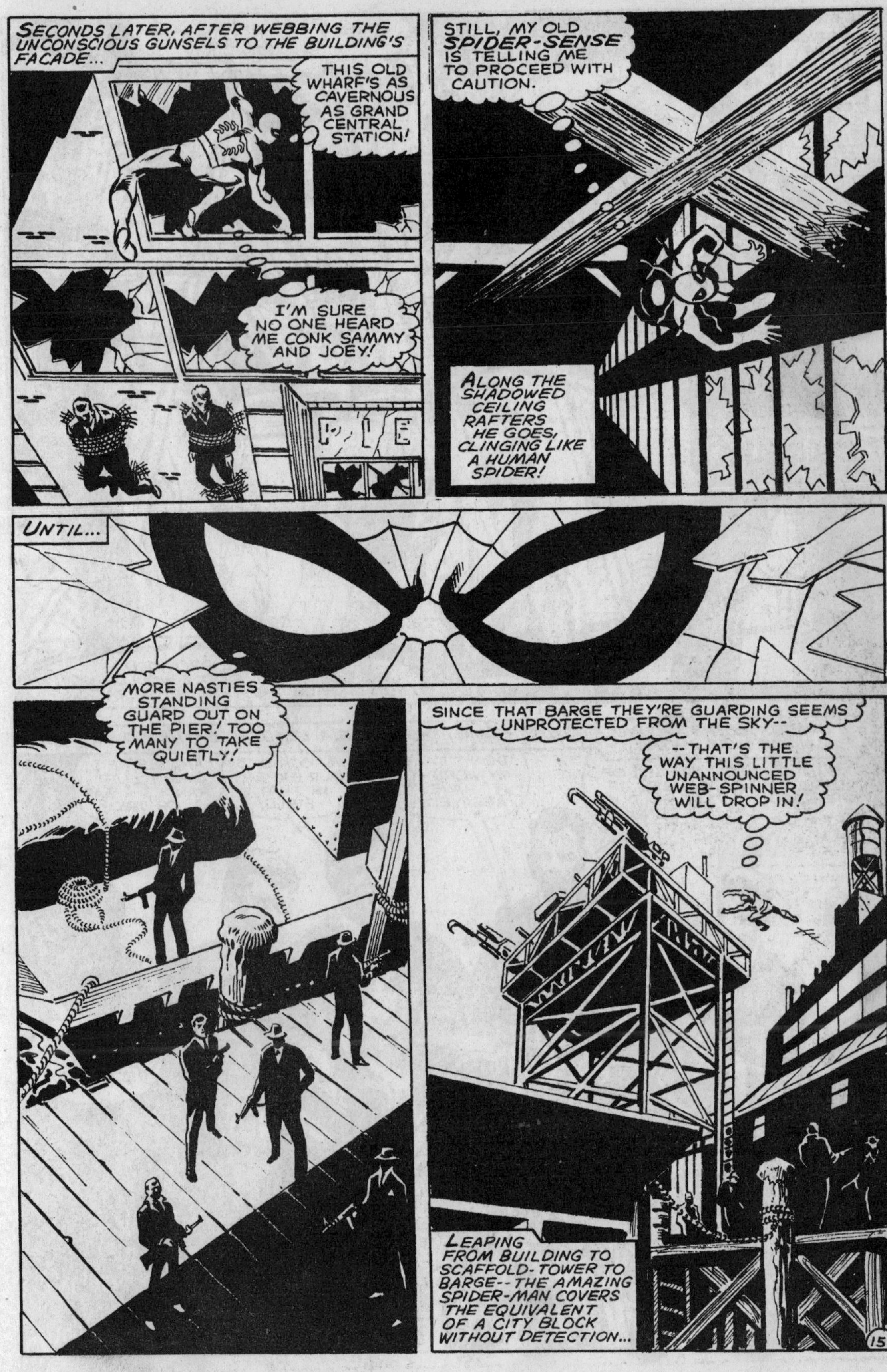
SECONDS LATER, AFTER WEBBING THE UNCONSCIOUS GUNSELS TO THE BUILDING'S FACADE...
THIS OLD WHARF'S AS CAVERNOUS AS GRAND CENTRAL STATION!
I'M SURE NO ONE HEARD ME CONK SAMMY AND JOEY!
PIE
STILL, MY OLD SPIDER-SENSE IS TELLING ME TO PROCEED WITH CAUTION.
ALONG THE SHADOWED CEILING RAFTERS HE GOES, CLINGING LIKE A HUMAN SPIDER!
UNTIL...
MORE NASTIES STANDING GUARD OUT ON THE PIER! TOO MANY TO TAKE QUIETLY!
SINCE THAT BARGE THEY'RE GUARDING SEEMS UNPROTECTED FROM THE SKY--
--THAT'S THE WAY THIS LITTLE UNANNOUNCED WEB-SPINNER WILL DROP IN!
LEAPING FROM BUILDING TO SCAFFOLD-TOWER TO BARGE--THE AMAZING SPIDER-MAN COVERS THE EQUIVALENT OF A CITY BLOCK WITHOUT DETECTION...
15

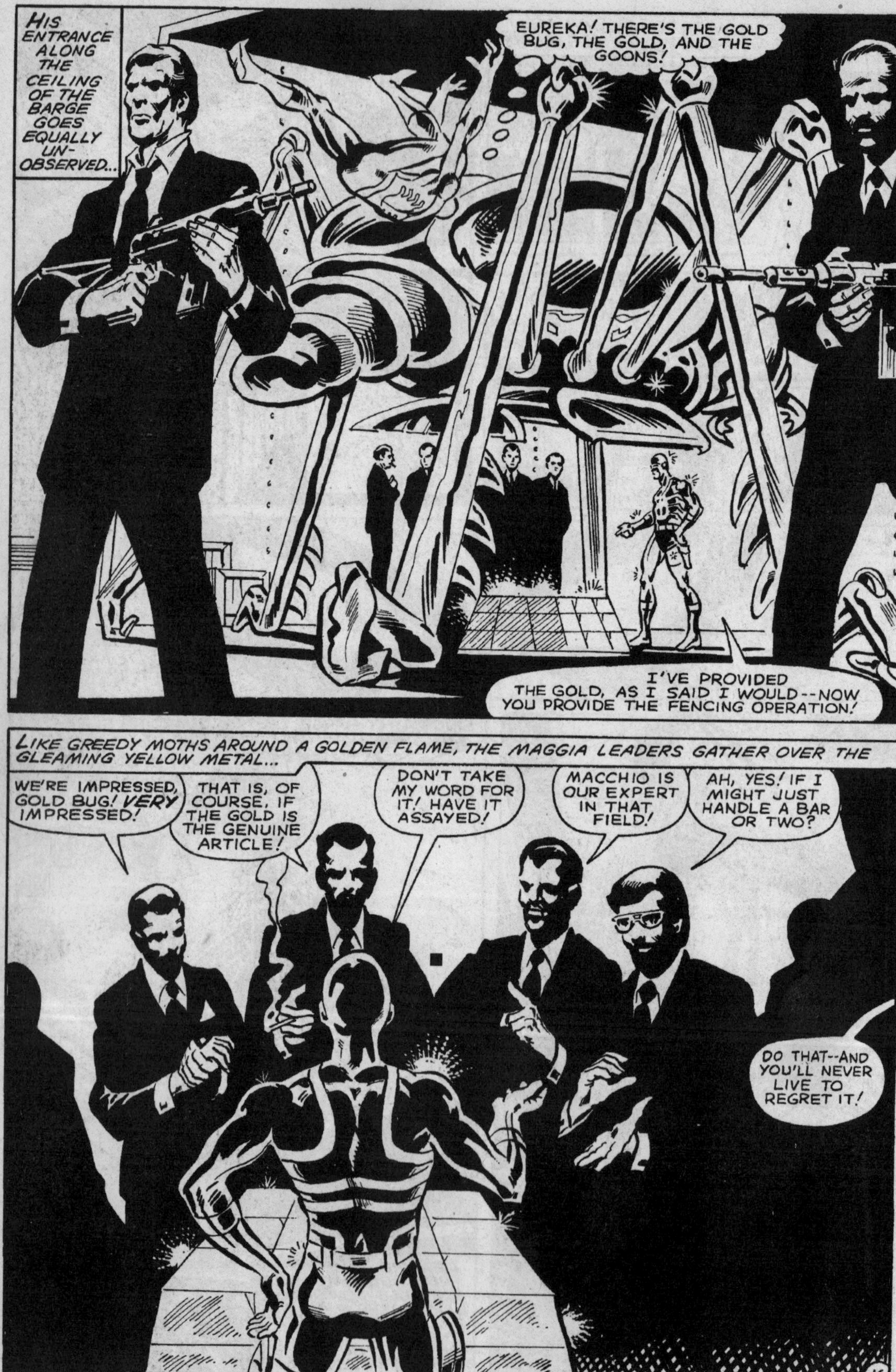
HIS ENTRANCE ALONG THE CEILING OF THE BARGE GOES EQUALLY UN-OBSERVED...
EUREKA! THERE'S THE GOLD BUG, THE GOLD, AND THE GOONS!
I'VE PROVIDED THE GOLD, AS I SAID I WOULD--NOW YOU PROVIDE THE FENCING OPERATION!
LIKE GREEDY MOTHS AROUND A GOLDEN FLAME, THE MAGGIA LEADERS GATHER OVER THE GLEAMING YELLOW METAL...
WE'RE IMPRESSED, GOLD BUG! VERY IMPRESSED!
THAT IS, OF COURSE, IF THE GOLD IS THE GENUINE ARTICLE!
DON'T TAKE MY WORD FOR IT! HAVE IT ASSAYED!
MACCHIO IS OUR EXPERT IN THAT FIELD!
AH, YES! IF I MIGHT JUST HANDLE A BAR OR TWO?
DO THAT--AND YOU'LL NEVER LIVE TO REGRET IT!
16

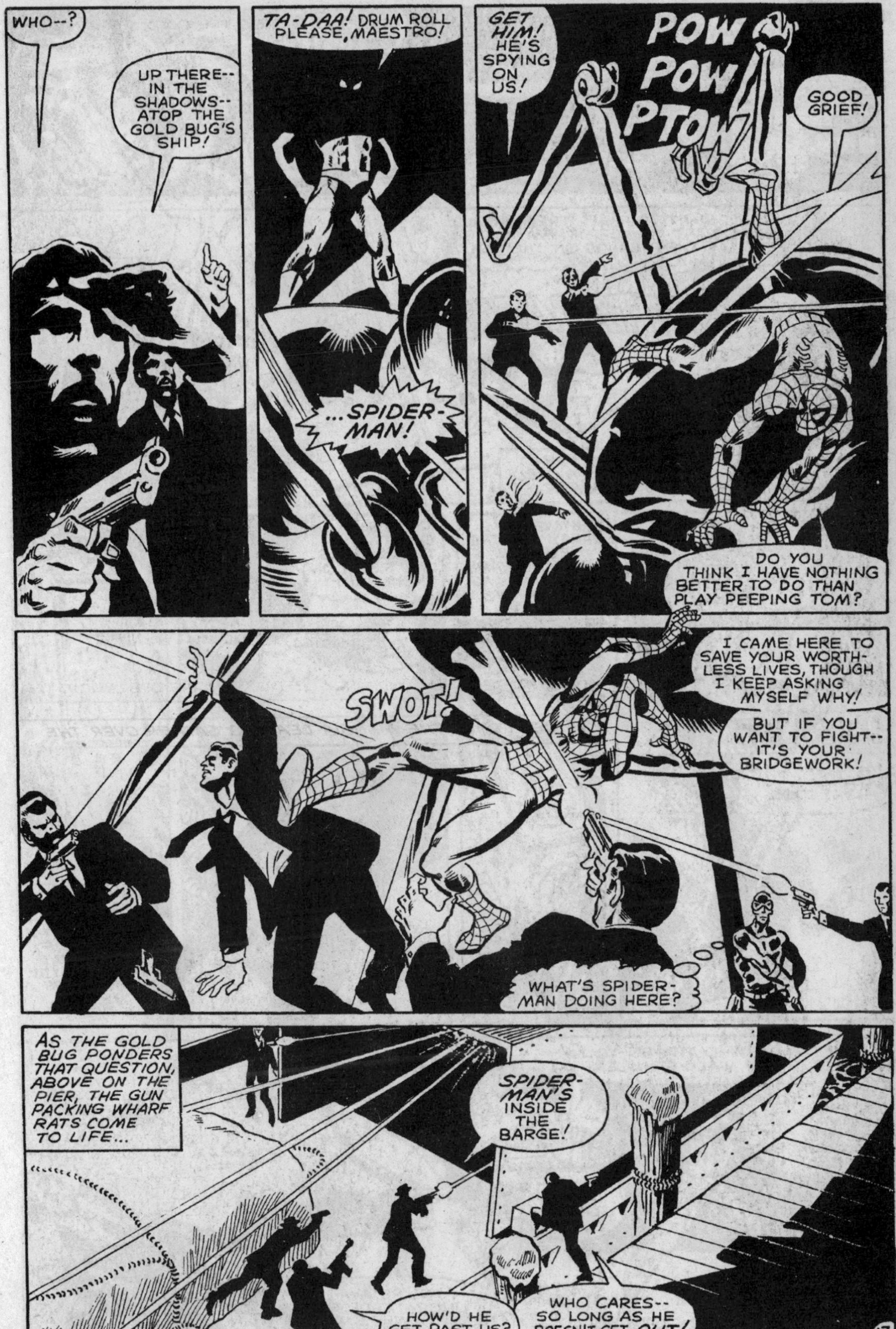
WHO--?
UP THERE-- IN THE SHADOWS-- ATOP THE GOLD BUG'S SHIP!
TA-DAA! DRUM ROLL PLEASE, MAESTRO!
...SPIDER-MAN!
GET HIM! HE'S SPYING ON US!
POW POW PTOW
GOOD GRIEF!
DO YOU THINK I HAVE NOTHING BETTER TO DO THAN PLAY PEEPING TOM?
I CAME HERE TO SAVE YOUR WORTHLESS LIVES, THOUGH I KEEP ASKING MYSELF WHY!
BUT IF YOU WANT TO FIGHT-- IT'S YOUR BRIDGEWORK!
SWOT!
WHAT'S SPIDER-MAN DOING HERE?
AS THE GOLD BUG PONDERS THAT QUESTION, ABOVE ON THE PIER, THE GUN PACKING WHARF RATS COME TO LIFE...
SPIDER-MAN'S INSIDE THE BARGE!
HOW'D HE GET PAST US?
WHO CARES-- SO LONG AS HE DOESN'T GET OUT!

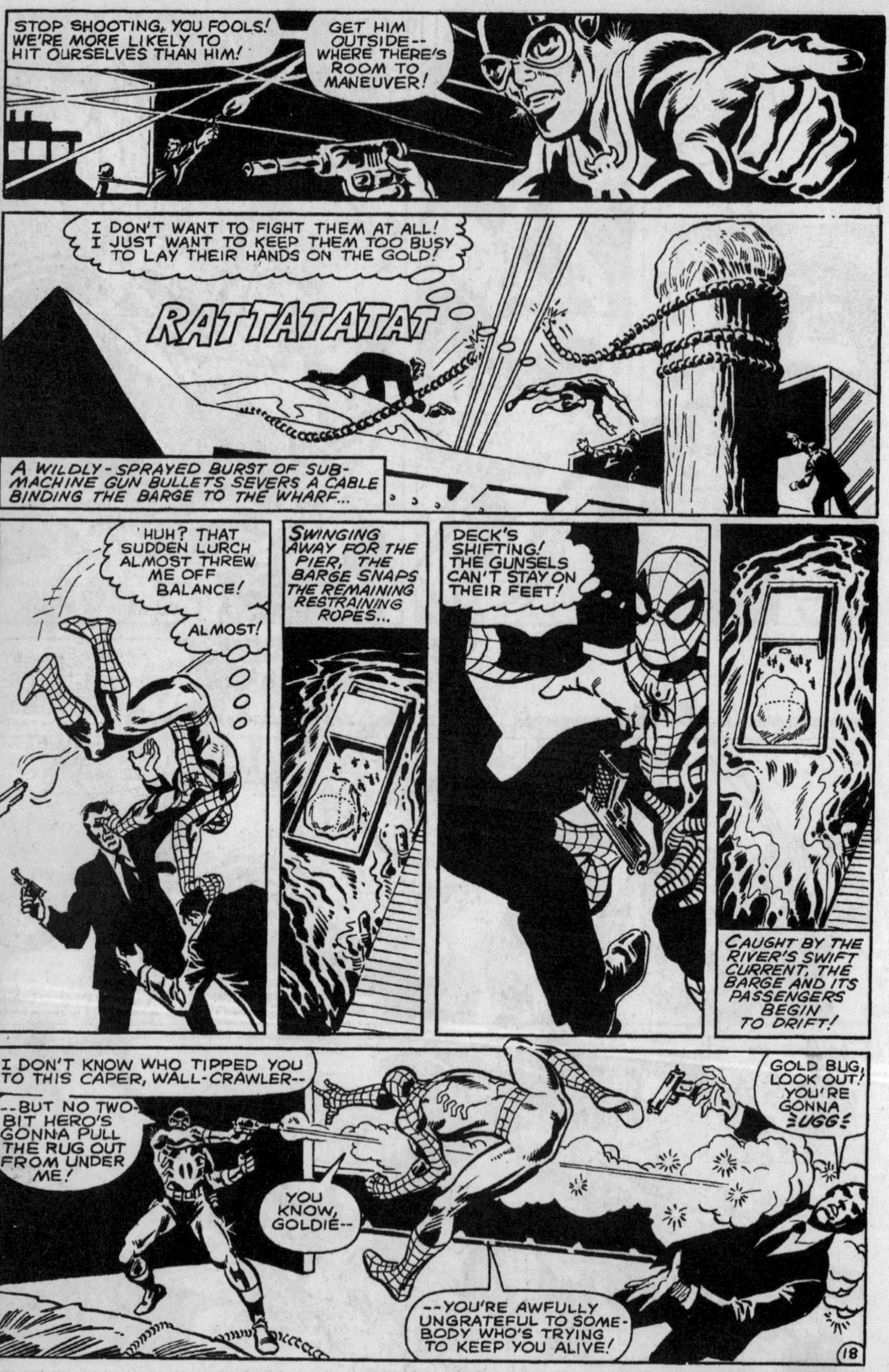

STOP SHOOTING, YOU FOOLS! WE'RE MORE LIKELY TO HIT OURSELVES THAN HIM!
GET HIM OUTSIDE-- WHERE THERE'S ROOM TO MANEUVER!
I DON'T WANT TO FIGHT THEM AT ALL! I JUST WANT TO KEEP THEM TOO BUSY TO LAY THEIR HANDS ON THE GOLD!
RATTATATAT
A WILDLY-SPRAYED BURST OF SUB-MACHINE GUN BULLETS SEVERS A CABLE BINDING THE BARGE TO THE WHARF...
HUH? THAT SUDDEN LURCH ALMOST THREW ME OFF BALANCE!
ALMOST!
SWINGING AWAY FOR THE PIER, THE BARGE SNAPS THE REMAINING RESTRAINING ROPES...
DECK'S SHIFTING! THE GUNSELS CAN'T STAY ON THEIR FEET!
CAUGHT BY THE RIVER'S SWIFT CURRENT, THE BARGE AND ITS PASSENGERS BEGIN TO DRIFT!
I DON'T KNOW WHO TIPPED YOU TO THIS CAPER, WALL-CRAWLER--
--BUT NO TWO-BIT HERO'S GONNA PULL THE RUG OUT FROM UNDER ME!
YOU KNOW, GOLDIE--
--YOU'RE AWFULLY UNGRATEFUL TO SOMEBODY WHO'S TRYING TO KEEP YOU ALIVE!
GOLD BUG, LOOK OUT! YOU'RE GONNA
UGG

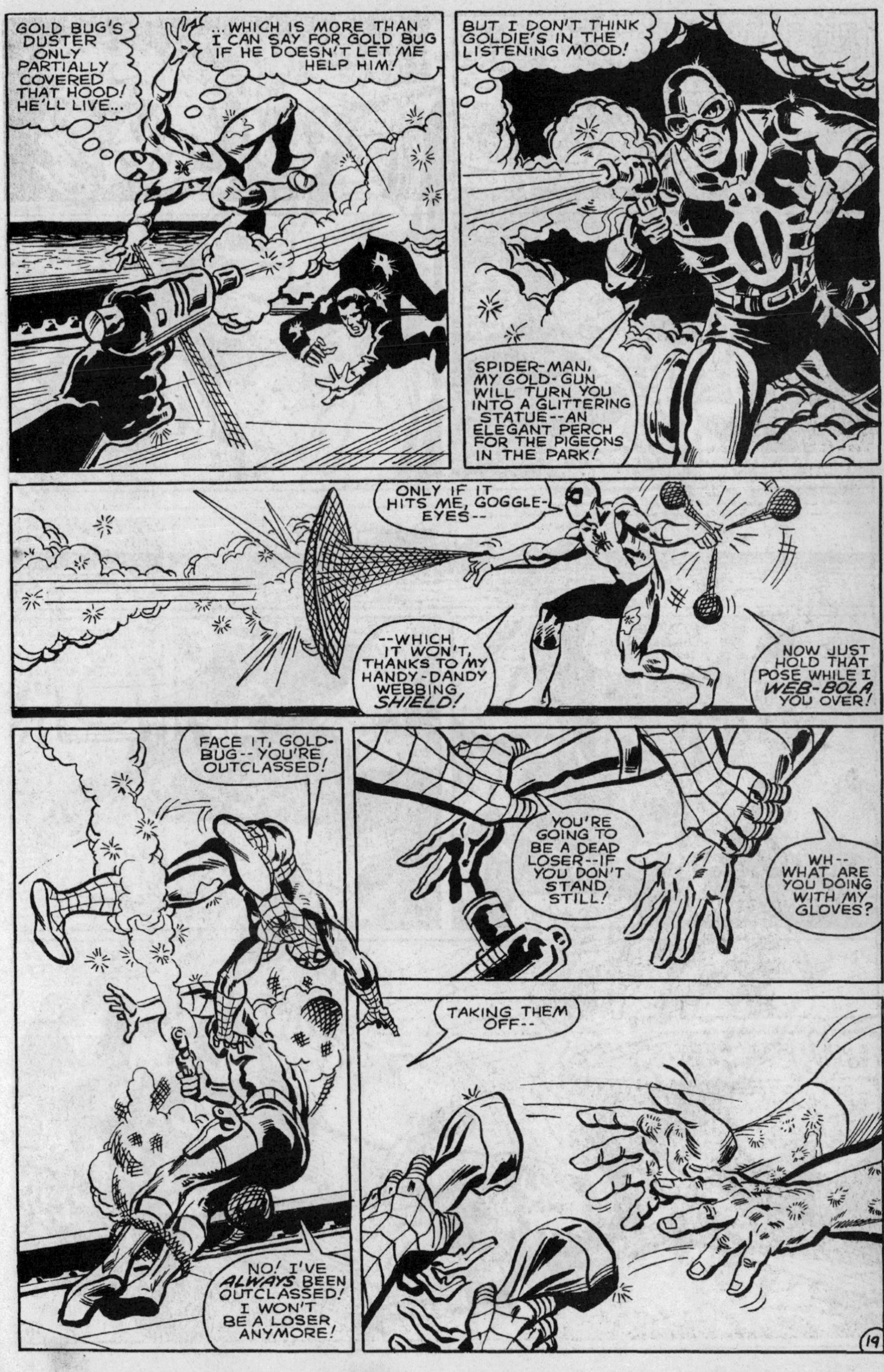
GOLD BUG'S DUSTER ONLY PARTIALLY COVERED THAT HOOD! HE'LL LIVE...
...WHICH IS MORE THAN I CAN SAY FOR GOLD BUG IF HE DOESN'T LET ME HELP HIM!
BUT I DON'T THINK GOLDIE'S IN THE LISTENING MOOD!
SPIDER-MAN, MY GOLD-GUN WILL TURN YOU INTO A GLITTERING STATUE--AN ELEGANT PERCH FOR THE PIGEONS IN THE PARK!
ONLY IF IT HITS ME, GOGGLE-EYES--
--WHICH IT WON'T, THANKS TO MY HANDY-DANDY WEBBING SHIELD!
NOW JUST HOLD THAT POSE WHILE I WEB-BOLA YOU OVER!
FACE IT, GOLD-BUG--YOU'RE OUTCLASSED!
NO! I'VE ALWAYS BEEN OUTCLASSED! I WON'T BE A LOSER ANYMORE!
YOU'RE GOING TO BE A DEAD LOSER--IF YOU DON'T STAND STILL!
WH--WHAT ARE YOU DOING WITH MY GLOVES?
TAKING THEM OFF--

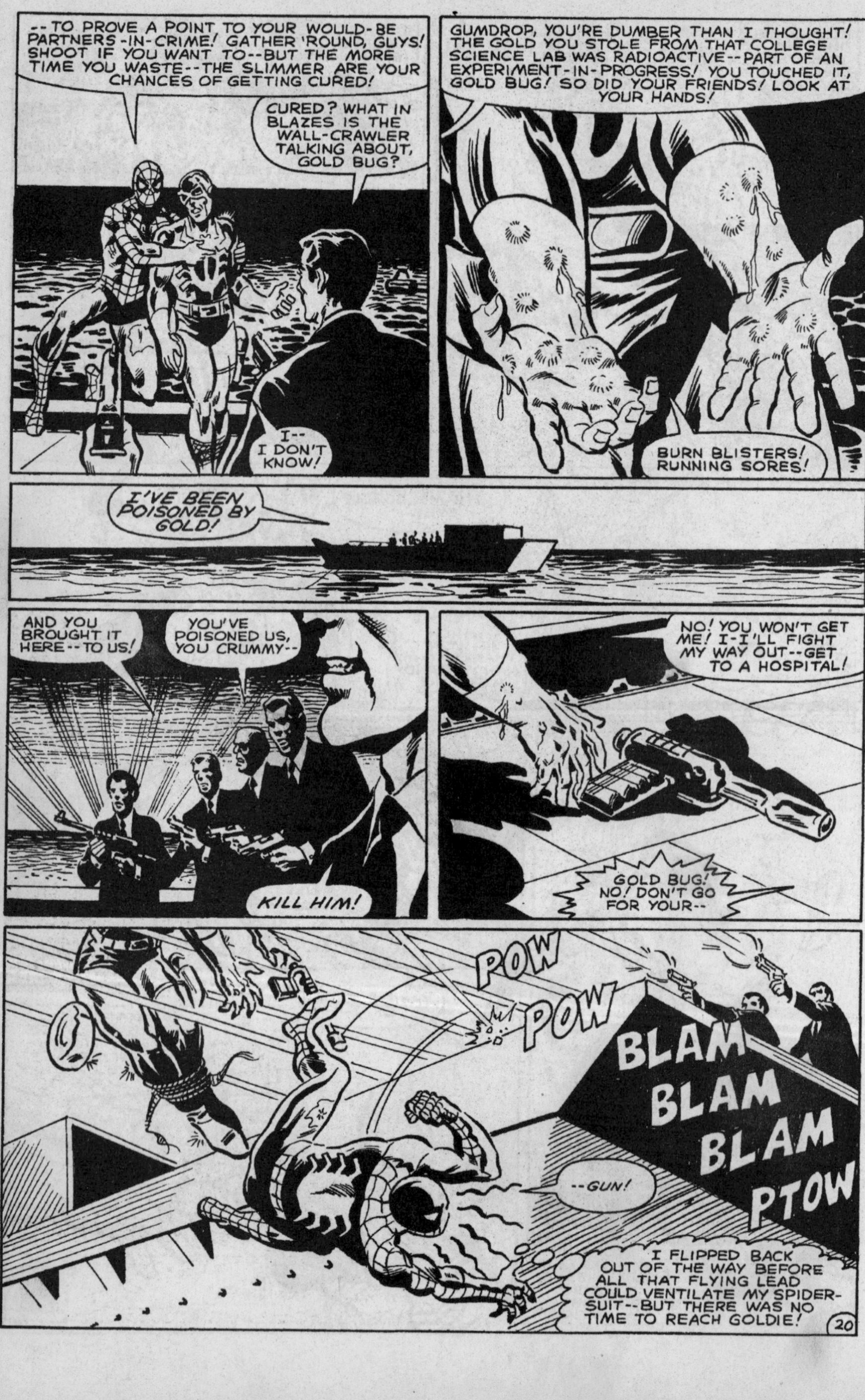
--TO PROVE A POINT TO YOUR WOULD-BE PARTNERS-IN-CRIME! GATHER 'ROUND, GUYS! SHOOT IF YOU WANT TO--BUT THE MORE TIME YOU WASTE--THE SLIMMER ARE YOUR CHANCES OF GETTING CURED!
CURED? WHAT IN BLAZES IS THE WALL-CRAWLER TALKING ABOUT, GOLD BUG?
I-- I DON'T KNOW!
GUMDROP, YOU'RE DUMBER THAN I THOUGHT! THE GOLD YOU STOLE FROM THAT COLLEGE SCIENCE LAB WAS RADIOACTIVE--PART OF AN EXPERIMENT-IN-PROGRESS! YOU TOUCHED IT, GOLD BUG! SO DID YOUR FRIENDS! LOOK AT YOUR HANDS!
BURN BLISTERS! RUNNING SORES!
I'VE BEEN POISONED BY GOLD!
AND YOU BROUGHT IT HERE--TO US!
YOU'VE POISONED US, YOU CRUMMY--
KILL HIM!
NO! YOU WON'T GET ME! I-I'LL FIGHT MY WAY OUT--GET TO A HOSPITAL!
GOLD BUG! NO! DON'T GO FOR YOUR--
POW
POW
BLAM
BLAM
BLAM
PTOW
--GUN!
I FLIPPED BACK OUT OF THE WAY BEFORE ALL THAT FLYING LEAD COULD VENTILATE MY SPIDER-SUIT--BUT THERE WAS NO TIME TO REACH GOLDIE!

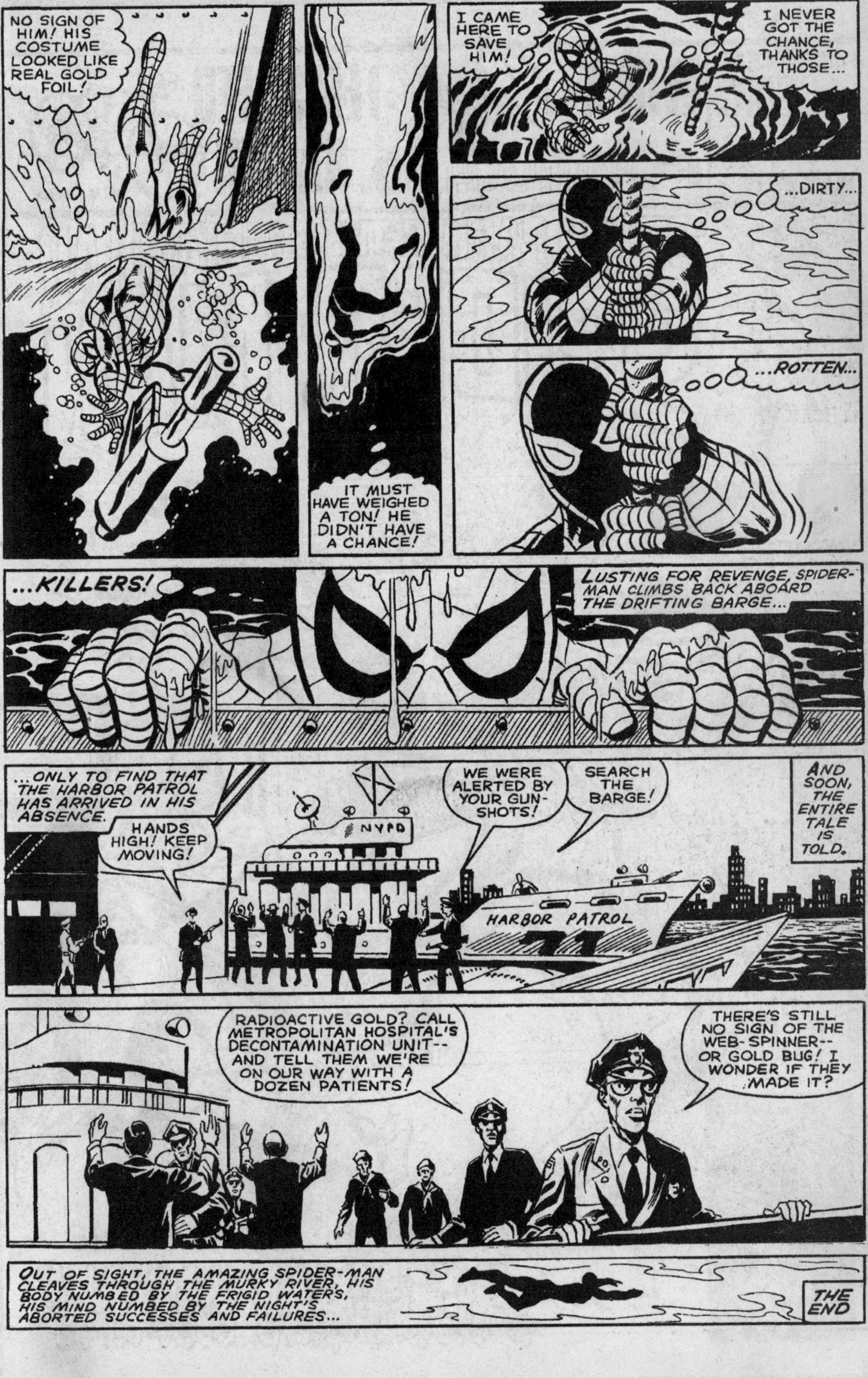

NO SIGN OF HIM! HIS COSTUME LOOKED LIKE REAL GOLD FOIL!
IT MUST HAVE WEIGHED A TON! HE DIDN'T HAVE A CHANCE!
I CAME HERE TO SAVE HIM!
I NEVER GOT THE CHANCE, THANKS TO THOSE...
...DIRTY...
...ROTTEN...
...KILLERS!
LUSTING FOR REVENGE, SPIDER-MAN CLIMBS BACK ABOARD THE DRIFTING BARGE...
...ONLY TO FIND THAT THE HARBOR PATROL HAS ARRIVED IN HIS ABSENCE.
HANDS HIGH! KEEP MOVING!
NYPD
WE WERE ALERTED BY YOUR GUN-SHOTS!
SEARCH THE BARGE!
HARBOR PATROL
AND SOON, THE ENTIRE TALE IS TOLD.
RADIOACTIVE GOLD? CALL METROPOLITAN HOSPITAL'S DECONTAMINATION UNIT-- AND TELL THEM WE'RE ON OUR WAY WITH A DOZEN PATIENTS!
THERE'S STILL NO SIGN OF THE WEB-SPINNER-- OR GOLD BUG! I WONDER IF THEY MADE IT?
OUT OF SIGHT, THE AMAZING SPIDER-MAN CLEAVES THROUGH THE MURKY RIVER, HIS BODY NUMBED BY THE FRIGID WATERS, HIS MIND NUMBED BY THE NIGHT'S ABORTED SUCCESSES AND FAILURES...
THE END

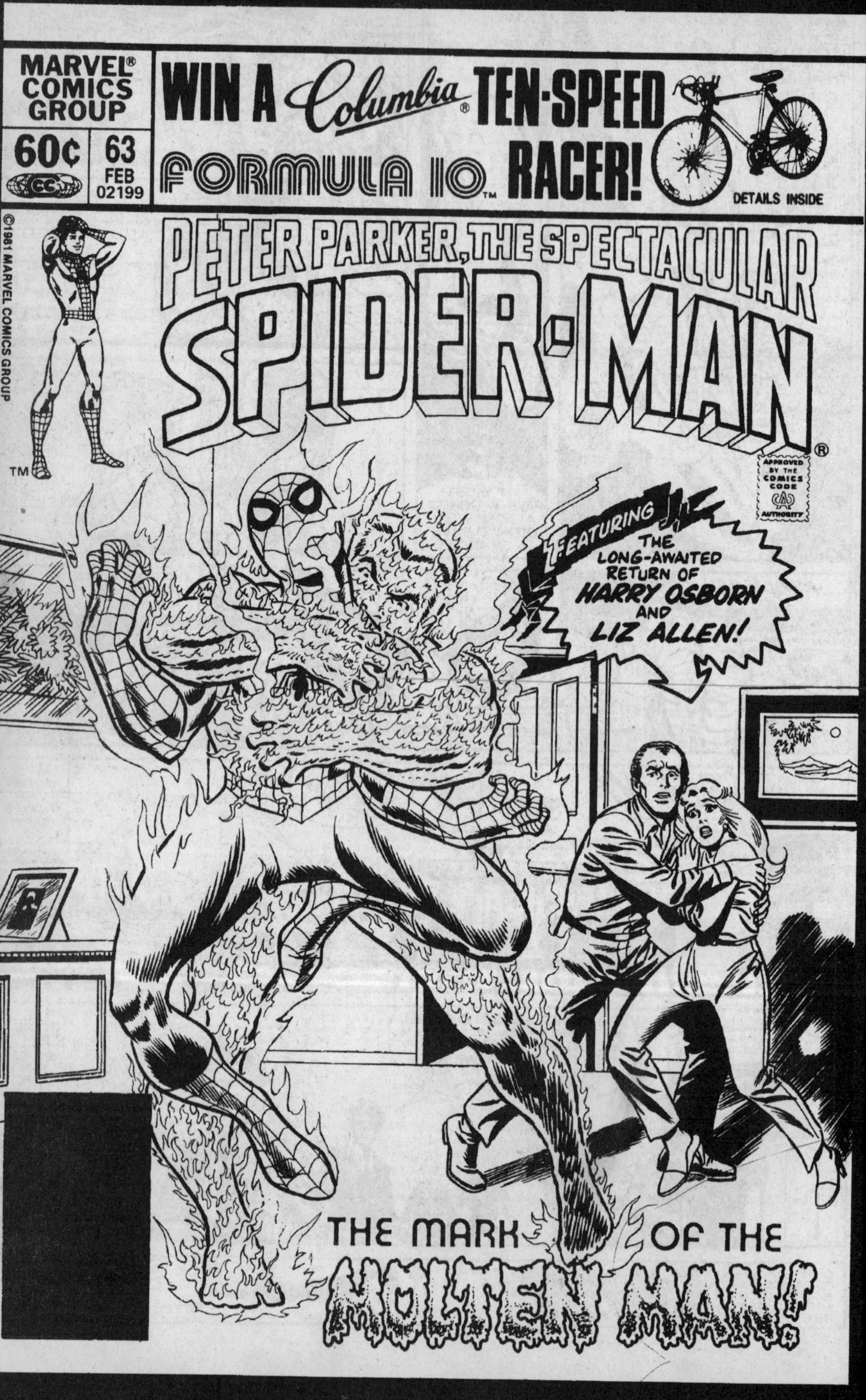
MARVEL® COMICS GROUP
60¢
63 FEB 02199
WIN A Columbia® TEN-SPEED
FORMULA 10™ RACER!
DETAILS INSIDE
PETER PARKER, THE SPECTACULAR SPIDER-MAN®
©1981 MARVEL COMICS GROUP
TM
APPROVED BY THE COMICS CODE AUTHORITY
FEATURING THE LONG-AWAITED RETURN OF HARRY OSBORN AND LIZ ALLEN!
THE MARK OF THE MOLTEN MAN!

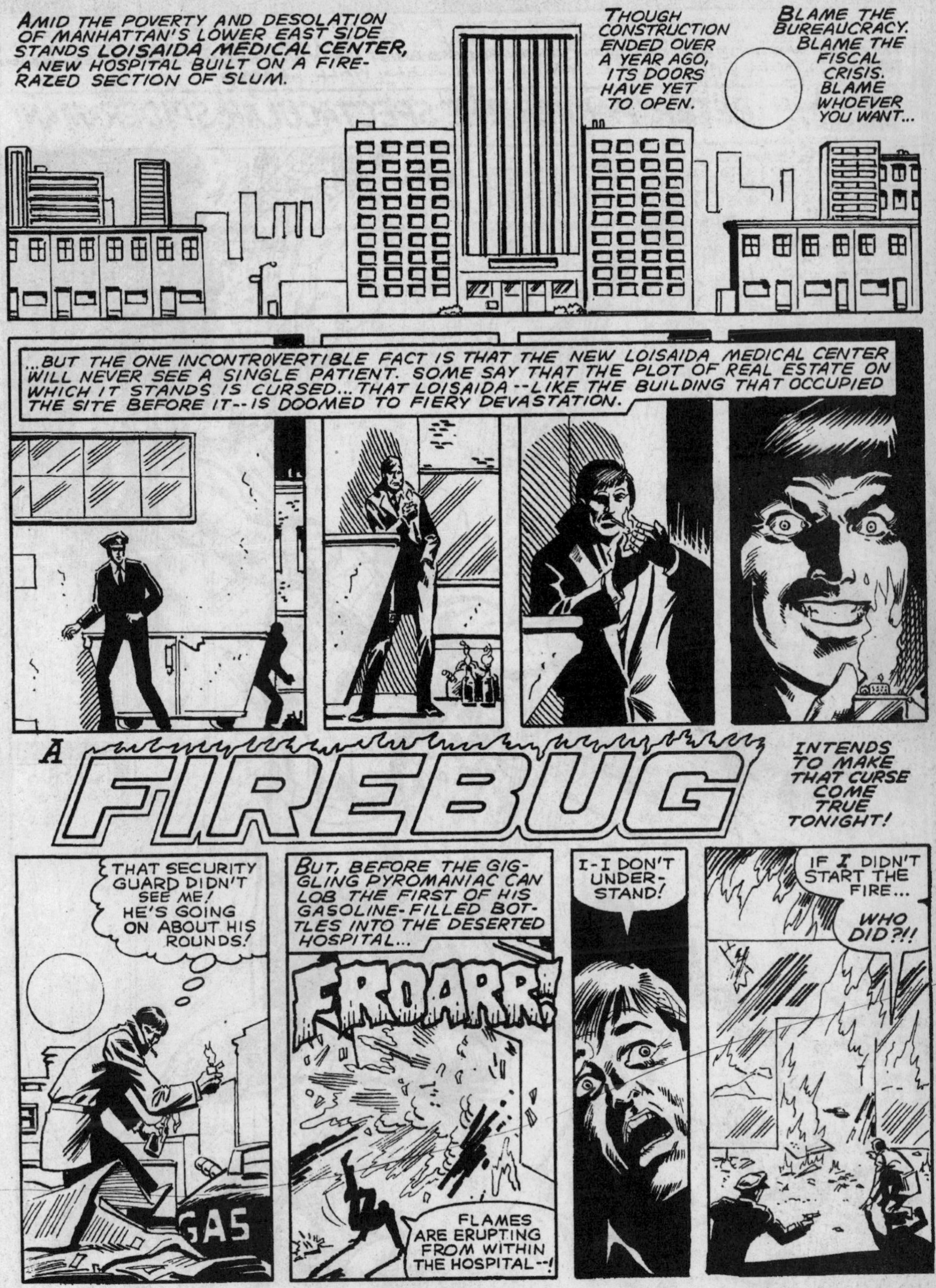
AMID THE POVERTY AND DESOLATION OF MANHATTAN'S LOWER EAST SIDE STANDS LOISAIDA MEDICAL CENTER, A NEW HOSPITAL BUILT ON A FIRE-RAZED SECTION OF SLUM.
THOUGH CONSTRUCTION ENDED OVER A YEAR AGO, ITS DOORS HAVE YET TO OPEN.
BLAME THE BUREAUCRACY. BLAME THE FISCAL CRISIS. BLAME WHOEVER YOU WANT...
...BUT THE ONE INCONTROVERTIBLE FACT IS THAT THE NEW LOISAIDA MEDICAL CENTER WILL NEVER SEE A SINGLE PATIENT. SOME SAY THAT THE PLOT OF REAL ESTATE ON WHICH IT STANDS IS CURSED...THAT LOISAIDA--LIKE THE BUILDING THAT OCCUPIED THE SITE BEFORE IT--IS DOOMED TO FIERY DEVASTATION.
A
FIREBUG
INTENDS TO MAKE THAT CURSE COME TRUE TONIGHT!
THAT SECURITY GUARD DIDN'T SEE ME! HE'S GOING ON ABOUT HIS ROUNDS!
GAS
BUT, BEFORE THE GIGGLING PYROMANIAC CAN LOB THE FIRST OF HIS GASOLINE-FILLED BOTTLES INTO THE DESERTED HOSPITAL...
FROARR!
FLAMES ARE ERUPTING FROM WITHIN THE HOSPITAL--!
I-I DON'T UNDERSTAND!
IF I DIDN'T START THE FIRE...
WHO DID?!!

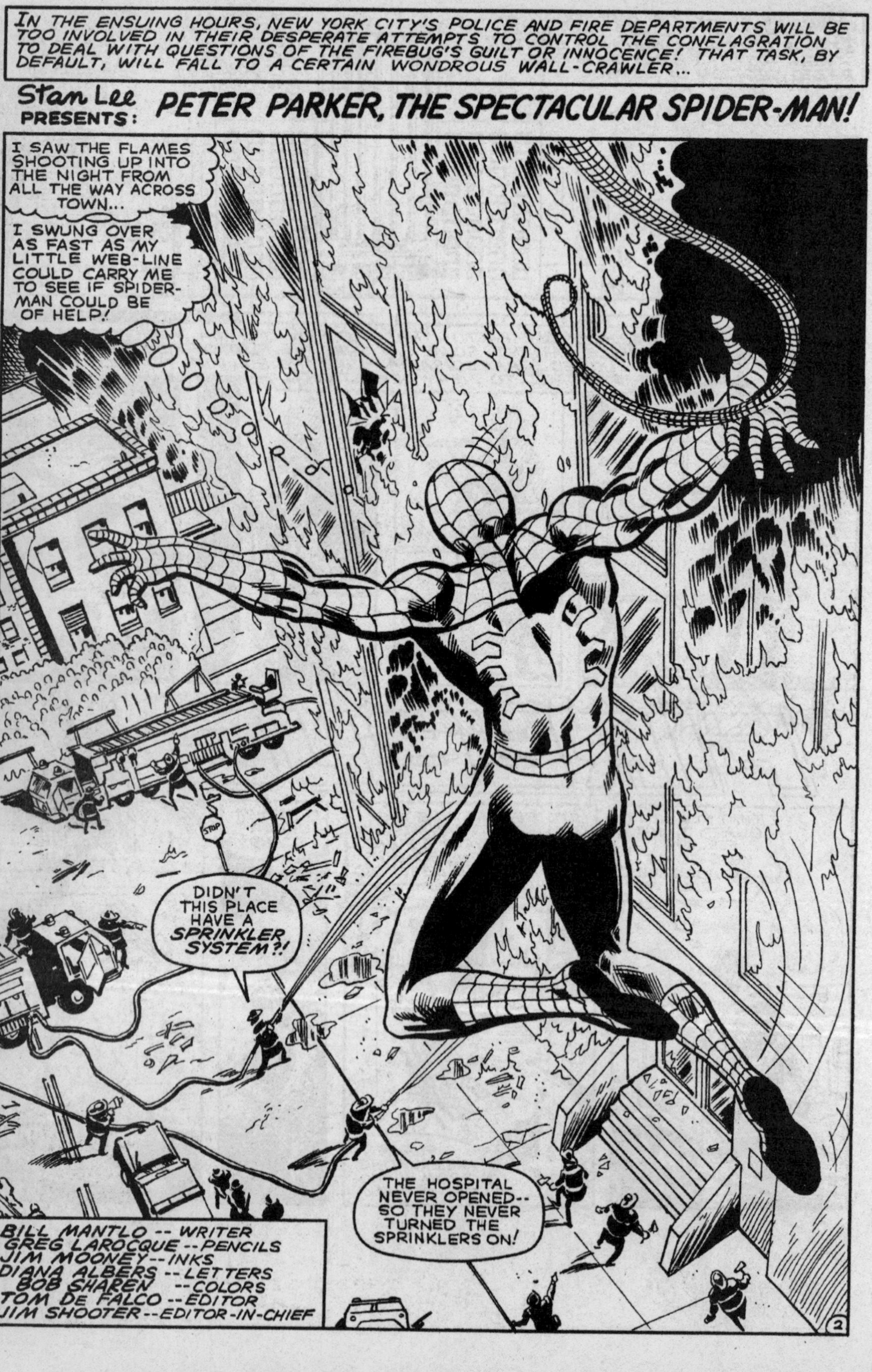
IN THE ENSUING HOURS, NEW YORK CITY'S POLICE AND FIRE DEPARTMENTS WILL BE TOO INVOLVED IN THEIR DESPERATE ATTEMPTS TO CONTROL THE CONFLAGRATION TO DEAL WITH QUESTIONS OF THE FIREBUG'S GUILT OR INNOCENCE! THAT TASK, BY DEFAULT, WILL FALL TO A CERTAIN WONDROUS WALL-CRAWLER...
Stan Lee PRESENTS: PETER PARKER, THE SPECTACULAR SPIDER-MAN!
I SAW THE FLAMES SHOOTING UP INTO THE NIGHT FROM ALL THE WAY ACROSS TOWN...
I SWUNG OVER AS FAST AS MY LITTLE WEB-LINE COULD CARRY ME TO SEE IF SPIDER-MAN COULD BE OF HELP!
DIDN'T THIS PLACE HAVE A SPRINKLER SYSTEM?!
THE HOSPITAL NEVER OPENED-- SO THEY NEVER TURNED THE SPRINKLERS ON!
STOP
BILL MANTLO -- WRITER
GREG LAROCQUE -- PENCILS
JIM MOONEY -- INKS
DIANA ALBERS -- LETTERS
BOB SHAREN -- COLORS
TOM DE FALCO -- EDITOR
JIM SHOOTER -- EDITOR-IN-CHIEF
2

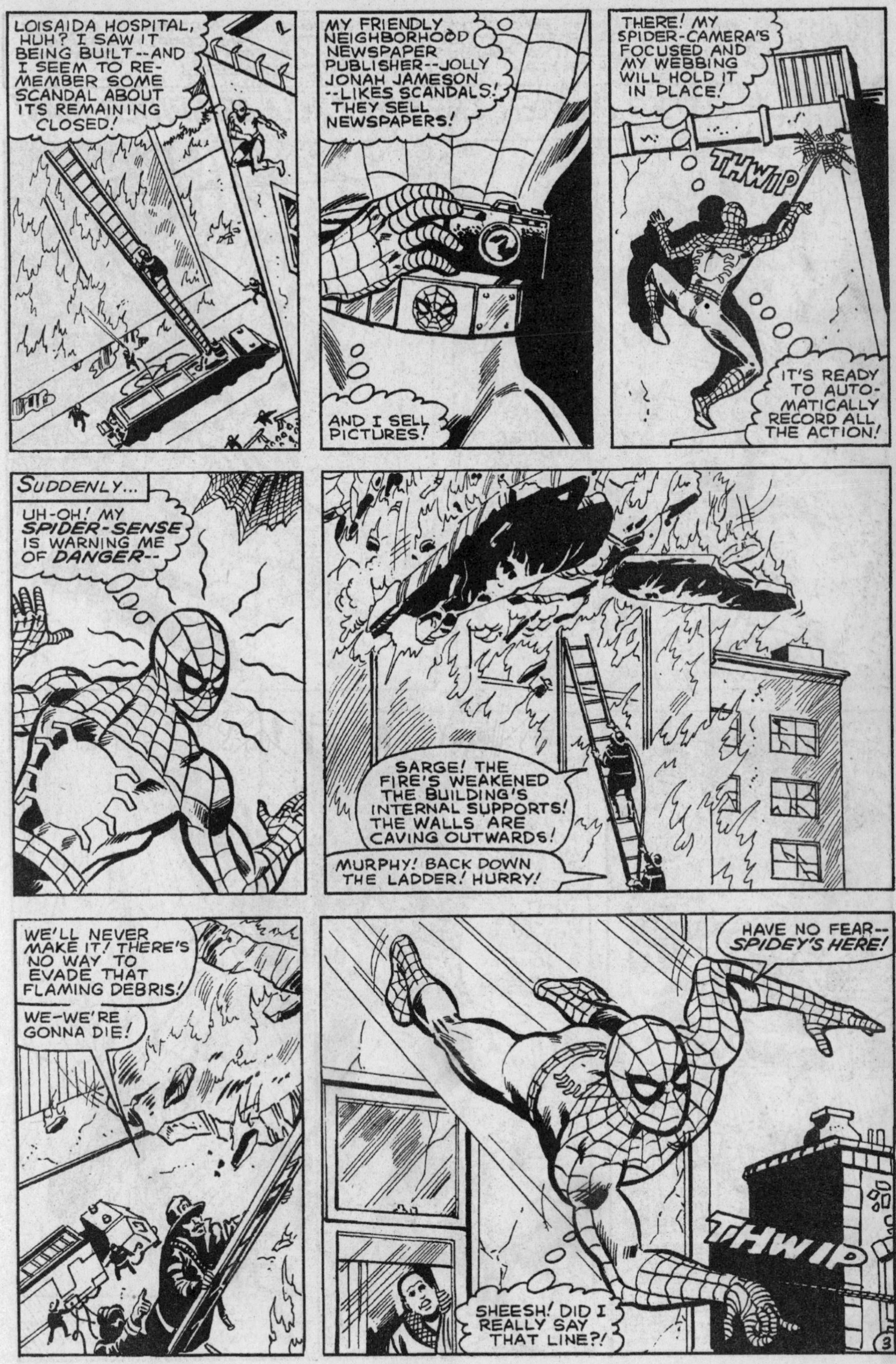
LOISAIDA HOSPITAL, HUH? I SAW IT BEING BUILT--AND I SEEM TO REMEMBER SOME SCANDAL ABOUT ITS REMAINING CLOSED!
MY FRIENDLY NEIGHBORHOOD NEWSPAPER PUBLISHER--JOLLY JONAH JAMESON--LIKES SCANDALS! THEY SELL NEWSPAPERS!
AND I SELL PICTURES!
THERE! MY SPIDER-CAMERA'S FOCUSED AND MY WEBBING WILL HOLD IT IN PLACE!
THWIP
IT'S READY TO AUTOMATICALLY RECORD ALL THE ACTION!
SUDDENLY...
UH-OH! MY SPIDER-SENSE IS WARNING ME OF DANGER--
SARGE! THE FIRE'S WEAKENED THE BUILDING'S INTERNAL SUPPORTS! THE WALLS ARE CAVING OUTWARDS!
MURPHY! BACK DOWN THE LADDER! HURRY!
WE'LL NEVER MAKE IT! THERE'S NO WAY TO EVADE THAT FLAMING DEBRIS!
WE-WE'RE GONNA DIE!
HAVE NO FEAR--SPIDEY'S HERE!
THWIP
SHEESH! DID I REALLY SAY THAT LINE?!
3

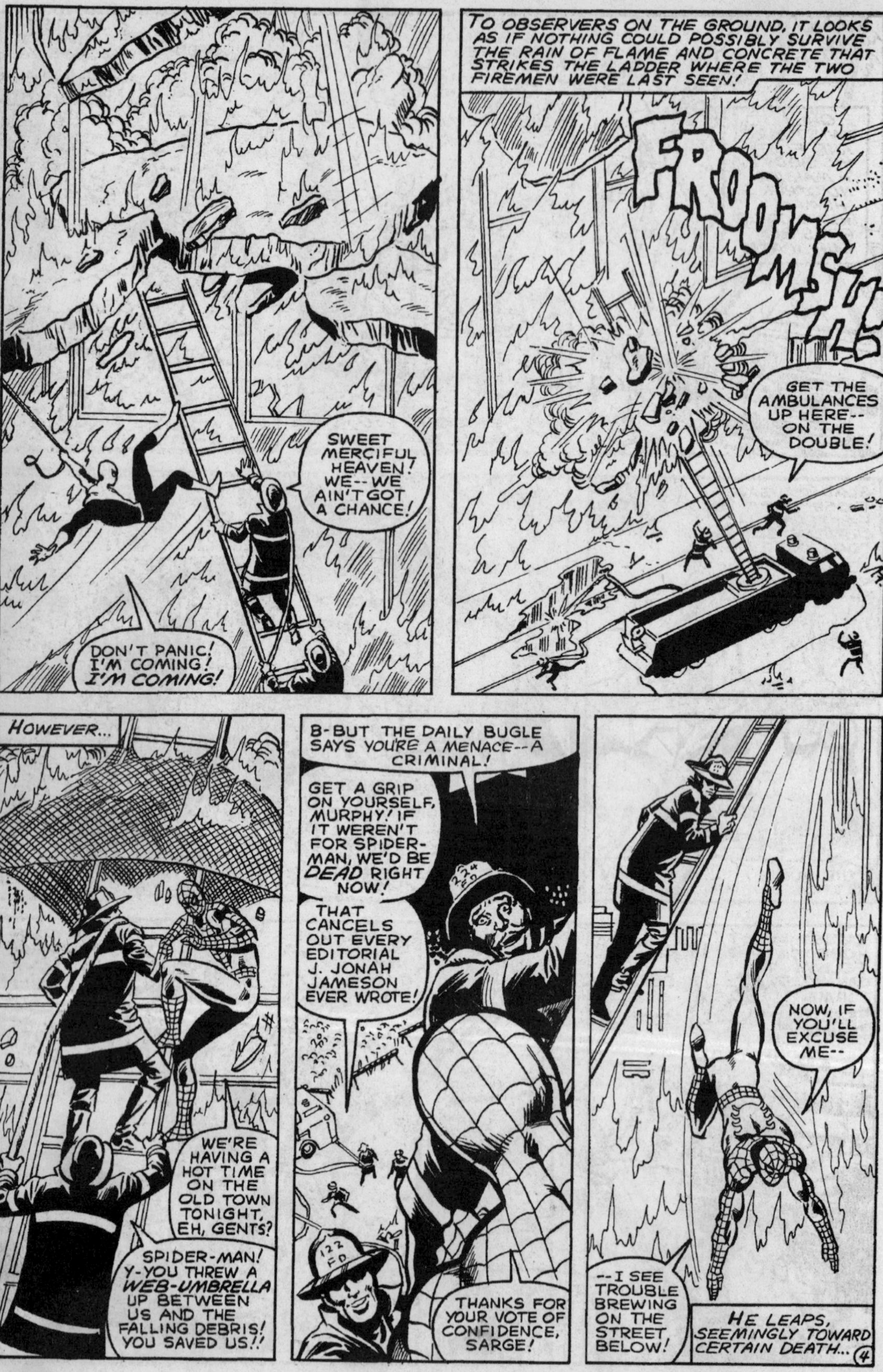

SWEET MERCIFUL HEAVEN! WE--WE AIN'T GOT A CHANCE!
DON'T PANIC! I'M COMING! I'M COMING!
TO OBSERVERS ON THE GROUND, IT LOOKS AS IF NOTHING COULD POSSIBLY SURVIVE THE RAIN OF FLAME AND CONCRETE THAT STRIKES THE LADDER WHERE THE TWO FIREMEN WERE LAST SEEN!
FROOMSH!
GET THE AMBULANCES UP HERE-- ON THE DOUBLE!
HOWEVER...
WE'RE HAVING A HOT TIME ON THE OLD TOWN TONIGHT, EH, GENTS?
SPIDER-MAN! Y-YOU THREW A WEB-UMBRELLA UP BETWEEN US AND THE FALLING DEBRIS! YOU SAVED US!!
B-BUT THE DAILY BUGLE SAYS YOU'RE A MENACE--A CRIMINAL!
GET A GRIP ON YOURSELF, MURPHY! IF IT WEREN'T FOR SPIDER-MAN, WE'D BE DEAD RIGHT NOW!
THAT CANCELS OUT EVERY EDITORIAL J. JONAH JAMESON EVER WROTE!
THANKS FOR YOUR VOTE OF CONFIDENCE, SARGE!
NOW, IF YOU'LL EXCUSE ME--
--I SEE TROUBLE BREWING ON THE STREET BELOW!
HE LEAPS, SEEMINGLY TOWARD CERTAIN DEATH...
4

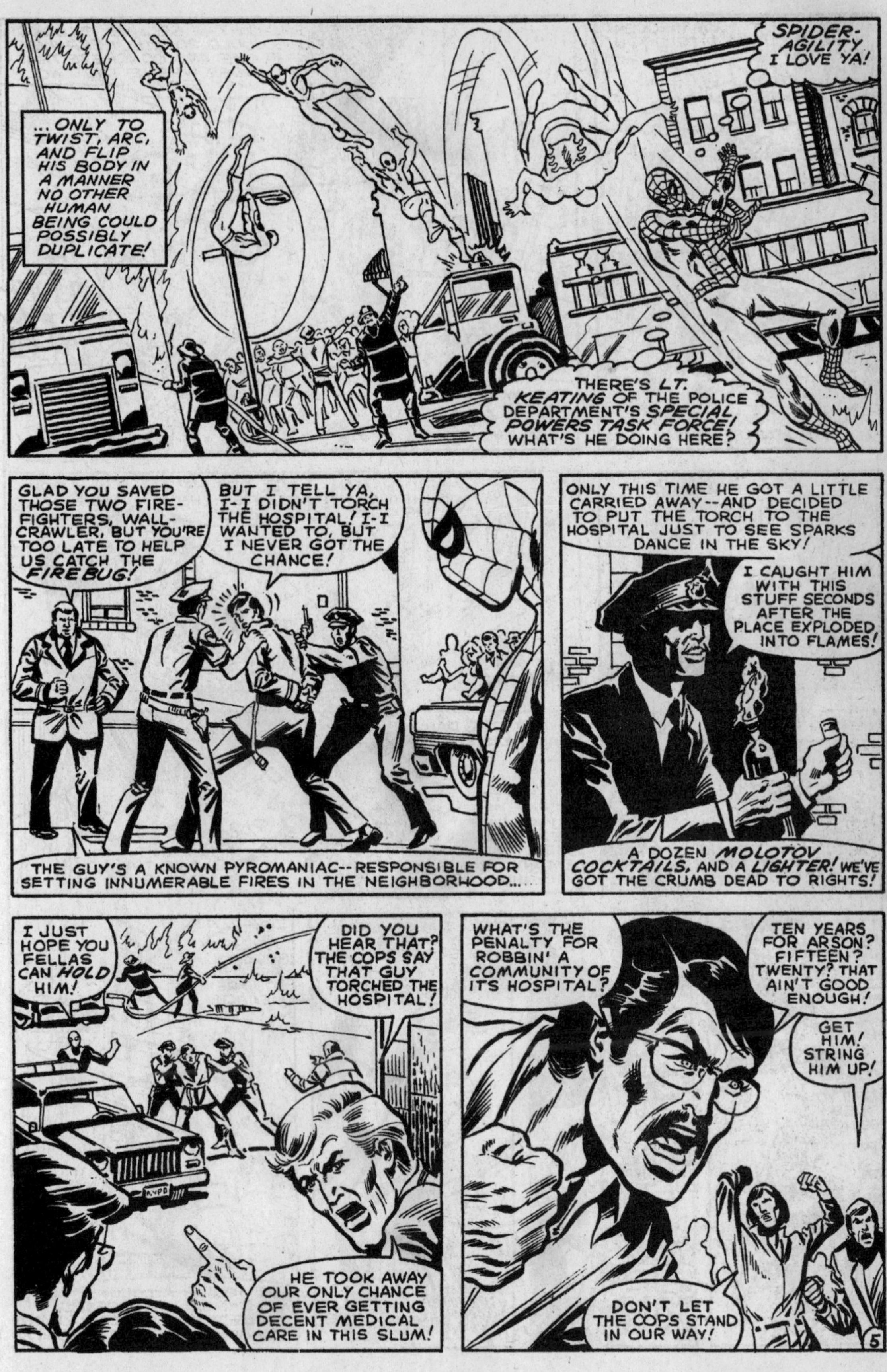
...ONLY TO TWIST, ARC, AND FLIP HIS BODY IN A MANNER NO OTHER HUMAN BEING COULD POSSIBLY DUPLICATE!
SPIDER-AGILITY I LOVE YA!
THERE'S LT. KEATING OF THE POLICE DEPARTMENT'S SPECIAL POWERS TASK FORCE! WHAT'S HE DOING HERE?
GLAD YOU SAVED THOSE TWO FIRE-FIGHTERS, WALL-CRAWLER, BUT YOU'RE TOO LATE TO HELP US CATCH THE FIREBUG!
BUT I TELL YA, I-I DIDN'T TORCH THE HOSPITAL! I-I WANTED TO, BUT I NEVER GOT THE CHANCE!
THE GUY'S A KNOWN PYROMANIAC--RESPONSIBLE FOR SETTING INNUMERABLE FIRES IN THE NEIGHBORHOOD...
ONLY THIS TIME HE GOT A LITTLE CARRIED AWAY--AND DECIDED TO PUT THE TORCH TO THE HOSPITAL JUST TO SEE SPARKS DANCE IN THE SKY!
I CAUGHT HIM WITH THIS STUFF SECONDS AFTER THE PLACE EXPLODED INTO FLAMES!
A DOZEN MOLOTOV COCKTAILS, AND A LIGHTER! WE'VE GOT THE CRUMB DEAD TO RIGHTS!
I JUST HOPE YOU FELLAS CAN HOLD HIM!
DID YOU HEAR THAT? THE COPS SAY THAT GUY TORCHED THE HOSPITAL!
NYPD
HE TOOK AWAY OUR ONLY CHANCE OF EVER GETTING DECENT MEDICAL CARE IN THIS SLUM!
WHAT'S THE PENALTY FOR ROBBIN' A COMMUNITY OF ITS HOSPITAL?
TEN YEARS FOR ARSON? FIFTEEN? TWENTY? THAT AIN'T GOOD ENOUGH!
GET HIM! STRING HIM UP!
DON'T LET THE COPS STAND IN OUR WAY!
5

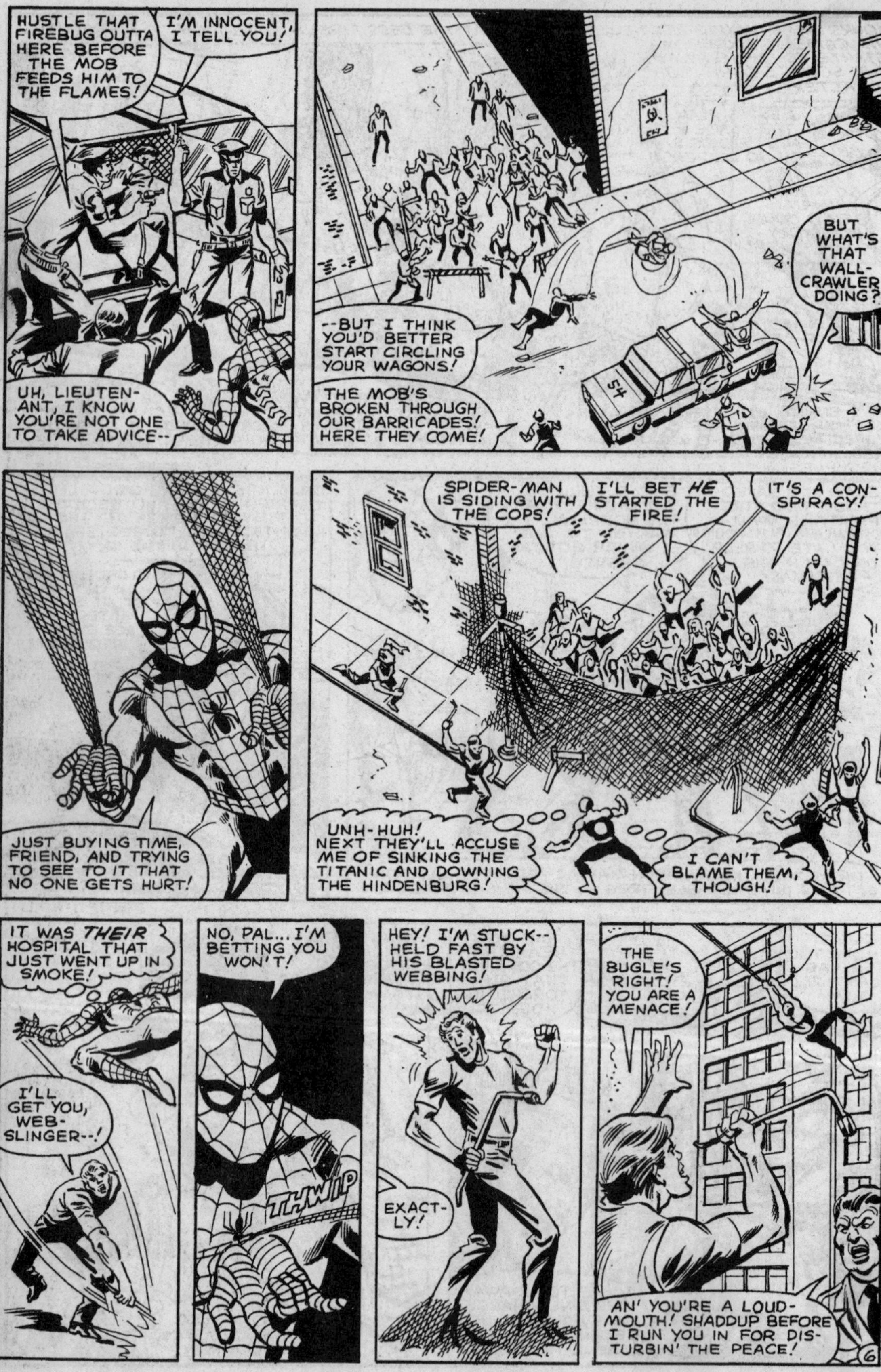

HUSTLE THAT FIREBUG OUTTA HERE BEFORE THE MOB FEEDS HIM TO THE FLAMES!
I'M INNOCENT, I TELL YOU!
UH, LIEUTENANT, I KNOW YOU'RE NOT ONE TO TAKE ADVICE--
--BUT I THINK YOU'D BETTER START CIRCLING YOUR WAGONS!
THE MOB'S BROKEN THROUGH OUR BARRICADES! HERE THEY COME!
BUT WHAT'S THAT WALL-CRAWLER DOING?
54
JUST BUYING TIME, FRIEND, AND TRYING TO SEE TO IT THAT NO ONE GETS HURT!
SPIDER-MAN IS SIDING WITH THE COPS!
I'LL BET HE STARTED THE FIRE!
IT'S A CONSPIRACY!
UNH-HUH! NEXT THEY'LL ACCUSE ME OF SINKING THE TITANIC AND DOWNING THE HINDENBURG!
I CAN'T BLAME THEM, THOUGH!
IT WAS THEIR HOSPITAL THAT JUST WENT UP IN SMOKE!
I'LL GET YOU, WEB-SLINGER--!
NO, PAL... I'M BETTING YOU WON'T!
THWIP
HEY! I'M STUCK-- HELD FAST BY HIS BLASTED WEBBING!
EXACTLY!
THE BUGLE'S RIGHT! YOU ARE A MENACE!
AN' YOU'RE A LOUDMOUTH! SHADDUP BEFORE I RUN YOU IN FOR DISTURBIN' THE PEACE!
6

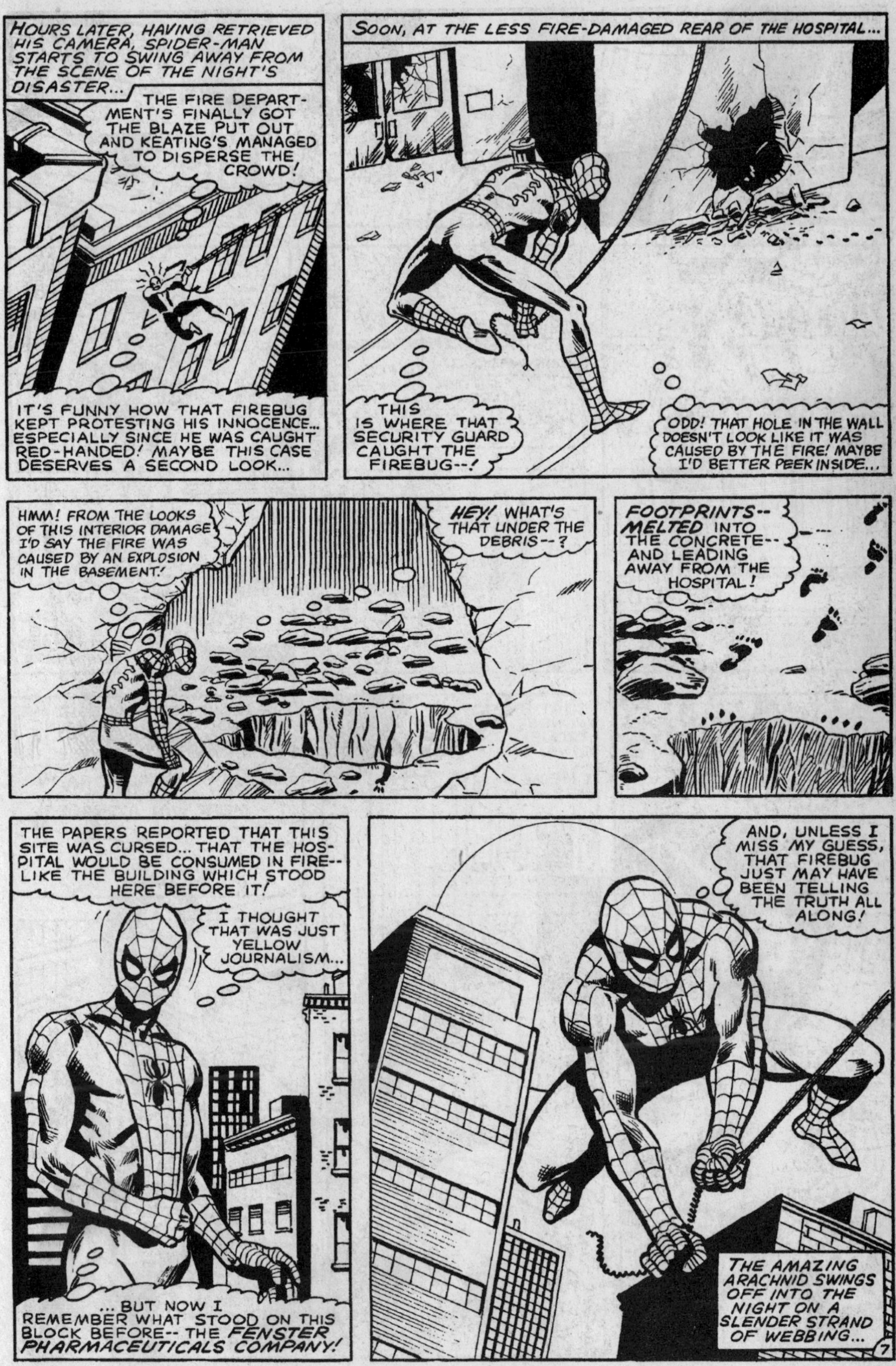
HOURS LATER, HAVING RETRIEVED HIS CAMERA, SPIDER-MAN STARTS TO SWING AWAY FROM THE SCENE OF THE NIGHT'S DISASTER...
THE FIRE DEPARTMENT'S FINALLY GOT THE BLAZE PUT OUT AND KEATING'S MANAGED TO DISPERSE THE CROWD!
IT'S FUNNY HOW THAT FIREBUG KEPT PROTESTING HIS INNOCENCE... ESPECIALLY SINCE HE WAS CAUGHT RED-HANDED! MAYBE THIS CASE DESERVES A SECOND LOOK...
SOON, AT THE LESS FIRE-DAMAGED REAR OF THE HOSPITAL...
THIS IS WHERE THAT SECURITY GUARD CAUGHT THE FIREBUG--!
ODD! THAT HOLE IN THE WALL DOESN'T LOOK LIKE IT WAS CAUSED BY THE FIRE! MAYBE I'D BETTER PEEK INSIDE...
HMM! FROM THE LOOKS OF THIS INTERIOR DAMAGE I'D SAY THE FIRE WAS CAUSED BY AN EXPLOSION IN THE BASEMENT!
HEY! WHAT'S THAT UNDER THE DEBRIS--?
FOOTPRINTS-- MELTED INTO THE CONCRETE-- AND LEADING AWAY FROM THE HOSPITAL!
THE PAPERS REPORTED THAT THIS SITE WAS CURSED... THAT THE HOSPITAL WOULD BE CONSUMED IN FIRE-- LIKE THE BUILDING WHICH STOOD HERE BEFORE IT!
I THOUGHT THAT WAS JUST YELLOW JOURNALISM...
... BUT NOW I REMEMBER WHAT STOOD ON THIS BLOCK BEFORE-- THE FENSTER PHARMACEUTICALS COMPANY!
AND, UNLESS I MISS MY GUESS, THAT FIREBUG JUST MAY HAVE BEEN TELLING THE TRUTH ALL ALONG!
THE AMAZING ARACHNID SWINGS OFF INTO THE NIGHT ON A SLENDER STRAND OF WEBBING...
7

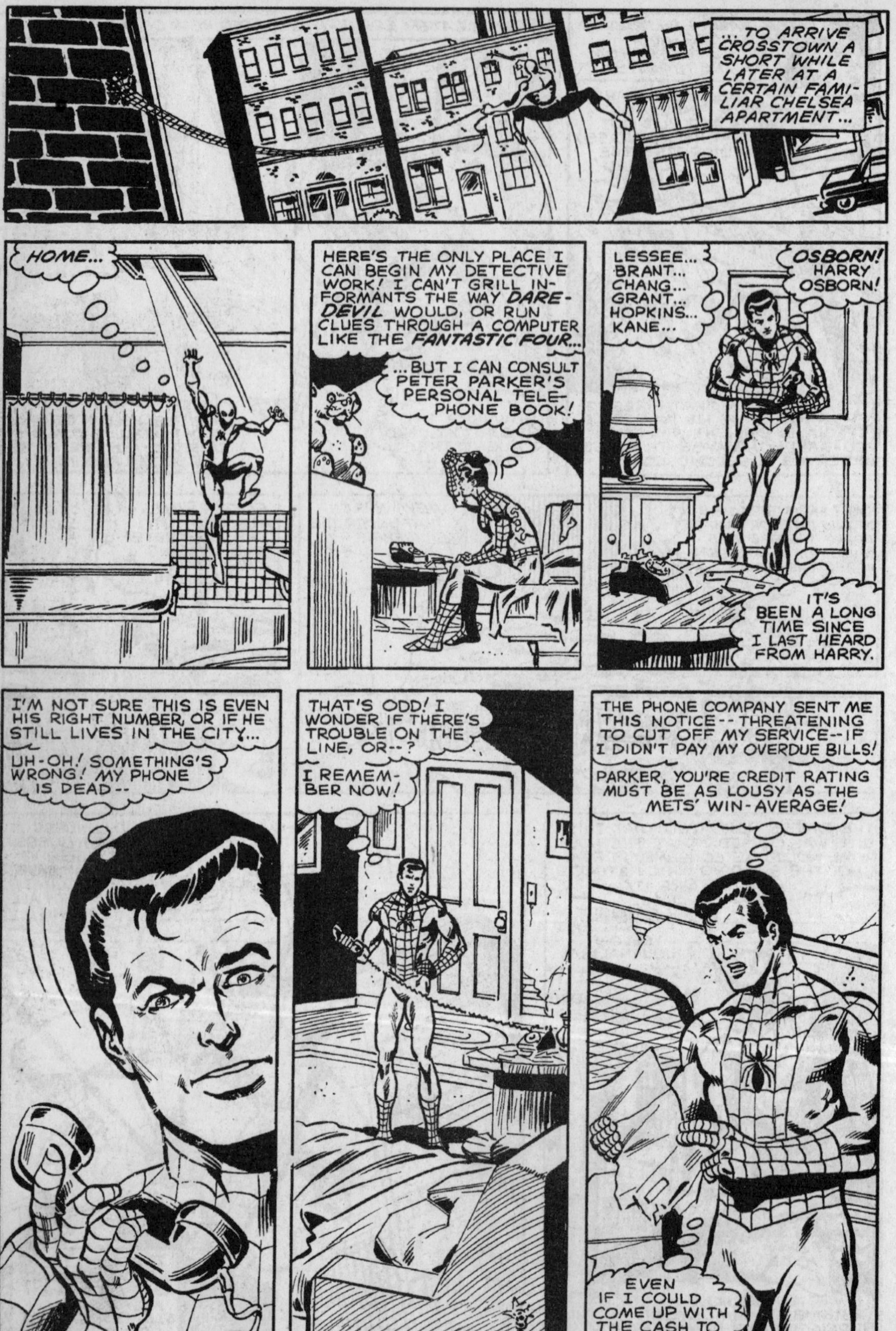
...TO ARRIVE CROSSTOWN A SHORT WHILE LATER AT A CERTAIN FAMILIAR CHELSEA APARTMENT...
HOME...
HERE'S THE ONLY PLACE I CAN BEGIN MY DETECTIVE WORK! I CAN'T GRILL INFORMANTS THE WAY DAREDEVIL WOULD, OR RUN CLUES THROUGH A COMPUTER LIKE THE FANTASTIC FOUR...
...BUT I CAN CONSULT PETER PARKER'S PERSONAL TELEPHONE BOOK!
LESSEE... BRANT... CHANG... GRANT... HOPKINS... KANE...
OSBORN! HARRY OSBORN!
IT'S BEEN A LONG TIME SINCE I LAST HEARD FROM HARRY.
I'M NOT SURE THIS IS EVEN HIS RIGHT NUMBER, OR IF HE STILL LIVES IN THE CITY...
UH-OH! SOMETHING'S WRONG! MY PHONE IS DEAD--
THAT'S ODD! I WONDER IF THERE'S TROUBLE ON THE LINE, OR--?
I REMEMBER NOW!
THE PHONE COMPANY SENT ME THIS NOTICE--THREATENING TO CUT OFF MY SERVICE--IF I DIDN'T PAY MY OVERDUE BILLS!
PARKER, YOU'RE CREDIT RATING MUST BE AS LOUSY AS THE METS' WIN-AVERAGE!
EVEN IF I COULD COME UP WITH THE CASH TO SQUARE ME--
8

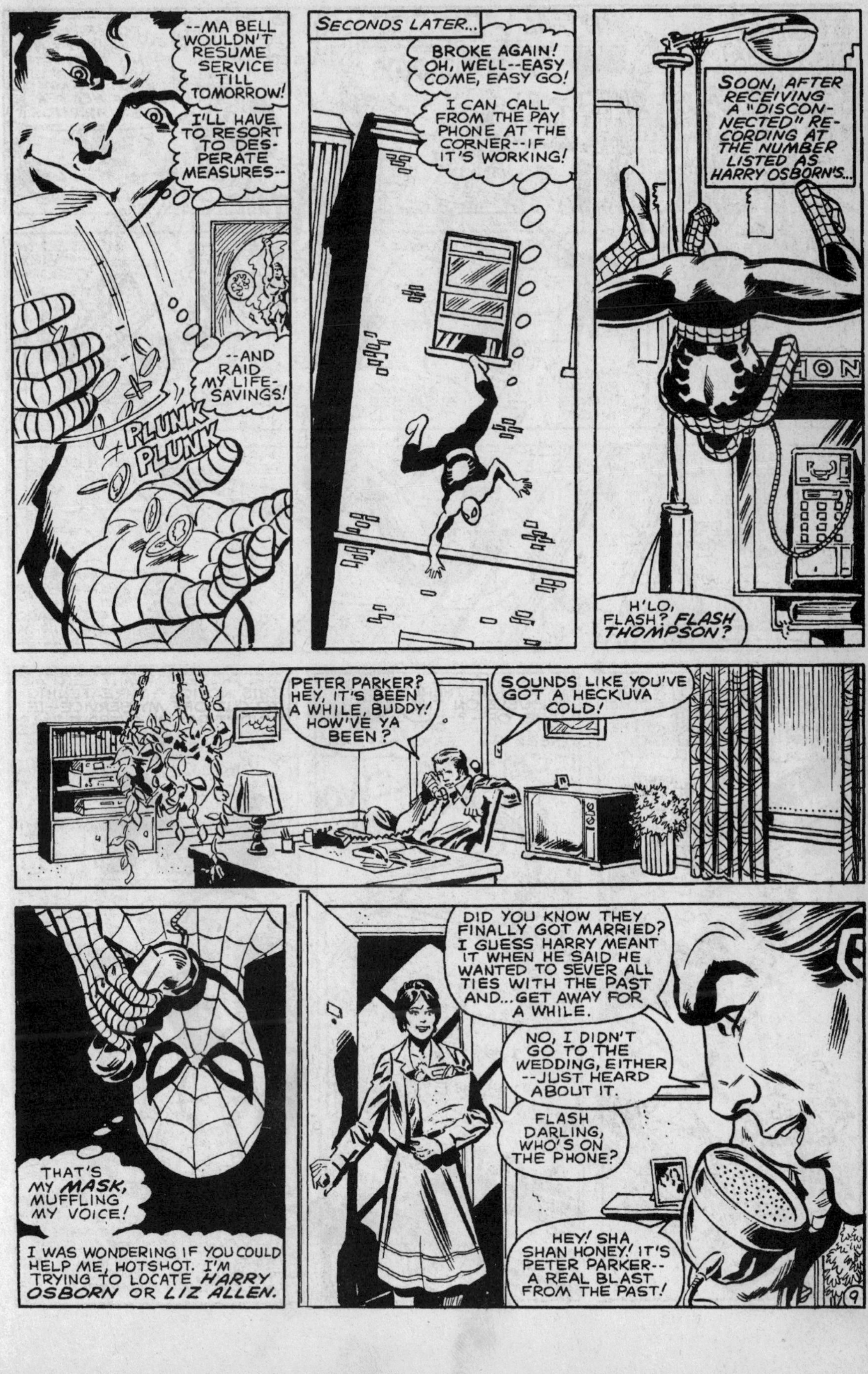
--MA BELL WOULDN'T RESUME SERVICE TILL TOMORROW!
I'LL HAVE TO RESORT TO DES-PERATE MEASURES--
--AND RAID MY LIFE-SAVINGS!
PLUNK PLUNK
SECONDS LATER...
BROKE AGAIN! OH, WELL--EASY COME, EASY GO!
I CAN CALL FROM THE PAY PHONE AT THE CORNER--IF IT'S WORKING!
SOON, AFTER RECEIVING A "DISCONNECTED" RECORDING AT THE NUMBER LISTED AS HARRY OSBORN'S...
H'LO, FLASH? FLASH THOMPSON?
PETER PARKER? HEY, IT'S BEEN A WHILE, BUDDY! HOW'VE YA BEEN?
SOUNDS LIKE YOU'VE GOT A HECKUVA COLD!
THAT'S MY MASK, MUFFLING MY VOICE!
I WAS WONDERING IF YOU COULD HELP ME, HOTSHOT. I'M TRYING TO LOCATE HARRY OSBORN OR LIZ ALLEN.
DID YOU KNOW THEY FINALLY GOT MARRIED? I GUESS HARRY MEANT IT WHEN HE SAID HE WANTED TO SEVER ALL TIES WITH THE PAST AND... GET AWAY FOR A WHILE.
NO, I DIDN'T GO TO THE WEDDING, EITHER --JUST HEARD ABOUT IT.
FLASH DARLING, WHO'S ON THE PHONE?
HEY! SHA SHAN HONEY! IT'S PETER PARKER-- A REAL BLAST FROM THE PAST!
9

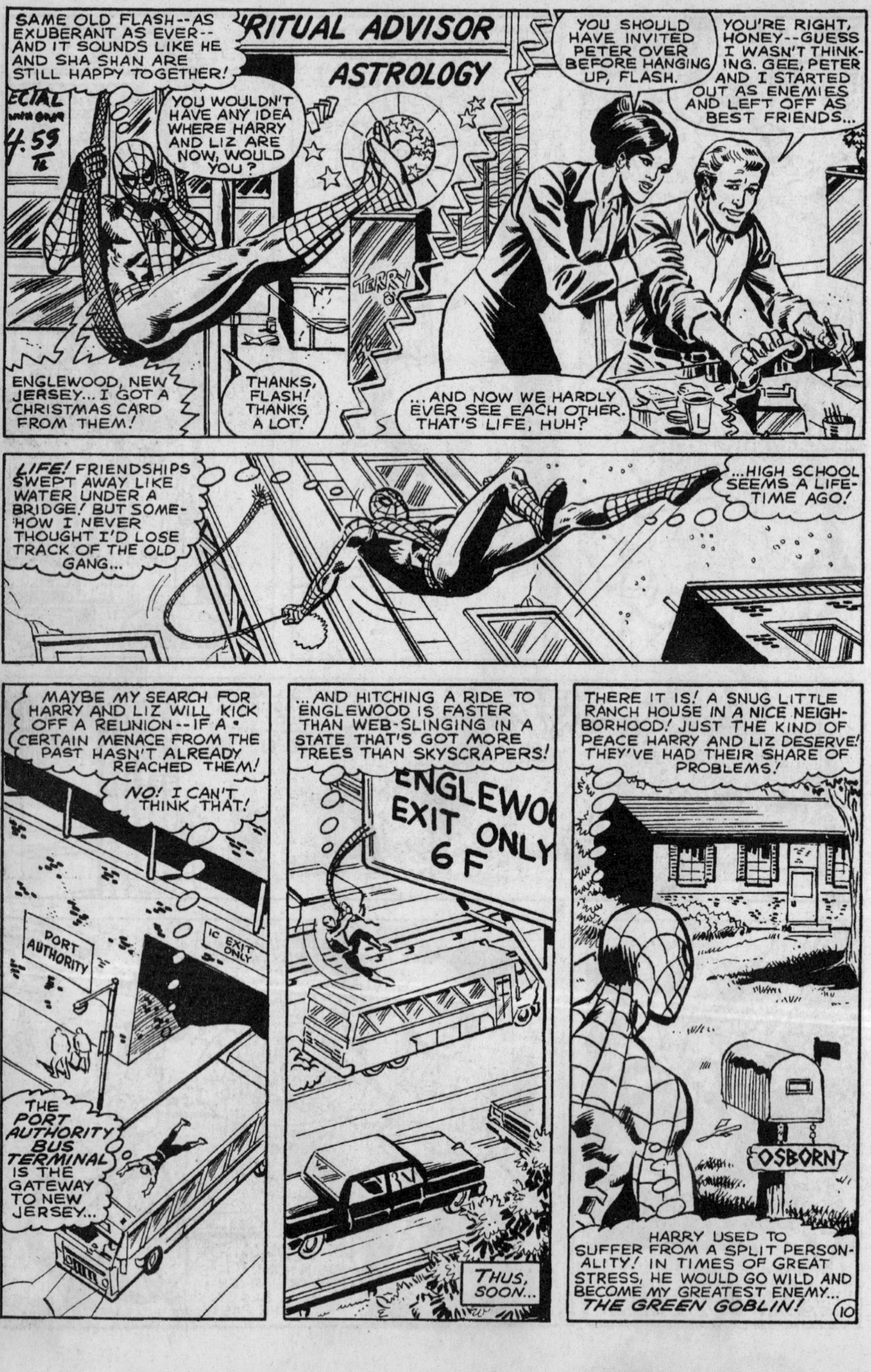

SAME OLD FLASH--AS EXUBERANT AS EVER--AND IT SOUNDS LIKE HE AND SHA SHAN ARE STILL HAPPY TOGETHER!
RITUAL ADVISOR
ASTROLOGY
YOU WOULDN'T HAVE ANY IDEA WHERE HARRY AND LIZ ARE NOW, WOULD YOU?
YOU SHOULD HAVE INVITED PETER OVER BEFORE HANGING UP, FLASH.
YOU'RE RIGHT, HONEY--GUESS I WASN'T THINKING. GEE, PETER AND I STARTED OUT AS ENEMIES AND LEFT OFF AS BEST FRIENDS...
ENGLEWOOD, NEW JERSEY... I GOT A CHRISTMAS CARD FROM THEM!
THANKS, FLASH! THANKS A LOT!
...AND NOW WE HARDLY EVER SEE EACH OTHER. THAT'S LIFE, HUH?
LIFE! FRIENDSHIPS SWEPT AWAY LIKE WATER UNDER A BRIDGE! BUT SOMEHOW I NEVER THOUGHT I'D LOSE TRACK OF THE OLD GANG...
...HIGH SCHOOL SEEMS A LIFETIME AGO!
MAYBE MY SEARCH FOR HARRY AND LIZ WILL KICK OFF A REUNION--IF A CERTAIN MENACE FROM THE PAST HASN'T ALREADY REACHED THEM!
NO! I CAN'T THINK THAT!
PORT AUTHORITY
IC EXIT ONLY
THE PORT AUTHORITY BUS TERMINAL IS THE GATEWAY TO NEW JERSEY...
...AND HITCHING A RIDE TO ENGLEWOOD IS FASTER THAN WEB-SLINGING IN A STATE THAT'S GOT MORE TREES THAN SKYSCRAPERS!
ENGLEWOO
EXIT ONLY
6 F
THUS, SOON...
THERE IT IS! A SNUG LITTLE RANCH HOUSE IN A NICE NEIGHBORHOOD! JUST THE KIND OF PEACE HARRY AND LIZ DESERVE! THEY'VE HAD THEIR SHARE OF PROBLEMS!
OSBORN
HARRY USED TO SUFFER FROM A SPLIT PERSONALITY! IN TIMES OF GREAT STRESS, HE WOULD GO WILD AND BECOME MY GREATEST ENEMY... THE GREEN GOBLIN!
10

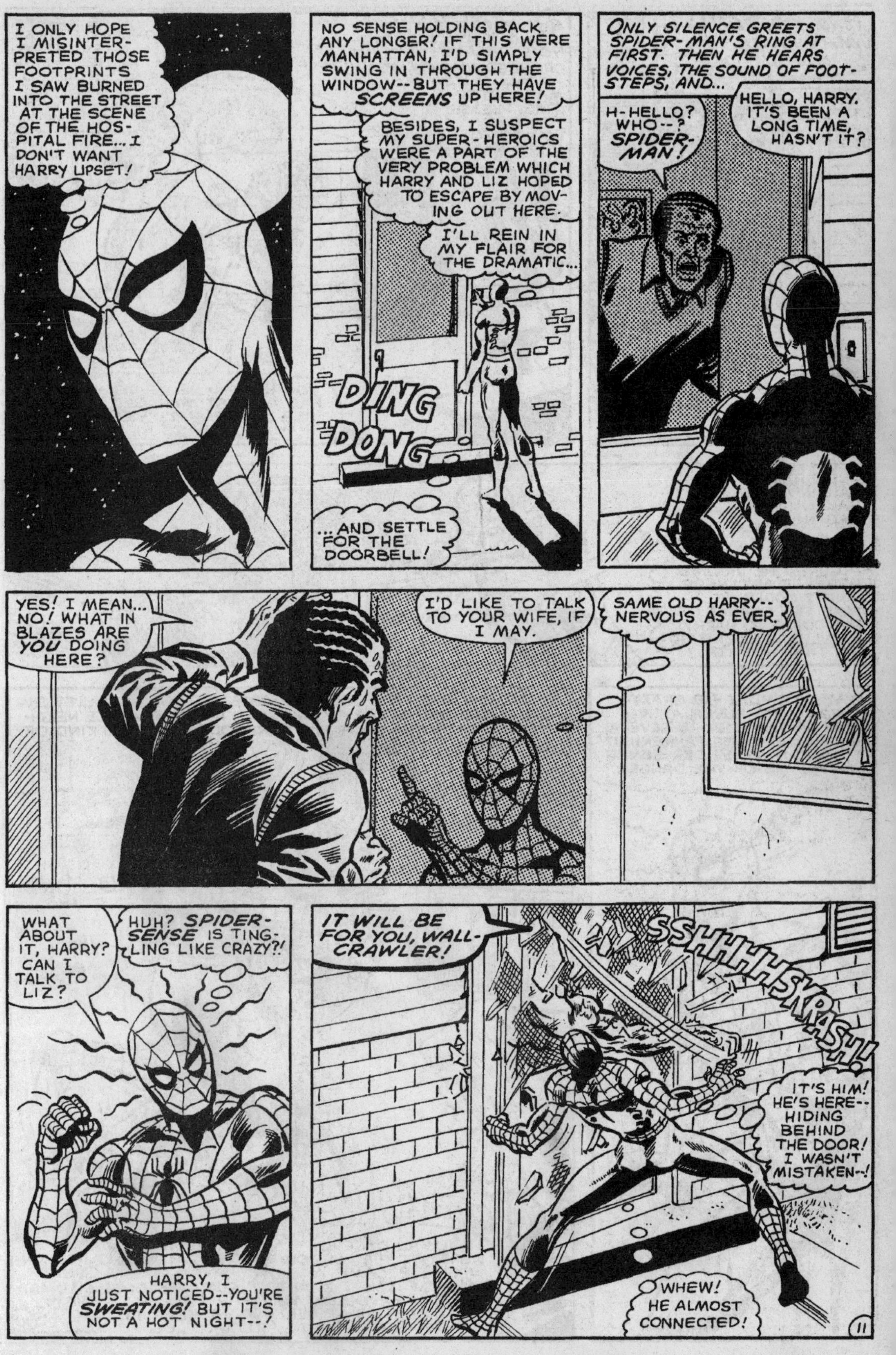
I ONLY HOPE I MISINTERPRETED THOSE FOOTPRINTS I SAW BURNED INTO THE STREET AT THE SCENE OF THE HOSPITAL FIRE... I DON'T WANT HARRY UPSET!
NO SENSE HOLDING BACK ANY LONGER! IF THIS WERE MANHATTAN, I'D SIMPLY SWING IN THROUGH THE WINDOW--BUT THEY HAVE SCREENS UP HERE!
BESIDES, I SUSPECT MY SUPER-HEROICS WERE A PART OF THE VERY PROBLEM WHICH HARRY AND LIZ HOPED TO ESCAPE BY MOVING OUT HERE.
I'LL REIN IN MY FLAIR FOR THE DRAMATIC...
DING DONG
...AND SETTLE FOR THE DOORBELL!
ONLY SILENCE GREETS SPIDER-MAN'S RING AT FIRST. THEN HE HEARS VOICES, THE SOUND OF FOOTSTEPS, AND...
H-HELLO? WHO--? SPIDER-MAN!
HELLO, HARRY. IT'S BEEN A LONG TIME, HASN'T IT?
YES! I MEAN... NO! WHAT IN BLAZES ARE YOU DOING HERE?
I'D LIKE TO TALK TO YOUR WIFE, IF I MAY.
SAME OLD HARRY-- NERVOUS AS EVER.
WHAT ABOUT IT, HARRY? CAN I TALK TO LIZ?
HUH? SPIDER-SENSE IS TINGLING LIKE CRAZY?!
HARRY, I JUST NOTICED--YOU'RE SWEATING! BUT IT'S NOT A HOT NIGHT--!
IT WILL BE FOR YOU, WALL-CRAWLER!
SSHHHHSKRASH!
IT'S HIM! HE'S HERE-- HIDING BEHIND THE DOOR! I WASN'T MISTAKEN--!
WHEW! HE ALMOST CONNECTED!
11

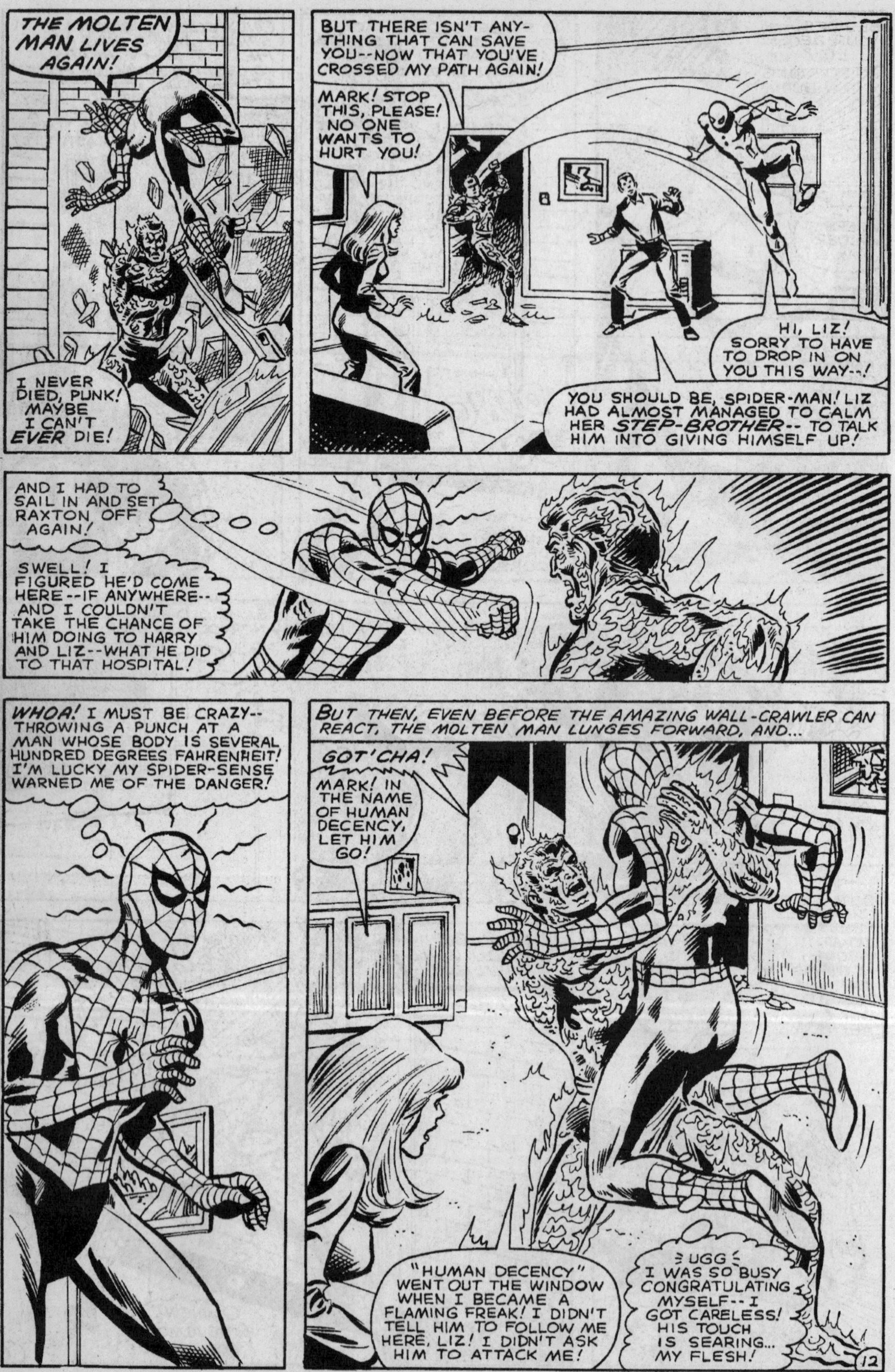
THE MOLTEN MAN LIVES AGAIN!
I NEVER DIED, PUNK! MAYBE I CAN'T EVER DIE!
BUT THERE ISN'T ANYTHING THAT CAN SAVE YOU--NOW THAT YOU'VE CROSSED MY PATH AGAIN!
MARK! STOP THIS, PLEASE! NO ONE WANTS TO HURT YOU!
HI, LIZ! SORRY TO HAVE TO DROP IN ON YOU THIS WAY--!
YOU SHOULD BE, SPIDER-MAN! LIZ HAD ALMOST MANAGED TO CALM HER STEP-BROTHER-- TO TALK HIM INTO GIVING HIMSELF UP!
AND I HAD TO SAIL IN AND SET RAXTON OFF AGAIN!
SWELL! I FIGURED HE'D COME HERE--IF ANYWHERE-- AND I COULDN'T TAKE THE CHANCE OF HIM DOING TO HARRY AND LIZ--WHAT HE DID TO THAT HOSPITAL!
WHOA! I MUST BE CRAZY-- THROWING A PUNCH AT A MAN WHOSE BODY IS SEVERAL HUNDRED DEGREES FAHRENHEIT! I'M LUCKY MY SPIDER-SENSE WARNED ME OF THE DANGER!
BUT THEN, EVEN BEFORE THE AMAZING WALL-CRAWLER CAN REACT, THE MOLTEN MAN LUNGES FORWARD, AND...
GOT'CHA!
MARK! IN THE NAME OF HUMAN DECENCY, LET HIM GO!
"HUMAN DECENCY" WENT OUT THE WINDOW WHEN I BECAME A FLAMING FREAK! I DIDN'T TELL HIM TO FOLLOW ME HERE, LIZ! I DIDN'T ASK HIM TO ATTACK ME!
UGG! I WAS SO BUSY CONGRATULATING MYSELF--I GOT CARELESS! HIS TOUCH IS SEARING... MY FLESH!
12

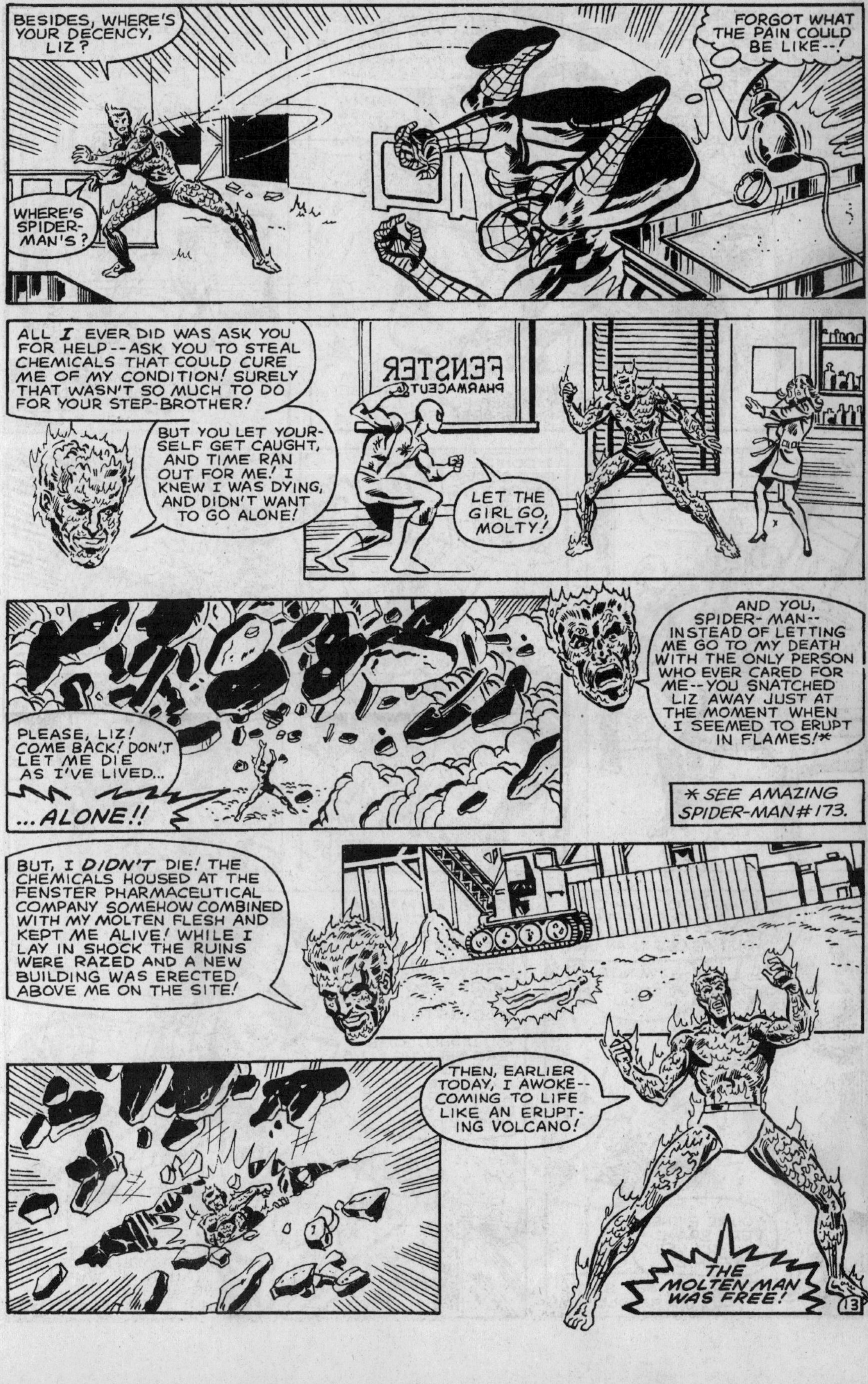

BESIDES, WHERE'S YOUR DECENCY, LIZ?
WHERE'S SPIDER-MAN'S?
FORGOT WHAT THE PAIN COULD BE LIKE--!
ALL I EVER DID WAS ASK YOU FOR HELP--ASK YOU TO STEAL CHEMICALS THAT COULD CURE ME OF MY CONDITION! SURELY THAT WASN'T SO MUCH TO DO FOR YOUR STEP-BROTHER!
BUT YOU LET YOURSELF GET CAUGHT, AND TIME RAN OUT FOR ME! I KNEW I WAS DYING, AND DIDN'T WANT TO GO ALONE!
FENSTER PHARMACEUT
LET THE GIRL GO, MOLTY!
PLEASE, LIZ! COME BACK! DON'T LET ME DIE AS I'VE LIVED...
...ALONE!!
AND YOU, SPIDER-MAN--INSTEAD OF LETTING ME GO TO MY DEATH WITH THE ONLY PERSON WHO EVER CARED FOR ME--YOU SNATCHED LIZ AWAY JUST AT THE MOMENT WHEN I SEEMED TO ERUPT IN FLAMES!*
*SEE AMAZING SPIDER-MAN #173.
BUT, I DIDN'T DIE! THE CHEMICALS HOUSED AT THE FENSTER PHARMACEUTICAL COMPANY SOMEHOW COMBINED WITH MY MOLTEN FLESH AND KEPT ME ALIVE! WHILE I LAY IN SHOCK THE RUINS WERE RAZED AND A NEW BUILDING WAS ERECTED ABOVE ME ON THE SITE!
THEN, EARLIER TODAY, I AWOKE--COMING TO LIFE LIKE AN ERUPTING VOLCANO!
THE MOLTEN MAN WAS FREE!
13

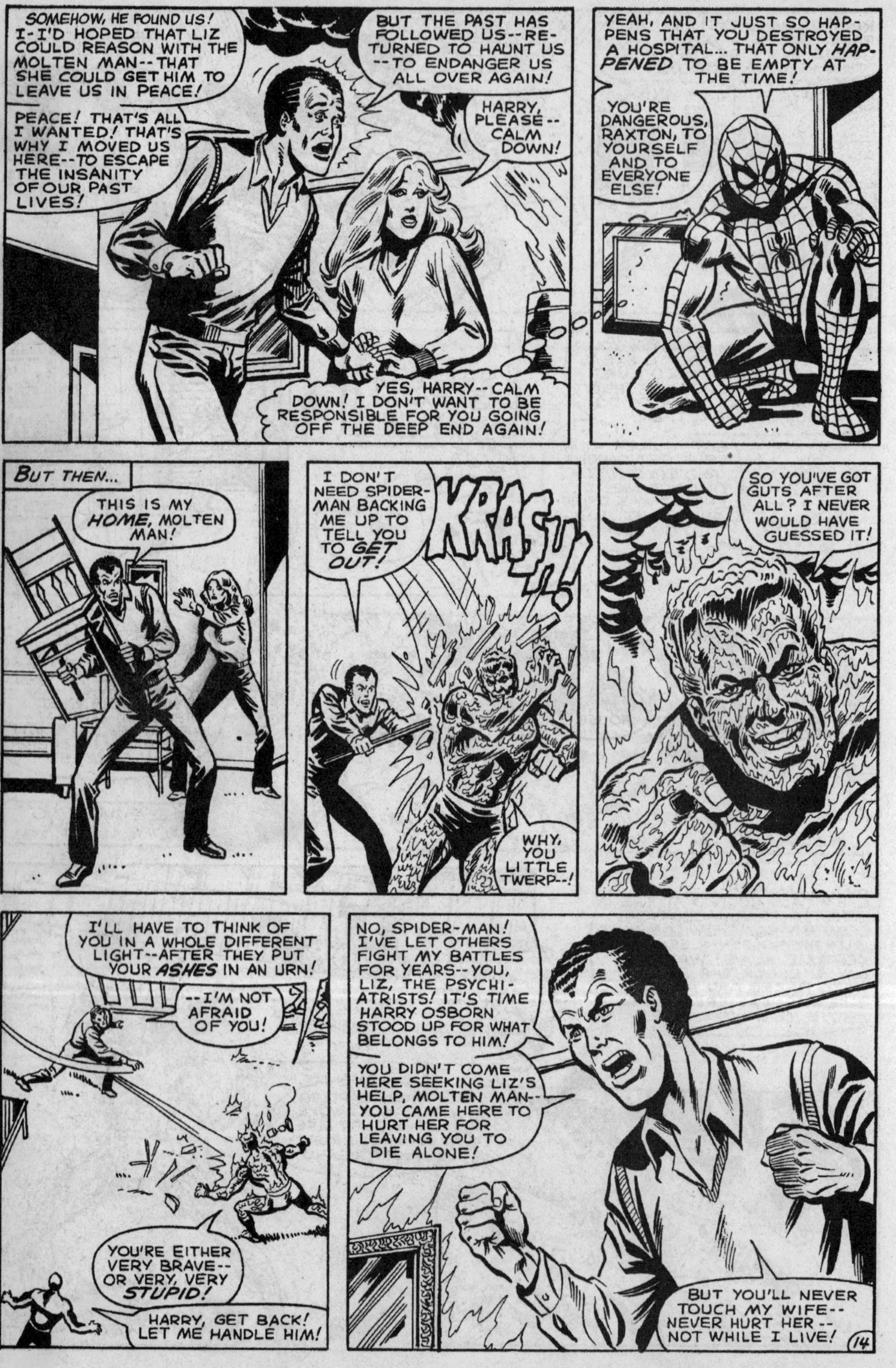
SOMEHOW, HE FOUND US! I-I'D HOPED THAT LIZ COULD REASON WITH THE MOLTEN MAN--THAT SHE COULD GET HIM TO LEAVE US IN PEACE!
PEACE! THAT'S ALL I WANTED! THAT'S WHY I MOVED US HERE--TO ESCAPE THE INSANITY OF OUR PAST LIVES!
BUT THE PAST HAS FOLLOWED US--RETURNED TO HAUNT US--TO ENDANGER US ALL OVER AGAIN!
HARRY, PLEASE--CALM DOWN!
YES, HARRY--CALM DOWN! I DON'T WANT TO BE RESPONSIBLE FOR YOU GOING OFF THE DEEP END AGAIN!
YEAH, AND IT JUST SO HAPPENS THAT YOU DESTROYED A HOSPITAL... THAT ONLY HAPPENED TO BE EMPTY AT THE TIME!
YOU'RE DANGEROUS, RAXTON, TO YOURSELF AND TO EVERYONE ELSE!
BUT THEN...
THIS IS MY HOME, MOLTEN MAN!
I DON'T NEED SPIDER-MAN BACKING ME UP TO TELL YOU TO GET OUT!
KRASH!
WHY, YOU LITTLE TWERP--!
SO YOU'VE GOT GUTS AFTER ALL? I NEVER WOULD HAVE GUESSED IT!
I'LL HAVE TO THINK OF YOU IN A WHOLE DIFFERENT LIGHT--AFTER THEY PUT YOUR ASHES IN AN URN!
--I'M NOT AFRAID OF YOU!
YOU'RE EITHER VERY BRAVE--OR VERY, VERY STUPID!
HARRY, GET BACK! LET ME HANDLE HIM!
NO, SPIDER-MAN! I'VE LET OTHERS FIGHT MY BATTLES FOR YEARS--YOU, LIZ, THE PSYCHIATRISTS! IT'S TIME HARRY OSBORN STOOD UP FOR WHAT BELONGS TO HIM!
YOU DIDN'T COME HERE SEEKING LIZ'S HELP, MOLTEN MAN--YOU CAME HERE TO HURT HER FOR LEAVING YOU TO DIE ALONE!
BUT YOU'LL NEVER TOUCH MY WIFE--NEVER HURT HER--NOT WHILE I LIVE!
14

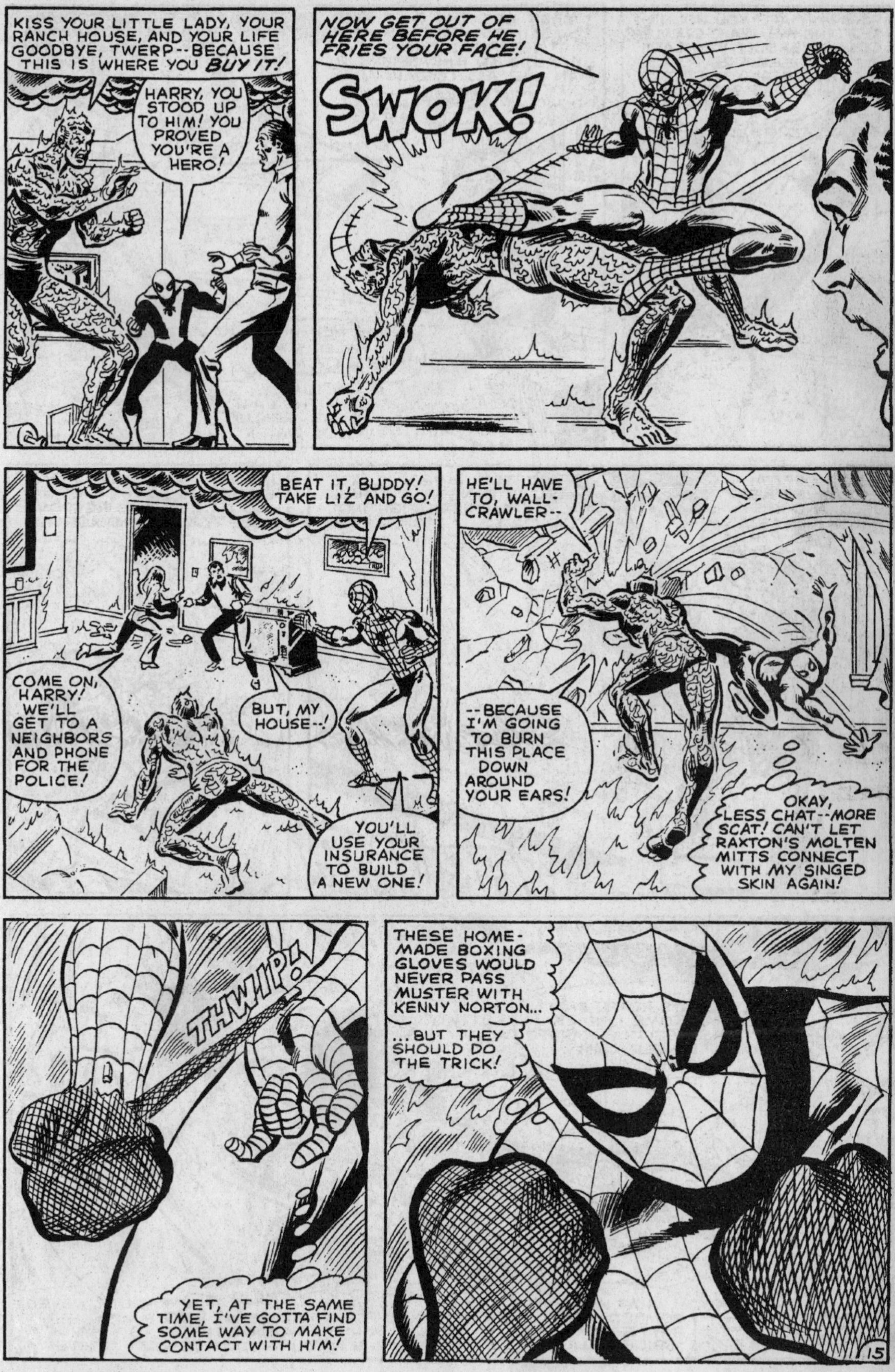
KISS YOUR LITTLE LADY, YOUR RANCH HOUSE, AND YOUR LIFE GOODBYE, TWERP--BECAUSE THIS IS WHERE YOU BUY IT!
HARRY, YOU STOOD UP TO HIM! YOU PROVED YOU'RE A HERO!
NOW GET OUT OF HERE BEFORE HE FRIES YOUR FACE!
SWOK!
BEAT IT, BUDDY! TAKE LIZ AND GO!
COME ON, HARRY! WE'LL GET TO A NEIGHBORS AND PHONE FOR THE POLICE!
BUT, MY HOUSE--!
YOU'LL USE YOUR INSURANCE TO BUILD A NEW ONE!
HE'LL HAVE TO, WALL-CRAWLER--
--BECAUSE I'M GOING TO BURN THIS PLACE DOWN AROUND YOUR EARS!
OKAY, LESS CHAT--MORE SCAT! CAN'T LET RAXTON'S MOLTEN MITTS CONNECT WITH MY SINGED SKIN AGAIN!
THWIP!
YET, AT THE SAME TIME, I'VE GOTTA FIND SOME WAY TO MAKE CONTACT WITH HIM!
THESE HOME-MADE BOXING GLOVES WOULD NEVER PASS MUSTER WITH KENNY NORTON...
...BUT THEY SHOULD DO THE TRICK!
15

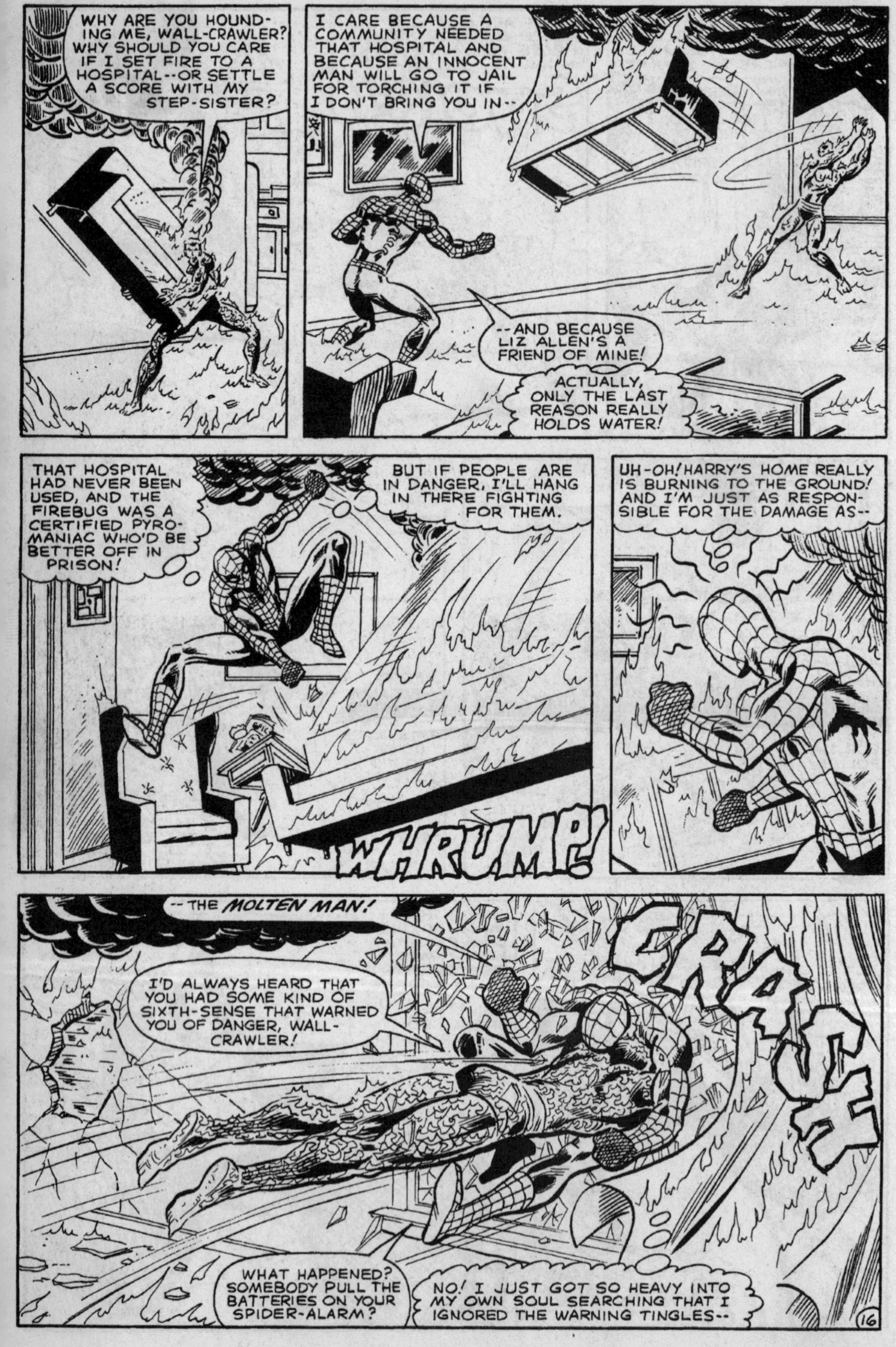
WHY ARE YOU HOUNDING ME, WALL-CRAWLER? WHY SHOULD YOU CARE IF I SET FIRE TO A HOSPITAL--OR SETTLE A SCORE WITH MY STEP-SISTER?
I CARE BECAUSE A COMMUNITY NEEDED THAT HOSPITAL AND BECAUSE AN INNOCENT MAN WILL GO TO JAIL FOR TORCHING IT IF I DON'T BRING YOU IN--
--AND BECAUSE LIZ ALLEN'S A FRIEND OF MINE!
ACTUALLY, ONLY THE LAST REASON REALLY HOLDS WATER!
THAT HOSPITAL HAD NEVER BEEN USED, AND THE FIREBUG WAS A CERTIFIED PYROMANIAC WHO'D BE BETTER OFF IN PRISON!
BUT IF PEOPLE ARE IN DANGER, I'LL HANG IN THERE FIGHTING FOR THEM.
WHRUMP!
UH-OH! HARRY'S HOME REALLY IS BURNING TO THE GROUND! AND I'M JUST AS RESPONSIBLE FOR THE DAMAGE AS--
--THE MOLTEN MAN!
CRASH
I'D ALWAYS HEARD THAT YOU HAD SOME KIND OF SIXTH-SENSE THAT WARNED YOU OF DANGER, WALL-CRAWLER!
WHAT HAPPENED? SOMEBODY PULL THE BATTERIES ON YOUR SPIDER-ALARM?
NO! I JUST GOT SO HEAVY INTO MY OWN SOUL SEARCHING THAT I IGNORED THE WARNING TINGLES--

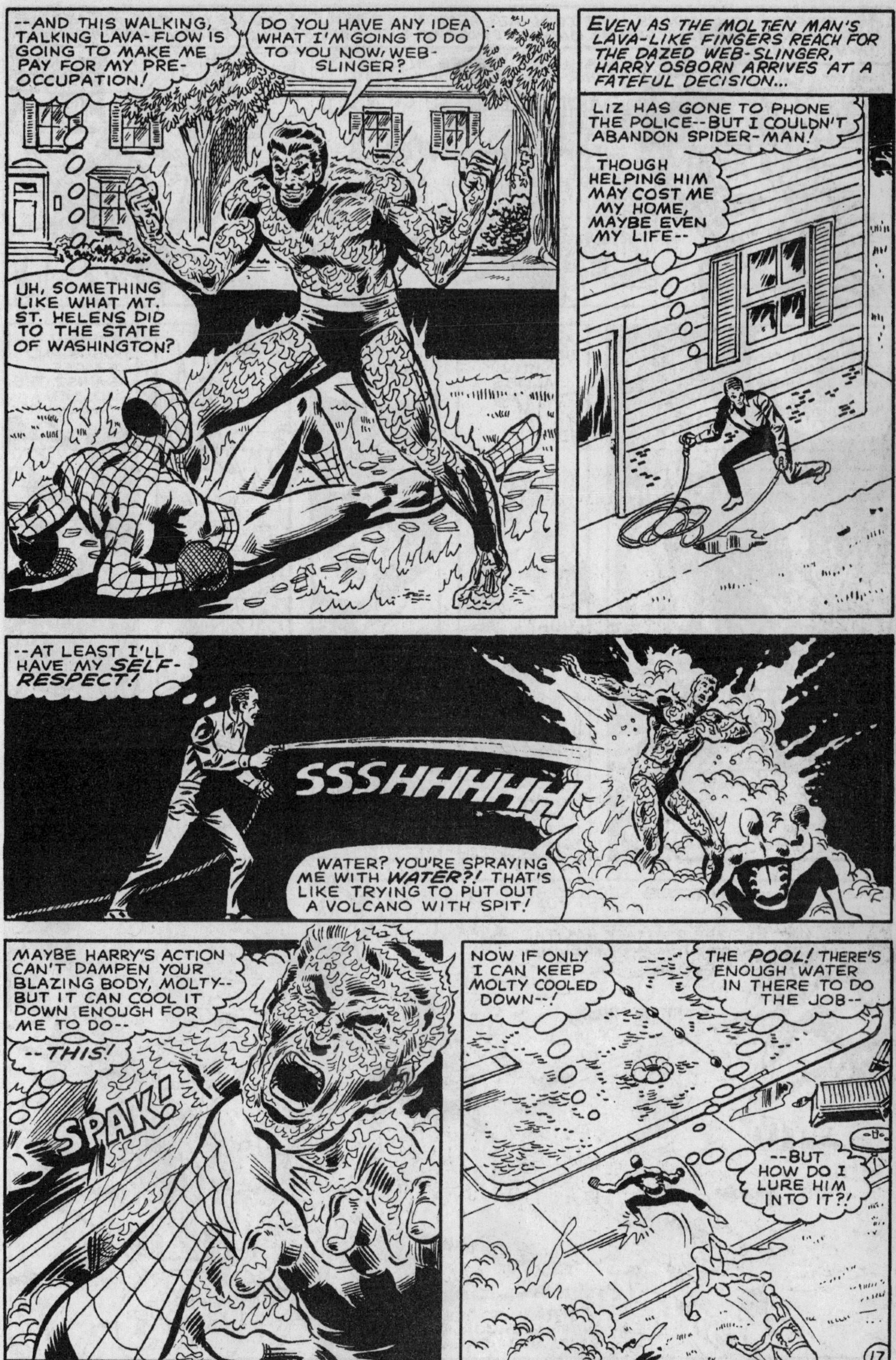
--AND THIS WALKING, TALKING LAVA-FLOW IS GOING TO MAKE ME PAY FOR MY PRE-OCCUPATION!
DO YOU HAVE ANY IDEA WHAT I'M GOING TO DO TO YOU NOW, WEB-SLINGER?
UH, SOMETHING LIKE WHAT MT. ST. HELENS DID TO THE STATE OF WASHINGTON?
EVEN AS THE MOLTEN MAN'S LAVA-LIKE FINGERS REACH FOR THE DAZED WEB-SLINGER, HARRY OSBORN ARRIVES AT A FATEFUL DECISION...
LIZ HAS GONE TO PHONE THE POLICE--BUT I COULDN'T ABANDON SPIDER-MAN!
THOUGH HELPING HIM MAY COST ME MY HOME, MAYBE EVEN MY LIFE--
--AT LEAST I'LL HAVE MY SELF-RESPECT!
SSSHHHHHH
WATER? YOU'RE SPRAYING ME WITH WATER?! THAT'S LIKE TRYING TO PUT OUT A VOLCANO WITH SPIT!
MAYBE HARRY'S ACTION CAN'T DAMPEN YOUR BLAZING BODY, MOLTY--BUT IT CAN COOL IT DOWN ENOUGH FOR ME TO DO--
--THIS!
SPAK!
NOW IF ONLY I CAN KEEP MOLTY COOLED DOWN--!
THE POOL! THERE'S ENOUGH WATER IN THERE TO DO THE JOB--
--BUT HOW DO I LURE HIM INTO IT?!

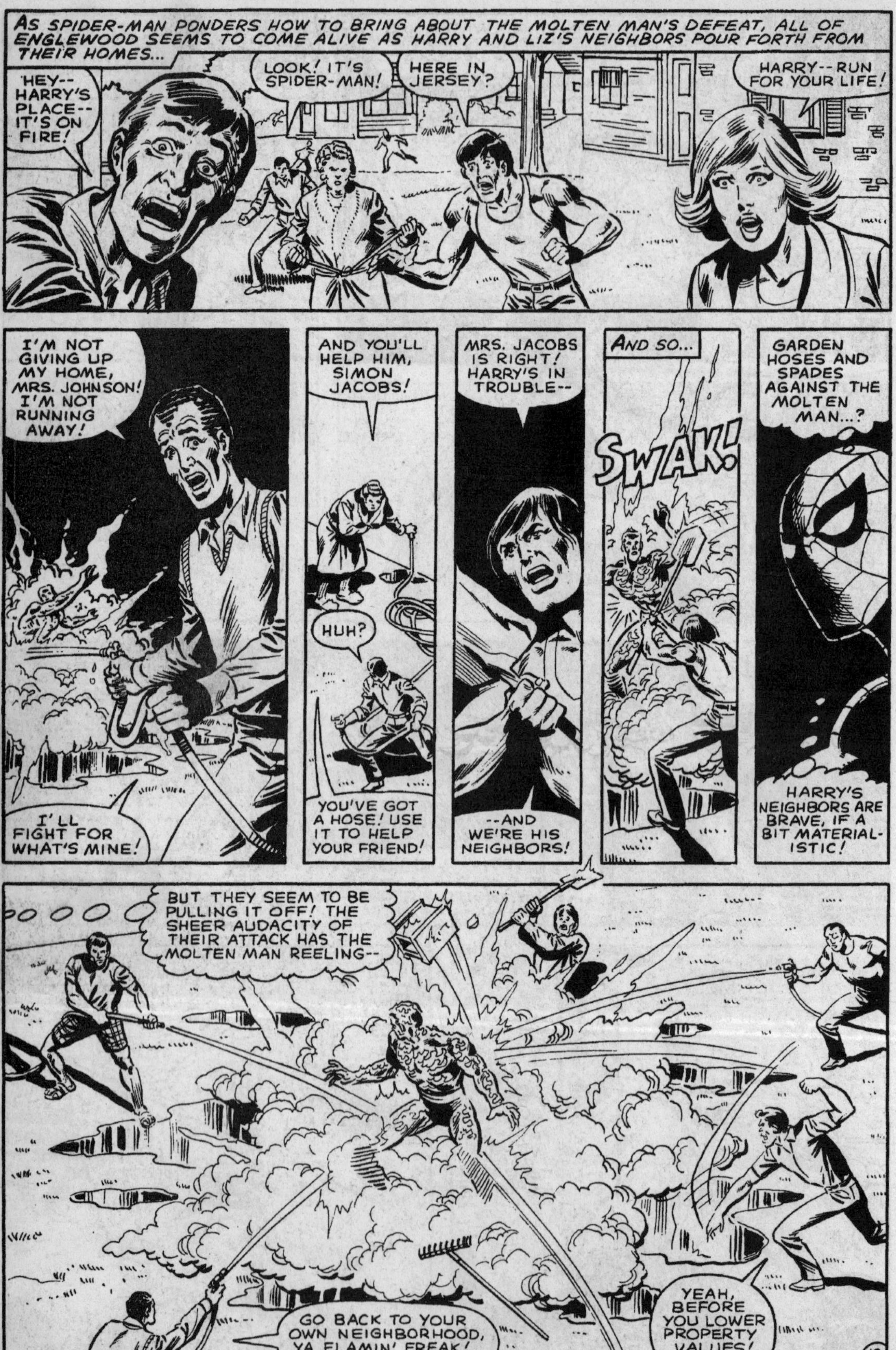
AS SPIDER-MAN PONDERS HOW TO BRING ABOUT THE MOLTEN MAN'S DEFEAT, ALL OF ENGLEWOOD SEEMS TO COME ALIVE AS HARRY AND LIZ'S NEIGHBORS POUR FORTH FROM THEIR HOMES...
HEY-- HARRY'S PLACE-- IT'S ON FIRE!
LOOK! IT'S SPIDER-MAN!
HERE IN JERSEY?
HARRY--RUN FOR YOUR LIFE!
I'M NOT GIVING UP MY HOME, MRS. JOHNSON! I'M NOT RUNNING AWAY!
I'LL FIGHT FOR WHAT'S MINE!
AND YOU'LL HELP HIM, SIMON JACOBS!
HUH?
YOU'VE GOT A HOSE! USE IT TO HELP YOUR FRIEND!
MRS. JACOBS IS RIGHT! HARRY'S IN TROUBLE--
--AND WE'RE HIS NEIGHBORS!
AND SO...
SWAK!
GARDEN HOSES AND SPADES AGAINST THE MOLTEN MAN...?
HARRY'S NEIGHBORS ARE BRAVE, IF A BIT MATERIAL-ISTIC!
BUT THEY SEEM TO BE PULLING IT OFF! THE SHEER AUDACITY OF THEIR ATTACK HAS THE MOLTEN MAN REELING--
GO BACK TO YOUR OWN NEIGHBORHOOD, YA FLAMIN' FREAK!
YEAH, BEFORE YOU LOWER PROPERTY VALUES!
18

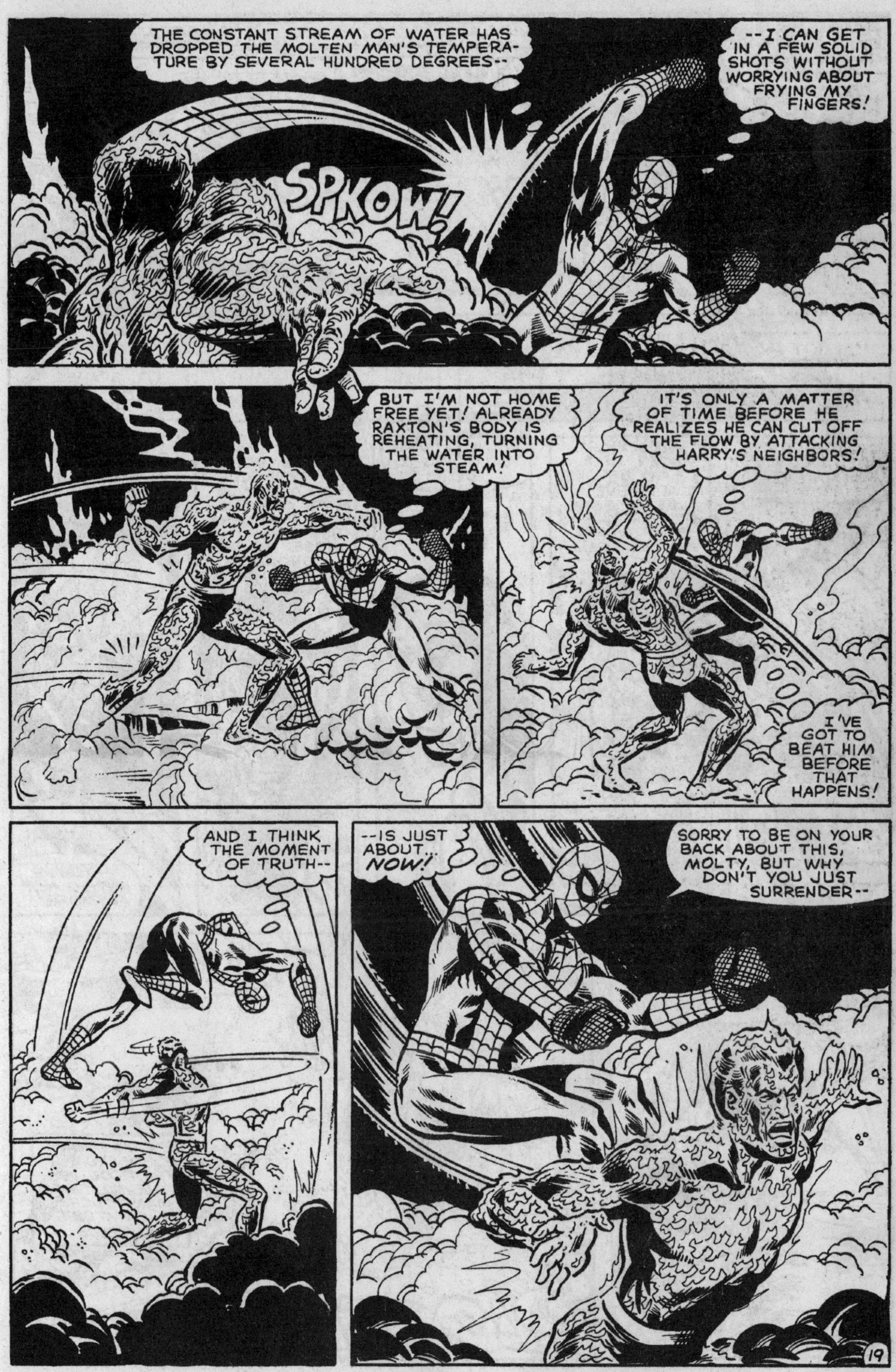
THE CONSTANT STREAM OF WATER HAS DROPPED THE MOLTEN MAN'S TEMPERATURE BY SEVERAL HUNDRED DEGREES--
--I CAN GET IN A FEW SOLID SHOTS WITHOUT WORRYING ABOUT FRYING MY FINGERS!
SPKOW!
BUT I'M NOT HOME FREE YET! ALREADY RAXTON'S BODY IS REHEATING, TURNING THE WATER INTO STEAM!
IT'S ONLY A MATTER OF TIME BEFORE HE REALIZES HE CAN CUT OFF THE FLOW BY ATTACKING HARRY'S NEIGHBORS!
I'VE GOT TO BEAT HIM BEFORE THAT HAPPENS!
AND I THINK THE MOMENT OF TRUTH--
--IS JUST ABOUT... NOW!
SORRY TO BE ON YOUR BACK ABOUT THIS, MOLTY, BUT WHY DON'T YOU JUST SURRENDER--
19

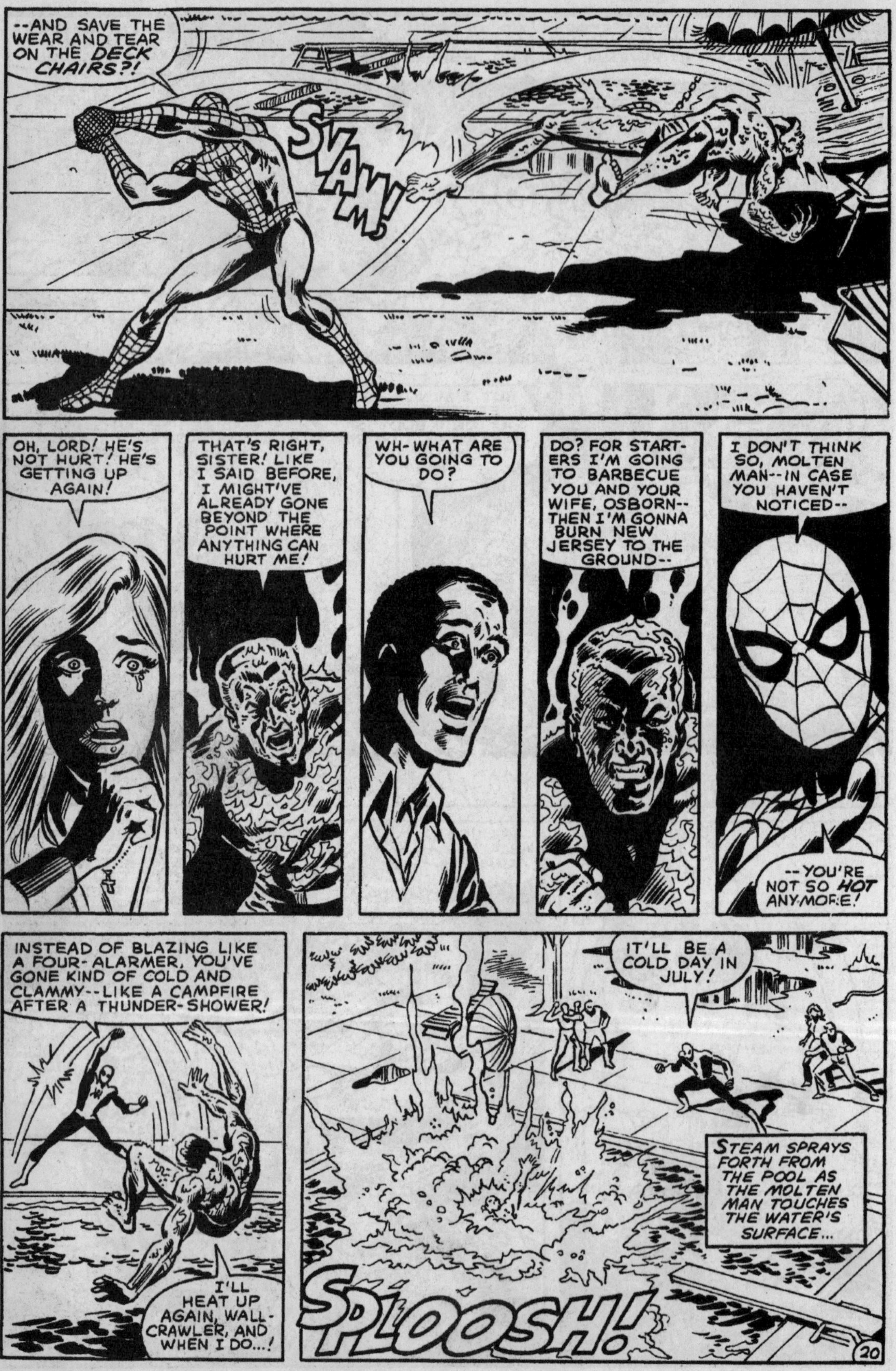
--AND SAVE THE WEAR AND TEAR ON THE DECK CHAIRS?!
SVAM!
OH, LORD! HE'S NOT HURT! HE'S GETTING UP AGAIN!
THAT'S RIGHT, SISTER! LIKE I SAID BEFORE, I MIGHT'VE ALREADY GONE BEYOND THE POINT WHERE ANYTHING CAN HURT ME!
WH-WHAT ARE YOU GOING TO DO?
DO? FOR STARTERS I'M GOING TO BARBECUE YOU AND YOUR WIFE, OSBORN--THEN I'M GONNA BURN NEW JERSEY TO THE GROUND--
I DON'T THINK SO, MOLTEN MAN--IN CASE YOU HAVEN'T NOTICED--
--YOU'RE NOT SO HOT ANYMORE!
INSTEAD OF BLAZING LIKE A FOUR-ALARMER, YOU'VE GONE KIND OF COLD AND CLAMMY--LIKE A CAMPFIRE AFTER A THUNDER-SHOWER!
I'LL HEAT UP AGAIN, WALL-CRAWLER, AND WHEN I DO...!
IT'LL BE A COLD DAY IN JULY!
STEAM SPRAYS FORTH FROM THE POOL AS THE MOLTEN MAN TOUCHES THE WATER'S SURFACE...
SPLOOSH!

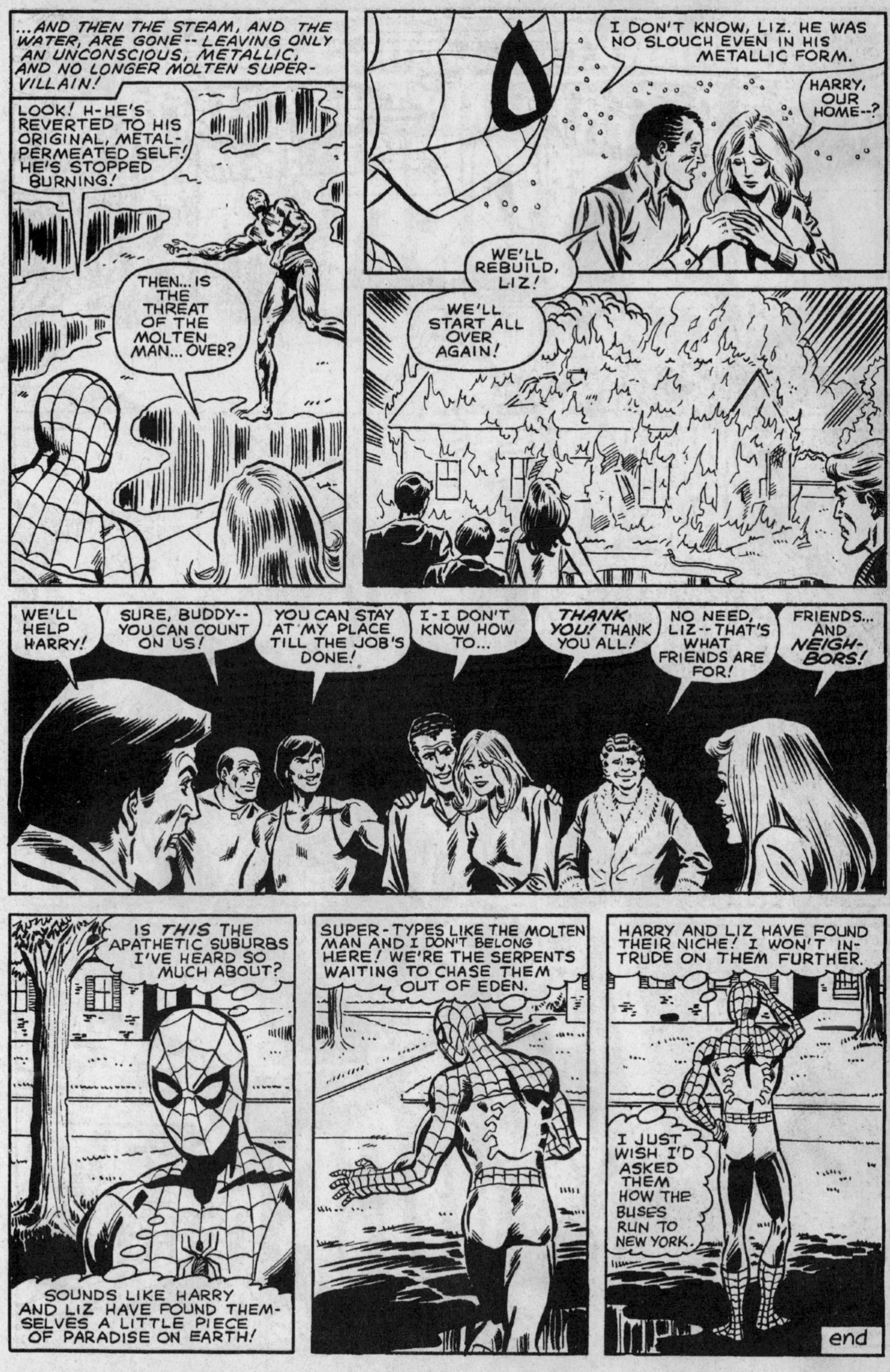

...AND THEN THE STEAM, AND THE WATER, ARE GONE -- LEAVING ONLY AN UNCONSCIOUS, METALLIC, AND NO LONGER MOLTEN SUPER-VILLAIN!
LOOK! H-HE'S REVERTED TO HIS ORIGINAL, METAL-PERMEATED SELF! HE'S STOPPED BURNING!
THEN... IS THE THREAT OF THE MOLTEN MAN... OVER?
I DON'T KNOW, LIZ. HE WAS NO SLOUCH EVEN IN HIS METALLIC FORM.
HARRY, OUR HOME--?
WE'LL REBUILD, LIZ!
WE'LL START ALL OVER AGAIN!
WE'LL HELP HARRY!
SURE, BUDDY-- YOU CAN COUNT ON US!
YOU CAN STAY AT MY PLACE TILL THE JOB'S DONE!
I-I DON'T KNOW HOW TO...
THANK YOU! THANK YOU ALL!
NO NEED, LIZ -- THAT'S WHAT FRIENDS ARE FOR!
FRIENDS... AND NEIGHBORS!
IS THIS THE APATHETIC SUBURBS I'VE HEARD SO MUCH ABOUT?
SOUNDS LIKE HARRY AND LIZ HAVE FOUND THEMSELVES A LITTLE PIECE OF PARADISE ON EARTH!
SUPER-TYPES LIKE THE MOLTEN MAN AND I DON'T BELONG HERE! WE'RE THE SERPENTS WAITING TO CHASE THEM OUT OF EDEN.
HARRY AND LIZ HAVE FOUND THEIR NICHE! I WON'T INTRUDE ON THEM FURTHER.
I JUST WISH I'D ASKED THEM HOW THE BUSES RUN TO NEW YORK.
end

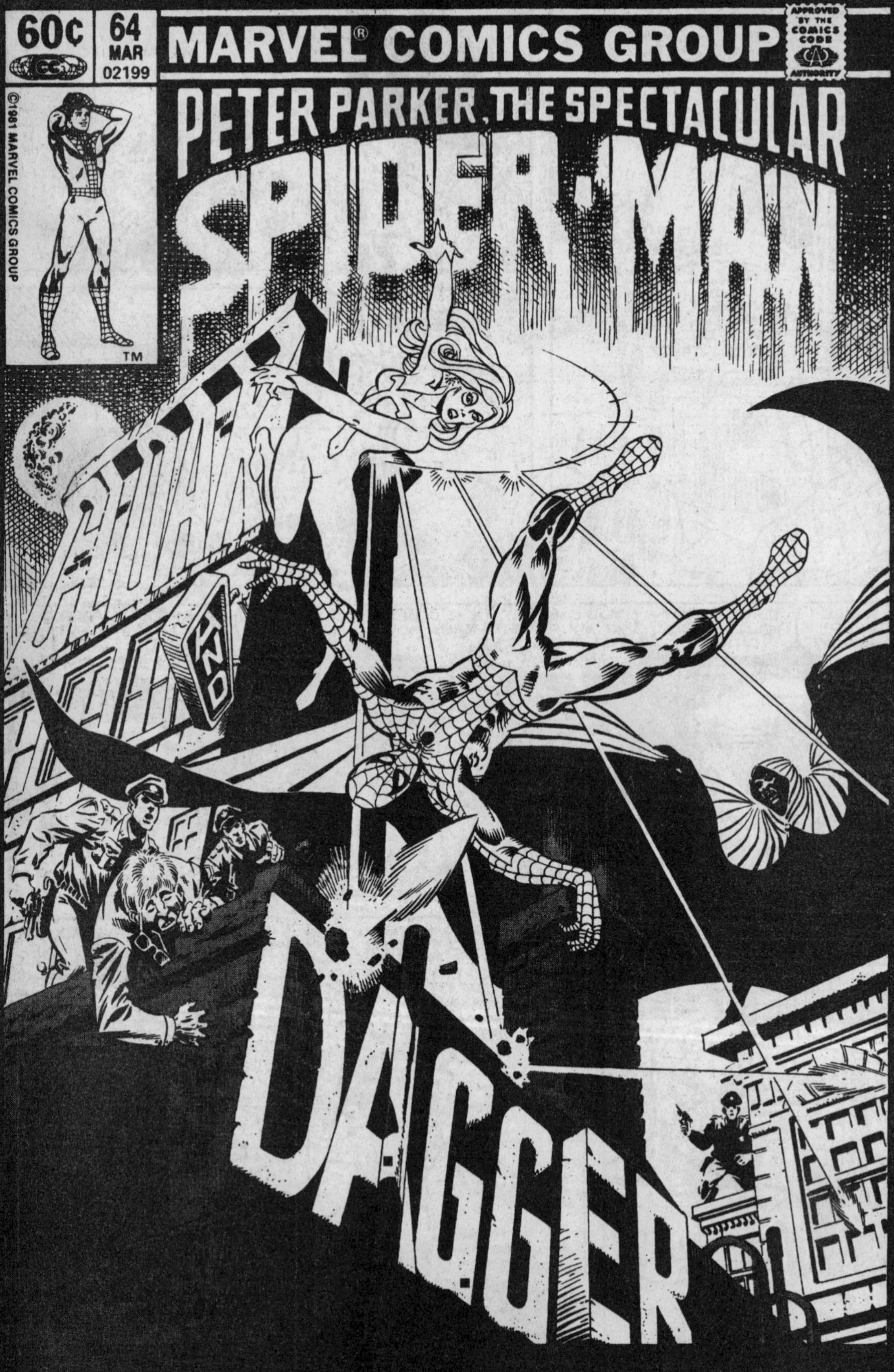
60¢
64
MAR
02199
MARVEL® COMICS GROUP
APPROVED BY THE COMICS CODE AUTHORITY
©1981 MARVEL COMICS GROUP
TM
PETER PARKER, THE SPECTACULAR
SPIDER-MAN®
CLOAK
AND
DAGGER

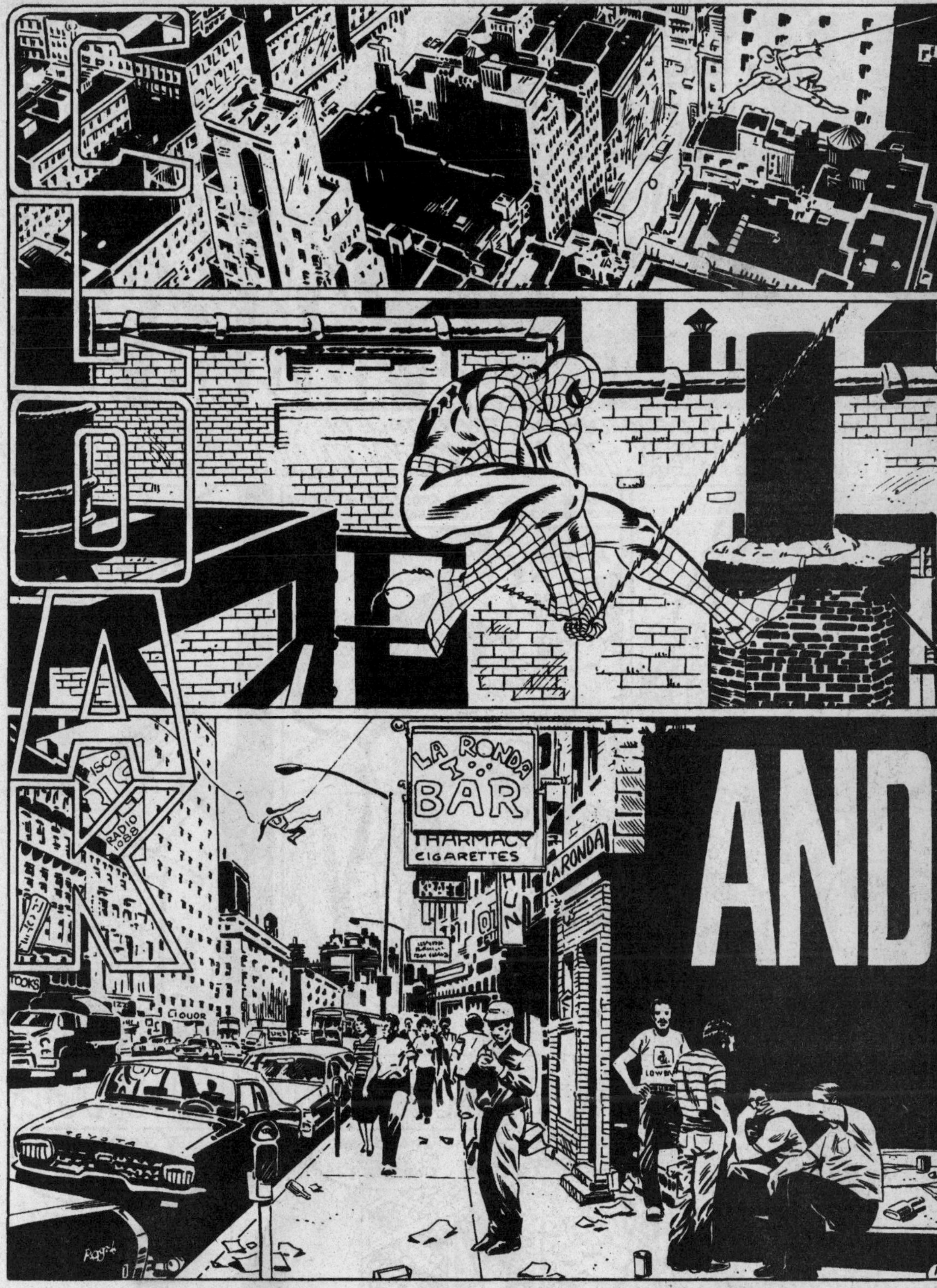

LA RONDA BAR
PHARMACY
CIGARETTES
LA RONDA
AND

DAGGER!

Stan Lee PRESENTS: A DECIDEDLY DIFFERENT TALE OF...

PETER PARKER, THE SPECTACULAR SPIDER-MAN!

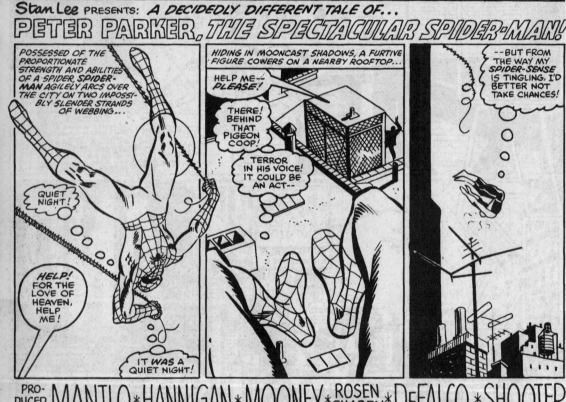

POSSESSED OF THE PROPORTIONATE STRENGTH AND ABILITIES OF A SPIDER, SPIDER-MAN AGILELY ARCS OVER THE CITY ON TWO IMPOSSIBLY SLENDER STRANDS OF WEBBING...

QUIET NIGHT!

HELP! FOR THE LOVE OF HEAVEN, HELP ME!

IT WAS A QUIET NIGHT!

HIDING IN MOONCAST SHADOWS, A FURTIVE FIGURE COWERS ON A NEARBY ROOFTOP...

HELP ME-- PLEASE!

THERE! BEHIND THAT PIGEON COOP!

TERROR IN HIS VOICE! IT COULD BE AN ACT--

--BUT FROM THE WAY MY SPIDER-SENSE IS TINGLING, I'D BETTER NOT TAKE CHANCES!

PRODUCED BY MANTLO * HANNIGAN * MOONEY * ROSEN SHAREN * DeFALCO * SHOOTER

HI! WHAT SEEMS TO BE THE TROUBLE?

SPIDER-MAN! Y-YOU CAME?! YOU'LL HELP ME?!!

2

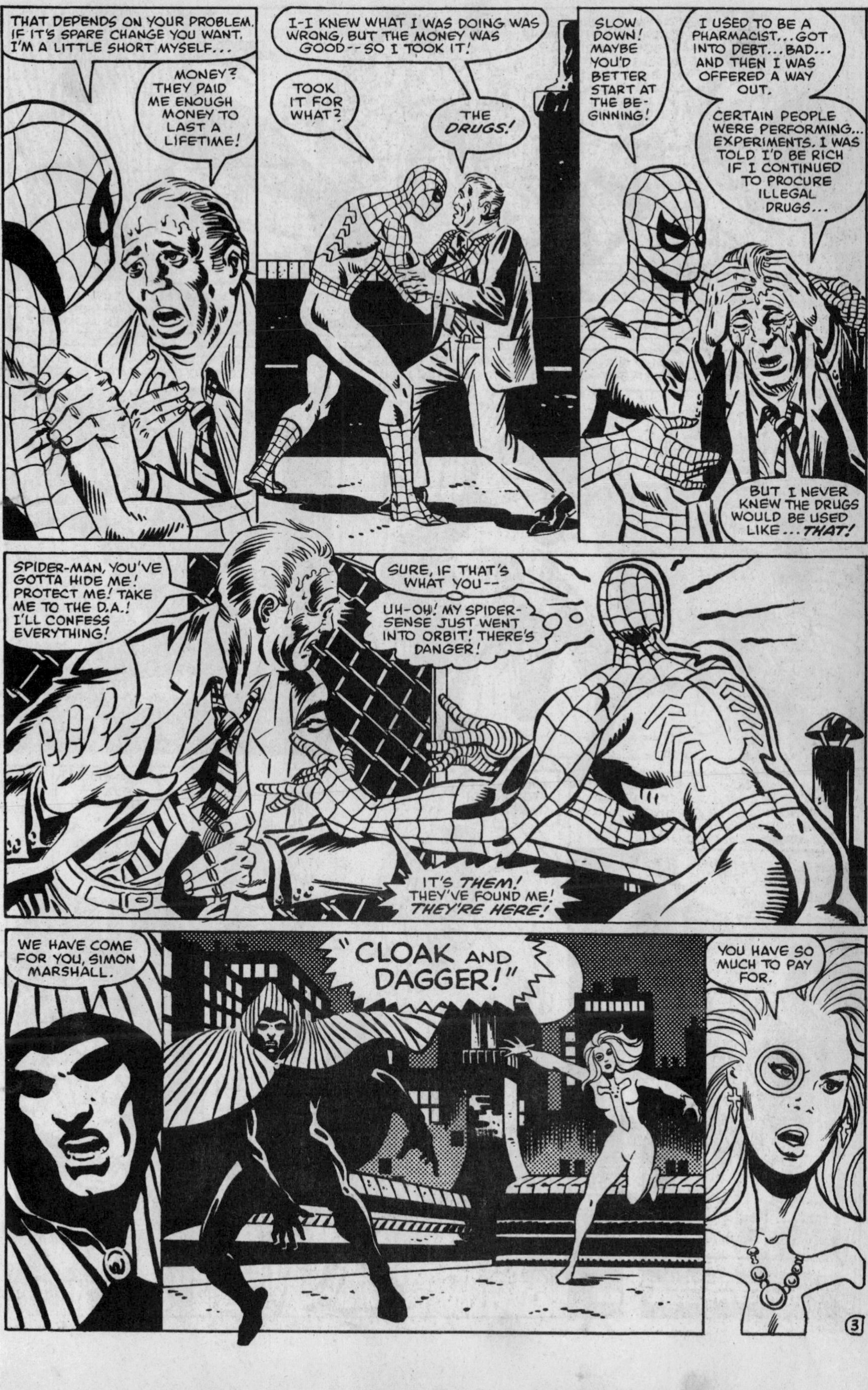
THAT DEPENDS ON YOUR PROBLEM. IF IT'S SPARE CHANGE YOU WANT, I'M A LITTLE SHORT MYSELF...
MONEY? THEY PAID ME ENOUGH MONEY TO LAST A LIFETIME!
I-I KNEW WHAT I WAS DOING WAS WRONG, BUT THE MONEY WAS GOOD--SO I TOOK IT!
TOOK IT FOR WHAT?
THE DRUGS!
SLOW DOWN! MAYBE YOU'D BETTER START AT THE BEGINNING!
I USED TO BE A PHARMACIST...GOT INTO DEBT...BAD... AND THEN I WAS OFFERED A WAY OUT.
CERTAIN PEOPLE WERE PERFORMING... EXPERIMENTS. I WAS TOLD I'D BE RICH IF I CONTINUED TO PROCURE ILLEGAL DRUGS...
BUT I NEVER KNEW THE DRUGS WOULD BE USED LIKE...THAT!
SPIDER-MAN, YOU'VE GOTTA HIDE ME! PROTECT ME! TAKE ME TO THE D.A.! I'LL CONFESS EVERYTHING!
SURE, IF THAT'S WHAT YOU--
UH-OH! MY SPIDER-SENSE JUST WENT INTO ORBIT! THERE'S DANGER!
IT'S THEM! THEY'VE FOUND ME! THEY'RE HERE!
WE HAVE COME FOR YOU, SIMON MARSHALL.
"CLOAK AND DAGGER!"
YOU HAVE SO MUCH TO PAY FOR.

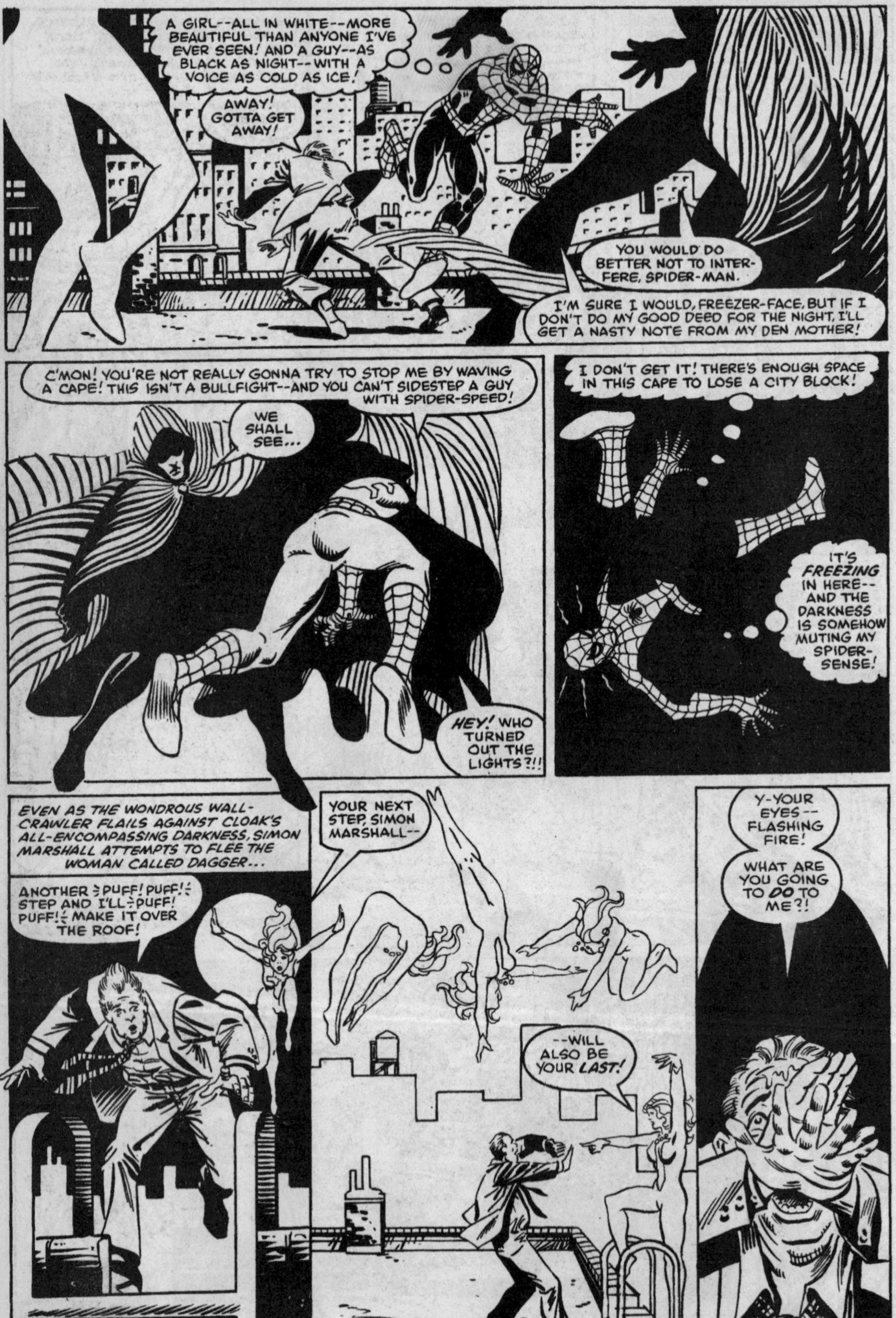

A GIRL--ALL IN WHITE--MORE BEAUTIFUL THAN ANYONE I'VE EVER SEEN! AND A GUY--AS BLACK AS NIGHT--WITH A VOICE AS COLD AS ICE!
AWAY! GOTTA GET AWAY!
YOU WOULD DO BETTER NOT TO INTERFERE, SPIDER-MAN.
I'M SURE I WOULD, FREEZER-FACE, BUT IF I DON'T DO MY GOOD DEED FOR THE NIGHT, I'LL GET A NASTY NOTE FROM MY DEN MOTHER!
C'MON! YOU'RE NOT REALLY GONNA TRY TO STOP ME BY WAVING A CAPE! THIS ISN'T A BULLFIGHT--AND YOU CAN'T SIDESTEP A GUY WITH SPIDER-SPEED!
WE SHALL SEE...
HEY! WHO TURNED OUT THE LIGHTS?!!
I DON'T GET IT! THERE'S ENOUGH SPACE IN THIS CAPE TO LOSE A CITY BLOCK!
IT'S FREEZING IN HERE--AND THE DARKNESS IS SOMEHOW MUTING MY SPIDER-SENSE!
EVEN AS THE WONDROUS WALL-CRAWLER FLAILS AGAINST CLOAK'S ALL-ENCOMPASSING DARKNESS, SIMON MARSHALL ATTEMPTS TO FLEE THE WOMAN CALLED DAGGER...
ANOTHER *PUFF! PUFF!* STEP AND I'LL *PUFF! PUFF!* MAKE IT OVER THE ROOF!
YOUR NEXT STEP, SIMON MARSHALL--
--WILL ALSO BE YOUR LAST!
Y-YOUR EYES--FLASHING FIRE!
WHAT ARE YOU GOING TO DO TO ME?!

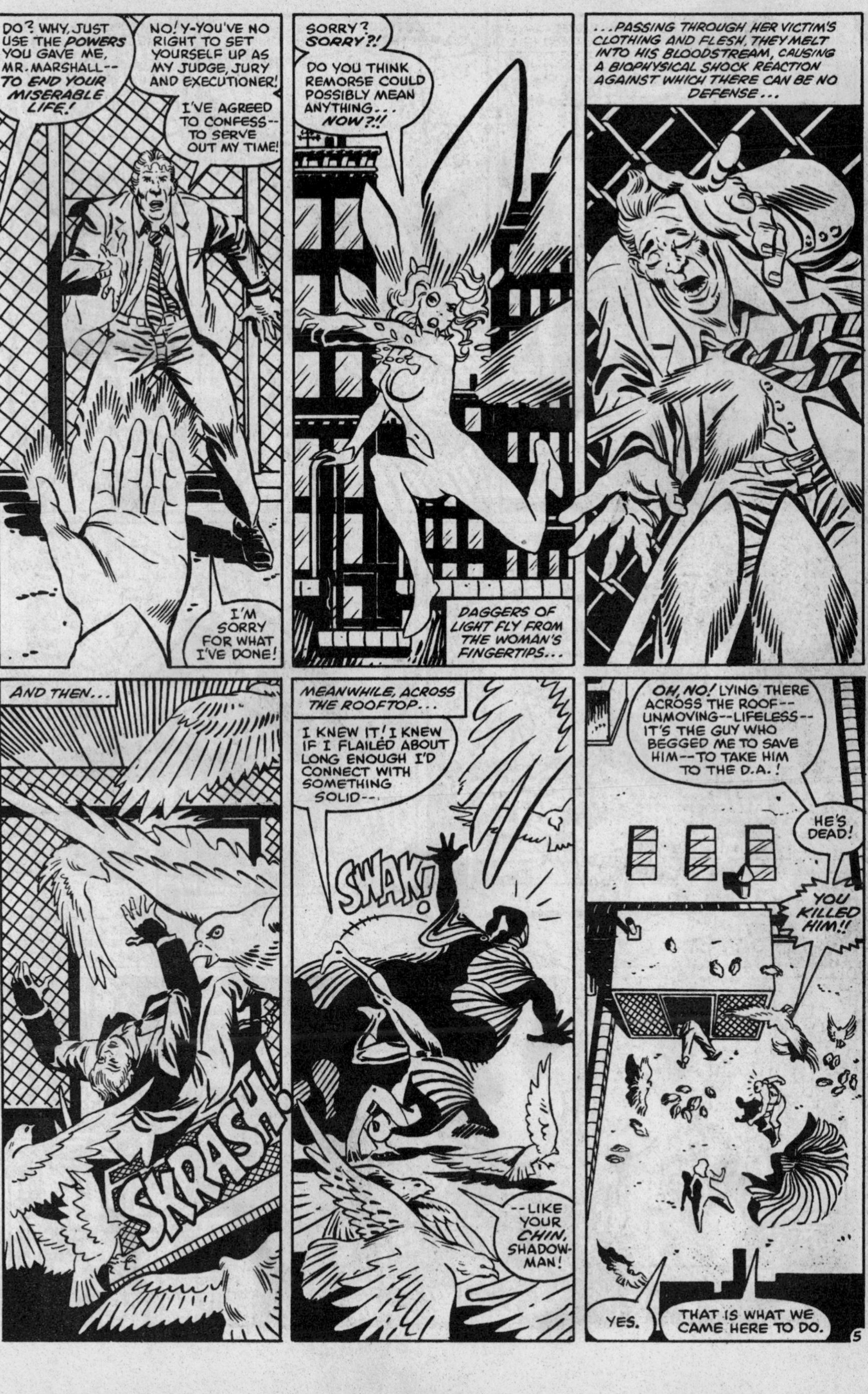
DO? WHY, JUST USE THE POWERS YOU GAVE ME, MR. MARSHALL-- TO END YOUR MISERABLE LIFE!
NO! Y-YOU'VE NO RIGHT TO SET YOURSELF UP AS MY JUDGE, JURY AND EXECUTIONER!
I'VE AGREED TO CONFESS-- TO SERVE OUT MY TIME!
I'M SORRY FOR WHAT I'VE DONE!
SORRY? SORRY?!
DO YOU THINK REMORSE COULD POSSIBLY MEAN ANYTHING... NOW?!!
DAGGERS OF LIGHT FLY FROM THE WOMAN'S FINGERTIPS...
...PASSING THROUGH HER VICTIM'S CLOTHING AND FLESH, THEY MELT INTO HIS BLOODSTREAM, CAUSING A BIOPHYSICAL SHOCK REACTION AGAINST WHICH THERE CAN BE NO DEFENSE...
AND THEN...
SKRASH!
MEANWHILE, ACROSS THE ROOFTOP...
I KNEW IT! I KNEW IF I FLAILED ABOUT LONG ENOUGH I'D CONNECT WITH SOMETHING SOLID--
SWAK!
--LIKE YOUR CHIN, SHADOW-MAN!
OH, NO! LYING THERE ACROSS THE ROOF-- UNMOVING--LIFELESS-- IT'S THE GUY WHO BEGGED ME TO SAVE HIM--TO TAKE HIM TO THE D.A.!
HE'S DEAD!
YOU KILLED HIM!!
YES.
THAT IS WHAT WE CAME HERE TO DO.

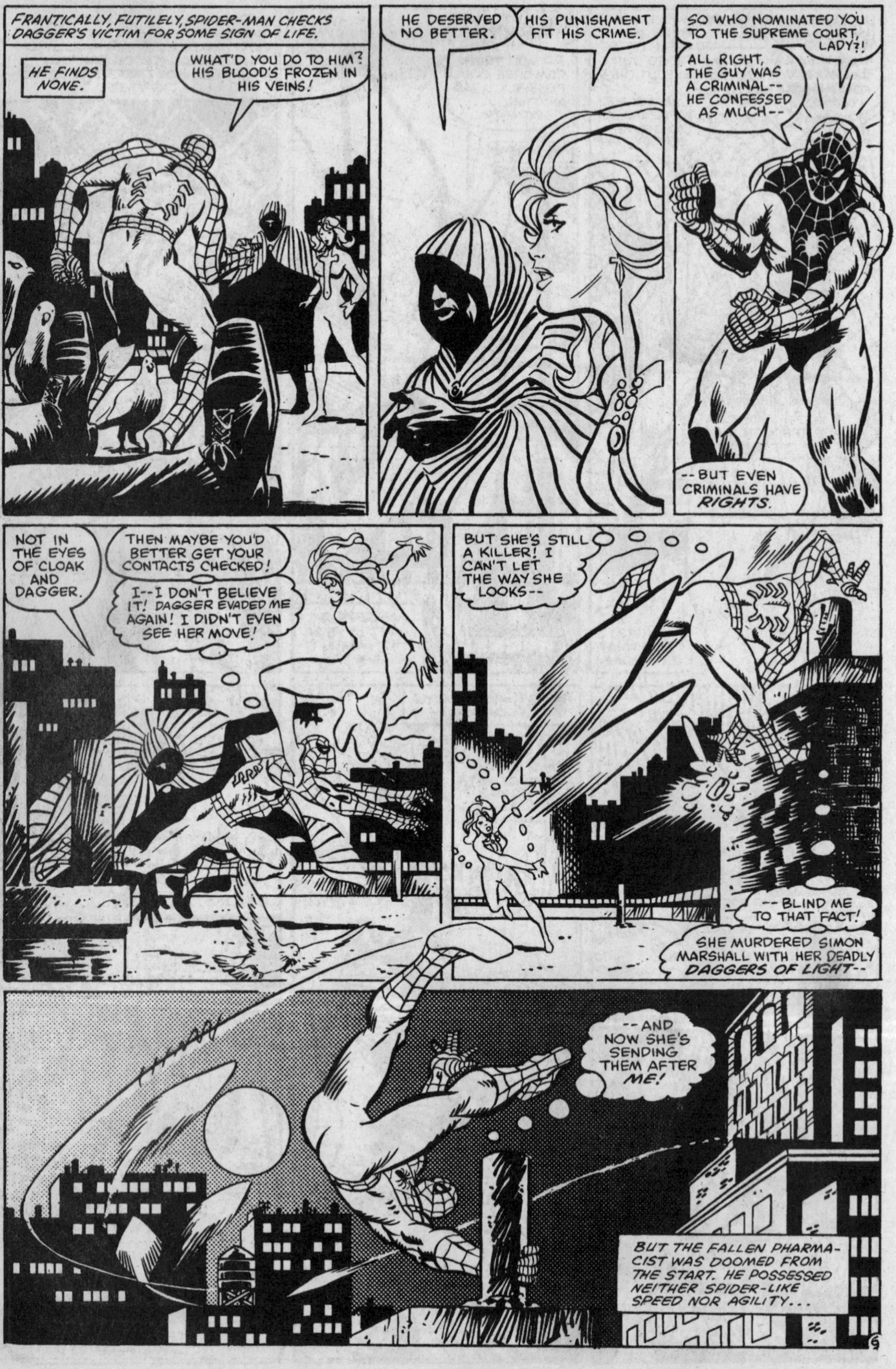
FRANTICALLY, FUTILELY, SPIDER-MAN CHECKS DAGGER'S VICTIM FOR SOME SIGN OF LIFE.
HE FINDS NONE.
WHAT'D YOU DO TO HIM? HIS BLOOD'S FROZEN IN HIS VEINS!
HE DESERVED NO BETTER.
HIS PUNISHMENT FIT HIS CRIME.
SO WHO NOMINATED YOU TO THE SUPREME COURT, LADY?!
ALL RIGHT, THE GUY WAS A CRIMINAL-- HE CONFESSED AS MUCH--
--BUT EVEN CRIMINALS HAVE RIGHTS.
NOT IN THE EYES OF CLOAK AND DAGGER.
THEN MAYBE YOU'D BETTER GET YOUR CONTACTS CHECKED!
I--I DON'T BELIEVE IT! DAGGER EVADED ME AGAIN! I DIDN'T EVEN SEE HER MOVE!
BUT SHE'S STILL A KILLER! I CAN'T LET THE WAY SHE LOOKS--
--BLIND ME TO THAT FACT!
SHE MURDERED SIMON MARSHALL WITH HER DEADLY DAGGERS OF LIGHT--
--AND NOW SHE'S SENDING THEM AFTER ME!
BUT THE FALLEN PHARMACIST WAS DOOMED FROM THE START. HE POSSESSED NEITHER SPIDER-LIKE SPEED NOR AGILITY...
6

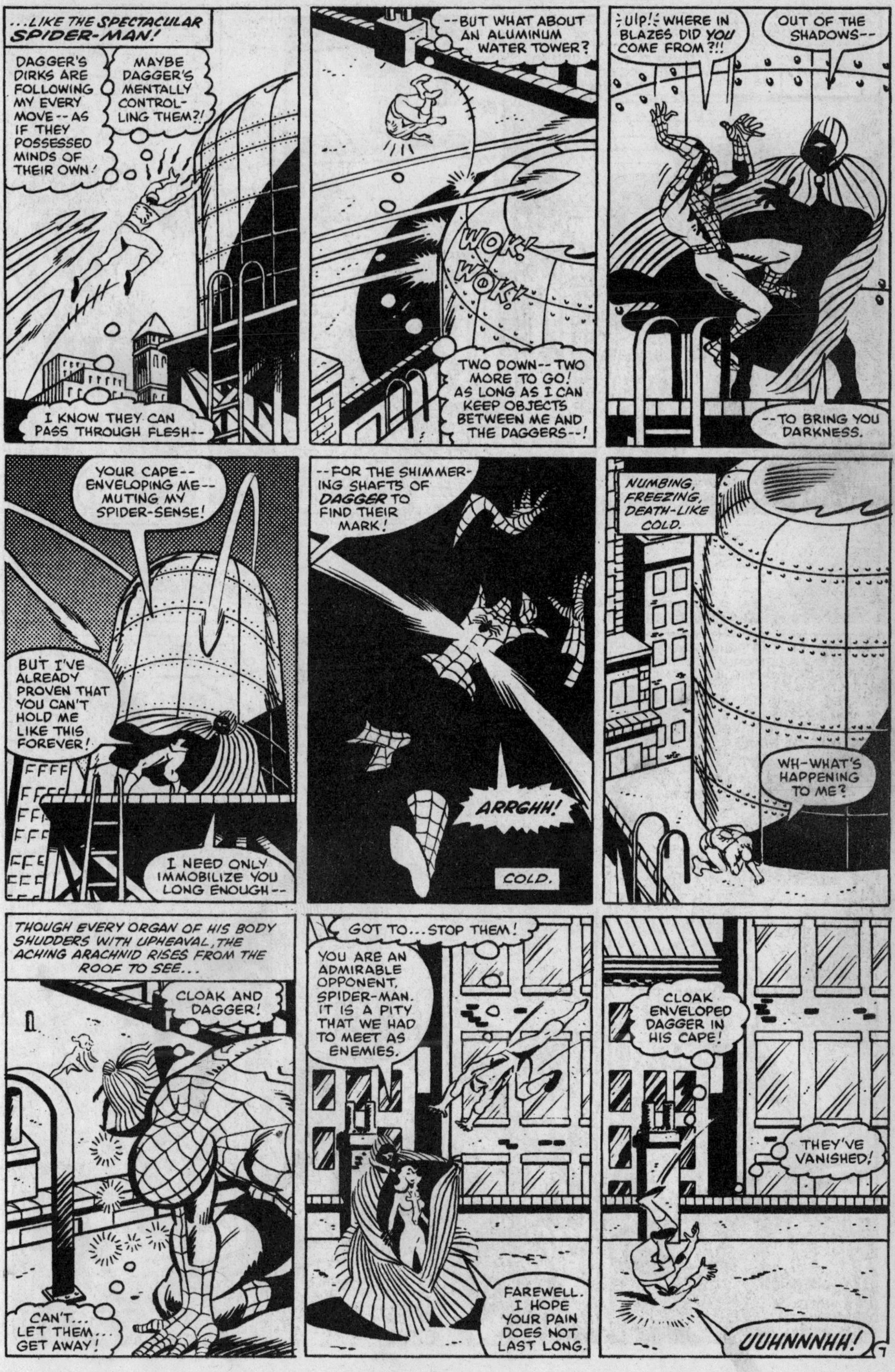

...LIKE THE SPECTACULAR SPIDER-MAN!
DAGGER'S DIRKS ARE FOLLOWING MY EVERY MOVE--AS IF THEY POSSESSED MINDS OF THEIR OWN!
MAYBE DAGGER'S MENTALLY CONTROL-LING THEM?!
I KNOW THEY CAN PASS THROUGH FLESH--
--BUT WHAT ABOUT AN ALUMINUM WATER TOWER?
WOK! WOK!
TWO DOWN--TWO MORE TO GO! AS LONG AS I CAN KEEP OBJECTS BETWEEN ME AND THE DAGGERS--!
ULP! WHERE IN BLAZES DID YOU COME FROM?!!
OUT OF THE SHADOWS--
--TO BRING YOU DARKNESS.
YOUR CAPE--ENVELOPING ME--MUTING MY SPIDER-SENSE!
BUT I'VE ALREADY PROVEN THAT YOU CAN'T HOLD ME LIKE THIS FOREVER!
I NEED ONLY IMMOBILIZE YOU LONG ENOUGH--
--FOR THE SHIMMER-ING SHAFTS OF DAGGER TO FIND THEIR MARK!
ARRGHH!
COLD.
NUMBING, FREEZING, DEATH-LIKE COLD.
WH-WHAT'S HAPPENING TO ME?
THOUGH EVERY ORGAN OF HIS BODY SHUDDERS WITH UPHEAVAL, THE ACHING ARACHNID RISES FROM THE ROOF TO SEE...
CLOAK AND DAGGER!
CAN'T... LET THEM... GET AWAY!
GOT TO... STOP THEM!
YOU ARE AN ADMIRABLE OPPONENT, SPIDER-MAN. IT IS A PITY THAT WE HAD TO MEET AS ENEMIES.
FAREWELL. I HOPE YOUR PAIN DOES NOT LAST LONG.
CLOAK ENVELOPED DAGGER IN HIS CAPE!
THEY'VE VANISHED!
UUHNNNHH!

Panel 1 (caption): SUDDENLY THE SCREAMING OF A SIREN -- AND THE SQUEALING OF TIRES ON THE STREET FAR BELOW -- INTRUDE UPON SPIDER-MAN'S AGONY...

Panel 2 (caption): AND THEN...

FRANK! ACROSS THE ROOF, IT'S... SPIDER-MAN!

LOOKS LIKE HE'S IN A BAD WAY!

YEAH, BUT THE STIFF LYING NEAR HIM LOOKS WORSE!

Panel 3: THE NEIGHBORS REPORTED A DISTURBANCE UP HERE! THEY DIDN'T SAY ANYTHING ABOUT MURDER!

I AM TAKING YOU INTO CUSTODY. YOU HAVE THE RIGHT TO REMAIN SILENT--

ENOUGH WITH THE MIRANDA WARNINGS, KOJAK! I DIDN'T KILL THAT GUY!

HE LOOKS LIKE HE'S BEEN FREEZE-DRIED -- FROM THE INSIDE OUT!

HEY! THIS IS SIMON MARSHALL! THERE'S AN A.P.B.* OUT ON HIM!

*ALL-POINTS BULLETIN.

Panel 4: MARSHALL -- THE DRUG-RUNNER? WE'VE BEEN LOOKING FOR THAT SNAKE FOR MONTHS, EVER SINCE...!

SPIDER-MAN, I DON'T KNOW WHETHER TO TAKE YOU IN -- OR TO TAKE YOU OUT TO DINNER!

IF YOU DON'T MIND, I'D JUST LIKE TO TAKE A POWDER!

HEY, WAIT! YOU REALLY LOOK SICK--!

Panel 5: BEFORE THE ASTONISHED PEACE OFFICERS CAN STOP HIM, SPIDER-MAN DIVES INTO DARKNESS, THEN...

HE'S GONE! WE HAD SPIDER-MAN DEAD-TO-RIGHTS, AND WE LET HIM GET AWAY!

DON'T WORRY! THE CHIEF'S GONNA GIVE US A MEDAL FOR HAULING IN MARSHALL!

I DON'T KNOW IF SPIDER-MAN SKRAGGED THAT DOPE-DEALER OR NOT--

Panel 6: --BUT IF SO, HE DID THIS CITY A SERVICE!

I HOPE THE WALL-CRAWLER MAKES IT HOME OKAY! FUNNY HOW HE VANISHED LIKE THAT...

8

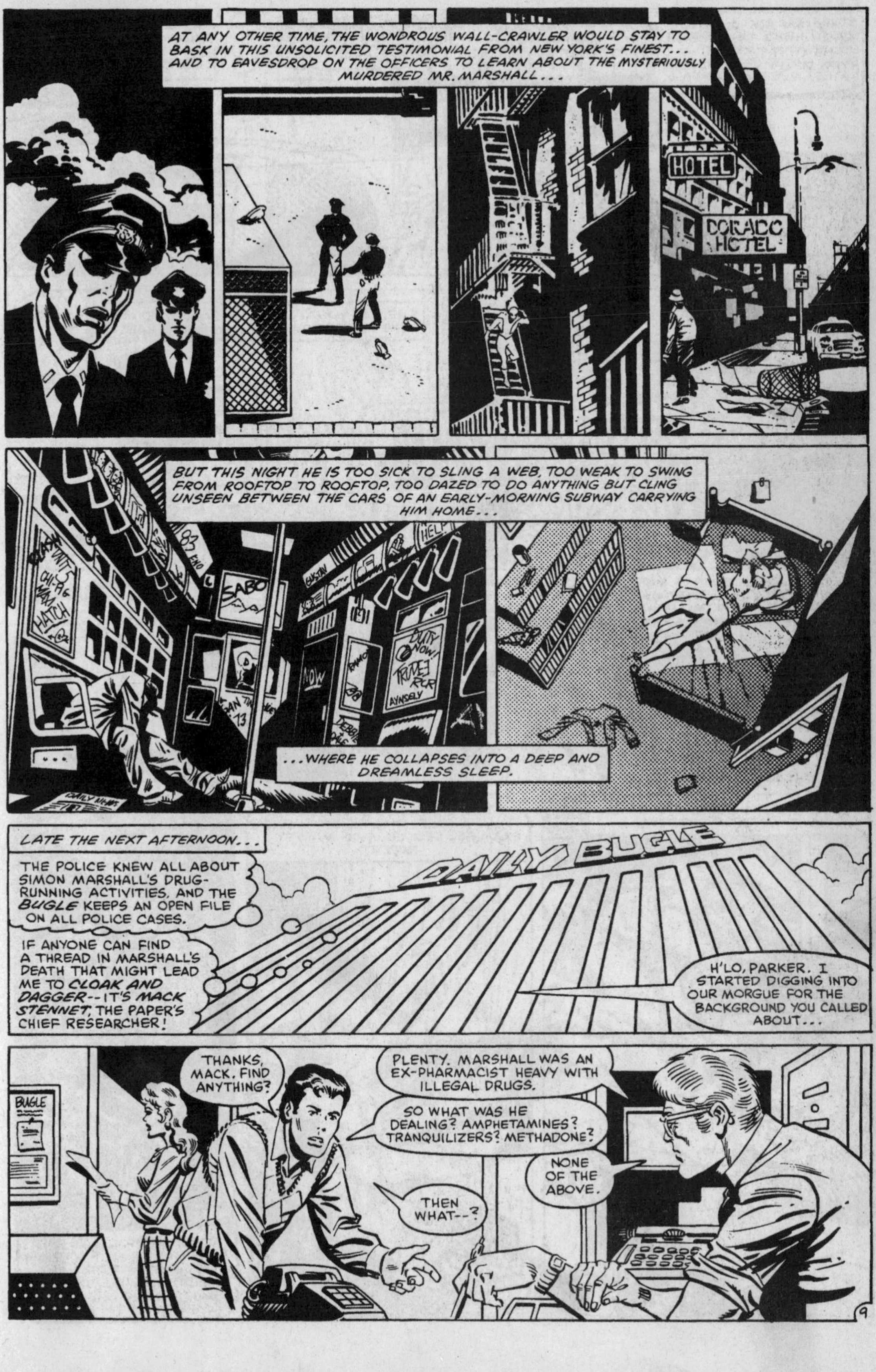
AT ANY OTHER TIME, THE WONDROUS WALL-CRAWLER WOULD STAY TO BASK IN THIS UNSOLICITED TESTIMONIAL FROM NEW YORK'S FINEST... AND TO EAVESDROP ON THE OFFICERS TO LEARN ABOUT THE MYSTERIOUSLY MURDERED MR. MARSHALL...
HOTEL
DORADO HOTEL
BUT THIS NIGHT HE IS TOO SICK TO SLING A WEB, TOO WEAK TO SWING FROM ROOFTOP TO ROOFTOP, TOO DAZED TO DO ANYTHING BUT CLING UNSEEN BETWEEN THE CARS OF AN EARLY-MORNING SUBWAY CARRYING HIM HOME...
...WHERE HE COLLAPSES INTO A DEEP AND DREAMLESS SLEEP.
LATE THE NEXT AFTERNOON...
THE POLICE KNEW ALL ABOUT SIMON MARSHALL'S DRUG-RUNNING ACTIVITIES, AND THE BUGLE KEEPS AN OPEN FILE ON ALL POLICE CASES.
IF ANYONE CAN FIND A THREAD IN MARSHALL'S DEATH THAT MIGHT LEAD ME TO CLOAK AND DAGGER--IT'S MACK STENNET, THE PAPER'S CHIEF RESEARCHER!
DAILY BUGLE
H'LO, PARKER. I STARTED DIGGING INTO OUR MORGUE FOR THE BACKGROUND YOU CALLED ABOUT...
THANKS, MACK. FIND ANYTHING?
PLENTY. MARSHALL WAS AN EX-PHARMACIST HEAVY WITH ILLEGAL DRUGS.
SO WHAT WAS HE DEALING? AMPHETAMINES? TRANQUILIZERS? METHADONE?
NONE OF THE ABOVE.
THEN WHAT--?
BUGLE

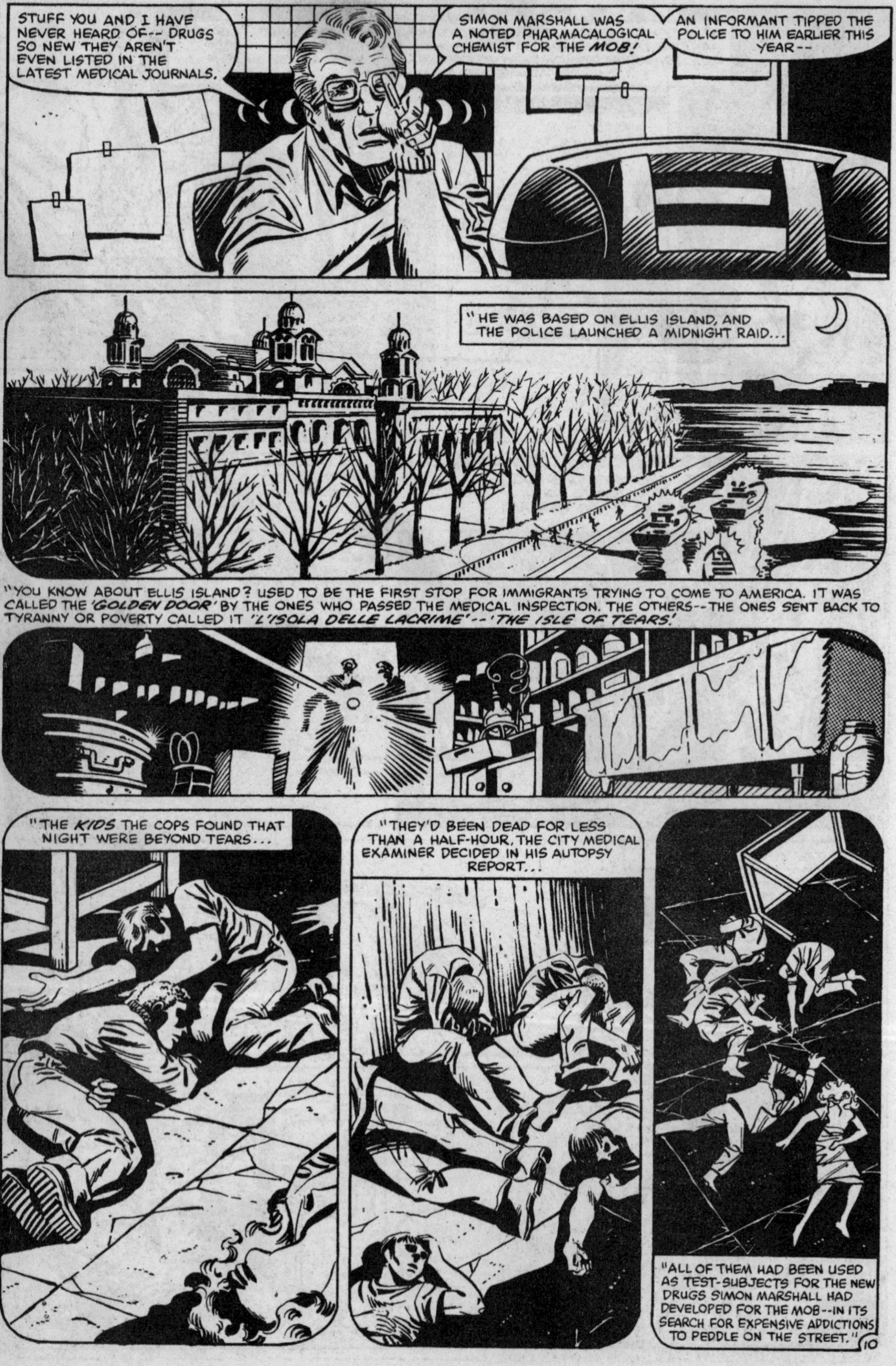
STUFF YOU AND I HAVE NEVER HEARD OF-- DRUGS SO NEW THEY AREN'T EVEN LISTED IN THE LATEST MEDICAL JOURNALS.
SIMON MARSHALL WAS A NOTED PHARMACALOGICAL CHEMIST FOR THE MOB!
AN INFORMANT TIPPED THE POLICE TO HIM EARLIER THIS YEAR--
"HE WAS BASED ON ELLIS ISLAND, AND THE POLICE LAUNCHED A MIDNIGHT RAID...
"YOU KNOW ABOUT ELLIS ISLAND? USED TO BE THE FIRST STOP FOR IMMIGRANTS TRYING TO COME TO AMERICA. IT WAS CALLED THE 'GOLDEN DOOR' BY THE ONES WHO PASSED THE MEDICAL INSPECTION. THE OTHERS--THE ONES SENT BACK TO TYRANNY OR POVERTY CALLED IT 'L'ISOLA DELLE LACRIME'--'THE ISLE OF TEARS.'
"THE KIDS THE COPS FOUND THAT NIGHT WERE BEYOND TEARS...
"THEY'D BEEN DEAD FOR LESS THAN A HALF-HOUR, THE CITY MEDICAL EXAMINER DECIDED IN HIS AUTOPSY REPORT...
"ALL OF THEM HAD BEEN USED AS TEST-SUBJECTS FOR THE NEW DRUGS SIMON MARSHALL HAD DEVELOPED FOR THE MOB--IN ITS SEARCH FOR EXPENSIVE ADDICTIONS TO PEDDLE ON THE STREET."
10

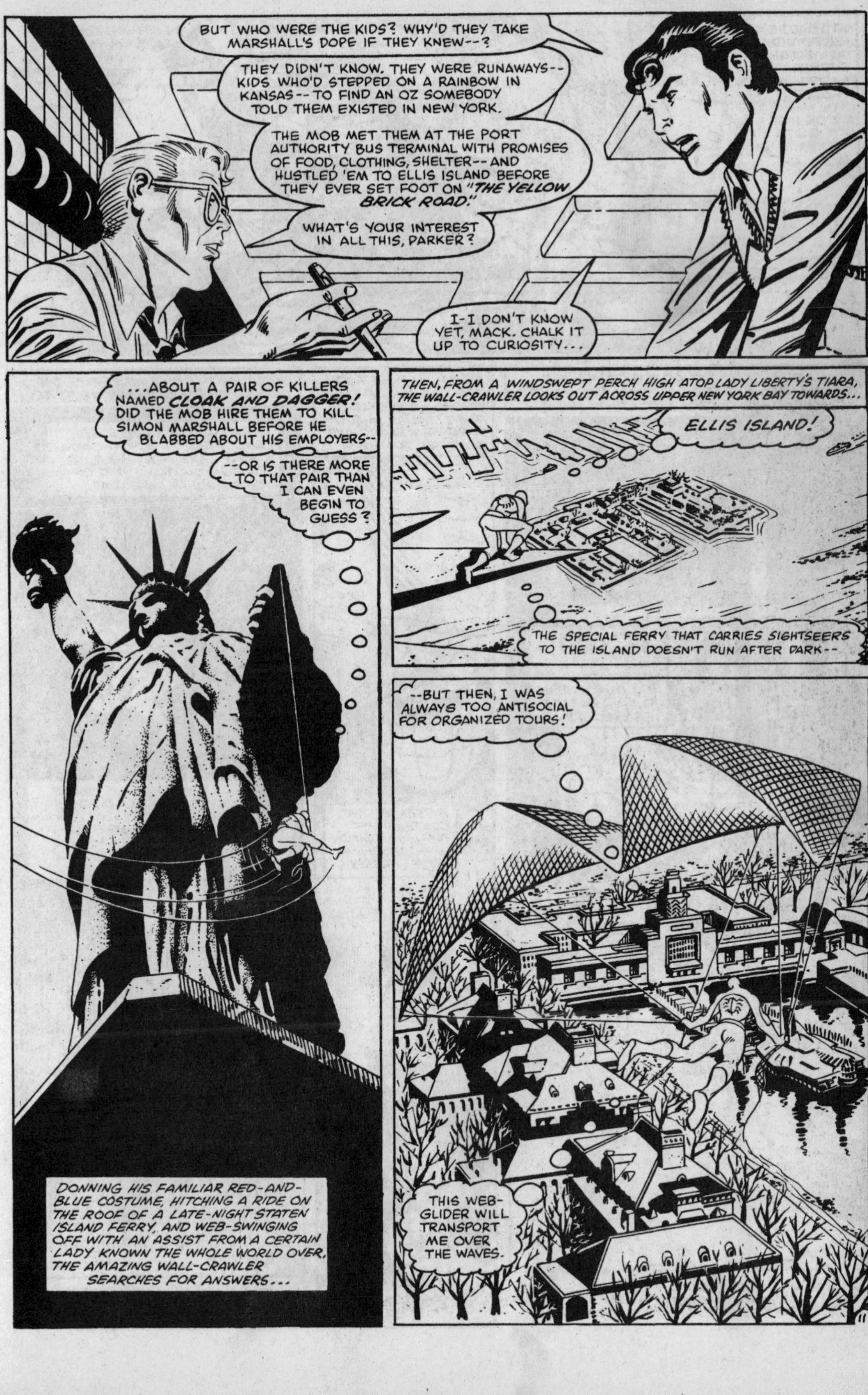

BUT WHO WERE THE KIDS? WHY'D THEY TAKE MARSHALL'S DOPE IF THEY KNEW--?
THEY DIDN'T KNOW. THEY WERE RUNAWAYS--KIDS WHO'D STEPPED ON A RAINBOW IN KANSAS--TO FIND AN OZ SOMEBODY TOLD THEM EXISTED IN NEW YORK.
THE MOB MET THEM AT THE PORT AUTHORITY BUS TERMINAL WITH PROMISES OF FOOD, CLOTHING, SHELTER--AND HUSTLED 'EM TO ELLIS ISLAND BEFORE THEY EVER SET FOOT ON "THE YELLOW BRICK ROAD."
WHAT'S YOUR INTEREST IN ALL THIS, PARKER?
I-I DON'T KNOW YET, MACK. CHALK IT UP TO CURIOSITY...
...ABOUT A PAIR OF KILLERS NAMED CLOAK AND DAGGER! DID THE MOB HIRE THEM TO KILL SIMON MARSHALL BEFORE HE BLABBED ABOUT HIS EMPLOYERS--
--OR IS THERE MORE TO THAT PAIR THAN I CAN EVEN BEGIN TO GUESS?
DONNING HIS FAMILIAR RED-AND-BLUE COSTUME, HITCHING A RIDE ON THE ROOF OF A LATE-NIGHT STATEN ISLAND FERRY, AND WEB-SWINGING OFF WITH AN ASSIST FROM A CERTAIN LADY KNOWN THE WHOLE WORLD OVER, THE AMAZING WALL-CRAWLER SEARCHES FOR ANSWERS...
THEN, FROM A WINDSWEPT PERCH HIGH ATOP LADY LIBERTY'S TIARA, THE WALL-CRAWLER LOOKS OUT ACROSS UPPER NEW YORK BAY TOWARDS...
ELLIS ISLAND!
THE SPECIAL FERRY THAT CARRIES SIGHTSEERS TO THE ISLAND DOESN'T RUN AFTER DARK--
--BUT THEN, I WAS ALWAYS TOO ANTISOCIAL FOR ORGANIZED TOURS!
THIS WEB-GLIDER WILL TRANSPORT ME OVER THE WAVES.
11

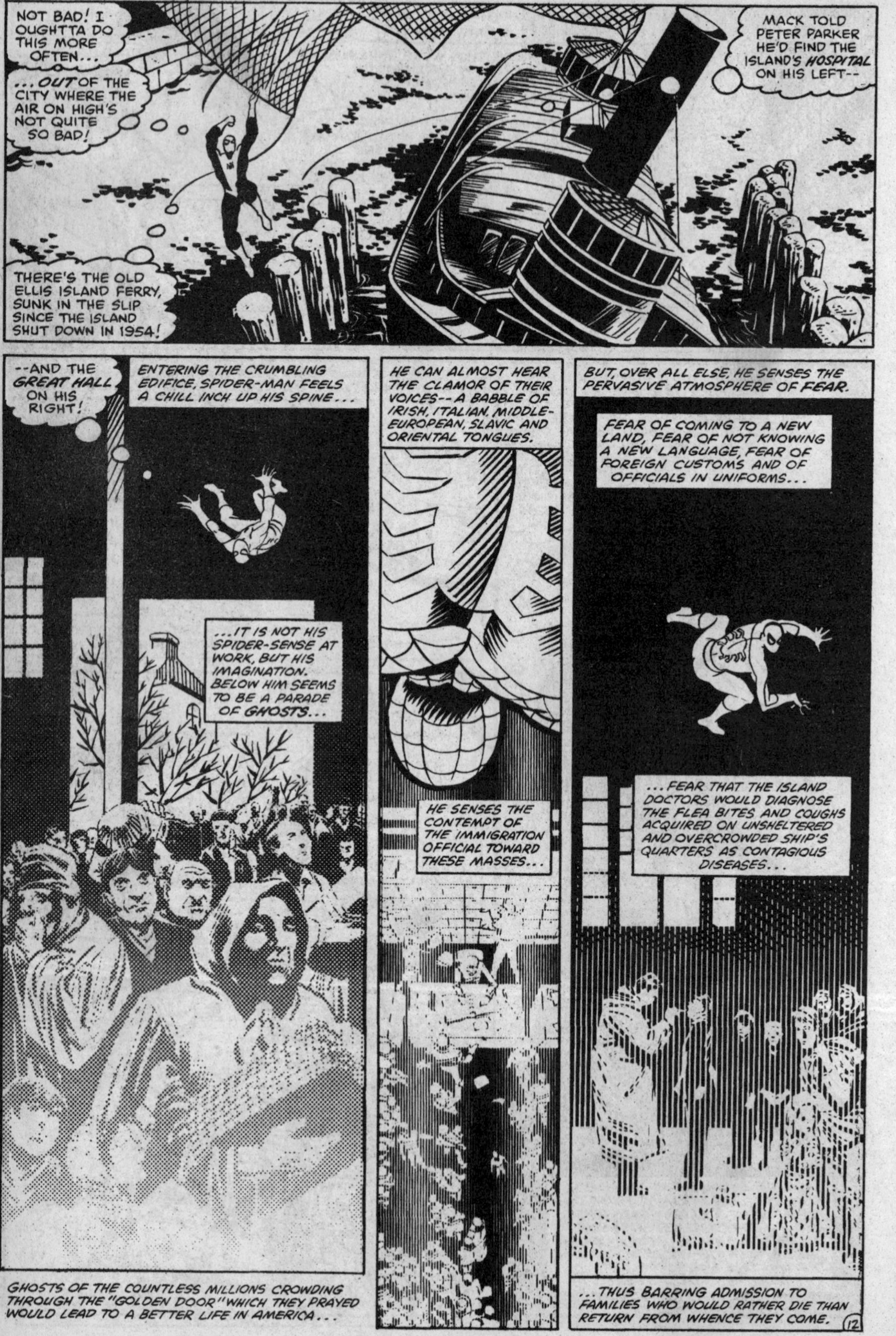
NOT BAD! I OUGHTTA DO THIS MORE OFTEN...
...OUT OF THE CITY WHERE THE AIR ON HIGH'S NOT QUITE SO BAD!
THERE'S THE OLD ELLIS ISLAND FERRY, SUNK IN THE SLIP SINCE THE ISLAND SHUT DOWN IN 1954!
MACK TOLD PETER PARKER HE'D FIND THE ISLAND'S HOSPITAL ON HIS LEFT--
--AND THE GREAT HALL ON HIS RIGHT!
ENTERING THE CRUMBLING EDIFICE, SPIDER-MAN FEELS A CHILL INCH UP HIS SPINE...
...IT IS NOT HIS SPIDER-SENSE AT WORK, BUT HIS IMAGINATION. BELOW HIM SEEMS TO BE A PARADE OF GHOSTS...
GHOSTS OF THE COUNTLESS MILLIONS CROWDING THROUGH THE "GOLDEN DOOR" WHICH THEY PRAYED WOULD LEAD TO A BETTER LIFE IN AMERICA...
HE CAN ALMOST HEAR THE CLAMOR OF THEIR VOICES-- A BABBLE OF IRISH, ITALIAN, MIDDLE-EUROPEAN, SLAVIC AND ORIENTAL TONGUES.
HE SENSES THE CONTEMPT OF THE IMMIGRATION OFFICIAL TOWARD THESE MASSES...
BUT, OVER ALL ELSE, HE SENSES THE PERVASIVE ATMOSPHERE OF FEAR.
FEAR OF COMING TO A NEW LAND, FEAR OF NOT KNOWING A NEW LANGUAGE, FEAR OF FOREIGN CUSTOMS AND OF OFFICIALS IN UNIFORMS...
...FEAR THAT THE ISLAND DOCTORS WOULD DIAGNOSE THE FLEA BITES AND COUGHS ACQUIRED ON UNSHELTERED AND OVERCROWDED SHIP'S QUARTERS AS CONTAGIOUS DISEASES...
...THUS BARRING ADMISSION TO FAMILIES WHO WOULD RATHER DIE THAN RETURN FROM WHENCE THEY COME.
12

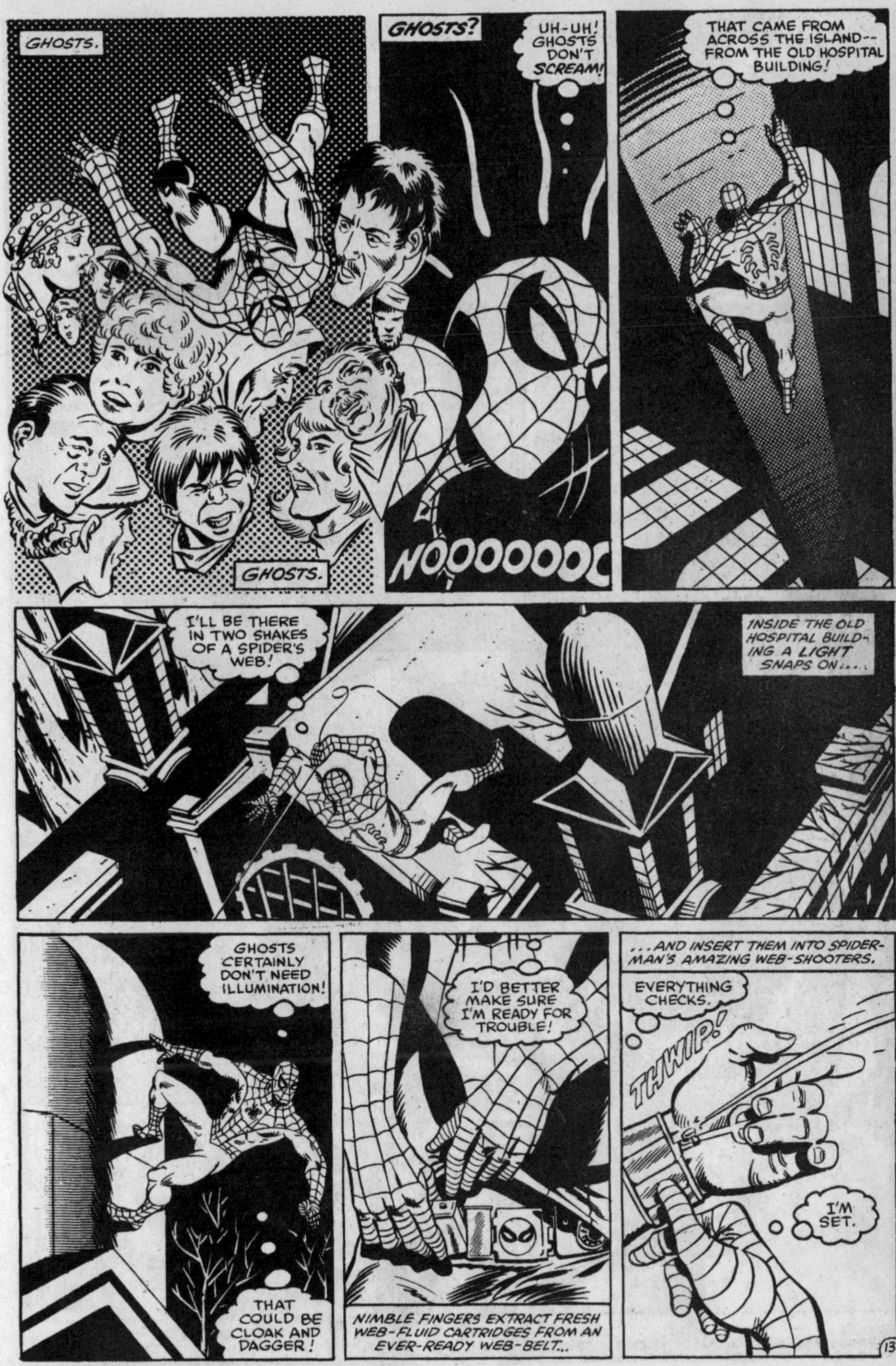
GHOSTS.
GHOSTS.
GHOSTS?
UH-UH! GHOSTS DON'T SCREAM!
NOOOOOOO
THAT CAME FROM ACROSS THE ISLAND-- FROM THE OLD HOSPITAL BUILDING!
I'LL BE THERE IN TWO SHAKES OF A SPIDER'S WEB!
INSIDE THE OLD HOSPITAL BUILDING A LIGHT SNAPS ON...
GHOSTS CERTAINLY DON'T NEED ILLUMINATION!
THAT COULD BE CLOAK AND DAGGER!
I'D BETTER MAKE SURE I'M READY FOR TROUBLE!
NIMBLE FINGERS EXTRACT FRESH WEB-FLUID CARTRIDGES FROM AN EVER-READY WEB-BELT...
...AND INSERT THEM INTO SPIDER-MAN'S AMAZING WEB-SHOOTERS.
EVERYTHING CHECKS.
THWIP!
I'M SET.

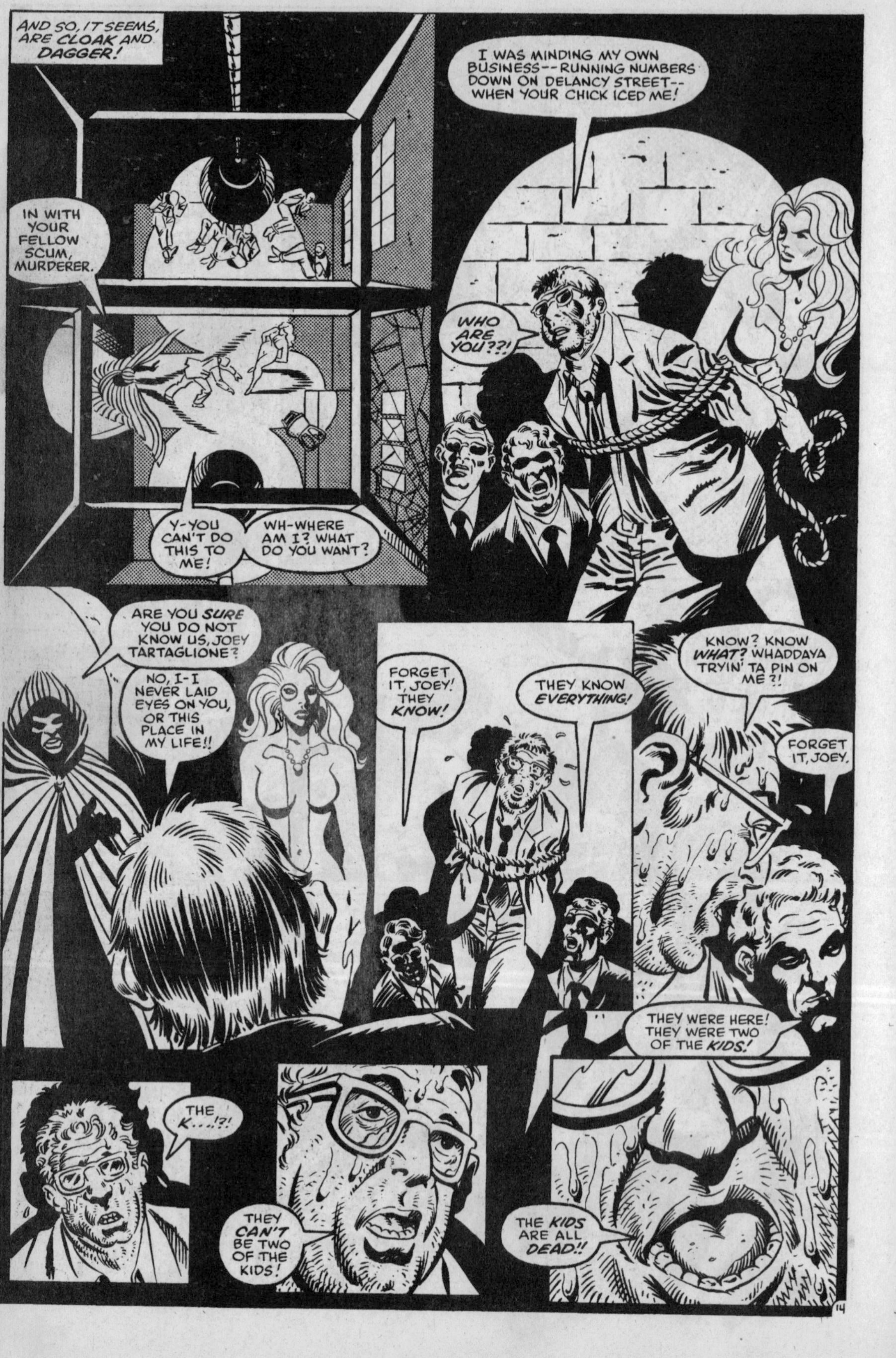
AND SO, IT SEEMS, ARE CLOAK AND DAGGER!
IN WITH YOUR FELLOW SCUM, MURDERER.
Y-YOU CAN'T DO THIS TO ME!
WH-WHERE AM I? WHAT DO YOU WANT?
I WAS MINDING MY OWN BUSINESS--RUNNING NUMBERS DOWN ON DELANCY STREET--WHEN YOUR CHICK ICED ME!
WHO ARE YOU??!
ARE YOU SURE YOU DO NOT KNOW US, JOEY TARTAGLIONE?
NO, I-I NEVER LAID EYES ON YOU, OR THIS PLACE IN MY LIFE!!
FORGET IT, JOEY! THEY KNOW!
THEY KNOW EVERYTHING!
KNOW? KNOW WHAT? WHADDAYA TRYIN' TA PIN ON ME?!
FORGET IT, JOEY.
THEY WERE HERE! THEY WERE TWO OF THE KIDS!
THE K...!?!
THEY CAN'T BE TWO OF THE KIDS!
THE KIDS ARE ALL DEAD!!

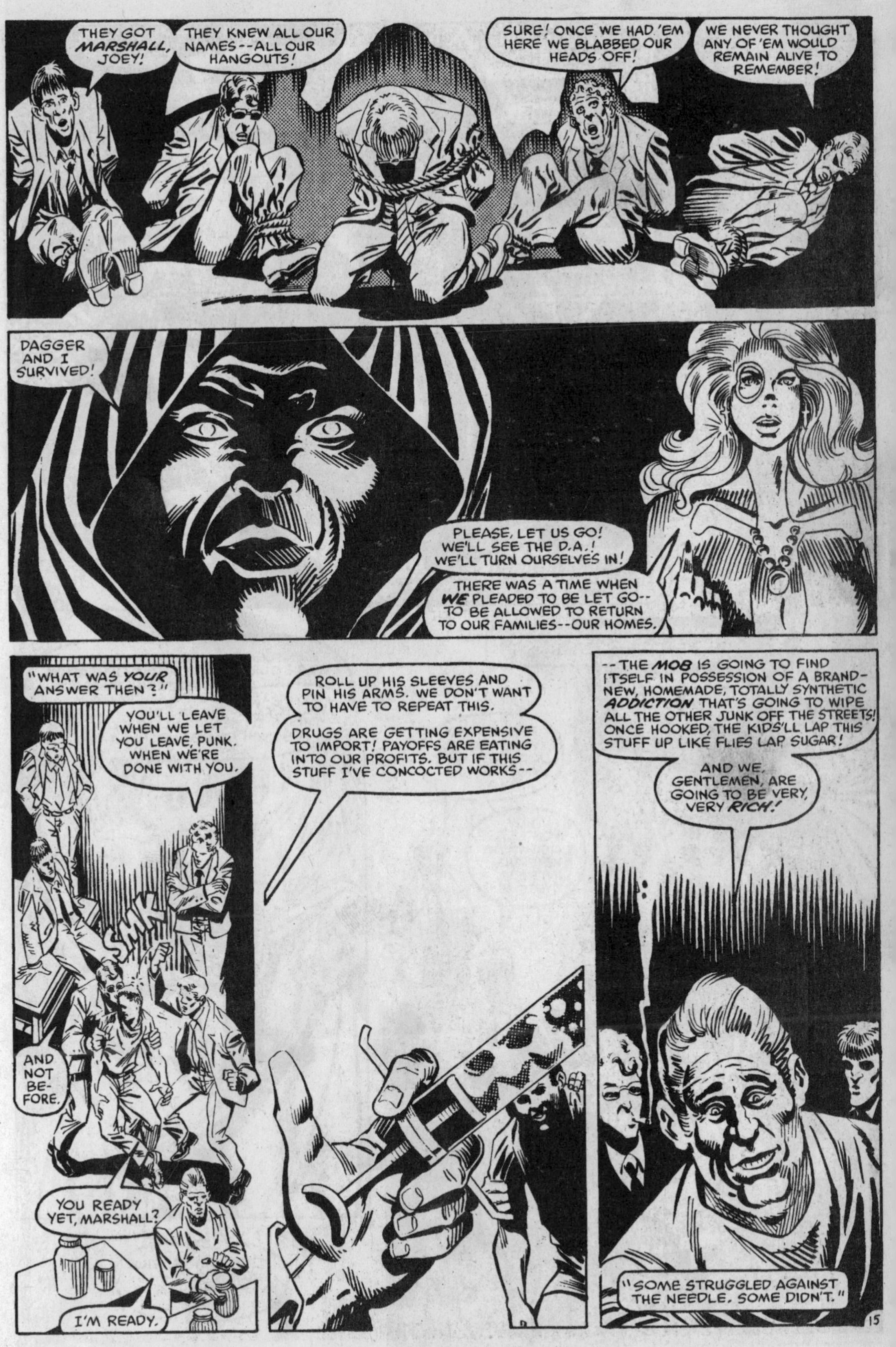
THEY GOT MARSHALL, JOEY!
THEY KNEW ALL OUR NAMES--ALL OUR HANGOUTS!
SURE! ONCE WE HAD 'EM HERE WE BLABBED OUR HEADS OFF!
WE NEVER THOUGHT ANY OF 'EM WOULD REMAIN ALIVE TO REMEMBER!
DAGGER AND I SURVIVED!
PLEASE, LET US GO! WE'LL SEE THE D.A.! WE'LL TURN OURSELVES IN!
THERE WAS A TIME WHEN WE PLEADED TO BE LET GO--TO BE ALLOWED TO RETURN TO OUR FAMILIES--OUR HOMES.
"WHAT WAS YOUR ANSWER THEN?"
YOU'LL LEAVE WHEN WE LET YOU LEAVE, PUNK. WHEN WE'RE DONE WITH YOU.
SMK
AND NOT BEFORE.
YOU READY YET, MARSHALL?
I'M READY.
ROLL UP HIS SLEEVES AND PIN HIS ARMS. WE DON'T WANT TO HAVE TO REPEAT THIS.
DRUGS ARE GETTING EXPENSIVE TO IMPORT! PAYOFFS ARE EATING INTO OUR PROFITS. BUT IF THIS STUFF I'VE CONCOCTED WORKS--
--THE MOB IS GOING TO FIND ITSELF IN POSSESSION OF A BRAND-NEW, HOMEMADE, TOTALLY SYNTHETIC ADDICTION THAT'S GOING TO WIPE ALL THE OTHER JUNK OFF THE STREETS! ONCE HOOKED, THE KIDS'LL LAP THIS STUFF UP LIKE FLIES LAP SUGAR!
AND WE, GENTLEMEN, ARE GOING TO BE VERY, VERY RICH!
"SOME STRUGGLED AGAINST THE NEEDLE. SOME DIDN'T."

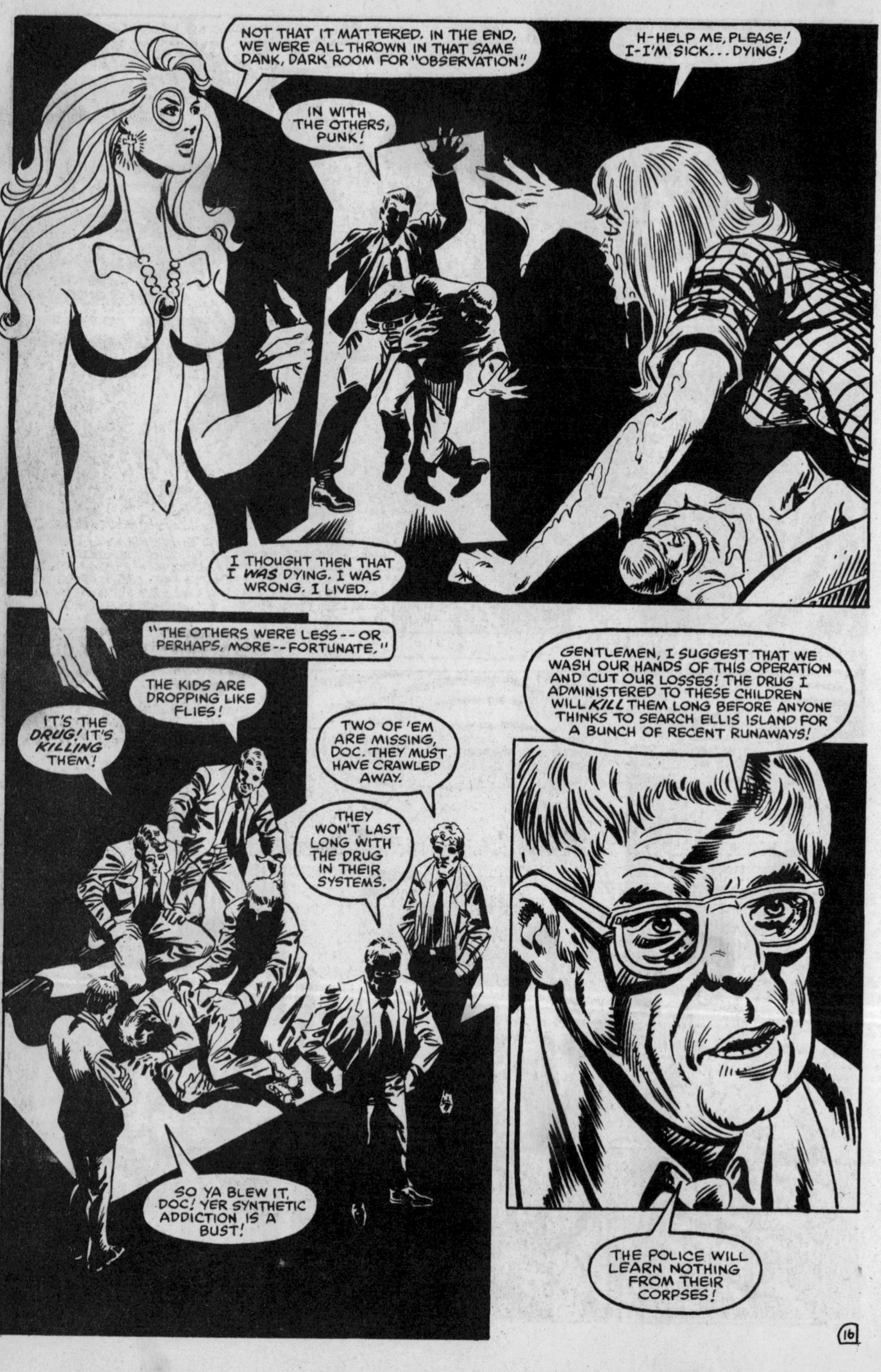

NOT THAT IT MATTERED. IN THE END, WE WERE ALL THROWN IN THAT SAME DANK, DARK ROOM FOR "OBSERVATION."
IN WITH THE OTHERS, PUNK!
H-HELP ME, PLEASE! I-I'M SICK... DYING!
I THOUGHT THEN THAT I WAS DYING. I WAS WRONG. I LIVED.
"THE OTHERS WERE LESS--OR PERHAPS, MORE--FORTUNATE."
THE KIDS ARE DROPPING LIKE FLIES!
IT'S THE DRUG! IT'S KILLING THEM!
TWO OF 'EM ARE MISSING, DOC. THEY MUST HAVE CRAWLED AWAY.
THEY WON'T LAST LONG WITH THE DRUG IN THEIR SYSTEMS.
SO YA BLEW IT, DOC! YER SYNTHETIC ADDICTION IS A BUST!
GENTLEMEN, I SUGGEST THAT WE WASH OUR HANDS OF THIS OPERATION AND CUT OUR LOSSES! THE DRUG I ADMINISTERED TO THESE CHILDREN WILL KILL THEM LONG BEFORE ANYONE THINKS TO SEARCH ELLIS ISLAND FOR A BUNCH OF RECENT RUNAWAYS!
THE POLICE WILL LEARN NOTHING FROM THEIR CORPSES!

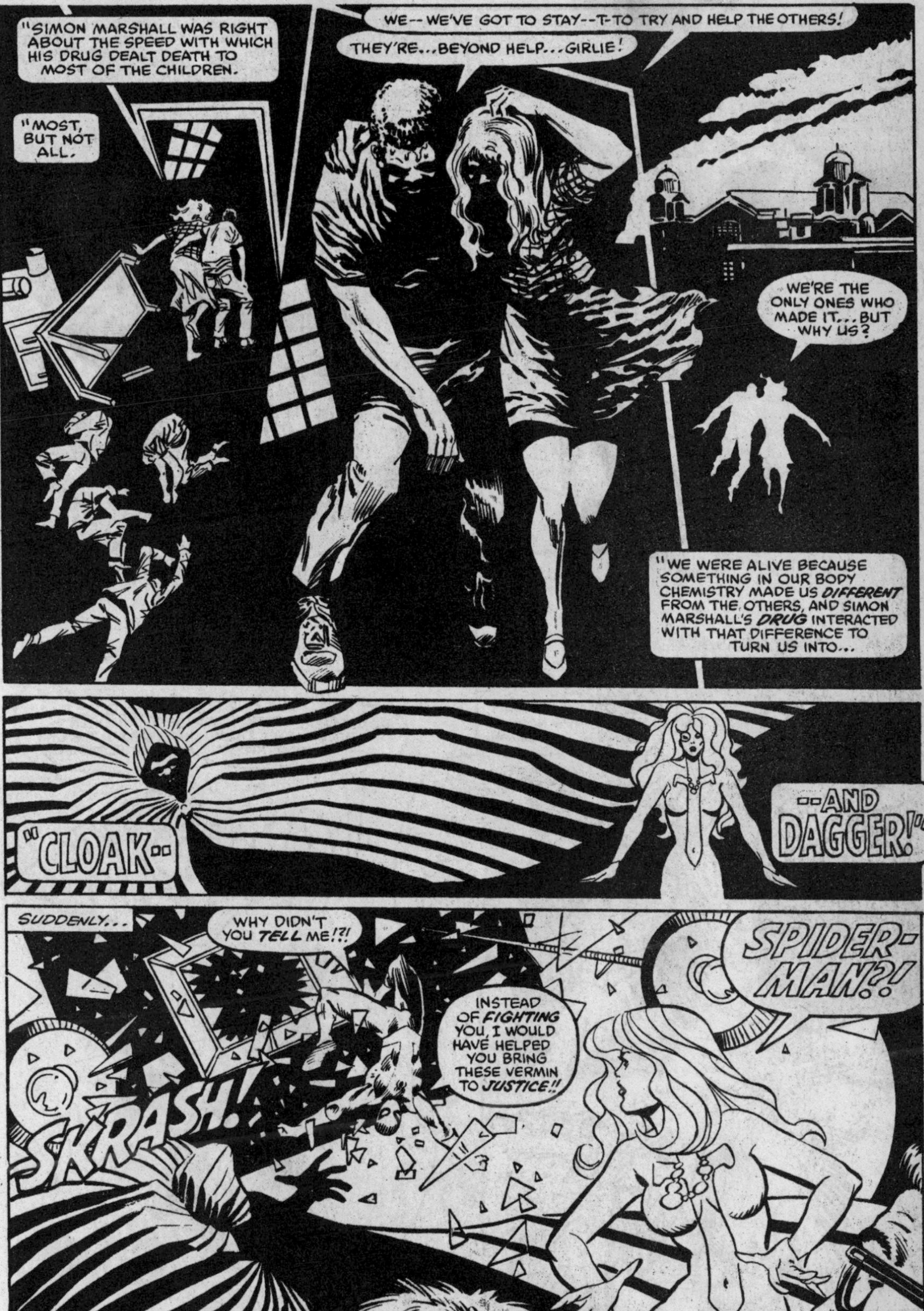
"SIMON MARSHALL WAS RIGHT ABOUT THE SPEED WITH WHICH HIS DRUG DEALT DEATH TO MOST OF THE CHILDREN.
"MOST, BUT NOT ALL.
WE-- WE'VE GOT TO STAY--T-TO TRY AND HELP THE OTHERS!
THEY'RE... BEYOND HELP... GIRLIE!
WE'RE THE ONLY ONES WHO MADE IT... BUT WHY US?
"WE WERE ALIVE BECAUSE SOMETHING IN OUR BODY CHEMISTRY MADE US DIFFERENT FROM THE OTHERS, AND SIMON MARSHALL'S DRUG INTERACTED WITH THAT DIFFERENCE TO TURN US INTO...
"CLOAK--
--AND DAGGER!"
SUDDENLY...
WHY DIDN'T YOU TELL ME!?!
SPIDER-MAN?!
INSTEAD OF FIGHTING YOU, I WOULD HAVE HELPED YOU BRING THESE VERMIN TO JUSTICE!!
SKRASH!

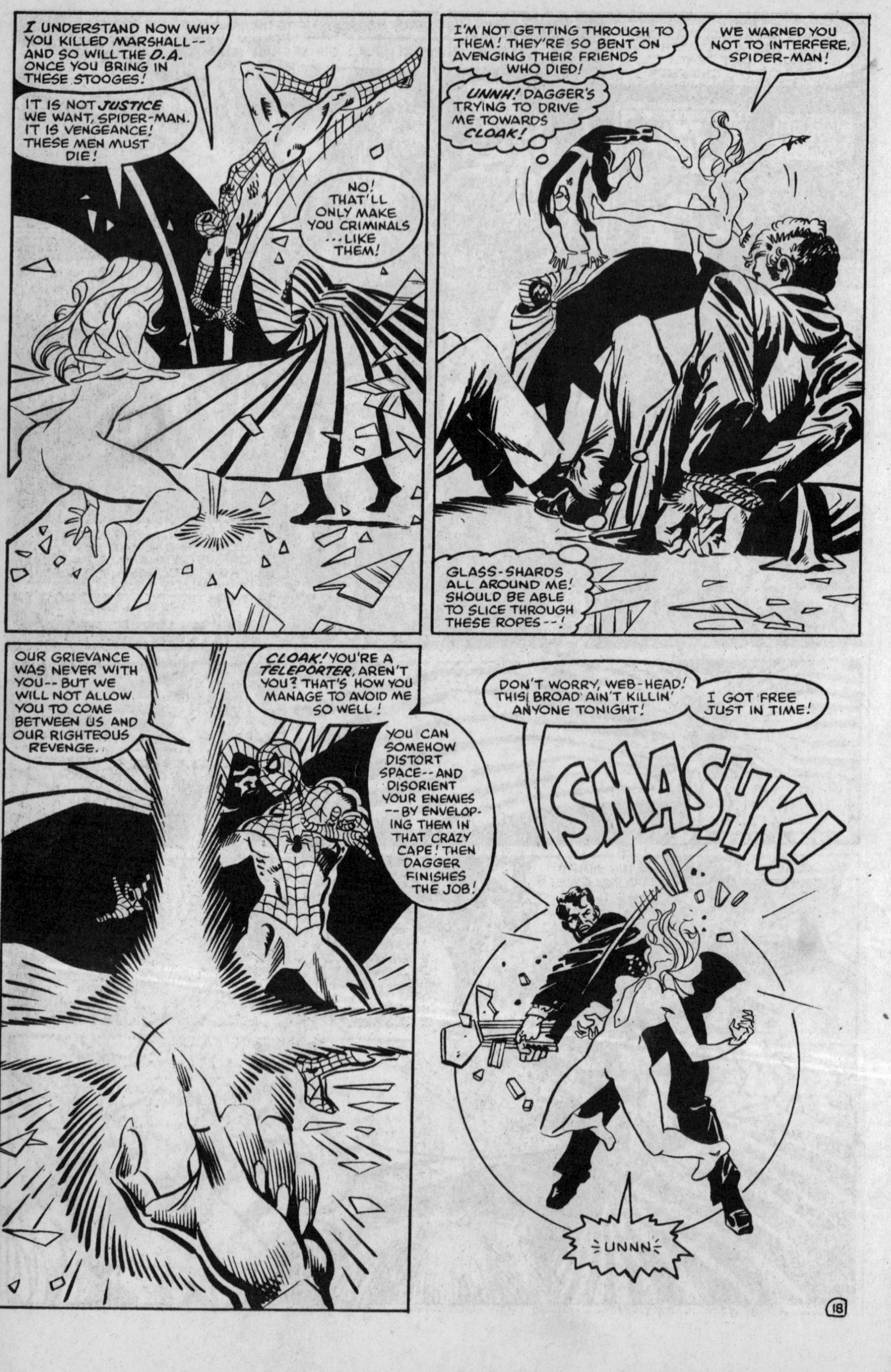

I UNDERSTAND NOW WHY YOU KILLED MARSHALL-- AND SO WILL THE D.A. ONCE YOU BRING IN THESE STOOGES!
IT IS NOT JUSTICE WE WANT, SPIDER-MAN. IT IS VENGEANCE! THESE MEN MUST DIE!
NO! THAT'LL ONLY MAKE YOU CRIMINALS ...LIKE THEM!
I'M NOT GETTING THROUGH TO THEM! THEY'RE SO BENT ON AVENGING THEIR FRIENDS WHO DIED!
WE WARNED YOU NOT TO INTERFERE, SPIDER-MAN!
UNNH! DAGGER'S TRYING TO DRIVE ME TOWARDS CLOAK!
GLASS-SHARDS ALL AROUND ME! SHOULD BE ABLE TO SLICE THROUGH THESE ROPES--!
OUR GRIEVANCE WAS NEVER WITH YOU-- BUT WE WILL NOT ALLOW YOU TO COME BETWEEN US AND OUR RIGHTEOUS REVENGE.
CLOAK! YOU'RE A TELEPORTER, AREN'T YOU? THAT'S HOW YOU MANAGE TO AVOID ME SO WELL!
YOU CAN SOMEHOW DISTORT SPACE--AND DISORIENT YOUR ENEMIES --BY ENVELOPING THEM IN THAT CRAZY CAPE! THEN DAGGER FINISHES THE JOB!
DON'T WORRY, WEB-HEAD! THIS BROAD AIN'T KILLIN' ANYONE TONIGHT!
I GOT FREE JUST IN TIME!
SMASHK!
UNNN

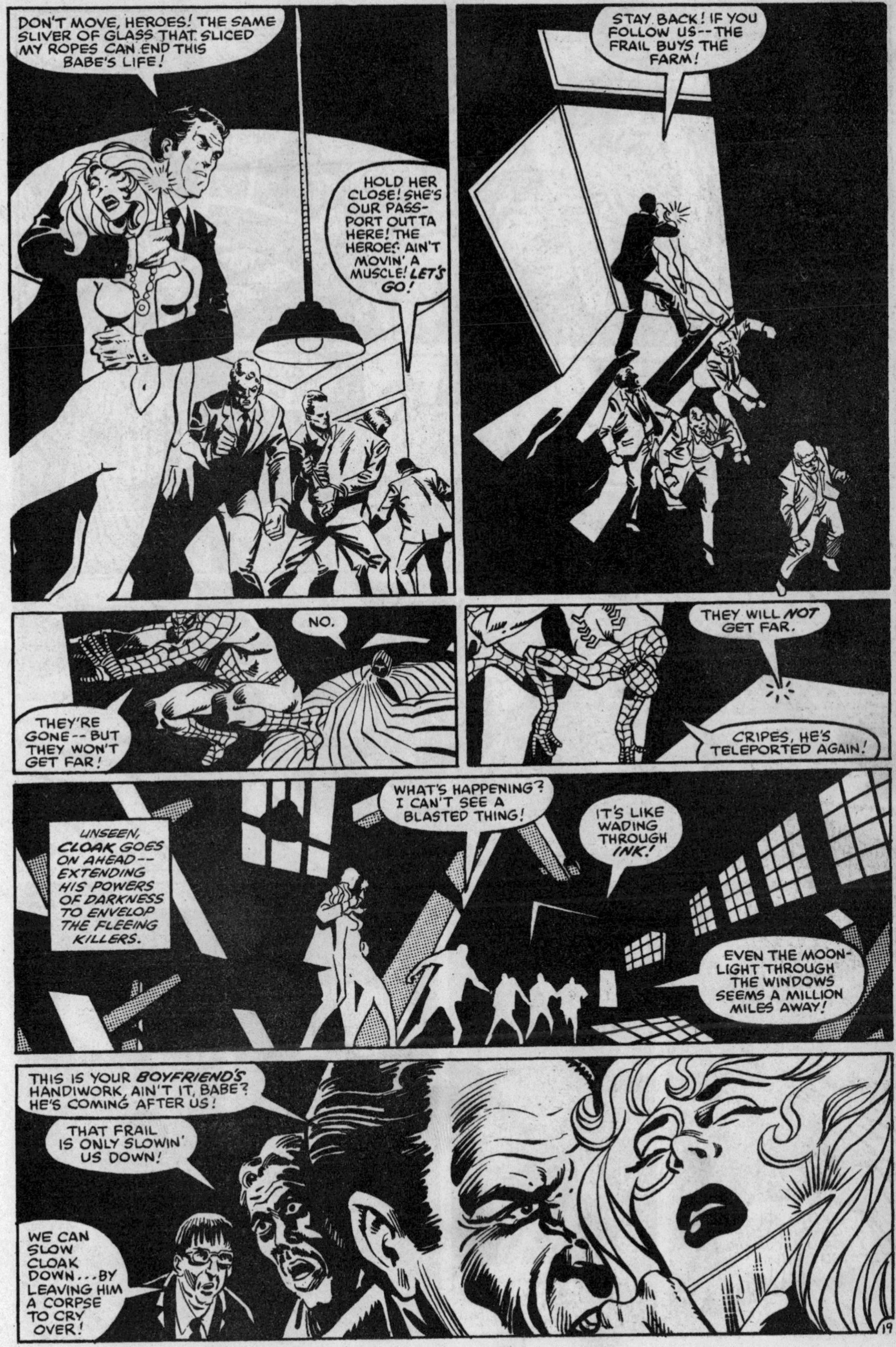
DON'T MOVE, HEROES! THE SAME SLIVER OF GLASS THAT SLICED MY ROPES CAN END THIS BABE'S LIFE!
HOLD HER CLOSE! SHE'S OUR PASSPORT OUTTA HERE! THE HEROES AIN'T MOVIN' A MUSCLE! LET'S GO!
STAY BACK! IF YOU FOLLOW US--THE FRAIL BUYS THE FARM!
NO.
THEY'RE GONE-- BUT THEY WON'T GET FAR!
THEY WILL NOT GET FAR.
CRIPES, HE'S TELEPORTED AGAIN!
UNSEEN, CLOAK GOES ON AHEAD-- EXTENDING HIS POWERS OF DARKNESS TO ENVELOP THE FLEEING KILLERS.
WHAT'S HAPPENING? I CAN'T SEE A BLASTED THING!
IT'S LIKE WADING THROUGH INK!
EVEN THE MOONLIGHT THROUGH THE WINDOWS SEEMS A MILLION MILES AWAY!
THIS IS YOUR BOYFRIEND'S HANDIWORK, AIN'T IT, BABE? HE'S COMING AFTER US!
THAT FRAIL IS ONLY SLOWIN' US DOWN!
WE CAN SLOW CLOAK DOWN... BY LEAVING HIM A CORPSE TO CRY OVER!
19

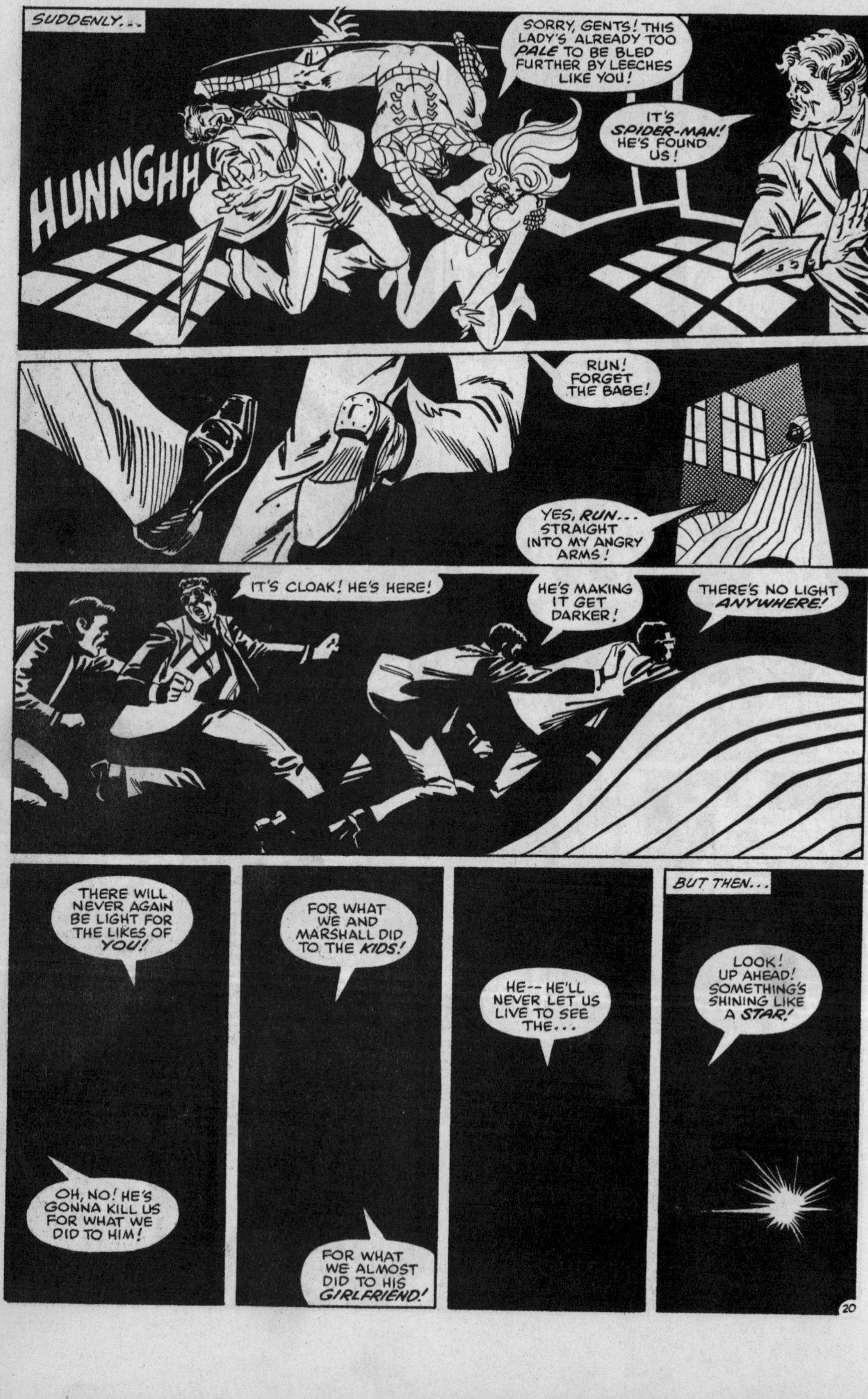
SUDDENLY...
SORRY, GENTS! THIS LADY'S ALREADY TOO PALE TO BE BLED FURTHER BY LEECHES LIKE YOU!
HUNNGHH
IT'S SPIDER-MAN! HE'S FOUND US!
RUN! FORGET THE BABE!
YES, RUN... STRAIGHT INTO MY ANGRY ARMS!
IT'S CLOAK! HE'S HERE!
HE'S MAKING IT GET DARKER!
THERE'S NO LIGHT ANYWHERE!
THERE WILL NEVER AGAIN BE LIGHT FOR THE LIKES OF YOU!
OH, NO! HE'S GONNA KILL US FOR WHAT WE DID TO HIM!
FOR WHAT WE AND MARSHALL DID TO THE KIDS!
FOR WHAT WE ALMOST DID TO HIS GIRLFRIEND!
HE-- HE'LL NEVER LET US LIVE TO SEE THE...
BUT THEN...
LOOK! UP AHEAD! SOMETHING'S SHINING LIKE A STAR!

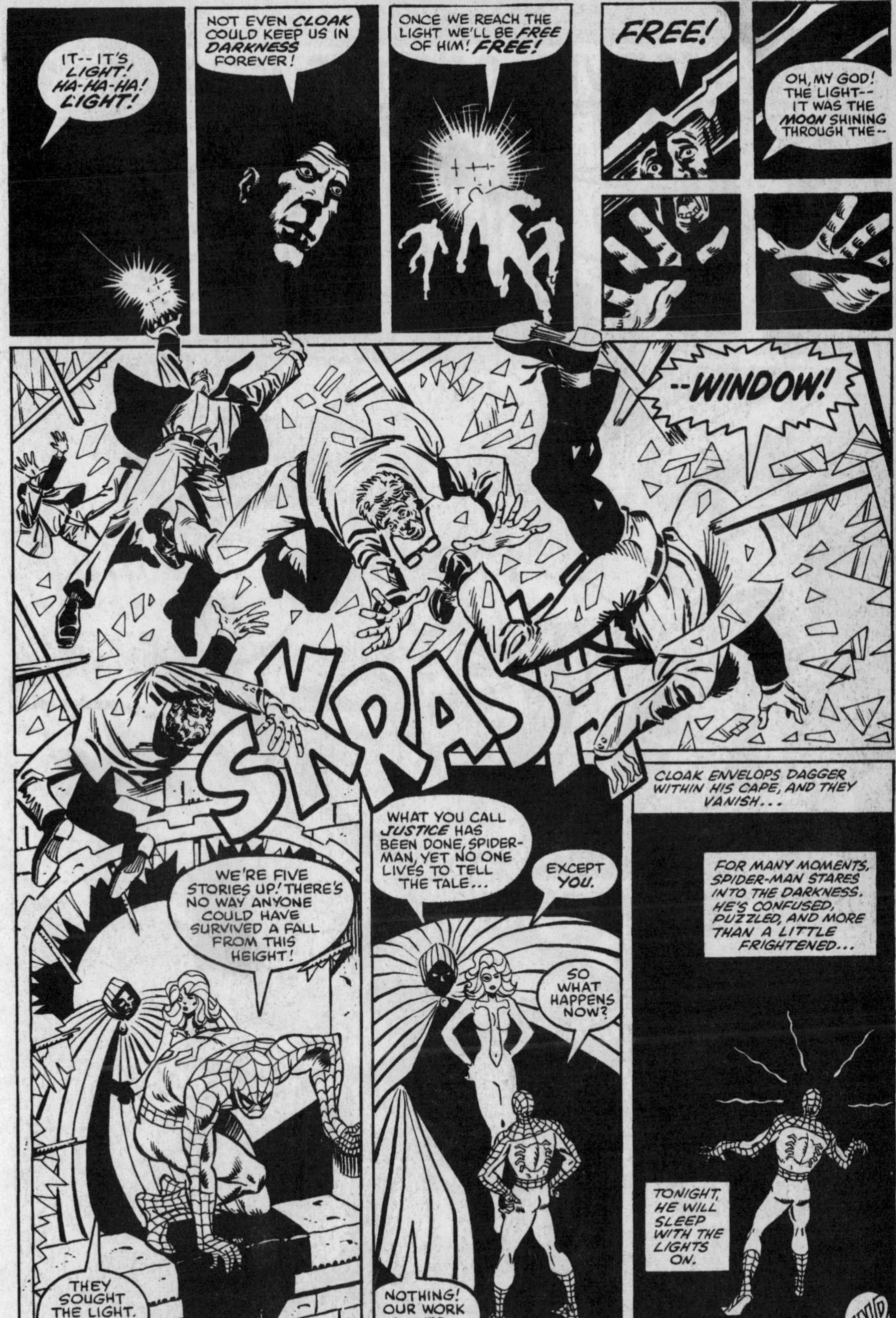
IT-- IT'S LIGHT! HA-HA-HA! LIGHT!
NOT EVEN CLOAK COULD KEEP US IN DARKNESS FOREVER!
ONCE WE REACH THE LIGHT WE'LL BE FREE OF HIM! FREE!
FREE!
OH, MY GOD! THE LIGHT-- IT WAS THE MOON SHINING THROUGH THE--
--WINDOW!
SMASH
WE'RE FIVE STORIES UP! THERE'S NO WAY ANYONE COULD HAVE SURVIVED A FALL FROM THIS HEIGHT!
THEY SOUGHT THE LIGHT. I LET THEM FIND IT.
WHAT YOU CALL JUSTICE HAS BEEN DONE, SPIDER-MAN, YET NO ONE LIVES TO TELL THE TALE...
EXCEPT YOU.
SO WHAT HAPPENS NOW?
NOTHING! OUR WORK IS OVER... FOR NOW!
CLOAK ENVELOPS DAGGER WITHIN HIS CAPE, AND THEY VANISH...
FOR MANY MOMENTS, SPIDER-MAN STARES INTO THE DARKNESS. HE'S CONFUSED, PUZZLED, AND MORE THAN A LITTLE FRIGHTENED...
TONIGHT, HE WILL SLEEP WITH THE LIGHTS ON.
END

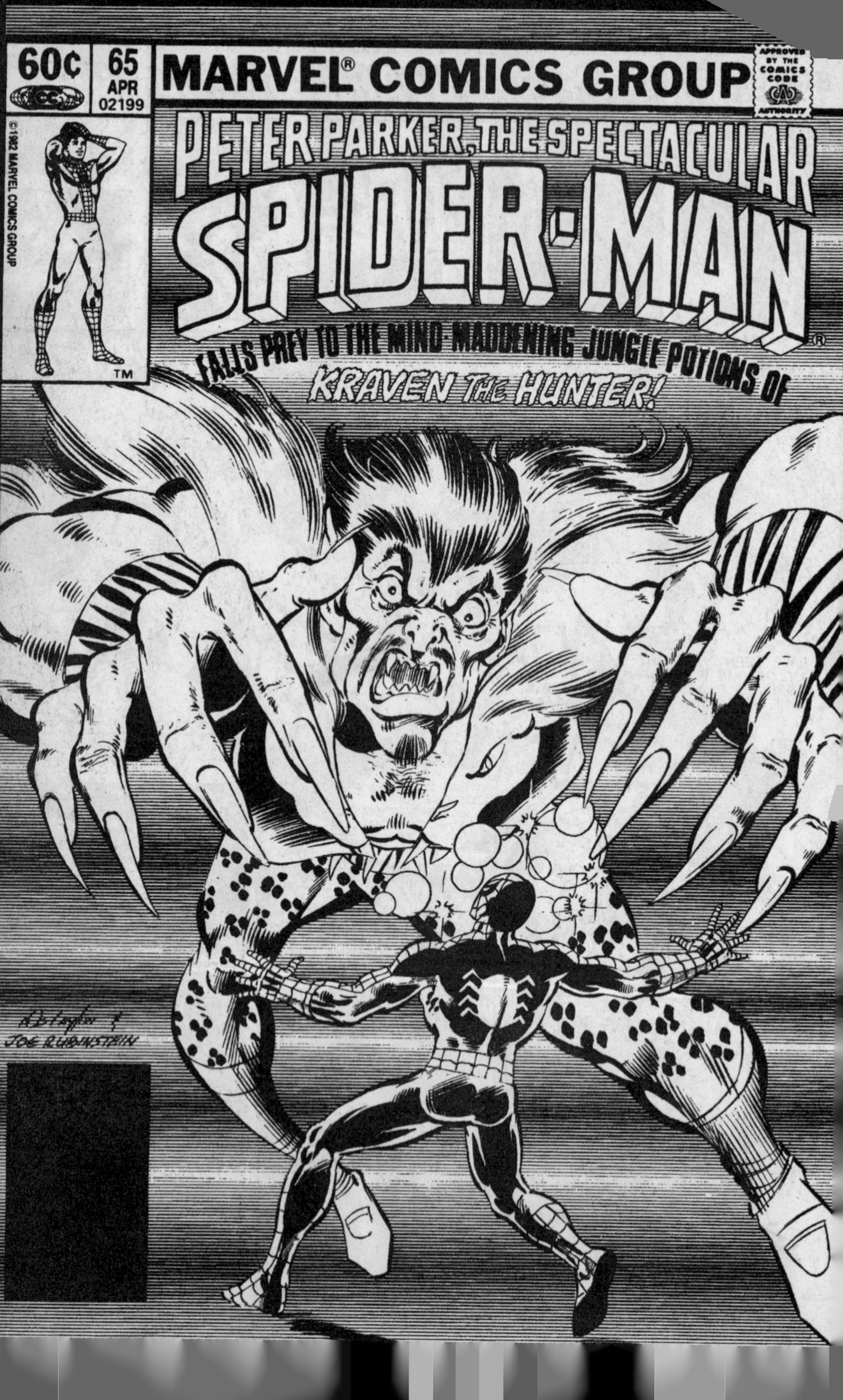
60¢
65
APR
02199
MARVEL® COMICS GROUP
APPROVED BY THE COMICS CODE AUTHORITY
©1982 MARVEL COMICS GROUP
PETER PARKER, THE SPECTACULAR
SPIDER-MAN®
TM
FALLS PREY TO THE MIND-MADDENING JUNGLE POTIONS OF
KRAVEN THE HUNTER!
JOE RUBINSTEIN

While attending a demonstration in radiology, student PETER PARKER was bitten by a spider which had accidentally been exposed to RADIOACTIVE RAYS. Through a miracle of science, Peter gained the arachnid's powers... and in effect, became a human spider...

Stan Lee Presents: THE SPECTACULAR SPIDER-MAN!®

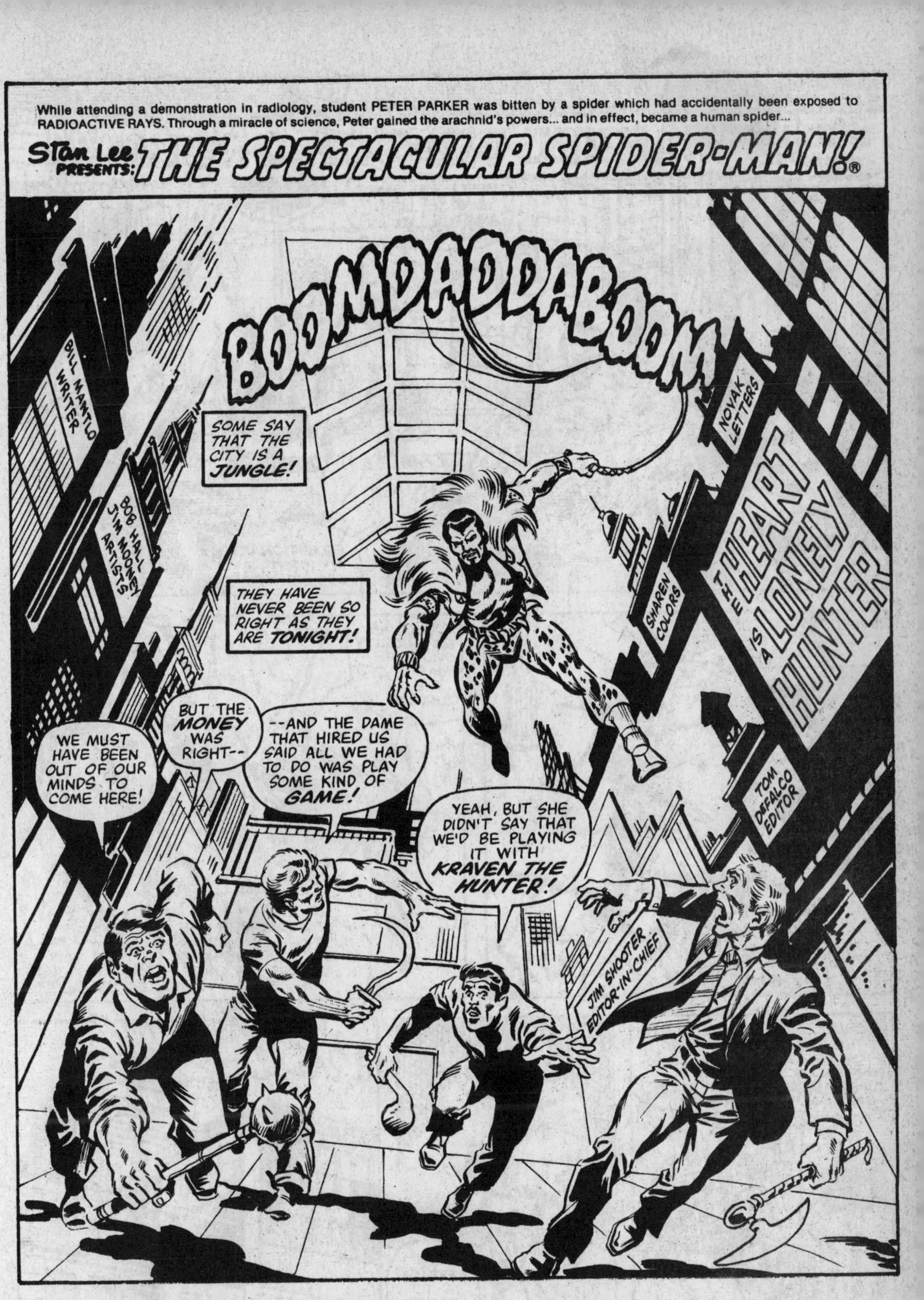

BOOMDADDABOOM
SOME SAY THAT THE CITY IS A JUNGLE!
THEY HAVE NEVER BEEN SO RIGHT AS THEY ARE TONIGHT!
THE HEART IS A LONELY HUNTER
BILL MANTLO WRITER
BOB HALL JIM MOONEY ARTISTS
NOVAK LETTERS
SHAREN COLORS
TOM DEFALCO EDITOR
JIM SHOOTER EDITOR-IN-CHIEF
WE MUST HAVE BEEN OUT OF OUR MINDS TO COME HERE!
BUT THE MONEY WAS RIGHT--
--AND THE DAME THAT HIRED US SAID ALL WE HAD TO DO WAS PLAY SOME KIND OF GAME!
YEAH, BUT SHE DIDN'T SAY THAT WE'D BE PLAYING IT WITH KRAVEN THE HUNTER!

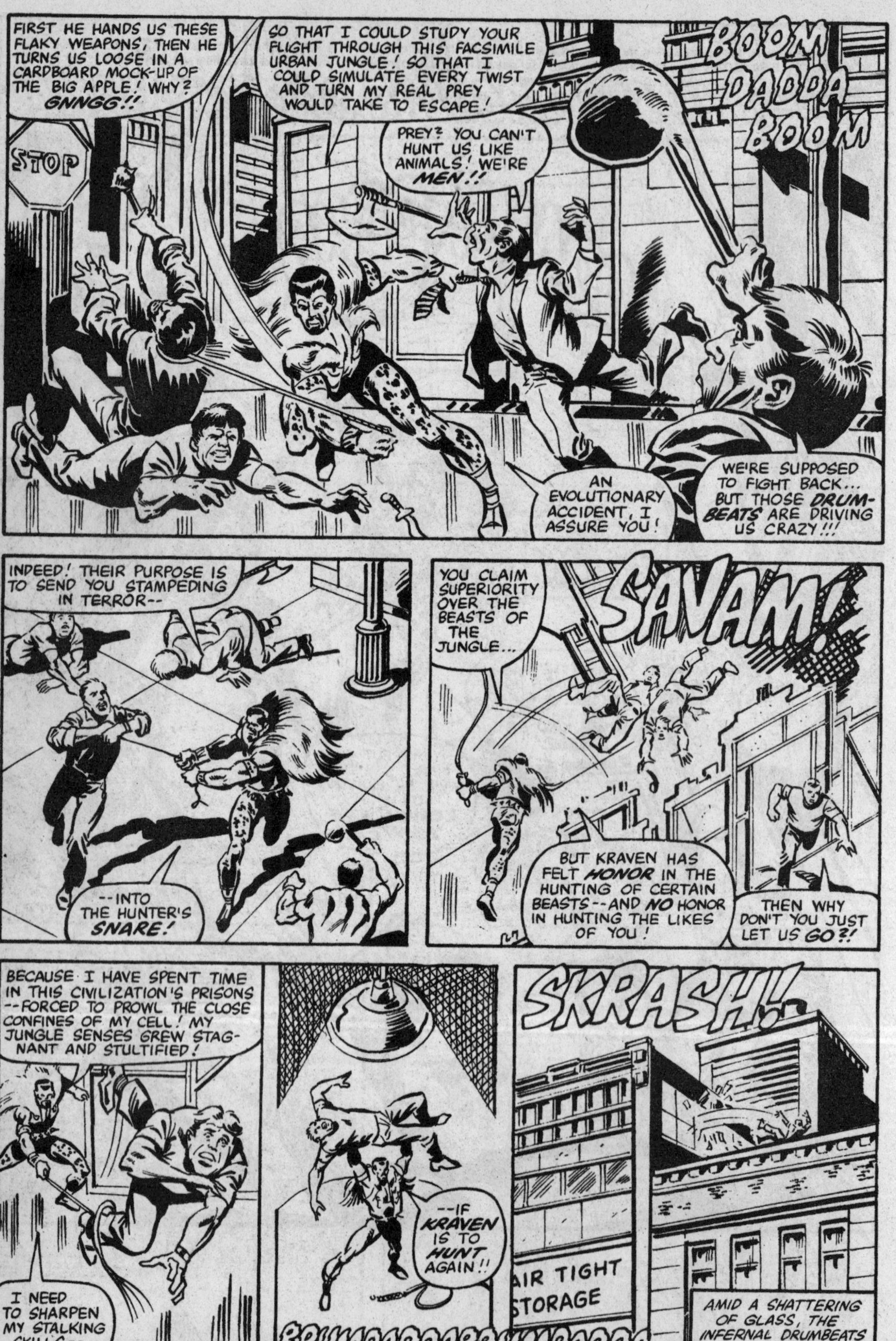

FIRST HE HANDS US THESE FLAKY WEAPONS, THEN HE TURNS US LOOSE IN A CARDBOARD MOCK-UP OF THE BIG APPLE! WHY? GNNGG!!
SO THAT I COULD STUDY YOUR FLIGHT THROUGH THIS FACSIMILE URBAN JUNGLE! SO THAT I COULD SIMULATE EVERY TWIST AND TURN MY REAL PREY WOULD TAKE TO ESCAPE!
BOOM DADDA BOOM
STOP
PREY? YOU CAN'T HUNT US LIKE ANIMALS! WE'RE MEN!!
AN EVOLUTIONARY ACCIDENT, I ASSURE YOU!
WE'RE SUPPOSED TO FIGHT BACK... BUT THOSE DRUMBEATS ARE DRIVING US CRAZY!!!
INDEED! THEIR PURPOSE IS TO SEND YOU STAMPEDING IN TERROR--
--INTO THE HUNTER'S SNARE!
YOU CLAIM SUPERIORITY OVER THE BEASTS OF THE JUNGLE...
SAVAM!
BUT KRAVEN HAS FELT HONOR IN THE HUNTING OF CERTAIN BEASTS--AND NO HONOR IN HUNTING THE LIKES OF YOU!
THEN WHY DON'T YOU JUST LET US GO?!
BECAUSE I HAVE SPENT TIME IN THIS CIVILIZATION'S PRISONS --FORCED TO PROWL THE CLOSE CONFINES OF MY CELL! MY JUNGLE SENSES GREW STAGNANT AND STULTIFIED!
I NEED TO SHARPEN MY STALKING SKILLS--
--IF KRAVEN IS TO HUNT AGAIN!!
BRUMDADDABRUMDADDA...
SKRASH!
AIR TIGHT STORAGE
AMID A SHATTERING OF GLASS, THE INFERNAL DRUMBEATS ...STOP!

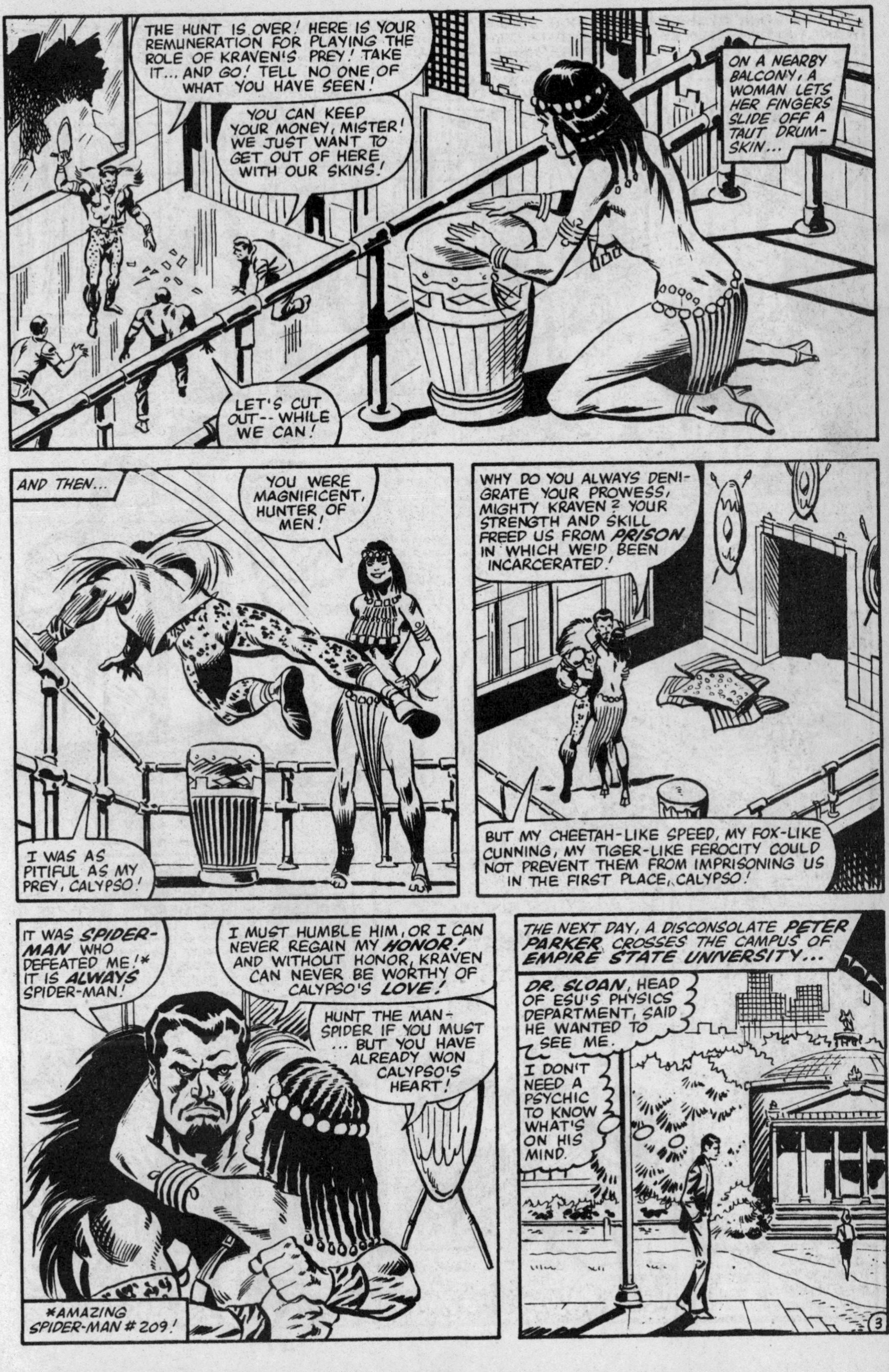
THE HUNT IS OVER! HERE IS YOUR REMUNERATION FOR PLAYING THE ROLE OF KRAVEN'S PREY! TAKE IT... AND GO! TELL NO ONE OF WHAT YOU HAVE SEEN!
YOU CAN KEEP YOUR MONEY, MISTER! WE JUST WANT TO GET OUT OF HERE WITH OUR SKINS!
ON A NEARBY BALCONY, A WOMAN LETS HER FINGERS SLIDE OFF A TAUT DRUM-SKIN...
LET'S CUT OUT-- WHILE WE CAN!
AND THEN...
YOU WERE MAGNIFICENT, HUNTER OF MEN!
I WAS AS PITIFUL AS MY PREY, CALYPSO!
WHY DO YOU ALWAYS DENIGRATE YOUR PROWESS, MIGHTY KRAVEN? YOUR STRENGTH AND SKILL FREED US FROM PRISON IN WHICH WE'D BEEN INCARCERATED!
BUT MY CHEETAH-LIKE SPEED, MY FOX-LIKE CUNNING, MY TIGER-LIKE FEROCITY COULD NOT PREVENT THEM FROM IMPRISONING US IN THE FIRST PLACE, CALYPSO!
IT WAS SPIDER-MAN WHO DEFEATED ME!* IT IS ALWAYS SPIDER-MAN!
I MUST HUMBLE HIM, OR I CAN NEVER REGAIN MY HONOR! AND WITHOUT HONOR, KRAVEN CAN NEVER BE WORTHY OF CALYPSO'S LOVE!
HUNT THE MAN-SPIDER IF YOU MUST ... BUT YOU HAVE ALREADY WON CALYPSO'S HEART!
*AMAZING SPIDER-MAN #209!
THE NEXT DAY, A DISCONSOLATE PETER PARKER CROSSES THE CAMPUS OF EMPIRE STATE UNIVERSITY...
DR. SLOAN, HEAD OF ESU'S PHYSICS DEPARTMENT, SAID HE WANTED TO SEE ME.
I DON'T NEED A PSYCHIC TO KNOW WHAT'S ON HIS MIND.
3

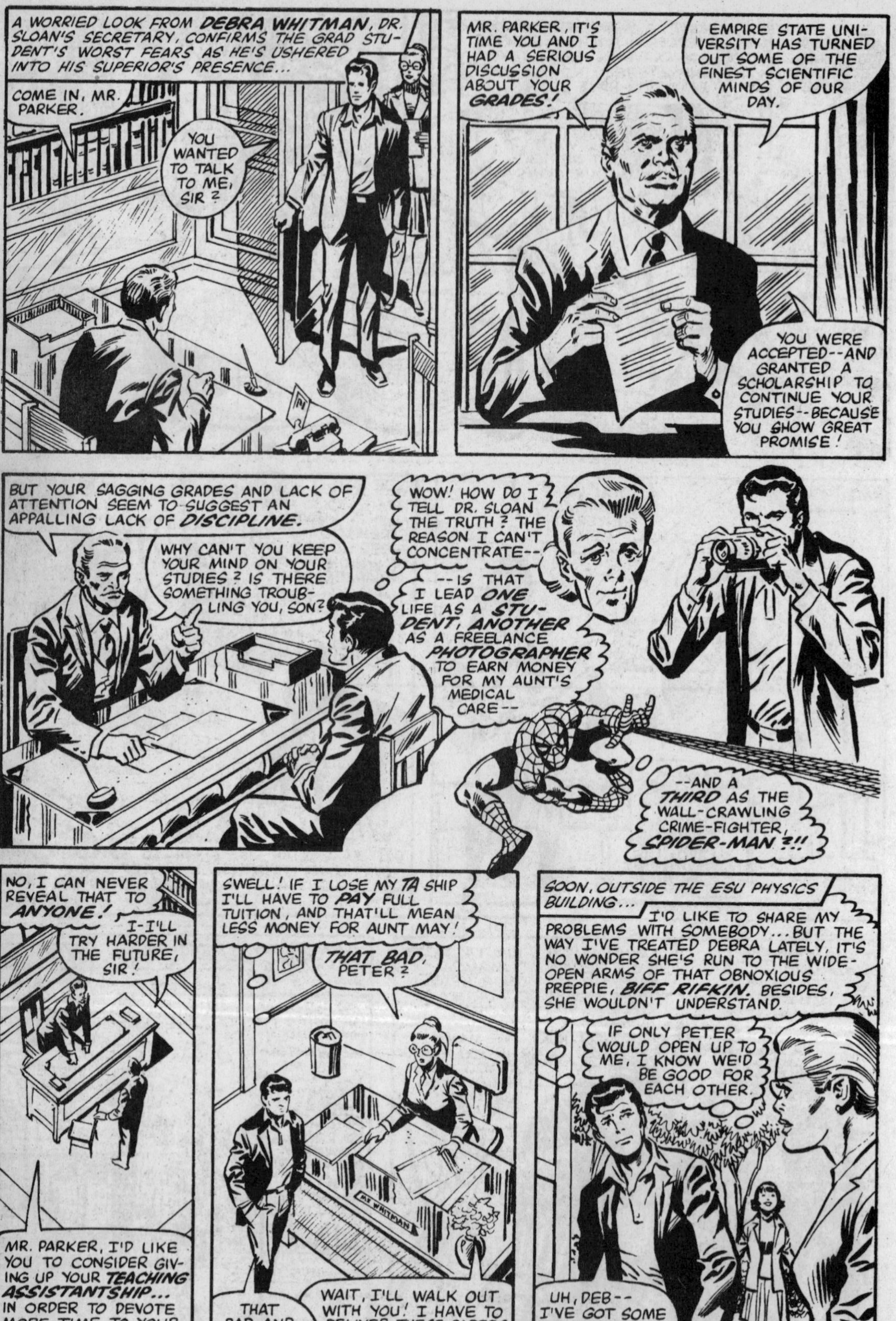
A WORRIED LOOK FROM DEBRA WHITMAN, DR. SLOAN'S SECRETARY, CONFIRMS THE GRAD STUDENT'S WORST FEARS AS HE'S USHERED INTO HIS SUPERIOR'S PRESENCE...
COME IN, MR. PARKER.
YOU WANTED TO TALK TO ME, SIR?
MR. PARKER, IT'S TIME YOU AND I HAD A SERIOUS DISCUSSION ABOUT YOUR GRADES!
EMPIRE STATE UNIVERSITY HAS TURNED OUT SOME OF THE FINEST SCIENTIFIC MINDS OF OUR DAY.
YOU WERE ACCEPTED--AND GRANTED A SCHOLARSHIP TO CONTINUE YOUR STUDIES--BECAUSE YOU SHOW GREAT PROMISE!
BUT YOUR SAGGING GRADES AND LACK OF ATTENTION SEEM TO SUGGEST AN APPALLING LACK OF DISCIPLINE.
WHY CAN'T YOU KEEP YOUR MIND ON YOUR STUDIES? IS THERE SOMETHING TROUBLING YOU, SON?
WOW! HOW DO I TELL DR. SLOAN THE TRUTH? THE REASON I CAN'T CONCENTRATE--
--IS THAT I LEAD ONE LIFE AS A STUDENT, ANOTHER AS A FREELANCE PHOTOGRAPHER TO EARN MONEY FOR MY AUNT'S MEDICAL CARE--
--AND A THIRD AS THE WALL-CRAWLING CRIME-FIGHTER, SPIDER-MAN?!!
NO, I CAN NEVER REVEAL THAT TO ANYONE!
I-I'LL TRY HARDER IN THE FUTURE, SIR!
MR. PARKER, I'D LIKE YOU TO CONSIDER GIVING UP YOUR TEACHING ASSISTANTSHIP... IN ORDER TO DEVOTE MORE TIME TO YOUR STUDIES.
SWELL! IF I LOSE MY TA SHIP I'LL HAVE TO PAY FULL TUITION, AND THAT'LL MEAN LESS MONEY FOR AUNT MAY!
THAT BAD, PETER?
THAT BAD AND WORSE, DEB.
WAIT, I'LL WALK OUT WITH YOU! I HAVE TO DELIVER THESE PAPERS FOR DR. SLOAN.
SOON, OUTSIDE THE ESU PHYSICS BUILDING...
I'D LIKE TO SHARE MY PROBLEMS WITH SOMEBODY... BUT THE WAY I'VE TREATED DEBRA LATELY, IT'S NO WONDER SHE'S RUN TO THE WIDE-OPEN ARMS OF THAT OBNOXIOUS PREPPIE, BIFF RIFKIN. BESIDES, SHE WOULDN'T UNDERSTAND.
IF ONLY PETER WOULD OPEN UP TO ME, I KNOW WE'D BE GOOD FOR EACH OTHER.
UH, DEB-- I'VE GOT SOME THINKING TO DO, OKAY?
4

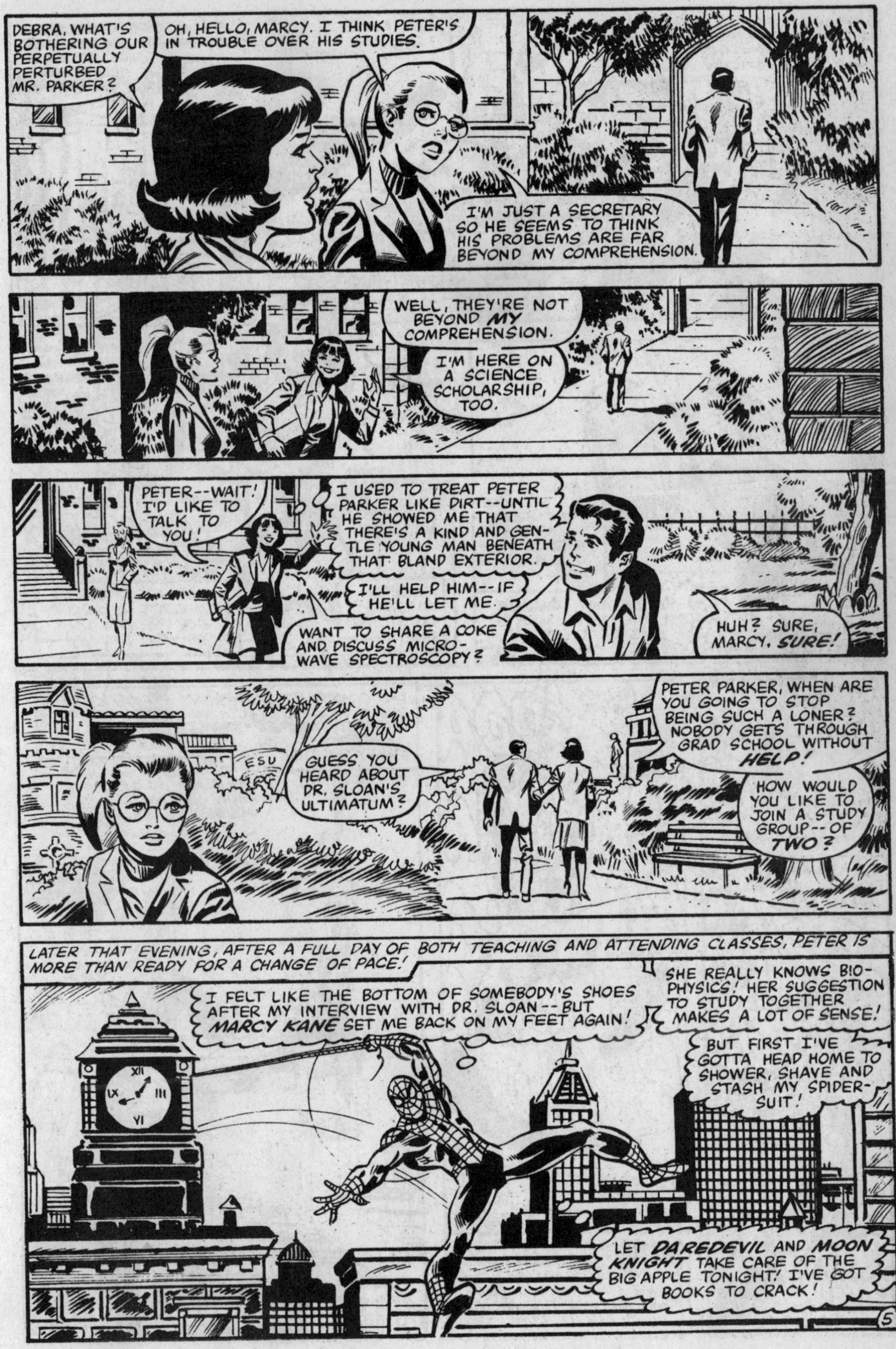

DEBRA, WHAT'S BOTHERING OUR PERPETUALLY PERTURBED MR. PARKER?
OH, HELLO, MARCY. I THINK PETER'S IN TROUBLE OVER HIS STUDIES.
I'M JUST A SECRETARY SO HE SEEMS TO THINK HIS PROBLEMS ARE FAR BEYOND MY COMPREHENSION.
WELL, THEY'RE NOT BEYOND MY COMPREHENSION.
I'M HERE ON A SCIENCE SCHOLARSHIP, TOO.
PETER--WAIT! I'D LIKE TO TALK TO YOU!
I USED TO TREAT PETER PARKER LIKE DIRT--UNTIL HE SHOWED ME THAT THERE'S A KIND AND GENTLE YOUNG MAN BENEATH THAT BLAND EXTERIOR.
I'LL HELP HIM--IF HE'LL LET ME.
WANT TO SHARE A COKE AND DISCUSS MICRO-WAVE SPECTROSCOPY?
HUH? SURE, MARCY. SURE!
ESU
GUESS YOU HEARD ABOUT DR. SLOAN'S ULTIMATUM?
PETER PARKER, WHEN ARE YOU GOING TO STOP BEING SUCH A LONER? NOBODY GETS THROUGH GRAD SCHOOL WITHOUT HELP!
HOW WOULD YOU LIKE TO JOIN A STUDY GROUP--OF TWO?
LATER THAT EVENING, AFTER A FULL DAY OF BOTH TEACHING AND ATTENDING CLASSES, PETER IS MORE THAN READY FOR A CHANGE OF PACE!
I FELT LIKE THE BOTTOM OF SOMEBODY'S SHOES AFTER MY INTERVIEW WITH DR. SLOAN--BUT MARCY KANE SET ME BACK ON MY FEET AGAIN!
SHE REALLY KNOWS BIO-PHYSICS! HER SUGGESTION TO STUDY TOGETHER MAKES A LOT OF SENSE!
BUT FIRST I'VE GOTTA HEAD HOME TO SHOWER, SHAVE AND STASH MY SPIDER-SUIT!
LET DAREDEVIL AND MOON KNIGHT TAKE CARE OF THE BIG APPLE TONIGHT! I'VE GOT BOOKS TO CRACK!
5

BUT, UNBEKNOWNST TO THE WEBBED WONDER, HIS CHELSEA HOMECOMING IS BEING OBSERVED...

AT LAST! MY NIGHTS SPENT STALKING MY PREY HAVE BORNE FRUIT!

A TRUE HUNTER ALWAYS STUDIES THE CREATURES HE HUNTS!

THUS I KNEW, FROM WEEKS OF OBSERVATION, THAT *SPIDER-MAN* IS OFTEN SEEN IN THIS PARTICULAR NEIGHBORHOOD!

RAISING HIGH HIS *AFRICAN WAR AXE,* KRAVEN GIVES A SIGNAL...

...TO THE *BEAUTEOUS CALYPSO,* WHO ARRANGES CEREMONIAL OBJECTS ON A NEARBY ROOFTOP.

THE *BIRA BELLS* AND *YORUBA SPIRIT DRUM* ARE INSTRUMENTS THAT ENABLE ONE AS ADEPT IN THEIR USE AS I AM--

--TO *BECLOUD* THE MIND OF AN ENEMY!

FINGERS CARESS STRETCHED SKIN...

...AND *MESMERIZING DRUMBEATS* REVERBER-ATE IN THE CANYONS OF MANHATTAN!

BRUM BRUDDA BRUM BRUDDA

WHAT THE HECK--? *DRUMS*?!

THE SOUNDS... DEAFENING-- MAKING IT HARD TO THINK!

CALYPSO'S RITUAL PLAYING OF THE *MYSTIC PERCUSSION INSTRUMENTS* HAS ANOTHER, MORE SINISTER PURPOSE THAN FILLING THE AIR WITH THEIR THUNDER.

THE *CONSTANT CACAPHONY HYPNOTICALLY DULLS* THE SPECTACULAR SPIDER-MAN'S VAUNTED *SPIDER-SENSE,* LEAVING HIM UNPREPARED FOR A SUDDEN *LIGHTNING-SWIFT ATTACK!*

SOMETHING CLEAVING THE AIR-- HURLED FROM BELOW! IT MISSED ME BY A HAIR!

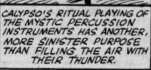

6

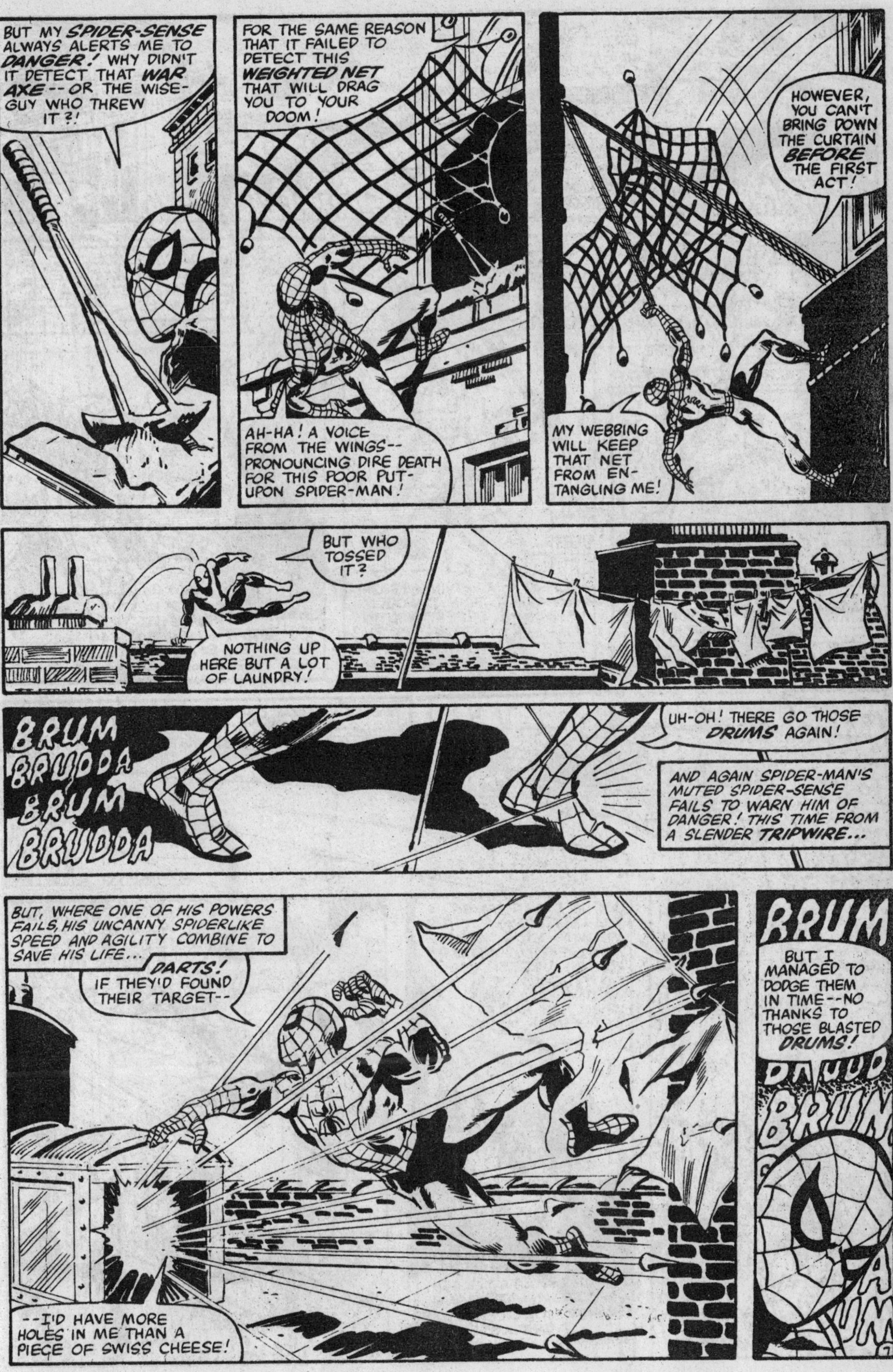
BUT MY SPIDER-SENSE ALWAYS ALERTS ME TO DANGER! WHY DIDN'T IT DETECT THAT WAR AXE--OR THE WISE-GUY WHO THREW IT?!
FOR THE SAME REASON THAT IT FAILED TO DETECT THIS WEIGHTED NET THAT WILL DRAG YOU TO YOUR DOOM!
AH-HA! A VOICE FROM THE WINGS--PRONOUNCING DIRE DEATH FOR THIS POOR PUT-UPON SPIDER-MAN!
HOWEVER, YOU CAN'T BRING DOWN THE CURTAIN BEFORE THE FIRST ACT!
MY WEBBING WILL KEEP THAT NET FROM EN-TANGLING ME!
BUT WHO TOSSED IT?
NOTHING UP HERE BUT A LOT OF LAUNDRY!
BRUM BRUDDA BRUM BRUDDA
UH-OH! THERE GO THOSE DRUMS AGAIN!
AND AGAIN SPIDER-MAN'S MUTED SPIDER-SENSE FAILS TO WARN HIM OF DANGER! THIS TIME FROM A SLENDER TRIPWIRE...
BUT, WHERE ONE OF HIS POWERS FAILS, HIS UNCANNY SPIDERLIKE SPEED AND AGILITY COMBINE TO SAVE HIS LIFE...
DARTS! IF THEY'D FOUND THEIR TARGET--
--I'D HAVE MORE HOLES IN ME THAN A PIECE OF SWISS CHEESE!
BRUM
BUT I MANAGED TO DODGE THEM IN TIME--NO THANKS TO THOSE BLASTED DRUMS!
7

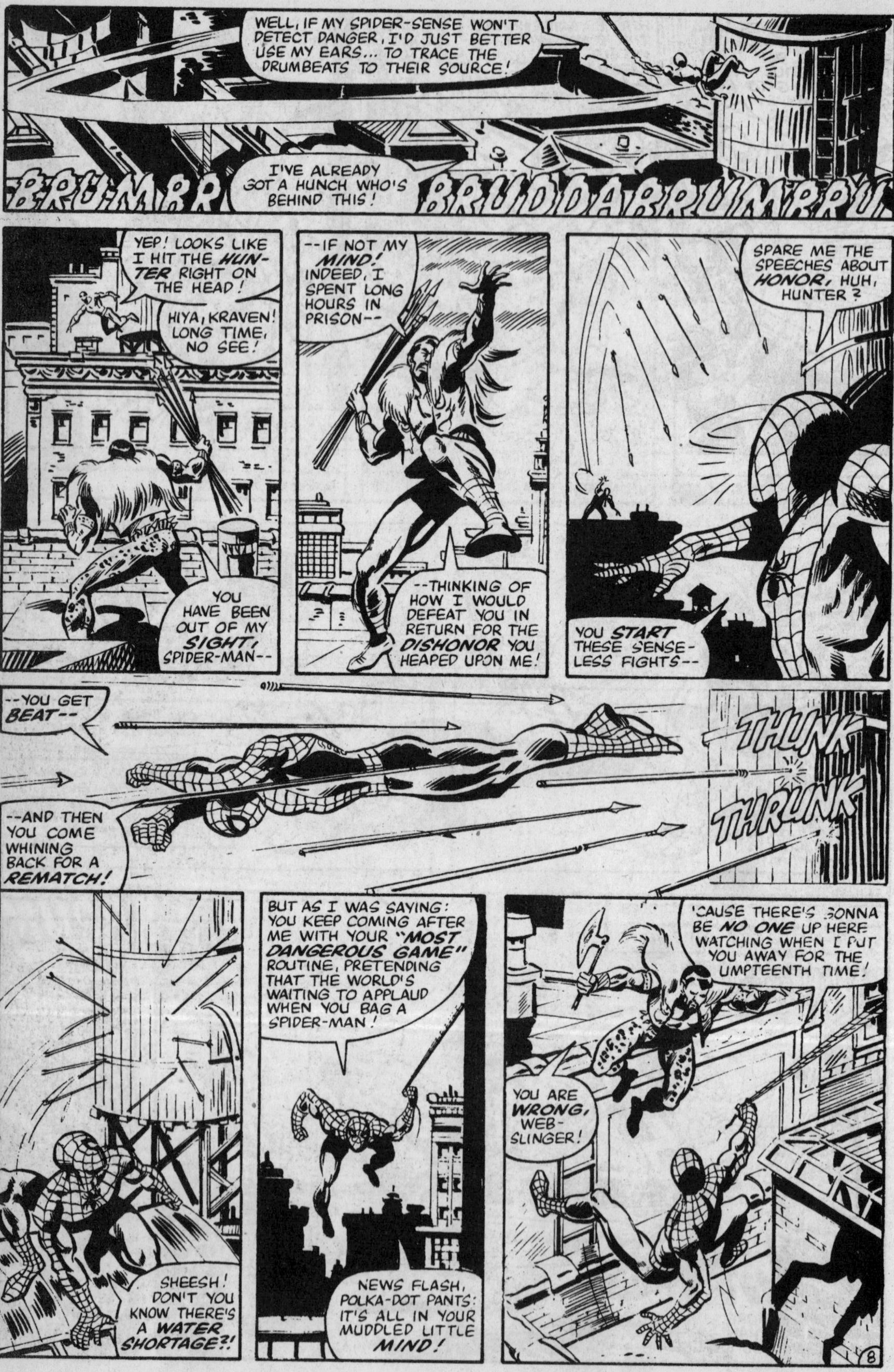

WELL, IF MY SPIDER-SENSE WON'T DETECT DANGER, I'D JUST BETTER USE MY EARS... TO TRACE THE DRUMBEATS TO THEIR SOURCE!
BRUMBR
I'VE ALREADY GOT A HUNCH WHO'S BEHIND THIS!
BRUDDABRRUMBRRU
YEP! LOOKS LIKE I HIT THE HUNTER RIGHT ON THE HEAD!
HIYA, KRAVEN! LONG TIME, NO SEE!
YOU HAVE BEEN OUT OF MY SIGHT, SPIDER-MAN--
--IF NOT MY MIND! INDEED, I SPENT LONG HOURS IN PRISON--
--THINKING OF HOW I WOULD DEFEAT YOU IN RETURN FOR THE DISHONOR YOU HEAPED UPON ME!
SPARE ME THE SPEECHES ABOUT HONOR, HUH, HUNTER?
YOU START THESE SENSE-LESS FIGHTS--
--YOU GET BEAT--
--AND THEN YOU COME WHINING BACK FOR A REMATCH!
THUNK
THRUNK
SHEESH! DON'T YOU KNOW THERE'S A WATER SHORTAGE?!
BUT AS I WAS SAYING: YOU KEEP COMING AFTER ME WITH YOUR "MOST DANGEROUS GAME" ROUTINE, PRETENDING THAT THE WORLD'S WAITING TO APPLAUD WHEN YOU BAG A SPIDER-MAN!
NEWS FLASH, POLKA-DOT PANTS: IT'S ALL IN YOUR MUDDLED LITTLE MIND!
'CAUSE THERE'S GONNA BE NO ONE UP HERE WATCHING WHEN I PUT YOU AWAY FOR THE UMPTEENTH TIME!
YOU ARE WRONG, WEB-SLINGER!
8

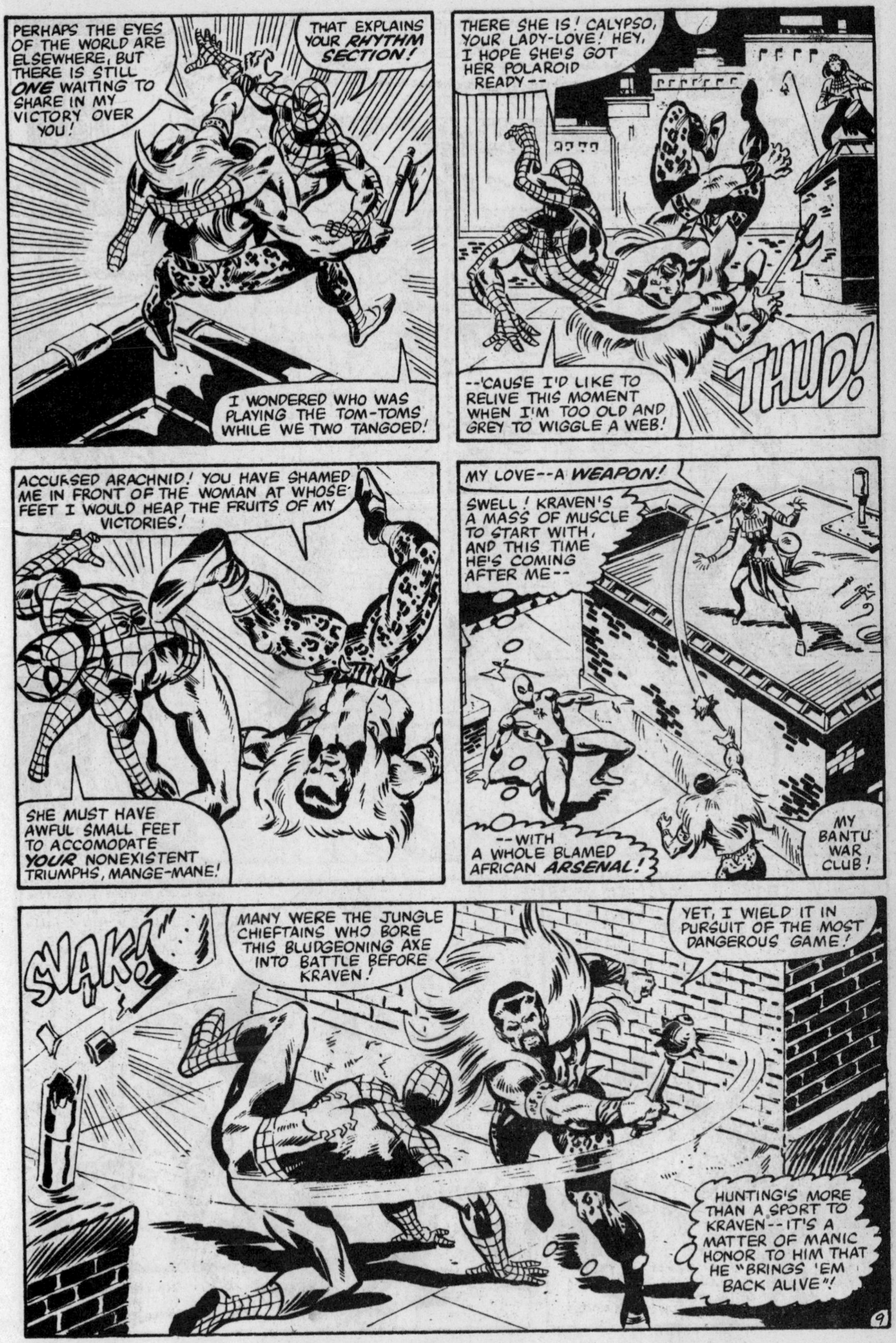
PERHAPS THE EYES OF THE WORLD ARE ELSEWHERE, BUT THERE IS STILL ONE WAITING TO SHARE IN MY VICTORY OVER YOU!
THAT EXPLAINS YOUR RHYTHM SECTION!
I WONDERED WHO WAS PLAYING THE TOM-TOMS WHILE WE TWO TANGOED!
THERE SHE IS! CALYPSO, YOUR LADY-LOVE! HEY, I HOPE SHE'S GOT HER POLAROID READY--
THUD!
--'CAUSE I'D LIKE TO RELIVE THIS MOMENT WHEN I'M TOO OLD AND GREY TO WIGGLE A WEB!
ACCURSED ARACHNID! YOU HAVE SHAMED ME IN FRONT OF THE WOMAN AT WHOSE FEET I WOULD HEAP THE FRUITS OF MY VICTORIES!
SHE MUST HAVE AWFUL SMALL FEET TO ACCOMODATE YOUR NONEXISTENT TRIUMPHS, MANGE-MANE!
MY LOVE--A WEAPON!
SWELL! KRAVEN'S A MASS OF MUSCLE TO START WITH, AND THIS TIME HE'S COMING AFTER ME--
--WITH A WHOLE BLAMED AFRICAN ARSENAL!
MY BANTU WAR CLUB!
SNAK!
MANY WERE THE JUNGLE CHIEFTAINS WHO BORE THIS BLUDGEONING AXE INTO BATTLE BEFORE KRAVEN!
YET, I WIELD IT IN PURSUIT OF THE MOST DANGEROUS GAME!
HUNTING'S MORE THAN A SPORT TO KRAVEN--IT'S A MATTER OF MANIC HONOR TO HIM THAT HE "BRINGS 'EM BACK ALIVE"!
9

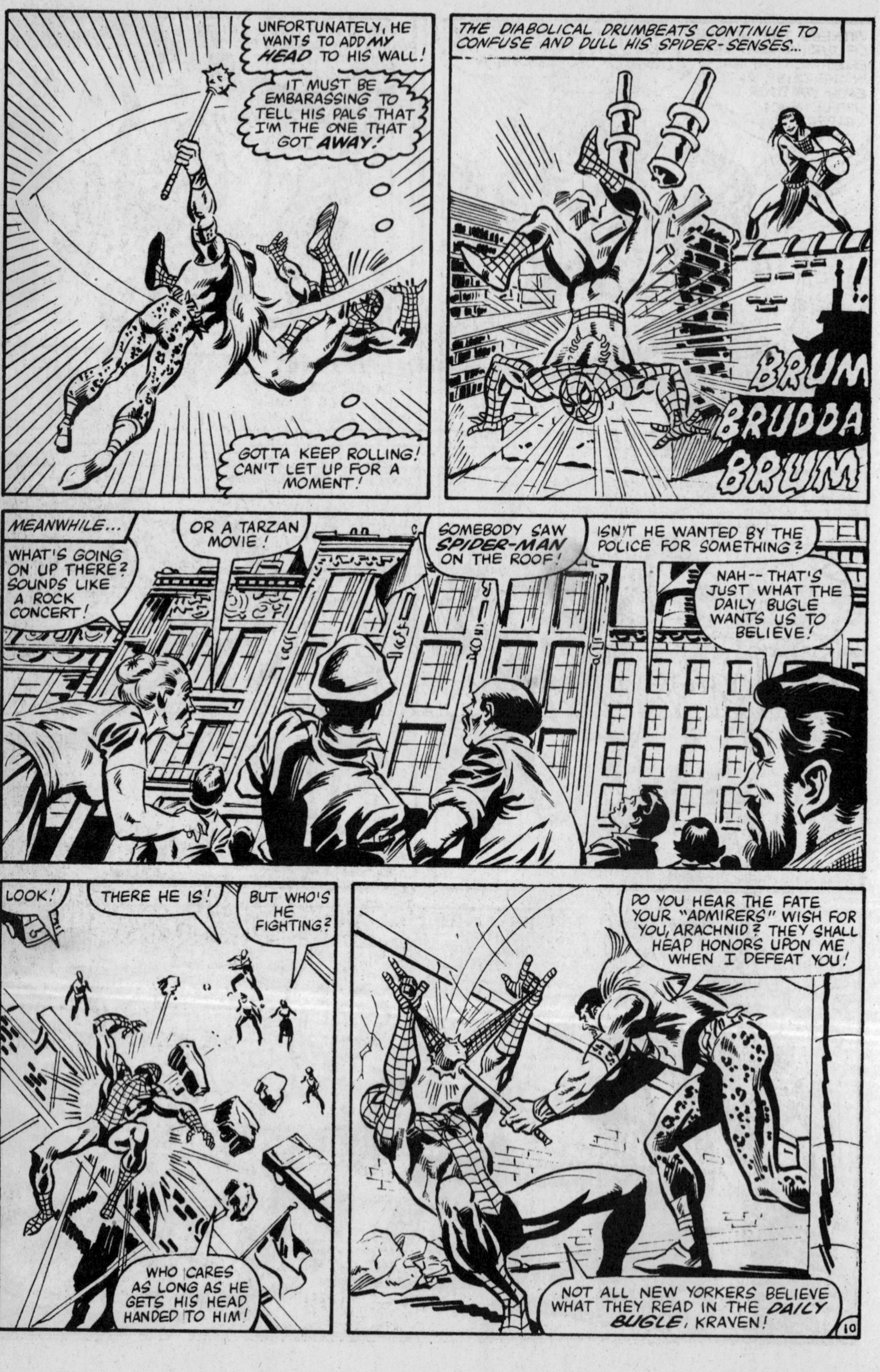
UNFORTUNATELY, HE WANTS TO ADD MY HEAD TO HIS WALL!
IT MUST BE EMBARASSING TO TELL HIS PALS THAT I'M THE ONE THAT GOT AWAY!
GOTTA KEEP ROLLING! CAN'T LET UP FOR A MOMENT!
THE DIABOLICAL DRUMBEATS CONTINUE TO CONFUSE AND DULL HIS SPIDER-SENSES...
BRUM BRUDDA BRUM
MEANWHILE...
WHAT'S GOING ON UP THERE? SOUNDS LIKE A ROCK CONCERT!
OR A TARZAN MOVIE!
SOMEBODY SAW SPIDER-MAN ON THE ROOF!
ISN'T HE WANTED BY THE POLICE FOR SOMETHING?
NAH-- THAT'S JUST WHAT THE DAILY BUGLE WANTS US TO BELIEVE!
LOOK!
THERE HE IS!
BUT WHO'S HE FIGHTING?
WHO CARES AS LONG AS HE GETS HIS HEAD HANDED TO HIM!
DO YOU HEAR THE FATE YOUR "ADMIRERS" WISH FOR YOU, ARACHNID? THEY SHALL HEAP HONORS UPON ME WHEN I DEFEAT YOU!
NOT ALL NEW YORKERS BELIEVE WHAT THEY READ IN THE DAILY BUGLE, KRAVEN!
10

WITNESS THE NUMBER OF JURIES WHO KEEP CHUCKING YOU BACK IN THE CLINK AFTER EACH OF YOUR LITTLE ESCAPADES!

THEIR LAWS ARE NOT THE *HUNTER'S LAWS* -- THE LAWS OF THE SAVAGE JUNGLE!

AMEN TO THAT! I'D HATE TO LIVE IN A SOCIETY THAT PUT UP WITH PEOPLE WHO HUNT PEOPLE FOR THE FUN OF IT!

SPRAK!

AND, NOW THAT I'VE GOT *YOU* OUT OF MY HAIR FOR A SECOND, LET'S SEE WHAT I CAN DO ABOUT THE CHICK... WHOSE PERCUSSION IS PARALYZING MY GREY MATTER!

NO! YOU SHALL NOT SULLY CALYPSO'S PERSON WITH YOUR INSECT-LIKE TOUCH!

ABRUMBRUDABRUMBRUDDARR

DESTROY THE MAN-SPIDER, MY LOVE!

FLAY HIM SENSELESS WITH THIS LOVEDU *WAR WHIP!*

LADY, I NEVER INTENDED TO LAY A FINGER ON YOU! ALL I WANT--

--IS THAT *DRUM* YOU'RE USING TO DRIVE ME BANANAS!

NO! WITHOUT THE RITUALISTIC BEATING OF THE *YORUBA SPIRIT* DRUM... YOUR ACCURSED SPIDER-SENSE WILL *RETURN!*

11

Panel 1: THAT'S THE TICKET, TOOTS!

BAH! EVEN WITH YOUR COWARDLY SPIDER-SENSE RETURNED TO YOU, KRAVEN WILL STILL TRIUMPH!

BOY, ARE YOU LIVING IN A DREAM-WORLD, TIGER-TIGHTS!

Panel 2: WITHOUT MY SPIDER-SENSE, YOU MAY HAVE GOTTEN IN A LICK OR TWO -- BUT YOU HARDLY MUSSED MY MASK!

NOW, THERE'S NO WAY YOU'RE GONNA LAY A GLOVE ON ME!

CURSE YOUR ARROGANCE, ARACHNID--!

THWAP!

AVOID ALLITERATION, KRAVEN! IT'LL ONLY GET YOU A FAT LIP!

SPKOW!

I DON'T BELIEVE IT! KRAVEN CAN STOP A CHARGING BULL RHINO WITH A SINGLE BLOW -- BUT HE HAS BEEN FELLED BY THE MUCH SMALLER *SPIDER-MAN!*

KRAVEN'S EGO DRIVES HIM TO ENGAGE THE MAN-SPIDER ALONE! BUT, PERHAPS I CAN SECRETLY AID HIM--

--SO THAT HE MAY TRIUMPH OVER SPIDER-MAN WITH HIS VANITY INTACT!

TWANG!

SINCE HIS SPIDER-SENSE IS TINGLING ALREADY AT THE DANGER POSED BY A WHIP-WIELDING KRAVEN, SPIDER-MAN FAILS TO DETECT THE TINY DART THAT PRICKS HIS CALF...

...INJECTING AN HERBAL HALLUCI-NOGEN INTO HIS BLOODSTREAM.

12

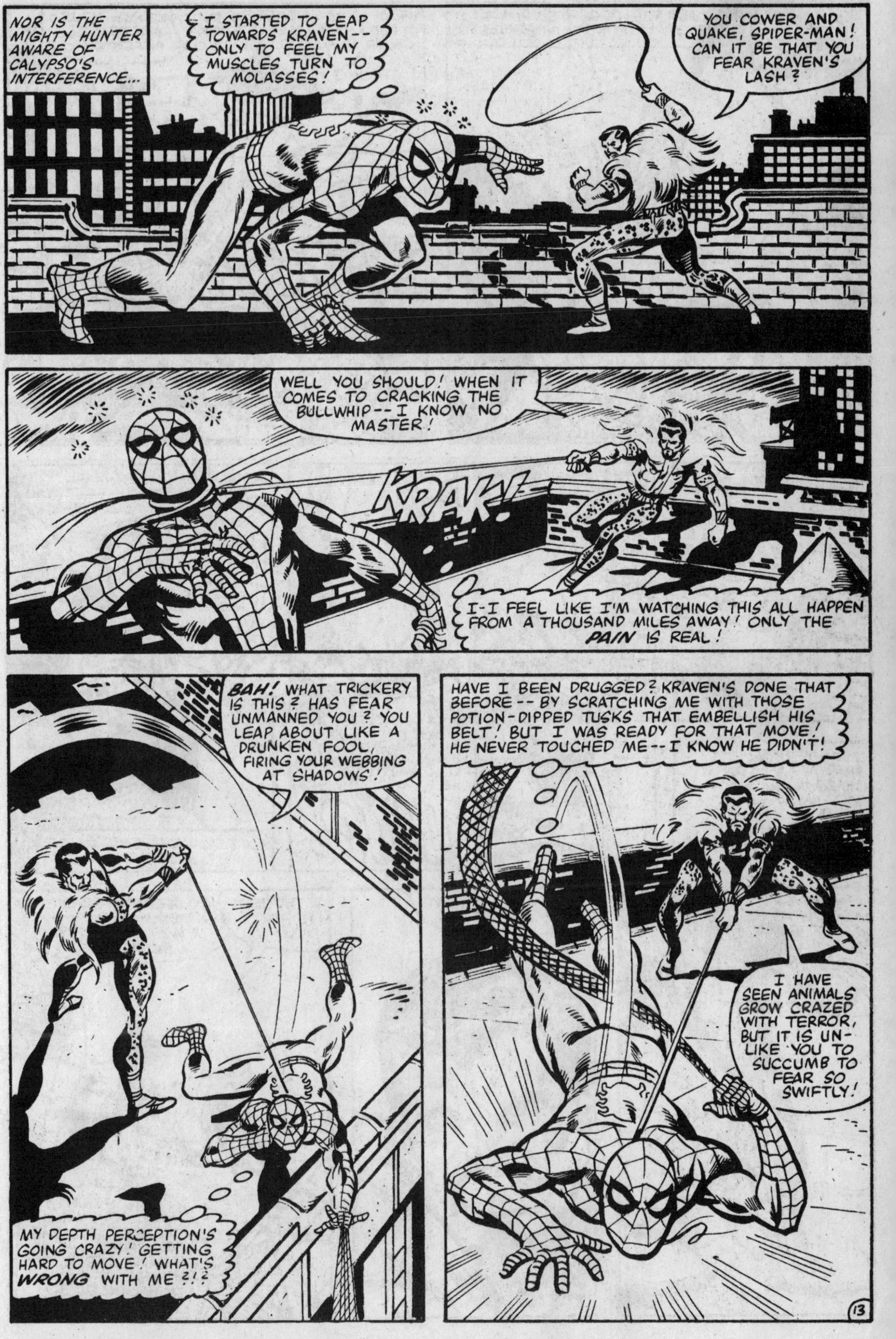

NOR IS THE MIGHTY HUNTER AWARE OF CALYPSO'S INTERFERENCE...
I STARTED TO LEAP TOWARDS KRAVEN-- ONLY TO FEEL MY MUSCLES TURN TO MOLASSES!
YOU COWER AND QUAKE, SPIDER-MAN! CAN IT BE THAT YOU FEAR KRAVEN'S LASH?
WELL YOU SHOULD! WHEN IT COMES TO CRACKING THE BULLWHIP-- I KNOW NO MASTER!
KRAK!
I-I FEEL LIKE I'M WATCHING THIS ALL HAPPEN FROM A THOUSAND MILES AWAY! ONLY THE PAIN IS REAL!
BAH! WHAT TRICKERY IS THIS? HAS FEAR UNMANNED YOU? YOU LEAP ABOUT LIKE A DRUNKEN FOOL, FIRING YOUR WEBBING AT SHADOWS!
MY DEPTH PERCEPTION'S GOING CRAZY! GETTING HARD TO MOVE! WHAT'S WRONG WITH ME?!?
HAVE I BEEN DRUGGED? KRAVEN'S DONE THAT BEFORE-- BY SCRATCHING ME WITH THOSE POTION-DIPPED TUSKS THAT EMBELLISH HIS BELT! BUT I WAS READY FOR THAT MOVE! HE NEVER TOUCHED ME-- I KNOW HE DIDN'T!
I HAVE SEEN ANIMALS GROW CRAZED WITH TERROR, BUT IT IS UNLIKE YOU TO SUCCUMB TO FEAR SO SWIFTLY!
13

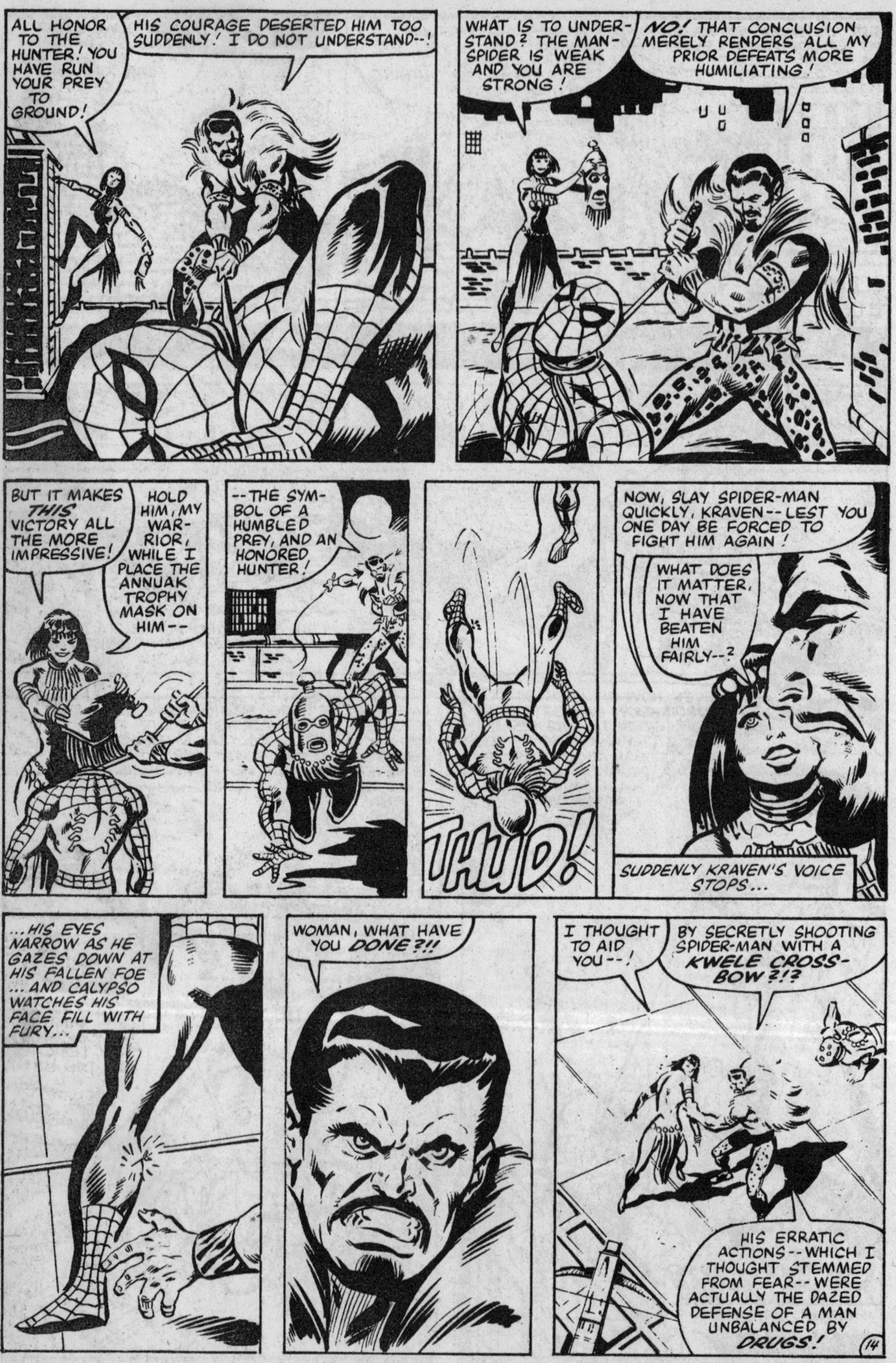
ALL HONOR TO THE HUNTER! YOU HAVE RUN YOUR PREY TO GROUND!
HIS COURAGE DESERTED HIM TOO SUDDENLY! I DO NOT UNDERSTAND--!
WHAT IS TO UNDERSTAND? THE MAN-SPIDER IS WEAK AND YOU ARE STRONG!
NO! THAT CONCLUSION MERELY RENDERS ALL MY PRIOR DEFEATS MORE HUMILIATING!
BUT IT MAKES THIS VICTORY ALL THE MORE IMPRESSIVE!
HOLD HIM, MY WARRIOR, WHILE I PLACE THE ANNUAK TROPHY MASK ON HIM--
--THE SYMBOL OF A HUMBLED PREY, AND AN HONORED HUNTER!
THUD!
NOW, SLAY SPIDER-MAN QUICKLY, KRAVEN--LEST YOU ONE DAY BE FORCED TO FIGHT HIM AGAIN!
WHAT DOES IT MATTER, NOW THAT I HAVE BEATEN HIM FAIRLY--?
SUDDENLY KRAVEN'S VOICE STOPS...
...HIS EYES NARROW AS HE GAZES DOWN AT HIS FALLEN FOE ...AND CALYPSO WATCHES HIS FACE FILL WITH FURY...
WOMAN, WHAT HAVE YOU DONE?!!
I THOUGHT TO AID YOU--!
BY SECRETLY SHOOTING SPIDER-MAN WITH A KWELE CROSS-BOW?!?
HIS ERRATIC ACTIONS--WHICH I THOUGHT STEMMED FROM FEAR--WERE ACTUALLY THE DAZED DEFENSE OF A MAN UNBALANCED BY DRUGS!

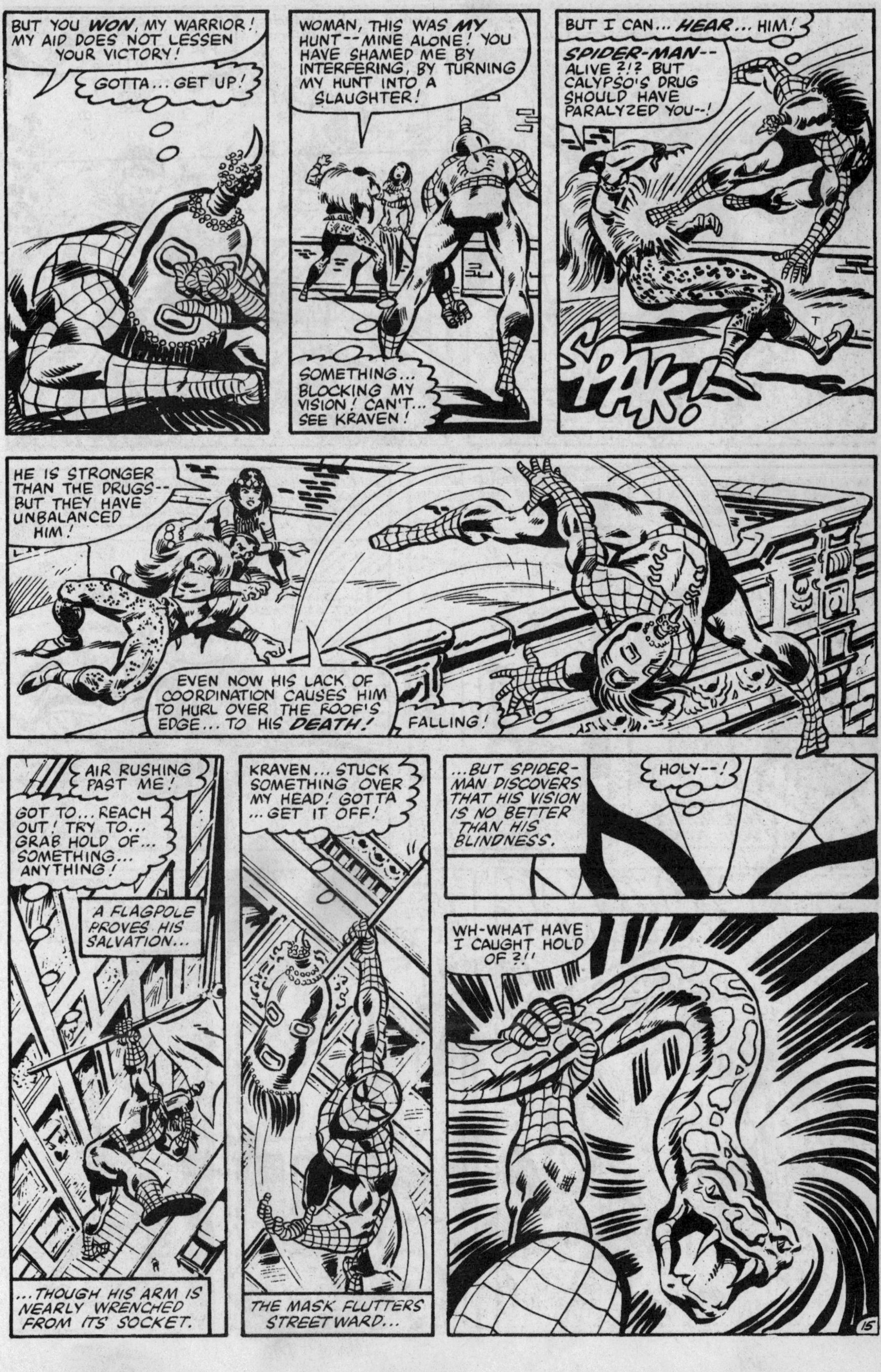
BUT YOU WON, MY WARRIOR! MY AID DOES NOT LESSEN YOUR VICTORY!
GOTTA... GET UP!
WOMAN, THIS WAS MY HUNT--MINE ALONE! YOU HAVE SHAMED ME BY INTERFERING, BY TURNING MY HUNT INTO A SLAUGHTER!
SOMETHING... BLOCKING MY VISION! CAN'T... SEE KRAVEN!
BUT I CAN... HEAR... HIM!
SPIDER-MAN--ALIVE?!? BUT CALYPSO'S DRUG SHOULD HAVE PARALYZED YOU--!
SPAK!
HE IS STRONGER THAN THE DRUGS--BUT THEY HAVE UNBALANCED HIM!
EVEN NOW HIS LACK OF COORDINATION CAUSES HIM TO HURL OVER THE ROOF'S EDGE... TO HIS DEATH!
FALLING!
AIR RUSHING PAST ME!
GOT TO... REACH OUT! TRY TO... GRAB HOLD OF... SOMETHING... ANYTHING!
A FLAGPOLE PROVES HIS SALVATION...
...THOUGH HIS ARM IS NEARLY WRENCHED FROM ITS SOCKET.
KRAVEN... STUCK SOMETHING OVER MY HEAD! GOTTA ...GET IT OFF!
THE MASK FLUTTERS STREETWARD...
...BUT SPIDER-MAN DISCOVERS THAT HIS VISION IS NO BETTER THAN HIS BLINDNESS.
HOLY--!
WH-WHAT HAVE I CAUGHT HOLD OF?!
15

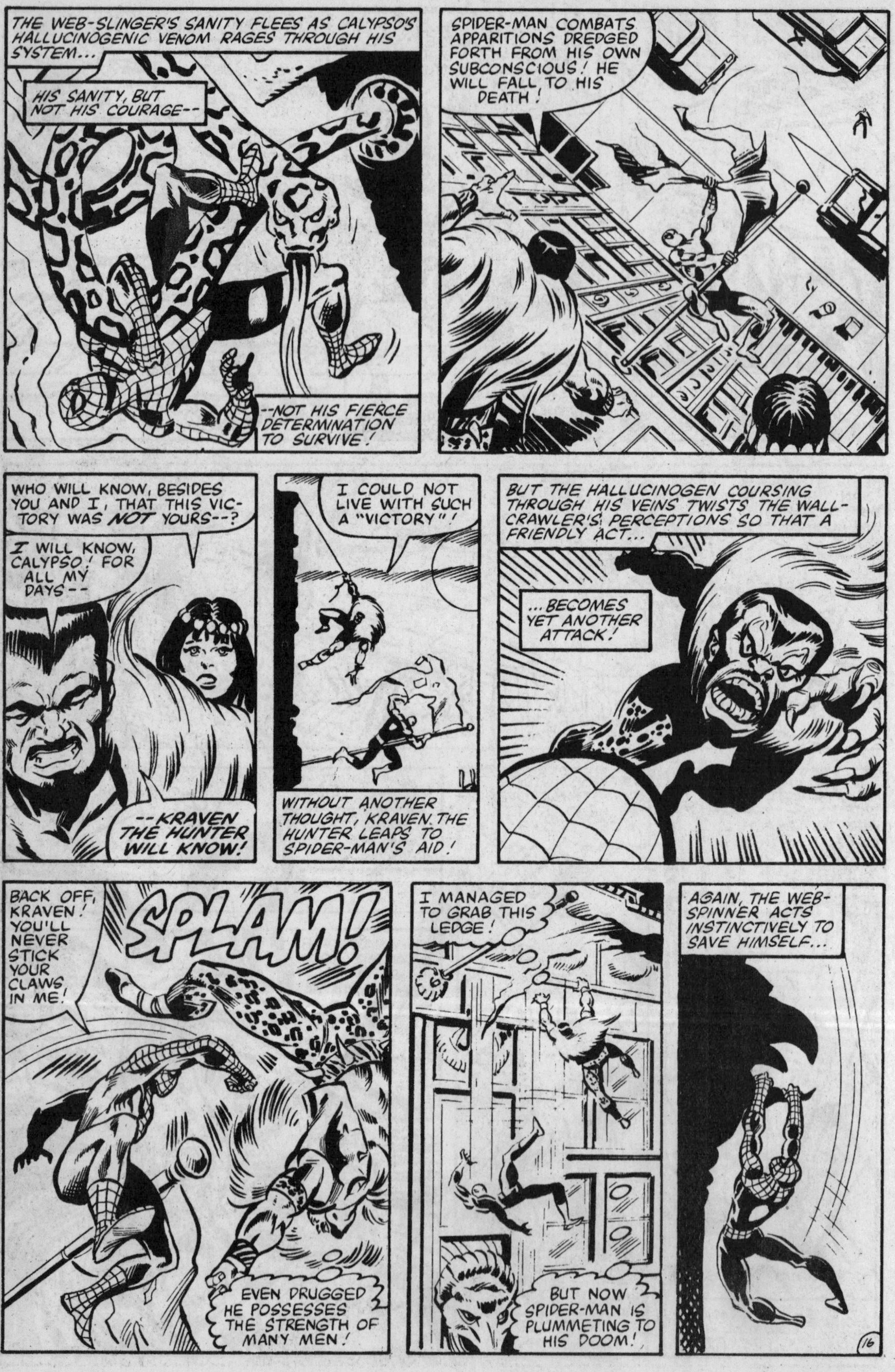
THE WEB-SLINGER'S SANITY FLEES AS CALYPSO'S HALLUCINOGENIC VENOM RAGES THROUGH HIS SYSTEM...
HIS SANITY, BUT NOT HIS COURAGE--
--NOT HIS FIERCE DETERMINATION TO SURVIVE!
SPIDER-MAN COMBATS APPARITIONS DREDGED FORTH FROM HIS OWN SUBCONSCIOUS! HE WILL FALL TO HIS DEATH!
WHO WILL KNOW, BESIDES YOU AND I, THAT THIS VICTORY WAS NOT YOURS--?
I WILL KNOW, CALYPSO! FOR ALL MY DAYS--
--KRAVEN THE HUNTER WILL KNOW!
I COULD NOT LIVE WITH SUCH A "VICTORY"!
WITHOUT ANOTHER THOUGHT, KRAVEN THE HUNTER LEAPS TO SPIDER-MAN'S AID!
BUT THE HALLUCINOGEN COURSING THROUGH HIS VEINS TWISTS THE WALL-CRAWLER'S PERCEPTIONS SO THAT A FRIENDLY ACT...
...BECOMES YET ANOTHER ATTACK!
BACK OFF, KRAVEN! YOU'LL NEVER STICK YOUR CLAWS IN ME!
SPLAM!
EVEN DRUGGED HE POSSESSES THE STRENGTH OF MANY MEN!
I MANAGED TO GRAB THIS LEDGE!
BUT NOW SPIDER-MAN IS PLUMMETING TO HIS DOOM!
AGAIN, THE WEB-SPINNER ACTS INSTINCTIVELY TO SAVE HIMSELF...
16

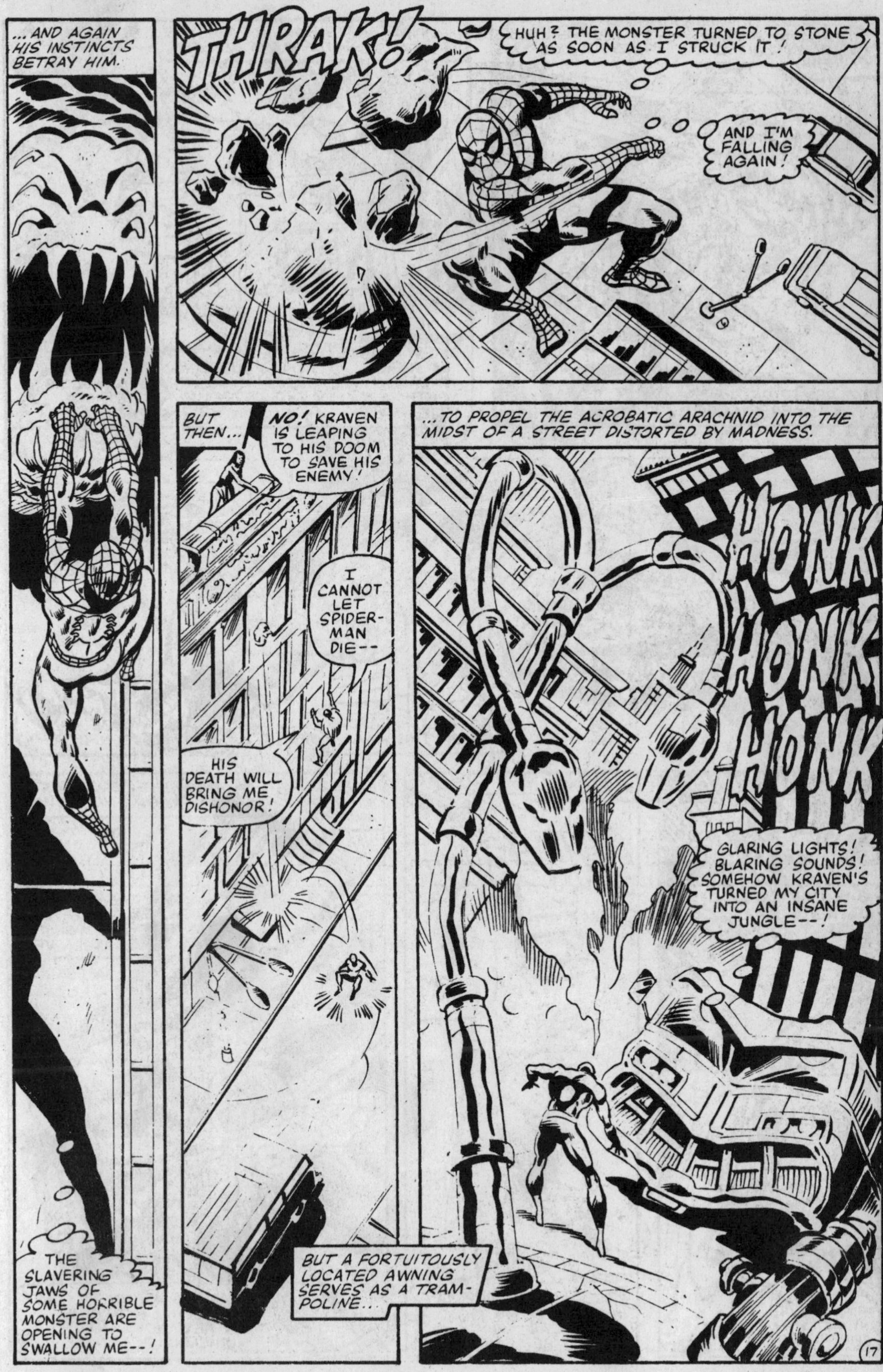
...AND AGAIN HIS INSTINCTS BETRAY HIM.
THE SLAVERING JAWS OF SOME HORRIBLE MONSTER ARE OPENING TO SWALLOW ME--!
THRAK!
HUH? THE MONSTER TURNED TO STONE AS SOON AS I STRUCK IT!
AND I'M FALLING AGAIN!
BUT THEN...
NO! KRAVEN IS LEAPING TO HIS DOOM TO SAVE HIS ENEMY!
I CANNOT LET SPIDER-MAN DIE--
HIS DEATH WILL BRING ME DISHONOR!
BUT A FORTUITOUSLY LOCATED AWNING SERVES AS A TRAMPOLINE...
...TO PROPEL THE ACROBATIC ARACHNID INTO THE MIDST OF A STREET DISTORTED BY MADNESS.
HONK HONK HONK
GLARING LIGHTS! BLARING SOUNDS! SOMEHOW KRAVEN'S TURNED MY CITY INTO AN INSANE JUNGLE--!
17

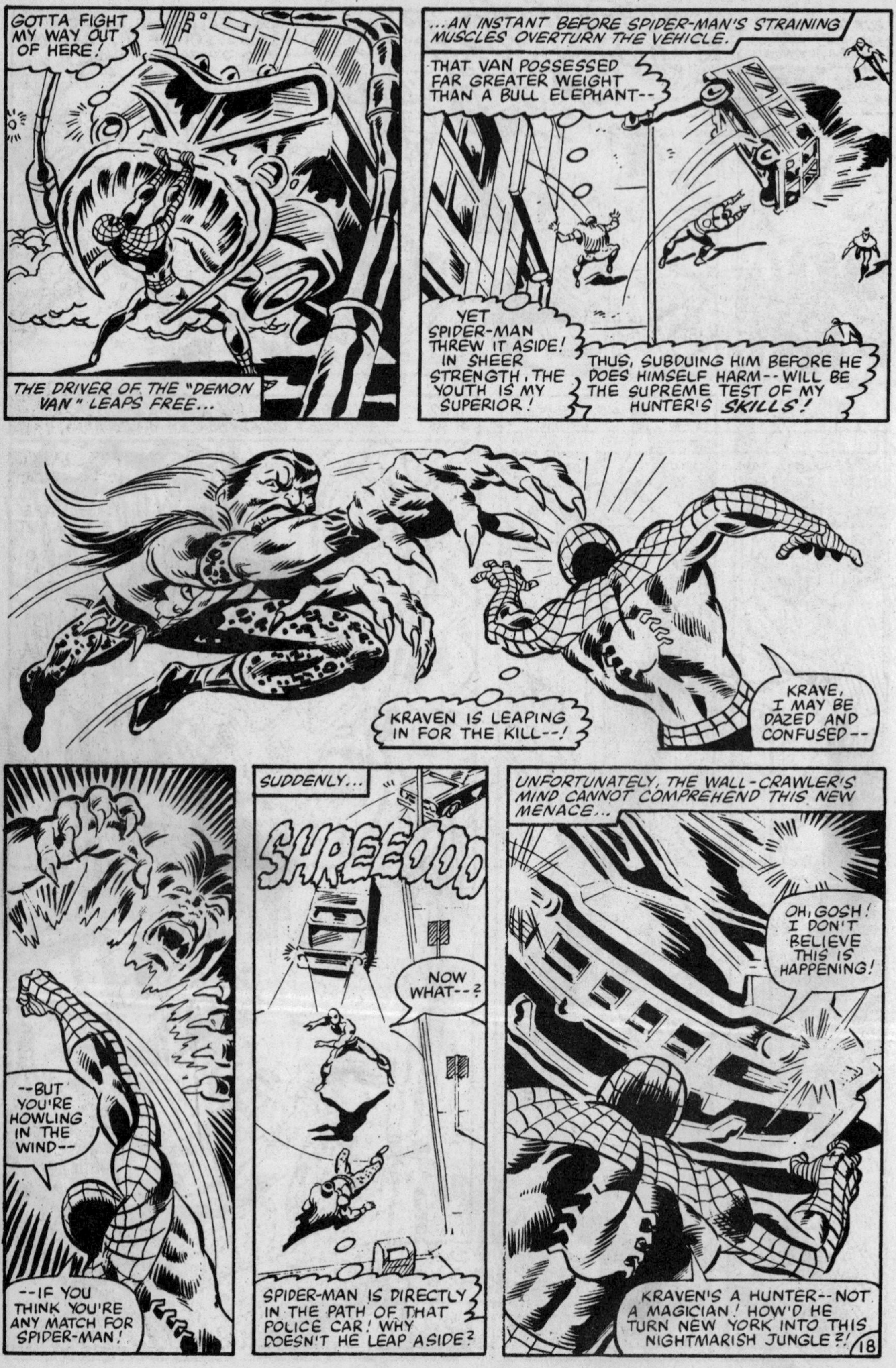
GOTTA FIGHT MY WAY OUT OF HERE!
THE DRIVER OF THE "DEMON VAN" LEAPS FREE...
...AN INSTANT BEFORE SPIDER-MAN'S STRAINING MUSCLES OVERTURN THE VEHICLE.
THAT VAN POSSESSED FAR GREATER WEIGHT THAN A BULL ELEPHANT--
YET SPIDER-MAN THREW IT ASIDE! IN SHEER STRENGTH, THE YOUTH IS MY SUPERIOR!
THUS, SUBDUING HIM BEFORE HE DOES HIMSELF HARM--WILL BE THE SUPREME TEST OF MY HUNTER'S SKILLS!
KRAVEN IS LEAPING IN FOR THE KILL--!
KRAVE, I MAY BE DAZED AND CONFUSED--
--BUT YOU'RE HOWLING IN THE WIND--
--IF YOU THINK YOU'RE ANY MATCH FOR SPIDER-MAN!
SUDDENLY...
SHREEOOO
NOW WHAT--?
SPIDER-MAN IS DIRECTLY IN THE PATH OF THAT POLICE CAR! WHY DOESN'T HE LEAP ASIDE?
UNFORTUNATELY, THE WALL-CRAWLER'S MIND CANNOT COMPREHEND THIS NEW MENACE...
OH, GOSH! I DON'T BELIEVE THIS IS HAPPENING!
KRAVEN'S A HUNTER--NOT A MAGICIAN! HOW'D HE TURN NEW YORK INTO THIS NIGHTMARISH JUNGLE?!
18

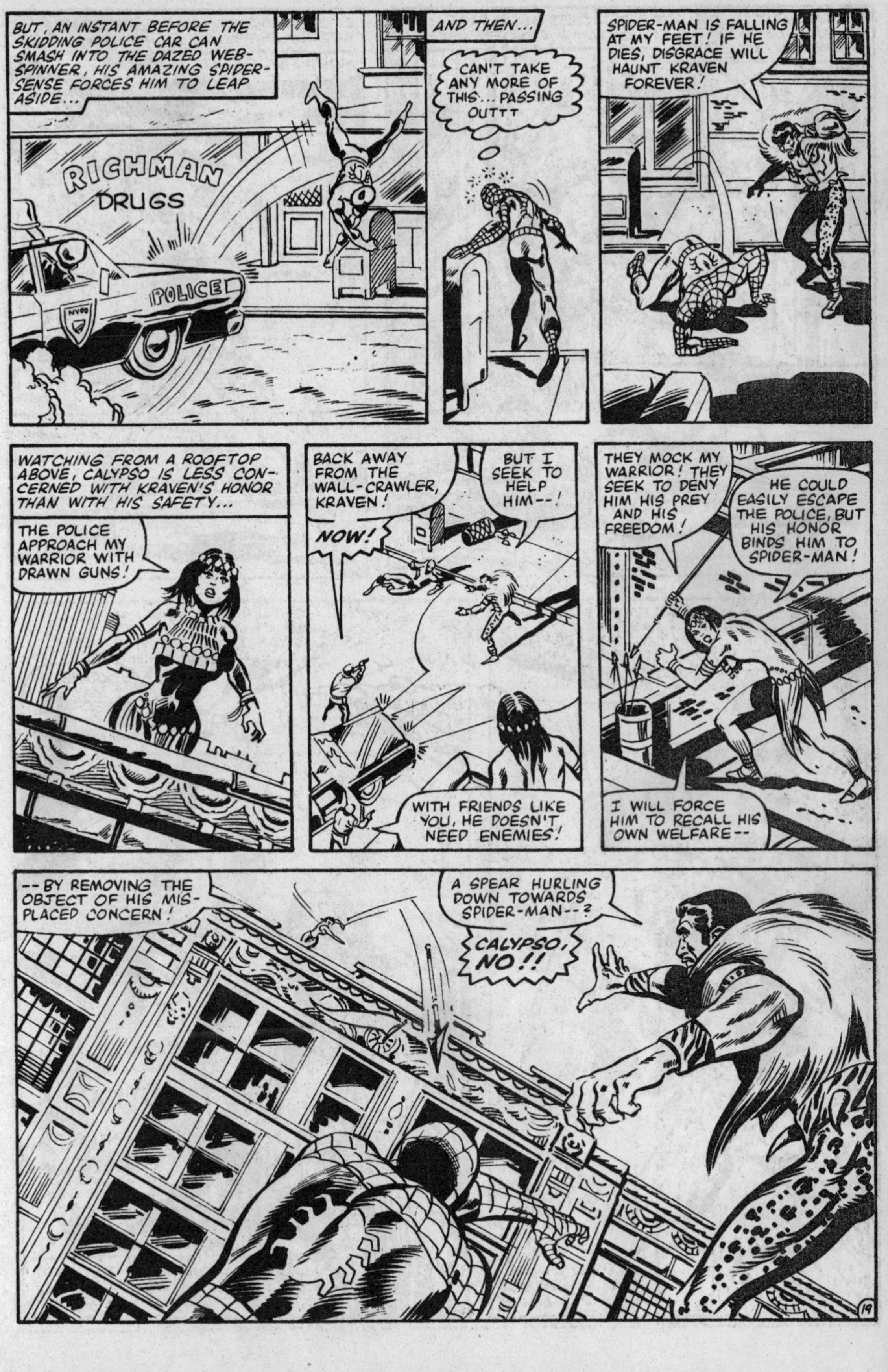

BUT, AN INSTANT BEFORE THE SKIDDING POLICE CAR CAN SMASH INTO THE DAZED WEB-SPINNER, HIS AMAZING SPIDER-SENSE FORCES HIM TO LEAP ASIDE...
RICHMAN DRUGS
POLICE
NYPD
AND THEN...
CAN'T TAKE ANY MORE OF THIS... PASSING OUTTT
SPIDER-MAN IS FALLING AT MY FEET! IF HE DIES, DISGRACE WILL HAUNT KRAVEN FOREVER!
WATCHING FROM A ROOFTOP ABOVE, CALYPSO IS LESS CONCERNED WITH KRAVEN'S HONOR THAN WITH HIS SAFETY...
THE POLICE APPROACH MY WARRIOR WITH DRAWN GUNS!
BACK AWAY FROM THE WALL-CRAWLER, KRAVEN!
BUT I SEEK TO HELP HIM--!
NOW!
WITH FRIENDS LIKE YOU, HE DOESN'T NEED ENEMIES!
THEY MOCK MY WARRIOR! THEY SEEK TO DENY HIM HIS PREY AND HIS FREEDOM!
HE COULD EASILY ESCAPE THE POLICE, BUT HIS HONOR BINDS HIM TO SPIDER-MAN!
I WILL FORCE HIM TO RECALL HIS OWN WELFARE--
--BY REMOVING THE OBJECT OF HIS MISPLACED CONCERN!
A SPEAR HURLING DOWN TOWARDS SPIDER-MAN--?
CALYPSO, NO!!
19

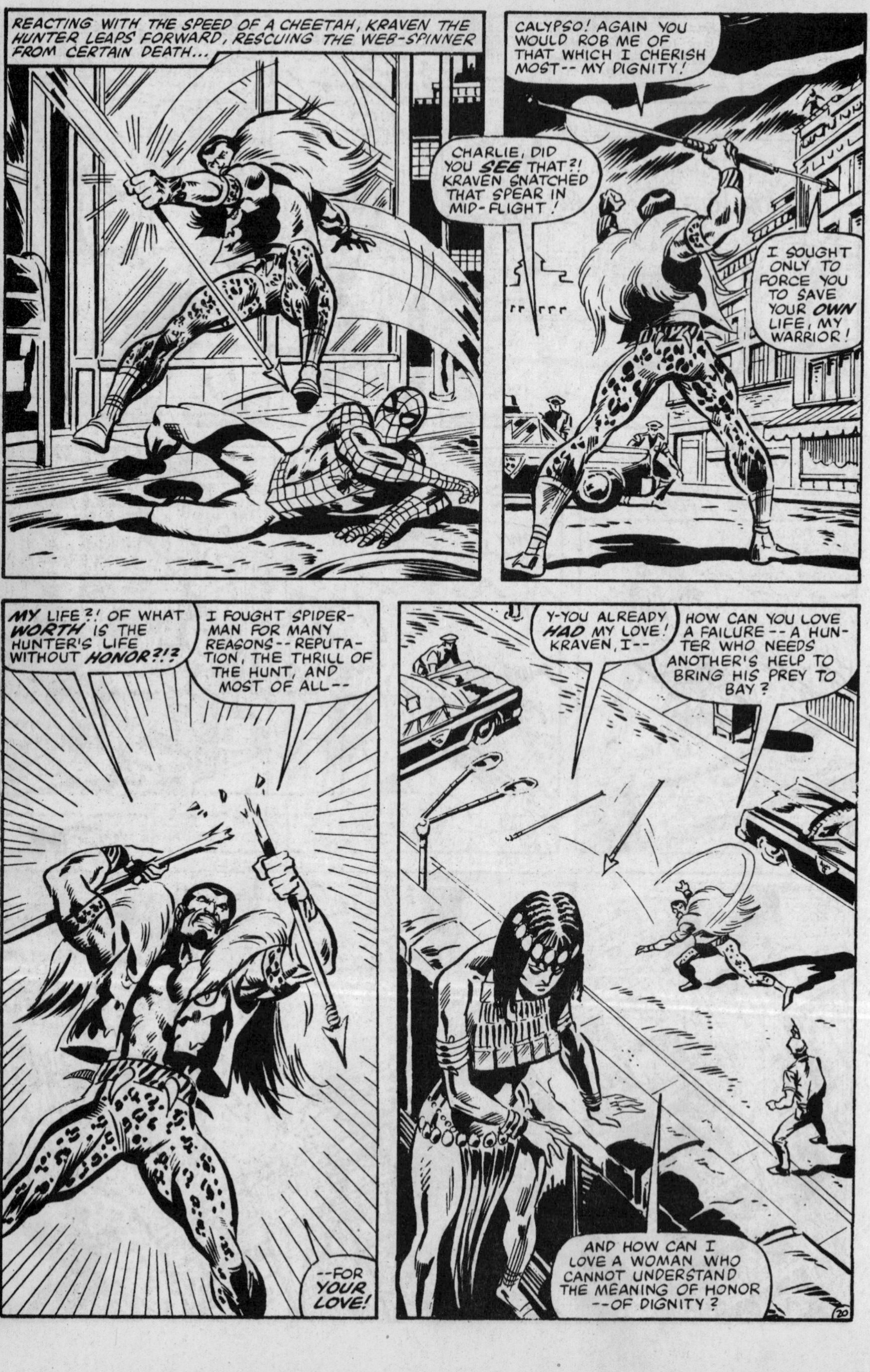
REACTING WITH THE SPEED OF A CHEETAH, KRAVEN THE HUNTER LEAPS FORWARD, RESCUING THE WEB-SPINNER FROM CERTAIN DEATH...
CALYPSO! AGAIN YOU WOULD ROB ME OF THAT WHICH I CHERISH MOST-- MY DIGNITY!
CHARLIE, DID YOU SEE THAT?! KRAVEN SNATCHED THAT SPEAR IN MID-FLIGHT!
I SOUGHT ONLY TO FORCE YOU TO SAVE YOUR OWN LIFE, MY WARRIOR!
MY LIFE?! OF WHAT WORTH IS THE HUNTER'S LIFE WITHOUT HONOR?!?
I FOUGHT SPIDER-MAN FOR MANY REASONS-- REPUTATION, THE THRILL OF THE HUNT, AND MOST OF ALL--
--FOR YOUR LOVE!
Y-YOU ALREADY HAD MY LOVE! KRAVEN, I--
HOW CAN YOU LOVE A FAILURE-- A HUNTER WHO NEEDS ANOTHER'S HELP TO BRING HIS PREY TO BAY?
AND HOW CAN I LOVE A WOMAN WHO CANNOT UNDERSTAND THE MEANING OF HONOR --OF DIGNITY?
20

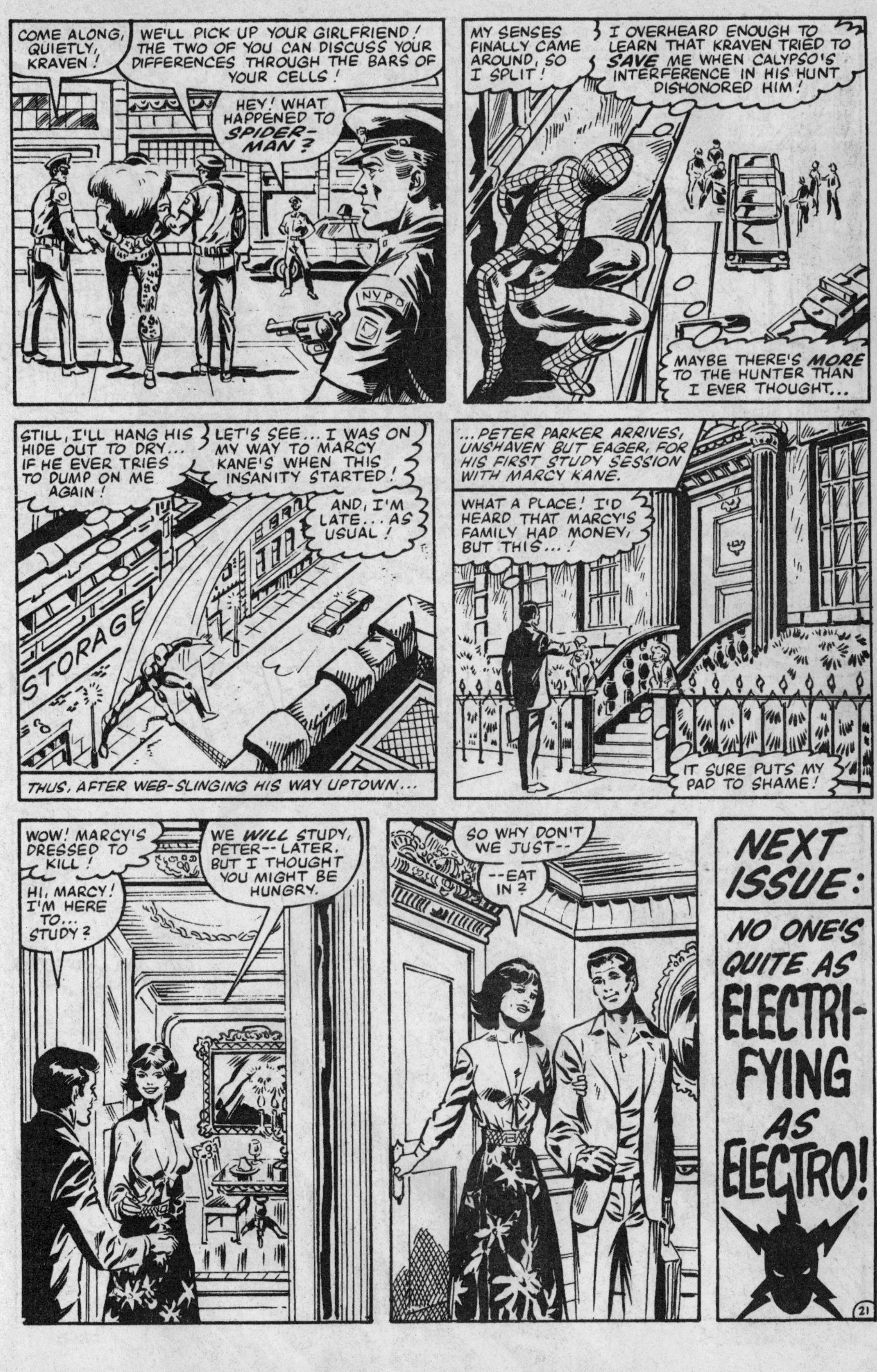
COME ALONG, QUIETLY, KRAVEN!
WE'LL PICK UP YOUR GIRLFRIEND! THE TWO OF YOU CAN DISCUSS YOUR DIFFERENCES THROUGH THE BARS OF YOUR CELLS!
HEY! WHAT HAPPENED TO SPIDER-MAN?
NYPD
MY SENSES FINALLY CAME AROUND, SO I SPLIT!
I OVERHEARD ENOUGH TO LEARN THAT KRAVEN TRIED TO SAVE ME WHEN CALYPSO'S INTERFERENCE IN HIS HUNT DISHONORED HIM!
MAYBE THERE'S MORE TO THE HUNTER THAN I EVER THOUGHT...
STILL, I'LL HANG HIS HIDE OUT TO DRY... IF HE EVER TRIES TO DUMP ON ME AGAIN!
LET'S SEE... I WAS ON MY WAY TO MARCY KANE'S WHEN THIS INSANITY STARTED!
AND, I'M LATE... AS USUAL!
STORAGE
THUS, AFTER WEB-SLINGING HIS WAY UPTOWN...
...PETER PARKER ARRIVES, UNSHAVEN BUT EAGER, FOR HIS FIRST STUDY SESSION WITH MARCY KANE.
WHAT A PLACE! I'D HEARD THAT MARCY'S FAMILY HAD MONEY, BUT THIS...!
IT SURE PUTS MY PAD TO SHAME!
WOW! MARCY'S DRESSED TO KILL!
HI, MARCY! I'M HERE TO... STUDY?
WE WILL STUDY, PETER--LATER. BUT I THOUGHT YOU MIGHT BE HUNGRY.
SO WHY DON'T WE JUST--
--EAT IN?
NEXT ISSUE:
NO ONE'S QUITE AS ELECTRI-FYING AS ELECTRO!
21

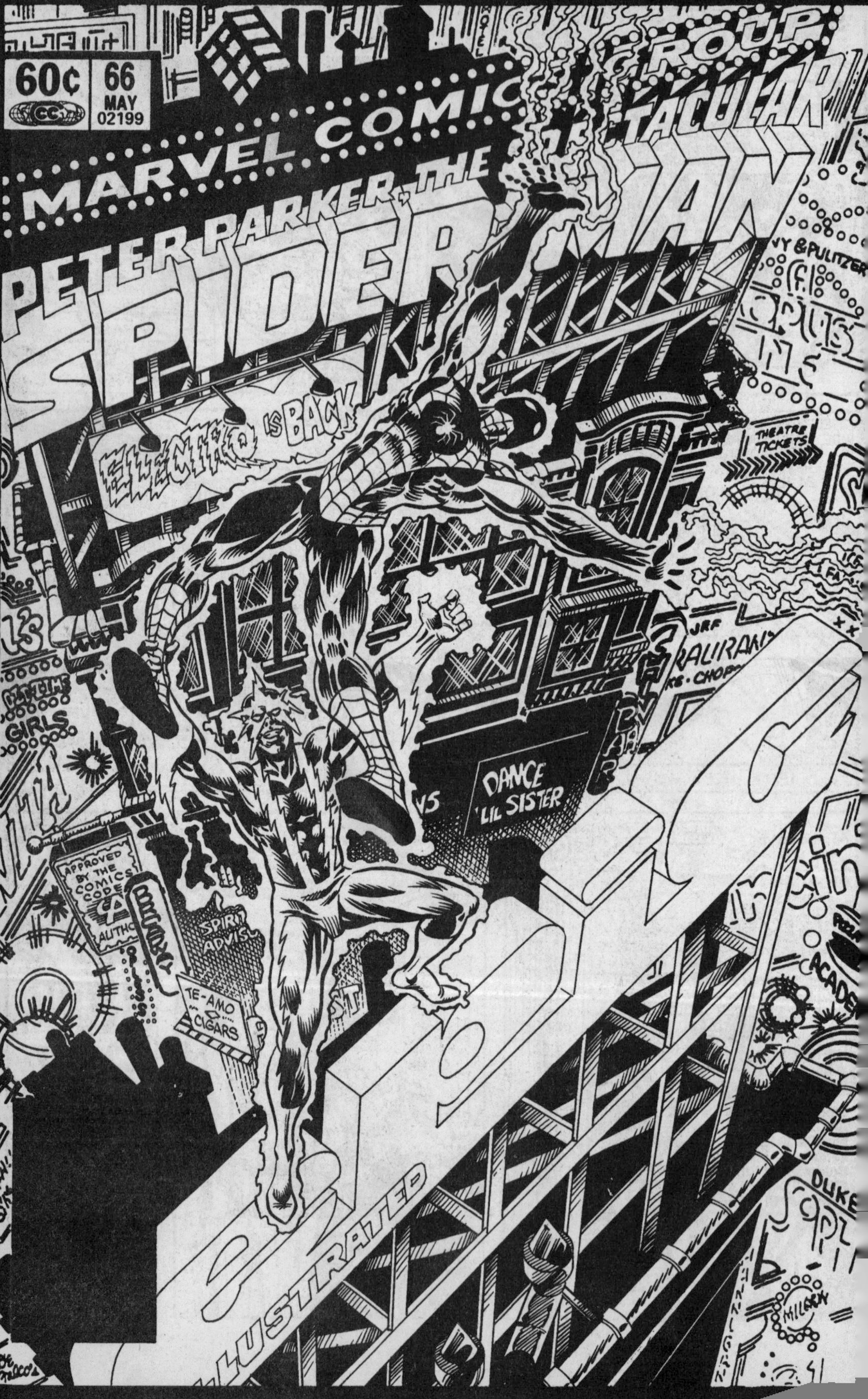

60¢
66
MAY
02199
MARVEL COMIC GROUP
PETER PARKER, THE SPECTACULAR
SPIDER-MAN
ELECTRO IS BACK
THEATRE TICKETS
DANCE 'LIL SISTER
GIRLS
APPROVED BY THE COMICS CODE
TE-AMO CIGARS
ILLUSTRATED

STan Lee PRESENTS: THE SPECTACULAR SPIDER-MAN!®

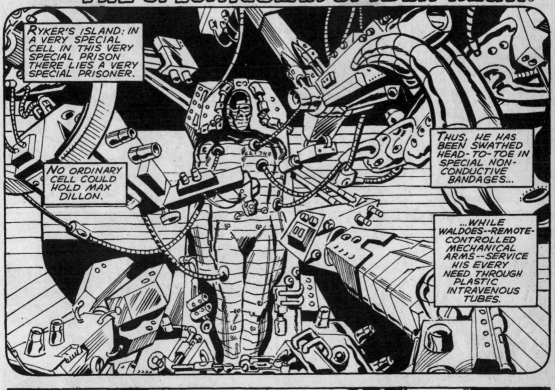

RYKER'S ISLAND: IN A VERY SPECIAL CELL IN THIS VERY SPECIAL PRISON THERE LIES A VERY SPECIAL PRISONER.

NO ORDINARY CELL COULD HOLD MAX DILLON.

THUS, HE HAS BEEN SWATHED HEAD-TO-TOE IN SPECIAL NON-CONDUCTIVE BANDAGES...

...WHILE WALDOES—REMOTE-CONTROLLED MECHANICAL ARMS—SERVICE HIS EVERY NEED THROUGH PLASTIC INTRAVENOUS TUBES.

MAX DILLON IS NOT GREATLY ENAMORED OF THE SITUATION.

IF LOOKS COULD KILL, WE'D BE COLD MEAT!

WE'RE LUCKY THAT DILLON'S AS HELPLESS AS A NEWBORN BABE!

DON'T LET OUR MUMMY RATTLE YOU, GEORGE!

BABYSITTING THIS TEN-TIME LOSER IS A PIECE OF CAKE!

Story: BILL MANTLO
Art: ED HANNIGAN and JIM MOONEY
Letters: DIANA ALBERS
Colors: BOB SHAREN
Editor: TOM DeFALCO
Chief: JIM SHOOTER

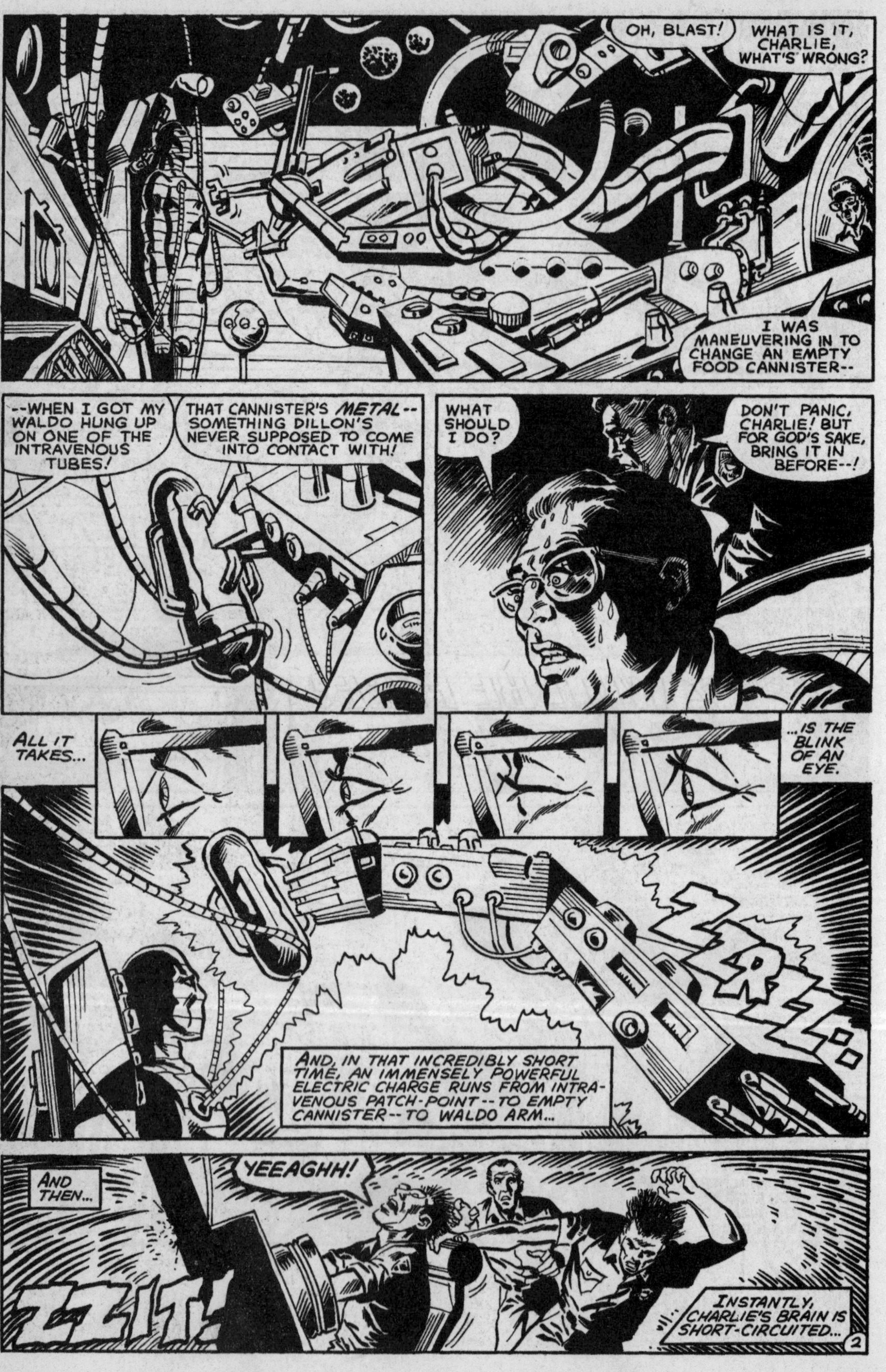
OH, BLAST!
WHAT IS IT, CHARLIE, WHAT'S WRONG?
I WAS MANEUVERING IN TO CHANGE AN EMPTY FOOD CANNISTER--
--WHEN I GOT MY WALDO HUNG UP ON ONE OF THE INTRAVENOUS TUBES!
THAT CANNISTER'S METAL-- SOMETHING DILLON'S NEVER SUPPOSED TO COME INTO CONTACT WITH!
WHAT SHOULD I DO?
DON'T PANIC, CHARLIE! BUT FOR GOD'S SAKE, BRING IT IN BEFORE--!
ALL IT TAKES...
...IS THE BLINK OF AN EYE.
ZRRZZ
AND, IN THAT INCREDIBLY SHORT TIME, AN IMMENSELY POWERFUL ELECTRIC CHARGE RUNS FROM INTRAVENOUS PATCH-POINT--TO EMPTY CANNISTER--TO WALDO ARM...
AND THEN...
YEEAGHH!
ZZIT!
INSTANTLY, CHARLIE'S BRAIN IS SHORT-CIRCUITED...
2

WWHHHHUURRRRRRG RRR

...AS ANOTHER, STRONGER WILL TAKES ELECTRICAL CONTROL OVER THE MECHANICAL SERVO-ARMS.

THIS HAS BEEN THE BREAK THAT MAX DILLON HAS PATIENTLY BIDED HIS TIME FOR THESE LONG MONTHS PAST. HE INTENDS TO MAKE THE MOST OF IT.

AT LAST! I CAN USE THE WALDOES TO TEAR AWAY MY BANDAGES, AND--

RRRRIIII PPPPP !!!!

-- ELECTRO WILL BE FREE!

WITHIN SECONDS, SHRILL ALARMS ROUSE THE AUTHORITIES IN CHARGE OF THIS VERY SPECIAL PRISON.

HURRY! BREAKOUT IN E-SECTION!

ELECTRO!

3

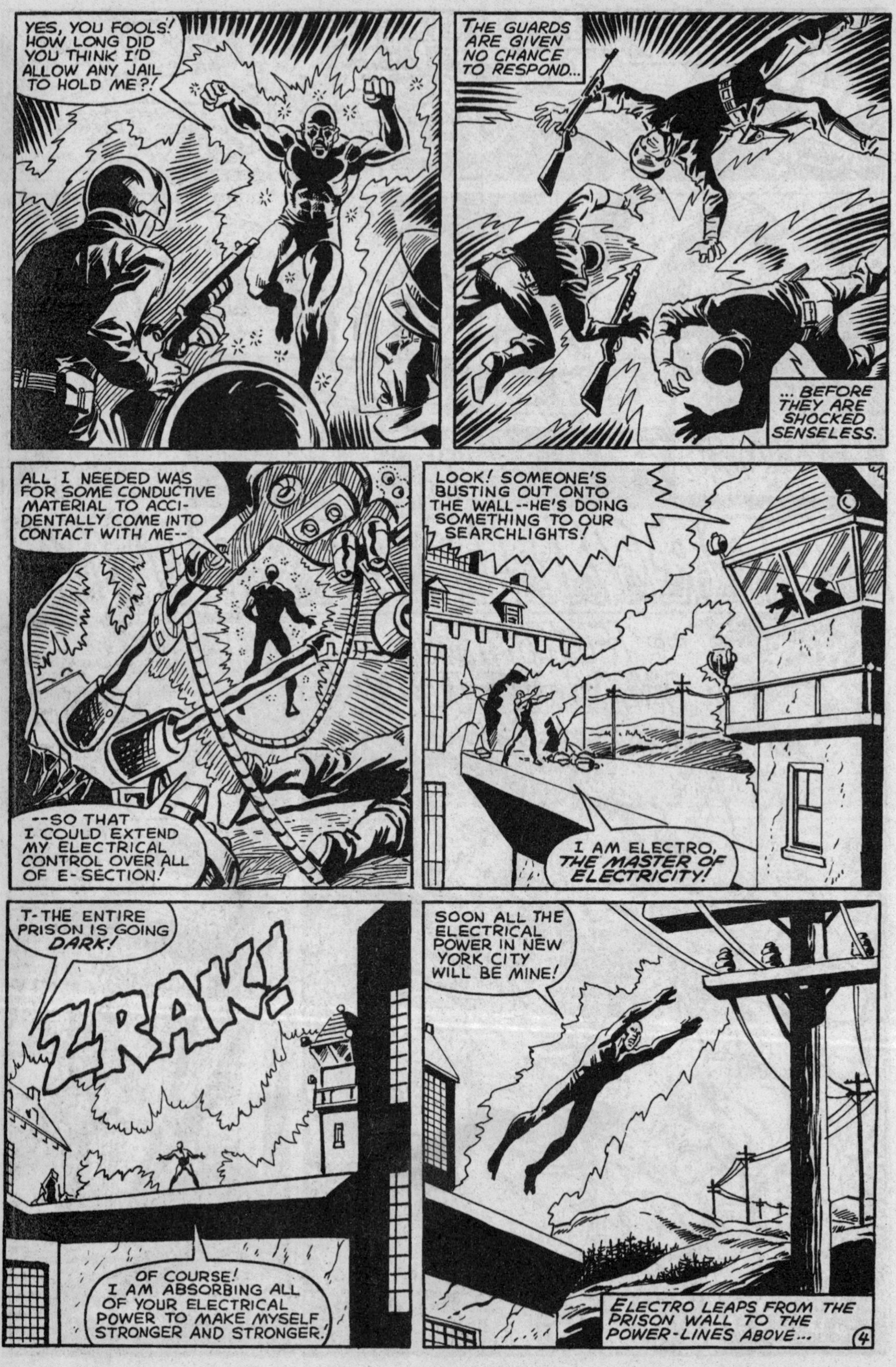

YES, YOU FOOLS! HOW LONG DID YOU THINK I'D ALLOW ANY JAIL TO HOLD ME?!
THE GUARDS ARE GIVEN NO CHANCE TO RESPOND...
... BEFORE THEY ARE SHOCKED SENSELESS.
ALL I NEEDED WAS FOR SOME CONDUCTIVE MATERIAL TO ACCIDENTALLY COME INTO CONTACT WITH ME--
--SO THAT I COULD EXTEND MY ELECTRICAL CONTROL OVER ALL OF E-SECTION!
LOOK! SOMEONE'S BUSTING OUT ONTO THE WALL--HE'S DOING SOMETHING TO OUR SEARCHLIGHTS!
I AM ELECTRO, THE MASTER OF ELECTRICITY!
T-THE ENTIRE PRISON IS GOING DARK!
ZRAK!
OF COURSE! I AM ABSORBING ALL OF YOUR ELECTRICAL POWER TO MAKE MYSELF STRONGER AND STRONGER.
SOON ALL THE ELECTRICAL POWER IN NEW YORK CITY WILL BE MINE!
ELECTRO LEAPS FROM THE PRISON WALL TO THE POWER-LINES ABOVE...
4

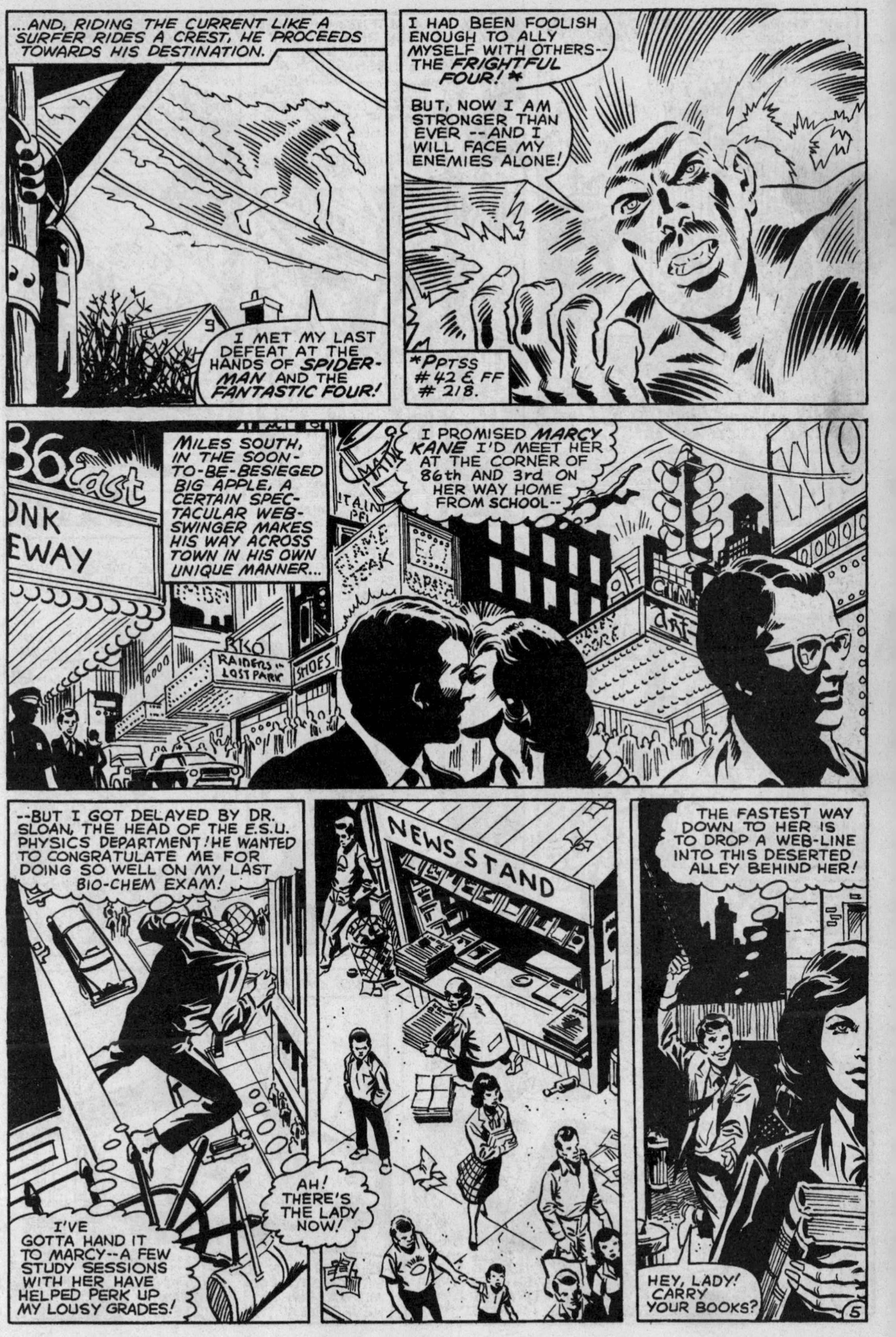
...AND, RIDING THE CURRENT LIKE A SURFER RIDES A CREST, HE PROCEEDS TOWARDS HIS DESTINATION.
I MET MY LAST DEFEAT AT THE HANDS OF SPIDER-MAN AND THE FANTASTIC FOUR!
I HAD BEEN FOOLISH ENOUGH TO ALLY MYSELF WITH OTHERS-- THE FRIGHTFUL FOUR! *
BUT, NOW I AM STRONGER THAN EVER --AND I WILL FACE MY ENEMIES ALONE!
*PPTSS #42 & FF #218.
MILES SOUTH, IN THE SOON-TO-BE-BESIEGED BIG APPLE, A CERTAIN SPECTACULAR WEB-SWINGER MAKES HIS WAY ACROSS TOWN IN HIS OWN UNIQUE MANNER...
I PROMISED MARCY KANE I'D MEET HER AT THE CORNER OF 86th AND 3rd ON HER WAY HOME FROM SCHOOL--
86 East
RAIDERS LOST PARK
SHOES
--BUT I GOT DELAYED BY DR. SLOAN, THE HEAD OF THE E.S.U. PHYSICS DEPARTMENT! HE WANTED TO CONGRATULATE ME FOR DOING SO WELL ON MY LAST BIO-CHEM EXAM!
I'VE GOTTA HAND IT TO MARCY--A FEW STUDY SESSIONS WITH HER HAVE HELPED PERK UP MY LOUSY GRADES!
NEWS STAND
AH! THERE'S THE LADY NOW!
THE FASTEST WAY DOWN TO HER IS TO DROP A WEB-LINE INTO THIS DESERTED ALLEY BEHIND HER!
HEY, LADY! CARRY YOUR BOOKS?
5

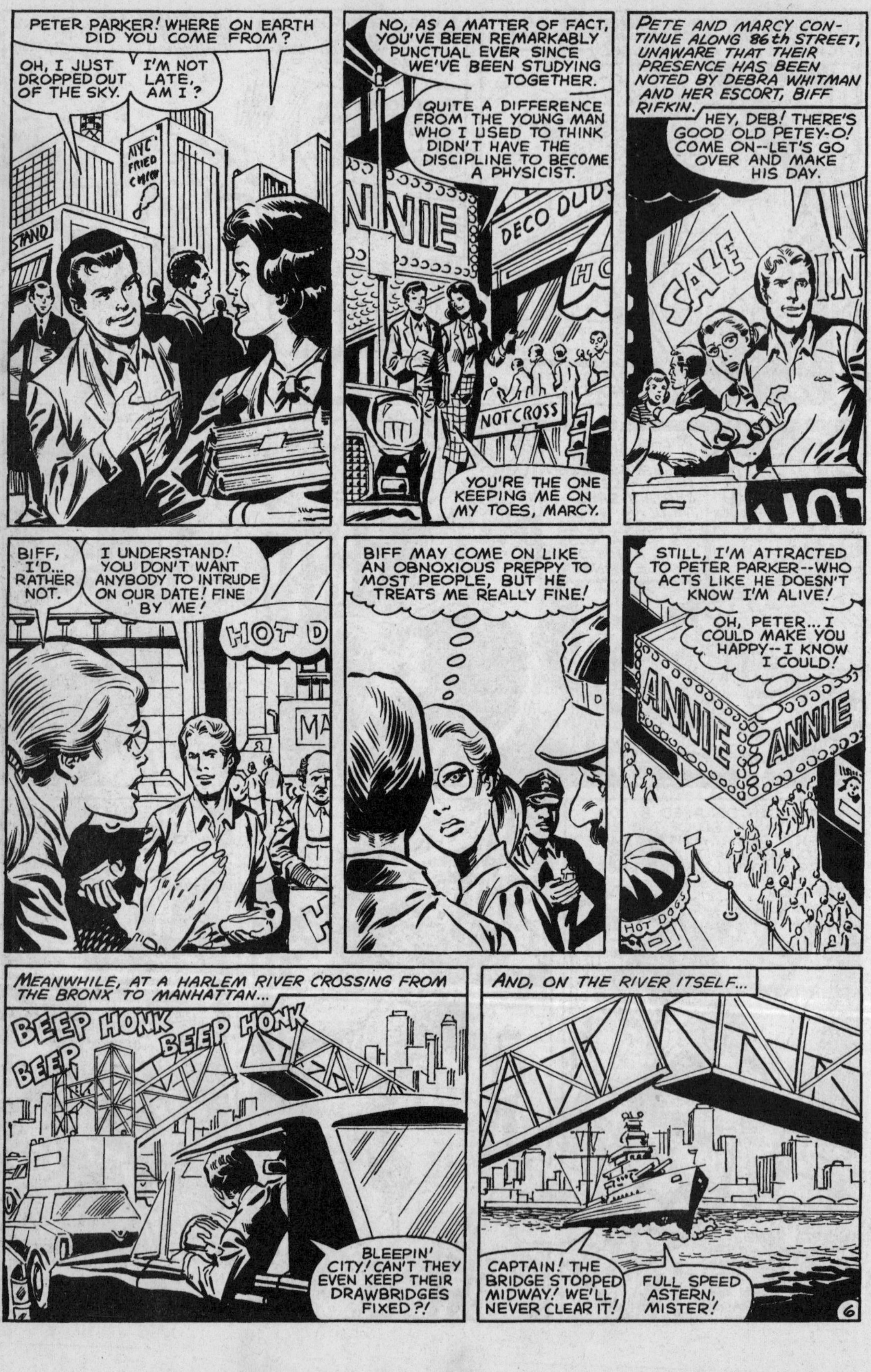
PETER PARKER! WHERE ON EARTH DID YOU COME FROM?
OH, I JUST DROPPED OUT OF THE SKY.
I'M NOT LATE, AM I?
NO, AS A MATTER OF FACT, YOU'VE BEEN REMARKABLY PUNCTUAL EVER SINCE WE'VE BEEN STUDYING TOGETHER.
QUITE A DIFFERENCE FROM THE YOUNG MAN WHO I USED TO THINK DIDN'T HAVE THE DISCIPLINE TO BECOME A PHYSICIST.
YOU'RE THE ONE KEEPING ME ON MY TOES, MARCY.
PETE AND MARCY CONTINUE ALONG 86th STREET, UNAWARE THAT THEIR PRESENCE HAS BEEN NOTED BY DEBRA WHITMAN AND HER ESCORT, BIFF RIFKIN.
HEY, DEB! THERE'S GOOD OLD PETEY-O! COME ON--LET'S GO OVER AND MAKE HIS DAY.
BIFF, I'D... RATHER NOT.
I UNDERSTAND! YOU DON'T WANT ANYBODY TO INTRUDE ON OUR DATE! FINE BY ME!
BIFF MAY COME ON LIKE AN OBNOXIOUS PREPPY TO MOST PEOPLE, BUT HE TREATS ME REALLY FINE!
STILL, I'M ATTRACTED TO PETER PARKER--WHO ACTS LIKE HE DOESN'T KNOW I'M ALIVE!
OH, PETER... I COULD MAKE YOU HAPPY--I KNOW I COULD!
MEANWHILE, AT A HARLEM RIVER CROSSING FROM THE BRONX TO MANHATTAN...
BEEP HONK BEEP BEEP HONK
BLEEPIN' CITY! CAN'T THEY EVEN KEEP THEIR DRAWBRIDGES FIXED?!
AND, ON THE RIVER ITSELF...
CAPTAIN! THE BRIDGE STOPPED MIDWAY! WE'LL NEVER CLEAR IT!
FULL SPEED ASTERN, MISTER!

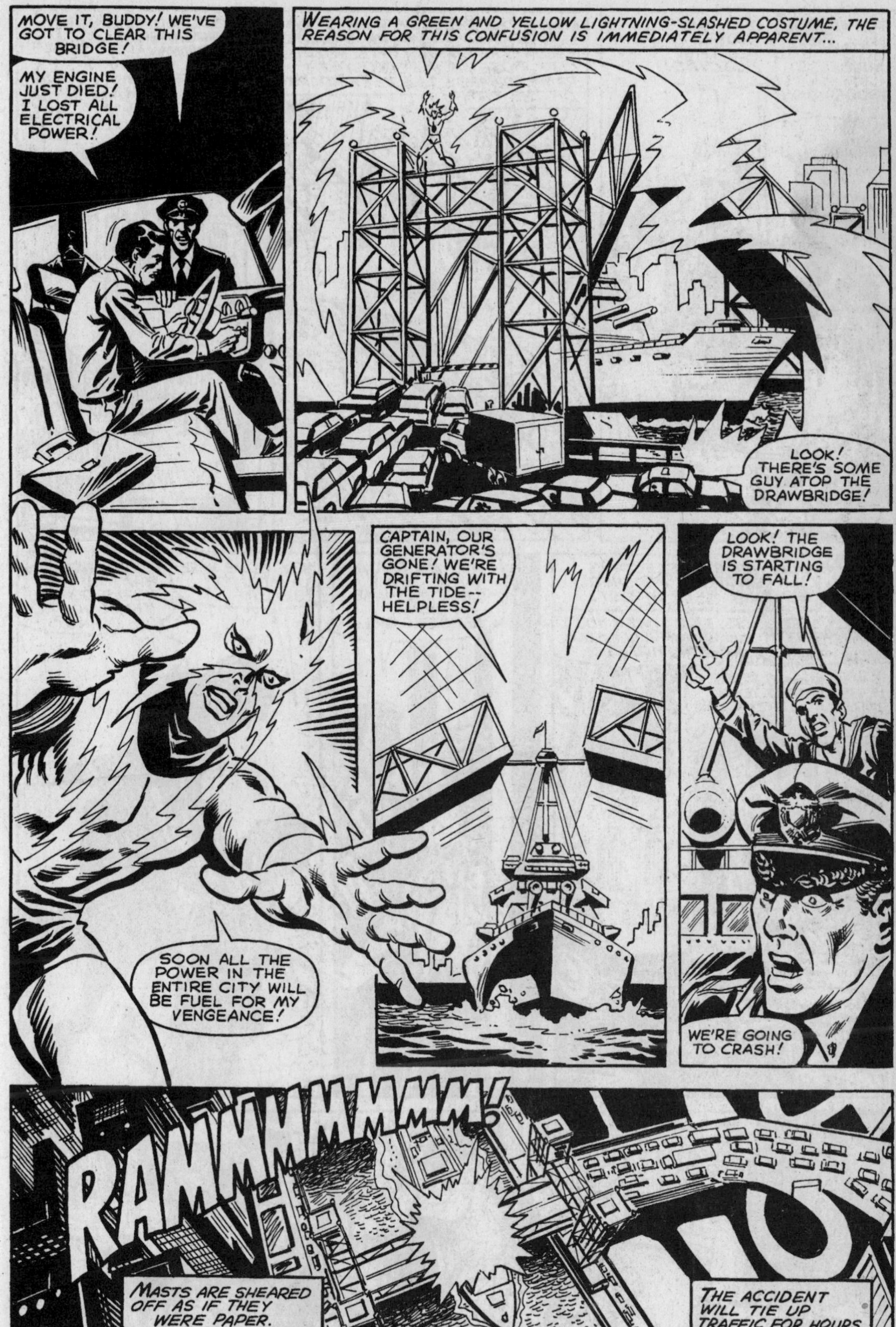
MOVE IT, BUDDY! WE'VE GOT TO CLEAR THIS BRIDGE!
MY ENGINE JUST DIED! I LOST ALL ELECTRICAL POWER!
WEARING A GREEN AND YELLOW LIGHTNING-SLASHED COSTUME, THE REASON FOR THIS CONFUSION IS IMMEDIATELY APPARENT...
LOOK! THERE'S SOME GUY ATOP THE DRAWBRIDGE!
SOON ALL THE POWER IN THE ENTIRE CITY WILL BE FUEL FOR MY VENGEANCE!
CAPTAIN, OUR GENERATOR'S GONE! WE'RE DRIFTING WITH THE TIDE-- HELPLESS!
LOOK! THE DRAWBRIDGE IS STARTING TO FALL!
WE'RE GOING TO CRASH!
RAMMMMMMMM!
MASTS ARE SHEARED OFF AS IF THEY WERE PAPER.
THE ACCIDENT WILL TIE UP TRAFFIC FOR HOURS.

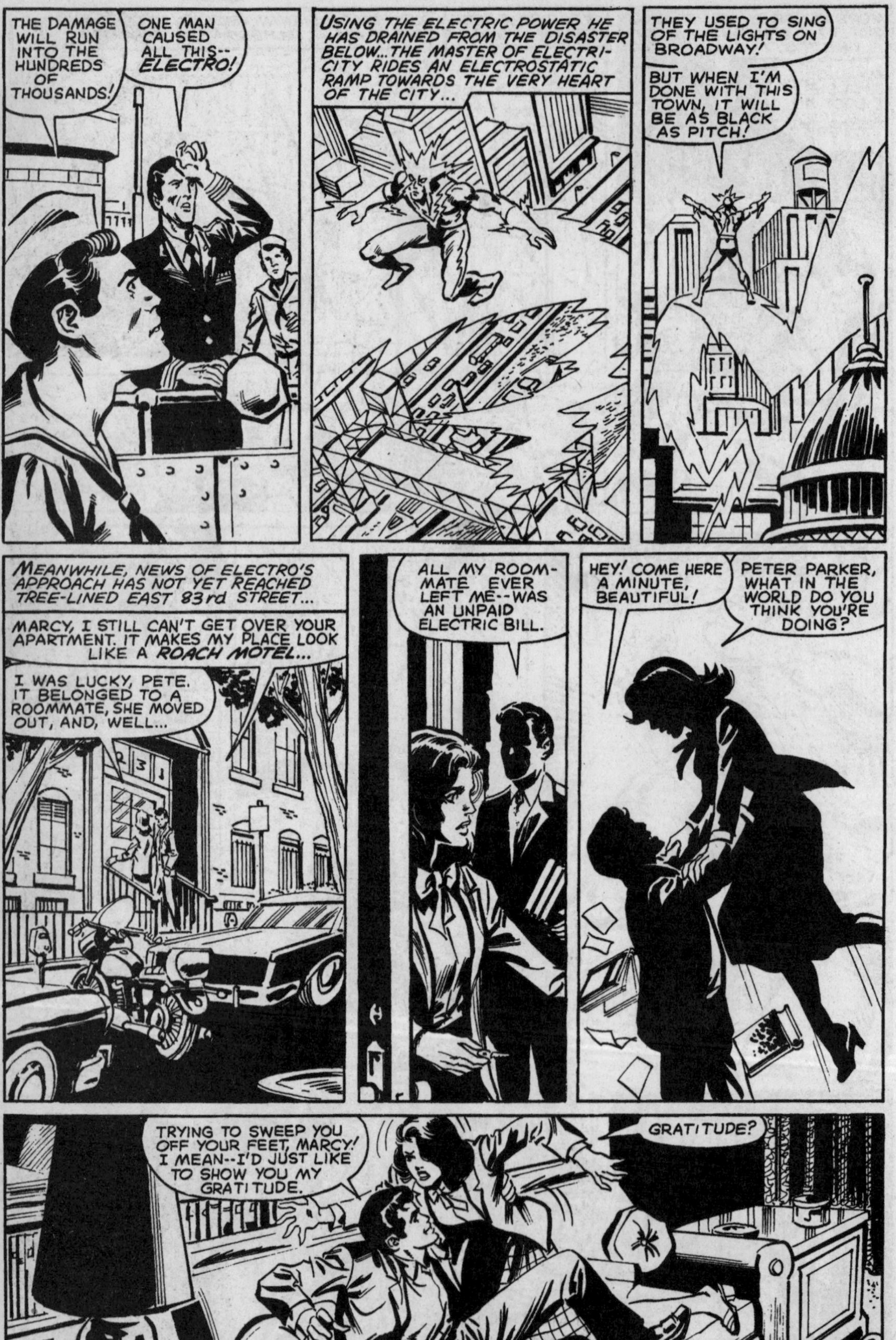
THE DAMAGE WILL RUN INTO THE HUNDREDS OF THOUSANDS!
ONE MAN CAUSED ALL THIS-- ELECTRO!
USING THE ELECTRIC POWER HE HAS DRAINED FROM THE DISASTER BELOW...THE MASTER OF ELECTRICITY RIDES AN ELECTROSTATIC RAMP TOWARDS THE VERY HEART OF THE CITY...
THEY USED TO SING OF THE LIGHTS ON BROADWAY!
BUT WHEN I'M DONE WITH THIS TOWN, IT WILL BE AS BLACK AS PITCH!
MEANWHILE, NEWS OF ELECTRO'S APPROACH HAS NOT YET REACHED TREE-LINED EAST 83rd STREET...
MARCY, I STILL CAN'T GET OVER YOUR APARTMENT. IT MAKES MY PLACE LOOK LIKE A ROACH MOTEL...
I WAS LUCKY, PETE. IT BELONGED TO A ROOMMATE, SHE MOVED OUT, AND, WELL...
ALL MY ROOMMATE EVER LEFT ME--WAS AN UNPAID ELECTRIC BILL.
HEY! COME HERE A MINUTE, BEAUTIFUL!
PETER PARKER, WHAT IN THE WORLD DO YOU THINK YOU'RE DOING?
TRYING TO SWEEP YOU OFF YOUR FEET, MARCY! I MEAN--I'D JUST LIKE TO SHOW YOU MY GRATITUDE.
GRATITUDE?
8

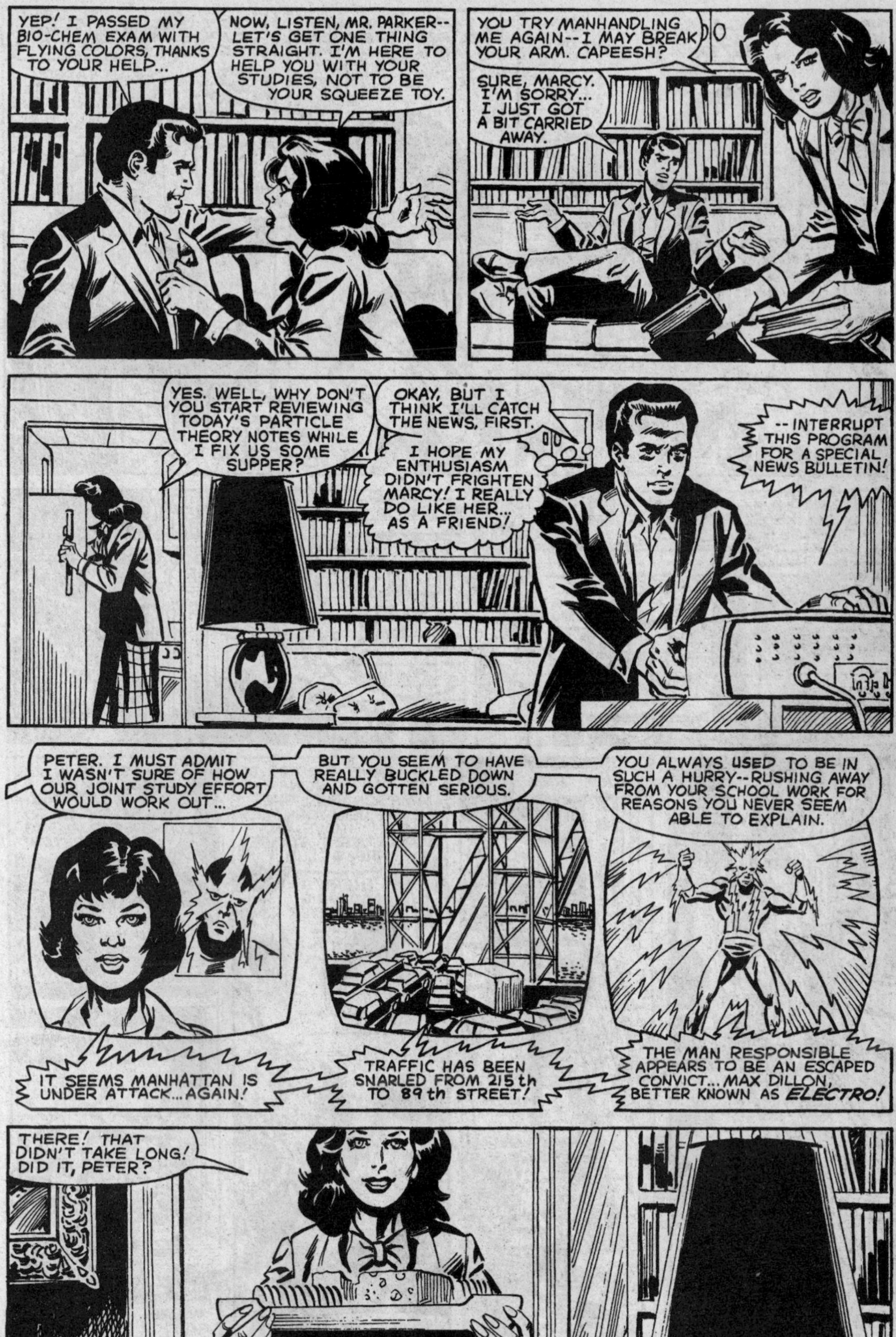
YEP! I PASSED MY BIO-CHEM EXAM WITH FLYING COLORS, THANKS TO YOUR HELP...
NOW, LISTEN, MR. PARKER-- LET'S GET ONE THING STRAIGHT. I'M HERE TO HELP YOU WITH YOUR STUDIES, NOT TO BE YOUR SQUEEZE TOY.
YOU TRY MANHANDLING ME AGAIN--I MAY BREAK YOUR ARM. CAPEESH?
SURE, MARCY. I'M SORRY... I JUST GOT A BIT CARRIED AWAY.
YES. WELL, WHY DON'T YOU START REVIEWING TODAY'S PARTICLE THEORY NOTES WHILE I FIX US SOME SUPPER?
OKAY, BUT I THINK I'LL CATCH THE NEWS, FIRST.
I HOPE MY ENTHUSIASM DIDN'T FRIGHTEN MARCY! I REALLY DO LIKE HER... AS A FRIEND!
--INTERRUPT THIS PROGRAM FOR A SPECIAL NEWS BULLETIN!
PETER. I MUST ADMIT I WASN'T SURE OF HOW OUR JOINT STUDY EFFORT WOULD WORK OUT...
BUT YOU SEEM TO HAVE REALLY BUCKLED DOWN AND GOTTEN SERIOUS.
YOU ALWAYS USED TO BE IN SUCH A HURRY--RUSHING AWAY FROM YOUR SCHOOL WORK FOR REASONS YOU NEVER SEEM ABLE TO EXPLAIN.
IT SEEMS MANHATTAN IS UNDER ATTACK...AGAIN!
TRAFFIC HAS BEEN SNARLED FROM 215th TO 89th STREET!
THE MAN RESPONSIBLE APPEARS TO BE AN ESCAPED CONVICT... MAX DILLON, BETTER KNOWN AS ELECTRO!
THERE! THAT DIDN'T TAKE LONG! DID IT, PETER?
9

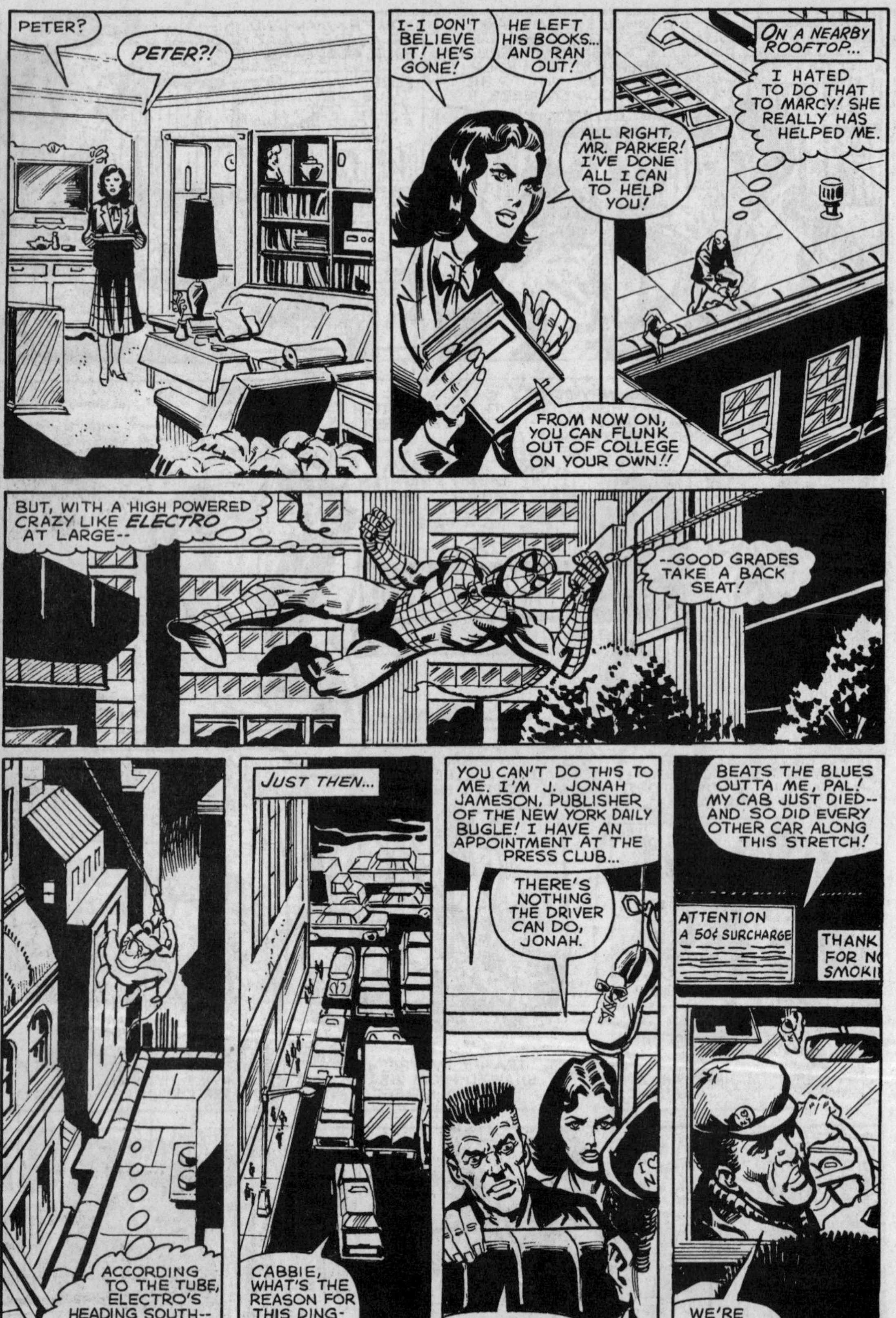
PETER?
PETER?!
I-I DON'T BELIEVE IT! HE'S GONE!
HE LEFT HIS BOOKS... AND RAN OUT!
ALL RIGHT, MR. PARKER! I'VE DONE ALL I CAN TO HELP YOU!
FROM NOW ON, YOU CAN FLUNK OUT OF COLLEGE ON YOUR OWN!!
ON A NEARBY ROOFTOP...
I HATED TO DO THAT TO MARCY! SHE REALLY HAS HELPED ME.
BUT, WITH A HIGH POWERED CRAZY LIKE ELECTRO AT LARGE--
--GOOD GRADES TAKE A BACK SEAT!
ACCORDING TO THE TUBE, ELECTRO'S HEADING SOUTH--STOPPING TRAFFIC ALONG THE WAY!
JUST THEN...
CABBIE, WHAT'S THE REASON FOR THIS DING-BLASTED DELAY?!
YOU CAN'T DO THIS TO ME. I'M J. JONAH JAMESON, PUBLISHER OF THE NEW YORK DAILY BUGLE! I HAVE AN APPOINTMENT AT THE PRESS CLUB...
THERE'S NOTHING THE DRIVER CAN DO, JONAH.
OF ALL THE INCOMPETENT--!
BEATS THE BLUES OUTTA ME, PAL! MY CAB JUST DIED--AND SO DID EVERY OTHER CAR ALONG THIS STRETCH!
ATTENTION
A 50¢ SURCHARGE
THANK
FOR NO
SMOKI
WE'RE STUCK BUT GOOD!
10

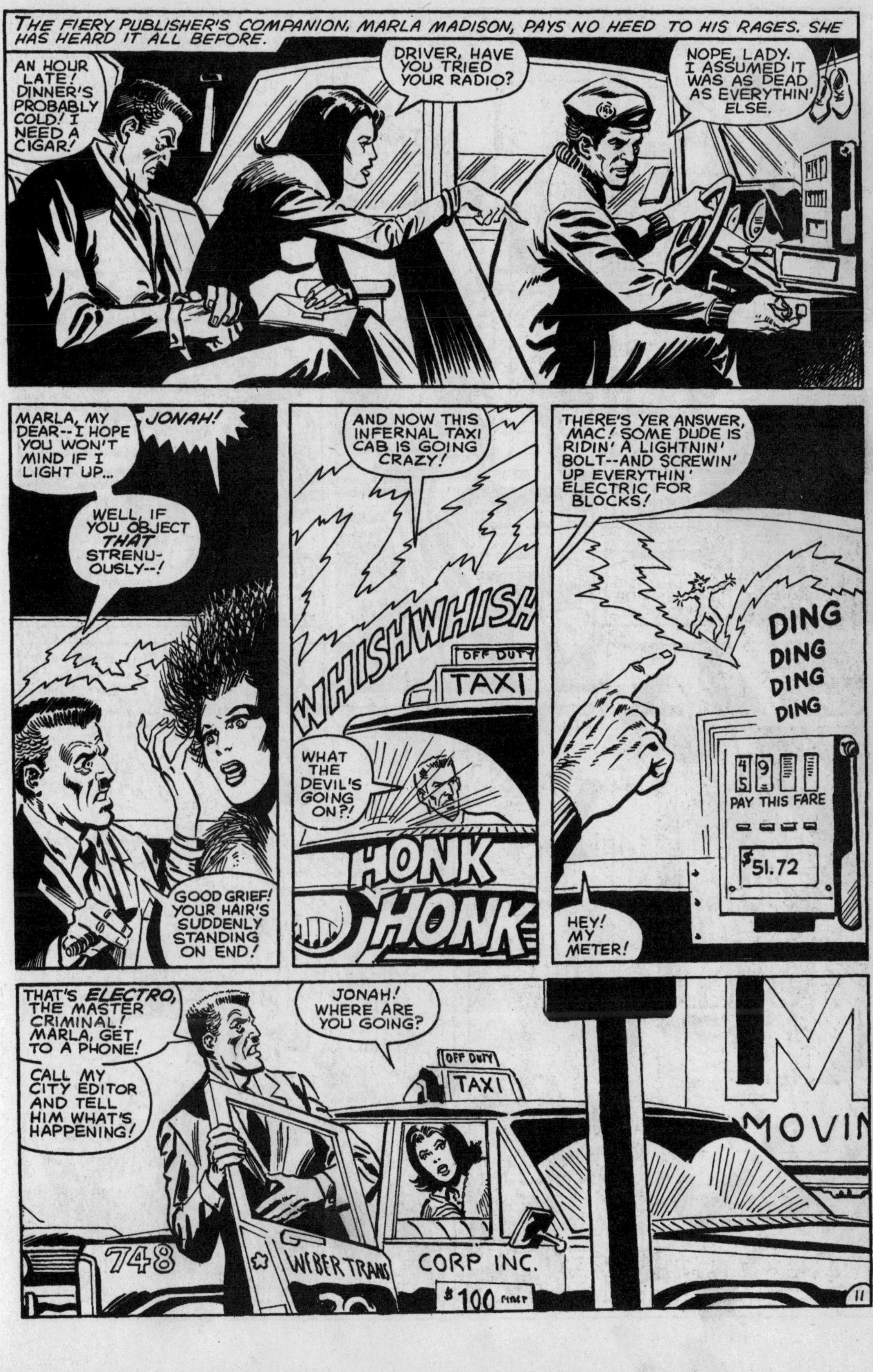
THE FIERY PUBLISHER'S COMPANION, MARLA MADISON, PAYS NO HEED TO HIS RAGES. SHE HAS HEARD IT ALL BEFORE.
AN HOUR LATE! DINNER'S PROBABLY COLD! I NEED A CIGAR!
DRIVER, HAVE YOU TRIED YOUR RADIO?
NOPE, LADY. I ASSUMED IT WAS AS DEAD AS EVERYTHIN' ELSE.
MARLA, MY DEAR-- I HOPE YOU WON'T MIND IF I LIGHT UP...
JONAH!
WELL, IF YOU OBJECT THAT STRENUOUSLY--!
GOOD GRIEF! YOUR HAIR'S SUDDENLY STANDING ON END!
AND NOW THIS INFERNAL TAXI CAB IS GOING CRAZY!
WHISHWHISH
OFF DUTY
TAXI
WHAT THE DEVIL'S GOING ON?!
HONK
HONK
THERE'S YER ANSWER, MAC! SOME DUDE IS RIDIN' A LIGHTNIN' BOLT--AND SCREWIN' UP EVERYTHIN' ELECTRIC FOR BLOCKS!
DING DING DING DING
PAY THIS FARE
$51.72
HEY! MY METER!
THAT'S ELECTRO, THE MASTER CRIMINAL! MARLA, GET TO A PHONE!
CALL MY CITY EDITOR AND TELL HIM WHAT'S HAPPENING!
JONAH! WHERE ARE YOU GOING?
OFF DUTY
TAXI
MOVIN
748
WEBER TRANS
CORP INC.
$100

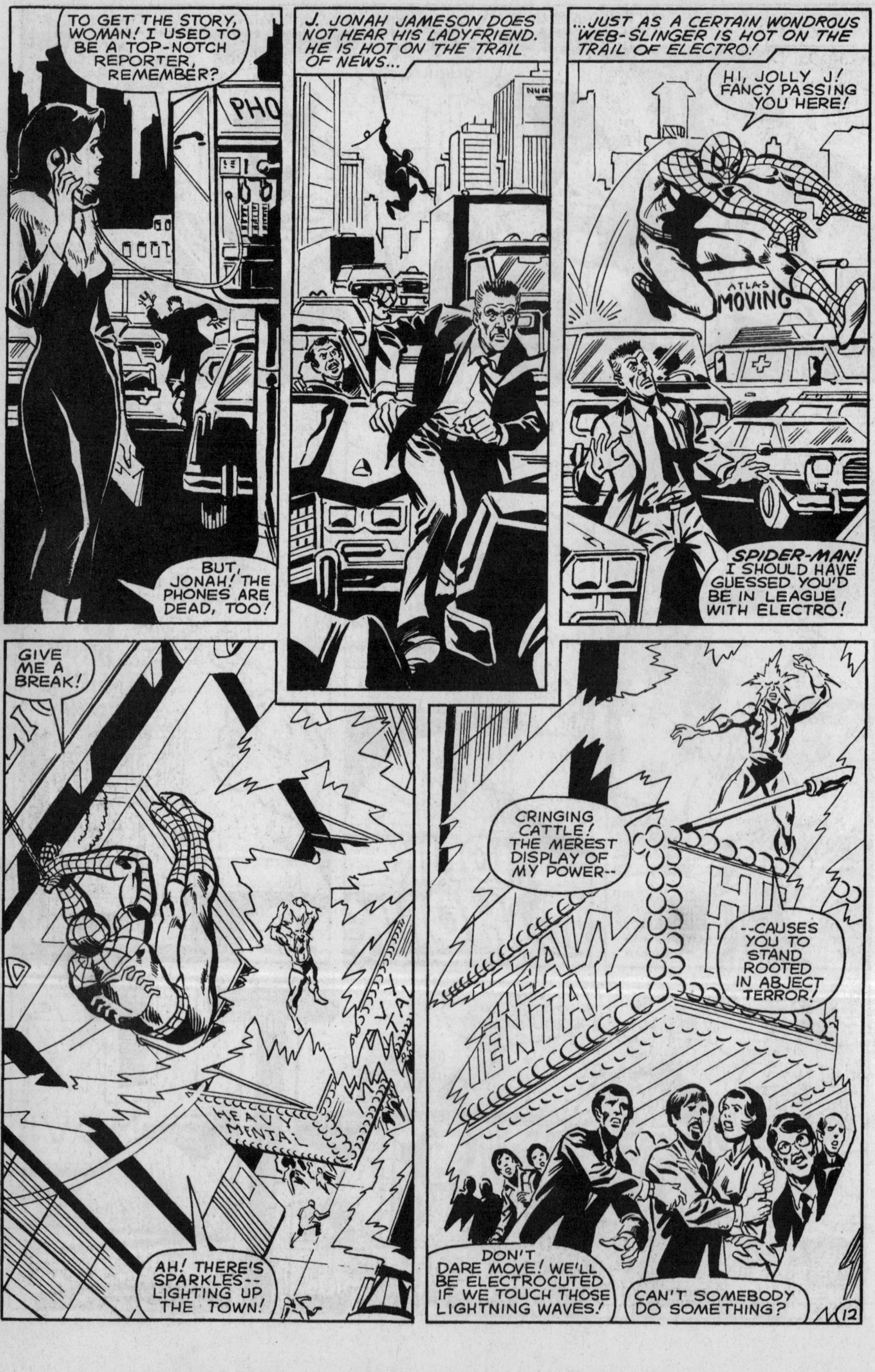
TO GET THE STORY, WOMAN! I USED TO BE A TOP-NOTCH REPORTER, REMEMBER?
PHO
BUT, JONAH! THE PHONES ARE DEAD, TOO!
J. JONAH JAMESON DOES NOT HEAR HIS LADYFRIEND. HE IS HOT ON THE TRAIL OF NEWS...
...JUST AS A CERTAIN WONDROUS WEB-SLINGER IS HOT ON THE TRAIL OF ELECTRO!
HI, JOLLY J! FANCY PASSING YOU HERE!
ATLAS MOVING
SPIDER-MAN! I SHOULD HAVE GUESSED YOU'D BE IN LEAGUE WITH ELECTRO!
GIVE ME A BREAK!
HEAVY MENTAL
AH! THERE'S SPARKLES-- LIGHTING UP THE TOWN!
CRINGING CATTLE! THE MEREST DISPLAY OF MY POWER--
--CAUSES YOU TO STAND ROOTED IN ABJECT TERROR!
HEAVY MENTAL
DON'T DARE MOVE! WE'LL BE ELECTROCUTED IF WE TOUCH THOSE LIGHTNING WAVES!
CAN'T SOMEBODY DO SOMETHING?
12

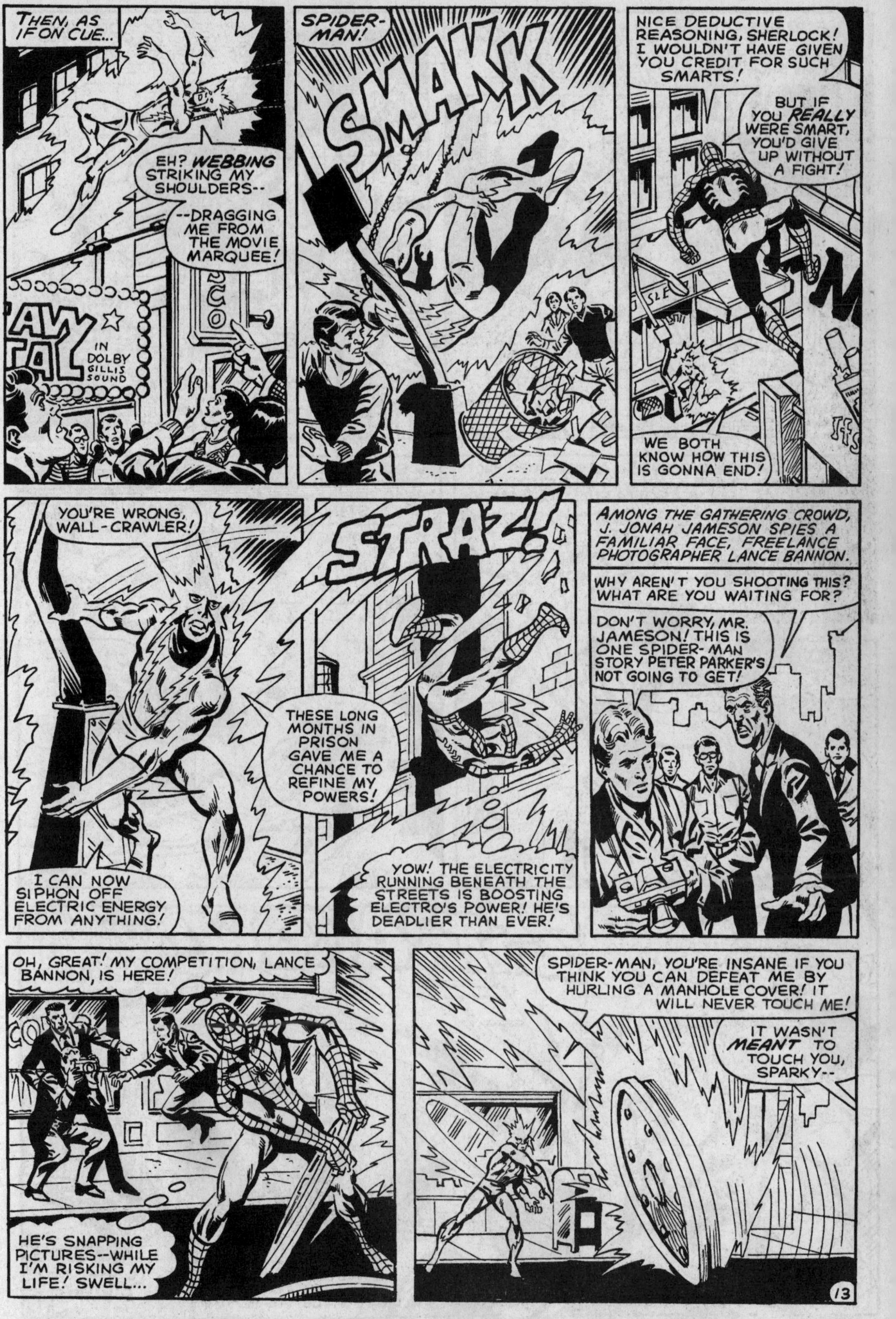
THEN, AS IF ON CUE...
EH? WEBBING STRIKING MY SHOULDERS--
--DRAGGING ME FROM THE MOVIE MARQUEE!
IN DOLBY GILLIS SOUND
SPIDER-MAN!
SMAKK
NICE DEDUCTIVE REASONING, SHERLOCK! I WOULDN'T HAVE GIVEN YOU CREDIT FOR SUCH SMARTS!
BUT IF YOU REALLY WERE SMART, YOU'D GIVE UP WITHOUT A FIGHT!
WE BOTH KNOW HOW THIS IS GONNA END!
YOU'RE WRONG, WALL-CRAWLER!
I CAN NOW SIPHON OFF ELECTRIC ENERGY FROM ANYTHING!
STRAZ!
THESE LONG MONTHS IN PRISON GAVE ME A CHANCE TO REFINE MY POWERS!
YOW! THE ELECTRICITY RUNNING BENEATH THE STREETS IS BOOSTING ELECTRO'S POWER! HE'S DEADLIER THAN EVER!
AMONG THE GATHERING CROWD, J. JONAH JAMESON SPIES A FAMILIAR FACE, FREELANCE PHOTOGRAPHER LANCE BANNON.
WHY AREN'T YOU SHOOTING THIS? WHAT ARE YOU WAITING FOR?
DON'T WORRY, MR. JAMESON! THIS IS ONE SPIDER-MAN STORY PETER PARKER'S NOT GOING TO GET!
OH, GREAT! MY COMPETITION, LANCE BANNON, IS HERE!
HE'S SNAPPING PICTURES--WHILE I'M RISKING MY LIFE! SWELL...
SPIDER-MAN, YOU'RE INSANE IF YOU THINK YOU CAN DEFEAT ME BY HURLING A MANHOLE COVER! IT WILL NEVER TOUCH ME!
IT WASN'T MEANT TO TOUCH YOU, SPARKY--

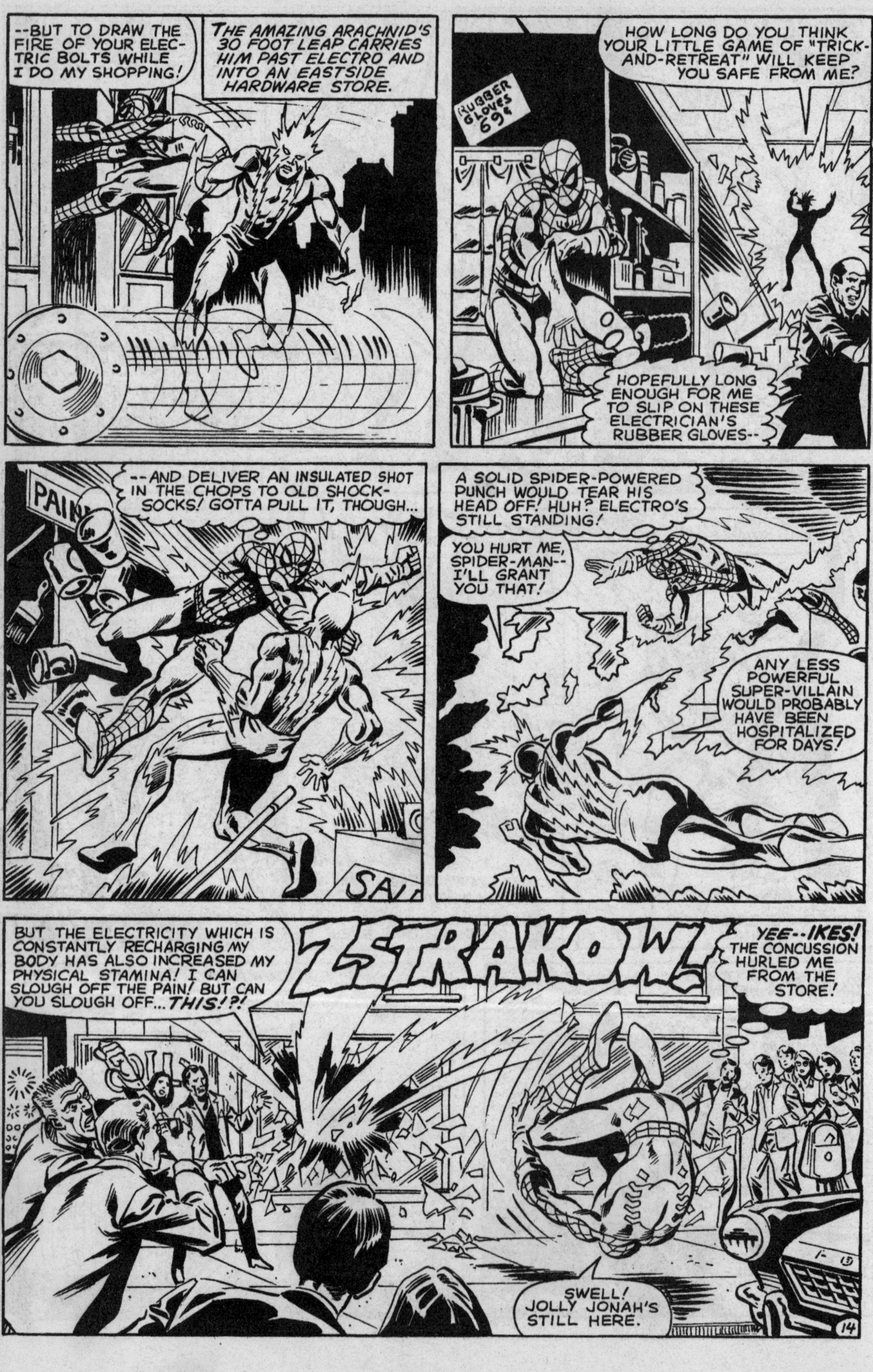
--BUT TO DRAW THE FIRE OF YOUR ELECTRIC BOLTS WHILE I DO MY SHOPPING!
THE AMAZING ARACHNID'S 30 FOOT LEAP CARRIES HIM PAST ELECTRO AND INTO AN EASTSIDE HARDWARE STORE.
HOW LONG DO YOU THINK YOUR LITTLE GAME OF "TRICK-AND-RETREAT" WILL KEEP YOU SAFE FROM ME?
RUBBER GLOVES 69¢
HOPEFULLY LONG ENOUGH FOR ME TO SLIP ON THESE ELECTRICIAN'S RUBBER GLOVES--
--AND DELIVER AN INSULATED SHOT IN THE CHOPS TO OLD SHOCK-SOCKS! GOTTA PULL IT, THOUGH...
A SOLID SPIDER-POWERED PUNCH WOULD TEAR HIS HEAD OFF! HUH? ELECTRO'S STILL STANDING!
YOU HURT ME, SPIDER-MAN--I'LL GRANT YOU THAT!
ANY LESS POWERFUL SUPER-VILLAIN WOULD PROBABLY HAVE BEEN HOSPITALIZED FOR DAYS!
BUT THE ELECTRICITY WHICH IS CONSTANTLY RECHARGING MY BODY HAS ALSO INCREASED MY PHYSICAL STAMINA! I CAN SLOUGH OFF THE PAIN! BUT CAN YOU SLOUGH OFF... THIS!?!
ZSTRAKOW!
YEE--IKES! THE CONCUSSION HURLED ME FROM THE STORE!
SWELL! JOLLY JONAH'S STILL HERE.
14

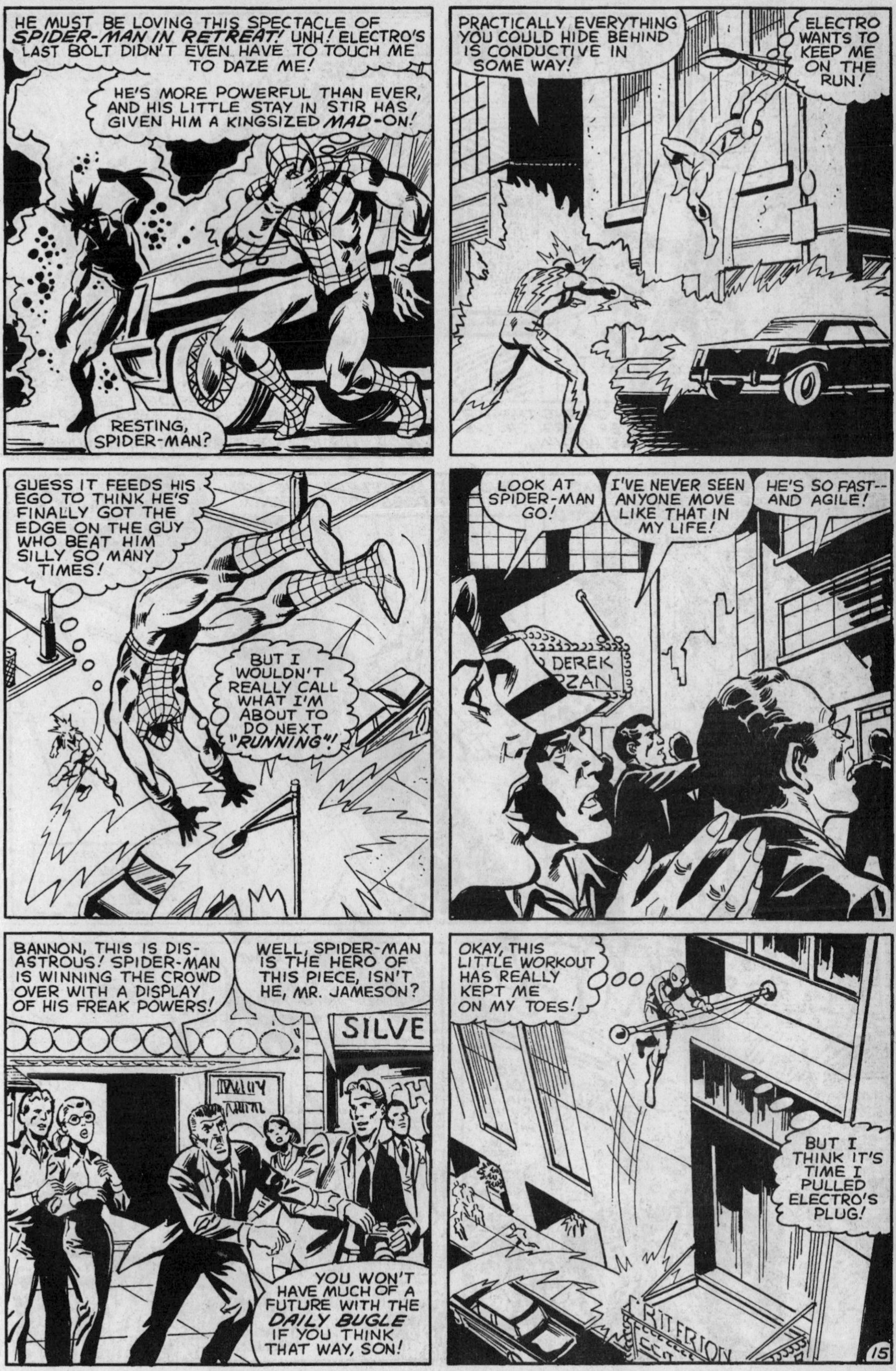
HE MUST BE LOVING THIS SPECTACLE OF SPIDER-MAN IN RETREAT! UNH! ELECTRO'S LAST BOLT DIDN'T EVEN HAVE TO TOUCH ME TO DAZE ME!
HE'S MORE POWERFUL THAN EVER, AND HIS LITTLE STAY IN STIR HAS GIVEN HIM A KINGSIZED MAD-ON!
RESTING, SPIDER-MAN?
PRACTICALLY EVERYTHING YOU COULD HIDE BEHIND IS CONDUCTIVE IN SOME WAY!
ELECTRO WANTS TO KEEP ME ON THE RUN!
GUESS IT FEEDS HIS EGO TO THINK HE'S FINALLY GOT THE EDGE ON THE GUY WHO BEAT HIM SILLY SO MANY TIMES!
BUT I WOULDN'T REALLY CALL WHAT I'M ABOUT TO DO NEXT "RUNNING"!
LOOK AT SPIDER-MAN GO!
I'VE NEVER SEEN ANYONE MOVE LIKE THAT IN MY LIFE!
HE'S SO FAST-- AND AGILE!
DEREK
RZAN
BANNON, THIS IS DIS-ASTROUS! SPIDER-MAN IS WINNING THE CROWD OVER WITH A DISPLAY OF HIS FREAK POWERS!
WELL, SPIDER-MAN IS THE HERO OF THIS PIECE, ISN'T HE, MR. JAMESON?
SILVE
YOU WON'T HAVE MUCH OF A FUTURE WITH THE DAILY BUGLE IF YOU THINK THAT WAY, SON!
OKAY, THIS LITTLE WORKOUT HAS REALLY KEPT ME ON MY TOES!
BUT I THINK IT'S TIME I PULLED ELECTRO'S PLUG!
RITERION

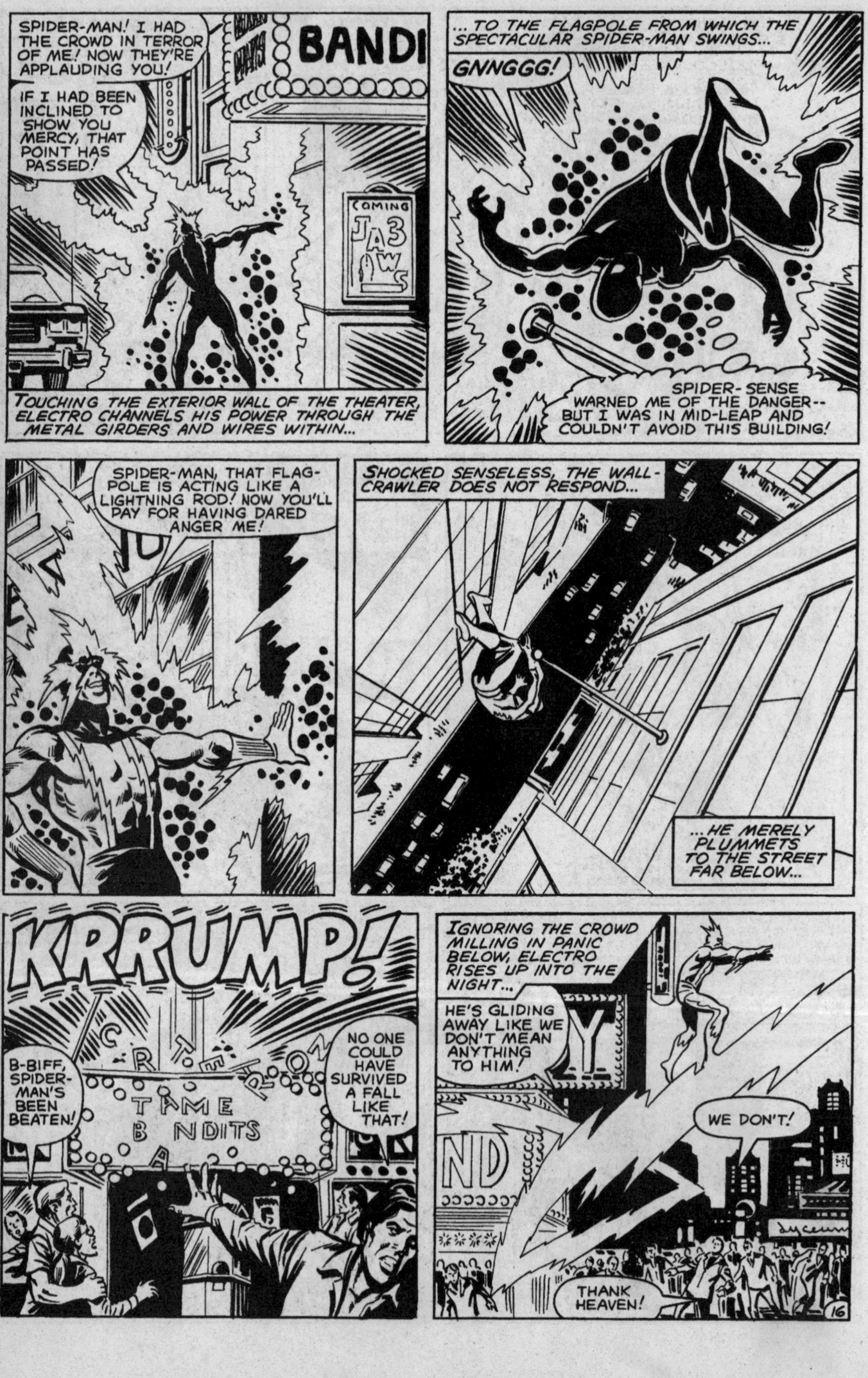
SPIDER-MAN! I HAD THE CROWD IN TERROR OF ME! NOW THEY'RE APPLAUDING YOU!
IF I HAD BEEN INCLINED TO SHOW YOU MERCY, THAT POINT HAS PASSED!
BANDI
COMING JAWS 3
TOUCHING THE EXTERIOR WALL OF THE THEATER, ELECTRO CHANNELS HIS POWER THROUGH THE METAL GIRDERS AND WIRES WITHIN...
...TO THE FLAGPOLE FROM WHICH THE SPECTACULAR SPIDER-MAN SWINGS...
GNNGGG!
SPIDER-SENSE WARNED ME OF THE DANGER-- BUT I WAS IN MID-LEAP AND COULDN'T AVOID THIS BUILDING!
SPIDER-MAN, THAT FLAG-POLE IS ACTING LIKE A LIGHTNING ROD! NOW YOU'LL PAY FOR HAVING DARED ANGER ME!
SHOCKED SENSELESS, THE WALL-CRAWLER DOES NOT RESPOND...
...HE MERELY PLUMMETS TO THE STREET FAR BELOW...
KRRUMP!
CRITERION
TIME BANDITS
B-BIFF, SPIDER-MAN'S BEEN BEATEN!
NO ONE COULD HAVE SURVIVED A FALL LIKE THAT!
IGNORING THE CROWD MILLING IN PANIC BELOW, ELECTRO RISES UP INTO THE NIGHT...
HE'S GLIDING AWAY LIKE WE DON'T MEAN ANYTHING TO HIM!
WE DON'T!
THANK HEAVEN!
16

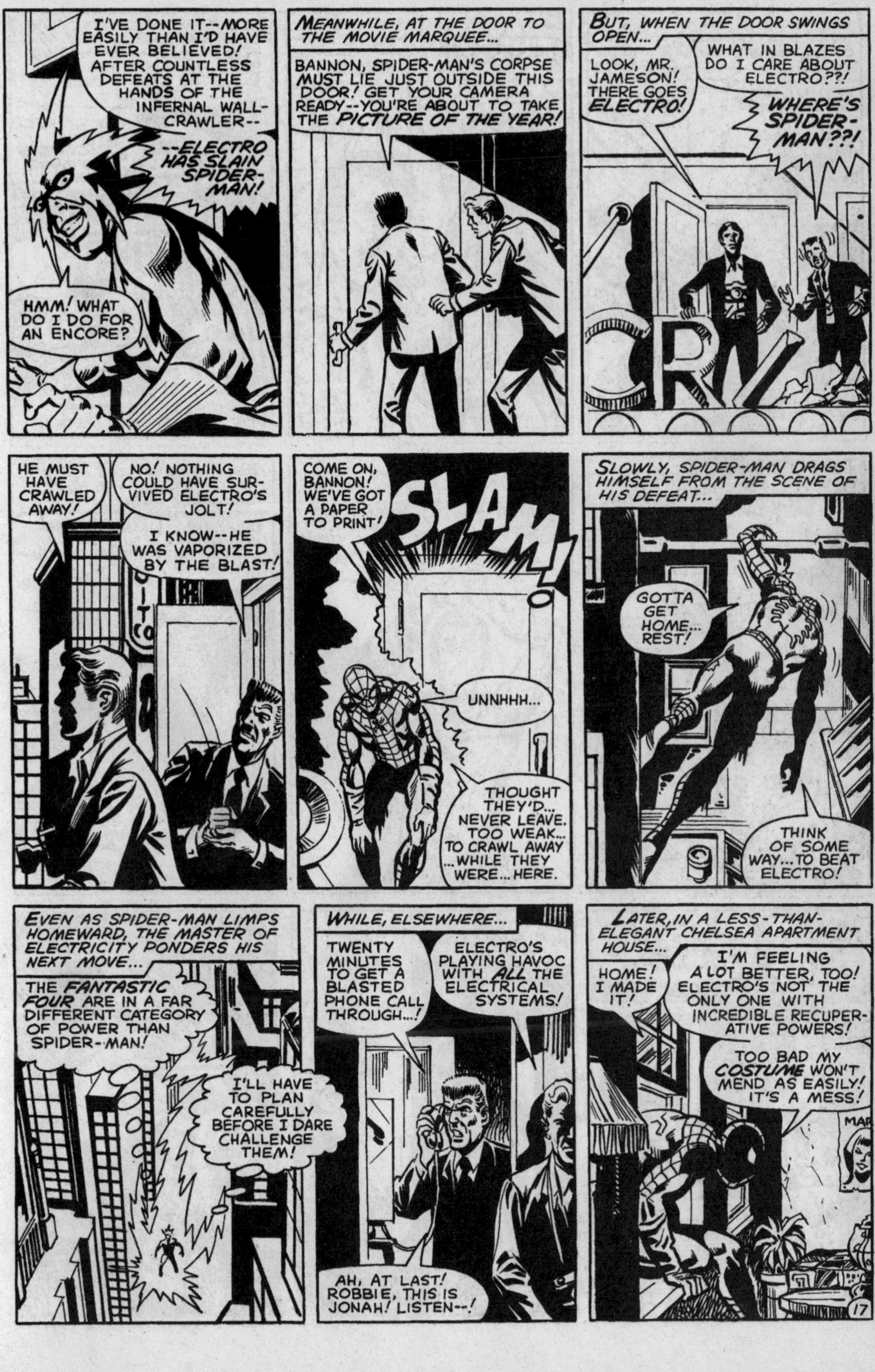
I'VE DONE IT--MORE EASILY THAN I'D HAVE EVER BELIEVED! AFTER COUNTLESS DEFEATS AT THE HANDS OF THE INFERNAL WALL-CRAWLER--
--ELECTRO HAS SLAIN SPIDER-MAN!
HMM! WHAT DO I DO FOR AN ENCORE?
MEANWHILE, AT THE DOOR TO THE MOVIE MARQUEE...
BANNON, SPIDER-MAN'S CORPSE MUST LIE JUST OUTSIDE THIS DOOR! GET YOUR CAMERA READY--YOU'RE ABOUT TO TAKE THE PICTURE OF THE YEAR!
BUT, WHEN THE DOOR SWINGS OPEN...
LOOK, MR. JAMESON! THERE GOES ELECTRO!
WHAT IN BLAZES DO I CARE ABOUT ELECTRO??!
WHERE'S SPIDER-MAN??!
HE MUST HAVE CRAWLED AWAY!
NO! NOTHING COULD HAVE SURVIVED ELECTRO'S JOLT!
I KNOW--HE WAS VAPORIZED BY THE BLAST!
COME ON, BANNON! WE'VE GOT A PAPER TO PRINT!
SLAM!
UNNHHH...
THOUGHT THEY'D... NEVER LEAVE. TOO WEAK... TO CRAWL AWAY ...WHILE THEY WERE... HERE.
SLOWLY, SPIDER-MAN DRAGS HIMSELF FROM THE SCENE OF HIS DEFEAT...
GOTTA GET HOME... REST!
THINK OF SOME WAY... TO BEAT ELECTRO!
EVEN AS SPIDER-MAN LIMPS HOMEWARD, THE MASTER OF ELECTRICITY PONDERS HIS NEXT MOVE...
THE FANTASTIC FOUR ARE IN A FAR DIFFERENT CATEGORY OF POWER THAN SPIDER-MAN!
I'LL HAVE TO PLAN CAREFULLY BEFORE I DARE CHALLENGE THEM!
WHILE, ELSEWHERE...
TWENTY MINUTES TO GET A BLASTED PHONE CALL THROUGH...!
ELECTRO'S PLAYING HAVOC WITH ALL THE ELECTRICAL SYSTEMS!
AH, AT LAST! ROBBIE, THIS IS JONAH! LISTEN--!
LATER, IN A LESS-THAN-ELEGANT CHELSEA APARTMENT HOUSE...
HOME! I MADE IT!
I'M FEELING A LOT BETTER, TOO! ELECTRO'S NOT THE ONLY ONE WITH INCREDIBLE RECUPERATIVE POWERS!
TOO BAD MY COSTUME WON'T MEND AS EASILY! IT'S A MESS!
MAR
17

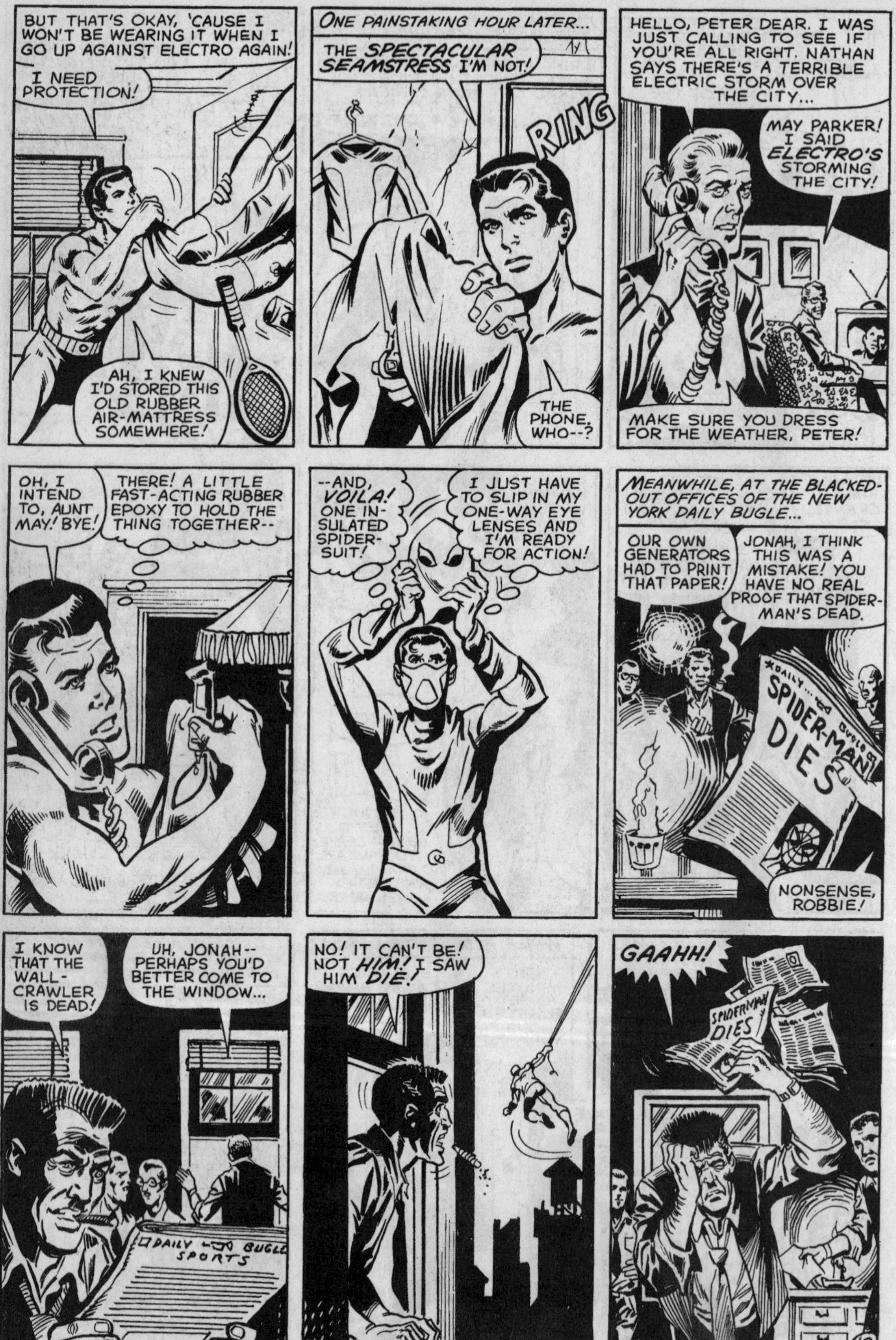

BUT THAT'S OKAY, 'CAUSE I WON'T BE WEARING IT WHEN I GO UP AGAINST ELECTRO AGAIN!
I NEED PROTECTION!
AH, I KNEW I'D STORED THIS OLD RUBBER AIR-MATTRESS SOMEWHERE!
ONE PAINSTAKING HOUR LATER...
THE SPECTACULAR SEAMSTRESS I'M NOT!
RING
THE PHONE, WHO--?
HELLO, PETER DEAR. I WAS JUST CALLING TO SEE IF YOU'RE ALL RIGHT. NATHAN SAYS THERE'S A TERRIBLE ELECTRIC STORM OVER THE CITY...
MAY PARKER! I SAID ELECTRO'S STORMING THE CITY!
MAKE SURE YOU DRESS FOR THE WEATHER, PETER!
OH, I INTEND TO, AUNT MAY! BYE!
THERE! A LITTLE FAST-ACTING RUBBER EPOXY TO HOLD THE THING TOGETHER--
--AND, VOILA! ONE INSULATED SPIDER-SUIT!
I JUST HAVE TO SLIP IN MY ONE-WAY EYE LENSES AND I'M READY FOR ACTION!
MEANWHILE, AT THE BLACKED-OUT OFFICES OF THE NEW YORK DAILY BUGLE...
OUR OWN GENERATORS HAD TO PRINT THAT PAPER!
JONAH, I THINK THIS WAS A MISTAKE! YOU HAVE NO REAL PROOF THAT SPIDER-MAN'S DEAD.
DAILY BUGLE
SPIDER-MAN DIES
NONSENSE, ROBBIE!
I KNOW THAT THE WALL-CRAWLER IS DEAD!
UH, JONAH-- PERHAPS YOU'D BETTER COME TO THE WINDOW...
DAILY BUGLE SPORTS
NO! IT CAN'T BE! NOT HIM! I SAW HIM DIE!
GAAHH!
SPIDERMAN DIES
18

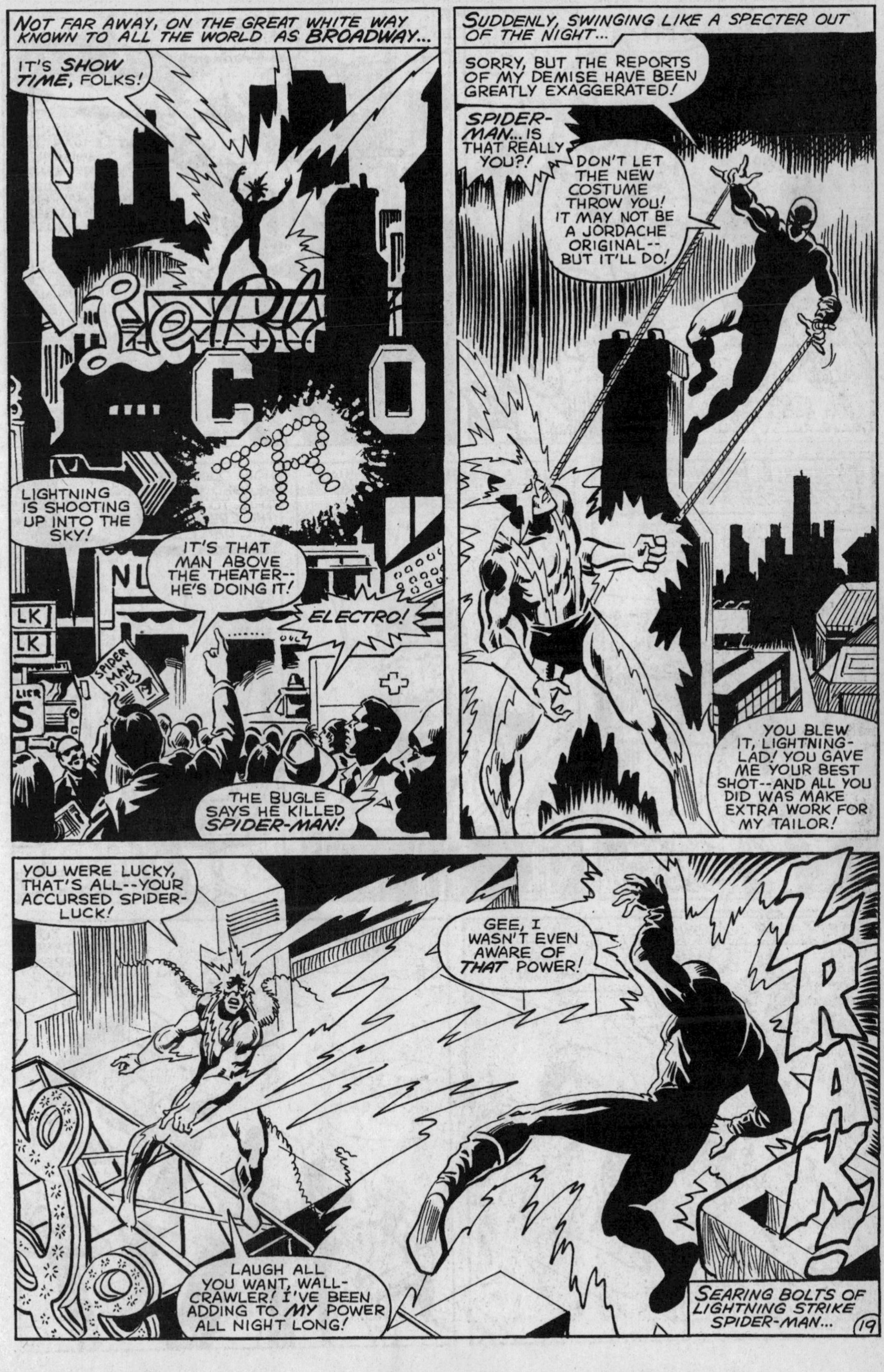
NOT FAR AWAY, ON THE GREAT WHITE WAY KNOWN TO ALL THE WORLD AS BROADWAY...
IT'S SHOW TIME, FOLKS!
LIGHTNING IS SHOOTING UP INTO THE SKY!
IT'S THAT MAN ABOVE THE THEATER--HE'S DOING IT!
ELECTRO!
THE BUGLE SAYS HE KILLED SPIDER-MAN!
SPIDER MAN
SUDDENLY, SWINGING LIKE A SPECTER OUT OF THE NIGHT...
SORRY, BUT THE REPORTS OF MY DEMISE HAVE BEEN GREATLY EXAGGERATED!
SPIDER-MAN... IS THAT REALLY YOU?!
DON'T LET THE NEW COSTUME THROW YOU! IT MAY NOT BE A JORDACHE ORIGINAL--BUT IT'LL DO!
YOU BLEW IT, LIGHTNING-LAD! YOU GAVE ME YOUR BEST SHOT--AND ALL YOU DID WAS MAKE EXTRA WORK FOR MY TAILOR!
YOU WERE LUCKY, THAT'S ALL--YOUR ACCURSED SPIDER-LUCK!
GEE, I WASN'T EVEN AWARE OF THAT POWER!
KRAK
LAUGH ALL YOU WANT, WALL-CRAWLER! I'VE BEEN ADDING TO MY POWER ALL NIGHT LONG!
SEARING BOLTS OF LIGHTNING STRIKE SPIDER-MAN...

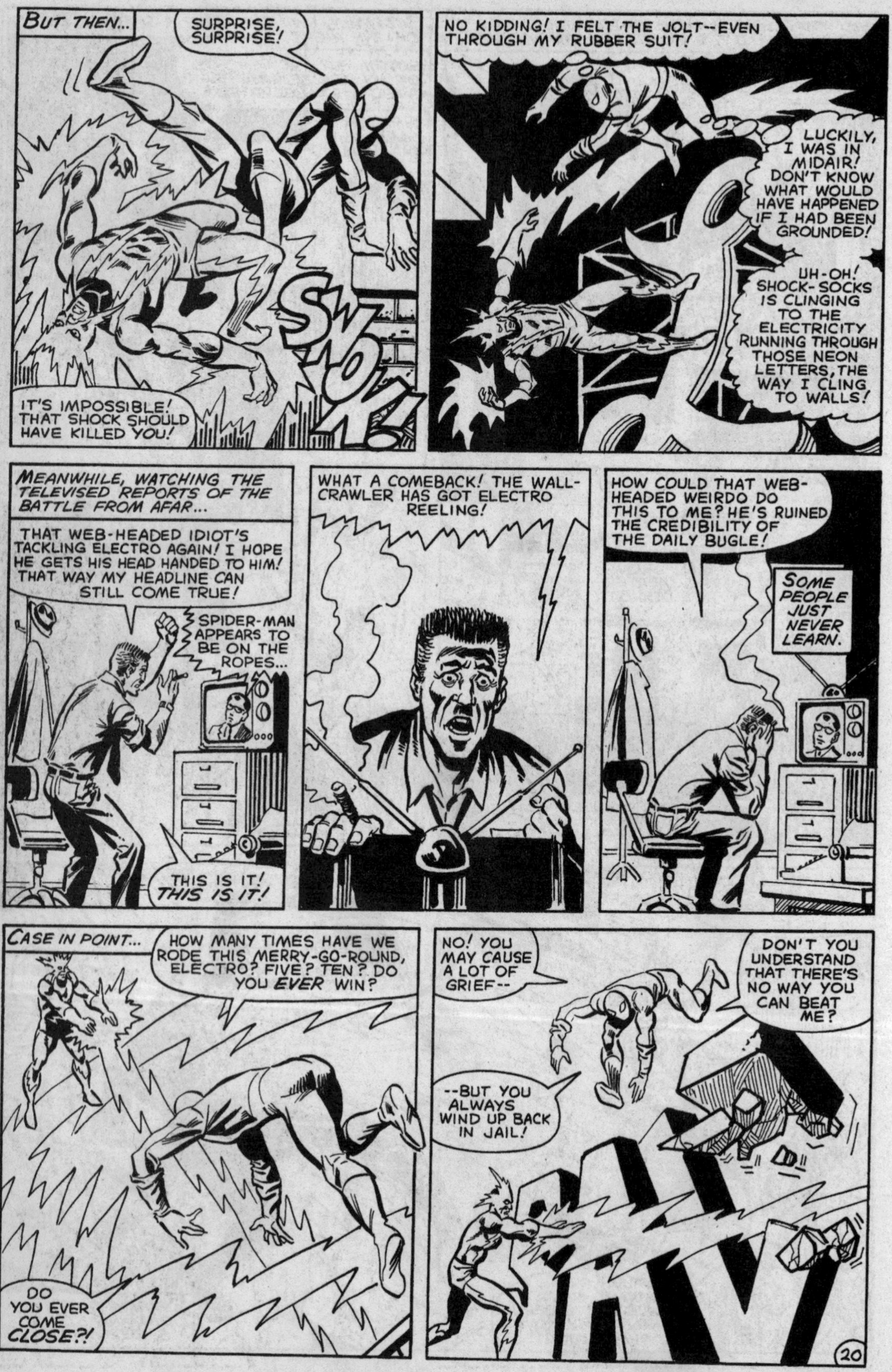
BUT THEN...
SURPRISE, SURPRISE!
SNOK!
IT'S IMPOSSIBLE! THAT SHOCK SHOULD HAVE KILLED YOU!
NO KIDDING! I FELT THE JOLT--EVEN THROUGH MY RUBBER SUIT!
LUCKILY, I WAS IN MIDAIR! DON'T KNOW WHAT WOULD HAVE HAPPENED IF I HAD BEEN GROUNDED!
UH-OH! SHOCK-SOCKS IS CLINGING TO THE ELECTRICITY RUNNING THROUGH THOSE NEON LETTERS, THE WAY I CLING TO WALLS!
MEANWHILE, WATCHING THE TELEVISED REPORTS OF THE BATTLE FROM AFAR...
THAT WEB-HEADED IDIOT'S TACKLING ELECTRO AGAIN! I HOPE HE GETS HIS HEAD HANDED TO HIM! THAT WAY MY HEADLINE CAN STILL COME TRUE!
SPIDER-MAN APPEARS TO BE ON THE ROPES...
THIS IS IT! THIS IS IT!
WHAT A COMEBACK! THE WALL-CRAWLER HAS GOT ELECTRO REELING!
HOW COULD THAT WEB-HEADED WEIRDO DO THIS TO ME? HE'S RUINED THE CREDIBILITY OF THE DAILY BUGLE!
SOME PEOPLE JUST NEVER LEARN.
CASE IN POINT...
HOW MANY TIMES HAVE WE RODE THIS MERRY-GO-ROUND, ELECTRO? FIVE? TEN? DO YOU EVER WIN?
DO YOU EVER COME CLOSE?!
NO! YOU MAY CAUSE A LOT OF GRIEF--
DON'T YOU UNDERSTAND THAT THERE'S NO WAY YOU CAN BEAT ME?
--BUT YOU ALWAYS WIND UP BACK IN JAIL!
20

ALL RIGHT, SPIDER-MAN-- LET'S SAY, FOR ARGUMENT'S SAKE, THAT POWER AGAINST POWER YOU'LL ALWAYS WIN! THEN, I'D HAVE TO FIND SOME *OTHER* WAY TO BEAT YOU, WOULDN'T I?

WHAT WAY?

WELL, I COULD THREATEN TO ELECTROCUTE THOSE PITIFUL WORMS SQUIRMING ON THE STREET BELOW--

--UNLESS YOU OFFERED YOURSELF IN THEIR PLACE!

YOU MERCILESS, MOTHERLESS--!

PLEASE! LET'S NOT GET PERSONAL! I'M TALKING ABOUT A BUSINESS ARRANGEMENT.

YOUR LIFE... FOR *THEIRS!*

IT... DOESN'T LOOK LIKE I HAVE ANY CHOICE.

NONE AT ALL.

GIVE ME YOUR HAND, SPIDER-MAN.

THEN WHAT?

IT...DOESN'T LOOK LIKE I HAVE ANY CHOICE.

THEN I'LL CONDUCT MY POWER THROUGH YOU--

--A *KILLING CURRENT* THAT CAN'T FAIL TO REDUCE YOU TO ASH!

YEEAGHH!

THUS, FOR THE *SECOND* TIME THIS NIGHT-- SPIDER-MAN DIES!

HUGHE

AND, FOR THE SECOND TIME TONIGHT, *YOU* BLEW IT!

POW!

21

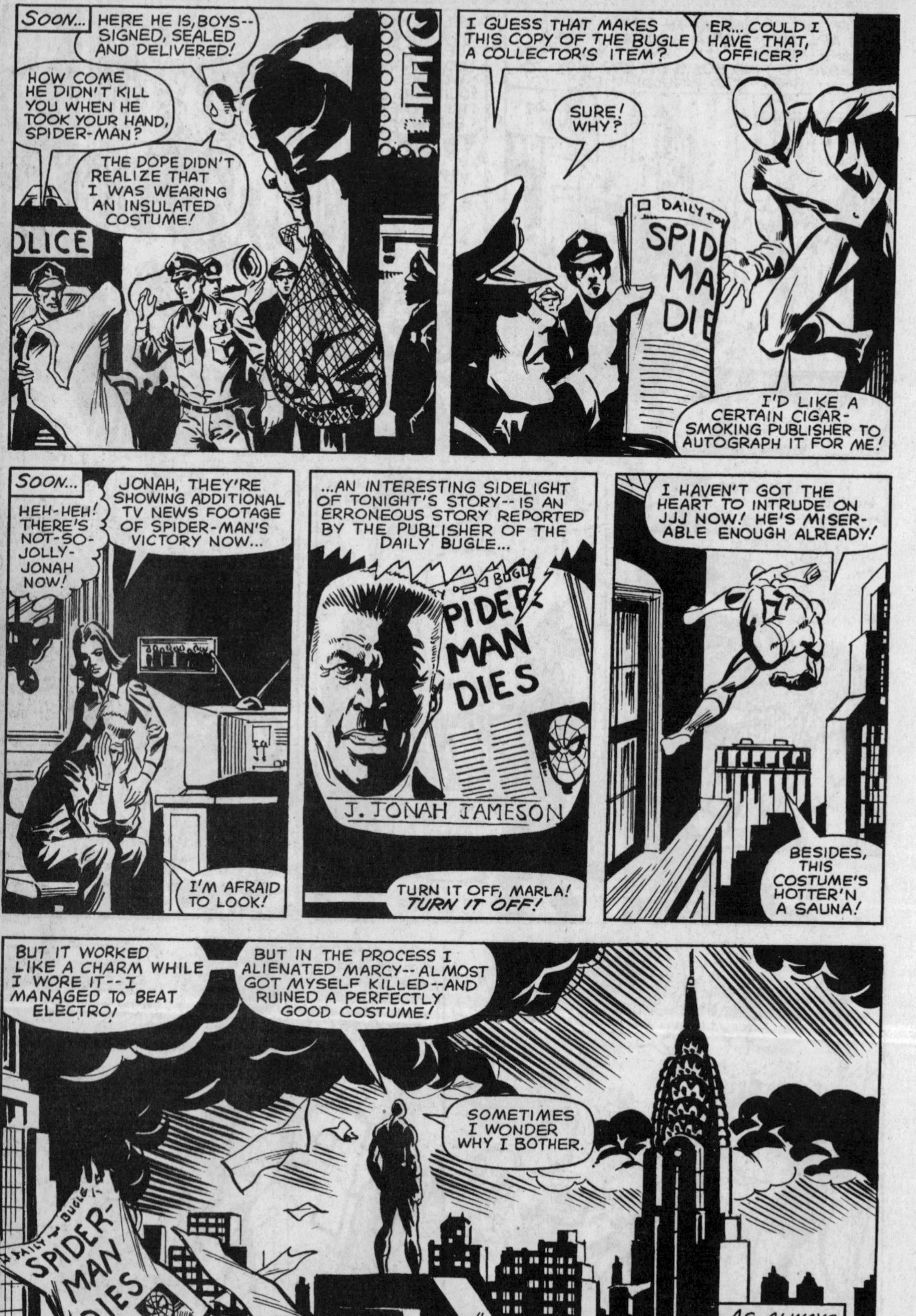

SOON...
HERE HE IS, BOYS-- SIGNED, SEALED AND DELIVERED!
HOW COME HE DIDN'T KILL YOU WHEN HE TOOK YOUR HAND, SPIDER-MAN?
THE DOPE DIDN'T REALIZE THAT I WAS WEARING AN INSULATED COSTUME!
OLICE
I GUESS THAT MAKES THIS COPY OF THE BUGLE A COLLECTOR'S ITEM?
ER... COULD I HAVE THAT, OFFICER?
SURE! WHY?
DAILY
SPID MA DIE
I'D LIKE A CERTAIN CIGAR-SMOKING PUBLISHER TO AUTOGRAPH IT FOR ME!
SOON...
HEH-HEH! THERE'S NOT-SO-JOLLY-JONAH NOW!
JONAH, THEY'RE SHOWING ADDITIONAL TV NEWS FOOTAGE OF SPIDER-MAN'S VICTORY NOW...
I'M AFRAID TO LOOK!
...AN INTERESTING SIDELIGHT OF TONIGHT'S STORY-- IS AN ERRONEOUS STORY REPORTED BY THE PUBLISHER OF THE DAILY BUGLE...
BUGLE
PIDER MAN DIES
J. JONAH JAMESON
TURN IT OFF, MARLA! TURN IT OFF!
I HAVEN'T GOT THE HEART TO INTRUDE ON JJJ NOW! HE'S MISERABLE ENOUGH ALREADY!
BESIDES, THIS COSTUME'S HOTTER'N A SAUNA!
BUT IT WORKED LIKE A CHARM WHILE I WORE IT-- I MANAGED TO BEAT ELECTRO!
BUT IN THE PROCESS I ALIENATED MARCY-- ALMOST GOT MYSELF KILLED--AND RUINED A PERFECTLY GOOD COSTUME!
SOMETIMES I WONDER WHY I BOTHER.
DAILY BUGLE
SPIDER-MAN DIES
AS ALWAYS, IT'S A LONG WAY HOME.
END.

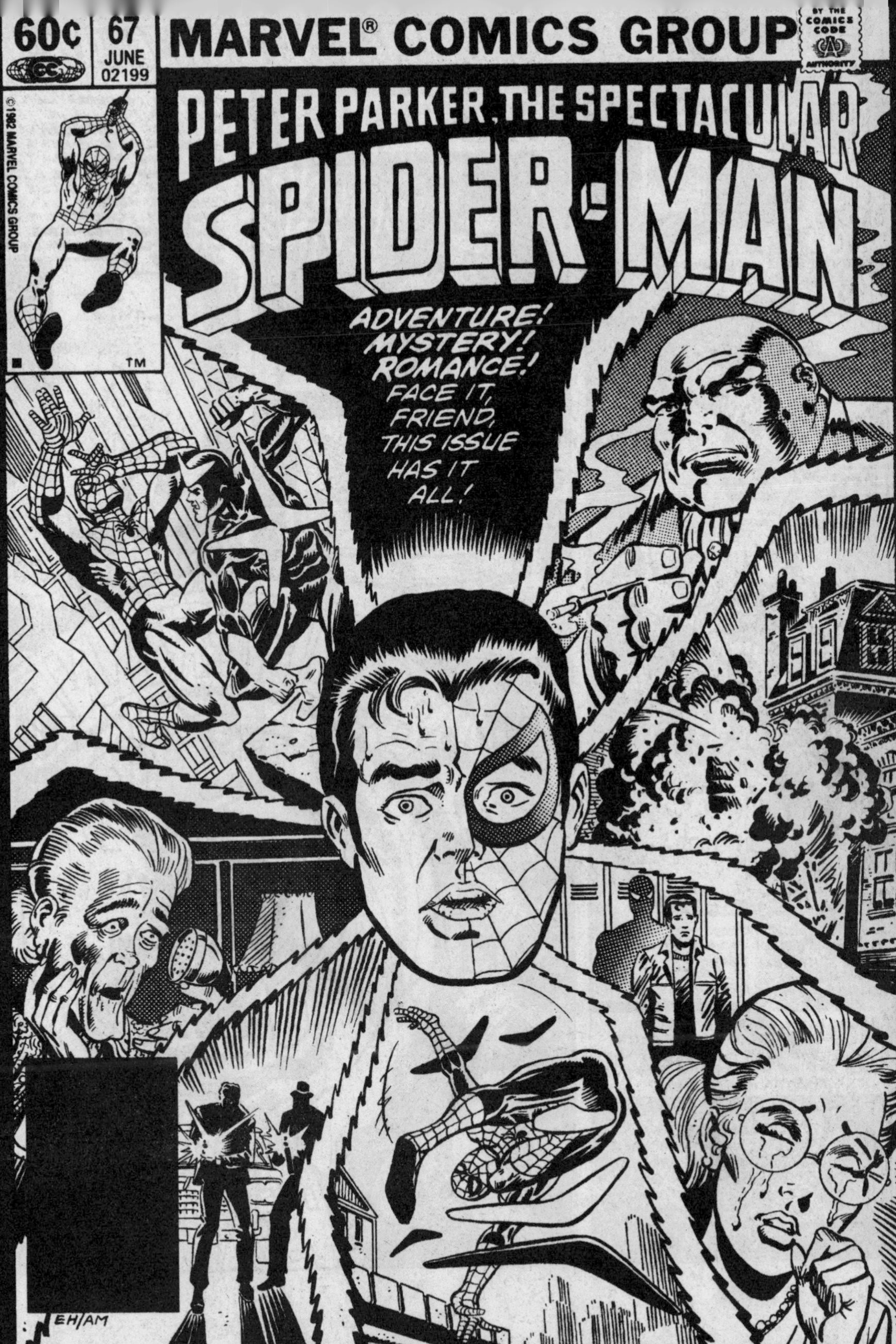
60¢
67
JUNE
02199
MARVEL® COMICS GROUP
BY THE COMICS CODE AUTHORITY
PETER PARKER, THE SPECTACULAR
SPIDER-MAN
©1982 MARVEL COMICS GROUP
TM
ADVENTURE!
MYSTERY!
ROMANCE!
FACE IT,
FRIEND,
THIS ISSUE
HAS IT
ALL!
EH/AM

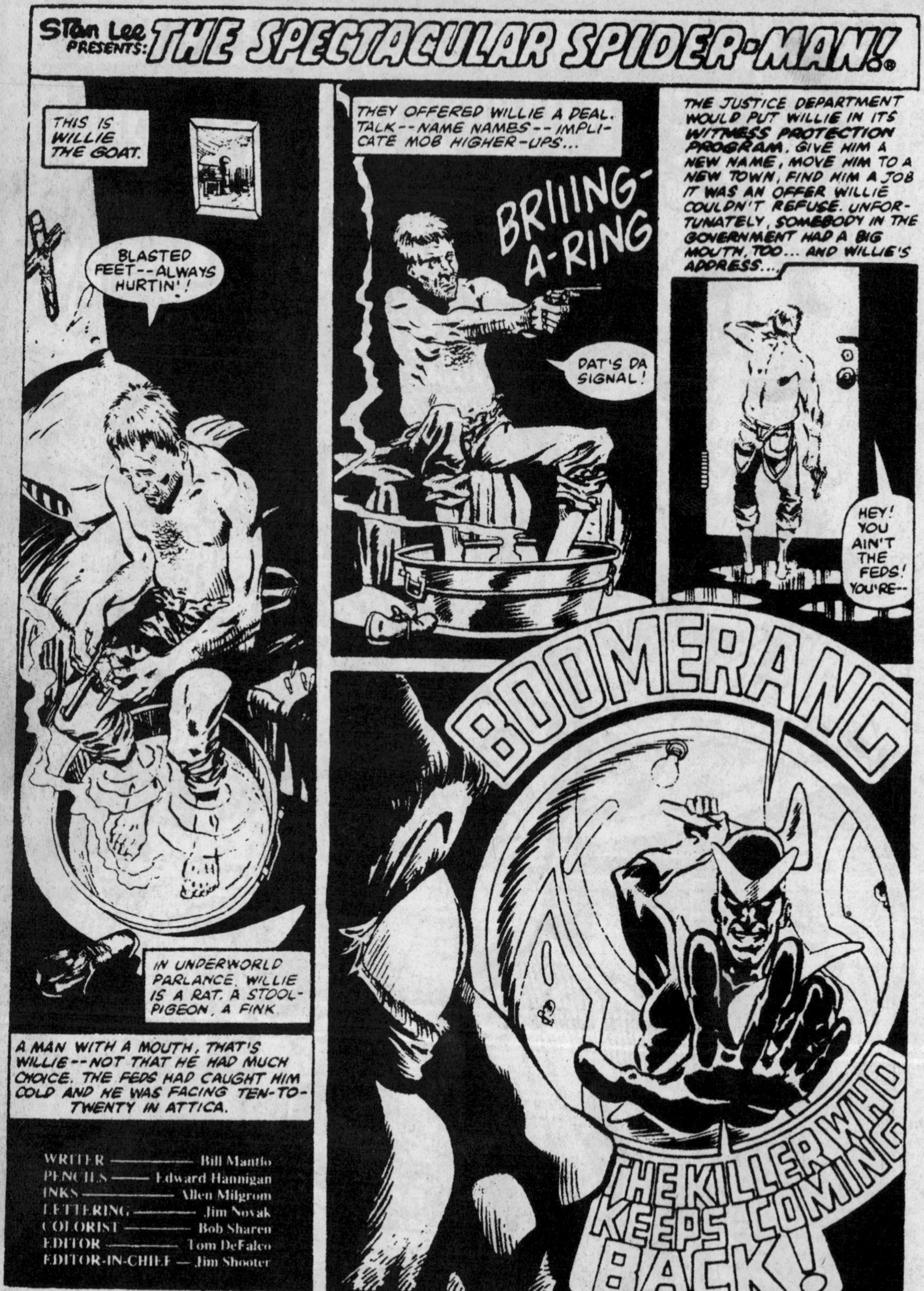
STAN LEE PRESENTS: THE SPECTACULAR SPIDER-MAN!
THIS IS WILLIE THE GOAT.
BLASTED FEET--ALWAYS HURTIN'!
IN UNDERWORLD PARLANCE, WILLIE IS A RAT, A STOOL-PIGEON, A FINK.
A MAN WITH A MOUTH, THAT'S WILLIE--NOT THAT HE HAD MUCH CHOICE. THE FEDS HAD CAUGHT HIM COLD AND HE WAS FACING TEN-TO-TWENTY IN ATTICA.
THEY OFFERED WILLIE A DEAL. TALK--NAME NAMBS--IMPLICATE MOB HIGHER-UPS...
BRIIING-A-RING
DAT'S DA SIGNAL!
THE JUSTICE DEPARTMENT WOULD PUT WILLIE IN ITS WITNESS PROTECTION PROGRAM. GIVE HIM A NEW NAME, MOVE HIM TO A NEW TOWN, FIND HIM A JOB. IT WAS AN OFFER WILLIE COULDN'T REFUSE. UNFORTUNATELY, SOMEBODY IN THE GOVERNMENT HAD A BIG MOUTH, TOO... AND WILLIE'S ADDRESS...
HEY! YOU AIN'T THE FEDS! YOU'RE--
BOOMERANG
THE KILLER WHO KEEPS COMING BACK!
WRITER — Bill Mantlo
PENCILS — Edward Hannigan
INKS — Allen Milgrom
LETTERING — Jim Novak
COLORIST — Bob Sharen
EDITOR — Tom DeFalco
EDITOR-IN-CHIEF — Jim Shooter

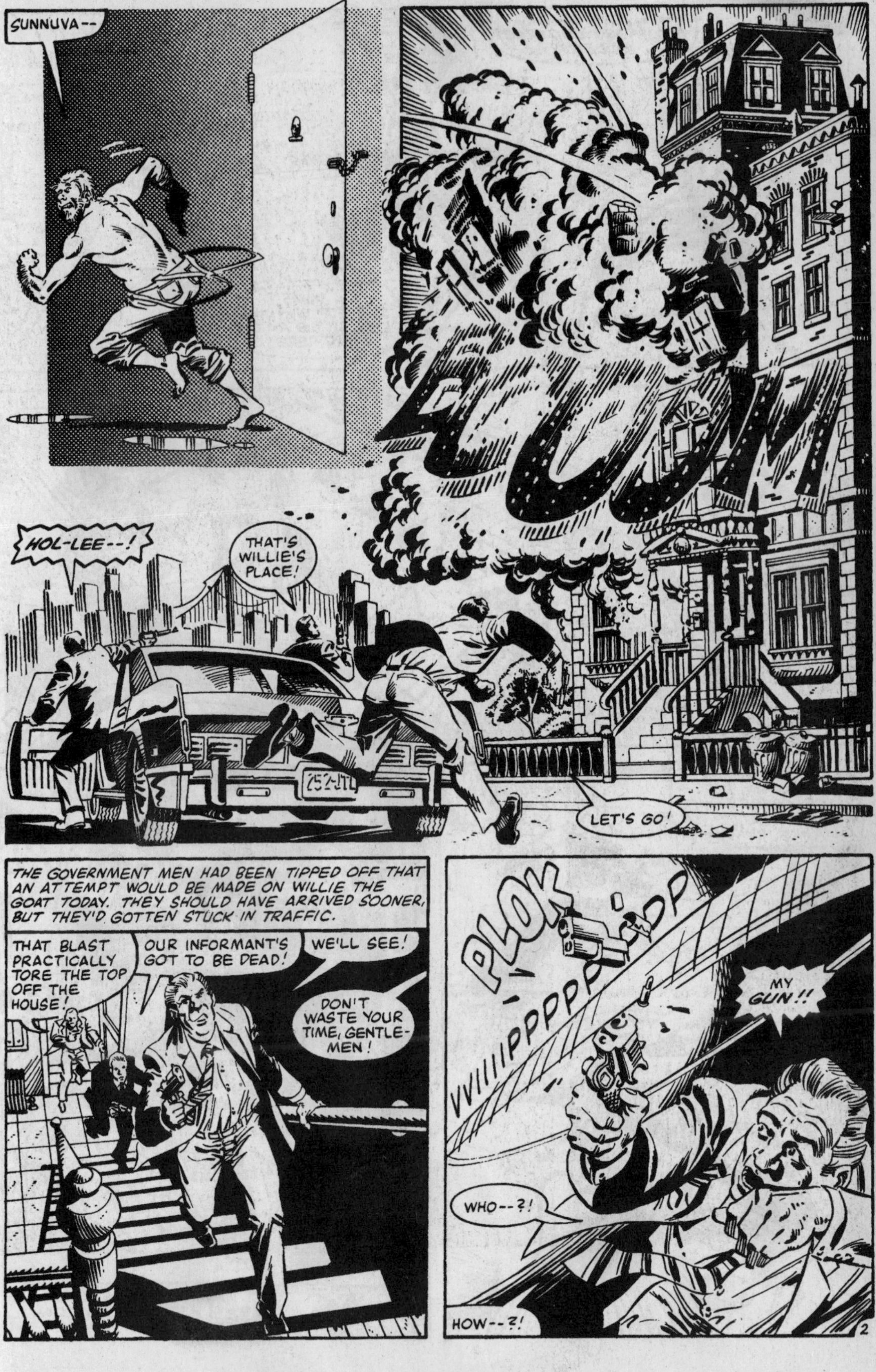
SUNNUVA--
HOL-LEE--!
THAT'S WILLIE'S PLACE!
LET'S GO!
THE GOVERNMENT MEN HAD BEEN TIPPED OFF THAT AN ATTEMPT WOULD BE MADE ON WILLIE THE GOAT TODAY. THEY SHOULD HAVE ARRIVED SOONER, BUT THEY'D GOTTEN STUCK IN TRAFFIC.
THAT BLAST PRACTICALLY TORE THE TOP OFF THE HOUSE!
OUR INFORMANT'S GOT TO BE DEAD!
WE'LL SEE!
DON'T WASTE YOUR TIME, GENTLEMEN!
PLOK
VVIIIIPPPPPP
MY GUN!!
WHO--?!
HOW--?!
2

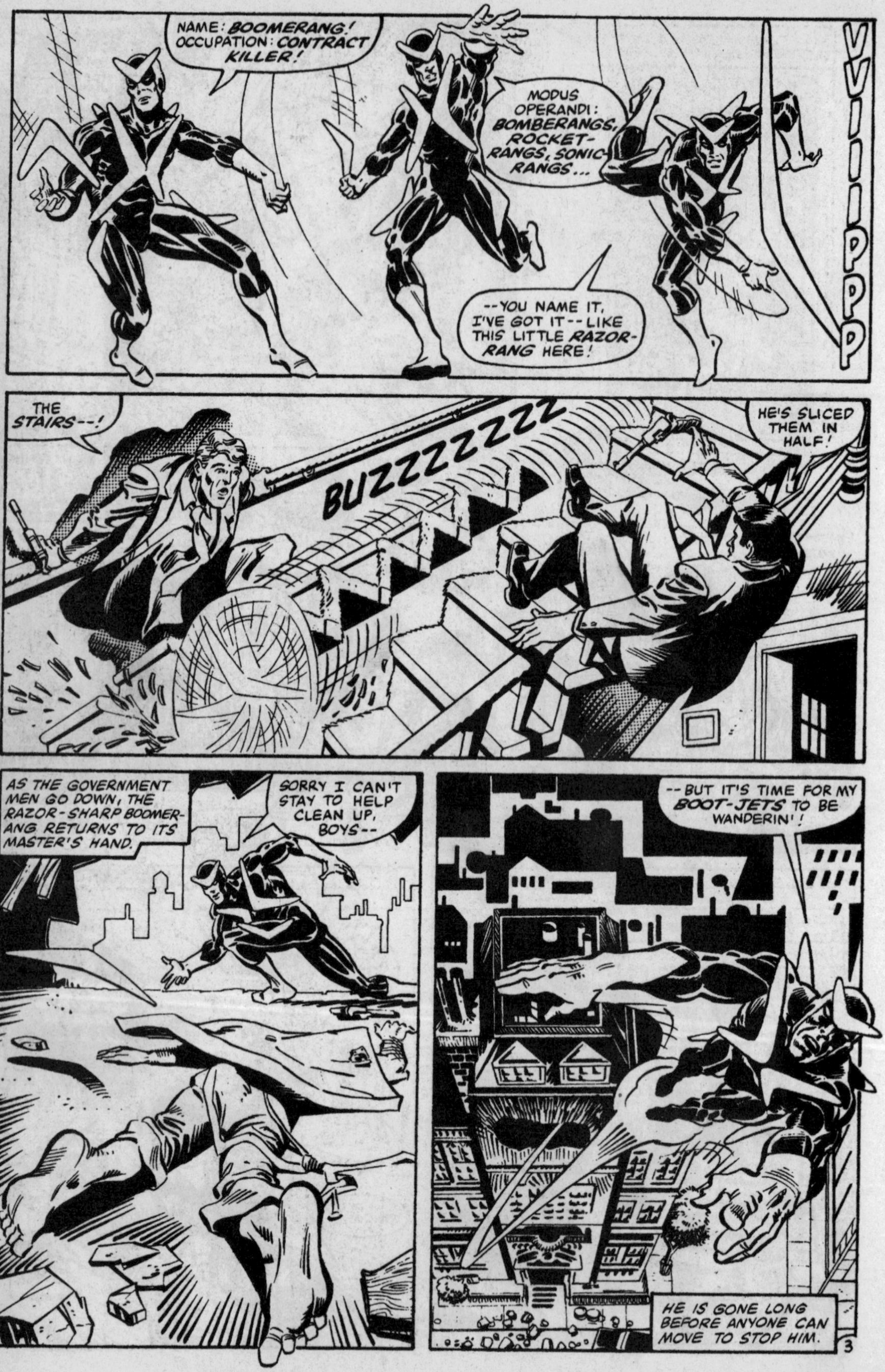
NAME: BOOMERANG! OCCUPATION: CONTRACT KILLER!
MODUS OPERANDI: BOMBERANGS, ROCKET-RANGS, SONIC-RANGS...
--YOU NAME IT, I'VE GOT IT--LIKE THIS LITTLE RAZOR-RANG HERE!
VVIIIPPP
THE STAIRS--!
BUZZZZZZZ
HE'S SLICED THEM IN HALF!
AS THE GOVERNMENT MEN GO DOWN, THE RAZOR-SHARP BOOMERANG RETURNS TO ITS MASTER'S HAND.
SORRY I CAN'T STAY TO HELP CLEAN UP, BOYS--
--BUT IT'S TIME FOR MY BOOT-JETS TO BE WANDERIN'!
HE IS GONE LONG BEFORE ANYONE CAN MOVE TO STOP HIM.
3

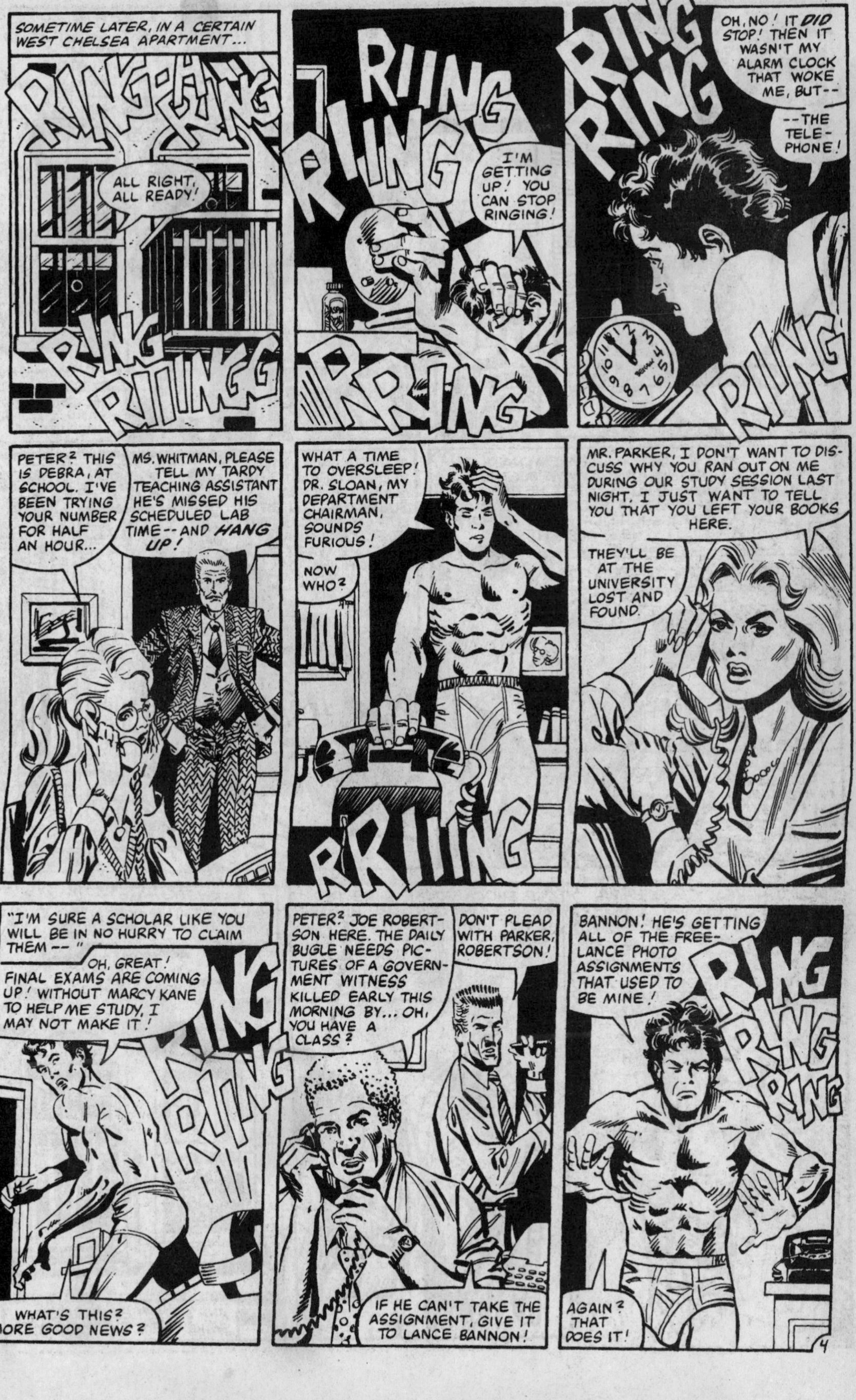
SOMETIME LATER, IN A CERTAIN WEST CHELSEA APARTMENT...
RING-A-RING
ALL RIGHT, ALL READY!
RING RIIINGG
RIING RING
I'M GETTING UP! YOU CAN STOP RINGING!
RRRING
RING RING
OH, NO! IT DID STOP! THEN IT WASN'T MY ALARM CLOCK THAT WOKE ME, BUT--
--THE TELE-PHONE!
RING
PETER? THIS IS DEBRA, AT SCHOOL. I'VE BEEN TRYING YOUR NUMBER FOR HALF AN HOUR...
MS. WHITMAN, PLEASE TELL MY TARDY TEACHING ASSISTANT HE'S MISSED HIS SCHEDULED LAB TIME--AND HANG UP!
WHAT A TIME TO OVERSLEEP! DR. SLOAN, MY DEPARTMENT CHAIRMAN, SOUNDS FURIOUS!
NOW WHO?
RRIIING
MR. PARKER, I DON'T WANT TO DISCUSS WHY YOU RAN OUT ON ME DURING OUR STUDY SESSION LAST NIGHT. I JUST WANT TO TELL YOU THAT YOU LEFT YOUR BOOKS HERE.
THEY'LL BE AT THE UNIVERSITY LOST AND FOUND.
"I'M SURE A SCHOLAR LIKE YOU WILL BE IN NO HURRY TO CLAIM THEM --"
OH, GREAT! FINAL EXAMS ARE COMING UP! WITHOUT MARCY KANE TO HELP ME STUDY, I MAY NOT MAKE IT!
RING RING
WHAT'S THIS? MORE GOOD NEWS?
PETER? JOE ROBERTSON HERE. THE DAILY BUGLE NEEDS PICTURES OF A GOVERNMENT WITNESS KILLED EARLY THIS MORNING BY... OH, YOU HAVE A CLASS?
DON'T PLEAD WITH PARKER, ROBERTSON!
IF HE CAN'T TAKE THE ASSIGNMENT, GIVE IT TO LANCE BANNON!
BANNON! HE'S GETTING ALL OF THE FREE-LANCE PHOTO ASSIGNMENTS THAT USED TO BE MINE!
RING RING RING
AGAIN? THAT DOES IT!

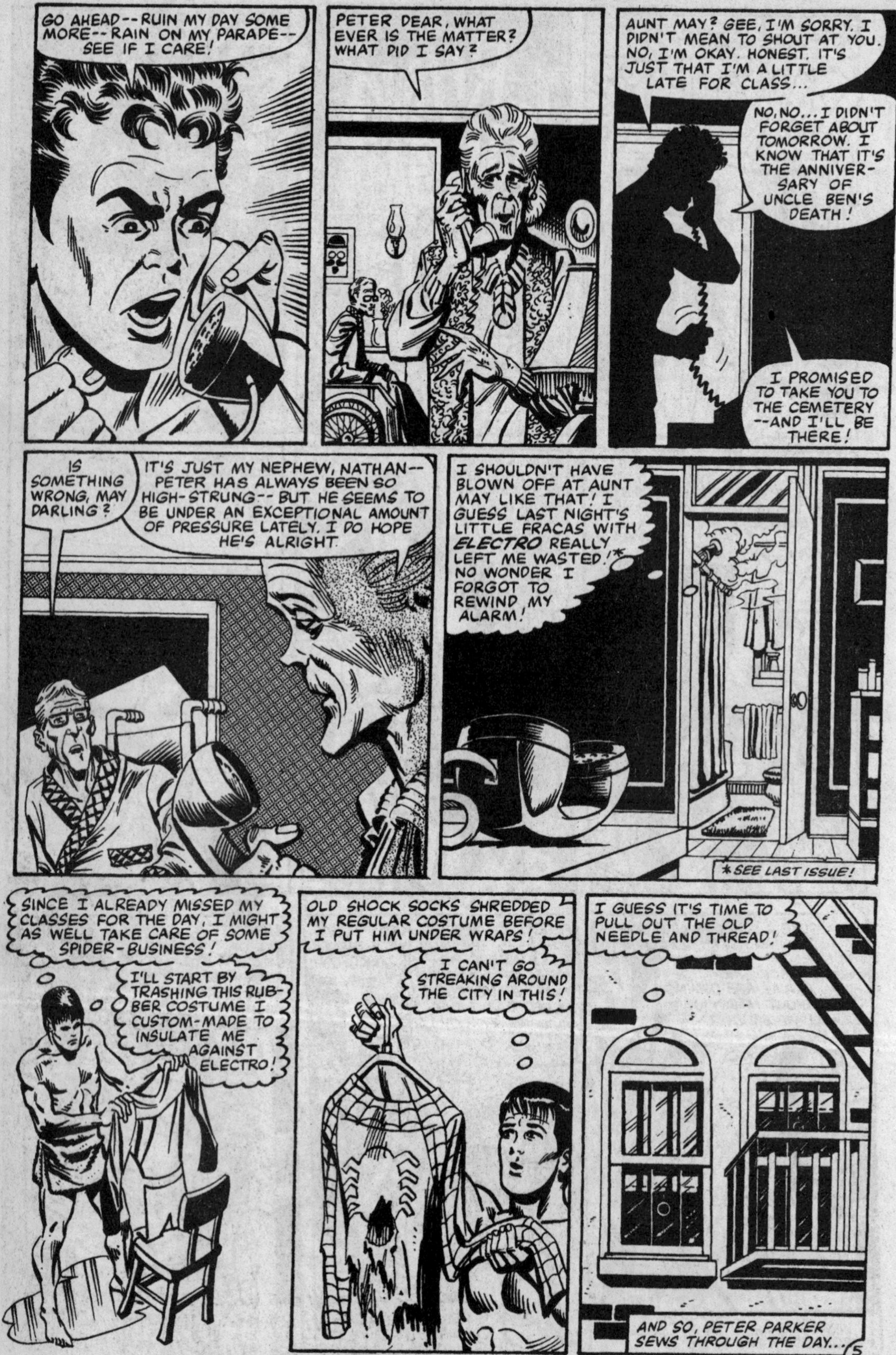
GO AHEAD--RUIN MY DAY SOME MORE--RAIN ON MY PARADE--SEE IF I CARE!
PETER DEAR, WHAT EVER IS THE MATTER? WHAT DID I SAY?
AUNT MAY? GEE, I'M SORRY. I DIDN'T MEAN TO SHOUT AT YOU. NO, I'M OKAY. HONEST. IT'S JUST THAT I'M A LITTLE LATE FOR CLASS...
NO, NO... I DIDN'T FORGET ABOUT TOMORROW. I KNOW THAT IT'S THE ANNIVER-SARY OF UNCLE BEN'S DEATH!
I PROMISED TO TAKE YOU TO THE CEMETERY --AND I'LL BE THERE!
IS SOMETHING WRONG, MAY DARLING?
IT'S JUST MY NEPHEW, NATHAN--PETER HAS ALWAYS BEEN SO HIGH-STRUNG--BUT HE SEEMS TO BE UNDER AN EXCEPTIONAL AMOUNT OF PRESSURE LATELY. I DO HOPE HE'S ALRIGHT.
I SHOULDN'T HAVE BLOWN OFF AT AUNT MAY LIKE THAT! I GUESS LAST NIGHT'S LITTLE FRACAS WITH ELECTRO REALLY LEFT ME WASTED!* NO WONDER I FORGOT TO REWIND MY ALARM!
*SEE LAST ISSUE!
SINCE I ALREADY MISSED MY CLASSES FOR THE DAY, I MIGHT AS WELL TAKE CARE OF SOME SPIDER-BUSINESS!
I'LL START BY TRASHING THIS RUB-BER COSTUME I CUSTOM-MADE TO INSULATE ME AGAINST ELECTRO!
OLD SHOCK SOCKS SHREDDED MY REGULAR COSTUME BEFORE I PUT HIM UNDER WRAPS!
I CAN'T GO STREAKING AROUND THE CITY IN THIS!
I GUESS IT'S TIME TO PULL OUT THE OLD NEEDLE AND THREAD!
AND SO, PETER PARKER SEWS THROUGH THE DAY...
5

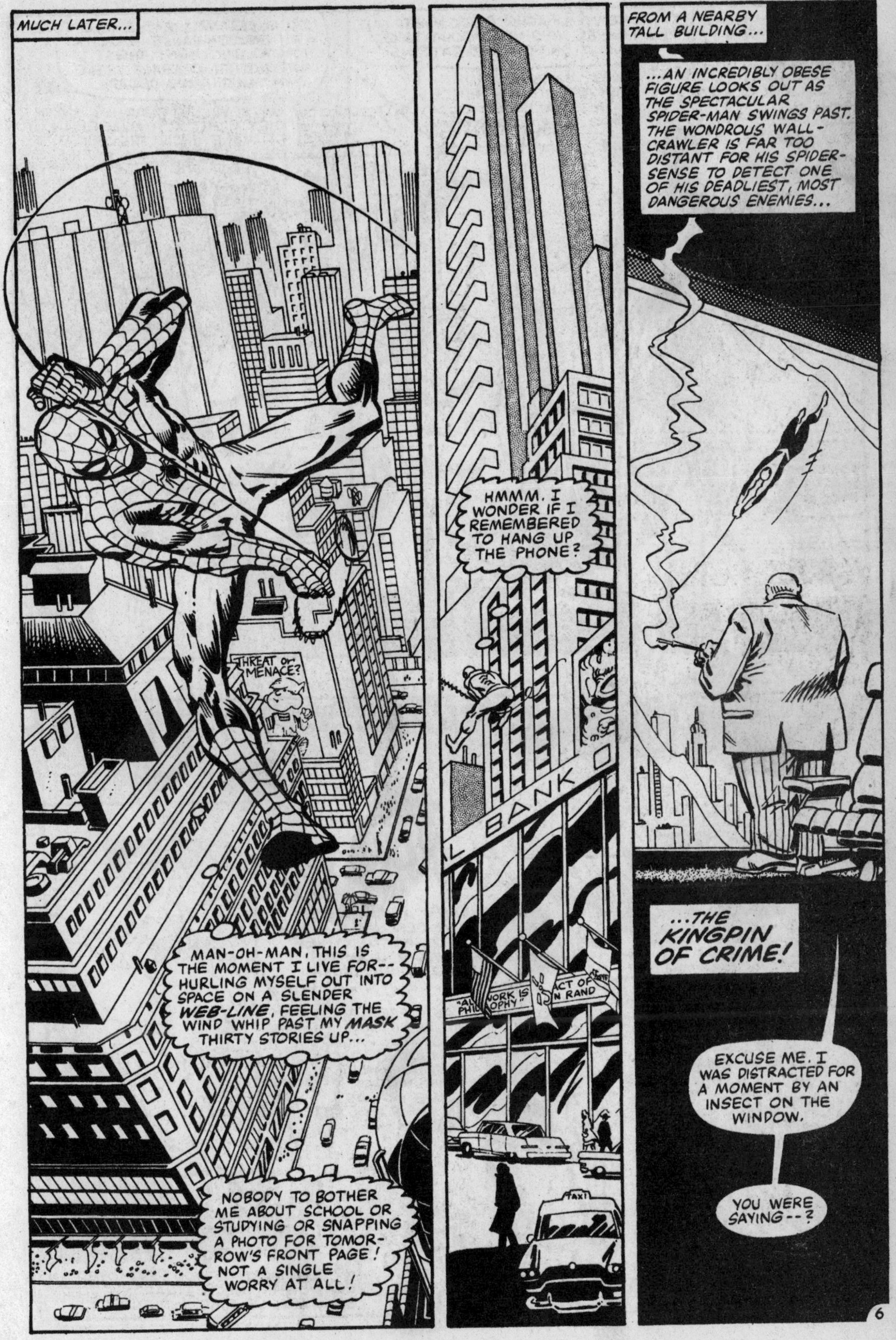
MUCH LATER...
MAN-OH-MAN, THIS IS THE MOMENT I LIVE FOR-- HURLING MYSELF OUT INTO SPACE ON A SLENDER WEB-LINE, FEELING THE WIND WHIP PAST MY MASK THIRTY STORIES UP...
NOBODY TO BOTHER ME ABOUT SCHOOL OR STUDYING OR SNAPPING A PHOTO FOR TOMORROW'S FRONT PAGE! NOT A SINGLE WORRY AT ALL!
THREAT OR MENACE?
HMMM. I WONDER IF I REMEMBERED TO HANG UP THE PHONE?
BANK
TAXI
FROM A NEARBY TALL BUILDING...
...AN INCREDIBLY OBESE FIGURE LOOKS OUT AS THE SPECTACULAR SPIDER-MAN SWINGS PAST. THE WONDROUS WALL-CRAWLER IS FAR TOO DISTANT FOR HIS SPIDER-SENSE TO DETECT ONE OF HIS DEADLIEST, MOST DANGEROUS ENEMIES...
...THE KINGPIN OF CRIME!
EXCUSE ME. I WAS DISTRACTED FOR A MOMENT BY AN INSECT ON THE WINDOW.
YOU WERE SAYING--?
6

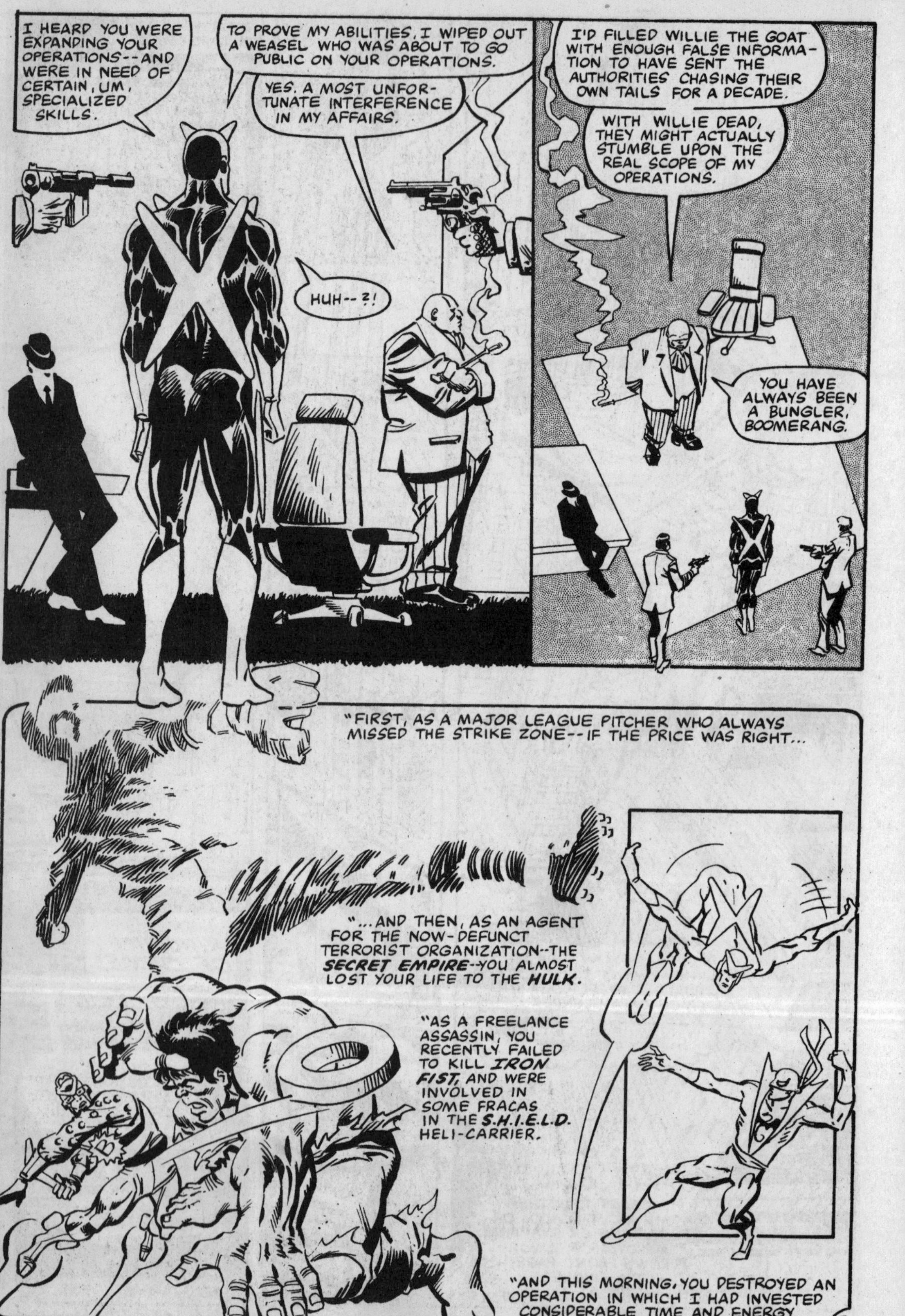
I HEARD YOU WERE EXPANDING YOUR OPERATIONS--AND WERE IN NEED OF CERTAIN, UM, SPECIALIZED SKILLS.
TO PROVE MY ABILITIES, I WIPED OUT A WEASEL WHO WAS ABOUT TO GO PUBLIC ON YOUR OPERATIONS.
YES. A MOST UNFORTUNATE INTERFERENCE IN MY AFFAIRS.
HUH--?!
I'D FILLED WILLIE THE GOAT WITH ENOUGH FALSE INFORMATION TO HAVE SENT THE AUTHORITIES CHASING THEIR OWN TAILS FOR A DECADE.
WITH WILLIE DEAD, THEY MIGHT ACTUALLY STUMBLE UPON THE REAL SCOPE OF MY OPERATIONS.
YOU HAVE ALWAYS BEEN A BUNGLER, BOOMERANG.
"FIRST, AS A MAJOR LEAGUE PITCHER WHO ALWAYS MISSED THE STRIKE ZONE--IF THE PRICE WAS RIGHT...
"...AND THEN, AS AN AGENT FOR THE NOW-DEFUNCT TERRORIST ORGANIZATION--THE SECRET EMPIRE--YOU ALMOST LOST YOUR LIFE TO THE HULK.
"AS A FREELANCE ASSASSIN, YOU RECENTLY FAILED TO KILL IRON FIST, AND WERE INVOLVED IN SOME FRACAS IN THE S.H.I.E.L.D. HELI-CARRIER.
"AND THIS MORNING, YOU DESTROYED AN OPERATION IN WHICH I HAD INVESTED CONSIDERABLE TIME AND ENERGY.

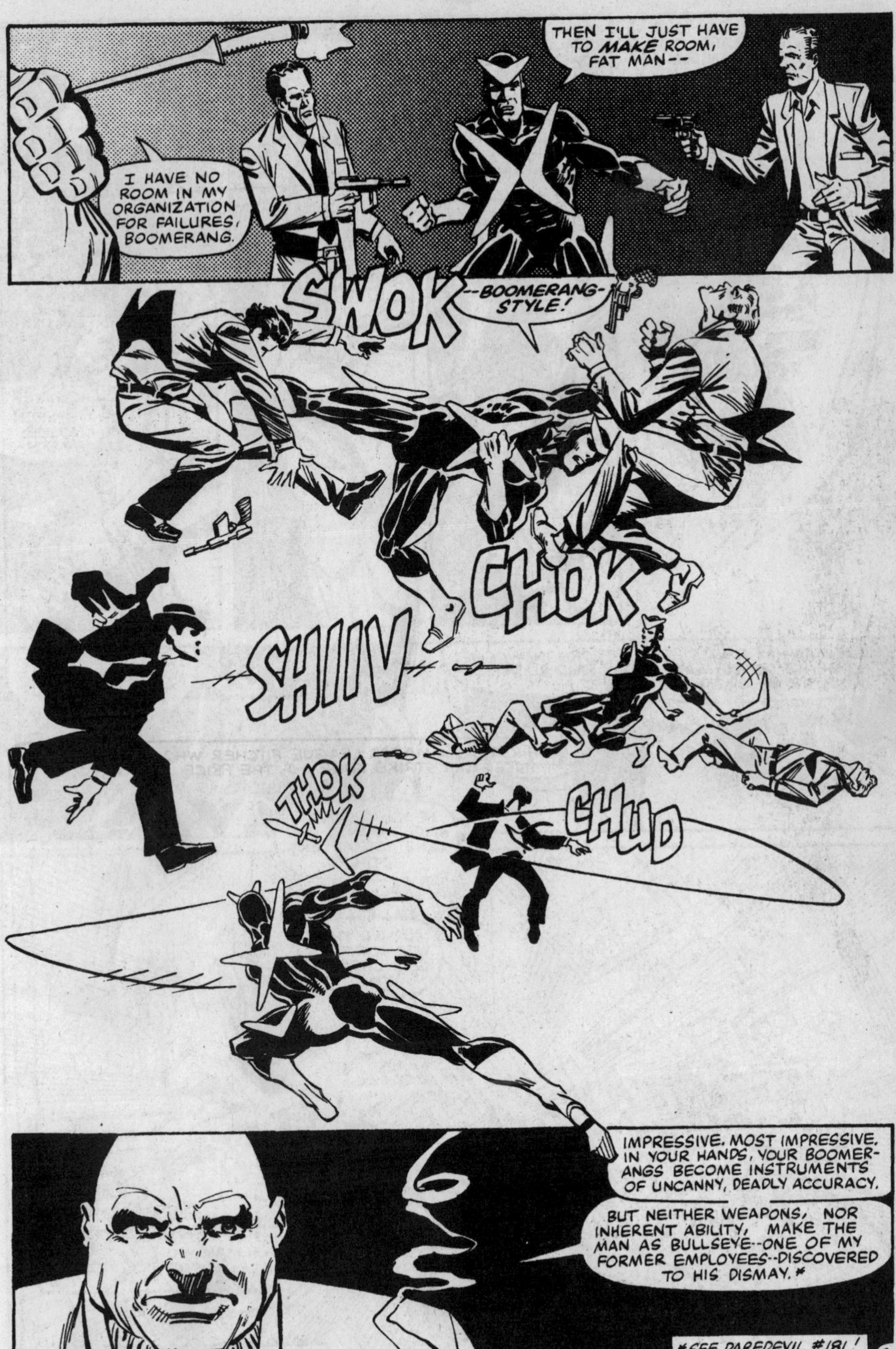
I HAVE NO ROOM IN MY ORGANIZATION FOR FAILURES, BOOMERANG.
THEN I'LL JUST HAVE TO MAKE ROOM, FAT MAN--
SWOK
--BOOMERANG-STYLE!
CHOK
SHIIV
THOK
CHUD
IMPRESSIVE. MOST IMPRESSIVE. IN YOUR HANDS, YOUR BOOMERANGS BECOME INSTRUMENTS OF UNCANNY, DEADLY ACCURACY.
BUT NEITHER WEAPONS, NOR INHERENT ABILITY, MAKE THE MAN AS BULLSEYE--ONE OF MY FORMER EMPLOYEES--DISCOVERED TO HIS DISMAY.*
*SEE DAREDEVIL #181!

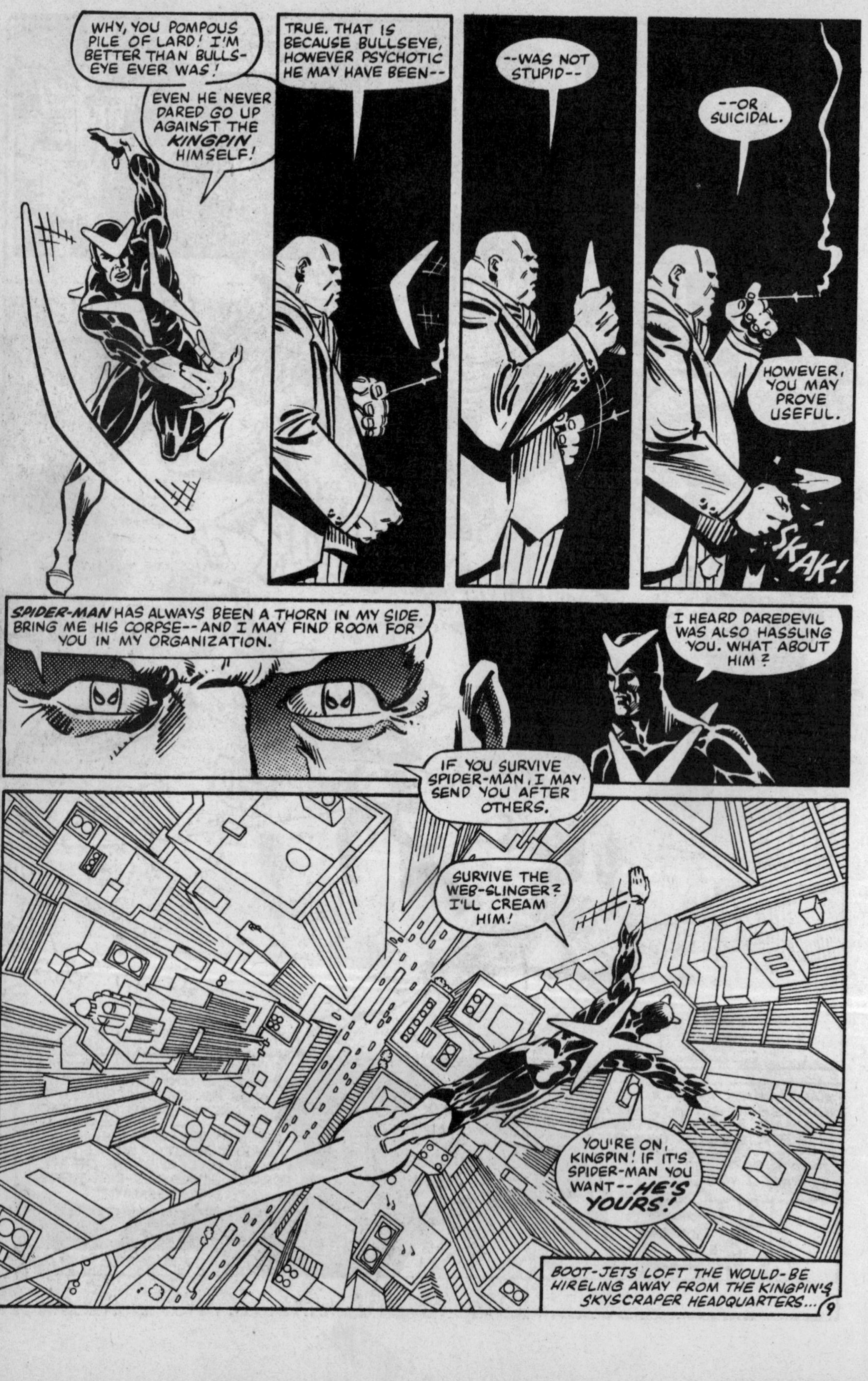
WHY, YOU POMPOUS PILE OF LARD! I'M BETTER THAN BULLS-EYE EVER WAS!
EVEN HE NEVER DARED GO UP AGAINST THE KINGPIN HIMSELF!
TRUE. THAT IS BECAUSE BULLSEYE, HOWEVER PSYCHOTIC HE MAY HAVE BEEN--
--WAS NOT STUPID--
--OR SUICIDAL.
HOWEVER, YOU MAY PROVE USEFUL.
SKAK!
SPIDER-MAN HAS ALWAYS BEEN A THORN IN MY SIDE. BRING ME HIS CORPSE--AND I MAY FIND ROOM FOR YOU IN MY ORGANIZATION.
I HEARD DAREDEVIL WAS ALSO HASSLING YOU. WHAT ABOUT HIM?
IF YOU SURVIVE SPIDER-MAN, I MAY SEND YOU AFTER OTHERS.
SURVIVE THE WEB-SLINGER? I'LL CREAM HIM!
YOU'RE ON, KINGPIN! IF IT'S SPIDER-MAN YOU WANT--HE'S YOURS!
BOOT-JETS LOFT THE WOULD-BE HIRELING AWAY FROM THE KINGPIN'S SKYSCRAPER HEADQUARTERS...

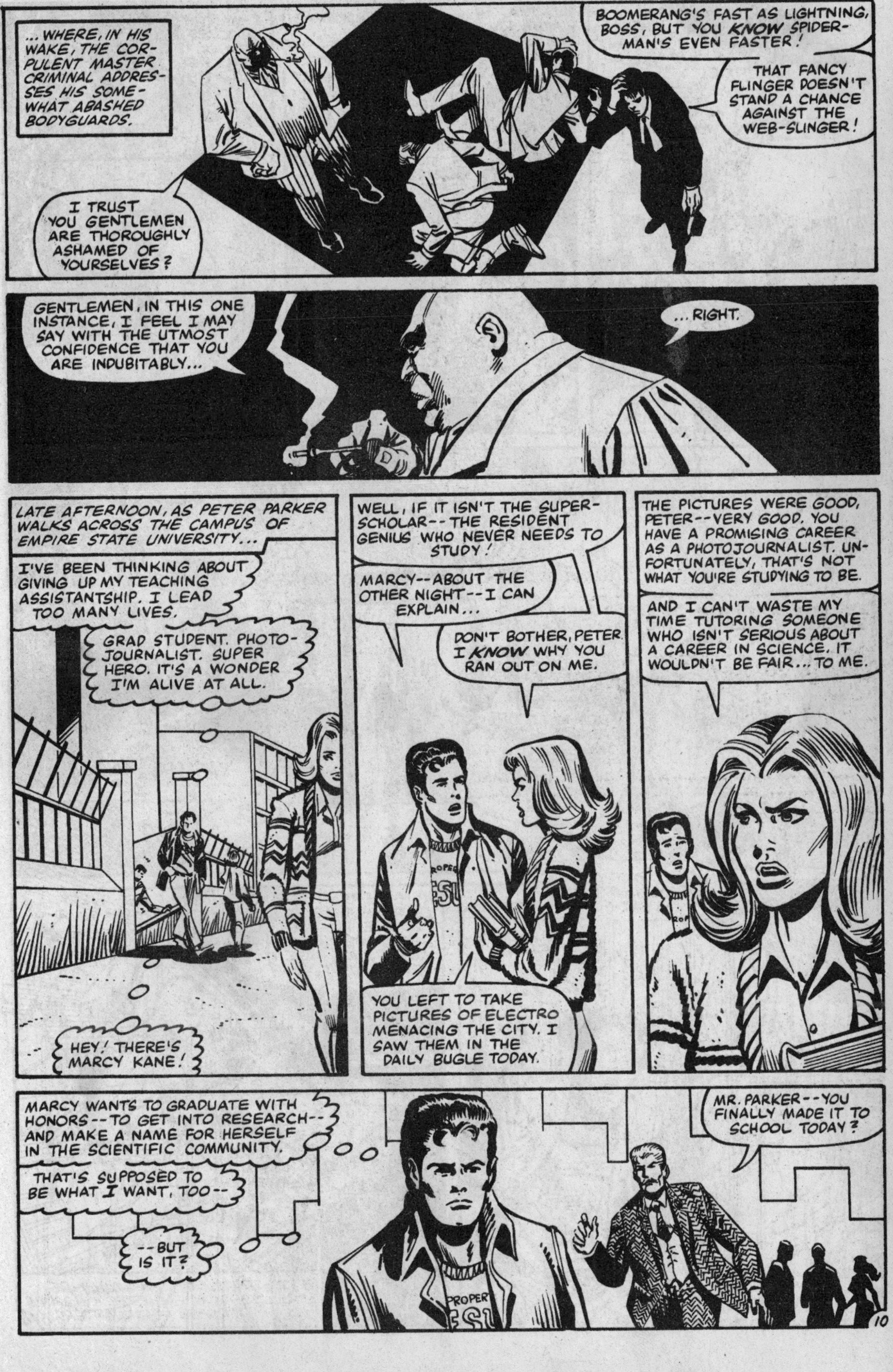

...WHERE, IN HIS WAKE, THE CORPULENT MASTER CRIMINAL ADDRESSES HIS SOMEWHAT ABASHED BODYGUARDS.
BOOMERANG'S FAST AS LIGHTNING, BOSS, BUT YOU KNOW SPIDER-MAN'S EVEN FASTER!
THAT FANCY FLINGER DOESN'T STAND A CHANCE AGAINST THE WEB-SLINGER!
I TRUST YOU GENTLEMEN ARE THOROUGHLY ASHAMED OF YOURSELVES?
GENTLEMEN, IN THIS ONE INSTANCE, I FEEL I MAY SAY WITH THE UTMOST CONFIDENCE THAT YOU ARE INDUBITABLY...
...RIGHT.
LATE AFTERNOON, AS PETER PARKER WALKS ACROSS THE CAMPUS OF EMPIRE STATE UNIVERSITY...
I'VE BEEN THINKING ABOUT GIVING UP MY TEACHING ASSISTANTSHIP. I LEAD TOO MANY LIVES.
GRAD STUDENT. PHOTOJOURNALIST. SUPER HERO. IT'S A WONDER I'M ALIVE AT ALL.
HEY! THERE'S MARCY KANE!
WELL, IF IT ISN'T THE SUPER-SCHOLAR--THE RESIDENT GENIUS WHO NEVER NEEDS TO STUDY!
MARCY--ABOUT THE OTHER NIGHT--I CAN EXPLAIN...
DON'T BOTHER, PETER. I KNOW WHY YOU RAN OUT ON ME.
YOU LEFT TO TAKE PICTURES OF ELECTRO MENACING THE CITY. I SAW THEM IN THE DAILY BUGLE TODAY.
THE PICTURES WERE GOOD, PETER--VERY GOOD. YOU HAVE A PROMISING CAREER AS A PHOTOJOURNALIST. UNFORTUNATELY, THAT'S NOT WHAT YOU'RE STUDYING TO BE.
AND I CAN'T WASTE MY TIME TUTORING SOMEONE WHO ISN'T SERIOUS ABOUT A CAREER IN SCIENCE. IT WOULDN'T BE FAIR... TO ME.
MARCY WANTS TO GRADUATE WITH HONORS--TO GET INTO RESEARCH--AND MAKE A NAME FOR HERSELF IN THE SCIENTIFIC COMMUNITY.
THAT'S SUPPOSED TO BE WHAT I WANT, TOO--
--BUT IS IT?
MR. PARKER--YOU FINALLY MADE IT TO SCHOOL TODAY?
10

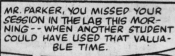

MR. PARKER, YOU MISSED YOUR *SESSION* IN THE LAB THIS MORNING -- WHEN ANOTHER STUDENT COULD HAVE USED THAT VALUABLE TIME.

I'M SORRY, DR. SLOAN. IT WON'T HAPPEN AGAIN!

INDEED IT WON'T.

YOU HAVE A NATURAL APTITUDE FOR SCIENCE, PARKER. YOU'VE COASTED UNTIL NOW. BUT GRADUATE WORK REQUIRES TOTAL ABSORPTION AND DISCIPLINE.

IF YOU CANNOT APPLY YOURSELF MORE DILIGENTLY, PERHAPS WE SHOULD CONSIDER MAKING ROOM FOR SOMEONE WHO CAN.

I WANT TO SUCCEED AT SCHOOL -- I REALLY DO!

BUT HOW CAN I POSSIBLY LIVE UP TO EVERYONE'S EXPECTATIONS OF ME?

I'M ONLY ONE PERSON -- OR I *WAS* -- UNTIL A RADIOACTIVE SPIDER WENT AND COMPLICATED THINGS!

NOW I'M JUGGLING MORE LIVES THAN A CAT --

-- AND IT'S ALL *YOUR* FAULT!

IF IT WEREN'T FOR YOU, I'D HAVE TIME TO STUDY -- TO MAKE FRIENDS -- TO GET SOMEWHERE IN THE WORLD! YOU HAVE IT EASY, DON'T YOU?

YOU SOLVE EVERYTHING WITH YOUR --

-- FISTS!

SPLAK

11

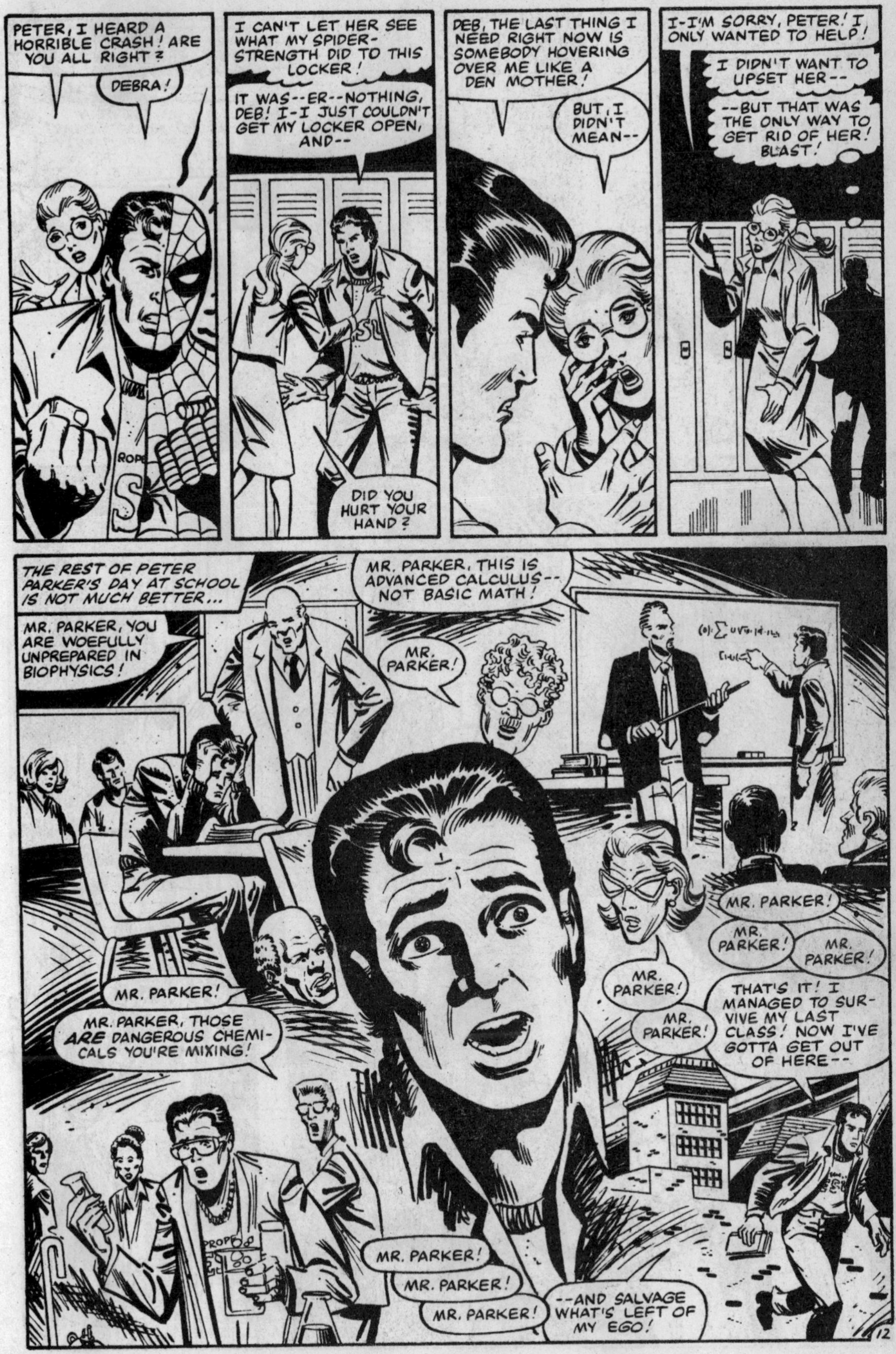
PETER, I HEARD A HORRIBLE CRASH! ARE YOU ALL RIGHT?
DEBRA!
I CAN'T LET HER SEE WHAT MY SPIDER-STRENGTH DID TO THIS LOCKER!
IT WAS--ER--NOTHING, DEB! I-I JUST COULDN'T GET MY LOCKER OPEN, AND--
DID YOU HURT YOUR HAND?
DEB, THE LAST THING I NEED RIGHT NOW IS SOMEBODY HOVERING OVER ME LIKE A DEN MOTHER!
BUT, I DIDN'T MEAN--
I-I'M SORRY, PETER! I ONLY WANTED TO HELP!
I DIDN'T WANT TO UPSET HER--
--BUT THAT WAS THE ONLY WAY TO GET RID OF HER! BLAST!
THE REST OF PETER PARKER'S DAY AT SCHOOL IS NOT MUCH BETTER...
MR. PARKER, YOU ARE WOEFULLY UNPREPARED IN BIOPHYSICS!
MR. PARKER, THIS IS ADVANCED CALCULUS--NOT BASIC MATH!
MR. PARKER!
MR. PARKER!
MR. PARKER!
MR. PARKER!
MR. PARKER!
MR. PARKER, THOSE ARE DANGEROUS CHEMICALS YOU'RE MIXING!
MR. PARKER!
MR. PARKER!
MR. PARKER!
THAT'S IT! I MANAGED TO SURVIVE MY LAST CLASS! NOW I'VE GOTTA GET OUT OF HERE--
MR. PARKER!
MR. PARKER!
MR. PARKER!
--AND SALVAGE WHAT'S LEFT OF MY EGO!
12

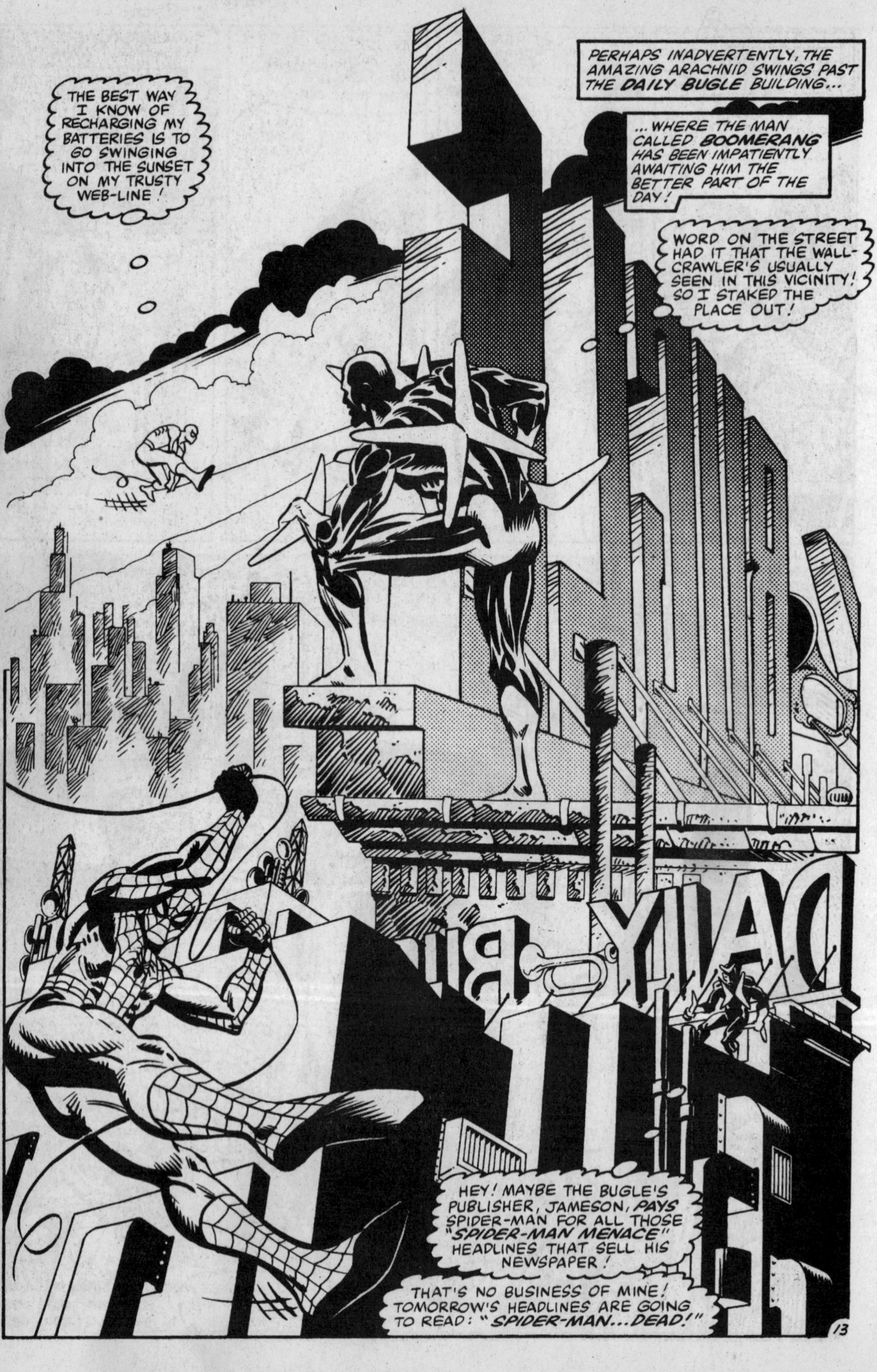
PERHAPS INADVERTENTLY, THE AMAZING ARACHNID SWINGS PAST THE DAILY BUGLE BUILDING...
THE BEST WAY I KNOW OF RECHARGING MY BATTERIES IS TO GO SWINGING INTO THE SUNSET ON MY TRUSTY WEB-LINE!
...WHERE THE MAN CALLED BOOMERANG HAS BEEN IMPATIENTLY AWAITING HIM THE BETTER PART OF THE DAY!
WORD ON THE STREET HAD IT THAT THE WALL-CRAWLER'S USUALLY SEEN IN THIS VICINITY! SO I STAKED THE PLACE OUT!
HEY! MAYBE THE BUGLE'S PUBLISHER, JAMESON, PAYS SPIDER-MAN FOR ALL THOSE "SPIDER-MAN MENACE" HEADLINES THAT SELL HIS NEWSPAPER!
THAT'S NO BUSINESS OF MINE! TOMORROW'S HEADLINES ARE GOING TO READ: "SPIDER-MAN...DEAD!"
13

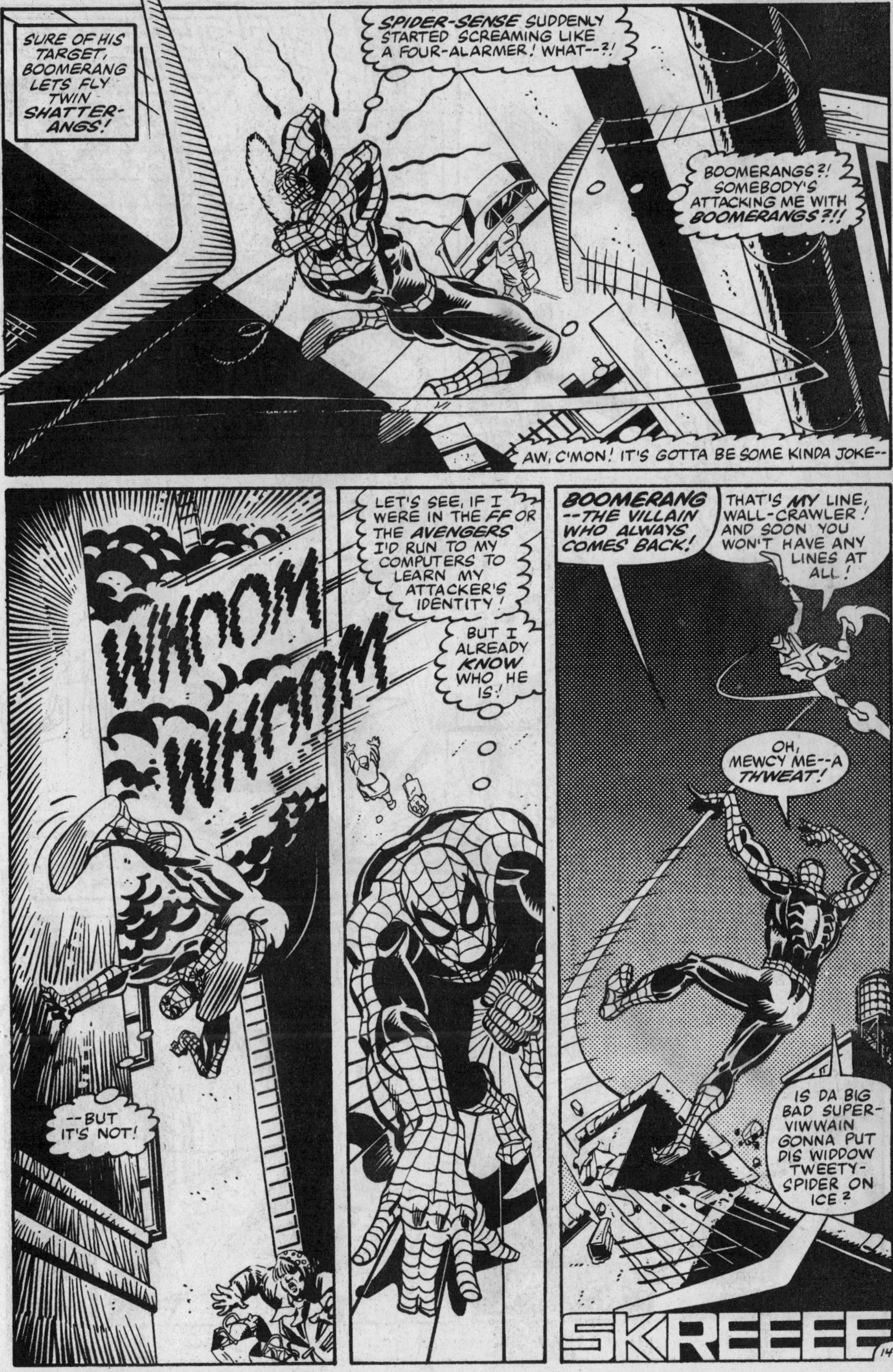
SURE OF HIS TARGET, BOOMERANG LETS FLY TWIN SHATTER-ANGS!
SPIDER-SENSE SUDDENLY STARTED SCREAMING LIKE A FOUR-ALARMER! WHAT--?!
BOOMERANGS?! SOMEBODY'S ATTACKING ME WITH BOOMERANGS?!!
AW, C'MON! IT'S GOTTA BE SOME KINDA JOKE--
WHOOM
WHOOM
--BUT IT'S NOT!
LET'S SEE, IF I WERE IN THE FF OR THE AVENGERS I'D RUN TO MY COMPUTERS TO LEARN MY ATTACKER'S IDENTITY!
BUT I ALREADY KNOW WHO HE IS!
BOOMERANG --THE VILLAIN WHO ALWAYS COMES BACK!
THAT'S MY LINE, WALL-CRAWLER! AND SOON YOU WON'T HAVE ANY LINES AT ALL!
OH, MEWCY ME--A THWEAT!
IS DA BIG BAD SUPER-VIWWAIN GONNA PUT DIS WIDDOW TWEETY-SPIDER ON ICE?
SKREEEE

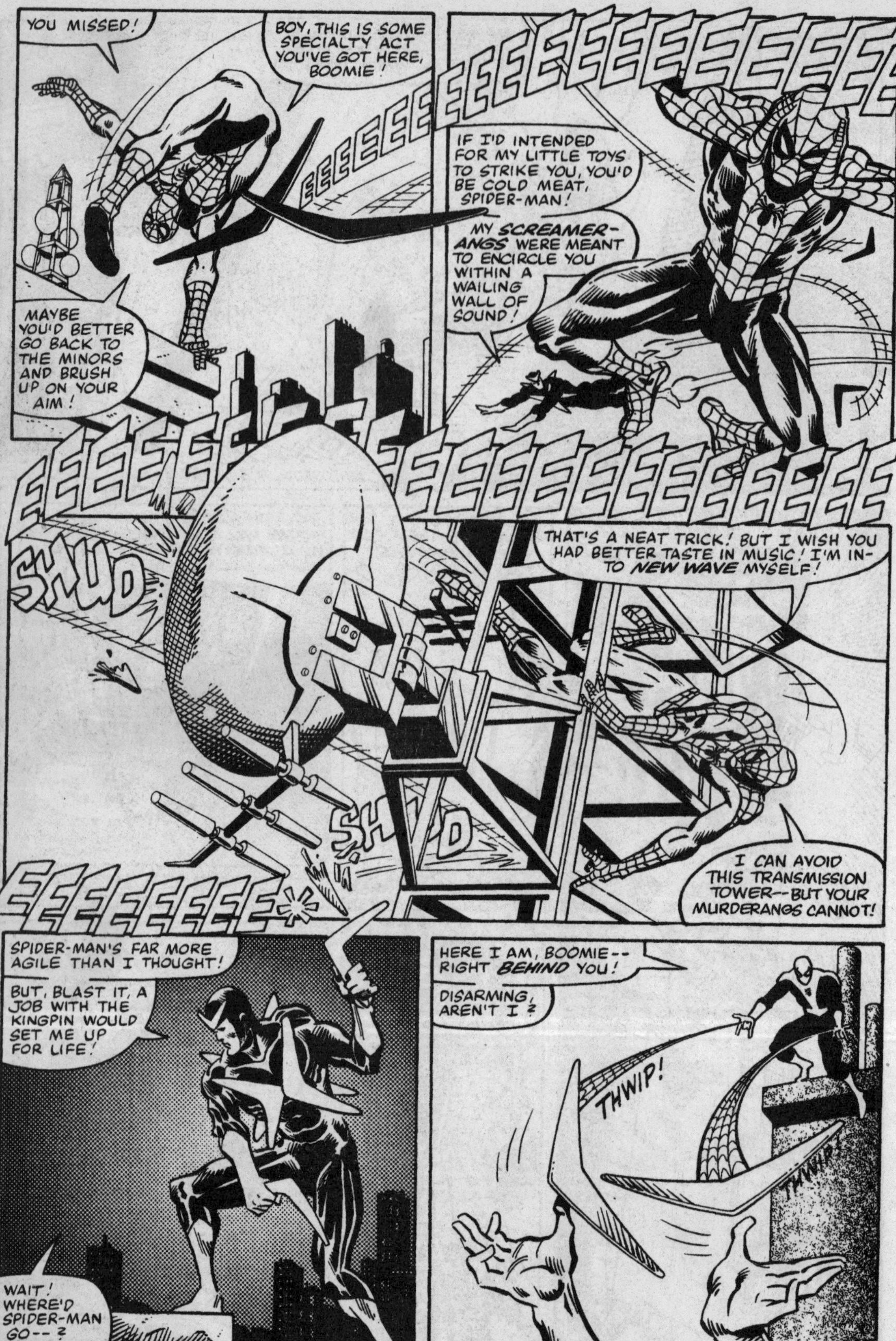
YOU MISSED!
BOY, THIS IS SOME SPECIALTY ACT YOU'VE GOT HERE, BOOMIE!
MAYBE YOU'D BETTER GO BACK TO THE MINORS AND BRUSH UP ON YOUR AIM!
IF I'D INTENDED FOR MY LITTLE TOYS TO STRIKE YOU, YOU'D BE COLD MEAT, SPIDER-MAN!
MY SCREAMER-ANGS WERE MEANT TO ENCIRCLE YOU WITHIN A WAILING WALL OF SOUND!
SHUD
THAT'S A NEAT TRICK! BUT I WISH YOU HAD BETTER TASTE IN MUSIC! I'M INTO NEW WAVE MYSELF!
I CAN AVOID THIS TRANSMISSION TOWER--BUT YOUR MURDERANGS CANNOT!
SPIDER-MAN'S FAR MORE AGILE THAN I THOUGHT!
BUT, BLAST IT, A JOB WITH THE KINGPIN WOULD SET ME UP FOR LIFE!
WAIT! WHERE'D SPIDER-MAN GO--?
HERE I AM, BOOMIE--RIGHT BEHIND YOU!
DISARMING, AREN'T I?
THWIP!
THWIP!

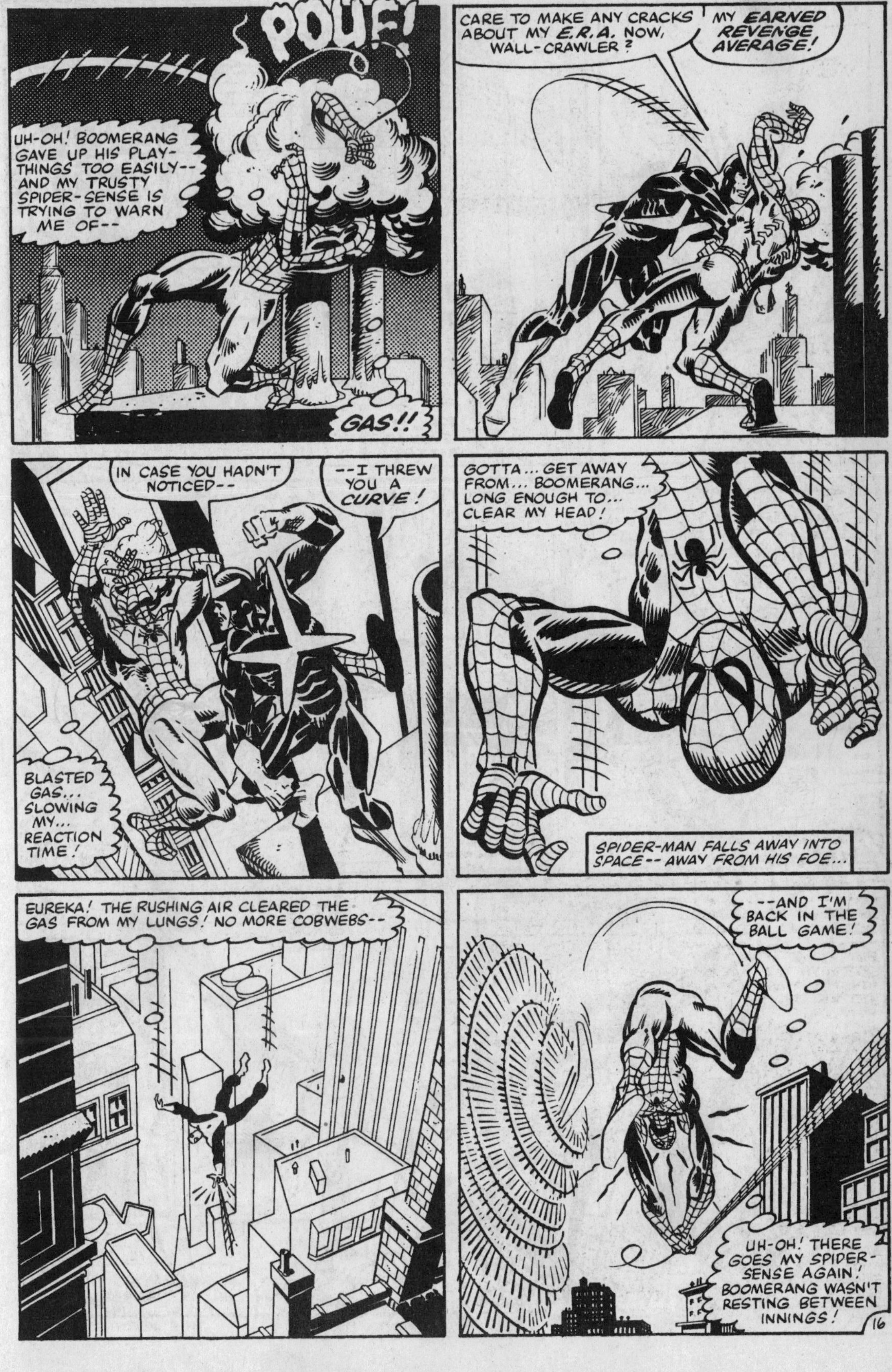
POUF!
UH-OH! BOOMERANG GAVE UP HIS PLAYTHINGS TOO EASILY--AND MY TRUSTY SPIDER-SENSE IS TRYING TO WARN ME OF--
GAS!!
CARE TO MAKE ANY CRACKS ABOUT MY E.R.A. NOW, WALL-CRAWLER?
MY EARNED REVENGE AVERAGE!
IN CASE YOU HADN'T NOTICED--
--I THREW YOU A CURVE!
BLASTED GAS... SLOWING MY... REACTION TIME!
GOTTA... GET AWAY FROM... BOOMERANG... LONG ENOUGH TO... CLEAR MY HEAD!
SPIDER-MAN FALLS AWAY INTO SPACE-- AWAY FROM HIS FOE...
EUREKA! THE RUSHING AIR CLEARED THE GAS FROM MY LUNGS! NO MORE COBWEBS--
--AND I'M BACK IN THE BALL GAME!
UH-OH! THERE GOES MY SPIDER-SENSE AGAIN! BOOMERANG WASN'T RESTING BETWEEN INNINGS!
16

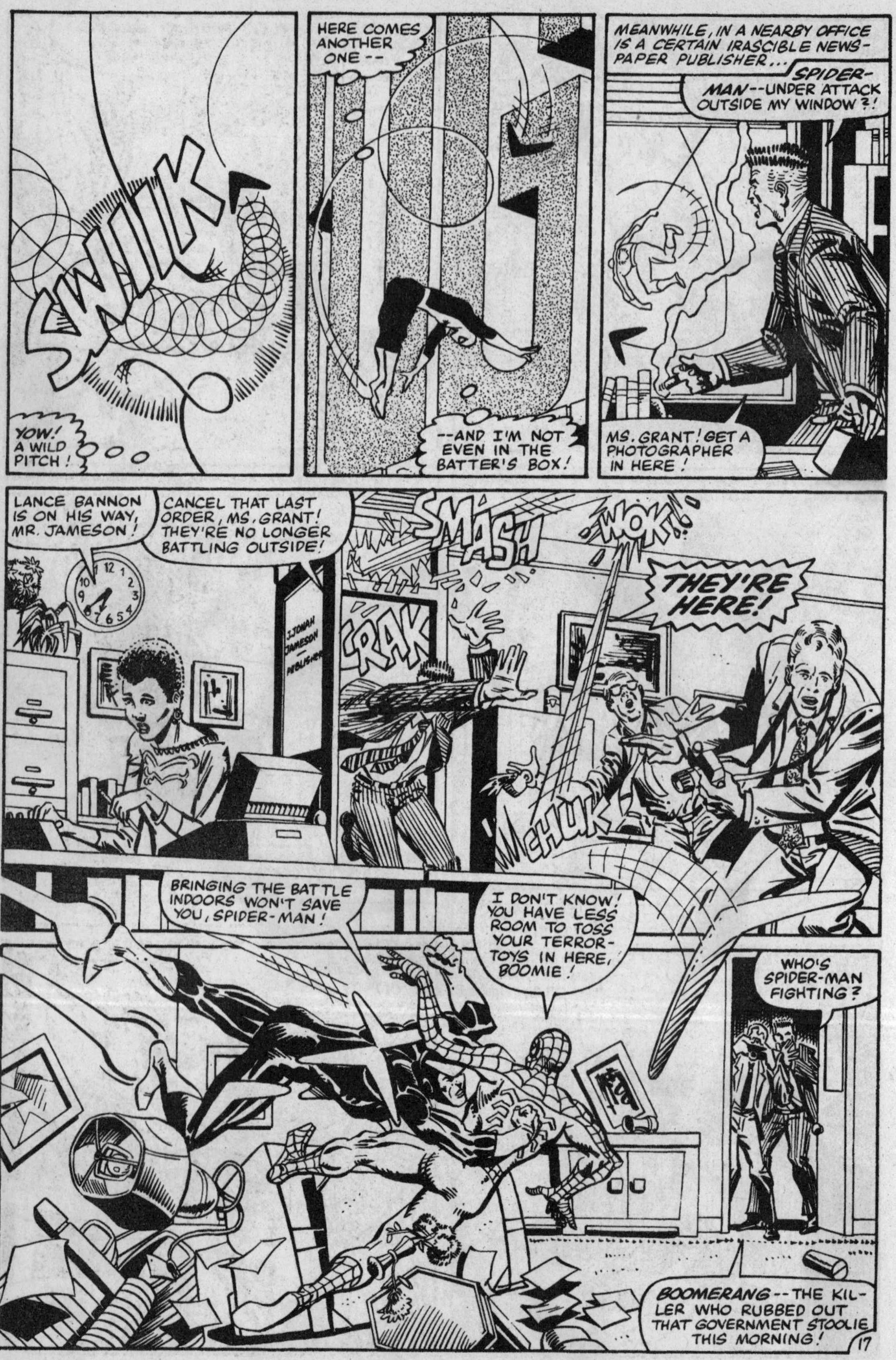
SWIIK
YOW! A WILD PITCH!
HERE COMES ANOTHER ONE --
--AND I'M NOT EVEN IN THE BATTER'S BOX!
MEANWHILE, IN A NEARBY OFFICE IS A CERTAIN IRASCIBLE NEWS-PAPER PUBLISHER...
SPIDER-MAN--UNDER ATTACK OUTSIDE MY WINDOW?!
MS. GRANT! GET A PHOTOGRAPHER IN HERE!
LANCE BANNON IS ON HIS WAY, MR. JAMESON!
CANCEL THAT LAST ORDER, MS. GRANT! THEY'RE NO LONGER BATTLING OUTSIDE!
SMASH
WOK!
CRAK
THEY'RE HERE!
CHUK
BRINGING THE BATTLE INDOORS WON'T SAVE YOU, SPIDER-MAN!
I DON'T KNOW! YOU HAVE LESS ROOM TO TOSS YOUR TERROR-TOYS IN HERE, BOOMIE!
WHO'S SPIDER-MAN FIGHTING?
BOOMERANG--THE KILLER WHO RUBBED OUT THAT GOVERNMENT STOOLIE THIS MORNING!

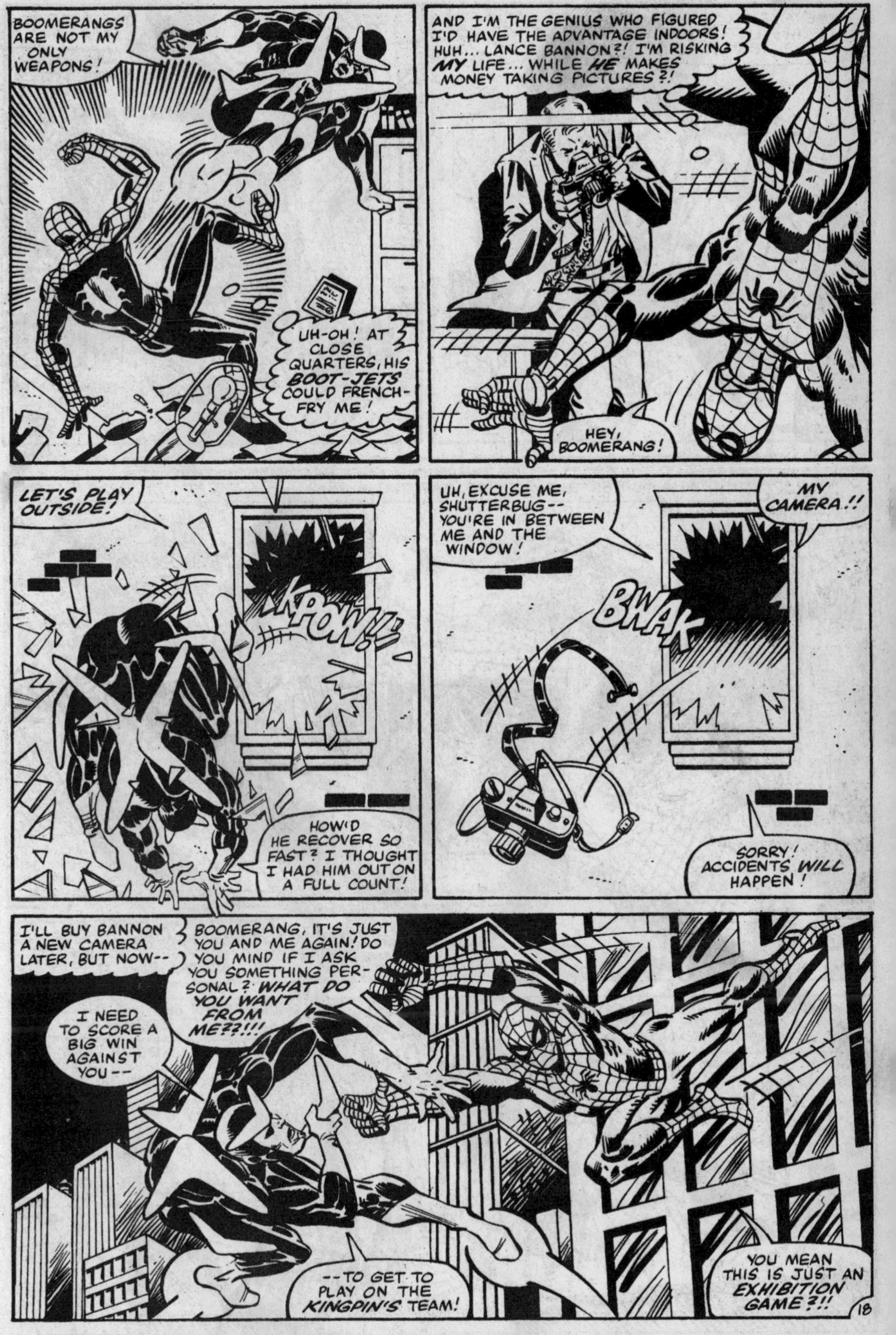
BOOMERANGS ARE NOT MY ONLY WEAPONS!
UH-OH! AT CLOSE QUARTERS, HIS BOOT-JETS COULD FRENCH-FRY ME!
AND I'M THE GENIUS WHO FIGURED I'D HAVE THE ADVANTAGE INDOORS! HUH... LANCE BANNON?! I'M RISKING MY LIFE... WHILE HE MAKES MONEY TAKING PICTURES?!
HEY, BOOMERANG!
LET'S PLAY OUTSIDE!
KPOW!!
HOW'D HE RECOVER SO FAST? I THOUGHT I HAD HIM OUT ON A FULL COUNT!
UH, EXCUSE ME, SHUTTERBUG-- YOU'RE IN BETWEEN ME AND THE WINDOW!
MY CAMERA!!
BWAK
SORRY! ACCIDENTS WILL HAPPEN!
I'LL BUY BANNON A NEW CAMERA LATER, BUT NOW--
BOOMERANG, IT'S JUST YOU AND ME AGAIN! DO YOU MIND IF I ASK YOU SOMETHING PERSONAL? WHAT DO YOU WANT FROM ME??!!!
I NEED TO SCORE A BIG WIN AGAINST YOU--
--TO GET TO PLAY ON THE KINGPIN'S TEAM!
YOU MEAN THIS IS JUST AN EXHIBITION GAME?!!

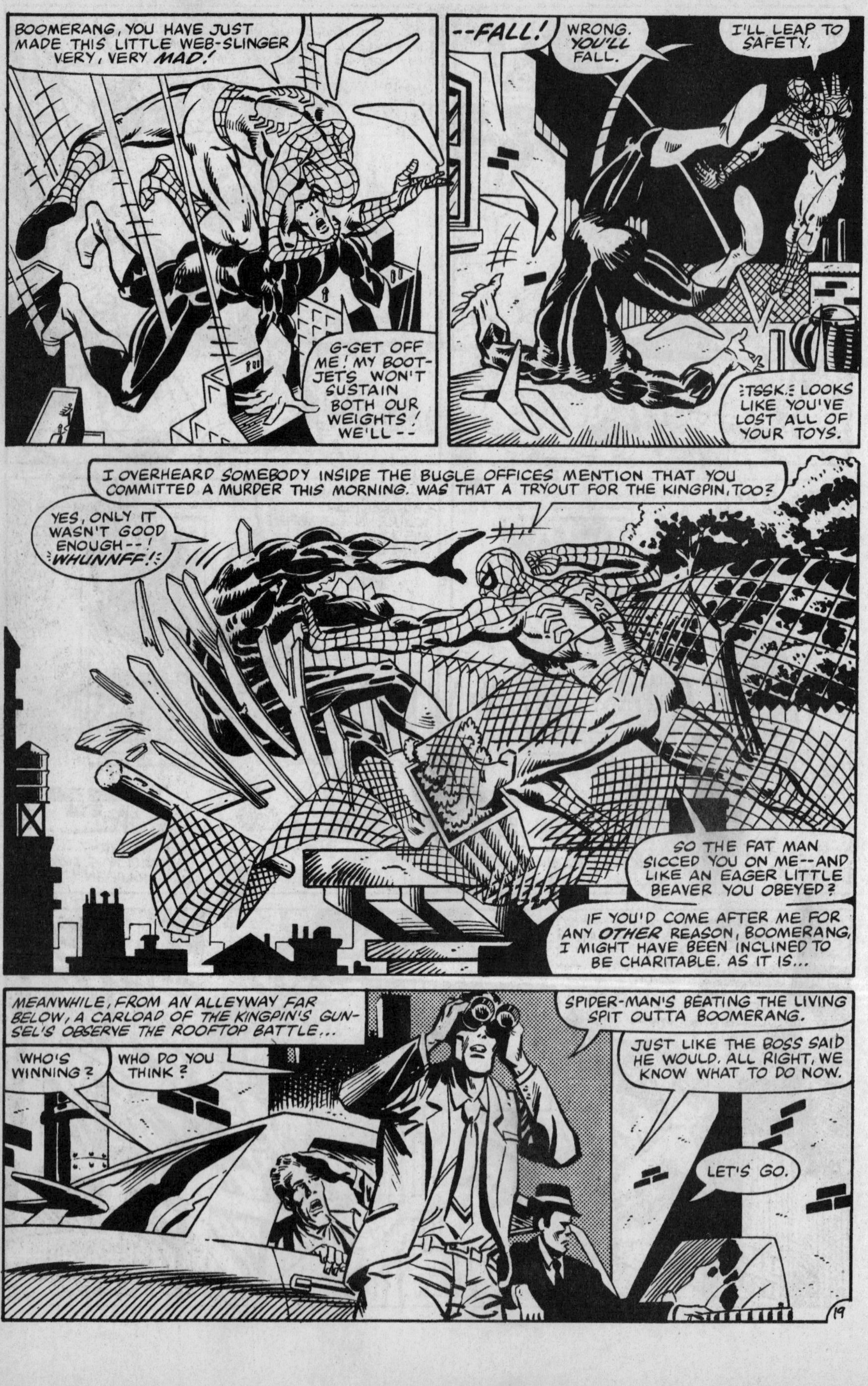
BOOMERANG, YOU HAVE JUST MADE THIS LITTLE WEB-SLINGER VERY, VERY *MAD!*
G-GET OFF ME! MY BOOT-JETS WON'T SUSTAIN BOTH OUR WEIGHTS! WE'LL --
--*FALL!*
WRONG. *YOU'LL* FALL.
I'LL LEAP TO SAFETY.
TSSK. LOOKS LIKE YOU'VE LOST ALL OF YOUR TOYS.
I OVERHEARD SOMEBODY INSIDE THE BUGLE OFFICES MENTION THAT YOU COMMITTED A MURDER THIS MORNING. WAS THAT A TRYOUT FOR THE KINGPIN, TOO?
YES, ONLY IT WASN'T GOOD ENOUGH--! *WHUNNFF!*
SO THE FAT MAN SICCED YOU ON ME--AND LIKE AN EAGER LITTLE BEAVER YOU OBEYED?
IF YOU'D COME AFTER ME FOR ANY *OTHER* REASON, BOOMERANG, I MIGHT HAVE BEEN INCLINED TO BE CHARITABLE. AS IT IS...
MEANWHILE, FROM AN ALLEYWAY FAR BELOW, A CARLOAD OF THE KINGPIN'S GUNSEL'S OBSERVE THE ROOFTOP BATTLE...
WHO'S WINNING?
WHO DO YOU THINK?
SPIDER-MAN'S BEATING THE LIVING SPIT OUTTA BOOMERANG.
JUST LIKE THE BOSS SAID HE WOULD. ALL RIGHT, WE KNOW WHAT TO DO NOW.
LET'S GO.
19

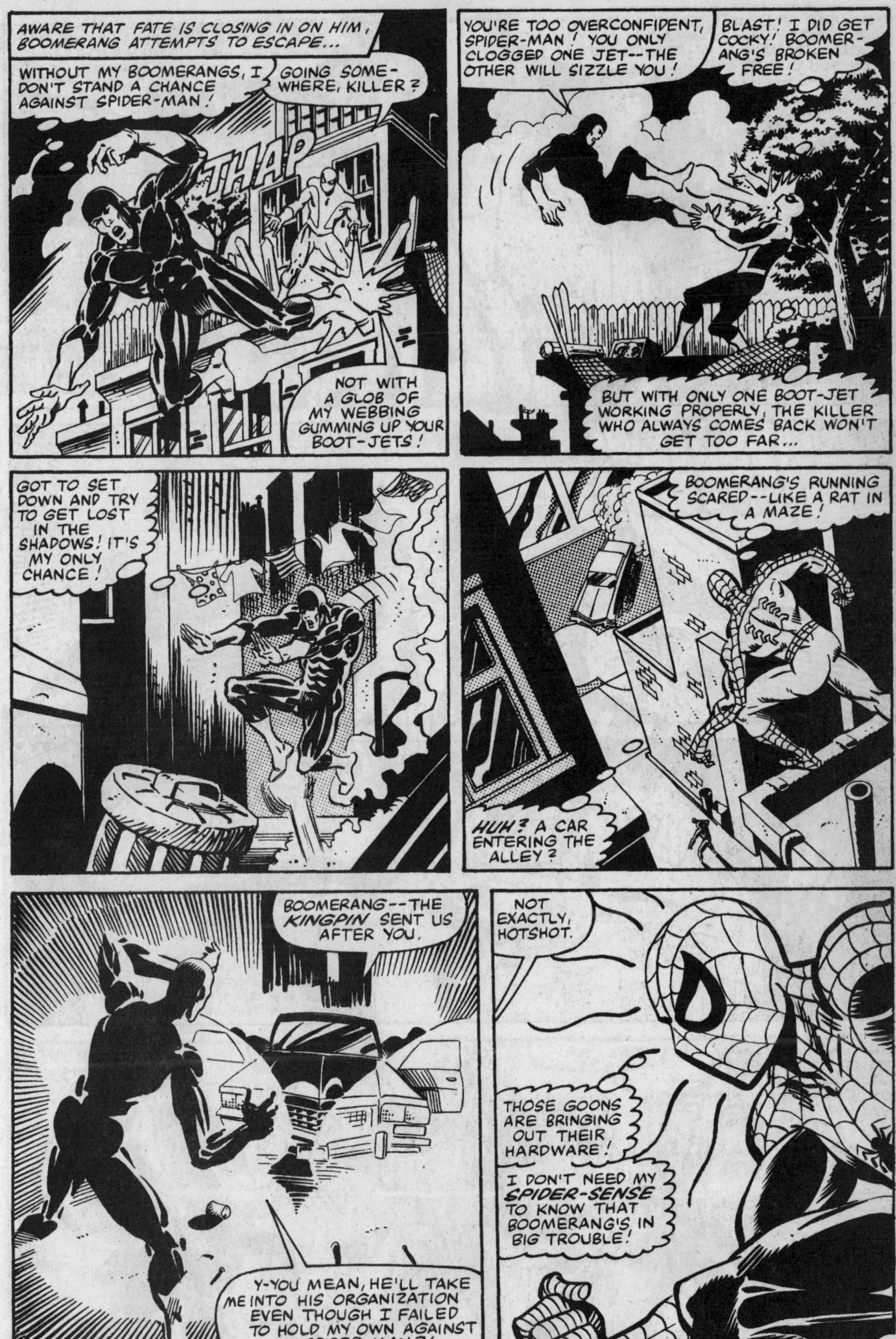
AWARE THAT FATE IS CLOSING IN ON HIM, BOOMERANG ATTEMPTS TO ESCAPE...
WITHOUT MY BOOMERANGS, I DON'T STAND A CHANCE AGAINST SPIDER-MAN!
GOING SOME-WHERE, KILLER?
THAP
NOT WITH A GLOB OF MY WEBBING GUMMING UP YOUR BOOT-JETS!
YOU'RE TOO OVERCONFIDENT, SPIDER-MAN! YOU ONLY CLOGGED ONE JET--THE OTHER WILL SIZZLE YOU!
BLAST! I DID GET COCKY! BOOMER-ANG'S BROKEN FREE!
BUT WITH ONLY ONE BOOT-JET WORKING PROPERLY, THE KILLER WHO ALWAYS COMES BACK WON'T GET TOO FAR...
GOT TO SET DOWN AND TRY TO GET LOST IN THE SHADOWS! IT'S MY ONLY CHANCE!
BOOMERANG'S RUNNING SCARED--LIKE A RAT IN A MAZE!
HUH? A CAR ENTERING THE ALLEY?
BOOMERANG--THE KINGPIN SENT US AFTER YOU.
Y-YOU MEAN, HE'LL TAKE ME INTO HIS ORGANIZATION EVEN THOUGH I FAILED TO HOLD MY OWN AGAINST SPIDER-MAN?!
NOT EXACTLY, HOTSHOT.
THOSE GOONS ARE BRINGING OUT THEIR HARDWARE!
I DON'T NEED MY SPIDER-SENSE TO KNOW THAT BOOMERANG'S IN BIG TROUBLE!

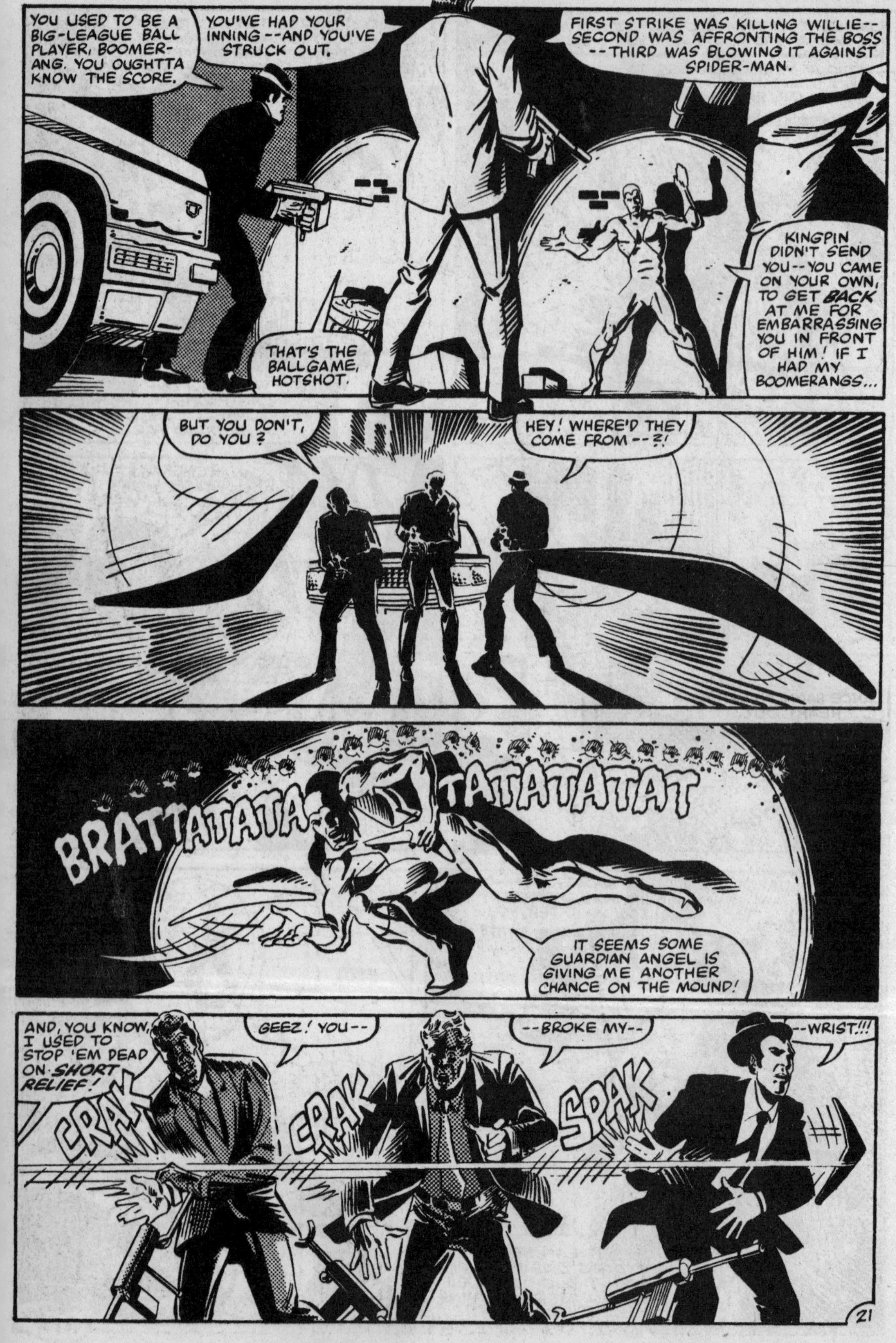
YOU USED TO BE A BIG-LEAGUE BALL PLAYER, BOOMERANG. YOU OUGHTTA KNOW THE SCORE.
YOU'VE HAD YOUR INNING--AND YOU'VE STRUCK OUT.
FIRST STRIKE WAS KILLING WILLIE--SECOND WAS AFFRONTING THE BOSS--THIRD WAS BLOWING IT AGAINST SPIDER-MAN.
THAT'S THE BALLGAME, HOTSHOT.
KINGPIN DIDN'T SEND YOU--YOU CAME ON YOUR OWN, TO GET BACK AT ME FOR EMBARRASSING YOU IN FRONT OF HIM! IF I HAD MY BOOMERANGS...
BUT YOU DON'T, DO YOU?
HEY! WHERE'D THEY COME FROM--?!
BRATTATATA
TATATATAT
IT SEEMS SOME GUARDIAN ANGEL IS GIVING ME ANOTHER CHANCE ON THE MOUND!
AND, YOU KNOW, I USED TO STOP 'EM DEAD ON SHORT RELIEF!
GEEZ! YOU--
--BROKE MY--
--WRIST!!!
CRAK
CRAK
SPAK

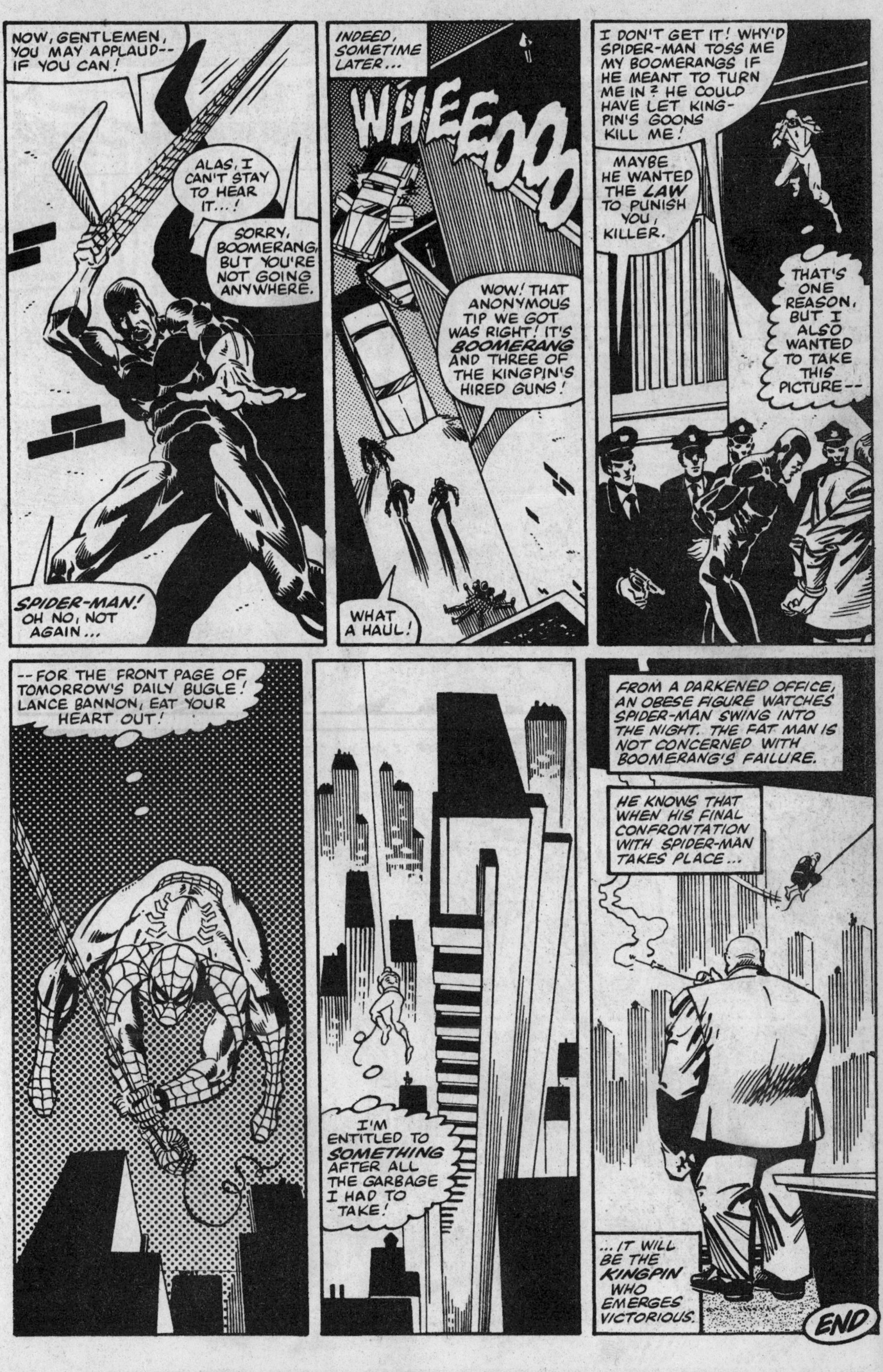
NOW, GENTLEMEN, YOU MAY APPLAUD-- IF YOU CAN!
ALAS, I CAN'T STAY TO HEAR IT...!
SORRY, BOOMERANG, BUT YOU'RE NOT GOING ANYWHERE.
SPIDER-MAN! OH NO, NOT AGAIN...
INDEED, SOMETIME LATER...
WHEEOOO
WOW! THAT ANONYMOUS TIP WE GOT WAS RIGHT! IT'S BOOMERANG AND THREE OF THE KINGPIN'S HIRED GUNS!
WHAT A HAUL!
I DON'T GET IT! WHY'D SPIDER-MAN TOSS ME MY BOOMERANGS IF HE MEANT TO TURN ME IN? HE COULD HAVE LET KING-PIN'S GOONS KILL ME!
MAYBE HE WANTED THE LAW TO PUNISH YOU, KILLER.
THAT'S ONE REASON, BUT I ALSO WANTED TO TAKE THIS PICTURE--
--FOR THE FRONT PAGE OF TOMORROW'S DAILY BUGLE! LANCE BANNON, EAT YOUR HEART OUT!
I'M ENTITLED TO SOMETHING AFTER ALL THE GARBAGE I HAD TO TAKE!
FROM A DARKENED OFFICE, AN OBESE FIGURE WATCHES SPIDER-MAN SWING INTO THE NIGHT. THE FAT MAN IS NOT CONCERNED WITH BOOMERANG'S FAILURE.
HE KNOWS THAT WHEN HIS FINAL CONFRONTATION WITH SPIDER-MAN TAKES PLACE...
...IT WILL BE THE KINGPIN WHO EMERGES VICTORIOUS.
END

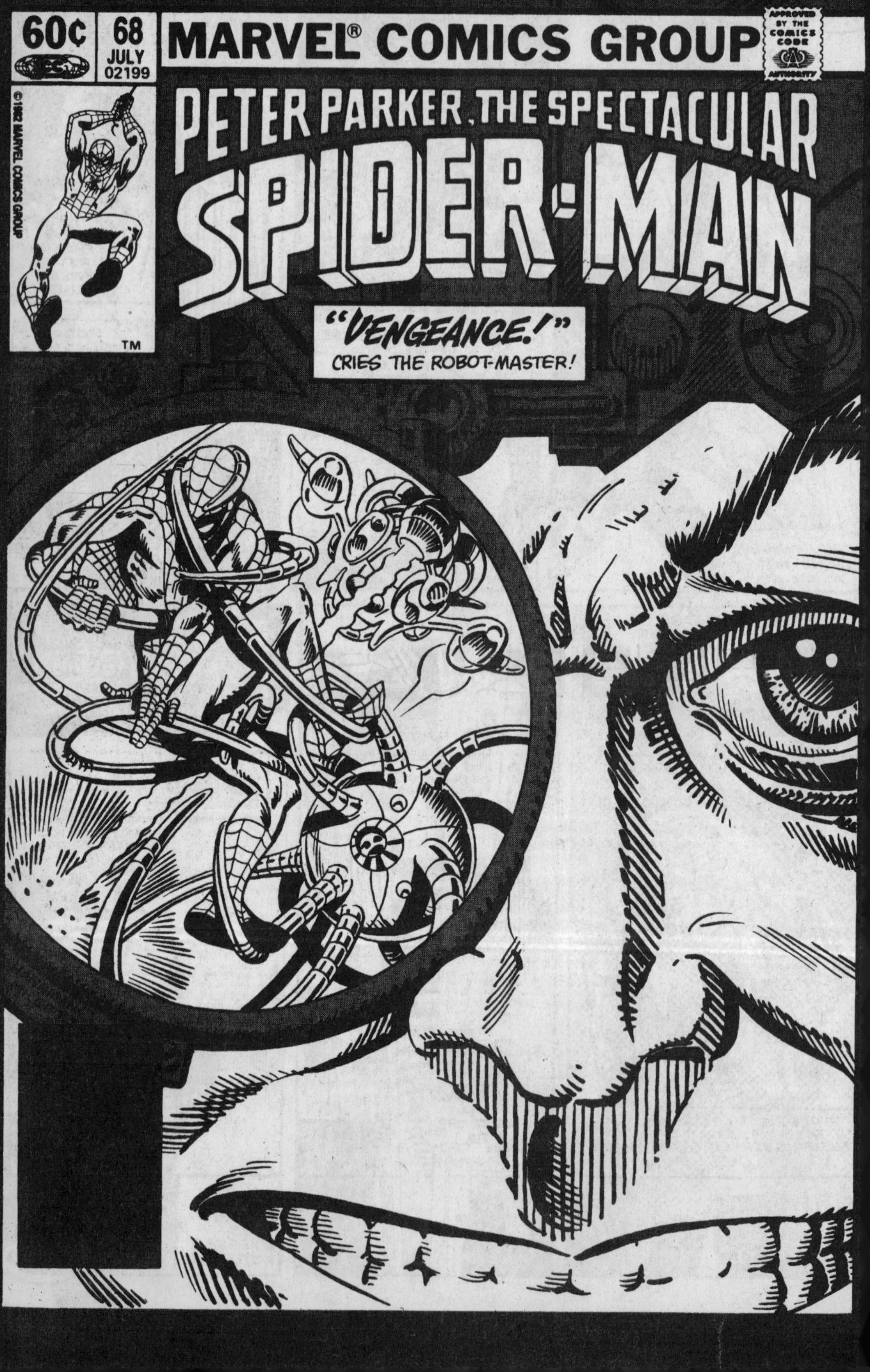
60¢
68
JULY
02199
MARVEL® COMICS GROUP
APPROVED BY THE COMICS CODE AUTHORITY
© 1982 MARVEL COMICS GROUP
PETER PARKER, THE SPECTACULAR
SPIDER-MAN
TM
"VENGEANCE!"
CRIES THE ROBOT-MASTER!

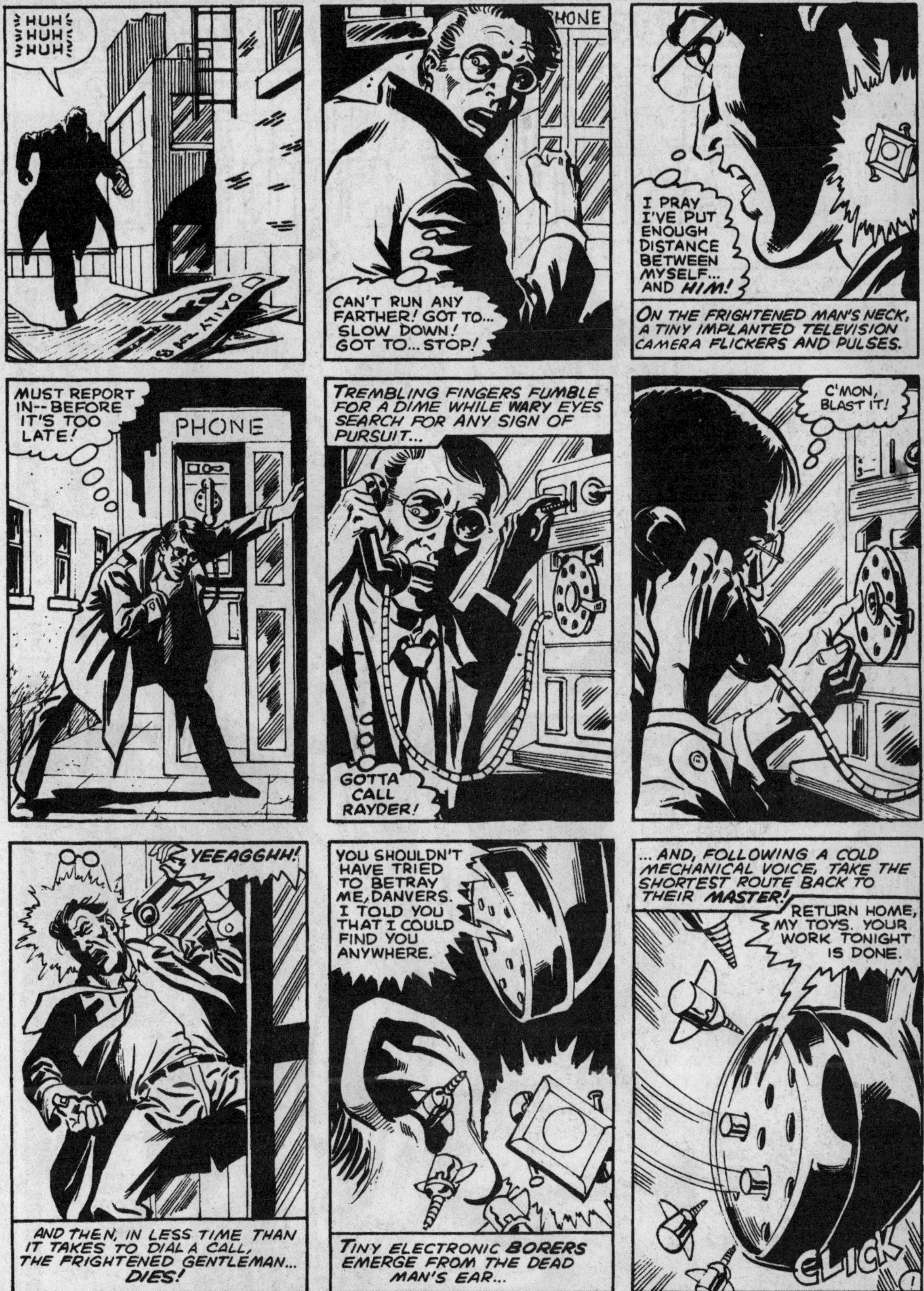
HUH HUH HUH
PHONE
CAN'T RUN ANY FARTHER! GOT TO... SLOW DOWN! GOT TO... STOP!
I PRAY I'VE PUT ENOUGH DISTANCE BETWEEN MYSELF... AND HIM!
ON THE FRIGHTENED MAN'S NECK, A TINY IMPLANTED TELEVISION CAMERA FLICKERS AND PULSES.
MUST REPORT IN-- BEFORE IT'S TOO LATE!
PHONE
TREMBLING FINGERS FUMBLE FOR A DIME WHILE WARY EYES SEARCH FOR ANY SIGN OF PURSUIT...
GOTTA CALL RAYDER!
C'MON, BLAST IT!
YEEAGGHH!
AND THEN, IN LESS TIME THAN IT TAKES TO DIAL A CALL, THE FRIGHTENED GENTLEMAN... DIES!
YOU SHOULDN'T HAVE TRIED TO BETRAY ME, DANVERS. I TOLD YOU THAT I COULD FIND YOU ANYWHERE.
TINY ELECTRONIC BORERS EMERGE FROM THE DEAD MAN'S EAR...
... AND, FOLLOWING A COLD MECHANICAL VOICE, TAKE THE SHORTEST ROUTE BACK TO THEIR MASTER!
RETURN HOME, MY TOYS. YOUR WORK TONIGHT IS DONE.
CLICK!

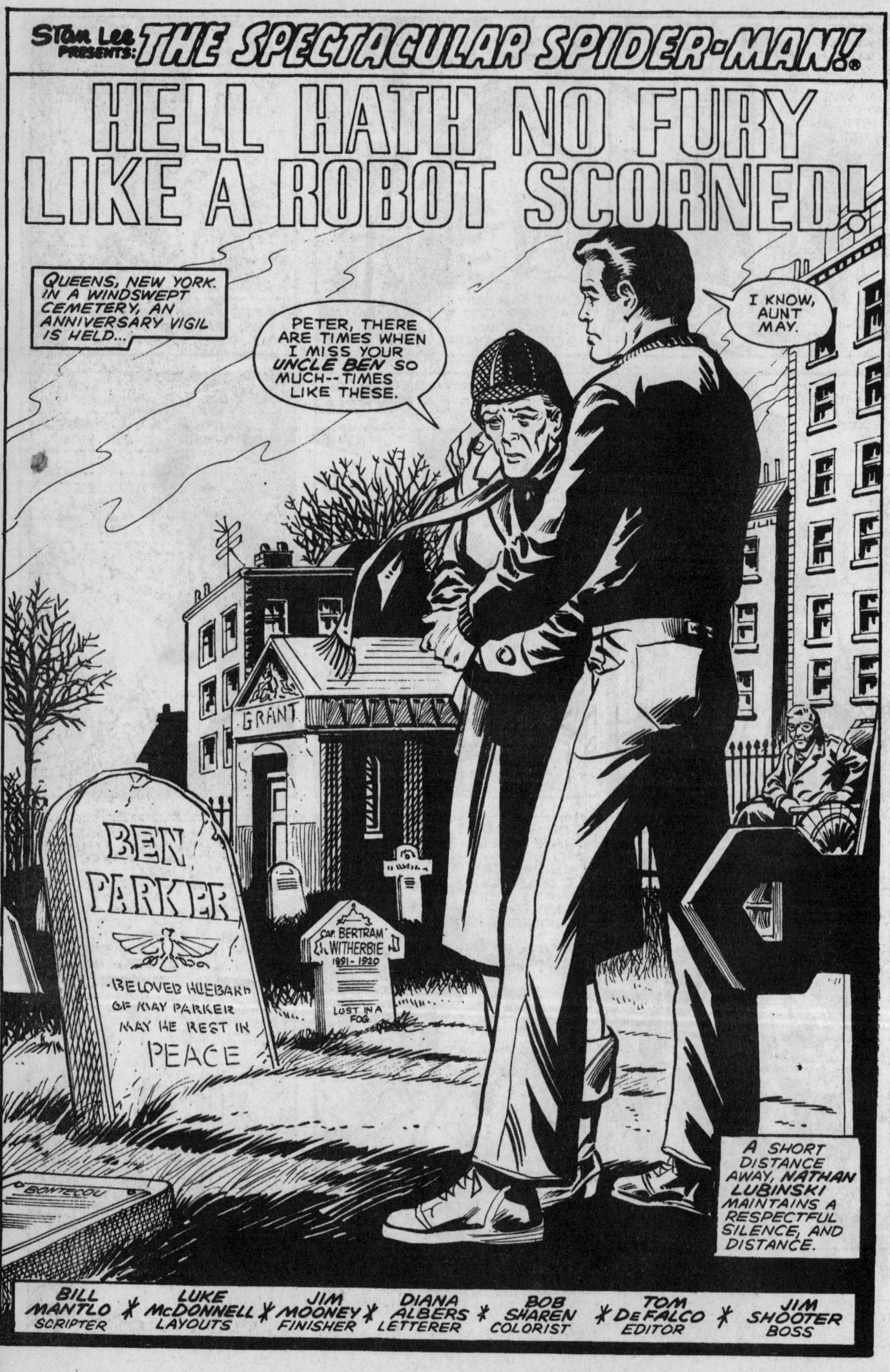

STAN LEE PRESENTS: THE SPECTACULAR SPIDER-MAN!®
HELL HATH NO FURY LIKE A ROBOT SCORNED!
QUEENS, NEW YORK. IN A WINDSWEPT CEMETERY, AN ANNIVERSARY VIGIL IS HELD...
PETER, THERE ARE TIMES WHEN I MISS YOUR UNCLE BEN SO MUCH--TIMES LIKE THESE.
I KNOW, AUNT MAY.
GRANT
BEN PARKER
BELOVED HUSBAND OF MAY PARKER MAY HE REST IN PEACE
CAP. BERTRAM WITHERBIE 1891-1920
LOST IN A FOG
BONTECOU
A SHORT DISTANCE AWAY, NATHAN LUBINSKI MAINTAINS A RESPECTFUL SILENCE, AND DISTANCE.
BILL MANTLO SCRIPTER * LUKE McDONNELL LAYOUTS * JIM MOONEY FINISHER * DIANA ALBERS LETTERER * BOB SHAREN COLORIST * TOM DeFALCO EDITOR * JIM SHOOTER BOSS

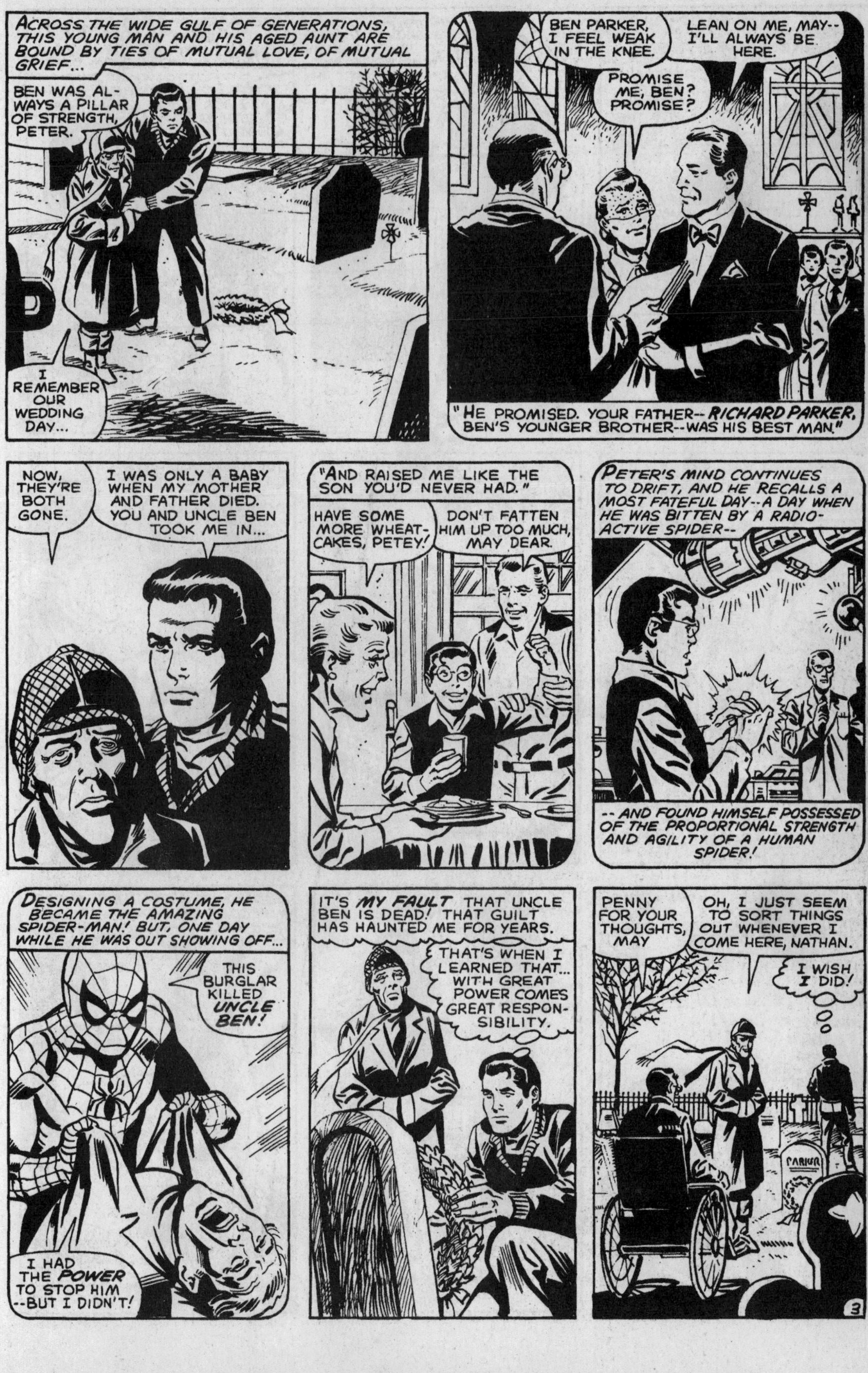
ACROSS THE WIDE GULF OF GENERATIONS, THIS YOUNG MAN AND HIS AGED AUNT ARE BOUND BY TIES OF MUTUAL LOVE, OF MUTUAL GRIEF...
BEN WAS ALWAYS A PILLAR OF STRENGTH, PETER.
I REMEMBER OUR WEDDING DAY...
BEN PARKER, I FEEL WEAK IN THE KNEE.
LEAN ON ME, MAY-- I'LL ALWAYS BE HERE.
PROMISE ME, BEN? PROMISE?
"HE PROMISED. YOUR FATHER-- RICHARD PARKER, BEN'S YOUNGER BROTHER--WAS HIS BEST MAN."
NOW, THEY'RE BOTH GONE.
I WAS ONLY A BABY WHEN MY MOTHER AND FATHER DIED. YOU AND UNCLE BEN TOOK ME IN...
"AND RAISED ME LIKE THE SON YOU'D NEVER HAD."
HAVE SOME MORE WHEATCAKES, PETEY!
DON'T FATTEN HIM UP TOO MUCH, MAY DEAR.
PETER'S MIND CONTINUES TO DRIFT, AND HE RECALLS A MOST FATEFUL DAY--A DAY WHEN HE WAS BITTEN BY A RADIO-ACTIVE SPIDER--
-- AND FOUND HIMSELF POSSESSED OF THE PROPORTIONAL STRENGTH AND AGILITY OF A HUMAN SPIDER!
DESIGNING A COSTUME, HE BECAME THE AMAZING SPIDER-MAN! BUT, ONE DAY WHILE HE WAS OUT SHOWING OFF...
THIS BURGLAR KILLED UNCLE BEN!
I HAD THE POWER TO STOP HIM --BUT I DIDN'T!
IT'S MY FAULT THAT UNCLE BEN IS DEAD! THAT GUILT HAS HAUNTED ME FOR YEARS.
THAT'S WHEN I LEARNED THAT... WITH GREAT POWER COMES GREAT RESPONSIBILITY.
PENNY FOR YOUR THOUGHTS, MAY
OH, I JUST SEEM TO SORT THINGS OUT WHENEVER I COME HERE, NATHAN.
I WISH I DID!
PARKER
3

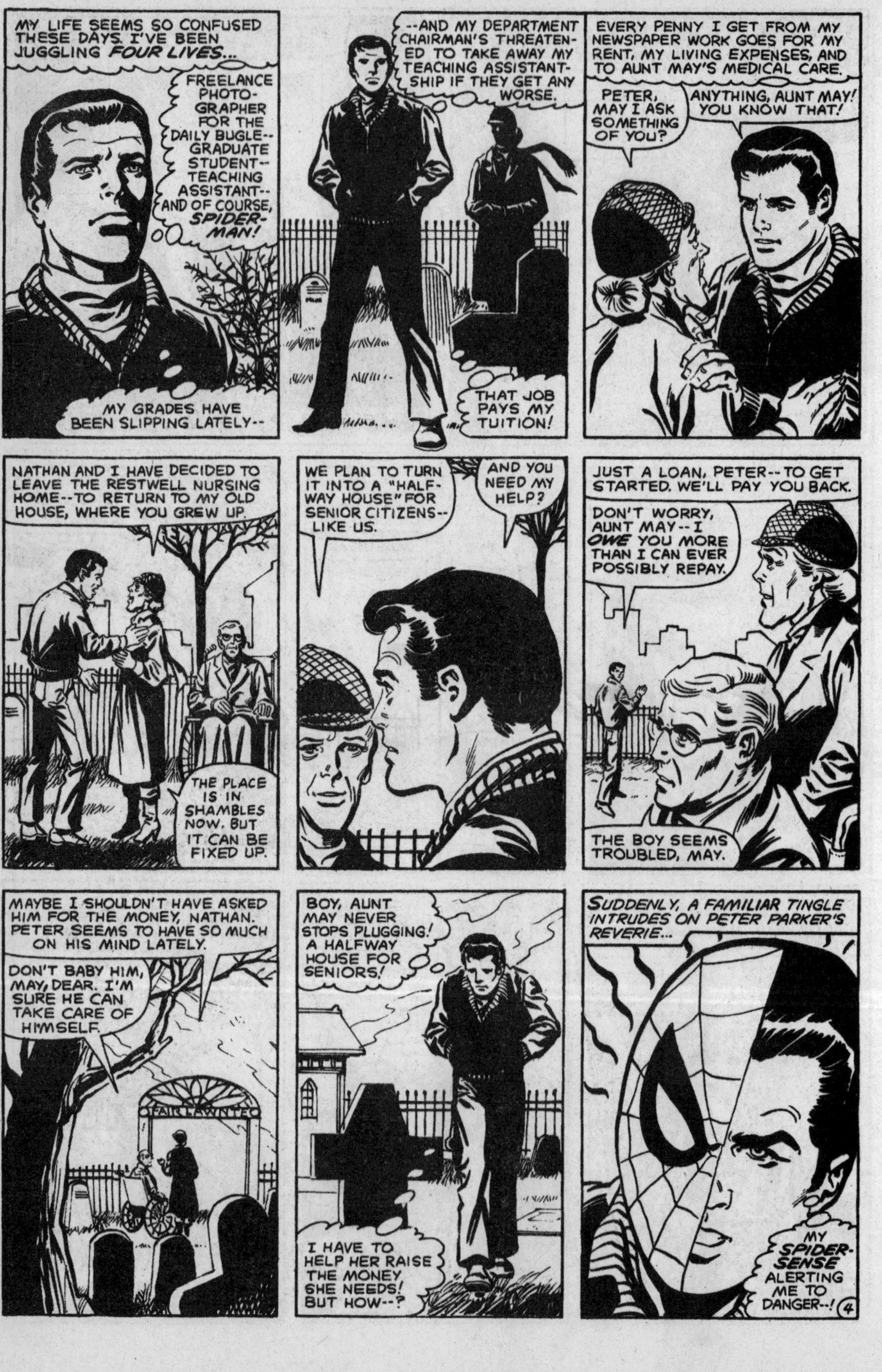
MY LIFE SEEMS SO CONFUSED THESE DAYS. I'VE BEEN JUGGLING FOUR LIVES...
FREELANCE PHOTOGRAPHER FOR THE DAILY BUGLE-- GRADUATE STUDENT-- TEACHING ASSISTANT-- AND OF COURSE, SPIDER-MAN!
MY GRADES HAVE BEEN SLIPPING LATELY--
--AND MY DEPARTMENT CHAIRMAN'S THREATENED TO TAKE AWAY MY TEACHING ASSISTANTSHIP IF THEY GET ANY WORSE.
THAT JOB PAYS MY TUITION!
EVERY PENNY I GET FROM MY NEWSPAPER WORK GOES FOR MY RENT, MY LIVING EXPENSES, AND TO AUNT MAY'S MEDICAL CARE.
PETER, MAY I ASK SOMETHING OF YOU?
ANYTHING, AUNT MAY! YOU KNOW THAT!
NATHAN AND I HAVE DECIDED TO LEAVE THE RESTWELL NURSING HOME--TO RETURN TO MY OLD HOUSE, WHERE YOU GREW UP.
THE PLACE IS IN SHAMBLES NOW. BUT IT CAN BE FIXED UP.
WE PLAN TO TURN IT INTO A "HALFWAY HOUSE" FOR SENIOR CITIZENS-- LIKE US.
AND YOU NEED MY HELP?
JUST A LOAN, PETER--TO GET STARTED. WE'LL PAY YOU BACK.
DON'T WORRY, AUNT MAY--I OWE YOU MORE THAN I CAN EVER POSSIBLY REPAY.
THE BOY SEEMS TROUBLED, MAY.
MAYBE I SHOULDN'T HAVE ASKED HIM FOR THE MONEY, NATHAN. PETER SEEMS TO HAVE SO MUCH ON HIS MIND LATELY.
DON'T BABY HIM, MAY, DEAR. I'M SURE HE CAN TAKE CARE OF HIMSELF.
FAIR LAWN
BOY, AUNT MAY NEVER STOPS PLUGGING! A HALFWAY HOUSE FOR SENIORS!
I HAVE TO HELP HER RAISE THE MONEY SHE NEEDS! BUT HOW--?
SUDDENLY, A FAMILIAR TINGLE INTRUDES ON PETER PARKER'S REVERIE...
MY SPIDER-SENSE ALERTING ME TO DANGER--!
4

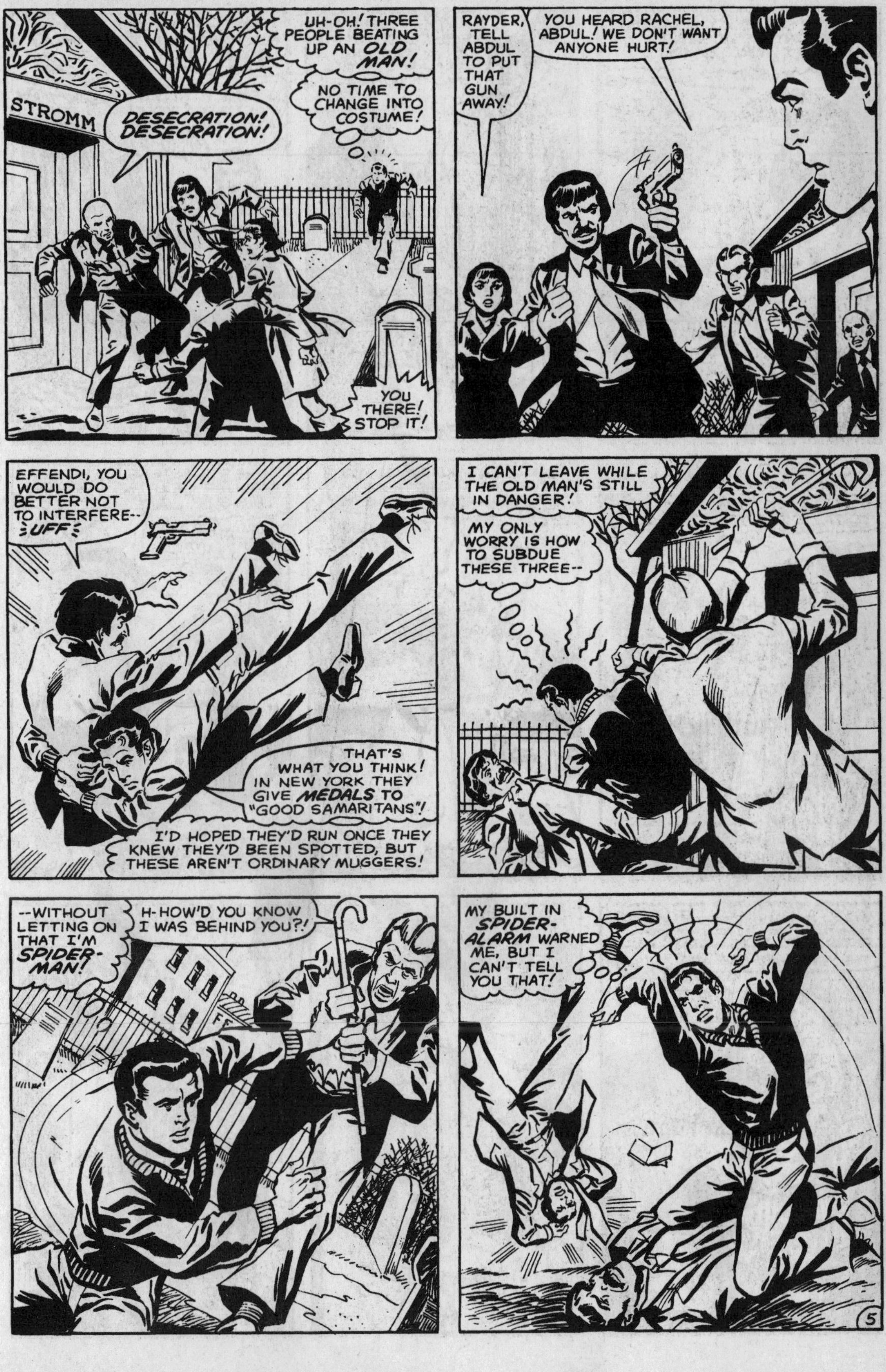
UH-OH! THREE PEOPLE BEATING UP AN OLD MAN!
NO TIME TO CHANGE INTO COSTUME!
STROMM
DESECRATION! DESECRATION!
YOU THERE! STOP IT!
RAYDER, TELL ABDUL TO PUT THAT GUN AWAY!
YOU HEARD RACHEL, ABDUL! WE DON'T WANT ANYONE HURT!
EFFENDI, YOU WOULD DO BETTER NOT TO INTERFERE-- UFF
THAT'S WHAT YOU THINK! IN NEW YORK THEY GIVE MEDALS TO "GOOD SAMARITANS"!
I'D HOPED THEY'D RUN ONCE THEY KNEW THEY'D BEEN SPOTTED, BUT THESE AREN'T ORDINARY MUGGERS!
I CAN'T LEAVE WHILE THE OLD MAN'S STILL IN DANGER!
MY ONLY WORRY IS HOW TO SUBDUE THESE THREE--
--WITHOUT LETTING ON THAT I'M SPIDER-MAN!
H-HOW'D YOU KNOW I WAS BEHIND YOU?!
MY BUILT IN SPIDER-ALARM WARNED ME, BUT I CAN'T TELL YOU THAT!
5

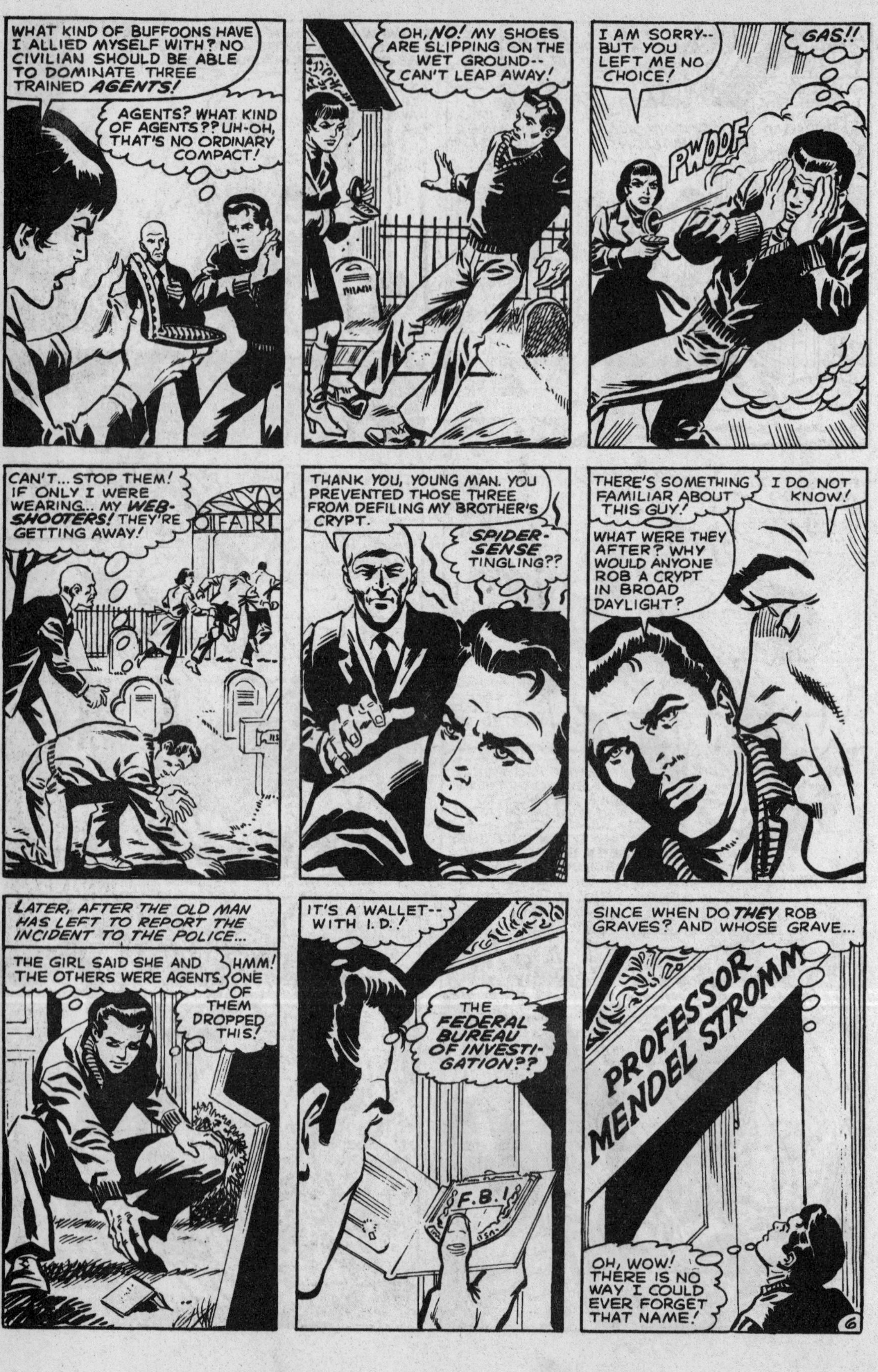
WHAT KIND OF BUFFOONS HAVE I ALLIED MYSELF WITH? NO CIVILIAN SHOULD BE ABLE TO DOMINATE THREE TRAINED AGENTS!
AGENTS? WHAT KIND OF AGENTS?? UH-OH, THAT'S NO ORDINARY COMPACT!
OH, NO! MY SHOES ARE SLIPPING ON THE WET GROUND-- CAN'T LEAP AWAY!
I AM SORRY-- BUT YOU LEFT ME NO CHOICE!
GAS!!
PWOOF
CAN'T... STOP THEM! IF ONLY I WERE WEARING... MY WEB-SHOOTERS! THEY'RE GETTING AWAY!
THANK YOU, YOUNG MAN. YOU PREVENTED THOSE THREE FROM DEFILING MY BROTHER'S CRYPT.
SPIDER-SENSE TINGLING??
THERE'S SOMETHING FAMILIAR ABOUT THIS GUY!
I DO NOT KNOW!
WHAT WERE THEY AFTER? WHY WOULD ANYONE ROB A CRYPT IN BROAD DAYLIGHT?
LATER, AFTER THE OLD MAN HAS LEFT TO REPORT THE INCIDENT TO THE POLICE...
THE GIRL SAID SHE AND THE OTHERS WERE AGENTS.
HMM! ONE OF THEM DROPPED THIS!
IT'S A WALLET-- WITH I.D.!
THE FEDERAL BUREAU OF INVESTI-GATION??
F.B.I.
SINCE WHEN DO THEY ROB GRAVES? AND WHOSE GRAVE...
PROFESSOR MENDEL STROMM
OH, WOW! THERE IS NO WAY I COULD EVER FORGET THAT NAME!
6

SOME HOURS LATER, ON THE CAMPUS OF *EMPIRE STATE UNIVERSITY*...

MENDEL STROMM. I NEVER THOUGHT I'D HEAR THAT NAME AGAIN!

STROMM WAS A SCIENTIFIC GENIUS WHO WAS CAUGHT EMBEZZLING FUNDS FROM THE COMPANY HE WORKED FOR...

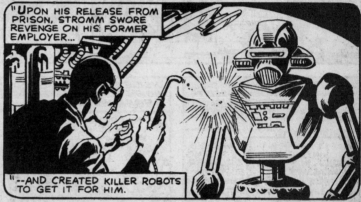

"UPON HIS RELEASE FROM PRISON, STROMM SWORE REVENGE ON HIS FORMER EMPLOYER...

"--AND CREATED KILLER ROBOTS TO GET IT FOR HIM.

"THAT'S WHEN I ENTERED THE PICTURE... AND PUT AN END TO STROMM'S PLANS...

"BUT THEN, JUST AS STROMM WAS ABOUT TO SURRENDER, MY SPIDER-SENSE ALERTED ME TO..."

DANGER! THERE'S SOMEONE AT THE WINDOW!

I SHOVED STROMM OUT OF THE LINE OF FIRE, BUT HIS FRIGHT CAUSED HIS WEAK HEART TO FAIL.*

*SPIDER-MAN #37!

⑦

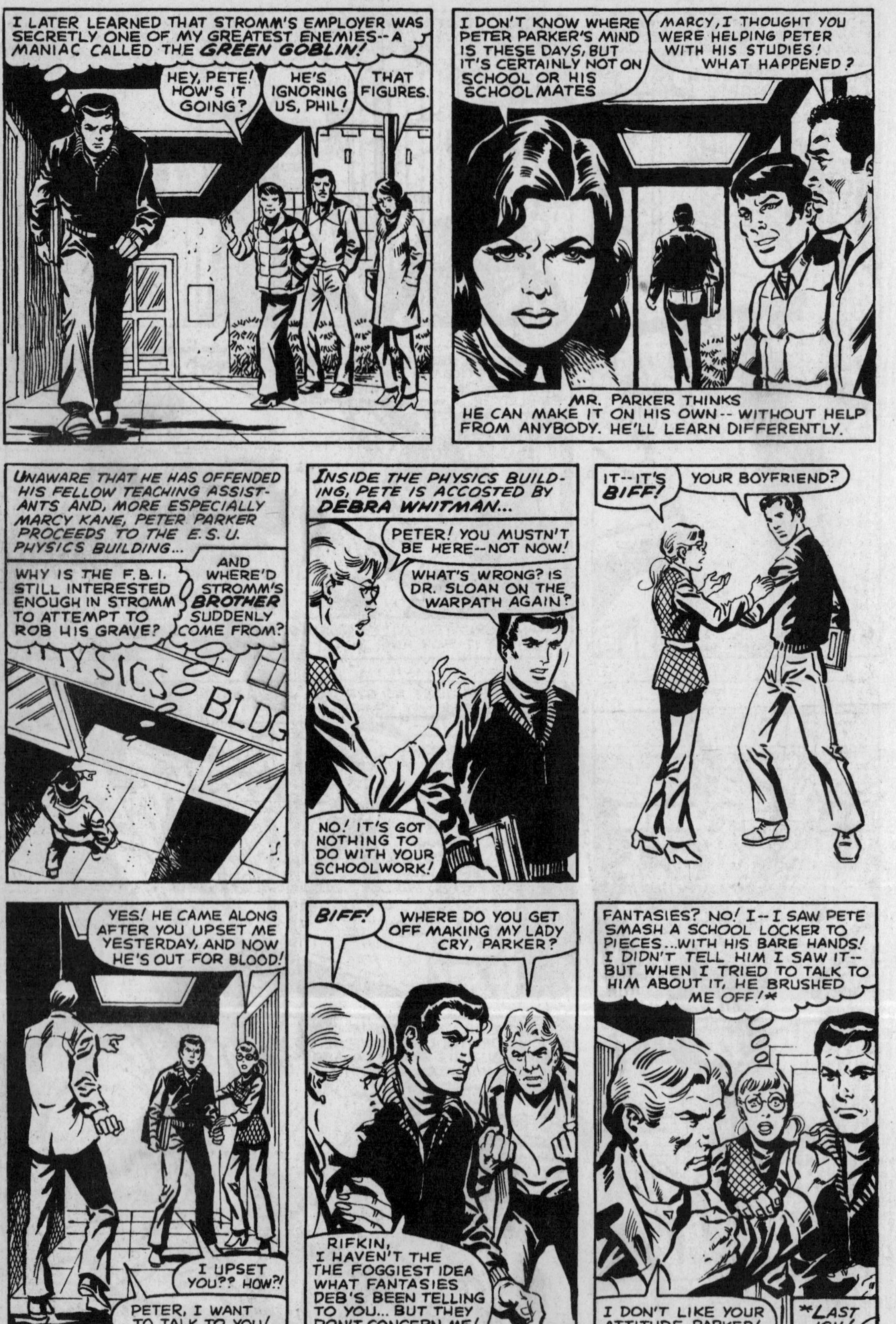
I LATER LEARNED THAT STROMM'S EMPLOYER WAS SECRETLY ONE OF MY GREATEST ENEMIES-- A MANIAC CALLED THE GREEN GOBLIN!
HEY, PETE! HOW'S IT GOING?
HE'S IGNORING US, PHIL!
THAT FIGURES.
I DON'T KNOW WHERE PETER PARKER'S MIND IS THESE DAYS, BUT IT'S CERTAINLY NOT ON SCHOOL OR HIS SCHOOLMATES
MARCY, I THOUGHT YOU WERE HELPING PETER WITH HIS STUDIES! WHAT HAPPENED?
MR. PARKER THINKS HE CAN MAKE IT ON HIS OWN -- WITHOUT HELP FROM ANYBODY. HE'LL LEARN DIFFERENTLY.
UNAWARE THAT HE HAS OFFENDED HIS FELLOW TEACHING ASSISTANTS AND, MORE ESPECIALLY MARCY KANE, PETER PARKER PROCEEDS TO THE E.S.U. PHYSICS BUILDING...
WHY IS THE F.B.I. STILL INTERESTED ENOUGH IN STROMM TO ATTEMPT TO ROB HIS GRAVE?
AND WHERE'D STROMM'S BROTHER SUDDENLY COME FROM?
INSIDE THE PHYSICS BUILDING, PETE IS ACCOSTED BY DEBRA WHITMAN...
PETER! YOU MUSTN'T BE HERE--NOT NOW!
WHAT'S WRONG? IS DR. SLOAN ON THE WARPATH AGAIN?
NO! IT'S GOT NOTHING TO DO WITH YOUR SCHOOLWORK!
IT--IT'S BIFF!
YOUR BOYFRIEND?
YES! HE CAME ALONG AFTER YOU UPSET ME YESTERDAY, AND NOW HE'S OUT FOR BLOOD!
I UPSET YOU?? HOW?!
PETER, I WANT TO TALK TO YOU!
BIFF!
WHERE DO YOU GET OFF MAKING MY LADY CRY, PARKER?
RIFKIN, I HAVEN'T THE THE FOGGIEST IDEA WHAT FANTASIES DEB'S BEEN TELLING TO YOU... BUT THEY DON'T CONCERN ME!
FANTASIES? NO! I--I SAW PETE SMASH A SCHOOL LOCKER TO PIECES...WITH HIS BARE HANDS! I DIDN'T TELL HIM I SAW IT-- BUT WHEN I TRIED TO TALK TO HIM ABOUT IT, HE BRUSHED ME OFF!*
I DON'T LIKE YOUR ATTITUDE, PARKER!
*LAST ISH!
8

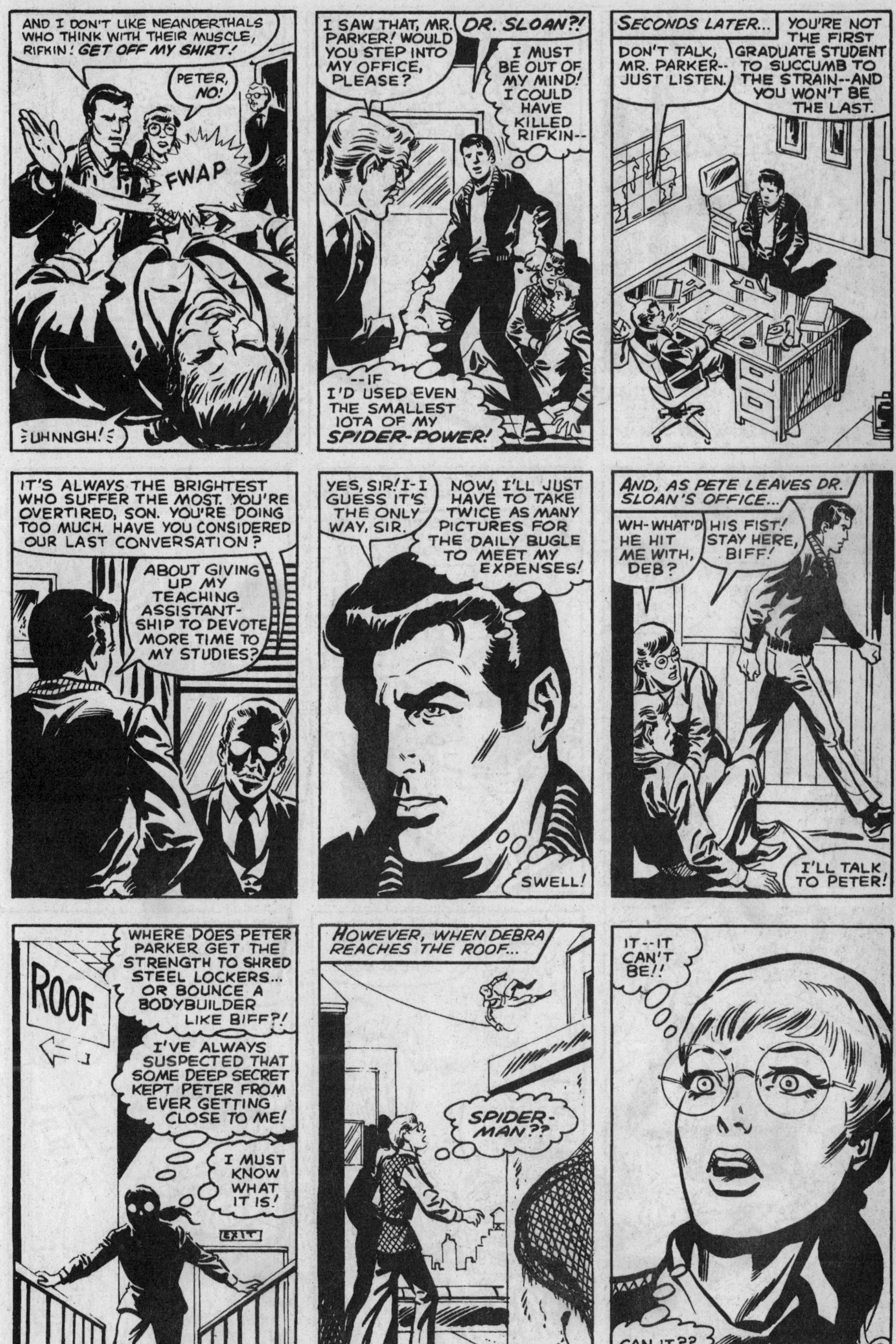
AND I DON'T LIKE NEANDERTHALS WHO THINK WITH THEIR MUSCLE, RIFKIN! GET OFF MY SHIRT!
PETER, NO!
FWAP
UHNNGH!
I SAW THAT, MR. PARKER! WOULD YOU STEP INTO MY OFFICE, PLEASE?
DR. SLOAN?!
I MUST BE OUT OF MY MIND! I COULD HAVE KILLED RIFKIN--
--IF I'D USED EVEN THE SMALLEST IOTA OF MY SPIDER-POWER!
SECONDS LATER...
DON'T TALK, MR. PARKER-- JUST LISTEN.
YOU'RE NOT THE FIRST GRADUATE STUDENT TO SUCCUMB TO THE STRAIN--AND YOU WON'T BE THE LAST.
IT'S ALWAYS THE BRIGHTEST WHO SUFFER THE MOST. YOU'RE OVERTIRED, SON. YOU'RE DOING TOO MUCH. HAVE YOU CONSIDERED OUR LAST CONVERSATION?
ABOUT GIVING UP MY TEACHING ASSISTANT-SHIP TO DEVOTE MORE TIME TO MY STUDIES?
YES, SIR! I-I GUESS IT'S THE ONLY WAY, SIR.
NOW, I'LL JUST HAVE TO TAKE TWICE AS MANY PICTURES FOR THE DAILY BUGLE TO MEET MY EXPENSES!
SWELL!
AND, AS PETE LEAVES DR. SLOAN'S OFFICE...
WH-WHAT'D HE HIT ME WITH, DEB?
HIS FIST! STAY HERE, BIFF!
I'LL TALK TO PETER!
ROOF
WHERE DOES PETER PARKER GET THE STRENGTH TO SHRED STEEL LOCKERS... OR BOUNCE A BODYBUILDER LIKE BIFF?!
I'VE ALWAYS SUSPECTED THAT SOME DEEP SECRET KEPT PETER FROM EVER GETTING CLOSE TO ME!
I MUST KNOW WHAT IT IS!
EXIT
HOWEVER, WHEN DEBRA REACHES THE ROOF...
SPIDER-MAN??
IT--IT CAN'T BE!!
CAN IT??

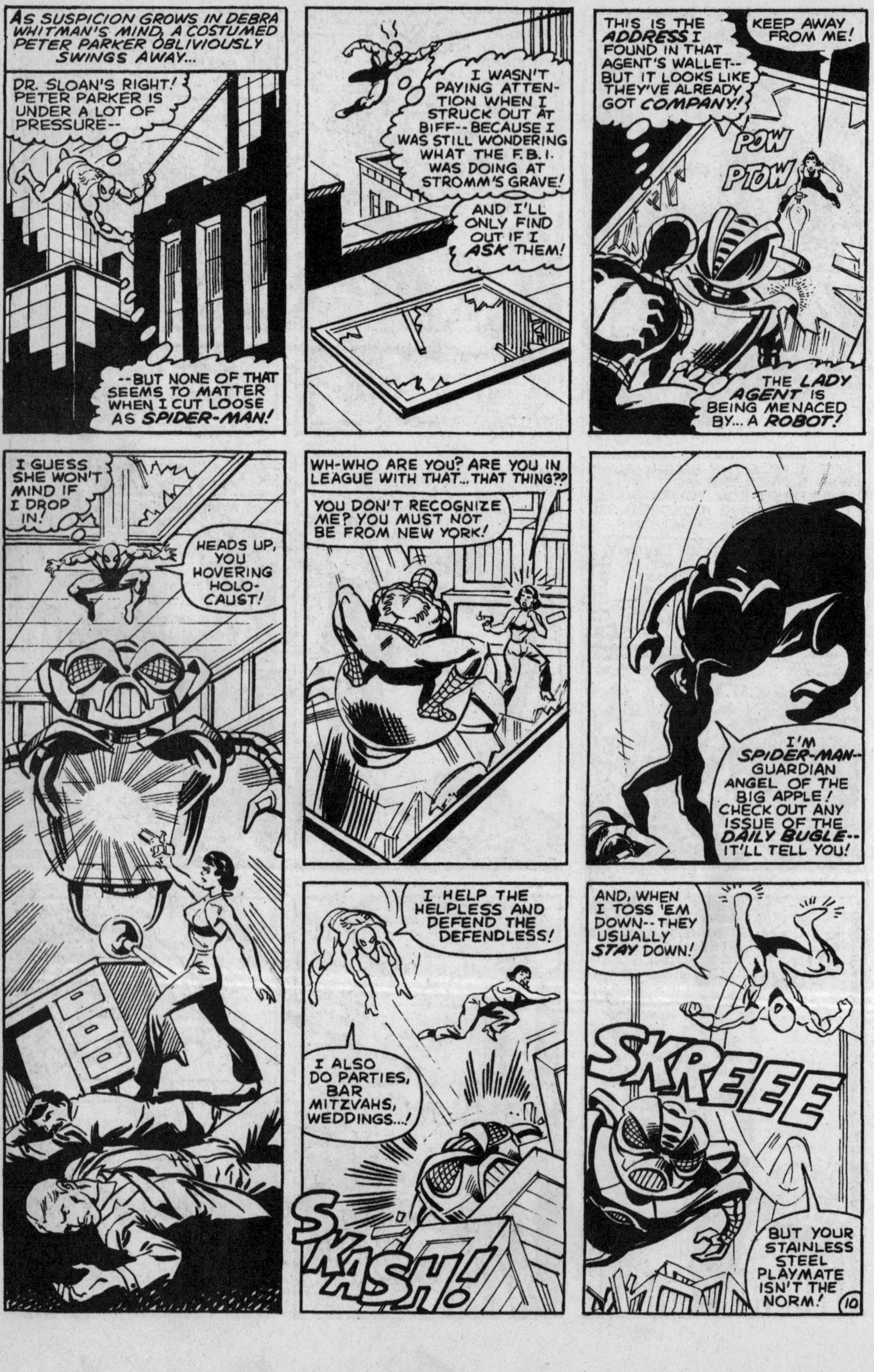
AS SUSPICION GROWS IN DEBRA WHITMAN'S MIND, A COSTUMED PETER PARKER OBLIVIOUSLY SWINGS AWAY...
DR. SLOAN'S RIGHT! PETER PARKER IS UNDER A LOT OF PRESSURE--
--BUT NONE OF THAT SEEMS TO MATTER WHEN I CUT LOOSE AS SPIDER-MAN!
I WASN'T PAYING ATTENTION WHEN I STRUCK OUT AT BIFF--BECAUSE I WAS STILL WONDERING WHAT THE F.B.I. WAS DOING AT STROMM'S GRAVE!
AND I'LL ONLY FIND OUT IF I ASK THEM!
THIS IS THE ADDRESS I FOUND IN THAT AGENT'S WALLET--BUT IT LOOKS LIKE THEY'VE ALREADY GOT COMPANY!
KEEP AWAY FROM ME!
POW
PTOW
THE LADY AGENT IS BEING MENACED BY... A ROBOT!
I GUESS SHE WON'T MIND IF I DROP IN!
HEADS UP, YOU HOVERING HOLO-CAUST!
WH-WHO ARE YOU? ARE YOU IN LEAGUE WITH THAT... THAT THING??
YOU DON'T RECOGNIZE ME? YOU MUST NOT BE FROM NEW YORK!
I'M SPIDER-MAN--GUARDIAN ANGEL OF THE BIG APPLE! CHECK OUT ANY ISSUE OF THE DAILY BUGLE--IT'LL TELL YOU!
I HELP THE HELPLESS AND DEFEND THE DEFENDLESS!
I ALSO DO PARTIES, BAR MITZVAHS, WEDDINGS...!
SKASH!
AND, WHEN I TOSS 'EM DOWN--THEY USUALLY STAY DOWN!
SKREEE
BUT YOUR STAINLESS STEEL PLAYMATE ISN'T THE NORM!
10

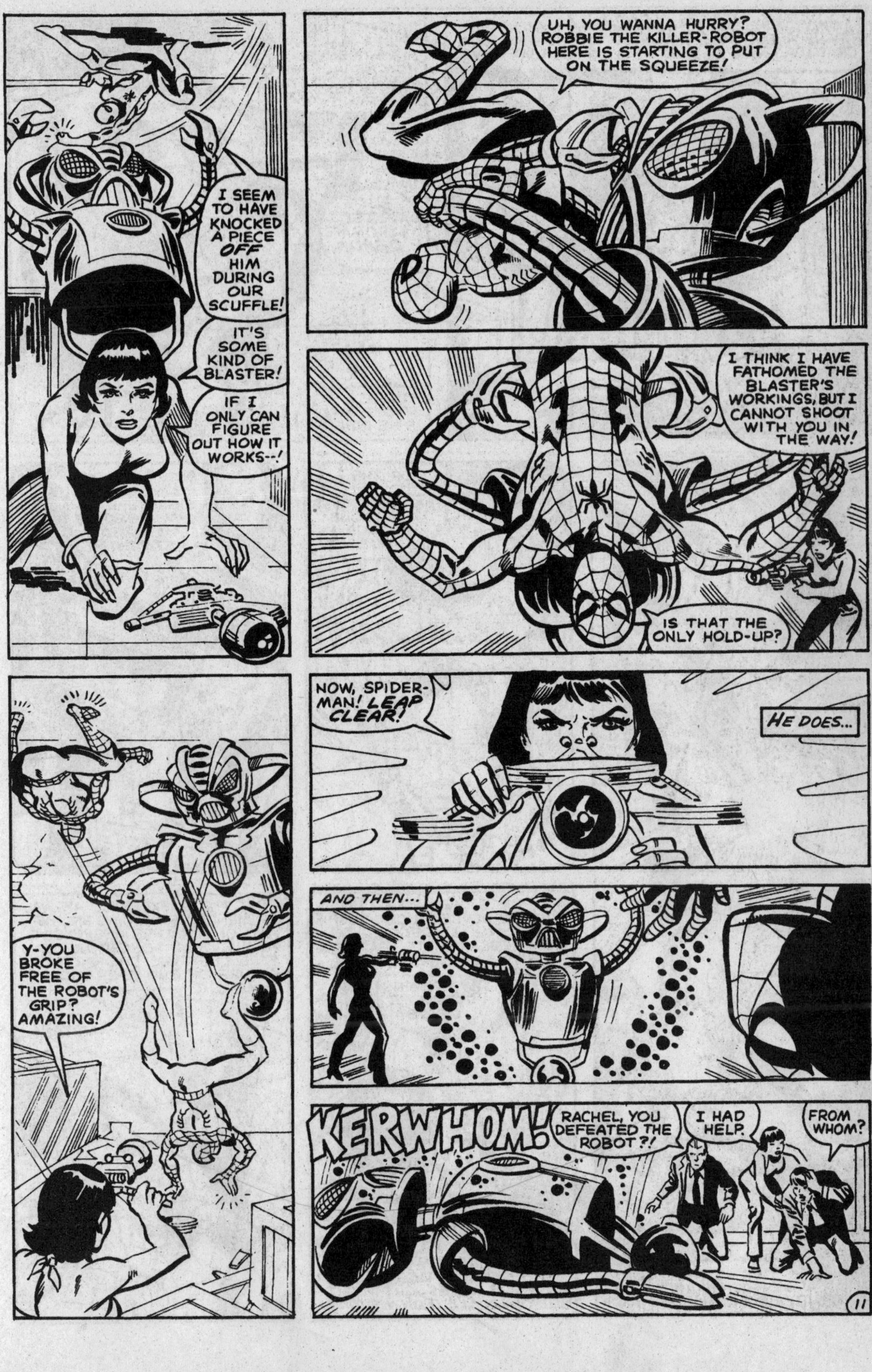
I SEEM TO HAVE KNOCKED A PIECE OFF HIM DURING OUR SCUFFLE!
IT'S SOME KIND OF BLASTER!
IF I ONLY CAN FIGURE OUT HOW IT WORKS--!
UH, YOU WANNA HURRY? ROBBIE THE KILLER-ROBOT HERE IS STARTING TO PUT ON THE SQUEEZE!
I THINK I HAVE FATHOMED THE BLASTER'S WORKINGS, BUT I CANNOT SHOOT WITH YOU IN THE WAY!
IS THAT THE ONLY HOLD-UP?
NOW, SPIDER-MAN! LEAP CLEAR!
HE DOES...
Y-YOU BROKE FREE OF THE ROBOT'S GRIP? AMAZING!
AND THEN...
KERWHOM!
RACHEL, YOU DEFEATED THE ROBOT?!
I HAD HELP.
FROM WHOM?
11

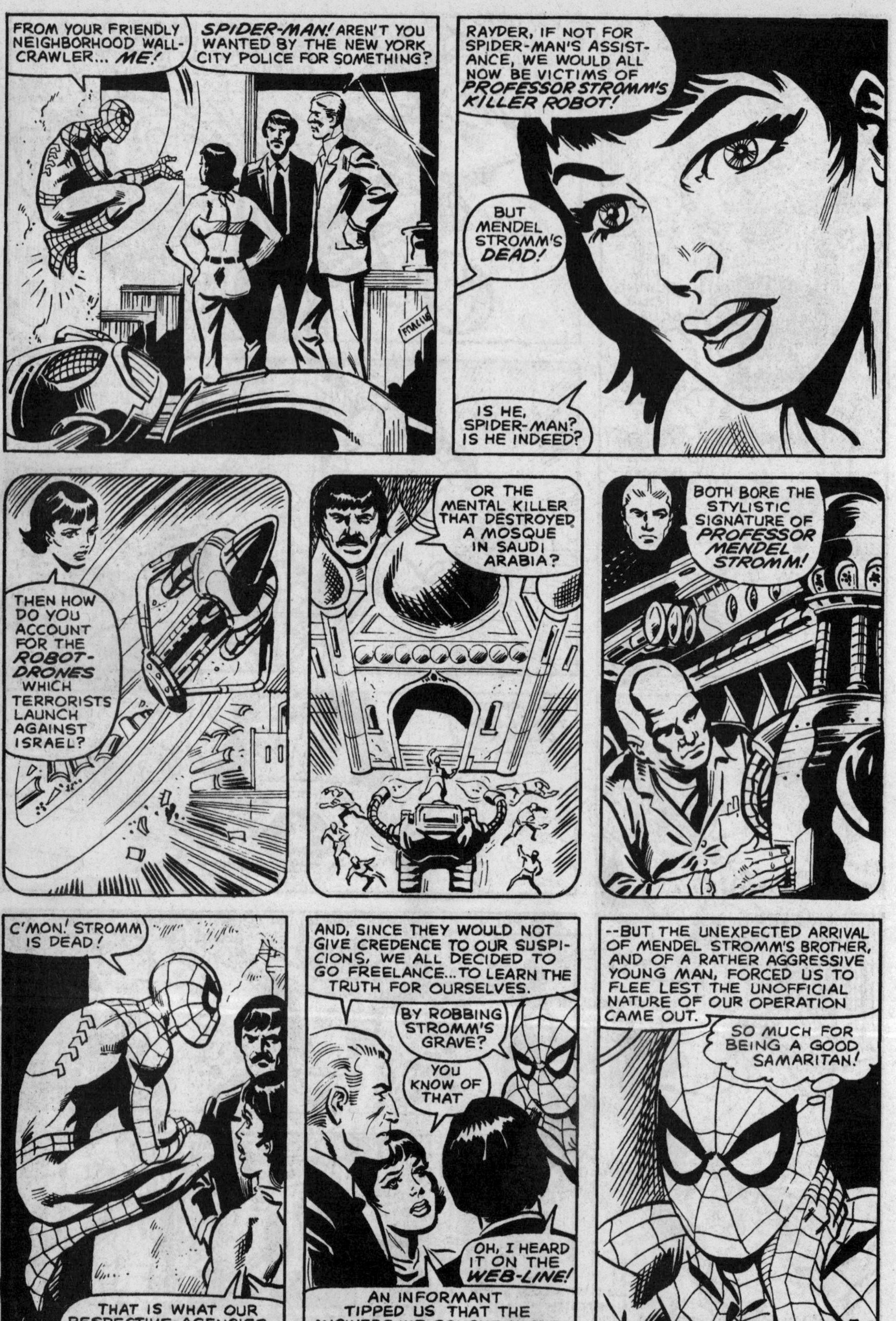
FROM YOUR FRIENDLY NEIGHBORHOOD WALL-CRAWLER... ME!
SPIDER-MAN! AREN'T YOU WANTED BY THE NEW YORK CITY POLICE FOR SOMETHING?
RAYDER, IF NOT FOR SPIDER-MAN'S ASSIST-ANCE, WE WOULD ALL NOW BE VICTIMS OF PROFESSOR STROMM'S KILLER ROBOT!
BUT MENDEL STROMM'S DEAD!
IS HE, SPIDER-MAN? IS HE INDEED?
THEN HOW DO YOU ACCOUNT FOR THE ROBOT-DRONES WHICH TERRORISTS LAUNCH AGAINST ISRAEL?
OR THE MENTAL KILLER THAT DESTROYED A MOSQUE IN SAUDI ARABIA?
BOTH BORE THE STYLISTIC SIGNATURE OF PROFESSOR MENDEL STROMM!
C'MON! STROMM IS DEAD!
THAT IS WHAT OUR RESPECTIVE AGENCIES BELIEVE, SPIDER-MAN.
AND, SINCE THEY WOULD NOT GIVE CREDENCE TO OUR SUSPI-CIONS, WE ALL DECIDED TO GO FREELANCE...TO LEARN THE TRUTH FOR OURSELVES.
BY ROBBING STROMM'S GRAVE?
YOU KNOW OF THAT
OH, I HEARD IT ON THE WEB-LINE!
AN INFORMANT TIPPED US THAT THE ANSWERS WE SOUGHT MIGHT BE FOUND IN STROMM'S TOMB-
--BUT THE UNEXPECTED ARRIVAL OF MENDEL STROMM'S BROTHER, AND OF A RATHER AGGRESSIVE YOUNG MAN, FORCED US TO FLEE LEST THE UNOFFICIAL NATURE OF OUR OPERATION CAME OUT.
SO MUCH FOR BEING A GOOD SAMARITAN!
12

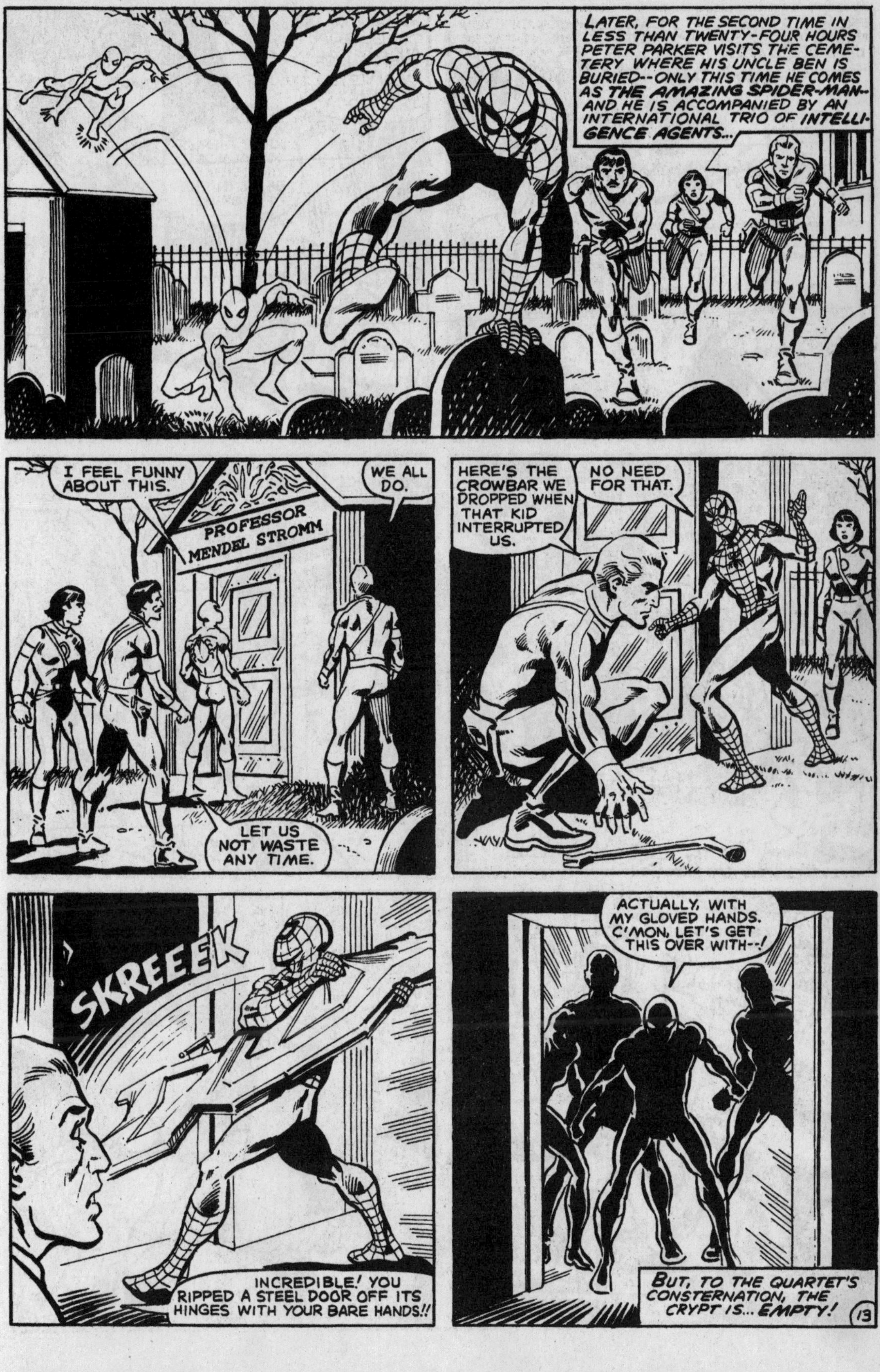
LATER, FOR THE SECOND TIME IN LESS THAN TWENTY-FOUR HOURS PETER PARKER VISITS THE CEMETERY WHERE HIS UNCLE BEN IS BURIED--ONLY THIS TIME HE COMES AS THE AMAZING SPIDER-MAN--AND HE IS ACCOMPANIED BY AN INTERNATIONAL TRIO OF INTELLIGENCE AGENTS...
I FEEL FUNNY ABOUT THIS.
WE ALL DO.
PROFESSOR MENDEL STROMM
LET US NOT WASTE ANY TIME.
HERE'S THE CROWBAR WE DROPPED WHEN THAT KID INTERRUPTED US.
NO NEED FOR THAT.
SKREEEEK
INCREDIBLE! YOU RIPPED A STEEL DOOR OFF ITS HINGES WITH YOUR BARE HANDS!!
ACTUALLY, WITH MY GLOVED HANDS. C'MON, LET'S GET THIS OVER WITH--!
BUT, TO THE QUARTET'S CONSTERNATION, THE CRYPT IS... EMPTY!
13

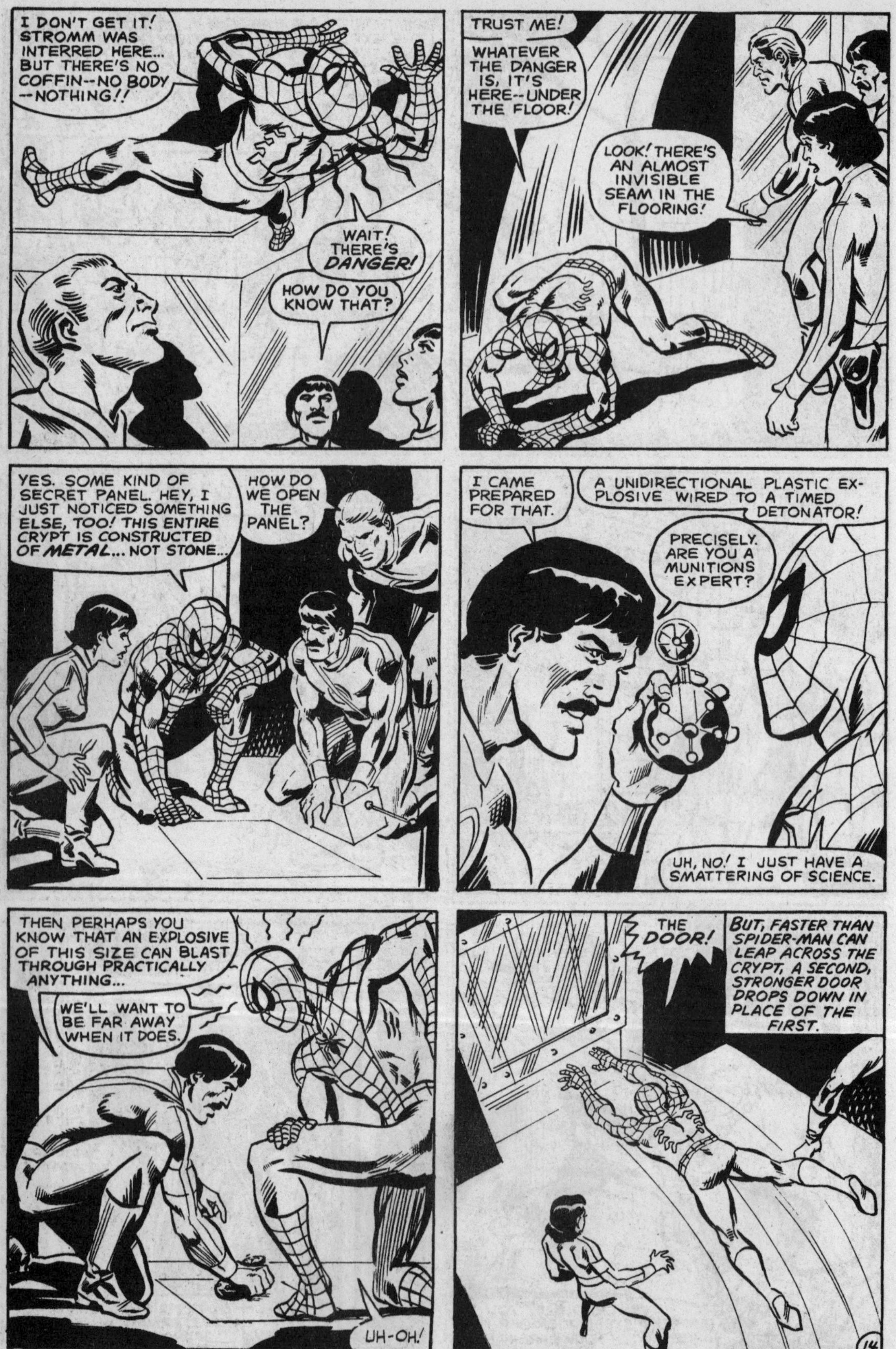
I DON'T GET IT! STROMM WAS INTERRED HERE... BUT THERE'S NO COFFIN--NO BODY--NOTHING!!
WAIT! THERE'S DANGER!
HOW DO YOU KNOW THAT?
TRUST ME!
WHATEVER THE DANGER IS, IT'S HERE--UNDER THE FLOOR!
LOOK! THERE'S AN ALMOST INVISIBLE SEAM IN THE FLOORING!
YES. SOME KIND OF SECRET PANEL. HEY, I JUST NOTICED SOMETHING ELSE, TOO! THIS ENTIRE CRYPT IS CONSTRUCTED OF METAL... NOT STONE...
HOW DO WE OPEN THE PANEL?
I CAME PREPARED FOR THAT.
A UNIDIRECTIONAL PLASTIC EXPLOSIVE WIRED TO A TIMED DETONATOR!
PRECISELY. ARE YOU A MUNITIONS EXPERT?
UH, NO! I JUST HAVE A SMATTERING OF SCIENCE.
THEN PERHAPS YOU KNOW THAT AN EXPLOSIVE OF THIS SIZE CAN BLAST THROUGH PRACTICALLY ANYTHING...
WE'LL WANT TO BE FAR AWAY WHEN IT DOES.
UH-OH!
THE DOOR!
BUT, FASTER THAN SPIDER-MAN CAN LEAP ACROSS THE CRYPT, A SECOND, STRONGER DOOR DROPS DOWN IN PLACE OF THE FIRST.
14

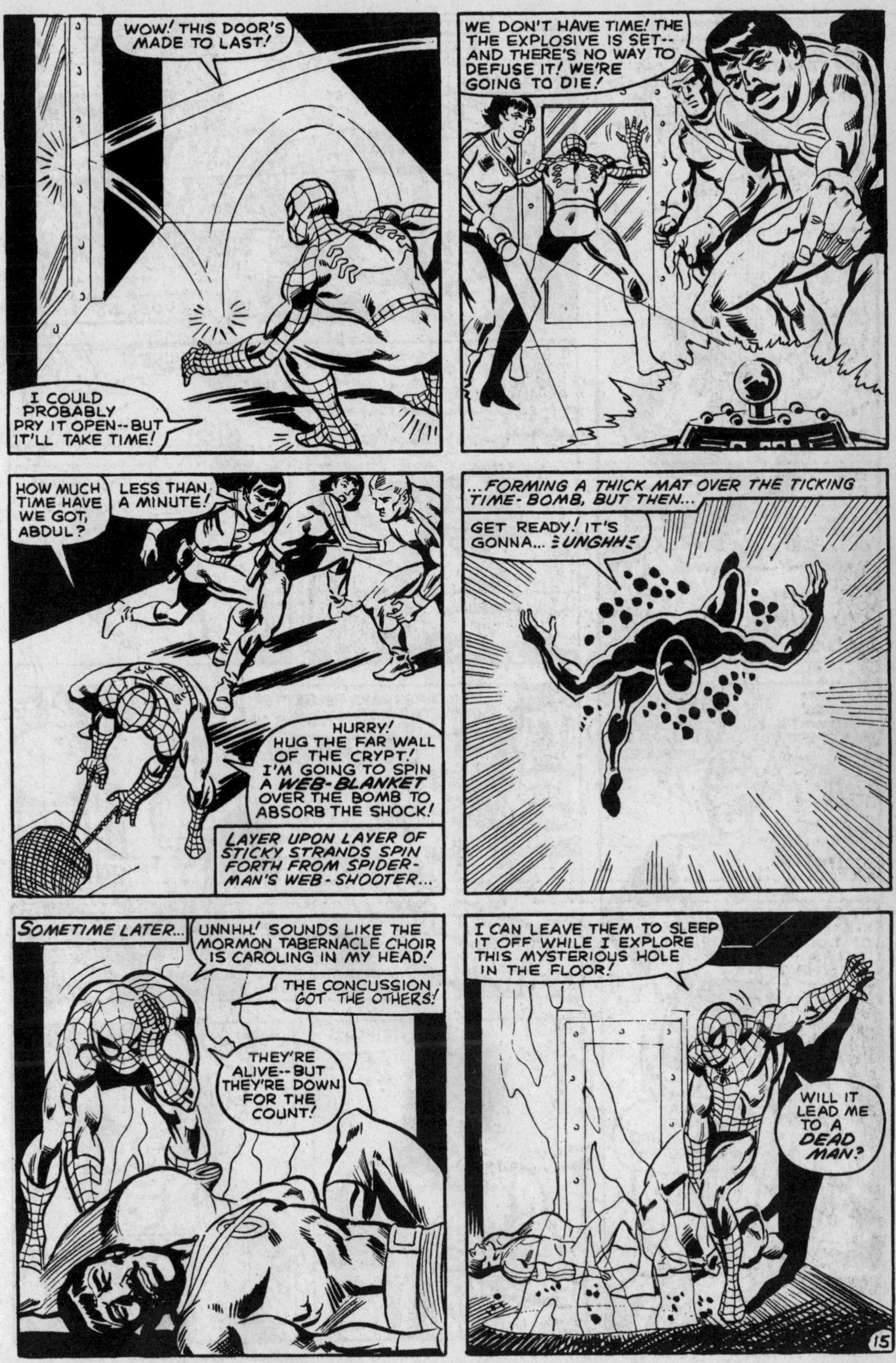
WOW! THIS DOOR'S MADE TO LAST!
I COULD PROBABLY PRY IT OPEN--BUT IT'LL TAKE TIME!
WE DON'T HAVE TIME! THE THE EXPLOSIVE IS SET--AND THERE'S NO WAY TO DEFUSE IT! WE'RE GOING TO DIE!
HOW MUCH TIME HAVE WE GOT, ABDUL?
LESS THAN A MINUTE!
HURRY! HUG THE FAR WALL OF THE CRYPT! I'M GOING TO SPIN A WEB-BLANKET OVER THE BOMB TO ABSORB THE SHOCK!
LAYER UPON LAYER OF STICKY STRANDS SPIN FORTH FROM SPIDER-MAN'S WEB-SHOOTER...
...FORMING A THICK MAT OVER THE TICKING TIME-BOMB, BUT THEN...
GET READY! IT'S GONNA... UNGHH!
SOMETIME LATER...
UNNHH! SOUNDS LIKE THE MORMON TABERNACLE CHOIR IS CAROLING IN MY HEAD!
THE CONCUSSION GOT THE OTHERS!
THEY'RE ALIVE--BUT THEY'RE DOWN FOR THE COUNT!
I CAN LEAVE THEM TO SLEEP IT OFF WHILE I EXPLORE THIS MYSTERIOUS HOLE IN THE FLOOR!
WILL IT LEAD ME TO A DEAD MAN?
15

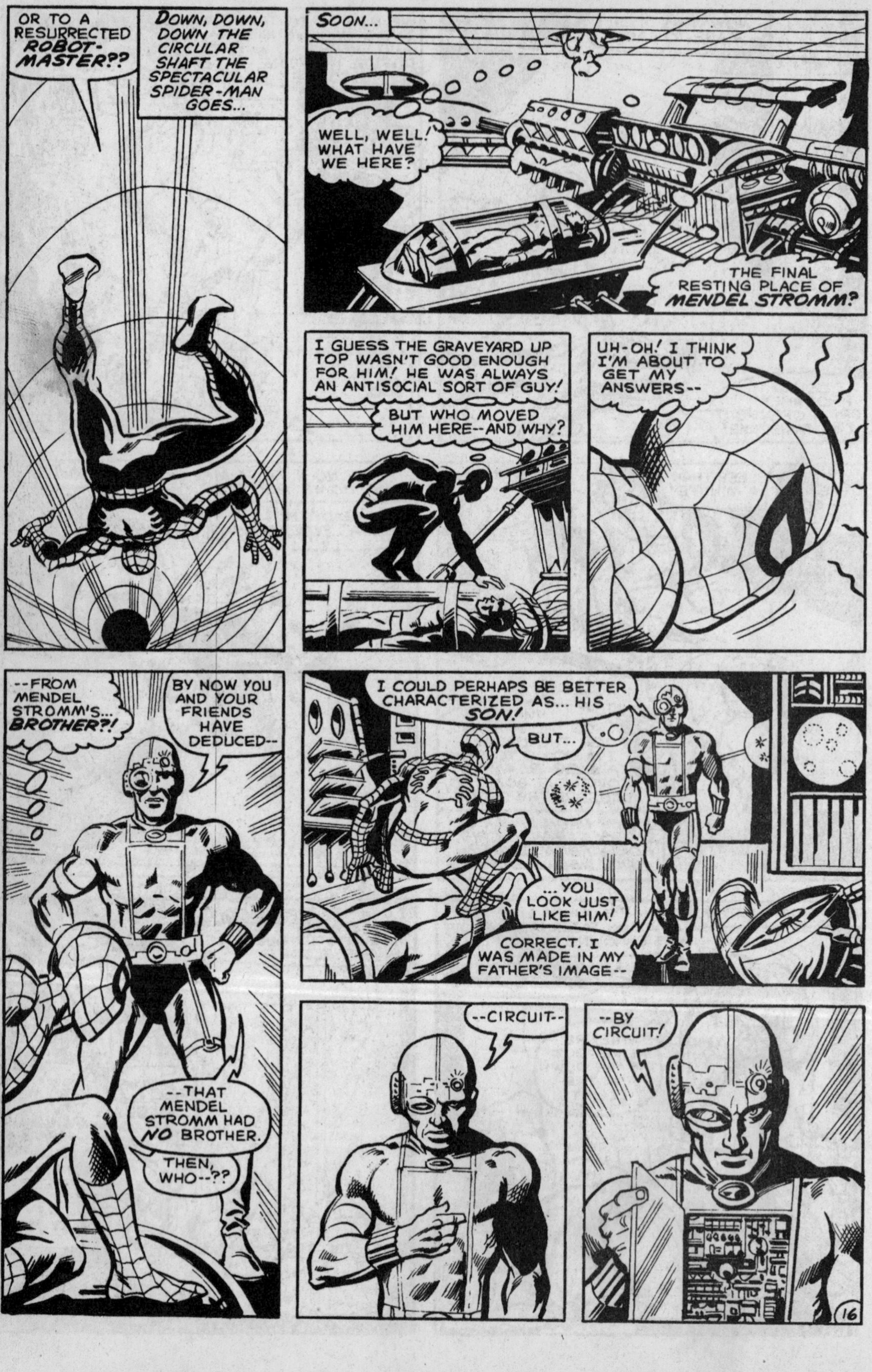
OR TO A RESURRECTED ROBOT-MASTER??
DOWN, DOWN, DOWN THE CIRCULAR SHAFT THE SPECTACULAR SPIDER-MAN GOES...
SOON...
WELL, WELL! WHAT HAVE WE HERE?
THE FINAL RESTING PLACE OF MENDEL STROMM?
I GUESS THE GRAVEYARD UP TOP WASN'T GOOD ENOUGH FOR HIM! HE WAS ALWAYS AN ANTISOCIAL SORT OF GUY!
BUT WHO MOVED HIM HERE--AND WHY?
UH-OH! I THINK I'M ABOUT TO GET MY ANSWERS--
--FROM MENDEL STROMM'S... BROTHER?!
BY NOW YOU AND YOUR FRIENDS HAVE DEDUCED--
--THAT MENDEL STROMM HAD NO BROTHER.
THEN, WHO--??
I COULD PERHAPS BE BETTER CHARACTERIZED AS... HIS SON!
BUT...
...YOU LOOK JUST LIKE HIM!
CORRECT. I WAS MADE IN MY FATHER'S IMAGE--
--CIRCUIT--
--BY CIRCUIT!
16

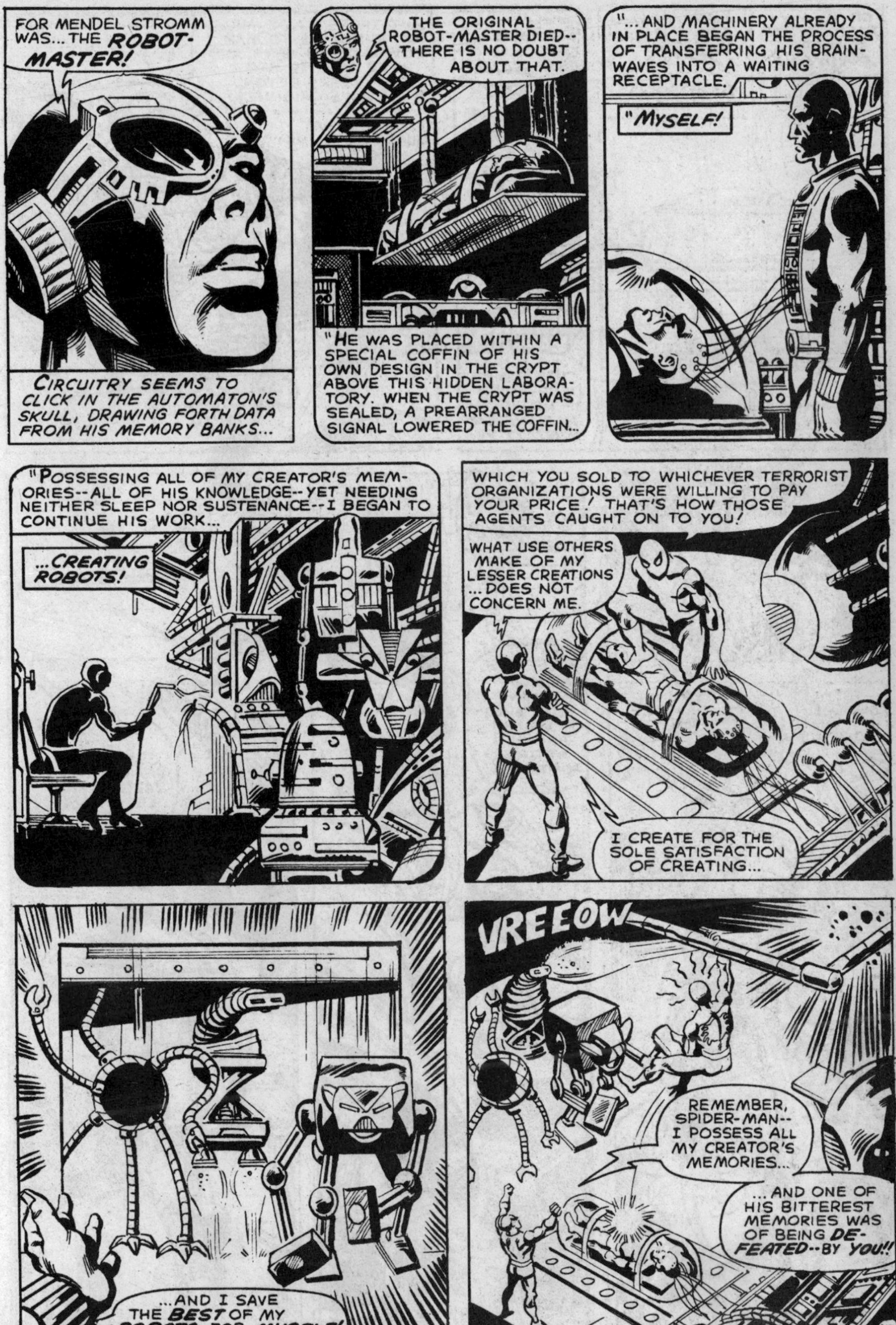
FOR MENDEL STROMM WAS... THE ROBOT-MASTER!
CIRCUITRY SEEMS TO CLICK IN THE AUTOMATON'S SKULL, DRAWING FORTH DATA FROM HIS MEMORY BANKS...
THE ORIGINAL ROBOT-MASTER DIED-- THERE IS NO DOUBT ABOUT THAT.
"HE WAS PLACED WITHIN A SPECIAL COFFIN OF HIS OWN DESIGN IN THE CRYPT ABOVE THIS HIDDEN LABORATORY. WHEN THE CRYPT WAS SEALED, A PREARRANGED SIGNAL LOWERED THE COFFIN...
"...AND MACHINERY ALREADY IN PLACE BEGAN THE PROCESS OF TRANSFERRING HIS BRAIN-WAVES INTO A WAITING RECEPTACLE.
"MYSELF!
"POSSESSING ALL OF MY CREATOR'S MEMORIES--ALL OF HIS KNOWLEDGE--YET NEEDING NEITHER SLEEP NOR SUSTENANCE--I BEGAN TO CONTINUE HIS WORK...
...CREATING ROBOTS!
WHICH YOU SOLD TO WHICHEVER TERRORIST ORGANIZATIONS WERE WILLING TO PAY YOUR PRICE! THAT'S HOW THOSE AGENTS CAUGHT ON TO YOU!
WHAT USE OTHERS MAKE OF MY LESSER CREATIONS ...DOES NOT CONCERN ME.
I CREATE FOR THE SOLE SATISFACTION OF CREATING...
...AND I SAVE THE BEST OF MY ROBOTS--FOR MYSELF!
VREEOW
REMEMBER, SPIDER-MAN-- I POSSESS ALL MY CREATOR'S MEMORIES...
...AND ONE OF HIS BITTEREST MEMORIES WAS OF BEING DEFEATED--BY YOU!!

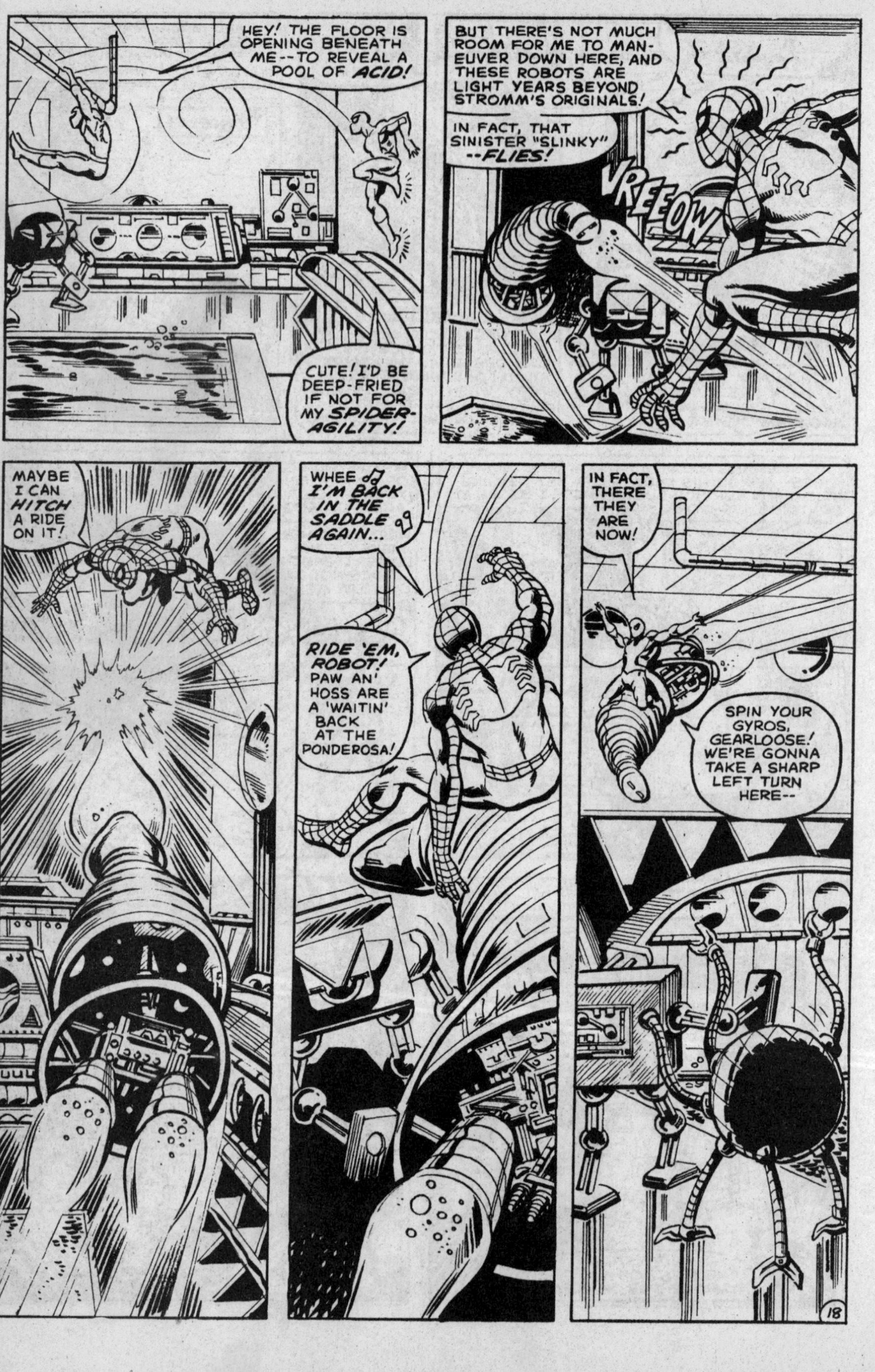
HEY! THE FLOOR IS OPENING BENEATH ME--TO REVEAL A POOL OF ACID!
CUTE! I'D BE DEEP-FRIED IF NOT FOR MY SPIDER-AGILITY!
BUT THERE'S NOT MUCH ROOM FOR ME TO MAN-EUVER DOWN HERE, AND THESE ROBOTS ARE LIGHT YEARS BEYOND STROMM'S ORIGINALS!
IN FACT, THAT SINISTER "SLINKY" --FLIES!
VREEOW
MAYBE I CAN HITCH A RIDE ON IT!
WHEE I'M BACK IN THE SADDLE AGAIN...
RIDE 'EM, ROBOT! PAW AN' HOSS ARE A 'WAITIN' BACK AT THE PONDEROSA!
IN FACT, THERE THEY ARE NOW!
SPIN YOUR GYROS, GEARLOOSE! WE'RE GONNA TAKE A SHARP LEFT TURN HERE--
18

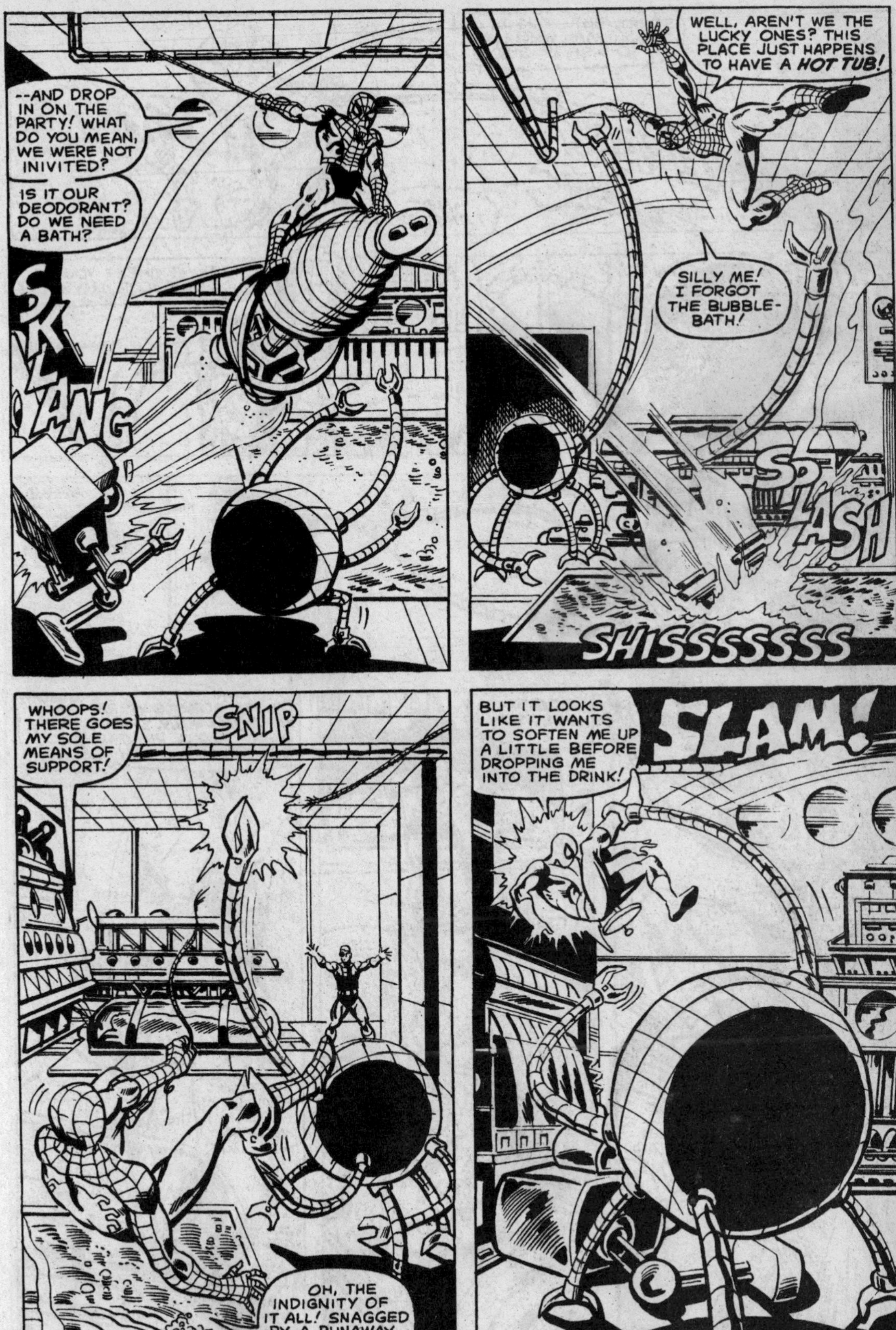
--AND DROP IN ON THE PARTY! WHAT DO YOU MEAN, WE WERE NOT INIVITED?
IS IT OUR DEODORANT? DO WE NEED A BATH?
SKLANG
WELL, AREN'T WE THE LUCKY ONES? THIS PLACE JUST HAPPENS TO HAVE A HOT TUB!
SILLY ME! I FORGOT THE BUBBLE-BATH!
SPLASH
SHISSSSSSS
WHOOPS! THERE GOES MY SOLE MEANS OF SUPPORT!
SNIP
OH, THE INDIGNITY OF IT ALL! SNAGGED BY A RUNAWAY TREE-PRUNER!
BUT IT LOOKS LIKE IT WANTS TO SOFTEN ME UP A LITTLE BEFORE DROPPING ME INTO THE DRINK!
SLAM!
19

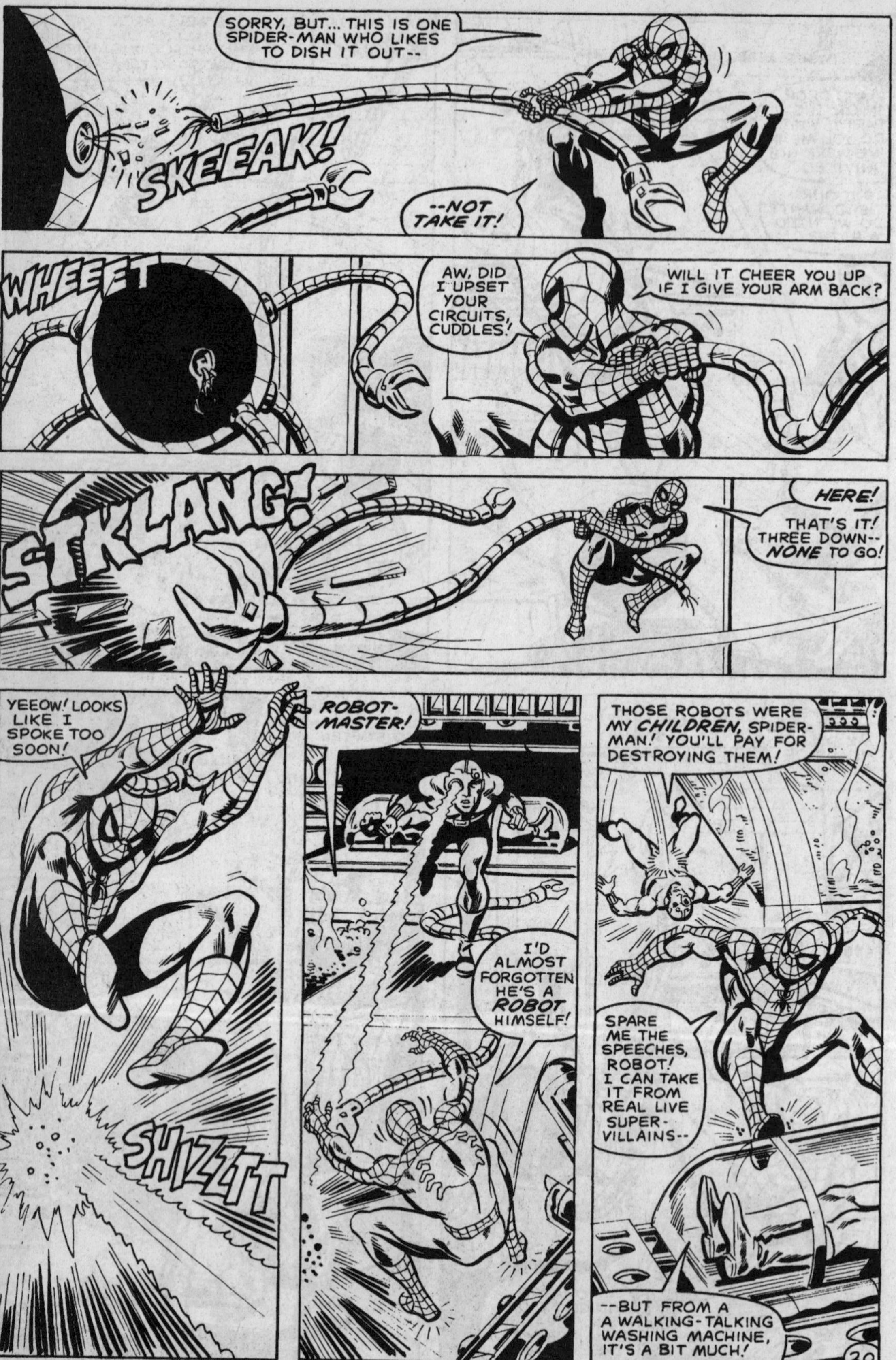
SORRY, BUT... THIS IS ONE SPIDER-MAN WHO LIKES TO DISH IT OUT--
SKEEAK!
--NOT TAKE IT!
WHEEET
AW, DID I UPSET YOUR CIRCUITS, CUDDLES!
WILL IT CHEER YOU UP IF I GIVE YOUR ARM BACK?
STKLANG!
HERE!
THAT'S IT! THREE DOWN-- NONE TO GO!
YEEOW! LOOKS LIKE I SPOKE TOO SOON!
SHIZZTT
ROBOT-MASTER!
I'D ALMOST FORGOTTEN HE'S A ROBOT HIMSELF!
THOSE ROBOTS WERE MY CHILDREN, SPIDER-MAN! YOU'LL PAY FOR DESTROYING THEM!
SPARE ME THE SPEECHES, ROBOT! I CAN TAKE IT FROM REAL LIVE SUPER-VILLAINS--
--BUT FROM A A WALKING-TALKING WASHING MACHINE, IT'S A BIT MUCH!
20

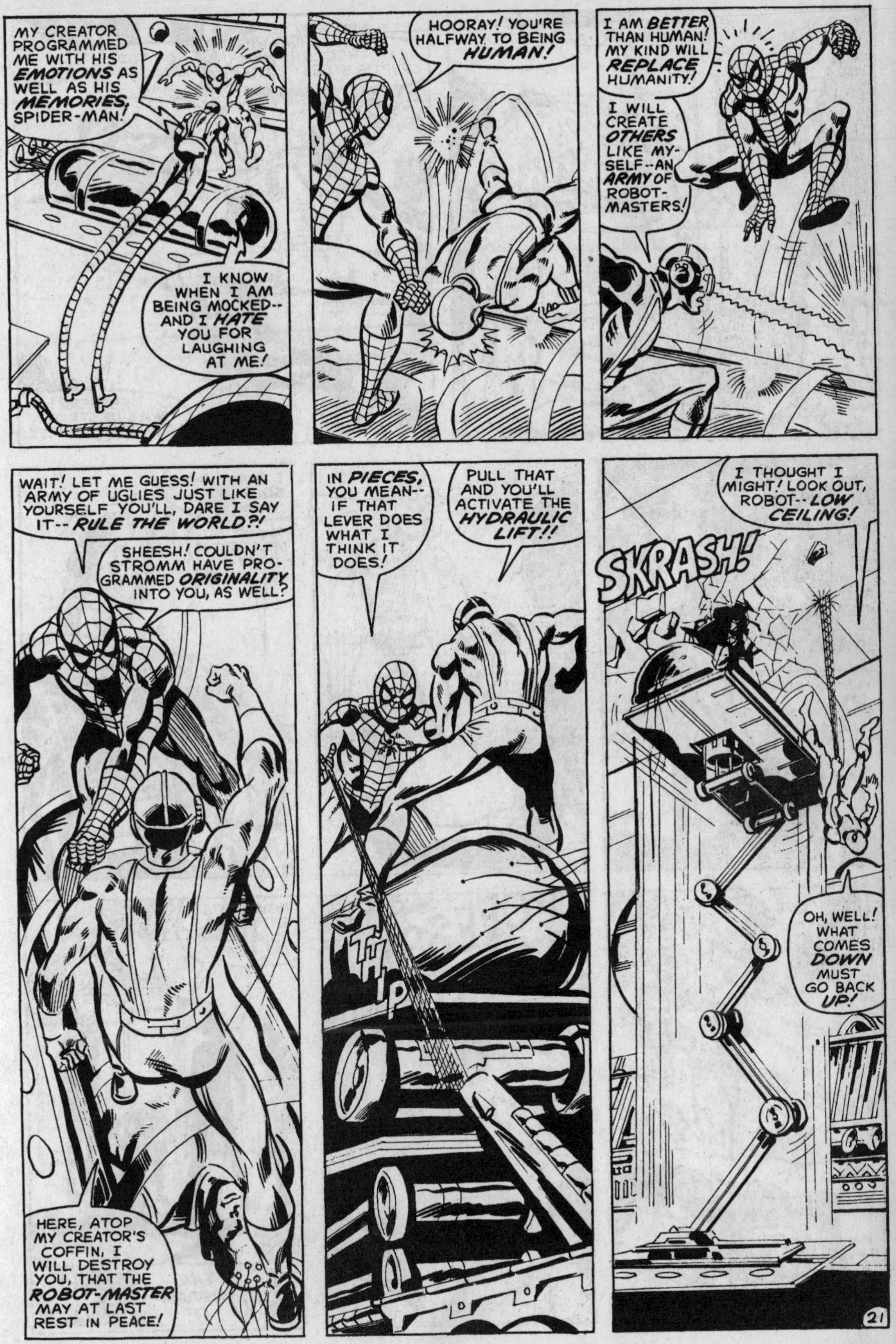
MY CREATOR PROGRAMMED ME WITH HIS EMOTIONS AS WELL AS HIS MEMORIES, SPIDER-MAN!
I KNOW WHEN I AM BEING MOCKED-- AND I HATE YOU FOR LAUGHING AT ME!
HOORAY! YOU'RE HALFWAY TO BEING HUMAN!
I AM BETTER THAN HUMAN! MY KIND WILL REPLACE HUMANITY!
I WILL CREATE OTHERS LIKE MYSELF--AN ARMY OF ROBOT-MASTERS!
WAIT! LET ME GUESS! WITH AN ARMY OF UGLIES JUST LIKE YOURSELF YOU'LL, DARE I SAY IT-- RULE THE WORLD?!
SHEESH! COULDN'T STROMM HAVE PROGRAMMED ORIGINALITY INTO YOU, AS WELL?
HERE, ATOP MY CREATOR'S COFFIN, I WILL DESTROY YOU, THAT THE ROBOT-MASTER MAY AT LAST REST IN PEACE!
PULL THAT AND YOU'LL ACTIVATE THE HYDRAULIC LIFT!!
IN PIECES, YOU MEAN-- IF THAT LEVER DOES WHAT I THINK IT DOES!
THIP
I THOUGHT I MIGHT! LOOK OUT, ROBOT-- LOW CEILING!
SKRASH!
OH, WELL! WHAT COMES DOWN MUST GO BACK UP!

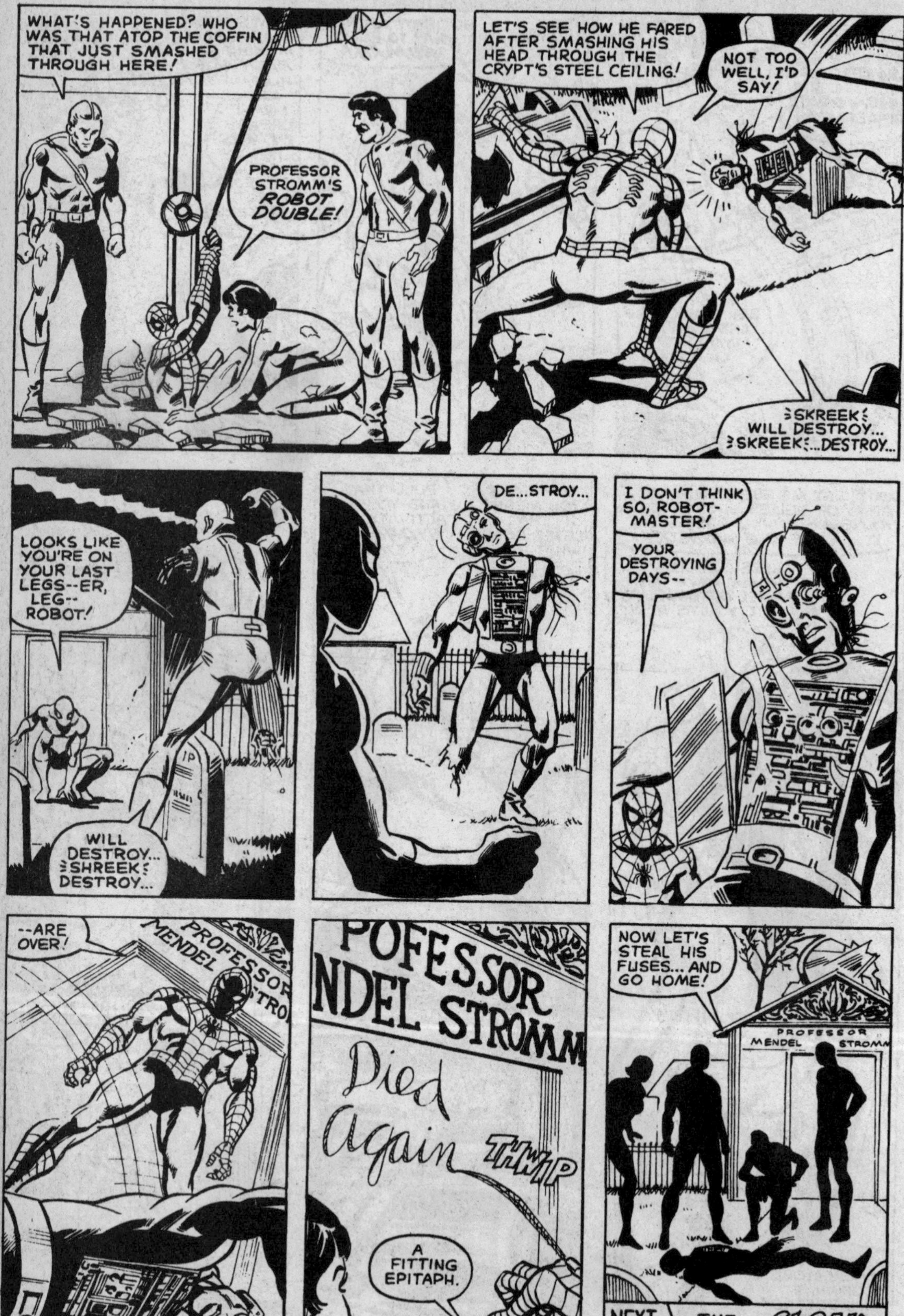
WHAT'S HAPPENED? WHO WAS THAT ATOP THE COFFIN THAT JUST SMASHED THROUGH HERE!
PROFESSOR STROMM'S ROBOT DOUBLE!
LET'S SEE HOW HE FARED AFTER SMASHING HIS HEAD THROUGH THE CRYPT'S STEEL CEILING!
NOT TOO WELL, I'D SAY!
SKREEK WILL DESTROY... SKREEK ...DESTROY...
LOOKS LIKE YOU'RE ON YOUR LAST LEGS--ER, LEG--ROBOT!
WILL DESTROY... SHREEK DESTROY...
DE...STROY...
I DON'T THINK SO, ROBOT-MASTER!
YOUR DESTROYING DAYS--
--ARE OVER!
PROFESSOR MENDEL STRO
SKLANG
POFESSOR NDEL STROMM
Died Again
THWIP
A FITTING EPITAPH.
NOW LET'S STEAL HIS FUSES... AND GO HOME!
PROFESSOR MENDEL STROMM
NEXT MONTH
THE RETURN OF CLOAK & DAGGER!

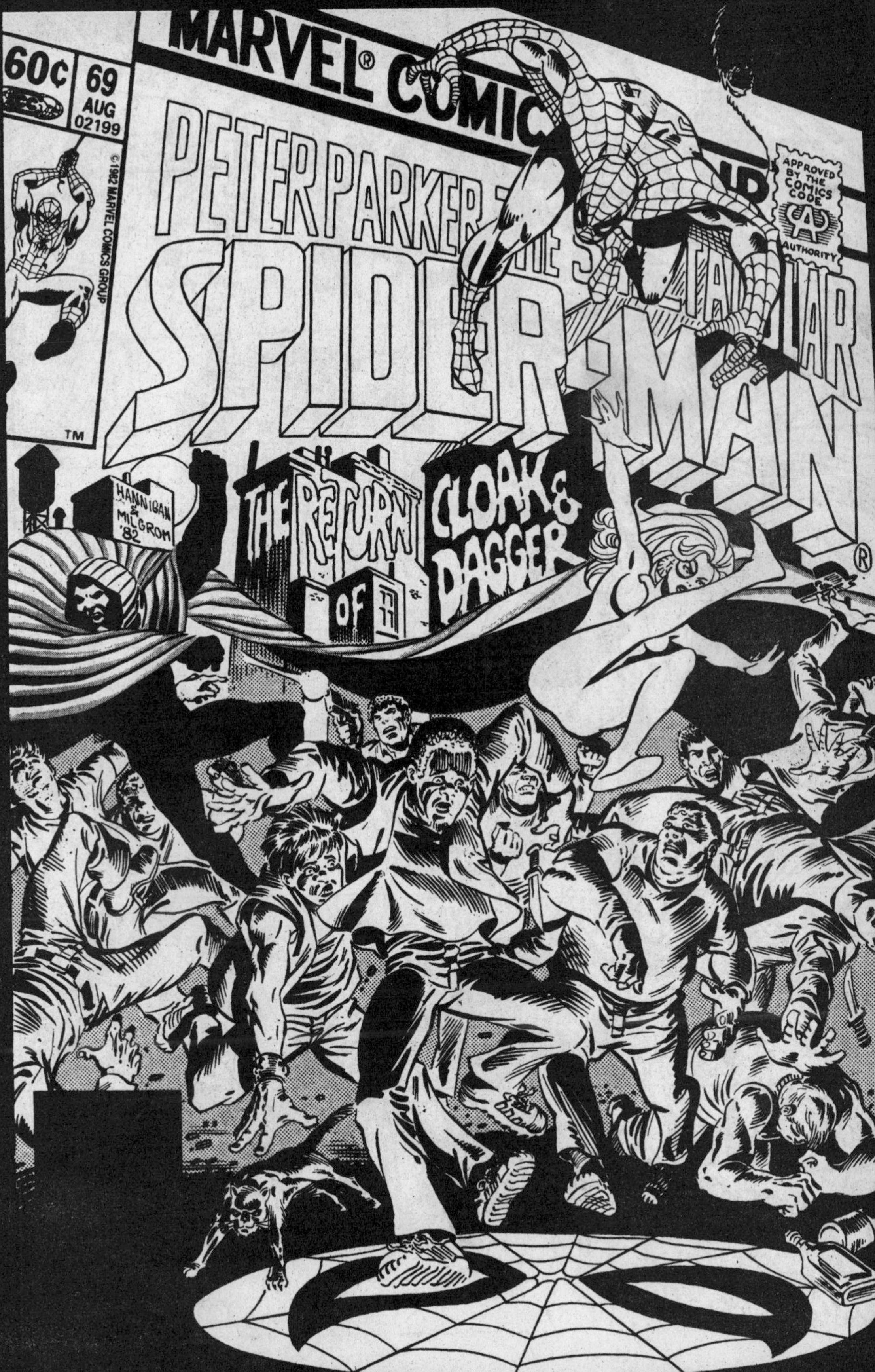
MARVEL® COMIC
60¢
69
AUG
02199
© 1982 MARVEL COMICS GROUP
PETER PARKER
SPIDER-MAN®
TM
APPROVED BY THE COMICS CODE AUTHORITY
HANNIGAN & MILGROM '82
THE RETURN OF
CLOAK & DAGGER

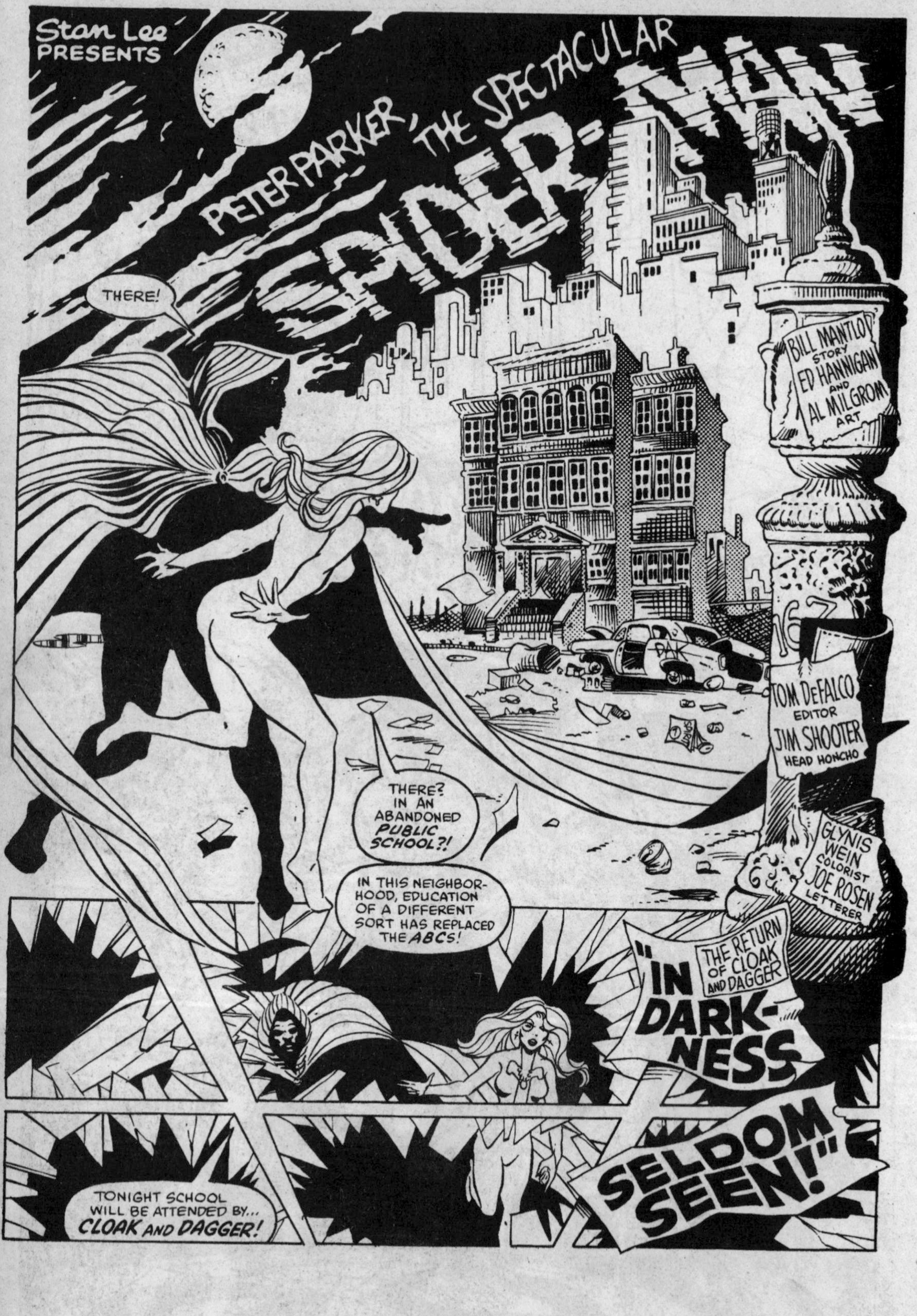
Stan Lee PRESENTS
PETER PARKER, THE SPECTACULAR SPIDER-MAN
THERE!
BILL MANTLO STORY
ED HANNIGAN AND AL MILGROM ART
TOM DeFALCO EDITOR
JIM SHOOTER HEAD HONCHO
GLYNIS WEIN COLORIST
JOE ROSEN LETTERER
THERE? IN AN ABANDONED PUBLIC SCHOOL?!
IN THIS NEIGHBORHOOD, EDUCATION OF A DIFFERENT SORT HAS REPLACED THE ABCs!
THE RETURN OF CLOAK AND DAGGER
"IN DARKNESS SELDOM SEEN!"
TONIGHT SCHOOL WILL BE ATTENDED BY... CLOAK AND DAGGER!

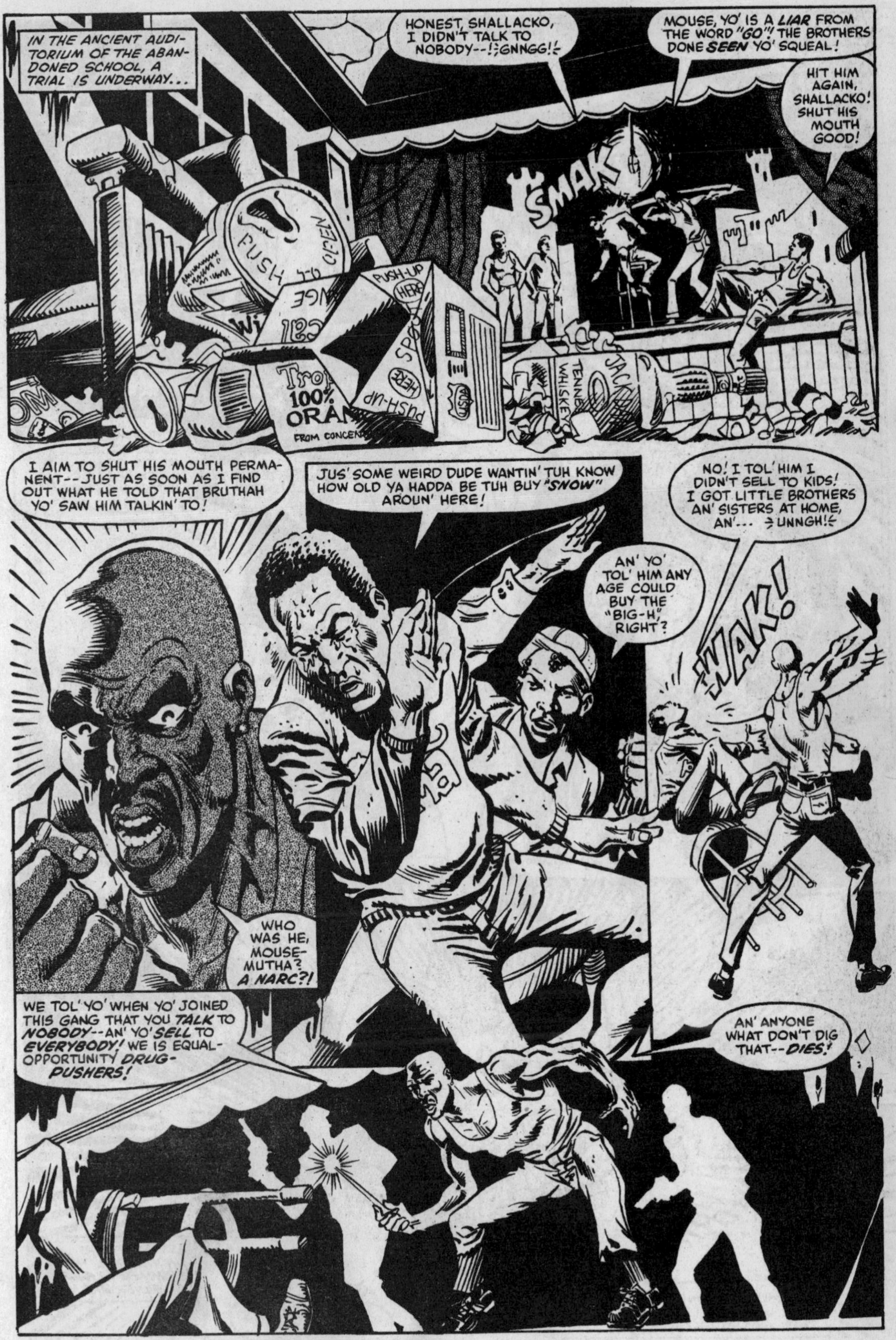
IN THE ANCIENT AUDITORIUM OF THE ABANDONED SCHOOL, A TRIAL IS UNDERWAY...
HONEST, SHALLACKO, I DIDN'T TALK TO NOBODY--!;GNNGG!
MOUSE, YO' IS A LIAR FROM THE WORD "GO"! THE BROTHERS DONE SEEN YO' SQUEAL!
HIT HIM AGAIN, SHALLACKO! SHUT HIS MOUTH GOOD!
SMAK
I AIM TO SHUT HIS MOUTH PERMANENT--JUST AS SOON AS I FIND OUT WHAT HE TOLD THAT BRUTHAH YO' SAW HIM TALKIN' TO!
WHO WAS HE, MOUSE-MUTHA? A NARC?!
JUS' SOME WEIRD DUDE WANTIN' TUH KNOW HOW OLD YA HADDA BE TUH BUY "SNOW" AROUN' HERE!
AN' YO' TOL' HIM ANY AGE COULD BUY THE "BIG-H," RIGHT?
NO! I TOL' HIM I DIDN'T SELL TO KIDS! I GOT LITTLE BROTHERS AN' SISTERS AT HOME, AN'... UNNGH!
WAK!
WE TOL' YO' WHEN YO' JOINED THIS GANG THAT YOU TALK TO NOBODY--AN' YO' SELL TO EVERYBODY! WE IS EQUAL-OPPORTUNITY DRUG-PUSHERS!
AN' ANYONE WHAT DON'T DIG THAT--DIES!

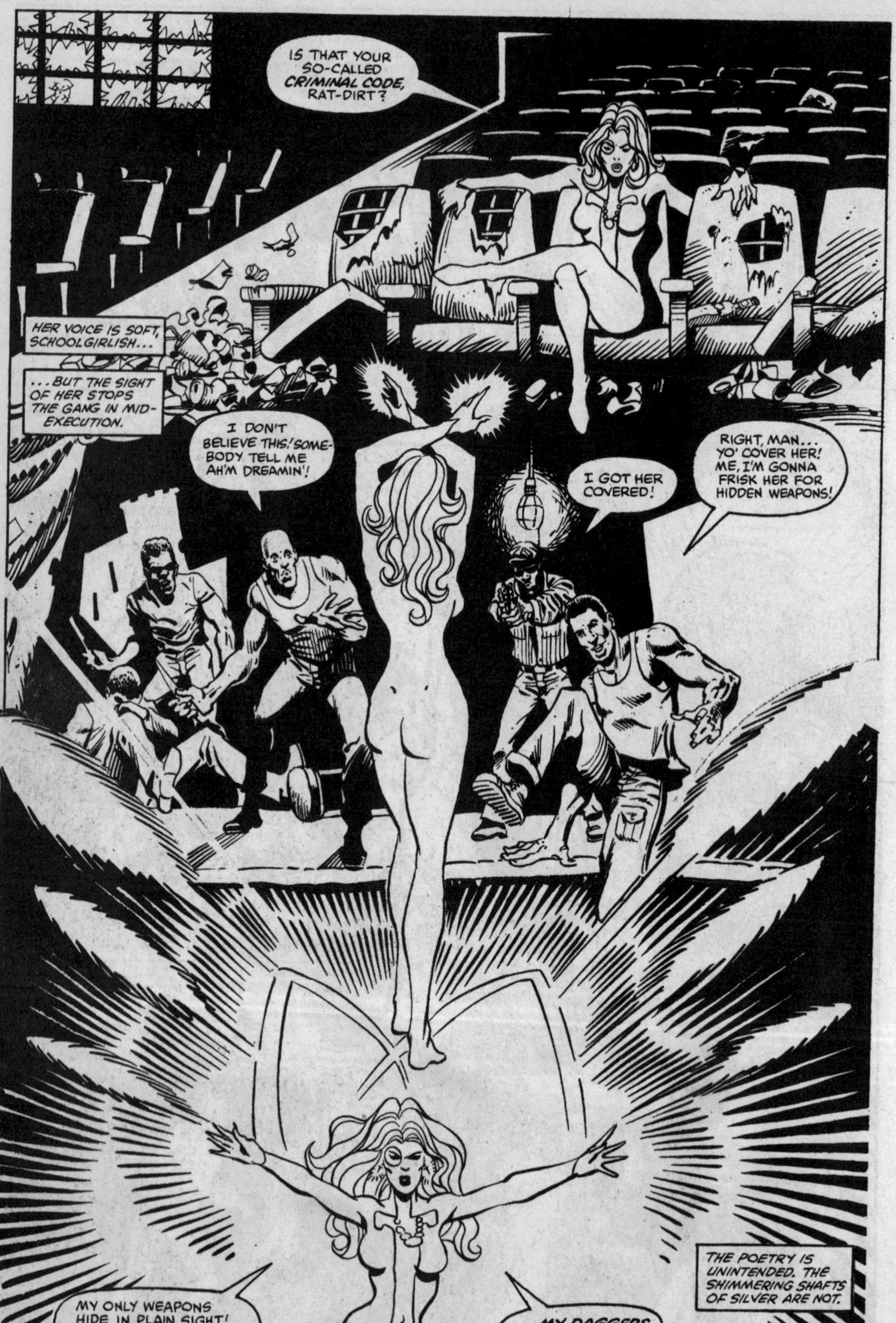
IS THAT YOUR SO-CALLED CRIMINAL CODE, RAT-DIRT?
HER VOICE IS SOFT, SCHOOLGIRLISH...
...BUT THE SIGHT OF HER STOPS THE GANG IN MID-EXECUTION.
I DON'T BELIEVE THIS! SOMEBODY TELL ME AH'M DREAMIN'!
I GOT HER COVERED!
RIGHT, MAN... YO' COVER HER! ME, I'M GONNA FRISK HER FOR HIDDEN WEAPONS!
MY ONLY WEAPONS HIDE IN PLAIN SIGHT! THEY ARE MY DAGGERS...
...MY DAGGERS OF LIGHT!
THE POETRY IS UNINTENDED. THE SHIMMERING SHAFTS OF SILVER ARE NOT.

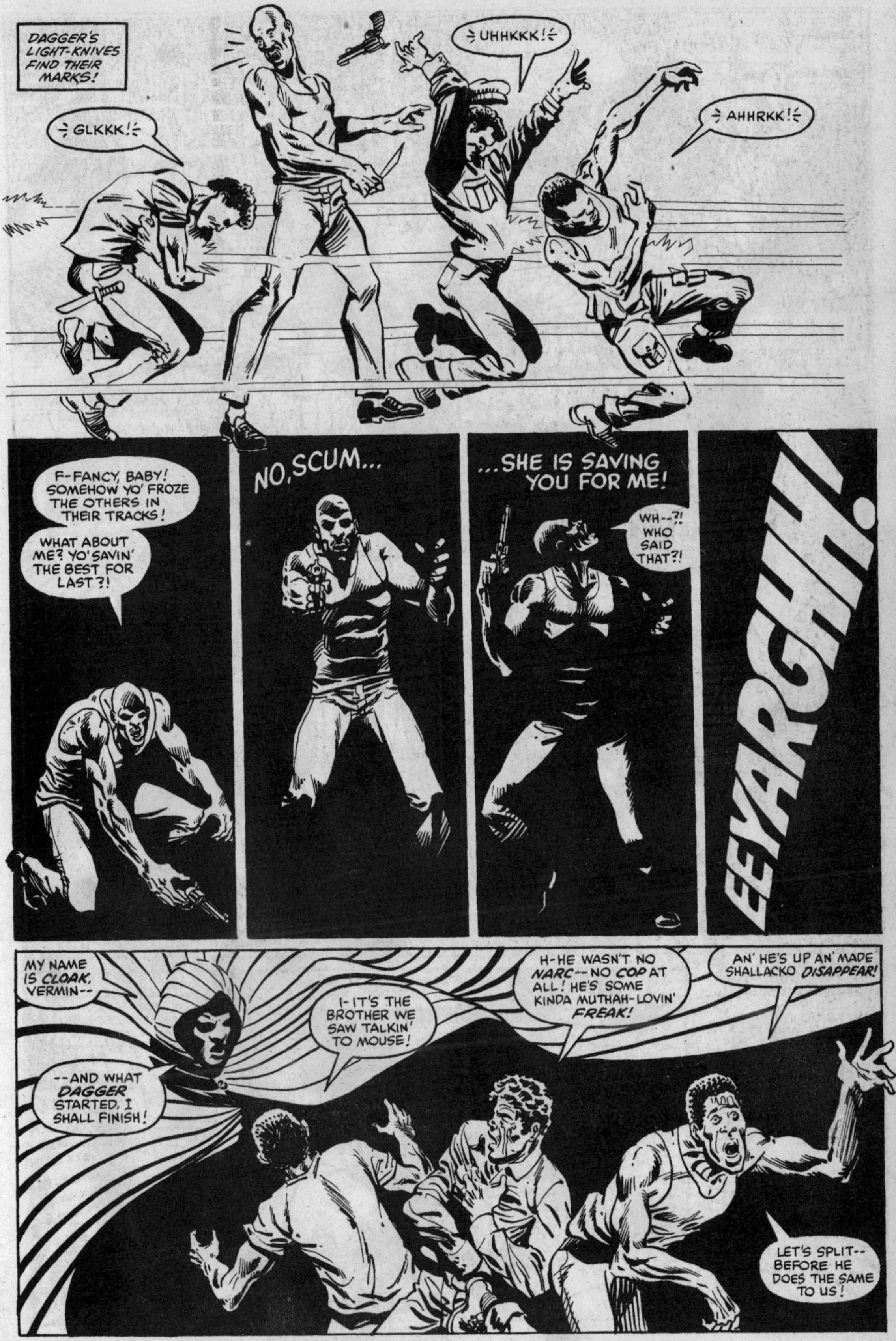
DAGGER'S LIGHT-KNIVES FIND THEIR MARKS!
GLKKK!
UHHKKK!
AHHRKK!
F-FANCY, BABY! SOMEHOW YO' FROZE THE OTHERS IN THEIR TRACKS!
WHAT ABOUT ME? YO' SAVIN' THE BEST FOR LAST?!
NO, SCUM...
...SHE IS SAVING YOU FOR ME!
WH--?! WHO SAID THAT?!
EEYARGH!
MY NAME IS CLOAK, VERMIN--
--AND WHAT DAGGER STARTED, I SHALL FINISH!
I-IT'S THE BROTHER WE SAW TALKIN' TO MOUSE!
H-HE WASN'T NO NARC--NO COP AT ALL! HE'S SOME KINDA MUTHAH-LOVIN' FREAK!
AN' HE'S UP AN' MADE SHALLACKO DISAPPEAR!
LET'S SPLIT-- BEFORE HE DOES THE SAME TO US!

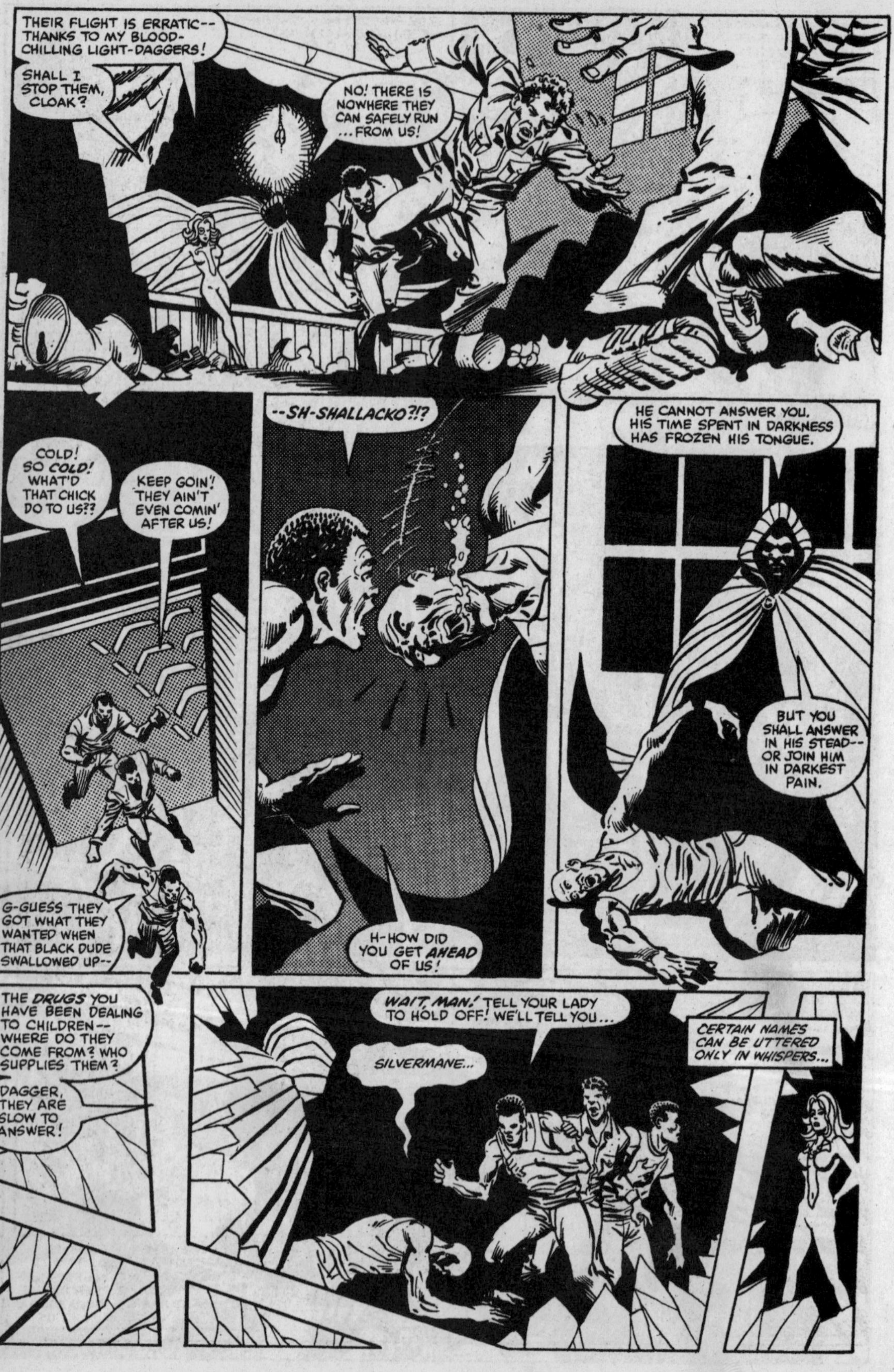
THEIR FLIGHT IS ERRATIC-- THANKS TO MY BLOOD-CHILLING LIGHT-DAGGERS!
SHALL I STOP THEM, CLOAK?
NO! THERE IS NOWHERE THEY CAN SAFELY RUN ...FROM US!
COLD! SO COLD! WHAT'D THAT CHICK DO TO US??
KEEP GOIN'! THEY AIN'T EVEN COMIN' AFTER US!
G-GUESS THEY GOT WHAT THEY WANTED WHEN THAT BLACK DUDE SWALLOWED UP--
--SH-SHALLACKO?!?
H-HOW DID YOU GET AHEAD OF US!
HE CANNOT ANSWER YOU. HIS TIME SPENT IN DARKNESS HAS FROZEN HIS TONGUE.
BUT YOU SHALL ANSWER IN HIS STEAD-- OR JOIN HIM IN DARKEST PAIN.
THE DRUGS YOU HAVE BEEN DEALING TO CHILDREN-- WHERE DO THEY COME FROM? WHO SUPPLIES THEM?
DAGGER, THEY ARE SLOW TO ANSWER!
WAIT, MAN! TELL YOUR LADY TO HOLD OFF! WE'LL TELL YOU...
SILVERMANE...
CERTAIN NAMES CAN BE UTTERED ONLY IN WHISPERS...

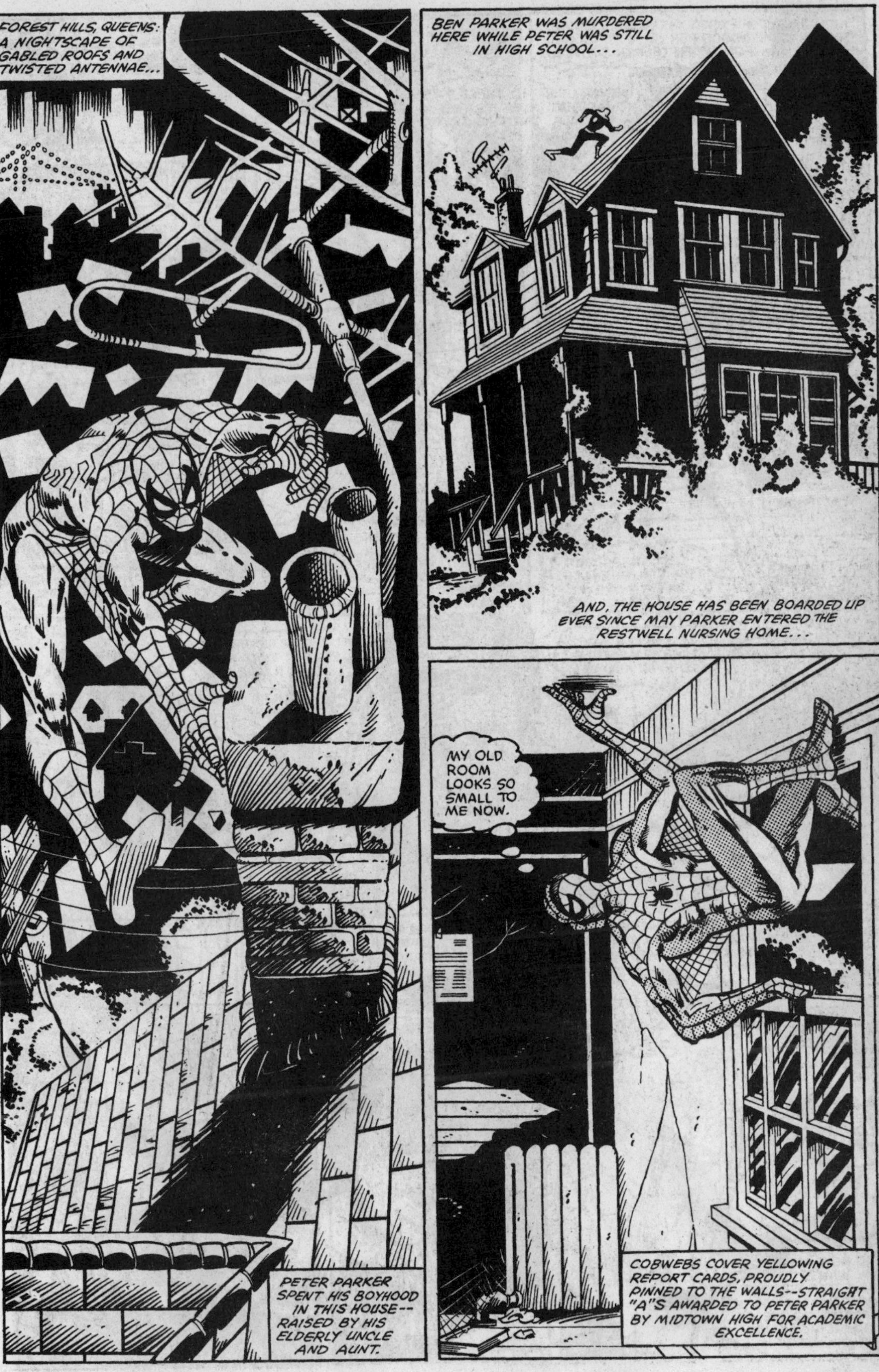
FOREST HILLS, QUEENS: A NIGHTSCAPE OF GABLED ROOFS AND TWISTED ANTENNAE...
PETER PARKER SPENT HIS BOYHOOD IN THIS HOUSE-- RAISED BY HIS ELDERLY UNCLE AND AUNT.
BEN PARKER WAS MURDERED HERE WHILE PETER WAS STILL IN HIGH SCHOOL...
AND, THE HOUSE HAS BEEN BOARDED UP EVER SINCE MAY PARKER ENTERED THE RESTWELL NURSING HOME...
MY OLD ROOM LOOKS SO SMALL TO ME NOW.
COBWEBS COVER YELLOWING REPORT CARDS, PROUDLY PINNED TO THE WALLS--STRAIGHT "A"S AWARDED TO PETER PARKER BY MIDTOWN HIGH FOR ACADEMIC EXCELLENCE.

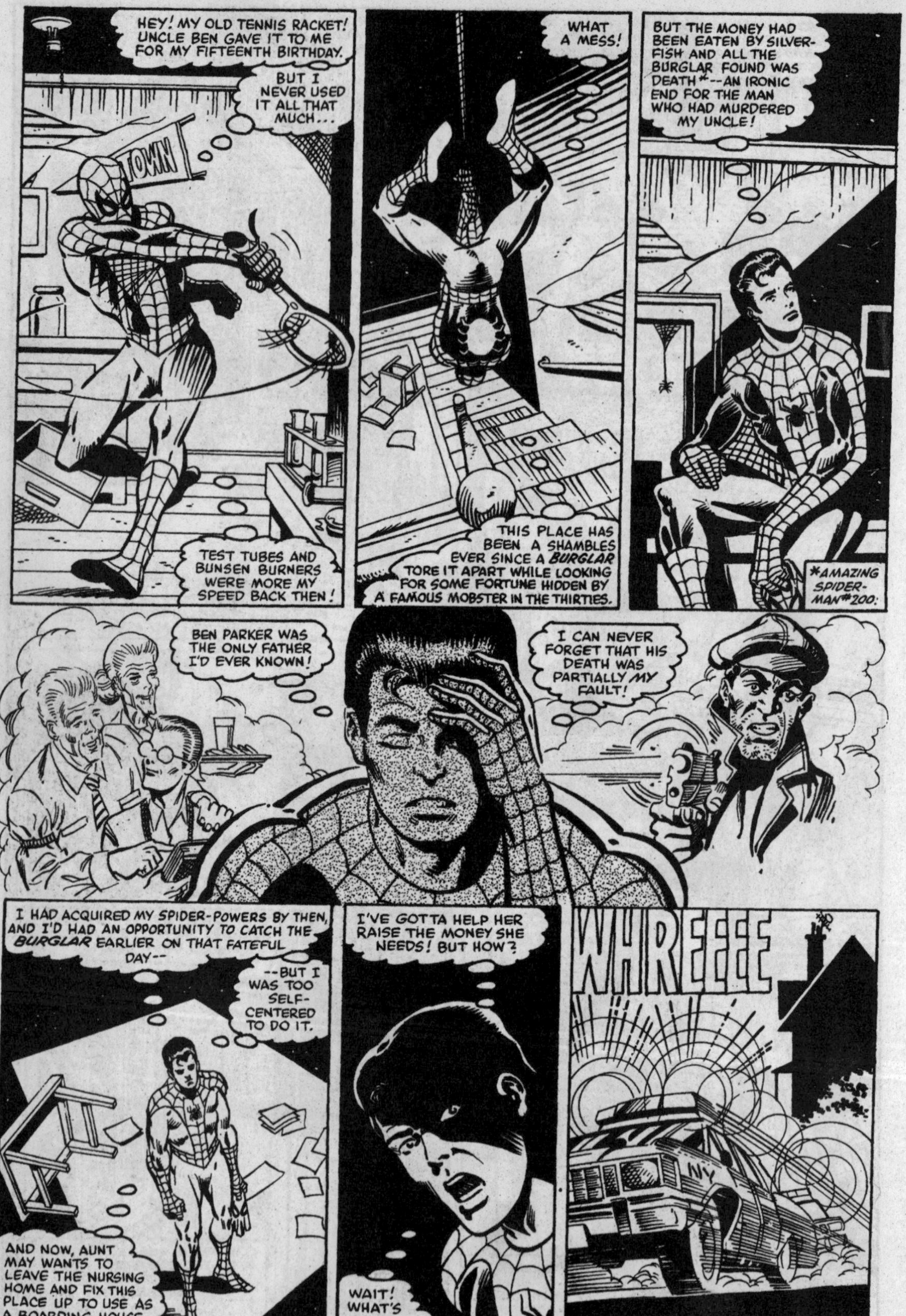
HEY! MY OLD TENNIS RACKET! UNCLE BEN GAVE IT TO ME FOR MY FIFTEENTH BIRTHDAY.
BUT I NEVER USED IT ALL THAT MUCH...
TOWN
TEST TUBES AND BUNSEN BURNERS WERE MORE MY SPEED BACK THEN!
WHAT A MESS!
THIS PLACE HAS BEEN A SHAMBLES EVER SINCE A BURGLAR TORE IT APART WHILE LOOKING FOR SOME FORTUNE HIDDEN BY A FAMOUS MOBSTER IN THE THIRTIES.
BUT THE MONEY HAD BEEN EATEN BY SILVER-FISH AND ALL THE BURGLAR FOUND WAS DEATH*--AN IRONIC END FOR THE MAN WHO HAD MURDERED MY UNCLE!
*AMAZING SPIDER-MAN #200.
BEN PARKER WAS THE ONLY FATHER I'D EVER KNOWN!
I CAN NEVER FORGET THAT HIS DEATH WAS PARTIALLY MY FAULT!
I HAD ACQUIRED MY SPIDER-POWERS BY THEN, AND I'D HAD AN OPPORTUNITY TO CATCH THE BURGLAR EARLIER ON THAT FATEFUL DAY--
--BUT I WAS TOO SELF-CENTERED TO DO IT.
AND NOW, AUNT MAY WANTS TO LEAVE THE NURSING HOME AND FIX THIS PLACE UP TO USE AS A BOARDING HOUSE FOR OLDSTERS.
I'VE GOTTA HELP HER RAISE THE MONEY SHE NEEDS! BUT HOW?
WAIT! WHAT'S THAT SOUND--?
WHREEEE
NY

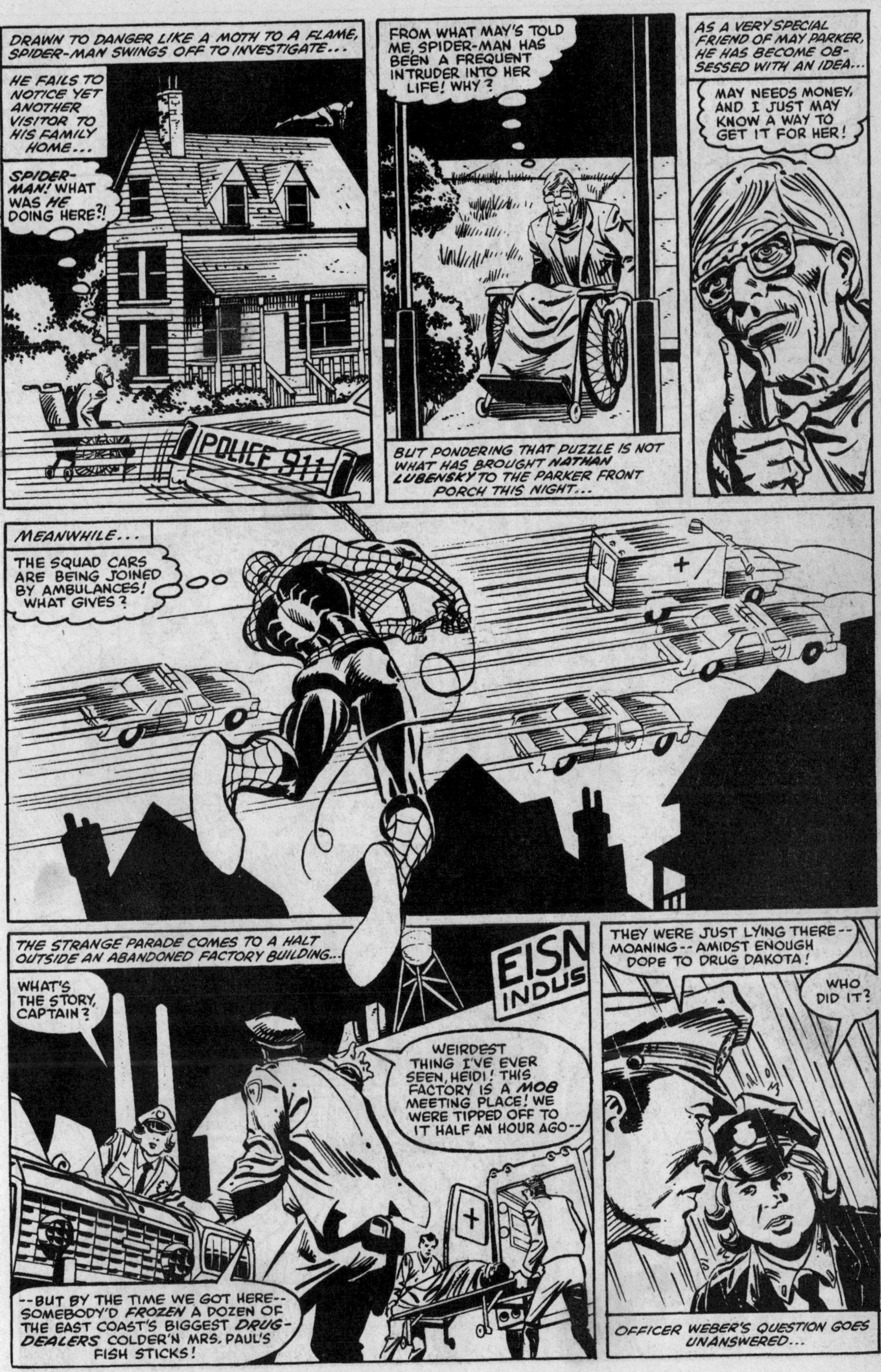
DRAWN TO DANGER LIKE A MOTH TO A FLAME, SPIDER-MAN SWINGS OFF TO INVESTIGATE...
HE FAILS TO NOTICE YET ANOTHER VISITOR TO HIS FAMILY HOME...
SPIDER-MAN! WHAT WAS HE DOING HERE?!
POLICE 911
FROM WHAT MAY'S TOLD ME, SPIDER-MAN HAS BEEN A FREQUENT INTRUDER INTO HER LIFE! WHY?
BUT PONDERING THAT PUZZLE IS NOT WHAT HAS BROUGHT NATHAN LUBENSKY TO THE PARKER FRONT PORCH THIS NIGHT...
AS A VERY SPECIAL FRIEND OF MAY PARKER, HE HAS BECOME OBSESSED WITH AN IDEA...
MAY NEEDS MONEY, AND I JUST MAY KNOW A WAY TO GET IT FOR HER!
MEANWHILE...
THE SQUAD CARS ARE BEING JOINED BY AMBULANCES! WHAT GIVES?
THE STRANGE PARADE COMES TO A HALT OUTSIDE AN ABANDONED FACTORY BUILDING...
EISN INDUS
WHAT'S THE STORY, CAPTAIN?
WEIRDEST THING I'VE EVER SEEN, HEIDI! THIS FACTORY IS A MOB MEETING PLACE! WE WERE TIPPED OFF TO IT HALF AN HOUR AGO--
--BUT BY THE TIME WE GOT HERE--SOMEBODY'D FROZEN A DOZEN OF THE EAST COAST'S BIGGEST DRUG-DEALERS COLDER'N MRS. PAUL'S FISH STICKS!
THEY WERE JUST LYING THERE--MOANING--AMIDST ENOUGH DOPE TO DRUG DAKOTA!
WHO DID IT?
OFFICER WEBER'S QUESTION GOES UNANSWERED...

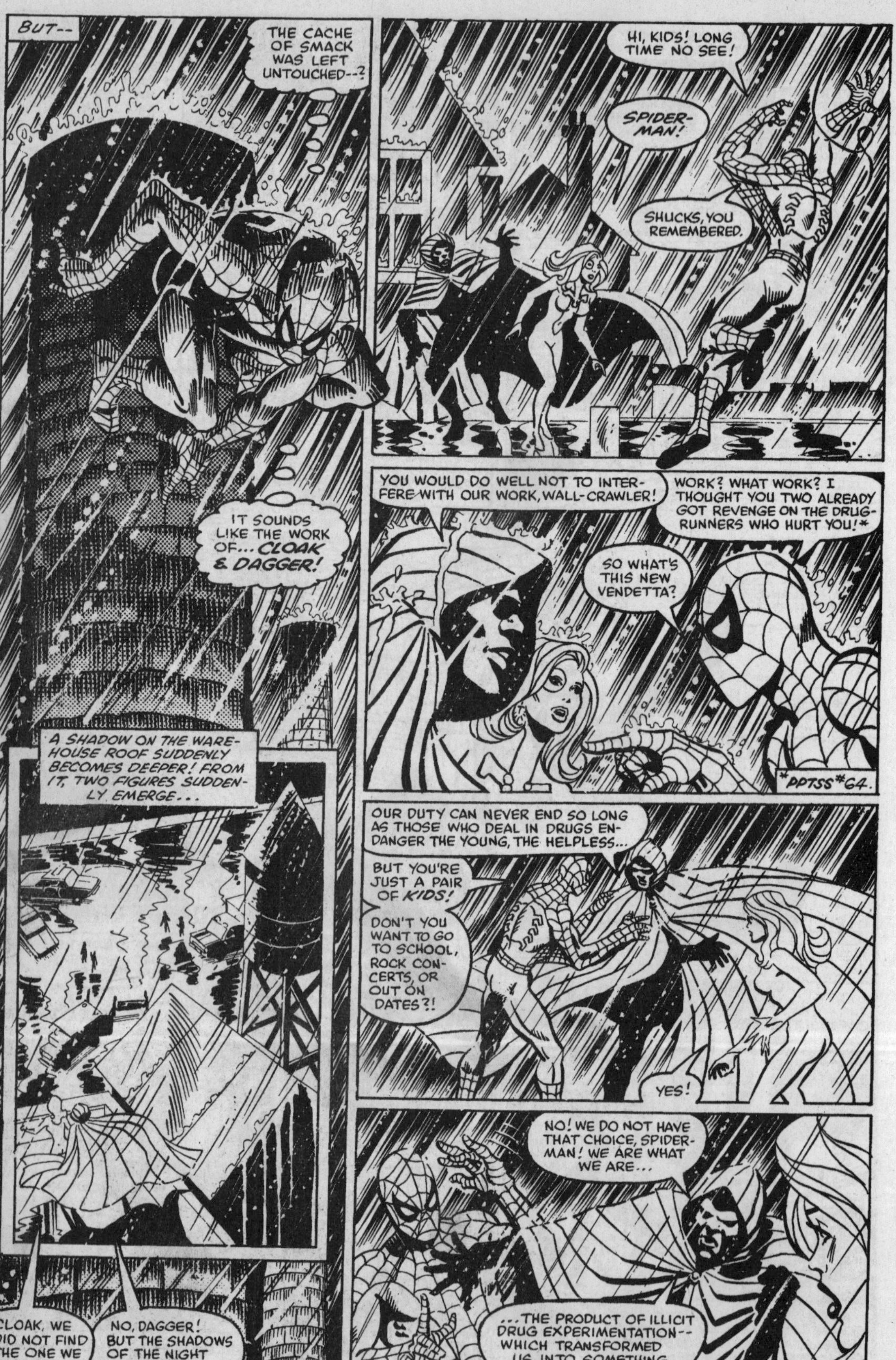
BUT--
THE CACHE OF SMACK WAS LEFT UNTOUCHED--?
IT SOUNDS LIKE THE WORK OF... CLOAK & DAGGER!
A SHADOW ON THE WAREHOUSE ROOF SUDDENLY BECOMES DEEPER! FROM IT, TWO FIGURES SUDDENLY EMERGE...
CLOAK, WE DID NOT FIND THE ONE WE SOUGHT.
NO, DAGGER! BUT THE SHADOWS OF THE NIGHT ARE STILL LONG!
HI, KIDS! LONG TIME NO SEE!
SPIDER-MAN!
SHUCKS, YOU REMEMBERED.
YOU WOULD DO WELL NOT TO INTERFERE WITH OUR WORK, WALL-CRAWLER!
WORK? WHAT WORK? I THOUGHT YOU TWO ALREADY GOT REVENGE ON THE DRUG-RUNNERS WHO HURT YOU!*
SO WHAT'S THIS NEW VENDETTA?
*PPTSS #64.
OUR DUTY CAN NEVER END SO LONG AS THOSE WHO DEAL IN DRUGS ENDANGER THE YOUNG, THE HELPLESS...
BUT YOU'RE JUST A PAIR OF KIDS!
DON'T YOU WANT TO GO TO SCHOOL, ROCK CONCERTS, OR OUT ON DATES?!
YES!
NO! WE DO NOT HAVE THAT CHOICE, SPIDER-MAN! WE ARE WHAT WE ARE...
...THE PRODUCT OF ILLICIT DRUG EXPERIMENTATION--WHICH TRANSFORMED US INTO SOMETHING OTHER THAN HUMAN!

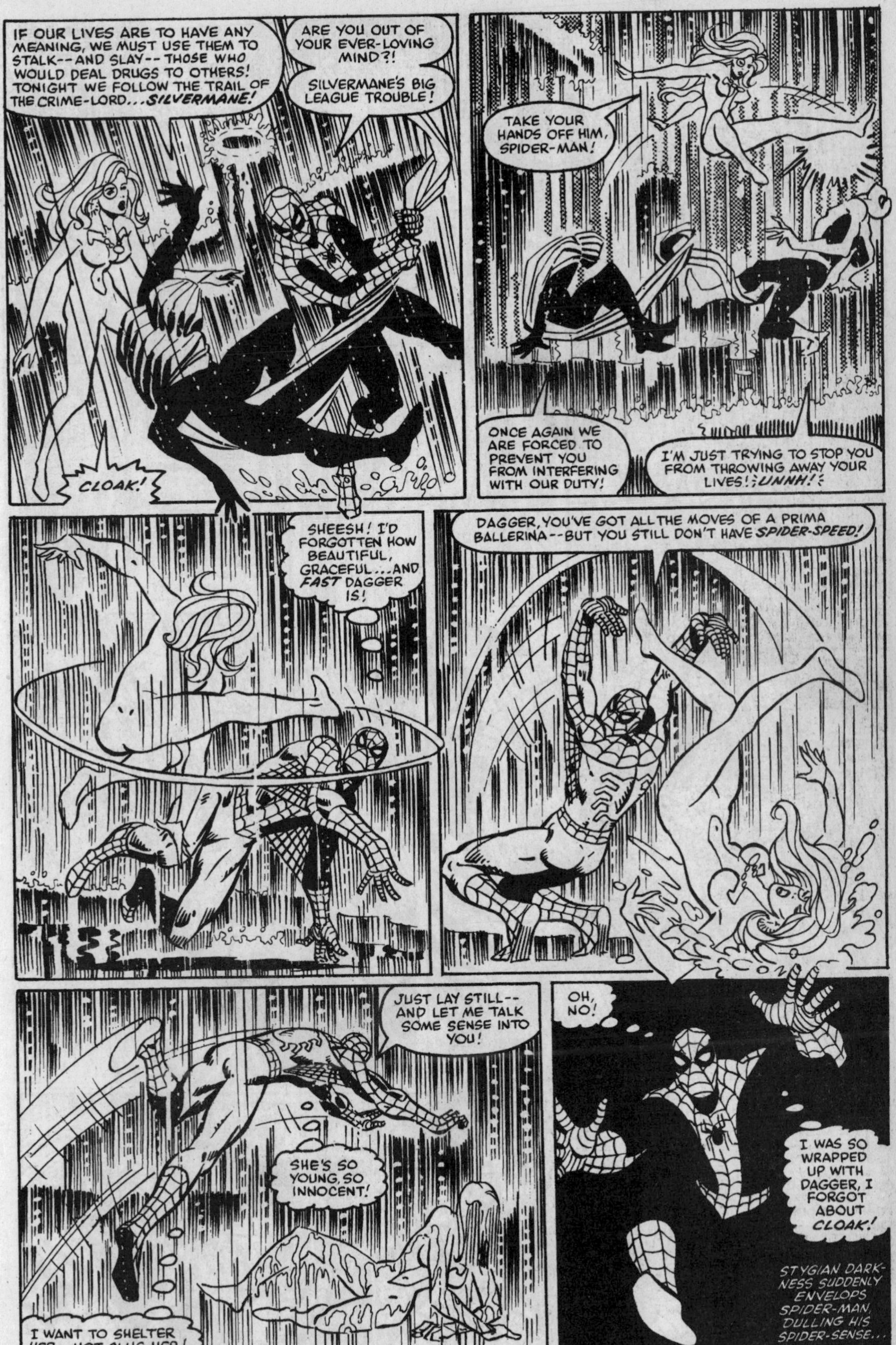

IF OUR LIVES ARE TO HAVE ANY MEANING, WE MUST USE THEM TO STALK--AND SLAY--THOSE WHO WOULD DEAL DRUGS TO OTHERS! TONIGHT WE FOLLOW THE TRAIL OF THE CRIME-LORD...SILVERMANE!
ARE YOU OUT OF YOUR EVER-LOVING MIND?!
SILVERMANE'S BIG LEAGUE TROUBLE!
CLOAK!
TAKE YOUR HANDS OFF HIM, SPIDER-MAN!
ONCE AGAIN WE ARE FORCED TO PREVENT YOU FROM INTERFERING WITH OUR DUTY!
I'M JUST TRYING TO STOP YOU FROM THROWING AWAY YOUR LIVES! UNNH!
SHEESH! I'D FORGOTTEN HOW BEAUTIFUL, GRACEFUL...AND FAST DAGGER IS!
DAGGER, YOU'VE GOT ALL THE MOVES OF A PRIMA BALLERINA--BUT YOU STILL DON'T HAVE SPIDER-SPEED!
JUST LAY STILL--AND LET ME TALK SOME SENSE INTO YOU!
SHE'S SO YOUNG, SO INNOCENT!
I WANT TO SHELTER HER--NOT SLUG HER!
OH, NO!
I WAS SO WRAPPED UP WITH DAGGER, I FORGOT ABOUT CLOAK!
STYGIAN DARKNESS SUDDENLY ENVELOPS SPIDER-MAN, DULLING HIS SPIDER-SENSE...

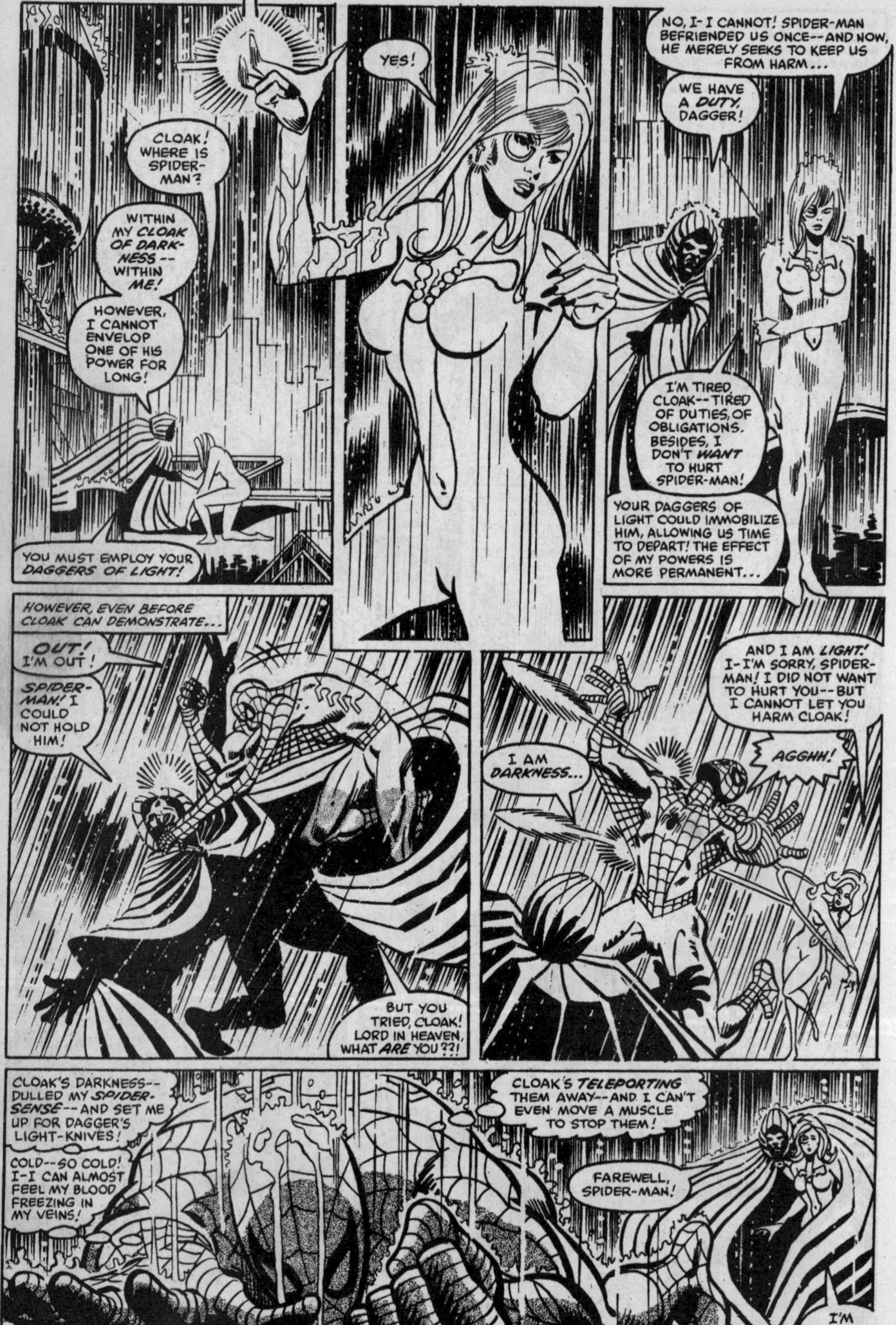
CLOAK! WHERE IS SPIDER-MAN?
WITHIN MY CLOAK OF DARKNESS-- WITHIN ME!
HOWEVER, I CANNOT ENVELOP ONE OF HIS POWER FOR LONG!
YOU MUST EMPLOY YOUR DAGGERS OF LIGHT!
YES!
NO, I- I CANNOT! SPIDER-MAN BEFRIENDED US ONCE--AND NOW, HE MERELY SEEKS TO KEEP US FROM HARM...
WE HAVE A DUTY, DAGGER!
I'M TIRED, CLOAK--TIRED OF DUTIES, OF OBLIGATIONS. BESIDES, I DON'T WANT TO HURT SPIDER-MAN!
YOUR DAGGERS OF LIGHT COULD IMMOBILIZE HIM, ALLOWING US TIME TO DEPART! THE EFFECT OF MY POWERS IS MORE PERMANENT...
HOWEVER, EVEN BEFORE CLOAK CAN DEMONSTRATE...
OUT! I'M OUT!
SPIDER-MAN! I COULD NOT HOLD HIM!
BUT YOU TRIED, CLOAK! LORD IN HEAVEN, WHAT ARE YOU??!
I AM DARKNESS...
AND I AM LIGHT! I- I'M SORRY, SPIDER-MAN! I DID NOT WANT TO HURT YOU--BUT I CANNOT LET YOU HARM CLOAK!
AGGHH!
CLOAK'S DARKNESS--DULLED MY SPIDER-SENSE--AND SET ME UP FOR DAGGER'S LIGHT-KNIVES!
COLD--SO COLD! I-I CAN ALMOST FEEL MY BLOOD FREEZING IN MY VEINS!
CLOAK'S TELEPORTING THEM AWAY--AND I CAN'T EVEN MOVE A MUSCLE TO STOP THEM!
FAREWELL, SPIDER-MAN!
I'M SORRY...

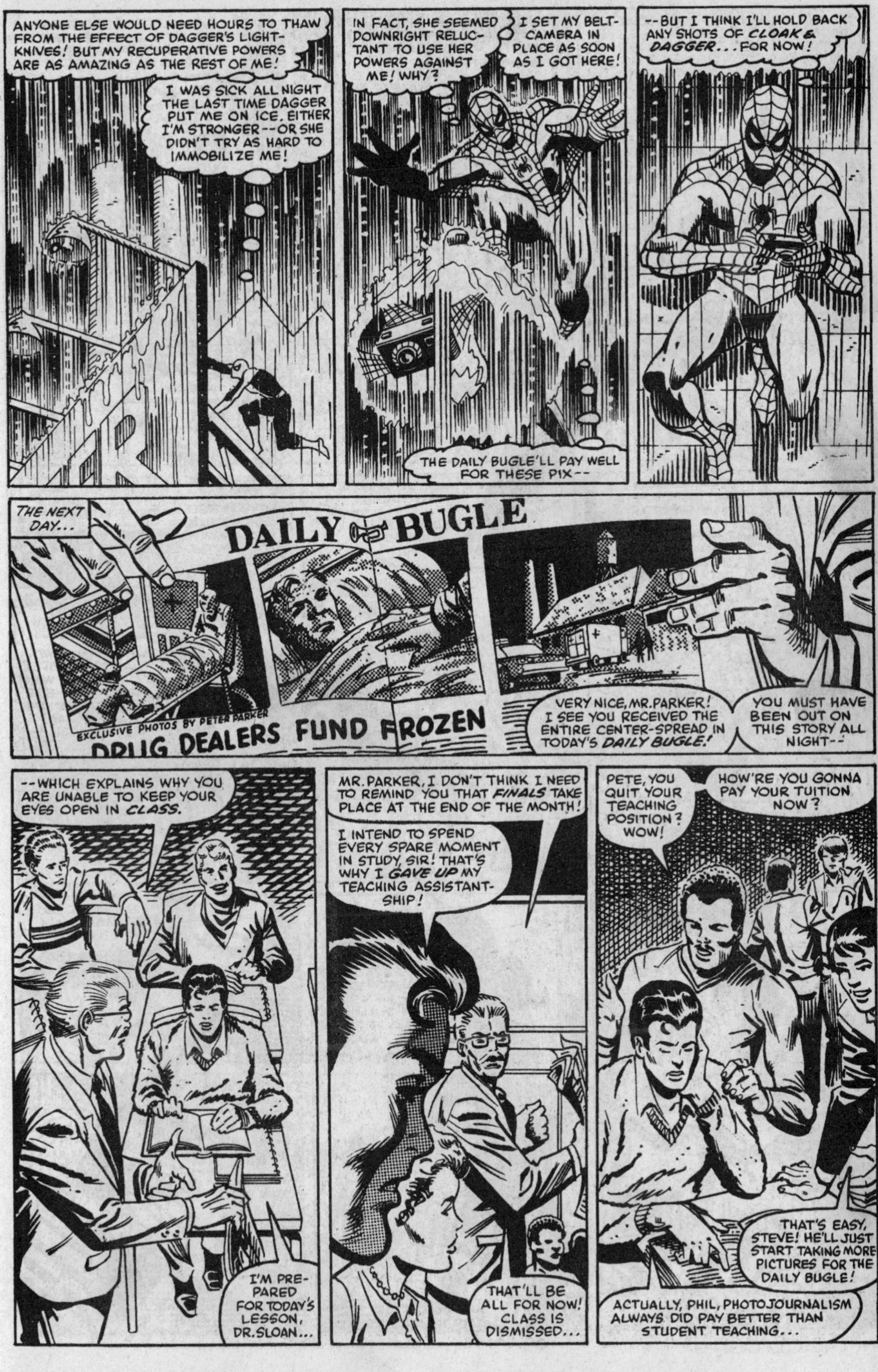
ANYONE ELSE WOULD NEED HOURS TO THAW FROM THE EFFECT OF DAGGER'S LIGHT-KNIVES! BUT MY RECUPERATIVE POWERS ARE AS AMAZING AS THE REST OF ME!
I WAS SICK ALL NIGHT THE LAST TIME DAGGER PUT ME ON ICE. EITHER I'M STRONGER--OR SHE DIDN'T TRY AS HARD TO IMMOBILIZE ME!
IN FACT, SHE SEEMED DOWNRIGHT RELUCTANT TO USE HER POWERS AGAINST ME! WHY?
I SET MY BELT-CAMERA IN PLACE AS SOON AS I GOT HERE!
THE DAILY BUGLE'LL PAY WELL FOR THESE PIX--
--BUT I THINK I'LL HOLD BACK ANY SHOTS OF CLOAK & DAGGER... FOR NOW!
THE NEXT DAY...
DAILY BUGLE
EXCLUSIVE PHOTOS BY PETER PARKER
DRUG DEALERS FUND FROZEN
VERY NICE, MR. PARKER! I SEE YOU RECEIVED THE ENTIRE CENTER-SPREAD IN TODAY'S DAILY BUGLE!
YOU MUST HAVE BEEN OUT ON THIS STORY ALL NIGHT--
--WHICH EXPLAINS WHY YOU ARE UNABLE TO KEEP YOUR EYES OPEN IN CLASS.
I'M PREPARED FOR TODAY'S LESSON, DR. SLOAN...
MR. PARKER, I DON'T THINK I NEED TO REMIND YOU THAT FINALS TAKE PLACE AT THE END OF THE MONTH!
I INTEND TO SPEND EVERY SPARE MOMENT IN STUDY, SIR! THAT'S WHY I GAVE UP MY TEACHING ASSISTANTSHIP!
THAT'LL BE ALL FOR NOW! CLASS IS DISMISSED...
PETE, YOU QUIT YOUR TEACHING POSITION? WOW!
HOW'RE YOU GONNA PAY YOUR TUITION NOW?
THAT'S EASY, STEVE! HE'LL JUST START TAKING MORE PICTURES FOR THE DAILY BUGLE!
ACTUALLY, PHIL, PHOTOJOURNALISM ALWAYS DID PAY BETTER THAN STUDENT TEACHING...

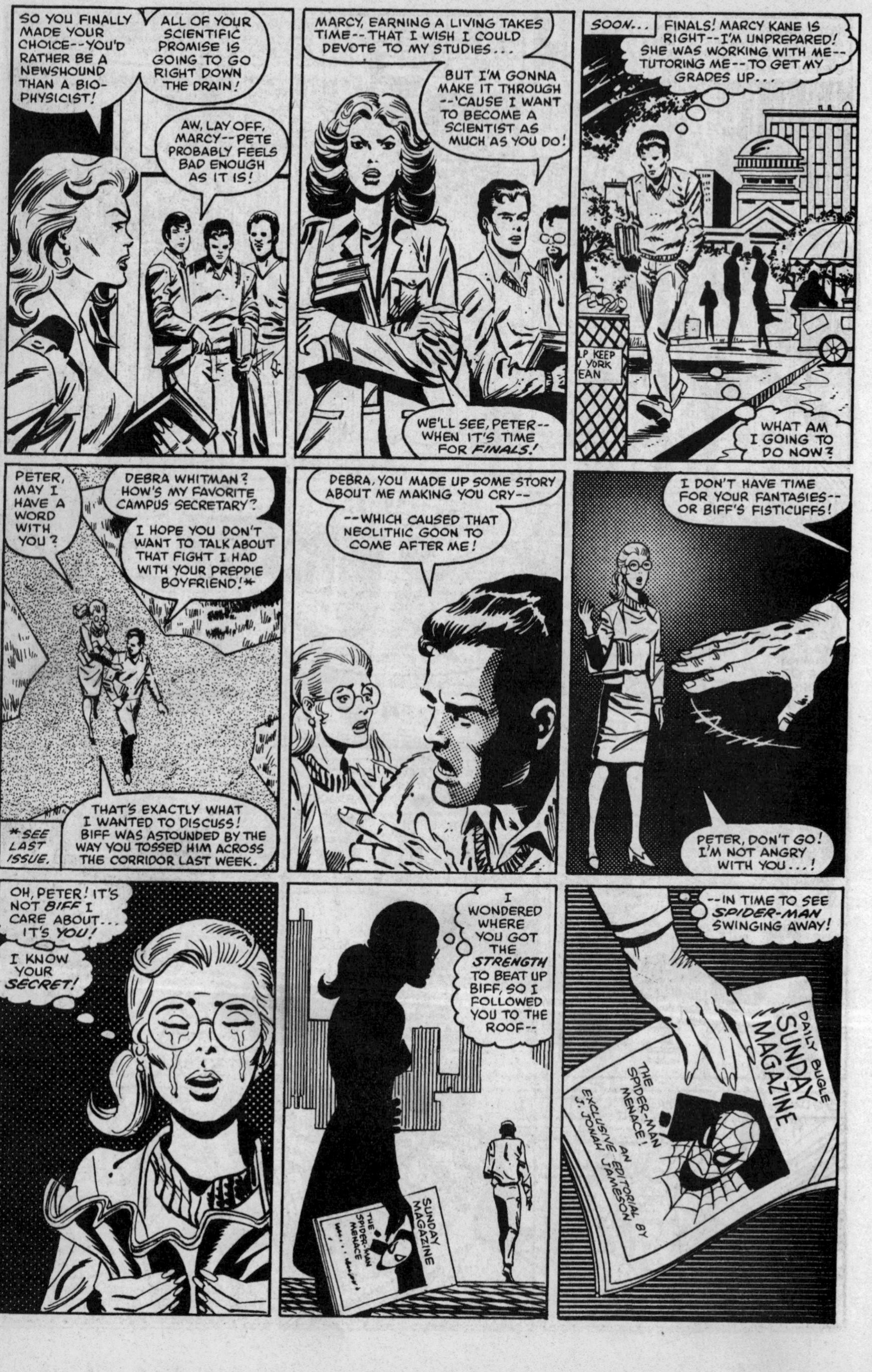
SO YOU FINALLY MADE YOUR CHOICE--YOU'D RATHER BE A NEWSHOUND THAN A BIO-PHYSICIST!
ALL OF YOUR SCIENTIFIC PROMISE IS GOING TO GO RIGHT DOWN THE DRAIN!
AW, LAY OFF, MARCY--PETE PROBABLY FEELS BAD ENOUGH AS IT IS!
MARCY, EARNING A LIVING TAKES TIME--THAT I WISH I COULD DEVOTE TO MY STUDIES...
BUT I'M GONNA MAKE IT THROUGH --'CAUSE I WANT TO BECOME A SCIENTIST AS MUCH AS YOU DO!
WE'LL SEE, PETER--WHEN IT'S TIME FOR FINALS!
SOON...
FINALS! MARCY KANE IS RIGHT--I'M UNPREPARED! SHE WAS WORKING WITH ME--TUTORING ME--TO GET MY GRADES UP...
LP KEEP Y YORK EAN
WHAT AM I GOING TO DO NOW?
PETER, MAY I HAVE A WORD WITH YOU?
DEBRA WHITMAN? HOW'S MY FAVORITE CAMPUS SECRETARY?
I HOPE YOU DON'T WANT TO TALK ABOUT THAT FIGHT I HAD WITH YOUR PREPPIE BOYFRIEND!*
THAT'S EXACTLY WHAT I WANTED TO DISCUSS! BIFF WAS ASTOUNDED BY THE WAY YOU TOSSED HIM ACROSS THE CORRIDOR LAST WEEK.
*SEE LAST ISSUE.
DEBRA, YOU MADE UP SOME STORY ABOUT ME MAKING YOU CRY--
--WHICH CAUSED THAT NEOLITHIC GOON TO COME AFTER ME!
I DON'T HAVE TIME FOR YOUR FANTASIES--OR BIFF'S FISTICUFFS!
PETER, DON'T GO! I'M NOT ANGRY WITH YOU...!
OH, PETER! IT'S NOT BIFF I CARE ABOUT... IT'S YOU!
I KNOW YOUR SECRET!
I WONDERED WHERE YOU GOT THE STRENGTH TO BEAT UP BIFF, SO I FOLLOWED YOU TO THE ROOF--
SUNDAY MAGAZINE
THE SPIDER-MAN MENACE
--IN TIME TO SEE SPIDER-MAN SWINGING AWAY!
DAILY BUGLE SUNDAY MAGAZINE
THE SPIDER-MAN MENACE!
AN EXCLUSIVE EDITORIAL BY J. JONAH JAMESON

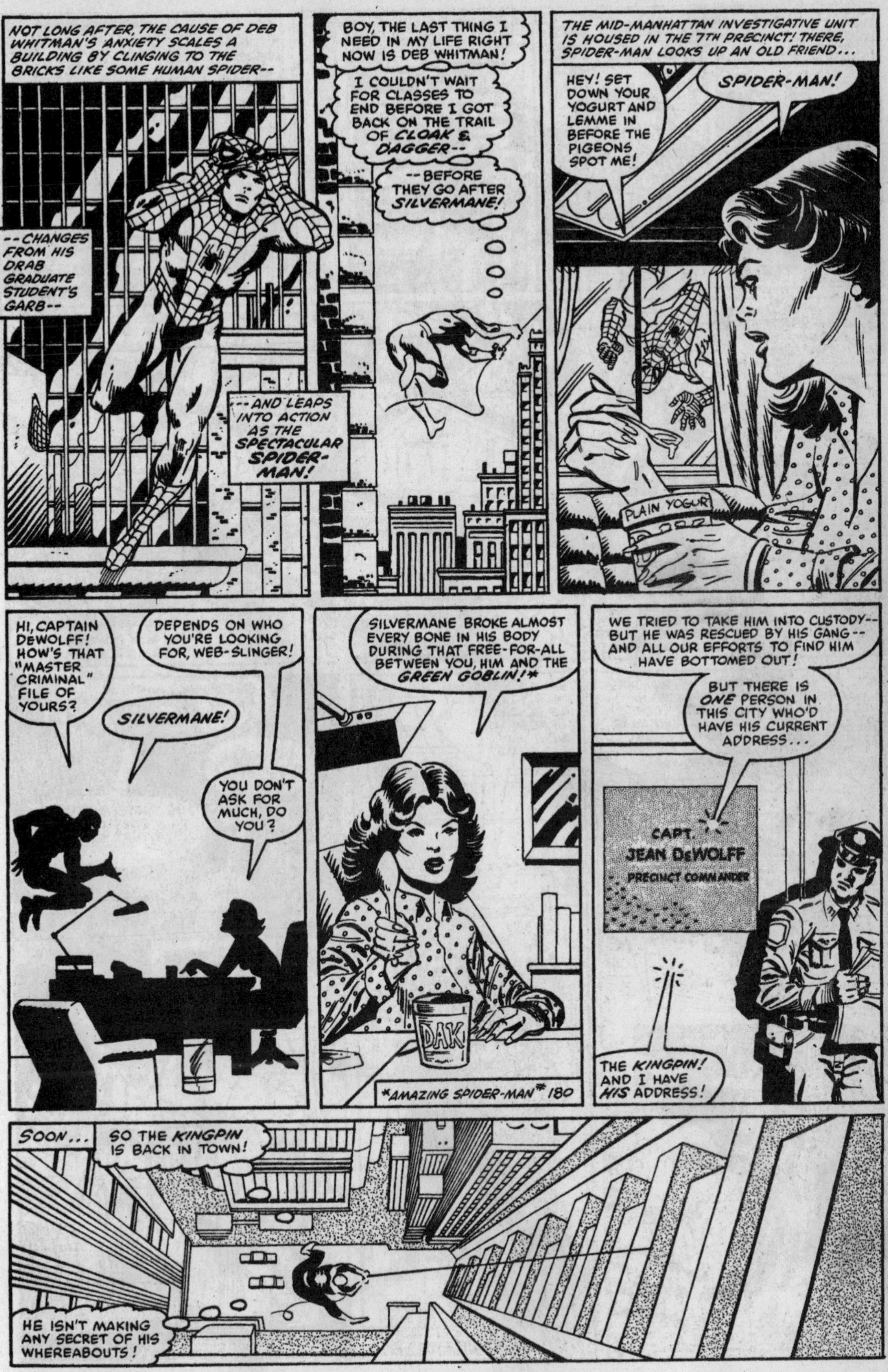
NOT LONG AFTER, THE CAUSE OF DEB WHITMAN'S ANXIETY SCALES A BUILDING BY CLINGING TO THE BRICKS LIKE SOME HUMAN SPIDER--
--CHANGES FROM HIS DRAB GRADUATE STUDENT'S GARB--
--AND LEAPS INTO ACTION AS THE SPECTACULAR SPIDER-MAN!
BOY, THE LAST THING I NEED IN MY LIFE RIGHT NOW IS DEB WHITMAN!
I COULDN'T WAIT FOR CLASSES TO END BEFORE I GOT BACK ON THE TRAIL OF CLOAK & DAGGER--
--BEFORE THEY GO AFTER SILVERMANE!
THE MID-MANHATTAN INVESTIGATIVE UNIT IS HOUSED IN THE 7TH PRECINCT! THERE, SPIDER-MAN LOOKS UP AN OLD FRIEND...
HEY! SET DOWN YOUR YOGURT AND LEMME IN BEFORE THE PIGEONS SPOT ME!
SPIDER-MAN!
PLAIN YOGURT
HI, CAPTAIN DEWOLFF! HOW'S THAT "MASTER CRIMINAL" FILE OF YOURS?
DEPENDS ON WHO YOU'RE LOOKING FOR, WEB-SLINGER!
SILVERMANE!
YOU DON'T ASK FOR MUCH, DO YOU?
SILVERMANE BROKE ALMOST EVERY BONE IN HIS BODY DURING THAT FREE-FOR-ALL BETWEEN YOU, HIM AND THE GREEN GOBLIN!*
DAK
*AMAZING SPIDER-MAN # 180
WE TRIED TO TAKE HIM INTO CUSTODY-- BUT HE WAS RESCUED BY HIS GANG-- AND ALL OUR EFFORTS TO FIND HIM HAVE BOTTOMED OUT!
BUT THERE IS ONE PERSON IN THIS CITY WHO'D HAVE HIS CURRENT ADDRESS...
CAPT. JEAN DeWOLFF PRECINCT COMMANDER
THE KINGPIN! AND I HAVE HIS ADDRESS!
SOON...
SO THE KINGPIN IS BACK IN TOWN!
HE ISN'T MAKING ANY SECRET OF HIS WHEREABOUTS!

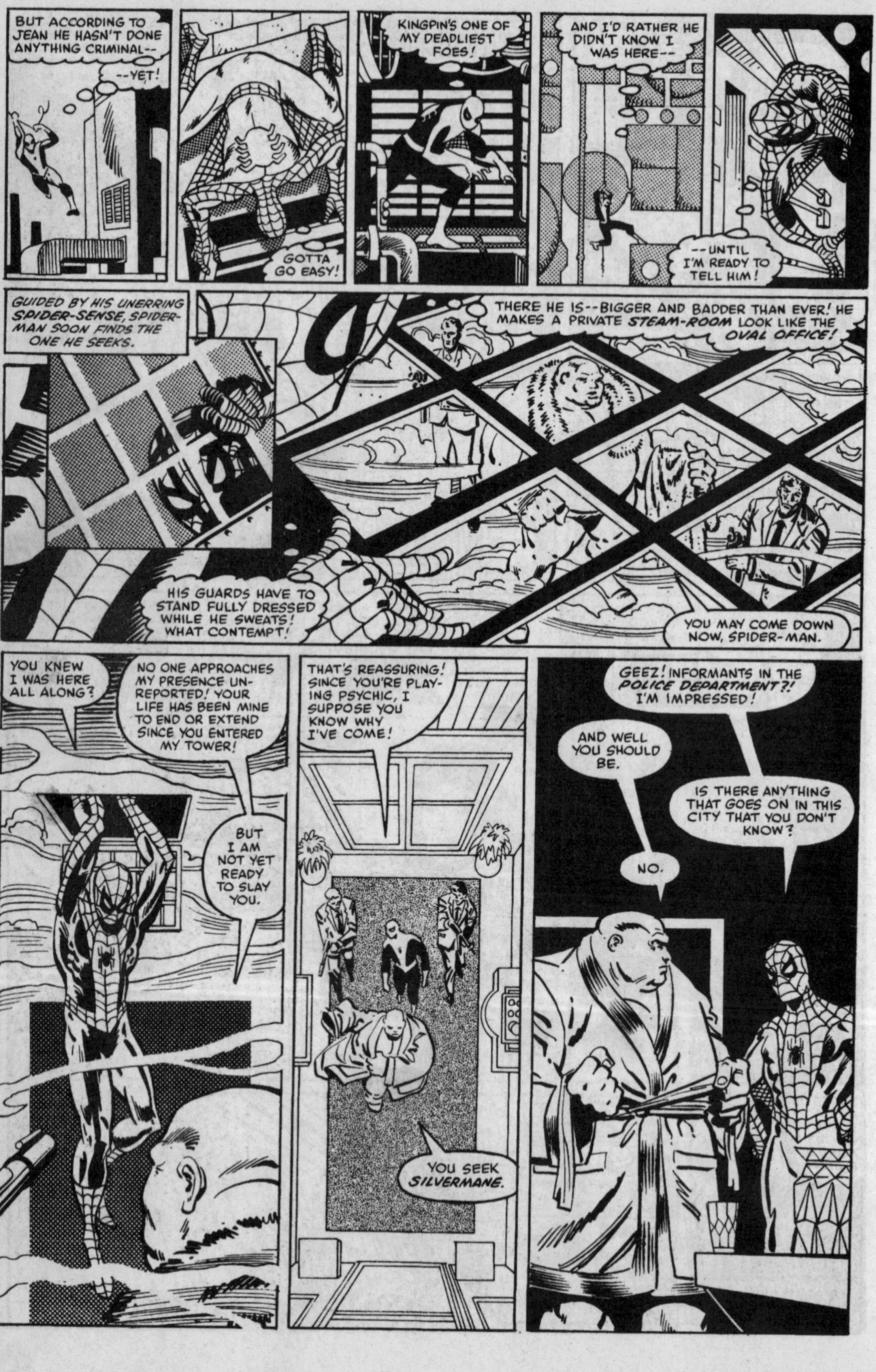
BUT ACCORDING TO JEAN HE HASN'T DONE ANYTHING CRIMINAL--
--YET!
KINGPIN'S ONE OF MY DEADLIEST FOES!
GOTTA GO EASY!
AND I'D RATHER HE DIDN'T KNOW I WAS HERE--
--UNTIL I'M READY TO TELL HIM!
GUIDED BY HIS UNERRING SPIDER-SENSE, SPIDER-MAN SOON FINDS THE ONE HE SEEKS.
THERE HE IS--BIGGER AND BADDER THAN EVER! HE MAKES A PRIVATE STEAM-ROOM LOOK LIKE THE OVAL OFFICE!
HIS GUARDS HAVE TO STAND FULLY DRESSED WHILE HE SWEATS! WHAT CONTEMPT!
YOU MAY COME DOWN NOW, SPIDER-MAN.
YOU KNEW I WAS HERE ALL ALONG?
NO ONE APPROACHES MY PRESENCE UN-REPORTED! YOUR LIFE HAS BEEN MINE TO END OR EXTEND SINCE YOU ENTERED MY TOWER!
BUT I AM NOT YET READY TO SLAY YOU.
THAT'S REASSURING! SINCE YOU'RE PLAY-ING PSYCHIC, I SUPPOSE YOU KNOW WHY I'VE COME!
YOU SEEK SILVERMANE.
GEEZ! INFORMANTS IN THE POLICE DEPARTMENT?! I'M IMPRESSED!
AND WELL YOU SHOULD BE.
IS THERE ANYTHING THAT GOES ON IN THIS CITY THAT YOU DON'T KNOW?
NO.

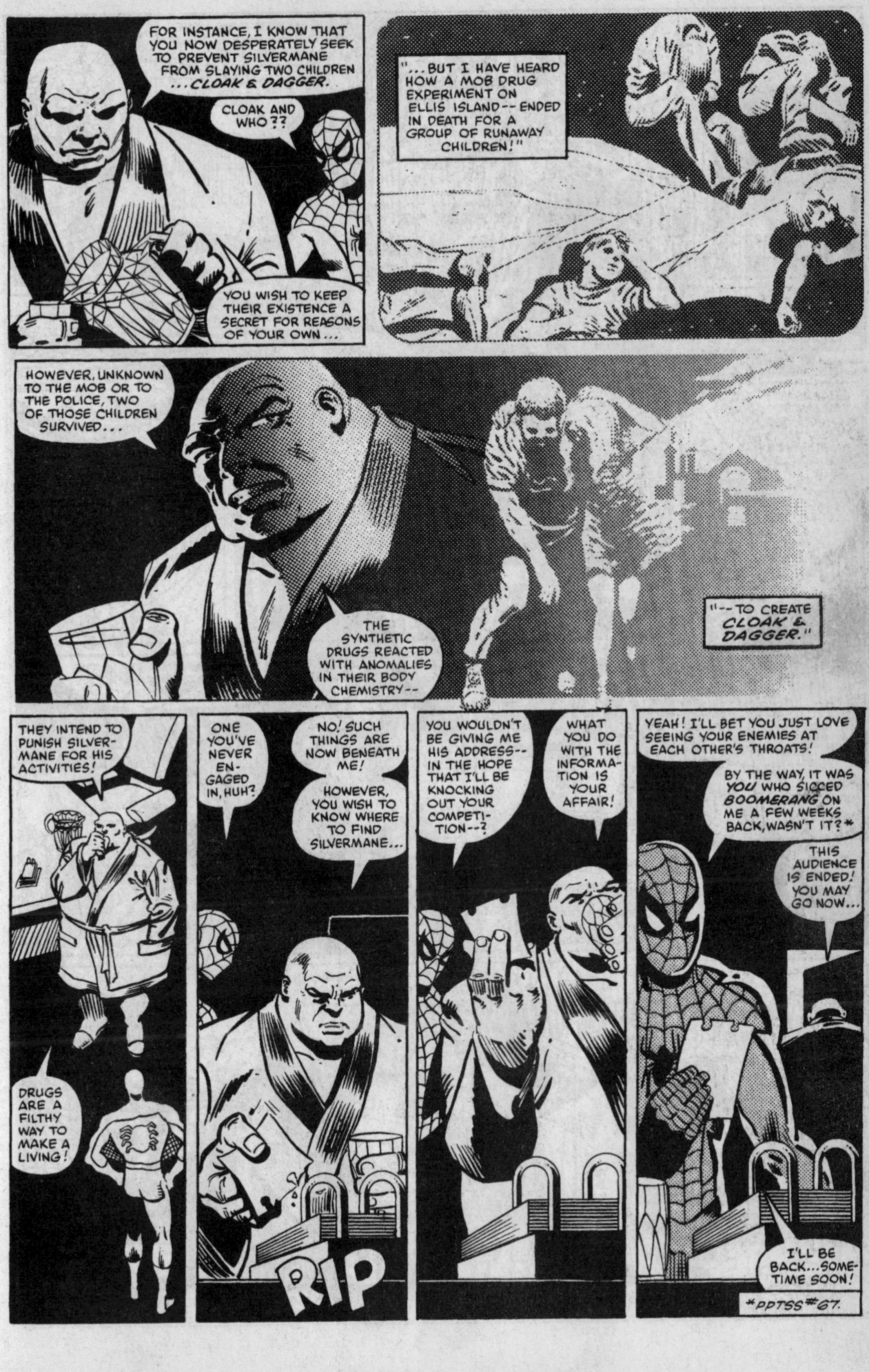

FOR INSTANCE, I KNOW THAT YOU NOW DESPERATELY SEEK TO PREVENT SILVERMANE FROM SLAYING TWO CHILDREN ...CLOAK & DAGGER.
CLOAK AND WHO??
YOU WISH TO KEEP THEIR EXISTENCE A SECRET FOR REASONS OF YOUR OWN...
"...BUT I HAVE HEARD HOW A MOB DRUG EXPERIMENT ON ELLIS ISLAND--ENDED IN DEATH FOR A GROUP OF RUNAWAY CHILDREN!"
HOWEVER, UNKNOWN TO THE MOB OR TO THE POLICE, TWO OF THOSE CHILDREN SURVIVED...
THE SYNTHETIC DRUGS REACTED WITH ANOMALIES IN THEIR BODY CHEMISTRY--
"--TO CREATE CLOAK & DAGGER."
THEY INTEND TO PUNISH SILVERMANE FOR HIS ACTIVITIES!
DRUGS ARE A FILTHY WAY TO MAKE A LIVING!
ONE YOU'VE NEVER ENGAGED IN, HUH?
NO! SUCH THINGS ARE NOW BENEATH ME!
HOWEVER, YOU WISH TO KNOW WHERE TO FIND SILVERMANE...
RIP
YOU WOULDN'T BE GIVING ME HIS ADDRESS--IN THE HOPE THAT I'LL BE KNOCKING OUT YOUR COMPETITION--?
WHAT YOU DO WITH THE INFORMATION IS YOUR AFFAIR!
YEAH! I'LL BET YOU JUST LOVE SEEING YOUR ENEMIES AT EACH OTHER'S THROATS!
BY THE WAY, IT WAS YOU WHO SICCED BOOMERANG ON ME A FEW WEEKS BACK, WASN'T IT?*
THIS AUDIENCE IS ENDED! YOU MAY GO NOW...
I'LL BE BACK...SOMETIME SOON!
*PPTSS #67.

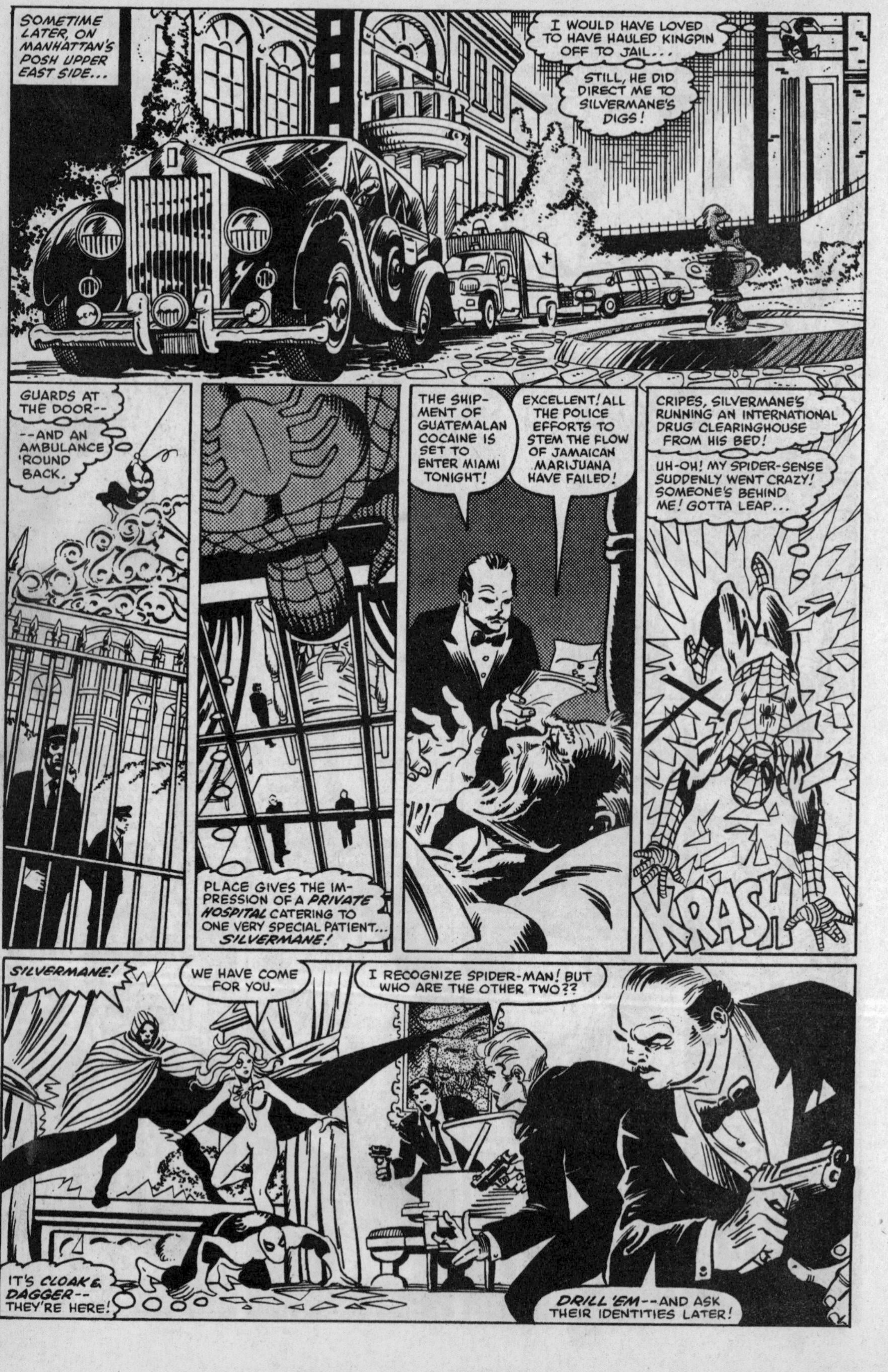
SOMETIME LATER, ON MANHATTAN'S POSH UPPER EAST SIDE...
I WOULD HAVE LOVED TO HAVE HAULED KINGPIN OFF TO JAIL...
STILL, HE DID DIRECT ME TO SILVERMANE'S DIGS!
GUARDS AT THE DOOR--
--AND AN AMBULANCE 'ROUND BACK.
PLACE GIVES THE IMPRESSION OF A PRIVATE HOSPITAL CATERING TO ONE VERY SPECIAL PATIENT... SILVERMANE!
THE SHIPMENT OF GUATEMALAN COCAINE IS SET TO ENTER MIAMI TONIGHT!
EXCELLENT! ALL THE POLICE EFFORTS TO STEM THE FLOW OF JAMAICAN MARIJUANA HAVE FAILED!
CRIPES, SILVERMANE'S RUNNING AN INTERNATIONAL DRUG CLEARINGHOUSE FROM HIS BED!
UH-OH! MY SPIDER-SENSE SUDDENLY WENT CRAZY! SOMEONE'S BEHIND ME! GOTTA LEAP...
KRASH
SILVERMANE!
WE HAVE COME FOR YOU.
I RECOGNIZE SPIDER-MAN! BUT WHO ARE THE OTHER TWO??
IT'S CLOAK & DAGGER-- THEY'RE HERE!
DRILL 'EM--AND ASK THEIR IDENTITIES LATER!

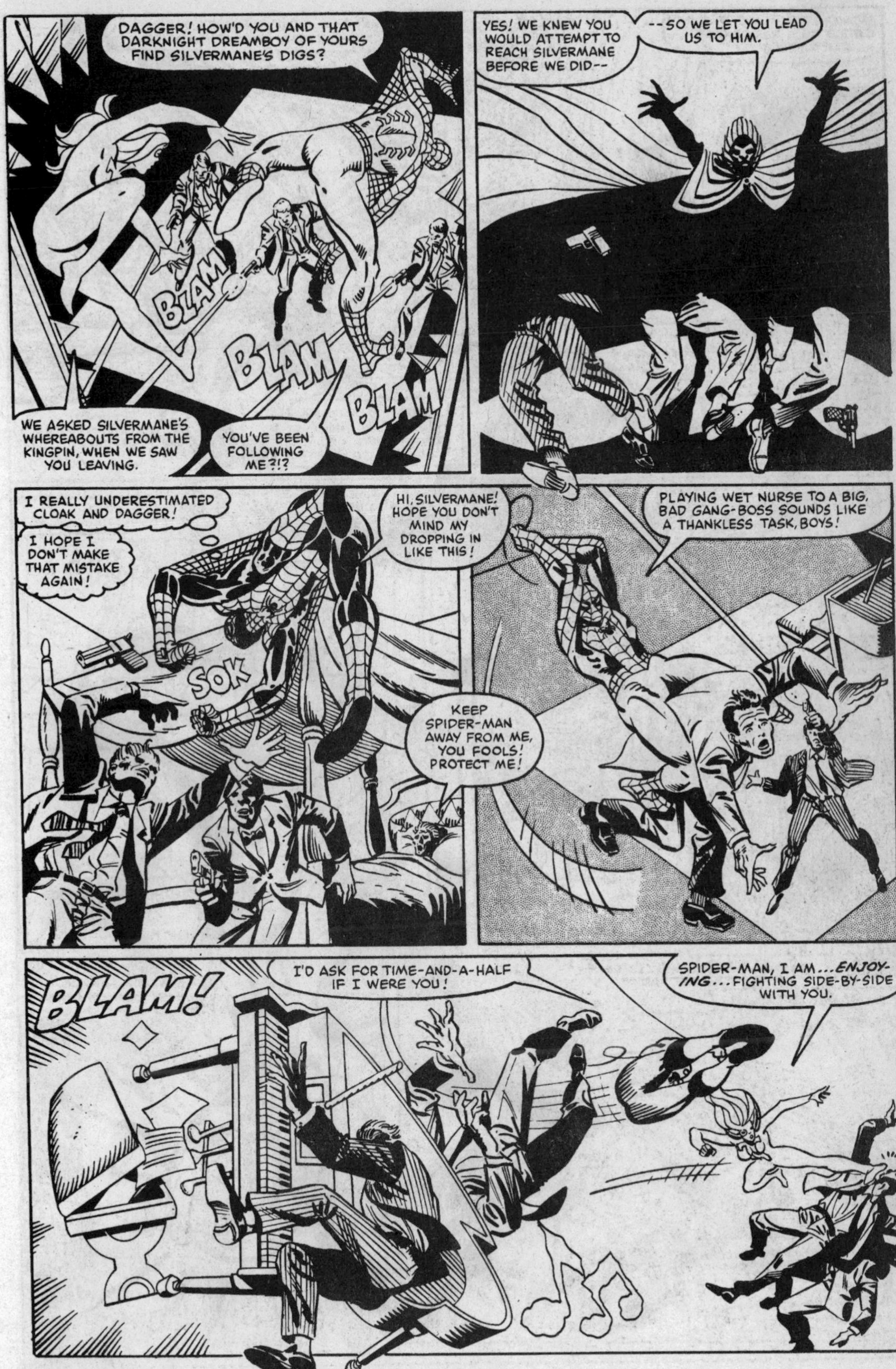
DAGGER! HOW'D YOU AND THAT DARKNIGHT DREAMBOY OF YOURS FIND SILVERMANE'S DIGS?
BLAM
BLAM
BLAM
WE ASKED SILVERMANE'S WHEREABOUTS FROM THE KINGPIN, WHEN WE SAW YOU LEAVING.
YOU'VE BEEN FOLLOWING ME?!?
YES! WE KNEW YOU WOULD ATTEMPT TO REACH SILVERMANE BEFORE WE DID--
--SO WE LET YOU LEAD US TO HIM.
I REALLY UNDERESTIMATED CLOAK AND DAGGER!
I HOPE I DON'T MAKE THAT MISTAKE AGAIN!
HI, SILVERMANE! HOPE YOU DON'T MIND MY DROPPING IN LIKE THIS!
SOK
KEEP SPIDER-MAN AWAY FROM ME, YOU FOOLS! PROTECT ME!
PLAYING WET NURSE TO A BIG, BAD GANG-BOSS SOUNDS LIKE A THANKLESS TASK, BOYS!
BLAM!
I'D ASK FOR TIME-AND-A-HALF IF I WERE YOU!
SPIDER-MAN, I AM... ENJOYING... FIGHTING SIDE-BY-SIDE WITH YOU.

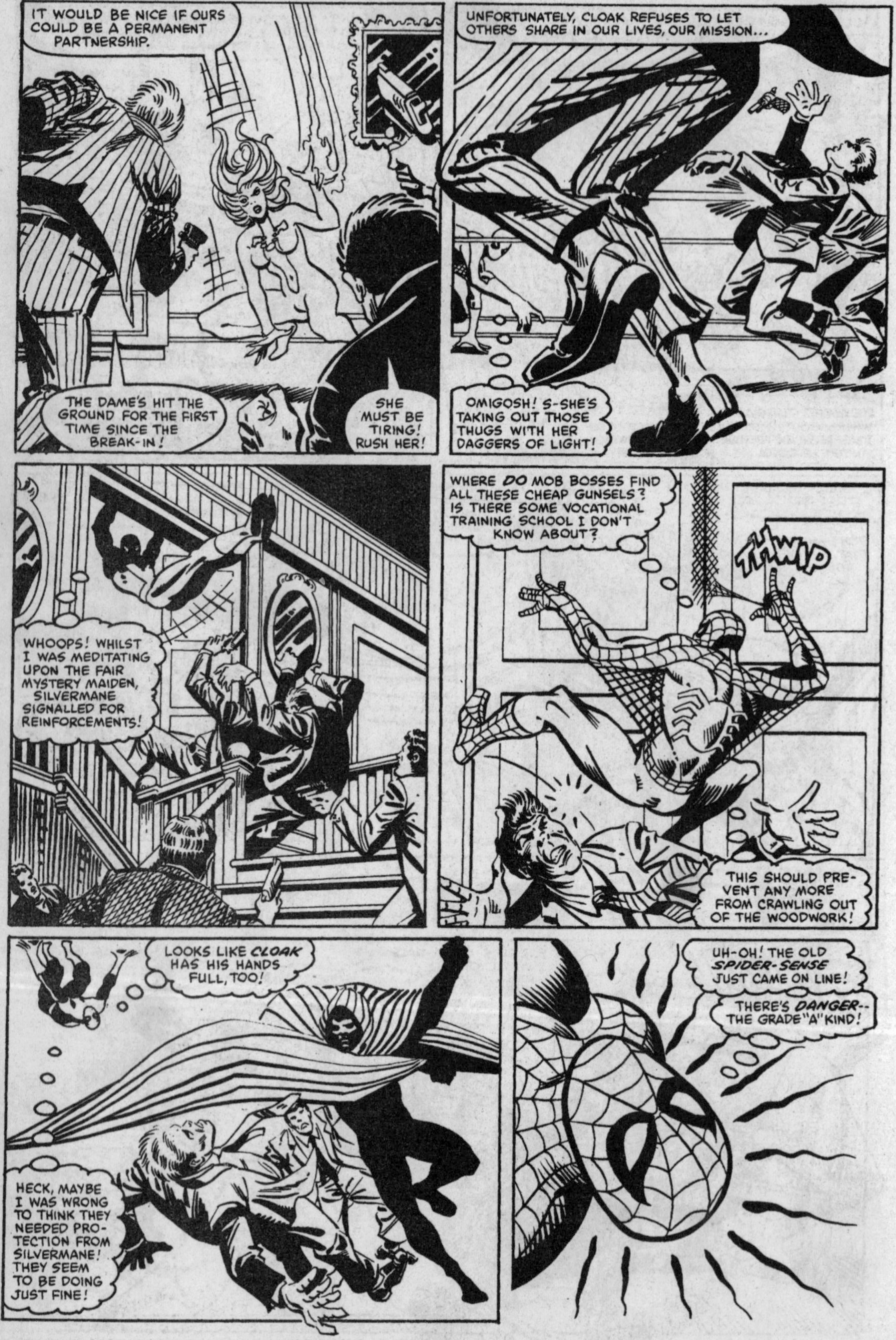
IT WOULD BE NICE IF OURS COULD BE A PERMANENT PARTNERSHIP.
THE DAME'S HIT THE GROUND FOR THE FIRST TIME SINCE THE BREAK-IN!
SHE MUST BE TIRING! RUSH HER!
UNFORTUNATELY, CLOAK REFUSES TO LET OTHERS SHARE IN OUR LIVES, OUR MISSION...
OMIGOSH! S-SHE'S TAKING OUT THOSE THUGS WITH HER DAGGERS OF LIGHT!
WHOOPS! WHILST I WAS MEDITATING UPON THE FAIR MYSTERY MAIDEN, SILVERMANE SIGNALLED FOR REINFORCEMENTS!
WHERE DO MOB BOSSES FIND ALL THESE CHEAP GUNSELS? IS THERE SOME VOCATIONAL TRAINING SCHOOL I DON'T KNOW ABOUT?
THWIP
THIS SHOULD PREVENT ANY MORE FROM CRAWLING OUT OF THE WOODWORK!
LOOKS LIKE CLOAK HAS HIS HANDS FULL, TOO!
HECK, MAYBE I WAS WRONG TO THINK THEY NEEDED PROTECTION FROM SILVERMANE! THEY SEEM TO BE DOING JUST FINE!
UH-OH! THE OLD SPIDER-SENSE JUST CAME ON LINE!
THERE'S DANGER-- THE GRADE "A" KIND!

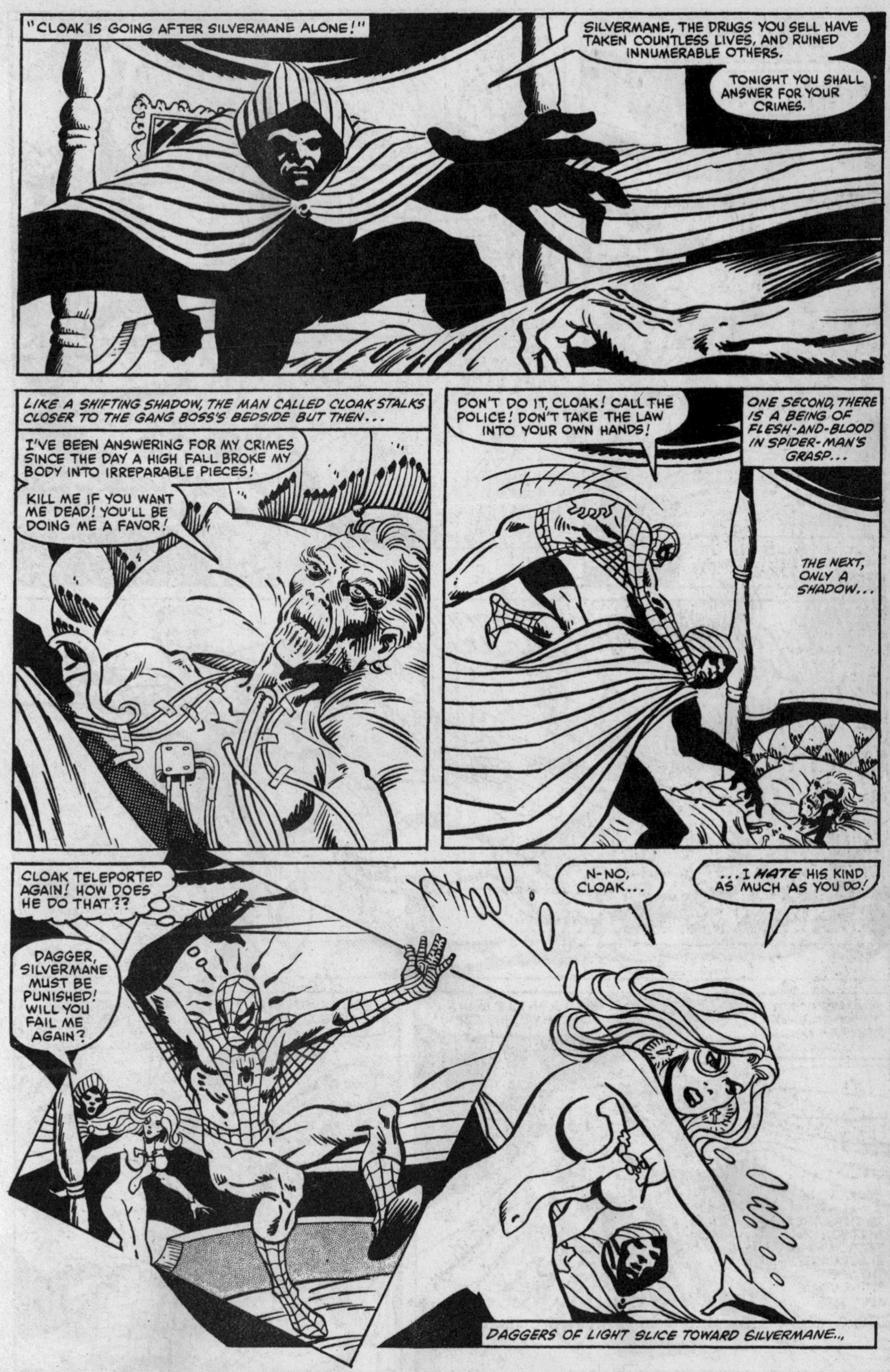
"CLOAK IS GOING AFTER SILVERMANE ALONE!"
SILVERMANE, THE DRUGS YOU SELL HAVE TAKEN COUNTLESS LIVES, AND RUINED INNUMERABLE OTHERS.
TONIGHT YOU SHALL ANSWER FOR YOUR CRIMES.
LIKE A SHIFTING SHADOW, THE MAN CALLED CLOAK STALKS CLOSER TO THE GANG BOSS'S BEDSIDE BUT THEN...
I'VE BEEN ANSWERING FOR MY CRIMES SINCE THE DAY A HIGH FALL BROKE MY BODY INTO IRREPARABLE PIECES!
KILL ME IF YOU WANT ME DEAD! YOU'LL BE DOING ME A FAVOR!
DON'T DO IT, CLOAK! CALL THE POLICE! DON'T TAKE THE LAW INTO YOUR OWN HANDS!
ONE SECOND, THERE IS A BEING OF FLESH-AND-BLOOD IN SPIDER-MAN'S GRASP...
THE NEXT, ONLY A SHADOW...
CLOAK TELEPORTED AGAIN! HOW DOES HE DO THAT??
DAGGER, SILVERMANE MUST BE PUNISHED! WILL YOU FAIL ME AGAIN?
N-NO, CLOAK...
...I HATE HIS KIND AS MUCH AS YOU DO!
DAGGERS OF LIGHT SLICE TOWARD SILVERMANE..,

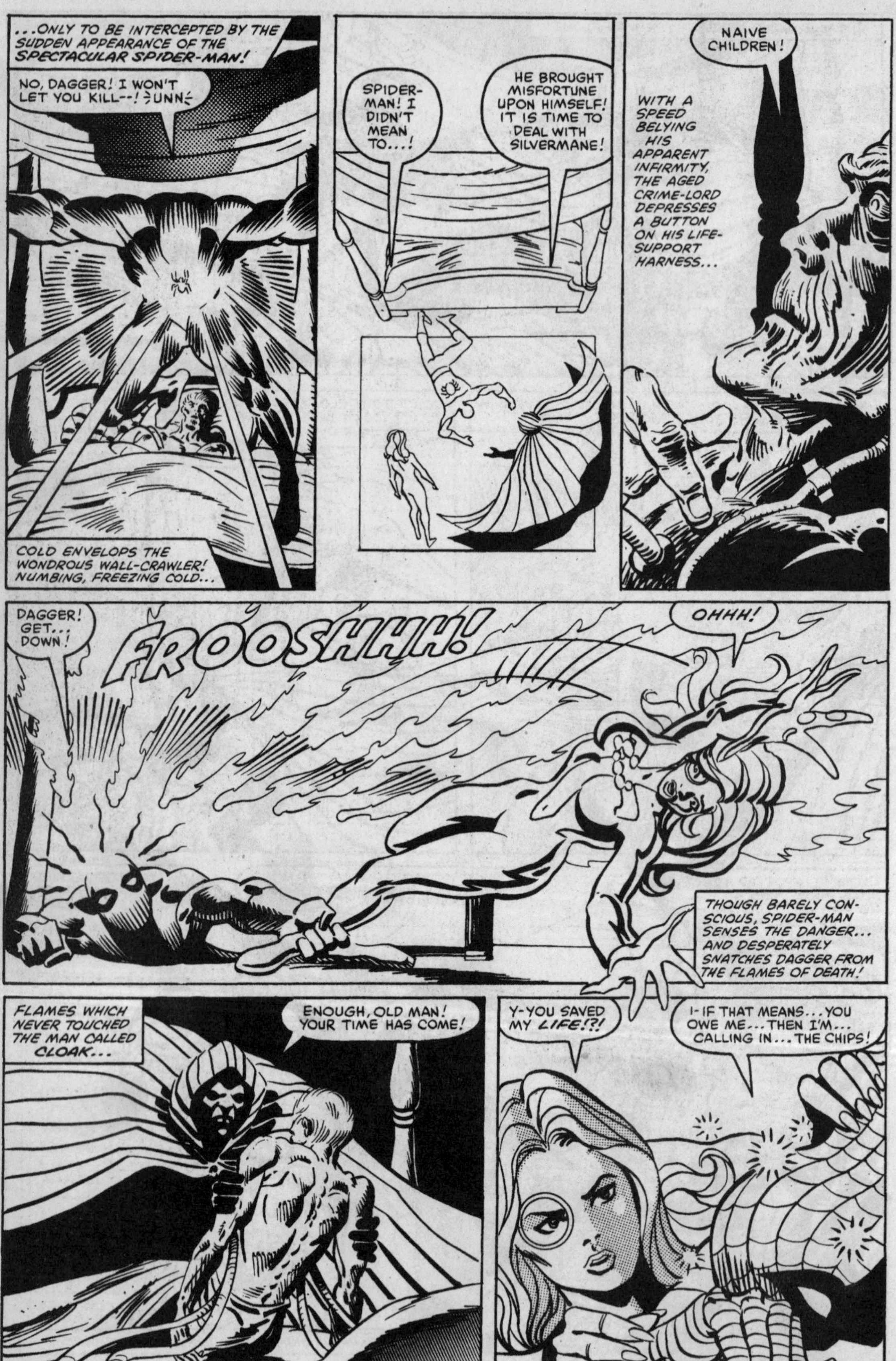

...ONLY TO BE INTERCEPTED BY THE SUDDEN APPEARANCE OF THE SPECTACULAR SPIDER-MAN!
NO, DAGGER! I WON'T LET YOU KILL--! UNN
COLD ENVELOPS THE WONDROUS WALL-CRAWLER! NUMBING, FREEZING COLD...
SPIDER-MAN! I DIDN'T MEAN TO...!
HE BROUGHT MISFORTUNE UPON HIMSELF! IT IS TIME TO DEAL WITH SILVERMANE!
NAIVE CHILDREN!
WITH A SPEED BELYING HIS APPARENT INFIRMITY, THE AGED CRIME-LORD DEPRESSES A BUTTON ON HIS LIFE-SUPPORT HARNESS...
DAGGER! GET... DOWN!
FROOSHHH!
OHHH!
THOUGH BARELY CONSCIOUS, SPIDER-MAN SENSES THE DANGER... AND DESPERATELY SNATCHES DAGGER FROM THE FLAMES OF DEATH!
FLAMES WHICH NEVER TOUCHED THE MAN CALLED CLOAK...
ENOUGH, OLD MAN! YOUR TIME HAS COME!
Y-YOU SAVED MY LIFE!?!
I- IF THAT MEANS... YOU OWE ME... THEN I'M... CALLING IN... THE CHIPS!

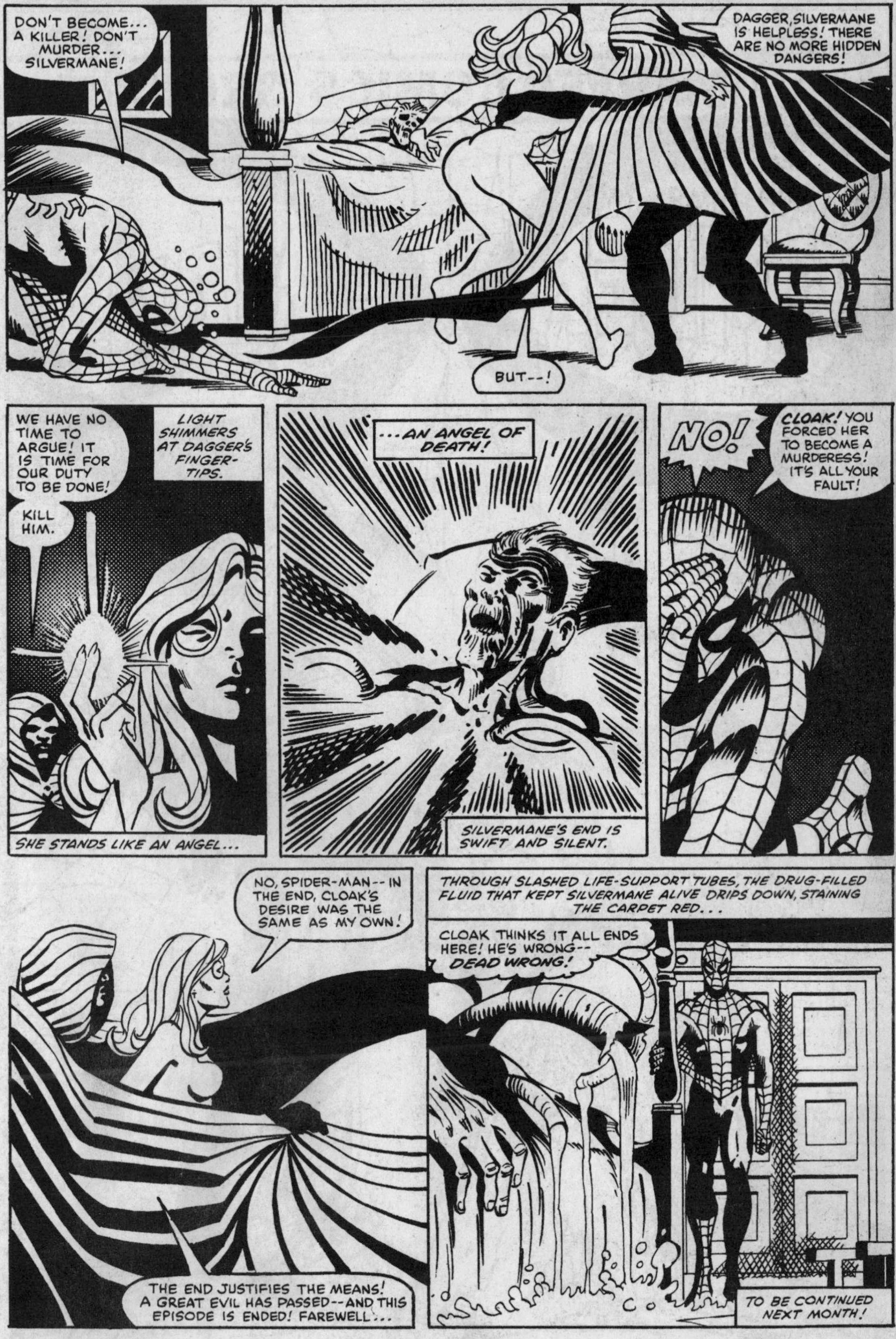
DON'T BECOME... A KILLER! DON'T MURDER... SILVERMANE!
DAGGER, SILVERMANE IS HELPLESS! THERE ARE NO MORE HIDDEN DANGERS!
BUT--!
WE HAVE NO TIME TO ARGUE! IT IS TIME FOR OUR DUTY TO BE DONE!
KILL HIM.
LIGHT SHIMMERS AT DAGGER'S FINGER-TIPS.
SHE STANDS LIKE AN ANGEL...
...AN ANGEL OF DEATH!
SILVERMANE'S END IS SWIFT AND SILENT.
NO!
CLOAK! YOU FORCED HER TO BECOME A MURDERESS! IT'S ALL YOUR FAULT!
NO, SPIDER-MAN-- IN THE END, CLOAK'S DESIRE WAS THE SAME AS MY OWN!
THE END JUSTIFIES THE MEANS! A GREAT EVIL HAS PASSED--AND THIS EPISODE IS ENDED! FAREWELL...
THROUGH SLASHED LIFE-SUPPORT TUBES, THE DRUG-FILLED FLUID THAT KEPT SILVERMANE ALIVE DRIPS DOWN, STAINING THE CARPET RED...
CLOAK THINKS IT ALL ENDS HERE! HE'S WRONG-- DEAD WRONG!
TO BE CONTINUED NEXT MONTH!

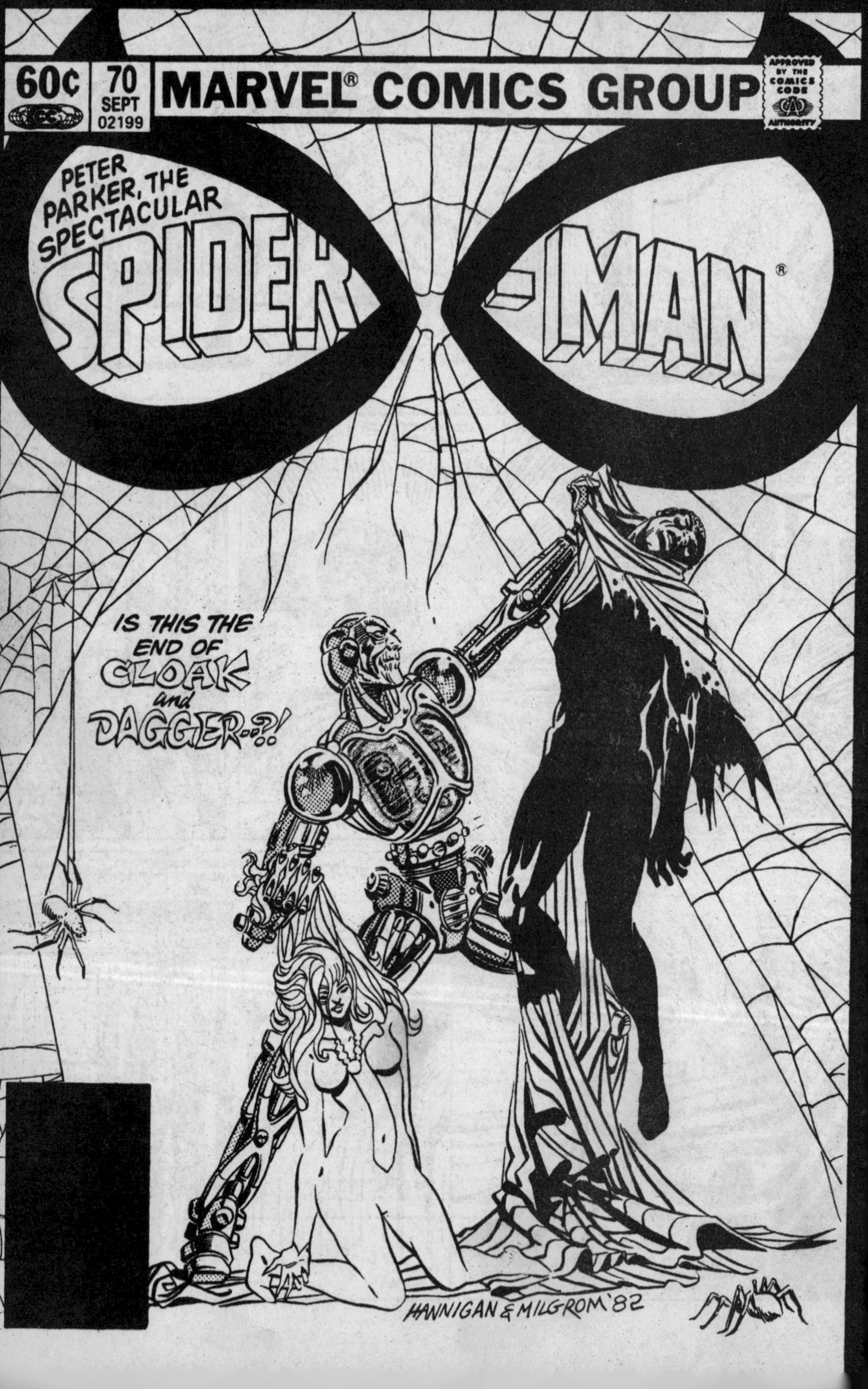
60¢
70
SEPT
02199
MARVEL® COMICS GROUP
APPROVED BY THE COMICS CODE AUTHORITY
PETER PARKER, THE SPECTACULAR
SPIDER-MAN®
IS THIS THE END OF CLOAK and DAGGER..?!
HANNIGAN & MILGROM '82

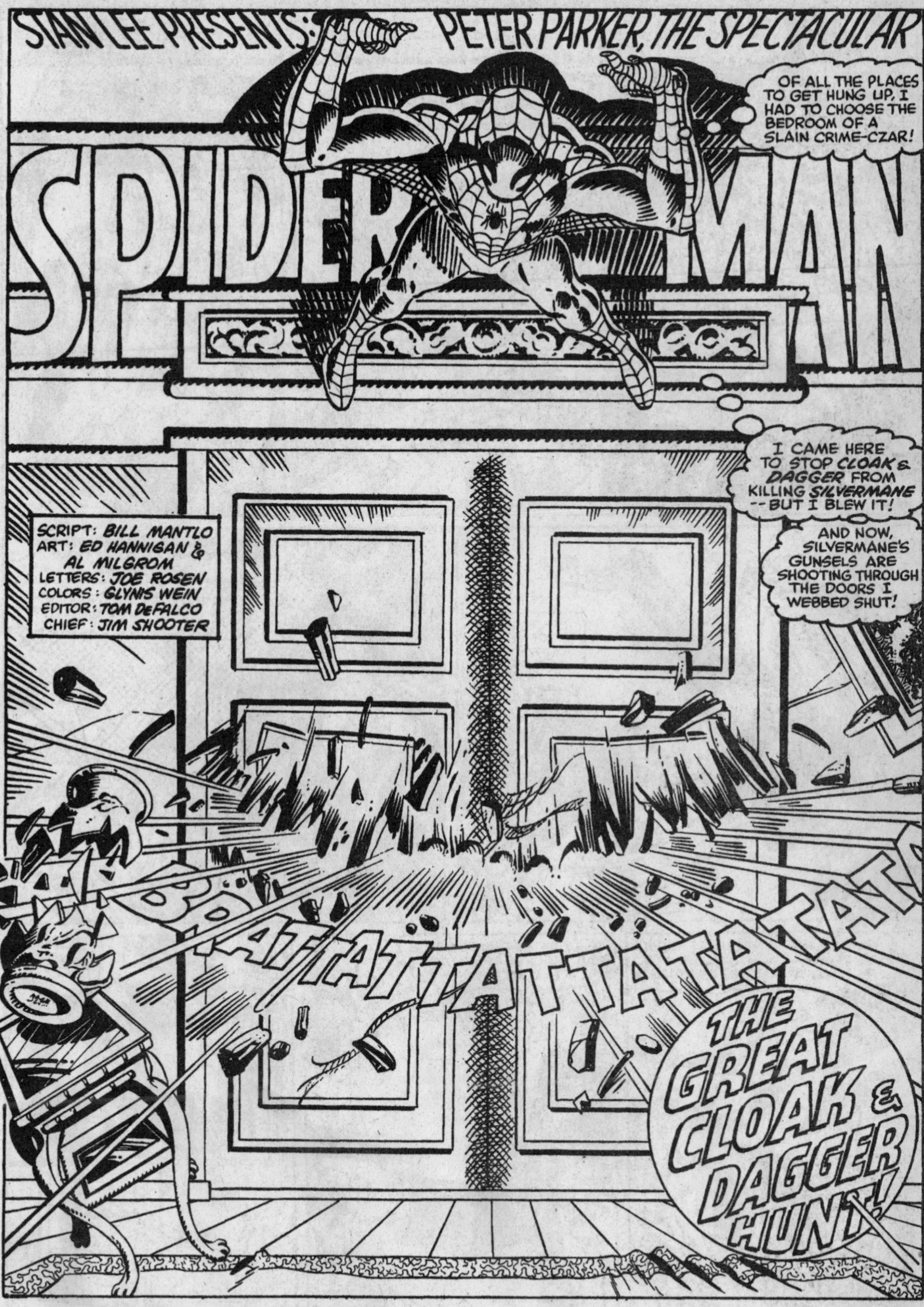
STAN LEE PRESENTS: PETER PARKER, THE SPECTACULAR
SPIDER-MAN
OF ALL THE PLACES TO GET HUNG UP, I HAD TO CHOOSE THE BEDROOM OF A SLAIN CRIME-CZAR!
I CAME HERE TO STOP CLOAK & DAGGER FROM KILLING SILVERMANE -- BUT I BLEW IT!
AND NOW, SILVERMANE'S GUNSELS ARE SHOOTING THROUGH THE DOORS I WEBBED SHUT!
SCRIPT: BILL MANTLO
ART: ED HANNIGAN & AL MILGROM
LETTERS: JOE ROSEN
COLORS: GLYNIS WEIN
EDITOR: TOM DeFALCO
CHIEF: JIM SHOOTER
BRATTATTATTATATATATA
THE GREAT CLOAK & DAGGER HUNT!

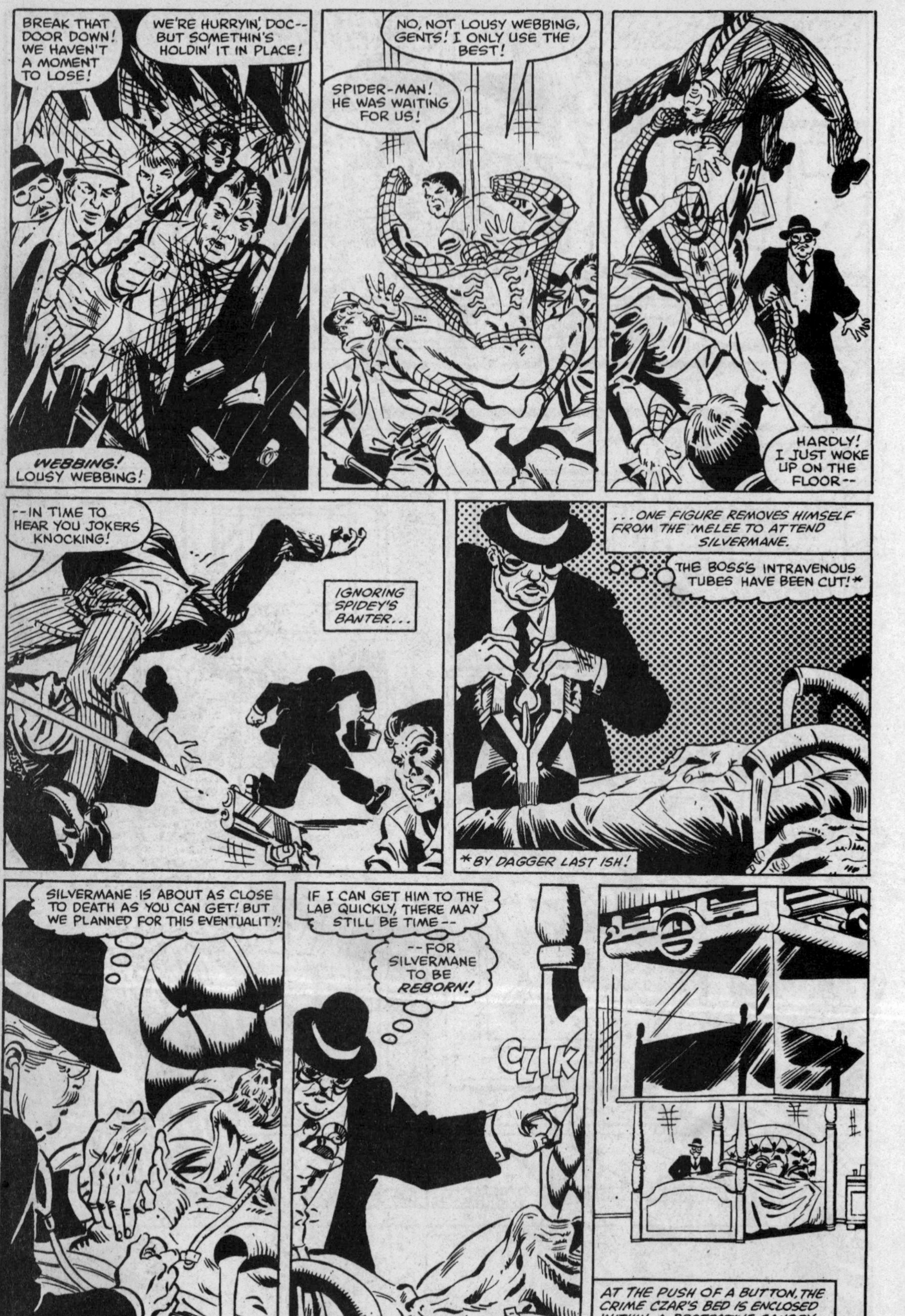
BREAK THAT DOOR DOWN! WE HAVEN'T A MOMENT TO LOSE!
WE'RE HURRYIN', DOC-- BUT SOMETHIN'S HOLDIN' IT IN PLACE!
WEBBING! LOUSY WEBBING!
NO, NOT LOUSY WEBBING, GENTS! I ONLY USE THE BEST!
SPIDER-MAN! HE WAS WAITING FOR US!
HARDLY! I JUST WOKE UP ON THE FLOOR--
--IN TIME TO HEAR YOU JOKERS KNOCKING!
IGNORING SPIDEY'S BANTER...
...ONE FIGURE REMOVES HIMSELF FROM THE MELEE TO ATTEND SILVERMANE.
THE BOSS'S INTRAVENOUS TUBES HAVE BEEN CUT!*
*BY DAGGER LAST ISH!
SILVERMANE IS ABOUT AS CLOSE TO DEATH AS YOU CAN GET! BUT WE PLANNED FOR THIS EVENTUALITY!
IF I CAN GET HIM TO THE LAB QUICKLY, THERE MAY STILL BE TIME--
--FOR SILVERMANE TO BE REBORN!
CLIK
AT THE PUSH OF A BUTTON, THE CRIME CZAR'S BED IS ENCLOSED WITHIN A PROTECTIVE CANOPY...

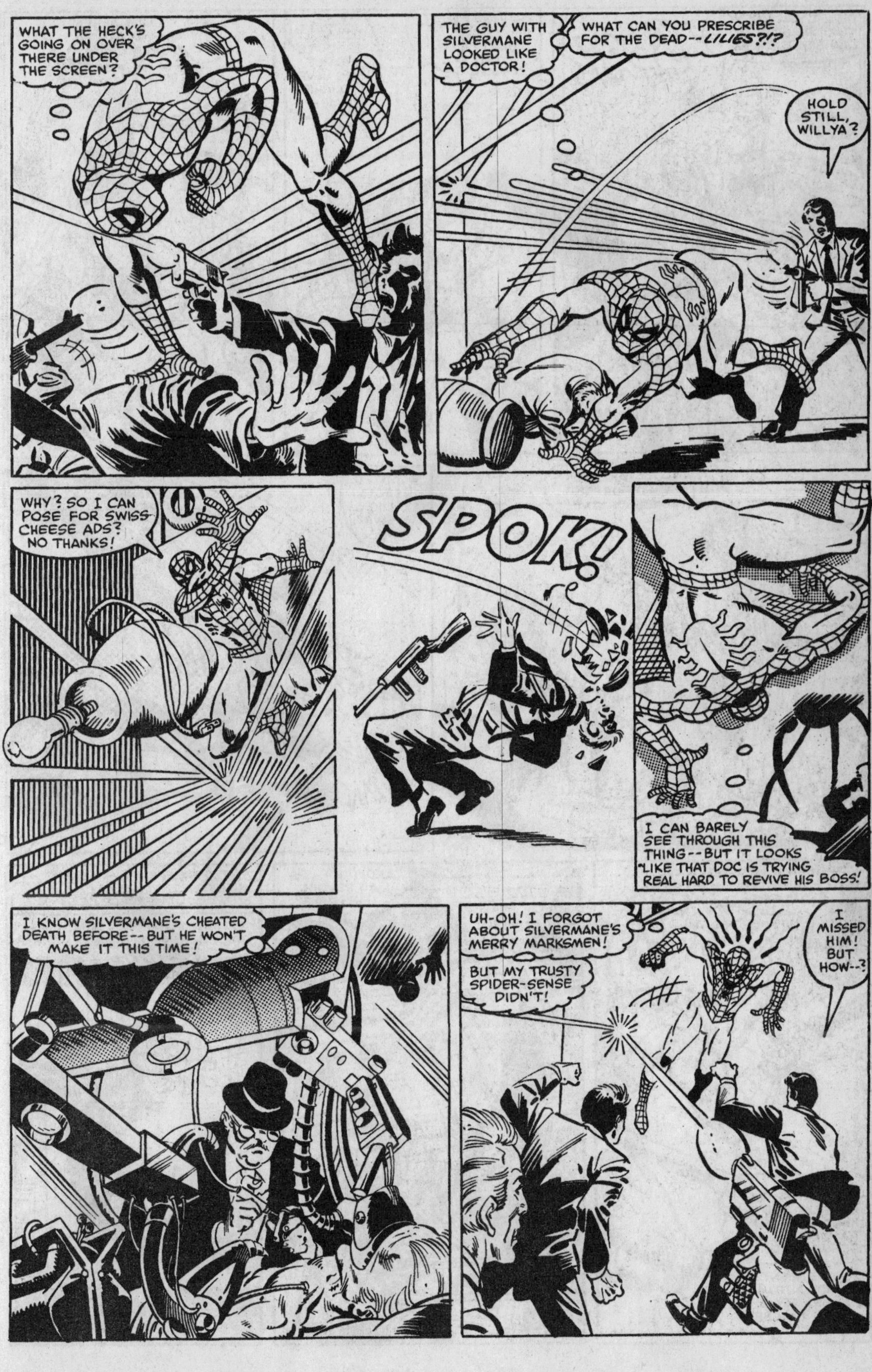
WHAT THE HECK'S GOING ON OVER THERE UNDER THE SCREEN?
THE GUY WITH SILVERMANE LOOKED LIKE A DOCTOR!
WHAT CAN YOU PRESCRIBE FOR THE DEAD--LILIES?!?
HOLD STILL, WILLYA?
WHY? SO I CAN POSE FOR SWISS-CHEESE ADS? NO THANKS!
SPOK!
I CAN BARELY SEE THROUGH THIS THING--BUT IT LOOKS LIKE THAT DOC IS TRYING REAL HARD TO REVIVE HIS BOSS!
I KNOW SILVERMANE'S CHEATED DEATH BEFORE--BUT HE WON'T MAKE IT THIS TIME!
UH-OH! I FORGOT ABOUT SILVERMANE'S MERRY MARKSMEN!
BUT MY TRUSTY SPIDER-SENSE DIDN'T!
I MISSED HIM! BUT HOW--?

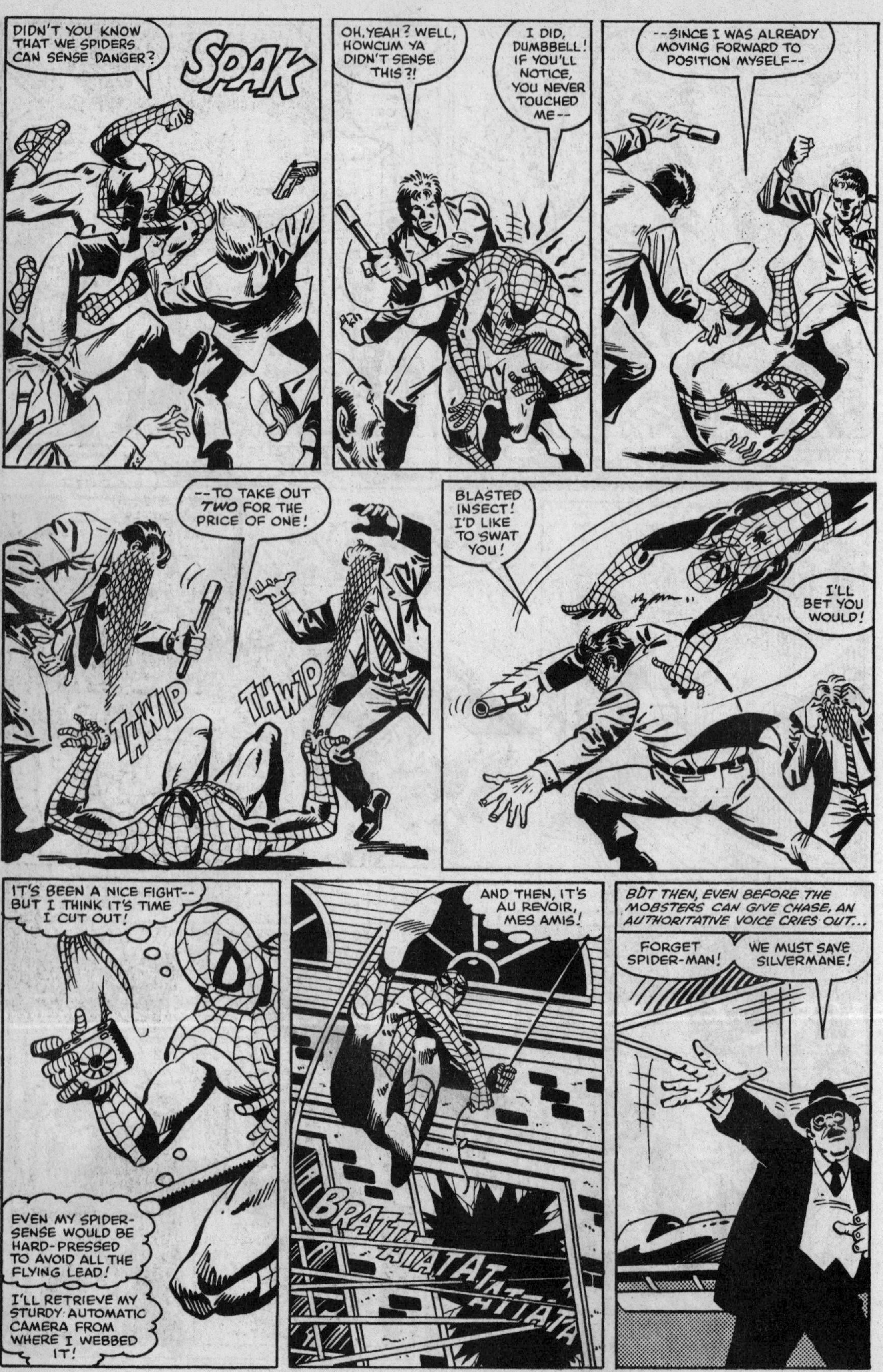
DIDN'T YOU KNOW THAT WE SPIDERS CAN SENSE DANGER?
SPAK
OH, YEAH? WELL, HOWCUM YA DIDN'T SENSE THIS?!
I DID, DUMBBELL! IF YOU'LL NOTICE, YOU NEVER TOUCHED ME--
--SINCE I WAS ALREADY MOVING FORWARD TO POSITION MYSELF--
--TO TAKE OUT TWO FOR THE PRICE OF ONE!
THWIP
THWIP
BLASTED INSECT! I'D LIKE TO SWAT YOU!
I'LL BET YOU WOULD!
IT'S BEEN A NICE FIGHT-- BUT I THINK IT'S TIME I CUT OUT!
EVEN MY SPIDER-SENSE WOULD BE HARD-PRESSED TO AVOID ALL THE FLYING LEAD!
I'LL RETRIEVE MY STURDY AUTOMATIC CAMERA FROM WHERE I WEBBED IT!
AND THEN, IT'S AU REVOIR, MES AMIS!
BRATTTHHATATATATTATA
BUT THEN, EVEN BEFORE THE MOBSTERS CAN GIVE CHASE, AN AUTHORITATIVE VOICE CRIES OUT...
FORGET SPIDER-MAN!
WE MUST SAVE SILVERMANE!

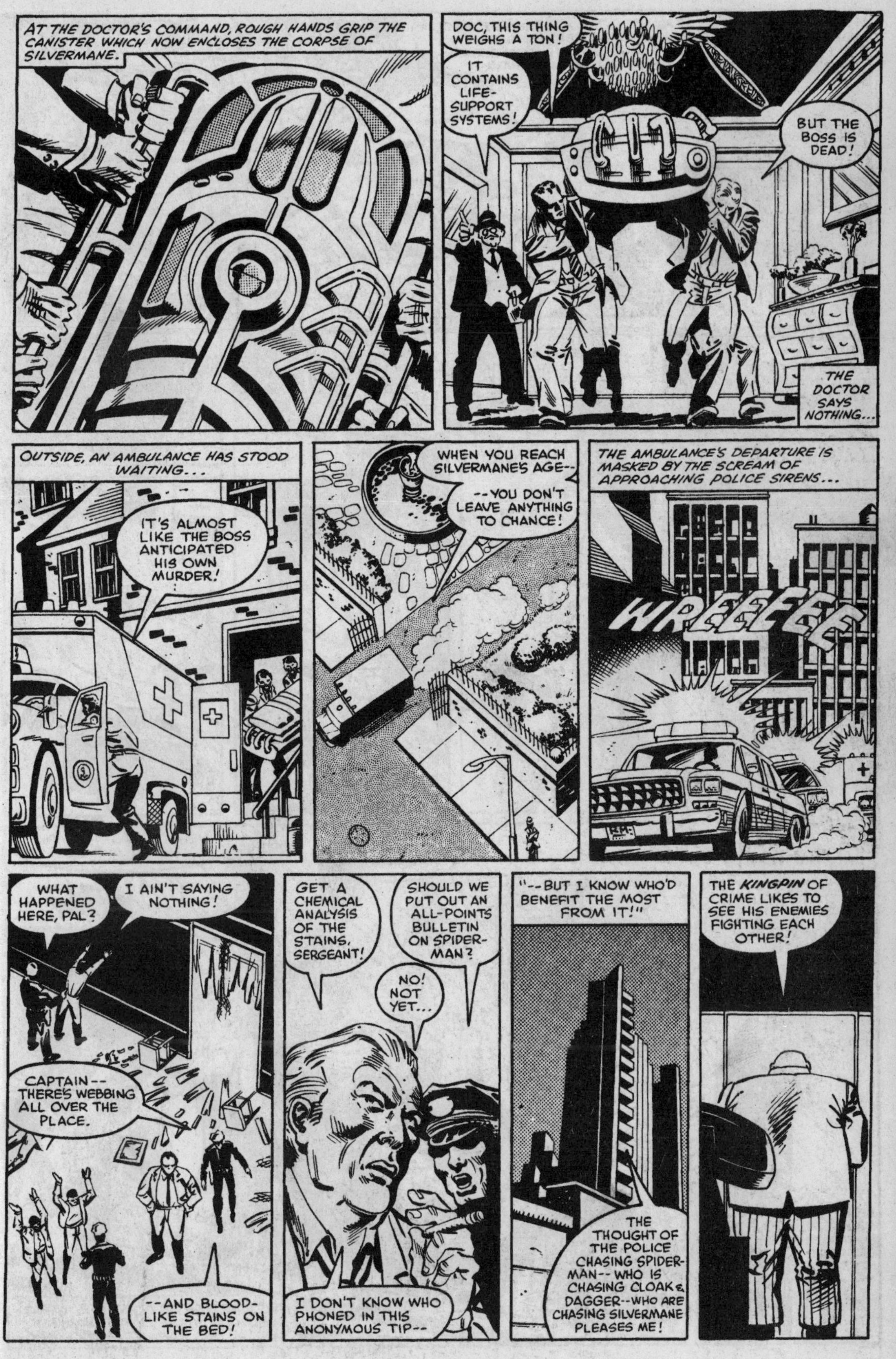
AT THE DOCTOR'S COMMAND, ROUGH HANDS GRIP THE CANISTER WHICH NOW ENCLOSES THE CORPSE OF SILVERMANE.
DOC, THIS THING WEIGHS A TON!
IT CONTAINS LIFE-SUPPORT SYSTEMS!
BUT THE BOSS IS DEAD!
THE DOCTOR SAYS NOTHING...
OUTSIDE, AN AMBULANCE HAS STOOD WAITING...
IT'S ALMOST LIKE THE BOSS ANTICIPATED HIS OWN MURDER!
WHEN YOU REACH SILVERMANE'S AGE--
--YOU DON'T LEAVE ANYTHING TO CHANCE!
THE AMBULANCE'S DEPARTURE IS MASKED BY THE SCREAM OF APPROACHING POLICE SIRENS...
WREEEEE
WHAT HAPPENED HERE, PAL?
I AIN'T SAYING NOTHING!
CAPTAIN-- THERE'S WEBBING ALL OVER THE PLACE.
--AND BLOOD-LIKE STAINS ON THE BED!
GET A CHEMICAL ANALYSIS OF THE STAINS, SERGEANT!
SHOULD WE PUT OUT AN ALL-POINTS BULLETIN ON SPIDER-MAN?
NO! NOT YET...
I DON'T KNOW WHO PHONED IN THIS ANONYMOUS TIP--
"--BUT I KNOW WHO'D BENEFIT THE MOST FROM IT!"
THE THOUGHT OF THE POLICE CHASING SPIDER-MAN-- WHO IS CHASING CLOAK & DAGGER--WHO ARE CHASING SILVERMANE PLEASES ME!
THE KINGPIN OF CRIME LIKES TO SEE HIS ENEMIES FIGHTING EACH OTHER!

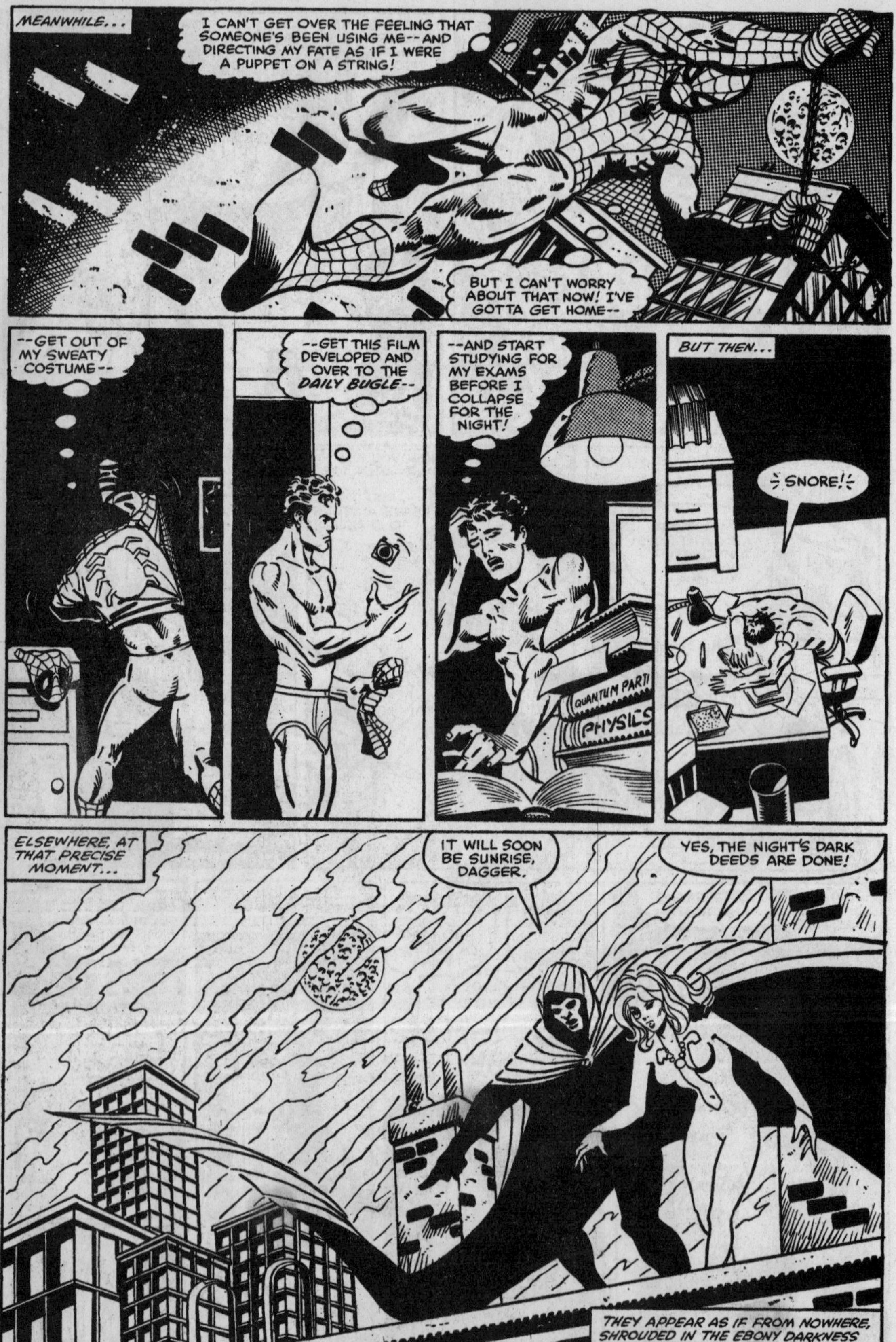
MEANWHILE...
I CAN'T GET OVER THE FEELING THAT SOMEONE'S BEEN USING ME--AND DIRECTING MY FATE AS IF I WERE A PUPPET ON A STRING!
BUT I CAN'T WORRY ABOUT THAT NOW! I'VE GOTTA GET HOME--
--GET OUT OF MY SWEATY COSTUME--
--GET THIS FILM DEVELOPED AND OVER TO THE DAILY BUGLE--
--AND START STUDYING FOR MY EXAMS BEFORE I COLLAPSE FOR THE NIGHT!
QUANTUM PARTI
PHYSICS
BUT THEN...
SNORE!
ELSEWHERE, AT THAT PRECISE MOMENT...
IT WILL SOON BE SUNRISE, DAGGER.
YES, THE NIGHT'S DARK DEEDS ARE DONE!
THEY APPEAR AS IF FROM NOWHERE, SHROUDED IN THE EBONY DARKNESS THAT IS THE YOUTH CALLED CLOAK.

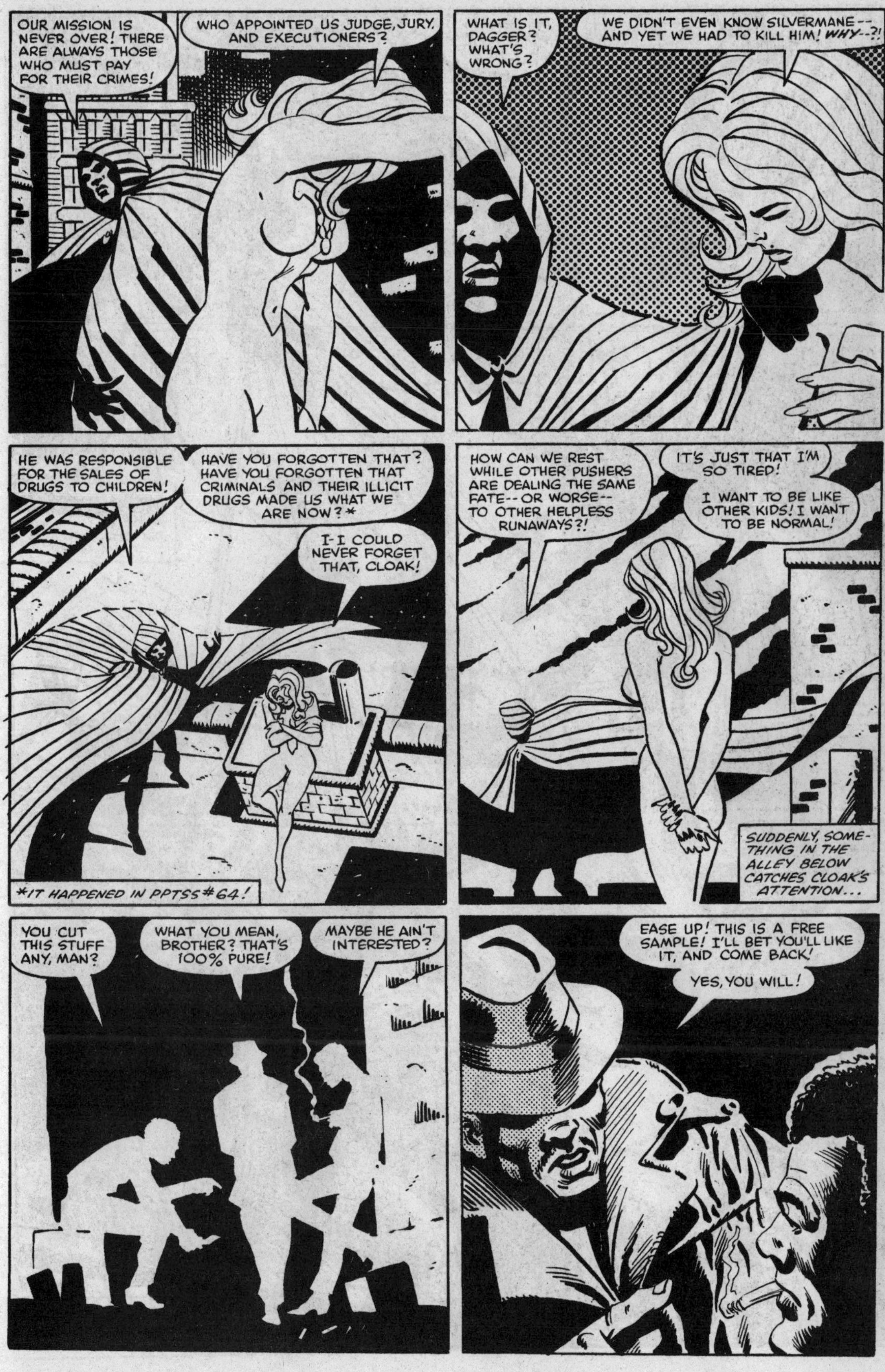

OUR MISSION IS NEVER OVER! THERE ARE ALWAYS THOSE WHO MUST PAY FOR THEIR CRIMES!
WHO APPOINTED US JUDGE, JURY, AND EXECUTIONERS?
WHAT IS IT, DAGGER? WHAT'S WRONG?
WE DIDN'T EVEN KNOW SILVERMANE-- AND YET WE HAD TO KILL HIM! WHY--?!
HE WAS RESPONSIBLE FOR THE SALES OF DRUGS TO CHILDREN!
HAVE YOU FORGOTTEN THAT? HAVE YOU FORGOTTEN THAT CRIMINALS AND THEIR ILLICIT DRUGS MADE US WHAT WE ARE NOW?*
I-I COULD NEVER FORGET THAT, CLOAK!
*IT HAPPENED IN PPTSS #64!
HOW CAN WE REST WHILE OTHER PUSHERS ARE DEALING THE SAME FATE--OR WORSE-- TO OTHER HELPLESS RUNAWAYS?!
IT'S JUST THAT I'M SO TIRED!
I WANT TO BE LIKE OTHER KIDS! I WANT TO BE NORMAL!
SUDDENLY, SOMETHING IN THE ALLEY BELOW CATCHES CLOAK'S ATTENTION...
YOU CUT THIS STUFF ANY, MAN?
WHAT YOU MEAN, BROTHER? THAT'S 100% PURE!
MAYBE HE AIN'T INTERESTED?
EASE UP! THIS IS A FREE SAMPLE! I'LL BET YOU'LL LIKE IT, AND COME BACK!
YES, YOU WILL!

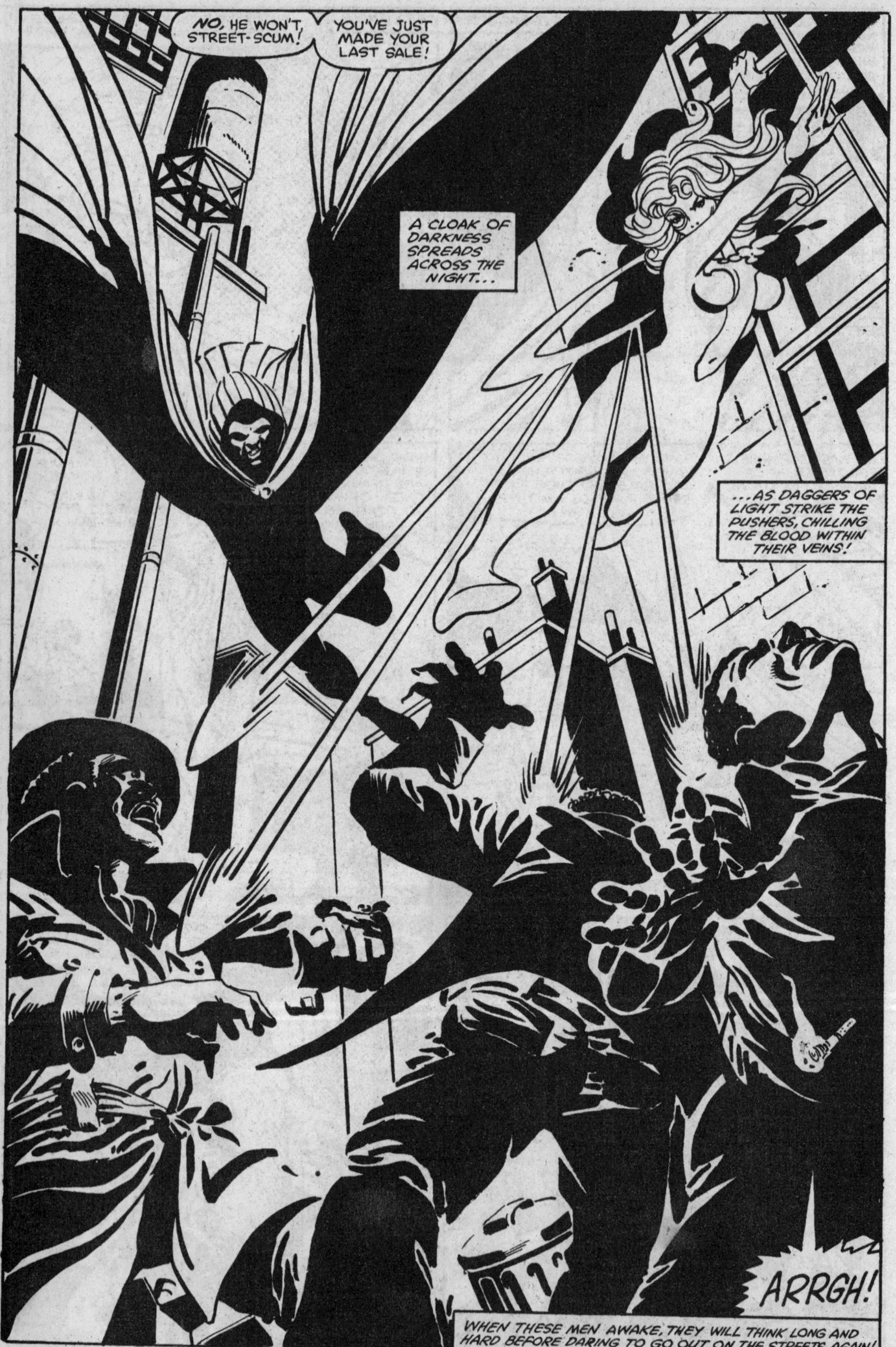
NO, HE WON'T, STREET-SCUM!
YOU'VE JUST MADE YOUR LAST SALE!
A CLOAK OF DARKNESS SPREADS ACROSS THE NIGHT...
...AS DAGGERS OF LIGHT STRIKE THE PUSHERS, CHILLING THE BLOOD WITHIN THEIR VEINS!
ARRGH!
WHEN THESE MEN AWAKE, THEY WILL THINK LONG AND HARD BEFORE DARING TO GO OUT ON THE STREETS AGAIN!

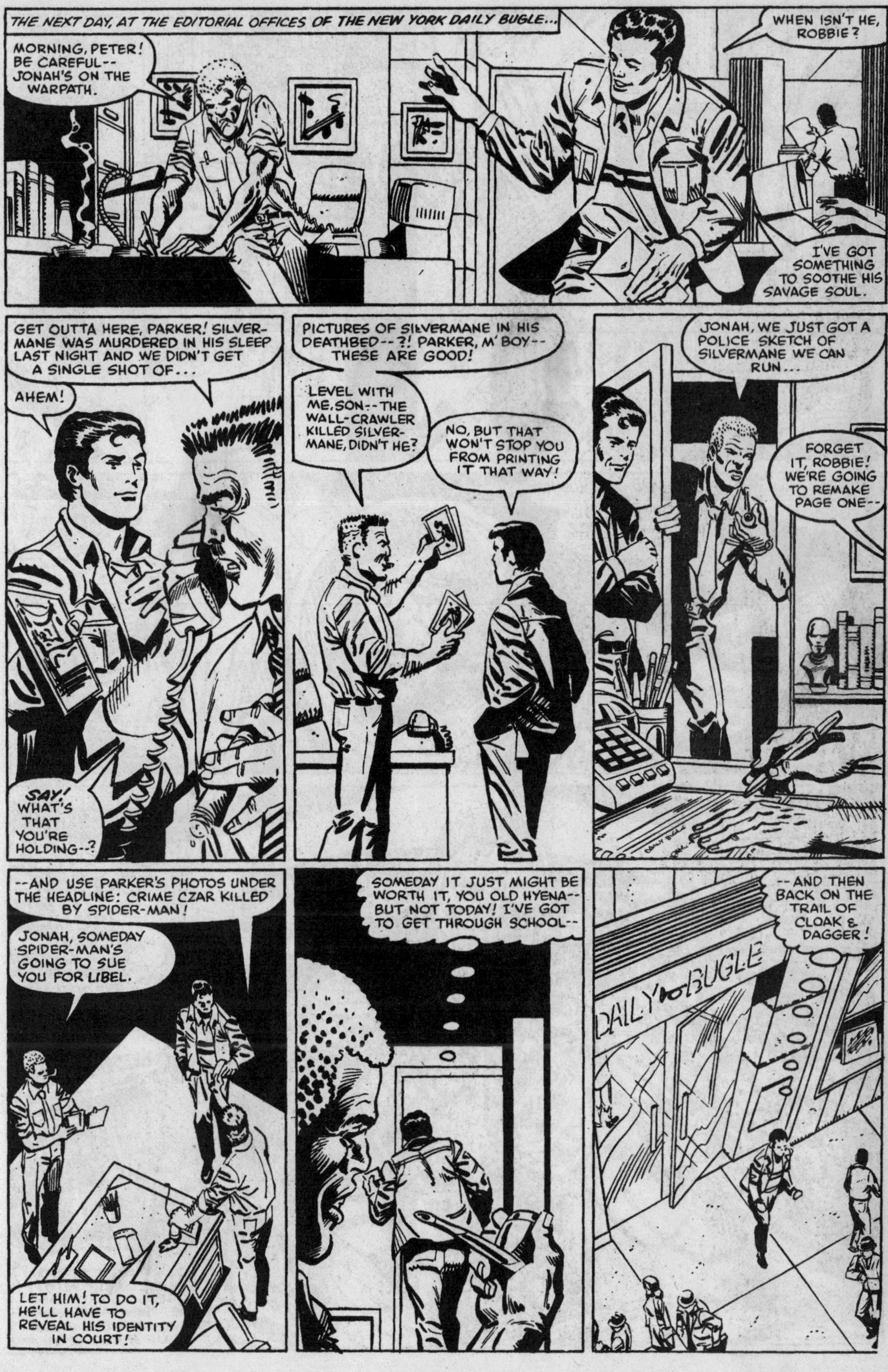
THE NEXT DAY, AT THE EDITORIAL OFFICES OF THE NEW YORK DAILY BUGLE...
MORNING, PETER! BE CAREFUL-- JONAH'S ON THE WARPATH.
WHEN ISN'T HE, ROBBIE?
I'VE GOT SOMETHING TO SOOTHE HIS SAVAGE SOUL.
GET OUTTA HERE, PARKER! SILVER-MANE WAS MURDERED IN HIS SLEEP LAST NIGHT AND WE DIDN'T GET A SINGLE SHOT OF...
AHEM!
SAY! WHAT'S THAT YOU'RE HOLDING--?
PICTURES OF SILVERMANE IN HIS DEATHBED--?! PARKER, M' BOY-- THESE ARE GOOD!
LEVEL WITH ME, SON-- THE WALL-CRAWLER KILLED SILVER-MANE, DIDN'T HE?
NO, BUT THAT WON'T STOP YOU FROM PRINTING IT THAT WAY!
JONAH, WE JUST GOT A POLICE SKETCH OF SILVERMANE WE CAN RUN...
FORGET IT, ROBBIE! WE'RE GOING TO REMAKE PAGE ONE--
--AND USE PARKER'S PHOTOS UNDER THE HEADLINE: CRIME CZAR KILLED BY SPIDER-MAN!
JONAH, SOMEDAY SPIDER-MAN'S GOING TO SUE YOU FOR LIBEL.
LET HIM! TO DO IT, HE'LL HAVE TO REVEAL HIS IDENTITY IN COURT!
SOMEDAY IT JUST MIGHT BE WORTH IT, YOU OLD HYENA-- BUT NOT TODAY! I'VE GOT TO GET THROUGH SCHOOL--
--AND THEN BACK ON THE TRAIL OF CLOAK & DAGGER!
DAILY BUGLE

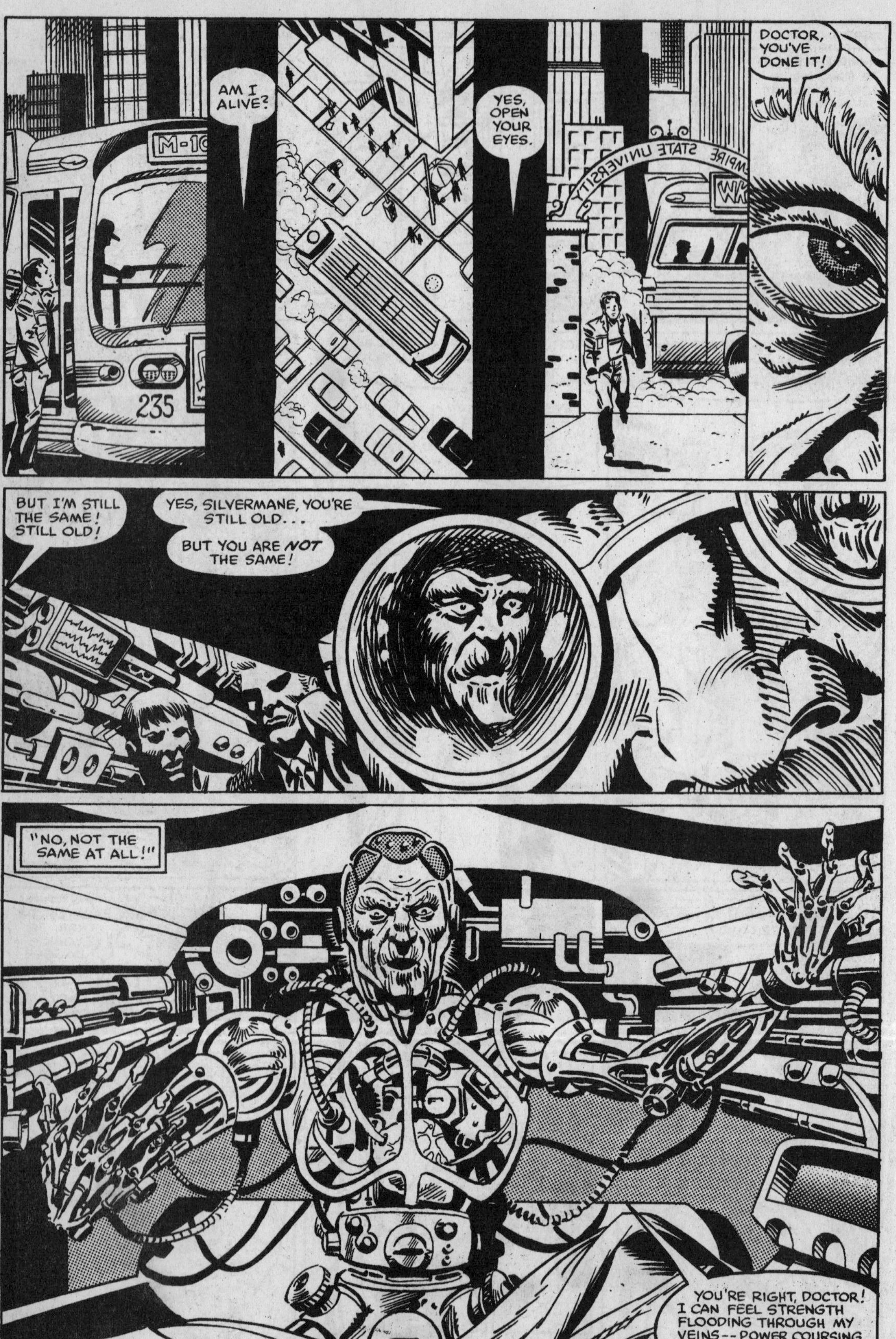

M-10
235
AM I ALIVE?
YES, OPEN YOUR EYES.
EMPIRE STATE UNIVERSITY
DOCTOR, YOU'VE DONE IT!
BUT I'M STILL THE SAME! STILL OLD!
YES, SILVERMANE, YOU'RE STILL OLD... BUT YOU ARE *NOT* THE SAME!
"NO, NOT THE SAME AT ALL!"
YOU'RE RIGHT, DOCTOR! I CAN FEEL STRENGTH FLOODING THROUGH MY VEINS--POWER COURSING THROUGH EVERY FIBER OF MY BEING!

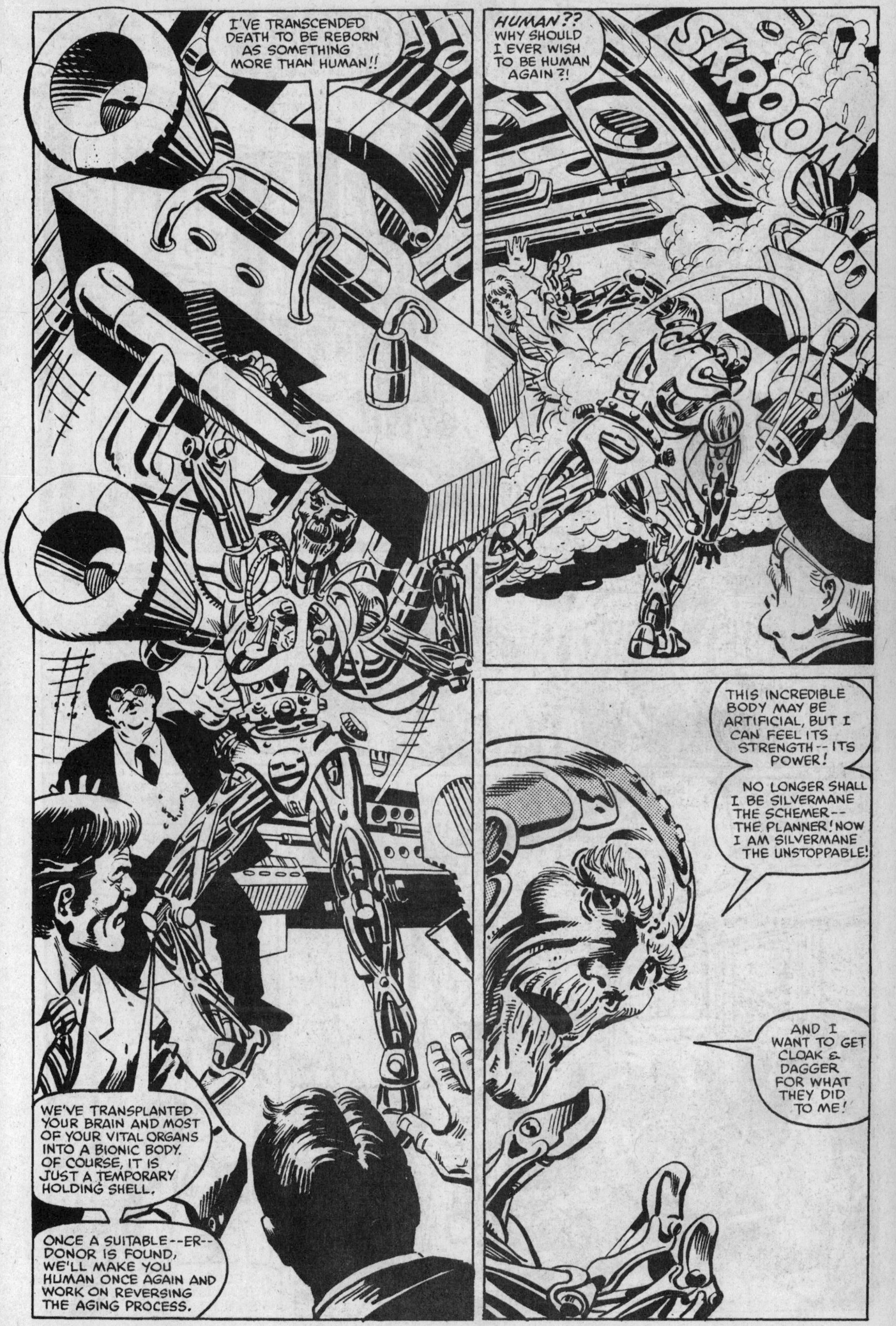
I'VE TRANSCENDED DEATH TO BE REBORN AS SOMETHING MORE THAN HUMAN!!
WE'VE TRANSPLANTED YOUR BRAIN AND MOST OF YOUR VITAL ORGANS INTO A BIONIC BODY. OF COURSE, IT IS JUST A TEMPORARY HOLDING SHELL.
ONCE A SUITABLE--ER--DONOR IS FOUND, WE'LL MAKE YOU HUMAN ONCE AGAIN AND WORK ON REVERSING THE AGING PROCESS.
HUMAN?? WHY SHOULD I EVER WISH TO BE HUMAN AGAIN?!
SKROOM
THIS INCREDIBLE BODY MAY BE ARTIFICIAL, BUT I CAN FEEL ITS STRENGTH--ITS POWER!
NO LONGER SHALL I BE SILVERMANE THE SCHEMER--THE PLANNER! NOW I AM SILVERMANE THE UNSTOPPABLE!
AND I WANT TO GET CLOAK & DAGGER FOR WHAT THEY DID TO ME!

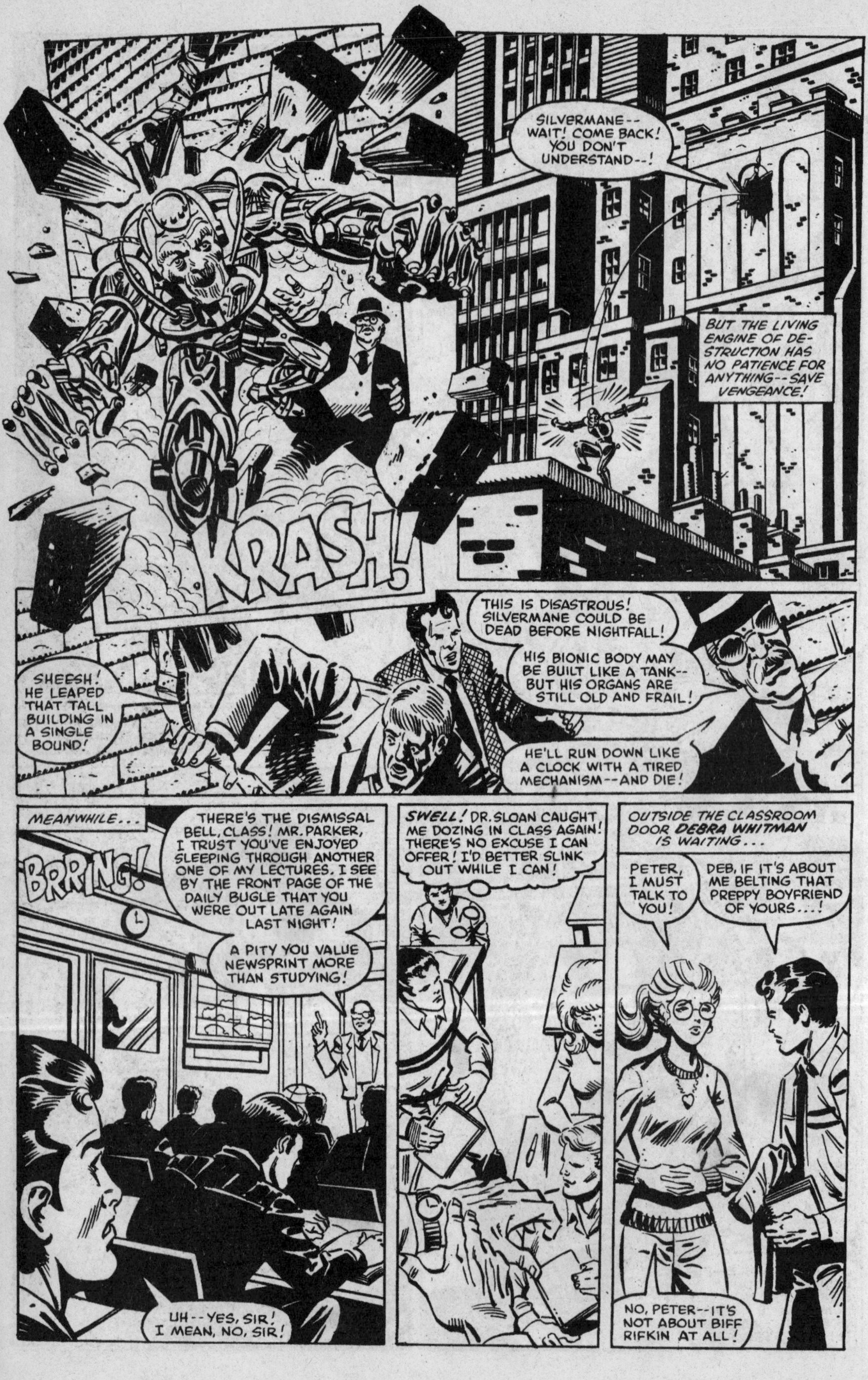
SILVERMANE-- WAIT! COME BACK! YOU DON'T UNDERSTAND--!
BUT THE LIVING ENGINE OF DESTRUCTION HAS NO PATIENCE FOR ANYTHING--SAVE VENGEANCE!
KRASH!
SHEESH! HE LEAPED THAT TALL BUILDING IN A SINGLE BOUND!
THIS IS DISASTROUS! SILVERMANE COULD BE DEAD BEFORE NIGHTFALL!
HIS BIONIC BODY MAY BE BUILT LIKE A TANK-- BUT HIS ORGANS ARE STILL OLD AND FRAIL!
HE'LL RUN DOWN LIKE A CLOCK WITH A TIRED MECHANISM--AND DIE!
MEANWHILE...
BRRING!
THERE'S THE DISMISSAL BELL, CLASS! MR. PARKER, I TRUST YOU'VE ENJOYED SLEEPING THROUGH ANOTHER ONE OF MY LECTURES. I SEE BY THE FRONT PAGE OF THE DAILY BUGLE THAT YOU WERE OUT LATE AGAIN LAST NIGHT!
A PITY YOU VALUE NEWSPRINT MORE THAN STUDYING!
UH--YES, SIR! I MEAN, NO, SIR!
SWELL! DR. SLOAN CAUGHT ME DOZING IN CLASS AGAIN! THERE'S NO EXCUSE I CAN OFFER! I'D BETTER SLINK OUT WHILE I CAN!
OUTSIDE THE CLASSROOM DOOR DEBRA WHITMAN IS WAITING...
PETER, I MUST TALK TO YOU!
DEB, IF IT'S ABOUT ME BELTING THAT PREPPY BOYFRIEND OF YOURS...!
NO, PETER--IT'S NOT ABOUT BIFF RIFKIN AT ALL!

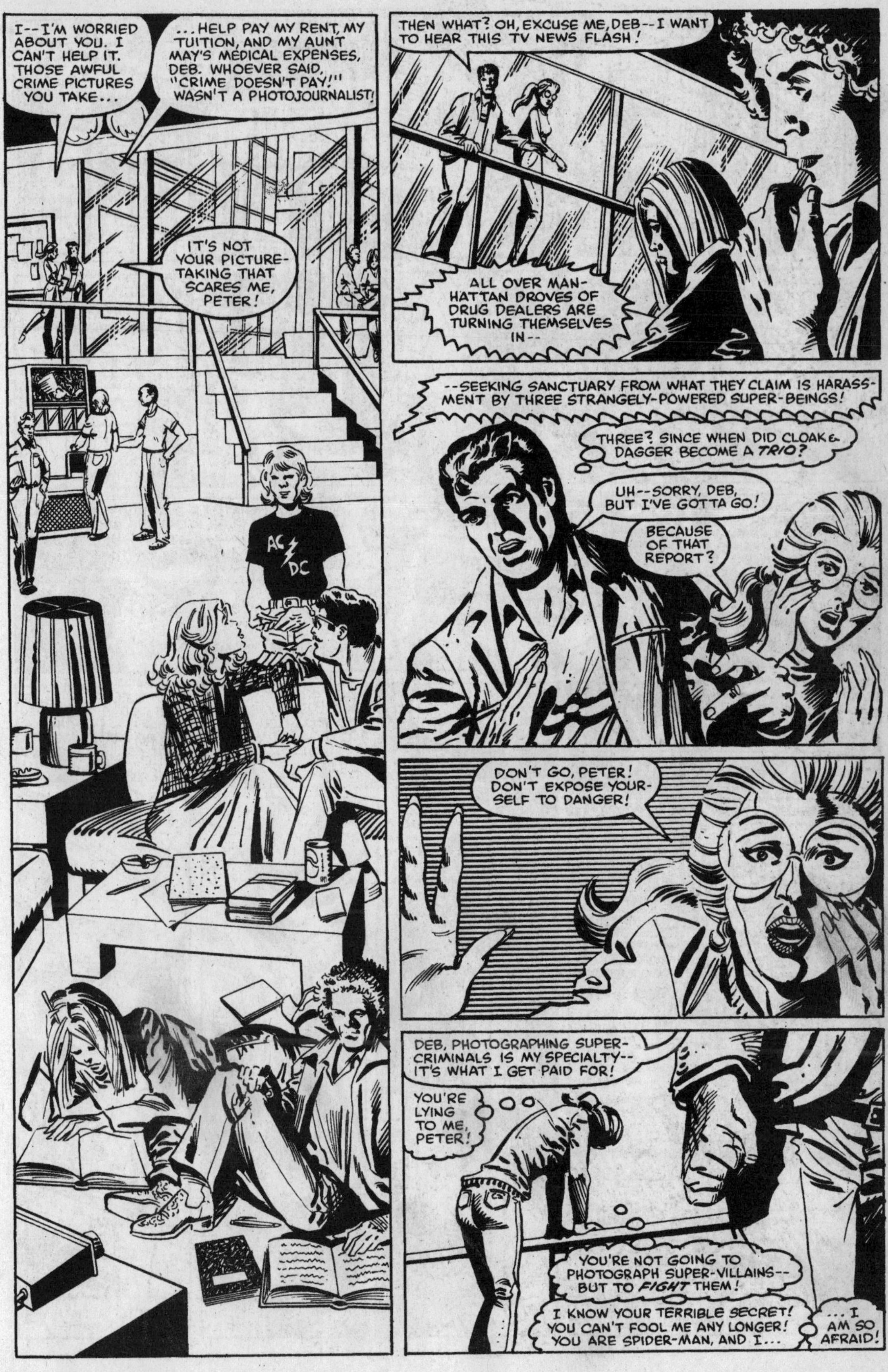
I--I'M WORRIED ABOUT YOU. I CAN'T HELP IT. THOSE AWFUL CRIME PICTURES YOU TAKE...
...HELP PAY MY RENT, MY TUITION, AND MY AUNT MAY'S MEDICAL EXPENSES, DEB. WHOEVER SAID, "CRIME DOESN'T PAY!" WASN'T A PHOTOJOURNALIST!
IT'S NOT YOUR PICTURE-TAKING THAT SCARES ME, PETER!
AC DC
THEN WHAT? OH, EXCUSE ME, DEB--I WANT TO HEAR THIS TV NEWS FLASH!
ALL OVER MANHATTAN DROVES OF DRUG DEALERS ARE TURNING THEMSELVES IN--
--SEEKING SANCTUARY FROM WHAT THEY CLAIM IS HARASSMENT BY THREE STRANGELY-POWERED SUPER-BEINGS!
THREE? SINCE WHEN DID CLOAK & DAGGER BECOME A *TRIO*?
UH--SORRY, DEB, BUT I'VE GOTTA GO!
BECAUSE OF THAT REPORT?
DON'T GO, PETER! DON'T EXPOSE YOURSELF TO DANGER!
DEB, PHOTOGRAPHING SUPER-CRIMINALS IS MY SPECIALTY--IT'S WHAT I GET PAID FOR!
YOU'RE LYING TO ME, PETER!
YOU'RE NOT GOING TO PHOTOGRAPH SUPER-VILLAINS--BUT TO *FIGHT* THEM!
I KNOW YOUR TERRIBLE SECRET! YOU CAN'T FOOL ME ANY LONGER! YOU ARE SPIDER-MAN, AND I...
...I AM SO AFRAID!

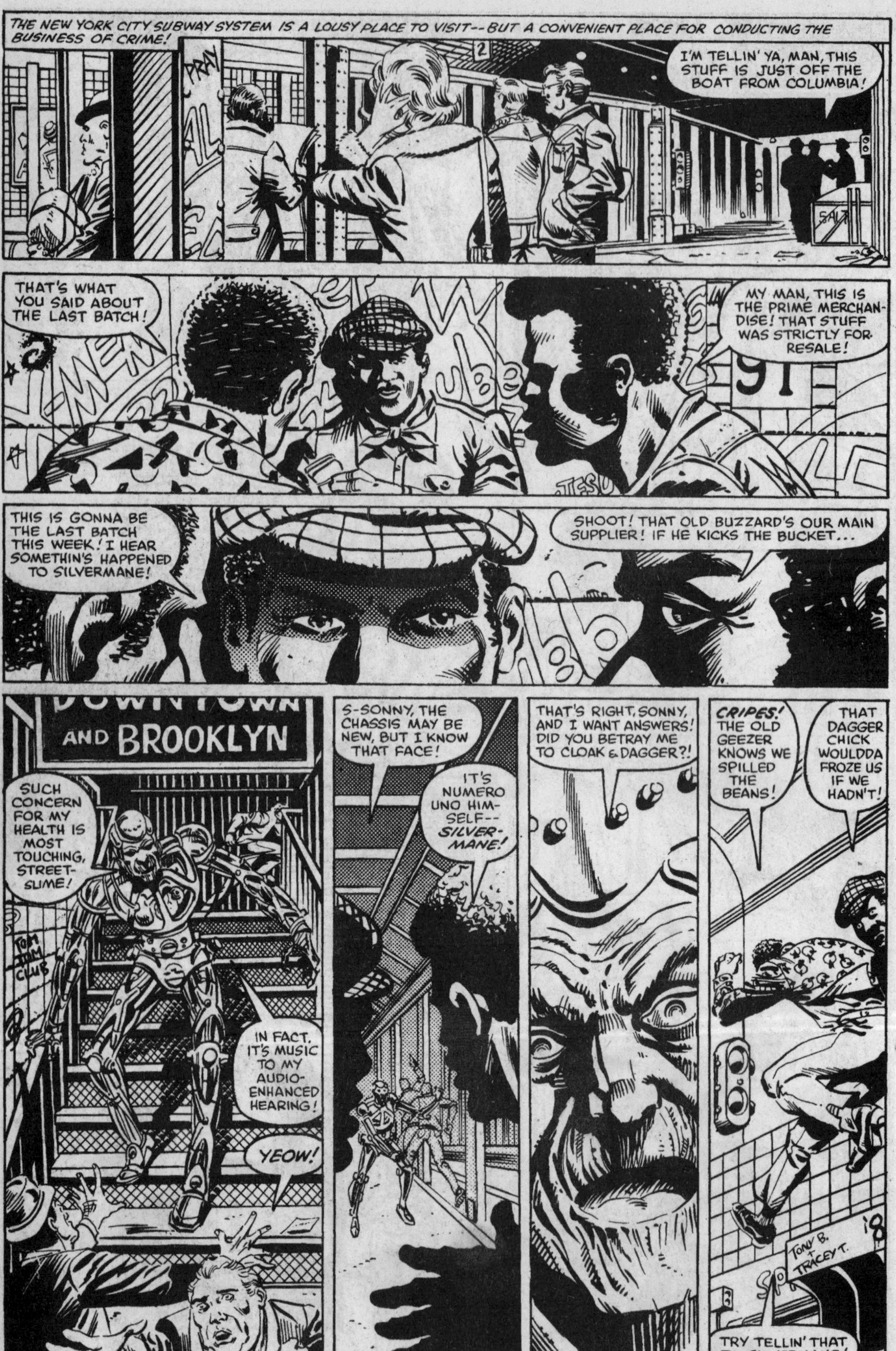
THE NEW YORK CITY SUBWAY SYSTEM IS A LOUSY PLACE TO VISIT-- BUT A CONVENIENT PLACE FOR CONDUCTING THE BUSINESS OF CRIME!
I'M TELLIN' YA, MAN, THIS STUFF IS JUST OFF THE BOAT FROM COLUMBIA!
THAT'S WHAT YOU SAID ABOUT THE LAST BATCH!
MY MAN, THIS IS THE PRIME MERCHANDISE! THAT STUFF WAS STRICTLY FOR RESALE!
THIS IS GONNA BE THE LAST BATCH THIS WEEK! I HEAR SOMETHIN'S HAPPENED TO SILVERMANE!
SHOOT! THAT OLD BUZZARD'S OUR MAIN SUPPLIER! IF HE KICKS THE BUCKET...
DOWNTOWN AND BROOKLYN
SUCH CONCERN FOR MY HEALTH IS MOST TOUCHING, STREET-SLIME!
IN FACT, IT'S MUSIC TO MY AUDIO-ENHANCED HEARING!
YEOW!
S-SONNY, THE CHASSIS MAY BE NEW, BUT I KNOW THAT FACE!
IT'S NUMERO UNO HIMSELF-- SILVERMANE!
THAT'S RIGHT, SONNY, AND I WANT ANSWERS! DID YOU BETRAY ME TO CLOAK & DAGGER?!
CRIPES! THE OLD GEEZER KNOWS WE SPILLED THE BEANS!
THAT DAGGER CHICK WOULDDA FROZE US IF WE HADN'T!
TRY TELLIN' THAT TO SILVERMANE!
TONY B. + TRACEY T.
18

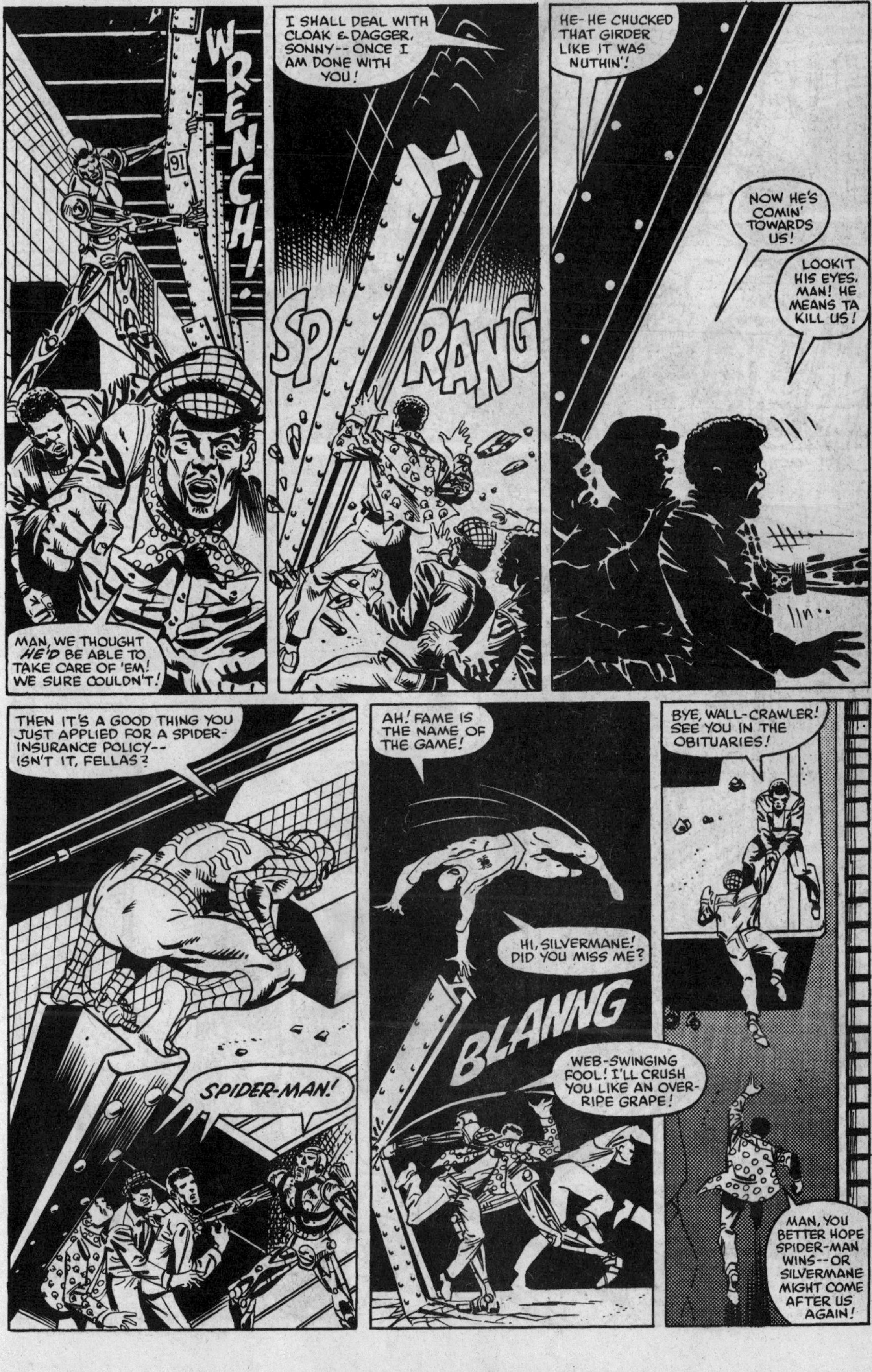
WRENCH!
91
MAN, WE THOUGHT *HE'D* BE ABLE TO TAKE CARE OF 'EM! WE SURE COULDN'T!
I SHALL DEAL WITH CLOAK & DAGGER, SONNY-- ONCE I AM DONE WITH YOU!
SPRANG
HE-HE CHUCKED THAT GIRDER LIKE IT WAS NUTHIN'!
NOW HE'S COMIN' TOWARDS US!
LOOKIT HIS EYES, MAN! HE MEANS TA KILL US!
THEN IT'S A GOOD THING YOU JUST APPLIED FOR A SPIDER-INSURANCE POLICY-- ISN'T IT, FELLAS?
SPIDER-MAN!
AH! FAME IS THE NAME OF THE GAME!
HI, SILVERMANE! DID YOU MISS ME?
BLANNG
WEB-SWINGING FOOL! I'LL CRUSH YOU LIKE AN OVER-RIPE GRAPE!
BYE, WALL-CRAWLER! SEE YOU IN THE OBITUARIES!
MAN, YOU BETTER HOPE SPIDER-MAN WINS--OR SILVERMANE MIGHT COME AFTER US AGAIN!

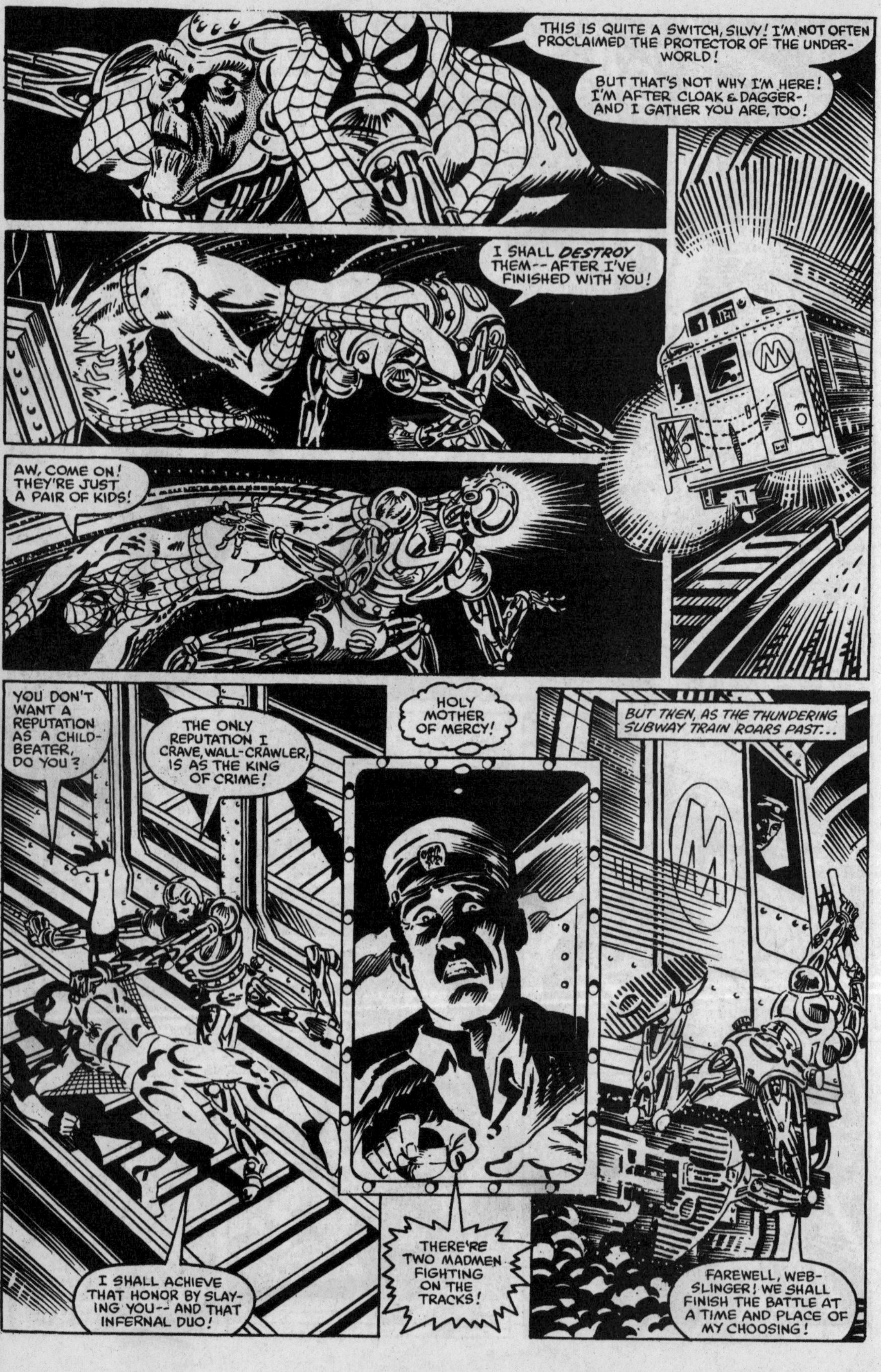
THIS IS QUITE A SWITCH, SILVY! I'M NOT OFTEN PROCLAIMED THE PROTECTOR OF THE UNDER-WORLD!
BUT THAT'S NOT WHY I'M HERE! I'M AFTER CLOAK & DAGGER-AND I GATHER YOU ARE, TOO!
I SHALL DESTROY THEM-- AFTER I'VE FINISHED WITH YOU!
AW, COME ON! THEY'RE JUST A PAIR OF KIDS!
YOU DON'T WANT A REPUTATION AS A CHILD-BEATER, DO YOU?
THE ONLY REPUTATION I CRAVE, WALL-CRAWLER, IS AS THE KING OF CRIME!
I SHALL ACHIEVE THAT HONOR BY SLAYING YOU-- AND THAT INFERNAL DUO!
HOLY MOTHER OF MERCY!
THERE'RE TWO MADMEN FIGHTING ON THE TRACKS!
BUT THEN, AS THE THUNDERING SUBWAY TRAIN ROARS PAST...
FAREWELL, WEB-SLINGER! WE SHALL FINISH THE BATTLE AT A TIME AND PLACE OF MY CHOOSING!

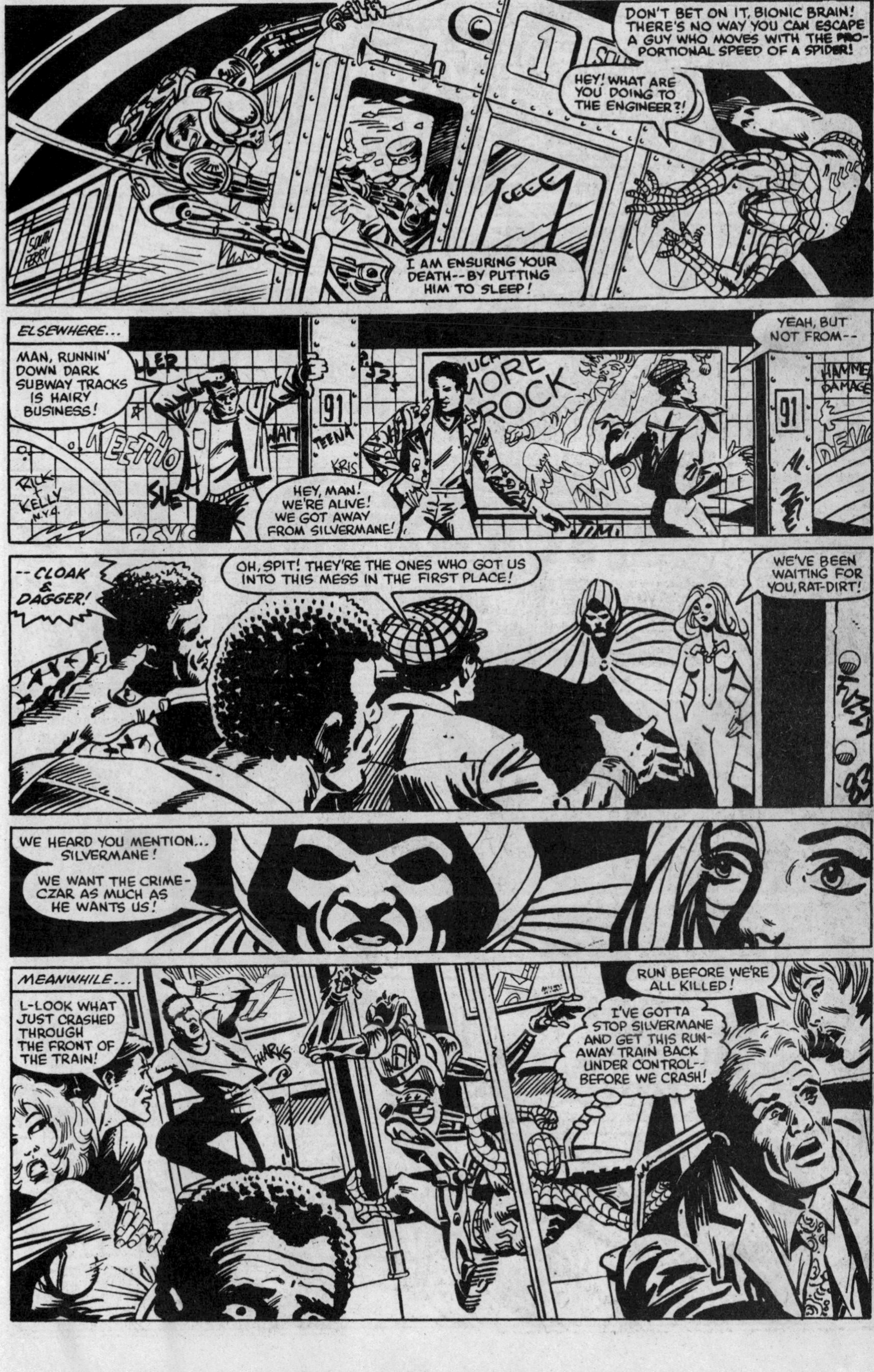
DON'T BET ON IT, BIONIC BRAIN! THERE'S NO WAY YOU CAN ESCAPE A GUY WHO MOVES WITH THE PROPORTIONAL SPEED OF A SPIDER!
HEY! WHAT ARE YOU DOING TO THE ENGINEER?!
I AM ENSURING YOUR DEATH--BY PUTTING HIM TO SLEEP!
ELSEWHERE...
MAN, RUNNIN' DOWN DARK SUBWAY TRACKS IS HAIRY BUSINESS!
HEY, MAN! WE'RE ALIVE! WE GOT AWAY FROM SILVERMANE!
YEAH, BUT NOT FROM--
--CLOAK & DAGGER!
OH, SPIT! THEY'RE THE ONES WHO GOT US INTO THIS MESS IN THE FIRST PLACE!
WE'VE BEEN WAITING FOR YOU, RAT-DIRT!
WE HEARD YOU MENTION... SILVERMANE!
WE WANT THE CRIME-CZAR AS MUCH AS HE WANTS US!
MEANWHILE...
L-LOOK WHAT JUST CRASHED THROUGH THE FRONT OF THE TRAIN!
RUN BEFORE WE'RE ALL KILLED!
I'VE GOTTA STOP SILVERMANE AND GET THIS RUNAWAY TRAIN BACK UNDER CONTROL--BEFORE WE CRASH!

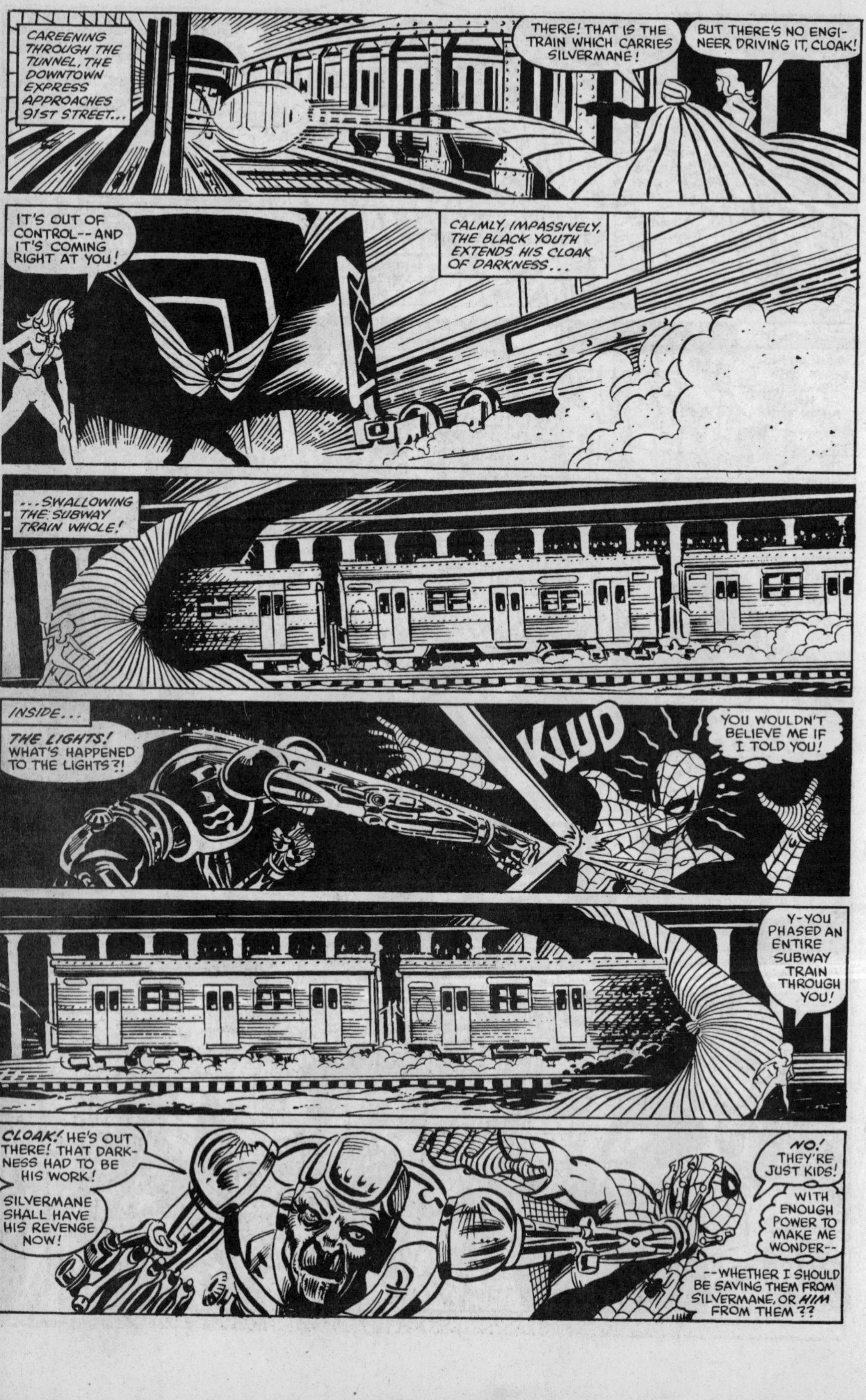

CAREENING THROUGH THE TUNNEL, THE DOWNTOWN EXPRESS APPROACHES 91ST STREET...
THERE! THAT IS THE TRAIN WHICH CARRIES SILVERMANE!
BUT THERE'S NO ENGINEER DRIVING IT, CLOAK!
IT'S OUT OF CONTROL--AND IT'S COMING RIGHT AT YOU!
CALMLY, IMPASSIVELY, THE BLACK YOUTH EXTENDS HIS CLOAK OF DARKNESS...
...SWALLOWING THE SUBWAY TRAIN WHOLE!
INSIDE...
THE LIGHTS! WHAT'S HAPPENED TO THE LIGHTS?!
KLUD
YOU WOULDN'T BELIEVE ME IF I TOLD YOU!
Y-YOU PHASED AN ENTIRE SUBWAY TRAIN THROUGH YOU!
CLOAK! HE'S OUT THERE! THAT DARKNESS HAD TO BE HIS WORK!
SILVERMANE SHALL HAVE HIS REVENGE NOW!
NO! THEY'RE JUST KIDS!
WITH ENOUGH POWER TO MAKE ME WONDER--
--WHETHER I SHOULD BE SAVING THEM FROM SILVERMANE, OR HIM FROM THEM??

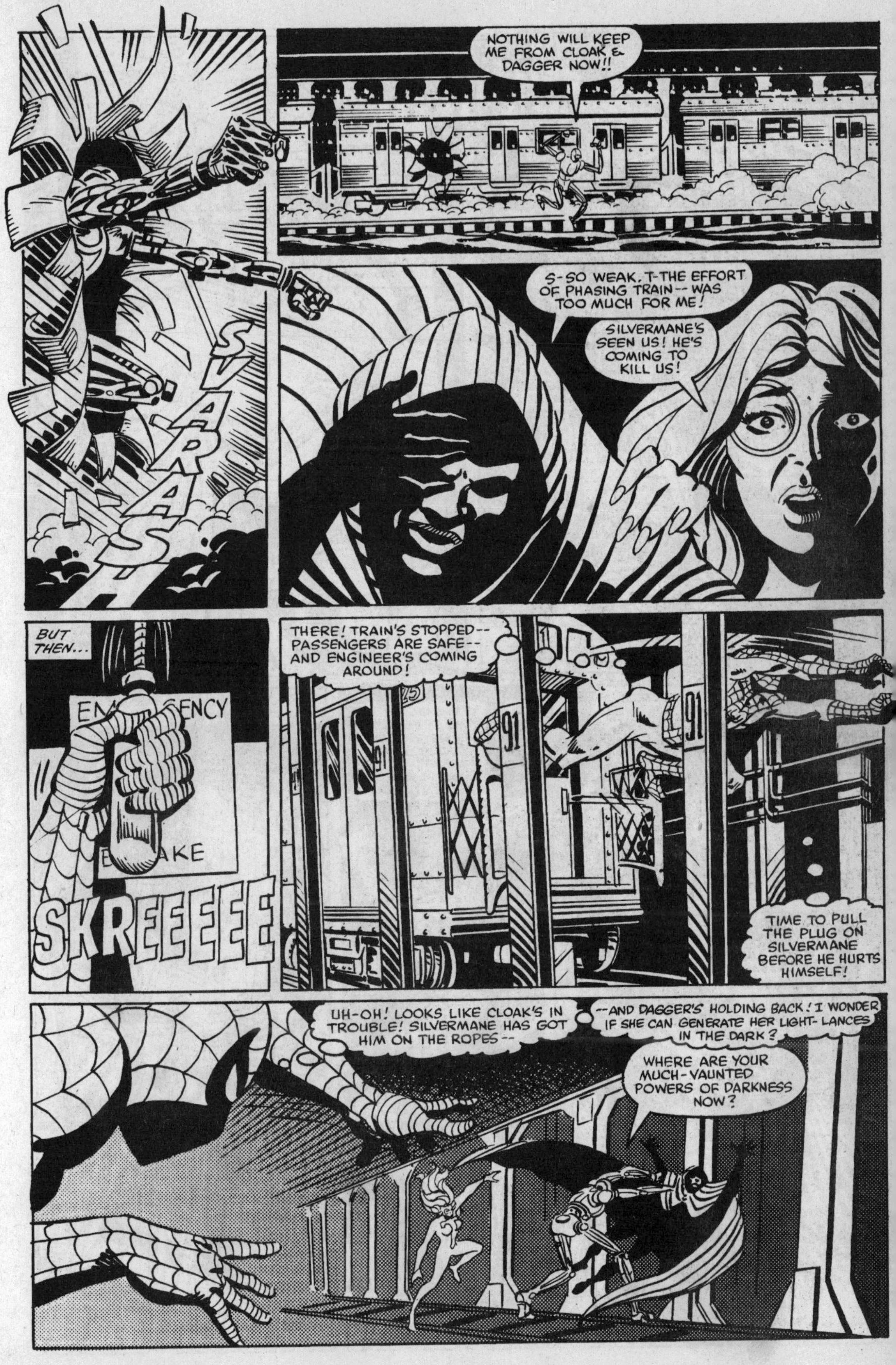
SVARASH
NOTHING WILL KEEP ME FROM CLOAK & DAGGER NOW!!
S-SO WEAK. T-THE EFFORT OF PHASING TRAIN--WAS TOO MUCH FOR ME!
SILVERMANE'S SEEN US! HE'S COMING TO KILL US!
BUT THEN...
EMERGENCY
BRAKE
SKREEEEE
THERE! TRAIN'S STOPPED-- PASSENGERS ARE SAFE-- AND ENGINEER'S COMING AROUND!
TIME TO PULL THE PLUG ON SILVERMANE BEFORE HE HURTS HIMSELF!
UH-OH! LOOKS LIKE CLOAK'S IN TROUBLE! SILVERMANE HAS GOT HIM ON THE ROPES--
--AND DAGGER'S HOLDING BACK! I WONDER IF SHE CAN GENERATE HER LIGHT-LANCES IN THE DARK?
WHERE ARE YOUR MUCH-VAUNTED POWERS OF DARKNESS NOW?

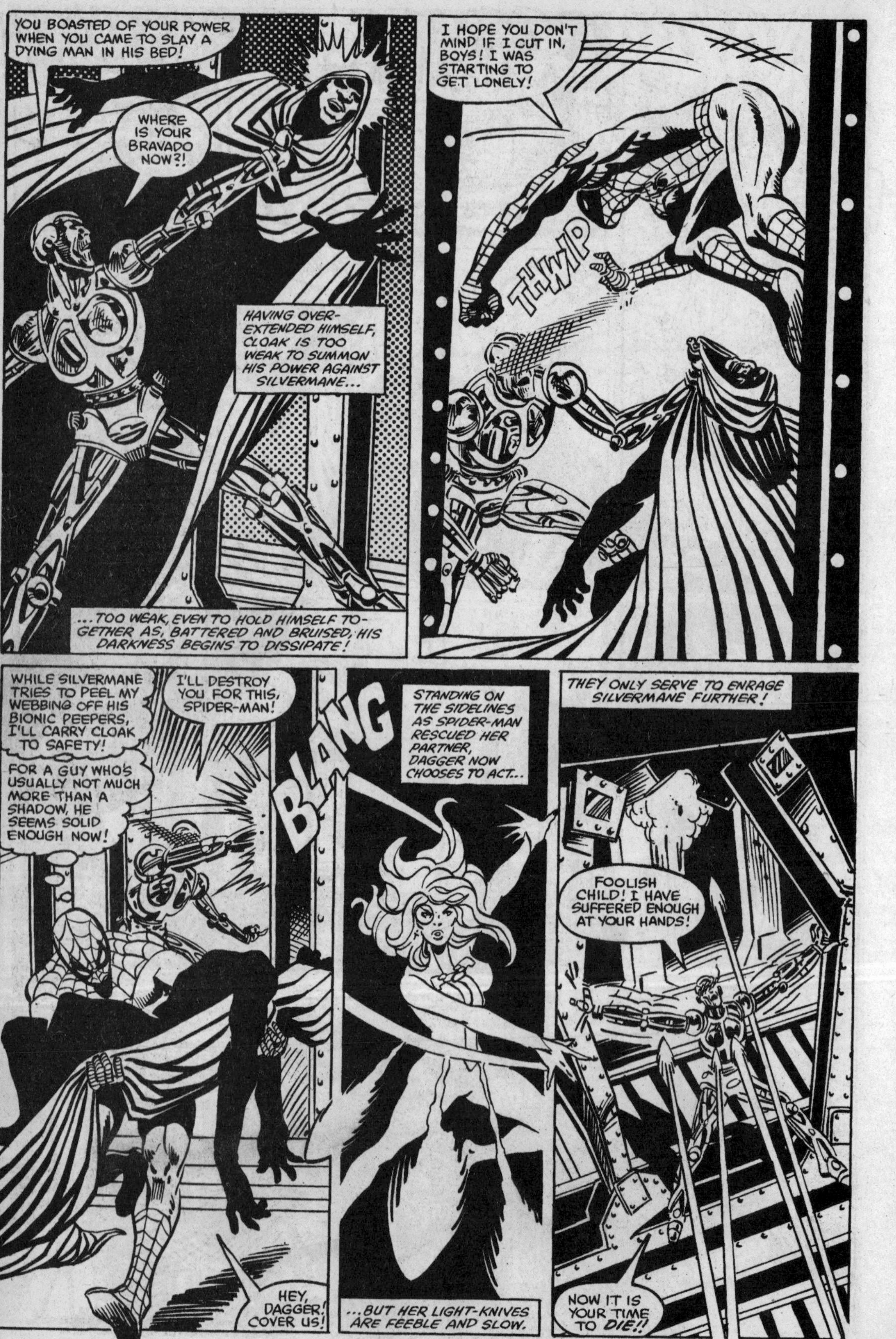
YOU BOASTED OF YOUR POWER WHEN YOU CAME TO SLAY A DYING MAN IN HIS BED!
WHERE IS YOUR BRAVADO NOW?!
HAVING OVER-EXTENDED HIMSELF, CLOAK IS TOO WEAK TO SUMMON HIS POWER AGAINST SILVERMANE...
...TOO WEAK, EVEN TO HOLD HIMSELF TO-GETHER AS, BATTERED AND BRUISED, HIS DARKNESS BEGINS TO DISSIPATE!
I HOPE YOU DON'T MIND IF I CUT IN, BOYS! I WAS STARTING TO GET LONELY!
THWIP
WHILE SILVERMANE TRIES TO PEEL MY WEBBING OFF HIS BIONIC PEEPERS, I'LL CARRY CLOAK TO SAFETY!
FOR A GUY WHO'S USUALLY NOT MUCH MORE THAN A SHADOW, HE SEEMS SOLID ENOUGH NOW!
I'LL DESTROY YOU FOR THIS, SPIDER-MAN!
BLANG
HEY, DAGGER! COVER US!
STANDING ON THE SIDELINES AS SPIDER-MAN RESCUED HER PARTNER, DAGGER NOW CHOOSES TO ACT...
...BUT HER LIGHT-KNIVES ARE FEEBLE AND SLOW.
THEY ONLY SERVE TO ENRAGE SILVERMANE FURTHER!
FOOLISH CHILD! I HAVE SUFFERED ENOUGH AT YOUR HANDS!
NOW IT IS YOUR TIME TO DIE!!

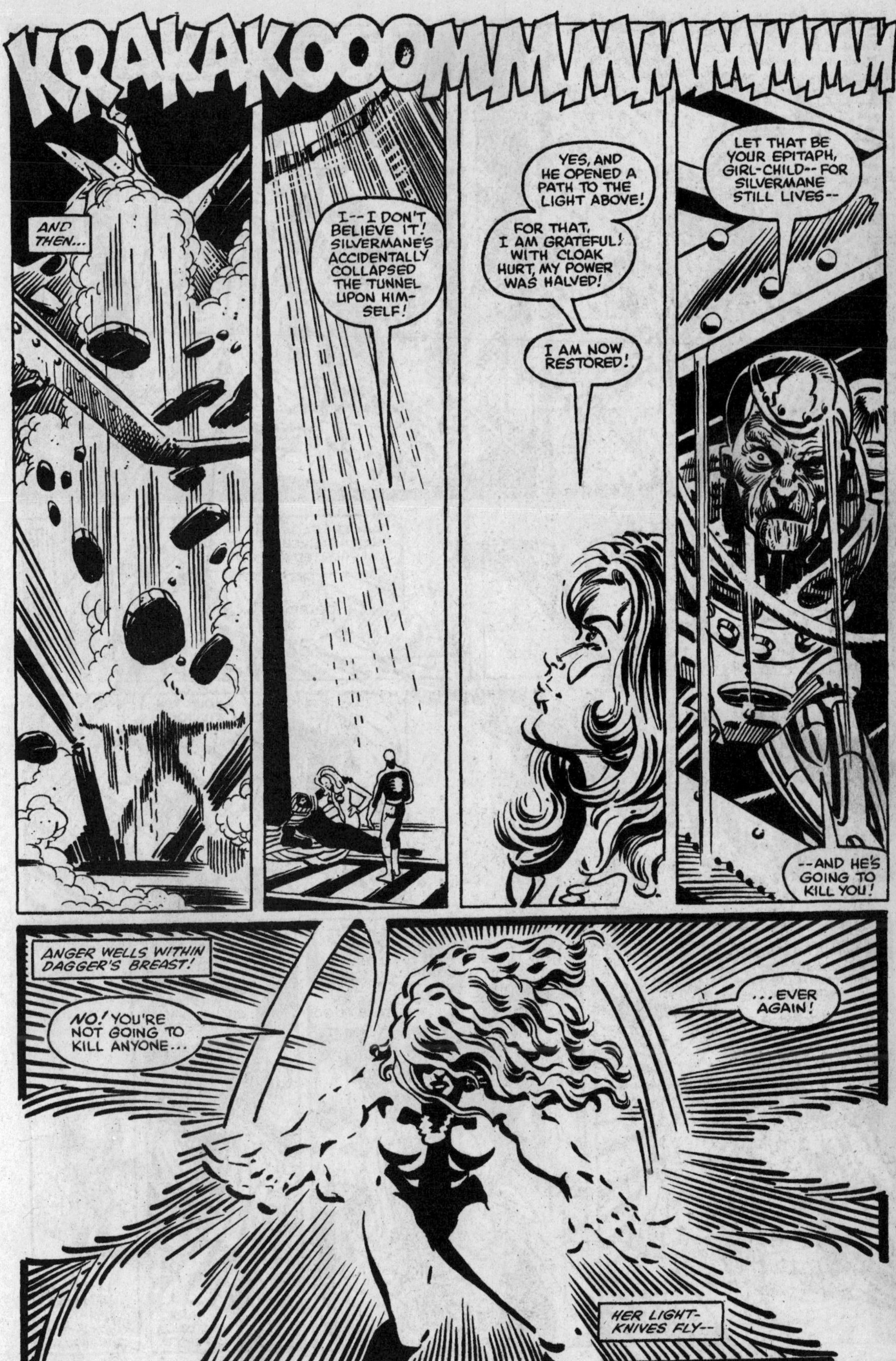
KRAKAKOOOOMMMMMMMMMH
AND THEN...
I-- I DON'T BELIEVE IT! SILVERMANE'S ACCIDENTALLY COLLAPSED THE TUNNEL UPON HIMSELF!
YES, AND HE OPENED A PATH TO THE LIGHT ABOVE!
FOR THAT, I AM GRATEFUL! WITH CLOAK HURT, MY POWER WAS HALVED!
I AM NOW RESTORED!
LET THAT BE YOUR EPITAPH, GIRL-CHILD-- FOR SILVERMANE STILL LIVES--
--AND HE'S GOING TO KILL YOU!
ANGER WELLS WITHIN DAGGER'S BREAST!
NO! YOU'RE NOT GOING TO KILL ANYONE...
...EVER AGAIN!
HER LIGHT-KNIVES FLY--

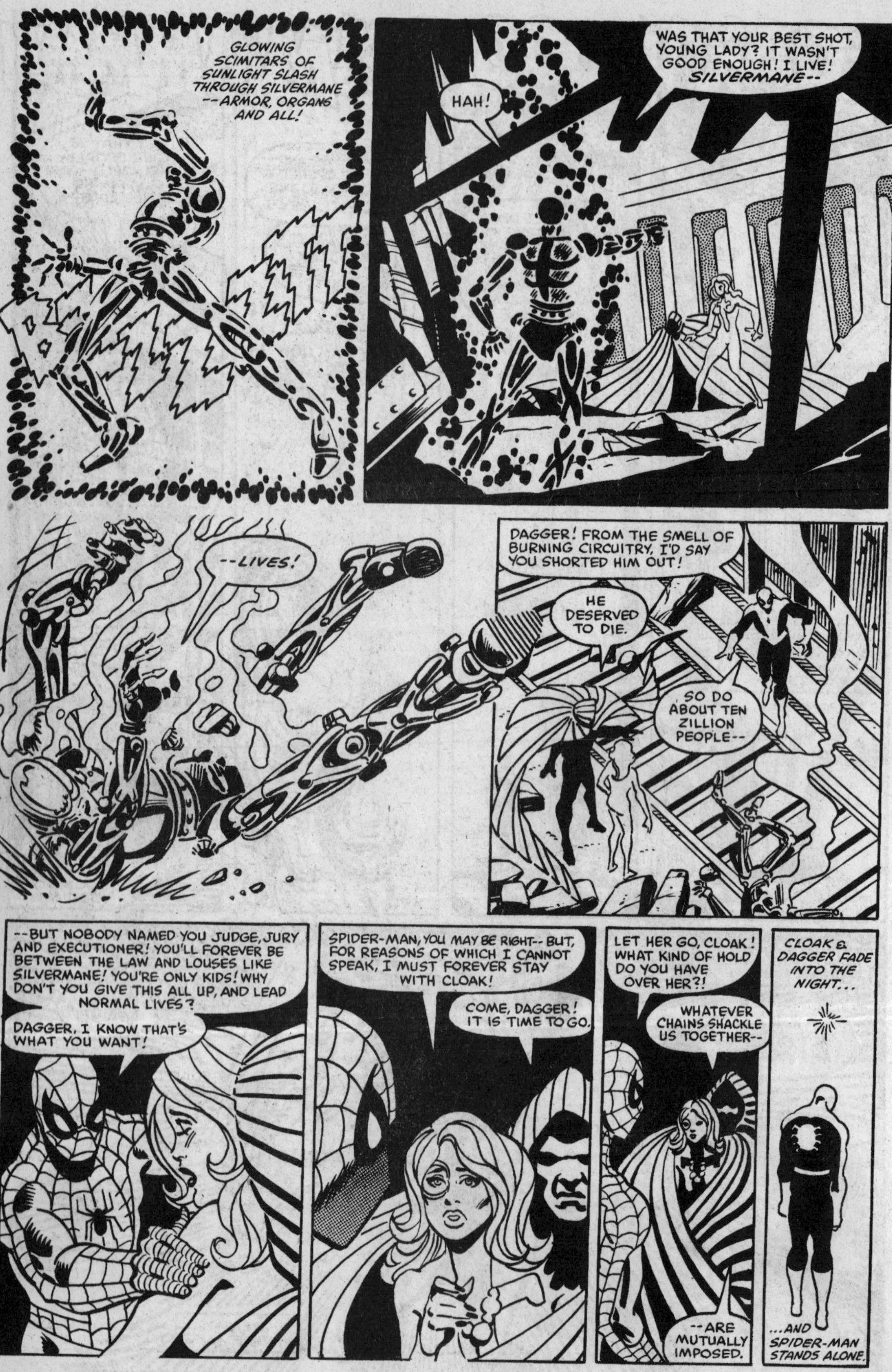
GLOWING SCIMITARS OF SUNLIGHT SLASH THROUGH SILVERMANE --ARMOR, ORGANS AND ALL!
HAH!
WAS THAT YOUR BEST SHOT, YOUNG LADY? IT WASN'T GOOD ENOUGH! I LIVE! SILVERMANE--
--LIVES!
DAGGER! FROM THE SMELL OF BURNING CIRCUITRY, I'D SAY YOU SHORTED HIM OUT!
HE DESERVED TO DIE.
SO DO ABOUT TEN ZILLION PEOPLE--
--BUT NOBODY NAMED YOU JUDGE, JURY AND EXECUTIONER! YOU'LL FOREVER BE BETWEEN THE LAW AND LOUSES LIKE SILVERMANE! YOU'RE ONLY KIDS! WHY DON'T YOU GIVE THIS ALL UP, AND LEAD NORMAL LIVES?
DAGGER, I KNOW THAT'S WHAT YOU WANT!
SPIDER-MAN, YOU MAY BE RIGHT-- BUT, FOR REASONS OF WHICH I CANNOT SPEAK, I MUST FOREVER STAY WITH CLOAK!
COME, DAGGER! IT IS TIME TO GO.
LET HER GO, CLOAK! WHAT KIND OF HOLD DO YOU HAVE OVER HER?!
WHATEVER CHAINS SHACKLE US TOGETHER--
--ARE MUTUALLY IMPOSED.
CLOAK & DAGGER FADE INTO THE NIGHT...
...AND SPIDER-MAN STANDS ALONE.

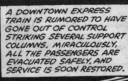

EPILOGUE: THE EVENING NEWS REPORTS A GIANT HOLE WHICH SNARLS WEST SIDE TRAFFIC FOR HOURS.

A DOWNTOWN EXPRESS TRAIN IS RUMORED TO HAVE GONE OUT OF CONTROL STRIKING SEVERAL SUPPORT COLUMNS. MIRACULOUSLY, ALL THE PASSENGERS ARE EVACUATED SAFELY, AND SERVICE IS SOON RESTORED.

BUT, THERE IS A MYSTERY HERE...

THE PASSENGERS SPEAK OF AN ALL-ENVELOPING DARKNESS AND A SOUL-NUMBING COLD THAT SEEMED TO SWALLOW THE TRAIN JUST BEFORE THE ACCIDENT...

...AND THE POLICE FIND TRACES OF SPIDER-MAN'S WEBBING ON THE TRACKS--

--ALONGSIDE AN UNCONSCIOUS FIGURE IDENTIFIED AS THAT OF THE ALLEGEDLY SLAIN CRIME CZAR...SILVERMANE!

SOMEWHERE, DEBRA WHITMAN TUNES OUT THE NIGHTLY NEWS...

I-I KNOW WE'VE GONE ALL OVER THIS BEFORE--MY FANTASIES--THE WAY I MIX UP WHAT'S REAL WITH WHAT ISN'T!

BUT THIS TIME I'M SURE I'M NOT IMAGINING ANYTHING!

OH, YOU'LL LAUGH! YOU'LL SAY, "DEBRA, YOU'RE BEING SILLY!"

BUT THERE'S NO OTHER ANSWER FOR IT!

EITHER THE BOY I THINK I'M IN LOVE WITH IS SPIDER-MAN--

--OR I'M IN MORE TROUBLE THAN I THOUGHT!

JOIN US NEXT MONTH...

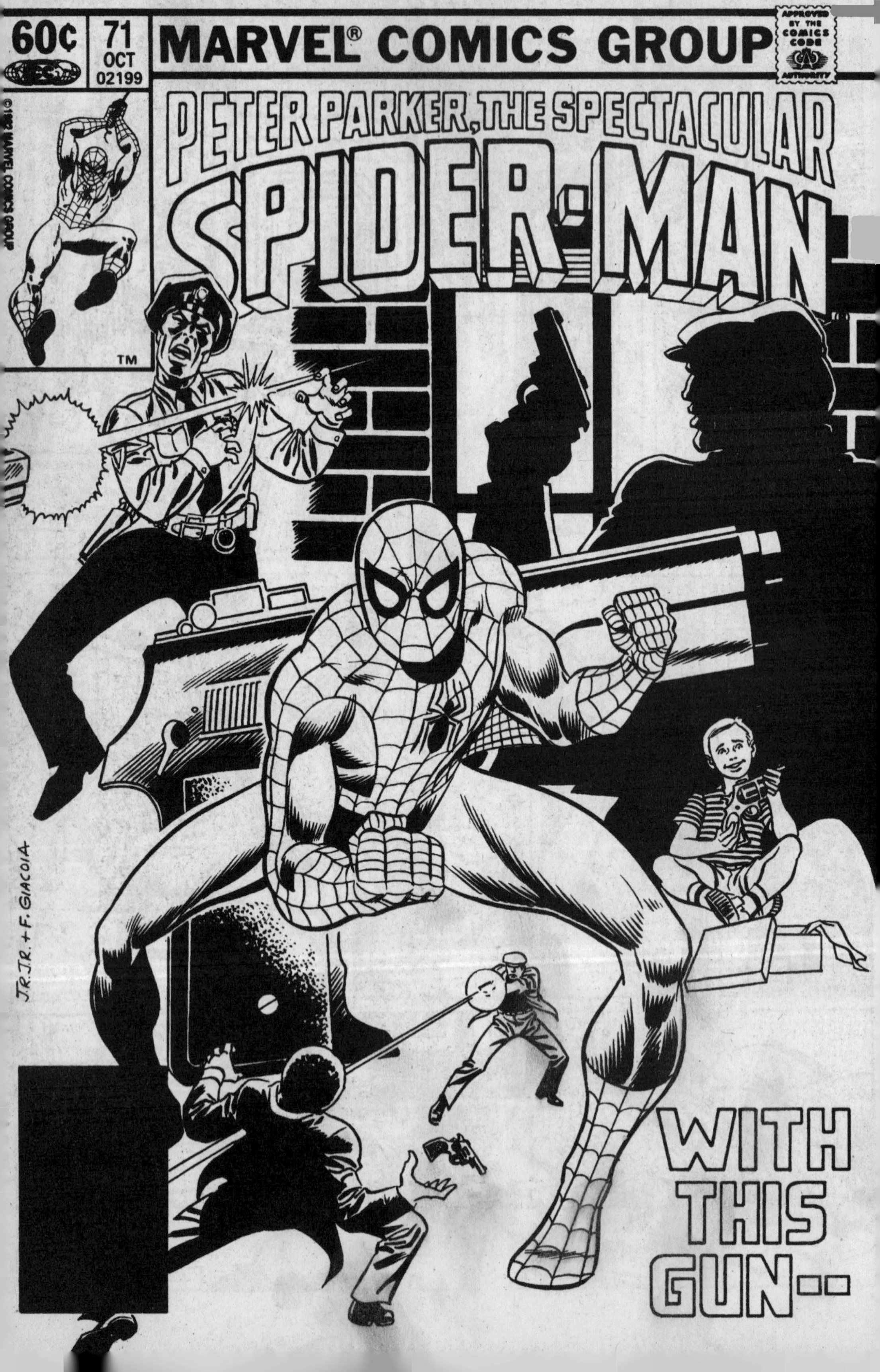

60¢
71
OCT
02199
MARVEL® COMICS GROUP
APPROVED BY THE COMICS CODE AUTHORITY
PETER PARKER, THE SPECTACULAR
SPIDER-MAN
TM
J.R.JR. + F. GIACOIA
WITH THIS GUN--

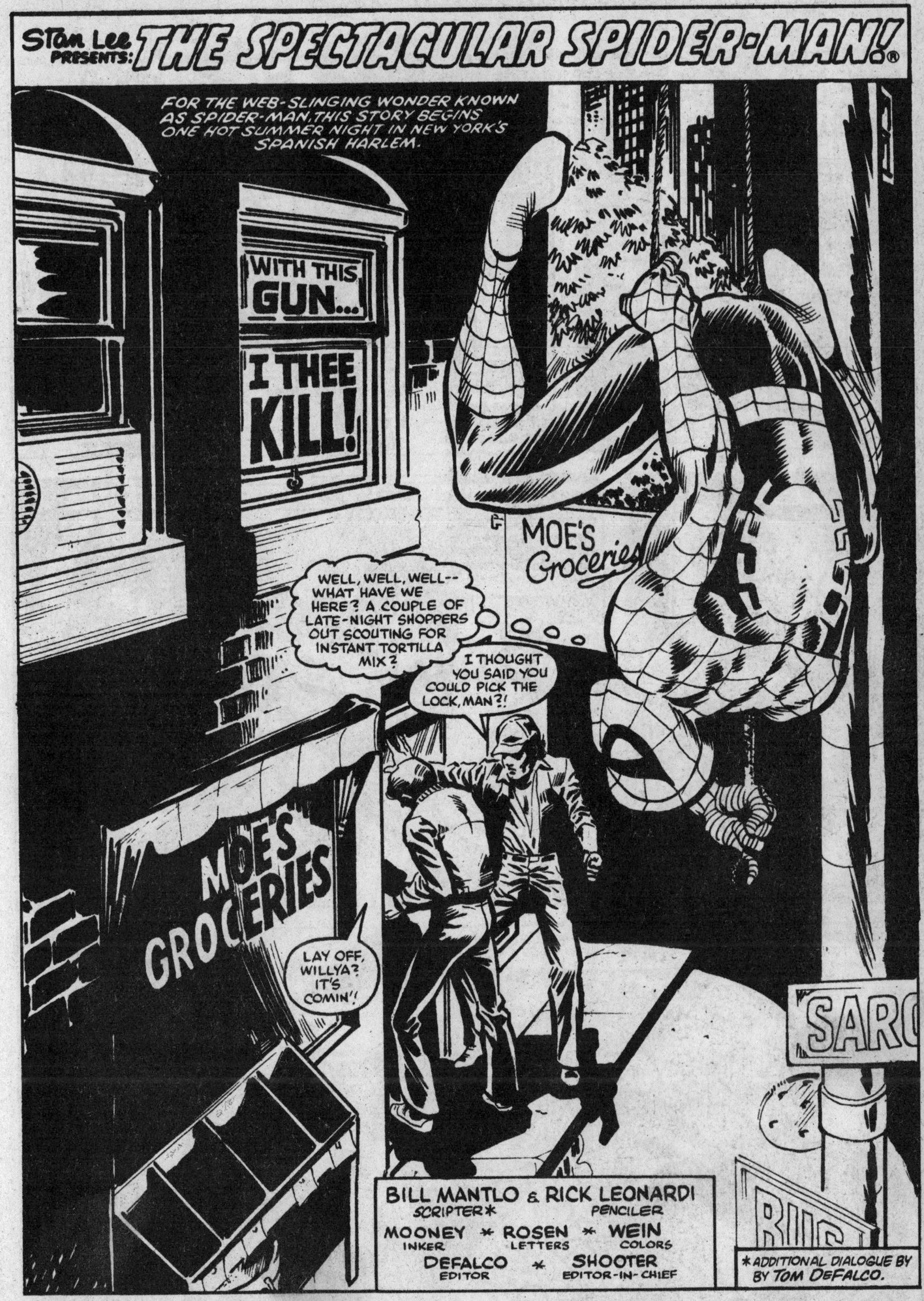
Stan Lee PRESENTS: THE SPECTACULAR SPIDER-MAN!®
FOR THE WEB-SLINGING WONDER KNOWN AS SPIDER-MAN, THIS STORY BEGINS ONE HOT SUMMER NIGHT IN NEW YORK'S SPANISH HARLEM.
WITH THIS GUN...
I THEE KILL!
MOE'S Groceries
WELL, WELL, WELL-- WHAT HAVE WE HERE? A COUPLE OF LATE-NIGHT SHOPPERS OUT SCOUTING FOR INSTANT TORTILLA MIX?
I THOUGHT YOU SAID YOU COULD PICK THE LOCK, MAN?!
MOES GROCERIES
LAY OFF, WILLYA? IT'S COMIN'!
SARG
BILL MANTLO & RICK LEONARDI
SCRIPTER* PENCILER
MOONEY * ROSEN * WEIN
INKER LETTERS COLORS
DEFALCO * SHOOTER
EDITOR EDITOR-IN-CHIEF
*ADDITIONAL DIALOGUE BY BY TOM DEFALCO.

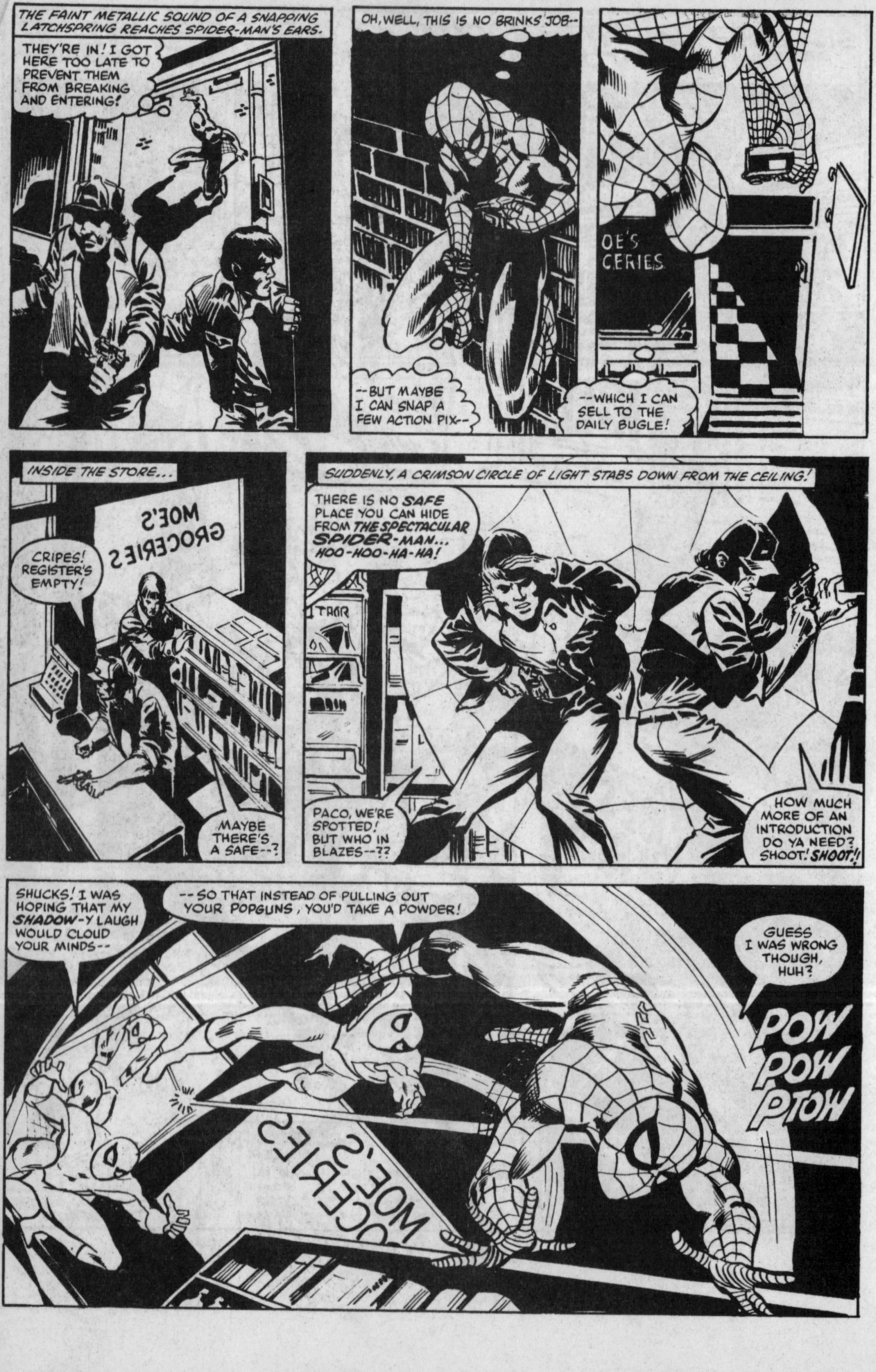
THE FAINT METALLIC SOUND OF A SNAPPING LATCHSPRING REACHES SPIDER-MAN'S EARS.
THEY'RE IN! I GOT HERE TOO LATE TO PREVENT THEM FROM BREAKING AND ENTERING!
OH, WELL, THIS IS NO BRINKS JOB--
--BUT MAYBE I CAN SNAP A FEW ACTION PIX--
OE'S CERIES
--WHICH I CAN SELL TO THE DAILY BUGLE!
INSIDE THE STORE...
MOE'S GROCERIES
CRIPES! REGISTER'S EMPTY!
MAYBE THERE'S A SAFE--?
SUDDENLY, A CRIMSON CIRCLE OF LIGHT STABS DOWN FROM THE CEILING!
THERE IS NO SAFE PLACE YOU CAN HIDE FROM THE SPECTACULAR SPIDER-MAN... HOO-HOO-HA-HA!
PACO, WE'RE SPOTTED! BUT WHO IN BLAZES--??
HOW MUCH MORE OF AN INTRODUCTION DO YA NEED? SHOOT! SHOOT!!
SHUCKS! I WAS HOPING THAT MY SHADOW-Y LAUGH WOULD CLOUD YOUR MINDS--
--SO THAT INSTEAD OF PULLING OUT YOUR POPGUNS, YOU'D TAKE A POWDER!
GUESS I WAS WRONG THOUGH, HUH?
POW
POW
PTOW
MOE'S CERIES

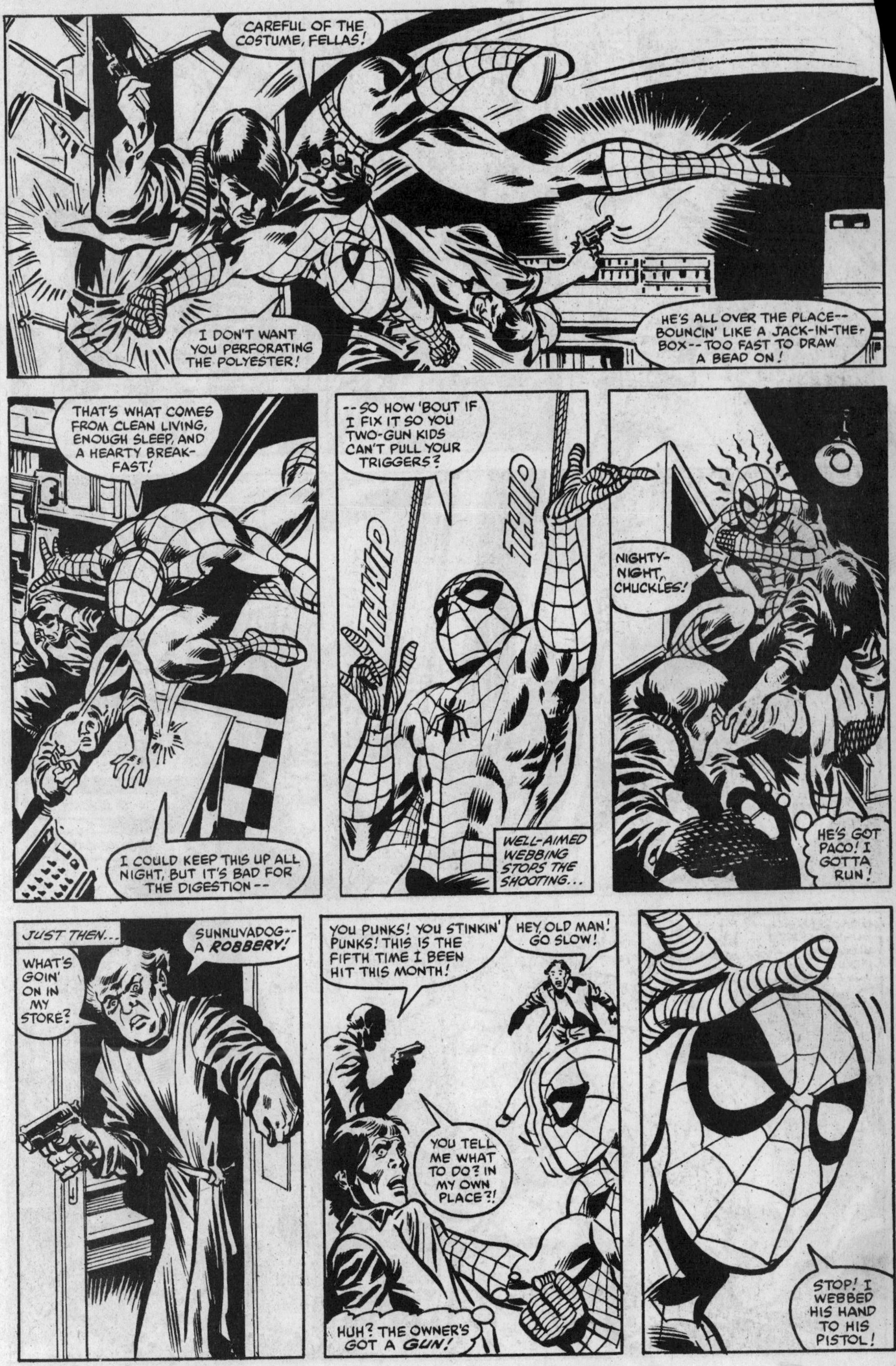
CAREFUL OF THE COSTUME, FELLAS!
I DON'T WANT YOU PERFORATING THE POLYESTER!
HE'S ALL OVER THE PLACE-- BOUNCIN' LIKE A JACK-IN-THE-BOX--TOO FAST TO DRAW A BEAD ON!
THAT'S WHAT COMES FROM CLEAN LIVING, ENOUGH SLEEP, AND A HEARTY BREAK-FAST!
I COULD KEEP THIS UP ALL NIGHT, BUT IT'S BAD FOR THE DIGESTION--
--SO HOW 'BOUT IF I FIX IT SO YOU TWO-GUN KIDS CAN'T PULL YOUR TRIGGERS?
THWIP
THWIP
WELL-AIMED WEBBING STOPS THE SHOOTING...
NIGHTY-NIGHT, CHUCKLES!
HE'S GOT PACO! I GOTTA RUN!
JUST THEN...
WHAT'S GOIN' ON IN MY STORE?
SUNNUVADOG-- A ROBBERY!
YOU PUNKS! YOU STINKIN' PUNKS! THIS IS THE FIFTH TIME I BEEN HIT THIS MONTH!
HEY, OLD MAN! GO SLOW!
YOU TELL ME WHAT TO DO? IN MY OWN PLACE?!
HUH? THE OWNER'S GOT A GUN!
STOP! I WEBBED HIS HAND TO HIS PISTOL!

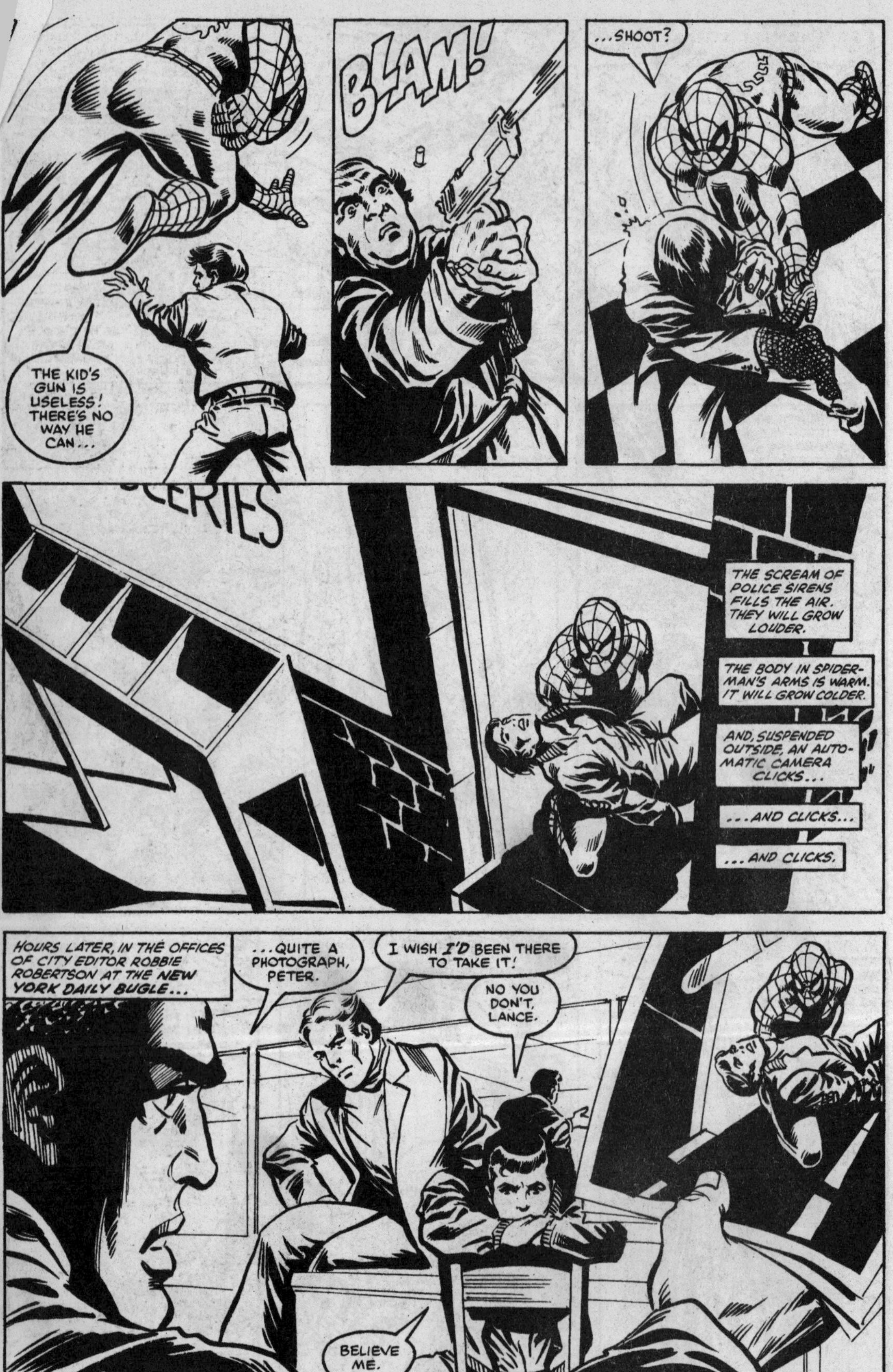
THE KID'S GUN IS USELESS! THERE'S NO WAY HE CAN...
BLAM!
...SHOOT?
CERIES
THE SCREAM OF POLICE SIRENS FILLS THE AIR. THEY WILL GROW LOUDER.
THE BODY IN SPIDER-MAN'S ARMS IS WARM. IT WILL GROW COLDER.
AND, SUSPENDED OUTSIDE, AN AUTOMATIC CAMERA CLICKS...
...AND CLICKS...
...AND CLICKS.
HOURS LATER, IN THE OFFICES OF CITY EDITOR ROBBIE ROBERTSON AT THE NEW YORK DAILY BUGLE...
...QUITE A PHOTOGRAPH, PETER.
I WISH I'D BEEN THERE TO TAKE IT!
NO YOU DON'T, LANCE.
BELIEVE ME.

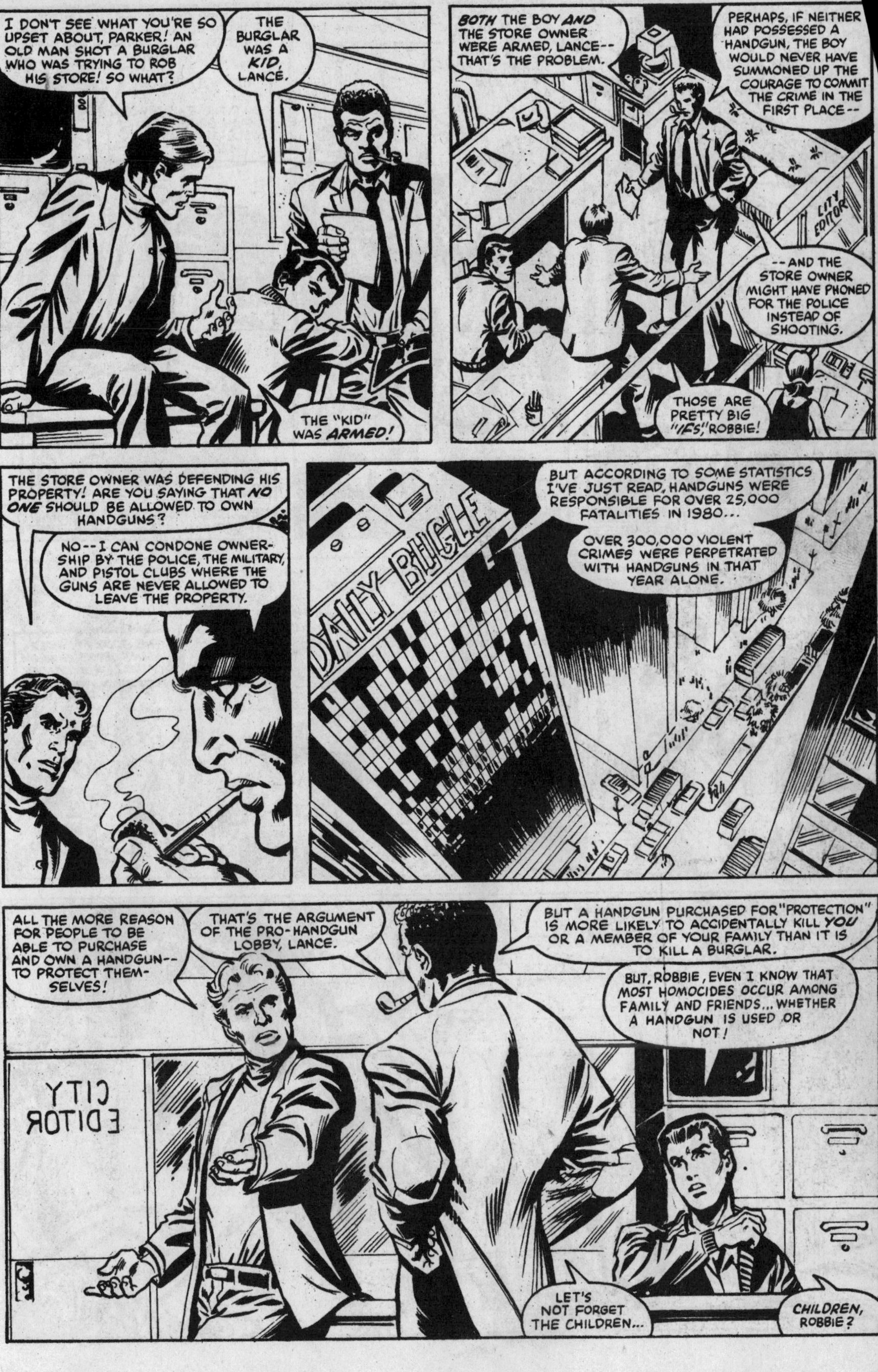
I DON'T SEE WHAT YOU'RE SO UPSET ABOUT, PARKER! AN OLD MAN SHOT A BURGLAR WHO WAS TRYING TO ROB HIS STORE! SO WHAT?
THE BURGLAR WAS A KID, LANCE.
THE "KID" WAS ARMED!
BOTH THE BOY AND THE STORE OWNER WERE ARMED, LANCE-- THAT'S THE PROBLEM.
PERHAPS, IF NEITHER HAD POSSESSED A HANDGUN, THE BOY WOULD NEVER HAVE SUMMONED UP THE COURAGE TO COMMIT THE CRIME IN THE FIRST PLACE--
CITY EDITOR
--AND THE STORE OWNER MIGHT HAVE PHONED FOR THE POLICE INSTEAD OF SHOOTING.
THOSE ARE PRETTY BIG "IFS," ROBBIE!
THE STORE OWNER WAS DEFENDING HIS PROPERTY! ARE YOU SAYING THAT NO ONE SHOULD BE ALLOWED TO OWN HANDGUNS?
NO--I CAN CONDONE OWNERSHIP BY THE POLICE, THE MILITARY, AND PISTOL CLUBS WHERE THE GUNS ARE NEVER ALLOWED TO LEAVE THE PROPERTY.
DAILY BUGLE
BUT ACCORDING TO SOME STATISTICS I'VE JUST READ, HANDGUNS WERE RESPONSIBLE FOR OVER 25,000 FATALITIES IN 1980...
OVER 300,000 VIOLENT CRIMES WERE PERPETRATED WITH HANDGUNS IN THAT YEAR ALONE.
ALL THE MORE REASON FOR PEOPLE TO BE ABLE TO PURCHASE AND OWN A HANDGUN--TO PROTECT THEMSELVES!
THAT'S THE ARGUMENT OF THE PRO-HANDGUN LOBBY, LANCE.
BUT A HANDGUN PURCHASED FOR "PROTECTION" IS MORE LIKELY TO ACCIDENTALLY KILL YOU OR A MEMBER OF YOUR FAMILY THAN IT IS TO KILL A BURGLAR.
BUT, ROBBIE, EVEN I KNOW THAT MOST HOMOCIDES OCCUR AMONG FAMILY AND FRIENDS... WHETHER A HANDGUN IS USED OR NOT!
CITY EDITOR
LET'S NOT FORGET THE CHILDREN...
CHILDREN, ROBBIE?

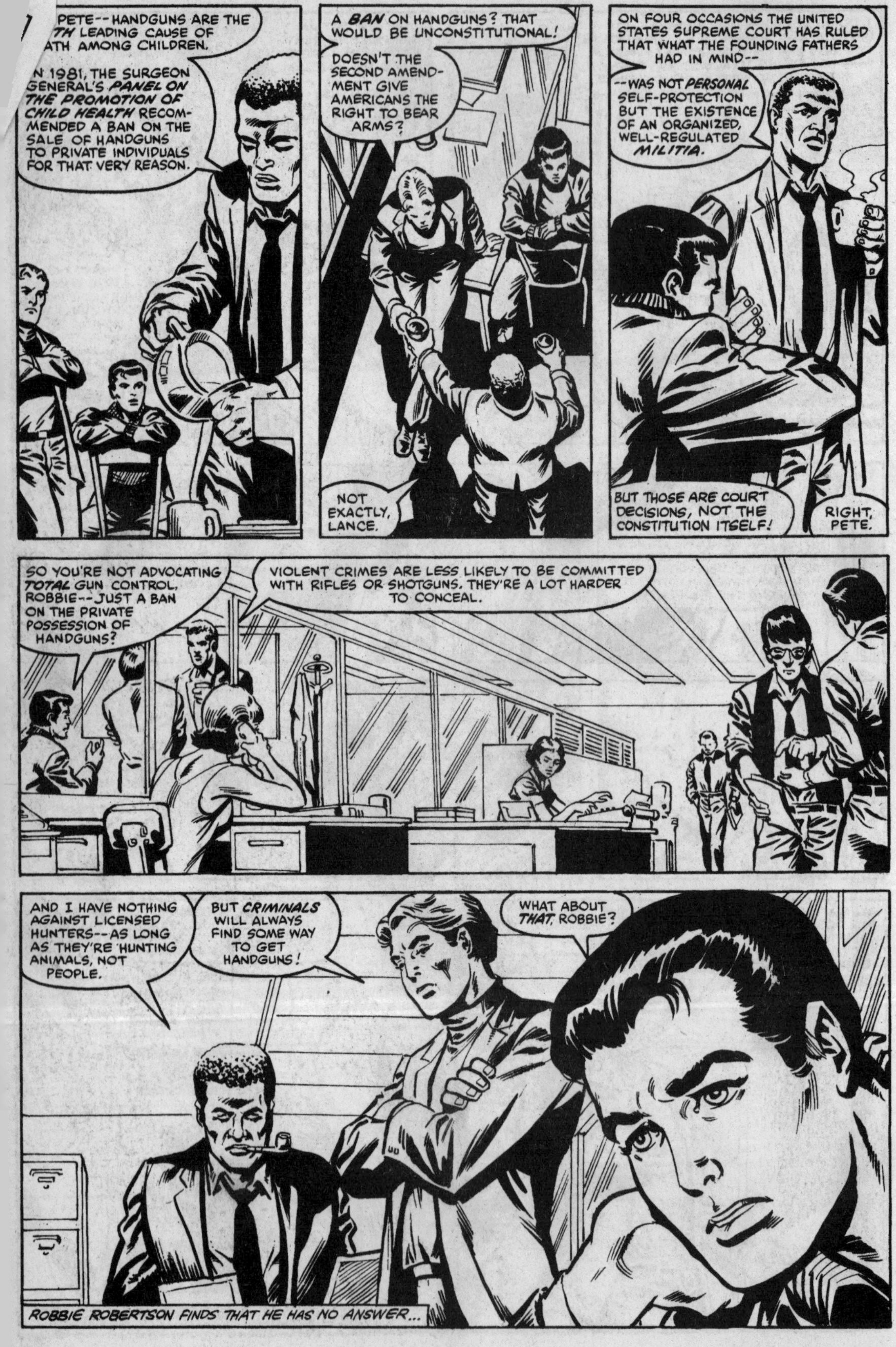

PETE--HANDGUNS ARE THE
TH LEADING CAUSE OF
ATH AMONG CHILDREN.
N 1981, THE SURGEON GENERAL'S *PANEL ON THE PROMOTION OF CHILD HEALTH* RECOMMENDED A BAN ON THE SALE OF HANDGUNS TO PRIVATE INDIVIDUALS FOR THAT VERY REASON.
A *BAN* ON HANDGUNS? THAT WOULD BE UNCONSTITUTIONAL!
DOESN'T THE SECOND AMENDMENT GIVE AMERICANS THE RIGHT TO BEAR ARMS?
NOT EXACTLY, LANCE.
ON FOUR OCCASIONS THE UNITED STATES SUPREME COURT HAS RULED THAT WHAT THE FOUNDING FATHERS HAD IN MIND--
--WAS NOT *PERSONAL* SELF-PROTECTION BUT THE EXISTENCE OF AN ORGANIZED, WELL-REGULATED *MILITIA*.
BUT THOSE ARE COURT DECISIONS, NOT THE CONSTITUTION ITSELF!
RIGHT, PETE.
SO YOU'RE NOT ADVOCATING *TOTAL* GUN CONTROL, ROBBIE--JUST A BAN ON THE PRIVATE POSSESSION OF HANDGUNS?
VIOLENT CRIMES ARE LESS LIKELY TO BE COMMITTED WITH RIFLES OR SHOTGUNS. THEY'RE A LOT HARDER TO CONCEAL.
AND I HAVE NOTHING AGAINST LICENSED HUNTERS--AS LONG AS THEY'RE HUNTING ANIMALS, NOT PEOPLE.
BUT *CRIMINALS* WILL ALWAYS FIND SOME WAY TO GET HANDGUNS!
WHAT ABOUT *THAT*, ROBBIE?
ROBBIE ROBERTSON FINDS THAT HE HAS NO ANSWER...

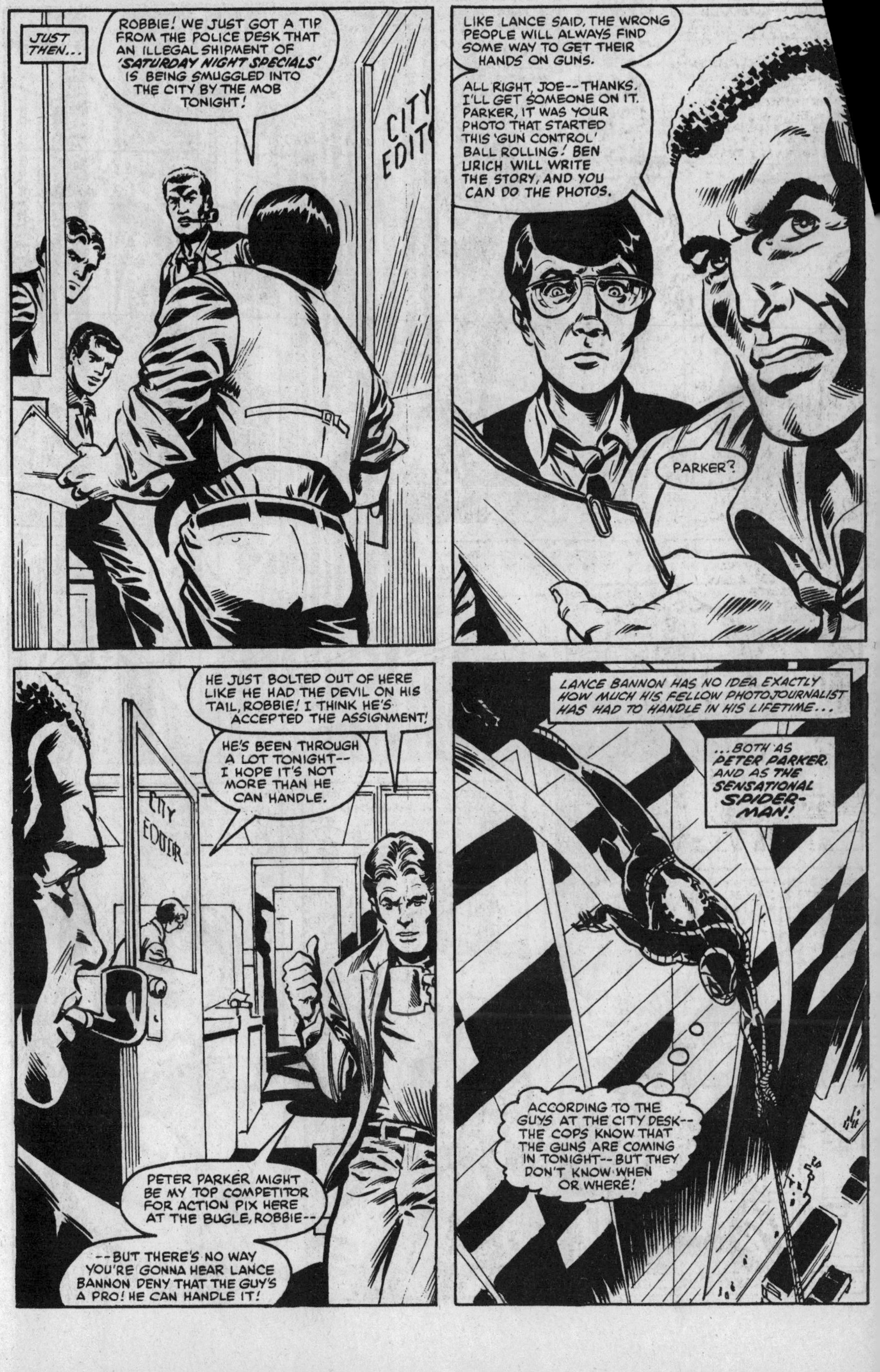
JUST THEN...
ROBBIE! WE JUST GOT A TIP FROM THE POLICE DESK THAT AN ILLEGAL SHIPMENT OF 'SATURDAY NIGHT SPECIALS' IS BEING SMUGGLED INTO THE CITY BY THE MOB TONIGHT!
CITY EDITO
LIKE LANCE SAID, THE WRONG PEOPLE WILL ALWAYS FIND SOME WAY TO GET THEIR HANDS ON GUNS.
ALL RIGHT, JOE--THANKS. I'LL GET SOMEONE ON IT. PARKER, IT WAS YOUR PHOTO THAT STARTED THIS 'GUN CONTROL' BALL ROLLING! BEN URICH WILL WRITE THE STORY, AND YOU CAN DO THE PHOTOS.
PARKER?
HE JUST BOLTED OUT OF HERE LIKE HE HAD THE DEVIL ON HIS TAIL, ROBBIE! I THINK HE'S ACCEPTED THE ASSIGNMENT!
HE'S BEEN THROUGH A LOT TONIGHT-- I HOPE IT'S NOT MORE THAN HE CAN HANDLE.
CITY EDITOR
PETER PARKER MIGHT BE MY TOP COMPETITOR FOR ACTION PIX HERE AT THE BUGLE, ROBBIE--
--BUT THERE'S NO WAY YOU'RE GONNA HEAR LANCE BANNON DENY THAT THE GUY'S A PRO! HE CAN HANDLE IT!
LANCE BANNON HAS NO IDEA EXACTLY HOW MUCH HIS FELLOW PHOTOJOURNALIST HAS HAD TO HANDLE IN HIS LIFETIME...
...BOTH AS PETER PARKER, AND AS THE SENSATIONAL SPIDER-MAN!
ACCORDING TO THE GUYS AT THE CITY DESK-- THE COPS KNOW THAT THE GUNS ARE COMING IN TONIGHT--BUT THEY DON'T KNOW WHEN OR WHERE!

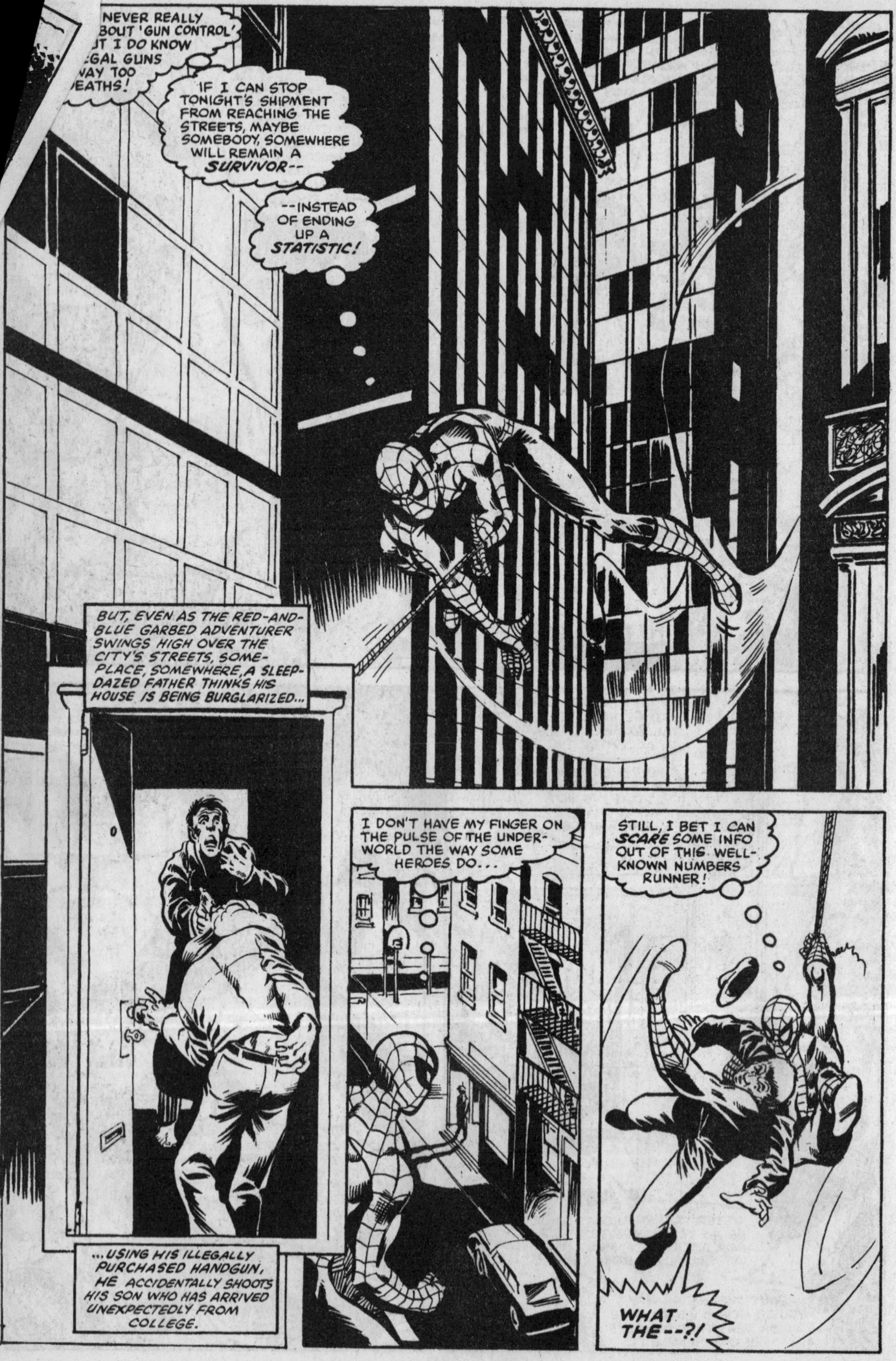
NEVER REALLY BOUT 'GUN CONTROL' UT I DO KNOW EGAL GUNS WAY TOO DEATHS!
IF I CAN STOP TONIGHT'S SHIPMENT FROM REACHING THE STREETS, MAYBE SOMEBODY, SOMEWHERE WILL REMAIN A SURVIVOR--
--INSTEAD OF ENDING UP A STATISTIC!
BUT, EVEN AS THE RED-AND-BLUE GARBED ADVENTURER SWINGS HIGH OVER THE CITY'S STREETS, SOME-PLACE, SOMEWHERE, A SLEEP-DAZED FATHER THINKS HIS HOUSE IS BEING BURGLARIZED...
...USING HIS ILLEGALLY PURCHASED HANDGUN, HE ACCIDENTALLY SHOOTS HIS SON WHO HAS ARRIVED UNEXPECTEDLY FROM COLLEGE.
I DON'T HAVE MY FINGER ON THE PULSE OF THE UNDER-WORLD THE WAY SOME HEROES DO...
STILL, I BET I CAN SCARE SOME INFO OUT OF THIS WELL-KNOWN NUMBERS RUNNER!
WHAT THE--?!

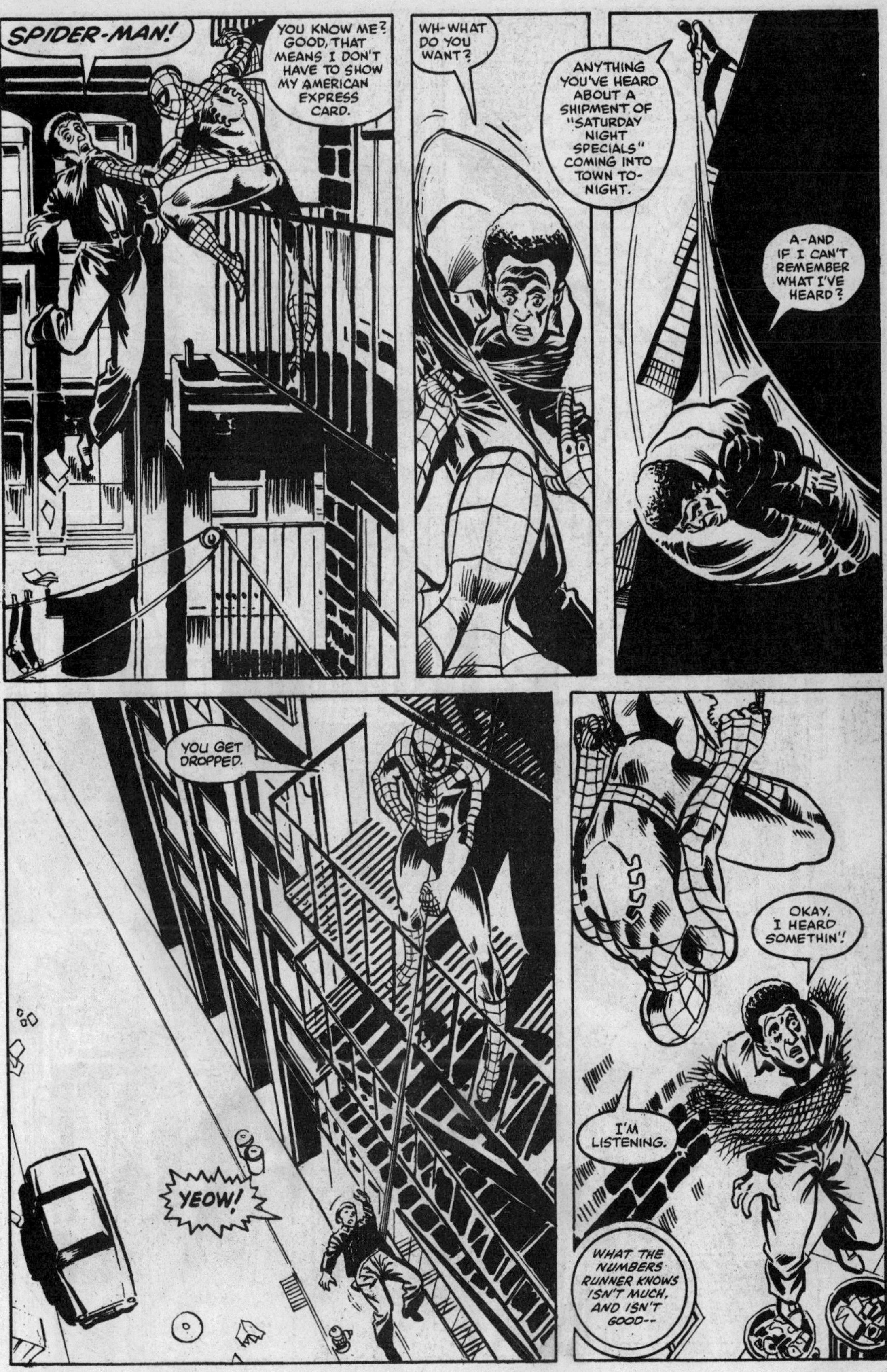
SPIDER-MAN!
YOU KNOW ME? GOOD, THAT MEANS I DON'T HAVE TO SHOW MY AMERICAN EXPRESS CARD.
WH-WHAT DO YOU WANT?
ANYTHING YOU'VE HEARD ABOUT A SHIPMENT OF "SATURDAY NIGHT SPECIALS" COMING INTO TOWN TO-NIGHT.
A-AND IF I CAN'T REMEMBER WHAT I'VE HEARD?
YOU GET DROPPED.
YEOW!
OKAY, I HEARD SOMETHIN'!
I'M LISTENING.
WHAT THE NUMBERS RUNNER KNOWS ISN'T MUCH, AND ISN'T GOOD--

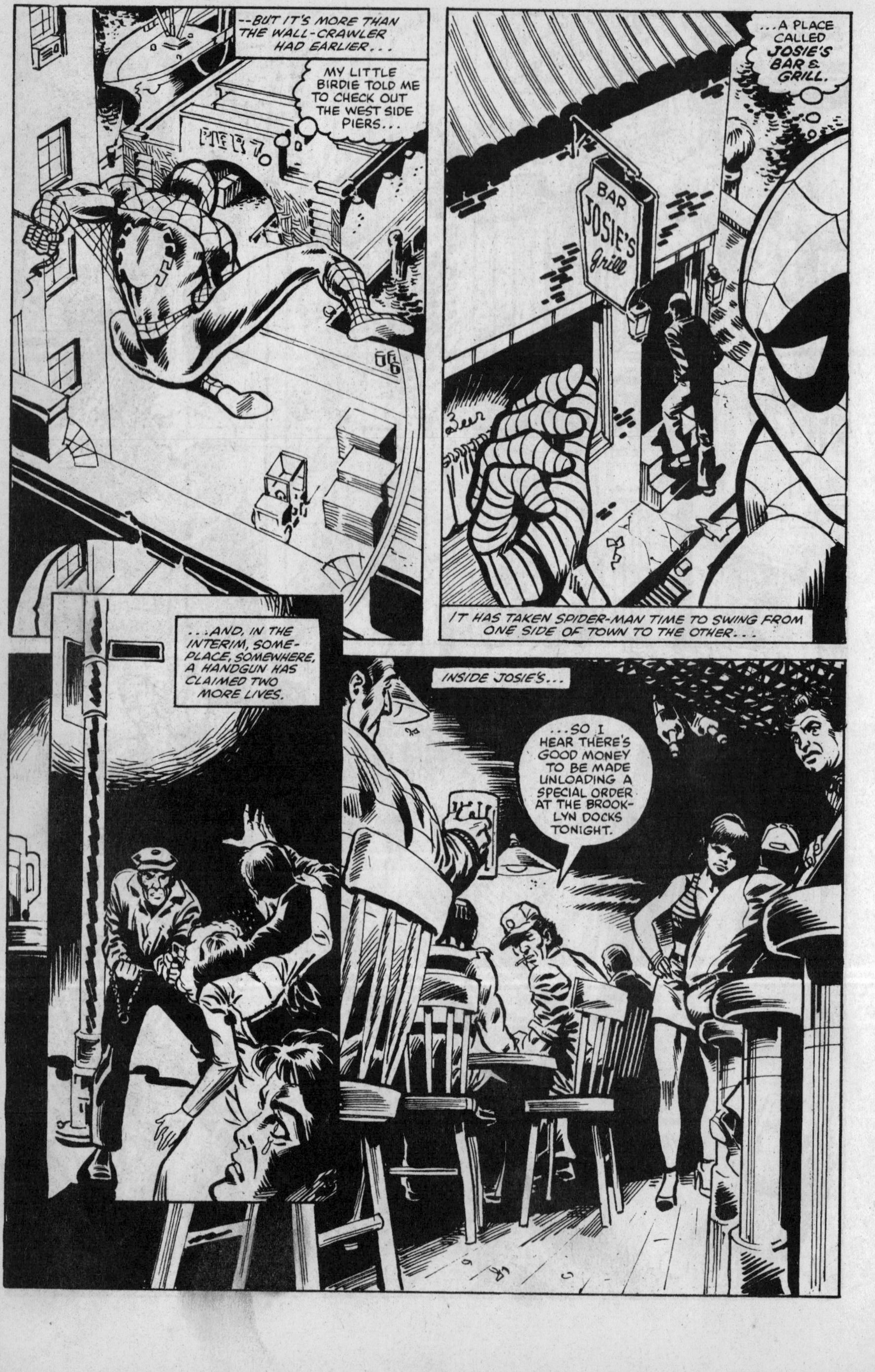
--BUT IT'S MORE THAN THE WALL-CRAWLER HAD EARLIER...
MY LITTLE BIRDIE TOLD ME TO CHECK OUT THE WEST SIDE PIERS...
PIER 7
...A PLACE CALLED JOSIE'S BAR & GRILL.
BAR JOSIE'S Grill
IT HAS TAKEN SPIDER-MAN TIME TO SWING FROM ONE SIDE OF TOWN TO THE OTHER...
...AND, IN THE INTERIM, SOME-PLACE, SOMEWHERE, A HANDGUN HAS CLAIMED TWO MORE LIVES.
INSIDE JOSIE'S...
...SO I HEAR THERE'S GOOD MONEY TO BE MADE UNLOADING A SPECIAL ORDER AT THE BROOK-LYN DOCKS TONIGHT.

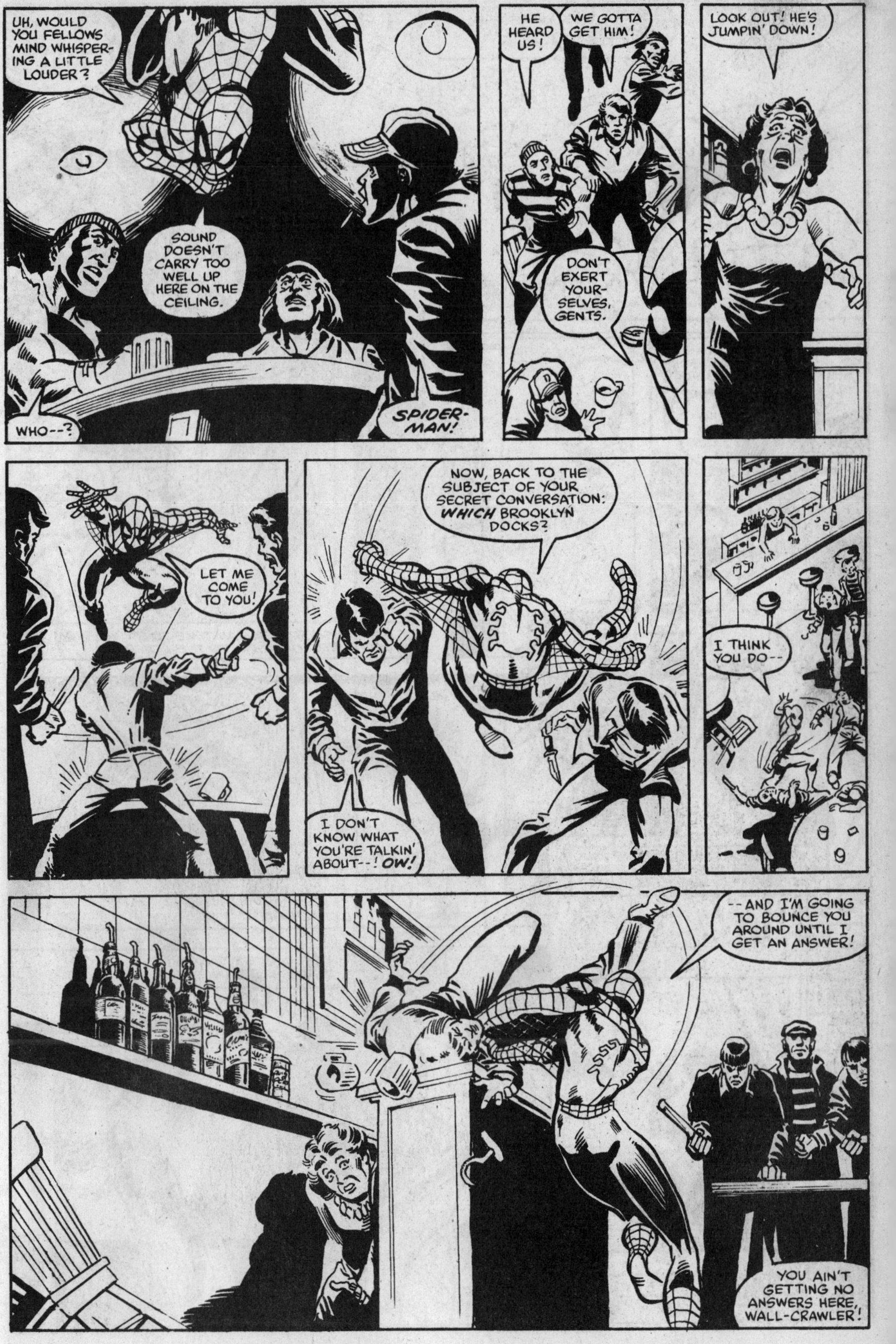
UH, WOULD YOU FELLOWS MIND WHISPERING A LITTLE LOUDER?
SOUND DOESN'T CARRY TOO WELL UP HERE ON THE CEILING.
WHO--?
SPIDER-MAN!
HE HEARD US!
WE GOTTA GET HIM!
DON'T EXERT YOURSELVES, GENTS.
LOOK OUT! HE'S JUMPIN' DOWN!
LET ME COME TO YOU!
NOW, BACK TO THE SUBJECT OF YOUR SECRET CONVERSATION: WHICH BROOKLYN DOCKS?
I DON'T KNOW WHAT YOU'RE TALKIN' ABOUT--! OW!
I THINK YOU DO--
9
--AND I'M GOING TO BOUNCE YOU AROUND UNTIL I GET AN ANSWER!
YOU AIN'T GETTING NO ANSWERS HERE, WALL-CRAWLER!

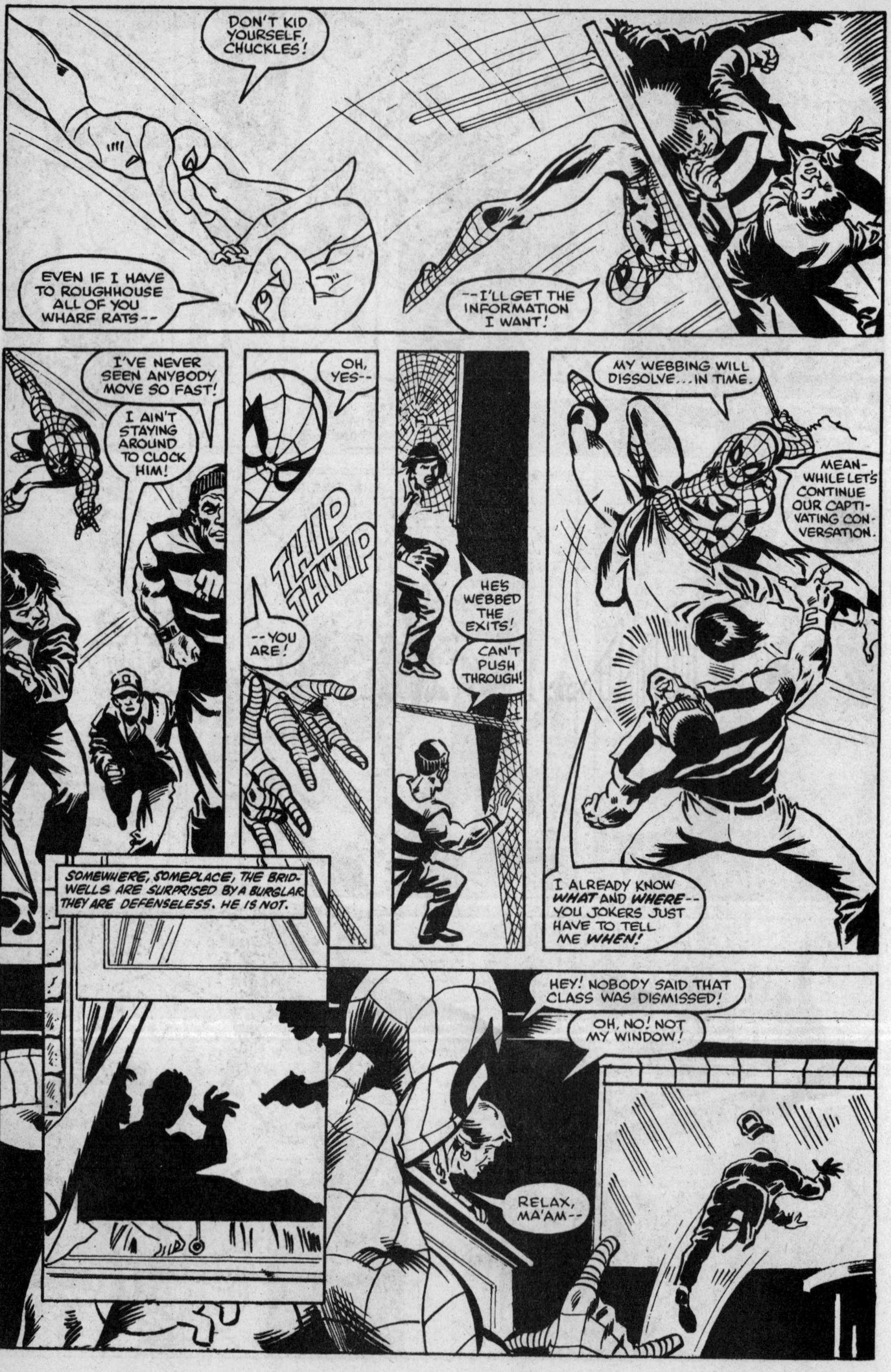
DON'T KID YOURSELF, CHUCKLES!
EVEN IF I HAVE TO ROUGHHOUSE ALL OF YOU WHARF RATS--
--I'LL GET THE INFORMATION I WANT!
I'VE NEVER SEEN ANYBODY MOVE SO FAST!
I AIN'T STAYING AROUND TO CLOCK HIM!
OH, YES--
THIP THWIP
--YOU ARE!
HE'S WEBBED THE EXITS!
CAN'T PUSH THROUGH!
MY WEBBING WILL DISSOLVE... IN TIME.
MEAN-WHILE LET'S CONTINUE OUR CAPTIVATING CON-VERSATION.
I ALREADY KNOW WHAT AND WHERE-- YOU JOKERS JUST HAVE TO TELL ME WHEN!
SOMEWHERE, SOMEPLACE, THE BRID-WELLS ARE SURPRISED BY A BURGLAR. THEY ARE DEFENSELESS. HE IS NOT.
HEY! NOBODY SAID THAT CLASS WAS DISMISSED!
OH, NO! NOT MY WINDOW!
RELAX, MA'AM--

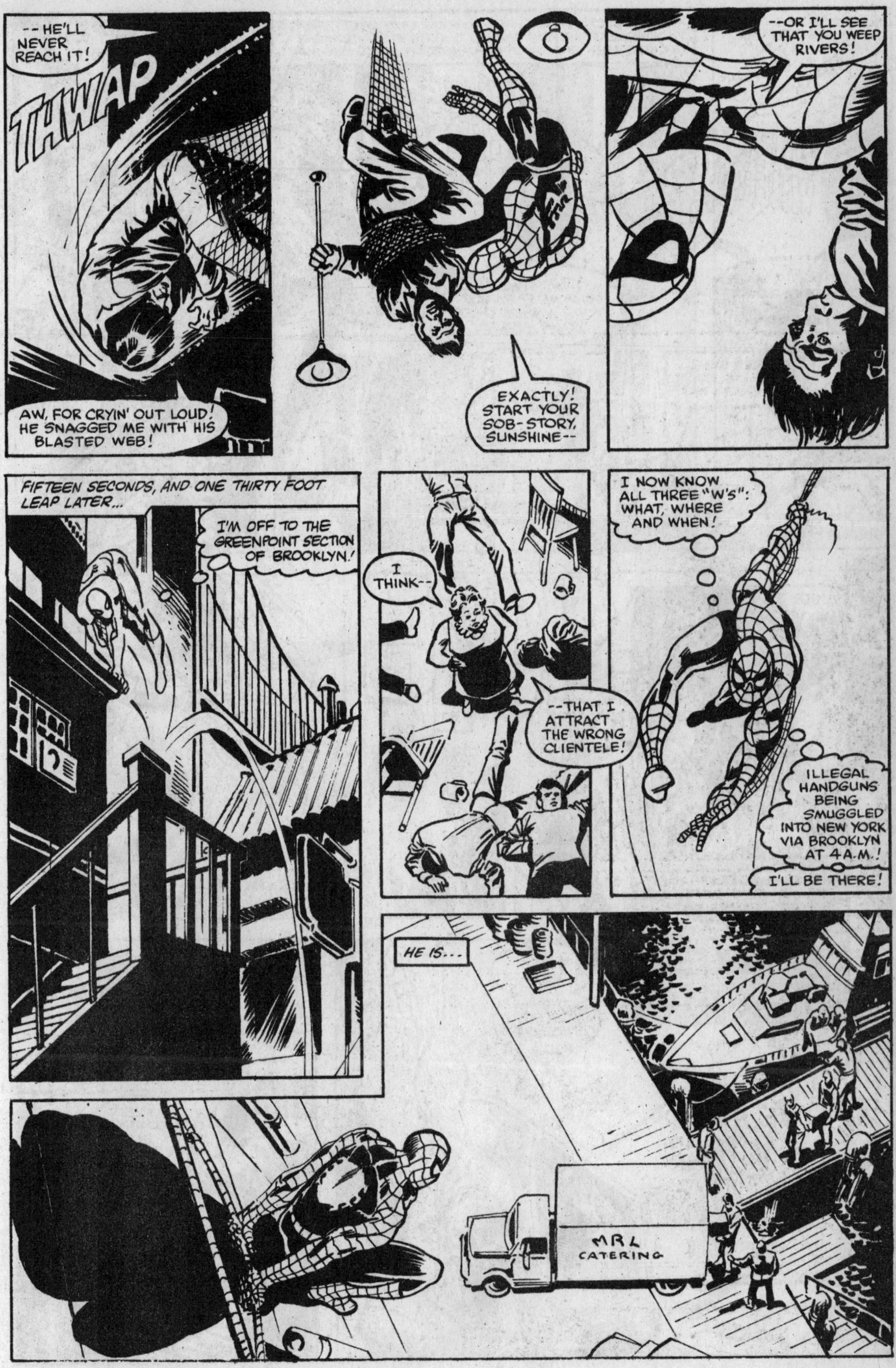
--HE'LL NEVER REACH IT!
THWAP
AW, FOR CRYIN' OUT LOUD! HE SNAGGED ME WITH HIS BLASTED WEB!
EXACTLY! START YOUR SOB-STORY, SUNSHINE--
--OR I'LL SEE THAT YOU WEEP RIVERS!
FIFTEEN SECONDS, AND ONE THIRTY FOOT LEAP LATER...
I'M OFF TO THE GREENPOINT SECTION OF BROOKLYN!
I THINK--
--THAT I ATTRACT THE WRONG CLIENTELE!
I NOW KNOW ALL THREE "W'S": WHAT, WHERE AND WHEN!
ILLEGAL HANDGUNS BEING SMUGGLED INTO NEW YORK VIA BROOKLYN AT 4 A.M.!
I'LL BE THERE!
HE IS...
MRL CATERING

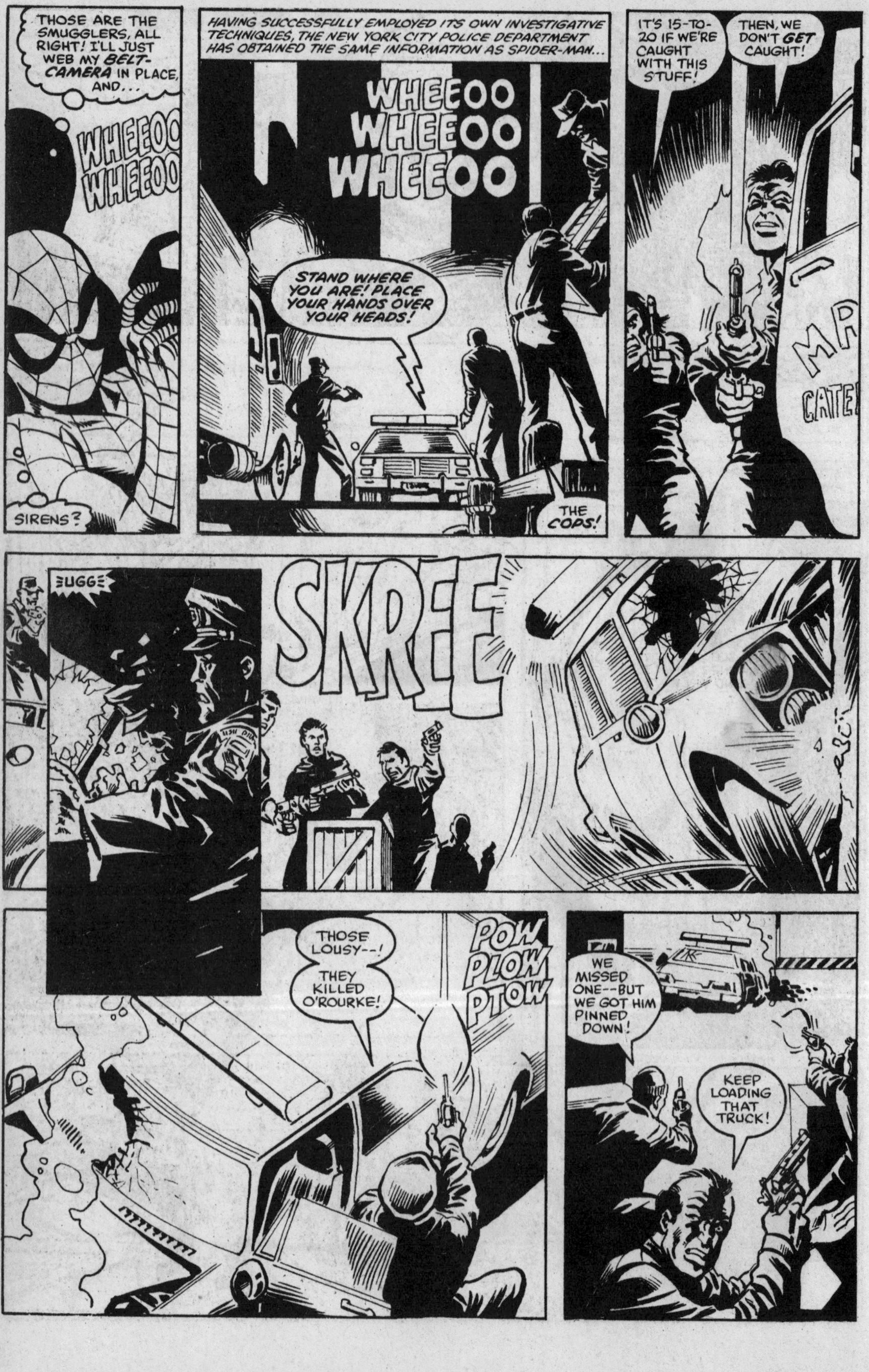
THOSE ARE THE SMUGGLERS, ALL RIGHT! I'LL JUST WEB MY BELT-CAMERA IN PLACE, AND...
WHEEOO WHEEOO
SIRENS?
HAVING SUCCESSFULLY EMPLOYED ITS OWN INVESTIGATIVE TECHNIQUES, THE NEW YORK CITY POLICE DEPARTMENT HAS OBTAINED THE SAME INFORMATION AS SPIDER-MAN...
WHEEOO WHEEOO WHEEOO
STAND WHERE YOU ARE! PLACE YOUR HANDS OVER YOUR HEADS!
THE COPS!
IT'S 15-TO-20 IF WE'RE CAUGHT WITH THIS STUFF!
THEN, WE DON'T GET CAUGHT!
SKREE
THOSE LOUSY--! THEY KILLED O'ROURKE!
POW PLOW PTOW
WE MISSED ONE--BUT WE GOT HIM PINNED DOWN!
KEEP LOADING THAT TRUCK!

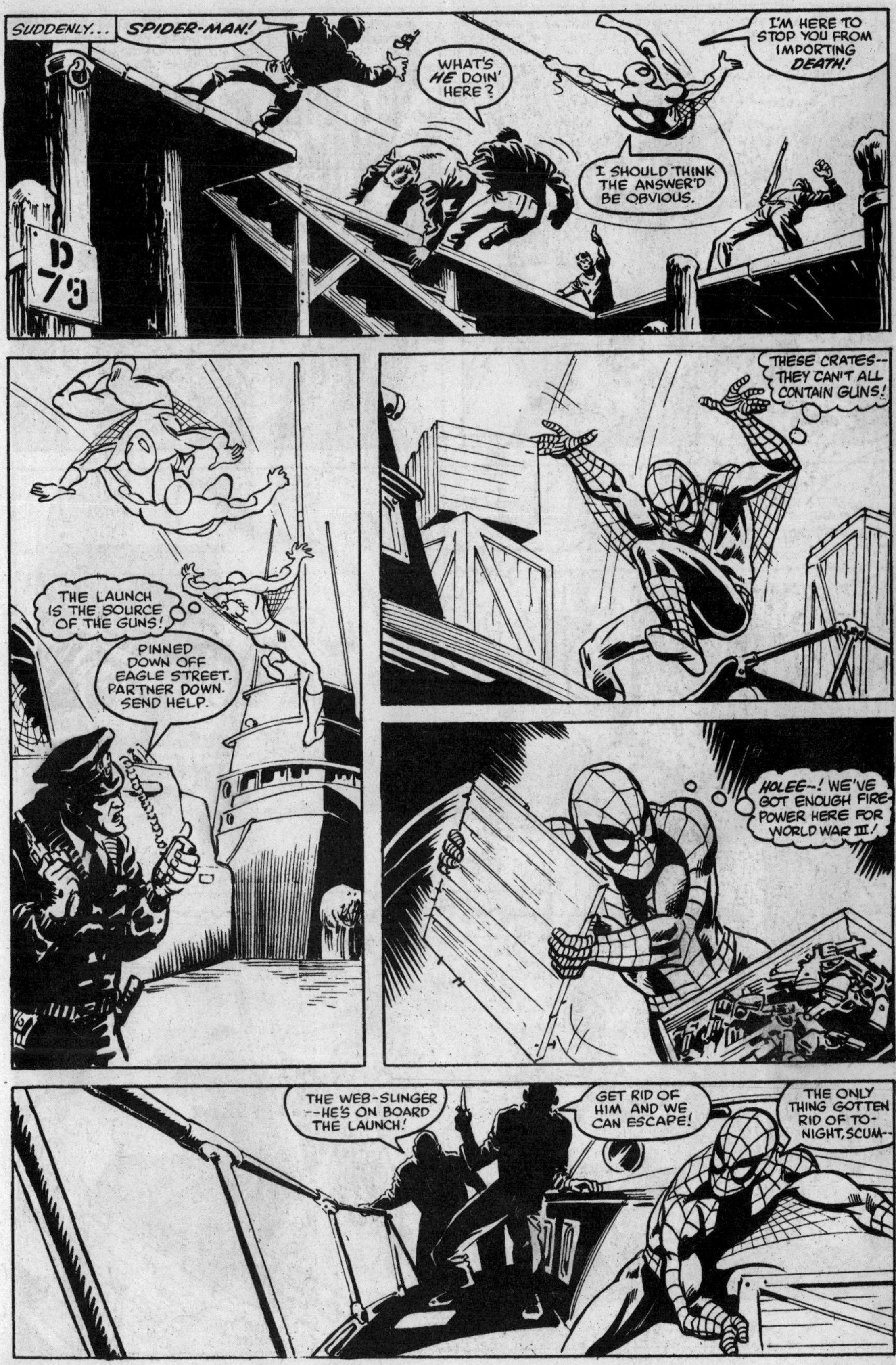
SUDDENLY...
SPIDER-MAN!
WHAT'S HE DOIN' HERE?
I'M HERE TO STOP YOU FROM IMPORTING DEATH!
I SHOULD THINK THE ANSWER'D BE OBVIOUS.
D 79
THE LAUNCH IS THE SOURCE OF THE GUNS!
PINNED DOWN OFF EAGLE STREET. PARTNER DOWN. SEND HELP.
THESE CRATES-- THEY CAN'T ALL CONTAIN GUNS!
HOLEE--! WE'VE GOT ENOUGH FIRE-POWER HERE FOR WORLD WAR III!
THE WEB-SLINGER --HE'S ON BOARD THE LAUNCH!
GET RID OF HIM AND WE CAN ESCAPE!
THE ONLY THING GOTTEN RID OF TO-NIGHT, SCUM--

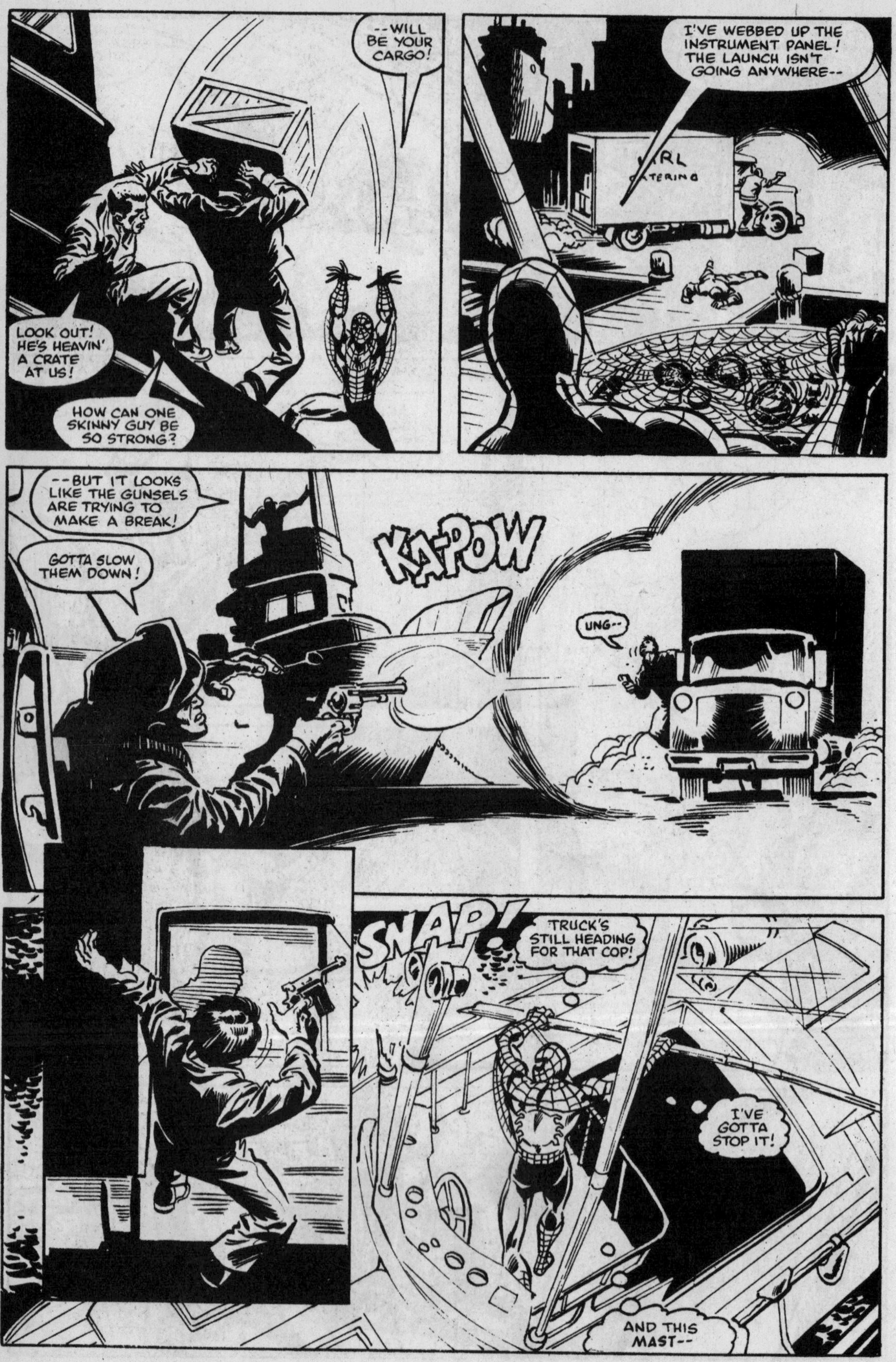
--WILL BE YOUR CARGO!
LOOK OUT! HE'S HEAVIN' A CRATE AT US!
HOW CAN ONE SKINNY GUY BE SO STRONG?
I'VE WEBBED UP THE INSTRUMENT PANEL! THE LAUNCH ISN'T GOING ANYWHERE--
--BUT IT LOOKS LIKE THE GUNSELS ARE TRYING TO MAKE A BREAK!
GOTTA SLOW THEM DOWN!
KA-POW
UNG--
SNAP!
TRUCK'S STILL HEADING FOR THAT COP!
I'VE GOTTA STOP IT!
AND THIS MAST--

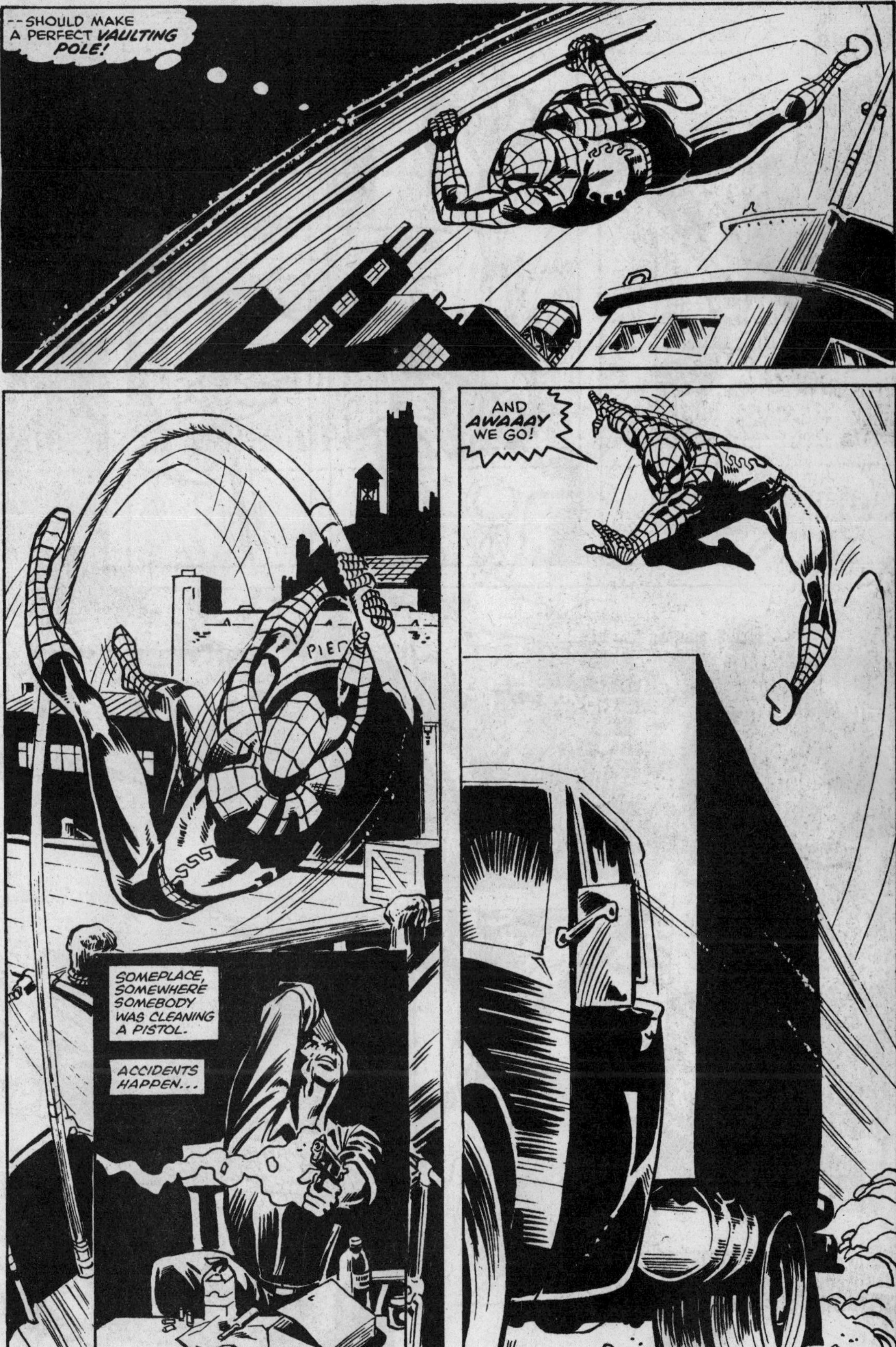
--SHOULD MAKE A PERFECT VAULTING POLE!
PIER
AND AWAAAY WE GO!
SOMEPLACE, SOMEWHERE SOMEBODY WAS CLEANING A PISTOL.
ACCIDENTS HAPPEN...

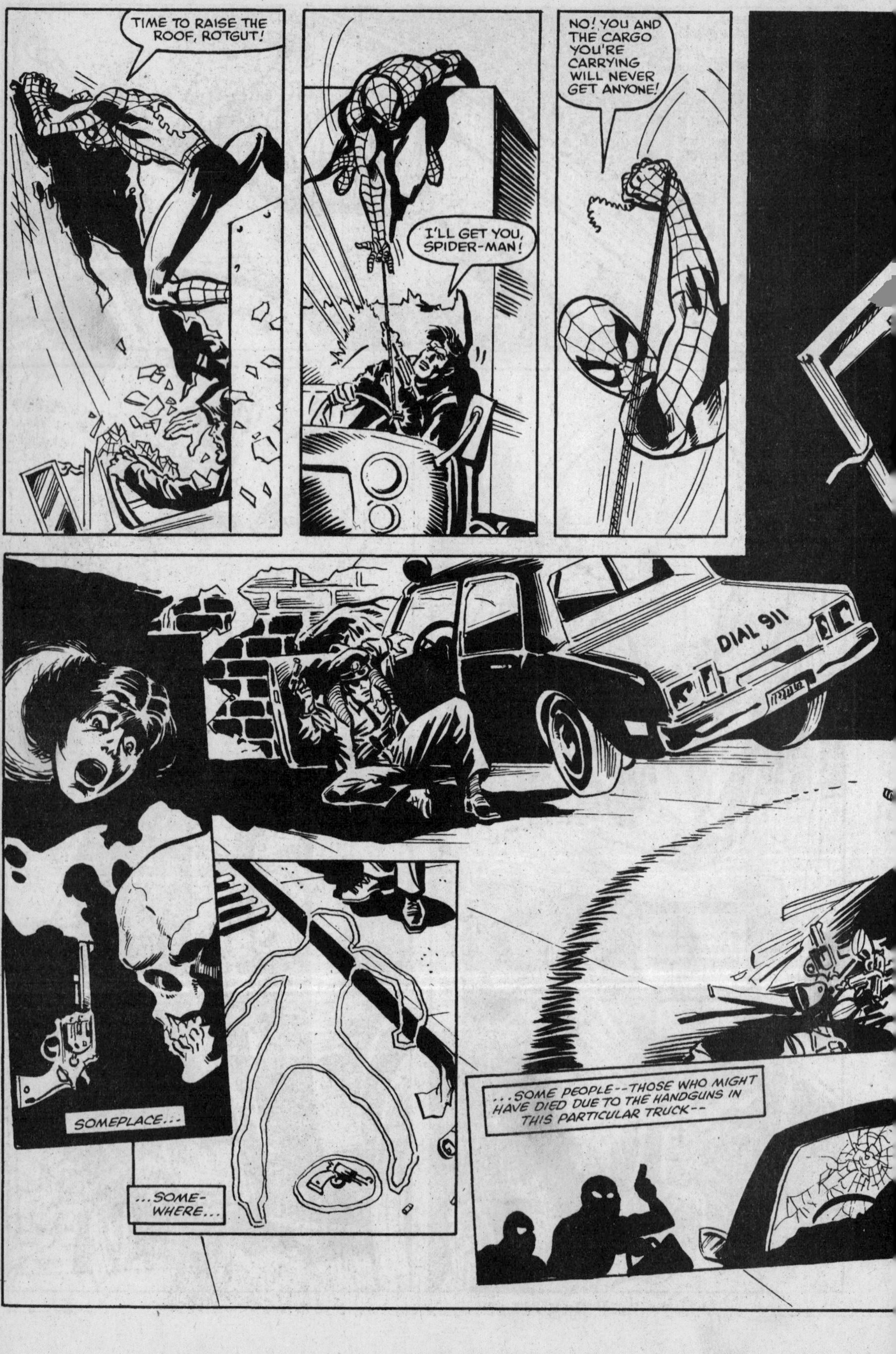
TIME TO RAISE THE ROOF, ROTGUT!
I'LL GET YOU, SPIDER-MAN!
NO! YOU AND THE CARGO YOU'RE CARRYING WILL NEVER GET ANYONE!
DIAL 911
SOMEPLACE...
...SOME-WHERE...
...SOME PEOPLE--THOSE WHO MIGHT HAVE DIED DUE TO THE HANDGUNS IN THIS PARTICULAR TRUCK--

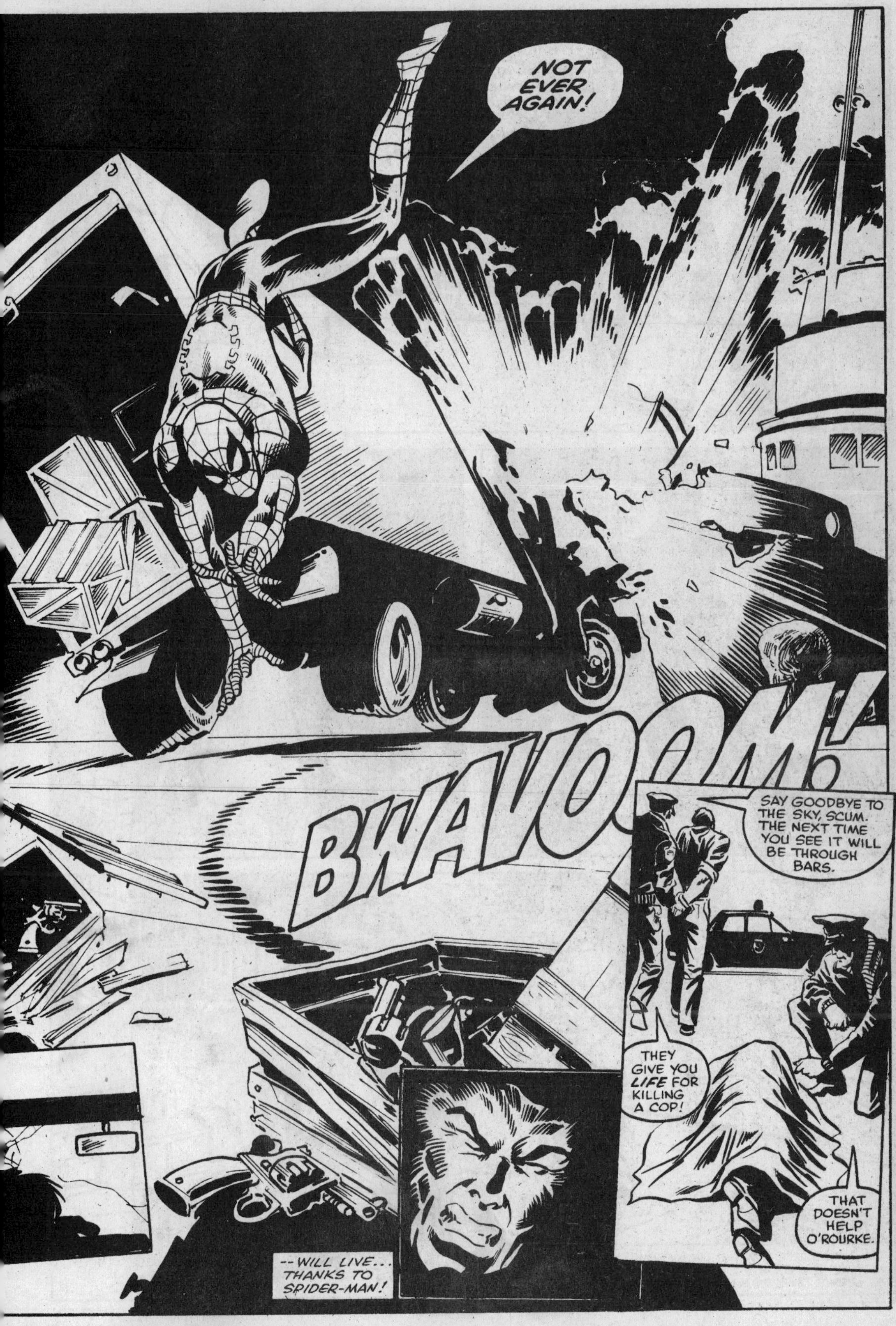
NOT EVER AGAIN!
BWAVOOM!
--WILL LIVE... THANKS TO SPIDER-MAN!
SAY GOODBYE TO THE SKY, SCUM. THE NEXT TIME YOU SEE IT WILL BE THROUGH BARS.
THEY GIVE YOU LIFE FOR KILLING A COP!
THAT DOESN'T HELP O'ROURKE.

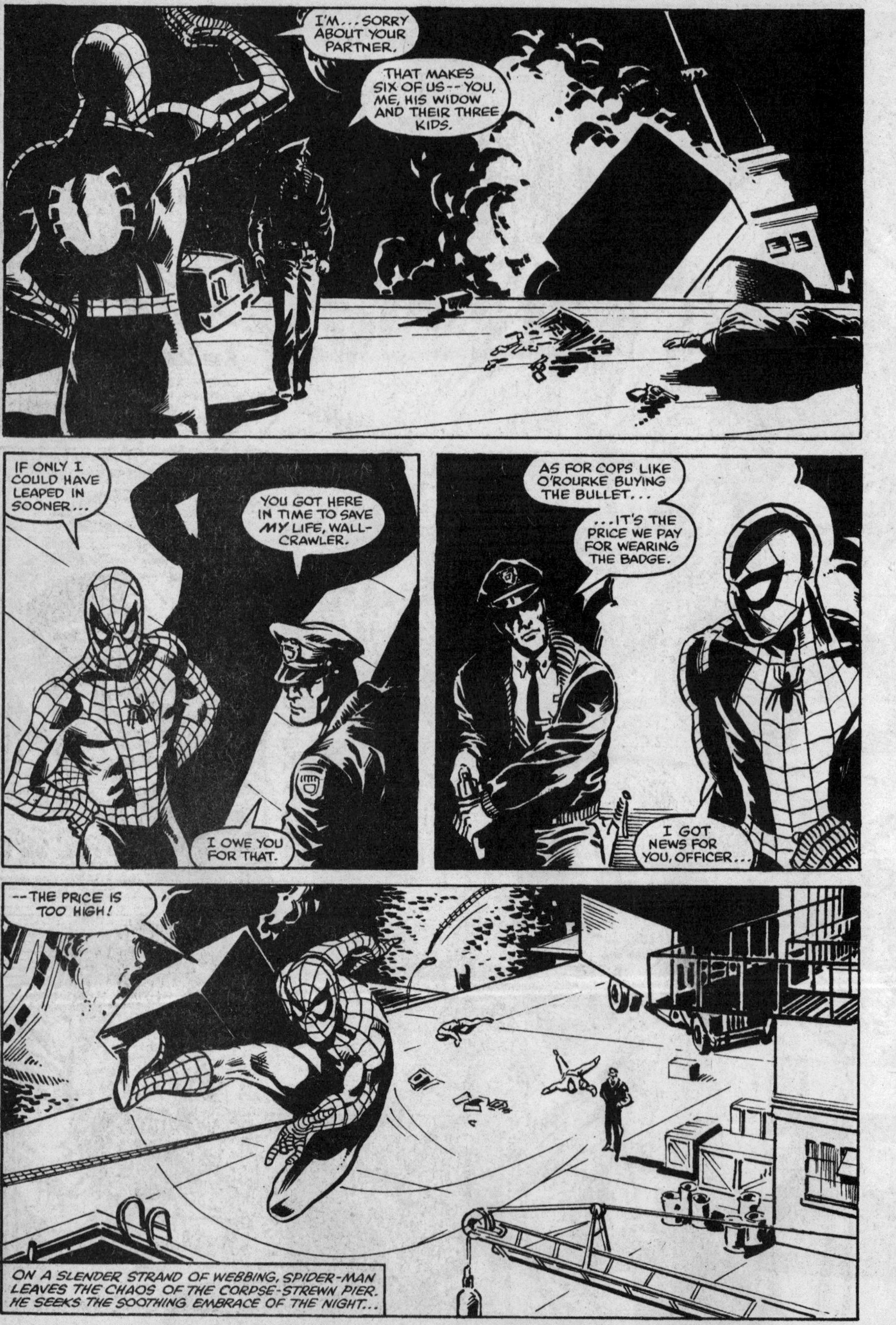
I'M... SORRY ABOUT YOUR PARTNER.
THAT MAKES SIX OF US--YOU, ME, HIS WIDOW AND THEIR THREE KIDS.
IF ONLY I COULD HAVE LEAPED IN SOONER...
YOU GOT HERE IN TIME TO SAVE MY LIFE, WALL-CRAWLER.
I OWE YOU FOR THAT.
AS FOR COPS LIKE O'ROURKE BUYING THE BULLET...
...IT'S THE PRICE WE PAY FOR WEARING THE BADGE.
I GOT NEWS FOR YOU, OFFICER...
--THE PRICE IS TOO HIGH!
ON A SLENDER STRAND OF WEBBING, SPIDER-MAN LEAVES THE CHAOS OF THE CORPSE-STREWN PIER. HE SEEKS THE SOOTHING EMBRACE OF THE NIGHT...

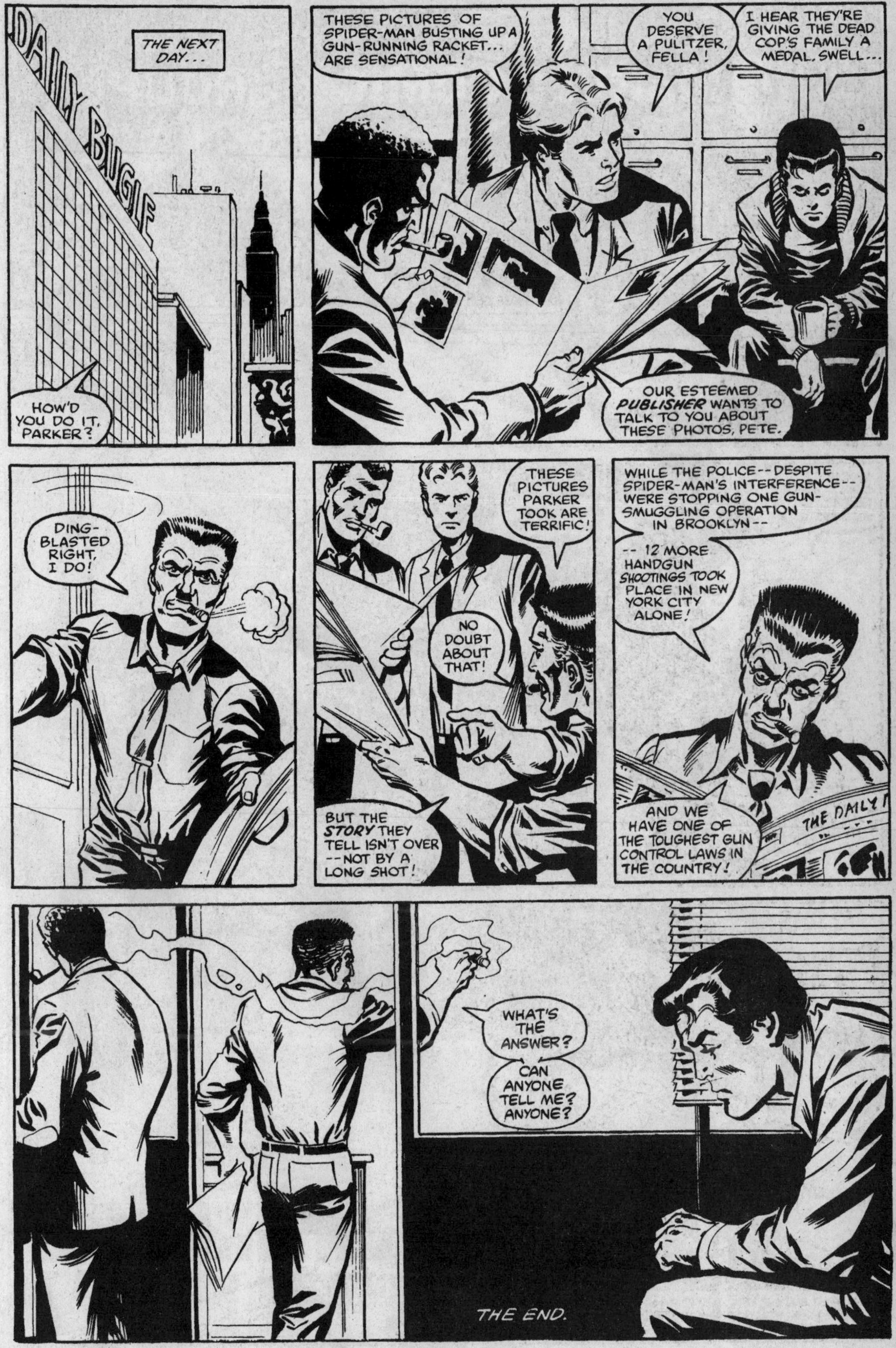
THE NEXT DAY...
DAILY BUGLE
HOW'D YOU DO IT, PARKER?
THESE PICTURES OF SPIDER-MAN BUSTING UP A GUN-RUNNING RACKET... ARE SENSATIONAL!
YOU DESERVE A PULITZER, FELLA!
I HEAR THEY'RE GIVING THE DEAD COP'S FAMILY A MEDAL. SWELL...
OUR ESTEEMED PUBLISHER WANTS TO TALK TO YOU ABOUT THESE PHOTOS, PETE.
DING-BLASTED RIGHT, I DO!
THESE PICTURES PARKER TOOK ARE TERRIFIC!
NO DOUBT ABOUT THAT!
BUT THE STORY THEY TELL ISN'T OVER --NOT BY A LONG SHOT!
WHILE THE POLICE--DESPITE SPIDER-MAN'S INTERFERENCE--WERE STOPPING ONE GUN-SMUGGLING OPERATION IN BROOKLYN--
--12 MORE HANDGUN SHOOTINGS TOOK PLACE IN NEW YORK CITY ALONE!
AND WE HAVE ONE OF THE TOUGHEST GUN CONTROL LAWS IN THE COUNTRY!
THE DAILY
WHAT'S THE ANSWER?
CAN ANYONE TELL ME? ANYONE?
THE END.

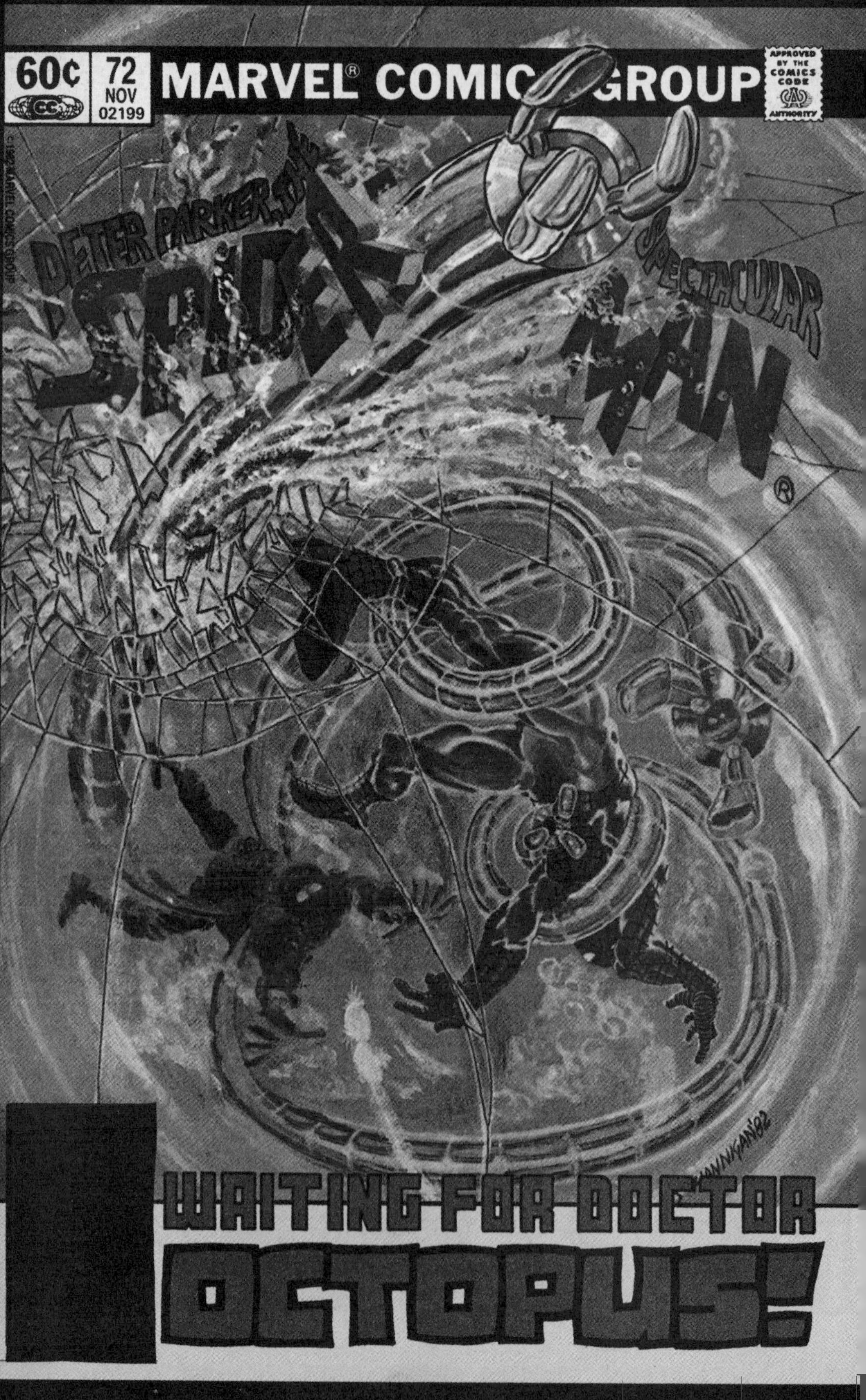
60¢
72
NOV
02199
MARVEL® COMICS GROUP
APPROVED BY THE COMICS CODE AUTHORITY
©1982 MARVEL COMICS GROUP
PETER PARKER, THE SPECTACULAR SPIDER-MAN®
HANNIGAN '82
WAITING FOR DOCTOR OCTOPUS!

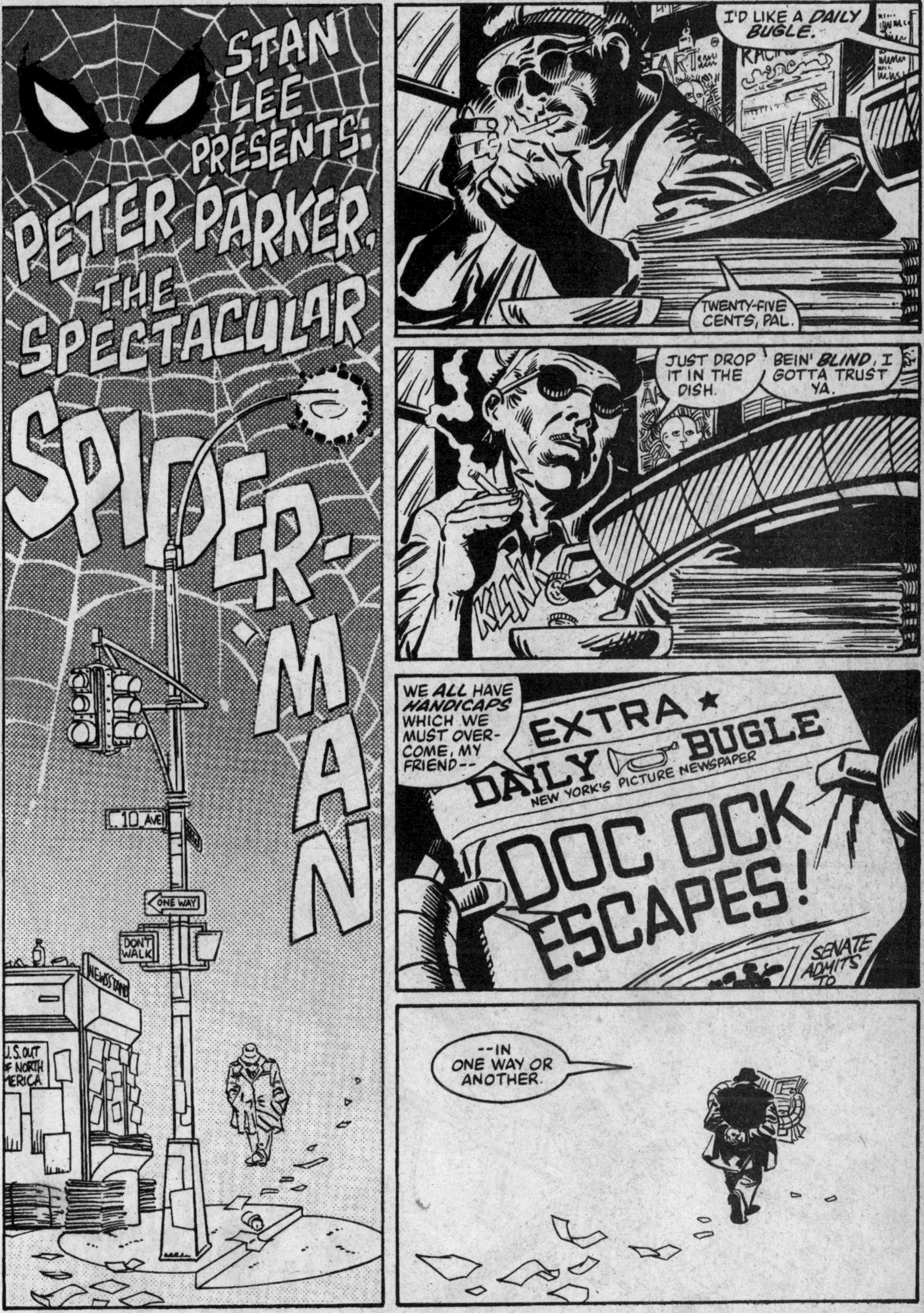
STAN LEE PRESENTS:
PETER PARKER, THE SPECTACULAR
SPIDER-MAN
10 AVE
ONE WAY
DON'T WALK
NEWSSTAND
U.S. OUT OF NORTH AMERICA
I'D LIKE A DAILY BUGLE.
TWENTY-FIVE CENTS, PAL.
JUST DROP IT IN THE DISH.
BEIN' BLIND, I GOTTA TRUST YA.
KLINK
WE ALL HAVE HANDICAPS WHICH WE MUST OVERCOME, MY FRIEND--
EXTRA
DAILY BUGLE
NEW YORK'S PICTURE NEWSPAPER
DOC OCK ESCAPES!
SENATE ADMITS TO
--IN ONE WAY OR ANOTHER.

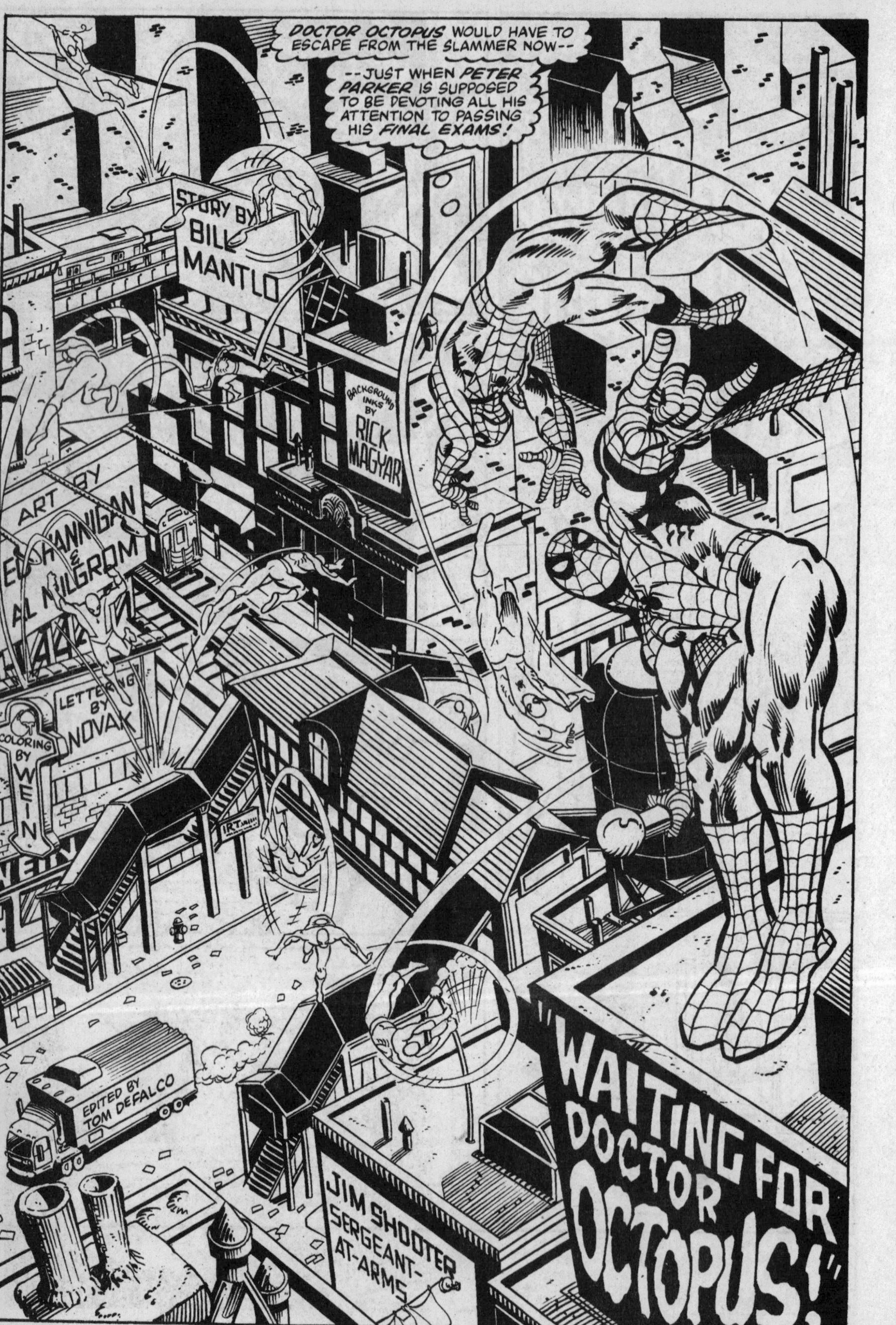
DOCTOR OCTOPUS WOULD HAVE TO ESCAPE FROM THE SLAMMER NOW--
--JUST WHEN PETER PARKER IS SUPPOSED TO BE DEVOTING ALL HIS ATTENTION TO PASSING HIS FINAL EXAMS!
STORY BY BILL MANTLO
BACKGROUND INKS BY RICK MAGYAR
ART BY ED HANNIGAN & AL MILGROM
LETTERING BY NOVAK
COLORING BY WEIN
EDITED BY TOM DEFALCO
JIM SHOOTER SERGEANT-AT-ARMS
"WAITING FOR DOCTOR OCTOPUS!"

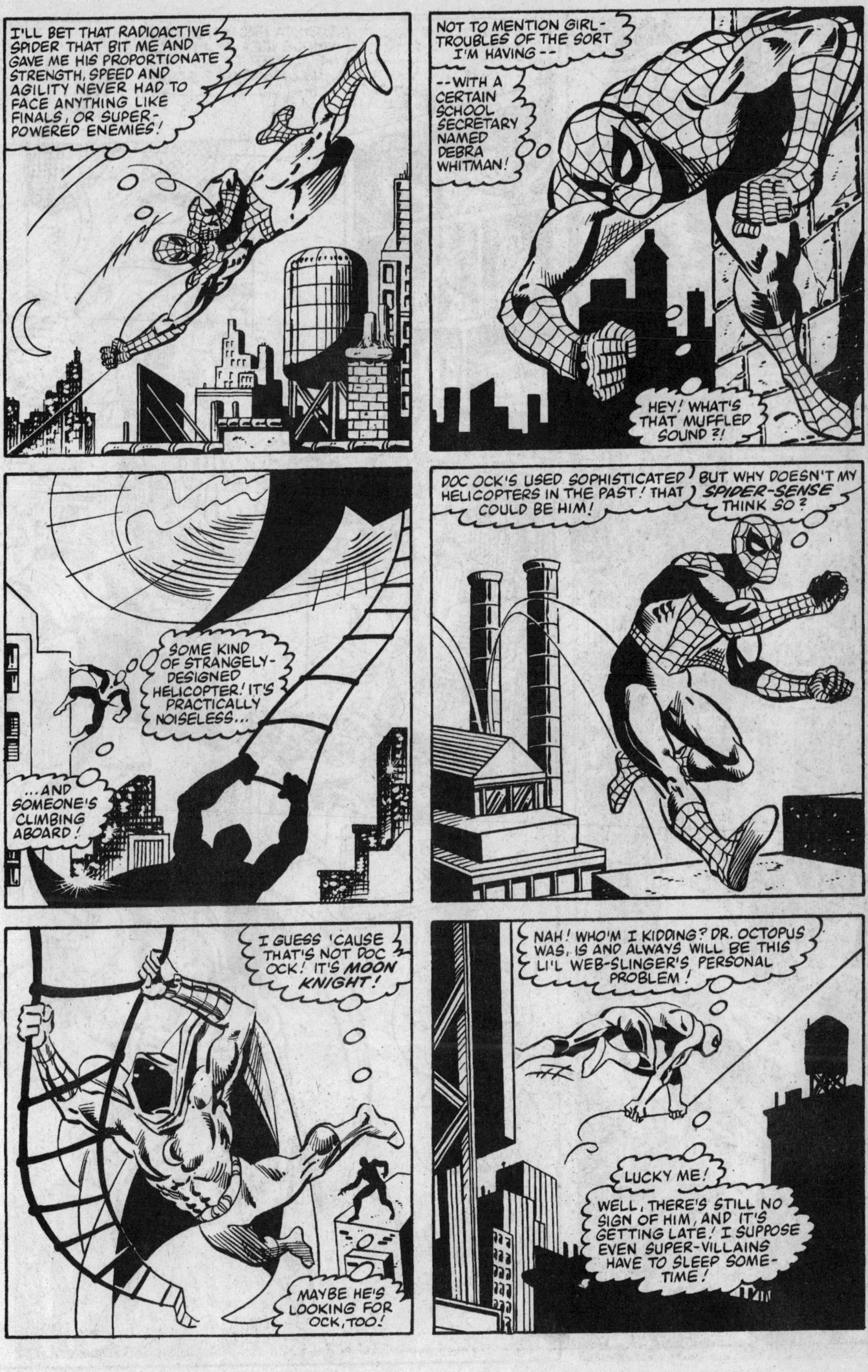
I'LL BET THAT RADIOACTIVE SPIDER THAT BIT ME AND GAVE ME HIS PROPORTIONATE STRENGTH, SPEED AND AGILITY NEVER HAD TO FACE ANYTHING LIKE FINALS, OR SUPER-POWERED ENEMIES!
NOT TO MENTION GIRL-TROUBLES OF THE SORT I'M HAVING--
--WITH A CERTAIN SCHOOL SECRETARY NAMED DEBRA WHITMAN!
HEY! WHAT'S THAT MUFFLED SOUND?!
SOME KIND OF STRANGELY-DESIGNED HELICOPTER! IT'S PRACTICALLY NOISELESS...
...AND SOMEONE'S CLIMBING ABOARD!
DOC OCK'S USED SOPHISTICATED HELICOPTERS IN THE PAST! THAT COULD BE HIM!
BUT WHY DOESN'T MY SPIDER-SENSE THINK SO?
I GUESS 'CAUSE THAT'S NOT DOC OCK! IT'S MOON KNIGHT!
MAYBE HE'S LOOKING FOR OCK, TOO!
NAH! WHO'M I KIDDING? DR. OCTOPUS WAS, IS AND ALWAYS WILL BE THIS LI'L WEB-SLINGER'S PERSONAL PROBLEM!
LUCKY ME!
WELL, THERE'S STILL NO SIGN OF HIM, AND IT'S GETTING LATE! I SUPPOSE EVEN SUPER-VILLAINS HAVE TO SLEEP SOME-TIME!

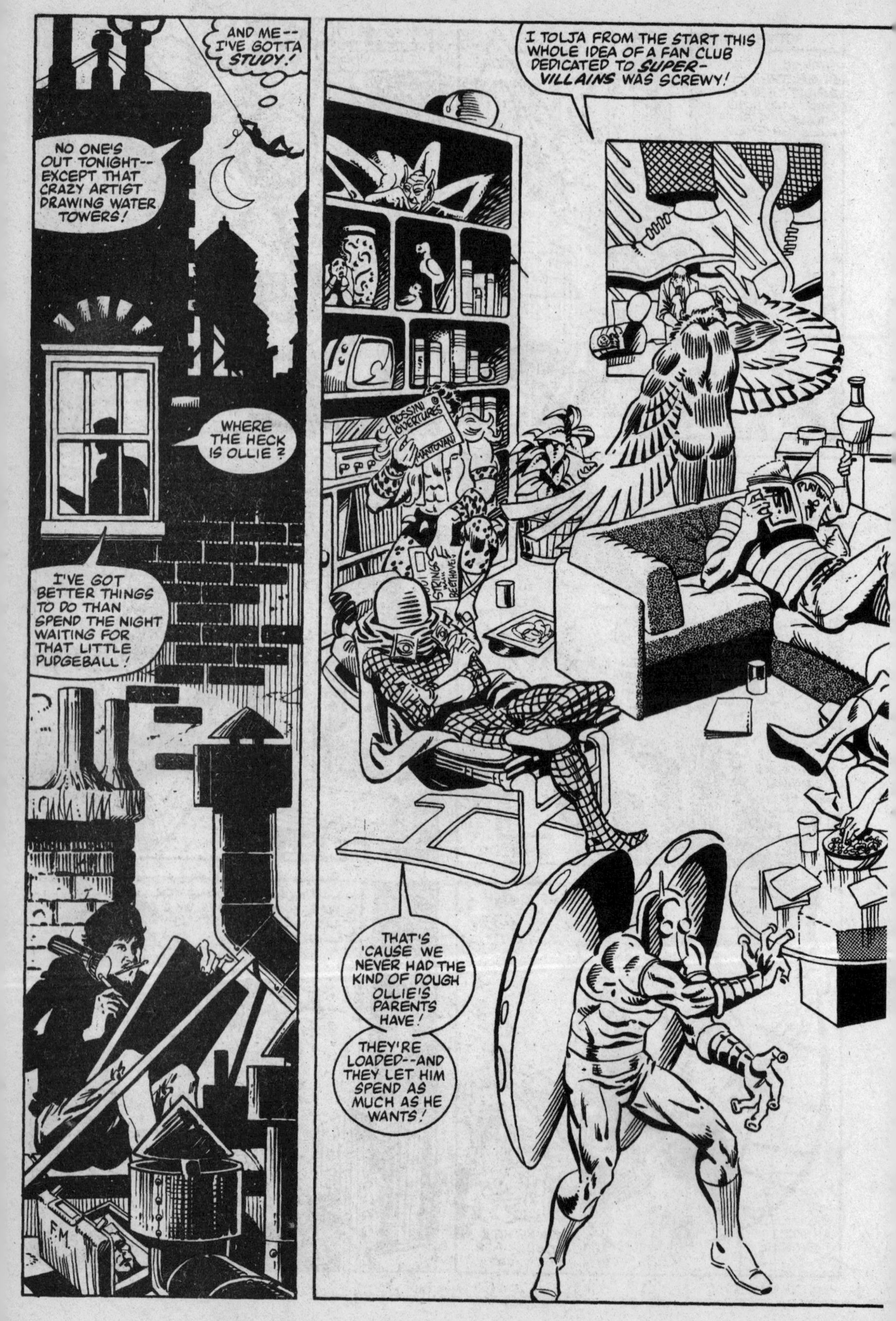
AND ME-- I'VE GOTTA STUDY!
NO ONE'S OUT TONIGHT-- EXCEPT THAT CRAZY ARTIST DRAWING WATER TOWERS!
WHERE THE HECK IS OLLIE?
I'VE GOT BETTER THINGS TO DO THAN SPEND THE NIGHT WAITING FOR THAT LITTLE PUDGEBALL!
F.M.
I TOLJA FROM THE START THIS WHOLE IDEA OF A FAN CLUB DEDICATED TO SUPER-VILLAINS WAS SCREWY!
ROSSINI OVERTURES
MANTOVANI
THAT'S 'CAUSE WE NEVER HAD THE KIND OF DOUGH OLLIE'S PARENTS HAVE!
THEY'RE LOADED--AND THEY LET HIM SPEND AS MUCH AS HE WANTS!

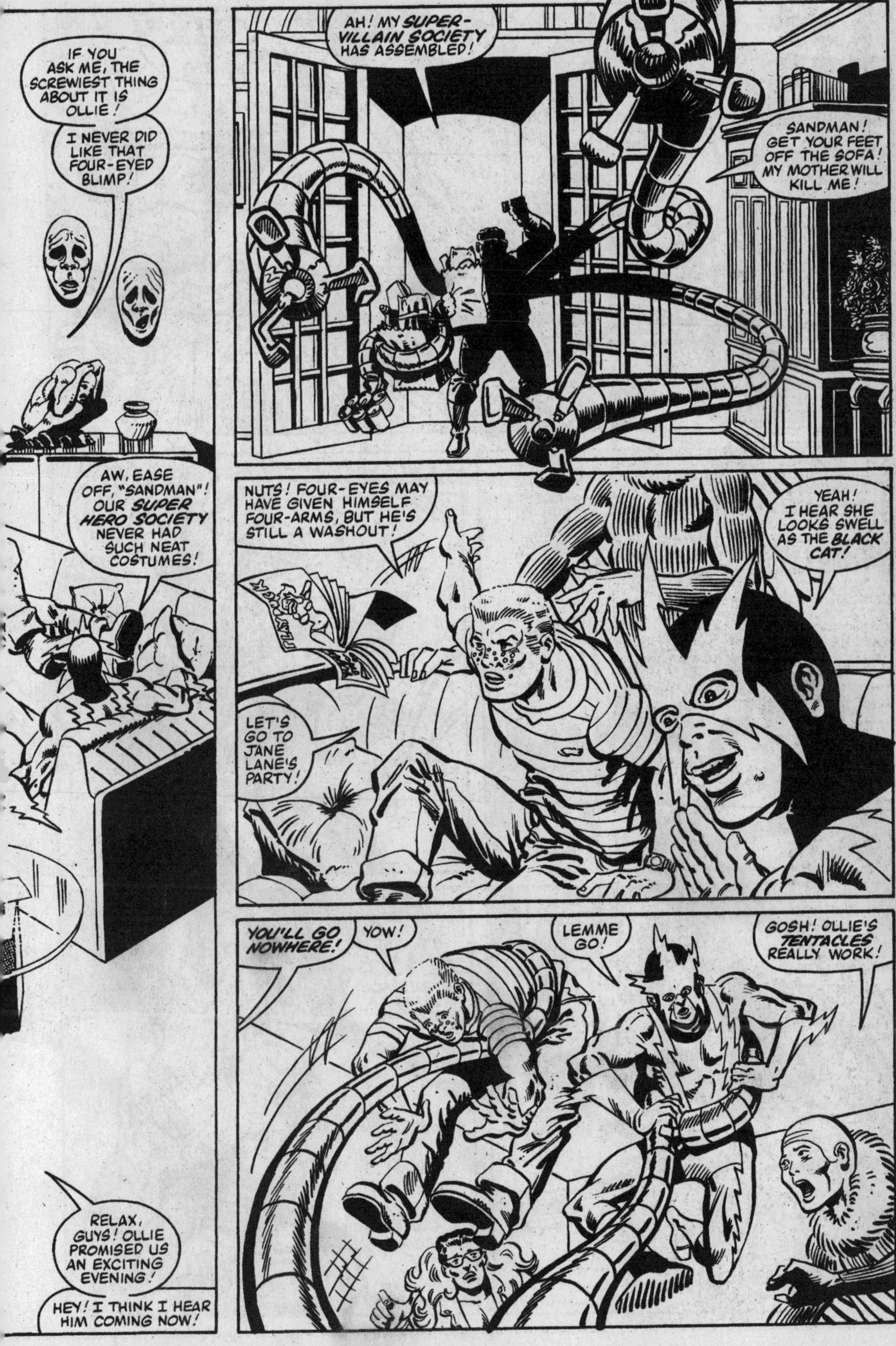
IF YOU ASK ME, THE SCREWIEST THING ABOUT IT IS OLLIE!
I NEVER DID LIKE THAT FOUR-EYED BLIMP!
AH! MY SUPER-VILLAIN SOCIETY HAS ASSEMBLED!
SANDMAN! GET YOUR FEET OFF THE SOFA! MY MOTHER WILL KILL ME!
AW, EASE OFF, "SANDMAN"! OUR SUPER HERO SOCIETY NEVER HAD SUCH NEAT COSTUMES!
NUTS! FOUR-EYES MAY HAVE GIVEN HIMSELF FOUR-ARMS, BUT HE'S STILL A WASHOUT!
YEAH! I HEAR SHE LOOKS SWELL AS THE BLACK CAT!
LET'S GO TO JANE LANE'S PARTY!
RELAX, GUYS! OLLIE PROMISED US AN EXCITING EVENING!
HEY! I THINK I HEAR HIM COMING NOW!
YOU'LL GO NOWHERE!
YOW!
LEMME GO!
GOSH! OLLIE'S TENTACLES REALLY WORK!

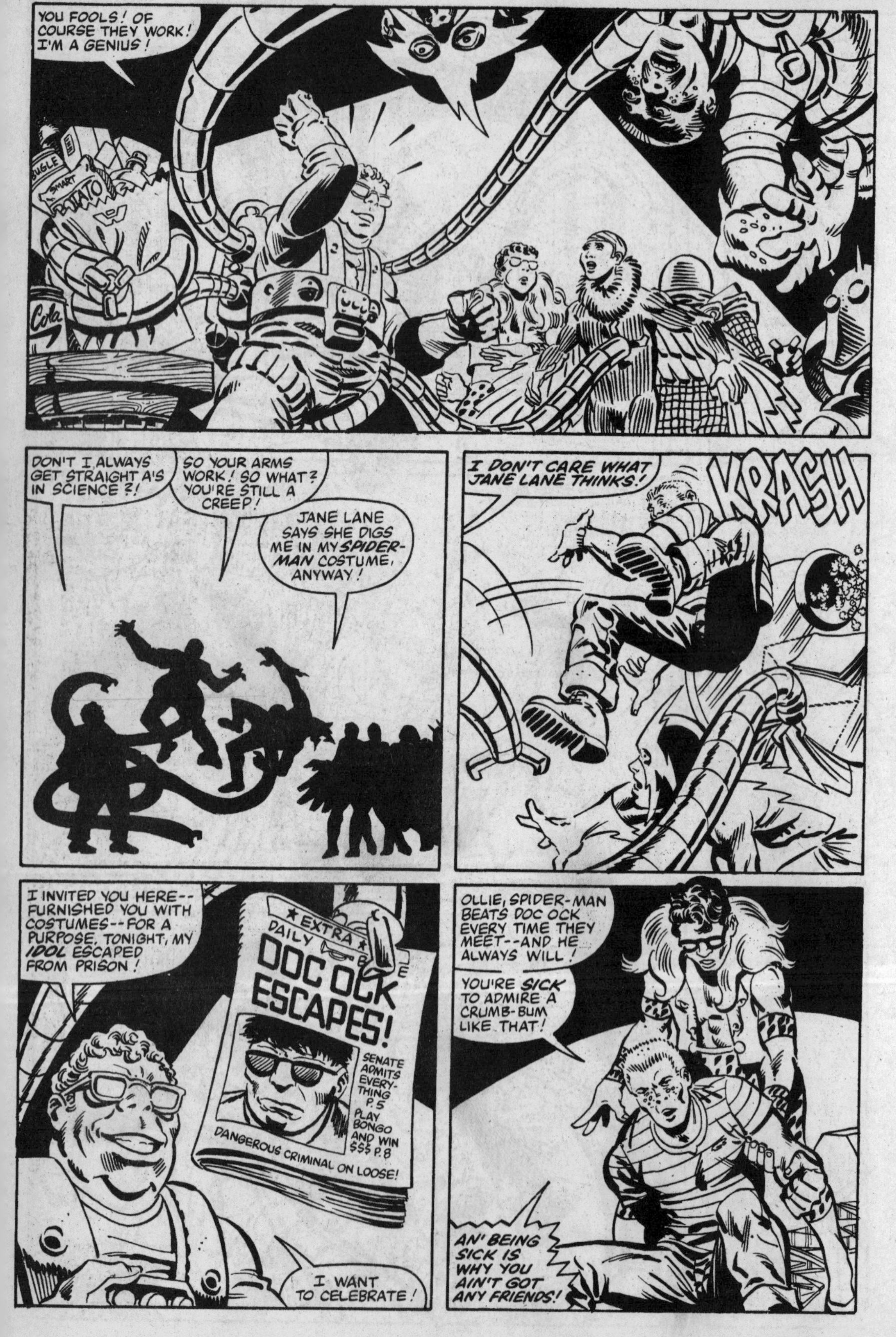
YOU FOOLS! OF COURSE THEY WORK! I'M A GENIUS!
BUGLE
SMART POTATO
Cola
DON'T I ALWAYS GET STRAIGHT A'S IN SCIENCE ?!
SO YOUR ARMS WORK! SO WHAT? YOU'RE STILL A CREEP!
JANE LANE SAYS SHE DIGS ME IN MY *SPIDER-MAN* COSTUME, ANYWAY!
I DON'T CARE WHAT JANE LANE THINKS!
KRASH
I INVITED YOU HERE-- FURNISHED YOU WITH COSTUMES--FOR A PURPOSE. TONIGHT, MY *IDOL* ESCAPED FROM PRISON!
★ EXTRA ★
DAILY
DOC OCK ESCAPES!
SENATE ADMITS EVERYTHING P.5
PLAY BONGO AND WIN $$$ P.8
DANGEROUS CRIMINAL ON LOOSE!
I WANT TO CELEBRATE!
OLLIE, SPIDER-MAN BEATS DOC OCK EVERY TIME THEY MEET--AND HE ALWAYS WILL!
YOU'RE *SICK* TO ADMIRE A CRUMB-BUM LIKE THAT!
AN' BEING SICK IS WHY YOU AIN'T GOT ANY FRIENDS!

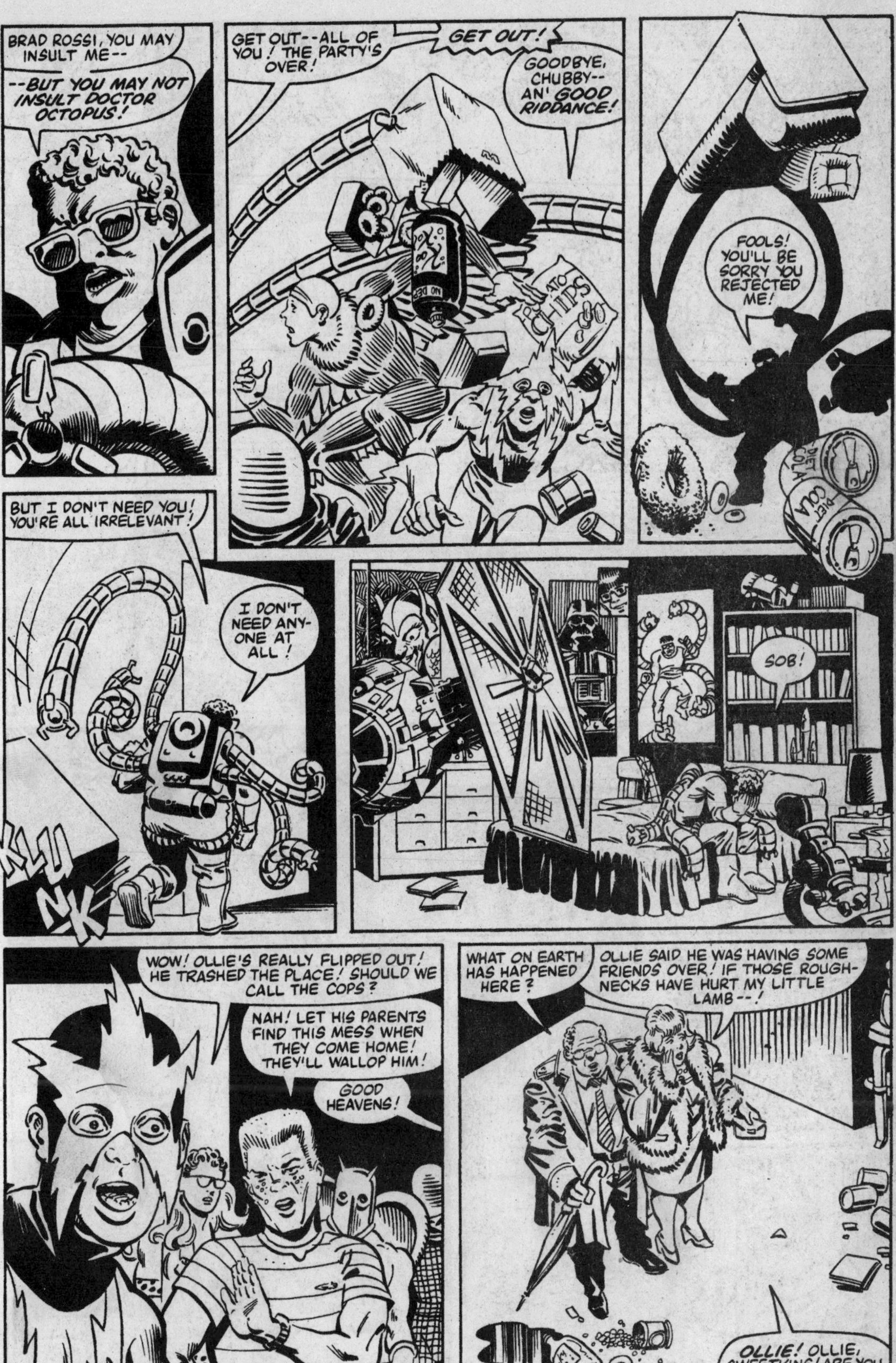
BRAD ROSSI, YOU MAY INSULT ME--
--BUT YOU MAY NOT INSULT DOCTOR OCTOPUS!
GET OUT--ALL OF YOU! THE PARTY'S OVER!
GET OUT!
GOODBYE, CHUBBY-- AN' GOOD RIDDANCE!
POTATO CHIPS
FOOLS! YOU'LL BE SORRY YOU REJECTED ME!
DIET COLA
DIET COLA
BUT I DON'T NEED YOU! YOU'RE ALL IRRELEVANT!
I DON'T NEED ANY-ONE AT ALL!
KLUNK
SOB!
WOW! OLLIE'S REALLY FLIPPED OUT! HE TRASHED THE PLACE! SHOULD WE CALL THE COPS?
NAH! LET HIS PARENTS FIND THIS MESS WHEN THEY COME HOME! THEY'LL WALLOP HIM!
GOOD HEAVENS!
WHAT ON EARTH HAS HAPPENED HERE?
OLLIE SAID HE WAS HAVING SOME FRIENDS OVER! IF THOSE ROUGH-NECKS HAVE HURT MY LITTLE LAMB--!
OLLIE! OLLIE, SWEETKINS! ARE YOU ALL RIGHT?

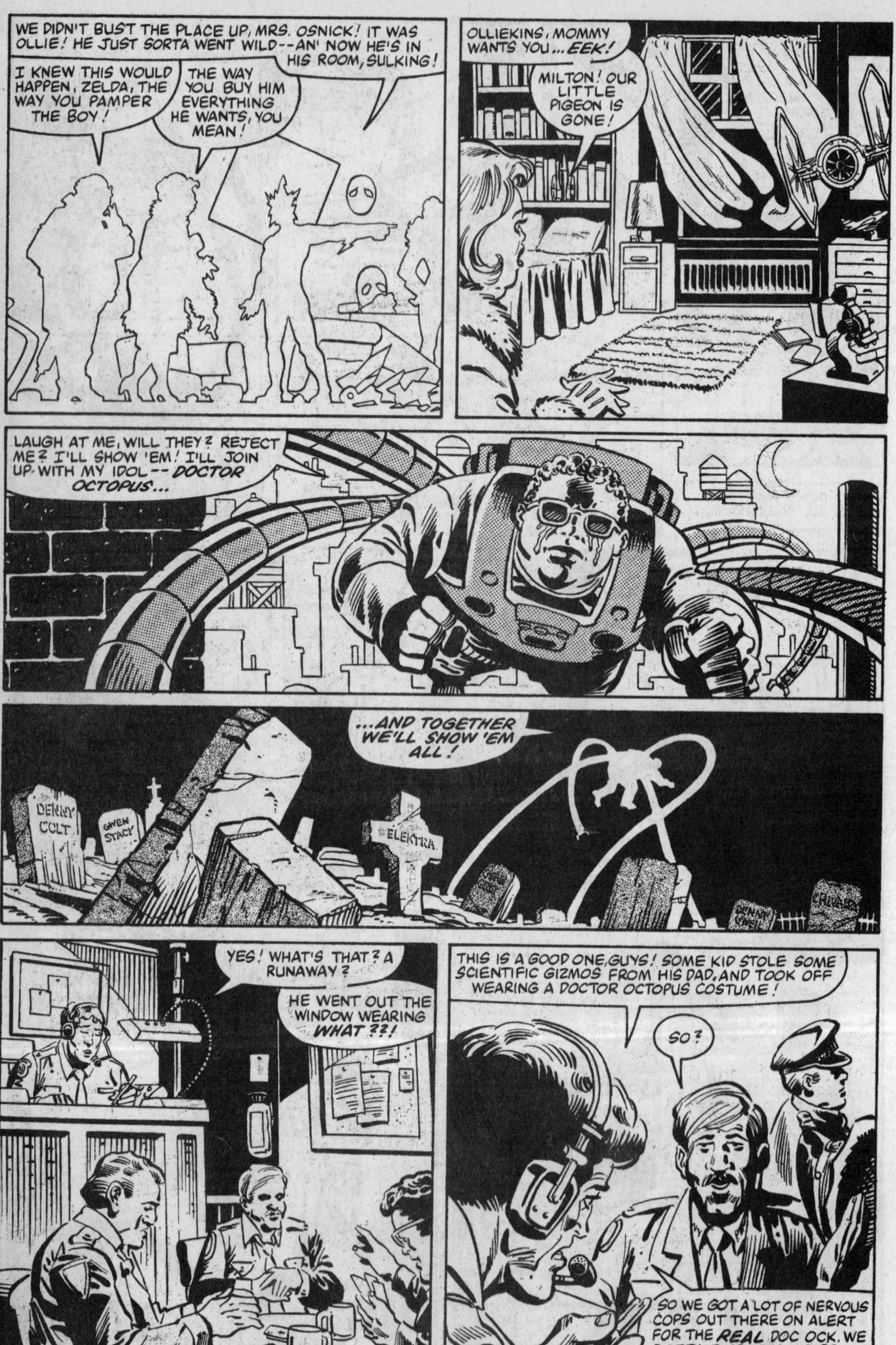
WE DIDN'T BUST THE PLACE UP, MRS. OSNICK! IT WAS OLLIE! HE JUST SORTA WENT WILD--AN' NOW HE'S IN HIS ROOM, SULKING!
I KNEW THIS WOULD HAPPEN, ZELDA, THE WAY YOU PAMPER THE BOY!
THE WAY YOU BUY HIM EVERYTHING HE WANTS, YOU MEAN!
OLLIEKINS, MOMMY WANTS YOU... EEK!
MILTON! OUR LITTLE PIGEON IS GONE!
LAUGH AT ME, WILL THEY? REJECT ME? I'LL SHOW 'EM! I'LL JOIN UP WITH MY IDOL--DOCTOR OCTOPUS...
...AND TOGETHER WE'LL SHOW 'EM ALL!
DENNY COLT
GWEN STACY
ELEKTRA
YES! WHAT'S THAT? A RUNAWAY?
HE WENT OUT THE WINDOW WEARING WHAT??!
THIS IS A GOOD ONE, GUYS! SOME KID STOLE SOME SCIENTIFIC GIZMOS FROM HIS DAD, AND TOOK OFF WEARING A DOCTOR OCTOPUS COSTUME!
SO?
SO WE GOT A LOT OF NERVOUS COPS OUT THERE ON ALERT FOR THE REAL DOC OCK. WE GOTTA FIND THIS KID BEFORE HE GETS...

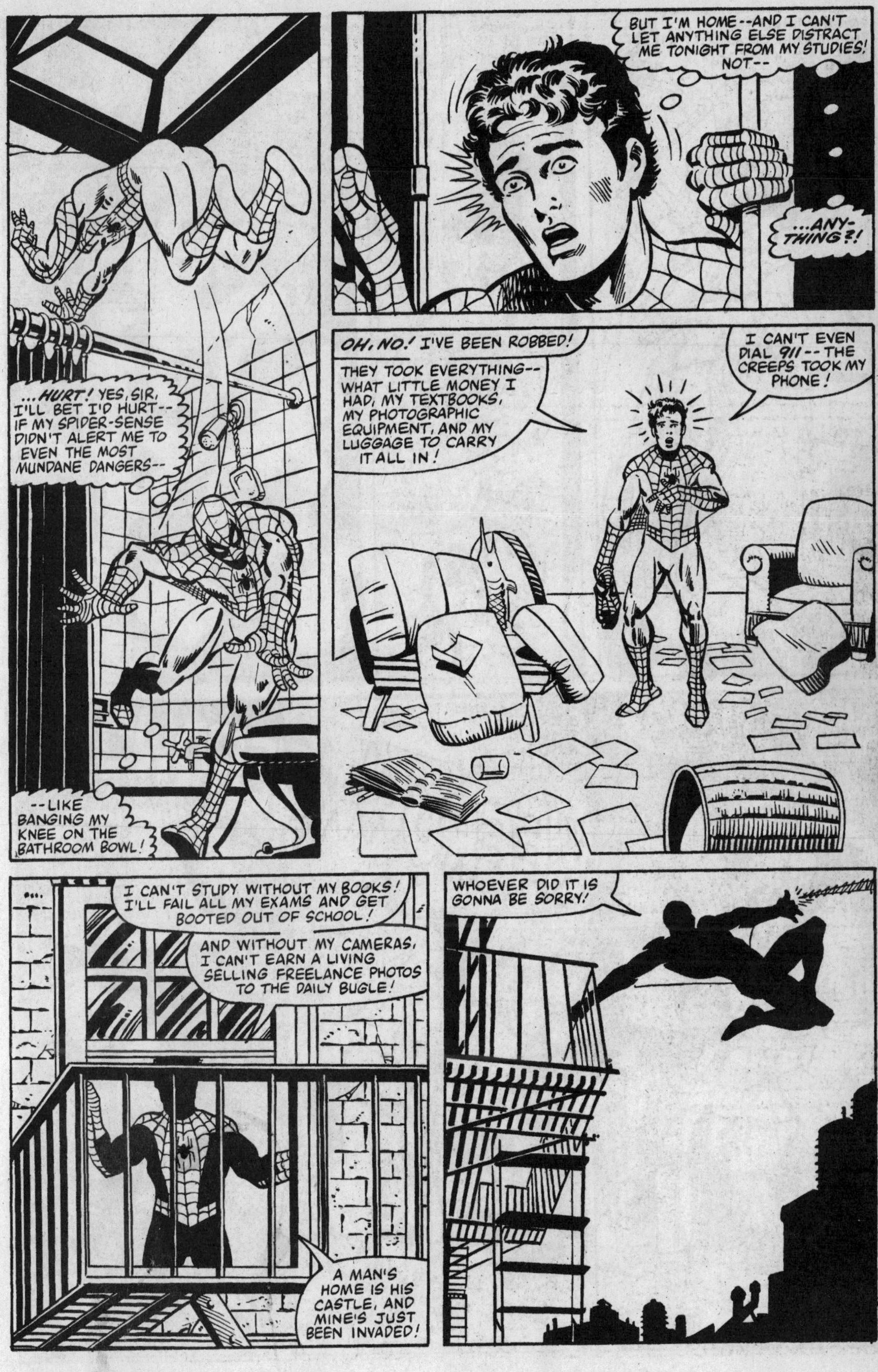
...HURT! YES, SIR, I'LL BET I'D HURT-- IF MY SPIDER-SENSE DIDN'T ALERT ME TO EVEN THE MOST MUNDANE DANGERS--
--LIKE BANGING MY KNEE ON THE BATHROOM BOWL!
BUT I'M HOME--AND I CAN'T LET ANYTHING ELSE DISTRACT ME TONIGHT FROM MY STUDIES! NOT--
...ANY-THING?!
OH, NO! I'VE BEEN ROBBED!
THEY TOOK EVERYTHING-- WHAT LITTLE MONEY I HAD, MY TEXTBOOKS, MY PHOTOGRAPHIC EQUIPMENT, AND MY LUGGAGE TO CARRY IT ALL IN!
I CAN'T EVEN DIAL 911 -- THE CREEPS TOOK MY PHONE!
...
I CAN'T STUDY WITHOUT MY BOOKS! I'LL FAIL ALL MY EXAMS AND GET BOOTED OUT OF SCHOOL!
AND WITHOUT MY CAMERAS, I CAN'T EARN A LIVING SELLING FREELANCE PHOTOS TO THE DAILY BUGLE!
A MAN'S HOME IS HIS CASTLE, AND MINE'S JUST BEEN INVADED!
WHOEVER DID IT IS GONNA BE SORRY!

BY SCOURING THE NEIGHBORHOOD AS ONLY A SPIDER-MAN CAN--

--I MIGHT FIND MY HAPPY HOME-WRECKERS FLEEING THE SCENE OF THE CRIME!

HEY, GUYS-- WAIT UP!

RUN FASTER, JERK! IT'S NOT OUR FAULT YOU SNATCHED THAT GUY'S WOODEN INDIAN!

MOST OF THE STUFF IN THAT PLACE WAS JUNK, ANY-WAY!

AH, BUT THE KIND OF JUNK FROM WHICH DREAMS ARE MADE!

SPIDER-MAN?! UNNN!

HEY! I GIVE UP! I'M NOT CRAZY ENOUGH TO FIGHT YOU! HERE'S THE MONEY WE STOLE! YOU CAN HAVE IT!

WHAT HAPPENED TO YOUR COURAGE? YOU GUYS ARE REAL BRAVE--WHEN NOBODY'S HOME!

WEEROWWWWEROWOWOW

I'LL CONFESS! I'LL TURN MYSELF IN!

SIRENS!

LOTS OF SIRENS! SOUNDS LIKE SOMETHING SERIOUS! I'D BETTER CHECK IT OUT!

BUT THERE'S NO WAY I'M LETTING THESE THIEVES GET AWAY!

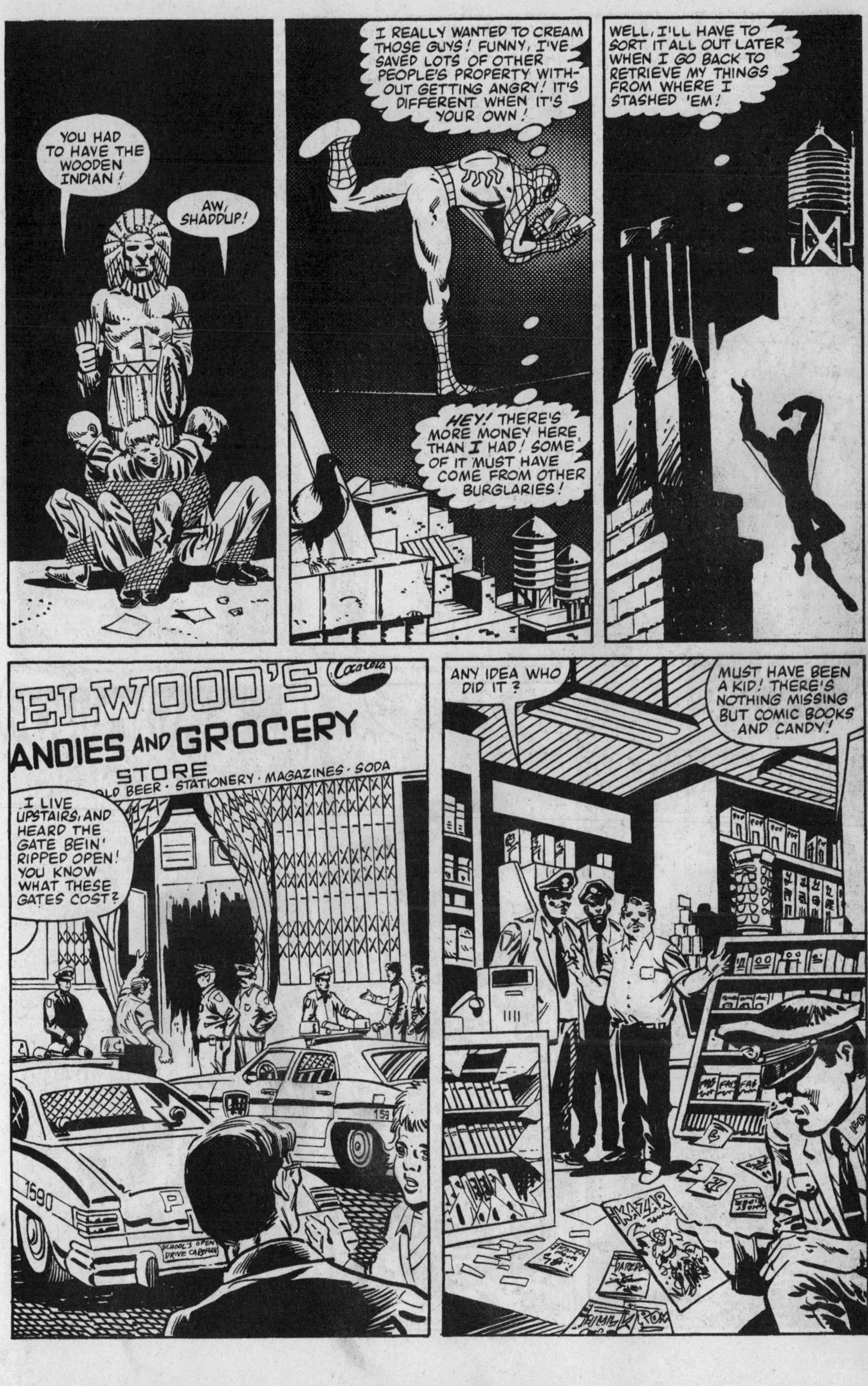
YOU HAD TO HAVE THE WOODEN INDIAN!
AW, SHADDUP!
I REALLY WANTED TO CREAM THOSE GUYS! FUNNY, I'VE SAVED LOTS OF OTHER PEOPLE'S PROPERTY WITH-OUT GETTING ANGRY! IT'S DIFFERENT WHEN IT'S YOUR OWN!
HEY! THERE'S MORE MONEY HERE THAN I HAD! SOME OF IT MUST HAVE COME FROM OTHER BURGLARIES!
WELL, I'LL HAVE TO SORT IT ALL OUT LATER WHEN I GO BACK TO RETRIEVE MY THINGS FROM WHERE I STASHED 'EM!
ELWOOD'S
ANDIES AND GROCERY
STORE
OLD BEER · STATIONERY · MAGAZINES · SODA
I LIVE UPSTAIRS, AND HEARD THE GATE BEIN' RIPPED OPEN! YOU KNOW WHAT THESE GATES COST?
SCHOOL'S OPEN DRIVE CAREFULLY
ANY IDEA WHO DID IT?
MUST HAVE BEEN A KID! THERE'S NOTHING MISSING BUT COMIC BOOKS AND CANDY!

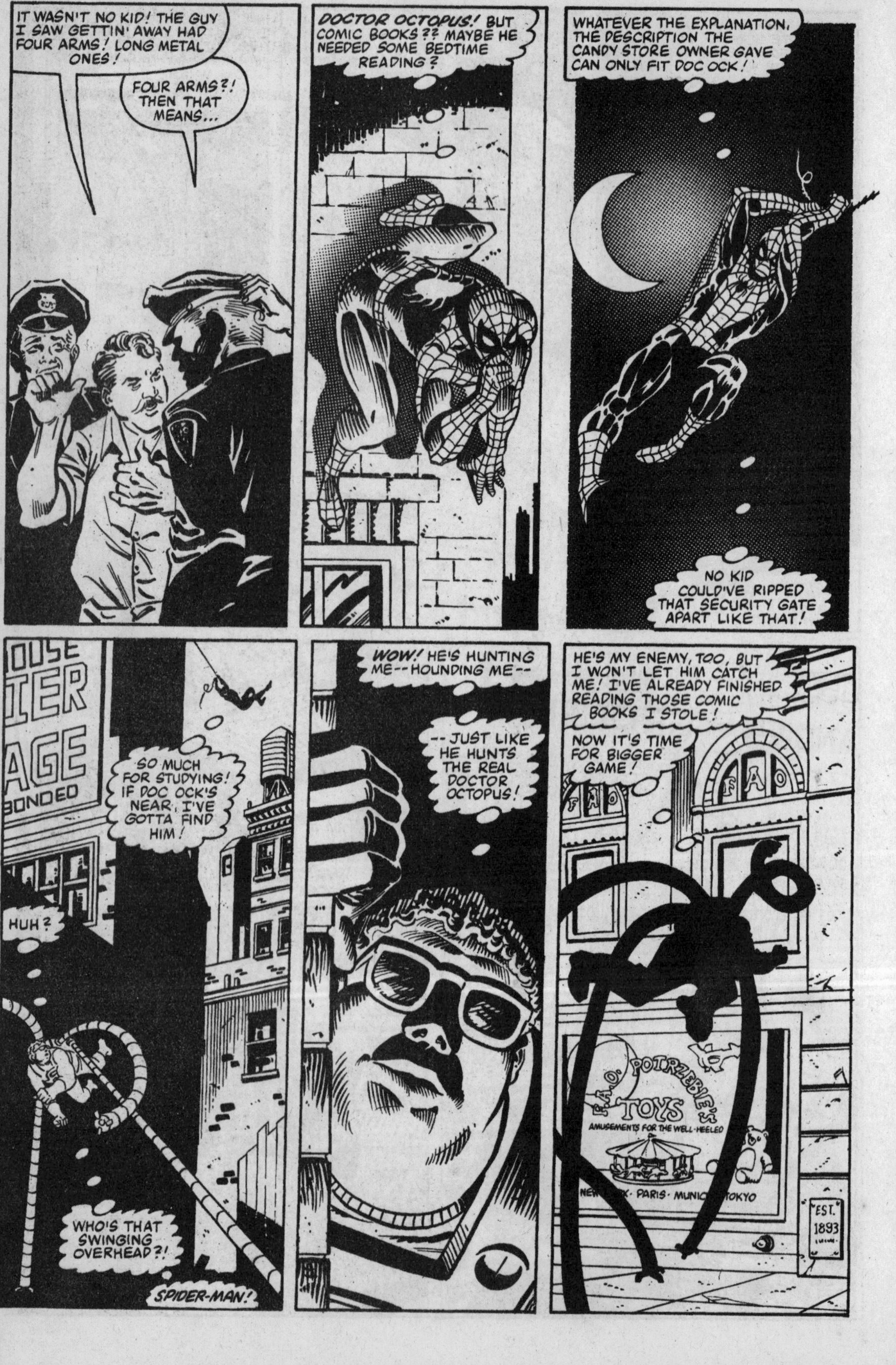
IT WASN'T NO KID! THE GUY I SAW GETTIN' AWAY HAD FOUR ARMS! LONG METAL ONES!
FOUR ARMS?! THEN THAT MEANS...
DOCTOR OCTOPUS! BUT COMIC BOOKS?? MAYBE HE NEEDED SOME BEDTIME READING?
WHATEVER THE EXPLANATION, THE DESCRIPTION THE CANDY STORE OWNER GAVE CAN ONLY FIT DOC OCK!
NO KID COULD'VE RIPPED THAT SECURITY GATE APART LIKE THAT!
SO MUCH FOR STUDYING! IF DOC OCK'S NEAR, I'VE GOTTA FIND HIM!
HUH?
WHO'S THAT SWINGING OVERHEAD?!
SPIDER-MAN!
WOW! HE'S HUNTING ME--HOUNDING ME--
--JUST LIKE HE HUNTS THE REAL DOCTOR OCTOPUS!
HE'S MY ENEMY, TOO, BUT I WON'T LET HIM CATCH ME! I'VE ALREADY FINISHED READING THOSE COMIC BOOKS I STOLE!
NOW IT'S TIME FOR BIGGER GAME!
F.A.O. POTRZEBIE'S TOYS
AMUSEMENTS FOR THE WELL-HEELED
PARIS
EST. 1893

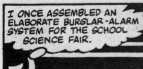

I ONCE ASSEMBLED AN ELABORATE BURGLAR-ALARM SYSTEM FOR THE SCHOOL SCIENCE FAIR.

THIS ONE IS EASY TO TAKE APART!

VOILA!

F.A.O. POTRZE TOYS NEW YORK

MEANWHILE...

I CAN SEE EVERY BANK AND JEWELRY STORE ON THE UPPER WEST SIDE FROM HERE!

DOC OCK MAY ATTEMPT A ROBBERY-- HE ALWAYS NEEDS COLD CASH TO FINANCE HIS BIZARRE SCHEMES!

SPEAKING OF MONEY-- WHAT AM I GONNA DO WITH THE EXTRA BUCKS I RECOVERED FROM THOSE BURGLARS?

CAN'T REALLY KEEP IT. THAT WOULD BE DISHONEST.

ELSEWHERE...

I'M IN!

AT LAST! I AM ABOUT TO FEAST UPON THE FRUITS OF CRIME!

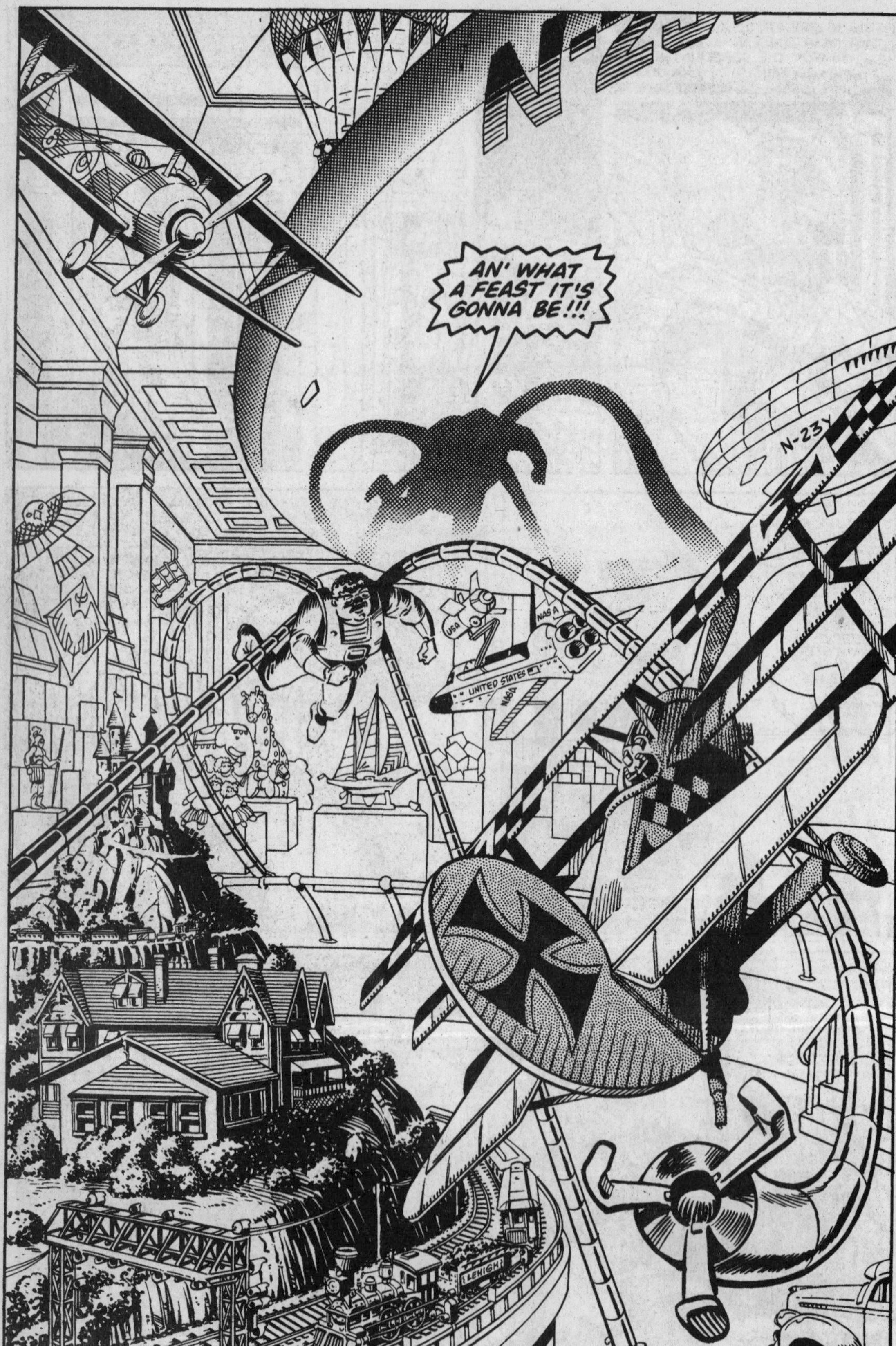

N-23Y
AN' WHAT A FEAST IT'S GONNA BE!!!
N-23Y
USA
NASA
UNITED STATES
NASA
LEHIGH

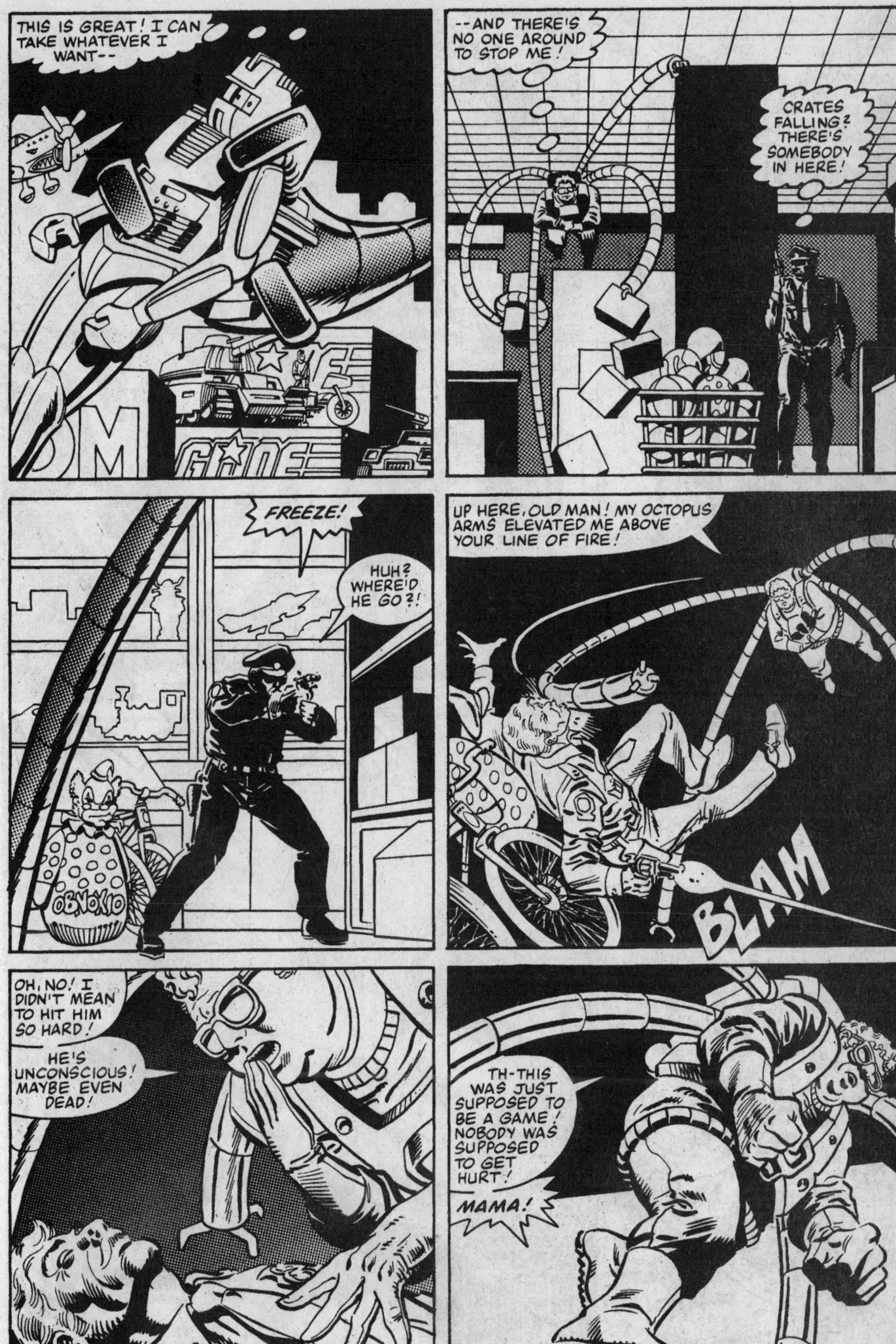
THIS IS GREAT! I CAN TAKE WHATEVER I WANT--
--AND THERE'S NO ONE AROUND TO STOP ME!
CRATES FALLING? THERE'S SOMEBODY IN HERE!
G.I. JOE
FREEZE!
HUH? WHERE'D HE GO?!
OBNOXIO
UP HERE, OLD MAN! MY OCTOPUS ARMS ELEVATED ME ABOVE YOUR LINE OF FIRE!
BLAM
OH, NO! I DIDN'T MEAN TO HIT HIM SO HARD!
HE'S UNCONSCIOUS! MAYBE EVEN DEAD!
TH-THIS WAS JUST SUPPOSED TO BE A GAME! NOBODY WAS SUPPOSED TO GET HURT!
MAMA!

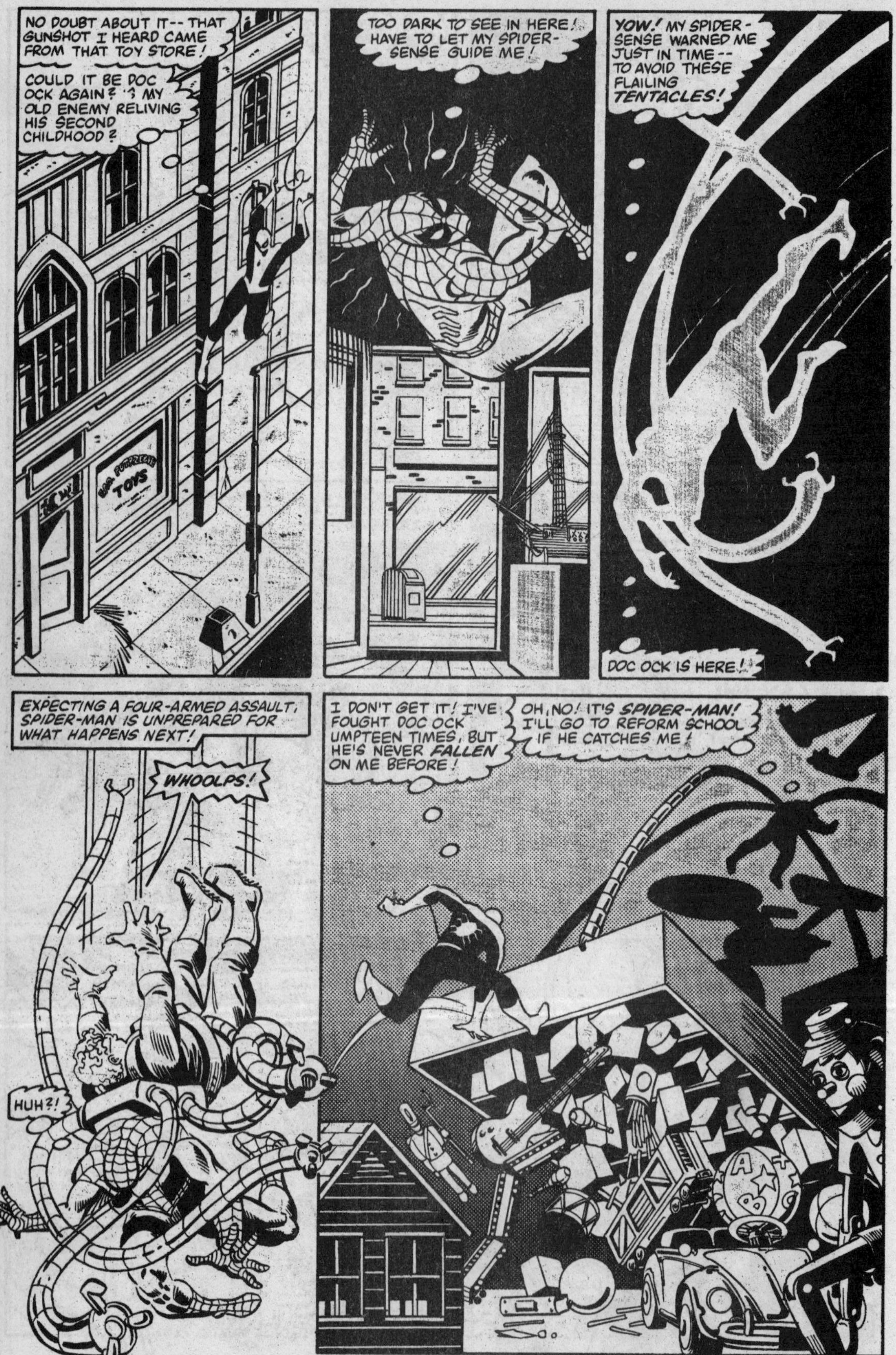
NO DOUBT ABOUT IT-- THAT GUNSHOT I HEARD CAME FROM THAT TOY STORE!
COULD IT BE DOC OCK AGAIN? 'N MY OLD ENEMY RELIVING HIS SECOND CHILDHOOD?
TOYS
TOO DARK TO SEE IN HERE! HAVE TO LET MY SPIDER-SENSE GUIDE ME!
YOW! MY SPIDER-SENSE WARNED ME JUST IN TIME-- TO AVOID THESE FLAILING TENTACLES!
DOC OCK IS HERE!
EXPECTING A FOUR-ARMED ASSAULT, SPIDER-MAN IS UNPREPARED FOR WHAT HAPPENS NEXT!
WHOOLPS!
HUH?!
I DON'T GET IT! I'VE FOUGHT DOC OCK UMPTEEN TIMES, BUT HE'S NEVER FALLEN ON ME BEFORE!
OH, NO! IT'S SPIDER-MAN! I'LL GO TO REFORM SCHOOL IF HE CATCHES ME!

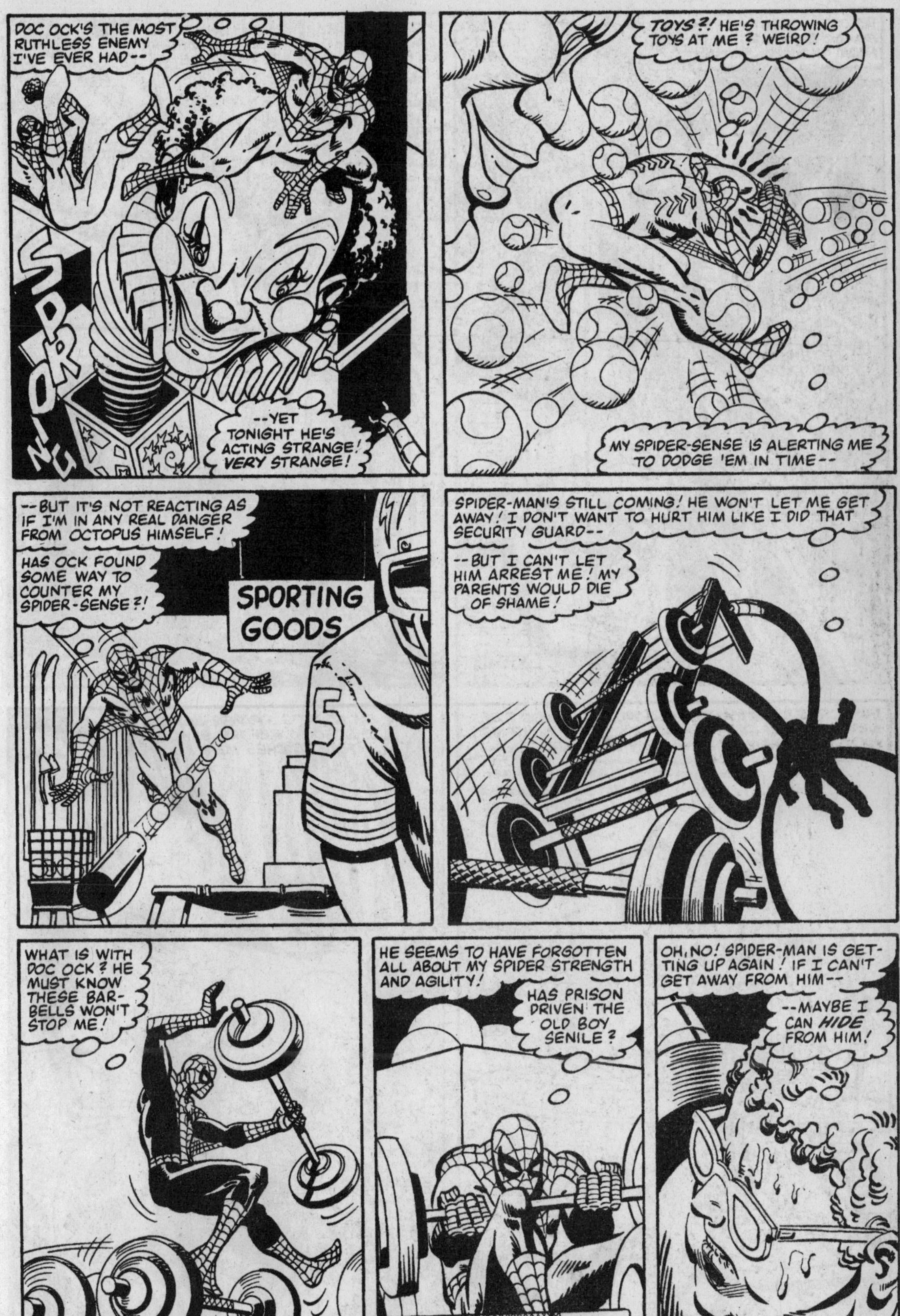
DOC OCK'S THE MOST RUTHLESS ENEMY I'VE EVER HAD--
SPRONG
--YET TONIGHT HE'S ACTING STRANGE! VERY STRANGE!
TOYS?! HE'S THROWING TOYS AT ME? WEIRD!
MY SPIDER-SENSE IS ALERTING ME TO DODGE 'EM IN TIME--
--BUT IT'S NOT REACTING AS IF I'M IN ANY REAL DANGER FROM OCTOPUS HIMSELF!
HAS OCK FOUND SOME WAY TO COUNTER MY SPIDER-SENSE?!
SPORTING GOODS
SPIDER-MAN'S STILL COMING! HE WON'T LET ME GET AWAY! I DON'T WANT TO HURT HIM LIKE I DID THAT SECURITY GUARD--
--BUT I CAN'T LET HIM ARREST ME! MY PARENTS WOULD DIE OF SHAME!
WHAT IS WITH DOC OCK? HE MUST KNOW THESE BAR-BELLS WON'T STOP ME!
HE SEEMS TO HAVE FORGOTTEN ALL ABOUT MY SPIDER STRENGTH AND AGILITY!
HAS PRISON DRIVEN THE OLD BOY SENILE?
OH, NO! SPIDER-MAN IS GETTING UP AGAIN! IF I CAN'T GET AWAY FROM HIM--
--MAYBE I CAN HIDE FROM HIM!

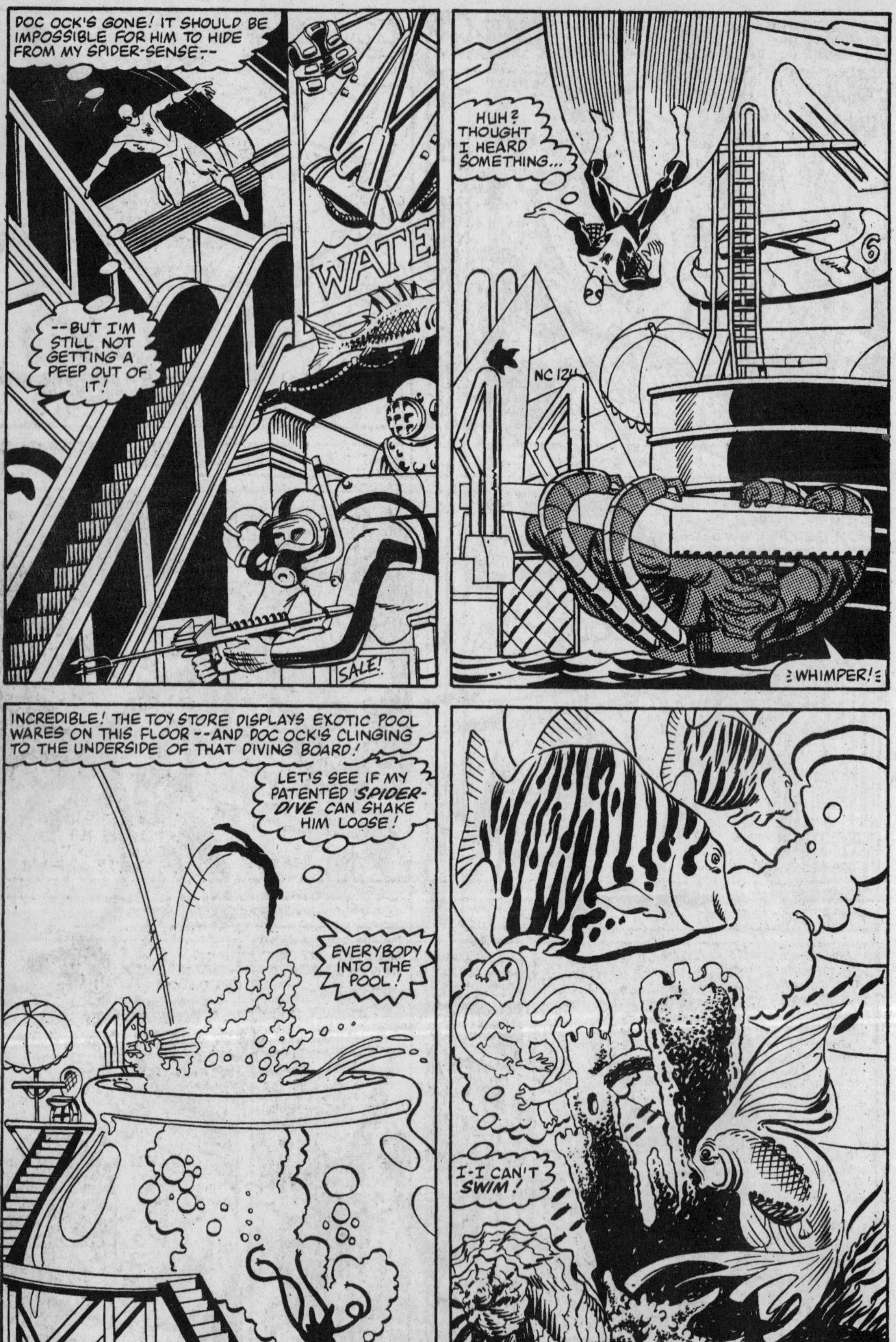
DOC OCK'S GONE! IT SHOULD BE IMPOSSIBLE FOR HIM TO HIDE FROM MY SPIDER-SENSE--
--BUT I'M STILL NOT GETTING A PEEP OUT OF IT!
SALE!
HUH? THOUGHT I HEARD SOMETHING...
NC 124
WHIMPER!
INCREDIBLE! THE TOY STORE DISPLAYS EXOTIC POOL WARES ON THIS FLOOR--AND DOC OCK'S CLINGING TO THE UNDERSIDE OF THAT DIVING BOARD!
LET'S SEE IF MY PATENTED SPIDER-DIVE CAN SHAKE HIM LOOSE!
EVERYBODY INTO THE POOL!
I-I CAN'T SWIM!

I'M OUT OF MY ELEMENT IN HERE!
THERE IS NOTHING TO CLING TO! NO WAY I CAN USE MY SPEED OR AGILITY!
WITH HIS TENTACLES FLAILING ALL OVER THE PLACE, DOC SHOULD FEEL RIGHT AT HOME!
SOK
HEY! THAT PUNCH FELT MORE LIKE A LOVE TAP THAN WHAT I'M USED TO FROM DOC!
WHAT THE--?! I'VE JUST SHREDDED ONE OF OCK'S TENTACLE-ARMS IN TWO!
DESPITE ALL MY SPIDER-POWER, I WAS NEVER ABLE TO DO *THAT* SO EASILY BEFORE!
WHAT'S THIS--SOME KIND OF BACKPACK?!
DR. OCTOPUS NEVER WORE A CONTRAPTION LIKE THIS BEFORE!
SOMETHING IS SERIOUSLY WRONG HERE--AND I'M GOING TO FIND OUT *WHAT* JUST AS SOON AS WE GET OUT OF THIS OVERGROWN FISHBOWL!

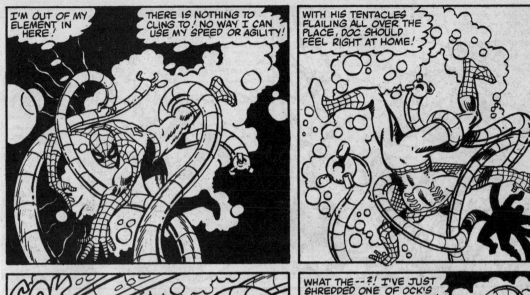

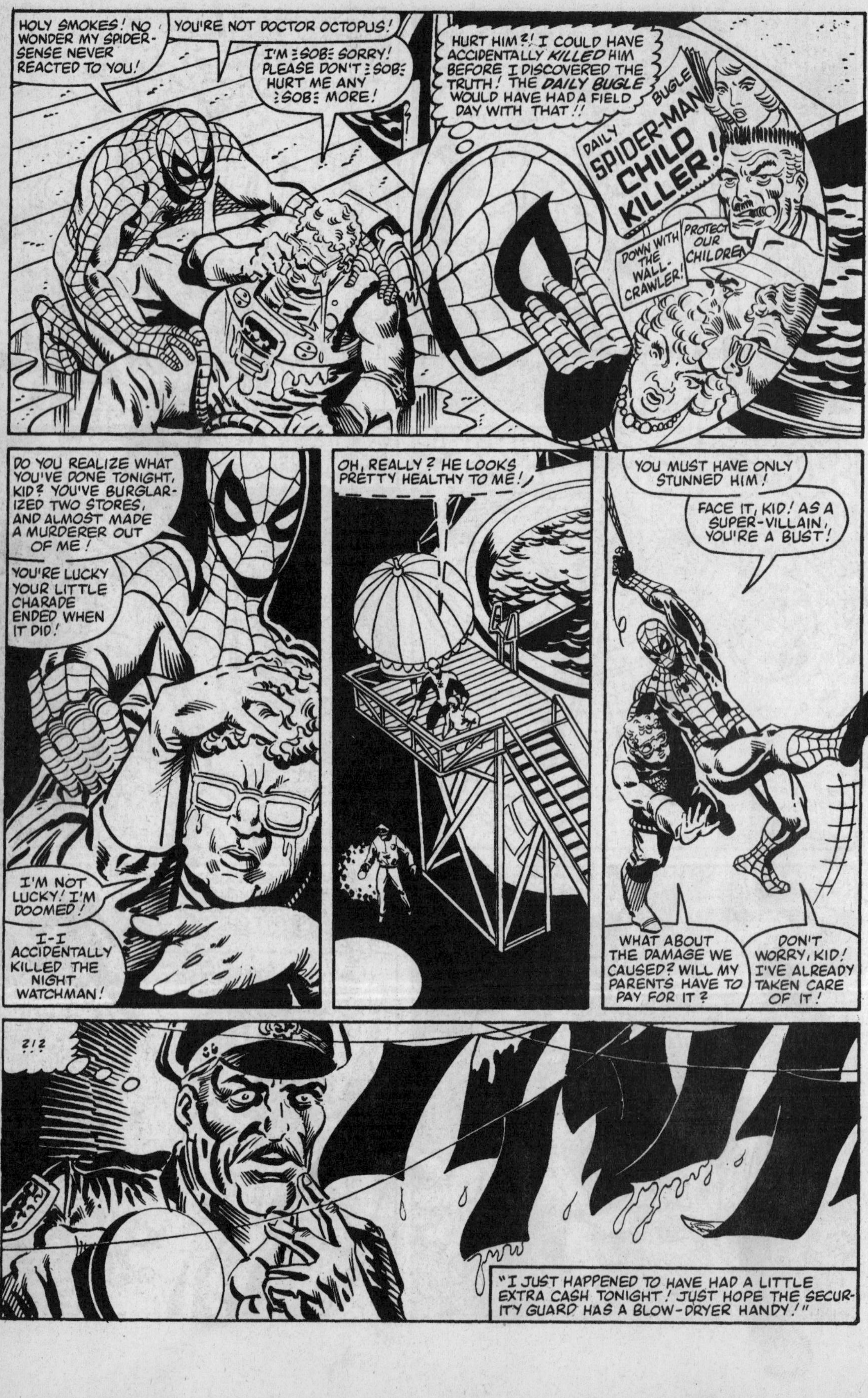
HOLY SMOKES! NO WONDER MY SPIDER-SENSE NEVER REACTED TO YOU!
YOU'RE NOT DOCTOR OCTOPUS!
I'M SOB SORRY! PLEASE DON'T SOB HURT ME ANY SOB MORE!
HURT HIM?! I COULD HAVE ACCIDENTALLY KILLED HIM BEFORE I DISCOVERED THE TRUTH! THE DAILY BUGLE WOULD HAVE HAD A FIELD DAY WITH THAT!!
DAILY BUGLE
SPIDER-MAN CHILD KILLER!
DOWN WITH THE WALL-CRAWLER!
PROTECT OUR CHILDREN
DO YOU REALIZE WHAT YOU'VE DONE TONIGHT, KID? YOU'VE BURGLARIZED TWO STORES, AND ALMOST MADE A MURDERER OUT OF ME!
YOU'RE LUCKY YOUR LITTLE CHARADE ENDED WHEN IT DID!
I'M NOT LUCKY! I'M DOOMED!
I-I ACCIDENTALLY KILLED THE NIGHT WATCHMAN!
OH, REALLY? HE LOOKS PRETTY HEALTHY TO ME!
YOU MUST HAVE ONLY STUNNED HIM!
FACE IT, KID! AS A SUPER-VILLAIN, YOU'RE A BUST!
WHAT ABOUT THE DAMAGE WE CAUSED? WILL MY PARENTS HAVE TO PAY FOR IT?
DON'T WORRY, KID! I'VE ALREADY TAKEN CARE OF IT!
?!?
"I JUST HAPPENED TO HAVE HAD A LITTLE EXTRA CASH TONIGHT! JUST HOPE THE SECURITY GUARD HAS A BLOW-DRYER HANDY!"

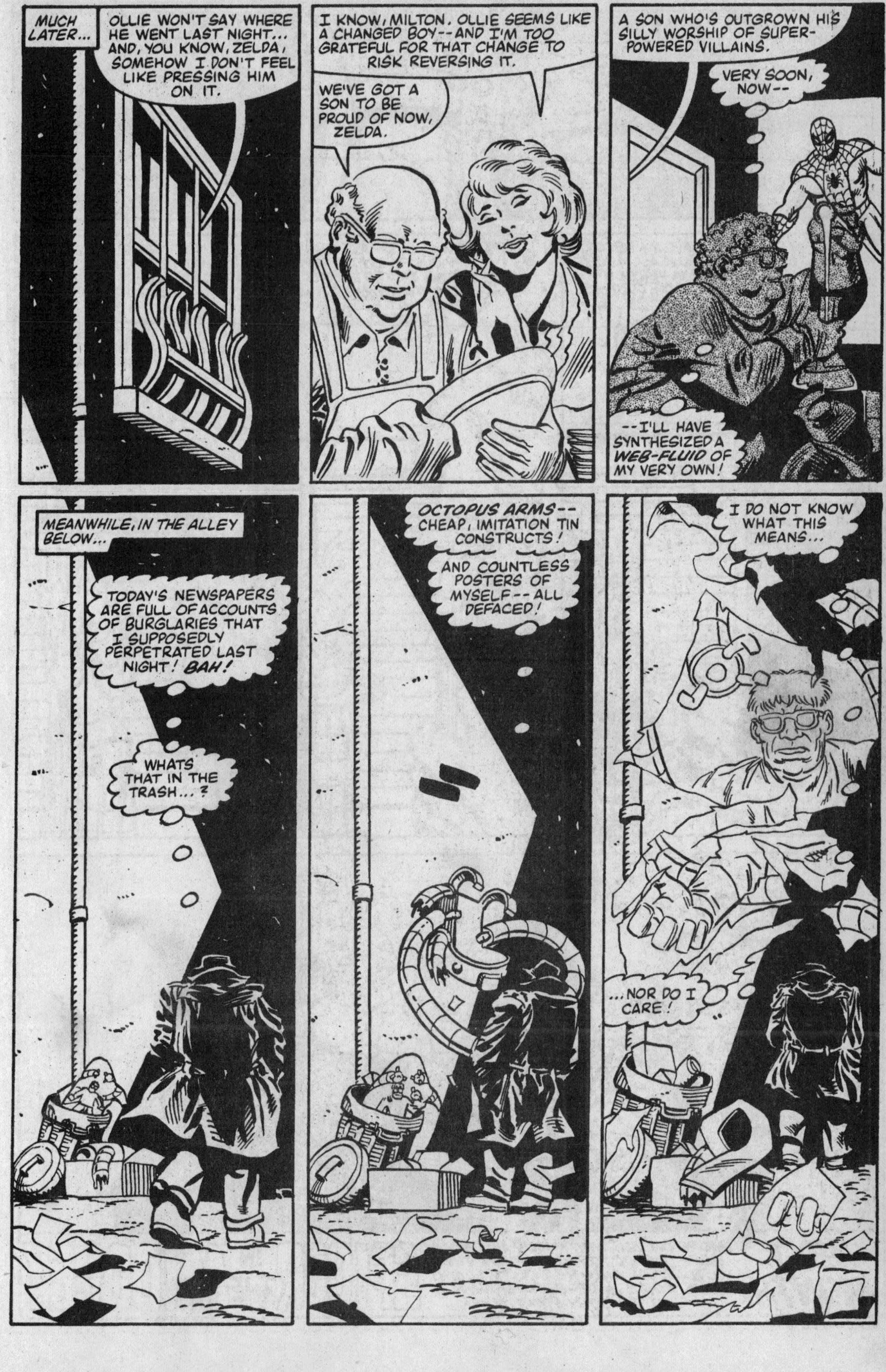
MUCH LATER...
OLLIE WON'T SAY WHERE HE WENT LAST NIGHT... AND, YOU KNOW, ZELDA, SOMEHOW I DON'T FEEL LIKE PRESSING HIM ON IT.
I KNOW, MILTON. OLLIE SEEMS LIKE A CHANGED BOY--AND I'M TOO GRATEFUL FOR THAT CHANGE TO RISK REVERSING IT.
WE'VE GOT A SON TO BE PROUD OF NOW, ZELDA.
A SON WHO'S OUTGROWN HIS SILLY WORSHIP OF SUPER-POWERED VILLAINS.
VERY SOON, NOW--
--I'LL HAVE SYNTHESIZED A WEB-FLUID OF MY VERY OWN!
MEANWHILE, IN THE ALLEY BELOW...
TODAY'S NEWSPAPERS ARE FULL OF ACCOUNTS OF BURGLARIES THAT I SUPPOSEDLY PERPETRATED LAST NIGHT! BAH!
WHATS THAT IN THE TRASH...?
OCTOPUS ARMS--CHEAP, IMITATION TIN CONSTRUCTS!
AND COUNTLESS POSTERS OF MYSELF--ALL DEFACED!
I DO NOT KNOW WHAT THIS MEANS...
...NOR DO I CARE!

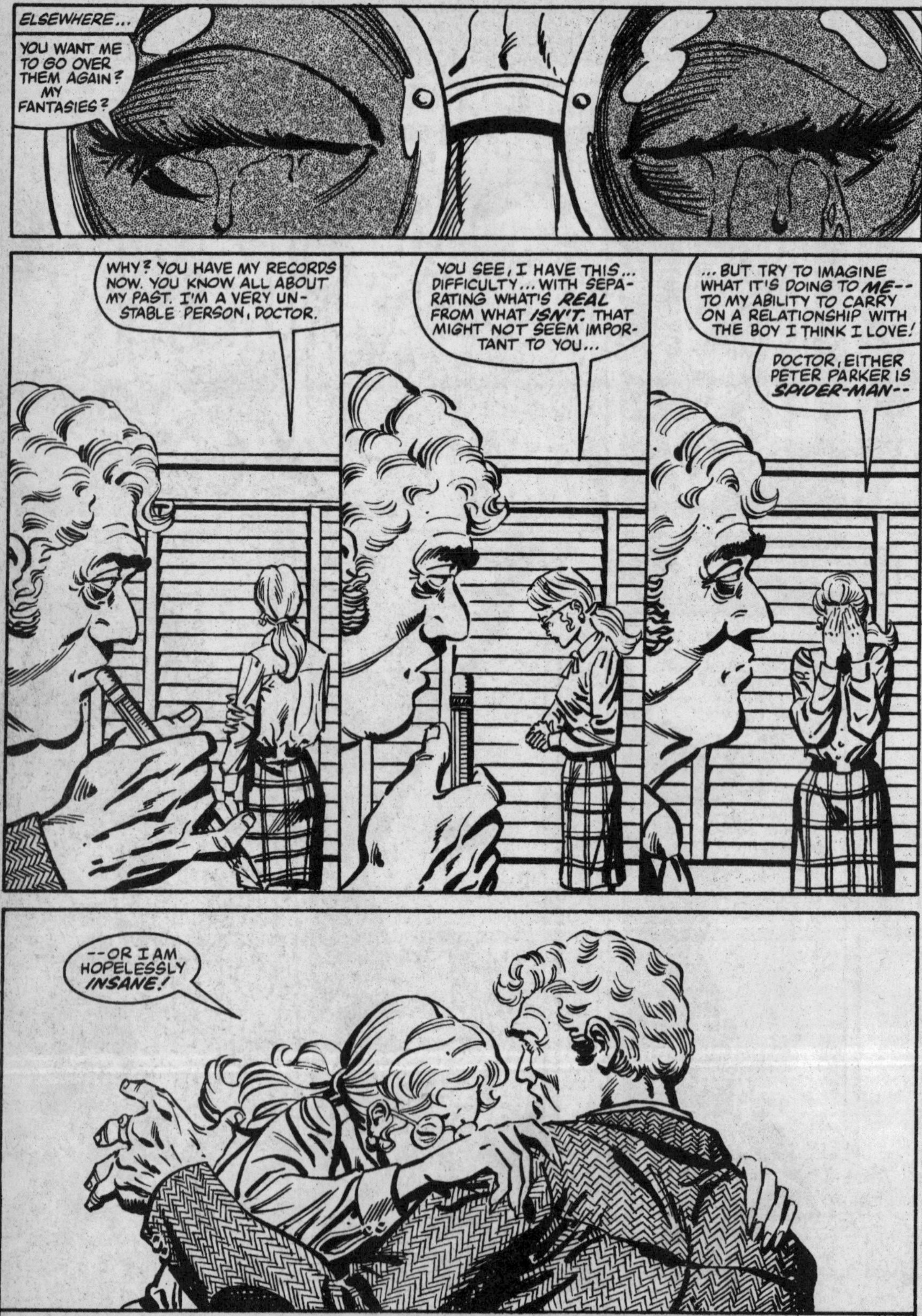
ELSEWHERE...
YOU WANT ME TO GO OVER THEM AGAIN? MY FANTASIES?
WHY? YOU HAVE MY RECORDS NOW. YOU KNOW ALL ABOUT MY PAST. I'M A VERY UNSTABLE PERSON, DOCTOR.
YOU SEE, I HAVE THIS... DIFFICULTY... WITH SEPARATING WHAT'S REAL FROM WHAT ISN'T. THAT MIGHT NOT SEEM IMPORTANT TO YOU...
...BUT TRY TO IMAGINE WHAT IT'S DOING TO ME-- TO MY ABILITY TO CARRY ON A RELATIONSHIP WITH THE BOY I THINK I LOVE!
DOCTOR, EITHER PETER PARKER IS SPIDER-MAN--
--OR I AM HOPELESSLY INSANE!
NEXT MONTH:
MORE ON DEB WHITMAN'S DILEMMA! MORE ON DOCTOR OCTOPUS! THE RETURN OF ANOTHER OLD VILLAIN! PLUS SOME INTERESTING NEW PLOT TWISTS! DON'T MISS...
SPIDER IN THE MIDDLE!

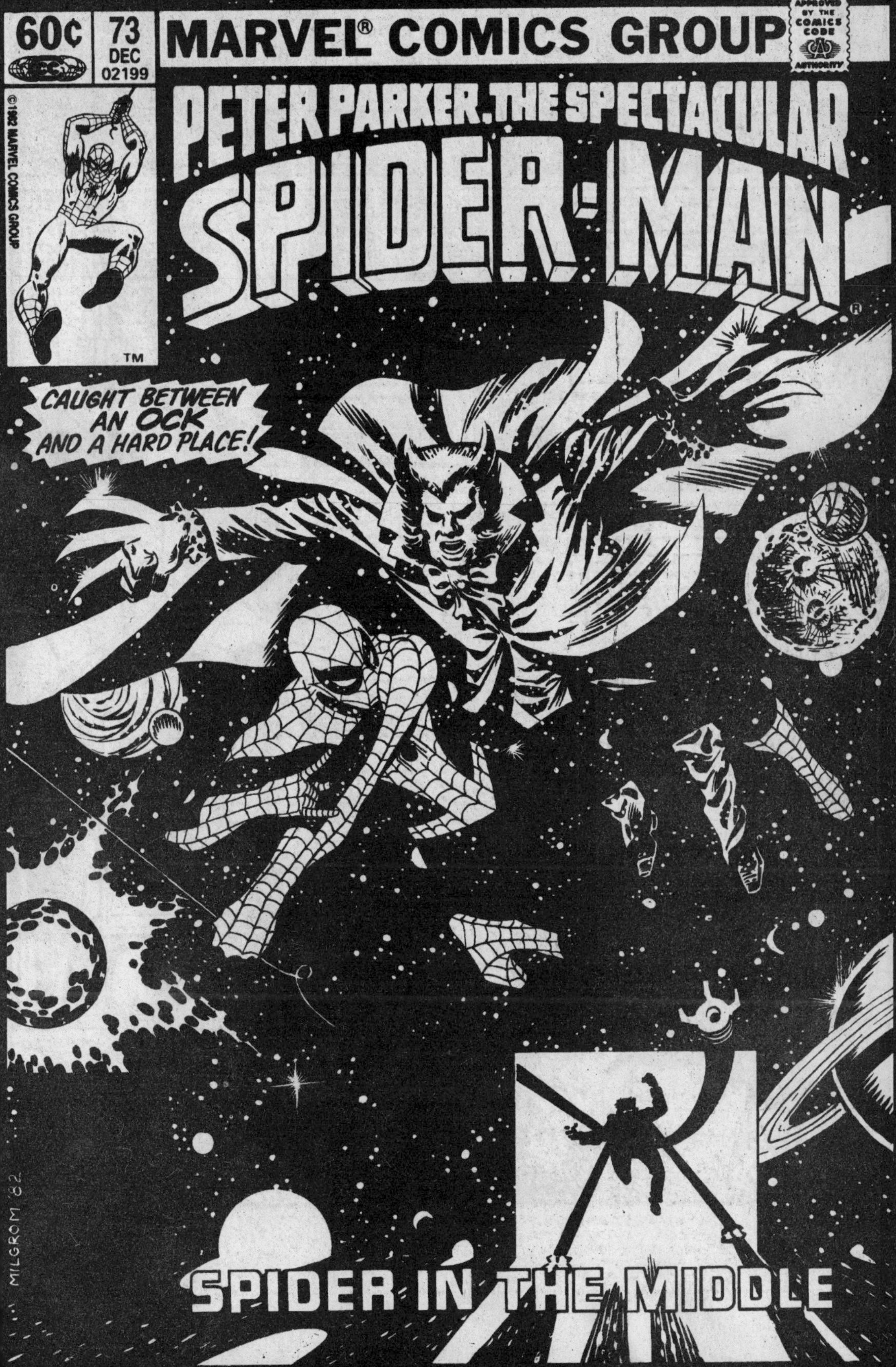

60¢
73
DEC
02199
MARVEL® COMICS GROUP
APPROVED BY THE COMICS CODE AUTHORITY
© 1982 MARVEL COMICS GROUP
PETER PARKER, THE SPECTACULAR
SPIDER-MAN®
TM
CAUGHT BETWEEN AN OCK AND A HARD PLACE!
MILGROM '82
SPIDER IN THE MIDDLE

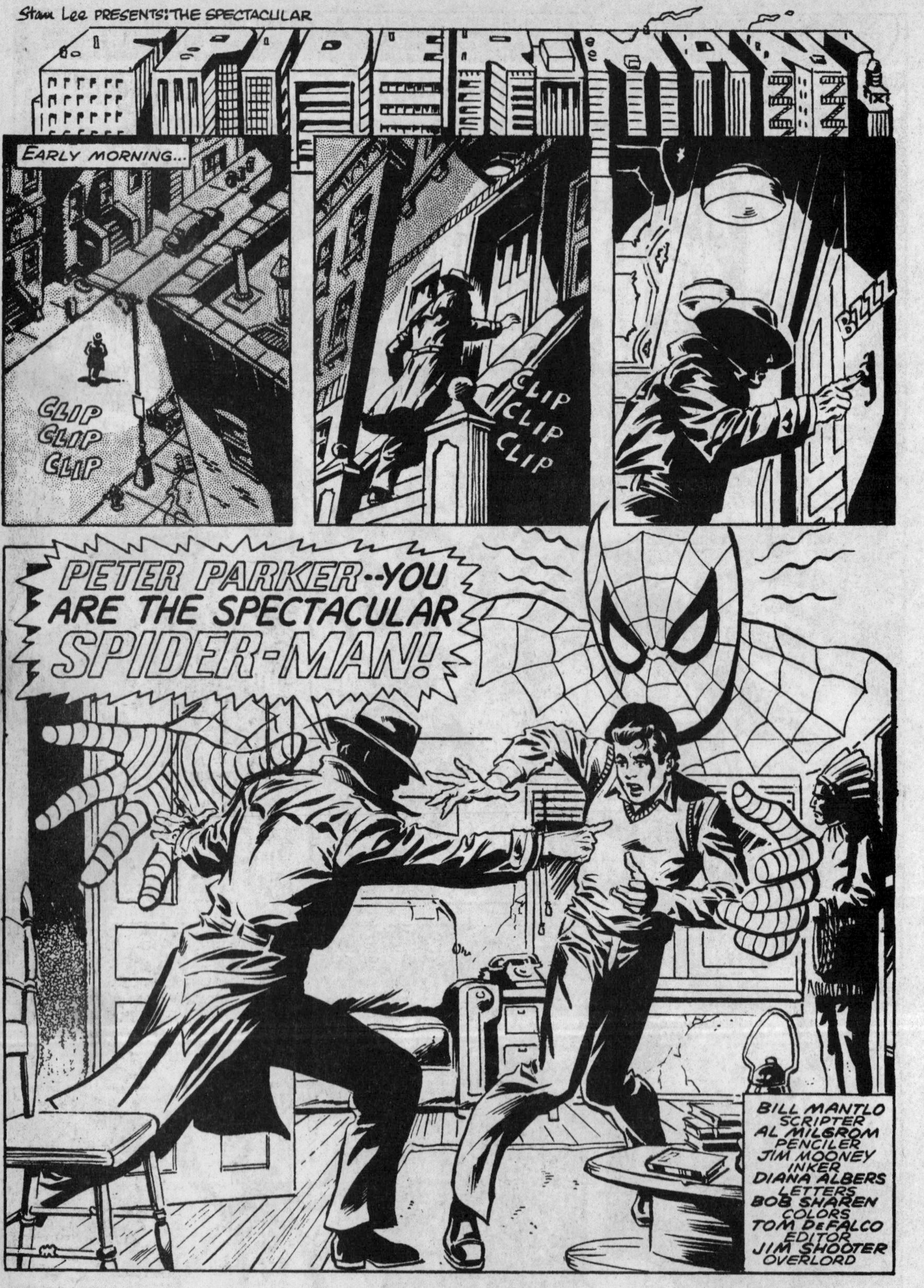
Stan Lee PRESENTS: THE SPECTACULAR
SPIDER-MAN
EARLY MORNING...
CLIP CLIP CLIP
CLIP CLIP CLIP
BZZZ
PETER PARKER--YOU ARE THE SPECTACULAR SPIDER-MAN!
BILL MANTLO SCRIPTER
AL MILGROM PENCILER
JIM MOONEY INKER
DIANA ALBERS LETTERS
BOB SHAREN COLORS
TOM DeFALCO EDITOR
JIM SHOOTER OVERLORD

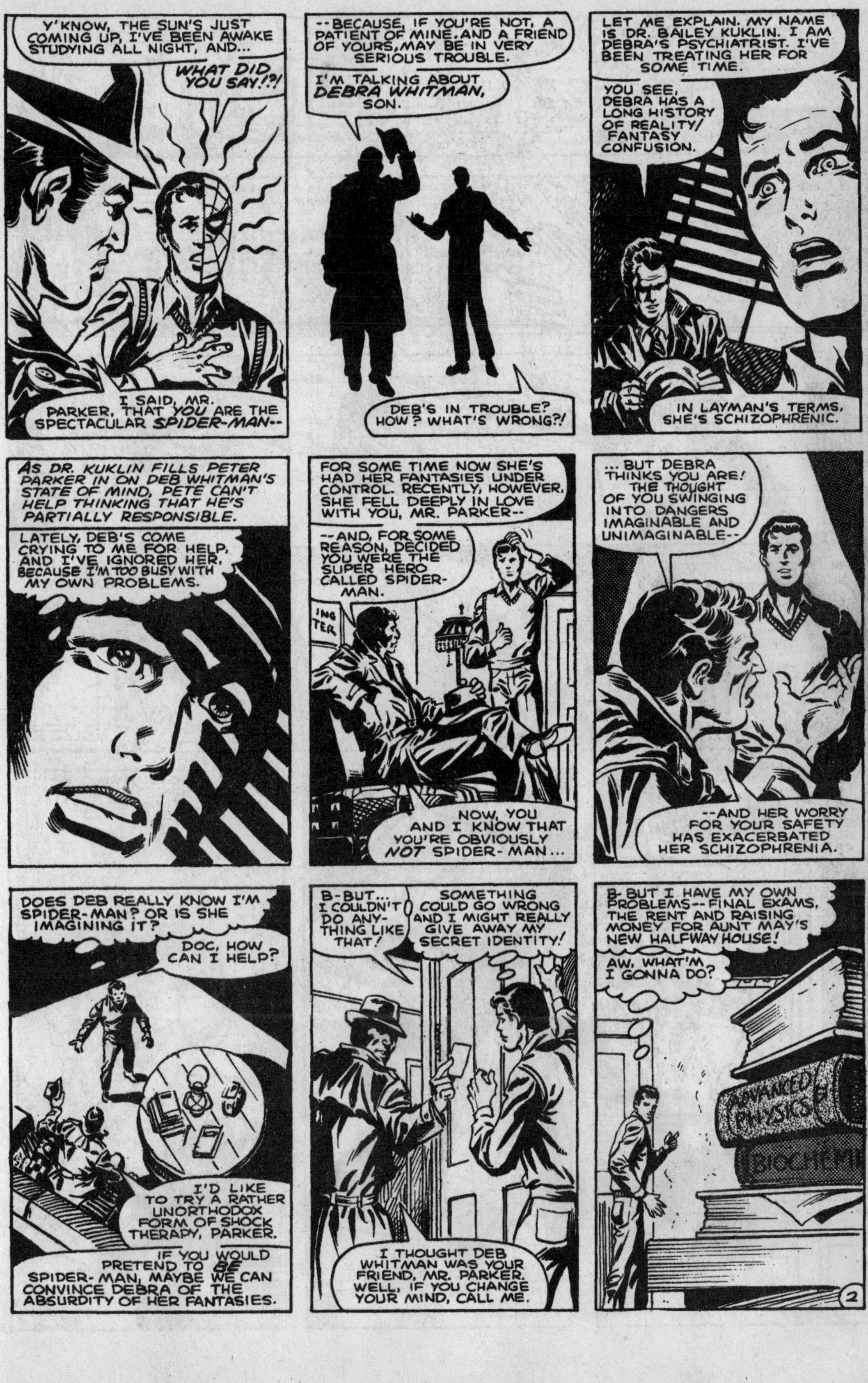

Y'KNOW, THE SUN'S JUST COMING UP, I'VE BEEN AWAKE STUDYING ALL NIGHT, AND...
WHAT DID YOU SAY!?!
I SAID, MR. PARKER, THAT YOU ARE THE SPECTACULAR SPIDER-MAN--
--BECAUSE, IF YOU'RE NOT, A PATIENT OF MINE, AND A FRIEND OF YOURS, MAY BE IN VERY SERIOUS TROUBLE.
I'M TALKING ABOUT DEBRA WHITMAN, SON.
DEB'S IN TROUBLE? HOW? WHAT'S WRONG?!
LET ME EXPLAIN. MY NAME IS DR. BAILEY KUKLIN. I AM DEBRA'S PSYCHIATRIST. I'VE BEEN TREATING HER FOR SOME TIME.
YOU SEE, DEBRA HAS A LONG HISTORY OF REALITY/ FANTASY CONFUSION.
IN LAYMAN'S TERMS, SHE'S SCHIZOPHRENIC.
AS DR. KUKLIN FILLS PETER PARKER IN ON DEB WHITMAN'S STATE OF MIND, PETE CAN'T HELP THINKING THAT HE'S PARTIALLY RESPONSIBLE.
LATELY, DEB'S COME CRYING TO ME FOR HELP, AND I'VE IGNORED HER, BECAUSE I'M TOO BUSY WITH MY OWN PROBLEMS.
FOR SOME TIME NOW SHE'S HAD HER FANTASIES UNDER CONTROL. RECENTLY, HOWEVER, SHE FELL DEEPLY IN LOVE WITH YOU, MR. PARKER--
--AND, FOR SOME REASON, DECIDED YOU WERE THE SUPER HERO CALLED SPIDER-MAN.
NOW, YOU AND I KNOW THAT YOU'RE OBVIOUSLY NOT SPIDER-MAN...
... BUT DEBRA THINKS YOU ARE! THE THOUGHT OF YOU SWINGING INTO DANGERS IMAGINABLE AND UNIMAGINABLE--
--AND HER WORRY FOR YOUR SAFETY HAS EXACERBATED HER SCHIZOPHRENIA.
DOES DEB REALLY KNOW I'M SPIDER-MAN? OR IS SHE IMAGINING IT?
DOC, HOW CAN I HELP?
I'D LIKE TO TRY A RATHER UNORTHODOX FORM OF SHOCK THERAPY, PARKER.
IF YOU WOULD PRETEND TO BE SPIDER-MAN, MAYBE WE CAN CONVINCE DEBRA OF THE ABSURDITY OF HER FANTASIES.
B-BUT... I COULDN'T DO ANYTHING LIKE THAT!
SOMETHING COULD GO WRONG AND I MIGHT REALLY GIVE AWAY MY SECRET IDENTITY!
I THOUGHT DEB WHITMAN WAS YOUR FRIEND, MR. PARKER. WELL, IF YOU CHANGE YOUR MIND, CALL ME.
B-BUT I HAVE MY OWN PROBLEMS--FINAL EXAMS, THE RENT AND RAISING MONEY FOR AUNT MAY'S NEW HALFWAY HOUSE!
AW, WHAT'M I GONNA DO?
ADVANCED PHYSICS
BIOCHEM
2

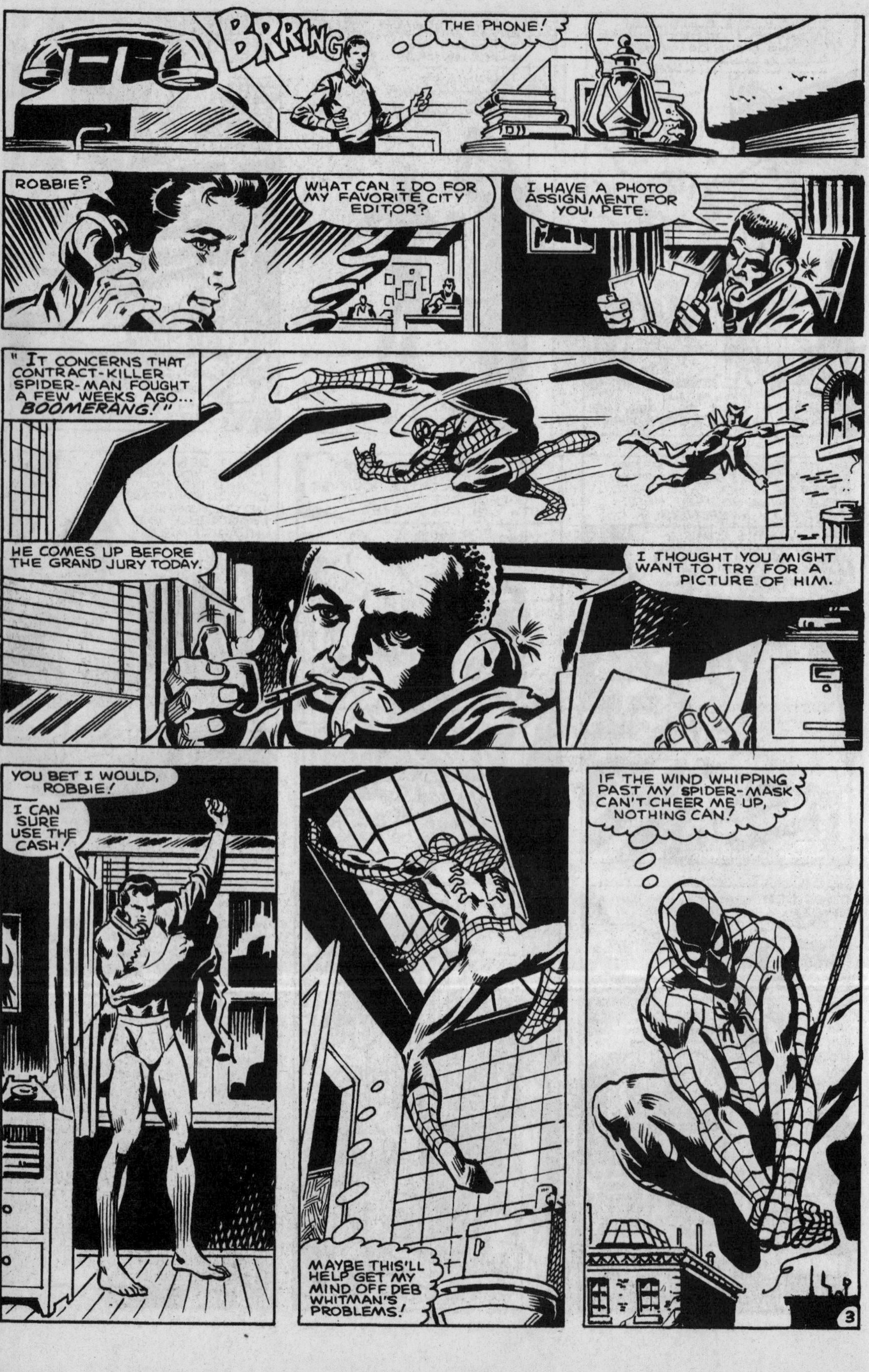
BRRING
THE PHONE!
ROBBIE?
WHAT CAN I DO FOR MY FAVORITE CITY EDITOR?
I HAVE A PHOTO ASSIGNMENT FOR YOU, PETE.
"IT CONCERNS THAT CONTRACT-KILLER SPIDER-MAN FOUGHT A FEW WEEKS AGO... BOOMERANG!"
HE COMES UP BEFORE THE GRAND JURY TODAY.
I THOUGHT YOU MIGHT WANT TO TRY FOR A PICTURE OF HIM.
YOU BET I WOULD, ROBBIE!
I CAN SURE USE THE CASH!
MAYBE THIS'LL HELP GET MY MIND OFF DEB WHITMAN'S PROBLEMS!
IF THE WIND WHIPPING PAST MY SPIDER-MASK CAN'T CHEER ME UP, NOTHING CAN!
3

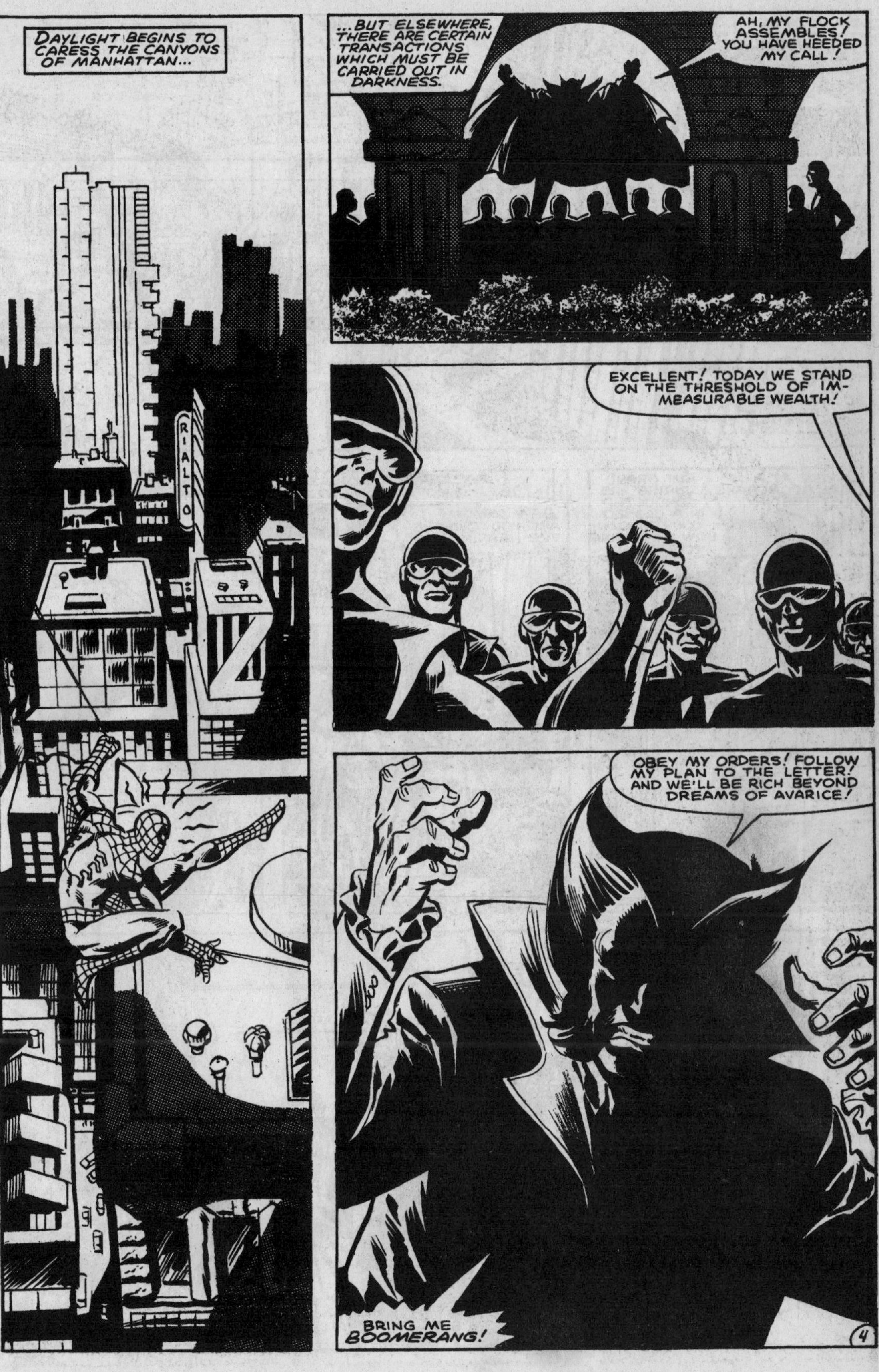
DAYLIGHT BEGINS TO CARESS THE CANYONS OF MANHATTAN...
RIALTO
...BUT ELSEWHERE, THERE ARE CERTAIN TRANSACTIONS WHICH MUST BE CARRIED OUT IN DARKNESS.
AH, MY FLOCK ASSEMBLES! YOU HAVE HEEDED MY CALL!
EXCELLENT! TODAY WE STAND ON THE THRESHOLD OF IM-MEASURABLE WEALTH!
OBEY MY ORDERS! FOLLOW MY PLAN TO THE LETTER! AND WE'LL BE RICH BEYOND DREAMS OF AVARICE!
BRING ME BOOMERANG!
4

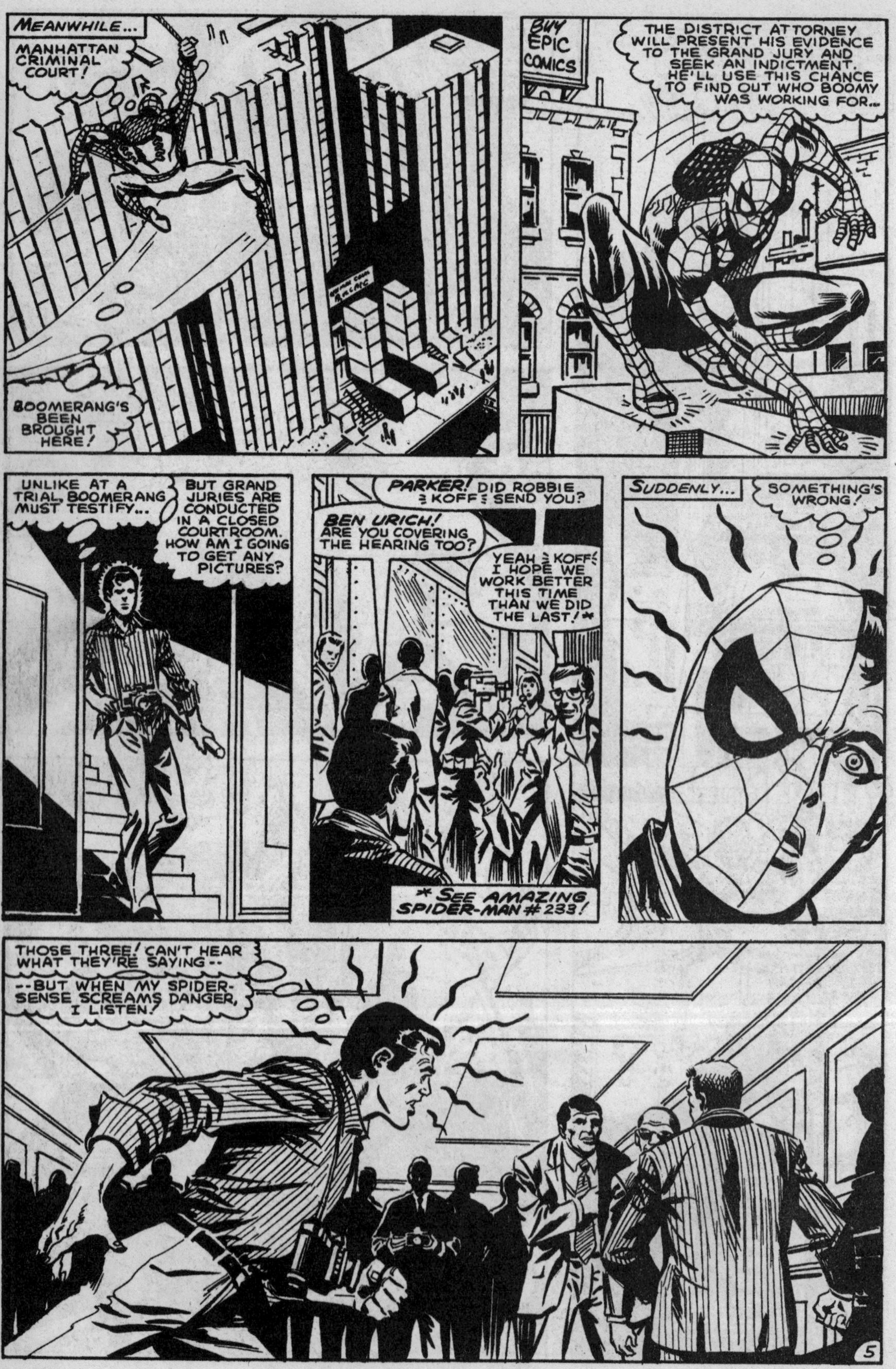

MEANWHILE...
MANHATTAN CRIMINAL COURT!
BOOMERANG'S BEEN BROUGHT HERE!
BUY EPIC COMICS
THE DISTRICT ATTORNEY WILL PRESENT HIS EVIDENCE TO THE GRAND JURY AND SEEK AN INDICTMENT. HE'LL USE THIS CHANCE TO FIND OUT WHO BOOMY WAS WORKING FOR...
UNLIKE AT A TRIAL, BOOMERANG MUST TESTIFY...
BUT GRAND JURIES ARE CONDUCTED IN A CLOSED COURTROOM. HOW AM I GOING TO GET ANY PICTURES?
PARKER! DID ROBBIE KOFF SEND YOU?
BEN URICH! ARE YOU COVERING THE HEARING TOO?
YEAH KOFF! I HOPE WE WORK BETTER THIS TIME THAN WE DID THE LAST! *
* SEE AMAZING SPIDER-MAN #233!
SUDDENLY...
SOMETHING'S WRONG!
THOSE THREE! CAN'T HEAR WHAT THEY'RE SAYING --
--BUT WHEN MY SPIDER-SENSE SCREAMS DANGER, I LISTEN!
5

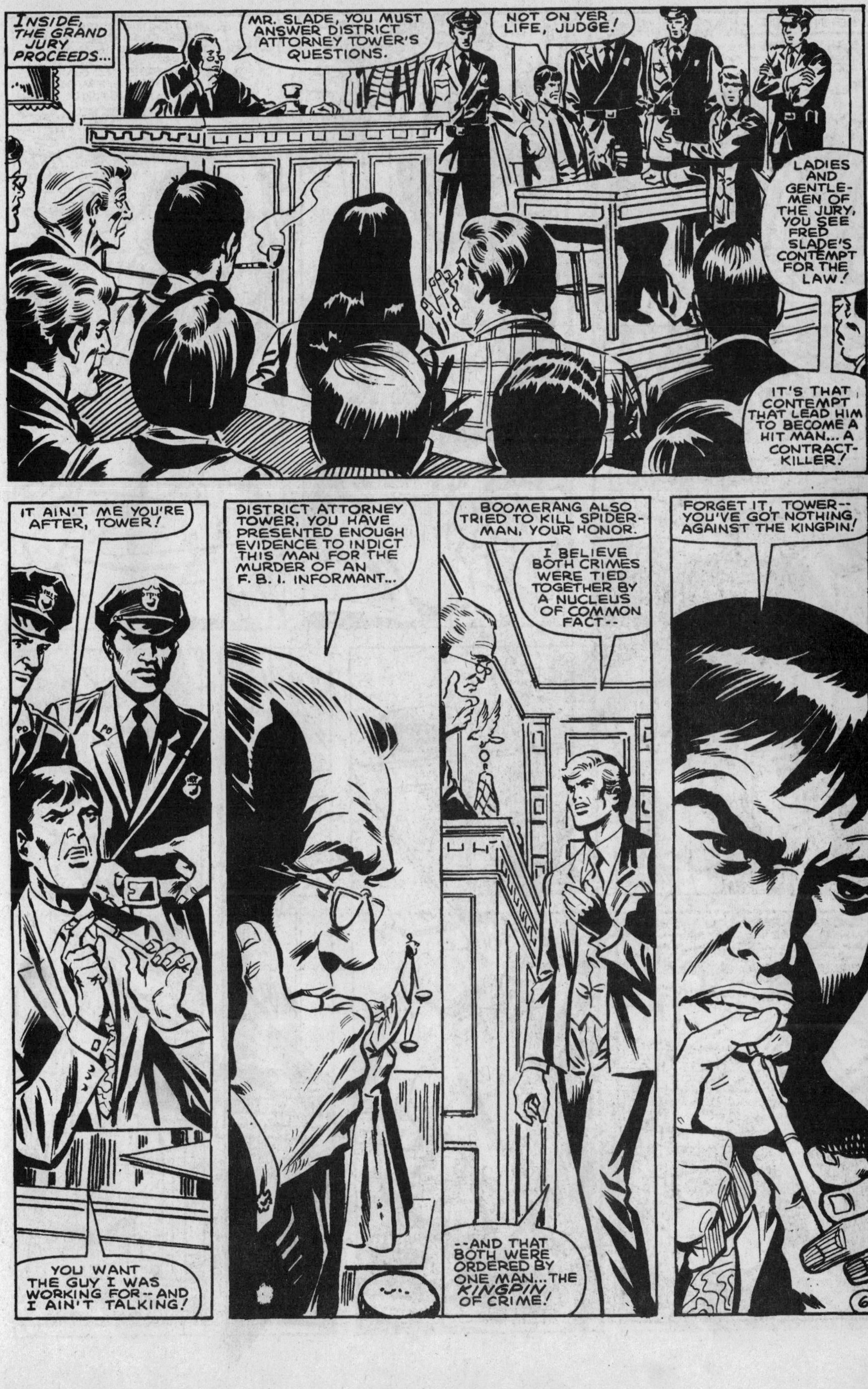
INSIDE, THE GRAND JURY PROCEEDS...
MR. SLADE, YOU MUST ANSWER DISTRICT ATTORNEY TOWER'S QUESTIONS.
NOT ON YER LIFE, JUDGE!
LADIES AND GENTLEMEN OF THE JURY, YOU SEE FRED SLADE'S CONTEMPT FOR THE LAW!
IT'S THAT CONTEMPT THAT LEAD HIM TO BECOME A HIT MAN... A CONTRACT-KILLER!
IT AIN'T ME YOU'RE AFTER, TOWER!
YOU WANT THE GUY I WAS WORKING FOR-- AND I AIN'T TALKING!
DISTRICT ATTORNEY TOWER, YOU HAVE PRESENTED ENOUGH EVIDENCE TO INDICT THIS MAN FOR THE MURDER OF AN F. B. I. INFORMANT...
BOOMERANG ALSO TRIED TO KILL SPIDER-MAN, YOUR HONOR.
I BELIEVE BOTH CRIMES WERE TIED TOGETHER BY A NUCLEUS OF COMMON FACT--
--AND THAT BOTH WERE ORDERED BY ONE MAN... THE KINGPIN OF CRIME!
FORGET IT, TOWER-- YOU'VE GOT NOTHING AGAINST THE KINGPIN!
6

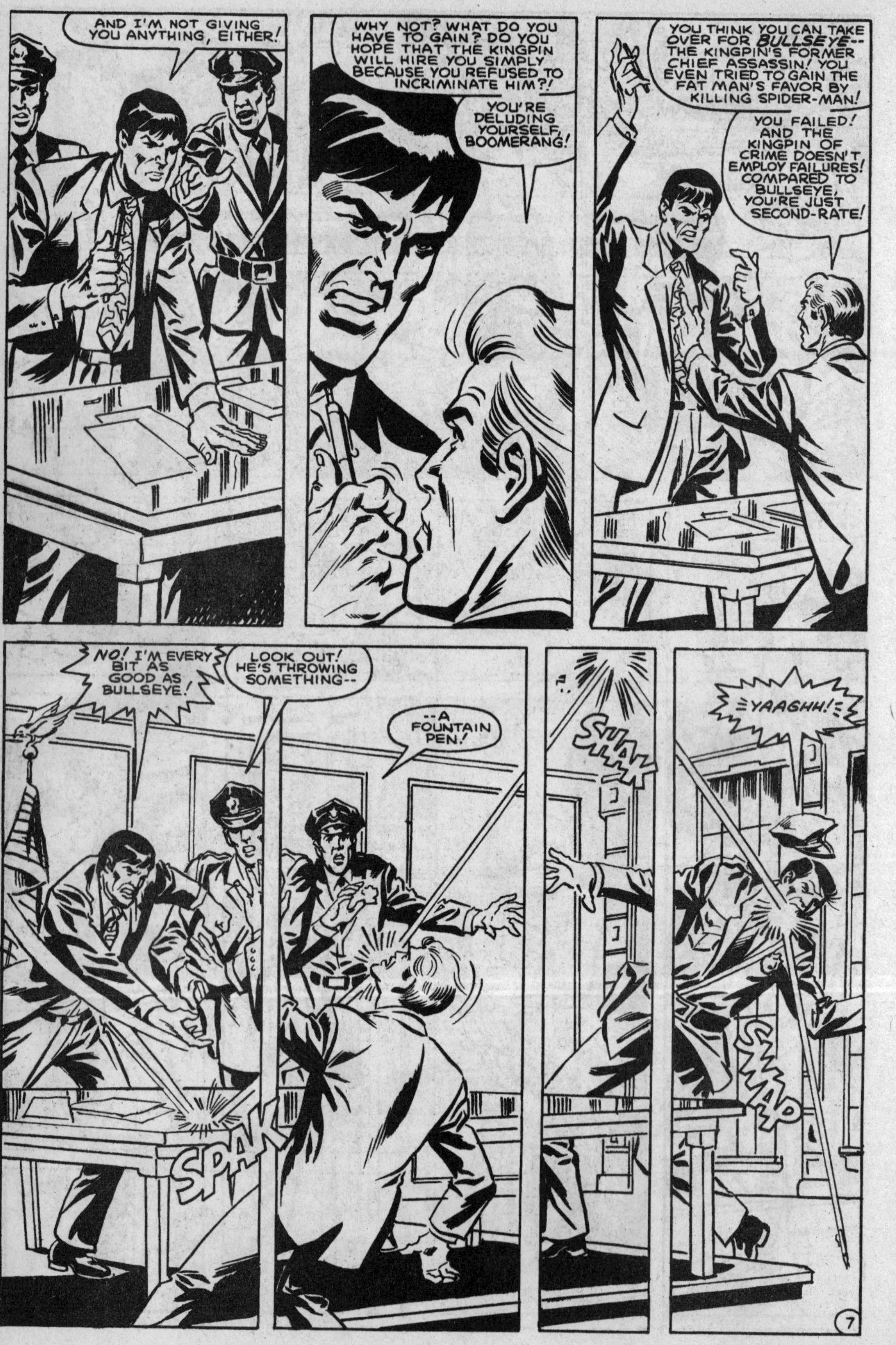
AND I'M NOT GIVING YOU ANYTHING, EITHER!
WHY NOT? WHAT DO YOU HAVE TO GAIN? DO YOU HOPE THAT THE KINGPIN WILL HIRE YOU SIMPLY BECAUSE YOU REFUSED TO INCRIMINATE HIM?!
YOU'RE DELUDING YOURSELF, BOOMERANG!
YOU THINK YOU CAN TAKE OVER FOR BULLSEYE-- THE KINGPIN'S FORMER CHIEF ASSASSIN! YOU EVEN TRIED TO GAIN THE FAT MAN'S FAVOR BY KILLING SPIDER-MAN!
YOU FAILED! AND THE KINGPIN OF CRIME DOESN'T EMPLOY FAILURES! COMPARED TO BULLSEYE, YOU'RE JUST SECOND-RATE!
NO! I'M EVERY BIT AS GOOD AS BULLSEYE!
LOOK OUT! HE'S THROWING SOMETHING--
--A FOUNTAIN PEN!
SPAK
SHAK
YAAGHH!
SNAP

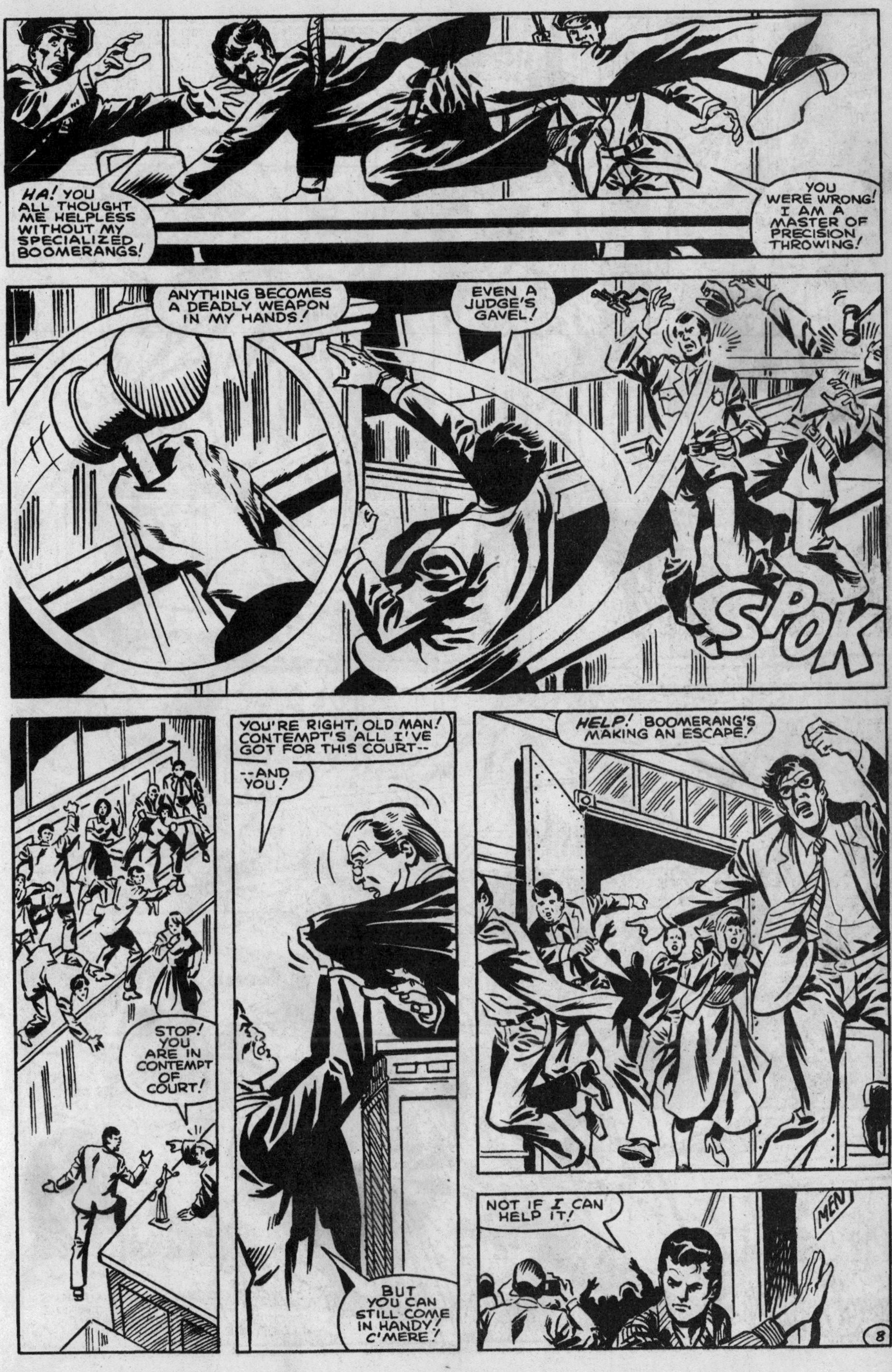
HA! YOU ALL THOUGHT ME HELPLESS WITHOUT MY SPECIALIZED BOOMERANGS!
YOU WERE WRONG! I AM A MASTER OF PRECISION THROWING!
ANYTHING BECOMES A DEADLY WEAPON IN MY HANDS!
EVEN A JUDGE'S GAVEL!
SPOK
STOP! YOU ARE IN CONTEMPT OF COURT!
YOU'RE RIGHT, OLD MAN! CONTEMPT'S ALL I'VE GOT FOR THIS COURT--
--AND YOU!
BUT YOU CAN STILL COME IN HANDY! C'MERE!
HELP! BOOMERANG'S MAKING AN ESCAPE!
NOT IF I CAN HELP IT!
MEN

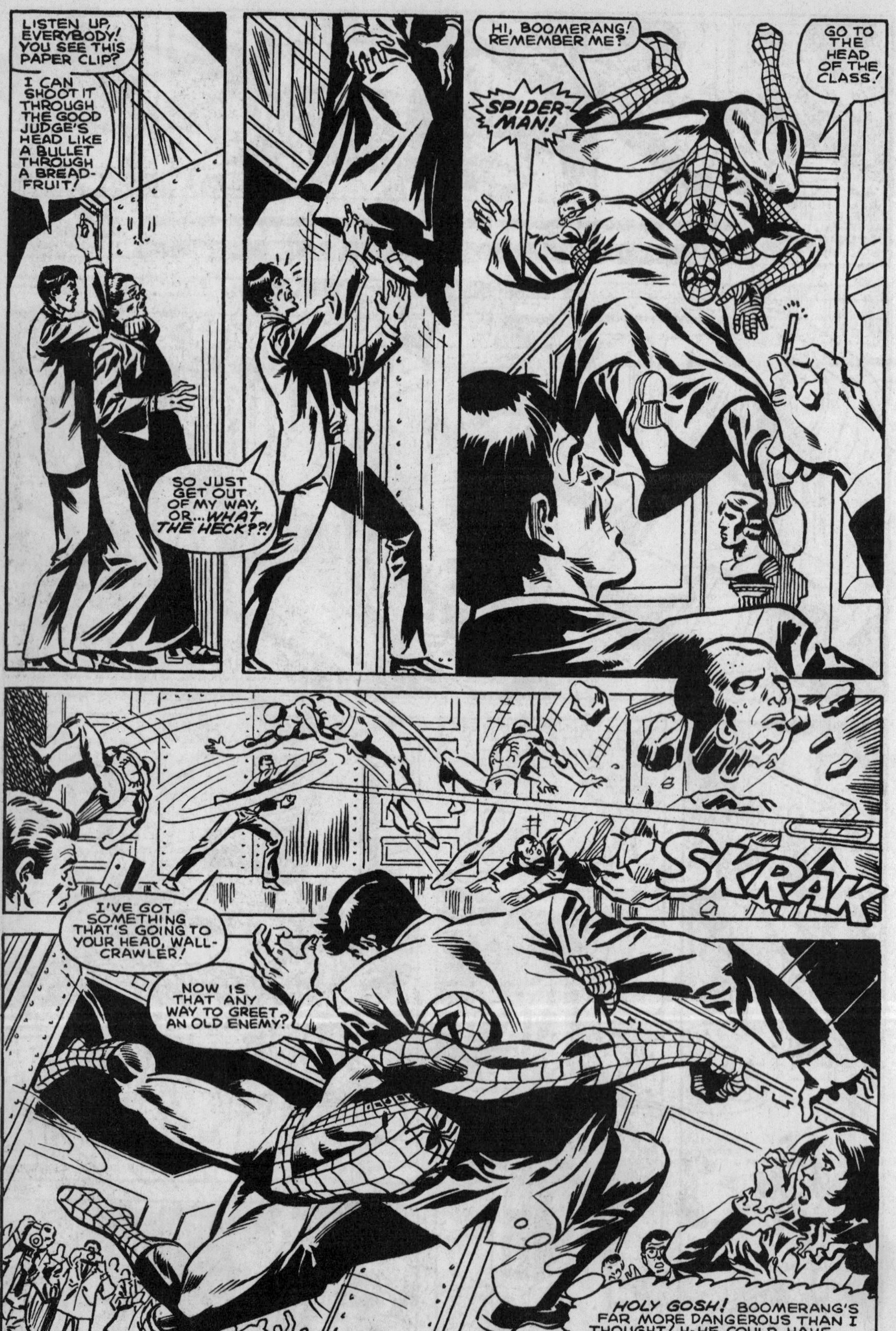
LISTEN UP, EVERYBODY! YOU SEE THIS PAPER CLIP?
I CAN SHOOT IT THROUGH THE GOOD JUDGE'S HEAD LIKE A BULLET THROUGH A BREAD-FRUIT!
SO JUST GET OUT OF MY WAY, OR... WHAT THE HECK??!
HI, BOOMERANG! REMEMBER ME?
SPIDER-MAN!
GO TO THE HEAD OF THE CLASS!
SKRAK
I'VE GOT SOMETHING THAT'S GOING TO YOUR HEAD, WALL-CRAWLER!
NOW IS THAT ANY WAY TO GREET AN OLD ENEMY?
HOLY GOSH! BOOMERANG'S FAR MORE DANGEROUS THAN I THOUGHT! H-HE COULD HAVE KILLED ME WITH THAT THING!
9

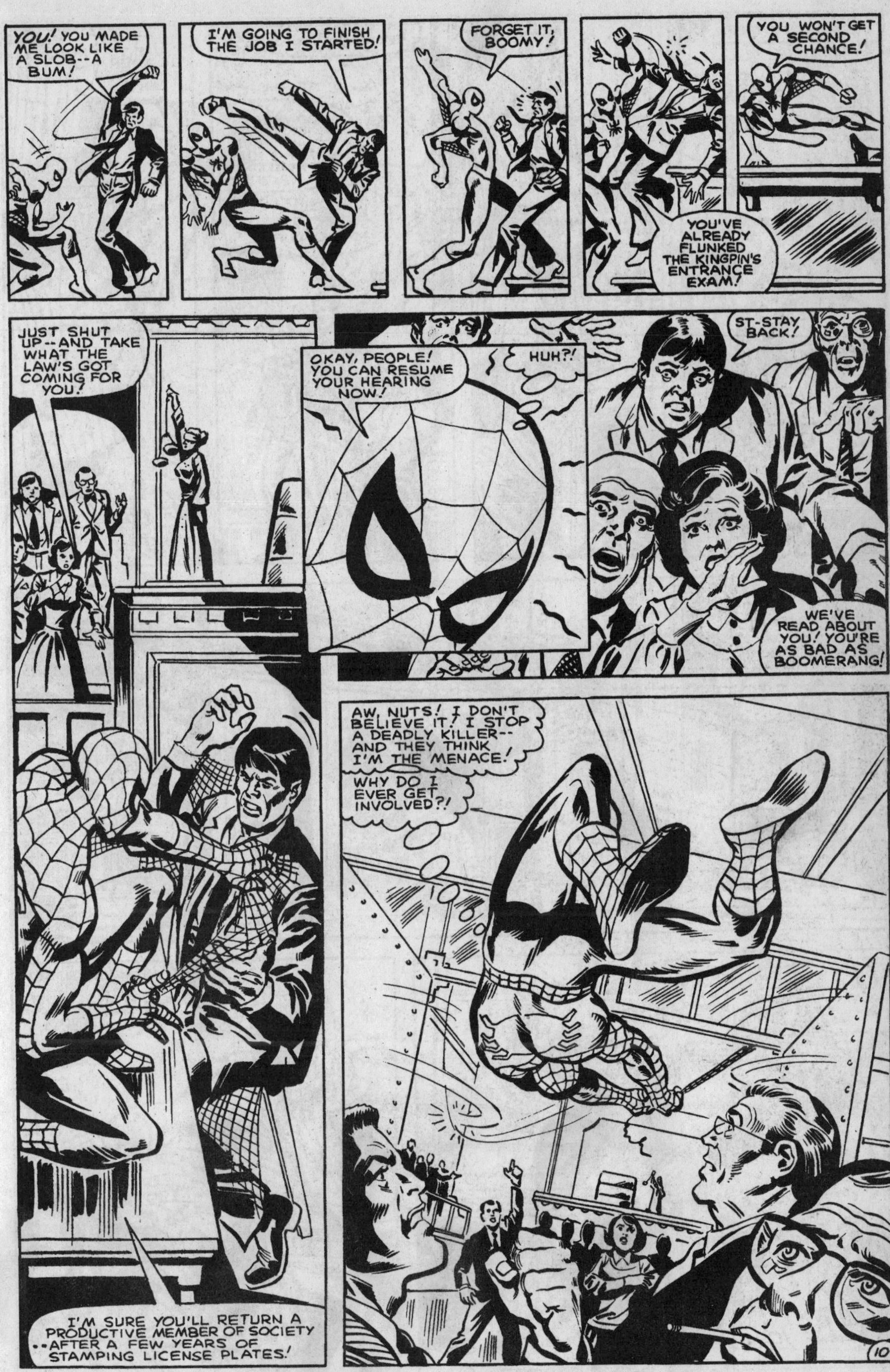

YOU! YOU MADE ME LOOK LIKE A SLOB--A BUM!
I'M GOING TO FINISH THE JOB I STARTED!
FORGET IT, BOOMY!
YOU WON'T GET A SECOND CHANCE!
YOU'VE ALREADY FLUNKED THE KINGPIN'S ENTRANCE EXAM!
JUST SHUT UP--AND TAKE WHAT THE LAW'S GOT COMING FOR YOU!
I'M SURE YOU'LL RETURN A PRODUCTIVE MEMBER OF SOCIETY --AFTER A FEW YEARS OF STAMPING LICENSE PLATES!
OKAY, PEOPLE! YOU CAN RESUME YOUR HEARING NOW!
HUH?!
ST-STAY BACK!
WE'VE READ ABOUT YOU! YOU'RE AS BAD AS BOOMERANG!
AW, NUTS! I DON'T BELIEVE IT! I STOP A DEADLY KILLER--AND THEY THINK I'M THE MENACE!
WHY DO I EVER GET INVOLVED?!
10

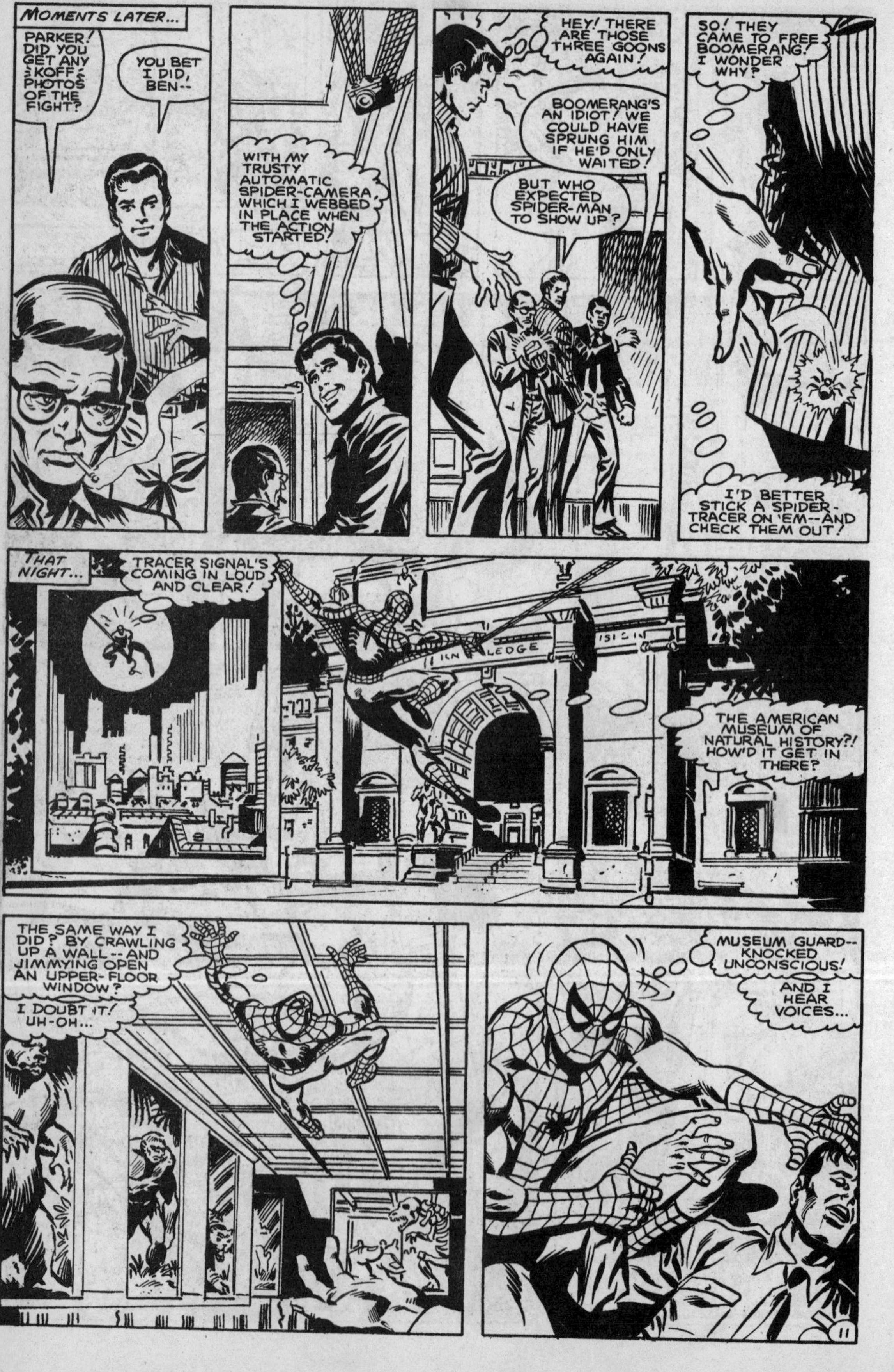
MOMENTS LATER...
PARKER! DID YOU GET ANY KOFF PHOTOS OF THE FIGHT?
YOU BET I DID, BEN--
WITH MY TRUSTY AUTOMATIC SPIDER-CAMERA, WHICH I WEBBED IN PLACE WHEN THE ACTION STARTED!
HEY! THERE ARE THOSE THREE GOONS AGAIN!
BOOMERANG'S AN IDIOT! WE COULD HAVE SPRUNG HIM IF HE'D ONLY WAITED!
BUT WHO EXPECTED SPIDER-MAN TO SHOW UP?
SO! THEY CAME TO FREE BOOMERANG! I WONDER WHY?
I'D BETTER STICK A SPIDER-TRACER ON 'EM--AND CHECK THEM OUT!
THAT NIGHT...
TRACER SIGNAL'S COMING IN LOUD AND CLEAR!
THE AMERICAN MUSEUM OF NATURAL HISTORY?! HOW'D IT GET IN THERE?
THE SAME WAY I DID? BY CRAWLING UP A WALL--AND JIMMYING OPEN AN UPPER-FLOOR WINDOW?
I DOUBT IT! UH-OH...
MUSEUM GUARD--KNOCKED UNCONSCIOUS!
AND I HEAR VOICES...

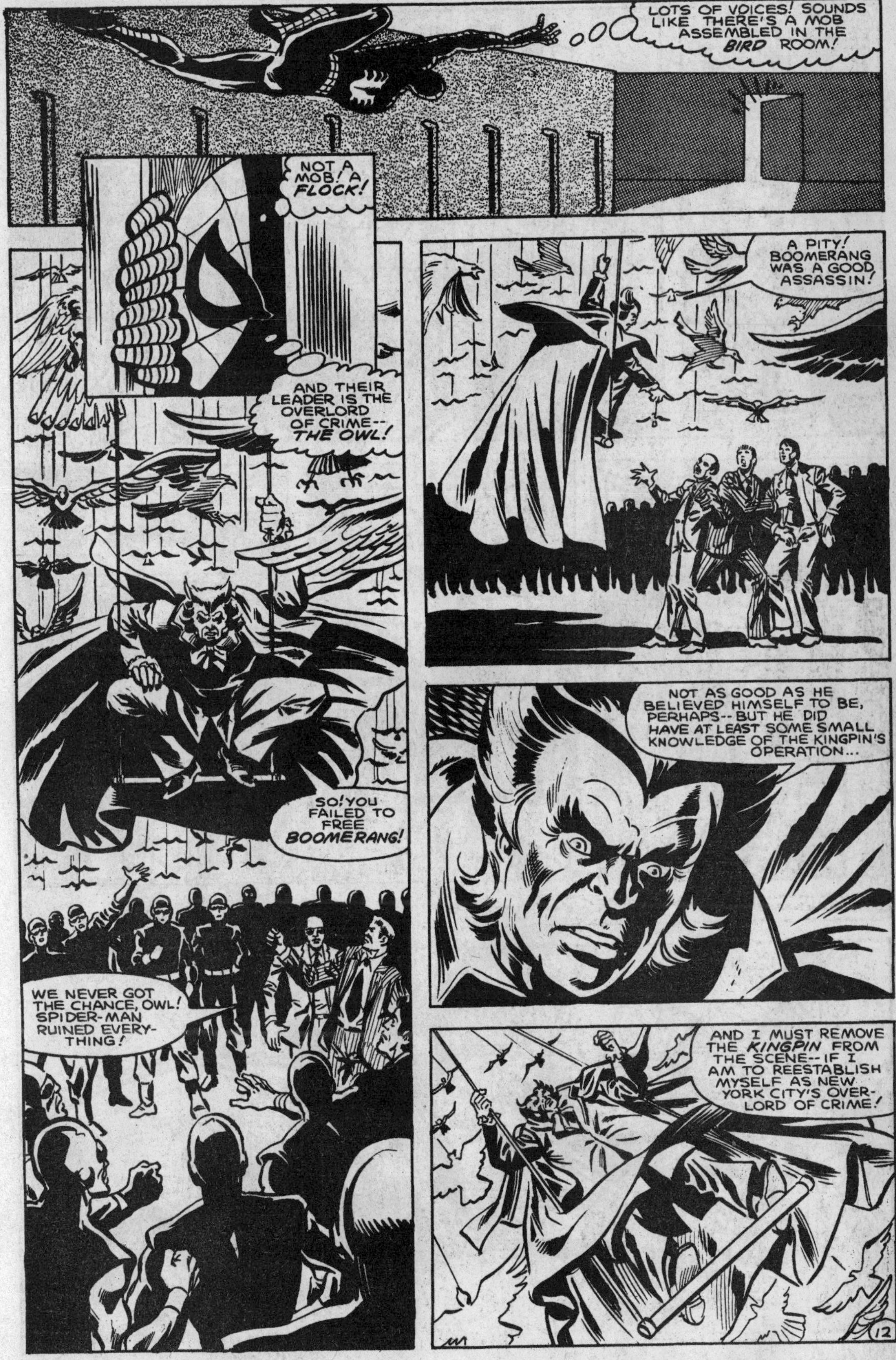
LOTS OF VOICES! SOUNDS LIKE THERE'S A MOB ASSEMBLED IN THE BIRD ROOM!
NOT A MOB! A FLOCK!
AND THEIR LEADER IS THE OVERLORD OF CRIME-- THE OWL!
SO! YOU FAILED TO FREE BOOMERANG!
WE NEVER GOT THE CHANCE, OWL! SPIDER-MAN RUINED EVERY-THING!
A PITY! BOOMERANG WAS A GOOD ASSASSIN!
NOT AS GOOD AS HE BELIEVED HIMSELF TO BE, PERHAPS-- BUT HE DID HAVE AT LEAST SOME SMALL KNOWLEDGE OF THE KINGPIN'S OPERATION...
AND I MUST REMOVE THE KINGPIN FROM THE SCENE-- IF I AM TO REESTABLISH MYSELF AS NEW YORK CITY'S OVER-LORD OF CRIME!
12

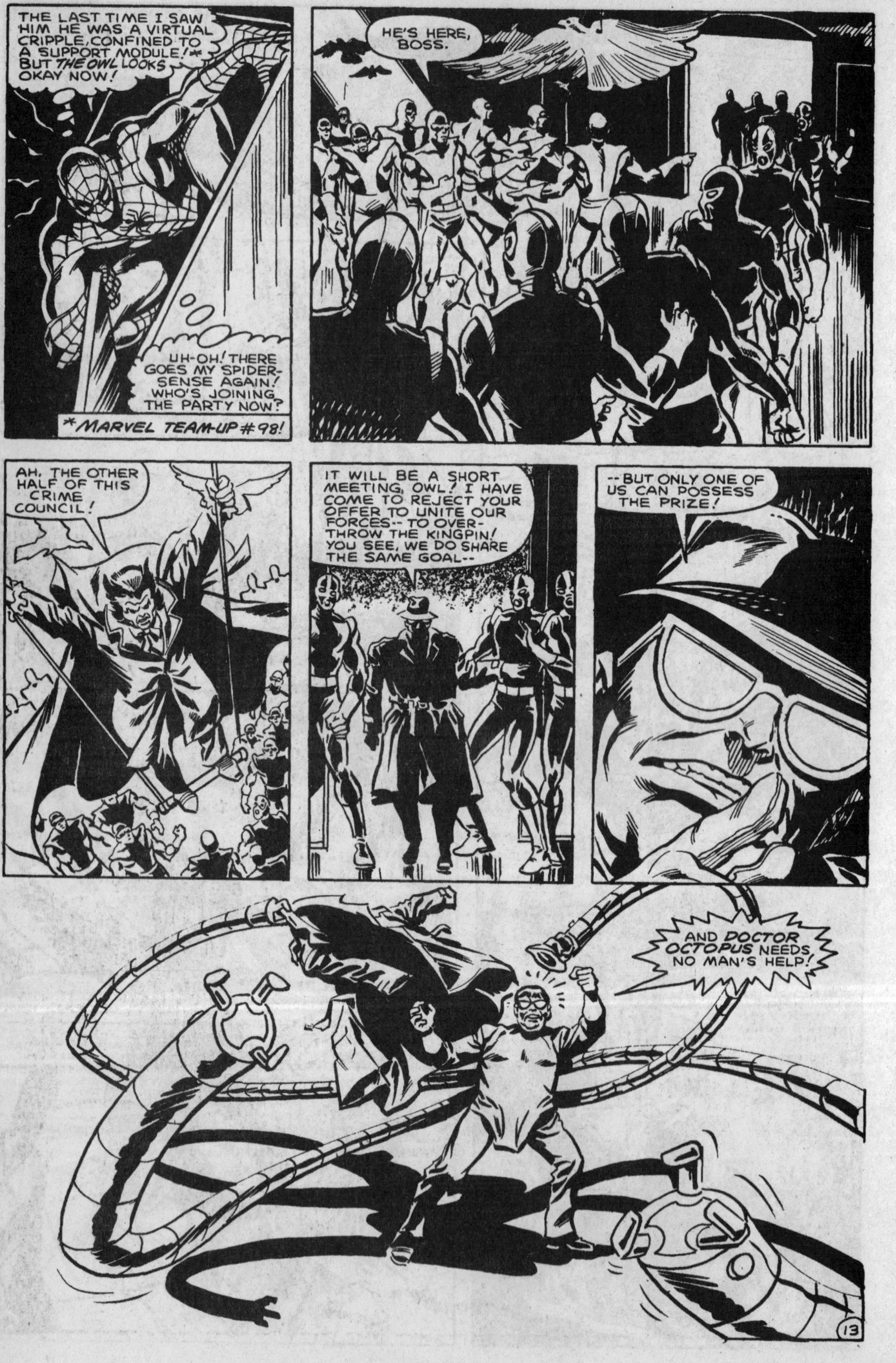
THE LAST TIME I SAW HIM HE WAS A VIRTUAL CRIPPLE, CONFINED TO A SUPPORT MODULE!* BUT THE OWL LOOKS OKAY NOW!
UH-OH! THERE GOES MY SPIDER-SENSE AGAIN! WHO'S JOINING THE PARTY NOW?
*MARVEL TEAM-UP #98!
HE'S HERE, BOSS.
AH, THE OTHER HALF OF THIS CRIME COUNCIL!
IT WILL BE A SHORT MEETING, OWL! I HAVE COME TO REJECT YOUR OFFER TO UNITE OUR FORCES-- TO OVERTHROW THE KINGPIN! YOU SEE, WE DO SHARE THE SAME GOAL--
--BUT ONLY ONE OF US CAN POSSESS THE PRIZE!
AND DOCTOR OCTOPUS NEEDS NO MAN'S HELP!
13

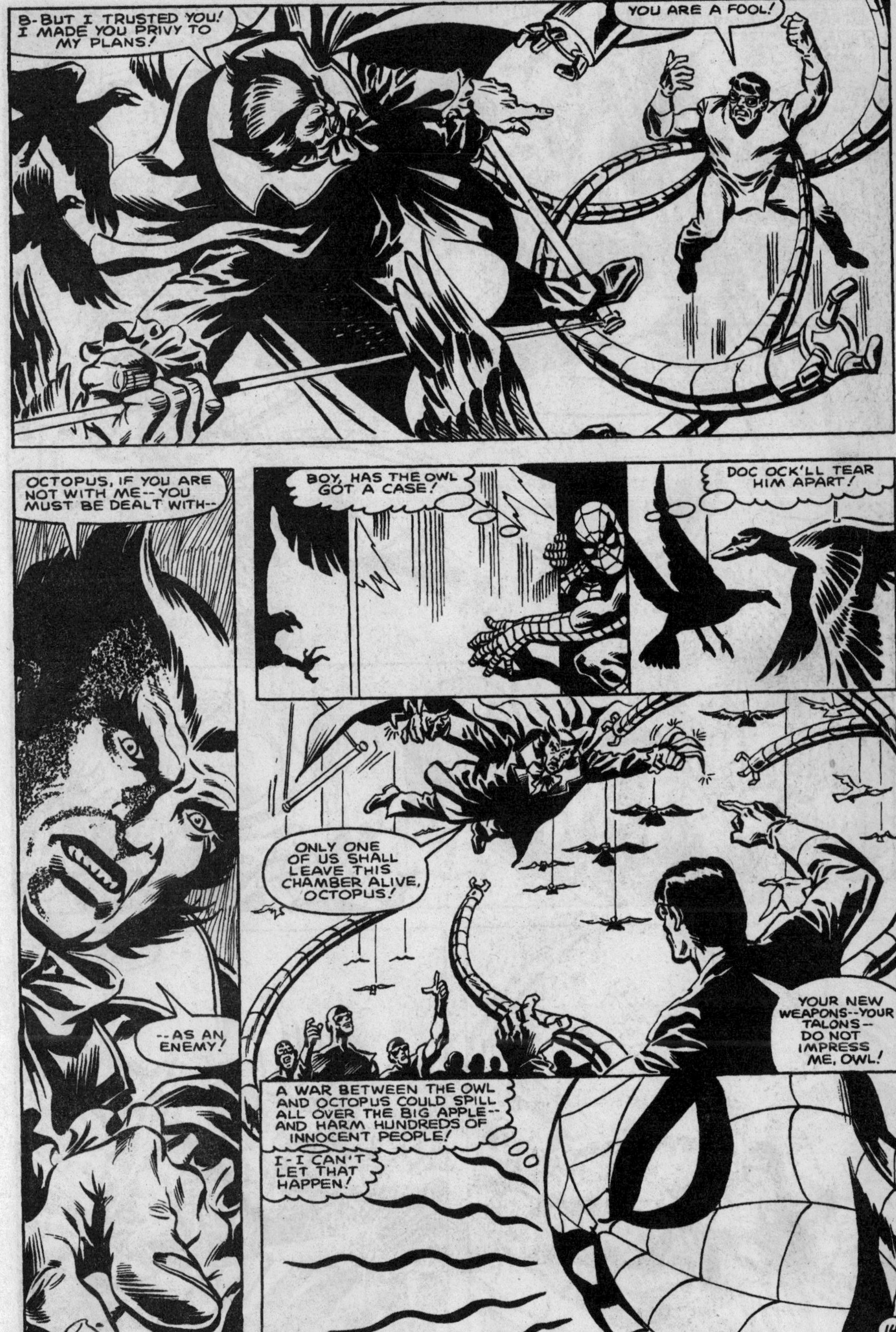
B-BUT I TRUSTED YOU! I MADE YOU PRIVY TO MY PLANS!
YOU ARE A FOOL!
OCTOPUS, IF YOU ARE NOT WITH ME--YOU MUST BE DEALT WITH--
--AS AN ENEMY!
BOY, HAS THE OWL GOT A CASE!
DOC OCK'LL TEAR HIM APART!
ONLY ONE OF US SHALL LEAVE THIS CHAMBER ALIVE, OCTOPUS!
YOUR NEW WEAPONS--YOUR TALONS--DO NOT IMPRESS ME, OWL!
A WAR BETWEEN THE OWL AND OCTOPUS COULD SPILL ALL OVER THE BIG APPLE--AND HARM HUNDREDS OF INNOCENT PEOPLE!
I-I CAN'T LET THAT HAPPEN!
14

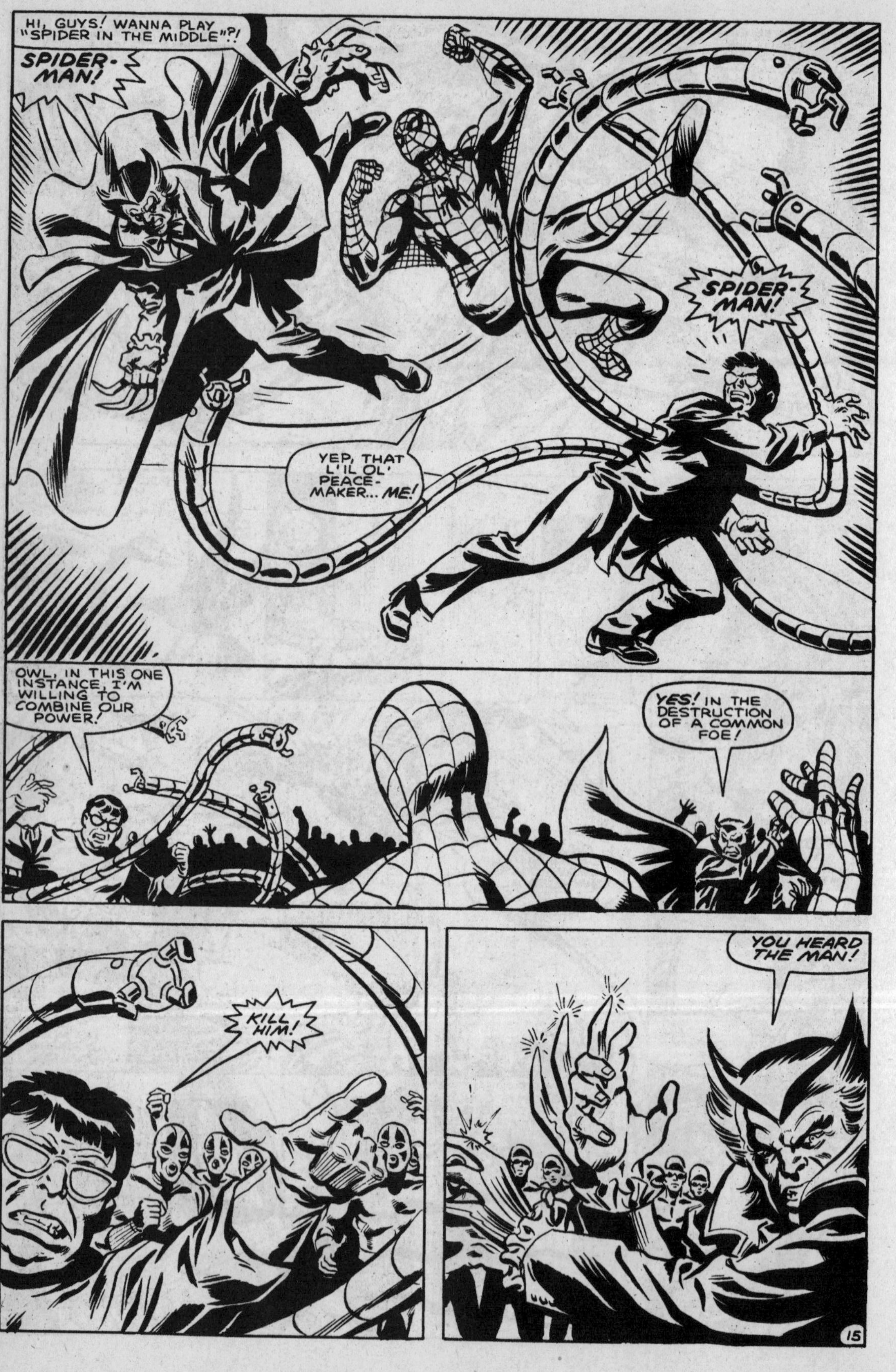
HI, GUYS! WANNA PLAY "SPIDER IN THE MIDDLE"?!
SPIDER-MAN!
SPIDER-MAN!
YEP, THAT L'IL OL' PEACE-MAKER... ME!
OWL, IN THIS ONE INSTANCE, I'M WILLING TO COMBINE OUR POWER!
YES! IN THE DESTRUCTION OF A COMMON FOE!
KILL HIM!
YOU HEARD THE MAN!

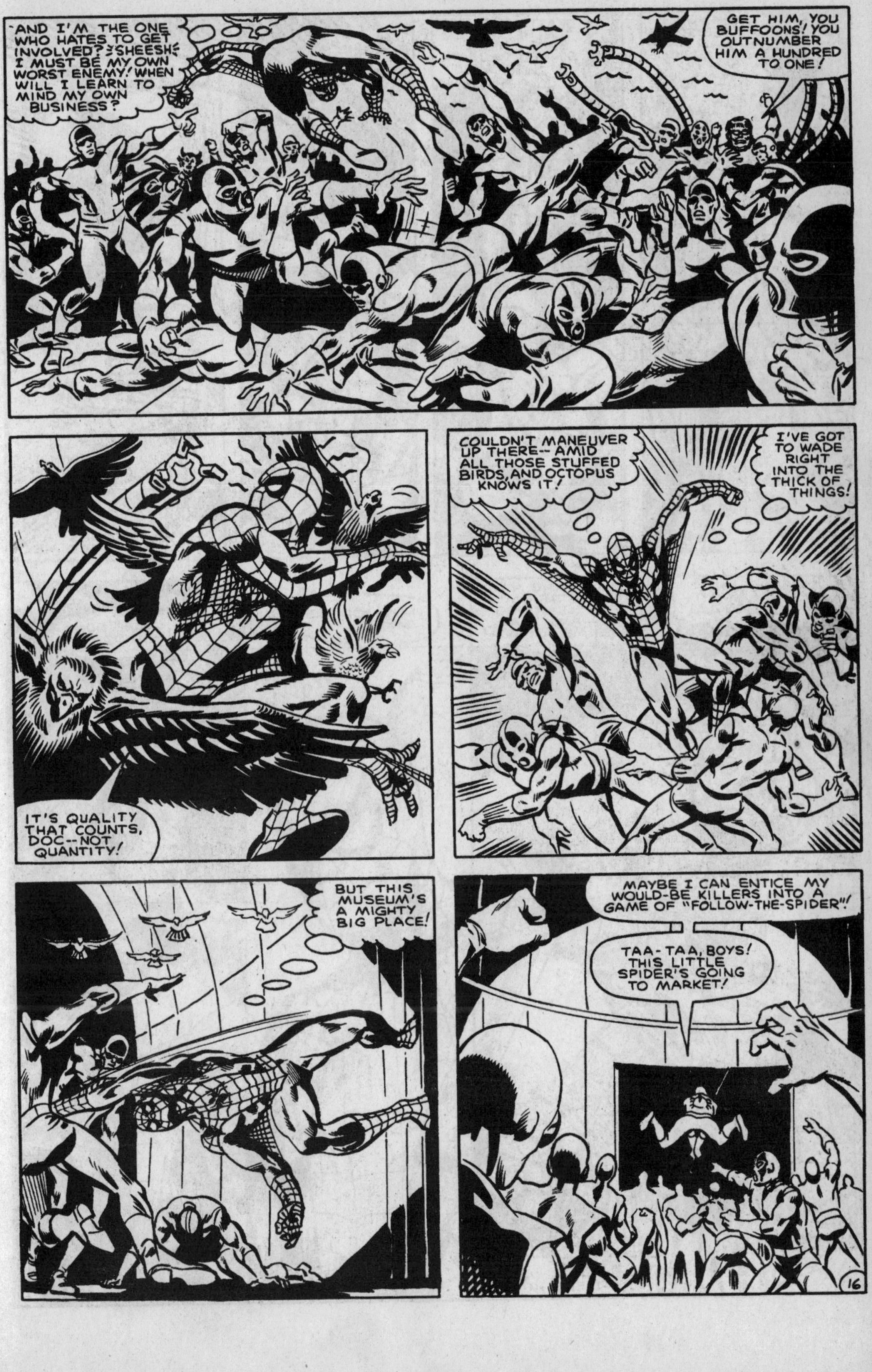
AND I'M THE ONE WHO HATES TO GET INVOLVED? SHEESH! I MUST BE MY OWN WORST ENEMY! WHEN WILL I LEARN TO MIND MY OWN BUSINESS?
GET HIM, YOU BUFFOONS! YOU OUTNUMBER HIM A HUNDRED TO ONE!
IT'S QUALITY THAT COUNTS, DOC--NOT QUANTITY!
COULDN'T MANEUVER UP THERE--AMID ALL THOSE STUFFED BIRDS, AND OCTOPUS KNOWS IT!
I'VE GOT TO WADE RIGHT INTO THE THICK OF THINGS!
BUT THIS MUSEUM'S A MIGHTY BIG PLACE!
MAYBE I CAN ENTICE MY WOULD-BE KILLERS INTO A GAME OF "FOLLOW-THE-SPIDER"!
TAA-TAA, BOYS! THIS LITTLE SPIDER'S GOING TO MARKET!
16

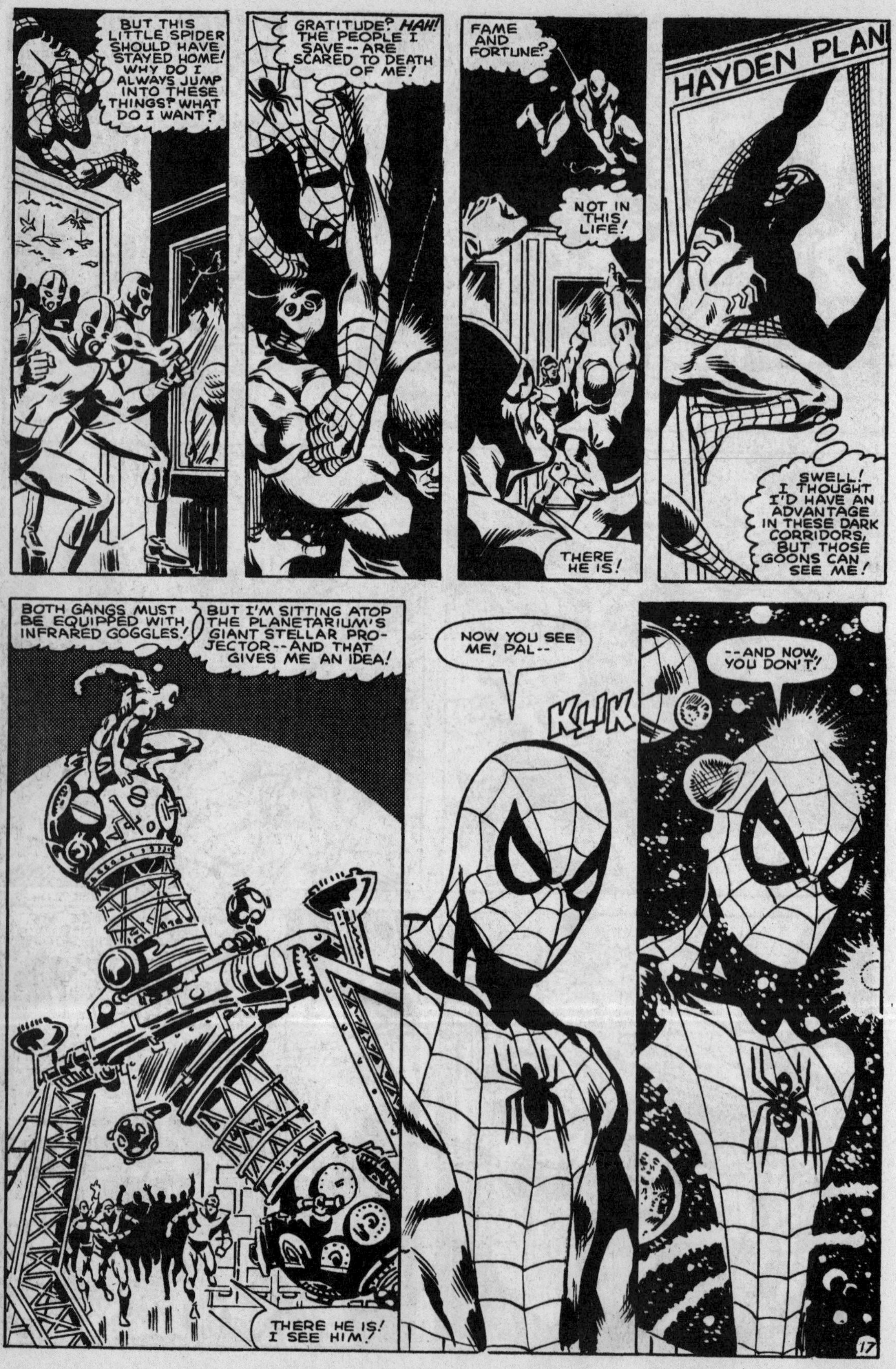

BUT THIS LITTLE SPIDER SHOULD HAVE STAYED HOME! WHY DO I ALWAYS JUMP INTO THESE THINGS? WHAT DO I WANT?
GRATITUDE? HAH! THE PEOPLE I SAVE--ARE SCARED TO DEATH OF ME!
FAME AND FORTUNE?
NOT IN THIS LIFE!
THERE HE IS!
HAYDEN PLAN
SWELL! I THOUGHT I'D HAVE AN ADVANTAGE IN THESE DARK CORRIDORS, BUT THOSE GOONS CAN SEE ME!
BOTH GANGS MUST BE EQUIPPED WITH INFRARED GOGGLES!
BUT I'M SITTING ATOP THE PLANETARIUM'S GIANT STELLAR PROJECTOR--AND THAT GIVES ME AN IDEA!
THERE HE IS! I SEE HIM!
NOW YOU SEE ME, PAL--
KLIK
--AND NOW, YOU DON'T!
17

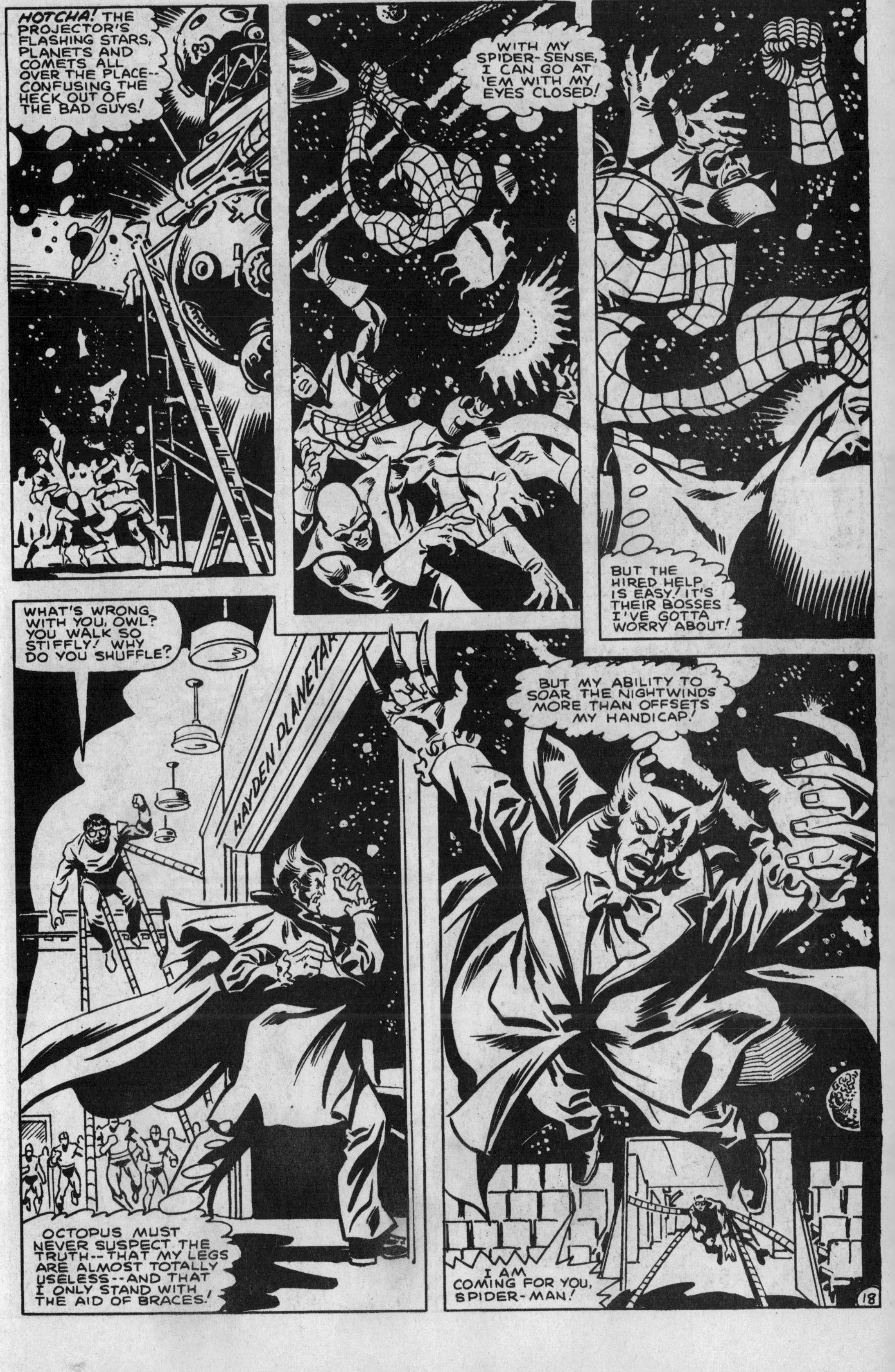

HOTCHA! THE PROJECTOR'S FLASHING STARS, PLANETS AND COMETS ALL OVER THE PLACE--CONFUSING THE HECK OUT OF THE BAD GUYS!
WITH MY SPIDER-SENSE, I CAN GO AT 'EM WITH MY EYES CLOSED!
BUT THE HIRED HELP IS EASY! IT'S THEIR BOSSES I'VE GOTTA WORRY ABOUT!
WHAT'S WRONG WITH YOU, OWL? YOU WALK SO STIFFLY! WHY DO YOU SHUFFLE?
HAYDEN PLANETAR
OCTOPUS MUST NEVER SUSPECT THE TRUTH--THAT MY LEGS ARE ALMOST TOTALLY USELESS--AND THAT I ONLY STAND WITH THE AID OF BRACES!
BUT MY ABILITY TO SOAR THE NIGHTWINDS MORE THAN OFFSETS MY HANDICAP!
I AM COMING FOR YOU, SPIDER-MAN!
18

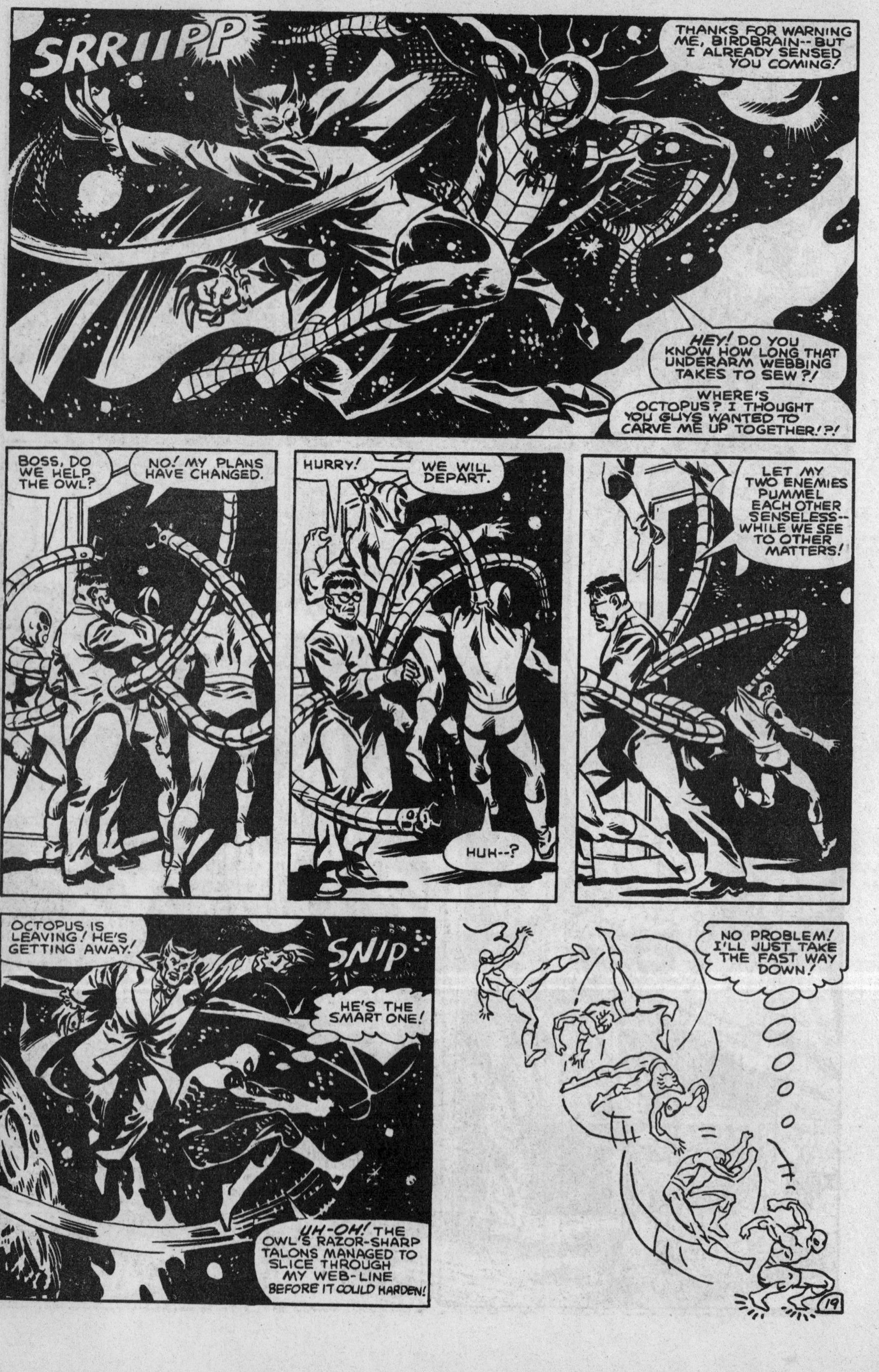
SRRIIPP
THANKS FOR WARNING ME, BIRDBRAIN-- BUT I ALREADY SENSED YOU COMING!
HEY! DO YOU KNOW HOW LONG THAT UNDERARM WEBBING TAKES TO SEW?!
WHERE'S OCTOPUS? I THOUGHT YOU GUYS WANTED TO CARVE ME UP TOGETHER!?!
BOSS, DO WE HELP THE OWL?
NO! MY PLANS HAVE CHANGED.
HURRY!
WE WILL DEPART.
HUH--?
LET MY TWO ENEMIES PUMMEL EACH OTHER SENSELESS-- WHILE WE SEE TO OTHER MATTERS!
OCTOPUS IS LEAVING! HE'S GETTING AWAY!
SNIP
HE'S THE SMART ONE!
UH-OH! THE OWL'S RAZOR-SHARP TALONS MANAGED TO SLICE THROUGH MY WEB-LINE BEFORE IT COULD HARDEN!
NO PROBLEM! I'LL JUST TAKE THE FAST WAY DOWN!
19

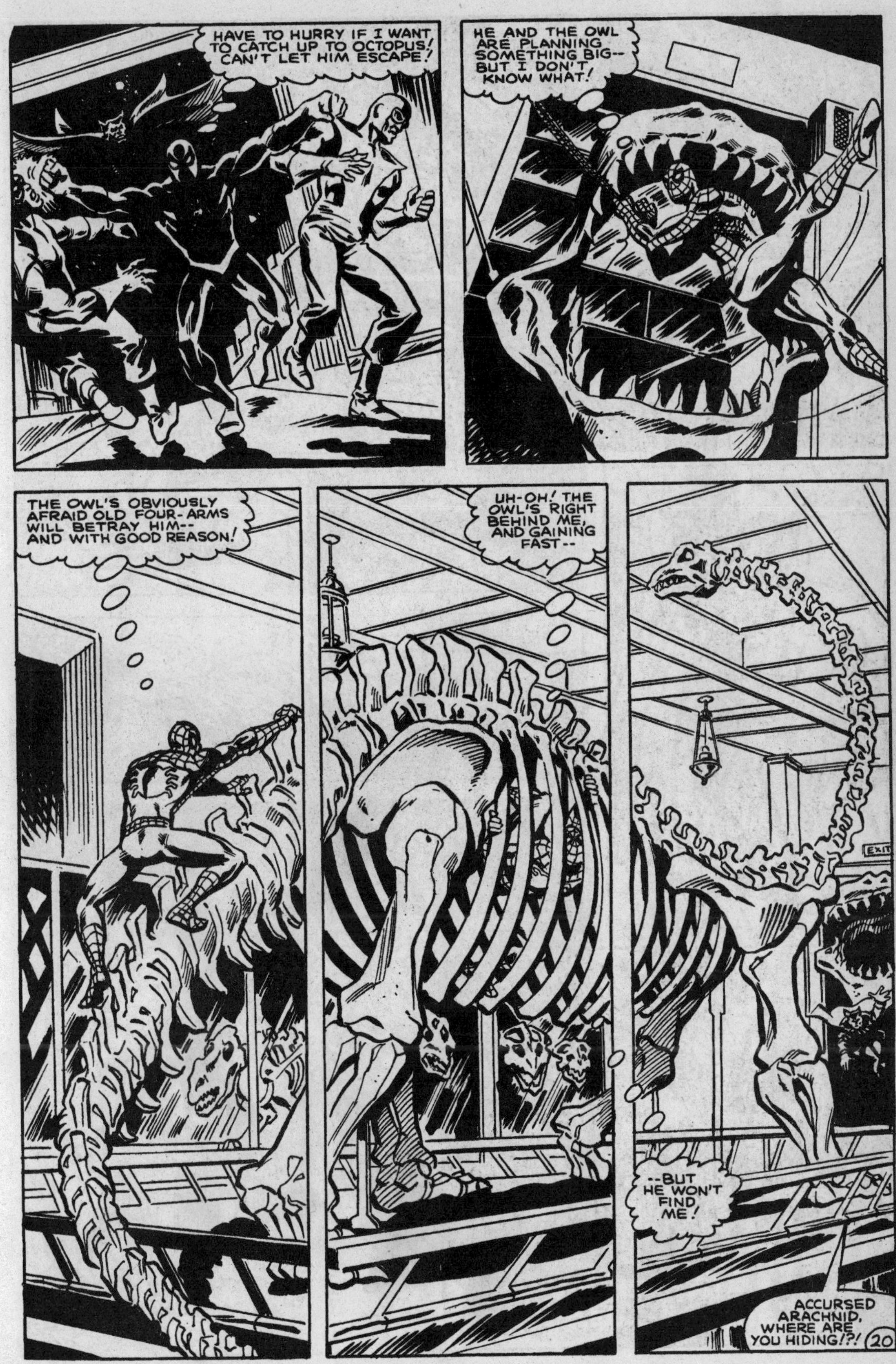
HAVE TO HURRY IF I WANT TO CATCH UP TO OCTOPUS! CAN'T LET HIM ESCAPE!
HE AND THE OWL ARE PLANNING SOMETHING BIG-- BUT I DON'T KNOW WHAT!
THE OWL'S OBVIOUSLY AFRAID OLD FOUR-ARMS WILL BETRAY HIM-- AND WITH GOOD REASON!
UH-OH! THE OWL'S RIGHT BEHIND ME, AND GAINING FAST--
--BUT HE WON'T FIND ME!
EXIT
ACCURSED ARACHNID, WHERE ARE YOU HIDING!?!
20

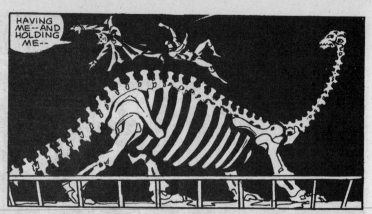

HAVING ME--AND HOLDING ME--

--ARE NOT THE SAME, SPIDER-MAN--

--AS YOU SHALL NOW LEARN!

INSIDE DEM BONES, DEM BONES, DEM DRY OLD BONES! *GOTCHA!*

THW!P!

ADIEU!

THE OWL'S GONE--

--AND THERE'S NO SIGN OF OCTOPUS!

I--I REALLY FLUSHED OUT! I LOST THEM BOTH!

21

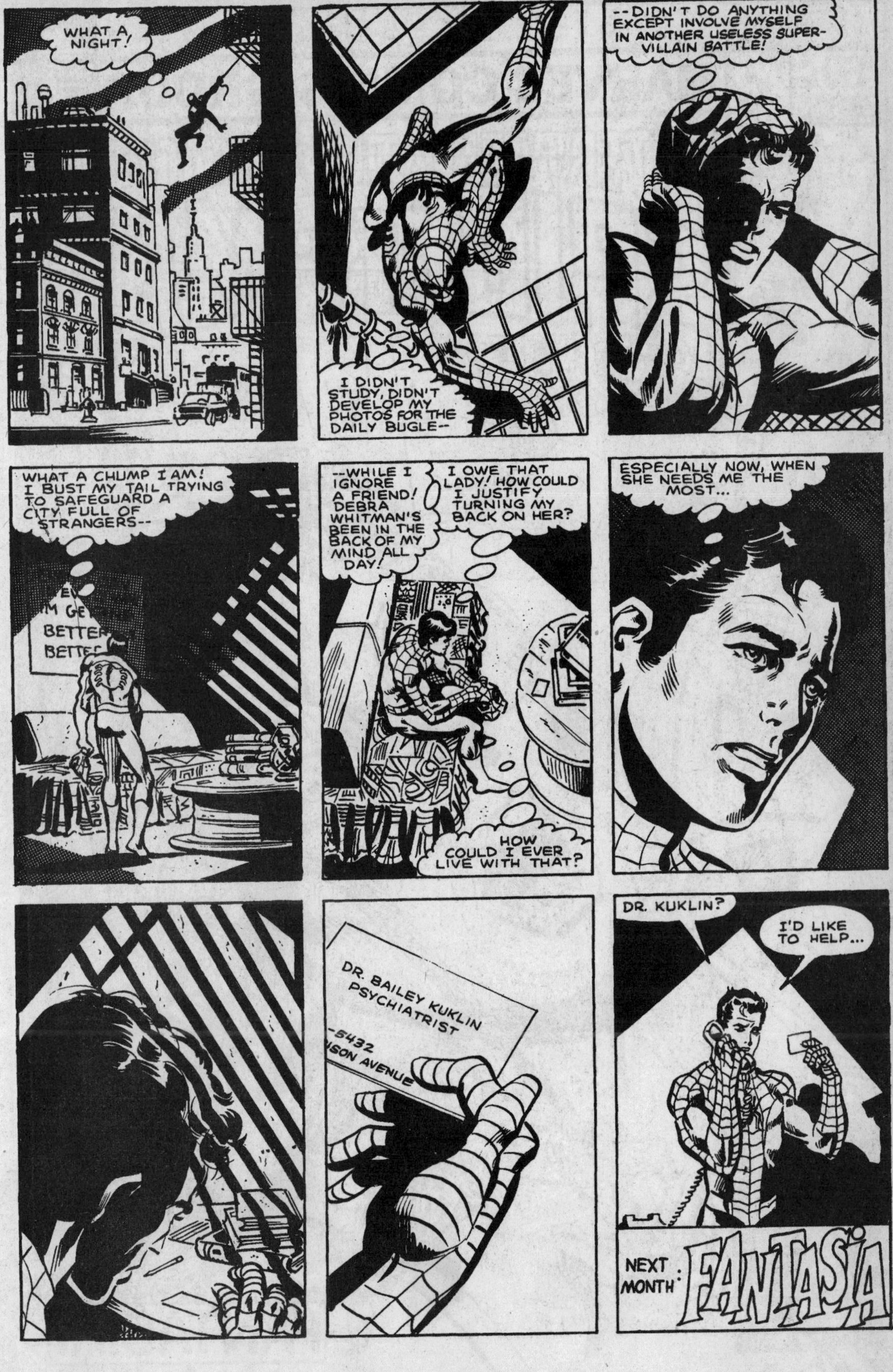
WHAT A NIGHT!
I DIDN'T STUDY, DIDN'T DEVELOP MY PHOTOS FOR THE DAILY BUGLE--
--DIDN'T DO ANYTHING EXCEPT INVOLVE MYSELF IN ANOTHER USELESS SUPER-VILLAIN BATTLE!
WHAT A CHUMP I AM! I BUST MY TAIL TRYING TO SAFEGUARD A CITY FULL OF STRANGERS--
--WHILE I IGNORE A FRIEND! DEBRA WHITMAN'S BEEN IN THE BACK OF MY MIND ALL DAY!
I OWE THAT LADY! HOW COULD I JUSTIFY TURNING MY BACK ON HER?
HOW COULD I EVER LIVE WITH THAT?
ESPECIALLY NOW, WHEN SHE NEEDS ME THE MOST...
DR. BAILEY KUKLIN
PSYCHIATRIST
-5432
ISON AVENUE
DR. KUKLIN?
I'D LIKE TO HELP...
NEXT MONTH: FANTASIA

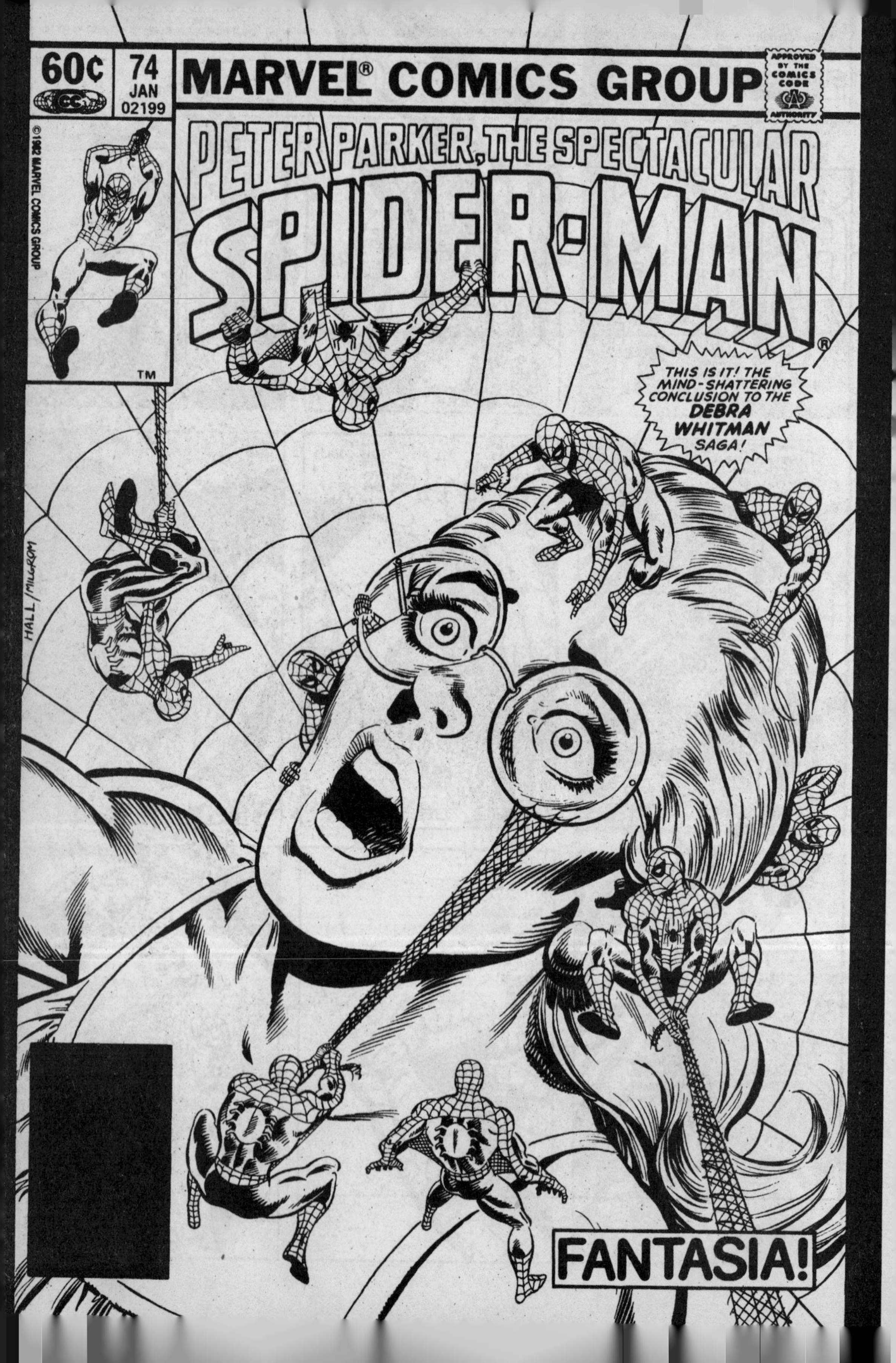

60¢
74
JAN
02199
MARVEL® COMICS GROUP
APPROVED BY THE COMICS CODE AUTHORITY
PETER PARKER, THE SPECTACULAR
SPIDER-MAN®
© 1982 MARVEL COMICS GROUP
TM
THIS IS IT! THE MIND-SHATTERING CONCLUSION TO THE DEBRA WHITMAN SAGA!
HALL / MILGROM
FANTASIA!

While attending a demonstration in radiology, student PETER PARKER was bitten by a spider which had accidentally been exposed to RADIOACTIVE RAYS. Through a miracle of science, Peter gained the arachnid's powers... and in effect, became a human spider...

Stan Lee PRESENTS: THE SPECTACULAR SPIDER-MAN!®

BILL MANTLO STORY / BOB HALL ART / JIM MOONEY INKS / DIANA ALBERS LETTERS / BOB SHAREN COLORS / TOM DeFALCO EDITOR / JIM SHOOTER HIGH MUCKAMUCK

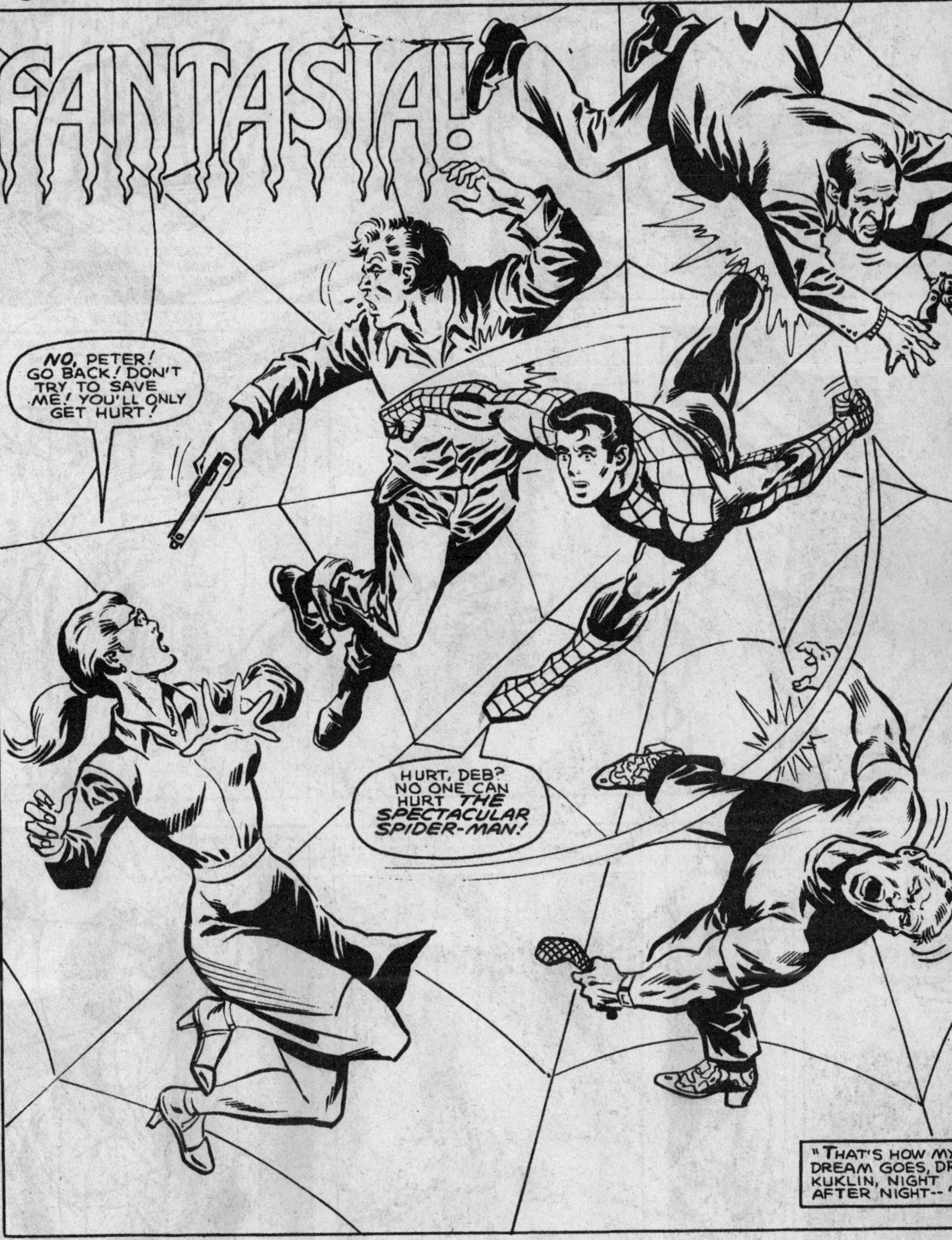
FANTASIA!
NO, PETER! GO BACK! DON'T TRY TO SAVE ME! YOU'LL ONLY GET HURT!
HURT, DEB? NO ONE CAN HURT THE SPECTACULAR SPIDER-MAN!
"THAT'S HOW MY DREAM GOES, DR. KUKLIN, NIGHT AFTER NIGHT--"

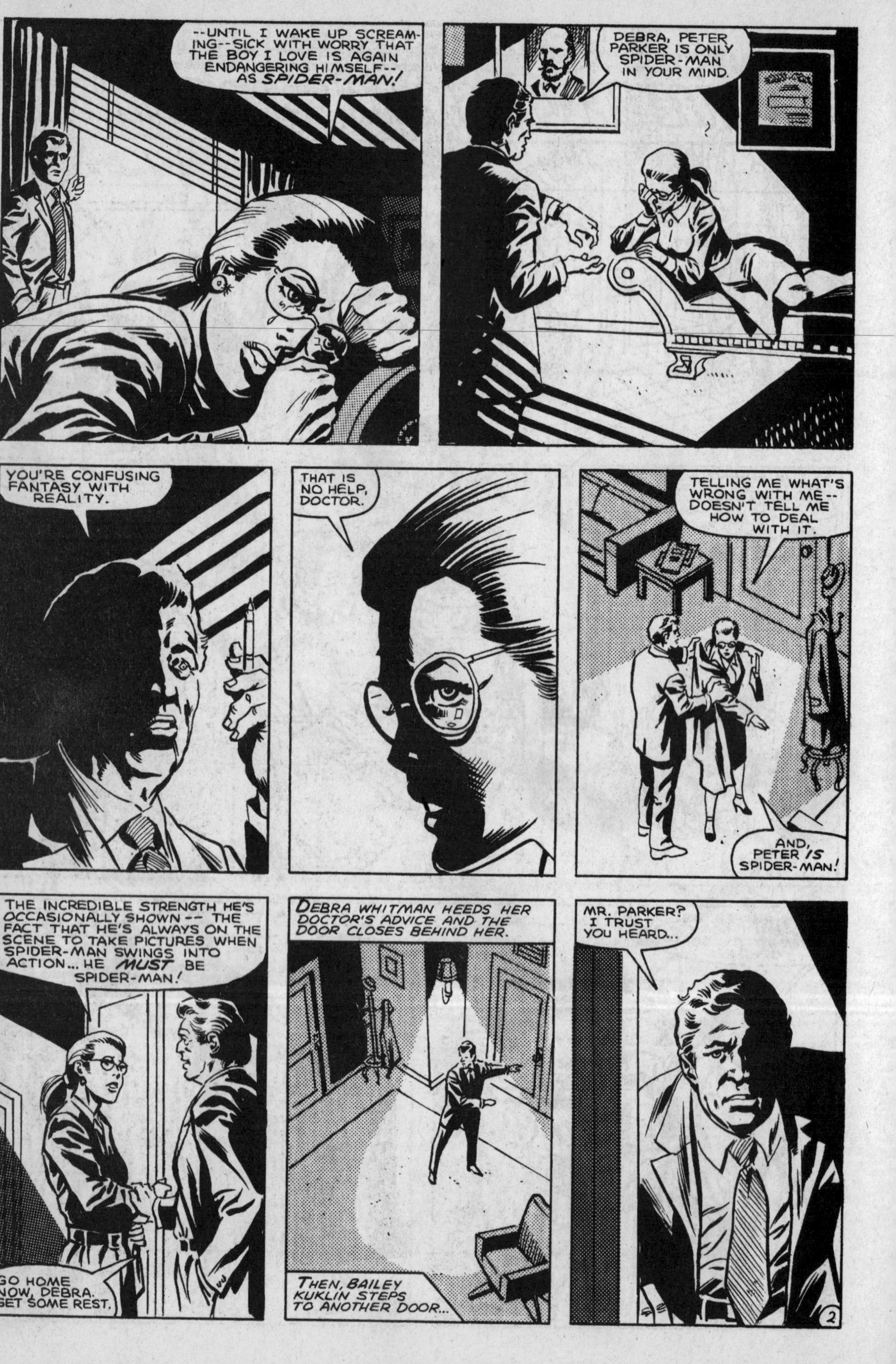
--UNTIL I WAKE UP SCREAMING--SICK WITH WORRY THAT THE BOY I LOVE IS AGAIN ENDANGERING HIMSELF-- AS SPIDER-MAN!
DEBRA, PETER PARKER IS ONLY SPIDER-MAN IN YOUR MIND.
YOU'RE CONFUSING FANTASY WITH REALITY.
THAT IS NO HELP, DOCTOR.
TELLING ME WHAT'S WRONG WITH ME-- DOESN'T TELL ME HOW TO DEAL WITH IT.
AND, PETER IS SPIDER-MAN!
THE INCREDIBLE STRENGTH HE'S OCCASIONALLY SHOWN -- THE FACT THAT HE'S ALWAYS ON THE SCENE TO TAKE PICTURES WHEN SPIDER-MAN SWINGS INTO ACTION... HE MUST BE SPIDER-MAN!
GO HOME NOW, DEBRA. GET SOME REST.
DEBRA WHITMAN HEEDS HER DOCTOR'S ADVICE AND THE DOOR CLOSES BEHIND HER.
THEN, BAILEY KUKLIN STEPS TO ANOTHER DOOR...
MR. PARKER? I TRUST YOU HEARD...
2

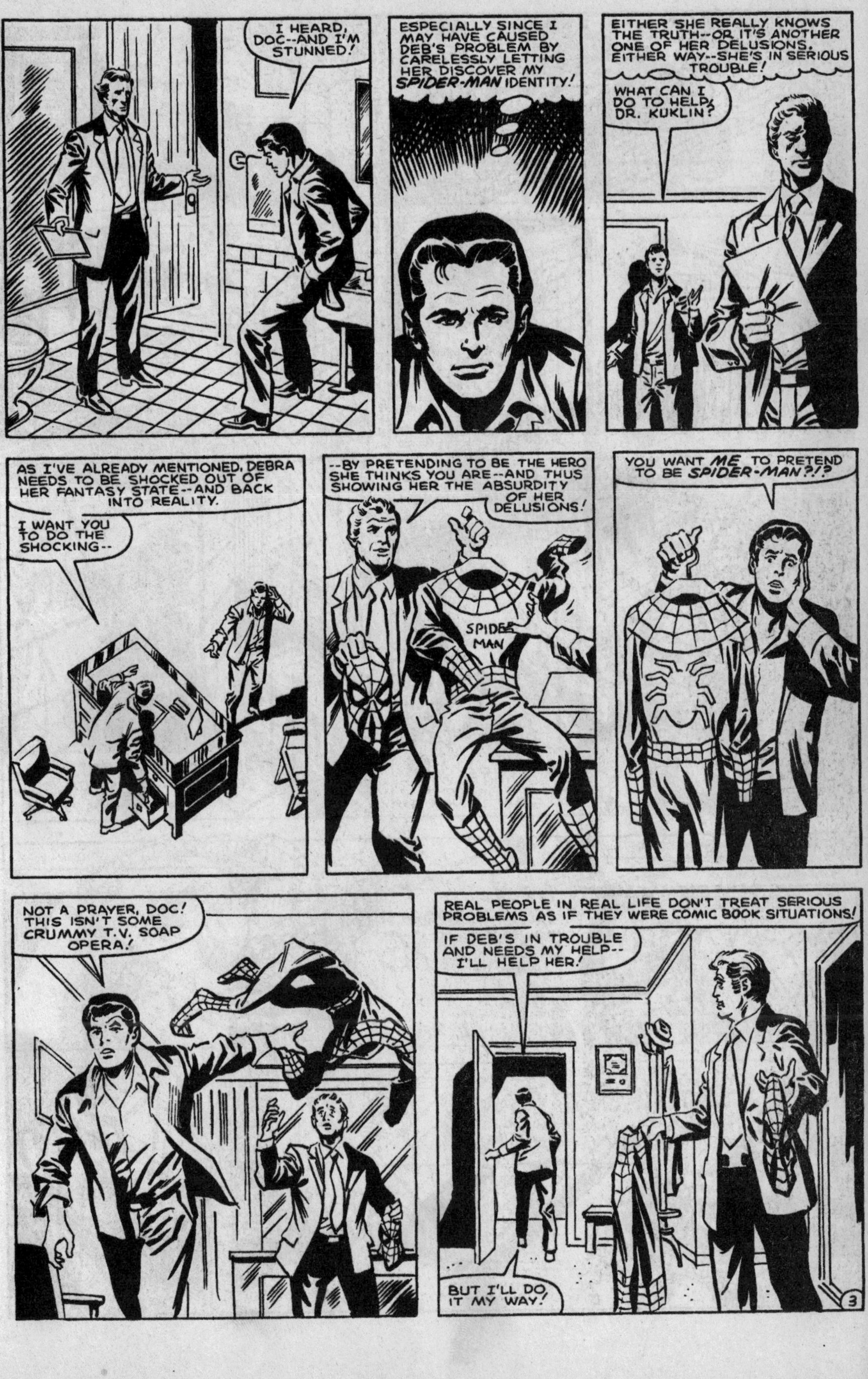
I HEARD, DOC--AND I'M STUNNED!
ESPECIALLY SINCE I MAY HAVE CAUSED DEB'S PROBLEM BY CARELESSLY LETTING HER DISCOVER MY SPIDER-MAN IDENTITY!
EITHER SHE REALLY KNOWS THE TRUTH--OR IT'S ANOTHER ONE OF HER DELUSIONS. EITHER WAY--SHE'S IN SERIOUS TROUBLE!
WHAT CAN I DO TO HELP, DR. KUKLIN?
AS I'VE ALREADY MENTIONED, DEBRA NEEDS TO BE SHOCKED OUT OF HER FANTASY STATE--AND BACK INTO REALITY.
I WANT YOU TO DO THE SHOCKING--
--BY PRETENDING TO BE THE HERO SHE THINKS YOU ARE--AND THUS SHOWING HER THE ABSURDITY OF HER DELUSIONS!
SPIDER MAN
YOU WANT ME TO PRETEND TO BE SPIDER-MAN?!?
NOT A PRAYER, DOC! THIS ISN'T SOME CRUMMY T.V. SOAP OPERA!
REAL PEOPLE IN REAL LIFE DON'T TREAT SERIOUS PROBLEMS AS IF THEY WERE COMIC BOOK SITUATIONS!
IF DEB'S IN TROUBLE AND NEEDS MY HELP-- I'LL HELP HER!
BUT I'LL DO IT MY WAY!
3

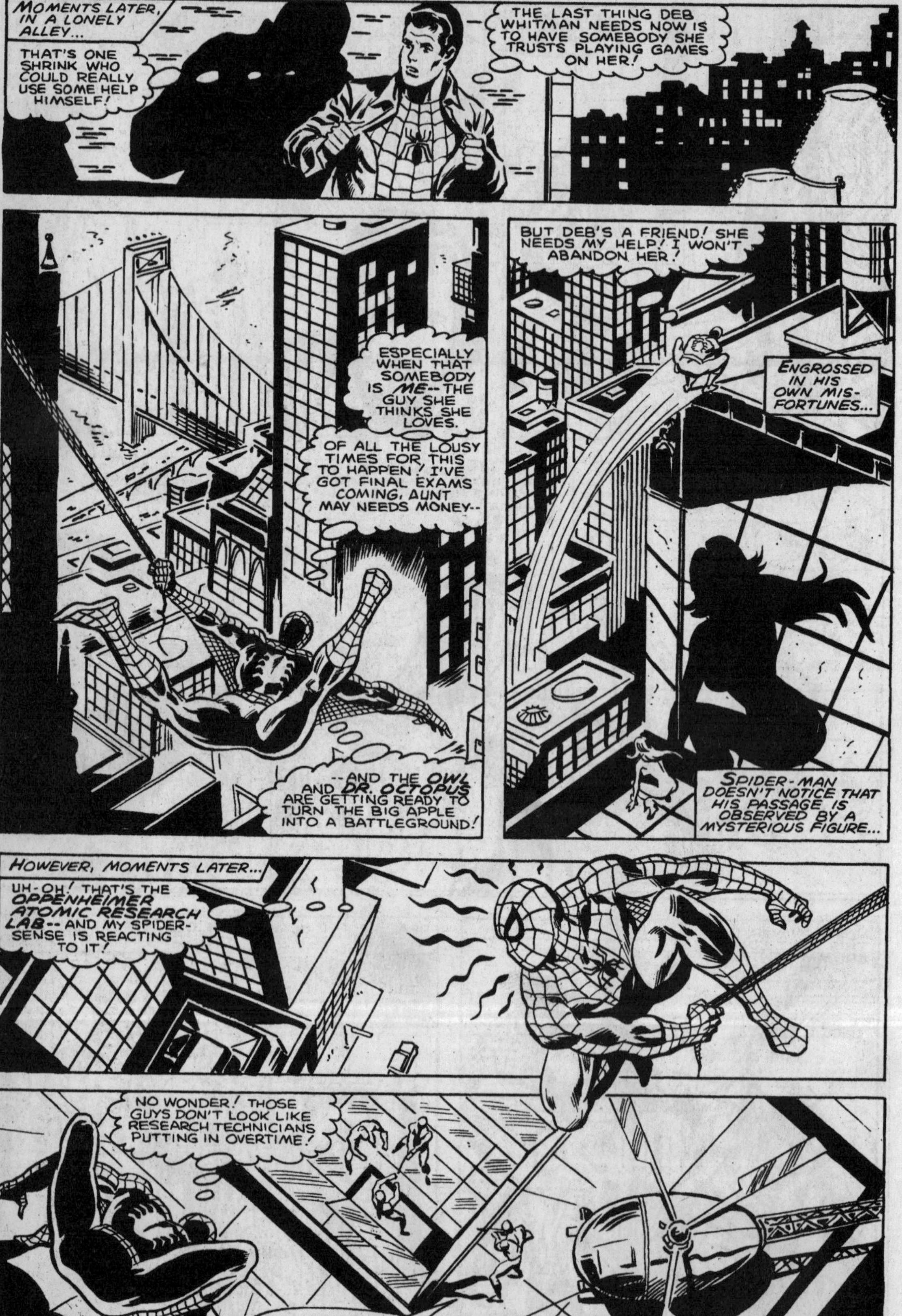
MOMENTS LATER, IN A LONELY ALLEY...
THAT'S ONE SHRINK WHO COULD REALLY USE SOME HELP HIMSELF!
THE LAST THING DEB WHITMAN NEEDS NOW IS TO HAVE SOMEBODY SHE TRUSTS PLAYING GAMES ON HER!
ESPECIALLY WHEN THAT SOMEBODY IS ME-- THE GUY SHE THINKS SHE LOVES.
OF ALL THE LOUSY TIMES FOR THIS TO HAPPEN! I'VE GOT FINAL EXAMS COMING, AUNT MAY NEEDS MONEY--
--AND THE OWL AND DR. OCTOPUS ARE GETTING READY TO TURN THE BIG APPLE INTO A BATTLEGROUND!
BUT DEB'S A FRIEND! SHE NEEDS MY HELP! I WON'T ABANDON HER!
ENGROSSED IN HIS OWN MIS-FORTUNES...
SPIDER-MAN DOESN'T NOTICE THAT HIS PASSAGE IS OBSERVED BY A MYSTERIOUS FIGURE...
HOWEVER, MOMENTS LATER...
UH-OH! THAT'S THE OPPENHEIMER ATOMIC RESEARCH LAB-- AND MY SPIDER-SENSE IS REACTING TO IT!
NO WONDER! THOSE GUYS DON'T LOOK LIKE RESEARCH TECHNICIANS PUTTING IN OVERTIME!
ALL RIGHT, WE MAKE OUR MOVE--
4

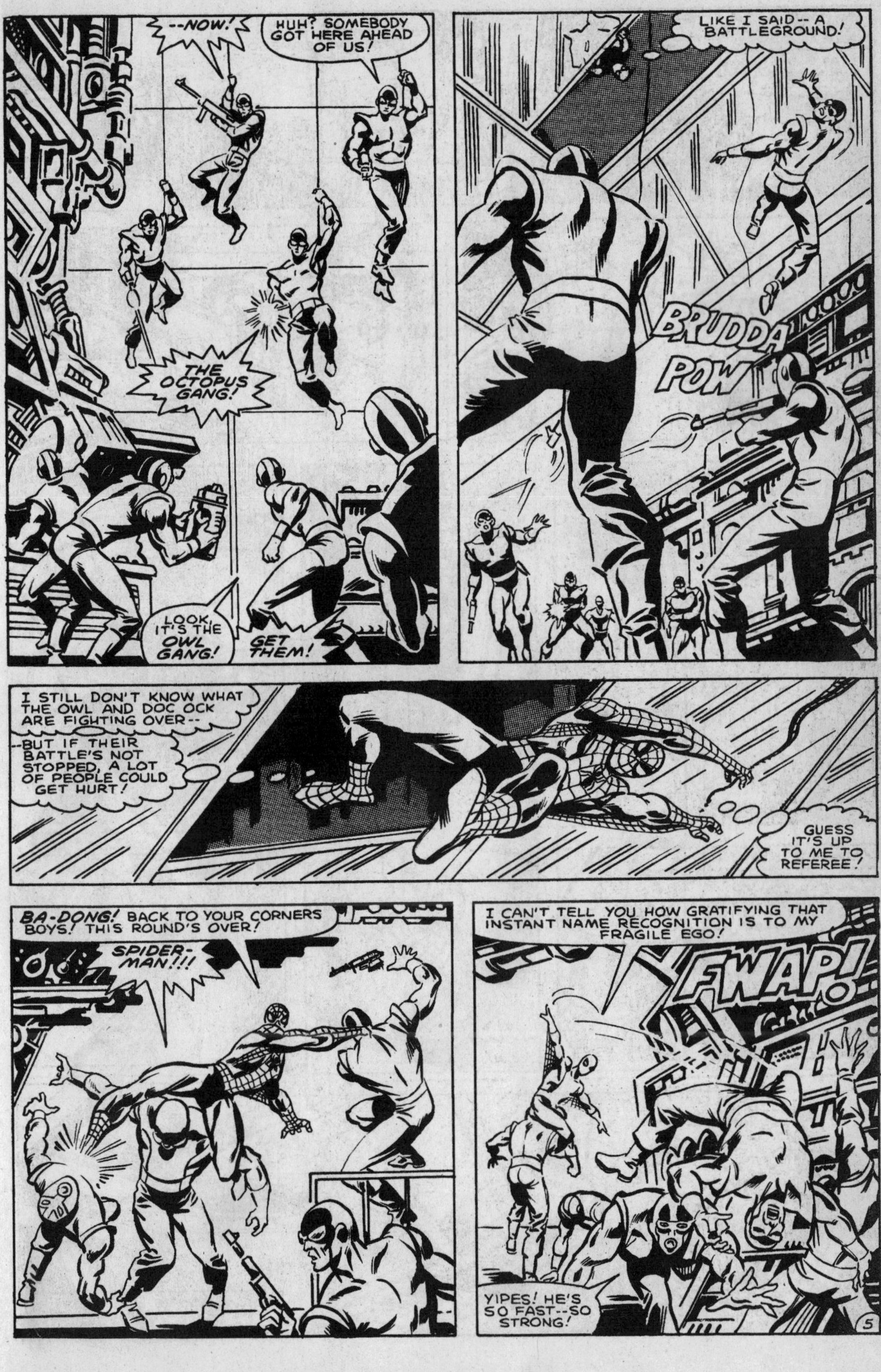
--NOW!
HUH? SOMEBODY GOT HERE AHEAD OF US!
THE OCTOPUS GANG!
LOOK, IT'S THE OWL GANG!
GET THEM!
LIKE I SAID--A BATTLEGROUND!
BRUDDA POW
I STILL DON'T KNOW WHAT THE OWL AND DOC OCK ARE FIGHTING OVER--
--BUT IF THEIR BATTLE'S NOT STOPPED, A LOT OF PEOPLE COULD GET HURT!
GUESS IT'S UP TO ME TO REFEREE!
BA-DONG! BACK TO YOUR CORNERS BOYS! THIS ROUND'S OVER!
SPIDER-MAN!!!
I CAN'T TELL YOU HOW GRATIFYING THAT INSTANT NAME RECOGNITION IS TO MY FRAGILE EGO!
FWAP!
YIPES! HE'S SO FAST--SO STRONG!

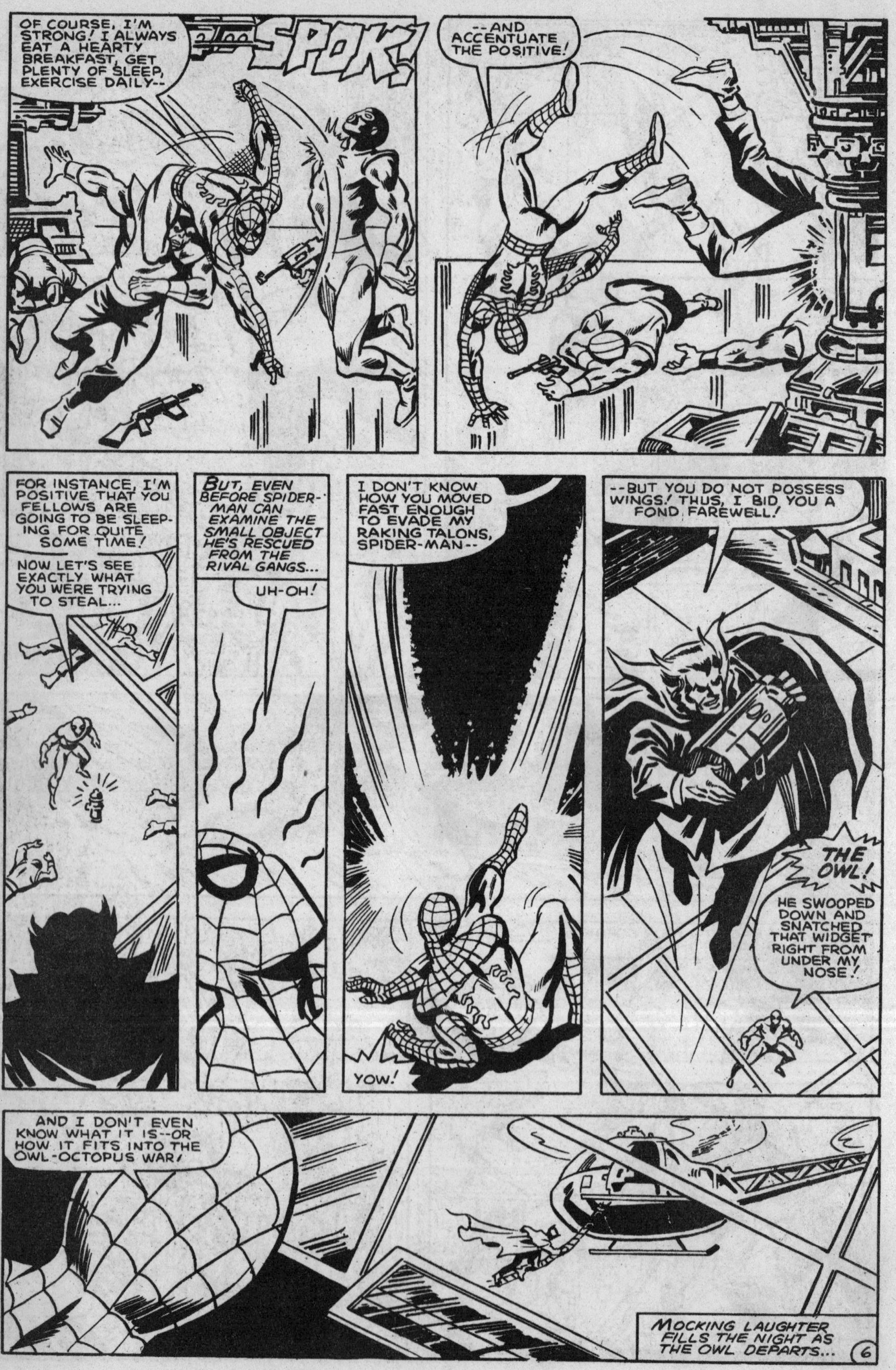
OF COURSE, I'M STRONG! I ALWAYS EAT A HEARTY BREAKFAST, GET PLENTY OF SLEEP, EXERCISE DAILY--
SPOK!
--AND ACCENTUATE THE POSITIVE!
FOR INSTANCE, I'M POSITIVE THAT YOU FELLOWS ARE GOING TO BE SLEEPING FOR QUITE SOME TIME!
NOW LET'S SEE EXACTLY WHAT YOU WERE TRYING TO STEAL...
BUT, EVEN BEFORE SPIDER-MAN CAN EXAMINE THE SMALL OBJECT HE'S RESCUED FROM THE RIVAL GANGS...
UH-OH!
I DON'T KNOW HOW YOU MOVED FAST ENOUGH TO EVADE MY RAKING TALONS, SPIDER-MAN--
YOW!
--BUT YOU DO NOT POSSESS WINGS! THUS, I BID YOU A FOND FAREWELL!
THE OWL!
HE SWOOPED DOWN AND SNATCHED THAT WIDGET RIGHT FROM UNDER MY NOSE!
AND I DON'T EVEN KNOW WHAT IT IS--OR HOW IT FITS INTO THE OWL-OCTOPUS WAR!
MOCKING LAUGHTER FILLS THE NIGHT AS THE OWL DEPARTS...
6

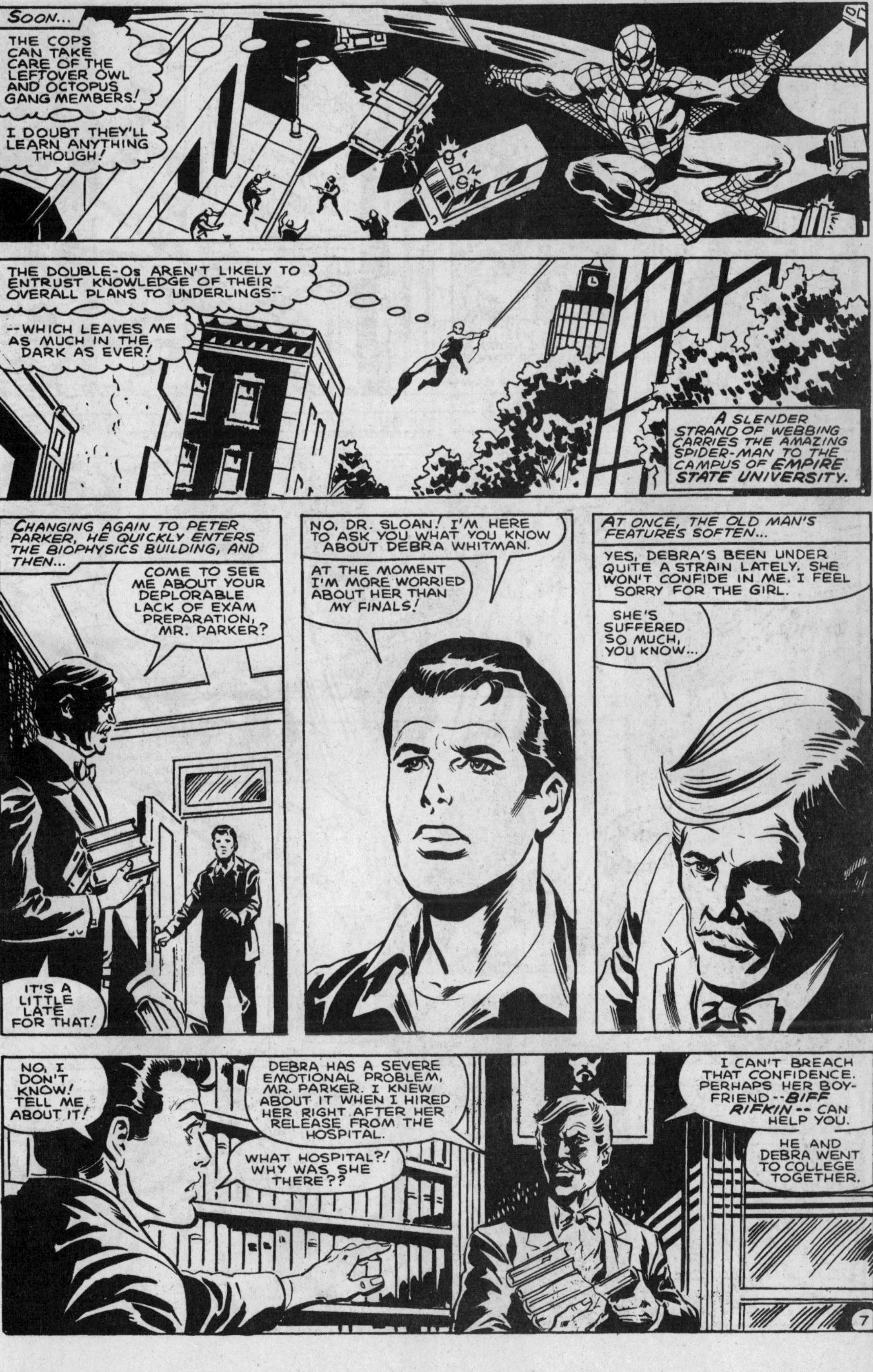
SOON...
THE COPS CAN TAKE CARE OF THE LEFTOVER OWL AND OCTOPUS GANG MEMBERS!
I DOUBT THEY'LL LEARN ANYTHING THOUGH!
THE DOUBLE-Os AREN'T LIKELY TO ENTRUST KNOWLEDGE OF THEIR OVERALL PLANS TO UNDERLINGS--
--WHICH LEAVES ME AS MUCH IN THE DARK AS EVER!
A SLENDER STRAND OF WEBBING CARRIES THE AMAZING SPIDER-MAN TO THE CAMPUS OF EMPIRE STATE UNIVERSITY.
CHANGING AGAIN TO PETER PARKER, HE QUICKLY ENTERS THE BIOPHYSICS BUILDING, AND THEN...
COME TO SEE ME ABOUT YOUR DEPLORABLE LACK OF EXAM PREPARATION, MR. PARKER?
IT'S A LITTLE LATE FOR THAT!
NO, DR. SLOAN! I'M HERE TO ASK YOU WHAT YOU KNOW ABOUT DEBRA WHITMAN.
AT THE MOMENT I'M MORE WORRIED ABOUT HER THAN MY FINALS!
AT ONCE, THE OLD MAN'S FEATURES SOFTEN...
YES, DEBRA'S BEEN UNDER QUITE A STRAIN LATELY. SHE WON'T CONFIDE IN ME. I FEEL SORRY FOR THE GIRL.
SHE'S SUFFERED SO MUCH, YOU KNOW...
NO, I DON'T KNOW! TELL ME ABOUT IT!
DEBRA HAS A SEVERE EMOTIONAL PROBLEM, MR. PARKER. I KNEW ABOUT IT WHEN I HIRED HER RIGHT AFTER HER RELEASE FROM THE HOSPITAL.
WHAT HOSPITAL?! WHY WAS SHE THERE??
I CAN'T BREACH THAT CONFIDENCE. PERHAPS HER BOY-FRIEND--BIFF RIFKIN--CAN HELP YOU.
HE AND DEBRA WENT TO COLLEGE TOGETHER.
7

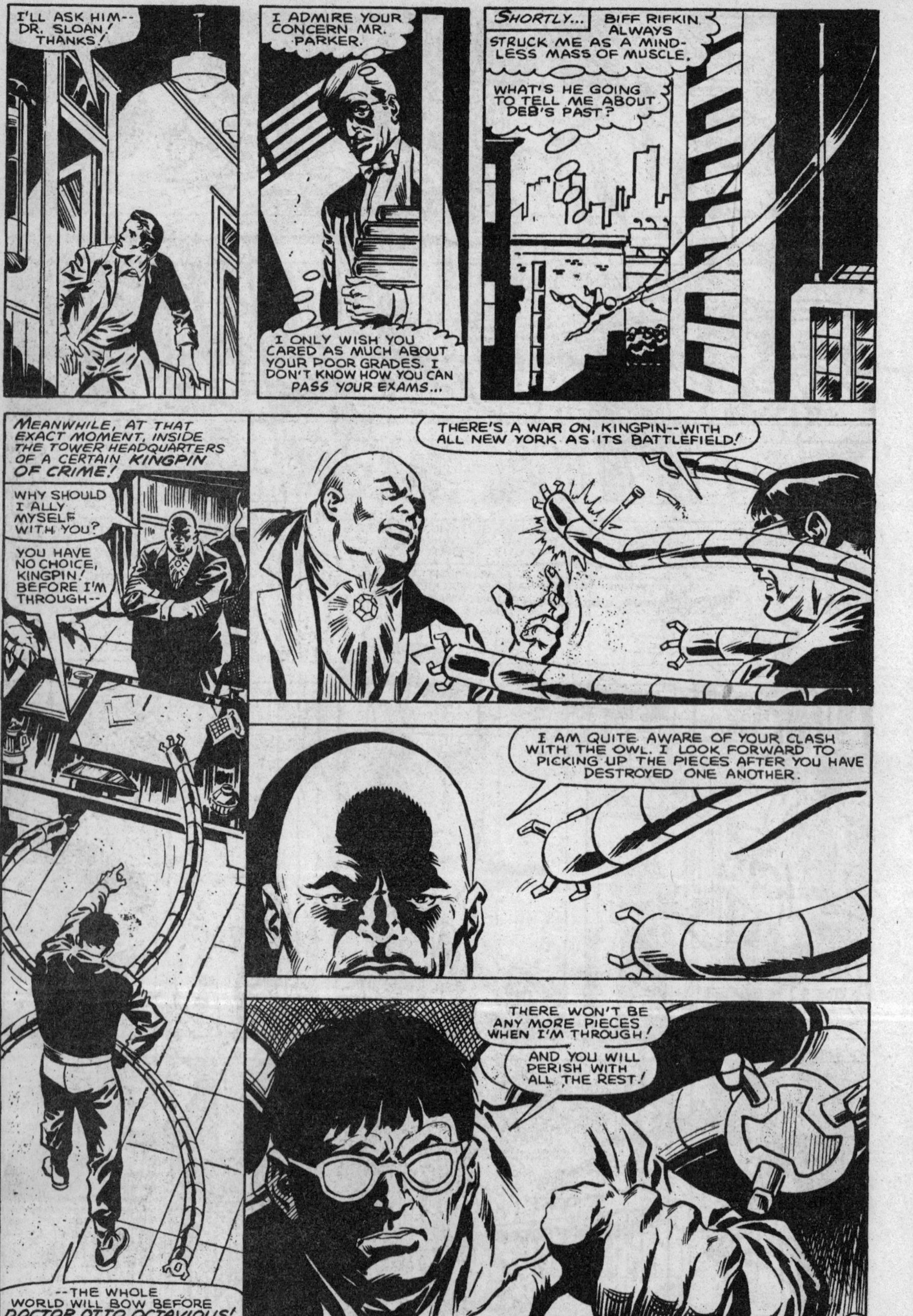

I'LL ASK HIM--DR. SLOAN! THANKS!
I ADMIRE YOUR CONCERN MR. PARKER.
I ONLY WISH YOU CARED AS MUCH ABOUT YOUR POOR GRADES. I DON'T KNOW HOW YOU CAN PASS YOUR EXAMS...
SHORTLY...
BIFF RIFKIN ALWAYS STRUCK ME AS A MINDLESS MASS OF MUSCLE.
WHAT'S HE GOING TO TELL ME ABOUT DEB'S PAST?
MEANWHILE, AT THAT EXACT MOMENT, INSIDE THE TOWER HEADQUARTERS OF A CERTAIN KINGPIN OF CRIME!
WHY SHOULD I ALLY MYSELF WITH YOU?
YOU HAVE NO CHOICE, KINGPIN! BEFORE I'M THROUGH--
--THE WHOLE WORLD WILL BOW BEFORE DOCTOR OTTO OCTAVIOUS!
THERE'S A WAR ON, KINGPIN--WITH ALL NEW YORK AS ITS BATTLEFIELD!
I AM QUITE AWARE OF YOUR CLASH WITH THE OWL. I LOOK FORWARD TO PICKING UP THE PIECES AFTER YOU HAVE DESTROYED ONE ANOTHER.
THERE WON'T BE ANY MORE PIECES WHEN I'M THROUGH!
AND YOU WILL PERISH WITH ALL THE REST!
8

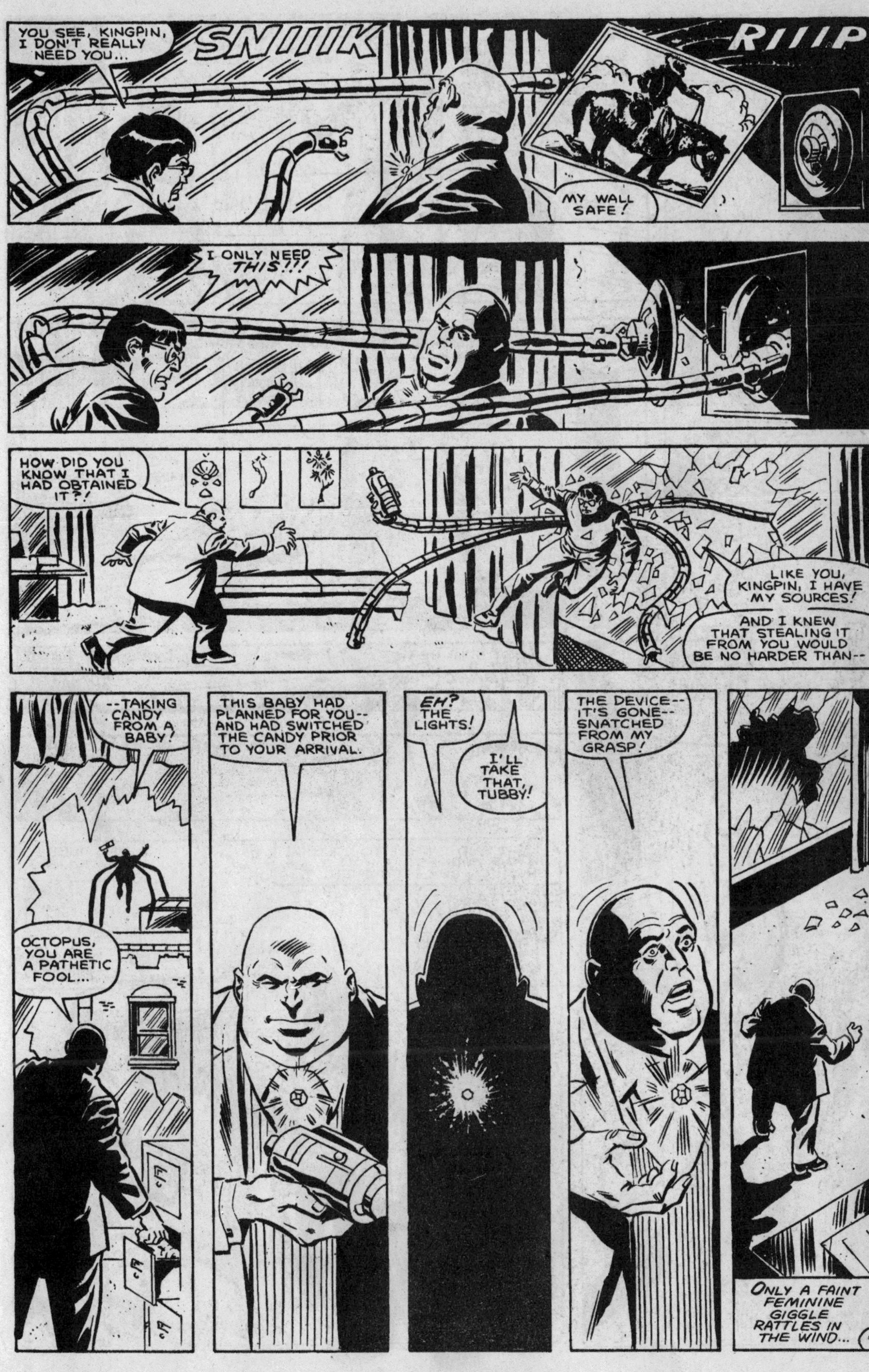
YOU SEE, KINGPIN, I DON'T REALLY NEED YOU...
SNIIIK
RIIIP
...MY WALL SAFE!
I ONLY NEED THIS!!!
HOW DID YOU KNOW THAT I HAD OBTAINED IT?!
LIKE YOU, KINGPIN, I HAVE MY SOURCES!
AND I KNEW THAT STEALING IT FROM YOU WOULD BE NO HARDER THAN--
--TAKING CANDY FROM A BABY!
OCTOPUS, YOU ARE A PATHETIC FOOL...
THIS BABY HAD PLANNED FOR YOU-- AND HAD SWITCHED THE CANDY PRIOR TO YOUR ARRIVAL.
EH? THE LIGHTS!
I'LL TAKE THAT, TUBBY!
THE DEVICE-- IT'S GONE-- SNATCHED FROM MY GRASP!
ONLY A FAINT FEMININE GIGGLE RATTLES IN THE WIND...
9

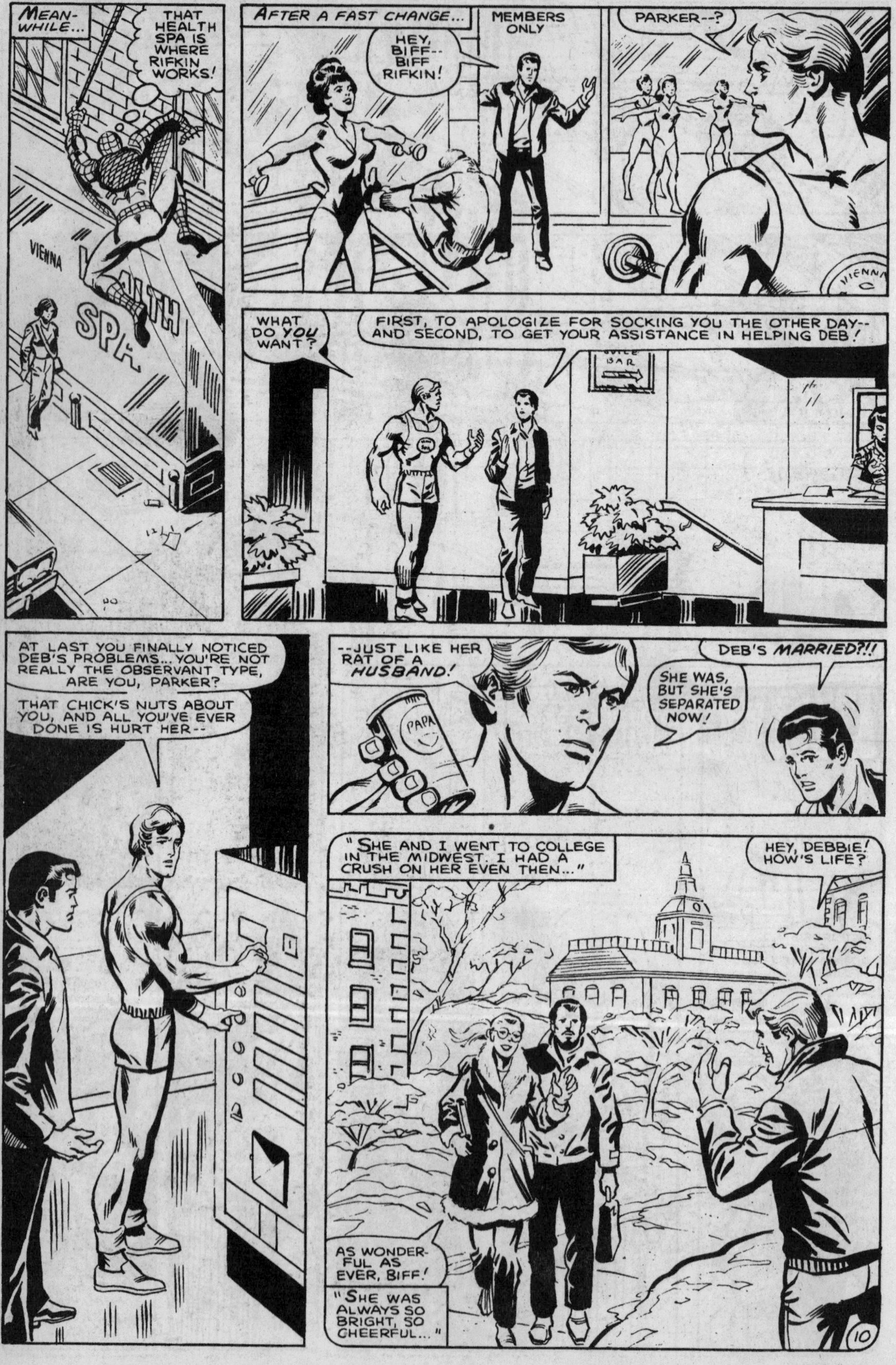
MEAN-WHILE...
THAT HEALTH SPA IS WHERE RIFKIN WORKS!
VIENNA
HEALTH SPA
AFTER A FAST CHANGE...
MEMBERS ONLY
HEY, BIFF-- BIFF RIFKIN!
PARKER--?
WHAT DO YOU WANT?
FIRST, TO APOLOGIZE FOR SOCKING YOU THE OTHER DAY-- AND SECOND, TO GET YOUR ASSISTANCE IN HELPING DEB!
AT LAST YOU FINALLY NOTICED DEB'S PROBLEMS... YOU'RE NOT REALLY THE OBSERVANT TYPE, ARE YOU, PARKER?
THAT CHICK'S NUTS ABOUT YOU, AND ALL YOU'VE EVER DONE IS HURT HER--
--JUST LIKE HER RAT OF A HUSBAND!
PAPA
DEB'S MARRIED?!!
SHE WAS, BUT SHE'S SEPARATED NOW!
"SHE AND I WENT TO COLLEGE IN THE MIDWEST. I HAD A CRUSH ON HER EVEN THEN..."
HEY, DEBBIE! HOW'S LIFE?
AS WONDER-FUL AS EVER, BIFF!
"SHE WAS ALWAYS SO BRIGHT, SO CHEERFUL..."
10

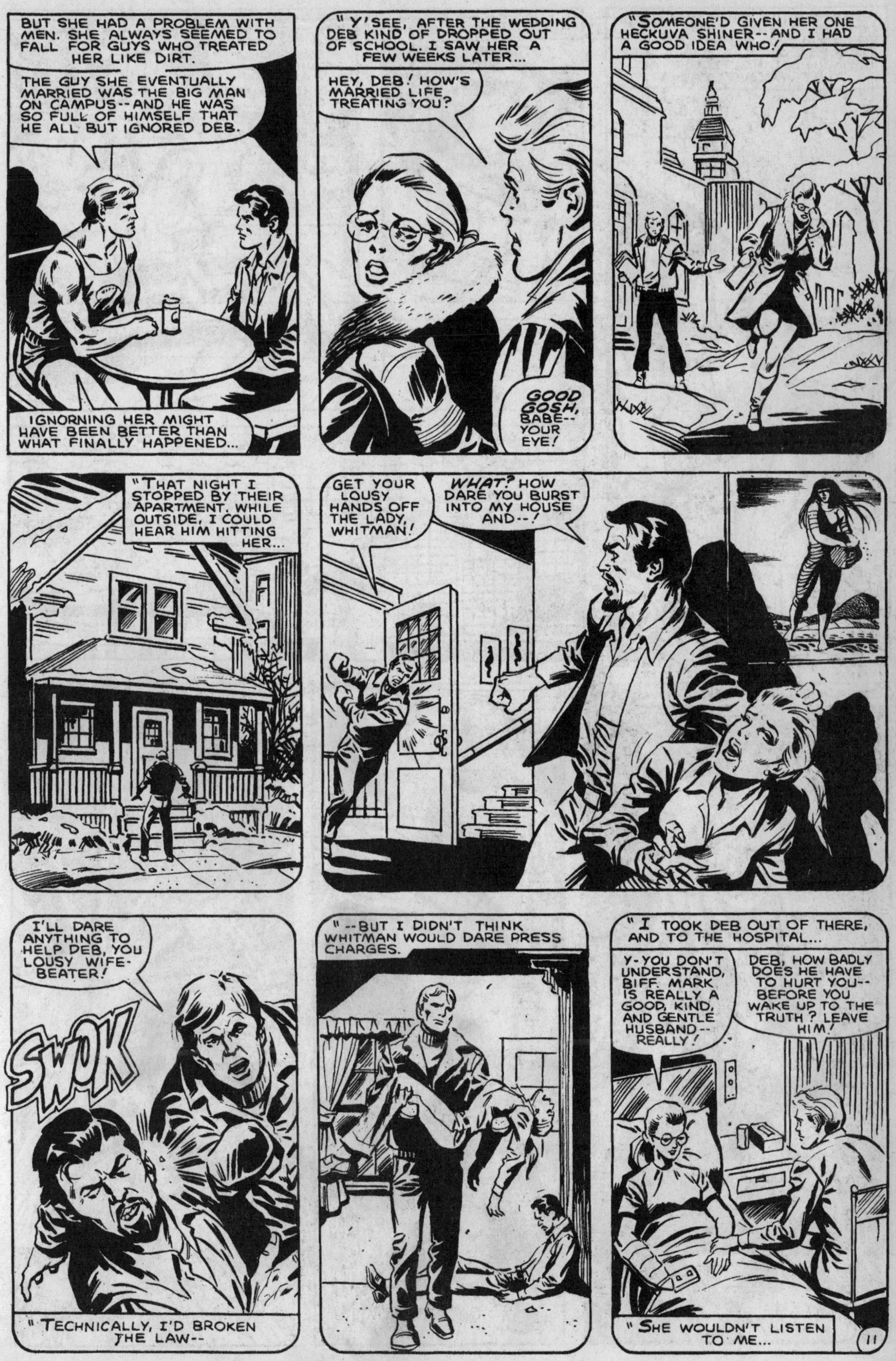
BUT SHE HAD A PROBLEM WITH MEN. SHE ALWAYS SEEMED TO FALL FOR GUYS WHO TREATED HER LIKE DIRT.
THE GUY SHE EVENTUALLY MARRIED WAS THE BIG MAN ON CAMPUS--AND HE WAS SO FULL OF HIMSELF THAT HE ALL BUT IGNORED DEB.
IGNORNING HER MIGHT HAVE BEEN BETTER THAN WHAT FINALLY HAPPENED...
"Y'SEE, AFTER THE WEDDING DEB KIND OF DROPPED OUT OF SCHOOL. I SAW HER A FEW WEEKS LATER...
HEY, DEB! HOW'S MARRIED LIFE TREATING YOU?
GOOD GOSH, BABE--YOUR EYE!
"SOMEONE'D GIVEN HER ONE HECKUVA SHINER--AND I HAD A GOOD IDEA WHO!
"THAT NIGHT I STOPPED BY THEIR APARTMENT. WHILE OUTSIDE, I COULD HEAR HIM HITTING HER...
GET YOUR LOUSY HANDS OFF THE LADY, WHITMAN!
WHAT? HOW DARE YOU BURST INTO MY HOUSE AND--!
I'LL DARE ANYTHING TO HELP DEB, YOU LOUSY WIFE-BEATER!
SWOK
"TECHNICALLY, I'D BROKEN THE LAW--
"--BUT I DIDN'T THINK WHITMAN WOULD DARE PRESS CHARGES.
"I TOOK DEB OUT OF THERE, AND TO THE HOSPITAL...
Y-YOU DON'T UNDERSTAND, BIFF. MARK IS REALLY A GOOD, KIND, AND GENTLE HUSBAND--REALLY!
DEB, HOW BADLY DOES HE HAVE TO HURT YOU--BEFORE YOU WAKE UP TO THE TRUTH? LEAVE HIM!
"SHE WOULDN'T LISTEN TO ME...

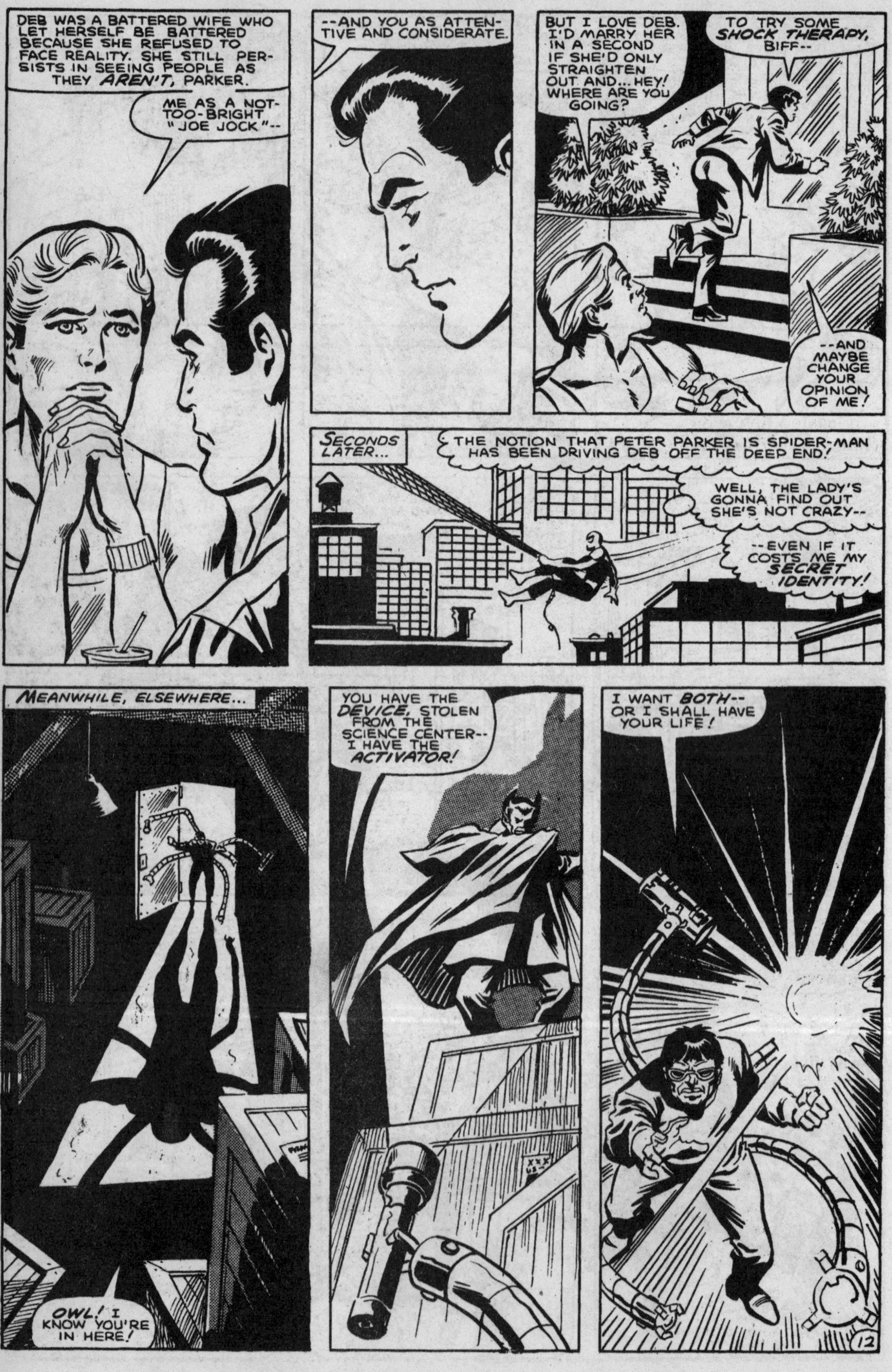
DEB WAS A BATTERED WIFE WHO LET HERSELF BE BATTERED BECAUSE SHE REFUSED TO FACE REALITY. SHE STILL PERSISTS IN SEEING PEOPLE AS THEY AREN'T, PARKER.
ME AS A NOT-TOO-BRIGHT "JOE JOCK"--
--AND YOU AS ATTENTIVE AND CONSIDERATE.
BUT I LOVE DEB. I'D MARRY HER IN A SECOND IF SHE'D ONLY STRAIGHTEN OUT. AND... HEY! WHERE ARE YOU GOING?
TO TRY SOME SHOCK THERAPY, BIFF--
--AND MAYBE CHANGE YOUR OPINION OF ME!
SECONDS LATER...
THE NOTION THAT PETER PARKER IS SPIDER-MAN HAS BEEN DRIVING DEB OFF THE DEEP END!
WELL, THE LADY'S GONNA FIND OUT SHE'S NOT CRAZY--
--EVEN IF IT COSTS ME MY SECRET IDENTITY!
MEANWHILE, ELSEWHERE...
OWL! I KNOW YOU'RE IN HERE!
YOU HAVE THE DEVICE, STOLEN FROM THE SCIENCE CENTER-- I HAVE THE ACTIVATOR!
I WANT BOTH-- OR I SHALL HAVE YOUR LIFE!
12

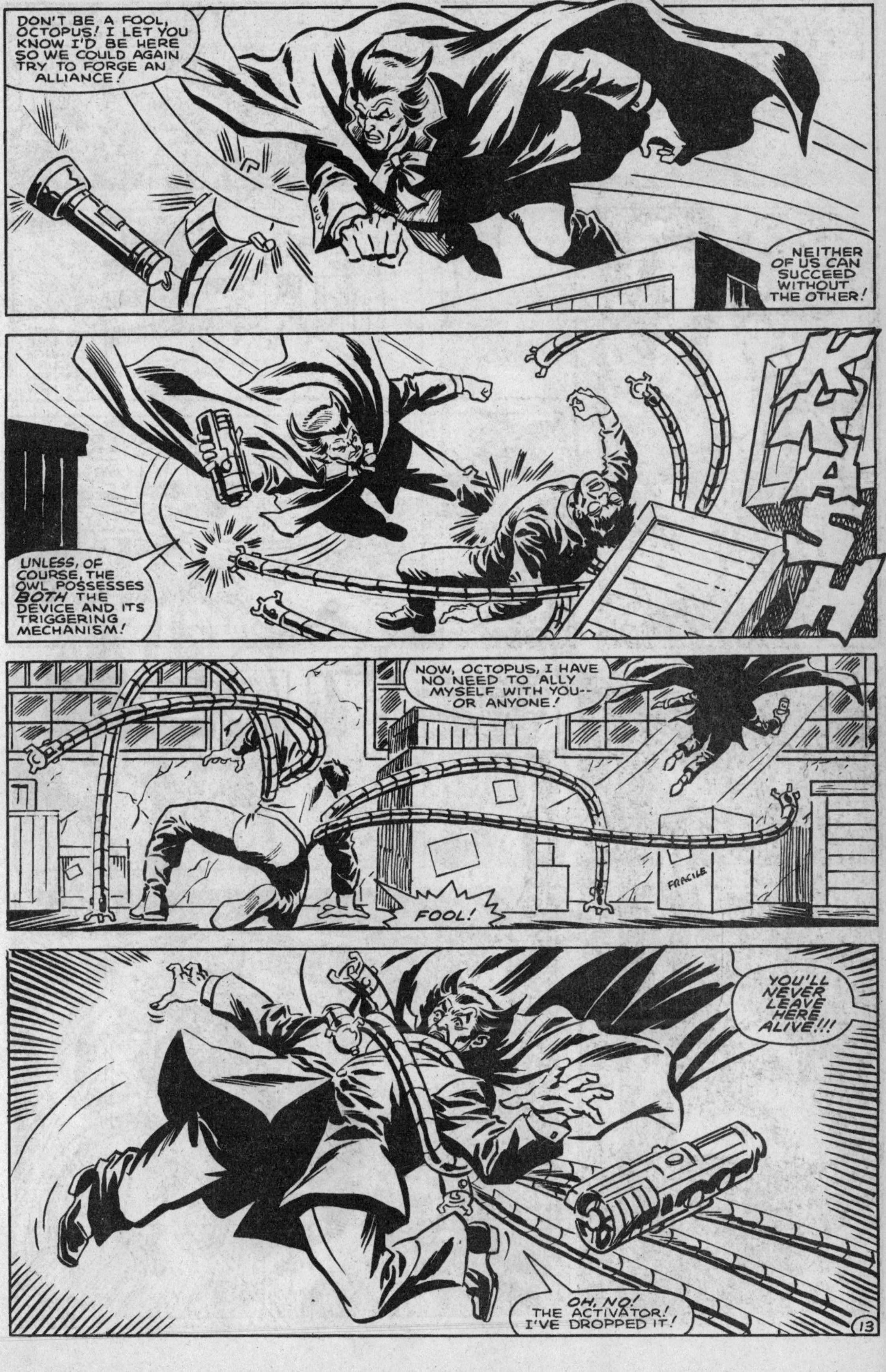

DON'T BE A FOOL, OCTOPUS! I LET YOU KNOW I'D BE HERE SO WE COULD AGAIN TRY TO FORGE AN ALLIANCE!
NEITHER OF US CAN SUCCEED WITHOUT THE OTHER!
KRASH
UNLESS, OF COURSE, THE OWL POSSESSES BOTH THE DEVICE AND ITS TRIGGERING MECHANISM!
NOW, OCTOPUS, I HAVE NO NEED TO ALLY MYSELF WITH YOU-- OR ANYONE!
FRAGILE
FOOL!
YOU'LL NEVER LEAVE HERE ALIVE!!!
OH, NO! THE ACTIVATOR! I'VE DROPPED IT!

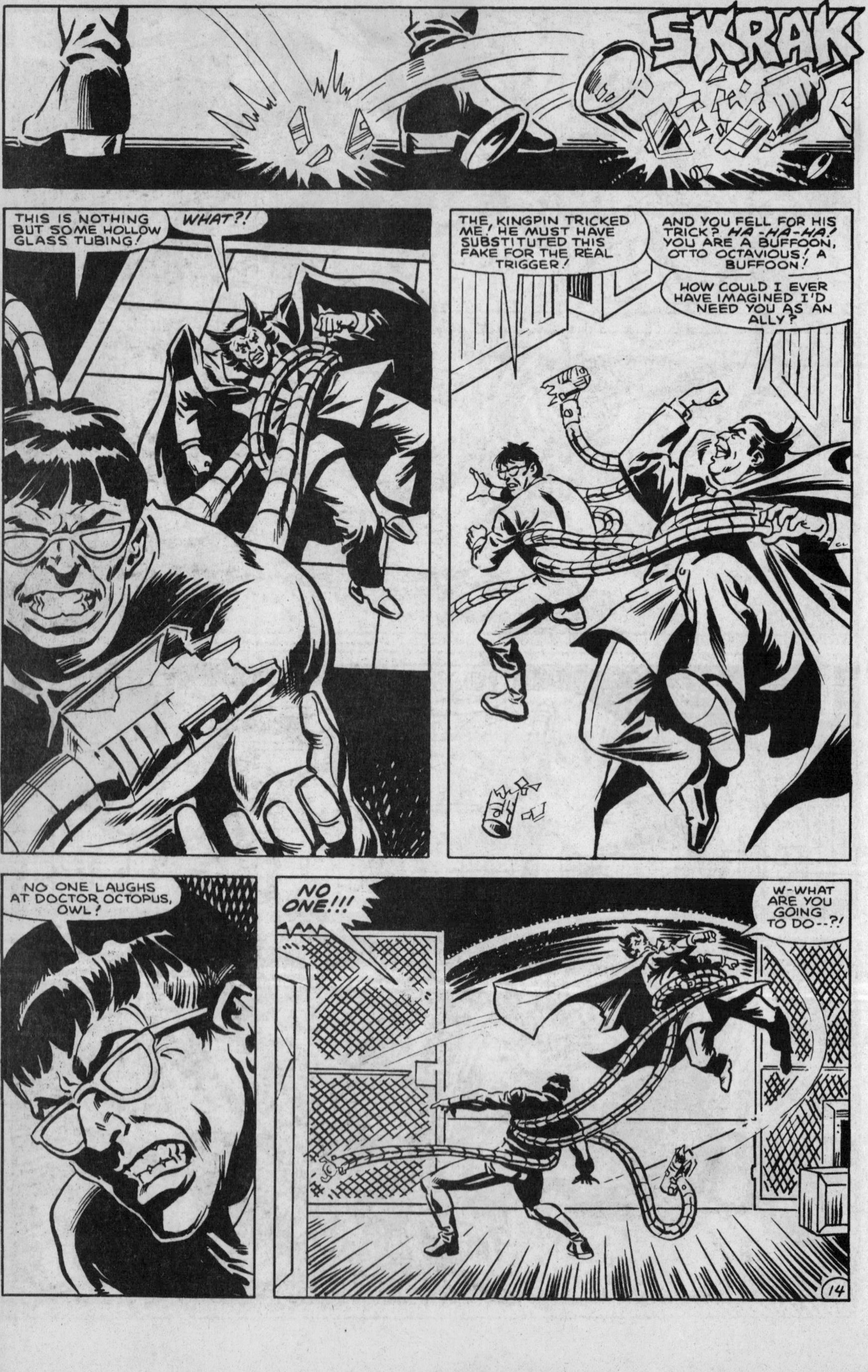
SKRAK
THIS IS NOTHING BUT SOME HOLLOW GLASS TUBING!
WHAT?!
THE KINGPIN TRICKED ME! HE MUST HAVE SUBSTITUTED THIS FAKE FOR THE REAL TRIGGER!
AND YOU FELL FOR HIS TRICK? HA-HA-HA! YOU ARE A BUFFOON, OTTO OCTAVIOUS! A BUFFOON!
HOW COULD I EVER HAVE IMAGINED I'D NEED YOU AS AN ALLY?
NO ONE LAUGHS AT DOCTOR OCTOPUS, OWL!
NO ONE!!!
W-WHAT ARE YOU GOING TO DO--?!
14

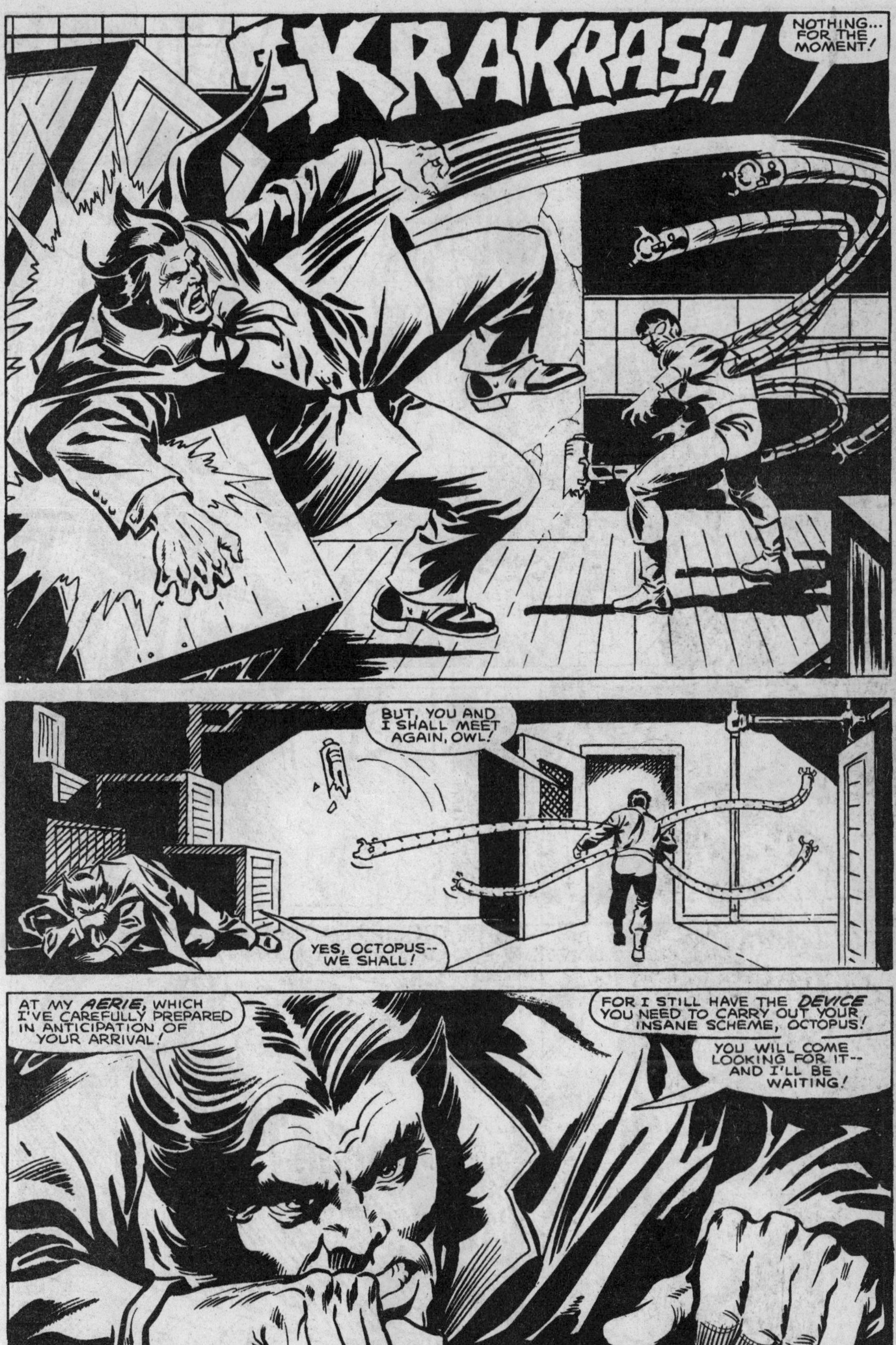
SKRAKRASH
NOTHING... FOR THE MOMENT!
BUT, YOU AND I SHALL MEET AGAIN, OWL!
YES, OCTOPUS-- WE SHALL!
AT MY AERIE, WHICH I'VE CAREFULLY PREPARED IN ANTICIPATION OF YOUR ARRIVAL!
FOR I STILL HAVE THE DEVICE YOU NEED TO CARRY OUT YOUR INSANE SCHEME, OCTOPUS!
YOU WILL COME LOOKING FOR IT-- AND I'LL BE WAITING!
15

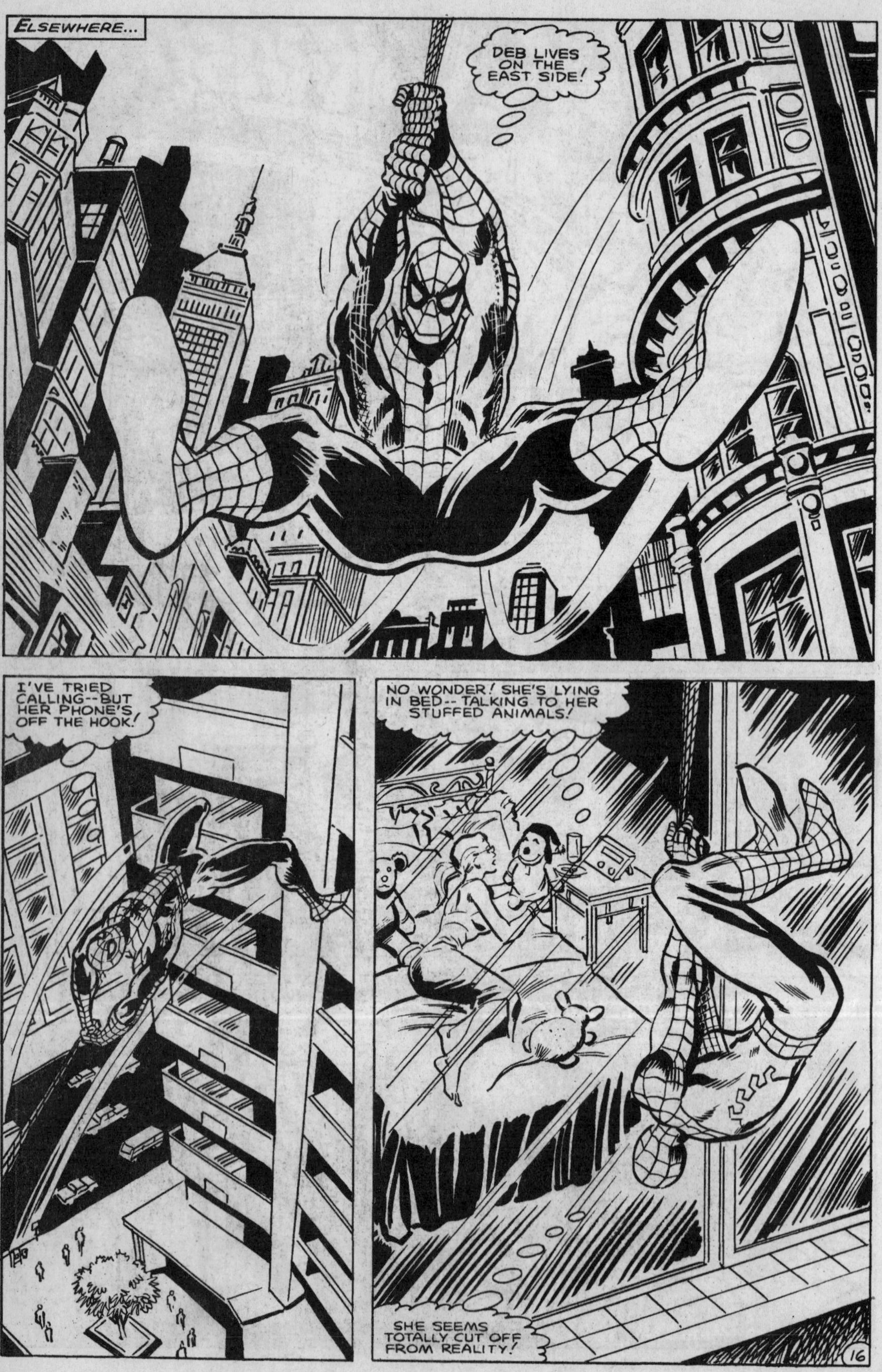
ELSEWHERE...
DEB LIVES ON THE EAST SIDE!
I'VE TRIED CALLING--BUT HER PHONE'S OFF THE HOOK!
NO WONDER! SHE'S LYING IN BED-- TALKING TO HER STUFFED ANIMALS!
SHE SEEMS TOTALLY CUT OFF FROM REALITY!
16

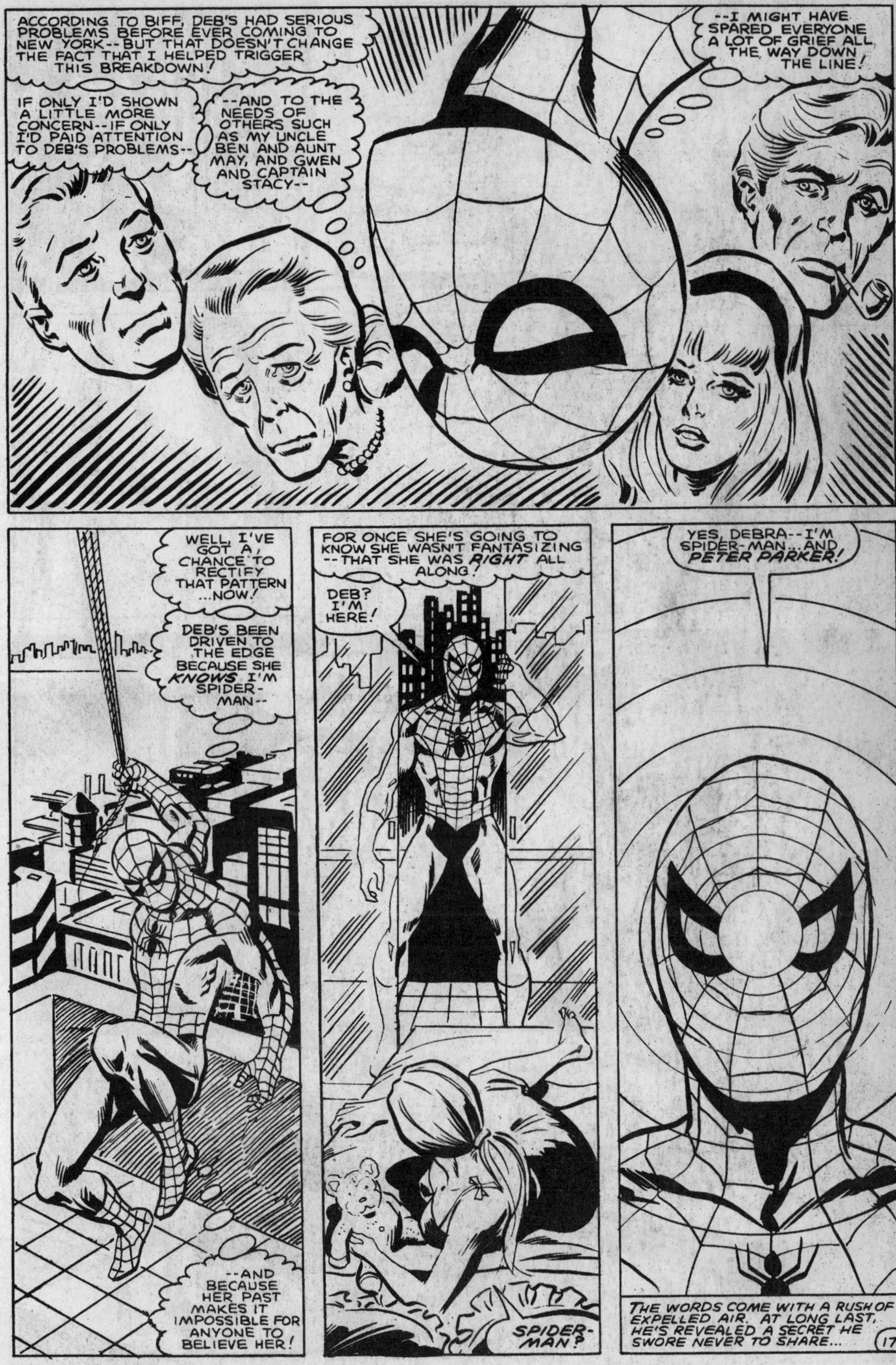

ACCORDING TO BIFF, DEB'S HAD SERIOUS PROBLEMS BEFORE EVER COMING TO NEW YORK--BUT THAT DOESN'T CHANGE THE FACT THAT I HELPED TRIGGER THIS BREAKDOWN!
IF ONLY I'D SHOWN A LITTLE MORE CONCERN--IF ONLY I'D PAID ATTENTION TO DEB'S PROBLEMS--
--AND TO THE NEEDS OF OTHERS SUCH AS MY UNCLE BEN AND AUNT MAY, AND GWEN AND CAPTAIN STACY--
--I MIGHT HAVE SPARED EVERYONE A LOT OF GRIEF ALL THE WAY DOWN THE LINE!
WELL, I'VE GOT A CHANCE TO RECTIFY THAT PATTERN ...NOW!
DEB'S BEEN DRIVEN TO THE EDGE BECAUSE SHE KNOWS I'M SPIDER-MAN--
--AND BECAUSE HER PAST MAKES IT IMPOSSIBLE FOR ANYONE TO BELIEVE HER!
FOR ONCE SHE'S GOING TO KNOW SHE WASN'T FANTASIZING --THAT SHE WAS RIGHT ALL ALONG!
DEB? I'M HERE!
SPIDER-MAN?
YES, DEBRA--I'M SPIDER-MAN...AND PETER PARKER!
THE WORDS COME WITH A RUSH OF EXPELLED AIR. AT LONG LAST, HE'S REVEALED A SECRET HE SWORE NEVER TO SHARE...

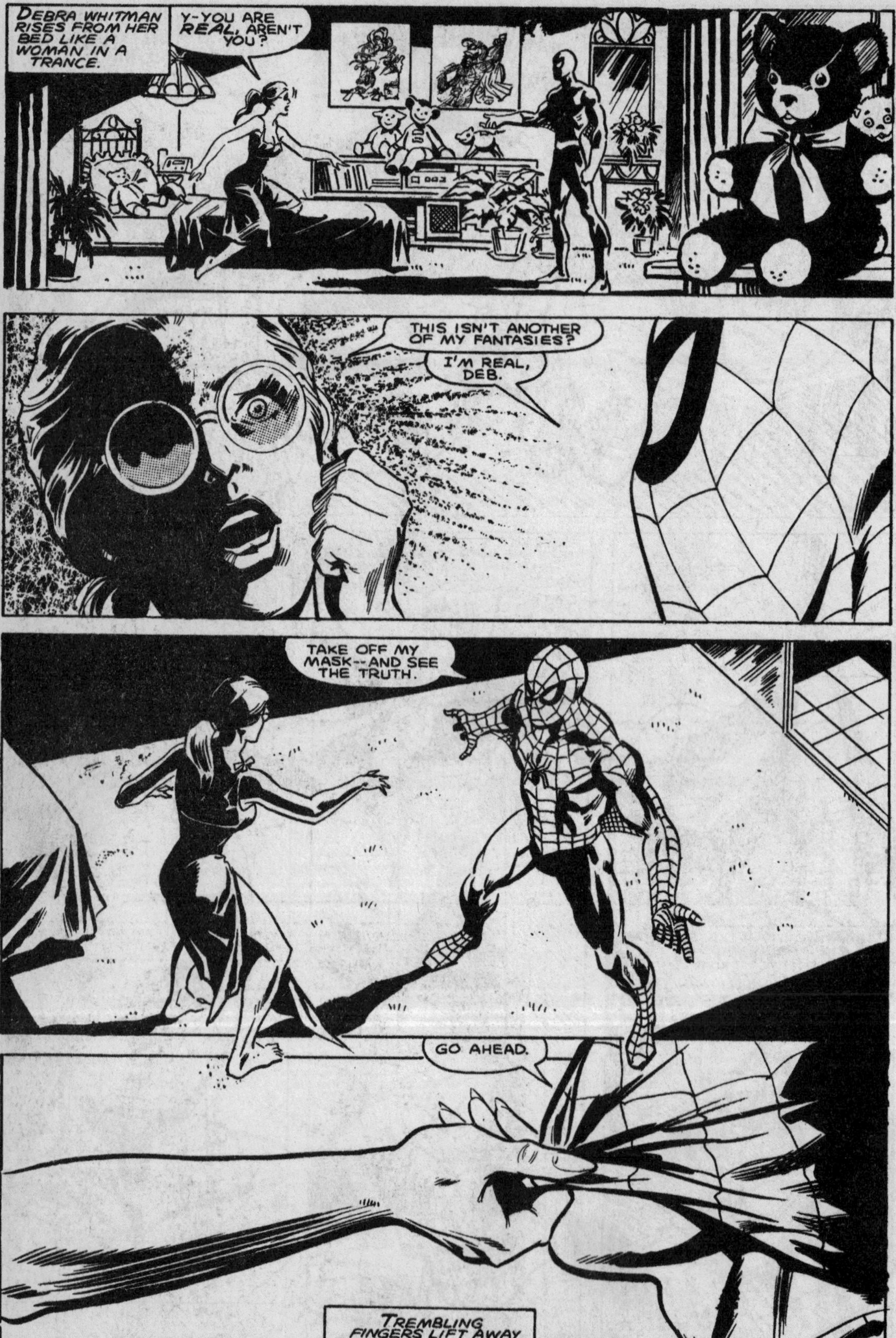
DEBRA WHITMAN RISES FROM HER BED LIKE A WOMAN IN A TRANCE.
Y-YOU ARE REAL, AREN'T YOU?
THIS ISN'T ANOTHER OF MY FANTASIES?
I'M REAL, DEB.
TAKE OFF MY MASK--AND SEE THE TRUTH.
GO AHEAD.
TREMBLING FINGERS LIFT AWAY THE CRIMSON MASK...
18

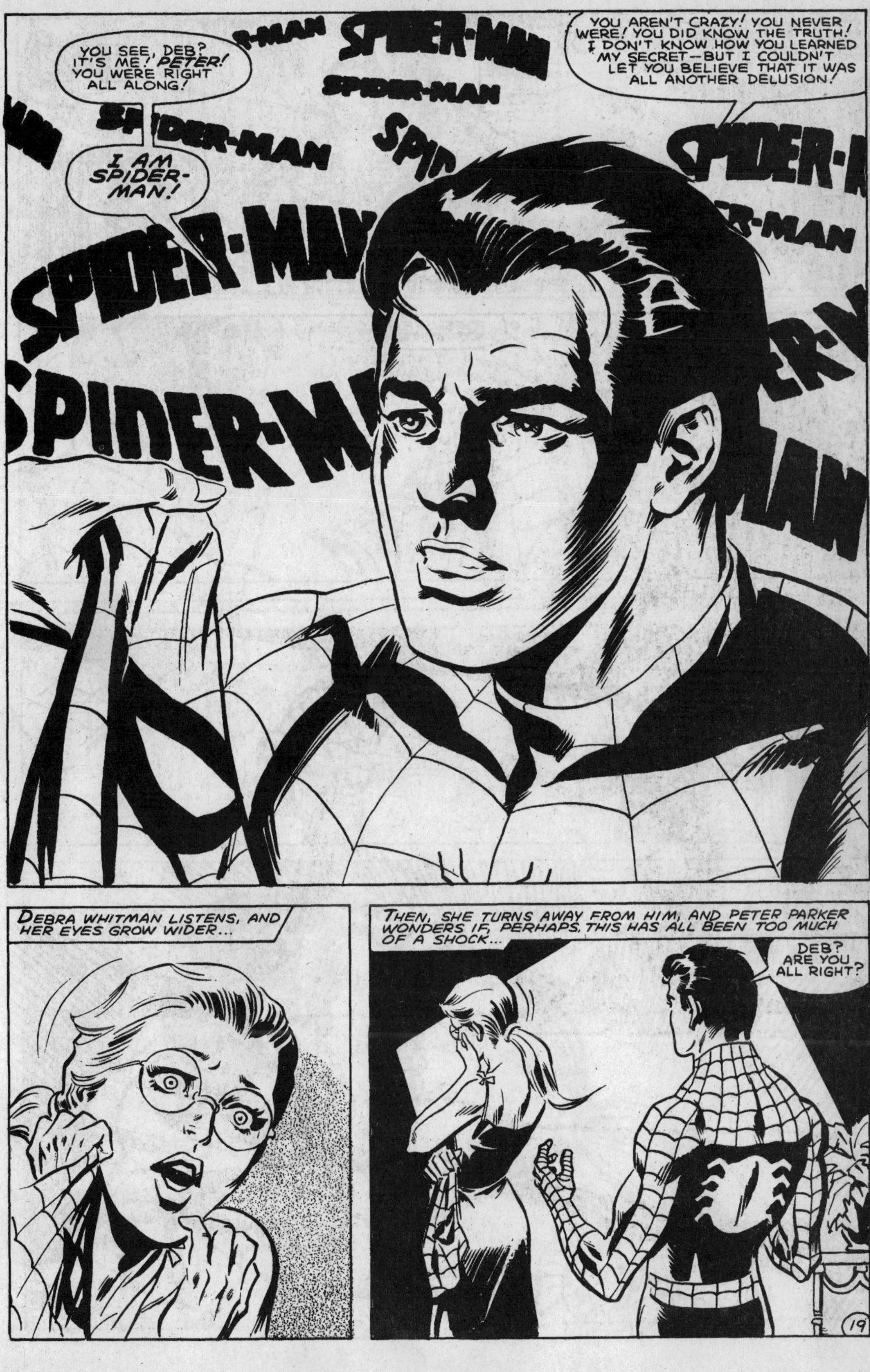
YOU SEE, DEB? IT'S ME! PETER! YOU WERE RIGHT ALL ALONG!
I AM SPIDER-MAN!
YOU AREN'T CRAZY! YOU NEVER WERE! YOU DID KNOW THE TRUTH! I DON'T KNOW HOW YOU LEARNED MY SECRET--BUT I COULDN'T LET YOU BELIEVE THAT IT WAS ALL ANOTHER DELUSION!
SPIDER-MAN
DEBRA WHITMAN LISTENS, AND HER EYES GROW WIDER...
THEN, SHE TURNS AWAY FROM HIM, AND PETER PARKER WONDERS IF, PERHAPS, THIS HAS ALL BEEN TOO MUCH OF A SHOCK...
DEB? ARE YOU ALL RIGHT?
19

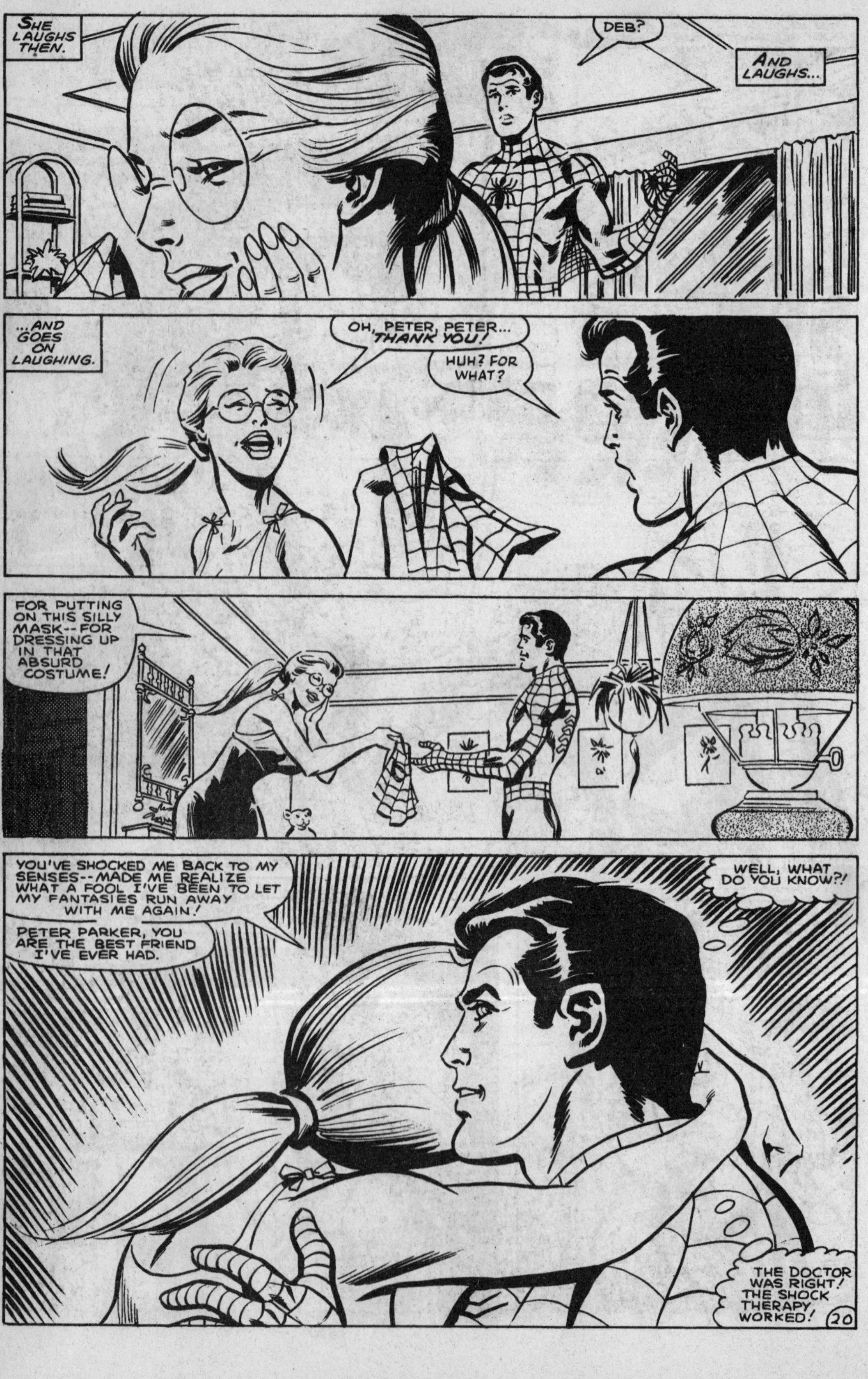
SHE LAUGHS THEN.
DEB?
AND LAUGHS...
...AND GOES ON LAUGHING.
OH, PETER, PETER... THANK YOU!
HUH? FOR WHAT?
FOR PUTTING ON THIS SILLY MASK--FOR DRESSING UP IN THAT ABSURD COSTUME!
YOU'VE SHOCKED ME BACK TO MY SENSES--MADE ME REALIZE WHAT A FOOL I'VE BEEN TO LET MY FANTASIES RUN AWAY WITH ME AGAIN!
PETER PARKER, YOU ARE THE BEST FRIEND I'VE EVER HAD.
WELL, WHAT DO YOU KNOW?!
THE DOCTOR WAS RIGHT! THE SHOCK THERAPY WORKED!
20

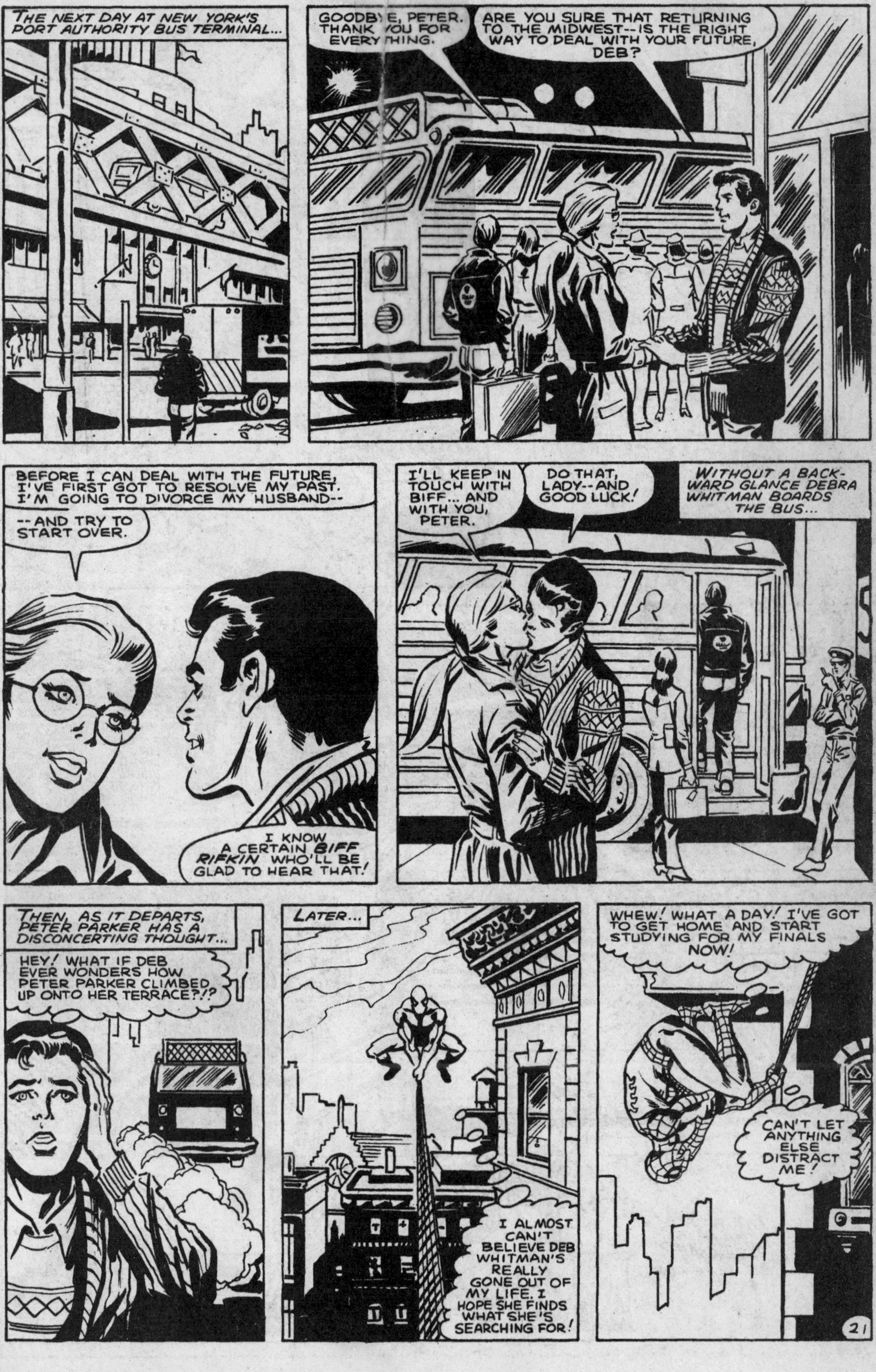
THE NEXT DAY AT NEW YORK'S PORT AUTHORITY BUS TERMINAL...
GOODBYE, PETER. THANK YOU FOR EVERYTHING.
ARE YOU SURE THAT RETURNING TO THE MIDWEST--IS THE RIGHT WAY TO DEAL WITH YOUR FUTURE, DEB?
BEFORE I CAN DEAL WITH THE FUTURE, I'VE FIRST GOT TO RESOLVE MY PAST. I'M GOING TO DIVORCE MY HUSBAND--
--AND TRY TO START OVER.
I KNOW A CERTAIN BIFF RIFKIN WHO'LL BE GLAD TO HEAR THAT!
I'LL KEEP IN TOUCH WITH BIFF... AND WITH YOU, PETER.
DO THAT, LADY--AND GOOD LUCK!
WITHOUT A BACKWARD GLANCE DEBRA WHITMAN BOARDS THE BUS...
THEN, AS IT DEPARTS, PETER PARKER HAS A DISCONCERTING THOUGHT...
HEY! WHAT IF DEB EVER WONDERS HOW PETER PARKER CLIMBED UP ONTO HER TERRACE?!?
LATER...
I ALMOST CAN'T BELIEVE DEB WHITMAN'S REALLY GONE OUT OF MY LIFE. I HOPE SHE FINDS WHAT SHE'S SEARCHING FOR!
WHEW! WHAT A DAY! I'VE GOT TO GET HOME AND START STUDYING FOR MY FINALS NOW!
CAN'T LET ANYTHING ELSE DISTRACT ME!
21

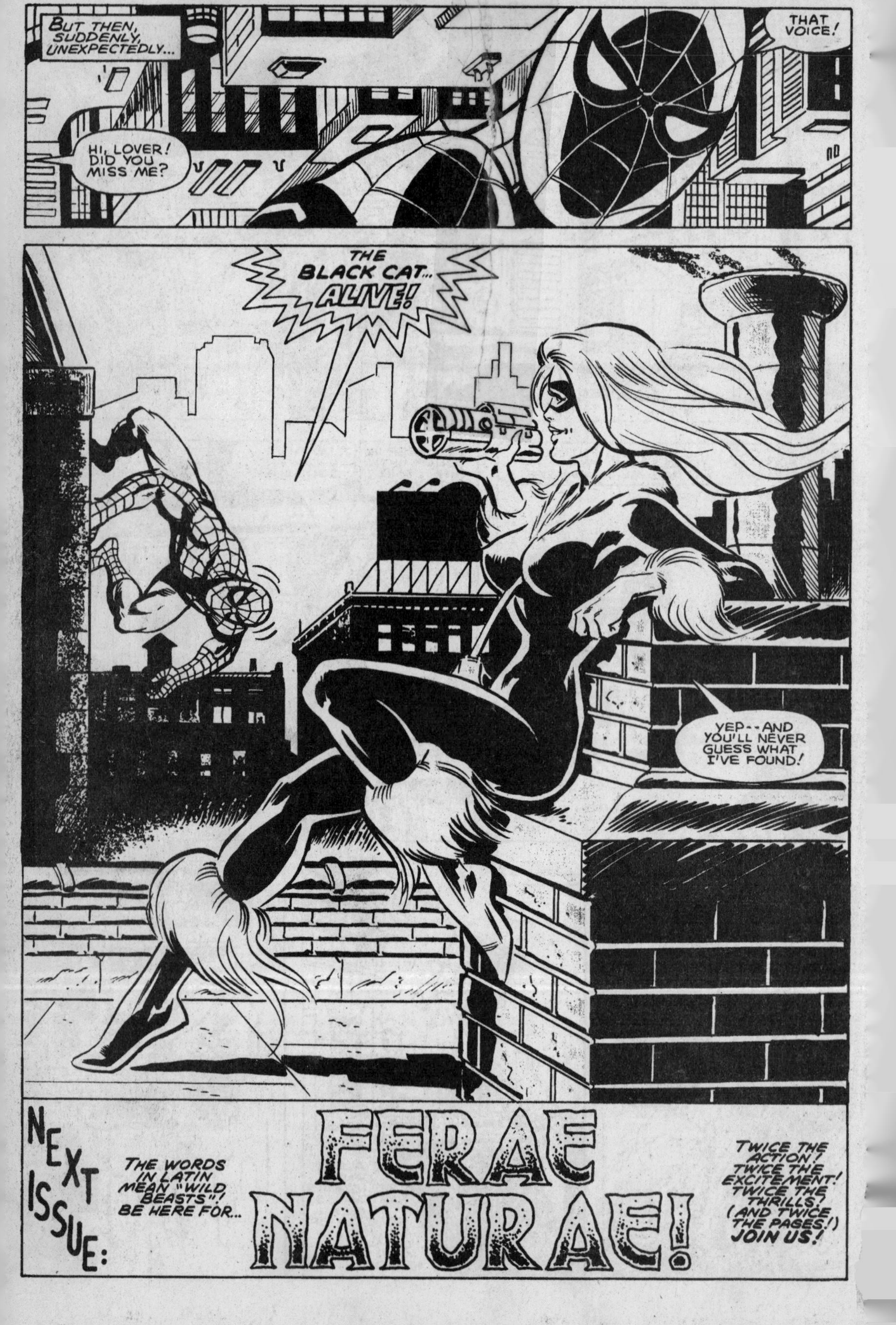

BUT THEN, SUDDENLY, UNEXPECTEDLY...
HI, LOVER! DID YOU MISS ME?
THAT VOICE!
THE BLACK CAT... ALIVE!
YEP--AND YOU'LL NEVER GUESS WHAT I'VE FOUND!
NEXT ISSUE:
THE WORDS IN LATIN MEAN "WILD BEASTS"! BE HERE FOR...
FERAE NATURAE!
TWICE THE ACTION! TWICE THE EXCITEMENT! TWICE THE THRILLS! (AND TWICE THE PAGES!) JOIN US!